D0356976

MARS & VENUS
365 WAYS TO KEEP
PASSION ALIVE

MARS & VENUS 365 WAYS TO KEEP PASSION ALIVE

JOHN GRAY

VERMILION

LONDON

3 5 7 9 10 8 6 4 2

Text © John Gray 1999

John Gray has asserted his right to be identified as the author of
this work under the Copyright, Designs and Patents Act 1988.

All rights reserved. No part of this publication may be
reproduced, stored in a retrieval system, or transmitted in any
form or by any means, electronic, mechanical, photocopying or
otherwise without the prior permission of the copyright owners.

First published in the United Kingdom in 2000 by Vermilion
Random House, 20 Vauxhall Bridge Road, London SW1V 2SA

Random House Australia (Pty) Limited
20 Alfred Street, Milsons Point, Sydney,
New South Wales 2061, Australia

Random House New Zealand Limited
18 Poland Road, Glenfield, Auckland 10, New Zealand

Random House South Africa (Pty) Limited
Endulini, 5a Jubilee Road, Parktown 2193, South Africa

Random House Group Ltd. Reg. No. 954009

Papers used by Vermilion are natural, recyclable products made
from wood grown in sustainable forests.

A CIP catalogue record for this book is available from the
British Library.

ISBN 0091826187
Printed and bound in the UK.

We want more from relationships than ever before. We want a lifetime of love; we want lasting passion with one special person.

If the flame of passion goes out, both men and women would rather risk the pain of divorce than the loss of feelings.

Deep inside, we sense that passionate monogamy is possible, but we do not have the skills to fully experience it.

♥

Generally speaking, when a man's emotional and passionate needs for love are not satisfied, he becomes entranced with sex, while a woman tends to become captivated with romance.

Since contemporary women increasingly can provide for themselves, they want more from a partner than helping to take care of the family.

If her husband needs another woman to be passionate, a woman today would rather start over with another man who wants her passionately.

For men or women, having an affair is ultimately an attempt to fulfil our need for love.

While it may satiate this need, an affair leads us farther and farther away from being able to have a truly fulfilling relationship with our mates.

When either a man or
a woman is having an affair, the
opportunity to grow together in
loving passion is greatly
restricted.

A relationship is like an
investment. We give to our
partner and hope over time to
get more and more in return.

Forgiveness is very powerful and can solidify a loving bond for ever.

Sometimes it takes the threat of permanent loss to make people appreciate what they have; sometimes the imminent death of a relationship must stare us in the face before we can feel our deep love and longing to live together.

Through forgiving and effectively communicating about the hurt and being motivated to make necessary changes, some couples are able to start completely over in love and experience greater passion and intimacy than ever before.

The most important aspect of attraction is that we are different.

Having to give up who
we are to please our partners
ultimately kills the passion.
By seeking to resolve our
differences without having to
deny our true selves, we ensure
lasting attraction.

By taking the time
to make sure that we avoid
emotional role reversal, we can
maintain the attraction we feel
to each other.

When passion is sustained,
our curiosity and interest in our
partners also grow over time.

Working with our differences
is a requirement for keeping the
passion alive.

For a woman to stay attracted
to a man, he must be in touch
with and express his male side.
But if he suppresses his male
side to be in a relationship with
her, she will eventually lose
her attraction for him.

Without taking deliberate steps to nurture her female side, a woman today will tend to automatically stay in her masculine side and unknowingly sabotage not only her relationships but her relationship with herself as well.

Living with the same person can, over time, eventually become very boring if they are not regularly changing. Staying fresh is crucial for both partners in a marriage.

Just as listening to a favourite
song a hundred times in a row
makes it grow stale, so also may
our partners become boring if
they do not grow and change.

Just as physical growth is so
obvious in our children, we must
always continue to grow
emotionally, mentally and
spiritually.

When a relationship does not allow us to grow, the passion between two people begins to fade.

Change is automatic if a relationship is to nurture us in being true to ourselves.

Loving your partner
does not mean spending all
your time together.

Too much time together
can also make a relationship
commonplace and devoid of
mystery. Enjoying other friends
and activities means that you can
always bring back something new
to the relationship.

If a woman doesn't feel safe
in talking about her feelings,
she will eventually have nothing
to say. Creating the safety for
her to talk freely without her
having to fear rejection,
interruption, or ridicule allows
a woman to thrive in a
relationship.

Over time, a woman can continue to trust and love her partner more if he is a good listener.

As a man begins to understand how to listen in an active way that his mate can appreciate, listening and sharing stops being a chore and becomes an important nurturing ritual.

With open lines of
communication, a woman will
continue to grow.

When a man does not feel
appreciated in a relationship,
he also stops growing.

It is important to schedule special occasions. If a man creates special times when a woman can get out of the routine, she is free to feel nurtured.

♥

Doing something special on those days for her frees her from feeling overwhelmed by life's repetitive responsibilities and assures her that she is loved.

One of the chief passion
assassins is routine.

Even if you are comfortable in
your rut, it is helpful to break
out of it from time to time.

All of our little efforts to
occasionally break the routine
make a difference.

Ultimately, what keeps passion alive in a relationship is growing in love.

When, as a result of living, laughing, crying and learning together, two people are able to love and trust each other more, the passion will continue.

When it is not safe to have
feelings or sensitivities, we quickly
lose touch with our passion.

While women need to talk more
about their feelings and be heard if
they are to feel vibrant in a
relationship, men need to be
appreciated for their actions if
they are to feel like doing things
for their partners.

When a man stops feeling a tender desire to please his partner, his tender feelings are automatically repressed.

When a woman stops feeling the safety to share her feelings, she also begins to close up by repressing emotions.

Slowly but surely, by
continuing to successfully
communicate and appreciate
each other, that wall of repressed
feelings can come down and
feelings can be fully
experienced again.

To continue feeling our love,
we need to feel.

When we are not getting
the love we need, but remain
vulnerable to our partners,
we feel pain.

Only by learning to reach out
for love and ask for what we
want in skilful ways can we really
heal our pain.

By turning off our feelings,
we lose touch with our inner
passion. We may not even know
what we actually need more of
because we have stopped feeling.

The challenge women face
in their relationships is to keep
opening up when feeling
disappointed or unloved.

Without having the skills
to get the love we need, we may
automatically begin to stop
feeling our needs. When this
happens, passion begins to
disappear.

It is of paramount importance
that we work on trusting our
partners more and more and
continue to be receptive.

The secret to growing in trust
is not to expect your partner to
be perfect but to believe that
you are growing in the skills
that help you help him
give you what you want.

To bring back passion, he needs
to remember that it will require
hard work and effort.

Through understanding how
men are different, a woman
enables herself to trust that he
loves her even when he doesn't
instinctively do the things she
would do to demonstrate caring.

Need and dependence become a
turn-on when we are needing
what our partner can give us.

A man can eventually come out
and overcome the inertia of not
caring if he is aware of the effort
required to open his heart again.
Eventually, he will be energised
as never before by pleasing
his partner.

As we grow together in love
and trust, open up and feel our
mutual needs more strongly, our

vulnerability increases too.
Passion is most powerfully
experienced when we know how
much we need someone.

With this kind of trust, even
when our partners let us down,
we will know that they did the
best they could and we can be
much more forgiving.

It is unwise as well as naive to expect our partners always to give us the love we need.

♥

Once we begin to need our partners in ways that they can't or don't support us, we will not only turn them off but will disappoint ourselves as well.

When we need our partners too much, we will eventually pull away our trust and caring.

As we continue to open up and have our emotional needs met in a relationship, our unresolved past feelings ultimately begin to surface.

Blaming your partner is looking
in the wrong direction and
aggravates the wound.

When a woman becomes
impatient, she will demand that
her partner make his changes
permanently instead of realising
that he is engaged in an ongoing
process to give her the support
she needs.

Whenever you feel you were
fine until your partner did one
thing that ruined your day, it is
generally something deep inside
you that needs to be healed.

It is an irony that when we feel
most loved, the unresolved
feelings from past experiences of
not being loved begin to affect
our moods.

When past feelings begin to surface they generally make us feel uncharacteristically negative.

When such feelings surface it is vital for us to work on taking responsibility for being more loving and forgiving.

When we start blaming our partners for our unhappiness, it is a clear signal that our own old stuff is coming up.

Although we feel especially entitled to demand more from our mates, we should demand nothing.

To expect our partners to make
us feel better is to put them in
the role of parents.

Whenever we feel out of
control and therefore seek to
control another, our childhood
is generally affecting us.

When our hearts are open, we are patient towards our partners' limitations and our own.

When we suddenly begin to feel impatient, we lose our realistic perspective and immediately demand more than is possible.

Instead of feeling good that progress is being achieved, we feel frustrated that not enough is happening fast enough.

When we feel blame towards our partner, it is difficult to accept, understand and forgive their limitations and imperfections.

Instead of giving up or demanding more, a woman needs to focus less on changing her partner and more on changing her own attitude.

The test of love is caring for a person even though we know them to be less than perfect and have experienced their daily limitations.

Only through learning to love them in stormy times can we grow together. Anybody can love somebody who's perfect.

Although we feel blame, by committing ourselves to finding forgiveness, we can bring ourselves back to being adults and release ourselves from immature feelings.

By taking responsibility for
re-parenting herself even if she
still blames her partner, she will
release herself from the spell of
past feelings and will remember
that she is cared for by a partner
who is doing his best.

A man needs to stop depending
on his partner's trust in him to
feel successful.

It is important that a man does not feel he has to surrender his sense of self in order to please his partner. Otherwise he would be weakened.

Making a small shift in behaviour does not mean that we can't be true to ourselves.

If we feel we are not getting the love we need and are blaming our partners, it is a clear sign that we need something our partners simply cannot presently give us.

Instead of drowning in negativity and reacting in unloving ways when our hearts are closed, we can use this downtime for self-healing.

Instead of looking to our
partners to change when we are
blaming them, we should focus
on changing ourselves.

When we are feeling open and
forgiving, we can refocus and
look for ways in which to solve
or correct the problem that
originally upset us.

Through taking responsibility
for our reactions and actions in a
relationship, we can truly begin
to give and receive love
successfully.

Without an awareness
of how our partners specifically
need love, we may be missing
priceless opportunities.

A woman feels loved
when she feels that a man's love
is consistent.

While good communication
provides a healthy basis for a
loving relationship, romance is
the dessert.

When a man does things
without a woman having to ask,
she feels deeply loved.

If he forgets to do them,
though, a wise woman graciously
persists in reminding him by
asking in a nondemanding
manner.

A man is happiest when a
woman is fulfilled.

Women generally do not realise
that the kind of love a man
needs most is her loving message
that he has fulfilled her.

The basis of almost all romantic
rituals is a male giving and a
female receiving.

The most important skill
for loving a man is to catch him
when he is doing something right
and notice and appreciate
him for it.
The most significant mistake is
taking him for granted.

Although women need romance
to feel loved, for passion to grow
over time their most important
requirement is monogamy.

Romance tells a woman that
she is special. And there is
nothing that makes a woman feel
more special than a man in
touch with his passions and
wanting only her.

As a woman ages,
her ability to feel and express
passion increases if she feels she
can fully trust her partner
to be there for her.
If she feels she is being
compared to another woman
or that she has to compete, she
cannot continue to open up.

Sexual monogamy strengthens
a man and makes him worthy of
the highest trust.

By clearly committing himself
and assuring a woman that they
are going to grow old together,
her mate gives her the special
support she needs to discover the
fires of sexual passion deep
within her soul.

Like a delicate rose she needs
the clear and clean water of
monogamy to gradually unfold,
one petal at a time.

Through creating and sustaining
a passionate monogamous
relationship, not only can a
woman grow in sexual passion but
a man can be more powerful and
effective in his work.

Just as communication and romance are the primary means for a woman to experience love, sex is the primary way for a man to connect with love and passion on an ongoing basis.

Just as romance is important to a woman, sexual gratification is important to a man. Sexual rejection is traumatic to a man's sense of self.

To be really good friends in a relationship requires a balance of autonomy and independence.

Friendship is a breeze if we suppress our feelings. If one partner is willing sacrifice who he or she is to the relationship, they will always get along – but the passion will die.

Without good communication skills, quite commonly a couple with a lot of love will choose to maintain the friendship and sacrifice their feelings.

Through practising personal responsibility and self-healing we can nurture ourselves at those times when our partners can't be our nurturers

Needing our partners is the basis of passion. However, if we are not also autonomous, at those times when our partners have little to give us, we will feel powerless to get what we need.

The real test of love is when we can be our partner's friend, and give without any expectation of return.

When we are confident that we can get what we need at other times, then we are not so demanding at those times when our partners have little to give.

For a woman to feel friendship for a man it means that he can be relaxed about her getting upset.

A man needs to feel that
sometimes he is on vacation in
the relationship and, in a sense,
can do no wrong. He wants to
feel that he is fine the way he is
and that he is not required
to change.

When a woman can be
lighthearted about her problems,
a man feels like a success.

Friendship for a woman means that her mate will, from time to time, go out of his way to support her or offer his help.

Friendship for a man means that a woman will go out of her way not to be demanding or expect too much.

Being our partner's friend
means never trying to change
their mood or taking personally
when they are not feeling the
way we want them to.

Partnership is the seventh secret
to creating a lasting and
passionate relationship.

When a man is skilled in loving a woman, there is no question that his love can sweep her off her feet. In a similar way, a woman's love can help plant a man's feet firmly on the ground.

When couples start out in love, they are always willing to do whatever it takes to make the relationship work.

By learning new skills
to express her love, she can be a
mirror to help him see and feel his
greatness. She can be a motivating
force that helps him succeed
in expressing his most competent
and loving self.

❤

We start relationships because we
are drawn to another person who
is different but complements us.

In our journey we must remember to nurture and respect our differences. Differences create passion.

A woman feels partnership when she and her partner are doing things together in a cooperative manner toward the same goal.

A man experiences partnership very differently. He likes to have his department, where he is in control, and he is happy for her to have her department, where she is in control. Together, doing different jobs with different responsibilities, they are a partnership teaming up to get the job done.

For a partnership to thrive and not be self-serving, it must have a purpose beyond itself. For the passion to grow, partners must share a common interest and work toward that end.

To fully open our hearts to each other and enjoy a lifetime of love and passion, the most important skill is forgiveness.

We all come into this world with gifts to share and purposes to fulfil beyond our personal happiness. For a relationship to grow in love and passion, the love we share with another needs to be directed in some loftier way.

Forgiving means letting go of hurt.

Forgiving your partner
for their mistakes not only frees
you to love again but allows
you to forgive yourself for
not being perfect.

When we don't forgive in one
relationship, our love is, to
various degrees, restricted in all
our life relationships.

The more you love someone,
the more you suffer when you
don't forgive them.

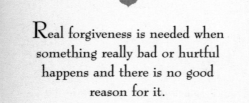

Real forgiveness is needed when
something really bad or hurtful
happens and there is no good
reason for it.

Real forgiveness acknowledges that a real mistake has been made and then affirms that the person who made it still deserves to be loved and respected.

We can begin to forgive our partners and others who hurt us when we can recognise that they really don't know what they are doing.

Mastering the new relationship skill of forgiveness takes time, but with practice, it becomes a natural response.

When you choose to love instead of closing your heart, you bring a little spark of divinity into our dark world of struggle. You lighten the load of others and help them to forgive as well.

Pleasing a woman is easier than
most men could ever imagine;
a woman can really love a man
and appreciate him for the
little things he does.

Be affectionate and touch each
other several times a day.

Through mastering the secrets of passion and practising forgiveness, we are not only creating a lifetime of love for ourselves, but we are making a difference in the world.

Practising new relationship skills and learning to harmonise dissonant values is not only the prerequisite for creating more

passionate relationships, but
directly contributes to a more
peaceful world.

Each time we take the
some-times painful or difficult
step to positive resolution in our
personal relationships, we are
paving the way for harmony in
the world.

Plan ahead and schedule regular romantic dates or getaways.

Romance for a woman can help her to rebuild her self-esteem after feeling ignored or unloved in a relationship. It is important for a woman to feel a man's desire to sustain a healthy self-esteem.

Sex ideally should be an expression of feeling good and having something to share.

Without an understanding of how to process any unresolved feelings that come up after sex, sexual release will leave us feeling bad, instead of making us feel good.

Regardless of what age we are, as we begin to feel more independent and autonomous, we want something more than just a good time or fun together. We want a deeper and richer opportunity to know someone and to be known.

Having an exclusive relationship provides the foundation for lasting intimacy.

Men need physical intimacy
in order to open up and feel
their love and desire,
to feel committed.

A woman creates intimacy by
honestly sharing more of who
she is, and a man experiences
increased intimacy by
successfully supporting and
nurturing more of who she is.

It is a mistake to think that
if a woman turns a man on,
fulfills his every need, and
happily accommodates his wishes
he will do the same for her.

♥

When a woman makes a man
feel masculine, his body is filled
with the fire of desire to get
close, and he becomes
purposeful. He feels inspired to

be better, and he is motivated to
fulfill her needs.

When a man is actively
interested in a woman, it gives
her an opportunity to explore
her true and authentic responses
to his pursuit.
This authenticity makes her
more attractive to the right kind
of guy for her.

When a man is actively interested in a woman, he is thinking about things like what he should do to impress her. When a woman is receptive, she gives the man the confidence to take the risks necessary to impress her.

When a man makes a woman
feel feminine, her mind is
stimulated and intrigued; she
feels warm, tender and vulnerable
inside; her heart begins to open
as she remembers that she is
special; and she is reassured by
the possibility of getting what
she wants and needs.

A man likes it when a woman reacts as if he is everything she wants, as if just being with him makes her happy, as if she is getting everything she needs and he is perfect for her just the way he is.

Men are interested in being successful. The opportunity to provide fulfillment to a woman is very interesting to any man.

Just as a man needs to put his best foot forward to impress a woman, she needs to put forth her most positively responsive self.

It is crucial that a man experience repeatedly that he can make and is making a difference in a woman's life.

Romantic rituals help a man
to stay on track. In most of the
traditional romantic rituals, the
man provides and the woman
graciously receives.

Romantic rituals are there
to make a woman feel special
and remind her to receive and
not give so much.

The purpose of having relationships has changed. We want more emotional fulfillment. We want romance. We want intimacy. And we want to find a deep and lasting love.

Romantic rituals remind men that to receive the love they want, they have to continue doing little things for a woman.

Men love it when a woman
lets go of being so responsible,
because then her receptive and
responsive feminine side can be
turned on.

It is only through understanding
and accepting our obvious and
less obvious differences that we
can achieve true intimacy
and great sex.

For many men, sexual arousal is the key for helping them connect with and realise their loving feelings.

Ironically it is sex that allows a man to feel his needs for love, while it is receiving love that helps a woman to feel her hunger for sex.

It is through sex that a man's heart opens, allowing him to experience both his loving feelings and his hunger for love as well.

A man does not instinctively realise that a woman generally needs to feel loved and romanced before she can feel her hunger for sex.

Sex allows a man to feel his needs for love, while receiving love helps a woman to feel her hunger for sex.

Just as a woman needs good communication with her partner to feel loved and loving, a man needs sex.

A man can feel loved in other ways, but the most powerful way a woman's love can touch his soul and open his heart is through great sex.

For sex to be great there must be loving and supportive communication in the relationship.

When sex gets better, suddenly the whole relationship gets better.

♥

Through great sex, the man begins to feel more love, and, as a result, the woman starts getting the love she may have been missing.

When a couple experiences relationship troubles, sometimes instead of focusing on the problems, taking a shortcut and creating great sex immediately reduces the problems and makes them easier to solve.

Great sex is your reward, and you deserve it.

The most effective way to jump start a relationship is to first learn the bedroom skills for making great sex.

Great sex softens a woman's heart and helps her to relax and receive her partner's support in other areas of the relationship.

One of the special rewards for learning and applying bedroom skills is that sex gets better and better.

♥

Loving sex, passionate sex, sensual sex, long sex, short sex, quickie sex, gourmet sex, playful sex, tender sex, rough sex, soft sex, hard sex, romantic sex, goal-orientated sex, erotic sex, simple sex, cool sex, and hot sex

are all an important part of
keeping the passion of love alive.

Great sex is not just a reward
but something that can rejuvenate
the body, mind and soul.

Good sex brightens our days
and strengthens our relationship
in the most basic ways.

A modern man wants his partner to value sex in a way that allows him to stay passionately connected to her and their relationship.

For sex and passion to grow over time, it is important that we do not feel judged or criticized for our wishes and desires.

A great sex life is not just the symptom of a passionate relationship, but also a major factor in creating it.

Great sex fills our hearts with love and can fulfill almost all our emotional needs.

Great sex softens a woman and opens her to experience the love in her heart and to remember her partner's love for her in a most definite way.

The hunger for love within a woman's soul is fulfilled with her partner's passionate and fully present attention.

Great sex releases a man from all his frustrations and allows him to rekindle his passion and commitment to a relationship.

Through a woman's fulfillment a man feels he has made his mark and that his love is appreciated.

Great sex reminds both men and women of the tender and highest love that originally drew them together.

Great sex is a special gift to those who work hard to make love a priority in their lives.

The one major characteristic
that makes a relationship more
than just a loving friendship
is sex.

Sex directly nurtures our male
and female sides more than any
other activity a couple can share.

Great sex is soothing to a woman and helps keep her in touch with her feminine side, while it strengthens a man and keeps him in touch with his masculine side.

A positive attitude to sex is essential for great sex.

To a woman, love is much more important than sex, but as the need for love is fulfilled, the importance of sex dramatically increases.

Even if a woman doesn't feel loved but feels the possibility of being loved, she can begin to feel her deep desire for sex.

A man wants love just as much as a woman, but before he can open his heart and let in his partner's love, sexual arousal is a prerequisite.

Just as a man needs love to open up to sex, a man needs sex to open up to love.

A woman's feelings
about a man's preoccupation
with sex can dramatically shift
when she understands why a man
needs sex.

Through sex, a man can feel,
and through feeling, he can
come back to his soul again.

A man is empowered and
nurtured most when he feels
appreciated, accepted, and
trusted.

When a woman is longing to
have sex with a man, she is most
open and trusting.

When a man's touch creates
a pleasurable response, he feels
greatly appreciated.

♥

Like a thirsty man wandering
in the desert, during sex a man
can finally relax and take a drink
from the oasis of his feelings.

Through touching a woman's softness and entering the warmth of her loving body, he is able to remain hard and masculine but also to experience his own softness and warmth.

Sex is an opportunity to share love in a way that nurtures men and women the most.

Sex is great when it is shared in
love and the love keeps growing.

For a woman to grow in sexual
fulfillment, she primarily needs
to feel emotionally supported in
a relationship.

A woman's pleasure corresponds to a gradual buildup of sexual tension.

To whatever extent his partner loves him, at the precious moment of orgasm, a man is able to receive her love the most.

As a man's heart opens during orgasm, he is able to feel the depth of his love and reaffirm his commitment to her.

Any resentments building up in a man are easily washed away when he experiences great sex.

When a woman feels relieved of her pressure to care for others, she can begin to feel her sexual desires.

By receiving the caring, nurturing, and sensuous support her female side craves, she begins to consciously feel her sexual yearnings.

A woman wants to be teased or gradually led to the place where she is longing to be touched.

♥

For a man, direct stimulation provides maximum pleasure.

♥

Sexual confidence is the ultimate turn-on for both men and women.

A woman's greatest ability to fulfill a man in sex is through helping him be successful in fulfilling her.

What makes sex fulfilling and memorable for a man is a woman's fulfillment.

To sustain passion and attraction in a relationship over the years a man needs clear messages that she loves sex with him.

A woman's acceptance of occasional quickies and a positive message whenever her partner initiates sex ensures lasting attraction and passion.

When a woman is unsure about
wanting sex, it means that she
needs a little time, attention,
and talking to find out.

A man does not realize that a
woman really does want sex, but
sometimes before she can feel
her desires, she first needs his
emotional support.

To keep a man attracted
to her, a woman does not need
to compete with the fantasy
women of the media and strive
to create a perfect body. Instead,
she needs to work toward
communicating positive and
nonrejecting messages
about sex.

A woman can better
understand a man's sexual
sensitivities by comparing them
to her sensitivities about feelings,
communication and intimacy.

A man loses his attraction
not because his partner doesn't
measure up to the ideal woman
but because he feels sexually
rejected and frustrated.

The primary reason for loss
of interest in sex is that men feel
rejected and women don't feel
romanced and understood in
the relationship.

A woman does not instinctively
understand how sensitive a man
is when she isn't in the mood
for sex.

A man does not instinctively
realise how much a woman needs
romance and good
communication to open up and
feel in the mood for sex.

If a woman doesn't feel safe to
say no to sex, she automatically
loses her ability to really say yes
to sex.

When a man repeatedly gets the message and truly believes that his partner loves sex with him, his sexual desires can remain healthy and strong.

When a woman feels a man is skilled in sex and he supports her in the relationship, her sexual desire can remain fresh.

Just as great communication opens a woman up to enjoy great sex, the possibility of great sex directly helps a man to be more loving in a relationship.

A man experiences pleasure primarily as a release of sexual tension.

One of the simplest and
most powerful ways to rekindle
passion is to get out of the house
on a romantic getaway. Spend
the night at a hotel. Enjoy a
change of scenery. Get away
from the routine and familiar.
Temporarily leave all domestic
responsibilities behind.
The more beautiful the new
environment is, the better.

If, for a long time, a woman
has not been able to get away
and feel free to be romantic and
sexual, her mood may become
increasingly asexual. To re-ignite
the passion and to feel like
a beautiful and loved woman,
she needs to get away from the
daily responsibilities and routine.
Just by scheduling a getaway,
a man can bring back her
romantic feelings.

Women particularly need
a change of environment to be
aroused. This change frees the
woman from feeling responsible
for the family and the home.
When the environment is
beautiful, it awakens her
to her inner beauty.

While spontaneous getaways can rekindle the romantic spirit, sometimes we are just too busy or responsible to others to get away easily. It is not always easy but it is worth it.

A man needs to remember that sometimes before a woman can feel romantic, she needs to

talk. If it is a long way to the
getaway spot she can talk the
whole way.

Sexy letters are not only good
for getting sex going but can also
help your partner understand
how you feel when you are
having sex.

When getaways are arranged,
a woman can stay in touch with
her sexual desires. That part of
her can look forward with
certainty to being fulfilled.

Sexy feelings are often there
inside us, but they need a little
extra help to come out
in the home.

If you find that when you are away from your partner, you are getting turned on, but when you are home you are not turned on, practice writing down your sexual feelings when they arise.

Another secret for bringing back sexual feelings is to write a sexy letter to your partner.

Of course not everyone is a writer, and expressing those delicate sentiments may be difficult. That does not mean that the feelings don't exist; it just means that you are not gifted in expressing them in words.

You can always find a greeting card that poetically expresses how you feel. It is perfectly okay to have loving feelings and not know how to articulate them and do justice to them. Picking the right

card to express your feelings is
just as good as writing the words
yourself.

This same principle holds true
with sexy letters. Feel free to
borrow many of the words and
expressions from romance novels
to get yours going. It is more
important to capture your
feelings than to be original.

When you are away from your
partner, feel your aroused mood
and imagine a romantic scene
acting out those sexual feelings
with your partner.

In a letter to your partner,
describe what you want to do and
then describe the scene and your
feelings as if it is really
happening.

Another secret for great sex and keeping the passion alive is understanding and working with our different sexual polarities. Just as the negative pole of a magnet strongly attracts the positive pole of a magnet, by expressing our opposite sexual polarities, we can increase attraction, desire, and pleasure. There are two sexual polarities, giving pleasure and receiving pleasure.

When one partner is giving
and the other partner is
receiving, the sexual pleasure can
easily build. In polarity sex,
partners take turns consciously
using these polarities to increase
desire and pleasure. One partner
gives while the other receives.
Then, later on, they switch,
and the giver stops giving and
just receives.

Polarity sex has two stages.
In the first stage, the man takes
and the woman gives.
Then, in the second stage,
he attends to her needs while
she relaxes and focuses
on receiving.

For the thought of sex to be a welcome idea, a woman needs to feel that she doesn't have to get turned on right away. Polarity sex is the solution to this problem.

A woman is generally open to occasional quickie sex when she feels emotionally supported in the relationship and knows that at other times she will experience

regular healthy home-cooked sex
and occasional gourmet sex.

Another secret of great sex is
variety. Women want sex to be a
little different every time.

Men are more goal-oriented
and his guiding principle is
'If it ain't broke, don't fix it.'

A man wants to find
a formula that will work each
time so he can relax in sex,
feeling confident that he knows
what he is doing.

A woman, however, feels most
excited when she doesn't know
what he is going to do next.
Predictability is a turnoff.

Shifting rhythms and
movements may seem
unimportant to a man,
but to a woman it makes
a big difference.

As a rule, a woman needs
about ten times more foreplay
than a man.

A man should remember that it is not what he does but how long he takes to do it that ensures a woman's fulfillment.

To assist a man in knowing what to do, it is helpful for a woman to give him clear feedback.

With a little reassuring
comment from a woman, a man
can keep going without worry that
he is doing the wrong things.

When a man is less mechanical
and non-predictable in sex, a
woman has the opportunity to
explore and express her unique
sexual moods or feelings that day.

When a woman feels free to change each time, and over time, like the weather, her sexual expression changes. If sex is to remain exciting, her natural changes are important.

The sexual act for a woman is a process of discovering what feels good that day.

Just as the seasons change,
so also will sex change and
continue to be interesting. For
this change to occur naturally,
a woman must feel supported
in discovering the different
expression of her sexual feelings.

A woman does not want
her partner to follow any
premeditated rigid plan.

Different expressions of
a woman's sexual nature are not
planned or thought out, but
instead are discovered in the
moment.

When a man can take the lead
in sex, he frees his partner to
think less and feel more. This
does not mean that she just lies

there passively. The freedom
to relax and stop thinking about
what 'should' happen allows her
to flow in the currents and
undulating rhythms of her
sensual and sexual nature. Like
dancing to a particular type of
music, she can move and dance
with him to the rhythm of her
mood that day.

When a woman has the freedom to be spontaneous, these different expressions and others will naturally come up and be expressed. When a man carefully takes the time to stimulate a woman with no expectations of how she is supposed to respond, over time she feels safer and safer in sex to do and express whatever she feels. This

uninhibited sexual expression frees
her to experience new heights of
sexual ecstasy.

Both men and woman need clear
and positive feedback to know
what brings their partners the
greatest fulfillment.

A woman wants sex to be a spontaneous creation each time, appropriate to how both partners are feeling.

In sex, like an artist, a man needs to be familiar with the basic colours of sex and then experiment with how they combine to create a new work of art.

A secret of great sex is to build
on the strengths you have and
not focus on the problems or
what you have missing.

It may surprise you to hear that
monogamy can help to keep sex
passionate and alive.

When you learn to make sex
spontaneous and not mechanical,
it can remain exciting.

Over time the sensations of sex
can continue to change and
passion can continue to grow.

Monogamy ensures that a woman continues to feel special and loved. If she is not feeling loved in this way, she cannot continue to open herself to him.

Trust is essential for a woman to continue getting turned on to her partner.

A man needs to repeatedly experience that he can make a woman happy if he is to stay attracted and turned on to her.

To remain a prisoner in a passionless relationship is not a choice that people today are willing to make.

Learning new skills to use in bed can ensure that passion stays alive and sex continues to get better and better.

Just as it is normal not to feel in love with your partner at times, it is also normal not to feel sexually attracted to your partner.

It is both healthy and natural
that the wave of passion in a
relationship rises and falls.

Times when you don't feel
sexual attraction are like cloudy
days when the sun doesn't shine.
A cloudy day does not mean the
sun is not there. It just means
that it is temporarily covered.

Cloudy days are the times when temptation knocks on our doors.

When attraction is blocked in a relationship, many times we feel attracted elsewhere.

Monogamy is essential for wild and uninhibited sex.

To maintain the possibility for
passion to come back to your
relationship, it is best not to
indulge your passions or
fantasies elsewhere.

It can take many years of
commitment before a man's
passions flow only in the
direction of his partner.

By containing your sexual feelings and repeatedly directing them to your partner, you increase your ability to be turned on to them.

When a man can feel both his passion and control it, a woman can begin to let go of control, release her inhibitions, and start to really feel her passions.

As a man learns to control his passions, not only does he help his partner reach higher levels of fulfillment, but he also can experience greater levels of sexual pleasure and love.

Don't feel bad for feeling attracted to someone else, but take that arousal back to your partner.

Every time a man is tempted by the possibility of sex and maintains his monogamous commitment, he is creating the safety for his partner to enjoy sex more.

Even tough minded, goal-orientated, high-powered executive women place great value on romance.

Romance has a magical effect
on women everywhere.

While men hunger for great
sex, women long for romance.

To fulfill a woman's need for
romance, a man first needs to
understand what romance is.

Receiving cards, cut flowers
and little presents; moonlit
nights; spontaneous decisions:
all spell romance.

A man is happy to be romantic
in the beginning to show her
how special she is, but once he
has behaved romantically, he
doesn't instinctively realise why
he has to keep doing it.

To feel romanced,
a woman doesn't want to
buy her own flowers.
She wants her lover to do it.

She doesn't want to have to ask
for romantic gestures. If she has
to ask, it doesn't count as
romance.

A man's self-motivated
purchase of cut flowers is, for a
woman, a symbol that he cares
for her and understands
her needs.

When a man plans a date,
handles the tickets, drives the
car, and takes care of all the
small details, that is romance.

When a man takes responsibility to take care of things, it allows a woman to relax and enjoy feeling taken care of.

Romance is like a mini-holiday that helps a woman come back to her female side.

Romantic moments are particularly helpful for women who don't feel comfortable sharing their feelings.

On a romantic date, without having to talk about her feelings, a woman can feel acknowledged, adored, understood, and supported.

A man's romantic
behaviour says repeatedly that
he acknowledges her, and by
anticipating her needs, he signals
that he understands and
respects her.

Romantic actions give her the
same support that talking does:
in both cases, she feels heard.

Romance clearly places a
woman in the feminine role of
being special and cared for.

♥

When a man passionately
focuses on fulfilling her needs,
she is able to release her
tendency to take care of others.

For romance to thrive
a woman needs to feel heard and
understood on a day-to-day basis.

When a man is untrained in
the skills of listening to and
understanding a woman, or when
the woman resists sharing the
feelings that naturally come up,
she eventually feels unheard and
is turned off.

When this happens, a man may make romantic overtures but they don't have the same magical feeling.

Creating romantic rituals that say, 'I love you and I care about you' can go a long way to communicate love without words.

With the support of romance, communication is much easier.

Romantic rituals are simple actions that acknowledge that he cares about her.

The same principle of asking for what you want applies to all romantic rituals.

It is more romantic if a man offers a hug to say hello, but if he forgets, it is better to ask than to miss out and feel resentful.

A woman can create some romance when they eat out simply by just having a good time and appreciating the food and the restaurant.

A romantic ritual when eating out is for the man to ask the woman what she is going to order and then order it for her when the waiter arrives.

♥

Although a man need not always do this, when he does, it makes dinner special. It gives the message that he is attentive to her.

When a man takes
a woman out, she has a golden
opportunity to make him feel
special. When she appreciates
what he provides for her, he feels
more intimate with her.

A man feels most romantic
when he feels successful in
providing for her happiness.

Just as little gifts and caring attention from a man to a woman make her feel loved and romantic, when a woman appreciates a man's efforts and what he provides for her, he feels more loved and romantically inclined.

With the support of romance, good communication becomes much easier.

It is attention to the little things that creates lasting romance. When men and women take each other for granted, the romance disappears.

Romantic rituals ensure that
a man can always do something
to win his partner's love and
the woman can get the special
attention and support she needs
to stay passionately attracted to
her partner.

When a man acts romantically
not only does he feel charming
and dashing , but she gets to feel
more fully that he cares.

Men want a woman to be
fulfilled but mistakenly assume
that what makes him happy
makes her happy.

A man reaching out to touch or hold hands is a turn-on for women. While men generally hold hands in the courting stage, they stop after a while. This is a big loss.

Start being more affectionate and touch more often, you'll be amazed at the difference.

A woman loves to feel
that a man wants to connect
with her in this way. She doesn't
feel loved if the only time he
wants to touch her is when he
wants sex.

If a man wants his partner to feel receptive to sex, he need to touch her in an affectionate way many times each day when he is not wanting sex. He can hold hands, put his arm around her, stroke her shoulders and arms, all without implying that he is wanting sex. If the only time he touches her is when he wants sex, she begins to feel used or taken for granted.

Not only is touching a great way to connect and feel close at any time, but it also softens the rough edges at times and brings us back to feeling our love for each other.

Although we may fall out of love, with patience and the right directions, we can find it again.

When we feel loved something very magical takes place; our hearts our filled with the warm glow of forgiveness and we are inspired by a new sense of power to realise our hopes and dreams.

Couples can grow together in love over a lifetime but it takes education and practice.

Even with the best intentions,
there will be times when we get
lost and lose touch with the love
in our hearts.

Like two best friends joyously
finding each other after a long
search, men and women can
magically fall in love again
and again.

May you always grow in love
and passion and enjoy God's
special gift. You deserve it.

LAROUSSE

MINI

ITALIAN-ENGLISH
ENGLISH-ITALIAN

DICTIONARY

LAROUSSE

Realizzato da / Produced by

LAROUSSE

Redazione/Editors

FRANCESCA LOGI   PETER BLANCHARD

RITA GAVA   WENDY LEE   DELIA PROSPERI   LESLIE RAY

CALLUM BRINES   CARMELA CELINO

Il dizionario MINI Larousse è stato realizzato per rispondere alle esigenze di chi viaggia o comincia a studiare l'inglese.

Con più di 30 000 parole ed espressioni e oltre 40 000 traduzioni, questo nuovo dizionario comprende non solo la terminologia generale di base, ma anche molte espressioni che permettono di decifrare cartelli, segnali stradali e menu.

Le divisioni semantiche sono accuratamente indicate e la consultazione delle voci complesse di uso più frequente è facilitata dai numerosi esempi e dalla presentazione chiara ed efficace.

Completo e allo stesso tempo praticissimo, questo dizionario si rivelerà un indispensabile compagno di studio e di viaggio. "Good luck", e non esitate ad inviarci i vostri suggerimenti.

L'EDITORE

The Larousse MINI dictionary has been designed with beginners and travellers in mind.

With over 30,000 references and 40,000 translations, this new dictionary gives thorough coverage of general vocabulary plus extensive treatment of the language found on street signs and menus.

Clear sense markers are provided throughout, while special emphasis has been placed on basic words, with many examples of usage and a particularly user-friendly layout.

Easy to use and comprehensive, this handy book packs a lot of wordpower for users at school, at home and on the move. "Buona fortuna", and don't hesitate to send us your comments.

THE PUBLISHER

ABBREVIATIONS

ABBREVIAZIONI

abbreviation	*abbr*	abbreviazione
adjective	*adj*	aggettivo
adverb	*adv*	avverbio
adjective	*agg*	aggettivo
American English	*Am*	inglese americano
anatomy	*ANAT*	anatomia
article	*art*	articolo
auxiliary	*aus*	ausiliare
automobile, cars	*AUT(O)*	automobile
auxiliary	*aux*	ausiliare
adverb	*avv*	avverbio
British English	*Br*	inglese britannico
commerce, business	*COMM*	commercio
comparative	*compar*	comparativo
computers	*COMPUT*	informatica
conjunction	*conj/cong*	congiunzione
continuous	*cont*	forma progressiva
culinary, cooking	*CULIN*	cucina, culinaria
before	*dav*	davanti a
juridical, legal	*DIR*	diritto
exclamation	*excl/esclam*	esclamazione
feminine	*f*	femminile
informal	*fam*	familiare
figurative	*fig*	figurato
finance, financial	*FIN*	finanza
formal	*fml/form*	formale
inseparable	*fus*	non separabile
generally	*gen*	generalmente
geography	*GEOG*	geografia
gerund	*ger*	gerundio
grammar	*GRAMM*	grammatica
informal	*inf*	familiare
computers	*INFORM*	informatica
interrogative	*interr*	interrogativo

invariable	*inv*	invariabile
juridical, legal	JUR	diritto
masculine	*m*	maschile
mathematics	MAT(H)	matematica
medicine	MED	medicina
military	MIL	militare
music	MUS	musica
noun	*n*	sostantivo
nautical, maritime	NAUT	nautica
numeral	*num*	numerale
oneself	*o.s.*	
pejorative	*pej*	spregiativo
plural	*pl*	plurale
politics	POL	politica
past participle	*pp*	participio passato
preposition	*prep*	preposizione
pronoun	*pron*	pronome
past tense	*pt*	passato
	qc	qualcosa
	qn	qualcuno
registered trademark	®	marchio registrato
religion	RELIG	religione
noun	*s*	sostantivo
someone, somebody	*sb*	
school	SCH/SCOL	scuola
Scottish English	Scot	scozzese
separable	*sep*	separabile
singular	*sg*	singolare
subject	*sog*	soggetto
pejorative	*spreg*	spregiativo
something	*sthg*	
subject	*subj*	soggetto
superlative	*superl*	superlativo
technology	TECH/TECNOL	tecnica, tecnologia
verb	*v, vb*	verbo

intransitive verb	*vi*	verbo intransitivo
impersonal verb	*v impers*	verbo impersonale
vulgar	*volg*	volgare
reflexive verb	*vr*	verbo riflessivo
transitive verb	*vt*	verbo transitivo
vulgar	*vulg*	volgare
cultural equivalent	$\simeq$	equivalenza culturale

TRADEMARKS

Words considered to be trademarks have been designated in this dictionary by the symbol ®. However, neither the presence nor the absence of such designation should be regarded as affecting the legal status of any trademark.

ENGLISH COMPOUNDS

A compound is a word or expression which has a single meaning but is made up of more than one word, e.g. **point of view, kiss of life, virtual reality** and **West Indies**. It is a feature of this dictionary that English compounds appear in the A–Z list in strict alphabetical order. The compound **blood test** will therefore come after **bloodshot** which itself follows **blood pressure**.

MARCHI REGISTRATI

Le parole considerate marchi registrati sono contrassegnate in questo dizionario con il simbolo ®. In ogni caso, né la presenza né l'assenza di tale simbolo implica alcuna valutazione del reale stato giuridico di un marchio.

COMPOSTI INGLESI

In inglese si definiscono composti quelle espressioni che, pur essendo formate da più di una parola, costituiscono un'unica unità di significato, come ad es. **point of view, kiss of life, virtual reality** e **West Indies**. In questo dizionario i composti inglesi seguono l'ordine alfabetico generale. Il composto **blood test** figura perciò dopo **bloodshot** che, a sua volta, segue **blood pressure**.

PHONETIC TRANSCRIPTION

English vowels

[ɪ] pit, big, rid
[e] pet, tend
[æ] pat, bag, mad
[ʌ] run, cut
[ɒ] pot, log
[ʊ] put, full
[ə] mother, suppose
[i:] bean, weed
[ɑ:] barn, car, laugh
[ɔ:] born, lawn
[u:] loop, loose
[ɜ:] burn, learn, bird

English diphthongs

[eɪ] bay, late, great
[aɪ] buy, light, aisle
[ɔɪ] boy, foil
[əʊ] no, road, blow
[aʊ] now, shout, town
[ɪə] peer, fierce, idea
[eə] pair, bear, share
[ʊə] poor, sure, tour

Semi-vowels

you, spaniel   [j]
wet, why, twin   [w]

Consonants

pop, people   [p]
bottle, bib   [b]
train, tip   [t]
dog, did   [d]
come, kitchen   [k]
gag, great   [g]
chain, wretched   [tʃ]
jet, fridge   [dʒ]

TRASCRIZIONE FONETICA

Vocali italiane

[a] pane, casa
[e] verde, entrare
[ɛ] letto, pezzo
[i] vino, isola
[o] monte, pozzo
[ɔ] corpo, sciocco
[u] una, cultura

Semivocali

ieri, viola
fuori, guasto

Consonanti

porta, sapore
barca, libro
torre, patata
dare, odore
cane, chiesa
gara, ghiro
cena, ciao
gente, gioco

fib, **ph**ysical	[f]	fine, afa
vine, livid	[v]	vero, ovvio
think, fif**th**	[θ]	
this, wi**th**	[ð]	
seal, peace	[s]	stella, casa
zip, his	[z]	sdraio, rosa
sheep, ma**ch**ine	[ʃ]	scimmia, ascia
usual, measure	[ʒ]	
how, perhaps	[h]	
metal, comb	[m]	mamma, amico
night, dinner	[n]	notte, anno
sung, parking	[ŋ]	
	[ɲ]	gnocchi, ogni
little, help	[l]	lana, pollo
	[ʎ]	gli, figlio
right, carry	[r]	re, dorato

The symbol ['] precedes a syllable carrying primary stress and the symbol [‚] precedes a syllable carrying secondary stress.

The symbol [ʳ] in English phonetics indicates that the final "r" is pronounced only when followed by a word beginning with a vowel. Note that it is nearly always pronounced in American English.

I simboli ['] e [‚] indicano rispettivamente un accento primario e uno secondario nella sillaba seguente.

Il simbolo [ʳ] nella trascrizione fonetica dell'inglese indica che la "r" in fine di parola viene pronunciata soltanto se seguita da una parola che comincia per vocale. Da notare che nell' inglese americano la "r" viene quasi sempre pronunciata.

XI

The position of the tonic stress in Italian is indicated by a dot immediately beneath the accented vowel on Italian headwords (**camera, valigia**). No dot is given on those words which end in an accented vowel, as Italian spelling allows for a written accent in these cases (**città, perché**). Full phonetics have been provided for words of foreign origin which do not follow Italian pronunciation rules (**cracker** ['krɛker], **brioche** [bri'ɔʃ]).

L'accento nelle voci italiane è segnalato da un punto sotto la vocale accentata (**camera, valigia**), con l'eccezione delle parole con l'accento sull'ultima sillaba, per le quali l'ortografia italiana prevede l'accento grafico (**città, perché**). Le parole di origine straniera sono seguite dalla trascrizione fonetica nei casi in cui la pronuncia generalmente adottata non rispetta le regole fonetiche dell'italiano (**cracker** ['krɛker], **brioche** [bri'ɔʃ]).

ITALIAN VERBS

Key: *pr ind* = presente indicativo, *imperf* = imperfetto, *fut* = futuro, *cond* = condizionale, *pr cong* = presente congiuntivo, *imperat* = imperativo, *ger* = gerundio, *pp* = participio passato

AMARE: *pr ind* amo, ami, ama, amiamo, amate, amano, *imperf* amavo, amavi, amava, amavamo, amavate, amavano, *fut* amerò, amerai, amerà, ameremo, amerete, ameranno, *cond* amerei, ameresti, amerebbe, ameremmo, amereste, amerebbero, *pr cong* ami, ami, ami, amiamo, amiate, amino, *imperat* ama, ami, amate, *ger* amando, *pp* amato

andare: *pr ind* vado, vai, va, andiamo, andate, vanno, *fut* andrò, *cond* andrei, *pr cong* vada, vada, vada, andiamo, andiate, vadano, *imperat* va', vada, andate, *ger* andando, *pp* andato

aprire: *pr ind* apro, *pr cong* apra, *pp* aperto

avere: *pr ind* ho, hai, ha, abbiamo, avete, hanno, *imperf* avevo, *fut* avrò, *cond* avrei, *pr cong* abbia, *imperat* abbi, abbia, abbiate, *ger* avendo, *pp* avuto

bere: *pr ind* bevo, *imperf* bevevo, *fut* berrò, *cond* berrei, *pr cong* beva, *imperat* bevi, beva, bevete, *ger* bevendo, *pp* bevuto

cadere: *fut* cadrò

correre: *pp* corso

cuocere: *pr ind* cuocio, cuoci, cuoce, cuociamo, cuocete, cuociono, *pp* cotto

dare: *pr ind* do, dai, dà, diamo, date, danno, *fut* darò, *pr cong* dia, *imperat* da', dia, date

dire: *pr ind* dico, dici, dice, diciamo, dite, dicono, *imperf* dicevo, *fut* dirò, *pr cong* dica, dica, dica, diciamo, diciate, dicano, *imperat* di', dica, dite, *ger* dicendo, *pp* detto

dovere: *pr ind* devo, devi, deve, dobbiamo, dovete, devono, *fut* dovrò, *cond* dovrei, *pr cong* deva, deva, deva, dobbiamo, dobbiate, devano

essere: *pr ind* sono, sei, è, siamo, siete, sono, *imperf* ero, eri, era, eravamo, eravate, erano, *fut* sarò, *cond* sarei, *pr cong* sia, *imperat* sii, sia, siate, *ger* essendo, *pp* stato

fare: *pr ind* faccio, fai, fa, facciamo, fate, fanno, *imperf* facevo, *pr cong* faccia, *imperat* fai, faccia, fate, *ger* facendo, *pp* fatto

FINIRE: *pr ind* finisco, finisci, finisce, finiamo, finite, finiscono, *imperf* finivo, finivi, finiva, finivamo, finivate, finivano, *fut* finirò, finirai, finirà, finiremo, finirete, finiranno, *cond* finirei, finiresti, finirebbe, finiremmo, finireste, finirebbero, *pr cong* finisca, finisca, finisca, finiamo, finiate, finiscano, *imperat* finisci, finisca, finite, *ger* finendo, *pp* finito

giungere: *pp* giunto

leggere: *pp* letto

mettere: *pp* messo

morire: *pr ind* muoio, muori, muore, moriamo, morite, muoiono, *fut* morirò, *pr cong* muoia, *imperat* muori, muoia, morite, *pp* morto

muovere: *pp* mosso

nascere: *pp* nato

piacere: *pr ind* piaccio, piaci, piace, piacciamo, piacete, piacciono, *pr cong* piaccia, *pp* piaciuto

porre: *pr ind* pongo, poni, pone, poniamo, ponete, pongono, *imperf* ponevo, *fut* porrò, *cond* porrei, *pr cong* ponga, *imperat* poni, ponga, ponete, *ger* ponendo, *pp* posto

potere: *pr ind* posso, puoi, può, possiamo, potete, possono, *fut* potrò, *pr cong* possa

prendere: *pp* preso

ridurre: *pr ind* riduco, *imperf* riducevo, *fut* ridurrò, *pr cong* riduca, *ger* riducendo, *pp* ridotto

riempire: *pr ind* riempio, riempi, riempie, riempiamo, riempite, riempiono, *ger* riempiendo

rimanere: *pr ind* rimango, rimani, rimane, rimaniamo, rimanete, rimangono, *fut* rimarrò, *pr cong* rimanga, *pp* rimasto

rispondere: *pp* risposto

salire: *pr ind* salgo, sali, sale, saliamo, salite, salgono, *pr cong* salga

sapere: *pr ind* so, sai, sa, sappiamo, sapete, sanno, *fut* saprò, *pr cong* sappia, *imperat* sappi, sappia, sappiate

scegliere: *pr ind* scelgo, scegli, sceglie, scegliamo, scegliete, scelgono, *pr cong* scelga, *imperat* scegli, scelga, scegliete, *pp* scelto

sciogliere: *pr ind* sciolgo, sciogli, scioglie, sciogliamo, sciogliete, sciolgono, *pr cong* sciolga, *imperat* sciogli, sciolga, sciogliete, *pp* sciolto

scrivere: *pp* scritto

sedere: *pr ind* siedo, siedi, siede, sediamo, sedete, siedono, *pr cong* sieda

SERVIRE: *pr ind* servo, servi, serve, serviamo, servite, servono, *imperf* servivo, servivi, serviva, servivamo, servivate, servivano, *fut* servirò, servirai, servirà, serviremo, servirete, serviranno, *cond* servirei, serviresti, servirebbe, serviremmo, servireste, servirebbero, *pr cong* serva, serva, serva, serviamo, serviate, servano, *imperat* servi, serva, servite, *ger* servendo, *pp* servito

spegnere: *pr ind* spengo, spegni, spegne, spegniamo, spegnete, spengono, *pr cong* spenga, *pp* spento

stare: *pr ind* sto, stai, sta, stiamo, state, stanno, *fut* starò, *pr cong* stia, *imperat* sta, stia, state, *pp* stato

tacere: *pr ind* taccio, taci, tace, tacciamo, tacete, tacciono, *pr cong* taccia, *pp* taciuto

TEMERE: *pr ind* temo, temi, teme, temiamo, temete, temono, *imperf* temevo, temevi, temeva, temevamo, temevate, temevano, *fut* temerò, temerai, temerà, temeremo, temerete, temeranno, *cond* temerei, temeresti, temerebbe, temeremmo, temereste, temerebbero, *pr cong* tema, tema, tema, temiamo, temiate, temano, *imperat* temi, tema, temete, *ger* temendo, *pp* temuto

tenere: *pr ind* tengo, tieni, tiene, teniamo, tenete, tengono, *fut* terrò, *pr cong* tenga

togliere: *pr ind* tolgo, togli, toglie, togliamo, togliete, tolgono, *pr cong* tolga, *imperat* togli, tolga, togliete, *pp* tolto

trarre: *pr ind* traggo, trai, trae, traiamo, traete, traggono, *fut* trarrò, *pr cong* tragga, *imperat* trai, tragga, traete, *ger* traendo, *pp* tratto

uscire: *pr ind* esco, esci, esce, usciamo, uscite, escono, *pr cong* esca

vedere: *fut* vedrò, *pp* visto

venire: *pr ind* vengo, vieni, viene, veniamo, venite, vengono, *fut* verrò, *pr cong* venga, *pp* venuto

vivere: *pp* vissuto

volere: *pr ind* voglio, vuoi, vuole, vogliamo, volete, vogliono, *fut* vorrò, *cond* vorrei, *pr cong* voglia

VERBI IRREGOLARI INGLESI

Infinitive	Past Tense	Past Participle	Infinitive	Past Tense	Past Participle
arise	arose	arisen	creep	crept	crept
awake	awoke	awoken	cut	cut	cut
be	was/were	been	deal	dealt	dealt
			dig	dug	dug
bear	bore	born(e)	do	did	done
beat	beat	beaten	draw	drew	drawn
begin	began	begun	dream	dreamed/dreamt	dreamed/dreamt
bend	bent	bent			
bet	bet/betted	bet/betted	drink	drank	drunk
			drive	drove	driven
bid	bid	bid	eat	ate	eaten
bind	bound	bound	fall	fell	fallen
bite	bit	bitten	feed	fed	fed
bleed	bled	bled	feel	felt	felt
blow	blew	blown	fight	fought	fought
break	broke	broken	find	found	found
breed	bred	bred	fling	flung	flung
bring	brought	brought	fly	flew	flown
build	built	built	forget	forgot	forgotten
burn	burnt/burned	burnt/burned	freeze	froze	frozen
			get	got	got (Am gotten)
burst	burst	burst			
buy	bought	bought	give	gave	given
can	could	–	go	went	gone
cast	cast	cast	grind	ground	ground
catch	caught	caught	grow	grew	grown
choose	chose	chosen	hang	hung/hanged	hung/hanged
come	came	come			
cost	cost	cost	have	had	had

Infinitive	Past Tense	Past Participle	Infinitive	Past Tense	Past Participle
hear	heard	heard	pay	paid	paid
hide	hid	hidden	put	put	put
hit	hit	hit	quit	quit	quit
hold	held	held		/quitted	/quitted
hurt	hurt	hurt			
keep	kept	kept	read	read	read
kneel	knelt	knelt	rid	rid	rid
	/kneeled	/kneeled	ride	rode	ridden
know	knew	known	ring	rang	rung
lay	laid	laid	rise	rose	risen
lead	led	led	run	ran	run
lean	leant	leant	saw	sawed	sawn
	/leaned	/leaned	say	said	said
leap	leapt	leapt	see	saw	seen
	/leaped	/leaped	seek	sought	sought
learn	learnt	learnt	sell	sold	sold
	/learned	/learned	send	sent	sent
leave	left	left	set	set	set
lend	lent	lent	shake	shook	shaken
let	let	let	shall	should	–
lie	lay	lain	shed	shed	shed
light	lit	lit	shine	shone	shone
	/lighted	/lighted	shoot	shot	shot
lose	lost	lost	show	showed	shown
make	made	made	shrink	shrank	shrunk
may	might	–	shut	shut	shut
mean	meant	meant	sing	sang	sung
meet	met	met	sink	sank	sunk
mow	mowed	mown	sit	sat	sat
		/mowed	sleep	slept	slept
			slide	slid	slid

sling	slung	slung
smell	smelt /smelled	smelt /smelled
sow	sowed	sown /sowed
speak	spoke	spoken
speed	sped /speeded	sped /speeded
spell	spelt /spelled	spelt /spelled
spend	spent	spent
spill	spilt /spilled	spilt /spilled
spin	spun	spun
spit	spat	spat
split	split	split
spoil	spoiled /spoilt	spoiled /spoilt
spread	spread	spread
spring	sprang	sprung
stand	stood	stood
steal	stole	stolen
stick	stuck	stuck
sting	stung	stung
stink	stank	stunk

strike	struck	struck /stricken
swear	swore	sworn
sweep	swept	swept
swell	swelled	swollen /swelled
swim	swam	swum
swing	swung	swung
take	took	taken
teach	taught	taught
tear	tore	torn
tell	told	told
think	thought	thought
throw	threw	thrown
tread	trod	trodden
wake	woke /waked	woken /waked
wear	wore	worn
weave	wove /weaved	woven /weaved
weep	wept	wept
win	won	won
wind	wound	wound
wring	wrung	wrung
write	wrote	written

a (ad + vocale) prep **1.** (complemento di termine) to; **dare qc a qn** to give sthg to sb, to give sb sthg; **chiedere qc a qn** to ask sb sthg.

2. (stato in luogo) at; **abito a Torino** I live in Turin; **stiamo a casa** let's stay (at) home; **la piscina è a due chilometri da qui** the swimming pool is two kilometres from here.

3. (moto a luogo) to; **andiamo a letto** let's go to bed; **torno a Roma** I'm going back to Rome; **mi porti allo stadio?** can you take me to the stadium?

4. (temporale) at; **c'è un volo alle 8.30** there's a flight at 8.30; **a domani!** see you tomorrow!; **al mattino** in the morning; **alla sera** in the evening.

5. (modo, mezzo): **alla milanese** in the Milanese style, the Milanese way; **riscaldamento a gas** gas heating; **a piedi** on foot; **vestire alla moda** to dress fashionably; **scrivere a matita** to write in pencil.

6. (con prezzi) at; **comprare qc a metà prezzo** to buy sthg half-price.

7. (per caratteristica): **camicia a maniche corte** short-sleeved shirt; **finestra a doppi vetri** double-glazed window.

8. (per rapporto) per, a; **50 chilometri all'ora** 50 kilometres per o an hour; **pagato a ore** paid by the hour.

A abbr = autostrada.

abbacchio sm spring lamb; **~ alla romana** lamb cooked slowly with white wine or vinegar, rosemary, anchovies and garlic.

abbaglianti smpl: **accendere gli ~** to put one's headlights on full beam (Br) o high beam (Am).

abbagliare vt (accecare) to dazzle.

abbaiare vi to bark.

abbandonare vt (persona, luogo) to abandon; (ricerche) to abandon, to give up.

abbandono sm (di persona, luogo) neglect; (rinuncia) abandonment.

abbassare vt to lower; (volume, radio, tv) to turn down □ **abbassarsi** vr (persona) to bend down; (livello) to drop; **abbassarsi a fare qc** to lower o.s. by doing sthg.

abbasso vt & compl: **~ la scuola!** down with school!

abbastanza avv (a sufficienza)

enough; *(piuttosto)* rather, quite; **averne ~ di** to have had enough of.

abbattere *vt (muro)* to knock down; *(albero)* to cut down; *(cavallo)* to destroy; *(aereo)* to shoot down; *(sconfiggere)* to defeat ❏ **abbattersi** *vr* to lose heart.

abbattuto, -a *agg (depresso)* depressed.

abbazia *sf* abbey.

abbeverare *vt (animali)* to water ❏ **abbeverarsi** *vr* to drink.

abbia → **avere**.

abbiente *agg* well-off.

abbigliamento *sm* clothes *(pl)*; **~ donna** women's wear; **~ sportivo** sportswear; **~ uomo** menswear.

abbinare *vt*: **~ qc (a qc)** to link sthg (to sthg).

abboccare *vi* to bite.

abboccato, -a *agg* sweetish.

abbonamento *sm (a giornale)* subscription; *(a autobus, teatro)* season ticket; **fare l'~ (a qc)** *(a giornale)* to take out a subscription (to sthg); *(a autobus, teatro)* to buy a season ticket (for sthg).

abbonarsi *vr*: **~ (a qc)** *(a autobus, teatro)* to buy a season ticket (for sthg); *(a giornale)* to subscribe (to sthg).

abbonato, -a *sm, f (a giornale)* subscriber; *(a autobus, teatro)* season ticket holder; *(a telefono)* subscriber; *(TV)* licence holder.

abbondante *agg* abundant.

abbondanza *sf* abundance.

abbordabile *agg (prezzo)* reasonable.

abbottonare *vt* to button up ❏ **abbottonarsi** *vr*: **abbottonarsi il cappotto** to button up one's coat.

abbottonatura *sf* buttons *(pl)*.

abbozzare *vt (disegno)* to sketch; **~ un sorriso** to smile faintly.

abbozzo *sm* sketch.

abbracciare *vt* to embrace, to hug; *(fede)* to embrace; *(professione)* to take up ❏ **abbracciarsi** *vr* to embrace, to hug one another.

abbraccio *sm* embrace, hug.

abbreviare *vt* to shorten.

abbreviazione *sf* abbreviation.

abbronzante *agg* suntan *(davs)* ◆ *sm* suntan cream.

abbronzare *vt* to tan ❏ **abbronzarsi** *vr* to get a tan.

abbronzato, -a *agg* tanned.

abbronzatura *sf* suntan.

abbrustolire *vt (pane)* to toast; *(caffè)* to roast.

abdicare *vi* to abdicate.

abete *sm* fir tree.

abile *agg (bravo)* capable; *(mossa, manovra)* skilful; *(idoneo)*: **~ (a qc)** fit (for sthg).

abilità *sf (bravura)* ability; *(astuzia)* cleverness.

abilmente *avv (con bravura)* skilfully; *(con astuzia)* cleverly.

abisso *sm* abyss.

abitacolo *sm (di auto)* inside; *(di aereo)* cockpit, cabin; *(di camion)* cab.

abitante *smf (di paese)* inhabitant; *(di casa)* occupant.

abitare *vi* to live ♦ *vt* to live in; **dove abita?** where do you live?; **abito a Roma** I live in Rome; **abito in Italia** I live in Italy.

abitato, -a *agg (casa)* occupied; *(paese)* inhabited ♦ *sm* built-up area.

abitazione *sf* house.

abito *sm (da donna)* dress; *(da uomo)* suit; **~ da sera** evening dress ❑ **abiti** *smpl* clothes.

abituale *agg* usual.

abitualmente *avv* usually.

abituare *vt* to accustom; **~ qn a fare qc** to accustom sb to doing sthg ❑ **abituarsi** *vr (adattarsi)*: **abituarsi a qc** to get used to sthg; **abituarsi a fare qc** to get used to doing sthg.

abitudine *sf* habit; **aver l'~ di fare qc** to be in the habit of doing sthg; **per ~** out of habit.

abolire *vt (tassa)* to abolish; *(legge)* to repeal; *(eliminare)* to eliminate.

aborigeno, -a *sm, f* aborigine.

abortire *vi (accidentalmente)* to miscarry; *(volontariamente)* to have an abortion.

aborto *sm (volontario)* abortion; **~ (spontaneo)** miscarriage.

abrogare *vt (legge)* to repeal.

Abruzzo *sm*: **l'~** the Abruzzo *(region of central Italy)*.

abside *sf* apse.

abusare : abusare di *v + prep (posizione, potere)* to take advantage of; *(persona)* to rape; **~ dell'alcool** to drink too much.

abusivo, -a *agg* unauthorized, unlawful.

abuso *sm (eccesso)* overindulgence; *(uso illecito)* abuse.

a.C. *(abbr di avanti Cristo)* BC.

accademia *sf* academy, school; **~ di belle arti** fine arts academy.

accadere *vi* to happen.

accaduto *sm*: **raccontare l'~** to describe what happened.

accalcarsi *vr* to crowd.

accampamento *sm* camp.

accampare *vt (truppe)* to encamp; *(richieste)* to make; *(diritti)* to assert ❑ **accamparsi** *vr (in tende)* to camp; *(fig: in alloggio)* to camp (out).

accanimento *sm (tenacia)* tenacity; *(odio)* fury.

accanito, -a *agg (odio)* fierce; *(lavoratore)* assiduous; **fumatore ~** chain smoker.

accanto *avv* nearby ♦ *agg inv* next door ♦ *prep*: **~ a** beside.

accaparrare *vt (fare incetta)* to buy up; *(voti, favore)* to secure, to gain; **accaparrarsi qc** to secure sthg for o.s.

accappatoio *sm* bathrobe.

accarezzare *vt (persona, animale)* to caress, to stroke; *(fig: idea)* to toy with.

accattone, -a *sm, f* beggar.

accavallare *vt (gambe)* to cross ❑ **accavallarsi** *vr (eventi)* to overlap.

accecare *vt (rendere cieco)* to blind; *(abbagliare)* to dazzle.

accedere *vi*: **~ a qc** to gain access to sthg.

accelerare *vi* to accelerate ♦ *vt* to speed up.

accelerato, -a agg quick ♦ sm stopping train.

acceleratore sm accelerator.

accendere vt (fuoco, sigaretta) to light; (radio, luce, fornello, motore) to turn on; (speranza, odio) to arouse; scusi, ha da ~? excuse me, have you got a light? □ **accendersi** vr (prendere fuoco) to catch fire; (entrare in funzione) to start up.

accendigas sm inv lighter for gas ring.

accendino sm (cigarette) lighter.

accennare vt (menzionare) to mention; (indicare) to point to; ~ un sorriso to half-smile □ **accennare a** v + prep (menzionare) to mention; (alludere a) to hint at; (dare segno di) to show signs of.

accensione sf ignition.

accentare vt (parola, sillaba) to stress.

accento sm accent; **mettere l'~ su qc** to stress sthg.

accentuare vt (differenze, difetto, pregio) to emphasize □ **accentuarsi** vr to become more marked.

accerchiare vt to encircle, to surround.

accertamento sm check.

accertare vt to check □ **accertarsi di** vr + prep to make sure of.

acceso, -a pp → **accendere** ♦ agg (fuoco, sigaretta) lighted; (radio, luce, motore) on; (colore) bright.

accessibile agg (luogo) accessible; (prezzo) affordable.

accesso sm (entrata) access; (MED) fit; (fig: impeto) outburst.

accessori smpl accessories.

accettare vt to accept; (proposta) to agree to; ~ **di fare qc** to agree to do sthg; **'si accettano carte di credito'** 'credit cards welcome'.

accettazione sf (locale) reception; **'~ bagagli'** 'check-in'.

acchiappare vt to catch.

acciacco, -chi sm ailment.

acciaio sm steel; ~ **inossidabile** stainless steel.

accidentale agg accidental.

accidentalmente avv accidentally.

accidentato, -a agg uneven.

accidenti esclam (con rabbia) blast!, damn!; (con stupore) good heavens!

acciuffare vt to catch.

acciuga, -ghe sf anchovy; **acciughe al limone** fresh anchovies marinated in lemon juice and dressed with oil.

acclamare vt (applaudire) to cheer, to applaud; (eleggere) to acclaim.

accludere vt to enclose.

accogliente agg cosy.

accoglienza sf welcome.

accogliere vt to receive; (dare il benvenuto) to welcome.

accoltellare vt to knife.

accomodare vt to repair □ **accomodarsi** vr (sedersi) to sit down; (venire avanti) to come in; **s'accomodi!** (si sieda) take a seat!; (venga avanti) come in!

accompagnamento sm accompaniment.

accompagnare vt (persona) to go/come with, to accompany; (piatto, abito) to go with; (con musica) to accompany.

accompagnatore, -trice sm, f companion; ~ **turistico** tourist guide.

acconsentire vi: ~ (a qc) to agree (to sthg).

accontentare vt to satisfy ❑ **accontentarsi: accontentarsi di** v + prep to be satisfied with.

acconto sm down payment; **dare un** ~ to pay a deposit; **in** ~ on account.

accorciare vt to shorten.

accordare vt (strumento) to tune; (concedere) to grant; (colori) to match ❑ **accordarsi** vr (mettersi d'accordo) to agree.

accordo sm (patto) agreement; (armonia) harmony; **d'~!** all right!; **andare d'~ con qn** to get on well with sb; **essere d'~ con** to agree; **mettersi d'~ con qn** (trovare un accordo) to reach an agreement with sb; (per appuntamento) to make an arrangement with sb.

accorgersi: accorgersi di v + prep to notice.

accorrere vi (in aiuto) to rush up; (verso un luogo) to rush.

accorto, -a pp → accorgersi ♦ agg shrewd.

accostare vt (persona) to approach; (porta) to leave ajar; (avvicinare): ~ **qc a qc** to move sthg near sthg ♦ vi to pull in; (nave) to come alongside; (cambiare rotta) to change course; (in auto) to draw up.

accreditare vt (fatto, notizia) to confirm; (denaro) to credit.

accrescere vt to increase ❑ **accrescersi** vr to grow.

accucciarsi vr (cane) to lie down.

accudire vt (malato, bambino) to look after ❑ **accudire a** v + prep (casa, faccende) to attend to.

accumulare vt to accumulate; (denaro) to save; (accatastare) to pile up.

accurato, -a agg (lavoro) careful; (persona) thorough.

accusa sf (di una colpa) accusation; (DIR) charge.

accusare vt: ~ **qn (di qc)** (incolpare) to accuse sb of sthg; (DIR) to charge.

acerbo, -a agg unripe.

acero sm maple.

aceto sm vinegar.

acetone sm (per unghie) nail varnish remover.

ACI sm (abbr di Automobile Club d'Italia) = AA (Br), = AAA (Am).

acidità sf: ~ **di stomaco** heartburn.

acido, -a agg (sapore) sour; (commento, persona) sharp ♦ sm acid.

acino sm grape.

acne sf acne.

acqua sf water; **sott'~** underwater; ~ **corrente** running water; ~ **cotta** Tuscan soup made from stale bread, onions and tomatoes; ~ **dolce** fresh water; ~ **minerale (gassata/naturale)** (carbonated/still) mineral water; ~ **ossigenata** hydrogen peroxide; ~ **del rubinetto** tap water; ~ **salata** salt water; ~

tonica tonic water; **acque termali** hot springs; **~ in bocca!** keep it to yourself!; **'~ non potabile'** 'not drinking water'.

acquaforte (*pl* **acqueforti**) *sf* etching.

acquaio *sm* sink.

acquamarina (*pl* **acquemarine**) *sf* aquamarine.

acquaragia *sf* turpentine.

acquario *sm* aquarium ▫ **Acquario** *sm* Aquarius.

acquasanta *sf* holy water.

acquàtico, -a, -ci, -che *agg* (*pianta, animale*) aquatic; (*SPORT*) water (*dav s*).

acquavite *sf* brandy.

acquazzone *sm* cloudburst.

acquedotto *sm* aqueduct.

acqueo *agg m* → **vapore**.

acquerello *sm* watercolour.

acquirente *smf* buyer.

acquisire *vt* (*ottenere*) to acquire.

acquistare *vt* (*comperare*) to buy; (*ottenere*) to acquire.

acquisto *sm* purchase; **fare acquisti** to shop.

acquolina *sf*: **far venire l'~ in bocca a qn** to make sb's mouth water.

acquoso, -a *agg* watery.

acrìlico, -a, -ci, -che *agg & sm* acrylic.

acròbata, -i, -e *smf* acrobat.

acrobazia *sf* (*di acrobata*) acrobatic feat; (*di aereo*) stunt.

acròpoli *sf inv* acropolis.

aculeo *sm* (*di vespa*) sting; (*di riccio*) spine; (*di pianta*) prickle.

acume *sm* acumen.

acùstico, -a, -ci, -che *agg* acoustic.

acuto, -a *agg* (*voce, suono*) high-pitched; (*intenso*) intense; (*appuntito*) pointed; (*intelligente*) sharp; (*MAT*) acute.

ad → **a**.

adagio *avv* slowly; **'entrare/uscire ~'** sign warning drivers to enter or leave side roads etc slowly.

adattamento *sm* (*adeguamento, di opera*) adaptation; (*modifica*) adjustment.

adattare *vt* to adapt ▫ **adattarsi** *vr*: **adattarsi (a qc)** (*adeguarsi*) to adapt (to sthg).

adatto, -a *agg*: **~ (a)** suitable (for); **~ a fare qc** suitable to do sthg.

addebitare *vt* to debit.

addestramento *sm* training.

addestrare *vt* to train.

addetto, -a *agg* (*persona*) responsible ♦ *sm, f* person responsible; **~ stampa** press attaché; **gli addetti ai lavori** (*fig*) the experts.

addio *esclam* goodbye!

addirittura *avv* (*perfino*) even (*direttamente*) directly ♦ *esclam* really?

addirsi : addirsi a *vr + prep* to be suitable for.

additivo *sm* additive.

addizionale *agg* additional.

addizione *sf* addition.

addobbo *sm* decoration; **addobbi natalizi** Christmas decorations.

addolcire *vt* to sweeten.

affanno

addolorare *vt* to sadden □
addolorarsi *vr* to upset o.s.

addome *sm* abdomen.

addomesticare *vt* to house-
train.

addormentare *vt* to send to
sleep □ **addormentarsi** *vr* to fall
asleep.

addossare *vt* (*al muro*) to lean;
(*attribuire*) to lay.

addosso *avv* (*sulla persona*) on ◆
prep: ~ **a** (*su*) on; (*contro* again);
mettersi qc ~ to put sth on; **dare**
~ **a** (*criticare*) to attack; **eravamo
uno** ~ **all'altro** we were right next
to each other.

adeguare *vt:* ~ **qc a qc** to adjust
sth to sth □ **adeguarsi** *vr:*
adeguarsi a qc to adapt to sth.

adeguato, -a *agg* adequate.

adempiere *vt* (*compiere*) to
carry out; (*esaudire*) to grant.

adenoidi *sfpl* adenoids.

aderente *agg* (*attillato*) close-
fitting; (*adesivo*) adhesive.

aderire *vi:* ~ **a qc** (*attaccarsi*) to
stick to sth; (*partito*) to join sth;
(*proposta*) to support sth; (*richiesta*) to agree to sth.

adesivo, -a *agg* adhesive ◆ *sm*
(*etichetta*) sticky label.

adesso *avv* (*ora*) now; (*tra poco*)
any moment now; (*poco fa*) just
now.

adiacente *agg* adjacent.

adibire *vt:* ~ **qc a qc** to use sth
as sth.

Adige *sm:* **l'**~ the River Adige.

adirarsi *vr* to get angry.

adocchiare *vt* (*scorgere*) to

glimpse; (*guardare*) to eye.

adolescente *smf* adolescent.

adolescenza *sf* adolescence.

adoperare *vt* to use.

adorabile *agg* adorable.

adorare *vt* (*persona, cosa*) to
adore; (*divinità*) to worship.

adottare *vt* (*bambino*) to adopt;
(*misure, decisione*) to take.

adottivo, -a *agg* (*figlio, patria*)
adopted; (*genitori*) adoptive.

adozione *sf* adoption.

adriatico, -a, -ci, -che *agg*
Adriatic ◆ **Adriatico** *sm:*
l'Adriatico the Adriatic (Sea).

adulterio *sm* adultery.

adulto, -a *agg & sm, f* (*di età*)
adult.

aerare *vt* to air.

aereo, -a *agg* air ◆ *sm*
(aero)plane, aircraft; ~ **da turismo**
light aircraft.

aerobica *sf* aerobics (*sg*).

aeronautica *sf* (*aviazione*) airforce.

aeroplano *sm* (aero)plane (*Br*),
airplane (*Am*).

aeroporto *sm* airport.

aerosol *sm* aerosol.

A.F. (*abbr di alta frequenza*) HF.

afa *sf* closeness.

affabile *agg* affable.

affacciarsi *vr* (*mostrarsi*) to
show o.s. □ **affacciarsi su** *vr +
prep* to show o.s. at.

affamato, -a *agg* starving.

affannarsi *vr* (*stancarsi*) to tire
o.s.; (*agitarsi*) to worry.

affanno *sm* (*di respiro*) breath-
lessness; (*ansia*) worry.

affare *sm* business; *(faccenda)* business, affair; *(occasione)* bargain; *(fam: cosa)* thing; **è un ~!** it's a bargain!; **affari** business *(sg)*; **per affari** on business; **fare affari con** to do business with; **Affari Esteri** Foreign Affairs.

affascinante *agg* charming.

affascinare *vt* to charm, to fascinate.

affaticarsi *vr* to get tired.

affatto *avv* completely; **non ... ~** not ... at all; **niente ~** not at all.

affermare *vt* to affirm ▢ **affermarsi** *vr* to make a name for o.s.

affermativo, -a *agg* affirmative.

affermazione *sf (dichiarazione)* affirmation; *(successo)* success.

afferrare *vt (prendere)* to seize; *(capire)* to grasp ▢ **afferrarsi a** *vr* + *prep* to grasp at.

affettare *vt* to slice.

affettato, -a *agg (a fette)* sliced; *(artificioso)* affected ♦ *sm* sliced cold meat.

affetto, -a *sm (attaccamento)* affection ♦ *agg*: **essere ~ da** *(malattia)* to suffer from.

affettuoso, -a *agg* affectionate.

affezionarsi *vr*: **~ a** to become fond of.

affezionato, -a *agg* fond.

affidamento *sm (DIR)* custody; *(fiducia)*: **fare ~ su** to rely on.

affidare *vt* to entrust; **~ qn/qc a qn** to entrust sb/sthg to sb.

affiggere *vt (cartello, poster)* to stick up.

affilare *vt* to sharpen.

affilato, -a *agg (lama, punta)* sharp.

affinché *cong* in order that, so that.

affinità *sf inv* affinity.

affissione *sf*: 'divieto di ~' 'post no bills'.

affisso, -a *pp* → **affiggere** ♦ *sm* poster.

affittare *vt (dare in affitto)* to let, to rent (out); *(prendere in affitto)* to rent; **'affittasi'** 'to let'.

affitto *sm* rent; **dare in ~** to let, to rent (out); **prendere in ~** to rent.

affliggere *vt* to torment ▢ **affliggersi** *vr* to torment o.s.

afflitto, -a *pp* → **affliggere** ♦ *agg* afflicted.

affluente *sm* tributary.

affluire *vi (fiume)* to flow; *(gente, merce)* to pour in.

affogare *vi & vt* to drown.

affogato *sm (gelato)* ice cream or 'semifreddo' with coffee, whisky or a liqueur poured over it.

affollato, -a *agg* crowded.

affondare *vi & vt* to sink.

affrancare *vt* to stamp.

affrancatura *sf* postage.

affresco, -schi *sm* fresco.

affrettare *vt* to hurry ▢ **affrettarsi** *vr* to hurry.

affrontare *vt (nemico)* to confront; *(spesa)* to meet; *(argomento)* to tackle.

affronto *sm* insult.

affumicato, -a *agg (cibo)* smoked; *(vetro)* tinted; *(annerito)* blackened.

afoso, -a *agg* close.

Africa *sf*: l'~ Africa.

africano, -a *agg & sm, f* African.

afta *sf* mouth ulcer.

agenda *sf* diary.

agente *sm* agent; ~ **di polizia** policeman (*f* policewoman); **gli agenti atmosferici** the elements.

agenzia *sf* (*impresa*) agency; (*succursale*) branch; ~ **di cambio** bureau de change; ~ **immobiliare** estate agent's (*Br*), real-estate office (*Am*); ~ **di viaggi** travel agency.

agevolare *vt* (*facilitare*) to facilitate; (*aiutare*) to help.

agevolazione *sf*: ~ **di pagamento** easy (payment) terms (*pl*).

aggeggio *sm* thing.

aggettivo *sm* adjective.

agghiacciante *agg* terrible.

aggiornare *vt* (*persona, opera*) to bring up-to-date; (*seduta*) to postpone ❑ **aggiornarsi** *vr* to bring o.s. up-to-date.

aggiornato, -a *agg* up-to-date.

aggirare *vt* to get round ❑ **aggirarsi** *vr* to wander; **aggirarsi su** *vr + prep* to be about.

aggiudicare *vt* to award ❑ **aggiudicarsi** *vr* to gain.

aggiungere *vt* to add.

aggiunta *sf*: **in** ~ in addition.

aggiunto, -a *pp* → **aggiungere**.

aggiustare *vt* to mend ❑ **aggiustarsi** *vr* to come to an agreement.

agglomerato *sm*: ~ **urbano** built-up area.

aggrapparsi *vr* to cling on; ~ **a** to cling to.

aggravare *vt* to make worse ❑ **aggravarsi** *vr* to get worse.

aggredire *vt* to attack.

aggressione *sf* attack.

aggressivo, -a *agg* aggressive.

agguato *sm* ambush.

agiato, -a *agg* (*persona*) well-off; (*vita*) comfortable.

agile *agg* agile, nimble.

agio *sm*: **essere a proprio** ~ to feel at ease; **mettersi a proprio** ~ to make o.s. at home.

agire *vi* (*comportarsi*) to act; ~ **da** (*fare da*) to act as.

agitare *vt* to shake; (*mano*) to wave; (*coda*) to wag; (*turbare*) to upset; '~ **prima dell'uso**' 'shake before use' ❑ **agitarsi** *vr* (*turbarsi*) to get worked up; (*muoversi*) to writhe; (*mare*) to get rough; **agitarsi nel letto** to toss and turn in bed.

agitato, -a *agg* (*inquieto*) worried; (*mare*) rough.

agitazione *sf* (*inquietudine*) agitation; (*subbuglio*) turmoil.

agli = **a + gli**, → **a**.

aglio *sm* garlic.

agnello *sm* lamb; ~ **alla norcina** leg of lamb larded with ham, garlic, parsley and marjoram.

agnolotti *smpl* ravioli stuffed with pork, salami, Parmesan cheese and spinach.

ago (*pl* **aghi**) *sm* needle.

agonia *sf* agony.

agopuntura *sf* acupuncture.

agosto *sm* August, → **settembre**.

agricolo, -a *agg* agricultural.

agricoltore *sm (contadino)* farm worker; *(imprenditore)* farmer.

agricoltura *sf* agriculture.

agriturismo *sm* farm holidays *(pl)*.

---

i ◆ **AGRITURISMO**

A form of tourism popular in Italy, "agriturismo" offers people the opportunity to spend their summer holiday on traditional farms in the Italian countryside. This type of holiday is particularly popular with those who enjoy the outdoors lifestyle, good home cooking and healthy exercise in beautiful rural surroundings. As well as participating in a range of sports such as horseriding, walking, tennis and bowls, holidaymakers also have the opportunity to help on the farm.

---

agrodolce *sm*: in ~ in a sweet and sour sauce.

agrume *sm* citrus fruit.

aguzzare *vt* to sharpen; ~ le orecchie to prick up one's ears.

aguzzo, -a *agg* sharp.

ahi *esclam* ouch!

ai = a + i, → a.

Aia *sf*: l'~ The Hague.

AIDS *sm o sf* AIDS.

A.I.G. *(abbr di Associazione Italiana Alberghi per la Gioventù)* = YHA.

air-terminal [ər 'tərminəl] *sm inv* air terminal.

aiuola *sf* flower bed.

aiutante *smf* assistant.

aiutare *vt* to help; ~ qn (a fare qc) to help sb (to do sthg).

aiuto *sm* help, assistance; *(assistente)* assistant; ~! help!; chiedere ~ to ask for help; essere di ~ a qn to be of help to sb; venire in ~ di qn to come to sb's aid.

al = a + il, → a.

ala *(pl* **ali)** *sf* wing; *(giocatore)* winger.

alano *sm* Great Dane.

alba *sf* dawn; all'~ at dawn.

albanese *agg & smf* Albanian.

Albania *sf*: l'~ Albania.

albergatore, -trice *sm, f* hotelier.

albergo, -ghi *sm* hotel; ~ diurno *public toilets where people can also wash, have a haircut, get their clothes ironed etc.*; ~ per la gioventù youth hostel.

albero *sm* tree; *(di nave)* mast; *(di macchina)* shaft; ~ genealogico family tree; ~ di Natale Christmas tree.

albese *sf thin slices of raw beef served with oil, lemon and mushrooms or Parmesan cheese.*

albicocca, -che *sf* apricot.

albino, -a *agg & sm, f* albino.

album *sm inv* album; ~ da disegno sketch book.

albume *sm* egg white.

alcol = alcool.

alcolico, -a, -ci, -che *agg* alcoholic ◆ *sm* alcoholic drink.

alcolizzato, -a *sm, f* alcoholic.

alcool *sm* alcohol.

alcuno, -a agg s: non ... ~ (nessuno) no, not any ☐ **alcuni, -e** agg pl some, a few ♦ pron pl some; alcuni di some of, a few of.

aldilà sm: l'~ the next life.

alfabeto sm alphabet.

alfiere sm (portabandiera) standard bearer; (negli scacchi) bishop.

alga, -ghe sf (di mare) seaweed.

algebra sf algebra.

Algeria sf: l'~ Algeria.

aliante sm glider.

alibi sm inv alibi.

alice sf anchovy; **alici areganate** anchovies cooked in oil, vinegar, garlic, parsley and oregano.

alienazione sf (pazzia) insanity; (DIR) transfer.

alieno, -a sm, f alien.

alimentare agg food (dav s) ♦ vt (nutrire) to feed; (fig: rafforzare) to strengthen; (rifornire) to supply ☐ **alimentari** smpl (cibi) foodstuffs; negozio di alimentari grocer's.

alimentazione sf (nutrimento) nutrition; (rifornimento) supply.

alimento sm food ☐ **alimenti** smpl alimony (sg).

aliscafo sm hydrofoil.

alito sm breath.

all' = a + l', → a.

alla = a + la, → a.

allacciare vt (scarpe) to tie up; (cintura, vestito) to fasten; (telefono, gas) to connect ☐ **allacciarsi** vr to fasten.

allagare vt to flood ☐ **allagarsi** vr to flood.

allargare vt (ampliare) to widen; (aprire) to open ☐ **allargarsi** vr to widen.

allarmare vt to alarm.

allarme sm alarm; ~ d'incendio fire alarm; **dare l'~** to give the alarm.

allattare vt (al seno) to breastfeed; (artificialmente) to bottle-feed.

alle = a + le, → a.

alleanza sf alliance.

allearsi vr to form an alliance.

allegare vt to enclose.

alleggerire vt to lighten.

allegria sf cheerfulness.

allegro, -a agg (contento) cheerful; (colore) bright; (vivace) lively ♦ sm (MUS) allegro.

allenamento sm training; tenersi in ~ to keep in training.

allenare vt to train ☐ **allenarsi** vr to train.

allenatore, -trice sm, f trainer, coach.

allentare vt (vite, nodo) to loosen; (sorveglianza, disciplina) to relax ☐ **allentarsi** vr to work loose.

allergia sf allergy.

allergico, -a, -ci, -che agg allergic; **essere ~ a qc** to be allergic to sthg.

allestire vt (mostra, spettacolo) to get ready.

allevamento sm (attività) breeding, rearing; (animali) stock.

allevare vt (animale) to breed; (bambino) to bring up.

allibratore sm bookmaker.

allievo, -a sm, f pupil, student.

alligatore sm alligator.

allineare vt to align ▫ **allinear-si** vr (mettersi in fila) to line up.

allo = a + lo, → **a**.

allodola sf skylark.

alloggiare vi to stay.

alloggio sm accommodation.

allontanare vt (mandare via) to send away; (pericolo) to avert ♦ **allontanarsi** vr to go away.

allora avv then ♦ cong (in tal caso) then; (ebbene) well; **da** ~ since then.

alloro sm laurel.

alluce sm big toe.

allucinante agg (spaventoso) terrifying; (incredibile) incredible.

allucinazione sf hallucination.

alludere : **alludere a** v + prep to allude to.

alluminio sm aluminium.

allungare vt (accrescere) to lengthen; (gambe) to stretch; (diluire) to water down ▫ **allungarsi** vr (accrescersi) to lengthen; (distendersi) to stretch out.

allusione sf allusion; **fare allusioni** to drop hints.

alluso pp → **alludere**

alluvione sf flood.

almeno avv at least.

Alpi sfpl: **le** ~ the Alps.

alpinismo sm climbing.

alpinista, -i, -e smf climber.

alpino, -a agg alpine.

alquanto avv somewhat.

alt esclam halt!

altalena sf (con funi) swing; (su asse) see-saw (Br), teeter-totter (Am).

altare sm altar.

alterare vt to affect ▫ **alterarsi** vr (merce) to be affected; (irritarsi) to get angry.

alternare vt: ~ **qn/qc a** to alternate sb/sthg with ▫ **alternarsi** vr to alternate.

alternativa sf alternative.

alternato, -a agg alternate; (corrente) alternating.

alterno, -a agg alternate.

altezza sf (statura, di cosa) height; (di acqua) depth; (altitudine) altitude.

altezzoso, -a agg haughty.

altipiano = altopiano.

altitudine sf altitude.

alto, -a agg high; (persona, edificio, albero) tall; (profondo) deep; (suono, voce) loud ♦ sm top ♦ avv high; (parlare) loud; **è** ~ **due metri** he's two metres tall; **ad alta voce** out loud, aloud; **alta moda** haute couture; **dall'**~ **in basso** from top to bottom; **alti e bassi** ups and downs; **in** ~ upwards.

altoparlante sm loudspeaker.

altopiano (pl altipiani) sm plateau.

altrettanto, -a agg (tempo, latte) as much; (persone, libri) as many ♦ pron the same ♦ avv equally; **auguri! – grazie, ~!** all the best! – thank you, the same to you!

altrimenti avv (se no) otherwise; (diversamente) differently.

altro, -a agg **1.** (diverso) other; **ha un** ~ **modello?** have you got another o a different model? **2.** (supplementare) other; **un** ~

caffè? another coffee?

3. *(rimanente)* other; **gli altri passeggeri sono pregati di restare al loro posto** would all remaining passengers please stay in their seats.

4. *(nel tempo):* **l'~ giorno** the other day; **l'altr'anno** last year; **l'~ ieri** the day before yesterday; **domani l'~** the day after tomorrow.

5. *(in espressioni):* **è tutt'~ che bello** it's far from being beautiful; **d'altra parte** on the other hand.

◆ *pron:* **l'~** the other (one); **un ~** another (one); **gli altri** *(il prossimo)* others, other people; **l'uno o l'~** one or the other; **se non** ~ at least; **senz'~** of course; **tra l'~** among other things.

altroché *esclam* and how!

altronde : d'altronde *avv* on the other hand.

altrove *avv* elsewhere.

altrui *agg inv* other people's.

altruista, -i, -e *agg* altruistic.

altura *sf* height.

alunno, -a *sm, f* pupil.

alveare *sm* beehive.

alzare *vt (oggetto)* to lift; *(prezzi, volume, voce)* to raise ❑ **alzarsi** *vr (dal letto, dalla sedia)* to get up; *(aumentare)* to rise; *(vento)* to get up.

amaca, -che *sf* hammock.

amalgamare *vt* to combine ◆

amalgamarsi *vr* to combine.

amante *smf* lover ◆ *agg:* **~ di qc** fond of sthg.

amare *vt (persona)* to love; *(cosa)* to be fond of.

amareggiato, -a *agg* embit-

tered.

amarena *sf* sour black cherry.

amaretto *sm (biscotto)* macaroon; *(liquore)* a liqueur made with almonds.

amarezza *sf* bitterness.

amaro, -a *agg (sapore)* bitter; *(spiacevole)* nasty.

ambasciata *sf* embassy.

ambasciatore, -trice *sm, f* ambassador.

ambedue *agg inv & pron* both.

ambientare *vt (film)* to set ❑ **ambientarsi** *vr* to get used to a place.

ambiente *sm (natura)* environment; *(cerchia)* surroundings *(pl)*.

ambiguo, -a *agg (parola, testo)* ambiguous; *(comportamento, persona)* dubious.

ambizione *sf* ambition.

ambizioso, -a *agg* ambitious.

ambra *sf* amber.

ambulante *agg* itinerant.

ambulanza *sf* ambulance.

ambulatorio *sm* surgery.

America *sf:* **l'~** America; **l'~ latina** Latin America.

americano, -a *agg & sm, f* American.

amianto *sm* asbestos.

amichevole *agg* friendly.

amicizia *sf* friendship; **fare ~ (con qn)** to make friends (with sb).

amico, -a, -ci, -che *sm, f* friend; **~ del cuore** best friend.

amido *sm* starch.

ammaccare *vt* to dent.

ammaccatura *sf (su metallo)* dent; *(su gamba)* bruise.

ammaestrare *vt* to train.

ammainare *vt* to lower.

ammalarsi *vr* to fall ill.

ammalato, -a *agg* ◆ *sm, f* patient.

ammassare *vt* to amass, to pile up.

ammazzare *vt* to kill □

ammazzarsi *vr* to kill o.s.

ammenda *sf* fine.

ammesso, -a *pp* → **ammettere**.

ammettere *vt* (*riconoscere*) to admit; (*permettere*) to allow; (*a esame, scuola*) to accept; (*supporre*) to suppose, to assume.

amministrare *vt* to run, to manage.

amministratore *sm* (*di condominio*) manager; **~ delegato** managing director.

ammirare *vt* to admire.

ammiratore, -trice *sm, f* admirer.

ammirazione *sf* admiration.

ammissione *sf* (*a esame*) admittance.

ammobiliato, -a *agg* furnished; **non ~** unfurnished.

ammollo *sm* soaking; **lasciare qc in ~** to leave sthg to soak.

ammoniaca *sf* ammonia.

ammonire *vt* (*rimproverare*) to warn; (*SPORT*) to book.

ammonizione *sf* (*rimprovero*) warning; (*SPORT*) booking.

ammontare : ammontare a *v + prep* to amount to.

ammorbidente *sm* fabric softener.

ammorbidire *vt* (*rendere morbido*) to soften.

ammortizzatore *sm* shock absorber.

ammucchiare *vt* to pile up.

ammuffito, -a *agg* mouldy.

ammutinamento *sm* mutiny.

amnistia *sf* amnesty.

amo *sm* bait.

amore *sm* love; **fare l'~** (con qn) to make love (with sb); **amor proprio** self-esteem.

ampio, -a *agg* (*vasto*) wide; (*spazioso*) spacious; (*abbondante*) abundant.

ampliare *vt* to widen.

amplificatore *sm* amplifier.

amputare *vt* to amputate.

amuleto *sm* amulet.

anabbaglianti *smpl* dipped headlights (*Br*), dimmed headlights (*Am*).

anagrafe *sf* (*ufficio*) registry office (*Br*), office of vital statistics (*Am*).

analcolico, -a, -ci, -che *agg* non-alcoholic ◆ *sm* soft drink.

analfabeta, -i, -e *agg & smf* illiterate.

analisi *sf inv* (*studio*) analysis; (*MED*) test; **~ del sangue** blood test.

analista, -i, -e *smf* analyst.

analizzare *vt* to analyse.

analogo, -a, -ghi, -ghe *agg* similar.

ananas *sm inv* pineapple.

anarchia *sf* anarchy.

ANAS *sf* (*abbr di Azienda Nazionale Autonoma delle Strade*) national road board.

anatomia *sf* anatomy.

anatomico, -a, -ci, -che *agg (sedile)* contoured.

anatra *sf* duck.

anca, -che *sf* hip.

anche *cong (pure)* too; *(persino)* even.

ancora¹ *sf* anchor.

ancora² *avv (tuttora)* still; *(persino)* even; *(di nuovo)* again; *(di più)* more, still; ~ **più bello** even more beautiful; ~ **un po' a bit more;** ~ **una volta** once more; **non** ~ not yet.

andare *vi* 1. *(muoversi)* to go; **scusi, per** ~ **alla stazione?** could you tell me the way to the station, please?; ~ **a Napoli** to go to Naples; ~ **avanti/indietro** to go forwards/backwards; ~ **in vacanza** to go on holiday *(Br)*, to go on vacation *(Am)*.

2. *(strada)* to go.

3. *(indica uno stato)*: **come va?** how are you?; ~ **bene/male (persona)** to be well/unwell; *(situazione)* to go well/badly.

4. *(piacere)*: **il suo modo di fare non mi va** I don't like the way he behaves; **non mi va di mangiare** I don't feel like eating.

5. *(funzionare)* to work.

6. *(con participio passato)*: **dove va messa la chiave?** where does the key go?; ~ **perso** *(essere smarrito)* to get lost.

7. *(in espressioni)*: ~ **bene a qn** *(come misura)*: **queste scarpe mi vanno bene** these shoes fit (me); **ti va bene andare al cinema?** do you feel like going to the cinema?; ~ **via** *(partire)* to leave; *(macchia)* to

come out.

♦ *sm*: **a lungo** ~ in time.

❑ **andarsene** *vr* to go away.

andata *sf*: **all'**~ on the way there; ~ **e ritorno** return (ticket) *(Br)*, round-trip ticket *(Am)*.

andatura *sf* walk.

andirivieni *sm inv* coming and going.

anello *sm (da dito)* ring; *(di catena)* link; ~ **di fidanzamento** engagement ring.

anemia *sf* anaemia.

anestesia *sf* anaesthesia.

anestetico *sm* anaesthetic.

anfiteatro *sm* amphitheatre.

anfora *sf* amphora.

angelo *sm* angel.

angina *sf* tonsillitis; ~ **pectoris** angina.

anglicano, -a *agg* Anglican.

angolo *sm* corner; ~ **cottura** kitchen area; **all'**~ on the corner.

angora *sf*: **d'**~ angora *(dav s)*.

angoscia *sf* anguish.

anguilla *sf* eel.

anguria *sf* watermelon.

anice *sm* aniseed.

anidride *sf*: ~ **carbonica** carbon dioxide.

anima *sf* soul.

animale *agg & sm* animal; ~ **domestico** pet.

animatore, -trice *sm, f*: ~ **turistico** entertainment organizer *(in holiday village)*.

animo *sm (mente)* mind; *(cuore)* heart; *(coraggio)*: **perdersi d'**~ to lose heart.

anitra = **anatra**.

annaffiare vt to water.

annaffiatoio sm watering can.

annata sf year; (di vino) vintage.

annegare vt & vi to drown ❑ **annegarsi** vr to drown o.s.

anniversario sm anniversary.

anno sm year; **buon ~!** Happy New Year!; **quanti anni hai?** how old are you?; **ho 21 anni** I'm 21; **un bambino di tre anni** a three-year-old; **~ accademico** academic year; **~ bisestile** leap year; **~ scolastico** school year.

annodare vt to tie.

annoiare vt to bore ❑ **annoiarsi** vr to get bored.

annotare vt (prendere nota) to note down; (commentare) to annotate.

annuale agg annual.

annuario sm yearbook.

annuire vi (con la testa) to nod.

annullare vt (partita, riunione, francobollo) to cancel; (matrimonio) to annul; (rendere vano) to destroy.

annunciare vt to announce; (indicare) to indicate.

annunciatore, -trice sm, f announcer.

Annunciazione sf: **l'~** the Annunciation.

annuncio sm announcement; **~ pubblicitario** advertisement; **annunci economici** classified ads.

annuo, -a agg annual, yearly.

annusare vt to smell.

annuvolamento sm clouding over.

ano sm anus.

anomalo, -a agg anomalous.

anonimo, -a agg anonymous.

anoressia sf anorexia.

anormale agg abnormal ♦ smf abnormal person.

ANSA sf (abbr di Agenzia Nazionale Stampa Associata) national press agency.

ansia sf anxiety.

ansimare vi to pant.

ansioso, -a agg (inquieto) anxious; (impaziente): **~ di fare qc** eager to do sthg.

anta sf (di finestra) shutter; (di armadio) door.

antagonista, -i, -e smf rival.

antartico, -a, -ci, -che agg Antarctic.

Antartide sf: **l'~** Antarctica.

anteguerra sm prewar period.

antenato, -a sm, f ancestor.

antenna sf aerial.

anteprima sf preview; **presentare qc in ~** to preview sthg.

anteriore agg (sedili, ruote) front (dav s); (nel tempo) previous.

antiabbaglianti = **anabbaglianti**.

antibiotico sm antibiotic.

anticamera sf anteroom.

antichità sf inv (passato) antiquity; (oggetto) antique.

anticipare vt (partenza) to bring forward; (denaro) to pay in advance.

anticipo sm (di denaro) advance; (di tempo): **il treno ha 10 minuti d'~** the train is 10 minutes early; **essere/arrivare in ~** to be/arrive early.

antico, -a, -chi, -che agg

(mobili) antique; *(dell'antichità)* ancient.

anticoncezionale *agg & sm* contraceptive.

anticonformista, -i, -e *agg & smf* nonconformist.

anticorpo *sm* antibody.

antidoto *sm* antidote.

antifascista, -i, -e *agg & smf* antifascist.

antifurto *agg inv* antitheft *(dav s)* ◆ *sm* antitheft device.

antigelo *sm inv* antifreeze.

Antille *sfpl*: **le ~** the West Indies.

antimafia *agg inv* anti-Mafia.

antincendio *agg inv* fire *(dav s)*.

antinebbia *agg inv* fog *(dav s)* ◆ *sm inv* fog lamp.

antiorario *agg m* → **senso**.

antipasto *sm* hors d'œuvre; **~ di mare** mixed seafood hors d'œuvre; **~ a scelta** hors d'œuvres chosen from a buffet of grilled or baked vegetables, pickled foods, cold meats etc.

antipatia *sf* antipathy.

antipatico, -a, -ci, -che *agg* unpleasant.

antiquariato *sm (commercio)* antique trade; **oggetti d'~** antiques.

antiquario, -a *sm, f* antique dealer.

antiquato, -a *agg* old-fashioned.

antiruggine *agg inv* rustproof.

antirughe *agg inv* antiwrinkle *(dav s)*.

antisettico, -a, -ci, -che *agg & sm* antiseptic.

antitetanica *sf* antitetanus injection.

antivipera *sm inv* antiviper serum.

antologia *sf* anthology.

anulare *agg* ring *(dav s)* ◆ *sm* ring finger.

anzi *cong (al contrario)* on the contrary; *(o meglio)* or rather.

anziano, -a *(di età)* elderly; *(di carica)* senior ◆ *sm, f (vecchio)* senior citizen.

anziché *cong* rather than.

anzitutto *avv* first of all.

apatia *sf* apathy.

apatico, -a, -ci, -che *agg* apathetic.

ape *sf* bee.

aperitivo *sm* aperitif.

---

i | **APERITIVO**

The tradition of taking an alcoholic or a non-alcoholic drink before lunch or dinner is common throughout Italy. Italians are especially fond of having an aperitif at some point during their Sunday stroll or "passeggiata". Although an aperitif is sometimes served at home, it is more usual to go out to a bar where, in addition to the usual range of drinks, there may be local or house specialities on offer. Drinks are generally accompanied by olives, crisps or other savoury snacks.

---

aperto, -a *pp* → **aprire** ◆ *agg* open ◆ *sm*: **all'~** in the open air.

apertura *sf* opening.

apice *sm* peak; **essere all'~ di** at

to be at the height of sthg.

apicoltura *sf* beekeeping.

apnea *sf*: in ~ *(subacqueo)* without breathing apparatus.

apolide *agg* stateless ◆ *smf* stateless person.

apostolo *sm* apostle.

apostrofo *sm* apostrophe.

appagare *vt* to satisfy.

appannare *vt (vetro)* to mist; *(fig: mente)* to dim □ **appannarsi** *vr (vetro)* to mist up; *(fig: vista, mente)* to grow dim.

apparato *sm (ANAT)* system; *(impianto)* apparatus.

apparecchiare *vt*: ~ la tavola to lay the table.

apparecchio *sm (congegno)* device; *(aereo)* aircraft; *(per i denti)* brace; ~ acustico hearing aid.

apparente *agg* apparent.

apparentemente *avv* apparently.

apparenza *sf*: in ○ all'~ apparently.

apparire *vi (mostrarsi)* to appear; *(sembrare)* to seem.

appariscente *agg* striking.

apparso, -a *pp →* apparire.

appartamento *sm* flat *(Br)*, apartment *(Am)*.

appartenere : appartenere a *v + prep* to belong to.

appassionato, -a *agg* passionate ◆ *sm, f* fan; essere ~ di qc to be keen on sthg.

appello *sm (chiamata)* rollcall; *(DIR)* appeal; fare ~ a to appeal to; fare l'~ to call the roll.

appena *avv (a fatica)* hardly; *(da*

poco) just; *(solo)* only, just ◆ *cong* as soon as; non ~ as soon as.

appendere *vt* to hang up.

appendice *sf* appendix.

appendicite *sf* appendicitis.

Appennini *smpl*: gli ~ the Apennines.

appeso, -a *pp →* appendere.

appetito *sm* appetite; buon ~! enjoy your meal!

appetitoso, -a *agg* appetizing.

appezzamento *sm* plot.

appiattire *vt* to flatten □ **appiattirsi** *vr (al suolo, contro il muro)* to flatten o.s.; *(diventare piatto)* to become flatter.

appiccare *vt*: ~ il fuoco a qc to set fire to sthg.

appiccicare *vt* to stick □ **appiccicarsi** *vr*: appiccicarsi (a) to stick (to); *(fig: persona)* to cling (to).

appieno *avv* fully.

appigliarsi : appigliarsi a *vr + prep (afferrarsi)* to hold on to; *(fig: pretesto)* to cling to.

appiglio *sm (appoggio)* hold; *(fig: pretesto)* pretext.

appisolarsi *vr* to doze off.

applaudire *vt* to applaud.

applauso *sm* applause; fare un ~ to give a round of applause.

applicare *vt* to apply □ **applicarsi** *vr* to apply o.s.

applicazione *sf (di cerotto, pomata)* application; *(attuazione)* enforcement.

appoggiare *vt (per terra, sul tavolo)* to put (down); *(sostenere)* to support; *(al muro)*: ~ qc a ○ contro

qc to lean sthg against sthg □ **appoggiarsi a** *vr + prep* to lean against.

appoggiatesta *sm inv* headrest.

apporre *vt (form)* to add.

appositamente *avv* on purpose; **~ per te** specially for you.

apposito, -a *agg* appropriate.

apposta *avv* deliberately; **fare qc ~** to do sthg on purpose.

apposto, -a *pp →* **apporre**.

apprendere *vt* to learn.

apprendista, -i, -e *smf* apprentice.

apprensivo, -a *agg* apprehensive.

appreso, -a *pp →* **apprendere**.

appretto *sm* starch.

apprezzamento *sm* appreciation.

apprezzare *vt* to appreciate.

approccio *sm* approach.

approdare *vi* to land; **non ~ a niente** to come to nothing.

approdo *sm (atto)* landing; *(luogo)* landing-place.

approfittare : approfittare di *v + prep* to take advantage of.

approfondire *vt (accentuare)* to deepen; *(studiare)* to study in depth.

appropriarsi : appropriarsi di *vr + prep* to appropriate.

approssimativo, -a *agg (calcolo)* approximate; *(conoscenza)* superficial.

approvare *vt (legge, proposta)* to pass; *(comportamento)* to approve of.

approvazione *sf* approval.

appuntamento *sm* appointment; *(amoroso)* date; **dare (un) ~ a qn** to arrange to meet sb; **prendere un ~ con ◆ da qn** to make an appointment with sb.

appuntare *vt (matita)* to sharpen; *(fissare)* to pin; *(annotare)* to note.

appunto *sm (annotazione)* note; *(rimprovero)* reprimand ◆ *avv* exactly.

apribottiglie *sm inv* bottle opener.

aprile *sm* April, → **settembre**.

aprire *vt* to open; *(gas, acqua)* to turn on ◆ *vi* to open; **vai tu ad ~?** can you answer the door?; **'non ~ prima che il treno sia fermo'** 'do not open before the train has stopped' □ **aprirsi** *vr (porta)* to open; *(inchiesta)* to start up; *(confidarsi)*: **aprirsi con qc** to open one's heart to sb.

apriscatole *sm inv* can opener.

aquila *sf* eagle.

aquilone *sm* kite.

Arabia Saudita *sf*: **l'~** Saudi Arabia.

arabo, -a *agg & sm, f* Arab ◆ *sm (lingua)* Arabic.

arachide *sf* peanut.

aragosta *sf* lobster.

arancia, -ce *sf* orange.

aranciata *sf* orange juice.

arancini *smpl* rice balls with a filling of tomatoes and mozzarella cheese (a Sicilian speciality).

arancio *sm* orange tree.

arancione

arancione *agg & sm* orange.

arare *vt* to plough.

aratro *sm* plough.

arazzo *sm* tapestry.

arbitrario, -a *agg* arbitrary.

arbitro *sm* referee.

arbusto *sm* shrub.

archeologia *sf* archaeology.

archeologico, -a, -ci, -che *agg* archaeological.

architetto *sm* architect.

architettura *sf* architecture.

archivio *sm (luogo)* archives *(pl)*; *(raccolta)* files *(pl)*; *(INFORM)* file.

arcipelago, -ghi *sm* archipelago.

arcivescovo *sm* archbishop.

arco, -chi *sm (volta)* arch; *(arma)* bow; *(durata):* **nell'~ di due mesi** in the space of two months.

arcobaleno *sm* rainbow.

ardere *vt & vi* to burn.

ardesia *sf (pietra)* slate.

ardire *vi* to dare ♦ *sm* daring.

ardore *sm* ardour.

area *sf* area; **'~ pedonale'** 'pedestrian precinct'; **~ di servizio** services *(pl)*.

arena *sf* arena.

arenarsi *vr* to run aground.

argenteria *sf* silverware.

Argentina *sf:* **l'~** Argentina.

argentino, -a *agg & sm, f* Argentinian.

argento *sm* silver; **d'~** silver.

argilla *sf* clay.

argine *sm* bank.

argomento *sm (tema)* subject; *(ragionamento)* argument.

arguto, -a *agg (persona)* quick-witted; *(discorso, battuta)* witty.

aria *sf* air; *(aspetto)* appearance; **ha l'~ familiare** he looks familiar; **mandare all'~ qc** to ruin sthg; **all'~ aperta** in the open air; **~ condizionata** air-conditioning; **darsi delle arie** to fancy o.s.

arido, -a *agg (secco)* arid; *(fig: persona, cuore)* cold.

ariete *sm (animale)* ram ❏ **Ariete** *sm* Aries.

aringa, -ghe *sf* herring.

arista *sf* saddle of pork.

aristocratico, -a, -ci, -che *agg* aristocratic ♦ *sm, f* aristocrat.

aritmetica *sf* arithmetic.

Arlecchino *sm* Harlequin.

arma, -i *sf (strumento)* weapon; *(di esercito)* division; **~ da fuoco** firearm.

armadio *sm* cupboard; **~ a muro** built-in cupboard.

armato, -a *agg* armed.

armatura *sf* armour.

armonia *sf* harmony.

arnese *sm (attrezzo)* tool; *(fam: oggetto)* thing.

arnia *sf* beehive.

Arno *sm:* **l'~** the Arno.

aroma, -i *sm (odore)* aroma; *(essenza)* flavouring ❏ **aromi** *mpl* spices.

arpa *sf* harp.

arpione *sm* harpoon.

arrabbiarsi *vr* to get angry.

arrabbiato, -a *agg* angry; **all'arrabbiata → penne.**

arrampicarsi *vr* to climb.

arrangiarsi *vr* to get by.

arredamento sm furnishings (pl).

arredare vt to furnish.

arrendersi vr to surrender.

arrestare vt (catturare) to arrest; (emorragia, flusso) to stop.

arresto sm (cattura) arrest; (fermata) stop; **~ cardiaco** cardiac arrest.

arretrato, -a agg (pagamento, giornale) back (dav s); (sottosviluppato) backward; (sorpassato) old-fashioned ❏ **arretrati** smpl arrears.

arricchire vt to enrich ❏ **arricchirsi** vr to get rich.

arricciacapelli sm inv curling tongs (pl).

arricciare vt (capelli, nastro) to curl; **~ il naso** to wrinkle one's nose.

arrivare vi to arrive; **arriverò a Firenze alle due** I'll get to Florence at two ❏ **arrivare a** v + prep (grado, livello) to reach; **~ a fare qc** (riuscire) to manage to do sthg; (giungere al punto di, osare) to go so far as to do sthg.

arrivederci esclam goodbye!

arrivederla esclam goodbye!

arrivista, -i, -e smf social climber.

arrivo sm arrival; (nello sport) finishing line; **essere in ~** to be arriving; **'arrivi (nazionali/internazionali)'** '(domestic/international) arrivals'.

arrogante agg arrogant.

arrossire vi to blush.

arrostire vt to roast.

arrosto sm roast.

arrotolare vt to roll up.

arrotondare vt (render tondo) to round; (numero) to round off; (stipendio) to add to.

arrugginito, -a agg rusty.

arruolarsi vr to enlist.

arsenale sm (di armi) arsenal; (cantiere) dockyard.

arte sf art; (abilità) skill.

arteria sf artery.

artico, -a, -ci, -che agg Arctic.

articolazione sf joint.

articolo sm article; (merce) article, item; **articoli da regalo** gifts.

Artide sf: **l'~** the Arctic.

artificiale agg artificial.

artigianato sm craftsmanship; **di ~** handcrafted.

artigiano, -a agg craft (dav s) ♦ sm, f craftsman (f craftswoman).

artiglio sm claw.

artista, -i, -e smf artist.

artistico, -a, -ci, -che agg artistic.

arto sm limb.

artrite sf arthritis.

artrosi sf osteoarthritis.

ascella sf armpit.

ascendente sm (influsso) ascendancy; (astrologico) ascendant.

Ascensione sf: **l'~** the Ascension.

ascensore sm lift (Br), elevator (Am).

ascesso sm abscess.

ascia (pl asce) sf axe.

asciugacapelli sm inv hairdryer.

asciugamano sm towel.

asciugare vt to dry ❑ **asciugarsi** vr (persona) to dry o.s.; (tinta, vestiti) to dry.

asciutto, -a agg (secco) dry; (magro) thin.

ascoltare vt to listen to.

ascoltatore, -trice sm, f listener.

ascolto sm: **dare** ○ **prestare ~ a** to pay attention to; **essere in ~ to** be listening.

asfaltato, -a agg asphalt (dav s).

asfalto sm asphalt.

asfissia sf asphyxia.

asfissiare vt & vi to suffocate.

Asia sf: l'~ Asia.

asiatico, -a, -ci, -che agg & sm, f Asian.

asilo sm (scuola) nursery; **~ nido** crèche; **~ politico** political asylum.

asino sm donkey.

asma sf asthma.

asola sf buttonhole.

asparago sm asparagus.

aspettare vt to wait for; **mi aspetto una risposta** I expect an answer; **~ un bambino** to be expecting a child.

aspettativa sf (previsione) expectation; (congedo) leave.

aspetto sm (apparenza) appearance; (punto di vista) point of view; (elemento) aspect.

aspirapolvere sm inv vacuum cleaner.

aspirare vt (inalare) to breathe in; (risucchiare) to suck up ❑ **aspi-**

rare a v + prep to aspire to.

aspiratore sm extractor.

aspirina® sf aspirin.

aspro, -a agg (sapore) sour.

assaggiare vt to taste.

assai avv (molto) very; (abbastanza) enough.

assalire vt to attack.

assassinare vt to murder.

assassinio sm murder.

assassino, -a sm, f murderer.

asse sm board ◆ sm (di auto) axle; (retta) axis.

assedio sm siege.

assegnare vt: **~ qc (a qn)** (casa, rendita) to allocate sthg (to sb); (incarico, compiti) to assign sthg (to sb); (premio) to award sthg (to sb).

assegno sm (bancario) cheque; (sussidio) benefit; **~ a vuoto** bounced cheque; **~ circolare** bank draft; **~ di studio** study grant; **~ di viaggio** ○ **turistico** traveller's cheque; **contro ~** cash on delivery.

assemblea sf meeting.

assente agg (da luogo) absent; (distratto) vacant ◆ smf absentee.

assenza sf (lontananza) absence; (mancanza) lack.

assetato, -a agg thirsty.

assicurare vt (auto, casa) to insure; (garantire) to ensure; (fissare) to secure ❑ **assicurarsi** vr to insure o.s.; **assicurarsi di fare qc** to be sure to do sthg; **assicurarsi che** to make sure that.

assicurata sf registered letter.

assicurato, -a agg insured.

assicurazione sf (contratto) insurance; (garanzia) assurance; **~**

sulla vita life assurance.

assillare *vt (infastidire)* to pester; *(sog: pensiero)* to torment.

Assisi *sf* Assisi.

assistente *smf* assistant; ~ **sociale** social worker; ~ **di volo** steward (*f* stewardess).

assistenza *sf* aid.

assistere *vt* to assist; *(malato)* to care for ◆ *vi:* ~ **(a qc)** *(a lezioni)* to attend (sthg); *(a scena)* to be present (at sthg).

assistito, -a *pp* → **assistere**.

asso *sm* ace.

associare *vt* to associate □

associarsi *vr:* **associarsi (a o con)** *(ditta)* to enter into a partnership (with); **associarsi a qc** *(club)* to join sthg.

associazione *sf* association.

assolto, -a *pp* → **assolvere**.

assolutamente *avv* absolutely.

assoluto, -a *agg* absolute.

assoluzione *sf (accusato)* acquittal; *(RELIG)* absolution.

assolvere *vt (accusato)* to acquit; *(RELIG)* to absolve; *(compito)* to carry out.

assomigliare : assomigliare a *v + prep* to resemble, to look like.

assonnato, -a *agg* sleepy.

assorbente *agg (tampone)* absorbent ◆ *sm:* ~ **(igienico)** (sanitary) towel; ~ **interno** tampon.

assorbire *vt* to absorb.

assordante *agg* deafening.

assortimento *sm* assortment.

assortito, -a *agg (vario)* assort-

ed; *(accordato)* matching.

assumere *vt (personale)* to take on; *(impegno)* to accept; *(atteggiamento)* to assume.

assunto, -a *pp* → **assumere**.

assurdità *sf inv* absurdity.

assurdo, -a *agg* absurd.

asta *sf (bastone)* pole; *(vendita)* auction.

astemio, -a *agg* teetotal.

astenersi : astenersi da *vr + prep* to abstain from.

asterisco, -schi *sm* asterisk.

astigmatico, -a, -ci, -che *agg* astigmatic.

astratto, -a *agg* abstract.

astrologia *sf* astrology.

astronauta, -i, -e *smf* astronaut.

astronomia *sf* astronomy.

astuccio *sm* case.

astuto, -a *agg (persona)* cunning; *(idea, azione)* shrewd.

astuzia *sf (furbizia)* shrewdness; *(stratagemma)* trick.

A.T. *abbr* = **alta tensione**.

ateo, -a *sm, f* atheist.

ATI *(abbr di Aerotrasporti Italiani)* Italian domestic airline.

atlante *sm (geografico)* atlas.

atlantico, -a, -ci, -che *agg* Atlantic.

Atlantico *sm:* l'(Oceano) ~ the Atlantic (Ocean).

atleta, -i, -e *smf* athlete.

atletica *sf* athletics (sg).

atletico, -a, -ci, -che *agg* athletic.

atmosfera *sf* atmosphere.

atmosferico, -a, -ci, -che
agg atmospheric.

atomico, -a, -ci, -che *agg*
atomic.

atomo *sm* atom.

atroce *agg* atrocious.

attaccante *sm* forward.

attaccapanni *sm inv* clothes
stand.

attaccare *vt (unire)* to attach;
(appendere) to hang up; *(assalire)* to
attack; *(trasmettere)* to give ❏
attaccarsi *vr* to stick.

attacco, -chi *sm* attack; *(presa)*
socket.

atteggiamento *sm* attitude.

attendere *vt* to wait for.

attentato *sm* attack.

attento, -a *agg (che presta attenzione)* attentive; *(prudente)* careful;
stai ~! *(non distrarti)* pay attention!;
(stai in guardia) be careful!; **'attenti
al cane'** 'beware of the dog';
'attenti al gradino' 'mind the step'.

attenzione *sf* attention; **~!** be
careful!; **fare ~** *(concentrarsi)* to pay
attention; *(essere prudente)* to be
careful.

atterraggio *sm* landing.

atterrare *vi* to land.

attesa *sf* wait; **essere in ~ di** to
be waiting for.

atteso, -a *pp* → attendere.

attestato *sm* certificate.

attico *sm* penthouse.

attillato, -a *agg* close-fitting.

attimo *sm* moment.

attirare *vt* to attract.

attitudine *sf* aptitude.

attività *sf inv* activity; *(occu-*

pazione) occupation; *(COMM)* assets
(pl).

attivo, -a *agg* active ◆ *sm*
assets *(pl)*.

atto *sm (azione, gesto)* act, deed;
(documento) document; *(di dramma)*
act; **mettere in ~** to put into
action.

attonito, -a *agg* astonished.

attorcigliare *vt* to twist.

attore, -trice *sm, f* actor *(f*
actress)*.

attorno *avv* around.

attracco, -chi *sm (manovra)*
docking; *(luogo)* mooring.

attraente *agg* attractive.

attrarre *vt (affascinare)* to
attract; *(richiamare)* to draw.

attrattiva *sf (richiamo)* attraction; *(qualità)* attractiveness.

attratto, -a *pp* → attrarre.

attraversamento *sm* crossing; **~ pedonale** pedestrian crossing.

attraversare *vt (strada, città)* to
cross; *(periodo)* to go through.

attraverso *prep (da parte a
parte)* across; *(per mezzo di)*
through.

attrazione *sf* attraction.

attrezzatura *sf* equipment.

attrezzo *sm* tool.

attribuire : attribuire a *v +
prep (opera)* to attribute to; **~ il
merito a qn** to give sb the credit.

attrice → attore.

attrito *sm* friction.

attuale *agg (presente)* present;
(moderno) topical.

attualità *sf inv* current events

(pl); **d'~** topical.

attualmente avv at present.

attuare vt to carry out.

attutire vt (colpo, rumore) to reduce.

audace agg bold.

audacia sf audacity.

audiovisivo, -a agg audiovisual.

auditorio sm auditorium.

audizione sf audition.

augurare vt: ~ **qc a qn** to wish sb sthg; **augurarsi di fare qc** to hope to do sthg; **mi auguro che tutto vada bene** I hope that all goes well.

augurio sm wish; **auguri** greetings; **(tanti) auguri!** all the best!; (per compleanno) happy birthday!; **fare gli auguri a qn** to give sb one's best wishes.

aula sf classroom.

aumentare vt & vi to increase.

aumento sm increase.

aureola sf halo.

auricolare sm earphone.

aurora sf dawn.

ausiliare agg & sm auxiliary.

austero, -a agg austere.

Australia sf: l'~ Australia.

australiano, -a agg & sm, f Australian.

Austria sf: l'~ Austria.

austriaco, -a, -ci, -che agg & sm, f Austrian.

autenticare vt to authenticate.

autentico, -a, -ci, -che agg (firma, quadro) authentic; (fatto) true; **è un ~ cretino** he's a real cretin.

autista, -i, -e smf driver.

auto sf inv car.

autoabbronzante agg selftanning ◆ sm fake tanning cream.

autoadesivo, -a agg selfadhesive ◆ sm sticker.

autoambulanza sf ambulance.

autobiografia sf autobiography.

autobus sm inv bus.

autocarro sm truck.

autocisterna sf tanker.

autocontrollo sm selfcontrol.

autodidatta, -i, -e smf selftaught person.

autodromo sm racing track.

autogol sm inv own goal.

autografo sm autograph.

autogrill® sm inv motorway restaurant.

autolinea sf bus service.

automa, -i sm automaton.

automatico, -a, -ci, -che agg automatic.

automazione sf automation.

automezzo sm motor vehicle.

automobile sf car (Br), automobile (Am).

automobilismo sm (sport) motor racing; (industria) car industry (Br), auto industry (Am).

automobilista, -i, -e smf motorist.

autonoleggio sm car hire.

autonomia sf (indipendenza) autonomy; (di veicolo) range.

autonomo, -a *agg* independent, autonomous.

autopsia *sf* autopsy.

autoradio *sf inv* car radio.

autore, -trice *sm, f* (*di libro*) author; (*di quadro*) painter; **l'~ del delitto** the person who committed the crime.

autorevole *agg* authoritative.

autorimessa *sf* garage.

autorità *sf inv* authority.

autoritario, -a *agg* authoritarian.

autorizzare *vt* to authorize.

autorizzazione *sf* authorization.

autoscatto *sm* timer.

autoscontro *sm* Dodgem® car.

autoscuola *sf* driving school.

autoservizi *smpl* bus services.

autostop *sm* hitchhiking; **fare l'~** to hitchhike.

autostoppista, -i, -e *smf* hitchhiker.

autostrada *sf* motorway (*Br*), freeway (*Am*).

autostradale *agg* motorway (*Br*) (*dav s*), freeway (*Am*) (*dav s*).

autoveicolo *sm* motor vehicle.

autovettura *sf* motorcar.

autunno *sm* autumn (*Br*), fall (*Am*).

avambraccio *sm* forearm.

avanguardia *sf:* **d'~** avant-garde; **essere all'~** to be in the vanguard.

avanti *avv* (*stato in luogo*) in front; (*moto*) forward ♦ *prep:* **~ a** (*stato in luogo*) ahead of; (*moto*)

ahead of, in front of; **~!** (*invito a entrare*) come in!; (*esortazione*) come on!; **'avanti!'** (*al semaforo*) 'cross now', 'walk' (*Am*); (*in banca*) 'enter'; **~ e indietro** backwards and forwards; **andare ~** to go on; **essere ~** (*nel lavoro, studio*) to be well ahead; **essere ~ negli anni** to be getting on (in years); **farsi ~** to come forward; **passare ~ a qn** to go in front of sb.

avanzare *vt* (*spostare avanti*) to move forward; (*proposta*) to put forward ♦ *vi* (*procedere*) to advance; (*restare*) to be left (over).

avanzo *sm* (*di cibo*) leftovers (*pl*); (*di stoffa*) remnant.

avaria *sf* (*meccanico*) breakdown.

avariato, -a *agg* (*cibo*) off.

avaro, -a *agg* mean ♦ *sm, f* miser.

avena *sf* oats (*pl*).

avere *vt* **1.** (*possedere*) to have; **ha due fratelli** he's got two brothers; **non ho più soldi** I haven't got any money left.

2. (*come caratteristica*) to have; **~ occhi e capelli scuri** to have dark eyes and hair; **~ molta immaginazione** to have a lot of imagination.

3. (*età*): **quanti anni hai?** how old are you?; **ho 18 anni** I'm 18 (years old).

4. (*portare addosso*) to have on, to wear; **ha un cappotto grigio** she's wearing a grey coat, she's got a grey coat on.

5. (*sentire*): **~ caldo/freddo** to be hot/cold; **~ sonno** to be sleepy; **~ fame** to be hungry; **ho mal di testa** I've got a headache.

6. (ottenere, ricevere) to get.

7. (in espressioni): **non ha niente a che fare** ○ **vedere con lui** that's got nothing to do with him; **non ne ho per molto** it won't take me long; **~ da fare** to have things to do; **avercela con qn** to be angry with sb; **quanti ne abbiamo oggi?** what's the date today?

◆ v aus to have; **non ho finito** I haven't finished; **gli ho parlato ieri** I spoke to him yesterday.

❑ **averi** smpl (beni) wealth (sg).

avi smpl ancestors.

aviazione sf aviation.

avido, -a agg greedy.

AVIS sf (abbr di Associazione Volontari Italiani del Sangue) blood donors' association.

avocado sm inv avocado.

avorio sm ivory.

avvallamento sm depression.

avvantaggiare vt to favour ◆ **avvantaggiarsi** vr: **avvantaggiarsi negli studi** to get ahead with one's studies; **avvantaggiarsi sui concorrenti** to get ahead of one's competitors; **avvantaggiarsi di** vr + prep to take advantage of.

avvelenamento sm poisoning.

avvelenare vt to poison; (aria) to pollute.

avvenente agg attractive.

avvenimento sm event.

avvenire sm future ◆ vi to happen.

avventarsi vr: **~ su** ○ **contro** to rush at.

avventato, -a agg rash.

avventura sf adventure; (amorosa) affair.

avventurarsi vr to venture.

avventuroso, -a agg adventurous.

avvenuto, -a pp → avvenire.

avverarsi vr to come true.

avverbio sm adverb.

avversario, -a agg opposing ◆ sm, f opponent.

avvertenza sf (avviso) notice ◆ **avvertenze** sfpl instructions.

avvertimento sm warning.

avvertire vt (avvisare) to warn; (dolore, fastidio) to feel.

avviamento sm (di motore) starting; (COMM) goodwill.

avviare vt (cominciare) to start; (indirizzare) to introduce ❑ **avviarsi** vr to set off.

avvicinare vt to move closer ❑ **avvicinarsi** vr: **avvicinarsi (a)** to move closer (to).

avvilirsi vr to lose heart.

avvincente agg enthralling.

avvisare vt (informare) to inform; (ammonire) to warn.

avviso sm (scritto) notice; (annuncio) announcement; (avvertimento) warning; **a mio ~** in my opinion.

avvistare vt to sight.

avvitare vt (lampadina) to screw in; (con viti) to screw.

avvizzire vi to wither.

avvocato sm lawyer.

avvolgere vt (fascia) to wrap round; (tappeto) to roll up; (avviluppare) to wrap up ❑ **avvolgersi** vr (aggrovigliarsi) to become tangled; (avvilupparsi) to wrap o.s. up.

avvolgibile sm roller blind.

avvolto, -a *pp* → **avvolgere.**

avvoltoio *sm* vulture.

azalea *sf* azalea.

azienda *sf* business, firm; ~ **agricola** farm.

azionare *vt* to operate.

azione *sf* action; (COMM) share.

azionista, -i, -e *smf* shareholder.

azoto *sm* nitrogen.

azzannare *vt* to sink one's teeth into.

azzardare *vt* to venture ❑ **azzardarsi** *vr*: **azzardarsi a fare qc** to dare to do sthg.

azzardo *sm* risk; **giocare d'~** to gamble.

azzeccare *vt* to get right.

azzuffarsi *vr* to scuffle.

azzurro, -a *agg* & *sm* blue ❑ **Azzurri** *smpl*: **gli Azzurri** the Italian national team.

babà *sm inv* rum baba.

babbo *sm* (fam) dad, daddy; **Babbo Natale** Father Christmas.

baby-sitter [bebi'sitter] *smf inv* babysitter.

bacca, -che *sf* (frutto) berry.

baccalà *sm inv* dried salt cod; ~ **alla fiorentina** dried salt cod cooked with garlic and tomato sauce; ~ **alla vicentina** dried salt cod poached in

milk with onions, anchovies and parsley.

bacheca, -che *sf* (pannello) notice board; (cassetta) display case.

baciare *vt* to kiss ❑ **baciarsi** *vr* to kiss (each other).

bacinella *sf* bowl.

bacino *sm* (in geografia, catino) basin; (ANAT) pelvis.

bacio *sm* kiss; **baci di dama** sweet pastries sandwiched together with chocolate cream.

badare *vi*: ~ **a** (prendersi cura di) to look after; (fare attenzione a) to pay attention to; ~ **a o di fare qc** to take care to do sthg; **mio fratello non bada a spese** money's no object where my brother's concerned.

badia *sf* abbey.

baffi *smpl* moustache (sg).

bagagliaio *sm* (di macchina) boot (Br), trunk (Am); (di treno) luggage van (Br), baggage car (Am).

bagaglio *sm* luggage, baggage; ~ **a mano** hand luggage; **ho un solo ~** I have only one piece of luggage ❑ **bagagli** *smpl* luggage (sg); **fare i bagagli** to pack.

bagliore *sm* (di lampi) flash; (di fari) glare.

bagna cauda *sf* oil, garlic and anchovy dip from Piedmont kept warm at the table and served with vegetables.

bagnare *vt* to wet; (tovaglia, vestiti) to get wet; (annaffiare) to water; (sog: fiume) to flow through; (sog: mare) to wash ❑ **bagnarsi** *vr* (in mare) to bathe; (di pioggia,

bar

spruzzi) to get wet.

bagnato, -a *agg* wet; **~ fradicio** soaked through.

bagnino, -a *sm, f* lifeguard.

bagno *sm (nella vasca)* bath; *(in piscina, mare)* swim; *(stanza)* bathroom; **fare il ~** *(nella vasca)* to have a bath; *(in mare)* to have a swim; **~ pubblico** public baths *(pl)* □ **bagni** *smpl (stabilimento)* bathing establishment.

bagnomaria *sm*: **cuocere a ~** to cook in a double saucepan.

bagnoschiuma *sm inv* bath foam.

baia *sf* bay.

baita *sf* chalet.

balaustra *sf* balustrade.

balbettare *vi* to stammer.

balcone *sm* balcony.

balena *sf* whale.

balla *sf (frottola)* fib; *(di merci)* bale.

ballare *vi & vt* to dance.

ballerino, -a *sf (scarpa)* pump, → ballerino.

ballerino, -a *sm, f* dancer; *(classico)* ballet-dancer • *f* ballerina).

balletto *sm* ballet.

ballo *sm* dance; *(festa)* dance, ball; **essere in ~** to be at stake; **tirare in ~** *(coinvolgere)* to involve; *(menzionare)* to mention.

balneare *agg* bathing *(dav s)*.

balneazione *sf* bathing; **'divieto di balneazione'** 'no bathing'.

balsamo *sm (per capelli)* conditioner; *(pomata)* ointment.

Baltico *sm*: **il (Mar) ~** the Baltic

(Sea).

balzare *vi* to leap.

bambinaia *sf* nanny.

bambino, -a *sm, f* child; *(neonato)* baby.

bambola *sf* doll.

banale *agg* banal.

banana *sf* banana.

banca, -che *sf* bank; **~ dati** data bank.

bancarella *sf* stall.

bancario, -a *agg* bank *(dav s)* • *sm, f* bank employee.

bancarotta *sf* bankruptcy.

banchina *sf (di porto)* quay; *(di stazione)* platform; **'~ non transitabile'** 'soft verges'.

banco, -chi *sm (di scuola)* desk; *(di negozio, bar)* counter; *(di mercato)* stall; *(banca)* bank; **~ di corallo** coral reef; **~ di nebbia** fog bank.

bancomat® *sm inv (sportello)* cash dispenser; *(tessera)* cash card; *(sistema)* automated banking.

bancone *sm* counter.

banconota *sf* bank note.

banda *sf (musicale)* band; *(striscia)* band, strip; *(di malviventi)* gang; *(di amici)* group.

bandiera *sf* flag.

bandito *sm* bandit.

bando *sm* announcement; **~ alle chiacchiere!** that's enough talking!

bar *sm inv* bar; **~tabacchi** *bar that also sells cigarettes and stamps.*

---

i	BAR

Italian bars are open throughout the day. You can have a coffee and a pastry for breakfast, a mid-morning snack, an aperitif or a toasted sandwich. You can eat standing at the counter, which is cheaper, but many bars also offer table service. Look out for the sign 'munirsi dello scontrino', as this means you have to pay at the cash desk before being served at the counter.

bara sf coffin.

baracca, -che sf hut; (spreg: casa) dump; **mandare avanti la ~** (fam) to keep things going.

baraccone sm booth.

baratro sm barter.

barattolo sm jar; (di latta) can.

barba sf beard; **farsi la ~ to shave; che ~!** what a bore!

barbaro, -a agg barbaric ♦ sm, f barbarian.

barbecue ['ba:bikju:] sm inv barbecue.

barbiere sm barber.

barbone, -a sm, f tramp.

barca, -che sf boat; **~ a remi** rowing boat (Br), rowboat (Am); **~ a vela** sailing boat (Br), sailboat (Am).

barcollare vi to stagger.

barella sf stretcher.

barista, -i, -e smf barman (f barmaid).

barman sm inv barman.

Barolo sm Barolo (full-bodied red wine from Piedmont).

barra sf rod, bar; (lineetta) stroke; (di barca) tiller.

barricare vt to barricade ❑ **barricarsi** vr: **barricarsi in/dietro** to barricade o.s. in/behind.

barriera sf barrier.

basare vt to base ❑ **basarsi su** vr + prep (persona) to base o.s. on.

base sf base; (fondamento) basis; **a ~ di whisky** whisky-based; **in ~ a** qc on the basis of sthg.

baseball ['beizbol] sm baseball.

basette sfpl sideboards.

basilica, -che sf basilica.

basilico sm basil.

basso, -a agg low; (persona) short; (acqua) shallow ♦ sm (fondo) bottom; (strumento, cantante) bass; **in ~** at the bottom.

basta esclam that's enough!

bastare vi & v impers to be enough; **~ a qn** to be enough for sb; **basta che** so long as; **basta così!** that's enough!

bastone sm stick; **~ da passeggio** walking stick.

battaglia sf battle.

battello sm boat.

battere vt to beat; (testa) to hit; (ore) to strike; (zona) to scour ♦ vi (cuore) to beat; (sole, pioggia) to beat down; (urtare): **~ contro ○ in** qc to hit sthg; **si batteva i denti dal freddo** our teeth were chattering with the cold; **~ a macchina** to type; **~ le mani** to clap; **in un batter d'occhio** in the twinkling of an eye ❑ **battersi** vr to fight.

batteria sf (elettrica) battery; (strumento) drums (pl).

battesimo sm baptism.

battezzare vt to baptize.

battigia sf water's edge.

battistrada sm inv tread.

bello

battito *sm* beat, beating; *(di orologio)* ticking; **~ cardiaco** heartbeat.

battuta *sf (spiritosaggine)* witty remark; *(teatrale)* cue; *(di tennis)* service.

baule *sm (da viaggio)* trunk; *(di auto)* boot *(Br)*, trunk *(Am)*.

bavaglino *sm* bib.

bavaglio *sm* gag.

bavarese *sf (dolce)* cold dessert made with eggs, milk and cream.

bavero *sm* collar.

bazzecola *sf (cosa poco importante)* trifle; *(cosa facile)*: **è una ~ it's** no problem.

beato, -a *agg (felice)* happy; *(RELIG)* blessed; **~ te!** lucky you!

beauty-case ['bjuːti keis] *sm inv* beauty case.

beccare *vt* to peck; *(fam: sorprendere)* to catch; **beccarsi qc** *(fam) (raffreddore)* to catch sthg; *(ceffone)* to get sthg.

becco, -chi *sm* beak.

Befana *sf (festa)* Epiphany; *(personaggio)* legendary old woman who brings children their presents at the Epiphany.

---

i BEFANA

According to legend, the "Befana" is a kindly old hag who delivers presents to children on the night before the Epiphany. Children leave out a stocking before going to bed, and the "Befana" comes down the chimney in the night, bringing sweets and other gifts to good boys and girls and lumps of coal to those who have been naughty.

beffa *sf* joke.

beffarsi : beffarsi di *vr + prep* to make fun of.

begli → bello.

bei → bello.

beige [beʒ] *agg inv & sm inv* beige.

bel → bello.

belga, -gi, -ghe *agg & smf* Belgian.

Belgio *sm*: **il ~** Belgium.

bella *sf (SPORT)* decider.

bellezza *sf* beauty; **che ~!** fantastic!

bello, -a *(dav sm* **bel** *(pl* **bei** *) + consonante;* **bello** *(pl* **begli** *) + s+consonante,* **gn, ps, z; bell'** *(pl* **begli** *) + vocale) agg* **1.** *(donna, cosa)* beautiful; *(uomo)* handsome; **farsi ~** to make o.s. beautiful; **le belle arti** fine arts.

2. *(piacevole)* pleasant, lovely.

3. *(tempo)* fine, beautiful; **la bella stagione** the summer months *(pl)*; **fa ~** it's lovely weather.

4. *(buono)* good.

5. *(lodevole)* good, kind.

6. *(grande)*: **un bel piatto di spaghetti** a nice big plate of spaghetti; **una bella dormita** a good sleep; **è una bella cifra** it's a considerable sum of money.

7. *(rafforzativo)*: **è bell'e (che) andato** he's already gone; **è una bugia bell'e buona** it's an absolute lie; **alla bell'e meglio** somehow or other; **un bel niente** absolutely nothing.

◆ *sm* **1.** *(bellezza)* beauty.

2. *(punto culminante)*: **sul più** ~ at that very moment; **il** ~ **è che** ... the best bit is that ...

belva sf wild beast.

belvedere sm inv scenic viewpoint.

benché cong although, though.

benda sf *(fasciatura)* bandage; *(per occhi)* blindfold.

bendare vt *(ferita)* to bandage; *(occhi)* to blindfold.

bene avv *(compar & superl* **meglio**)
1. *(in modo soddisfacente)* well; **avete mangiato** ~? did you enjoy your meal?

2. *(nel modo giusto)* well; **hai fatto** ~ you did the right thing.

3. *(in buona salute)*: **stare/sentirsi** ~ to be/feel well.

4. *(a proprio agio)*: **stare** ~ to be o feel comfortable.

5. *(esteticamente)*: **stare** ~ to look good.

6. *(rafforzativo)*: **è ben difficile** it's very difficult; **è ben più difficile del previsto** it's much more difficult than we thought; **lo credo** ~ I can well believe it; **spero** ~ **che** I very much hope that.

7. *(in espressioni)*: **è** ~ **che lo sappiate** it's as well that you know; **sarebbe** ~ **aspettare** it would be better to wait; **dire** ~ **di qn** to speak well of sb; **ti sta** ~! it serves you right!; **va** ~ all right, OK.
♦ esclam fine!, OK!
♦ sm good; **è per il tuo** ~ it's for your own good; **è un** ~ **per tutti** it is a good thing for everyone.
❏ **beni** smpl *(proprietà)* property *(sg)*.

benedire vt to bless.

benedizione sf blessing.

beneducato, -a agg well-mannered.

beneficenza sf charity.

benessere sm wellbeing.

benestante agg well-to-do.

benevolo, -a agg benevolent.

beninteso avv certainly, of course.

benvenuto, -a agg & sm welcome; **benvenuti a Roma!** welcome to Rome!; **dare il** ~ **a qn** to welcome sb.

benzina sf petrol *(Br)*, gas *(Am)*; **fare** ~ to get petrol *(Br)*, to get gas *(Am)*.

benzinaio, -a sm, f forecourt attendant.

bere vt to drink; **bevi qualcosa?** would you like something to drink?; **offrire da** ~ **a qn** to offer sb a drink.

bermuda smpl bermuda shorts.

bernoccolo sm bump.

bersaglio sm target.

besciamella sf béchamel sauce.

bestemmiare vi to curse, to swear.

bestia sf animal; **andare in** ~ to fly into a rage.

bestiame sm livestock.

bevanda sf drink.

bevuto, -a pp → **bere**.

biancheria sf linen; ~ **intima** underwear.

bianchetto sm correcting fluid.

bianco, -a, -chi, -che agg & sm white ♦ sm, f *(persona)* white man (*f* white woman); **riso in ~** plain rice; **pesce in ~** boiled fish; **in ~ e nero** black and white.

biasimare *vt* to blame.

bibbia *sf* bible.

biberon *sm inv* baby's bottle.

bibita *sf* drink.

biblioteca, -che *sf* library.

bicarbonato *sm:* **~ (di sodio)** bicarbonate (of soda).

bicchiere *sm* glass.

bici *sf inv (fam)* bike.

bicicletta *sf* bicycle; **andare in ~** to cycle.

bidè *sm inv* bidet.

bidone *sm* bin; *(fam) (imbroglio)* swindle; **fare un ~ a qn** *(fam) (imbrogliare)* to cheat sb; *(mancare a un appuntamento)* to stand sb up

biennale *agg (ogni due anni)* two-yearly; *(per due anni)* two-year *(dav s)* ❑ **Biennale** *sf:* **la Biennale** the Venice Arts Festival.

BIENNALE

Established in 1895, this international art festival takes place every two years in the gardens of the International Gallery of Modern Art in Venice. The selection of paintings and sculptures on view reflects the avant-garde emphasis of the festival, a trend which has become more pronounced in recent years and is not without its critics. Alongside the art festival there are festivals of music, theatre and architecture, as well as an annual film festival.

---

biforcarsi *vr* to fork.

BIGE *sm reduced-price train ticket for people under 26.*

bigiotteria *sf* costume jewellery; *(negozio)* costume jeweller's.

biglia = **bilia**.

bigliardo = **biliardo**.

bigliettaio, -a *sm, f* ticket inspector.

biglietteria *sf* ticket office; *(al teatro)* box office; **~ automatica** ticket machine.

biglietto *sm (scontrino)* ticket; *(messaggio)* note; *(banconota)* (bank) note; **fare il ~** to buy one's ticket; **~ d'andata e ritorno** return (ticket); **~ di (sola) andata** single (ticket); **~ collettivo** party ticket; **~ cumulativo** group ticket; **~ gratuito** complimentary ticket; **~ intero** full-price ticket; **~ ridotto** reduced-price ticket; **~ d'auguri** greetings card; **~ da visita** visiting card.

bignè *sm inv* choux bun filled with custard or chocolate.

bigodino *sm* curler.

bigoli *smpl:* **~ coi rovinazzi** *large spaghetti from Veneto in a sauce made with duck giblets.*

bikini® *sm inv* bikini.

bilancia, -ce *sf* scales *(pl)* ❑ **Bilancia** *sf* Libra.

bilancio *sm (COMM)* balance sheet; **~ preventivo** budget.

bilia *sf (di vetro)* marble; *(da biliardo)* billiard ball.

biliardo *sm (gioco)* billiards *(sg);* *(tavolo)* billiard table.

bilico : **in bilico** *avv* balanced.

bilingue agg bilingual.

bimbo, -a sm, f little boy (f little girl).

binario sm (rotaie) railway track; (marciapiede) platform; **'ai binari'** 'to the trains'.

binocolo sm binoculars (pl).

biologia sf biology.

biondo, -a agg blond (f blonde).

birichino, -a agg cheeky ♦ sm, f little rascal.

birillo sm skittle.

biro® sf inv Biro.

birra sf beer; **~ chiara** lager; **~ scura** stout; **~ alla spina** draught beer.

birreria sf pub.

bis esclam encore!

bisbigliare vi & vt to whisper.

biscotto sm biscuit.

bisessuale agg bisexual.

bisestile agg → **anno**.

bisnonno, -a sm, f greatgrandfather (f great-grandmother).

bisognare v impers: **bisogna stare attenti** we/I must be careful; **bisogna che tu venga subito** you have to come at once.

bisogno sm need, necessity; **aver ~ di** to need.

bistecca, -che sf steak; **~ al sangue** rare steak; **~ alla fiorentina** T-bone steak grilled or cooked over charcoal.

bisticciare vi to bicker.

bitter sm inv bitters (pl).

bivio sm fork, junction.

bizza sf tantrum.

bizzarro, -a agg odd, eccentric.

bloccare vt to block; (città) to cut off; (meccanismo) to jam; (prezzi) to freeze ❑ **bloccarsi** vr (ascensore) to get stuck; (porta) to jam.

blocchetto sm (quaderno) notebook.

blocco, -chi sm block; (quaderno) notebook; (di meccanismo) blockage; (di attività) stoppage; **~ stradale** roadblock; **in ~** en bloc.

blu agg inv & sm inv blue.

blue-jeans [blu'dʒins] smpl jeans.

blusa sf blouse.

boa sm inv (serpente) boa ♦ sf (galleggiante) buoy.

bobina sf (di auto) coil; (di pellicola) reel.

bocca, -che sf mouth; **in ~ al lupo!** good luck!

boccaccia, -ce sf: **fare le boccacce** to pull faces.

boccale sm jug.

boccia, -ce sf bowl.

bocciare vt (studente) to fail; (proposta, progetto) to reject.

boccone sm mouthful; **mangiare un ~** to have a bite to eat.

bocconi avv face downwards.

boicottare vt to boycott.

bolla sf (di bubble; (vescica) blister; (COMM) bill.

bollente agg boiling.

bolletta sf (di bill; (ricevuta) receipt.

bollettino sm bulletin; **~ meteorologico** weather forecast.

bollire vt & vi to boil.

bollito, -a *agg* boiled ♦ *sm* beef, veal or chicken, served with a parsley sauce.

bollitore *sm* kettle.

bollo *sm (marchio)* stamp.

Bologna *sf* Bologna.

bolognese *agg* of/from Bologna; **alla ~** with meat and tomato sauce.

bomba *sf* bomb.

bombardare *vt* to bomb.

bombola *sf* cylinder.

bombolone *sm* doughnut.

bonaccia *sf* (dead) calm.

bonario, -a *agg* good-natured.

bonet *sm inv* chocolate-flavoured egg custard.

bontà *sf* goodness.

borbottare *vi* to grumble ♦ *vt* to mutter.

bordeaux [bor'do] *agg inv* maroon.

bordo *sm (orlo)* edge; *(guarnizione)* trim, border; *(di nave)* (ship's) side; **a ~ di** *(nave, aereo)* on board; *(auto)* in; *(moto)* on.

borghese *agg* middle-class; **in ~** in plain clothes.

borghesia *sf* middle classes *(pl)*.

borgo, -ghi *sm (paesino)* hamlet; *(quartiere)* district.

borotalco® *sm* talcum powder.

borraccia, -ce *sf* flask.

borsa *sf* bag; **~ dell'acqua calda** hot-water bottle; **~ del ghiaccio** ice bag; **~ della spesa** shopping bag; **~ di studio** grant ♦ **Borsa** *sf* Stock Exchange.

borsaiolo *sm* pickpocket.

borsellino *sm* purse.

borsetta *sf* handbag.

bosco, -schi *sm* wood.

botanico, -a, -ci, -che *agg* botanic ♦ *sm, f* botanist.

botta *sf* blow; *(rumore)* bang; **fare a botte** to come to blows.

botte *sf* barrel.

bottega, -ghe *sf* shop; *(laboratorio)* workshop.

bottegaio, -a *sm, f* shopkeeper.

bottiglia *sf* bottle.

bottiglione *sm* large bottle.

bottone *sm* button; **attaccare un ~ a qn** to buttonhole sb.

boutique [bu'tik] *sf inv* boutique.

box *sm inv (garage)* lock-up (garage); *(per bambini)* playpen; *(per animali)* pen.

boxe [boks] *sf* boxing.

boy-scout [bɔi'skaut] *sm inv* boy scout.

braccetto : a braccetto *avv* arm in arm.

bracciale *sm* bracelet.

braccialetto *sm* bracelet.

braccio *sm (arto: pl f* braccia*)* arm; *(di edificio: pl m* bracci*)* wing; *(di gru, fiume: pl m* bracci*)* arm; **~ di ferro** arm wrestling; **sotto ~** arm in arm.

bracciolo *sm* arm.

brace *sf* embers *(pl)*; **alla ~** charcoal-grilled.

braciola *sf* steak; *(con osso)* chop.

braille ['braj] *sm* braille.

branco, -chi sm (di animali) herd; (spreg: di persone) gang, bunch.

branda sf camp bed.

brasato sm braised beef.

Brasile sm: il ~ Brazil.

bravo, -a agg good; ~! well done!; ~ a fare qc good at doing sthg; ~ in qc good at sthg.

bresaola sf dried salt beef served thinly sliced.

bretelle sfpl (per pantaloni) braces; (spalline) straps.

breve agg short, brief; **in** ~ briefly; **tra** ~ shortly.

brevetto sm (di invenzione) patent; (patente) licence.

brezza sf breeze.

bricco, -chi sm jug.

briciola sf crumb.

briciolo sm: un ~ di qc a bit of sthg.

brillante agg brilliant; (lucente) bright ◆ sm diamond.

brillare vi to shine.

brillo, -a agg tipsy.

brindisi sm inv toast; fare un ~ a to toast.

brioche [bri'ɔʃ] sf inv round, sweet bread roll made with butter and eaten for breakfast.

britannico, -a, -ci, -che agg British.

brivido sm shiver, shudder.

brocca, -che sf jug.

brodo sm broth; pasta in ~ noodle soup; riso in ~ rice soup.

bronchite sf bronchitis.

brontolare vi to grumble; (stomaco, tuono) to rumble.

bronzo sm bronze.

bruciapelo : a bruciapelo avv point-blank.

bruciare vt to burn; (distruggere) to burn down ◆ vi to burn; (produrre bruciore) to sting ❑ **bruciarsi** vr (persona) to burn o.s.; (oggetto) to burn.

bruciato, -a agg burnt.

bruciatura sf burn.

bruno, -a agg dark.

bruschetta sf bread toasted with garlic and olive oil.

brusio sm buzz.

brutale agg brutal.

brutto, -a agg (di aspetto) ugly; (tempo, giornata, strada) bad; (situazione, sorpresa, malattia) nasty; (rafforzativo): ~ **imbroglione!** you rotten cheat!; **brutti ma buoni** almond and hazelnut meringues.

Bruxelles [bru'ksɛl] sf Brussels.

buca, -che sf hole; ~ **delle lettere** letterbox.

bucare vt to make a hole o holes in; ~ **una gomma** to puncture a tyre ❑ **bucarsi** vr (forarsi) to have a puncture; (pungersi) to prick o.s.; (fam: drogarsi) to mainline.

bucatini smpl: ~ **all'amatriciana** dish from Lazio consisting of long, thin pasta tubes in a sauce of tomatoes, bacon, chillies and pecorino cheese.

bucato sm washing.

buccellato sm light, ring-shaped sponge cake from Sarzana and Lucca.

buccia, -ce sf skin.

buco, -chi sm hole.

budino sm type of egg custard

baked in a mould; **~ di riso** egg custard made with rice, sultanas and sometimes rum.

bufera sf storm.

buffet [byfɛ] sm inv buffet.

buffo, -a agg funny.

bugia sf lie; (candeliere) candleholder.

bugiardo, -a agg lying ♦ sm, f liar.

buio, -a agg dark ♦ sm darkness; far ~ to get dark.

Bulgaria sf: la ~ Bulgaria.

bulgaro, -a agg Bulgarian.

bullone sm bolt.

buonanotte esclam good night!

buonasera esclam good evening!

buongiorno esclam (in mattinata) good morning!; (nel pomeriggio) good afternoon!

buongustaio, -a sm, f gourmet.

buono, -a agg (dav sm buon + consonante o vocale; **buono** + s + consonante, gn, ps, x, z) 1. (di qualità) good.

2. (gradevole) good.

3. (generoso): ~ (con) good (to), kind (to).

4. (bravo, efficiente) good; **non essere ~ a nulla** to be no good at anything; **è ~ solo a criticare** all he can do is criticize.

5. (valido: biglietto, passaporto) valid.

6. (temperamento) good; **avere un buon carattere** to be goodnatured; **essere di buon umore** to be in a good mood.

7. (occasione, momento) right.

8. (negli auguri): **buon appetito**

enjoy your meal!; **buon compleanno!** Happy Birthday!; **buona fortuna!** good luck!; **fate buon viaggio!** have a good journey!

9. (rafforzativo): **ci vuole un'ora buona** it takes a good hour.

10. (in espressioni): **~ a sapersi** that's nice to know; **a buon mercato** to cheap; **di buon'ora** early; **alla buona** (cena) simple; (vestirsi) simply; **farai i compiti, con le buone o con le cattive** like it or not, you'll do your homework.

♦ sm 1. (aspetto positivo) good; **il ~ è che ...** the good thing is that ...

2. (tagliando) voucher; (invece di rimborso) credit note; **~ sconto** voucher; **~ del tesoro** treasury bill.

buonsenso sm common sense.

buonumore sm good humour.

burattino sm puppet.

burla sf prank, trick.

burocrazia sf bureaucracy.

burrasca, -sche sf storm.

burrida sf Sardinian dish made from dogfish cooked with garlic, vinegar, pine kernels and walnuts and served cold.

burro sm butter; **~ di cacao** cocoa butter.

burrone sm ravine.

bus [bʌs] sm inv (abbr di autobus) bus.

bussare vi to knock.

bussola sf compass.

busta sf (per lettera) envelope; (di plastica, carta) bag; **~ paga** pay packet.

busto sm bust; (indumento) corset.

butano sm butane.

buttafuori

buttafuori *sm inv* bouncer.

buttare *vt (gettare)* to throw; ~ **all'aria** **qc** to turn sthg upside down; ~ **fuori** **qn** to throw sb out; ~ **giù** *(abbattere)* to knock down; *(inghiottire)* to gulp down; ~ *(via)* *(gettare)* to throw away; *(sprecare)* to waste ❑ **buttarsi** *vr (gettarsi)* to jump; *(fig: tentare)* to have a go.

by-pass [bai'pas] *sm inv* bypass.

C

cabina *sf (di nave)* cabin; *(in spiaggia)* beach hut; *(in piscina)* cubicle; *(di camion)* cab; ~ **telefonica** telephone box.

cacao *sm* cocoa.

cacca *sf (fam)* poo.

caccia, -ce *sf (di animali)* hunting; *(inseguimento)* chase; ~ **al tesoro** treasure hunt.

cacciare *vt (animale)* to hunt; *(mandar via)* to get rid of; ~ **fuori** **qc** to throw sb out ❑ **cacciarsi** *vr:* **dove si sarà cacciato?** where has he got to?; **cacciarsi nei guai** to get into trouble.

cacciatora *sf →* **pollo**.

cacciavite *sm inv* screwdriver.

cacciucco, -chi *sm* fish soup from Livorno, served with toast rubbed with garlic.

cachemire [kaʃ'mir] *sm* cashmere.

caciocavallo *sm* hard pear-

shaped cheese from southern Italy.

cadavere *sm* corpse, dead body.

cadere *vi* to fall; *(capelli)* to fall out; *(abito)* to hang; **far** ~ to knock over.

caduta *sf* fall; **la** ~ **dei capelli** hair loss; '~ **massi**' 'beware falling rocks'.

caffè *sm inv* coffee; *(locale)* cafe; **prendere un** ~ to have a coffee; ~ **corretto** coffee with a dash of spirits; ~ **macchiato** coffee with a dash of milk.

i CAFFÈ

Drunk at any time of day, "caffè" (coffee) or "espresso", served in the traditional "tazzina" (little cup), is the typical Italian drink. In bars and restaurants, you can choose from a number of different versions: "normale" (normal), "ristretto" (concentrated), "lungo" (more diluted), "macchiato caldo" or "macchiato freddo" (with a drop of hot or cold milk), or "corretto" (with a drop of your chosen spirit). If you prefer coffee without caffeine, you can order a "hag®", a "decaffeinato" or, a recent addition, "caffè d'orzo" (made with barley).

caffeina *sf* caffeine.

caffellatte *sm inv* hot milk with coffee.

caffettiera *sf* coffeepot.

cagna *sf* bitch.

CAI *(abbr di Club Alpino Italiano)* Italian mountaineering association.

cala *sf* bay.

calabrone sm hornet.

calamaretti smpl squid (sg).

calamaro sm squid; **calamari ripieni** squid stuffed with anchovies, capers, breadcrumbs and parsley, and cooked in white wine.

calamita sf magnet.

calare vt to lower ♦ vi (prezzo, peso) to go down; (vento) to drop; (sole) to set.

calca, -che sf throng.

calcagno sm heel.

calce sf lime.

calciatore, -trice sm, f footballer.

calcio sm (pedata) kick; (sport) football (Br), soccer; (elemento chimico) calcium; (di arma) butt; **dare un ~ a** to kick; **prendere a calci** to kick.

calcolare vt to calculate; (prevedere) to reckon on, to take into account.

calcolatrice sf calculator.

calcolo sm (conteggio) calculation; (MED) stone; **fare i calcoli** to do one's calculations; **è andato tutto secondo i calcoli** everything went according to plan.

caldaia sf boiler.

caldo, -a agg warm; (a temperatura elevata) hot ♦ sm (di calore) heat; **avere ~** to be hot; **è o fa ~** it's hot.

calendario sm calendar.

calma sf calm ♦ esclam calm down!

calmante sm tranquillizer.

calmare vt to calm; (dolore) to soothe ❑ **calmarsi** vr (persona) to

calm down; (mare) to become calm; (vento) to drop.

calmo, -a agg (tranquillo) peaceful, calm; (mare) calm.

calore sm warmth.

caloria sf (di cibo) calorie.

calorifero sm radiator.

caloroso, -a agg warm.

calpestare vt to tread on.

calunnia sf slander.

calvizie sf baldness.

calvo, -a agg bald.

calza sf (da donna) stocking; (da uomo) sock; **fare la ~** to knit.

calzagatto sm dish from Emilia Romagna consisting of polenta with beans, onions and bacon.

calzamaglia (pl **calzamaglie**) sf tights (pl) (Br), panty hose (pl) (Am).

calzante sm shoehorn.

calzare vt to put on ♦ vi to fit.

calzature sfpl footwear (sg).

calzettone sm knee(-length) sock.

calzino sm (short) sock.

calzolaio sm (riparatore) cobbler; (fabbricante) shoemaker.

calzoleria sf shoe shop.

calzoncini smpl shorts.

calzone sm (cibo) pasty made from pizza dough stuffed with cheese, tomato, ham and egg ❑ **calzoni** smpl trousers.

camaleonte sm chameleon.

cambiale sf bill.

cambiamento sm change.

cambiare vt & vi to change; **le lire in sterline** to change lire into sterling; **~ un biglietto da centomi**

la to change a hundred thousand lire note ◻ **cambiarsi** vr to change (one's clothes).

cambio sm (sostituzione) change; (di denaro) exchange; (di automobile) gears (pl); **dare il ~ a qn** to take over from sb; **fare a ~ (con qn)** to swap (with sb); **in ~ di qc** in exchange for sthg; **~ automatico** automatic gearbox.

camera sf (stanza, ~ da letto) bedroom; **~ d'aria** inner tube; **~ con bagno** room with a bath; **~ blindata** vault; **Camera di Commercio** Chamber of Commerce; **Camera dei Deputati** = House of Commons (Br), = House of Representatives (Am); **~ con doccia** room with a shower; **~ doppia** double room; **~ a due letti** twin-bedded room; **~ matrimoniale** room with a double bed; **~ degli ospiti** guestroom, spare room; **~ singola** single room.

cameriere, -a sm, f waiter (f waitress).

camice sm white coat.

camicetta sf blouse.

camicia sf (da uomo) shirt; (da donna) blouse, shirt; **~ da notte** (da donna) nightdress; (da uomo) nightshirt.

caminetto sm fireplace, hearth.

camino sm (focolare) fireplace, hearth; (comignolo) chimney.

camion sm inv truck.

camioncino sm van.

cammello sm camel; (tessuto) camelhair.

cammeo sm cameo.

camminare vi to walk.

camminata sf walk.

cammino sm way; **mettersi in ~** to set off.

camomilla sf camomile.

camorra sf Camorra.

camoscio sm chamois; **giacca di ~** suede jacket.

campagna sf country; (propaganda, guerra) campaign; **in ~** in the country; **andare in ~** to go to the country.

campana sf bell; **a ~** bell-shaped.

campanello sm bell; **suonare il ~** to ring the bell.

campanile sm bell-tower.

campare vi to get by.

campato, -a agg: **~ in aria** unfounded.

campeggiare vi to camp.

campeggiatore, -trice sm, f camper.

campeggio sm (luogo) campsite; (attività) camping.

camper sm inv camper van.

Campidoglio sm: **il ~** the Capitol.

camping sm inv campsite.

campionario sm (collection of) samples (pl).

campionato sm championship.

campione, -essa sm, f champion ◆ sm (esemplare) sample.

campo sm field; (accampamento) camp; **~ da tennis** tennis court; **~ di golf** golf course; **~ profughi** refugee camp.

camposanto (pl campisanti)

sm cemetery.

Canada *sm:* il ~ Canada.

canadese *agg & smf* Canadian
◆ *sf (tenda)* ridge tent.

canaglia *sf* rogue.

canale *sm* channel; *(artificiale)* canal; ~ **navigabile** ship canal.

canapa *sf* hemp.

canarino *sm* canary.

canasta *sf* canasta.

cancellare *vt (con gomma)* to rub out; *(con penna)* to cross out; *(annullare)* to cancel.

cancelleria *sf (materiale)* stationery.

cancello *sm* gate.

cancerogeno, -a *agg* carcinogenic.

cancrena *sf* (MED) gangrene.

cancro *sm* cancer ▢ **Cancro** *sm* Cancer.

candeggina *sf* bleach.

candela *sf* candle; ~ **(di accensione)** spark plug.

candelabro *sm* candelabra.

candeliere *sm* candlestick.

candidato, -a *sm, f* candidate.

candido, -a *agg (bianco)* (pure) white; *(puro)* pure, innocent.

candito, -a *agg* candied ◆ *sm* candied fruit.

cane *sm* dog; ~ **da guardia** guard dog; ~ **guida** guide dog; ~ **lupo** Alsatian; ~ **poliziotto** police dog; **non c'era un** ~ there wasn't a soul there; **solo come un** ~ all alone; **tempo da cani** lousy weather; **una vita da cani** a dog's life; **'cani al guinzaglio'** 'dogs must be kept on a lead'.

canestro *sm* basket.

cangiante *agg* iridescent.

canguro *sm* kangaroo.

canicola *sf* heat.

canile *sm (cuccia)* kennel; *(allevamento)* kennels *(pl)*; ~ **municipale** dog pound.

canino *sm* canine.

canna *sf (pianta)* reed; *(di bicicletta)* crossbar; *(di fucile)* barrel; ~ **fumaria** chimney flue; ~ **da pesca** fishing rod; ~ **da zucchero** sugar cane.

cannariculi *smpl* thin curved pastry covered in honey.

cannella *sf (spezia)* cinnamon; *(rubinetto)* tap.

cannello *sm* blowlamp.

cannelloni *smpl* cannelloni *(sg)*.

cannibale *smf* cannibal.

cannocchiale *sm* telescope.

cannolo *sm:* ~ **alla crema** pastry tube filled with custard; ~ **siciliano** 'cannolo' filled with sweetened ricotta cheese, candied fruit and chocolate.

cannone *sm* gun.

cannuccia, -ce *sf* straw.

canoa *sf* canoe.

canone *sm (quota)* rent; *(regola)* rule.

canottaggio *sm* rowing.

canottiera *sf (biancheria)* vest (Br), undershirt (Am); *(per esterno)* sleeveless T-shirt.

canotto *sm* rubber dinghy; ~ **di salvataggio** lifeboat.

cantante *smf* singer.

cantare *vt & vi* to sing.

cantautore, -trice *sm, f* singer-songwriter.

cantiere sm (edile) building site; (navale) shipyard.

cantina sf (seminterrato) cellar; (per il vino) wine cellar; (negozio) wine shop.

canto sm (ARTE) singing; (canzone) song; (di uccello) chirping; **d'altro ~** on the other hand.

cantonata sf: **prendere una ~** to make a blunder.

cantone sm (in Svizzera) canton.

Canton Ticino sm: **il ~** the canton of Ticino.

cantucci smpl wedge-shaped almond biscuits.

canzonare vt to tease.

canzone sf song.

caos sm chaos.

CAP abbr = **codice di avviamento postale**.

capace agg (esperto) able, capable; (ampio) capacious; **essere ~ di fare qc** to be able to do sthg; **essere ~ di tutto** to be capable of anything.

capacità sf inv (abilità) ability; (capienza) capacity.

capanna sf hut.

capannone sm (industriale) shed; (agricolo) barn.

caparbio, -a agg stubborn.

caparra sf deposit.

capello sm hair □ **capelli** smpl hair (sg); **averne fin sopra i capelli** to be fed up to the back teeth.

capezzolo sm nipple.

capillare sm capillary.

capire vt & vi to understand; **non capisco** I don't understand; **scusi, non ho capito** I'm sorry, I don't understand; **si capisce!** certainly! □ **capirsi** vr to understand each other.

capitale sf & sm capital ◆ agg (pena, peccato) capital; (fondamentale) fundamental.

capitaneria sf: **~ di porto** port authorities (pl).

capitano sm captain.

capitare vi (accadere) to happen; (giungere) to turn up ◆ v impers to happen; **~ a qn** to happen to sb; **~ a proposito** to come at the right time.

capitello sm capital.

capitolino, -a agg Capitoline.

capitolo sm chapter.

capitombolo sm tumble.

capo sm (principale) boss; (testa, estremità) head; (di gruppo) leader; (di tribù) chief; **~ di vestiario** item of clothing; **andare a ~** to start a new paragraph; **venire a ~ di qc** to get through sthg; **da ~** over again; **da un ~ all'altro (di qc)** from end to end (of sthg); **in ~ a un mese** within a month.

Capodanno sm New Year.

capofitto: **a capofitto** avv headfirst.

capolavoro sm masterpiece.

capolinea (pl capilinea) sm terminus.

capolino sm: **fare ~** to peep in/out.

capoluogo, -ghi sm: **~ di provincia** provincial capital, county town (Br); **~ di regione** regional capital.

capostazione (pl capistazione) smf station master.

capotavola (*mpl* **capitavola**, *fpl inv*) *smf* head of the table; **a ~** at the head of the table.

capoufficio (*mpl* **capiuffico**, *fpl inv*) *smf* office manager (*f* manageress).

capoverso *sm* paragraph.

capovolgere *vt* (*barca, oggetto*) to overturn; (*fig: situazione*) to reverse ❏ **capovolgersi** *vr* (*barca*) to capsize; (*macchina*) to overturn; (*fig: situazione*) to be reversed.

capovolto, -a *pp* → **capovolgere**.

cappa *sf* (*di camino*) hood; (*mantello*) cape.

cappella *sf* chapel.

cappello *sm* hat; **~ di paglia** straw hat.

cappero *sm* caper.

cappone *sm* capon; **~ ripieno al forno** capon stuffed with beef, Parmesan cheese and breadcrumbs.

cappotto *sm* coat.

cappuccino *sm* cappuccino.

cappuccio *sm* hood; (*di penna*) cap.

capra *sf* goat.

Capri *sf* Capri.

capriccio *sm* tantrum; (*voglia*) whim; **fare i capricci** to be naughty.

capriccioso, -a *agg* naughty.

Capricorno *sm* Capricorn.

capriola *sf* somersault.

capriolo *sm* roe deer.

capro *sm*: **~ espiatorio** scapegoat.

capsula *sf* (*di farmaco*) capsule; (*di bottiglia*) cap.

carica

carabiniere *sm* member of the Italian police force responsible for civil and military matters.

caraffa *sf* carafe, jug.

Caraibi *smpl*: **i ~** the Caribbean.

caramella *sf* sweet.

carato *sm* carat.

carattere *sm* character.

caratteristica, -che *sf* characteristic.

caratteristico, -a, -ci, -che *agg* characteristic.

caratterizzare *vt* to characterize.

carboidrato *sm* carbohydrate.

carbone *sm* coal.

carburante *sm* fuel.

carburatore *sm* carburettor.

carcerato, -a *sm, f* prisoner.

carcere (*pl f* **carceri**) *sm* prison.

carciofo *sm* artichoke; **carciofi alla romana** sautéed or baked artichokes with parsley, mint and garlic.

cardiaco, -a, -ci, -che *agg* cardiac, heart (*dav s*).

cardigan *sm inv* cardigan.

cardinale *agg* → **numero, punto** ♦ *sm* cardinal.

cardine *sm* hinge.

cardo *sm* thistle.

carenza *sf* lack, deficiency.

carestia *sf* famine.

carezza *sf* caress; (*a animale*) stroke.

carezzare *vt* to caress; (*animale*) to stroke.

carica, -che *sf* (*incarico*) position, office; (*elettrica, di arma*) charge; **in ~** in office.

caricare vt (mettere su) to load; (sveglia) to wind up; ~ qc di qc to load sthg with sthg; ~ qn di qc to weigh sb down with sthg.

carico, -a, -chi, -che agg (arma, macchina fotografica) loaded; (batteria) charged; (orologio) wound up ♦ sm load; ~ (di qc) weighed down (with sthg); **a ~ di** (spesa) charged to.

carie sf inv (dei denti) decay.

carino, -a agg (grazioso) pretty, lovely; (gentile) nice.

carnagione sf complexion.

carne sf meat; (ANAT) flesh; ~ **di maiale/vitello** pork/veal; ~ **macinata** o **tritata** mince.

carneficina sf massacre.

carnevale sm carnival.

---

i CARNEVALE

The period before Lent, from the Epiphany to Ash Wednesday, is carnival time in Italy. Most festivities take place during the last week of this period, Shrovetide. Both children and adults don masks, go to parties, play tricks on each other, and throw confetti ("coriandoli") and streamers. In some cities special organized events are held: Viareggio is particularly famous for its carnival procession, whilst in Venice the city gives itself over to open-air parties, theatre and concerts.

---

caro, -a agg expensive, dear; (amato) dear; **costare ~** to be expensive; **Caro Luca** Dear Luca.

carota sf carrot.

carovita sm high cost of living.

carpaccio sm thin slices of raw beef served with oil, lemon and shavings of Parmesan cheese.

carpire vt: ~ qc a qn (segreto) to get sthg out of sb.

carponi avv on all fours.

carrabile agg → passo.

carraio agg m → passo.

carreggiata sf carriageway.

carrello sm trolley.

carriera sf career; **far ~** to get on.

carro sm cart, wagon; ~ **armato** tank; ~ **attrezzi** breakdown truck (Br), tow truck (Am).

carrozza sf (cocchio) coach, carriage; (vagone) carriage (Br), car (Am); '~ **letto**' sleeping car; '~ **ristorante**' restaurant car.

carrozzeria sf bodywork.

carrozziere sm coachbuilder.

carrozzina sf pram (Br), baby carriage (Am).

carta sf paper; (tessera) card; **alla ~ à** la carte; ~ **d'argento** senior citizens' railcard; ~ **automobilistica** o **stradale** road map; ~ **da bollo** paper carrying a government duty stamp; ~ **di credito** credit card; ~ **geografica** map; ~ **d'identità** identity card; ~ **igienica** toilet paper; ~ **d'imbarco** boarding pass; ~ **da lettere** notepaper; ~ **da pacchi** brown paper, wrapping paper; ~ **da parati** wallpaper; ~ **stagnola** silver foil; ~ **verde** green card; ~ **dei vini** wine list; **carte da gioco** playing cards.

i | **CARTA D'IDENTITÀ**

Every Italian citizen is issued with an identity card, an official document listing details such as place and date of birth, home address, profession, colour of eyes and hair, and marital status. It also contains a photograph of the bearer. By law Italians must show their identity card when asked to do so by the police, and when booking in at hotels. The card can be used instead of a passport for travel inside the European Union.

cartacarbone *sf* carbon paper.

cartaccia, -ce *sf* waste paper.

cartapesta *sf* papier-mâché.

cartella *sf (di scolaro)* schoolbag; *(di professionista)* briefcase; *(per fogli)* folder; *(scheda)* file; **~ clinica** case history.

cartello *sm (avviso)* notice; *(in dimostrazioni)* placard; **~ stradale** road sign.

cartellone *sm (teatrale)* playbill; **~ (pubblicitario)** poster.

cartina *sf:* **~ (geografica)** map.

cartoccio *sm* paper bag; **al ~ in** tin foil.

cartoleria *sf* stationer's.

cartolibreria *sf* stationer's and bookseller's.

cartolina *sf (illustrata)* (picture) postcard; **~ postale** postcard.

cartone *sm* cardboard ❑ **cartoni animati** *smpl* cartoons.

casa *sf (costruzione)* house; *(dimora)* house, home; *(ditta)* firm;

andare a **~** to go home; **essere a** o **in ~** to be at home; **fatto in ~** homemade; **~ di cura** nursing home.

casalinga, -ghe *sf* housewife.

casalingo, -a, -ghi, -ghe *agg* homemade; *(amante della casa)* home-loving ❑ **casalinghi** *smpl* household articles.

cascare *vi* to fall down.

cascata *sf* waterfall.

cascina *sf* farmstead.

casco, -schi *sm (protettivo)* helmet; *(per capelli)* dryer; *(di banane)* bunch.

casella *sf (riquadro)* square; *(scomparto)* compartment; **~ postale** post office box.

casello *sm* tollbooth.

caserma *sf* barracks *(pl)*.

casino *sm (fam: confusione)* mess.

casinò *sm inv* casino.

caso *sm* chance; *(eventualità)* event; *(poliziesco, medico)* case; **fare ~ a** to pay attention to; **non è il ~ di offendersi** you shouldn't take offence; **a ~** at random; **in contrario** otherwise; **in ogni ~** in any case; **nel ~ venisse** should he come; **per ~** by chance; **in tutti i casi** at any rate; **'in ~ d'emergenza rompere il vetro'** 'in case of emergency break glass'.

casomai *cong* if by any chance.

cassa *sf (contenitore)* case, box; *(di negozio)* cash register; *(di supermercato)* checkout; *(di banca)* counter; *(amplificatore)* speaker; *(di orologio)* case; **~ automatica prelievi** cash dispenser; **~ continua** night safe; **~ toracica** chest.

cassaforte (*pl* **casseforti**) *sf* safe.

cassata *sf* ice cream dessert containing candied fruit, served in slices like a cake; **~ siciliana** Sicilian dessert made with sponge, ricotta cheese, candied fruit and liqueur.

casseruola *sf* saucepan.

cassetta *sf* (*contenitore*) box; (*di musica, film*) tape; **~ delle lettere** letterbox (*Br*), mailbox (*Am*); **~ di sicurezza** strongbox.

cassetto *sm* drawer.

cassettone *sm* chest of drawers.

cassiere, -a *sm, f* (*di negozio*) cashier; (*di banca*) teller.

cassoela *sf* pork ribs with salami and savoy cabbage (a speciality of Lombardy).

cassonetto *sm* large dustbin on wheels.

castagna *sf* chestnut.

castagnaccio *sm* Tuscan cake made from chestnut flour, pine kernels and sometimes sultanas and rosemary.

castagno *sm* chestnut.

castano, -a *agg* chestnut.

castello *sm* castle.

castigo, -ghi *sm* punishment; **mettere qn in ~** to punish sb.

castoro *sm* beaver.

castrare *vt* to castrate.

casual ['kaʃwal] *agg inv* casual.

casuale *agg* chance (*dav s*).

catacomba *sf* catacomb.

catalogare *vt* to catalogue.

catalogo, -ghi *sm* catalogue.

catamarano *sm* catamaran.

catarifrangente *sm* reflector.

catarro *sm* catarrh.

catasta *sf* stack.

catastrofe *sf* catastrophe.

categoria *sf* (*gruppo*) category; (*di albergo*) class.

catena *sf* chain; **~ di montaggio** assembly line; **a ~ chain** (*dav s*); **catene (da neve)** (snow) chains.

catinella *sf* basin; **piovere a catinelle** to pour down.

catino *sm* basin.

catrame *sm* tar.

cattedra *sf* teacher's desk.

cattedrale *sf* cathedral.

cattiveria *sf* (*qualità*) wickedness; (*commento*) spiteful remark; (*atto*) spiteful act.

cattività *sf* captivity.

cattivo, -a *agg* bad; (*bambino*) naughty; (*sapore, odore*) bad, nasty; (*incapace*) poor.

cattolico, -a, -ci, -che *agg & sm, f* Catholic.

cattura *sf* capture.

catturare *vt* to capture.

caucciù *sm* rubber.

causa *sf* cause; (*DIR*) case; **a o per ~ di** because of.

causare *vt* to cause.

cautela *sf* caution, prudence.

cautelare *vt* to protect □ **cautelarsi da** *vr* + *prep* to take precautions against.

cauto, -a *agg* cautious, prudent.

cauzione *sf* security; (*DIR*) bail.

cava *sf* quarry.

cavalcare *vt* to ride.

cavalcavia *sm inv* flyover.

cavalcioni *avv*: **a ~ di** astride.

cavaliere *sm (chi cavalca)* rider; *(medioevale, titolo)* knight; *(in balli)* partner.

cavalleria *sf (MIL)* cavalry; *(cortesia)* chivalry.

cavallerizzo, -a *sm, f (istruttore)* riding instructor; *(di circo)* bareback rider.

cavalletta *sf* grasshopper.

cavalletto *sm* easel.

cavallo *sm* horse; *(di pantaloni)* crotch; *(negli scacchi)* knight; **andare a ~ to** ride; **~ (vapore)** horsepower.

cavallone *sm (ondata)* breaker.

cavare *vt* to extract; **cavarsela** to manage, to cope.

cavatappi *sm inv* corkscrew.

cavatelli *smpl*: **~ alla foggiana** flat 'gnocchi' in a vegetable, cheese or meat sauce.

caverna *sf* cave.

cavia *sf* guinea pig; **fare da ~ to** be a guinea pig.

caviale *sm* caviar.

caviglia *sf* ankle.

cavità *sf inv (buca)* hollow; *(ANAT)* chamber.

cavo, -a *agg* hollow ♦ *sm* cable; *(corda)* rope.

cavolfiore *sm* cauliflower.

cavolo *sm* cabbage; **che ~ vuole?** *(fam)* what the hell does he want?

cazzotto *sm (fam)* punch.

cc *abbr di centimetro cubico* cc.

c/c *abbr di conto corrente)* a/c.

C.C. *abbr* = Carabinieri.

C.D. *sm inv* CD.

ce → ci.

cece *sm* chickpea.

Cecoslovacchia *sf*: **la ~** Czechoslovakia.

cedere *vt*: **~ qc (a qn)** to give sthg up (to sb) ♦ *vi (soffitto, pavimento)* to give way; **~ (a qc)** *(fig: persona)* to give in (to sthg), to yield (to sthg).

cedola *sf* coupon.

cedro *sm* lime.

CEE *sf (abbr di Comunità Economica Europea)* EEC.

ceffone *sm* slap.

celebrare *vt* to celebrate.

celebre *agg* famous.

celebrità *sf inv* fame.

celeste *agg* & *sm* sky-blue.

celibe *agg* single ♦ *sm* bachelor.

cella *sf* cell.

cellophane®   ['tʃɛlofan]   *sm* Cellophane®.

cellula *sf* cell; **~ fotoelettrica** photoelectric cell.

cellulare *sm (telefono)* mobile phone; *(furgone)* Black Maria.

cemento *sm* cement; **~ armato** reinforced concrete.

cena *sf* dinner.

cenare *vi* to have dinner.

cencio *sm (straccio)* rag ❑ **cenci** *smpl (CULIN)* Tuscan speciality of deep-fried sticks of dough sprinkled with sugar.

cenere *sf* ash.

cenno *sm (con la mano)* gesture; *(col capo)* nod; *(allusione)* hint; *(sintomo)* sign; **fare ~ a qn** to beckon to sb; **fare ~ di sì/no** to nod/shake one's head.

cenone *sm* New Year's Eve

dinner.

censimento *sm* census.

censura *sf* (*controllo*) censorship.

centenario, -a *agg* (*di età*) hundred-year-old; (*ogni cento anni*) centenary (*dav*) ◆ *sm* centenary.

centerbe *sm inv* type of liqueur made from herbs.

centesimo, -a *num* hundredth, → **sesto**.

centigrado *agg m* → **grado**.

centimetro *sm* centimetre.

centinaio (*pl f* **centinaia**) *sm*: un ~ (di) a hundred.

cento *num a* o one hundred; ~ per ~ 100 per cent, → **sei**.

centomila *num a* o one hundred thousand, → **sei**.

centotredici *sm* (*numero telefonico*) = 999 (*Br*), = 911 (*Am*); (*polizia*) police (*pl*).

centrale *agg* (*nel centro*) central; (*principale*) main ◆ *sf* head office; ~ **elettrica** electric power station.

centralinista, -i, -e *smf* operator.

centralino *sm* telephone exchange; (*di albergo, ditta*) switchboard.

centrare *vt* to hit the centre of.

centrifuga, -ghe *sf* spin-dryer.

centro *sm* centre; **fare** ~ (*colpire*) to hit the bull's eye; (*fig: risolvere*) to hit the nail on the head; ~ **abitato** built-up area; ~ **commerciale** shopping centre; ~ **storico** old town.

ceppo *sm* (*di albero*) stump; (*ciocco*) log.

cera *sf* wax.

ceramica *sf* pottery.

cerbiatto *sm* fawn.

cerca *sf*: **essere in** ~ **di qc** to be in search of sthg.

cercare *vt* to look for ❑ **cercare di** ◆ *vt* + *prep*: ~ **di fare qc** to try to do sthg.

cerchio *sm* circle; **mettersi in** ~ (**intorno a**) to form a circle (around).

cereale *sm* cereal.

cerimonia *sf* ceremony.

cerino *sm* match.

cernia *sf* grouper.

cerniera *sf* (*di porte, finestre*) hinge; ~ (**lampo**) zip.

cerotto *sm* plaster.

certamente *avv* certainly.

certezza *sf* certainty; **sapere qc con** ~ to know sthg for sure.

certificato *sm* certificate; ~ **medico** medical certificate; ~ **di nascita** birth certificate.

certo, -a *agg* **1.** (*convinto*) certain; **essere** ~ **di qc** to be certain of sthg; **sono** ~ **di aver prenotato** I'm positive I booked; **siete certi che sia lui?** are you sure it's him?

2. (*assicurato, evidente*) certain; **la vittoria è data per certa** victory is certain.

3. (*non specificato*) certain; **un** ~ **signor Rossi** a (certain) Mr Rossi; **c'è un** ~ **Paolo al telefono** there's someone called Paolo on the phone; **ho certe cose da fare** I have some things I need to do; **in certi casi** in some o certain cases.

4. (*qualche*) certain; **certi(-e)** some.

5. (*limitativo*) some; **avere un** ~

chitarra *sf* guitar.

chiudere *vt* to close, to shut; *(acqua, gas)* to turn off; *(strada)* to close; *(definitivamente)* to close down, to shut down; *(concludere)* to end ◆ *vi* to close, to shut; *(definitivamente)* to close down, to shut down; **~ a chiave** to lock ◆ **chiudersi** *vr* to close, to shut; **chiudersi in casa** to lock o.s. in; **'si chiude da sé'** 'automatic door'.

chiunque *pron (indefinito)* anyone; *(relativo)* whoever; **~ sia** whoever it may be.

chiuso, -a *pp* → **chiudere** ◆ *agg* closed; *(persona)* reserved; **'~ per ferie'** 'closed for holidays'; **'~ per riposo settimanale'** 'weekly closing day'.

chiusura *sf (di negozio, ufficio, scuole)* closing; *(definitiva)* closure; *(termine)* end; *(dispositivo)* fastener.

ci *(diventa ce se precede lo, la, li, le, ne)* **pron personale 1.** *(complemento oggetto)* us; **~ vedono** they can see us; **ascoltaci** listen to us.

2. *(complemento di termine)* (to) us; **~ può fare un favore?** can you do us a favour?; **non ce lo ha detto** he didn't tell us.

3. *(riflessivo)* ourselves; **~ laviamo** we wash ourselves.

4. *(reciproco)* each other; **~ vediamo stasera** see you tonight.

◆ *pron dimostrativo (a ciò, in ciò, su ciò)*: **~ penso io** I'll take care of it; **mettici un po' d'impegno!** put a bit of effort into it!; **quella sedia è vuota: posso appoggiarci la borsa?** that seat is empty: can I put my bag on it?; **~ puoi scommettere** you can bet on it.

◆ *avv* **1.** *(stato in luogo: qui)* here; *(stato in luogo: lì)* there; **~ fermiamo una sola notte** we are staying (here/there) for just one night.

2. *(moto a luogo: qui)* here; *(moto a luogo: lì)* there; **~ si può andare a piedi** you can walk there; **~ vengono spesso** they come here often.

3. *(moto per luogo)*: **~ passa l'autostrada** the motorway runs through it; **non ~ passa nessuno** nobody ever goes this/that way.

4. *(in espressioni)*: **c'è** there is; **~ sono** there are; **~ vuole un po' (di tempo)** it takes a bit of time; **~ sto** I agree; **non ~ sento/vedo** I can't hear/see.

ciabatta *sf (pantofola)* slipper; *(pane)* type of long, flat bread.

cialda *sf* wafer.

ciambella *sf (dolce)* ring-shaped cake; *(salvagente)* rubber ring; **~ di salvataggio** life buoy, life belt.

ciao *esclam (all'incontro)* hello!; *(di commiato)* bye!

ciascuno, -a *agg & pron* each; **~ di noi** each of us.

cibo *sm* food.

cicala *sf* cicada.

cicatrice *sf* scar.

cicca, -che *sf* cigarette end.

ciccione, -a *sm, f (fam)* fatty.

cicerone *sm* guide.

ciclabile *agg* → **pista**

ciclamino *sm* cyclamen.

ciclismo *sm* cycling.

ciclista, -i, -e *smf* cyclist.

ciclo *sm* cycle.

ciclomotore *sm* moped.

ciclone *sm* cyclone.

cicogna *sf* stork.

cieco, -a, -chi, -che *agg* blind ◆ *sm, f* blind man (f woman).

cielo *sm* sky; *(paradiso)* heaven.

cifra *sf (numero)* figure; *(di denaro)* sum, figure.

ciglio *sm (di palpebra: pl f ciglia)* eyelash; *(di strada: pl m cigli)* edge.

cigno *sm* swan.

cigolare *vi* to squeak, to creak.

Cile *sm:* **il ~** Chile.

cilecca *sf:* **fare ~** to fail.

ciliegia, -gie o **-ge** *sf* cherry.

cilindro *sm (di motore)* cylinder; *(cappello)* top hat.

cima *sf* top; *(estremità)* end; **in ~ (a qc)** at the top (of sthg); **da ~ a fondo** from top to bottom, from beginning to end; **~ alla genovese** veal stuffed with bacon, sweetbreads, brains, mushrooms, peas and grated cheese, served cold in slices.

cimice *sf (insetto)* bug; *(puntina)* drawing pin (Br), thumbtack (Am).

ciminiera *sf* chimney; *(di nave)* funnel.

cimitero *sm* cemetery.

Cina *sf:* **la ~** China.

cin cin *esclam* cheers!

Cinecittà *sf* film studios in Rome.

ℹ️ **CINECITTÀ**

Meaning "city of cinema", the name "Cinecittà" has been given to the film complex built in the suburbs of Rome in 1937. "Cinecittà" was most productive in the 1950s, when films like Fellini's *La dolce vita* were shot there, and it continues to be widely used by the Italian film industry.

cinema *sm inv* cinema.

cinepresa *sf* cine-camera.

cinese *agg, smf & sm* Chinese.

cingere *vt* to surround.

cinghia *sf* belt.

cinghiale *sm* wild boar.

cinguettare *vi* to chirp.

cinico, -a, -ci, -che *agg* cynical.

ciniglia *sf* chenille.

cinquanta *num* fifty, → **sei**.

cinquantesimo, -a *agg* fiftieth, → **sesto**.

cinquantina *sf (di età)*: **essere sulla ~** to be about 50; **una ~ (di)** about 50.

cinque *num* five, → **sei**.

cinquecento *num* five hundred, → **sei** ▫ **Cinquecento** *sm:* **il Cinquecento** the sixteenth century.

cinto, -a *pp* → **cingere**.

cintura *sf* belt; *(punto vita)* waist; **~ di sicurezza** safety ◇ seat belt; **'allacciare le cinture di sicurezza'** 'fasten your seat belts'.

ciò *pron* this, that; **~ che** what; **~ nonostante** nevertheless.

cioccolata *sf* chocolate; *(bevanda)* hot chocolate.

cioccolatino *sm* chocolate.

cioccolato *sm* chocolate.

cioè *avv* that is ◆ *cong (vale a dire)* that is; *(anzi)* or rather.

ciondolo *sm* pendant.

ciotola *sf* bowl.

ciottolo *sm* pebble.

cipolla *sf* onion.

cipresso *sm* cypress.

cipria *sf* face powder.

circa *avv & prep* about.

circo, -chi *sm* circus.

circolare *agg & sf* circular ◆ *vi* to circulate; *(veicoli)* to drive; *(persone)* to move along; *(notizia)* to go round.

circolazione *sf (di merce, moneta, giornali)* circulation; **mettere in ~** *(notizia)* to spread; *(merce, moneta)* to put into circulation; **~ sanguigna** circulation; **~ stradale** traffic.

circolo *sm* circle.

circondare *vt* to surround.

circonferenza *sf* circumference.

circonvallazione *sf* ring road.

circoscrizione *sf* district.

circostante *agg* surrounding.

circostanza *sf* circumstance; **date le circostanze** in o under the circumstances.

circuito *sm* circuit.

ciste = **cisti**.

cisterna *sf* tank.

cisti *sf inv* cyst.

citare *vt (DIR)* to summon; *(menzionare)* to cite; *(opera, autore)* to quote.

citofono *sm* entry phone.

città *sf inv* town; *(importante)* city; **~ universitaria** (university) campus □ **Città del Vaticano** *sf* Vatican City.

cittadinanza *sf* citizenship; *(abitanti)* citizens *(pl)*.

cittadino, -a *sm, f* citizen ◆ *agg* town, city *(dav s)*.

ciuco, -chi *sm* ass, donkey.

ciuffo *sm* tuft.

civetta *sf* owl; *(fig: donna)* flirt.

civico, -a, -ci, -che *agg* civic.

civile *agg* civic; *(civilizzato)* civilized ◆ *sm* civilian.

civiltà *sf inv* civilization.

clacson *sm inv* horn.

clamoroso, -a *agg* sensational.

clandestino, -a *agg (illegale)* illegal; *(segreto)* clandestine ◆ *sm, f* stowaway.

classe *sf* class; *(aula)* classroom; **~ turistica** tourist class; **prima/seconda ~** first/second class; **che fai?** what year are you in?

classico, -a, -ci, -che *agg (letteratura, arte, musica)* classical; *(moda, esempio)* classic.

classifica, -che *sf (sportiva)* league table; *(d'esame)* results *(pl)*; *(musicale)* charts *(pl)*.

classificare *vt (ordinare)* to classify; *(valutare)* to mark □ **classificarsi** *vr*: **classificarsi primo** to come first.

claudicante *agg (zoppicante)* limping.

clausola *sf (DIR)* clause.

clavicola *sf* clavicle.

claxon = **clacson**.

clero *sm* clergy.

cliente *smf (di negozio, bar)* customer; *(di professionista)* client.

clientela *sf (di negozio, bar)* clientele; *(di professionista)* clients *(pl)*.

clima, -i sm climate.

clinica, -che sf clinic.

cloro sm chlorine.

club [klab] sm inv club.

cm (abbr di centimetro) cm.

coagulare vt (sangue) to coagulate; (latte) to curdle ❑ **coagularsi** vr (sangue) to clot; (latte) to curdle.

coca sf (fam: bibita) Coke®.

Coca-Cola® sf Coca-Cola®.

cocaina sf cocaine.

coccinella sf ladybird.

coccio sm (terracotta) earthenware; (frammento) shard.

cocciuto, -a agg stubborn.

cocco, -chi sm (albero) coconut palm; (frutto) coconut.

coccodrillo sm crocodile.

coccolare vt to cuddle.

cocomero sm watermelon.

coda sf (fila) queue (Br), line (Am); (di animale) tail; **fare la ~** to queue (Br), to stand in line (Am); **mettersi in ~** to join the queue (Br) O line (Am); **~ (di cavallo)** ponytail.

codardo, -a agg cowardly.

codesto, -a agg & pron this.

codice sm code; **~ (di avviamento) postale** postcode; **~ fiscale** tax code; **~ della strada** highway code.

coerente agg consistent.

coetaneo, -a agg: **siamo coetanei** we are the same age.

cofano sm bonnet (Br), hood (Am).

cogliere vt to pick; (fig: occasione, momento) to seize; **~ qn sul fatto** to catch sb redhanded.

cognac sm inv cognac.

cognato, -a sm, f brother-in-law (f sister-in-law).

cognome sm surname.

coi = **con + i**, → **con**.

coincidenza sf (caso) coincidence; (aereo, treno) connection.

coincidere vi: **~ (con qc)** (oggetti) to coincide (with sthg); (versione dei fatti) to agree (with sthg); (date, eventi) to clash (with sthg).

coinciso, -a pp → **coincidere**.

coinvolgere vt: **~ qn (in qc)** to involve sb (in sthg).

coinvolto, -a pp → **coinvolgere**.

col = **con + il**, → **con**.

colapasta = **scolapasta**.

colare vt (filtrare) to filter; (pasta) to drain ♦ vi (liquido) to drip; (contenitore) to leak; (cera, burro) to melt; **~ a picco** to sink.

colazione sf (pranzo) lunch; (prima) **~** breakfast; **fare ~** (al mattino) to have breakfast.

colera sm cholera.

colica, -che sf colic.

colino sm colander.

colla sf glue.

collaborare vi to cooperate.

collaboratore, -trice sm, f collaborator.

collana sf necklace; (serie) series.

collant [kol'lan] smpl tights.

collare sm collar.

collasso sm collapse.

collaudo sm test.

colle sm hill.

collega, -ghi, -ghe smf colleague.

comandante

collegare vt to connect ❏ **collegarsi** vr to link up; **collegarsi con** vr + prep (per telefono, radio, TV) to link up with.

collegio sm boarding school.

collera sf anger; **essere in ~ (con qn)** to be angry (with sb).

colletta sf collection.

collettivo, -a agg (comune) common; (di gruppo) group (dav s).

colletto sm collar.

collezionare vt to collect.

collezione sf collection; **fare la ~ di qc** to collect sthg.

collina sf hill.

collirio sm eyewash.

collisione sf impact.

collo sm neck; (di abito) collar, neck; (pacco) package.

collocamento sm employment.

collocare vt (disporre) to place.

colloquio sm (conversazione) talk; (esame) oral exam; **~ di lavoro** interview.

colmo, -a agg full ♦ sm: **è il ~!** it's the last straw!

colomba sf dove; (dolce) Easter cake.

Colombia sf: **la ~** Colombia.

colonia sf colony; (per bambini) summer camp; **(acqua di) ~** (eau de) cologne.

colonna sf column; **~ vertebrale** spine, spinal column.

colorante sm (per alimenti) food colouring; (per tessuti) dye.

colorare vt to colour.

colore sm colour; **di che ~?** what colour?; **di ~** coloured; **a colori** colour (dav s).

coloro pron mpl: **~ che ...** those who ...

colosseo sm: **il Colosseo** the Colosseum.

IL COLOSSEO

One of Rome's most visited monuments, the Colosseum was built between 75 and 80 AD. In its arena spectators watched gladiatorial contests, fights between men and animals, chariot races and simulated naval battles. Pillaged over the centuries, and attacked more recently by pollution, the amphitheatre nevertheless still retains some of its outer walls.

---

colpa sf (responsabilità) fault; (reato) offence; **dare la ~ (di qc) a qn/qc** to blame sb/sthg (for sthg); **per ~** di through, owing to.

colpire vt to hit; (impressionare, sog: malattia) to strike.

colpo sm blow; (sparo) shot; (alla porta) knock; (fam: infarto) stroke; (fam: rapina) raid; **di ~** suddenly; **fare ~** to make a strong impression; **un ~ di fulmine** love at first sight; **~ di sole** sunstroke; **~ di stato coup** (d'état); **~ di telefono** phone call; **~ di testa** impulse; **~ di vento** gust of wind.

coltello sm knife.

coltivare vt to cultivate.

colto, -a pp → **cogliere** ♦ agg cultured.

coma sm inv coma.

comandante sm (di nave) captain; *(di esercito)* commanding officer.

comandare *vi* to be in command.

comando *sm* command; *(congegno)* control.

combaciare *vi* to fit together.

combattere *vt & vi* to fight.

combinare *vt (accordare)* to combine; *(organizzare)* to arrange; *(fam: fare)* to do.

combinazione *sf* combination; *(caso)* coincidence; **per ~ by** chance.

combustibile *agg* combustibile ◆ *sm* fuel.

come *avv* 1. *(comparativo)* like; **ho dormito ~ un ghiro** I slept like a log; **~ me like me; ~ sempre as** always; **~ se niente fosse** as if nothing had happened.

2. *(interrogativo)* how; **non so ~ fare** I don't know what to do; **~ sarebbe?** what do you mean?; **~ stai?** how are you?; **~ mai?** how come?

3. *(in qualità di)* as; **viaggiare ~ turista** to travel as a tourist.

4. *(in esclamazioni)* how; **~ mi dispiace!** I'm so sorry!

5. *(per esempio)* like; **mi piacciono i colori accesi ~ il rosso** I like bright colours like red.

◆ *cong* 1. *(nel modo in cui)* how; **mi ha spiegato ~ lo ha conosciuto** she told me how she met him; **fai ~ ti dico** do as I tell you; **~ vuole** as you like.

2. *(comparativa)* as; **non è caldo ~ pensavo** it's not as hot as I thought.

3. *(quanto)* how; **sai ~ mi piace il** cioccolato you know how much I like chocolate.

cometa *sf* comet.

comfort *sm inv* comfort; **l'hotel dispone di tutti i ~** the hotel offers a wide range of amenities.

comico, -a, -ci, -che *agg* funny; *(genere)* comic ◆ *sm (attore)* comedian.

cominciare *vt & vi* to begin, to start; **~ a fare qc** to begin to do sthg, to begin doing sthg; **~ col fare qc** to begin by doing sthg.

comitiva *sf* group.

comizio *sm* meeting.

commedia *sf* play.

commemorare *vt* to commemorate.

commentare *vt* to comment on.

commento *sm* comment; *(a un testo, programma)* commentary.

commerciale *agg* commercial.

commerciante *smf (mercante)* trader; *(negoziante)* shopkeeper.

commerciare : commerciare in *v + prep* to deal in.

commercio *sm (vendita)* trade; **essere fuori ~** not to be for sale; **essere in ~** to be on the market.

commesso, -a *pp* ◆ **commettere** ◆ *sm, f* shop assistant.

commestibile *agg* edible ❑ **commestibili** *smpl* foodstuffs.

commettere *vt (crimine)* to commit; *(errore)* to make.

commissario *sm (di polizia)* superintendent; *(d'esami)* member of an examining board; **~ tecnico** national coach.

commissione sf commission ❑ **commissioni** sfpl errands.

commosso, -a pp → **commuovere** ♦ agg moved.

commovente agg touching.

commozione sf (emozione) emotion; ~ **cerebrale** concussion.

commuovere vt to move, to touch ❑ **commuoversi** vr to be moved, to be touched.

comò sm inv chest of drawers.

comodino sm bedside table.

comodità sf inv comfort.

comodo, -a agg comfortable; (conveniente) convenient; (utile) handy ♦ sm: **fare** ~ **a qn** to be handy for sb; **fare il proprio** ~ to do as one pleases; **con** ~ at one's convenience.

compact disc ['kɔmpæt 'disk] sm inv compact disc.

compagnia sf company; (di amici) group; **fare** ~ **a qn** to keep sb company; ~ **aerea** airline; ~ **d'assicurazione** insurance company.

compagno, -a sm, f companion; (convivente) partner; ~ **di scuola** school friend; ~ **di squadra** team mate.

comparire vi to appear.

compartimento sm (di locale, spazio) section; (di treno) compartment.

compasso sm pair of compasses.

compatibile agg compatible; **un comportamento non** ~ inexcusable behaviour.

compatire vt (aver compassione di) to feel sorry for; (scusare) to

make allowances for.

compatto, -a agg (ben unito) compact; (folla) dense; (fig: solidale) united.

compensare vt to compensate; ~ **qn di qc** to compensate sb for sthg.

compenso sm (paga) payment; (risarcimento) compensation; (ricompensa) recompense; **in** ~ on the other hand.

comperare = **comprare**.

compere sfpl: **far** ~ to do the shopping.

competente agg competent.

competere vi to compete ❑ **competere a** v + prep to be up to.

competizione sf competition.

compiacere vt to please ❑ **compiacersi** vr: **compiacersi di** o **per qc** to be delighted at sthg; **compiacersi con qn** to congratulate sb.

compiaciuto, -a pp → **compiacere**.

compiere vt (eseguire) to fulfil; (concludere) to complete; **quando compi gli anni?** when is your birthday?; **compie 15 anni a maggio** he'll be 15 in May.

compilare vt to fill in.

compito sm (incarico) task; (dovere) duty; (in classe) test ❑ **compiti** smpl homework (sg); **fare i compiti** to do one's homework.

compleanno sm birthday; **buon** ~! Happy Birthday!

complessivo, -a agg overall.

complesso, -a agg complex ♦ sm complex; (musicale) band, group; **in ○ nel ~** on the whole.

completamente *avv* completely.

completare *vt* to complete.

completo, -a *agg* complete; *(pieno)* full ◆ *sm (vestiario)* suit; *(di oggetti)* set; **al ~** *(hotel, aereo)* fully booked; **c'era la famiglia al ~** the whole family was there.

complicare *vt* to complicate □ **complicarsi** *vr* to become complicated.

complicato, -a *agg* complicated.

complicazione *sf (difficoltà)* snag; *(di malattia)* complication.

complice *smf* accomplice.

complimentarsi *vr*: **~ con qn** to congratulate sb.

complimento *sm* compliment; **complimenti!** congratulations!; **non fare complimenti** don't stand on ceremony.

componente *smf (membro)* member ◆ *sf (aspetto)* element.

componibile *agg* fitted.

comporre *vt (musica, poesia)* to compose; *(parola)* to make up; *(numero di telefono)* to dial.

comportamento *sm* behaviour.

comportare *vt* to involve □ **comportarsi** *vr* to behave.

compositore, -trice *sm, f* composer.

composizione *sf* composition; **'~ principali treni'** board showing the position of compartments, restaurant car etc making up main line trains.

composto, -a *pp* → **comporre** ◆ *agg (persona, contegno)* composed; *(sostanza, parola)* compound ◆ *sm* compound; **~ da** composed of.

comprare *vt* to buy.

comprendere *vt (includere)* to include; *(capire)* to understand.

comprensione *sf* understanding.

comprensivo, -a *agg (tollerante)* understanding; *(inclusivo)* inclusive.

compreso, -a *pp* → **comprendere** ◆ *agg* inclusive; **~ nel prezzo** included in the price.

compressa *sf* tablet.

compromesso *sm* compromise.

compromettere *vt* to compromise.

computer [kom'pjuter] *sm inv* computer.

comunale *agg* municipal.

comune *agg* common; *(a più persone)* shared; *(ordinario)* ordinary ◆ *sm (edificio)* town hall; *(ente)* town council; *(area)* = borough; **avere qc in ~ (con qn)** to have sthg in common (with sb); **mettere qc in ~** to share sthg; **fuori del ~** out of the ordinary.

comunicare *vt* to communicate ◆ *vi (parlare, corrispondere)* to communicate; *(porta)*: **~ con** to lead to.

comunicazione *sf (atto)* communication; *(annuncio)* announcement; *(telefonica)* call; **dare la ~ a qn** to put a call through to sb.

comunione *sf (eucaristia)* Communion; ~ **dei beni** *(DIR)* joint ownership of property.

comunismo *sm* communism.

comunista, -i, -e *agg & smf* communist.

comunità *sf inv* community; **la Comunità (Economica) Europea** the European (Economic) Community.

comunque *avv* anyway ♦ *cong* *(tuttavia)* however; *(in qualsiasi modo)* no matter how.

con *prep* with; ~ **piacere!** with pleasure!; **viaggiare** ~ **il treno/la macchina** to travel by train/car.

concavo, -a *agg* concave.

concedere *vt (dare, accordare)* to grant; *(ammettere)* to concede; ~ **a qn di fare qc** to allow sb to do sthg; **concedersi qc** to treat o.s. to sthg.

concentrare *vt* to concentrate; *(riassumere)* to condense ❑ **concentrarsi** *vr* to concentrate.

concentrato, -a *agg* concentrated, concentrating ♦ *sm* concentrate.

concentrazione *sf* concentration.

concepimento *sm* conception.

concepire *vt (figlio)* to conceive; *(idea)* to devise.

concerto *sm* concert.

concessionario *sm* agent.

concesso, -a *pp →* **concedere**.

concetto *sm* concept; *(opinione)* opinion.

conchiglia *sf* shell.

conciliare *vt (impegni, attività)* to reconcile; *(sonno)* to be conducive to; *(contravvenzione)* to settle on the spot.

concime *sm* fertilizer.

concludere *vt* to conclude ❑ **concludersi** *vr* to conclude.

conclusione *sf* conclusion; **in** ~ in conclusion.

concluso, -a *pp →* **concludere**.

concordare *vt (stabilire)* to agree on; *(GRAMM)* to make agree ♦ *vi* to agree.

concorde *agg* in agreement.

concorrente *smf (in gara, affari)* competitor; *(ad un concorso)* contestant.

concorrenza *sf* competition.

concorso *sm* competition; *(esame)* competitive examination; ~ **di bellezza** beauty contest.

concreto, -a *agg* concrete.

condanna *sf (sentenza)* sentence; *(pena)* conviction; *(disapprovazione)* condemnation.

condannare *vt (DIR)* to sentence; *(disapprovare)* to condemn.

condimento *sm (per insalata)* dressing; *(per carne)* seasoning.

condire *vt (insalata)* to dress; *(carne)* to season.

condividere *vt* to share.

condizionale *agg & sm* conditional ♦ *sf (DIR)* suspended sentence.

condizionatore *sm* air-conditioner.

condizione *sf* condition; **a** ~ **che** on condition that.

condoglianze *sfpl* condolences.

condominio *sm* (*edificio*) block of flats (*jointly owned*); (*persone*) joint owners (*pl*).

condotta *sf* conduct.

condotto, -a *pp* → **condurre** ♦ *sm* conduit; (ANAT) duct.

conducente *sm* driver; '**non parlare al ~**' 'please do not speak to the driver whilst the vehicle is in motion'.

condurre *vt* (*affare, azienda*) to run; (*bambino, prigioniero*) to take; (*vita*) to lead; (*gas, acqua*) to carry.

conduttore, -trice *sm, f* driver ♦ *sm* (*di calore, elettricità*) conductor.

confarsi : confarsi a *vr + prep* to suit.

confederazione *sf* confederation.

conferenza *sf* (*riunione*) conference; (*discorso*) lecture; **~ stampa** press conference.

conferire *vt* (*form*): **~ qc a qn** to confer sthg on sb.

conferma *sf* confirmation.

confermare *vt* to confirm.

confessare *vt* to confess.

confessarsi *vr* (RELIG) to confess; (*dichiarare*): **confessarsi colpevole** to plead guilty.

confessione *sf* confession.

confetto *sm* (*dolciume*) sugared almond; (*pastiglia*) pill.

confezionare *vt* (*merce*) to package; (*pacco*) to make up; (*vestiario*) to make.

confezione *sf* (*involucro*) packaging; (*di vestiario*) tailoring; **~ regalo** gift pack.

confidare *vt*: **~ qc a qn** to confide sthg to sb □ **confidare in** *v + prep* to have confidence in; **confidarsi** *vr*: **confidarsi con qn** to open one's heart to sb.

confidenziale *agg* confidential.

confinare : confinare con *v + prep* to border on; **confinarsi in** *vr + prep* to shut o.s. away in.

confine *sm* (*frontiera*) border; (*limite*) boundary.

confiscare *vt* to confiscate.

conflitto *sm* (*guerra*) conflict; (*contrasto*) clash.

confondere *vt* to confuse, to mix up; **~ le idee a qn** to confuse sb □ **confondersi** *vr* (*mescolarsi*) to merge; (*sbagliarsi*) to get mixed up; (*turbarsi*) to become confused.

conformità *sf* conformity; **in ~ con** in accordance with.

confortare *vt* to comfort.

confortevole *agg* comfortable.

confrontare *vt* to compare.

confronto *sm* comparison; **in ~ (a)** in comparison (with); **nei miei confronti** towards me.

confusione *sf* (*caos*) confusion; (*disordine*) mess; (*chiasso*) racket, noise; **far ~** (*confondersi*) to get mixed up; (*far rumore*) to make a racket.

confuso, -a *pp* → **confondere** ♦ *agg* confused.

congedare *vt* (*lasciar andare*) to dismiss; (MIL) to demobilize □ **congedarsi** *vr* (*andar via*) to take one's leave; (MIL) to be demobilized.

congedo *sm* leave; (*MIL*) discharge.

congegno *sm* device.

congelare *vt* to freeze ❑ **congelarsi** *vr* to freeze; (*fig: persona, mani*) to be frozen.

congelato, -a *agg* frozen.

congelatore *sm* freezer.

congeniale *agg* congenial.

congenito, -a *agg* congenital.

congestione *sf* congestion.

congettura *sf* conjecture.

congiungere *vt* to join (together) ❑ **congiungersi** *vr* (*strade*) to meet.

congiuntivo *sm* subjunctive.

congiunto, -a *pp* → **congiungere** ♦ *sm, f* relative.

congiunzione *sf* conjunction.

congiura *sf* conspiracy.

congratularsi *vr* ~ **con qn per qc** to congratulate sb on sthg.

congratulazioni *sfpl* congratulations.

congresso *sm* congress.

coniglio *sm* rabbit.

coniugato, -a *agg* married.

coniuge *smf* spouse.

connazionale *smf* fellow countryman (f fellow countrywoman).

connettere *vt* to connect.

connotati *smpl* description (sg).

cono *sm* cone; ~ **gelato** ice-cream cone.

conoscente *smf* acquaintance.

conoscenza *sf* knowledge; (*persona*) acquaintance; **perdere** ~

to lose consciousness.

conoscere *vt* to know; (*incontrare*) to meet.

conosciuto, -a *pp* → **conoscere** ♦ *agg* well-known.

conquista *sf* (*azione*) conquest; (*risultato, cosa ottenuta*) achievement.

conquistare *vt* (*impadronirsi di*) to conquer; (*ottenere*) to gain; (*persona*) to win over.

consanguineo, -a *sm, f* blood relation.

consapevole *agg*: ~ **di qc** aware of sthg.

conscio, -a, -sci, -sce *agg*: ~ **di qc** conscious of sthg.

consegna *sf* (*recapito*) delivery; (*custodia*): **dare qc in** ~ **a qn** to entrust sb with sthg.

consegnare *vt* (*recapitare*) to deliver; (*affidare*) to entrust.

conseguenza *sf* consequence; **di** ~ consequently.

conseguire *vt* to obtain ♦ *vi*: **ne consegue che …** it follows that …

consenso *sm* consent.

consentire *vt* to allow ❑ **consentire a** *v* + *prep* to agree to.

conserva *sf* preserve; ~ **di frutta** jam; ~ **di pomodoro** tomato sauce.

conservante *sm* preservative.

conservare *vt* (*tenere*) to keep; (*monumento, resti*) to preserve; '~ **in frigo**' 'keep refrigerated' ❑ **conservarsi** *vr* (*cibo*) to keep; (*monumento, resti*) to keep.

conservatore, -trice *sm, f* conservative.

considerare vt to consider □
considerarsi vt to consider o.s.

considerazione sf: **prendere in ~** to take into consideration.

considerevole agg considerable.

consigliare vt (persona) to advise; (locale, metodo) to recommend; **~ a qn di fare qc** to advise sb to do sthg □ **consigliarsi con** vr + prep: **consigliarsi con qn** to ask sb's advice.

consigliere sm (funzionario) adviser; (politico) councillor.

consiglio sm (suggerimento) piece of advice; (riunione) meeting; (organo) council; **dare un ~ a qn** to give sb some advice; **~ d'amministrazione** board; **il Consiglio dei Ministri** = the Cabinet.

consistere : **consistere di** v + prep to consist of; **consistere in** v + prep to consist in.

consistito, -a pp → **consistere**.

consolare vt (confortare) to console; (sollevare) to cheer up □ **consolarsi** vr to console o.s.

consolato sm consulate.

console sm consul.

consonante sf consonant.

constatare vt to notice.

consueto, -a agg usual.

consulente smf consultant.

consultare vt to consult □ **consultarsi** vr to confer; **consultarsi con** vr + prep to consult with.

consultorio sm advice bureau.

consumare vt to consume; (logorare) to wear out □ **con-**

sumarsi vr to wear out.

consumatore sm consumer.

consumazione sf (bibita) drink; (spuntino) snack; **la ~ al tavolo è più cara** it's more expensive to eat/drink sitting at a table; **'~ obbligatoria'** 'minimum charge'.

consumismo sm consumerism.

consumo sm consumption.

contabile smf accountant.

contabilità sf inv (operazioni) accountancy; (libri) accounts (pl); (ufficio) accounts department.

contachilometri sm inv = milemeter.

contadino, -a sm, f farmer.

contagiare vt to infect.

contagocce sm inv dropper.

contante agg → **denaro** ♦ sm cash; **pagare in contanti** to pay in cash.

contare vt & vi to count; **avere i soldi contati** not to have a penny to spare □ **contare di** v + prep: **~ di fare qc** to intend to do sthg; **contare su** v + prep to count on.

contatore sm meter.

contattare vt to contact.

contatto sm contact.

conte, -essa sm, f count (f countess).

contegno sm attitude.

contemporaneamente avv simultaneously.

contemporaneo, -a agg (dello stesso tempo) contemporaneous; (attuale) contemporary.

contendere vt: **~ qc a qn** to

compete with sb for sthg.

contenere vt to contain ❑ **contenersi** vr to contain o.s.

contenitore sm container.

contento, -a agg (lieto) happy, glad; (soddisfatto): ~ **(di)** pleased (with).

contenuto sm (cosa racchiusa) contents (pl); (argomento) content.

contestare vt to object to.

contestazione sf (obiezione) objection; (protesta) protest.

contesto sm context.

contiguo, -a agg: ~ **(a qc)** adjacent (to sthg).

continentale agg continental.

continente sm (geografico) continent; (terraferma) mainland.

contingente sm contingent.

continuamente avv (senza interruzioni) continuously; (di frequente) continually.

continuare vt & vi to continue ♦ v impers: **continua a piovere** it's still raining; ~ **a fare qc** to continue doing sthg.

continuazione sf continuation.

continuo, -a agg (incessante) continuous; (serie, fila) continual; **di** ~ continually.

conto sm (calcolo) calculation; (di ristorante, albergo) bill; (bancario) account; **mi porta il** ~, **per favore?** could you bring me the bill, please?; **fare** ~ **su** to rely on; **rendersi** ~ **di qc** to realize sthg; **tenere** ~ **di qc** to take account of sthg; ~ **corrente** current account; **alla rovescia** countdown; **per** ~ **di qn** on behalf of sb; **fare i conti con qn**

(fam) to sort sb out; **in fin dei conti** all things considered.

contorno sm (di pietanza) vegetables (pl); (linea) outline.

contrabbando sm smuggling.

contrabbasso sm double bass.

contraccambiare vt to return.

contraccolpo sm rebound.

contraddire vt to contradict ❑ **contraddirsi** vr to contradict o.s.

contraddizione sf contradiction.

contraffare vt to falsify; (firma) to forge.

contrapporre vt to set against.

contrariamente avv: ~ **a** contrary to.

contrario, -a agg (opposto) opposite; (sfavorevole) unfavourable; ♦ sm opposite; **essere** ~ **a qc** to be against sthg; **avere qualcosa in** ~ to have an objection; **al** ~ on the contrary.

contrarre vt to contract ❑ **contrarsi** vr (muscolo) to contract.

contrassegno sm (marchio) mark; **spedire qc (in)** ~ to send sthg cash on delivery.

contrastare vt to hinder ♦ vi: ~ **(con)** to clash (with).

contrasto sm contrast; **essere** **in** ~ **con qc** (opinione, esigenza) to be in contrast with sthg.

contrattare vt to negotiate.

contrattempo sm hitch.

contratto, -a pp → **contrarre** ♦ sm contract.

contravvenzione *sf* fine.

contribuire : contribuire a *v* + *prep* to contribute to.

contributo *sm (partecipazione)* contribution; *(tassa)* levy.

contro *prep* against; ~ di me against me; prendere qc ~ il mal di gola to take sthg for one's sore throat.

controfigura *sf* stuntman (f stuntwoman).

controllare *vt* to control; *(verificare)* to check; '~ il resto' 'please check your change' ❑ **controllarsi** *vr* to control o.s.

controllo *sm (verifica)* check; *(sorveglianza)* supervision; *(dominio)* control; perdere il ~ to lose control; ~ **doganale** customs inspection; '~ elettronico della velocita' 'speed checks'; '~ passaporti' 'passport control'.

controllore *sm (di autobus, treni)* (ticket) inspector; ~ **di volo** air-traffic controller.

contromano *avv* in the wrong direction.

controproducente *agg* counterproductive.

controsenso *sm* contradiction in terms.

controvoglia *avv* reluctantly.

contusione *sf* bruise.

convalescenza *sf* convalescence.

convalidare *vt (biglietto)* to validate; *(dubbio, sospetto)* to confirm; '~ all'inizio del viaggio' 'stamp your ticket at the start of your journey'.

convegno *sm* conference.

convenevoli *smpl* civilities.

conveniente *agg* favourable; *(prezzo)* cheap; *(affare)* advantageous.

convenire *vi (riunirsi)* to gather; *(concordare)* to agree; *(tornare utile)* to be worthwhile ❖ *v impers (essere consigliabile)*: conviene avvertirli it is advisable to inform them; ti conviene aspettare you'd better wait.

convento *sm* convent.

convenuto *pp* → **convenire**.

convenzionale *agg* conventional.

convenzioni *sfpl* conventions.

conversazione *sf (chiacchierata)* conversation.

convertire *vt* to convert ❑ **convertirsi** *vr*: convertirsi (a qc) to convert (to sthg).

convincere *vt*: ~ qn di qc to convince sb of sthg; ~ qn a fare qc to persuade sb to do sthg.

convinto, -a *pp* → **convincere** ❖ *agg* convinced.

convivere *vi* to live together.

convocare *vt* to convene.

convoglio *sm* convoy.

convulsioni *sfpl* convulsions.

cooperativa *sf* cooperative.

coordinare *vt* to coordinate.

coperchio *sm* lid.

coperta *sf (da letto)* blanket; *(di nave)* deck.

copertina *sf* cover.

coperto, -a *pp* → **coprire** ❖ *agg (piscina, campo)* indoor *(dav s)*; *(persona)* wrapped up; *(cielo)* overcast ❖ *sm (a tavola)* place; *(al ri-*

storante) cover charge; **~ di qc** covered with sthg; **al ~** under cover.

copertone *sm (pneumatico)* tyre.

copia *sf* copy; **bella ~** final draft; **brutta ~** rough draft.

copiare *vt* to copy.

copione *sm* script.

coppa *sf (bicchiere)* goblet; *(di gelato)* tub; *(ciotola)* bowl; *(di reggiseno, trofeo)* cup; **~ dell'olio** oil sump.

coppia *sf (paio)* pair; *(di sposi, amanti)* couple; **a coppie** in pairs.

copricostume *sm inv* beach robe.

coprifuoco, -chi *sm* curfew.

copriletto *sm inv* bedspread.

coprire *vt* to cover; **~ qn di qc** to cover sb with sthg; *(insulti)* to shower sb with sthg □ **coprirsi** *vr (con indumenti)* to cover o.s.; **coprirsi di qc** *(muffa, fango)* to be covered in sthg.

coraggio *sm (forza d'animo)* courage; *(faccia tosta)* cheek ♦ *esclam* cheer up!; *(forza)* come on!; **avere il ~ di fare qc** *(avere l'animo)* to have the nerve to do sthg; *(avere faccia tosta)* to have the cheek to do sthg.

coraggioso, -a *agg* courageous, brave.

corallo *sm* coral.

Corano *sm*: **il ~** the Koran.

corazzieri *smpl* the President's guard.

corda *sf (fune)* rope; *(spago, di trumento)* string; **tagliare la ~** to sneak off; **corde vocali** vocal ords.

cordiale *agg* warm.

cordone *sm* cord; *(di persone)* cordon; **~ ombelicale** umbilical cord.

coreografia *sf* choreography.

coriandolo *sm (spezia, pianta)* coriander □ **coriandoli** *smpl* confetti *(sg)*.

coricarsi *vr* to go to bed.

cornamusa *sf* bagpipes *(pl)*.

cornetta *sf* receiver.

cornetto *sm (pasta)* croissant; *(gelato)* cone.

cornice *sf* frame.

cornicione *sm* cornice.

corno *(pl f* **corna)** *sm* horn; **facciamo le corna!** *(fam)* = touch wood!; **fare le corna a qn** *(fam)* to cheat on sb.

Cornovaglia *sf*: **la ~** Cornwall.

coro *sm* chorus; *(di chiesa)* choir.

corona *sf (reale)* crown; *(di fiori)* wreath.

corpo *sm* body; *(militare)* corps *(sg)*; **~ insegnante** teaching staff; **(a) ~ a ~** hand to hand.

corporatura *sf* build.

corporeo, -a *agg* bodily.

corredare *vt*: **~ qc di qc** to equip sthg with sthg.

corredo *sm (da sposa)* trousseau; *(attrezzatura)* kit.

correggere *vt* to correct.

corrente *agg (moneta)* valid; *(mese, anno)* current; *(comune)* everyday ♦ *sf* current; *(tendenza)* trend ♦ *sm*: **essere al ~ (di qc)** to be informed (about sthg); **mettere qn al ~ (di qc)** to inform sb (about sthg); **~ alternata** alternating current; **~ continua** direct current.

correntemente *avv (speditamente)* fluently; *(comunemente)* commonly.

correre *vi* to run; *(affrettarsi)* to rush ♦ *vt* to run; **~ dietro a qn** to run after sb.

corretto, -a *pp* → **correggere** ♦ *agg (esatto)* correct; *(onesto)* proper.

correzione *sf* correction; *(di compiti)* marking.

corridoio *sm* corridor.

corridore *sm (atleta)* runner; *(pilota)* racer.

corriera *sf* coach, bus.

corriere *sm* courier.

corrimano *sm* handrail.

corrispondente *agg* corresponding ♦ *smf* correspondent.

corrispondenza *sf* correspondence.

corrispondere *vt* to return □ **corrispondere a** *v + prep* to correspond to.

corrisposto, -a *pp* → **corrispondere.**

corrodere *vt* to corrode.

corrompere *vt (comprare)* to bribe; *(traviare)* to corrupt.

corroso, -a *pp* → **corrodere.**

corrotto, -a *pp* → **corrompere** ♦ *agg (disonesto)* corrupt.

corruzione *sf (disonestà)* corruption; *(con denaro)* bribery.

corsa *sf (a piedi)* running; *(gara)* race; *(di mezzo pubblico)* journey; **fare una ~** *(correre)* to run; *(sbrigarsi)* to dash; **di ~** in a rush; **corse dei cavalli** horse races.

corsia *sf (di strada)* lane; *(di ospedale)* ward; **~ preferenziale** bus and taxi lane; **~ di sorpasso** overtaking lane; **'~ chiusa'** 'lane closed'.

Corsica *sf:* **la ~** Corsica.

corso, -a *pp* → **correre** ♦ *sm* course; *(strada)* main street; **fare un ~ (di qc)** to take a course (in sthg); **~ accelerato** crash course; **~ d'acqua** watercourse; **corsi estivi** summer courses; **corsi serali** evening classes; **in ~** *(denaro)* in circulation; *(riunione, lavori)* in progress; **fuori ~** out of circulation.

corte *sf (reale)* court; **fare la ~ a qn** to court sb.

corteccia, -ce *sf* bark.

corteggiare *vt* to court.

corteo *sm (manifestazione)* demonstration; *(processione)* procession.

cortese *agg* polite.

cortesia *sf (qualità)* politeness; *(atto)* favour; **per ~** please.

cortile *sm* courtyard.

corto, -a *agg* short; **essere a ~ di qc** to be short of sthg.

cortocircuito *sm* short circuit.

corvo *sm* raven.

cosa *sf* thing; *(faccenda)* matter; **una ~ da niente** it's nothing; **~ c'è?** what's the matter?; **~ per prima** firstly.

coscia, -sce *sf (di uomo)* thigh; *(di pollo, agnello)* leg.

cosciente *agg (sveglio)* conscious; *(consapevole)* **~ di qc** conscious of sthg.

coscienza *sf* conscience; **avere qc sulla ~** to have sthg on one's conscience.

coscio *sm* leg.

cosciotto *sm* leg.

così *avv* **1.** *(in questo modo)* like this/like that; **fai ~** do it this way; **~ ~** so-so; **per ~ dire** so to speak; **meglio ~** it's better like this; **proprio ~!** just like that!; **e ~ via** and so on.

2. *(per descrivere misure)* so; **una scatola larga ~ e lunga ~** a box so wide and so long.

3. *(talmente)* so; **è ancora ~ presto!** it's still so early!; **poco/tanto ~** little/much; **una ragazza ~ bella** such a beautiful girl.

4. *(conclusivo)* so; **~, non hai ancora deciso** so you haven't decided yet.

♦ *cong* **1.** *(perciò)* so, therefore.

2. *(a tal punto)*: **~ ... che so ...** (that); **sono ~ stanco che non sto in piedi** I'm so tired I can hardly stand up; **~ ... da** enough ... to; **è ~ sciocco da dire di no** he's silly enough to say no.

♦ *agg inv*: **non ho mai visto una macchina ~** I've never seen a car like that.

❑ **così che** *cong*: *(affinché)* so (that).

cosicché *cong* so that.

cosiddetto, -a *agg* so-called.

cosmetici *smpl* cosmetics.

coso *sm* (*fam*) thing.

cospargere *vt*: **~ qc di qc** to sprinkle sthg with sthg.

cosparso, -a *pp* → **cospargere**.

cospicuo, -a *agg* sizeable.

cospirare *vi* to conspire.

costa *sf* coast.

costante *agg* *(stabile, durevole)* constant; *(persona)* steadfast.

costare *vi* to cost; **quanto costa?** how much does it cost?; **~ caro** to be expensive.

costata *sf* chop.

costare = **constatare**.

costeggiare *vt* *(fiancheggiare)* to go alongside; *(navigare)* to hug the coast of.

costellazione *sf* constellation.

costernato, -a *agg* dismayed.

costì *avv* there.

costiero, -a *agg* coastal.

costituire *vt* *(formare)* to constitute; *(fondare)* to set up ❑ **costituirsi** *vr* to give o.s. up.

costituzione *sf* constitution; *(formazione)* setting-up.

costo *sm* cost; **a tutti i costi** at all costs.

costola *sf* rib.

costoletta *sf* cutlet.

costoso, -a *agg* expensive.

costretto, -a *pp* → **costringere**.

costringere *vt*: **~ qn (a fare qc)** to force sb (to do sthg).

costruire *vt* *(fabbricare)* to build.

costruzione *sf* construction.

costume *sm* *(uso)* custom; *(abito)* costume; **~ da bagno** swimsuit.

cotechino *sm* pork sausage.

cotoletta *sf* chop; *(di vitello)* cutlet; **~ alla milanese** escalope of veal.

cotone *sm* cotton; ~ **idrofilo** cotton wool.

cotta *sf*: **prendersi una ~ per qn** *(fam)* to have a crush on sb.

cotto, -a *pp* → **cuocere** ♦ *agg* cooked; *(fam: innamorato)* head over heels in love; **ben ~** well-done.

cottura *sf* cooking.

coupon [ku'pɔn] *sm inv* coupon.

cozza *sf* mussel.

C.P. *(abbr di casella postale)* P.O. Box.

cracker ['krɛkər] *sm inv* cracker.

crampo *sm* cramp.

cranio *sm* skull.

cratere *sm* crater.

crauti *smpl* sauerkraut flavoured with cumin and juniper, a speciality of Trento.

cravatta *sf* tie.

creare *vt* to create.

creativo, -a *agg* creative.

creatore, -trice *sm, f* creator; **il Creatore** the Creator.

creatura *sf* creature.

credente *smf* believer.

credenza *sf* *(convinzione)* belief; *(mobile)* sideboard.

credere *vt* to believe; **credo di si/no** I think/don't think so; **credo (che) sia vero** I think that's true; **credo di fare la cosa giusta** I think I'm doing the right thing □ **credere a** *v + prep* to believe; **non ci credo!** I don't believe it!; **credere in** *v + prep* to believe in; **credersi** *vr* to consider o.s.

credito *sm* *(COMM)* credit; *(fiducia)* trust.

crema *sf* cream; *(liquida)* custard; ~ **di asparagi** cream of asparagus soup; ~ **depilatoria** hair-removing cream; ~ **pasticcera** confectioner's custard; ~ **solare** suntan cream; **gelato alla ~** vanilla ice-cream.

crematorio *sm* crematorium.

cremazione *sf* cremation.

crème caramel ['krɛm 'karamɛl] *sm inv* ○ *sf inv* crème caramel.

cremisi *agg inv* crimson.

cremoso, -a *agg* creamy.

crepaccio *sm* crevice.

crepapelle : a crepapelle *avv*: **ridere a ~** to split one's sides laughing.

crepare *vi* *(fam: morire)* to snuff it; ~ **dal ridere** to die laughing.

crêpe [krɛp] *sf inv* pancake.

crepuscolo *sm* *(tramonto)* twilight.

crescere *vi* to grow; *(diventare adulto)* to grow up ♦ *vt* to bring up.

crescita *sf* growth.

cresima *sf* confirmation.

crespo, -a *agg* frizzy.

cresta *sf* crest.

creta *sf* clay.

cretino, -a *agg* idiot.

cric *sm inv* *(attrezzo)* jack.

criminale *agg & smf* *(criminoso)* criminal.

crimine *sm* crime.

criniera *sf* mane.

cripta *sf* crypt.

crisi *sf inv* *(fase difficile)* crisi *(attacco)* fit; **in ~** in a state of crisi

cristallo *sm* crystal.

cristianesimo *sm* Christianity.

cristiano, -a *agg & sm, f* Christian.

Cristo *sm* Christ; **avanti ~** BC; **dopo ~** AD.

criterio *sm (regola)* criterion; *(buon senso)* common sense.

critica *sf (biasimo)* criticism; *(i critici)* critics *(pl)*, → **critico**.

criticare *vt* to criticize.

critico, -a, -ci, -che *agg* critical ◆ *sm, f (persona)* critic.

croccante *agg* crisp ◆ *sm* almond crunch.

crocchetta *sf* croquette.

croce *sf* cross; **la Croce Rossa** the Red Cross.

crocevia *sm inv* crossroads *(sg)*.

crociera *sf* cruise.

crocifisso *sm* crucifix.

crollare *vi (edificio, ponte)* to collapse; *(fig: per stanchezza, dolore)* to break down.

crollo *sm (di edificio, ponte)* collapse; *(di prezzi)* slump.

cronaca, -che *sf (attualità)* news *(sg)*; *(di partita)* commentary; **~ nera** crime news *(sg)*.

cronico, -a, -ci, -che *agg* chronic.

cronista, -i, -e *smf* reporter.

cronologico, -a, -ci, -che *agg* chronological.

crosta *sf (di pane)* crust; *(di formaggio)* rind; *(di ferita)* scab.

crostacei *smpl* shellfish.

crostata *sf* fruit or jam tart with a pastry lattice topping.

crostino *sm (per minestra)* crouton; *(tartina)* canapé; **crostini di fegato** small pieces of toast spread with chicken liver pâté.

croupier [kru'pje] *sm inv* croupier.

cruciale *agg* crucial.

cruciverba *sm inv* crossword.

crudele *agg* cruel.

crudo, -a *agg* raw.

crusca *sf* bran.

cruscotto *sm* dashboard.

cubo *sm* cube.

cuccetta *sf (di treno)* couchette; *(di nave)* berth.

cucchiaiata *sf* spoonful.

cucchiaino *sm* teaspoon.

cucchiaio *sm* spoon.

cuccia, -ce *sf* dog's bed; **a ~!** down!

cucciolo *sm* cub; *(di cane)* puppy.

cucina *sf (stanza)* kitchen; *(attività, cibi)* cooking; *(elettrodomestico)* cooker; **~ casalinga** home cooking; **~ a gas** gas cooker.

cucinare *vt* to cook.

cucire *vt* to sew.

cucitura *sf* stitching.

cuculo *sm* cuckoo.

cuffia *sf* cap; *(per l'ascolto)* headphones *(pl)*; **'è obbligatorio l'uso della ~'** 'swimming caps must be worn'.

cugino, -a *sm, f* cousin.

cui *pron relativo* **1.** *(in complemento indiretto: persona)* who, whom; **l'amico a ~ ho prestato il libro** the friend I lent the book to, the friend to whom I lent the book; **l'amico di ~ ti ho parlato** the friend I told you about; **la ragazza con ~ esco** the girl I'm going out with.

2. *(in complemento indiretto: cosa)* which; **il film a ~ mi riferisco** the film (which) I'm referring to; **l'appartamento in ~ vivo** the flat (which) I live in; **il motivo per ~ ti chiamo** the reason (that) I'm calling you.

3. *(tra articolo e sostantivo)*: **la città il ~ nome mi sfugge** the town whose name escapes me; **la persona alla ~ domanda rispondo** the person whose question I'm answering □ **per cui** *cong (perciò)* so; **sono stanco, per ~ vado a letto** I'm tired, so I'm going to bed.

culla *sf* cradle.

culmine *sm* peak.

culo *sm (volg)* arse *(Br)*, ass *(Am)*.

culto *sm* cult; *(adorazione)* worship.

cultura *sf* culture.

culturismo *sm* body-building.

cumulativo *agg m* → **biglietto**.

cumulo *sm (mucchio)* heap, pile.

cunetta *sf (avvallamento)* bump.

cuocere *vt & vi* to cook.

cuoco, -a, -chi, -che *sm, f* cook.

cuoio *sm* leather; **~ capelluto** scalp.

cuore *sm* heart; **avere a ~ qc** to care about sthg; **nel ~ della notte** in the middle of the night.

cupo, -a *agg (scuro)* dark; *(voce)* deep.

cupola *sf* dome.

cura *sf* care; *(trattamento, terapia)*

treatment; **avere ~ di** to take care of; **prendersi ~ di** to look after; **dimagrante** diet.

curare *vt (trattare)* to treat *(guarire)* to cure.

curiosare *vi* to look around.

curiosità *sf inv* curiosity.

curioso, -a *agg (insolito)* curious; *(indiscreto)* inquisitive.

curva *sf* bend; **in ~** on a bend; '**~ pericolosa**' 'dangerous bend'.

curvare *vi (veicolo, autista)* to turn; *(strada)* to bend ♦ *vt* to bend.

curvo, -a *agg (linea)* curved; *(persona, spalle)* bent.

cuscino *sm (da divano)* cushion; *(guanciale)* pillow.

custode *smf* attendant; *(di scuola)* janitor.

custodia *sf (cura, controllo)* custody; *(astuccio)* case.

custodire *vt (assistere)* to look after; *(conservare)* to keep.

cute *sf* skin.

D

da *prep* 1. *(con verbo passivo)* by; **viaggio è pagato dalla ditta** the tr is paid for by the company.

2. *(stato in luogo)* at; **abito ~ una z** I'm living at an aunt's.

3. *(moto a luogo)* to; **andare ~ medico/dal parrucchiere** to go the doctor's/the hairdresser's.

4. *(moto per luogo)* through; **è entr**

to dall'ingresso principale he came in through the main entrance; **il treno passa ~ Roma** the train goes via Rome.

5. (indica l'origine, la provenienza) from; **venire ~ Roma** to come from Rome; **ricevere una lettera ~ un amico** to get a letter from a friend.

6. (indica tempo) for; **aspetto ~** I've been waiting for hours; **lavoro dalle 9 alle 5** I work from 9 to 5; **non lo vedo ~ ieri** I haven't seen him since yesterday; **comincerò ~ domani** I'll start from tomorrow.

7. (indica condizione, funzione) as; **~ grande voglio fare il pompiere** when I grow up I want to be a fireman; **fare ~ guida** to act as a guide.

8. (indica la causa) with; **tremare dal freddo** to shiver; **piangere dalla felicità** to cry for joy.

9. (indica una caratteristica) with; **una ragazza dagli occhi verdi** a girl with green eyes, a green-eyed girl; **una stanza ~ 200 000 lire a notte** a 200,000 lira a night room; **una bottiglia ~ un litro** a litre bottle.

10. (indica il fine): **occhiali ~ sole** sunglasses; **qualcosa ~ mangiare** something to eat.

11. (indica separazione) from; **vedere ~ lontano/vicino** to see from a distance/close up; **essere lontano ~ casa** to be far from home; **la piscina è a 3 chilometri ~ qui** the swimming pool is 3 kilometres from here; **isolarsi ~ tutti** to cut o.s. off from everyone; **mettere qc ~ parte** to save sthg.

12. (indica modo) like; **trattare qn ~** amico to treat sb like o as a friend; **puoi farlo ~ te** you can do it (for) yourself; **non è cosa ~ te!** it's not like you!

13. (indica la conseguenza): **essere stanco ~ morire** to be dead tired.

daccapo avv from the beginning.

dado sm (per gioco) dice; (estratto) stock cube; (per vite) nut.

dagli = da + gli, → da.

dai[1] = da + i, → da.

dai[2] esclam go on!

daino sm (animale) deer.

dal = da + il, → da.

dall' = da + l', → da.

dalla = da + la, → da.

dalle = da + le, → da.

dallo = da + lo, → da.

daltonico, -a, -ci, -che agg colour-blind.

dama sf (gioco) draughts (sg); (nel ballo) partner.

damigiana sf demijohn.

danaro = denaro.

dancing [´densin] sm inv dance hall.

danese agg & sm Danish ◆ smf Dane.

Danimarca sf: **la ~** Denmark.

danneggiare vt (rovinare) to damage; (nuocere a) to harm.

danno sm (materiale) damage; (morale) harm; **i danni** (DIR) damages.

dannoso, -a agg harmful.

danza sf dance.

dappertutto avv everywhere.

dappoco agg inv (persona) inept; (questione) insignificant.

dapprima

dapprima *avv* at first.

dare *vt* to give; *(risultati)* to produce; *(film):* **cosa danno all'Odeon?** what's on at the Odeon?; **~ qc a qn** to give sthg to sb, to give sb sthg; **~ la mano a qn** to shake hands with sb; **~ la nausea a qn** to make sb feel sick; **~ la buonanotte a qn** to say goodnight to sb; **~ da bere a qn** to give sb something to drink; **~ una festa** to throw a party; **~ del lei a qn** to address sb as 'lei'; **~ del tu a qn** to address sb as 'tu'; **~ qn per morto** to give sb up for dead; **~ qc per scontato** to take sthg for granted; **darsi il cambio** to take it in turns; **~ alla testa a qn** *(sog: alcool, successo)* to go to sb's head □ **dare su** *v + prep (finestra)* to look out onto; *(porta)* to lead to; **darsi a** *v + prep (dedicarsi a)* to devote o.s. to; **darsi al bere** to take to drink.

data *sf* date; **~ di nascita** date of birth.

dato, -a *pp → dare* ♦ *agg* particular ♦ *sm* datum; **~ che** given that; **un ~ di fatto** a fact; **i dati** the data.

datore, -trice *sm, f:* **~ di lavoro** employer.

dattero *sm* date.

dattilografo, -a *sm, f* typist.

davanti *avv* in front; *(avanti)* ahead; *(nella parte anteriore)* at the front ♦ *agg inv* front *(dav s)* ♦ *sm* front ♦ *prep:* **~ a** in front of; *(dirimpetto)* opposite.

davanzale *sm* windowsill.

davvero *avv* really.

d.C. *(abbr di dopo Cristo)* A.D.

dea *sf* goddess.

debito *sm* debt.

debole *agg* weak ♦ *sm:* **avere un ~ per** to have a weakness for.

debolezza *sf* weakness.

debuttare *vi* to make one's debut.

decaffeinato, -a *agg* decaffeinated.

decapitare *vt* to decapitate.

decappottabile *agg & sf* convertible.

deceduto, -a *agg* deceased.

decennio *sm* decade.

decente *agg* decent.

decesso *sm (form)* death.

decidere *vt* to decide on ♦ *vi* to decide; **~ di fare qc** to decide to do sthg □ **decidersi** *vr:* **decidersi (a fare qc)** to make up one's mind (to do sthg).

decimale *agg* decimal.

decimo, -a *num* tenth, → **sesto**.

decina *sf* ten; *(circa dieci)* about ten; **decine di** dozens of.

decisione *sf* decision; **prendere una ~** to make a decision.

deciso, -a *pp → decidere* ♦ *agg* decisive; **~ a fare qc** determined to do sthg.

decollare *vi* to take off.

decollo *sm* takeoff.

decorare *vt* to decorate.

decotto *sm* decoction.

decreto *sm* decree.

dedica, -che *sf* dedication.

dedicare *vt:* **~ qc a qn** *(poesia, canzone)* to dedicate sthg to sb; *(fig: consacrare)* to devote sthg to

❏ **dedicarsi a** *vr* + *prep* to devote o.s. to.

dedito, -a *agg*: ~ **a qc** *(studio)* devoted to sthg; *(droga, alcool)* addicted to sthg.

dedotto, -a *pp* → **dedurre**.

dedurre *vt* *(concludere)* to deduce; *(detrarre)* to deduct.

deduzione *sf* deduction.

deficiente *agg* *(spreg)* idiotic.

deficit *sm inv* deficit.

definire *vt* to define.

definitivo, -a *agg* definitive.

definizione *sf* definition.

deformare *vt* to deform; *(fig: travisare)* to distort ❏ **deformarsi** *vr* to become deformed.

defunto, -a *sm, f* deceased.

degenerare *vi* to degenerate.

degli = **di** + **gli**, → **di**.

degnarsi *vr*: ~ **di fare qc** to condescend to do sthg.

degno, -a *agg*: ~ **di** worthy of.

degradare *vt* *(peggiorare)* to degrade; *(MIL)* to demote.

degustazione *sf* *(assaggio)* tasting; *(negozio)* specialist shop where beverages, especially wine or coffee, are tasted.

dei = **di** + **i**, → **di**.

delegare *vt*: ~ **qn (a fare qc)** to delegate sb (to do sthg); ~ **qc a qn** to delegate sthg to sb.

delegazione *sf* delegation.

delfino *sm* dolphin.

delicatezza *sf* *(l'essere delicato)* delicacy; *(gentilezza)* consideration; *(atto gentile)* considerate act.

delicato, -a *agg* delicate; *(gentile)* considerate.

delineare *vt* to outline ❏ **delinearsi** *vr* *(essere visibile)* to be outlined; *(fig: presentarsi)* to take shape.

delinquente *smf* delinquent.

delirio *sm* *(MED)* delirium; *(esaltazione)* frenzy.

delitto *sm* crime.

delizioso, -a *agg* *(cibo)* delicious; *(gradevole)* delightful.

dell' = **di** + **l'**, → **di**.

della = **di** + **la**, → **di**.

delle = **di** + **le**, → **di**.

dello = **di** + **lo**, → **di**.

delta *sm inv* delta.

deltaplano *sm* hang glider.

deludere *vt* to disappoint.

delusione *sf* disappointment.

deluso, -a *pp* → **deludere** ♦ *agg* disappointed.

democratico, -a, -ci, -che *agg* democratic.

democrazia *sf* democracy.

demolire *vt* to demolish.

demonio *sm* devil.

demoralizzare *vt* to demoralize ❏ **demoralizzarsi** *vr* to become demoralized.

denaro *sm* money; ~ **contante** cash.

denigrare *vt* to denigrate.

denominare *vt* to name.

denominazione *sf* name, denomination; ~ **d'origine controllata** a mark guaranteeing that the product, especially wine, is of a good quality.

densità *sf* density.

denso, -a *agg* thick.

dente *sm* tooth; ~ **da latte** milk

tooth; **~ del giudizio** wisdom tooth; **al ~** al dente *(cooked enough to be still firm when bitten)*; **mettere qc sotto i denti** to have a bite to eat; **armato fino ai denti** armed to the teeth.

dentiera *sf (denti finti)* dentures *(pl)*.

dentifricio *sm* toothpaste.

dentista, -i, -e *smf* dentist.

dentro *avv & prep* inside; **darci ~** *(fam)* to put one's back into it; **~ di sé** inwardly, inside; **qui/là ~** in here/there; **dal di ~** from the inside; **in ~** inwards.

denuncia, -ce o **-cie** *sf:* **fare la ~** to make a statement to the police; **~ dei redditi** income tax return.

denunciare *vt (sporgere denuncia contro)* to report; *(rendere noto)* to declare.

deodorante *sm (per il corpo)* deodorant; *(per ambiente)* air freshener.

deperibile *agg* perishable.

depilazione *sf* hair removal.

dépliant [depli'an] *sm inv* brochure.

deplorevole *agg* deplorable.

depositare *vt* to deposit; *(persona)* to leave ▫ **depositarsi** *vr* to settle.

deposito *sm* deposit; *(per autobus)* depot; *(per merci)* warehouse; *(di liquido)* sediment; **~ bagagli** left luggage office.

depravato, -a *sm, f* degenerate.

depressione *sf* depression.

depresso, -a *pp* → **deprimere**

♦ *agg* depressed.

deprimente *agg* depressing.

deprimere *vt* to depress ▫ **deprimersi** *vr* to become depressed.

deputato, -a *sm, f* = Member of Parliament *(Br)*, = Representative *(Am)*.

derattizzazione *sf* rodent control.

deriva *sf:* **andare alla ~** to drift.

derivare : derivare da *v + prep* to derive from.

dermatologo, -a, -gi o **-ghi, -ghe** *sm, f* dermatologist.

derubare *vt* to rob.

descritto, -a *pp* → **descrivere**.

descrivere *vt* to describe.

descrizione *sf* description.

deserto, -a *agg (disabitato)* deserted; *(senza vegetazione)* barren ♦ *sm* desert.

desiderare *vt* to want, to desire; *(sessualmente)* to desire; **desidera?** can I help you?; **~ fare qc** to wish to do sthg; **lasciare a ~** to leave much to be desired.

desiderio *sm* wish.

desideroso, -a *agg:* **~ di fare qc** eager to do sthg.

designare *vt* to designate.

desistere : desistere da *v + prep (form)* to give up.

desistito *pp* → **desistere**.

destinare *vt (assegnare, riservare)* to assign; *(indirizzare)* to address.

destinatario, -a *sm, f* addressee.

destinazióne *sf* destination; **arrivare a ~** to reach one's destination.

destìno *sm* destiny, fate.

dèstra *sf (mano)* right hand; *(lato)* right; **la ~** (POL) the right wing; **tenere la ~** to keep to the right; **a ~** *(stato in luogo)* on the right; *(moto a luogo)* right; **di ~** *(dal lato destro)* right-hand.

destreggiàrsi *vr (nel traffico)* to manoeuvre; *(fig: tra difficoltà)* to manage.

dèstro, -a *agg (opposto a sinistra)* right.

detenùto, -a *sm, f* prisoner.

detenzióne *sf* detention.

detergènte *agg* cleansing ♦ *sm (cosmetico)* cleansing cream; *(detersivo)* detergent.

deteriorare *vt* to impair □ **deteriorarsi** *vr* to deteriorate.

determinànte *agg* decisive.

determinàre *vt (stabilire)* to determine.

determinazióne *sf* determination.

detersìvo *sm* detergent.

detestàre *vt* to detest.

detràrre *vt* to deduct.

detràtto, -a *pp* → **detrarre**.

dettagliàto, -a *agg* detailed.

dettàglio *sm* detail; **al ~** (COMM) retail.

dettàre *vt* to dictate; **~ legge** to lay down the law.

dettàto *sm* dictation.

détto, -a *pp* → **dire** ♦ *agg (soprannominato)* known as ♦ *sm* saying.

devastàre *vt* to devastate.

deviàre *vi* to divert ♦ *vi (di direzione)*: **~ da qc** to turn off sthg.

deviazióne *sf (del traffico)* detour; *(di fiume)* deviation.

devòto, -a *agg* devoted.

di *prep* 1. *(indica appartenenza)* of; **il libro ~ Marco** Marco's book; **la porta della camera** the bedroom door.

2. *(indica l'autore)* by; **un quadro ~ Giotto** a painting by Giotto.

3. *(partitivo)* of; **alcuni ~ noi** some of us.

4. *(nei paragoni)*: **sono più alto ~ te** I'm taller than you; **il migliore ~ tutti** the best of all.

5. *(indica argomento)* about, of; **un libro ~ storia** a history book; **parlare ~** to talk about.

6. *(temporale)* in; **d'estate** in (the) summer; **~ mattina** in the morning; **~ notte** at/by night; **~ sabato** on Saturdays.

7. *(indica provenienza)* from; **~ dove sei?** where are you from?; **sono ~ Messina** I'm from Messina.

8. *(indica una caratteristica)*: **un bambino ~ due anni** a two-year-old child, a child of two; **una statua ~ marmo** a marble statue; **una torre ~ 40 metri** a 40-metre tower; **un film ~ due ore** a two-hour film.

9. *(indica la causa)*: **urlare ~ dolore** to scream with pain; **sto morendo ~ fame!** I'm starving!; **soffrire ~ mal di testa** to suffer from headaches; **morire ~ vecchiaia** to die of old age.

10. *(indica contenuto)* of; **una bottiglia ~ vino** a bottle of wine.

11. *(seguito da infinito)*: **mi ha detto**

~ **non aspettare** he told me not to wait; **pensavo ~ uscire** I was thinking of going out; **capita ~ sbagliare** anyone can make a mistake; **mi sembra ~ conoscerlo** I think I know him.

12. (in espressioni): **a causa ~** because of; **~ modo che** so as to; **dare del bugiardo a qn** to call sb a liar.

♦ art some; (in negative) any; **vorrei del pane** I'd like some bread; **ha degli spiccioli?** have you got any change?

diabete sm diabetes.

diabetico, -a, -ci, -che agg diabetic.

diaframma, -i sm diaphragm.

diagnosi sf diagnosis.

diagonale agg & sf diagonal.

diagramma, -i sm diagram.

dialetto sm dialect.

dialisi sf (MED) dialysis.

dialogo, -ghi sm dialogue.

diamante sm diamond.

diametro sm diameter.

diamine esclam (certo) absolutely!; (che ~ stai facendo? what on earth are you doing?

diapositiva sf slide.

diario sm diary; (a scuola) homework book; (calendario) timetable.

diarrea sf diarrhoea.

diavolo sm devil; **che ~ vuole?** (fam) what the hell does he want?; **va al ~!** (fam) go to hell!

dibattito sm debate.

dica → dire.

dicembre sm December, → settembre.

diceria sf piece of gossip, rumour.

dichiarare vt to declare.

dichiarazione sf declaration.

diciannove num nineteen, → sei.

diciannovesimo, -a num nineteenth, → sesto.

diciassette num seventeen, → sei.

diciassettesimo, -a num seventeenth, → sesto.

diciottesimo, -a num eighteenth, → sesto.

diciotto num eighteen, → sei.

dieci num ten, → sei.

diecina = decina.

diesel ['dizel] agg inv & sm inv diesel.

dieta sf diet; **essere a ~** to be on a diet.

dietetico, -a, -ci, -che agg diet (dav s).

dietro avv (nella parte posteriore) at/in the back; (indietro) behind ♦ sm back ♦ prep: **~ (a)** (dopo) after; (di là da) behind; **~ di me** behind me; **di ~** back (dav s); **qui/li ~** behind here/there; **~ pagamento** on payment.

difatti cong in fact.

difendere vt to defend □ **difendersi** vr to defend o.s.

difensore sm defender.

difesa sf defence.

difeso, -a pp → **difendere.**

difetto sm defect; (morale) fault; **~ di fabbricazione** manufacturing defect.

difettoso, -a agg (meccanismo)

faulty; *(vista, abito)* defective.

diffamare *vt (a parole)* to slander; *(per iscritto)* to libel.

differente *agg* different.

differenza *sf* difference; **non fa ~** it doesn't make any difference; **a ~ di** unlike.

difficile *agg* difficult; **è ~ che esca** *(poco probabile)* it's unlikely that he'll go out.

difficoltà *sf inv* difficulty.

diffidare : **diffidare di** *v + prep* to mistrust.

diffidente *agg* mistrustful.

diffondere *vt* to spread □ **diffondersi** *vr* to spread.

diffusione *sf* diffusion.

diffuso, -a *pp* → **diffondere** ♦ *agg* widespread.

diga, -ghe *sf* dam.

digeribile *agg* digestible.

digerire *vt* to digest.

digestione *sf* digestion.

digestivo, -a *agg* digestive ♦ *sm* liqueur drunk to aid digestion, after meals.

digitale *agg* digital.

digitare *vt (INFORM)* to key in.

digiunare *vi* to fast.

digiuno, -a *sm* fasting ♦ *agg*: **essere ~** not to have eaten; **a ~ on** an empty stomach.

dignità *sf* dignity.

dilagante *agg (fenomeno)* rampant.

dilagare *vi* to be rampant.

dilaniare *vt* to tear to pieces.

dilapidare *vt* to squander.

dilatare *vt (pupille)* to dilate; *(gas, metallo, corpo)* to expand □

dilatarsi *vr (pupille)* to dilate; *(gas, metallo, corpo)* to expand.

dilazionare *vt* to defer.

dilemma *-i sm* dilemma.

dilettante *smf* amateur.

diligente *agg* diligent.

diluire *vt (allungare)* to dilute; *(sciogliere)* to dissolve.

dilungarsi *vr*: **~ su** *(argomento)* to dwell upon; **~ in spiegazioni** to give a longwinded explanation.

diluvio *sm* downpour.

dimagrire *vi* to lose weight.

dimenare *vt (fianchi)* to swing; *(corpo)* to shake; *(coda)* to wag □ **dimenarsi** *vr* to fling o.s. about.

dimensione *sf* dimension.

dimenticanza *sf* oversight.

dimenticare *vt* to forget; *(lasciare)* to leave; **dimenticarsi qc** to leave sthg □ **dimenticarsi di** *vr + prep* to forget about; **dimenticarsi di fare qc** to forget to do sthg.

dimesso, -a *pp* → **dimettere** ♦ *agg* humble.

dimestichezza *sf* familiarity.

dimettere *vt* to discharge □ **dimettersi** *vr* to resign.

dimezzare *vt* to halve.

diminuire *vt* to reduce ♦ *vi* to decrease; *(prezzi)* to drop.

diminuzione *sf* fall; *(di prezzi)* drop.

dimissioni *sfpl* resignation *(sg)*; **dare le ~** to hand in one's resignation.

dimostrare *vt (manifestare)* to show; *(provare)* to prove; **dimostra meno di vent'anni** he doesn't look twenty □ **dimostrarsi** *vr* to

dimostrazione

prove to be.

dimostrazione *sf* (*d'affetto, simpatia*) show; (*di teoria*) proof; (*protesta, per prodotto*) demonstration.

dinàmico, -a, -ci, -che *agg* dynamic.

dinamite *sf* dynamite.

dìnamo *sf inv* dynamo.

dinanzi *prep*: ~ a (*davanti a*) in front of; (*alla presenza di*) before.

dinosauro *sm* dinosaur.

dintorni *smpl* outskirts; nei ~ di in the vicinity of.

dìo (*pl* **dèi**) *sm* god ❑ **Dìo** *sm* God; **mio Dìo!** my God!

diòcesi *sf inv* diocese.

dipartimento *sm* department.

dipendènte *agg* subordinate ♦ *smf* employee.

dipendènza *sf* (*subordinazione*) dependence; (*assuefazione*) addiction; **essere alle dipendènze di qn** to be employed by sb.

dipèndere *vi*: ~ **da** to depend on; (*derivare*) to be due to; **dipende** it depends.

dipéso, -a *pp* → **dipendere**.

dipìngere *vt* to paint.

dipìnto, -a *pp* → **dipingere** ♦ *sm* painting.

diplòma, -i *sm* diploma.

diplomàrsi *vr* to obtain a diploma.

diplomàtico, -a, -ci, -che *agg* diplomatic ♦ *sm* (*funzionario*) diplomat; (*pasta*) pastry made of layers of liqueur-soaked sponge, puff pastry and confectioner's custard, topped

with icing sugar.

diplomazìa *sf* diplomacy.

diradàre *vt* to cut down on ❑

diradàrsi *vr* (*nebbia, nubi*) to clear; (*vegetazione*) to thin out.

dìre *vt* 1. (*pronunciare*) to say; ~ **dì si/no** to say yes/no.

2. (*esprimere, raccontare*) to say; ~ **qc a qn** to tell sb sthg; ~ **a qn che/perché** to tell sb that/why; ~ **la verità** to tell the truth; **dimmi tutto** tell me everything; **dica pure** (*in un negozio*) can I help you?

3. (*ordinare*) to say; ~ **a qn di fare qc** to tell sb to do sthg.

4. (*sostenere*) to say; **dice che non è vero** he says it isn't true.

5. (*tradurre*): **come si dice 'scusi' in inglese?** what's the English for 'scusi'?

6. (*pensare*) to think; **che ne dite di ...?** how about ...?; **e ~ che ...!** to think that ...!

7. (*in espressioni*): **diciamo che ...** let's say that ...; **a ~ il vero ...** to tell the truth ...; **vuol ~ che ...** it means (that) ...; **non c'è che ~** there's no doubt about it; **il nome non mi dice niente** the name doesn't mean much to me; **dico davvero** O **sul serio!** I'm serious!; **a dir poco** at least; **a dir tanto** at most; **volevo ben ~!** I thought so! ♦ *v impers*: **si dice che ...** they say (that) ...; **si direbbe che ...** it seems (that) ...

direttaménte *avv* (*per via diretta*) straight; (*senza intermediari*) directly.

direttìssimo *sm* express train.

dirètto, -a *pp* → **dirigere** ♦ *agg* direct ♦ *sm* (*treno*) through train; **essere ~ a** *(aereo, passeggero)* to be bound for; *(indirizzato)* to be intended for.

direttore, -trice *sm, f* manager *(f* manageress); *(di scuola elementare)* head (teacher) *(Br)*, principal *(Am)*; **~ d'orchestra** conductor.

direzione *sf* direction; *(di azienda)* management.

dirigente *smf* executive.

dirigere *vt (attenzione, sguardo)* to direct; *(scuola, azienda)* to run; *(orchestra)* to conduct* ◻ **dirigersi** *vr* to head.

dirimpetto *avv* opposite.

diritto, -a *agg & avv* straight ◆ *sm* right; *(leggi)* law; *(di abito, stoffa)* right side; *(nel tennis)* forehand; *(nella maglia)* plain stitch; **andare ~** *(in linea retta)* to go straight on; **vai ~ a casa** go straight home; **sempre (a) ~** straight on; **avere ~ a qc** to be entitled to sthg.

dirittura *sf:* **~ d'arrivo** home straight.

diroccato, -a *agg* in ruins.

dirottare *vt* to hijack; *(traffico)* to divert.

dirotto, -a *agg:* **piovere a ~** to pour.

dirupo *sm* precipice.

disabitato, -a *agg* uninhabited.

disaccordo *sm* disagreement.

disadattato, -a *agg* maladjusted.

disagio *sm (scomodità)* discomfort; *(imbarazzo)* uneasiness; **essere a ~** to be ill at ease.

disapprovare *vt* to disap-

prove.

disarmare *vt* to disarm.

disarmo *sm* disarmament.

disastro *sm* disaster; *(danno)* damage.

disastroso, -a *agg* disastrous.

disattento, -a *agg* inattentive.

disavanzo *sm* deficit.

disavventura *sf* mishap.

discapito *sm:* **a ~ di** to the detriment of.

discarica, -che *sf* dump.

discendente *smf* descendant.

discepolo, -a *sm, f* disciple.

discesa *sf* slope; *(movimento)* descent; **in ~** downhill; **~ libera** downhill race; **'~ a mare'** 'this way down to the sea'.

dischetto *sm* diskette.

disciplina *sf (ubbidienza)* discipline; *(materia)* subject.

disciplinato, -a *agg* disciplined.

disc-jockey [disk 'dʒɔkei] *smf inv* disc jockey.

disco, -schi *sm (musicale)* record; *(per computer)* disk; **~ orario** parking disc; **~ volante** flying saucer.

discolpare *vt* to clear.

discorde *agg* conflicting.

discorrere: **discorrere di** *v + prep* to talk about.

discorso *pp →* **discorrere** ◆ *sm* speech; *(conversazione)* conversation, talk.

discoteca, -che *sf* disco.

discretamente *avv (abbastanza bene)* fairly well; *(con tatto)* discreetly.

discreto, -a *agg (persona)* discreet; *(abbastanza buono)* reasonably good.

discrezione *sf (tatto)* discretion; *(moderazione)* moderation.

discriminare *vt* to discriminate.

discussione *sf (dibattito)* discussion; *(litigio)* argument.

discusso, -a *pp* → discutere.

discutere *vt (parlare di)* to discuss; *(contestare)* to question ♦ *vi* to argue; ~ **di** o **su** *(dibattere)* to discuss.

disdetto, -a *pp* → disdire.

disdire *vt* to cancel.

disegnare *vt* to draw; *(progettare)* to design ♦ *vi* to draw.

disegno *sm* drawing; *(motivo)* design; *(progetto)* project; ~ **di legge** bill.

diseredare *vt* to disinherit.

disertare *vt & vi* to desert.

disertore *sm* deserter.

disfare *vt* to undo; *(valigia)* to unpack; *(maglia)* to unravel; *(sciogliere)* to melt.

disfatto, -a *pp* → disfare.

disgelo *sm* thaw.

disgrazia *sf (incidente)* accident.

disgraziato, -a *agg (persona)* wretched; *(viaggio)* ill-fated; *(anno)* unlucky ♦ *sm, f (sfortunato)* poor wretch; *(canaglia)* rogue.

disguido *sm* error.

disgustare *vt* to disgust.

disgusto *sm* disgust.

disgustoso, -a *agg* disgusting.

disidratare *vt* to dehydrate.

disinfestare *vt* to disinfest.

disinfettante *agg & sm* disinfectant.

disinfettare *vt* to disinfect.

disinibito, -a *agg* uninhibited.

disintegrare *vt* to cause to disintegrate.

disinteressarsi : disinteressarsi di *vr + prep* to take no interest in.

disinteresse *sm (indifferenza)* indifference; *(generosità)* unselfishness.

disintossicare *vt* to detoxify; ~ **l'organismo** to clear out one's system ❑ **disintossicarsi** *vr (da droga)* to be treated for drug addiction.

disintossicazione *sf (da droga)* treatment for drug addiction.

disinvolto, -a *agg* free and easy.

disinvoltura *sf* ease.

dislivello *sm (di quota)* difference in height; *(fig: differenza)* gap.

disoccupato, -a *agg* unemployed ♦ *sm, f* unemployed person.

disoccupazione *sf* unemployment.

disonesto, -a *agg* dishonest.

disopra *avv* above; *(al piano superiore)* upstairs ♦ *agg inv* above.

disordinato, -a *agg* untidy; *(vita)* disorderly.

disordine *sm (materiale)* untidiness; *(mentale)* confusion; **in** ~ in a mess.

disorganizzazione *sf* disorganization.

disorientato, -a agg disorientated.

disossare vt to bone.

disotto avv below; (al piano inferiore) downstairs ◆ agg inv below.

dispari agg inv odd.

disparte avv: tenersi O starsene in ~ to keep to o.s.

dispendioso, -a agg expensive.

dispensa sf (stanza) larder; (mobile) sideboard; (fascicolo) instalment.

disperarsi vr to despair.

disperatamente avv desperately.

disperato, -a agg desperate.

disperazione sf desperation.

disperdere vt to disperse.

disperso, -a pp → **disperdere** ◆ sm, f missing person.

dispetto sm (atto) spiteful trick; (stizza) vexation; **fare un ~ a qn** to play a spiteful trick on sb; **fare qc per ~** to do sthg out of spite; **a ~ di** despite.

dispiacere sm (dolore) grief; (rammarico) regret ◆ v impers: le dispiace se aspetto qui? do you mind if I wait here?; **mi dispiace che sia andata così** I'm sorry it worked out that way; **mi dispiace di non potermi trattenere** I'm afraid I can't stop.

dispiaciuto, -a pp → **dispiacere** ◆ agg sorry.

disponibile agg available; (persona) willing to help.

disponibilità sf (di posto, camere) availability; (di persona) willingness to help; (di denaro) liquid assets (pl).

disporre vt to arrange ❏ **disporre di** + prep (poter usare) to have at one's disposal; (avere) to have.

dispositivo sm device.

disposizione sf (di mobili, oggetti) arrangement; (comando) order; (attitudine) disposition; (DIR) provision; **essere a ~ di qn** to be at sb's disposal; **mettere qc a ~ di qn** to make sthg available to sb.

disposto, -a pp → **disporre** ◆ agg: ~ **a fare qc** prepared to do sthg.

disprezzare vt to despise.

disprezzo sm contempt.

disputa sf argument.

dissanguare vt (fig: persona) to bleed white.

disseminare vt to spread.

dissenso sm (disapprovazione) dissent; (contrasto) disagreement.

dissenteria sf dysentery.

disservizio sm inefficiency.

dissestato, -a agg uneven.

dissidente smf dissident.

dissidio sm disagreement.

dissimulare vt to conceal.

dissoluto, -a pp → **dissolvere** ◆ agg dissolute.

dissolvere vt (sciogliere) to dissolve; (nebbia, fumo) to disperse.

dissuadere vt: ~ **qn dal fare qc** to dissuade sb from doing sthg.

dissuaso, -a pp → **dissuadere**

distaccare vt (oggetti) to

distacco

remove; *(dipendente)* to transfer; *(SPORT)* to outdistance ❑ **distaccarsi da** *vr + prep (fig: allontanarsi)* to withdraw from.

distacco, -chi *sm* separation; *(indifferenza)* detachment.

distante *agg & avv* far away; ~ **da** far from.

distanza *sf* distance; *(temporale)*: **a ~ di due mesi** after two months; **tenere le distanze** to keep one's distance.

distanziare *vt (separare)* to space out; *(SPORT)* to outdistance.

distare *vi*: **quanto dista da qui?** how far is it from here?

distendere *vt (gamba, mano)* to stretch out; *(telo, coperta)* to spread; *(rilassare)* to relax ❑ **distendersi** *vr (sdraiarsi)* to lie down; *(rilassarsi)* to relax.

distesa *sf* expanse.

disteso, -a *pp* → **distendere**.

distillare *vt* to distil.

distilleria *sf* distillery.

distinguere *vt* to distinguish.

distintivo, -a *agg* distinctive ♦ *sm* badge.

distinto, -a *agg* → **distinguere** ♦ *agg (diverso)* different; *(immagine)* distinct; *(persona)* distinguished; **Distinti saluti** *(in lettera)* Yours faithfully.

distinzione *sf* distinction.

distogliere *vt*: ~ **qc da qn** to take sthg away from sb; ~ **qn da qc** to deter sb from sthg.

distolto, -a *pp* → **distogliere**.

distorsione *sf (MED)* sprain; *(di suono, immagine)* distortion.

distrarre *vt* to distract; *(divertire)* to amuse ❑ **distrarsi** *vr* to be distracted; *(divertirsi)* to amuse o.s.

distratto, -a *pp* → **distrarre** ♦ *agg (sbadato)* absent-minded; *(disattento)* inattentive.

distrazione *sf* distraction; *(svago)* amusement.

distretto *sm* district.

distribuire *vt (assegnare compiti)* to allocate; *(posta, giornali)* to distribute.

distributore *sm*: ~ **automatico** vending machine; ~ **(di benzina)** petrol pump *(Br)*, gasoline pump *(Am)*.

distribuzione *sf* distribution; *(ripartizione)* allocation.

distruggere *vt* to destroy.

distrutto, -a *pp* → **distruggere** ♦ *agg* shattered.

distruzione *sf* destruction.

disturbare *vt* to disturb; **'non ~ il conducente'** 'do not distract the driver' ❑ **disturbarsi** *vr* to bother.

disturbo *sm (fastidio)* bother; *(malessere)* disorder; *(di comunicazione)* interference.

disubbidiente *agg* disobedient.

disubbidire *vi*: ~ **(a qn)** to disobey (sb).

disumano, -a *agg* inhuman.

disuso *sm*: **in ~** obsolete.

ditale *sm* thimble.

dito *(pl f* **dita)** *sm* finger; *(misura)* drop; ~ **(del piede)** toe.

ditta *sf* company, firm.

dittatura *sf* dictatorship.

dittongo, -ghi sm diphthong.

diurno, -a agg daytime (dav s).

diva → **divo**.

divampare vi to flare up.

divano sm sofa; **~ letto** sofa-bed.

divaricare vt to open wide.

divenire vi to become.

diventare vi to become; **~ rosso** (persona) to go red.

diversificare vt to diversify.

diversità sf inv diversity; (l'esser diverso) difference.

diversivo sm diversion.

diverso, -a agg different; **~ da** different from □ **diversi, -e** agg pl various, several ♦ pron pl several; (varie persone) several (people).

divertente agg amusing.

divertimento sm amusement.

divertire vt to amuse □ **divertirsi** vr to enjoy o.s.

dividere vt to divide; (spartire) to share out; (separare) to separate; (condividere) to share □ **dividersi** vr (ripartirsi) to split up; (coppia) to separate.

divieto sm prohibition; **'~ di sosta'** 'no waiting'; **'~ di transito'** 'no thoroughfare'.

divinità sf inv divinity.

divino, -a agg divine.

divisa sf uniform.

divisione sf division.

diviso, -a pp → **dividere**.

divisorio, -a agg dividing.

divo sm, f star.

divorare vt to devour.

divorziare vi to divorce.

divorziato, -a agg divorced ♦ sm, f divorced person.

divorzio sm divorce.

divulgare vt (notizia) to divulge; (scienza, dottrina) to popularize □ **divulgarsi** vr to spread.

dizionario sm dictionary.

D.J. [di'dʒɛɪ] smf (abbr di disc-jockey) DJ.

D.N.A. sm DNA.

DOC (abbr di Denominazione di Origine Controllata) label guaranteeing the quality of an Italian wine.

doccia, -ce sf shower; **fare la ~** to take o to have a shower.

docente agg teaching ♦ smf teacher; (di università) lecturer.

docile agg (animale) docile.

documentare vt to document □ **documentarsi** vr to gather information.

documentario sm documentary.

documento sm document □ **documenti** smpl documents.

dodicesimo, -a num twelfth, → **sesto**.

dodici num twelve, → **sei**.

dogana sf customs (pl); **passare la ~** to go through customs.

doganale agg customs (dav s).

doganiere sm customs officer.

dolce agg sweet; (persona, carattere) gentle; (suono, musica, voce) soft ♦ sm (torta) cake; (portata) dessert.

dolcezza sf sweetness.

dolcificante sm sweetener.

dolciumi smpl confectionery (sg).

dolere *vi* to hurt ❑ **dolersi di** *vr* + *prep (essere spiacente di)* to regret; *(lamentarsi di)* to complain of.

dollaro *sm* dollar.

dolo *sm (DIR)* malice.

Dolomiti *sfpl*: **le ~** the Dolomites.

dolore *sm (fisico)* pain; *(morale)* sorrow.

doloroso, -a *agg (intervento)* painful; *(situazione)* distressing.

domanda *sf (per sapere)* question; *(per ottenere)* request; *(COMM)* demand; **fare una ~ a qn** to ask sb a question; **fare ~** to apply.

domandare *vt (per sapere)* to ask; *(per ottenere)* to ask for; **~ qc a qn** to ask sb sthg ❑ **domandarsi** *vr* to wonder.

domani *avv* tomorrow ♦ *sm (giorno seguente)* tomorrow; **a ~!** see you tomorrow!; **~ l'altro** the day after tomorrow; **il ~** the future; **~ mattina** tomorrow morning; **~ sera** tomorrow evening.

domare *vt (animale)* to tame; *(rivolta)* to put down; *(incendio)* to control.

domattina *avv* tomorrow morning.

domenica, -che *sf* Sunday, → sabato.

domestico, -a, -ci, -che *agg & sm, f* domestic.

domicilio *sm* domicile; **a ~** home *(dav s)*.

dominante *agg* dominant.

dominare *vt* to dominate; *(paese, popolo)* to rule; *(situazione, impulso)* to control ❑ **dominarsi** *vr* to control o.s.

dominio *sm (potere)* power; *(controllo)* control; *(territorio)* dominion; **essere di ~ pubblico** to be common knowledge.

domino *sm* dominoes *(pl)*.

donare *vt* to give ♦ *vi*: **questo colore ti dona** this colour suits you; **~ il sangue** to give blood.

donatore, -trice *sm, f* giver; *(di sangue, organi)* donor.

dondolare *vt* to rock ♦ *vi* to sway ❑ **dondolarsi** *vr* to sway.

dondolo *sm* swing hammock; **cavallo/sedia a ~** rocking horse/chair.

donna *sf* woman; *(nelle carte)* queen; **~ di servizio** maid.

dono *sm* gift.

doping *sm* doping.

dopo *avv* afterwards; *(più tardi)* later; *(nello spazio)* after ♦ *prep (di tempo)* after; *(di luogo)* past, after ♦ *agg inv* after ♦ *cong*: **~ aver fatto qc** after doing sthg; **il giorno ~** the following day; **un giorno ~** a day later; **a ~!** see you later!; **~ di me** after me.

dopobarba *sm inv* aftershave.

dopodiché *avv* after which.

dopodomani *avv* the day after tomorrow.

dopoguerra *sm* post-war period.

dopolavoro *sm* workers' recreational club.

dopopranzo *avv* in the early afternoon.

doposci *sm inv* après-ski.

doposcuola *sm inv* supervised

dovuto

after-school activities.

dopotutto *avv* after all.

doppiaggio *sm* dubbing.

doppiare *vt (film)* to dub; *(SPORT)* to lap; *(NAUT)* to round.

doppiato, -a *agg* dubbed.

doppio, -a *agg e avv* double ♦ *sm (SPORT)* doubles; **ne ha il ~ di me** *(quantità)* he has twice as much as me; *(numero)* he has twice as many as me.

doppione *sm* duplicate.

doppiopetto *sm* double-breasted jacket.

dorato, -a *agg (di colore)* golden; *(ricoperto d'oro)* gilt.

dormiglione, -a *sm, f* sleepyhead.

dormire *vi* to sleep.

dormitorio *sm* dormitory.

dorso *sm* back; *(di libro)* spine.

dosaggio *sm* dosage.

dosare *vt* to measure out; *(MED)* to dose.

dose *sf* amount; *(MED)* dose.

dosso *sm* bump; **togliersi o levarsi qc di ~** to take sthg off.

dotare *vt*: **~ qc di qc** to equip sthg with sthg.

dotato, -a *agg* gifted.

dote *sf (qualità)* gift; *(di sposa)* dowry.

Dott. *(abbr di dottore)* Dr.

dottorato *sm* doctorate.

dottore, -essa *sm, f (medico)* doctor; *(laureato)* graduate.

dottrina *sf* doctrine.

Dott.ssa *(abbr di dottoressa)* Dr.

dove *avv* where; **da ~ vieni?** where do you come from?; **di ~**

sei? where are you from?; **dov'è?** where is it?; **~ vai?** where are you going?; **siediti ~ vuoi** sit wherever you like.

dovere *vt* 1. *(essere debitore di)*: **~ qc a qn** to owe sb sthg; **gli devo dei soldi/un favore** I owe him some money/a favour; **quanto le devo?** *(in negozio)* how much does it come to?

2. *(esprime l'obbligo di)*: **~ fare qc** to have to do sthg; **comportarsi come si deve** to behave o.s. properly; **ora devo andare** I have to o must go now.

3. *(aver bisogno di)*: **~ fare qc** to have to do sthg; **devo dormire almeno otto ore** I need at least eight hours' sleep; **devi sapere che ...** you should know that ...

4. *(esprime un rimprovero)*: **avreste dovuto pensarci prima** you should have thought of it earlier; **avrei dovuto saperlo** I should have known.

5. *(per suggerire)*: **dovrebbe prendersi delle vacanze** he should o ought to take a holiday.

6. *(esprime probabilità)*: **devono essere già le sette** it must be seven o'clock already; **il tempo dovrebbe rimettersi** the weather should improve.

7. *(esprime intenzione)*: **dovevamo partire ieri, ma ...** we were due to leave yesterday, but ...

♦ *sm* duty; **avere dei doveri verso qn** to have a duty to sb.

dovunque *avv (in qualunque luogo)* wherever; *(dappertutto)* everywhere.

dovuto, -a *agg*: **~ a** due to.

dozzina *sf* dozen; **una ~ di rose** a dozen roses.

drago, -ghi *sm* dragon.

dramma, -i *sm* drama.

drammatico, -a, -ci, -che *agg* dramatic.

drastico, -a, -ci, -che *agg* drastic.

drenare *vt* to drain.

dritto, -a *agg & avv* = diritto.

drizzare *vt* (*raddrizzare*) to straighten; **~ le orecchie** to prick up one's ears □ **drizzarsi** *vr*: **drizzarsi (in piedi)** to stand up.

droga, -ghe *sf* drug.

drogare *vt* to drug □ **drogarsi** *vr* to take drugs.

drogato, -a *sm, f* drug addict.

drogheria *sf* grocer's.

droghiere *sm* grocer.

dromedario *sm* dromedary.

dubbio, -a *agg* (*incerto*) doubtful; (*equivoco*) questionable ♦ *sm* doubt; **ho il ~ che menta** I suspect that he's lying; **essere in ~** to be in doubt; **mettere in ~ qc** to question sthg; **senza ~** without a doubt.

dubbioso, -a *agg* uncertain.

dubitare : **dubitare di** *v + prep* to doubt; (*mettere in discussione*) to question; **dubito che venga** I doubt whether he'll come.

duca, -chi *sm* duke.

duchessa *sf* duchess.

due *num* two, → **sei**.

duecento *num* two hundred, → **sei** □ **Duecento** *sm*: **il Duecento** the thirteenth century.

duemila *num* two thousand □ **il Duemila** *sm* the year two thou-

sand, → **sei**.

duepezzi *sm inv* (*bikini*) bikini; (*abito*) two-piece suit.

duna *sf* dune.

dunque *cong* (*perciò*) so; (*allora*) well ♦ *sm*: **venire al ~** to get to the point.

duomo *sm* cathedral.

duplex *sm inv* party line.

duplicato *sm* duplicate.

duplice *agg* double; **in ~ copia** in duplicate.

durante *prep* during.

durare *vi* to last ♦ *vt*: **~ fatica** (a fare qc) to tire o.s. out (doing sthg).

durata *sf* (*periodo*) duration.

durezza *sf* (*di materiale*) hardness; (*insensibilità*) severity.

duro, -a *agg* hard; (*carne*) tough; (*ostinato*) stubborn; (*severo*) harsh ♦ *sm, f* tough person; **tieni ~!** don't give in!

durone *sm* callus.

E

e (*spesso* **ed** *+ vocale*) *cong* and; **~ io?** what about me?; **~ vacci!** well then, go!

è → **essere**.

E (*abbr di est*) E.

ebano *sm* ebony.

ebbene *cong* (*allora*) well.

ebbrezza *sf* (*ubriachezza*) intox-

stato di ~ drunk.

ebete *agg* idiotic.

ebollizione *sf* boiling.

ebraico, -a, -ci, -che *agg &* *sm* Hebrew.

ebreo, -a *agg* Jewish ◆ *sm, f* Jew.

Ebridi *sfpl:* **le (isole)** ~ the Hebrides.

ecc. *(abbr da eccetera)* etc.

eccedenza *sf* excess.

eccedere *vt* to exceed ❑ **eccedere in** *v + prep:* ~ **nel bere/mangiare** to drink/eat too much.

eccellente *agg* excellent.

eccellenza *sf* excellence; *(titolo)* Excellency.

eccellere *vi:* ~ **(in qc)** to excel (at sthg).

eccelso *pp* → **eccellere.**

eccentrico, -a, -ci, -che *agg* eccentric.

eccessivo, -a *agg* excessive.

eccesso *sm* excess; ~ **di velocità** speeding; **all'**~ excessively; **bagaglio in** ~ excess baggage.

eccetera *avv* etcetera.

eccetto *prep* except ◆ *cong:* ~ **che** unless.

eccettuare *vt* to except.

eccezionale *agg* exceptional.

eccezione *sf* exception; **a** ~ **di** with the exception of; **d'**~ exceptional; **senza** ~ without exception.

eccidio *sm* massacre.

eccitante *agg (stimolante)* stimulating; *(provocante)* exciting.

eccitare *vt (curiosità)* to arouse ❑ **eccitarsi** *vr* to get excited; *(ses-*

sualmente) to become aroused.

eccitazione *sf* excitement.

ecclesiastico, -a, -ci, -che *agg* ecclesiastical ◆ *sm* ecclesiastic.

ecco *avv* here is; ~ **a lei** here you are; ~ **fatto!** there, that's that!; **eccolo!** there he is!; **eccone uno!** there's one!

eccome *avv* you bet!

eclissi *sf inv* eclipse.

eco *(pl m* **echi)** *sf* echo.

ecologia *sf* ecology.

ecologico, -a, -ci, -che *agg* ecological.

economia *sf* economy; *(scienza)* economics *(sg);* **fare** ~ to economize.

economico, -a, -ci, -che *agg (dell'economia)* economic; *(poco costoso)* economical.

ecosistema, -i *sm* ecosystem.

ECU *sm inv* ECU.

eczema, -i *sm* eczema.

ed → **e.**

edera *sf* ivy.

edicola *sf* newsstand.

edificare *vt* to build.

edificio *sm* building.

edile *agg* building *(dav s).*

Edimburgo *sf* Edinburgh.

editore, -trice *agg* publishing *(dav s)* ◆ *sm* publisher.

editoria *sf* publishing (industry).

edizione *sf* edition; ~ **speciale** special edition.

educare *vt (formare)* to educate; *(bambino)* to bring up.

educato, -a *agg* polite.

educazione

educazione *sf (maniere)* (good) manners *(pl)*; *(formazione)* training; ~ **fisica** physical education.

effervescente *agg* effervescent.

effettivamente *avv* in fact.

effettivo, -a *agg* actual, real.

effetto *sm* effect; **in effetti** in fact, actually.

effettuare *vt* to carry out.

efficace *agg* effective.

efficacia *sf* effectiveness.

efficiente *agg* efficient.

efficienza *sf* efficiency.

effimero, -a *agg (gioia, successo)* short-lived.

egemonia *sf (supremazia)* hegemony.

Egitto *sm*: l' ~ Egypt.

egli *pron* he; ~ **stesso** he himself.

egocentrico, -a, -ci, -che *agg* egocentric.

egoismo *sm* selfishness.

egoista, -i, -e *agg* selfish.

egregio, -a, -gi, -gie *agg (nelle lettere)*: **Egregio Signore** Dear Sir.

eguagliare = uguagliare.

ehi *esclam* hey!

E.I. *abbr* = **Esercito Italiano**.

elaborare *vt (progetto, piano)* to work out; *(con computer)* to process.

elaborato, -a *agg* elaborate.

elaboratore *sm*: ~ **(elettronico)** computer.

elaborazione *sf*: ~ **dei dati** data processing.

elasticità *sf* elasticity; *(di mente)* flexibility.

elasticizzato, -a *agg* stretch *(dav s)*.

elastico, -a, -ci, -che *agg* elastic; *(momento)* flexible ♦ *sm (gommino)* rubber band; *(da cucito)* elastic.

Elba *sf*: l'**(isola d')** ~ Elba.

elefante *sm* elephant.

elegante *agg* elegant.

eleganza *sf* elegance.

eleggere *vt* to elect.

elementare *agg* elementary.

elementari *sfpl*: **le (scuole) elementari** primary school *(sg)* (Br), grade school *(sg)* (Am).

elemento *sm (fattore)* element; *(di cucina)* unit; *(persona)* individual.

elemosina *sf* alms *(pl)*; **chiedere l'**~ to beg.

elencare *vt* to list.

elenco, -chi *sm* list; ~ **telefonico** telephone directory.

eletto, -a *pp* → **eleggere**.

elettorale *agg* electoral.

elettore, -trice *sm, f* voter.

elettrauto *sm inv (officina)* workshop for electrical repairs on cars; *(persona)* car electrician.

elettricista, -i *sm* electrician.

elettricità *sf* electricity.

elettrico, -a, -ci, -che *agg* electric.

elettrodomestico, -ci *sm* electrical household appliance.

elettronico, -a, -ci, -che *agg* electronic.

elezione *sf* election.

elica, -che *sf* propeller.

elicottero *sm* helicopter.

eliminare *vt* to eliminate.

eliminatoria *sf* qualifying round.

ella *pron* she.

elmetto *sm* helmet.

elogio *sm* praise.

eloquente *agg* eloquent.

eludere *vt* to evade.

elusivo, -a *agg* elusive.

elvetico, -a, -ci, -che *agg* Swiss.

emaciato, -a *agg* emaciated.

emanare *vt* (*luce*) to send out; (*calore*) to give off; (*legge*) to issue.

emancipato, -a *agg* emancipated.

emarginato, -a *sm, f* social outcast.

ematoma, -i *sm* haematoma.

embrione *sm* embryo.

emergenza *sf* emergency.

emergere *vi* to emerge.

emerso, -a *pp* → **emergere**

emicrania *sf* migraine.

emigrante *smf* emigrant.

emigrare *vi* (*persona*) to emigrate; (*animale*) to migrate.

Emilia Romagna *sf*: l'~ Emilia Romagna (*region in eastern central Italy*).

emisfero *sm* hemisphere.

emittente *sf* broadcasting station.

emorragia *sf* hemorrhage.

emozionante *agg* thrilling.

emozione *sf* emotion.

emulsione *sf* emulsion.

enciclopedia *sf* encyclopedia.

ENEL *abbr* Italian national electricity company.

energia *sf* energy; ~ **elettrica** electrical energy.

energico, -a, -ci, -che *agg* energetic.

enfasi *sf inv* emphasis.

enigma, -i *sm* enigma.

ennesimo, -a *agg* umpteenth.

enorme *agg* enormous.

enoteca, -che *sf* (*negozio*) vintage wine store; (*bar*) wine bar.

ente *sm* body, organization.

entrambi, -e *pron pl* both (of them) ♦ *agg pl*: **entrambe le città** both towns.

entrare *vi* to enter, to go in; ~ **in qc** (*trovar posto*) to fit into sthg; (*essere ammesso*) to join sthg; **entra!** come in!; **questo non c'entra niente** this has nothing to do with it; ~ **in una stanza** to enter a room; ~ **in guerra** to go to war; **far** ~ **qn** to let sb in.

entrata *sf* entrance; '~ **libera**' (*in museo*) 'admission free'; (*in negozio*) 'browsers welcome' ❑ **entrate** *sfpl* (*incasso*) takings; (*guadagno*) income (*sg*).

entro *prep* (*periodo*) in, within; (*scadenza*) by.

entusiasmare *vt* to enthral ❑ **entusiasmarsi** *vr*: **entusiasmarsi (per)** to get excited (about).

entusiasmo *sm* enthusiasm.

entusiasta, -i, -e *agg* enthusiastic.

enunciare *vt* to enunciate.

Eolie *sfpl*: **le (isole)** ~ the Aeolian Islands.

epatite *sf* hepatitis.

epidemia sf epidemic.

epidermide sf epidermis.

Epifania sf: l'~ the Epiphany.

epilessia sf epilepsy.

episodio sm episode.

epoca, -che sf (era, età) age; (tempo) time; **d'~** (mobile, costume) period (dav s).

eppure cong and yet, nevertheless.

equatore sm equator.

equazione sf equation.

equestre agg equestrian.

equilibrare vt to balance.

equilibrato, -a agg (proporzionato) balanced; (persona) well-balanced.

equilibrio sm (stabilità) balance; (posizione, stato) equilibrium; **perdere l'~** to lose one's balance.

equino, -a agg equine, horse (dav s).

equipaggiamento sm (di nave, aereo) fitting out; (sportivo) equipment.

equipaggio sm crew.

equitazione sf horse riding.

equivalente agg & sm equivalent.

equivalere : equivalere a v + prep to be equivalent to.

equivalso, -a pp → equivalere.

equivoco, -a, -ci, -che agg (ambiguo) equivocal; (poco onesto) dubious ♦ sm misunderstanding.

era sf age.

erba sf (prato) grass; (pianta) herb; **erbe aromatiche** herbs.

erbazzone sm spinach and

Parmesan cheese tart topped with bacon and parsley (a speciality of Emilia Romagna).

erboristeria sf herbalist's.

erede smf heir (f heiress).

eredità sf inv inheritance; (biologica) heredity; **lasciare qc in ~ (a qn)** to bequeath sthg (to sb).

ereditare vt to inherit.

ereditario, -a agg hereditary.

eresia sf heresy.

eretico, -a, -ci, -che sm, f heretic.

eretto, -a pp → erigere ♦ agg erect.

ergastolo sm life imprisonment.

erigere vt to erect.

ernia sf hernia.

ero → essere.

eroe, eroina sm, f hero (f heroine).

erogare vt to supply.

eroico, -a, -ci, -che agg heroic.

eroina sf (droga) heroin, → eroe.

erosione sf erosion.

erotico, -a, -ci, -che agg erotic.

errare vi (vagare) to wander; (sbagliare) to be mistaken.

errore sm (di ortografia, calcolo) mistake; (colpa) error; **per ~** by mistake.

erta sf: **stare all'~** to be on the alert.

eruzione sf (di vulcano) eruption; (MED) rash.

esagerare vt & vi to exaggerate.

esagerato, -a *agg* excessive.

esalazione *sf* exhalation.

esaltare *vt* (*lodare*) to extol; (*entusiasmare*) to excite.

esame *sm* examination; **fare o dare un ~** to take an exam; **~ del sangue** blood test.

esaminare *vt* (*analizzare*) to examine; (*candidato*) to interview.

esattamente *avv & esclam* exactly.

esattezza *sf* accuracy.

esatto, -a *agg* (*giusto*) correct; (*preciso*) exact ♦ *esclam* exactly!

esattore *sm* collector.

esauriente *agg* exhaustive.

esaurimento *sm* exhaustion; **~ (nervoso)** nervous breakdown.

esaurire *vt* to exhaust □ **esaurirsi** *vr* (*merce*) to run out; (*persona*) to wear o.s. out.

esaurito, -a *agg* (*provviste, pozzo*) exhausted; (*merce*) sold out; (*persona*) worn out; **'tutto ~'** 'sold out'.

esausto, -a *agg* worn out.

esca (*pl* esche) *sf* bait.

escandescenza *sf*: **dare in escandescenze** to lose one's temper.

eschimese *smf* Eskimo.

esclamare *vi* to exclaim.

esclamazione *sf* exclamation.

escludere *vt* to exclude.

esclusiva *sf* (*di notizia*) scoop; (*DIR*) exclusive rights (*pl*).

esclusivo, -a *agg* exclusive.

escluso, -a *pp* → **escludere**.

esco → **uscire**.

escogitare *vt* to come up with.

escursione *sf* excursion; **~ termica** temperature range.

esecutivo, -a *agg & sm* executive.

esecuzione *sf* execution; (*di concerto*) performance.

eseguire *vt* to carry out; (*in musica*) to perform.

esempio *sm* example; **ad o per ~** for example; **fare un ~** to give an example.

esentare *vt*: **~ qn/qc da qc** to exempt sb/sthg from sthg.

esente *agg*: **~ da** (*esonerato da*) exempt from; (*libero da*) free from.

esequie *sfpl* funeral rites.

esercitare *vt* to exercise; (*professione*) to practise □ **esercitarsi** *vr* to practise.

esercito *sm* army.

esercizio *sm* exercise; (*di professione*) practice; (*azienda, negozio*) business; **essere fuori ~** to be out of practice.

esibire *vt* to show □ **esibirsi** *vr* to perform.

esigente *agg* demanding.

esigenza *sf* (*bisogno*) requirement; (*pretesa*) demand.

esigere *vt* (*pretendere*) to demand; (*richiedere*) to require; (*riscuotere*) to collect.

esile *agg* (*sottile*) thin; (*persona*) slim.

esilio *sm* exile.

esistente *agg* existing.

esistenza *sf* existence.

esistere *vi* to exist.

esitare *vi* to hesitate.

esitazione *sf* hesitation.

esito *sm* outcome.

esorbitante *agg* exorbitant.

esordio *sm* debut.

esortare *vt:* ~ qn a fare qc to urge sb to do sthg.

esotico, -a, -ci, -che *agg* exotic.

espandere *vt* to expand ❑ **espandersi** *vr (ingrandirsi)* to expand; *(odori, liquidi)* to spread.

espansione *sf (allargamento)* expansion; *(di attività)* growth.

espansivo, -a *agg* expansive.

espanso, -a *pp →* espandere.

espediente *sm* expedient.

espellere *vt (da scuola)* to expel; *(MED)* to excrete.

esperienza *sf* experience.

esperimento *sm (prova)* test; *(scientifico)* experiment.

esperto, -a *agg (con esperienza)* experienced; *(bravo)* skilful ♦ *sm* expert.

espiare *vt* to expiate.

esplicito, -a *agg* explicit.

esplodere *vi* to explode ♦ *vt* to fire.

esplorare *vt* to explore.

esploratore, -trice *sm, f* explorer.

esplosione *sf* explosion; *(di gioia, ira)* outburst.

esplosivo, -a *agg & sm* explosive.

esploso, -a *pp →* esplodere.

esporre *vt (merce)* to display; *(opera d'arte)* to show; *(pellicola)* to expose; *(idea, fatto)* to explain.

esportare *vt* to export.

esportazione *sf (spedizione)* exportation; *(merce)* exports *(pl)*.

esposizione *sf (di merce)* display; *(mostra)* exhibition; *(di pellicola)* exposure; *(resoconto)* account.

esposto, -a *pp →* esporre ♦ *sm* petition ♦ *agg:* ~ a sud facing south.

espressione *sf* expression.

espressivo, -a *agg* expressive.

espresso, -a *pp →* esprimere ♦ *sm (treno)* express; *(caffè)* espresso; *(lettera)* express letter.

esprimere *vt (pensiero, sentimento)* to express ❑ **esprimersi** *vr (spiegarsi)* to express o.s.; *(parlare)* to speak.

espulso, -a *pp →* espellere.

essenziale *agg* essential.

essere *vi* 1. *(per descrivere)* to be; **sono italiano** I'm Italian; **sei solo?** are you alone?; **siamo di Torino** we're from Turin; **Franco è (un) medico** Franco is a doctor.

2. *(trovarsi)* to be; **dove siete?** where are you?; **il museo è in centro** the museum is in the town centre; **sono a casa** I'm at home; **sono stato in Scozia tre volte** I've been to Scotland three times.

3. *(esistere)*: **c'è** there is; **c'è un'altra possibilità** there's another possibility; **ci sono** there are; **ci sono vari alberghi** there are various hotels.

4. *(con data, ora)* to be; **oggi è martedì** today is Tuesday; **è l'una** it's one o'clock; **sono le due** it's two o'clock.

5. *(con prezzo, peso)*: **quant'è?** — **(sono) 10 000 lire** how much is

it? – (that's) 10,000 lira; **sono due chili e mezzo** that's two and a half kilos.

6. *(indica appartenenza):* ~ **di qn** to belong to sb; **questa macchina è di Paolo** this car is Paolo's.

7. *(indica bisogno, obbligo):* **è da fare** it's still to be done; **la camera è da prenotare** the room is to be booked.

♦ *v impers* to be; **è tardi** it's late; **è vero che …** it's true that …; **oggi è freddo** it's cold today; **è meglio telefonare** it's better to phone.

♦ *v aus* **1.** *(in tempi passati)* to have, to be; **sono tornato ieri** I came back yesterday; **erano già usciti** they'd already gone out; **sono nata a Roma** I was born in Rome; **ti sei lavato?** did you wash yourself?

2. *(in passivi)* to be; **questo oggetto è fatto a mano** this object is hand-made; **sono stato pagato ieri** I was paid yesterday.

♦ *sm (creatura)* being; ~ **umano** human being; **gli esseri viventi** the living.

essi, -e → **esso**.

esso, -a *pron* it □ **essi, -e** *pron pl (soggetto)* they; *(con preposizione)* them.

est *sm* east; **a** ~ **di Milano** east of Milan.

estate *sf* summer.

estendere *vt* to extend.

esteriore *agg (esterno)* external, outward; *(apparente)* superficial.

esterno, -a *agg* exterior *(muro)* outer; *(pericolo)* external ♦ *sm* outside; **all'~** on the outside.

estero, -a *agg* foreign ♦ *sm*: **l'~** foreign countries *(pl)*; **all'~**

abroad.

esteso, -a *pp* → **estendere** ♦ *agg* extensive.

estetista, -i, -e *smf* beautician.

estinguere *vt (fuoco)* to extinguish; *(debito)* to settle □ **estinguersi** *vr (fuoco)* to go out; *(specie)* to become extinct.

estinto, -a *pp* → **estinguere**.

estintore *sm (fire)* extinguisher.

estivo, -a *agg* summer *(dav s)*.

estorcere *vt* to extort.

estraneo, -a *agg* unconnected ♦ *sm, f* stranger.

estrarre *vt* to extract; *(sorteggiare)* to draw.

estratto, -a *pp* → **estrarre** ♦ *sm (di sostanza)* essence; *(di libro)* extract; ~ **conto** bank statement.

estrazione *sf* extraction; ~ **a sorte** draw; ~ **sociale** social class.

estremità *sf inv* end ♦ *sfpl* extremities.

estremo, -a *agg (grande)* extreme; *(drastico)* drastic; *(ultimo)* final, last ♦ *sm (punto)* extreme; *(fig: limite)* limit □ **estremi** *smpl* details.

estroverso, -a *agg* extrovert.

estuario *sm* estuary.

esuberante *agg* exuberant.

età *sf inv* age; **abbiamo la stessa** ~ we are the same age; **la maggiore** ~ the legal age; **di mezza** ~ middle-aged; **la terza** ~ old age.

etere *sm* ether.

eternità *sf* eternity.

eterno, -a *agg* eternal.

eterogeneo, -a *agg* heterogeneous.

eterosessuale *agg & smf* heterosexual.

etica *sf* ethics.

etichetta *sf (di prodotto)* label; *(cerimoniale)* etiquette.

Etna *sm*: l'~ Mount Etna.

etrusco, -a, -schi, -sche *agg* Etruscan □ **Etruschi** *smpl*: gli **Etruschi** the Etruscans.

ettaro *sm* hectare.

etto *sm* = 100 grams.

ettogrammo *sm* hectogram.

eucaristia *sf*: l'~ the Eucharist.

euforia *sf* euphoria.

EUR *sm* residential area of Rome built on the site of the Rome Exhibition.

Europa *sf*: l'~ Europe.

europeo, -a *agg & sm, f* European.

eurovisione *sf*: in ~ Eurovision *(dav s)*.

eutanasia *sf* euthanasia.

evacuare *vt* to evacuate.

evacuazione *sf* evacuation.

evadere *vt (tasse, fisco)* to evade; *(corrispondenza)* to deal with ♦ *vi*: ~ **(da qc)** to escape (from sthg).

evaporare *vi* to evaporate.

evasione *sf* escape; ~ **fiscale** tax evasion; **d'~** escapist.

evasivo, -a *agg* evasive.

evaso, -a *pp* → **evadere** ♦ *sm, f* escapee.

evenienza *sf*: in ogni ~ should the need arise.

evento *sm* event.

eventuale *agg* possible.

eventualità *sf inv* possibility.

eventualmente *avv* if necessary.

evidente *agg (chiaro)* clear; *(ovvio)* obvious.

evidenza *sf* evidence; **mettere in** ~ to highlight.

evitare *vt* to avoid; ~ **di fare qc** to avoid doing sthg; ~ **qc a qn** to spare sb sthg.

evocare *vt (ricordare)* to recall; *(spiriti)* to evoke.

evoluto, -a *agg (tecnica, paese)* advanced; *(persona)* broadminded.

evoluzione *sf (biologica)* evolution; *(progresso)* progress.

evviva *esclam* hurrah!

ex *prep*: l'~ **presidente** the former president; **la sua** ~ **moglie** his ex-wife.

extra *agg inv & sm inv* extra.

extracomunitario, -a *agg* from outside the EU ♦ *sm, f immigrant from a non-EU country*.

extraconiugale *agg* extramarital.

extraterrestre *smf* alien.

F

fa¹ → **fare**.

fa² *avv*: **un anno** ~ a year ago **tempo** ~ some time ago.

fabbisogno *sm* needs *(pl)*.

fabbrica *sf* factory.

fabbricare *vt (costruire)* to build; *(produrre)* to make.

faccenda sf (questione) affair, matter □ **faccende** sfpl: **faccende (domestiche)** housework (sg).

facchino sm porter.

faccia, -ce sf face; **di ~ a** opposite; **~ a ~** face to face; **che ~ tosta!** what a nerve!

facciata sf (di edificio) facade; (di pagina) side.

faccio →**fare**.

facile agg easy; **è ~ che il treno sia in ritardo** the train is likely to be late.

facilità sf (caratteristica) easiness; (attitudine) ease.

facilitare vt to make easier.

facoltà sf inv faculty; (potere) power.

facoltativo, -a agg optional.

facsimile sm inv facsimile.

fagiano sm pheasant.

fagiolino sm French bean (Br), string bean (Am).

fagiolo sm bean; **fagioli all'uccelletto** white beans cooked with tomatoes and pepper (a Tuscan speciality).

fagotto sm bundle; (strumento) bassoon; **far ~** to pack one's bags and leave.

fai da te sm inv do-it-yourself.

falange sf finger bone.

falciare vt to mow.

falda sf (di cappello) brim; (d'acqua) water table; (di monte) slope.

falegname sm carpenter.

falla sf leak.

fallimento sm failure; (DIR) bankruptcy.

fallire vi (DIR) to go bankrupt; (non riuscire): **~ (in qc)** to fail (in

sthg) ♦ vt to miss.

fallo sm foul.

falò sm inv bonfire.

falsificare vt to forge.

falso, -a agg false; (gioiello) fake; (banconota, quadro) forged ♦ sm forgery.

fama sf fame; (reputazione) reputation.

fame sf hunger; **aver ~** to be hungry.

famiglia sf family.

familiare agg (della famiglia) family (dav s); (noto) familiar; (atmosfera) friendly; (informale) informal ♦ smf familiar.

familiari smpl relations.

famoso, -a agg famous.

fanale sm light.

fanatico, -a, -ci, -che agg fanatical.

fango, -ghi sm mud.

fanno →**fare**.

fannullone, -a sm, f loafer.

fantascienza sf science fiction.

fantasia sf (immaginazione) imagination ♦ agg inv patterned.

fantasma, -i sm ghost.

fantastico, -a, -ci, -che agg fantastic; (immaginario) fantasy (dav s).

fantino sm jockey.

fantoccio sm puppet.

farabutto sm crook.

faraglione sm stack.

faraona sf guinea fowl.

farcito, -a agg (pollo) stuffed; (torta) filled.

fard sm inv blusher.

fare vt 1. (fabbricare, preparare) to

farfalla

make; **~ progetti** to make plans; **~ da mangiare** to cook.

2. (attuare) to make; **~ un viaggio** to go on a trip; **~ un sogno** to dream.

3. (essere occupato in) to do; **cosa fai stasera?** what are you doing tonight?; **fa il meccanico** he's a mechanic; **~ l'università** to go to university; **faccio tennis** I play tennis.

4. (percorrere) to do; **che percorso facciamo per rientrare?** which route shall we take to go back?

5. (suscitare) to make; **mi fa pena** I feel sorry for him; **farsi male** to hurt o.s.; **~ paura** to be frightening; **~ chiasso** to be noisy.

6. (atteggiarsi a) to play, to act; **~ lo scemo** to behave like an idiot.

7. (indica il risultato): **2 più 2 fa 4** 2 and 2 makes 4; **quanto fa?** what's the total?

8. (credere): **ti facevo più furbo** I thought you were smarter than that.

9. (acquisire): **farsi degli amici** to make friends; **farsi la macchina nuova** (fam) to get a new car.

10. (con infinito) to make; **far credere qc a qn** to make sb believe sthg; **far vedere qc a qn** to show sb sthg; **far costruire qc** to have sthg built.

11. (in espressioni): **non ~ caso a** not to pay attention to; **non fa niente** (non importa) it doesn't matter; **farcela** to manage; **non ce la faccio più** I can't go on; **far bene/male (a qn)** to be good/bad (for sb).

♦ **vi 1.** (agire) to do; **come si fa a uscire?** how do you get out?; **fai come ti pare** do as you like; **non fa che ripetere le stesse cose** all he does is repeat the same things; **darsi da ~** to get busy.

2. (fam: dire) to say.

♦ **v impers** to be; **fa bello/brutto** it's lovely/awful weather; **fa caldo/freddo** it's hot/cold.

❑ **farsi** vr (diventare): **farsi grande** to grow up; **farsi furbo** (fam) to get smart; **farsi vivo** to get in touch; **farsi avanti/indietro** (spostarsi) to move forward/back.

farfalla sf butterfly; **cravatta a ~** bow tie.

farina sf flour; **~ gialla** maize flour.

farinata sf type of bread similar to a very thin 'focaccia' but made from chickpea flour (a speciality of Liguria).

faringite sf pharyngitis.

farmacia sf (negozio) chemist's (Br), drugstore (Am); (scienza) pharmacy; **'farmacie di turno'** 'duty chemists'.

farmacista, -i, -e smf pharmacist.

farmaco, -ci sm medicine.

faro sm (per navi) lighthouse; (di veicoli) headlight; (per aerei) beacon.

farsa sf farce.

farsumagru sm inv beef roll stuffed with mince, pecorino cheese, sausage and boiled eggs, cooked in Marsala and tomato puree (a Sicilian speciality).

fascia, -sce sf (striscia) strip, band; (medica) bandage; (di territorio) strip; (di popolazione) band; **~ elastica** elastic bandage; **~ oraria**

time band.

fasciare *vt* to bandage.

fasciatura *sf* bandage.

fascicolo *sm (di rivista)* issue; *(di documenti)* file.

fascino *sm* charm.

fascio *sm (d'erba, di fibri)* bunch; *(di legna)* bundle; *(di luce)* beam.

fascismo *sm* Fascism.

fascista, -i, -e *agg & smf* Fascist.

fase *sf* phase; *(di motore)* stroke.

fast food [fast'fud] *sm inv* fast-food restaurant.

fastidio *sm* bother, trouble; **dare ~ a qn** to annoy sb; **le dà ~ se fumo?** do you mind if I smoke?

fastidioso, -a *agg* inconvenient.

fastoso, -a *agg* sumptuous.

fasullo, -a *agg (falso)* fake.

fata *sf* fairy.

fatale *agg (mortale)* fatal; *(inevitabile)* inevitable; *(sguardo)* irresistible.

fatalità *sf inv (inevitabilità)* inevitability; *(destino)* fate; *(disgrazia)* misfortune.

fatica *sf* hard work; *(stanchezza)* fatigue; **fare ~ a fare qc** to have difficulty doing sthg; **a ~** hardly.

faticoso, -a *agg (stancante)* exhausting; *(difficile)* hard.

fatidico, -a, -ci, -che *agg* fateful.

fato *sm* fate.

fatto, -a *pp* → **fare** ◆ *sm (cosa concreta)* fact; *(avvenimento)* event ◆ *agg:* **~ a mano** hand-made; **~ in casa** home-made; **il ~ è che ...** the

fact is that ...; **cogliere qn sul ~** to catch sb in the act; **in ~ di vini ...** when it comes to wine ...; **sono fatti miei** that's my business.

fattoria *sf* farm.

fattorino *sm (per consegne)* delivery man; *(d'albergo)* messenger.

fattura *sf* invoice; *(magia)* spell.

fauna *sf* fauna.

favola *sf* fairy tale; *(cosa bella)* dream.

favoloso, -a *agg* fabulous.

favore *sm* favour; **per ~** please.

favorevole *agg* favourable; *(voto)* in favour.

favorire *vt (promuovere)* to promote; *(aiutare)* to favour; **vuoi ~?** would you like some?

favorito, -a *agg* favourite.

fazzoletto *sm (da naso)* handkerchief; *(per la testa)* headscarf.

febbraio *sm* February, → **settembre**.

febbre *sf* fever; **avere la ~** to have a temperature.

feci *sfpl* excrement *(sg)*.

fecondazione *sf* fertilization.

fede *sf* faith; *(anello)* wedding ring; **aver ~ in** to have faith in; **essere in buona/cattiva ~** to act in good/bad faith.

fedele *agg* faithful; *(cliente)* loyal; *(preciso)* accurate ◆ *smf* believer.

fedeltà *sf (lealtà)* faithfulness, loyalty; *(precisione)* accuracy.

federa *sf* pillowcase.

federazione *sf* federation.

fegato *sm* liver; *(fig: coraggio)* guts *(pl)*; **~ alla veneziana** thinly *sliced calves' liver and onions.*

felice *agg* happy.

felicità *sf* happiness.

felicitarsi *vr:* ~ **con qn per qc** to congratulate sb on sthg.

felino, -a *agg & sm* feline.

felpa *sf (maglia)* sweatshirt; *(tessuto)* plush.

femmina *sf (animale)* female; *(figlia, ragazza)* girl.

femminile *agg* female; *(rivista, modi)* women's *(dav s)*; *(GRAMM)* feminine ♦ *sm* feminine.

femminismo *sm* feminism.

fenomenale *agg* phenomenal.

fenomeno *sm* phenomenon.

feriale *agg* working *(dav s)*.

ferie *sfpl* holidays *(Br)*, vacation *(sg) (Am)*; **andare in** ~ to go on holiday *(Br)*, to go on vacation *(Am)*; **essere in** ~ to be on holiday *(Br)*, to be on vacation *(Am)*.

ferire *vt (colpire)* to injure; *(addolorare)* to hurt □ **ferirsi** *vr* to injure o.s.

ferita *sf* wound.

ferito, -a *agg* injured ♦ *sm, f* injured person.

fermaglio *sm* clip.

fermare *vt* to stop; *(bottone)* to fasten; *(sospetto)* to detain ♦ *vi* to stop □ **fermarsi** *vr* to stop; *(sostare)* to stay; **fermarsi a fare qc** to stop to do sthg.

fermata *sf* stop; **dell'autobus** bus stop; **'~ prenotata** 'bus stopping'; **'~ a richiesta** 'request stop'.

fermento *sm* ferment.

fermo, -a *agg (persona)* still; *(veicolo)* stationary; *(mano, voce)*

steady; *(orologio)* stopped; *(saldo)* firm; **stare** ~ to keep still.

fermo posta *avv & sm inv* poste restante *(Br)*, general delivery *(Am)*.

feroce *agg (animale)* ferocious; *(dolore)* terrible.

ferragosto *sm (giorno)* Italian public holiday which falls on 15 August; *(periodo)* August holidays *(pl)*.

---

i | **FERRAGOSTO**

August 15, the feast of the Assumption, is a national holiday in Italy and marks the peak of the holiday season. The Italian name, "Ferragosto", comes from the Latin "feriae augustae", meaning "August holidays". Cities become ghost towns, as families and groups of friends flock to the coast, the mountains and the lakes, and most factories and businesses close down.

---

ferramenta *sf* ironmonger's *(Br)*, hardware store *(Am)*.

ferro *sm* iron; **toccare** ~ to touch wood; ~ **battuto** wrought iron; ~ **da calza** knitting needle; ~ **da stiro** iron; **carne ai ferri** grilled meat.

ferrovia *sf* railway *(Br)*, railroad *(Am)*; **Ferrovie dello Stato** *Italian railway system,* ≃ British Rail *(Br),* ≃ Amtrak *(Am)*.

ferroviario, -a *agg* railway *(Br)* *(dav s)*, railroad *(Am)* *(dav s)*.

fertile *agg* fertile.

fervido, -a *agg* fervent, ardent.

fesso, -a *agg (fam)* stupid.

fessura *sf* crack; *(per gettone, moneta)* slot.

festa *sf (religiosa)* feast; *(giorno festivo)* holiday; *(ricevimento)* party; *(ricorrenza):* **la ~ della mamma** Mother's Day; **far ~** to have a holiday; **far ~ a qn** to give sb a warm welcome; **buone feste!** *(a Natale)* Merry Christmas!

 FESTA DELLE DONNE

Since the 1970s, March 8 has been celebrated as National Women's Day in Italy. Meetings, debates and conferences on women's issues are held, and there is now a tradition of presenting women with the gift of a bunch of mimosa.

festeggiare *vt (ricorrenza)* to celebrate; *(persona)* to throw a party for.

festival *sm inv* festival.

i **FESTIVAL DI SPOLETO**

Also known as the "Festival dei Due Mondi" (Festival of the Two Worlds), the Festival of Spoleto has been held every June and July since 1958. It hosts top-class performances of opera, theatre, music and ballet, attracting internationally renowned artists and a cosmopolitan audience.

festivo, -a *agg* festive; **giorno ~** holiday; **orario ~** *timetable for Sundays and public holidays.*

festone *sm* festoon.

festoso, -a *agg* merry.

feto *sm* foetus.

fetta *sf* slice.

fettuccine *sfpl* ribbons of egg pasta.

fettunta *sf* toast flavoured with garlic and olive oil (a Tuscan speciality).

FF.SS. *abbr* = BR *(Br)*, = Amtrak *(Am)*.

fiaba *sf* fairy tale.

fiaccola *sf* torch.

fiamma *sf* flame; **dare alle fiamme** to set on fire.

fiammeggiare *vt* to border.

fiammifero *sm* match.

fiancheggiare *vt* to border.

fianco, -chi *sm (di persona)* hip; *(di edificio, collina)* side; **di ~ a** next to.

fiasco, -schi *sm* flask; **fare ~** to flop.

fiato *sm (respiro)* breath; *(resistenza)* stamina; **avere il ~ grosso** to be out of breath.

fibbia *sf* buckle.

fibra *sf* fibre.

ficcanaso *(pl m* ficcanasi, *pl f inv)* *smf* busybody.

ficcare *vt* to put ♦ **ficcarsi** *vr:* **dove ti eri ficcato?** where did you get to?

fico, -chi *sm* fig; **~ d'India** prickly pear.

fidanzamento *sm* engagement.

fidanzarsi *vr* to get engaged.

fidanzato, -a *agg* engaged ♦ *sm, f* fiancé *(*fiancée).

fidarsi *vr:* **~ di** to trust.

fidato, -a *agg* trustworthy.

fiducia *sf* confidence.

fiducioso, -a *agg* confident.

fieno *sm* hay.

fiera *sf* fair.

fiero, -a *agg* proud.

fifa *sf (fam)* fright.

figlio, -a *sm, f* son *(f* daughter), child; ~ **unico** only child.

figura *sf* figure; *(illustrazione)* illustration, picture; **fare bella/ brutta ~** to create a good/bad impression.

figurare *vi* to appear ◆ *vt:* **figurarsi qc** to imagine sthg □ **figurarsi** *vr:* **figurati!** of course not!

figurina *sf* picture card.

fila *sf (coda)* queue *(Br),* line *(Am); (di macchine)* line; *(di posti)* row; *(serie)* series; **fare la ~** to queue *(Br),* to stand in line *(Am);* **di ~** in succession.

filare *vt (lana)* to spin ◆ *vi (ragno, baco)* to spin; *(formaggio)* to go stringy; *(discorso)* to be coherent; *(fam: andarsene)* to split; **fila!** off you go!; ~ **diritto** to toe the line.

filastrocca, -che *sf* nursery rhyme.

filatelia *sf* philately, stamp-collecting.

filatelli *smpl* thin strips of egg pasta served with a sauce made from pork, tomatoes, chillis and pecorino cheese (a speciality of Calabria).

filatieddi = **filatelli**.

filetto *sm* fillet; ~ **al pepe verde** fillet steak with green peppercorns.

film *sm inv* film *(Br),* movie *(Am).*

filo *sm* thread; *(cavo)* wire; *(di lama, rasoio)* edge; *(di pane)* stick; ~ **d'erba** blade of grass; ~ **spinato** barbed wire; **fil di ferro** wire; **per ~ e per segno** word for word.

filobus *sm inv* trolleybus.

filosofia *sf* philosophy.

filtrare *vt & vi* to filter.

filtro *sm (apparecchio)* filter; *(di sigarette)* filter tip.

fin → **fino**.

finale *agg & sf* final ◆ *sm* end, ending.

finalmente *avv* at (long) last.

finanza *sf* finance; *(di frontiera)* = Customs and Excise □ **finanze** *sfpl* finances.

finanziere *sm (banchiere)* financier; *(di frontiera)* customs officer; *(per tasse)* = Inland Revenue officer *(Br),* = Internal Revenue officer *(Am).*

finché *cong (per tutto il tempo)* as long as; *(fino a quando)* until.

fine *agg (sottile)* thin; *(polvere)* fine; *(elegante)* refined; *(vista, udito)* keen, sharp ◆ *sf (conclusione)* end ◆ *sm (scopo)* aim; **lieto ~** happy ending; ~ **settimana** weekend; **alla ~** in the end.

finestra *sf* window.

finestrino *sm* window.

fingere *vt (simulare)* to feign; ~ **di fare qc** to pretend to do sthg □ **fingersi** *vr:* **fingersi malato** to pretend to be ill.

finimondo *sm* pandemonium.

finire *vt* to finish ◆ *vi* to finish; *(avere esito)* to end; *(cacciarsi)* to end up; ~ **col fare qc** to end up doing sthg; ~ **di fare qc** to finish doing sthg.

finlandese agg & sm Finnish ♦ smf Finn.

Finlandia sf: la ~ Finland.

fino, -a agg (sottile) thin; (oro, argento) pure; (udito, vista) keen, sharp ♦ avv even ♦ prep: ~ a (di tempo) until; (di luogo) as far as; ~ a (luogo) as far as; **fin da domani** from tomorrow; **fin da ieri** since yesterday; ~ **qui/lì** as far as here/there.

finocchio sm fennel.

finora avv so far.

finta sf (finzione) pretence; (nel pugilato) feint; (nel calcio) dummy; **fare ~ di fare qc** to pretend to do sthg.

finto, -a pp → **fingere** ♦ agg false.

fiocco, -chi sm (di nastro) bow; (di neve) flake; **coi fiocchi** (ottimo) excellent, first-rate.

fiocina sf harpoon.

fioco, -a, -chi, -che agg (voce) faint; (luce) dim.

fioraio, -a sm, f florist.

fiore sm flower; **a fior d'acqua** on the surface of the water; **a fiori** (stoffa) with a floral pattern; **fiori di zucca ripieni** fried courgette flowers stuffed with breadcrumbs, parsley and anchovies ▫ **fiori** smpl (nelle carte) clubs.

fiorentino, -a agg & sm, f Florentine.

fiorire vi (albero) to blossom; (fiore) to bloom.

Firenze sf Florence.

firma sf (sottoscrizione) signature; (marca) designer brand.

firmare vt to sign.

fiscale agg tax (dav s).

fischiare vi to whistle ♦ vt to whistle; (disapprovare) to boo.

fischio sm whistle.

fisco sm = Inland Revenue (Br), = Internal Revenue (Am).

fisica sf (materia) physics (sg), → fisico.

fisico, -a, -ci, -che agg physical ♦ sm (corpo) physique ♦ sm, f physician.

fisionomia sf face.

fissare vt (guardare) to stare at; (rendere fisso) to fix; (appuntamento) to arrange; (camera, volo) to book ▫ **fissarsi** vr: **fissarsi di fare qc** to set one's heart on doing sthg.

fisso, -a agg (fissato) fixed; (impiego) permanent; (reddito) regular ♦ avv: **guardare ~** to stare.

fitta sf sharp pain.

fitto, -a agg thick ♦ sm (affitto) rent.

fiume sm river.

fiutare vt (sog: cane) to smell; (fig: accorgersi di) to get wind of.

flacone sm bottle.

flagrante agg: **cogliere qc in** ~ to catch sb in the act.

flash [flɛʃ] sm inv flash.

flessibile agg flexible.

flessione sf (sulle gambe) knee-bend; (a terra) sit-up; (calo) dip.

flesso, -a pp → **flettere**.

flettere vt to bend.

flipper sm inv pinball machine.

F.lli abbr Bros.

flora sf flora.

flotta sf fleet.

fluido 102

fluido, -a agg & sm fluid.

fluire vi to flow.

flusso sm flow; (in fisica) flux.

fluttuare vi (ondeggiare) to rise and fall; (FIN) to fluctuate.

F.M. (abbr di Modulazione di frequenza) FM.

focaccia, -ce sf (dolce) bun; (pane) type of flat salted bread made with olive oil; ~ **alla valdostana** 'focaccia' filled with fontina cheese.

foce sf mouth.

focolare sm hearth.

fodera sf (interna) lining; (esterna) cover.

foglia sf leaf.

foglio sm (di carta, di metallo) sheet; (documento) document; (banconota) note; ~ **rosa** provisional driving licence; ~ **di via** expulsion order.

fogna sf sewer.

fognature sfpl sewers.

föhn [fɔn] = fon.

folclore sm folklore.

folcloristico, -a, -ci, -che agg folk (dav s).

folgorare vt (sog: fulmine) to strike; (sog: alta tensione) to electrocute.

folla sf crowd.

folle agg (pazzo) mad; (TECNOL) idle; **in ~** (di auto) in neutral.

follia sf (pazzia) madness; (atto) act of madness.

folto, -a agg thick.

fon sm inv hairdryer.

fondale sm bottom (of the sea).

fondamentale agg fundamental, basic.

fondamento sm foundation □ **fondamenta** sfpl foundations.

fondare vt to found; (basare): ~ **qc su qc** to base sthg on sthg □ **fondarsi su** vr + prep to be based on.

fondazione sf foundation.

fondere vt to melt; (aziende) to merge ♦ vi to melt □ **fondersi** vr to melt.

fondo, -a agg (profondo) deep ♦ sm bottom; (di strada) surface; (di liquido) dregs (pl); (sfondo) background; (SPORT) long distance race; (proprietà) property; **andare a ~** (affondare) to sink; **conoscere a ~** to know very well; **in ~** (fig: tutto sommato) after all; **andare fino in ~ a qc** (approfondire) to get to the bottom of sthg; **in ~ (a qc)** at the bottom (of sthg); (stanza) at the back (of sthg); (libro, mese) at the end (of sthg) □ **fondi** smpl (denaro) funds.

fonduta sf fondue.

fonetica sf phonetics (sg).

fontana sf fountain.

fonte sf (sorgente) spring; (origine) source ♦ sm: ~ **battesimale** font.

fontina sf a hard cheese made from cow's milk (a speciality of the Valle d'Aosta).

foraggio sm fodder.

forare vt (praticare un foro in) to pierce; (gomma) to puncture; (biglietto) to punch; (pallone) to burst.

forbici sfpl scissors.

forca, -che sf (attrezzo) pitchfork; (patibolo) gallows (pl).

forchetta sf fork.

forcina sf hairpin.

foresta sf forest.

forza

forestiero, -a agg foreign ◆ sm, f foreigner.

forfora sf dandruff.

forma sf shape; (tipo) form; (stampo) mould; **essere in ~** to be fit; **a ~ di** in the shape of ❑ **forme** sfpl (del corpo) figure (sg).

formaggino sm processed cheese.

formaggio sm cheese.

FORMAGGIO

Cheese is a mainstay of the Italian diet, whether used as a filling for a roll, eaten as part of a main course, or served as a course in its own right. The cheese course in Italy comes after the main course and before fruit or dessert. Between 250 and 300 varieties of cheese may be found: soft ones, like "mozzarella", "ricotta", "robiola", "gorgonzola" and "bel paese"; and hard ones, like "caciocavallo", "provolone", "grana", "parmigiano" and "pecorino". These last three are grated onto pasta dishes and sprinkled on top of soups.

formale agg formal.

formalità sf inv formality.

formare vt to form; (comporre) to make up; (persona) to train ❑ **formarsi** vr to form.

formato sm size.

formazione sf formation; (istruzione) education; **~ professionale** professional training.

formica[1] sf Formica®.

formica[2], **-che** sf ant.

formicolio sm (intorpidimento) pins and needles (pl).

formidabile agg fantastic, amazing.

formula sf (chimica) formula; (frase rituale) set phrase; **~ uno** formula one.

fornaio, -a sm, f baker.

fornello sm (di elettrodomestico) ring; **~ elettrico** hotplate.

fornire vt: **~ qc a qn** to supply sb with sthg; **~ qn/qc di qc** to supply sb/sthg with sthg.

fornitore, -trice sm, f supplier.

forno sm oven; **~ a legna** wood-burning stove; **~ a microonde** microwave (oven).

foro sm (buco) hole; (romano) forum.

forse avv perhaps, maybe; (circa) about.

forte agg strong; (suono) loud; (luce, colore) bright ◆ avv (vigorosamente) hard; (ad alta voce) loudly; (velocemente) fast ◆ sm (fortezza) fort; (specialità) strong point.

fortezza sf fortress.

fortuito, -a agg chance (dav s), fortuitous.

fortuna sf luck; (patrimonio) fortune; **buona ~!** good luck!; **portare ~** to bring luck; **per ~** luckily, fortunately.

fortunatamente avv luckily, fortunately.

fortunato, -a agg (persona) lucky; (evento) successful.

forviare = **fuorviare**.

forza sf strength; (in fisica, violenza) force; **a ~ di** by dint of; **per ~**

(naturalmente) of course; (contro la volontà) against one's will; **le forze armate** the armed forces.

forzare vt (porta, finestra) to force open; (obbligare): ~ **qn a fare qc** to force sb to do sthg.

foschia sf haze.

fossa sf (buca) pit, hole; (tomba) grave.

fossato sm ditch; (di castello) moat.

fossile sm fossil.

fosso sm ditch.

foto sf inv photo.

fotocopia sf photocopy.

fotocopiare vt to photocopy.

fotogenico, -a, -ci, -che agg photogenic.

fotografare vt to photograph.

fotografia sf (ARTE) photography; (immagine) photograph; ~ **a colori** colour photograph; ~ **in bianco e nero** black and white photograph.

fotografo, -a sm, f photographer.

fototessera sf passport-size photograph.

fra = **tra**.

fracassare vt to smash.

fracasso sm crash.

fradicio, -a, -ci, -ce agg soaked.

fragile agg fragile; (persona) delicate.

fragola sf strawberry.

fragore sm loud noise.

fraintendere vt to misunderstand.

frammento sm fragment.

frana sf landslide; (fig: persona): **essere una ~** to be useless.

francese agg & sm French ♦ smf (abitante) Frenchman (f Frenchwoman); **i francesi** the French.

Francia sf: **la ~** France.

franco, -a, -chi, -che agg (sincero) frank; (COMM) free ♦ sm franc; **farla franca** to get away with it.

francobollo sm stamp.

frangia, -ge sf fringe.

frantumare vt to smash ❑ **frantumarsi** vr to smash.

frantumi smpl: **andare in ~** to smash; (sogno) to be shattered.

frappé sm inv (milk) shake.

frase sf (GRAMM) sentence; (espressione) expression.

frastuono sm din.

frate sm (monaco) friar; (pasta) ring doughnut.

fratellastro sm stepbrother.

fratello sm brother.

frattempo sm: **nel ~** in the meantime, meanwhile.

frattura sf fracture.

frazione sf (parte) fraction; (di comune) village.

freccia, -ce sf arrow; ~ **di direzione** indicator; **mettere la ~** to put the indicator on.

freddo, -a agg & sm cold; **aver ~** to be cold; **è o fa ~** it's cold.

freddoloso, -a agg: **essere ~** to feel the cold.

freezer ['fridzer] sm inv freezer.

fregare vt (strofinare) to rub; (fam: imbrogliare) to trick; ~ **qc a qn** (fam: rubare) to nick sthg from sb;

fregarsene (di qc) *(volg)* not to give a damn (about sthg).

frenare *vi* to brake ◆ *vt (rabbia, entusiasmo)* to curb; *(lacrime)* to hold back; *(avanzata, progresso)* to hold up.

frenata *sf* braking; **fare una ~** to brake.

frenetico, -a, -ci, -che *agg* hectic.

freno *sm (di veicolo)* brake; *(per cavallo)* bit; **~ a mano** handbrake.

frequentare *vt (corso, scuola)* to attend; *(locale)* to go to; *(persona)* to mix with.

frequente *agg* frequent.

fresco, -a, -schi, -sche *agg* fresh; *(temperatura)* cool; *(notizie)* recent ◆ *sm (temperatura)* cool; **è fa ~** it's cool; **mettere al ~** to put in a cool place; **stare ~** to be way out.

fretta *sf (urgenza)* hurry; *(rapidità)* haste; **avere ~** to be in a hurry; **in ~ e furia** in a hurry.

fricassea *sf* stewed meat and vegetables in an egg and lemon sauce.

friggere *vt* to fry ◆ *vi* to sizzle.

frigo *sm inv* fridge.

frigobar *sm inv* minibar.

frigorifero *sm* refrigerator.

frittata *sf* omelette.

frittella *sf* fritter; **frittelle di mele** apple fritters.

fritto, -a *pp* → **friggere** ◆ *agg* fried ◆ *sm*: **~ misto** mixed deep-fried fish and seafood.

frittura *sf*: **~ di pesce** deep-fried fish and seafood.

frivolo, -a *agg* frivolous.

frizione *sf (di auto)* clutch; *(massaggio)* massage.

frizzante *agg* fizzy; *(vino)* sparkling.

frode *sf* fraud.

frontale *agg* frontal; *(scontro)* head-on.

fronte *sf* forehead ◆ *sm* front; **di ~** opposite; **di ~ a** *(faccia a faccia)* opposite; *(in una fila)* in front of; *(in confronto a)* compared with.

frontiera *sf* frontier.

frottola *sf (bugia)* lie.

frugare *vi & vt* to search.

frullare *vt* to whisk.

frullato *sm* milk shake.

frullatore *sm* blender, liquidizer.

frullino *sm* whisk.

frusta *sf (per animali)* whip.

frustino *sm (riding)* crop.

frutta *sf* fruit; **~ secca** dried fruit and nuts.

fruttivendolo *sm (negozio)* greengrocer's.

frutto *sm* fruit; *(profitto)* profit; **frutti di mare** seafood *(sg)*.

F.S. = FF.SS.

fucile *sm* rifle.

fuga, -ghe *sf* escape; **~ di gas** gas leak.

fuggire *vi (allontanarsi)* to escape; *(rifugiarsi)* to run away.

fulmine *sm* bolt of lightning.

fumare *vi* to smoke ◆ *vi* to smoke; *(emettere vapore)* to steam; '**vietato ~**' 'no smoking'.

fumatore, -trice *sm, f* smoker; **fumatori o non fumatori?** smoking or non-smoking?

fumetti *smpl (vignette)* cartoon strip *(sg); (giornalino)* comics.

fumo *sm* smoke; *(vapore)* steam.

fune *sf* rope.

funebre *agg* funeral *(dav s); (lugubre)* funereal.

funerale *sm* funeral.

fungo, -ghi *sm* mushroom; *(MED)* fungus; **~ mangereccio** edible mushroom.

funicolare *sf* funicular railway.

funivia *sf* cable way.

funzionamento *sm* functioning.

funzionare *vi* to work ◻ **funzionare da** *v + prep* to act as.

funzione *sf* function; *(compito)* duty; *(religiosa)* service; **essere in ~** to be working; **in ~ di** *(secondo)* according to.

fuoco, -chi *sm* fire; *(fornello)* ring; *(in ottica)* focus; **al ~!** fire!; **dar ~ a qc** to set fire to sthg; **fare ~** to fire; **prender ~** to catch fire; **fuochi d'artificio** fireworks.

fuorché *cong* except.

fuori *avv* out, outside; *(fuori di casa)* out; *(all'aperto)* outdoors, outside ◆ *prep:* **~ (di)** out of, outside; **far ~ qn** *(fam)* to kill sb; **essere ~ di sé** to be beside oneself; **lasciare ~** to leave out; **tirare ~** to get out; **~ luogo** uncalled for; **~ mano** out of the way; **andare ~ strada** to leave the road; **'~ servizio'** 'out of order'.

fuoribordo *sm inv* outboard.

fuorilegge *smf inv* outlaw.

fuoristrada *sm inv* Jeep® ◆ *agg inv:* **moto ~** trail bike.

fuorviare *vt* to mislead.

furbo, -a *agg* clever, smart; *(spreg)* cunning.

furgone *sm* van.

furia *sf (ira)* fury; *(impeto)* violence; **a ~ di fare qc** by (means of) doing sthg; **andare su tutte le furie** to get into a towering rage.

furioso, -a *agg* furious.

furore *sm* fury; **far ~** to be all the rage.

furto *sm* theft; **~ con scasso** burglary.

fusa *sfpl:* **fare le ~** to purr.

fusione *sf (di cera, metallo)* melting; *(unione)* fusion.

fuso, -a *pp* → **fondere** ◆ *sm:* **~ orario** time zone.

fustino *sm* tub.

fusto *sm (di pianta)* stem; *(contenitore)* drum; *(fam: ragazzo)* hunk.

futile *agg* futile.

futuro, -a *agg & sm* future.

G

gabbia *sf* cage.

gabbiano *sm* seagull.

gabinetto *sm (bagno)* toilet; *(ministero)* cabinet; *(di dentista)* surgery.

gaffe [gaf] *sf inv* blunder.

gala *sf (sfarzo)* pomp; *(festa)* gala.

galassia *sf* galaxy.

galateo *sm* etiquette.

galera *sf* prison.

galla *sf:* **stare a ~** to float; **venire a ~** *(fig)* to come out.

galleggiante *agg* floating ◆ *sm (boa)* buoy; *(per la pesca)* float.

galleria *sf (traforo)* tunnel; *(museo)* gallery; *(di teatro)* circle; *(di cinema)* balcony; *(strada coperta)* arcade.

galletta *sf* cracker.

gallina *sf* hen.

gallo *sm* cock.

gamba *sf* leg; **essere in ~** to be smart.

gamberetto *sm* shrimp.

gambero *sm* prawn.

gamberoni *smpl:* **~ alla griglia** grilled crayfish.

gambo *sm* stem.

gancio *sm* hook.

gangheri *smpl:* **essere fuori dai ~** to fly off the handle.

gara *sf (nello sport)* race; *(concorso)* competitive bidding; **fare a ~** to compete.

garage [ga'raʒ] *sm inv* garage.

garantire *vt* to guarantee.

garanzia *sf (di merce)* guarantee; *(di debito)* guarantee, security.

gareggiare *vi* to compete.

gargarismo *sm:* **fare i gargarismi** to gargle.

garza *sf* gauze.

garzone *sm* boy.

gas *sm inv* gas; **dare ~** to step on the gas; **~ lacrimogeno** tear gas.

gasato, -a = **gassato**.

gasolio *sm* diesel (oil).

gassato, -a *agg (bevanda)* fizzy.

gassosa *sf* fizzy drink.

gastronomia *sf* gastronomy; *(negozio)* delicatessen.

gastronomico, -a, -ci, -che *agg* gastronomic.

gattino, -a *sm, f* kitten.

gatto, -a *sm, f* cat; **~ delle nevi** snow cat; **eravamo in quattro gatti** there were only a few of us.

gazzetta *sf* gazette.

G.d.F. *abbr* = **Guardia di Finanza.**

gel *sm inv* gel.

gelare *vi, vt & v impers* to freeze.

gelateria *sf* ice-cream shop *(Br)*, ice-cream parlour *(Am)*.

gelatina *sf* gelatine; **~ di frutta** fruit jelly.

gelato, -a *agg* frozen ◆ *sm* ice cream.

ⓘ GELATO

Although ice cream is associated with the summer months, it is eaten in Italy all year round and at any time of day. "Gelaterie", or ice-cream shops, specialize in the production and sale of a seemingly endless variety of flavours, ranging from traditional fruit, chocolate and coffee to the more exotic. "Gelato artigianale" means that the ice cream has been made on the premises.

gelido, -a *agg* freezing, icy.

gelo *sm (freddo)* intense cold; *(ghiaccio)* ice.

gelosia *sf* jealousy.

geloso, -a *agg* jealous.

gemello, -a *agg* twin ❑ **gemel-**

li *smpl (di camicia)* cuff links;
Gemelli *smpl* Gemini *(sg)*.

gemere *vi* to moan.

gemma *sf (pietra)* gem; *(di pianta)* bud.

generale *agg & sm* general; **in ~** in general.

generalità *sfpl* particulars.

generalmente *avv* generally.

generare *vt (produrre)* to generate, to produce.

generatore *sm* generator.

generazione *sf* generation.

genere *sm (tipo)* kind, type; *(di arte)* genre; (GRAMM) gender; *(di animali, vegetali)* genus; **il ~ umano** mankind; **in ~** generally □ **generi** *smpl:* **generi alimentari** foodstuffs.

generico, -a, -ci, -che *agg (generale)* generic; *(vago)* vague; **medico ~** general practitioner.

genero *sm* son-in-law.

generoso, -a *agg* generous.

gengiva *sf* gum.

geniale *agg* brilliant.

genio *sm* genius; **andare a ~ a qn** to be liked by sb.

genitali *smpl* genitals.

genitore *sm* parent; **i nostri genitori** our parents.

gennaio *sm* January, → **settembre**.

Genova *sf* Genoa.

gente *sf* people *(pl)*.

gentile *agg* kind, nice; **Gentile Signore** Dear Sir; **Gentile Signor G. Paoli** Mr G. Paoli.

gentilezza *sf* kindness; **per ~** please.

gentiluomo *(pl* gentiluomini*)*

sm gentleman.

genuino, -a *agg* genuine.

geografia *sf* geography.

geologia *sf* geology.

geometria *sf* geometry.

geranio *sm* geranium.

gerarchia *sf* hierarchy.

gergo, -ghi *sm (di giovani)* slang; *(specialistico)* jargon.

Germania *sf:* **la ~** Germany.

germe *sm* germ.

gerundio *sm* gerund.

gesso *sm* chalk; *(per frattura)* plaster.

gestione *sf* management.

gestire *vt* to run.

gesto *sm* gesture.

gestore *sm* manager.

Gesù *sm* Jesus.

gettare *vt (lanciare)* to throw; *(buttar via)* to throw away; *(grido)* to utter; *(acqua)* to spout; *(scultura)* to cast; **'non ~ alcun oggetto dal finestrino'** 'do not throw objects out of the window' □ **gettarsi** *vr:* **gettarsi da/in** to throw o.s. from/ into; **gettarsi in** *(fiume)* to flow into.

getto *sm (d'acqua, gas)* jet; *(vapore)* puff; **di ~** *(scrivere)* in one go.

gettone *sm* token; **~ telefonico** telephone token.

ghiacciaio *sm* glacier.

ghiacciato, -a *agg* frozen; *(freddo)* ice-cold.

ghiaccio *sm* ice.

ghiacciolo *sm (gelato)* ice lolly *(Br)*, Popsicle® *(Am)*; *(di fontana)* icicle.

ghiaia sf gravel.

ghiandola sf gland.

ghiotto, -a agg (persona) greedy; (cibo) appetizing.

già avv already; (precedentemente) already, before ◆ esclam of course!, yes!; **di ~?** already?

giacca, -che sf jacket; **~ a vento** windcheater.

giacché cong as, since.

giaccone sm heavy jacket.

giacere vi to lie.

giallo, -a agg (colore) yellow; (carnagione) sallow ◆ sm (colore) yellow; (romanzo) detective story; **film ~** thriller; **~ dell'uovo** yolk.

gianduiotto sm hazelnut chocolate.

Giappone sm: **il ~** Japan.

giapponese agg, smf & sm Japanese.

giardinaggio sm gardening.

giardiniera sf (verdure) starter of mixed pickled vegetables, → **giardiniere**.

giardiniere, -a sm, f gardener.

giardino sm garden; **~ botanico** botanical gardens (pl); **~ d'infanzia** nursery, kindergarten; **~ pubblico** park; **~ zoologico** zoo.

gigante agg (enorme) gigantic ◆ sm giant.

gigantesco, -a, -schi, -sche agg gigantic.

gilè sm inv waistcoat.

gin [dʒin] sm inv gin.

ginecologo, -a, -gi, -ghe sm, f gynaecologist.

ginestra sf broom.

Ginevra sf Geneva.

ginnastica sf gymnastics (sg); **fare ~** to do exercises.

ginocchio (pl m **ginocchi** o pl f **ginocchia**) sm knee; **stare in ~** to be on one's knees, to kneel.

giocare vi to play; (scommettere) to gamble ◆ vt to play; (scommettere) to gamble; (ingannare) to take in; **sai ~ a tennis?** can you play tennis?; **giocarsi il posto** to lose one's job.

giocatore, -trice sm, f player; **~ d'azzardo** gambler.

giocattolo sm toy.

gioco, -chi sm game; (divertimento) play; **mettere in ~ qc** to risk sthg; **~ d'azzardo** game of chance; **~ di parole** pun; **per ~** as a joke.

giocoliere sm juggler.

gioia sf of joy; (gioiello) jewel; **darsi alla pazza ~** to live it up.

gioielleria sf jeweller's shop.

gioiello sm jewel, piece of jewellery.

giornalaio, -a sm, f newsagent (Br), newsdealer (Am).

giornale sm (quotidiano) newspaper; (rivista) magazine; **~ radio** news bulletin.

giornaliero, -a agg daily.

giornalista, -i, -e smf journalist.

giornata sf day; **oggi è una bella ~** it's lovely today; **~ lavorativa** working day; **vivere alla ~** to live for the day.

giorno sm (ventiquattro ore) day; (opposto alla notte) day, daytime; (periodo di luce) daylight; **a giorni alterni** on alternate days; **l'altro ~** the other day; **~ feriale** working

giostra

day; **~ festivo** holiday; **~ libero** day off; **al ~** by the day, per day; **di ~** by day, during the day.

giostra *sf* merry-go-round.

giovane *agg* young; **da ~** as a young man/woman; **i giovani** young people.

giovanile *agg* youthful.

giovanotto *sm* young man.

giovare : **giovare a** *v + prep* to be good for ❑ **giovarsi di** *vr + prep* to make use of.

giovedì *sm inv* Thursday; **~ grasso** *last Thursday of Carnival, before Lent,* → **sabato**.

gioventù *sf (età)* youth; *(giovani)* young people *(pl)*.

giovinezza *sf* youth.

giradischi *sm inv* record player.

giraffa *sf* giraffe.

giramento *sm*: **~ di testa** dizziness.

girare *vt* to turn; *(visitare)* to go round; *(filmare)* to shoot; *(assegno, cambiale)* to endorse ♦ *vi* to turn; *(velocemente)* to spin; *(terra)* to revolve; *(andare in giro)* to go around ❑ **girarsi** *vr* to turn around.

girarrosto *sm* spit.

girasole *sm* sunflower.

girata *sf (passeggiata)* stroll; *(in macchina)* drive; *(FIN)* endorsement.

girello *sm (di carne)* topside; *(per bambini)* baby-walker.

girevole *agg* turning, revolving.

giro *sm (viaggio)* tour; *(rotazione)* turn; *(di amici, colleghi)* circle; *(di pista)* lap; **fare un ~** *(a piedi)* to go for a walk; *(in macchina)* to go for a

drive; *(in bicicletta)* to go for a ride; **fare il ~ di** *(città, negozi)* to go round; **~ d'affari** turnover; **~ di parole** circumlocution; **~ di prova** test drive; **in ~** around; **nel ~ di un anno** in the space of a year; **prendere in ~ qn** to tease sb, to pull sb's leg; **essere su di giri** to be excited.

girotondo *sm* ring-a-ring-o'-roses.

gita *sf* trip; **andare in ~ a Roma** to go on a trip to Rome.

giù *avv* down; *(al piano di sotto)* downstairs; **in ~** down, downwards; **~ di lì** thereabouts; **~ per le scale** down the stairs; **essere ~** *(fig: essere depresso)* to be low.

giubbotto *sm* jacket.

giudicare *vt (valutare)* to judge; *(reputare)* to consider; *(DIR)* to find ♦ *vi* to judge.

giudice *sm* judge; *(nello sport)* umpire.

giudizio *sm* judgment; *(opinione)* opinion; *(a scuola)* report; **a mio ~** in my opinion.

giugno *sm* June, → **settembre**.

giungere *vi*: **~ a/in** to reach.

giungla *sf* jungle.

giunta *sf* committee; **per ~** in addition.

giunto, -a *pp* → **giungere**.

giuramento *sm* oath.

giurare *vt* to swear ♦ *vi* to take an oath.

giuria *sf (di gare, concorsi)* judges *(pl)*; *(di tribunale)* jury.

giustificare *vt* to justify.

giustificazione *sf (scusa)* excuse; *(SCOL)* note (of absence).

giustizia *sf* justice.

giusto, -a *agg (equo)* fair, just; *(vero, adeguato)* right; *(esatto)* correct ♦ *avv (esattamente)* correctly; *(proprio)* just; **cercavo ~ te!** you're just the person I was looking for!

gli *art mpl (dav s + consonante, gn, ps, z, vocale e h)* the, → **il** ♦ *pron (a lui)* (to) him; *(a esso)* (to) it; *(a loro)* (to) them; **glielo hai detto?** have you told him/her?; **gliene devo due** I owe him/her two (of them).

gliela → **gli**.

gliele → **gli**.

glieli → **gli**.

glielo → **gli**.

gliene → **gli**.

globale *agg* global.

globo *sm* globe.

globulo *sm*: **~ rosso/bianco** red/white corpuscle.

gloria *sf* glory.

gnocchi *smpl* gnocchi *(small dumplings made from potatoes and flour or from semolina).*

goal [gɔl] *sm inv* goal.

gobba *sf (su schiena)* hump; *(rigonfiamento)* bump.

gobbo, -a *agg* hunchbacked; *(curvo)* round-shouldered ♦ *sm* hunchback.

goccia, -ce *sf* drop.

gocciolare *vi & vt* to drip.

godere *vt*: **godersi qc** to enjoy sthg □ **godere di** *v + prep (avere)* to enjoy; **~ di una riduzione** to benefit from a reduction.

goffo, -a *agg* clumsy.

gola *sf* throat; *(golosità)* greed; *(di monte)* gorge.

golf *sm inv (maglia)* sweater, jumper; *(sport)* golf.

golfo *sm* gulf.

goloso, -a *agg* greedy.

gomito *sm* elbow.

gomma *sf* rubber; *(per cancellare)* rubber (Br), eraser (Am); *(pneumatico)* tyre; **bucare** o **forare una ~** to have a puncture; **~ a terra** flat tyre; **~ (da masticare)** chewing gum.

gommapiuma® *sf* foam rubber.

gommone *sm* rubber dinghy.

gondola *sf* gondola.

gondoliere *sm* gondolier.

gonfiare *vt (pallone, gomme)* to inflate; *(dilatare, ingrossare)* to swell; *(notizia, impresa)* to exaggerate □ **gonfiarsi** *vr* to swell; *(fiume)* to rise.

gonfio, -a *agg (piede, occhi)* swollen; *(stomaco)* bloated.

gonna *sf* skirt; **~ a pieghe** pleated skirt; **~ pantalone** culottes *(pl).*

gorgogliare *vi* to gurgle.

gorgonzola *sm* Gorgonzola *(a strong green-veined cheese made from cow's milk).*

gorilla *sm inv (animale)* gorilla; *(guardia del corpo)* bodyguard.

goulash [ˈɡulaʃ] *sm* goulash.

governante *sf (per bambini)* governess; *(di casa)* housekeeper.

governare *vt* to govern; *(animale)* to look after.

governatore *sm* governor.

governo *sm* government.

gracile *agg* delicate.

gradazione *sf (di colori)* scale;

(sfumatura) shade; ~ **alcolica** alcoholic strength.

gradevole agg pleasant.

gradinata sf (scalinata) (flight of) steps; (in stadi, teatri) tiers (pl).

gradino sm step.

gradire vt (regalo) to like, to appreciate; (desiderare) to like; **gradisce un caffè?** would you like a coffee?

grado sm degree; (sociale) level; (MIL) rank; **quanti gradi ha questo vino?** how strong is this wine?; **essere in ~ di fare qc** to be able to do sthg; ~ **centigrado** centigrade.

graduale agg gradual.

graduatoria sf (ranked) list.

graffetta sf (fermaglio) clip; (di pinzatrice) staple.

graffiare vt to scratch.

graffio sm scratch.

grafica sf graphics (pl).

grafico, -a, -ci, -che agg (rappresentazione, arti) graphic ◆ sm, f (pubblicitario) designer ◆ sm graph.

grammatica, -che sf (disciplina) grammar; (libro) grammar book.

grammo sm gram.

grana sf (fam) (seccatura) trouble; (soldi) cash ◆ sm inv a hard cheese similar to Parmesan.

granaio sm granary, barn.

Gran Bretagna sf: **la ~** Great Britain.

granché pron: **non ne so (un) ~** I don't know much about it; **non è (un) ~** it's nothing special.

granchio sm crab; **prendere un**

~ (fig) to blunder.

grande (a volte **gran**) agg (ge ... big; (albero) tall; (rumore) lou ... (scrittore, affetto, capacità) great ◆ (adulto) grown-up, adult; ~ **mag** ... **zino** department store; **cosa fa** ... **da ~?** what will you do when y ... grow up?; **fare le cose in ~** to ... things on a grand scale; **è un gr** ... **bugiardo** he's such a liar; **fa** ... **gran caldo** it's very hot.

grandezza sf (dimensioni) siz ... (eccellenza) greatness.

grandinare v impers to hail.

grandine sf hail.

granello sm (di sale, sabbia, p ... vere) grain.

granita sf (crushed ... with syrup, fruit juice or coffee pou ... over).

grano sm wheat.

granturco sm maize.

grappa sf (acquavite) grap ... (spirit distilled from grape marc).

grappolo sm bunch.

grasso, -a agg (persona) ... (cibo) fatty; (pelle, capelli) greasy ... sm fat; (unto) grease.

grassoccio, -a, -ci, -ce ... plump.

grata sf grating.

gratis avv free.

gratitudine sf gratitude.

grato, -a agg grateful.

grattacielo sm skyscraper.

grattare vt to scratch; (form ... gio) to grate; (fam: rubare) to pin ... **grattarsi il naso/la gamba** ... scratch one's nose/leg ◻ **gratt** ... vr to scratch o.s.

grattugia sf grater.

grattugiare vt to grate.

gratuito, -a agg free.

grave agg (malattia, ferita) serious; (danno, perdite) serious, great; (responsabilità) heavy; (sacrificio) great; (voce, suono) deep; (contegno) solemn.

gravemente avv seriously.

gravidanza sf pregnancy.

gravità sf (in fisica) gravity; (serietà) seriousness.

grazia sf grace; (DIR) pardon.

grazie esclam thank you!; ~ tante ○ mille! thank you so much!; ~ dei fiori ○ per i fiori thank you for the flowers; ~ a thanks to.

grazioso, -a agg pretty, charming.

Grecia sf: la ~ Greece.

greco, -a, -ci, -che agg & sm, f Greek.

gregge (pl f greggi) sm flock.

greggio, -a, -gi, -ge agg raw, unrefined; (tessuto) unbleached; (diamante) rough, uncut ♦ sm crude oil.

grembiule sm (da cucina) apron; (per bambini) smock.

grezzo = greggio.

gridare vi to shout; (di dolore) to yell, to cry out ♦ vt to shout.

grido (pl f grida) sm (di persona) shout, cry; di ~ famous.

grigio, -a, -gi, -gie agg & sm grey.

griglia sf grill; alla ~ grilled.

grigliata sf mixed grill (of meat or fish).

grill sm = griglia.

grilletto sm trigger.

grillo sm cricket.

grinta sf determination.

grinzoso, -a agg (tessuto) creased; (pelle) wrinkled.

grissini smpl bread-sticks.

grolla sf wooden goblet or bowl, typical of the Valle d'Aosta.

grondare vi to stream □ grondare di v + prep to drip with.

groppa sf rump.

groppo sm tangle; avere un ~ alla gola to have a lump in one's throat.

grossista, -i, -e smf wholesaler.

grosso, -a agg big, large; (spesso) thick; (importante) important; (grave) great ♦ sm majority; dirla grossa to tell a whopping lie; questa volta l'hai fatta grossa! you've really done it this time!; sbagliarsi di ~ to make a big mistake; mare ~ rough sea; pezzo ~ big shot; sale ~ coarse salt.

grossolano, -a agg (persona) coarse; (lavoro) crude; (errore) gross.

grossomodo avv roughly, approximately.

grotta sf cave.

grottesco, -a, -schi, -sche agg grotesque.

groviera sm o sf Gruyère cheese.

groviglio sm tangle.

gru sf inv (macchina) crane.

gruccia, -ce sf (stampella) crutch; (per abiti) coat hanger.

grugnire vi to grunt.

grumo *sm (di sangue)* clot; *(di farina)* lump.

gruppo *sm* group; **~ sanguigno** blood group.

gruviera = groviera.

guadagnare *vt (soldi)* to earn; *(ottenere)* to gain; **guadagnarsi da vivere** to earn one's living.

guadagno *sm (denaro)* earnings *(pl); (tornaconto)* profit.

guado *sm* ford.

guai *esclam:* **~ a te!** you'll be for it!

guaio *sm (pasticcio)* trouble; *(inconveniente)* problem; **essere nei guai** to be in trouble; **mettere qn nei guai** to get sb into trouble.

guancia, -ce *sf* cheek.

guanciale *sm* pillow.

guanto *sm* glove.

guardaboschi *sm inv* forest ranger.

guardacoste *sm inv (persona)* coastguard; *(nave)* (coastguard's) patrol boat.

guardalinee *sm inv* linesman.

guardamacchine *sm inv* car park attendant.

guardare *vt (osservare)* to look at, to watch; *(televisione, film)* to watch; *(bambini, borsa)* to look after ♦ *vi (edificio)* to look, to face; *(badare):* **non ~ a spese** to spare no expense; **guarda!** look! ▭ **guardarsi** *vr* to look at o.s.; **guardarsi da** + *prep* to be wary of; **guardarsi dal fare qc** to be careful not to do sthg.

guardaroba *sm inv* wardrobe; *(di locale)* cloakroom.

guardia *sf* guard; *(attività)* watch, guard duty; **fare la ~ a** to guard; **mettere qn in ~ contro qc** to warn sb about sthg; **~ del corpo** bodyguard; **Guardia di Finanza** *military body responsible for customs and fiscal matters;* **~ forestale** forest ranger; **~ medica** first-aid station; **di ~** on duty.

guardiano *sm* caretaker; **~ notturno** night watchman.

guardrail [gar'dreil] *sm inv* crash barrier.

guarire *vi* to recover; *(ferita)* to heal ♦ *vt* to cure; *(ferita)* to heal.

guarnizione *sf (ornamento)* trim; *(contorno)* accompaniment, garnish; *(per recipienti)* seal; *(di auto)* gasket.

guastafeste *smf inv* spoilsport.

guastare *vt* to spoil □ **guastarsi** *vr (meccanismo)* to break down; *(cibo)* to go bad; *(tempo)* to change for the worse.

guasto, -a *agg (radio)* broken; *(ascensore, telefono)* out of order; *(cibo)* bad ♦ *sm* breakdown; **un ~ al motore** engine trouble.

guerra *sf* war; **essere in ~** to be at war; **~ mondiale** World War.

guerriglia *sf* guerrilla warfare.

gufo *sm* owl.

guglia *sf* spire.

guida *sf* guide; *(di veicolo)* driving; **~ a destra** right-hand drive; **~ a sinistra** left-hand drive.

guidare *vt (veicolo)* to drive; *(accompagnare)* to guide; **sai ~?** can you drive?

guidatore, -trice *sm, f* driver.

guinzaglio *sm* lead.

guscio *sm (di lumaca)* shell.

gustare *vt (cibo)* to taste; *(godersi)* to enjoy.

gusto *sm* taste; **al ~ di banana** banana-flavoured; **mangiare di ~** to enjoy one's food; **ridere di ~** to laugh heartily; **ci ha preso ~** he's come to like it.

gustoso, -a *agg* tasty.

ha → **avere**.

habitat *sm inv* habitat.

hai → **avere**.

hall [ɔl] *sf inv* hall, foyer.

hamburger [am'burger] *sm inv* hamburger.

handicap [ˈɛndikap] *sm inv* handicap.

handicappato, -a *agg* handicapped ♦ *sm, f* handicapped person, disabled person.

hanno → **avere**.

henné *sm inv* henna.

hg *(abbr di ettogrammo)* hg.

hi-fi [aiˈfai] *sm inv* hi-fi.

hippy *agg inv & smf inv* hippy.

ho → **avere**.

hobby *sm inv* hobby.

hockey *sm* hockey *(Br)*, field hockey *(Am)*; **~ su ghiaccio** ice hockey.

hostess *sf inv (di volo)* airhostess.

hotel *sm inv* hotel.

i *art mpl* the, → **il**.

iceberg [ˈaizberg] *sm inv* iceberg.

Iddio *sm* God.

idea *sf* idea; *(opinione, impressione)* impression; *(progetto)*: **avere ~ di fare qc** to think of doing sthg; **neanche per ~!** don't even think about it!; **non avere la più pallida ~ di qc** not to have the slightest idea about sthg; **non ne ho ~** I've no idea; **cambiare ~** to change one's mind.

ideale *agg & sm* ideal.

ideare *vt (metodo, sistema)* to devise; *(viaggio)* to plan.

idem *avv (fam: lo stesso)* the same.

identico, -a, -ci, -che *agg* identical.

identità *sf inv* identity.

ideologia, -gie *sf* ideology.

idiota, -i, -e *agg* idiotic, stupid ♦ *smf* idiot.

idolo *sm* idol.

idoneo, -a *agg (adatto)*: **~ a** suitable for; *(MIL)* fit for.

idrante *sm* hydrant.

idratante *agg* moisturizing.

idratare *vt* to moisturize.

idraulico, -a, -ci, -che *agg* hydraulic ♦ *sm* plumber; **impianto ~** plumbing.

idrofilo *agg m* → **cotone**.

idrogeno *sm* hydrogen.

idroscalo *sm* seaplane base.

idrosolubile

idrosolubile *agg* soluble (in water).

iella *sf (fam)* bad luck.

ieri *avv* yesterday; ~ **mattina** yesterday morning; ~ **notte** last night; **l'altro ~**, ~ **l'altro** the day before yesterday; **la posta di ~** yesterday's mail.

igiene *sf* hygiene.

igienico, -a, -ci, -che *agg* hygienic.

ignorante *agg* ignorant.

ignorare *vt (non sapere)* not to know; *(trascurare)* to ignore.

ignoto, -a *agg* unknown.

il *(mpl* **i**; *dav sm* **lo** *(pl* **gli**) *+ s+consonante, gn, ps, z; f* **la**, *fpl* **le**; *dav sm o sf* **l'** *+ vocale e h) art* **1.** *(gen)* the. **2.** *(con nome comune)* the; ~ **lago** the lake; ~ **la finestra** the window; **lo studente** the student; **l'isola** the island. **3.** *(con nome astratto)*: ~ **tempo** time; **la vita** life. **4.** *(con titolo)*: ~ **Signor Pollini** Mr Pollini; **la regina Elisabetta** Queen Elizabeth. **5.** *(con nomi geografici)*: ~ **Po** the Po; **le Dolomiti** the Dolomites. **6.** *(indica possesso)*: **si è rotto ~ naso** he broke his nose; **ha i capelli biondi** she has fair hair. **7.** *(indica il tempo)*: ~ **sabato** *(tutti i sabati)* on Saturdays; *(quel sabato)* on Saturday; **la sera** in the evening; **è ~ 29 dicembre** it's the 29th of December; **dopo le tre** after three o'clock. **8.** *(ciascuno)*: **5 000 lire l'uno** 5,000 lira each.

illazione *sf* inference.

illecito, -a *agg* illicit.

illegale *agg* illegal.

illegittimo, -a *agg* illegitimate.

illeso, -a *agg* unhurt.

illimitato, -a *agg (spazio, tempo)* unlimited; *(fiducia)* absolute.

illudere *vt* to deceive ☐ **illudersi** *vr* to deceive o.s.

illuminare *vt* to light up, to illuminate.

illuminazione *sf* lighting; *(fig: intuizione)* enlightenment.

illusione *sf (falsa apparenza)* illusion; *(falsa speranza)* delusion.

illusionista, -i, -e *smf* conjurer.

illuso, -a *pp* → **illudere** ◆ *sm, f*: **essere un ~** to be fooling o.s.

illustrare *vt* to illustrate.

illustrazione *sf* illustration, picture.

imballaggio *sm* packaging.

imballare *vt* to pack (up).

imbalsamare *vt* to embalm.

imbarazzante *agg* embarrassing.

imbarazzare *vt* to embarrass.

imbarazzato, -a *agg* embarrassed.

imbarcadero *sm* landing stage.

imbarcare *vt (passeggero)* to board; *(merce)* to load ☐ **imbarcarsi** *vr* to board.

imbarcazione *sf* boat; **imbarcazioni da diporto** pleasure boats.

imbarco, -chi *sm (salita bordo)* boarding; *(carico)* loading.

(luogo) point of departure.

imbàttersi : imbàttersi in *vr* + *prep* to run into.

imbecìlle *agg* stupid, idiotic ◆ *smf* imbecile, idiot.

imbellìre *vt* to embellish ◆ *vi* to become more beautiful.

imbiancàre *vt* to whitewash ◆ *vi (diventare bianco)* to turn white.

imbianchìno *sm* decorator.

imboccàre *vt (bambino)* to feed; *(strada)* to turn into.

imboccatùra *sf (di condotto)* mouth; *(di strada)* entrance; *(di strumento musicale)* mouthpiece.

imbòcco, -chi *sm* entrance.

imbottigliàre *vt (liquido)* to bottle; *(nave)* to blockade; **è rimasto imbottigliato** he got stuck in a traffic jam.

imbottìre *vt (cuscino)* to stuff; *(giacca)* to pad.

imbottìto, -a *agg* stuffed; *(indumento)* padded, quilted; **panino ~** filled roll.

imbranàto, -a *agg (fam)* clumsy.

imbrattàre *vt* to dirty.

imbrogliàre *vt (ingannare)* to deceive; *(ingarbugliare)* to entangle.

imbròglio *sm* swindle.

imbroglióne, -a *sm, f* swindler.

imbronciàto, -a *agg* sulky.

imbucàre *vt* to post *(Br)*, to mail *(Am)*.

imburràre *vt* to butter.

imbùto *sm* funnel.

imitàre *vt* to imitate.

imitazióne *sf* imitation.

immacolàto, -a *agg (bianco)* pure white; *(puro)* immaculate, pure.

immaginàre *vt (rappresentarsi)* to imagine; *(supporre)* to suppose; **si immagini!** don't mention it!; **~ di fare qc** to imagine doing sthg.

immaginazióne *sf* imagination.

immàgine *sf* image.

immatricolàre *vt (auto)* to register; *(studente)* to enrol.

immatùro, -a *agg* immature.

immedesimàrsi : immedesimàrsi in *vr* + *prep* to identify with.

immediatamènte *avv* immediately.

immediàto, -a *agg* immediate.

immènso, -a *agg* immense, enormous.

immèrgere *vt* to immerse ❑ **immèrgersi** *vr* to dive; **immèrgersi in** *vr* + *prep (dedicarsi a)* to immerse o.s. in.

immersióne *sf* dive.

immèrso, -a *pp* → **immèrgere**.

immèsso, -a *pp* → **immèttere**.

immèttere *vt* to introduce.

immigrànte *smf* immigrant.

immigràto, -a *sm, f* immigrant.

imminènte *agg* imminent.

immòbile *agg* immobile ◆ *sm* property *(Br)*, real estate *(Am)*.

immobiliàre *agg* property *(dav*

s) (Br), real estate (dav s) (Am).

immodesto, -a agg immodest.

immondizia sf rubbish.

immorale agg immoral.

immortale agg immortal.

immunità sf immunity.

immunizzare vt to immunize.

impacchettare vt to wrap.

impacciato, -a agg (goffo) awkward; (imbarazzato) embarrassed.

impacco, -chi sm compress.

impadronirsi : impadronirsi di vr + prep (città, beni) to take possession of; (lingua) to master.

impalcatura sf scaffolding.

impallidire vi to go pale.

impalpabile agg impalpable.

impappinarsi vr to stumble.

imparare vt to learn; ~ **a fare qc** to learn to do sthg.

imparziale agg impartial, unbiased.

impassibile agg impassive.

impastare vt (pane) to knead; (mescolare) to mix.

impasto sm (di farina) dough; (amalgama) mixture.

impatto sm impact.

impaurire vt to frighten □ **impaurirsi** vr to get frightened.

impaziente agg impatient; **essere ~ di fare qc** to be impatient to do sthg.

impazzire vi to go mad.

impedimento sm obstacle.

impedire vt (ostacolare) to obstruct; (vietare) : ~ **a qn di fare qc** to prevent sb from doing sthg.

impegnare vt (occupare) to keep busy; (dare in pegno) to pawn □ **impegnarsi** vr to commit to s.s.; **impegnarsi a fare qc** to undertake to do sthg; **impegnarsi in qc** to commit o.s. to sthg.

impegnativo, -a agg (lavoro) demanding, exacting; (promessa) binding.

impegnato, -a agg (occupato) busy; (militante) committed.

impegno sm commitment; (incombenza) engagement, appointment.

impellente agg pressing, urgent.

impenetrabile agg impenetrable.

impennarsi vr (cavallo) to rear (up); (moto) to do a wheelie; (aereo) to climb.

impennata sf (di cavallo) rearing; (di moto) wheelie; (di aereo) climb.

impensabile agg unthinkable, inconceivable.

impepata sf: ~ **di cozze** mussels cooked with lots of pepper or chilli (a speciality of Naples).

imperativo sm imperative.

imperatore, -trice sm, f emperor (f empress).

imperfezione sf imperfection.

impermeabile agg waterproof ◆ sm raincoat.

impero sm empire.

impersonale agg impersonal.

impersonare vt to play.

impertinente agg impertinent.

imperturbabile *agg* imperturbable.

imperversare *vi* (*calamità*) to rage; (*fam: moda*) to be all the rage.

impervio, -a *agg* passable with difficulty.

impeto *sm* (*forza*) force; (*slancio*) surge.

impianto *sm* (*installazione*) installation; (*elettrico, del gas, antifurto*) system; (*macchinario*) plant; ~ **di riscaldamento** heating system; ~ **sportivo** sports complex; **impianti di risalita** ski lifts.

impiccare *vt* to hang □ **impiccarsi** *vr* to hang o.s.

impiccione, -a *sm, f* busybody.

impiegare *vt* (*tempo*) to take; (*utilizzare*) to use; (*assumere*) to employ □ **impiegarsi** *vr* to get a job.

impiegato, -a *sm, f* employee; ~ **di banca** bank clerk.

impiego, -ghi *sm* (*lavoro*) work, employment; (*uso*) use.

impigliare *vt* to entangle □ **impigliarsi** *vr*: **impigliarsi in qc** to get entangled in sthg.

impigrire *vt* to make lazy ♦ *vi* to become lazy □ **impigrirsi** *vr* to become lazy.

implacabile *agg* implacable, relentless.

implicare *vt* (*comportare*) to imply, to entail; (*coinvolgere*) to involve.

implicato, -a *agg*: **essere ~ in qc** to be implicated in sthg.

implicazione *sf* implication.

implicito, -a *agg* implicit.

implorare *vt* to implore.

impolverare *vt* to cover with dust □ **impolverarsi** *vr* to get dusty.

imponente *agg* imposing.

impopolare *agg* unpopular.

imporre *vt* (*volontà, silenzio*) to impose; (*costringere*): ~ **a qn di fare qc** to make sb do sthg □ **imporsi** *vr* (*farsi ubbidire*) to impose o.s., to assert o.s.; (*avere successo*) to be successful; **imporsi di fare qc** to make o.s. do sthg.

importante *agg* important.

importanza *sf* importance; **avere ~** to be important, to matter; **dare ~ a qc** to give weight to sthg.

importare *vt* to import ♦ *vi* to matter, to be important ♦ *v impers* to matter; **non importa!** it doesn't matter!; **non mi importa** I don't care.

importato, -a *agg* imported.

importazione *sf* importation; (*prodotto*) import.

importo *sm* amount.

importunare *vt* to bother.

impossessarsi : **impossessarsi di** *vr* + *prep* to take possession of.

impossibile *agg* impossible ♦ *sm*: **fare l'~** to do all one can.

imposta, -a *pp* → **imporre** ♦ *sf* (*tassa*) tax, duty; (*di finestra*) shutter.

impostare *vt* (*lettera*) to post (*Br*), to mail (*Am*); (*lavoro*) to plan; (*domanda*) to formulate.

imposto, -a *pp* → **imporre**.

impostore, -a *sm, f* impostor.

impotente *agg* powerless; *(MED)* impotent.

impraticàbile *agg* impassable.

imprecare *vi* to curse.

imprecazione *sf* curse.

impregnare *vt*: ~ **qc (di qc)** *(inzuppare)* to soak sthg (with sthg); *(di fumo, odore)* to impregnate sthg (with sthg).

imprenditore, -trice *sm, f (industriale)* entrepreneur; *(appaltatore)* contractor.

impreparato, -a *agg* unprepared.

impresa *sf (azione)* undertaking; *(ditta)* business.

impresario, -a *sm, f (teatrale)* impresario; ~ **edile** building constructor.

impressionante *agg* impressive.

impressionare *vt (turbare)* to disturb; *(colpire)* to impress ❑ **impressionarsi** *vr* to get upset.

impressione *sf* impression; *(sensazione)* impression, feeling; **ho l'~ di conoscerlo** I have the impression o feeling I know him; **fare ~** *(colpire)* to impress; *(turbare)* to upset; **fare buona/cattiva ~ to** make a good/bad impression.

impresso, -a *pp* → **imprimere**.

imprestare *vt*: ~ **qc a qn** to lend sthg to sb.

imprevisto, -a *agg* unexpected ♦ *sm* unexpected event; **salvo imprevisti** circumstances permitting.

imprigionare *vt (incarcerare)* to imprison; *(tenere chiuso)* to confine.

imprimere *vt* to print; *(movimento)* to transmit.

improbàbile *agg* improbable, unlikely.

impronta *sf (di piede, mano, zampa)* print; ~ **digitale** fingerprint.

improvvisamente *avv* suddenly, unexpectedly.

improvvisare *vt* to improvise ❑ **improvvisarsi** *vr*: **si è improvvisato cuoco** he acted as cook.

improvvisata *sf* surprise.

improvviso, -a *agg (inatteso)* sudden, unexpected; *(istantaneo)* sudden; **all'~** suddenly.

imprudente *agg (persona)* unwise, imprudent; *(azione)* rash.

imprudenza *sf* rash action.

impudente *agg* impudent.

impugnare *vt (stringere)* to grasp; *(DIR)* to contest.

impugnatura *sf* handle.

impulsivo, -a *agg* impulsive.

impulso *sm* impulse; **d'~** on impulse.

impuntarsi *vr (bambino)* to stop dead; *(cavallo)* to jib; *(ostinarsi)* to dig one's heels in.

imputare *vt*: ~ **qc a qn** to attribute sthg to sb; ~ **qn di qc** to accuse sb of sthg.

imputato, -a *sm, f* defendant.

in *prep* 1. *(stato in luogo)* in; **abitare ~ campagna** to live in the country; **essere ~ casa** to be at home; **l'ho lasciato ~ macchina/nella borsa** I left it in the car/in the bag; **vivo ~ Italia** I live in Italy; **avere qc ~**

incalcolabile

mente to have sthg in mind.

2. (*moto a luogo*) to; andare ~ Italia to go to Italy; andare ~ montagna to go to the mountains; mettersi qc ~ testa to get sthg into one's head; entrare ~ macchina to get into the car; entrare nella stanza to go into the room.

3. (*indica un momento*) in; ~ primavera in spring; nel 1995 in 1995.

4. (*indica durata*) in; l'ho fatto ~ cinque minuti I did it in five minutes; ~ giornata within the day.

5. (*indica modo*): parlare ~ italiano to speak in Italian; ~ silenzio in silence; sono ancora in pigiama I'm still in my pyjamas; quant'è ~ lire? how much is that in lira?; ~ vacanza on holiday (Br), on vacation (Am).

6. (*indica mezzo*) by; pagare ~ contanti to pay cash; viaggiare ~ macchina to travel by car.

7. (*indica materia*) made of; statua ~ bronzo bronze statue.

8. (*indica fine*): ha speso un capitale in libri he spent a fortune on books; dare ~ omaggio to give as a free gift; ~ onore di in honour of.

9. (*con valore distributivo*): siamo partiti ~ tre three of us left; ~ tutto sono 10 000 lire it's 10,000 lira in total.

inabile *agg*: ~ (a qc) unfit (for sthg).

inaccessibile *agg* (*luogo*) inaccessible; (*persona*) unapproachable.

inaccettabile *agg* unacceptable.

inadatto, -a *agg* unsuitable.

inadeguato, -a *agg* (*insuffi-*

ciente) inadequate; (*non idoneo*) unsuitable.

inagibile *agg* unfit for use.

inalare *vt* to inhale.

inalberarsi *vr* to get angry.

inalterato, -a *agg* unchanged.

inamidare *vt* to starch.

inammissibile *agg* inadmissible.

inappetenza *sf* lack of appetite.

inappuntabile *agg* (*persona*) faultless, irreproachable; (*lavoro, vestito*) impeccable.

inarcare *vt* (*schiena*) to arch; ~ le sopracciglia to raise one's eyebrows ❑ **inarcarsi** *vr* to arch.

inaridire *vt* to dry (up) ❑ **inaridirsi** *vr* to dry up.

inaspettato, -a *agg* unexpected.

inasprire *vt* to make worse ❑ **inasprirsi** *vr* to become bitter.

inattendibile *agg* unbelievable, unreliable.

inatteso, -a *agg* unexpected.

inattività *sf* inactivity.

inattuabile *agg* impractical, unfeasible.

inaudito, -a *agg* unheard-of, unprecedented.

inaugurare *vt* (*luogo, mostra*) to open; (*monumento*) to unveil.

inavvertenza *sf* carelessness.

inavvertitamente *avv* inadvertently.

incagliarsi *vr* (*nave*) to run aground; (*fig: trattative*) to break down.

incalcolabile *agg* incalculable.

incallito, -a agg (mani, piedi) calloused; (fig: fumatore, giocatore) inveterate.

incalzare vt (inseguire) to pursue; (fig: premere) to press ♦ vi to be imminent.

incamminarsi vr to set out.

incantevole agg enchanting.

incanto sm (incantesimo) enchantment; (asta) auction; **come per ~** as if by magic.

incapace agg incapable.

incapacità sf (inettitudine) incapacity; (DIR) incompetence.

incappare : incappare in v + prep to run into.

incaricare vt to entrust; **~ qn di qc** to entrust sb with sthg; **~ qn di fare qc** to ask sb to do sthg □ **incaricarsi di** vr + prep to undertake to.

incaricato, -a agg: **~ di qc** entrusted with sthg ♦ sm, f representative.

incarico, -chi sm task.

incarnare vt to embody.

incarnirsi vr to become ingrown.

incartare vt to wrap up; **me lo può ~?** can you wrap it up for me?

incassare vt (denaro) to receive; (assegno) to cash; (colpo, offesa) to take; (mobile) to build in.

incasso sm takings (pl).

incastrare vt (connettere) to join; (fam: intrappolare) to catch □ **incastrarsi** vr (rimanere bloccato) to get stuck; (combaciare) to fit together.

incastro sm joint; **a ~** interlocking.

incatenare vt (legare) to chain.

incauto, -a agg imprudent, rash.

incavato, -a agg hollow; (occhi) sunken.

incavo sm hollow.

incavolarsi vr (fam) to lose one's temper.

incendiare vt (dare fuoco a) to set fire to □ **incendiarsi** vr to catch fire.

incendio sm fire.

incenerire vt to incinerate.

incenso sm incense.

incensurato, -a agg: **essere ~** to have no previous convictions.

incentivo sm incentive.

inceppare vt to block, to obstruct □ **incepparsi** vr to jam.

incerata sf (tela) oilcloth; (giaccone) oilskin.

incertezza sf uncertainty.

incerto, -a agg uncertain; (tempo) variable.

incetta sf: **fare ~ di qc** to buy sthg up.

inchiesta sf enquiry.

inchinarsi vr (uomo) to bow; (donna) to curtsy.

inchino sm (di uomo) bow; (di donna) curtsy.

inchiodare vt to nail.

inchiostro sm ink.

inciampare vi to trip; **~ in qc** to trip over sthg.

incidente sm accident; **~ stradale** road accident.

incidere vt (intagliare) to engrave; (canzone) to record; (ascesso) to lance □ **incidere su** v +

prep to affect.

incinta *agg f* pregnant.

incirca *avv* **all'~** approximately, about.

incisione *sf (taglio)* cut; *(in arte)* engraving; *(di disco, canzone)* recording; *(MED)* incision.

incisivo, -a *agg* incisive ◆ *sm* incisor.

inciso, -a *pp → incidere* ◆ *sm*: **per ~** incidentally.

incitare *vt* to incite.

incivile *agg (non civilizzato)* uncivilized; *(maleducato)* rude.

inclinazione *sf* inclination.

includere *vt (accludere)* to enclose; *(comprendere)* to include.

incluso, -a *pp → includere* ◆ *agg (accluso)* enclosed; *(compreso)* included; **~ nel prezzo** included in the price.

incognito *sm*: **in ~** incognito.

incollare *vt (sovrapporre)* to stick; *(unire)* to stick, to glue □ **incollarsi** *(stare vicino)*: **incollarsi a qn** to stick close to sb.

incolpare *vt*: **~ qn (di qc)** to blame sb (for sth).

incolume *agg* unhurt.

incominciare *vt & vi* to begin, to start; **~ a fare qc** to begin to do sthg o doing sthg, to start to do sthg o doing sthg.

incompatibile *agg* incompatible.

incompetente *agg* incompetent.

incompiuto, -a *agg* unfinished, incomplete.

incompleto, -a *agg* incom-

plete.

incomprensibile *agg* incomprehensible.

inconcepibile *agg* inconceivable.

inconcludente *agg (persona)* ineffectual; *(discorsi)* inconclusive.

incondizionato, -a *agg* unconditional.

inconfondibile *agg* unmistakable.

inconsapevole *agg* unaware.

inconscio, -a, -sci, -sce *agg* unconscious.

incontaminato, -a *agg* uncontaminated.

incontentabile *agg* impossible to please.

incontinenza *sf* incontinence.

incontrare *vt* to meet; *(difficoltà, favore)* to meet with □ **incontrarsi** *vr* to meet.

incontrario : **all'incontrario** *avv (fam) (alla rovescia)* back to front; *(all'indietro)* backwards.

incontro *sm* meeting; *(casuale)* encounter; *(sportivo)* match ◆ *avv* towards; **andare/venire ~ a qn** *(avanzare verso)* to go/to come towards sb; *(incontrare)* to go/to come to meet sb; *(fig: con compromesso)* to meet sb halfway; **andare ~ a qc** *(spese)* to incur; *(difficoltà)* to encounter.

inconveniente *sm* setback, problem.

incoraggiare *vt* to encourage.

incosciente *agg (privo di coscienza)* unconscious; *(irresponsabile)* irresponsible.

incredibile agg incredible.

incrementare vt to increase.

incremento sm increase.

incrociare vt to cross; (persona, veicolo) to pass; ~ **le gambe/braccia** to cross one's legs/arms; ~ **le dita** to cross one's fingers ◻ **incrociarsi** vr (strade, linee) to cross; (persone, veicoli) to pass each other.

incrocio sm (crocevia) crossroads (sg); (combinazione) cross-breed.

incubatrice sf incubator.

incubo sm nightmare.

incurabile agg incurable.

incurante agg: ~ **di** careless of, indifferent to.

incuriosire vt to make curious ◻ **incuriosirsi** vr to become curious.

incustodito, -a agg unattended.

indaco sm indigo.

indaffarato, -a agg busy.

indagine sf (di polizia) investigation; (studio) research.

indebolire vt to weaken ◻ **indebolirsi** vr to weaken, to become weak.

indecente agg indecent.

indecifrabile agg indecipherable.

indeciso, -a agg uncertain.

indefinito, -a agg indefinite.

indegno, -a agg disgraceful.

indelebile agg indelible.

indenne agg unhurt.

indennità sf inv (rimborso) payment; (risarcimento) compensation.

indescrivibile agg indescribable.

indeterminativo, -a agg indefinite.

indeterminato, -a agg indeterminate, vague.

India sf: l'~ India.

indiano, -a agg & sm, f Indian.

indicare vt (mostrare) to show; (col dito) to point to; (suggerire) to recommend.

indicatore sm (TECNOL) gauge; ~ **della benzina** petrol gauge; ~ **di direzione** indicator; ~ **di velocità** speedometer.

indicazione sf (segnalazione) indication; (informazione) piece of information; (prescrizione) direction.

indice sm (dito) index finger; (di libro) index; (lancetta) needle; (indizio) rating.

indietro avv back; (moto a luogo) backwards; (col lavoro) to be behind; (orologio) to be slow; **rimandare** ~ to send back; **tornare** ~ to go back; **all'**~ backwards.

indifeso, -a agg defenceless.

indifferente agg (insensibile) indifferent; (irrilevante) insignificant; **mi è** ~ it's all the same to me.

indigeno, -a sm, f native.

indigente agg destitute.

indigestione sf indigestion.

indigesto, -a agg indigestible.

indimenticabile agg unforgettable.

indipendente agg independent.

indipendenza sf independence.

inesistente

indire vt (concorso) to announce; (elezioni) to call.

indiretto, -a agg indirect.

indirizzare vt (lettera, discorso) to address; (mandare) to refer.

indirizzo sm address; **scuola a ~ tecnico** ≈ technical college.

indisciplinato, -a agg undisciplined.

indiscreto, -a agg indiscreet.

indiscrezione sf (invadenza) indiscretion; (notizia) unconfirmed report.

indiscusso, -a agg undisputed.

indiscutibile agg unquestionable.

indispensabile agg indispensable.

indispettire vt to annoy □ **indispettirsi** vr to become annoyed.

indisponente agg annoying.

indistruttibile agg indestructible.

individuale agg individual.

individuare vt to identify.

individuo sm individual.

indiziato, -a agg suspected ♦ sm, f suspect.

indizio sm (segno) sign; (per polizia) clue; (DIR) piece of evidence.

indole sf nature.

indolenzito, -a agg aching, stiff.

indolore agg painless.

indomani sm: l'~ the next day.

indossare vt (mettere addosso) to put on; (avere addosso) to wear.

indossatore, -trice sm, f model.

indotto, -a pp → **indurre**.

indovinare vt to guess; (prevedere) to predict; (azzeccare) to get right.

indovinello sm riddle.

indovino, -a sm, f fortuneteller.

indubbiamente avv undoubtedly.

indugiare vi (temporeggiare) to take one's time.

indugio sm delay; **senza ~** without delay.

indulgente agg indulgent.

indumento sm garment; **indumenti** (abiti) clothes.

indurire vt to harden □ **indurirsi** vr to harden.

indurre vt: ~ **qn a fare qc** to induce sb to do sthg.

industria sf industry; (stabilimento) industrial plant.

industriale agg industrial ♦ sm industrialist.

inebetito, -a agg stunned.

inebriante agg intoxicating.

ineccepibile agg unexceptionable.

inedito, -a agg unpublished.

inefficiente agg inefficient.

ineluttabile agg inescapable.

inerente agg: ~ a concerning.

inerme agg unarmed, defenceless.

inerzia sf inactivity.

inesatto, -a agg inaccurate.

inesauribile agg inexhaustible.

inesistente agg nonexistent.

inesperienza sf inexperience.

inesperto, -a agg inexperienced.

inestimabile agg inestimable.

inevaso, -a agg outstanding.

inevitabile agg inevitable.

inevitabilmente avv inevitably.

in extremis avv in extremis.

infallibile agg infallible.

infantile agg (di, per bambini) child (dav s); (immaturo) infantile.

infanzia sf (periodo) childhood; (bambini) children (pl); prima ~ infancy.

infarinare vt (di farina) to cover with flour; (cospargere) to sprinkle.

infarto sm heart attack.

infastidire vt to annoy □ **infastidirsi** vr to get annoyed.

infatti cong in fact.

infatuarsi : infatuarsi di vr + prep to become infatuated with.

infatuazione sf infatuation.

infedele agg unfaithful.

infedeltà sf inv infidelity.

infelice agg unhappy; (sfavorevole) unsuccessful; (mal riuscito) poor; (inopportuno) unfortunate.

infelicità sf unhappiness.

inferiore agg (sottostante) lower; (per qualità) inferior ♦ smf inferior; ~ a (minore) below; (peggiore) inferior to.

infermeria sf infirmary; (di scuola) sickbay.

infermiere, -a sm, f nurse.

infermo, -a agg infirm.

infernale agg (fam: terribile) terrible; (diabolico) diabolical.

inferno sm hell.

inferriata sf grating.

infestare vt to infest.

infettare vt to infect □ **infettarsi** vr to become infected.

infettivo, -a agg infectious; malattie infettive infectious diseases.

infezione sf infection.

infiammabile agg flammable.

infiammare vt (incendiare) to set alight; (MED) to inflame □ **infiammarsi** vr (incendiarsi) to catch fire; (MED) to become inflamed.

infiammazione sf inflammation.

infilare vt (introdurre) to insert; (ago) to thread; (anello, vestito) to slip on □ **infilarsi in** vr + prep to slip into.

infine avv (alla fine) finally; (insomma) in short.

infinità sf infinity; un'~ di countless.

infinito, -a agg (illimitato) infinite; (enorme, innumerevole) countless ♦ sm (spazio, tempo) infinite; (GRAMM) infinitive.

infischiarsi : infischiarsene di vr + prep not to care about.

inflazione sf inflation.

inflessibile agg inflexible.

infliggere vt to inflict.

inflitto, -a pp → infliggere.

influente agg influential.

influenza sf influence; (malattia) flu; avere ~ su to have an influence on; avere l'~ to have flu.

influenzare vt to influence.

influire : influire su v + prep to

have an effect on.

influsso *sm* influence.

infondato, -a *agg* unfounded.

infondere *vt* to instil.

inforcare *vt (fieno)* to fork up; *(bicicletta, moto)* to get onto; *(occhiali)* to put on.

informale *agg* informal.

informare *vt*: ~ **qn (di qc)** to inform sb (of sthg) □ **informarsi** *vr*: informarsi di o su to find out about.

informatica *sf* information technology.

informativo, -a *agg* informative.

informatore *sm* informer.

informazione *sf* piece of information; **chiedere informazioni (a qn)** to ask (sb) for information; **'informazioni'** 'information'.

informicolirsi *vr*: mi si è informicolita una gamba I've got pins and needles in my leg.

infortunio *sm* accident.

infossarsi *vr (terreno)* to sink; *(guance)* to become hollow.

infradito *sm inv* o *sf inv* flip-flop.

infrangere *vt* to break □ **infrangersi** *vr* to break.

infrangibile *agg* unbreakable.

infranto, -a *pp* → infrangere ♦ *agg* broken.

infrazione *sf* infringement.

infreddolito, -a *agg* chilled.

infuori *avv*: **all'~** outwards; **all'~ di** apart from.

infusione *sf* infusion.

infuso, -a *pp* → infondere ♦ *sm* herb tea.

ingannare *vt (imbrogliare)* to deceive; *(tempo)* to while away □ **ingannarsi** *vr* to be mistaken.

inganno *sm* deception.

ingarbugliare *vt* to tangle; *(situazione, conti)* to muddle □ **ingarbugliarsi** *vr* to become tangled; *(situazione)* to become muddled; *(impappinarsi)* to falter.

ingegnere *sm* engineer.

ingegneria *sf* engineering.

ingegno *sm (intelligenza)* intelligence; *(creatività)* ingenuity.

ingegnoso, -a *agg* ingenious.

ingelosire *vt* to make jealous □ **ingelosirsi** *vr* to become jealous.

ingente *agg* huge.

ingenuo, -a *agg* naive.

ingerire *vt* to ingest.

ingessare *vt* to put in plaster.

Inghilterra *sf*: l'~ England.

inghiottire *vt* to swallow; *(sopportare)* to put up with.

ingiallire *vi* to yellow.

ingigantire *vt (foto)* to enlarge; *(fig: problema)* to exaggerate.

inginocchiarsi *vr* to kneel down.

ingiù *avv*: **(all')~** downwards.

ingiustizia *sf (qualità)* injustice; *(atto)* unjust act.

ingiusto, -a *agg* unfair.

inglese *agg* English ♦ *smf* Englishman (*f* Englishwoman) ♦ *sm (lingua)* English.

ingoiare *vt (inghiottire)* to swallow; *(fig: sopportare)* to put up with.

ingolfare *vt* to flood □ **ingolfarsi** *vr* to flood.

ingombrante *agg* cumbersome.

ingombrare *vt (passaggio, strada)* to obstruct; *(tavolo, stanza)* to clutter up.

ingombro, -a *agg* obstructed ◆ *sm*: **essere d'~** to be in the way.

ingordo, -a *agg* greedy.

ingorgo, -ghi *sm* traffic jam.

ingranaggio *sm (meccanismo)* gear; *(fig: operazioni, attività)* machinery.

ingranare *vt* to engage ◆ *vi (ingranaggio)* to engage; *(fam: prendere avvio)* to get going.

ingrandimento *sm* enlargement; *(ottico)* magnification.

ingrandire *vt* to enlarge; *(con microscopio, lente)* to magnify ❏ **ingrandirsi** *vr (di misura)* to get bigger; *(d'importanza)* to become more important.

ingrassare *vi* to put on weight ◆ *vt (animali)* to fatten up; *(motore)* to grease.

ingrediente *sm* ingredient.

ingresso *sm (porta)* entrance; *(stanza)* hall; *(permesso di entrare)* admission; **'~ gratuito'** 'admission free'; **'~ libero'** 'admission free'.

ingrossare *vt (gambe, fegato)* to cause to swell ❏ **ingrossarsi** *vr (gambe, fegato)* to swell.

ingrosso *avv*: **all'~** *(vendita)* wholesale; *(grossomodo)* about, roughly.

inguine *sm* groin.

inibire *vt* to inhibit.

iniettare *vt* to inject.

iniezione *sf* injection.

inimicare *vt*: **inimicarsi qn** to make an enemy of sb.

inimitabile *agg* inimitable.

ininterrottamente *avv* nonstop.

ininterrotto, -a *agg* continuous, unbroken.

iniziale *agg & sf* initial.

inizialmente *avv* initially.

iniziare *vt & vi* to begin, to start; **~ qn a qc** to introduce sb to sthg; **~ a fare qc** to begin O start to do sthg.

iniziativa *sf* initiative; **prendere l'~** to take the initiative.

inizio *sm* start, beginning; **all'~** at the start, at the beginning; **dare ~ a qc** to start O begin sthg; **avere ~** to start, to begin.

innaffiare = **annaffiare**.

innalzare *vt* to erect.

innamorarsi *vr*: **~ (di qn)** to fall in love (with sb).

innamorato, -a *agg*: **~ (di qn)** in love (with sb).

innanzi *avv* in front ◆ *prep (davanti a)* in front of; *(prima di)* before.

innanzitutto *avv* first of all.

innato, -a *agg* innate.

innervosire *vt* to make nervous ❏ **innervosirsi** *vr* to get nervous.

innescare *vt (bomba)* to prime; *(fig: fenomeno, meccanismo)* to trigger.

innestare *vt (pianta)* to graft; *(meccanismo, marcia)* to engage.

inno *sm* hymn; **~ nazionale** national anthem.

innocente *agg* innocent.

innocuo, -a *agg* harmless.

innovazione *sf* innovation.

innumerevole *agg* countless.

inodore *agg* odourless.

inoffensivo, -a *agg* inoffensive.

inoltrare *vt* to forward □ **inoltrarsi** *vr* to advance.

inoltrato, -a *agg* late.

inoltre *avv* besides.

inondazione *sf* flood.

inopportuno, -a *agg* inappropriate.

inorridire *vt* to horrify ♦ *vi* to be horrified.

inosservato, -a *agg*: **passare ~** to go unnoticed.

inquadrare *vt* (*personaggio, avvenimento*) to place; (*con telecamera*): ~ **qn/qc** to get sb/sthg in the shot.

inquadratura *sf* shot.

inqualificabile *agg* contemptible.

inquietante *agg* disturbing.

inquilino, -a *sm, f* tenant.

inquinamento *sm* pollution.

inquinare *vt* (*contaminare*) to pollute; (*fig: prove*) to corrupt.

inquinato, -a *agg* polluted.

insabbiare *vt* to shelve □ **insabbiarsi** *vr* (*nave*) to run aground; (*pratica, progetto*) to be shelved.

insaccato *sm* sausage.

insalata *sf* (*di verdure*) salad; (*lattuga*) lettuce; ~ **mista** mixed salad; ~ **di mare** seafood salad; ~ **di riso** rice salad; ~ **russa** Russian salad

(*cold diced cooked vegetables mixed with mayonnaise*).

insalatiera *sf* salad bowl.

insaponare *vt* to soap □ **insaponarsi** *vr* to soap o.s.

insapore *agg* tasteless.

insaporire *vt* to flavour.

insaputa *sf*: **all'~ di qn** without sb's knowledge.

inscenare *vt* to stage.

insegna *sf* sign.

insegnamento *sm* teaching.

insegnante *smf* teacher.

insegnare *vt & vi* to teach; ~ **qc a qn** to teach sb sthg; ~ **a qn a fare qc** to teach sb to do sthg.

inseguire *vt* to pursue.

insenatura *sf* inlet, creek.

insensato, -a *agg* (*persona*) foolish; (*discorso, idea*) senseless.

insensibile *agg* insensitive.

inseparabile *agg* inseparable.

inserire *vt* (*introdurre*) to insert; (*includere*) to put in □ **inserirsi** *vr*: **inserirsi in qc** (*entrare a far parte di*) to become part of sthg.

inserto *sm* insert.

inserviente *smf* attendant.

inserzione *sf* advertisement.

insetticida, -i *sm* insecticide.

insetto *sm* insect.

insicurezza *sf* insecurity.

insicuro, -a *agg* insecure.

insidia *sf* hidden danger.

insieme *avv* together ♦ *sm* (*totalità*) whole; (*MAT*) set ♦ *prep*: ~ **a** con with; **mettere** ~ (*raccogliere*) to put together; **tutto** ~ all together; **tutti** ~ all together; **nell'~** taken as a whole.

insignificante _agg_ insignificant.

insinuare _vt_ to insinuate.

insinuazione _sf_ insinuation.

insipido, -a _agg_ insipid.

insistente _agg (persona, richieste)_ insistent; _(pioggia, dolore)_ persistent.

insistere _vi_ to insist; ~ **a** o **col fare qc** to persist in doing sthg.

insoddisfacente _agg_ unsatisfactory.

insoddisfatto, -a _agg_: ~ **di** dissatisfied with.

insolazione _sf_ sunstroke.

insolente _agg_ insolent.

insolito, -a _agg_ unusual.

insoluto, -a _agg (non risolto)_ unsolved; _(non pagato)_ outstanding.

insomma _avv_ well ◆ _esclam_ for Heaven's sake!

insonne _agg (persona)_ unable to sleep; _(notte)_ sleepless.

insonnia _sf_ insomnia.

insonnolito, -a _agg_ sleepy.

insopportabile _agg_ unbearable.

insorgere _vi (popolo)_ to rise up; _(difficoltà)_ to arise.

insospettire _vt_ to arouse suspicions in ❑ **insospettirsi** _vr_ to become suspicious.

insozzare _vt_ to dirty.

insperato, -a _agg_ unhoped-for.

inspiegabile _agg_ inexplicable.

inspirare _vt_ to breathe in.

installare _vt_ to install.

instaurare _vt_ to establish.

insù _avv_: **(all')**~ upwards.

insuccesso _sm_ failure.

insudiciare _vt_ to dirty ❑ **insudiciarsi** _vr_ to get dirty.

insufficiente _agg_ insufficient.

insulina _sf_ insulin.

insultare _vt_ to insult.

insulto _sm_ insult.

intaccare _vt_ to attack; _(fare tacche in)_ to cut into; _(risparmi)_ to break into.

intanto _avv (nel frattempo)_ meanwhile.

intarsio _sm_ inlay.

intasare _vt_ to block ❑ **intasarsi** _vr_ to become blocked.

intatto, -a _agg (intero)_ intact; _(mai toccato)_ untouched.

integrale _agg (totale)_ complete; _(pane, farina)_ wholemeal.

integrare _vt_ to integrate ❑ **integrarsi** _vr_ to integrate.

integrità _sf_ integrity.

integro, -a _agg (intero)_ intact; _(onesto)_ honest.

intelaiatura _sf_ framework.

intelletto _sm_ intellect.

intellettuale _agg & smf_ intellectual.

intelligente _agg_ intelligent.

intelligenza _sf_ intelligence.

intemperie _sfpl_ bad weather _(sg)_.

intendere _vt (capire)_ to understand; _(udire)_ to hear; _(avere intenzione di)_: ~ **fare qc** to intend to do sthg; **non intende ragioni** he won't listen to reason; **intendersela co**[n] **qn** to have an affair with sb ❑ **intendersi di** _vr + prep_ to know about.

intenditore, -trice *sm, f* expert.

intensificare *vt* to intensify □ **intensificarsi** *vr* to intensify.

intensità *sf* intensity.

intensivo, -a *agg* intensive.

intenso, -a *agg* intense.

intento, -a *sm* intention ♦ *agg*: ~ **(a fare qc)** intent (on doing sthg).

intenzione *sf* intention; **aver ~ di fare qc** to intend to do sthg.

interamente *avv* completely.

intercalare *sm* catchphrase ♦ *vt* to insert.

intercettare *vt* to intercept.

intercity [inter'siti] *sm inv* fast train connecting major Italian cities.

interdetto, -a *agg* taken aback.

interessamento *sm* (*interesse*) interest; (*intervento*) intervention.

interessante *agg* interesting; **in stato** ~ (*incinta*) expecting.

interessare *vt* (*destare l'interesse di*) to interest; (*riguardare*) to concern ♦ *vi*: ~ **a qn** to interest sb; **ciò non mi interessa** I'm not interested in it □ **interessarsi a** *vr + prep* to be interested in; **interessarsi di** *vr + prep* (*per informazioni*) to find out about; (*per lavoro, hobby*) to be interested in.

interessato, -a *agg* (*partecipe*) interested; (*calcolatore*) self-interested.

interesse *sm* interest; (*tornaconto*) self-interest □ **interessi** *smpl* nterests.

interferire *vi* to interfere.

interiezione *sf* interjection.

interiora *sfpl* entrails.

interiore *agg* (*lato, parte*) interior.

interlocutore, -trice *sm, f* interlocutor.

intermezzo *sm* interval.

interminabile *agg* endless.

intermittente *agg* intermittent.

internazionale *agg* international.

interno, -a *agg* (*di dentro*) interior, internal; (*nazionale*) domestic ♦ *sm* interior; (*telefono*) extension; (*in indirizzo*): ~ **20** flat 20; **all'~** inside □ **interni** *smpl*: **ministero degli Interni** = Home Office (*Br*), Department of the Interior (*Am*).

intero, -a *agg* whole; (*prezzo*) full; (*latte*) full-cream; **per ~** in full.

interpretare *vt* to interpret; (*recitare*) to perform.

interprete *smf* (*traduttore*) interpreter; (*attore, musicista*) performer.

interrogare *vt* (*studente*) to examine; (*sospetto*) to question.

interrogativo, -a *agg* (*sguardo*) enquiring; (*GRAMM*) interrogative ♦ *sm* question.

interrogazione *sf* oral examination.

interrompere *vt* to interrupt; (*linea telefonica, strada*) to cut off □ **interrompersi** *vr* to stop.

interrotto, -a *pp* → **interrompere** ♦ *agg* cut off.

interruttore *sm* switch.

intersecare vt to intersect.

interurbana sf long-distance call.

interurbano, -a agg (trasporti) intercity; (chiamata) long-distance.

intervallo sm interval.

intervenire vi to intervene; (partecipare) to take part; (MED) to operate.

intervento sm (intromissione) intervention; (partecipazione) participation; (discorso) speech; (MED) operation.

intervenuto, -a pp → intervenire.

intervista sf interview.

intesa sf (tra persone) understanding; (tra stati) agreement.

inteso, -a pp → intendere ♦ agg: **resta ~ che** it is understood that; **siamo intesi?** are we agreed?

intestare vt (lettera) to address; **~ qc a qn** (casa, auto) to register sthg in sb's name; (assegno) to make sthg out to sb.

intestino sm intestine.

intimare vt to order.

intimidire vt to intimidate.

intimità sf (spazio privato) privacy; (familiarità) intimacy.

intimo, -a agg intimate; (cerimonia, parti) private; (interiore) innermost; (igiene) personal ♦ sm (persona) close friend.

intimorire vt to frighten.

intingolo sm sauce.

intitolare vt (libro, film) to entitle; (via, piazza): **~ a** to name after □ **intitolarsi** vr to be entitled.

intollerabile agg unbearable.

intollerante agg intolerant.

intolleranza sf intolerance.

intonaco, -ci o **-chi** sm plaster.

intonare vt (canto) to intone; (vestiti): **~ qc a qc** to match sthg with sthg □ **intonarsi** vr to go together.

intontire vt to stun.

intorno avv around, round ♦ prep: **~ a** around.

intossicare vt to poison.

intossicato, -a agg poisoned.

intossicazione sf poisoning.

intraducibile agg untranslatable.

intralciare vt to hamper.

intramontabile agg timeless.

intramuscolare agg → iniezione.

intransigente agg intransigent.

intransitivo, -a agg intransitive.

intraprendente agg enterprising.

intraprendere vt to undertake.

intrapreso, -a pp → intraprendere.

intrattabile agg (persona) intractable; (prezzo) non-negotiable.

intrattenere vt (persona) to entertain; (relazioni, rapporti) to maintain □ **intrattenersi** vr: **intrattenersi su qc** to dwell on sthg.

intrecciare vt (capelli) to plait o braid; (nastri) to intertwine o to braid; (nastri) to intertwine □ **intrecciarsi** vr (fili) to intertwine.

intrigante *agg* scheming.

intrigo, -ghi *sm (macchinazione)* intrigue.

introdurre *vt* to introduce; *(moneta)* to insert; **'vietato ~ cani'** 'dogs not allowed' □ **introdursi** *vr (uso, tecnica)* to be introduced; *(entrare)* to enter.

introduzione *sf* introduction.

introito *sm (incasso)* income.

intromettersi *vr (immischiarsi)* to interfere; *(interporsi)* to intervene.

introvabile *agg* not to be found.

introverso, -a *agg* introverted.

intruso, -a *sm, f* intruder.

intuire *vt (cogliere)* to grasp; *(accorgersi)* to realize.

intuito *sm* intuition.

intuizione *sf* intuition.

inumidire *vt* to dampen □ **inumidirsi** *vr* to become damp.

inutile *agg* useless; *(superfluo)* pointless.

inutilmente *avv* in vain.

invadente *agg* intrusive.

invadere *vt* to invade.

invaghirsi : **invaghirsi di** *vr* + *prep* to take a fancy to.

invalido, -a *agg* disabled ♦ *sm, f* disabled person.

invano *avv* in vain.

invasione *sf* invasion.

invasore *sm* invader.

invecchiare *vi (persona)* to grow old; *(vino)* to age ♦ *vt (vino, formaggio)* to age; *(persona)* to make look older.

invece *avv* but ♦ *prep*: ~ **di** instead of.

inveire *vi*: ~ **(contro)** to rail (against).

inventare *vt* to invent; **si è inventato tutto** he made it all up.

inventario *sm (registrazione)* stocktaking; *(lista)* inventory.

inventore, -trice *sm, f* inventor.

invenzione *sf* invention.

invernale *agg* winter *(dav s)*.

inverno *sm* winter; **in** o **d'~** in (the) winter.

inverosimile *agg* unbelievable.

inversione *sf (di ordine, tendenza)* inversion; *(di marcia)* U-turn.

inverso, -a *agg & sm* opposite; **fare qc all'~** to do sthg the wrong way round.

invertire *vt (ordine)* to invert; ~ **la marcia** to do a U-turn.

investimento *sm* investment.

investire *vt (denaro)* to invest; *(persona, animale)* to knock down.

inviare *vt* to send.

inviato, -a *sm, f (incaricato)* envoy; *(giornalista)* correspondent.

invidia *sf* envy.

invidiare *vt* to envy; ~ **qc a qn** to envy sb sthg.

invidioso, -a *agg* envious.

invincibile *agg (imbattibile)* invincible.

invio *sm (spedizione)* dispatching; *(merci)* consignment.

inviperito, -a *agg* furious.

invischiarsi : **invischiarsi in** *vr* + *prep* to get involved in.

invisibile *agg* invisible.

invitare *vt* to invite; **~ qn a fare qc** *(proporre di)* to invite sb to do sthg; *(sollecitare)* to request sb to do sthg.

invitato, -a *sm, f* guest.

invito *sm* invitation.

invocare *vt* *(Dio)* to invoke; *(chiedere)* to beg for; *(legge, diritto)* to cite.

invogliare *vt* to tempt.

involontario, -a *agg* involuntary.

involtino *sm* thin slice of meat, rolled up and sometimes stuffed; **~ primavera** spring roll.

involucro *sm* covering.

inzaccherare *vt* to splash with mud.

inzuppare *vt* to soak; *(biscotto)* to dip.

io *pron* I; **sono ~** it's me; **~ stesso** I myself.

iodio *sm* iodine.

iogurt *sm* yogurt.

Ionio *sm*: **lo ~, il mar ~** the Ionian (Sea).

ipertensione *sf* hypertension.

ipnosi *sf* hypnosis.

ipnotizzare *vt* to hypnotize.

ipocrisia *sf* hypocrisy.

ipocrita, -i, -e *agg* hypocritical ♦ *smf* hypocrite.

ipoteca, -che *sf* mortgage.

ipotesi *sf inv* hypothesis.

ippica *sf* horse racing.

ippico, -a, -ci, -che *agg* horse *(dav s)*.

ippodromo *sm* racecourse.

ippopotamo *sm* hippopotamus.

Iran *sm*: **l'~** Iran.

Iraq *sm*: **l'~** Iraq.

iride *sf* *(di occhio)* iris; *(arcobaleno)* rainbow.

iris *sf inv* iris.

Irlanda *sf*: **l'~** Ireland; **l'~ del Nord** Northern Ireland.

irlandese *agg* Irish ♦ *smf* Irishman *(f Irishwoman)*.

ironia *sf* irony.

ironico, -a, -ci, -che *agg* ironic.

irradiare *vt* to light up ♦ *vi* to radiate.

irraggiungibile *agg* unreachable.

irragionevole *agg* unreasonable.

irrazionale *agg* irrational.

irreale *agg* unreal.

irrecuperabile *agg* *(oggetto)* irretrievable; *(fig: persona)* irredeemable.

irregolare *agg* irregular; *(discontinuo)* uneven.

irregolarità *sf inv* irregularity; *(discontinuità)* unevenness.

irremovibile *agg* inflexible.

irreparabile *agg* irreparable.

irrequieto, -a *agg* restless.

irresponsabile *agg* irresponsible.

irreversibile *agg* irreversible.

irriducibile *agg* unyielding.

irrigare *vt* to irrigate.

irrigidirsi *vr* to stiffen.

irrilevante *agg* insignificant.

irrisorio, -a *agg* ridiculous.

irritabile *agg* irritable.

irritante *agg* irritating.

irritare *vt* to irritate ❑ **irritarsi** *vr* to become irritated.

irrompere : **irrompere in** *v + prep* to burst into.

irrotto, -a *pp* → **irrompere**.

irruente *agg* impetuous.

irruzione *sf* raid.

iscritto, -a *pp* → **iscrivere** ♦ *agg*: **essere ~ a qc** (*ad un circolo, partito*) to be a member of sthg; (*all'università*) to be enrolled in sthg; (*ad un esame*) to be entered for sthg; **per ~** in writing.

iscrivere *vt*: ~ **qn (a qc)** (*scuola*) to register sb (at sthg), to enrol sb (at sthg); (*corso*) to register sb (for sthg), to enrol sb (for sthg) ❑ **iscriversi** *vr*: **iscriversi (a)** (*circolo, partito*) to become a member (of); (*university*) to enrol (in); (*esame*) to enter.

iscrizione *sf* (*a università*) enrolment; (*a esame*) entry; (*a partito*) membership; (*funeraria*) inscription.

Islanda *sf*: **l'~** Iceland.

islandese *agg* Icelandic ♦ *smf* Icelander.

isola *sf* island; ~ **pedonale** pedestrian precinct.

isolamento *sm* (*solitudine*) isolation; (*elettrico, termico*) insulation; (*acustico*) soundproofing.

isolante *agg* insulating ♦ *sm* insulator.

isolare *vt* (*tenere lontano*) to isolate; (*da freddo, corrente elettrica*) to insulate; (*da rumore*) to soundproof ❑ **isolarsi** *vr* to cut o.s. off.

isolato, -a *agg* isolated ♦ *sm* block.

ispettore *sm* inspector.

ispezionare *vt* to inspect.

ispezione *sf* inspection.

ispirare *vt* to inspire ❑ **ispirarsi a** *vr + prep* to draw one's inspiration from.

Israele *sm* Israel.

issare *vt* to hoist.

istantanea *sf* snapshot.

istantaneo, -a *agg* instantaneous, instant.

istante *sm* instant; **all'~** instantly, at once.

isterico, -a, -ci, -che *agg* hysterical.

istigare *vt*: ~ **qn a fare qc** to incite sb to do sthg.

istinto *sm* instinct.

istituire *vt* to institute.

istituto *sm* (*organismo*) institute; (*universitario*) department; ~ **di bellezza** beauty salon.

istituzione *sf* institution; **le istituzioni** (*le autorità*) the Establishment.

istmo *sm* (GEOG) isthmus.

istrice *sm* (*animale*) porcupine.

istruire *vt* (*insegnare a*) to teach; (*informare*) to instruct.

istruito, -a *agg* educated.

istruttore, -trice *sm, f* instructor.

istruzione *sf* (*insegnamento*) education; (*cultura*) learning ❑ **istruzioni** *sfpl*: **istruzioni (per l'uso)** instructions (for use).

Italia *sf*: **l'~** Italy.

italiano, -a *agg & sm, f* Italian.

itinerario

itinerario *sm (percorso)* route; *(descrizione)* itinerary; **~ turistico** *(percorso)* tourist route.

lugoslavia *sf:* **la ~** Yugoslavia.

IVA *sf (abbr di imposta sul valore aggiunto)* VAT.

kiwi ['kiwi] *sm inv* kiwi fruit.

km *(abbr di chilometro)* km.

k.o. *avv:* **mettere qn ~ to** knock sb out.

koala *sm inv* koala.

K-way® [ki'wei] *sm inv* cagoule.

J

jazz [dʒɛts] *sm* jazz.

jeans [dʒins] *smpl* jeans ◆ *sm (tessuto)* denim.

jeep® [dʒip] *sf inv* Jeep®.

jolly ['dʒɔlli] *sm inv* joker.

Jonio = **Ionio**.

jota *sf* bean soup with onions and turnips marinated in wine (a speciality of Friuli).

Jugoslavia = **Iugoslavia**.

juke-box [dʒu'bɔks] *sm inv* juke-box.

K

karaoke *sm inv (gioco)* karaoke; *(locale)* karaoke bar.

karatè *sm* karate.

Kenia *sm:* **il ~** Kenya.

kg *(abbr di chilogrammo)* kg.

killer *smf inv* killer.

kitsch [kitʃ] *agg inv* kitsch.

L

l' → **la, lo.**

la **(l'** *dav vocale e h)* *art f* the, → **il** ◆ *pron (persona)* her; *(animale, cosa)* it; *(forma di cortesia)* you.

là *avv* there; **di ~** *(nella stanza accanto)* in there; *(moto da luogo)* from there; *(nei paraggi)* over there; **al di ~ di** beyond.

labbro *(pl f* **labbra)** *sm (ANAT)* lip.

labirinto *sm (di strade, corridoi)* labyrinth; *(giardino)* maze.

laboratorio *sm (scientifico)* laboratory; *(artigianale)* workshop; **~ linguistico** language laboratory.

lacca, -che *sf (per capelli)* lacquer, hair spray; *(vernice)* lacquer.

laccio *sm* lace.

lacerare *vt* to tear, to rip ❑ **lacerarsi** *vr* to tear.

lacero, -a *agg* torn.

lacrima *sf* tear; **in lacrime** in tears.

lacrimogeno *agg m* → **gas.**

lacuna *sf* gap.

ladro, -a *sm, f* thief.

laggiù *avv (in basso)* down there; *(lontano)* over there.

lagnarsi *vr (piagnucolare)* to moan, to groan; *(protestare)*: ~ **(di)** to complain (about).

lago, -ghi *sm* lake.

ℹ️ I LAGHI

The most famous of the many Italian lakes are undoubtedly those in northern Italy: Lake Garda (the largest), Lake Maggiore and Lake Como. Millions of Italian and foreign tourists alike visit them every year, attracted by their scenic splendour and pleasant climate, the grand villas and lush gardens lining their shores, and the many varieties of wild flower to be found in the area. In summer the lakes attract swimmers, sunbathers and water-sports enthusiasts looking for an alternative to the coastal resorts.

laguna *sf* lagoon.

laico, -a, -ci, -che *agg* lay *(dav s)*.

lama *sf* blade.

lamentarsi *vr (emettere lamenti)* to groan, to moan; ~ **(di)** *(dimostrarsi insoddisfatto)* to complain (about).

lamentela *sf* complaint, complaining *(sg)*.

lametta *sf* razor blade.

lamiera *sf* sheet metal.

lampada *sf* lamp; **fare la** ~ **to** use a sunlamp; ~ **da tavolo** table lamp.

lampadario *sm* chandelier.

lampadina *sf* light bulb; ~ **ta-**

---

largo

scabile torch *(Br)*, flashlight *(Am)*.

lampeggiare *vi* to flash.

lampeggiatore *sm (freccia)* indicator; *(di ambulanza)* flashing light.

lampione *sm* streetlight.

lampo *sm (fulmine)* flash of lightning; *(bagliore)* flash ◆ *sf inv (cerniera)* zip *(Br)*, zipper *(Am)*.

lampone *sm* raspberry.

lana *sf* wool; **pura** ~ **vergine** pure new wool.

lancetta *sf* hand.

lancia, -ce *sf (arma)* lance; *(imbarcazione)* launch.

lanciare *vt (pietra, palla)* to throw; *(missile)* to launch; *(grido)* to give; *(insulto)* to hurl; *(fig: appello, moda, prodotto)* to launch ❑ **lanciarsi** *vr* to throw o.s.; **lanciarsi in** *qc (mare)* to throw o.s. into sthg; *(impresa)* to embark on sthg.

lancinante *agg* piercing, shooting.

lancio *sm (tiro)* throw; *(di prodotti, missile)* launch.

languido, -a *agg* languid.

languore *sm (di stomaco)* hunger pangs *(pl)*.

lapide *sf (funeraria)* tombstone; *(commemorativa)* plaque.

lapis *sm inv* pencil.

lapsus *sm inv* slip.

lardo *sm* lard, bacon fat.

larghezza *sf (dimensione)* width, breadth; *(abbondanza)* generosity.

largo, -a, -ghi, -ghe *agg* wide, broad; *(indumento)* loose; *(percentuale, parte)* large ◆ *sm* width; *(piazza)* square; *(alto mare)*

andare al ~ to take to the open sea; **è ~ 10 metri** it's 10 metres wide; **stare** ○ **tenersi alla larga (da)** to keep one's distance (from); **farsi ~ to** push one's way.

larva *sf (insetto)* larva.

lasagne *sfpl* lasagne *(sg)*.

lasciare *vt* to leave; *(cessare di tenere)* to let go of; **posso ~ i bagagli in camera?** can I leave the luggage in the room?; **~ la porta aperta** to leave the door open; **~ qn in pace** to leave sb in peace; **lasciar detto a qn che ...** to leave sb word that ...; **~ a desiderare** to leave a lot to be desired; **prendere o ~ take** it or leave it; **~ la presa** to let go ♦ *vb aus*: **lasciami vedere** let me see; **lascia che faccia come vuole** let him do as he wants; **lasciar perdere!** forget it!; **lasciar credere qc a qn** to let sb believe sthg; **lascialo stare!** leave him alone! ❑ **lasciarsi** *vr (separarsi)* to leave each other; **lasciarsi andare** to let o.s. go; **lasciarsi convincere** to allow o.s. to be persuaded.

laser *sm inv & agg inv* laser.

lassativo *sm* laxative.

lassù *avv* up there.

lastra *sf (di ghiaccio, vetro)* sheet; *(di pietra)* slab; *(radiografia)* plate.

laterale *agg* lateral, side *(dav s)*.

latino, -a *agg & sm* Latin.

latino-americano, -a *agg* Latin-American.

latitudine *sf* latitude.

lato *sm* side; **a ~ (di qc)** beside (sthg); **da un ~ ... dall'altro ...** on the one hand ... on the other hand ...

latta *sf* tin.

lattaio, -a *sm, f* milkman (f milkwoman).

lattante *smf* baby.

latte *sm* milk; **~ detergente** cleansing milk; **~ intero** full cream milk; **~ magro** ○ **scremato** skimmed milk; **~ in polvere** powdered milk; **~ di soia** soya milk.

latteria *sf* dairy.

latticini *smpl* dairy products.

lattina *sf* can.

lattuga, -ghe *sf* lettuce.

laurea *sf* degree.

laurearsi *vr* to graduate; **~ in qc** to graduate in sthg.

laureato, -a *agg & sm, f* graduate; **è ~ in legge** he has a law degree.

lava *sf* lava.

lavaggio *sm* washing; **~ automatico** *(per auto)* car wash.

lavagna *sf* blackboard.

lavanda *sf* lavender; **fare una ~ gastrica a qn** to pump sb's stomach.

lavanderia *sf* laundry; **~ automatica** launderette; **~ a secco** dry cleaner's.

lavandino *sm* sink.

lavapiatti *sf inv* dishwasher.

lavare *vt* to wash; **~ a secco qc** to dry-clean sthg; **lavarsi le mani** to wash one's hands; **lavarsi i denti** to clean one's teeth ❑ **lavarsi** *vr* to wash o.s.

lavasecco *sm inv o sf inv* dry cleaner's.

lavastoviglie *sf inv* dishwasher.

lavatrice sf washing machine.

lavorare vi & vt to work; ~ **a maglia** to knit.

lavorativo, -a agg working (dav s).

lavorato, -a agg (mobile, tessuto) elaborate; (terreno) cultivated.

lavoratore, -trice sm, f worker.

lavorazione sf (di legno) carving; (di cotone) manufacture.

lavoro sm work; (occupazione) work, job; **'lavori in corso'** 'men at work'; **lavori stradali** road works.

le art fpl the, → **il** ◆ pron (complemento oggetto) them; (a lei) (to) her; (forma di cortesia) (to) you.

leader ['lider] smf inv leader.

leale agg loyal.

lecca lecca sm inv lollipop.

leccare vt to lick.

lecito, -a agg permitted.

lega, -ghe sf (associazione) league; (alleanza politica) alliance; (di metalli) alloy.

legale agg legal ◆ smf (avvocato) lawyer.

legalizzare vt to legalize.

legame sm (sentimentale) tie; (nesso) link.

legare vt (con catena, laccio) to tie (up); (sog: sentimento, interesse) to bind.

legge sf law.

leggenda sf (favola) legend; (didascalia) key.

leggendario, -a agg legendary.

leggere vt & vi to read.

leggerezza sf (di materiale, corpo) lightness; (fig: sconsideratezza) thoughtlessness.

leggero, -a agg light; (caffè, tè) weak; (di poca importanza) slight.

legittimo, -a agg legitimate; **legittima difesa** self-defence.

legna sf firewood.

legname sm wood.

legno sm (materia) wood; (pezzo) piece of wood, stick.

legumi smpl pulses.

lei pron (soggetto) she; (complemento oggetto, con preposizione) her; (forma di cortesia) you; è ~ it's her; **io sto bene, e ~?** I'm fine, and you?; ~ **stessa** she herself/you yourself.

lentamente avv slowly.

lente sf lens; ~ **di ingrandimento** magnifying glass; **lenti a contatto** contact lenses.

lentezza sf slowness.

lenticchie sfpl lentils.

lento, -a agg slow; (allentato) loose ◆ sm slow dance.

lenza sf fishing line.

lenzuolo (pl f **lenzuola**) sm sheet.

leone sm lion ❑ **Leone** sm Leo.

leopardo sm leopard.

lepre sf hare; ~ **in salmì** marinated hare in a sauce made from its offal.

lesbica, -che sf lesbian.

lesione sf lesion.

lesso, -a agg boiled ◆ sm boiled beef.

letale agg lethal.

letame sm manure.

lettera sf letter; **alla ~** literally ❑ **lettere** sfpl (facoltà) = arts.

letteratura sf literature.

lettino *sm* (del medico) couch; (per bambini) cot.

letto, -a *pp* → **leggere** ♦ *sm* bed; **andare a ~** to go to bed; **~ matrimoniale** o **a due piazze** double bed; **~ a una piazza** single bed; **letti a castello** bunk beds; **letti gemelli** twin beds.

lettore, -trice *sm, f* (di libro, giornale) reader; (di università) foreign language assistant ♦ *sm*: **~ di compact** CD player.

lettura *sf* reading.

leva *sf* lever; (militare) conscription; **fare ~ su qc** (fig) to play on sthg; **~ del cambio** gear lever (Br), gear shift (Am).

levante *sm* east.

levare *vt* (togliere) to remove; (alzare) to raise ❏ **levarsi** *vr* (vento) to get up, to rise.

levata *sf* collection.

levatoio *agg m* → **ponte**.

levigare *vt* to smooth.

lezione *sf* lesson; (all'università) lecture.

lezioso, -a *agg* affected.

lezzo *sm* stink.

li *pron mpl* them.

lì *avv* there; **essere ~ (~) per fare qc** to be on the point of doing sthg; **da ~ in poi** (tempo) from then on; (spazio) from that point onwards.

Libano *sm*: **il ~** Lebanon.

libeccio *sm* southwest wind.

libellula *sf* dragonfly.

liberale *agg* liberal.

liberamente *avv* freely.

liberare *vt* (prigioniero) to free, to release; (camera, posto) to vacate ❏ **liberarsi** (annullare un impegno) to free o.s.; **liberarsi di** to get rid of.

libero, -a *agg* free; **essere ~ di fare qc** to be free to do sthg; **~ professionista** self-employed professional; **'libero'** (su taxi) 'for hire'; (in toilette) 'vacant'.

libertà *sf inv* freedom; (permesso) liberty; **mettere in ~ qn** to free sb.

Libia *sf*: **la ~** Libya.

libreria *sf* (negozio) bookshop; (mobile) bookcase.

libretto *sm* (MUS) libretto; **~ degli assegni** cheque book; **~ di circolazione** log book; **~ di risparmio** savings book; **~ universitario** university report card.

libro *sm* book; **~ giallo** thriller.

licenza *sf* (autorizzazione) licence; (militare) leave; **~ media** school-leaving certificate.

licenziamento *sm* dismissal.

licenziare *vt* to dismiss ❏ **licenziarsi** *vr* to resign.

liceo *sm* secondary school (Br), high school (Am).

lido *sm* beach; **il Lido di Venezia** the Venice Lido.

lieto, -a *agg* (contento): **~ di conoscerla!** pleased to meet you!; **molto ~!** pleased to meet you!

lievitare *vi* to rise.

lievito *sm* yeast; **~ di birra** brewer's yeast.

Liguria *sf*: **la ~** Liguria.

lillà *agg inv & sm inv* lilac.

lima *sf* file.

limetta *sf*: ~ per unghie nail file.

limitare *vt* to limit, to restrict ☐

limitarsi *vr*: limitarsi a fare qc to limit o.s. to doing sth; **limitarsi nel bere** to restrict one's drinking.

limitato, -a *agg* limited.

limite *sm* (confine) border; (punto estremo) limit; ~ **di velocità** speed limit; **entro certi limiti** within certain limits; **al** ~ if the worst comes to the worst.

limitrofo, -a *agg* neighbouring.

limonata *sf* lemonade.

limone *sm* lemon.

limpido, -a *agg* clear.

linea *sf* line; (itinerario) route; **mantenere la** ~ to look after one's figure; **avere qualche** ~ **di febbre** to have a slight temperature; **linee urbane** local buses; **in** ~ **d'aria** as the crow flies; **in** ~ **di massima** as a general rule; **a grandi linee** in broad outline; **è caduta la** ~ we have been cut off.

lineare *agg* linear.

lineetta *sf* dash.

lingua *sf* (ANAT & CULIN) tongue; (linguaggio) language; ~ **madre** mother tongue; ~ **straniera** foreign language.

linguaggio *sm* language; ~ **dei segni** sign language.

linguetta *sf* tongue.

linguistico, -a, -ci, -che *agg* linguistic.

lino *sm* linen.

linoleum *sm* linoleum.

liofilizzato, -a *agg* freeze-dried.

liquefare *vt* to melt ♦ **liquefarsi** *vr* to melt.

liquefatto, -a *pp* → liquefare.

liquidare *vt* (società, beni) to liquidate; (merce) to sell off; (sbarazzarsi di) to get rid of; (fig: questione, problema) to solve.

liquidazione *sf* (di merci) selling off, clearance; (indennità) severance pay.

liquido, -a *agg* liquid ♦ *sm* liquid; (denaro) cash.

liquirizia *sf* liquorice.

liquore *sm* liqueur.

lira *sf* lira; **non avere una** ~ not to have a penny (Br), not to have a dime (Am).

lirica *sf* opera.

lirico, -a, -ci, -che *agg* (musica) lyric(al); (opera) lyric.

lisca, -sche *sf* fishbone.

liscio, -a, -sci, -sce *agg* (pietra, pelle) smooth; (capelli) straight; (whisky) neat ♦ *sm* (ballo) ballroom dance; **andar** ~ to go smoothly.

lista *sf* list; **essere in** ~ **d'attesa** to be on a waiting list; ~ **dei vini** wine list.

listino *sm*: ~ **(dei) prezzi** price list; ~ **dei cambi** exchange rate.

Lit *abbr* = lira.

lite *sf* quarrel.

litigare *vi* to quarrel.

litigio *sm* quarrel.

litorale *sm* coast.

litoraneo, -a *agg* coastal.

litro *sm* litre.

livello *sm* (altezza, piano) level;

del mare sea level.

livido, -a agg (per percosse) black and blue ♦ sm bruise; **~ per il freddo** blue with cold.

lo art the, → **il** ♦ pron (persona) him; (animale, cosa) it; **~ so** I know.

locale agg local ♦ sm (stanza) room; (luogo pubblico) premises (pl); **~ notturno** night club.

località sf inv locality.

locanda sf inn.

locandina sf theatre poster.

locomotiva sf locomotive.

lodare vt to praise.

lode sf (elogio) praise; **laurearsi con 110 e ~ to graduate with first-class honours** (Br), **to graduate summa cum laude** (Am).

loggia, -ge sf loggia.

loggione sm: **il ~ the gods** (pl).

logica sf logic.

logico, -a, -ci, -che agg logical.

logorare vt to wear out □ **logorarsi** vr to wear out.

logorio sm wear and tear.

Lombardia sf: **la ~ Lombardy.**

lombardo, -a agg Lombard.

lombata sf loin.

lombrico, -chi sm earthworm.

Londra sf London.

longitudine sf longitude.

lontananza sf (distanza) distance; (di persona) absence; **in ~ in the distance.**

lontano, -a agg (luogo) distant, faraway; (nel tempo) far off; (assente) absent; (parente) distant ♦ avv far; **è ~?** is it far?; **è ~ 3**

chilometri it's 3 kilometres from here; **~ da** far (away) from; **da ~ from far away; più ~ farther.**

loquace agg talkative.

lordo, -a agg gross.

loro pron (soggetto) they; (complemento oggetto, con preposizione) them; (form: complemento di termine) (to) them; **~ stessi** they themselves □ **il loro** (f **la loro**, mpl **i loro**, fpl **le loro**) agg their ♦ pron theirs.

losco, -a, -schi, -sche agg suspicious, shady.

lotta sf struggle, fight.

lottare vi to fight.

lotteria sf lottery.

lotto sm (gioco) lottery; (di terreno) lot.

lozione sf lotion.

L.P. sm inv LP.

lubrificante sm lubricant.

lucchetto sm padlock.

luccicare vi to sparkle.

lucciola sf glow-worm, firefly.

luce sf light; (elettricità) electricity; **dare alla ~ to give birth to; mettere in ~ qc** to highlight sthg; **~ del sole** sunlight; **luci d'arresto** brake lights; **luci di direzione** indicators; **luci di posizione** parking lights; **film a luci rosse** porno film.

lucernario sm skylight.

lucertola sf lizard.

lucidare vt to polish.

lucidatrice sf floor polisher.

lucido, -a agg (pavimento, tessuto) shiny; (fig: mente, persona) lucid ♦ sm (da proiettore) acetate; **~ da scarpe** shoe polish.

macchiare

lucro *sm* profit.

luganega, -ghe *sf type of sausage (a speciality of Veneto and Lombardy)*.

luglio *sm* July, → **settembre**.

lugubre *agg* gloomy.

lui *pron (soggetto)* he; *(complemento oggetto, con preposizione)* him; **è** ~ it's him; ~ **stesso** he himself.

lumaca, -che *sf* snail.

lume *sm* lamp; **a ~ di candela** by candlelight.

luminaria *sf* illuminations *(pl)*.

luminoso, -a *agg* luminous, bright.

luna *sf* moon; ~ **di miele** honeymoon; ~ **park** funfair; ~ **piena** full moon.

lunario *sm*: **sbarcare il ~** to make ends meet.

lunedì *sm inv* Monday, → **sabato**.

lunghezza *sf* length; ~ **d'onda** wavelength.

lungo, -a, -ghi, -ghe *agg* long; *(caffè)* weak; **è ~ 3 metri** it's 3 metres long; **saperla lunga** to know what's what; **a ~ for** a long time; **di gran lunga** by far; **in ~ e in largo** far and wide; **andare per le lunghe** to drag on.

lungofiume *sm* embankment.

lungolago, -ghi *sm* road around a lake.

lungomare *sm* promenade.

lunotto *sm* rear window.

luogo, -ghi *sm* place; *(di delitto, incidente)* scene; **aver ~** to take place; **dare ~ a qc** to give rise to sthg; ~ **comune** commonplace; ~

di culto place of worship; ~ **di nascita** place of birth; **del ~** local; **in primo ~** in the first place.

lupini *smpl* lupins.

lupo *sm* wolf.

lurido, -a *agg* filthy.

lusinga, -ghe *sf* flattery.

lusingare *vt* to flatter.

lussare *vt* to dislocate.

Lussemburgo *sm*: **il ~** Luxembourg.

lusso *sm* luxury; **di ~** de luxe, luxury.

lussuoso, -a *agg* luxurious.

lussureggiante *agg* luxuriant.

lussuria *sf* lust.

lustrare *vt* to polish.

lustrino *sm* sequin.

lustro, -a *agg* shiny.

lutto *sm* mourning; **essere in ~** to be in mourning.

ma *cong* but.

macabro, -a *agg* macabre.

macché *esclam* of course not!

maccheroni *smpl* macaroni *(sg)*; ~ **alla chitarra** *flat ribbons of egg pasta in a sauce of either tomatoes and chillis, or lamb (a speciality of Abruzzo)*.

macchia *sf (chiazza)* spot, stain; *(di colore)* spot; *(bosco)* scrub.

macchiare *vt* to stain, to mark

❑ **macchiarsi** *vr (persona)* to get stains o marks on one's clothes; *(abiti, tappeto)* to become stained o marked.

macchiato, -a *agg* stained.

macchina *sf (automobile)* car; *(apparecchio)* machine; **andare in ~** to go by car, to drive; **~ fotografica** camera; **~ da scrivere** typewriter.

macchinario *sm* machinery.

macchinetta *sf (caffettiera)* percolator; **~ mangiasoldi** slot machine.

macchinista, -i *sm (di treno)* driver; *(di nave)* engineer.

macedonia *sf* fruit salad.

macellaio, -a *sm, f* butcher.

macelleria *sf* butcher's.

macerie *sfpl* rubble (sg).

macigno *sm* rock, boulder.

macinacaffè *sm inv* coffee grinder.

macinapepe *sm inv* pepper grinder.

macinare *vt (grano)* to mill, to grind; *(caffè, pepe)* to grind; *(carne)* to mince (Br), to grind (Am).

macinato, -a *agg* minced (Br), ground (Am) ◆ *sm* mince (Br), ground beef (Am).

macrobiotico, -a, -ci, -che *agg* macrobiotic.

Madonna *sf* Madonna.

madre *sf* mother.

madrelingua *agg inv* mother tongue *(dav s)* ◆ *sf* mother tongue.

madreperla *sf* mother-of-pearl.

madrina *sf* godmother.

maestrale *sm* northwest wind.

maestro, -a *sm, f* teacher ◆ *sm (MUS)* maestro; *(artigiano, artista)* master; **~ di tennis** tennis coach.

mafia *sf* Mafia.

mafioso, -a *agg* of the Mafia, Mafia *(dav s)* ◆ *sm, f* member of the Mafia.

magari *esclam* if only! ◆ *avv* maybe.

magazzino *sm* warehouse.

maggio *sm* May; **il primo ~** May Day, → **settembre**.

---

i **IL PRIMO MAGGIO**

Since the end of the Second World War, May 1 has been celebrated all over Italy as a workers' festival. It is a national holiday and is the occasion of trade union meetings and marches in the cities.

---

maggioranza *sf* majority; **nella ~ dei casi** in the majority of cases.

maggiore *agg (comparativo: più grande, più numeroso)* larger, bigger; *(di quantità)* greater; *(più importante)* major, more important; *(più vecchio)* elder, older; *(superlativo: più grande, più numeroso)* largest, biggest; *(di quantità)* greatest; *(più importante)* most important; *(più vecchio)* eldest, oldest ◆ *sm (MIL)* major; **andare per la ~** to be very popular; **la ~ età** the age of majority; **la maggior parte (di)** the majority (of).

maggiorenne *agg* of age ◆ *smf* person who has come of age.

maggiormente *avv* much more.

magia *sf* magic.

magico, -a, -ci, -che agg magic.

magistratura sf magistracy.

maglia sf (indumento) sweater, jersey; (di sportivo, tessuto) jersey; (di catena) link; **lavorare a ~** to knit.

maglieria sf knitwear.

maglietta sf T-shirt; (canottiera) vest (Br), undershirt (Am).

maglione sm sweater, jumper.

magnate sm magnate.

magnetico, -a, -ci, -che agg magnetic.

magnifico, -a, -ci, -che agg magnificent.

mago, -a, -ghi, -ghe sm, f (stregone) sorcerer (f sorceress); (illusionista) magician.

magro, -a agg (persona) thin; (formaggio, yogurt) low-fat; (carne) lean; (fig: scarso) meagre.

mai avv never; (qualche volta): **l'hai ~ visto?** have you ever seen him?; **non ... ~** never; **~ più** never again.

maiale sm (animale) pig; (carne) pork; **~ alle mele** pork with brandy-flavoured apple sauce.

maiolica sf majolica.

maionese sf mayonnaise.

mais sm maize.

maiuscola sf capital letter.

maiuscolo, -a agg capital.

mal = **male**.

malafede sf bad faith.

malaga sm: gelato al ~ rum and raisin ice cream.

malandato, -a agg (persona) in poor shape; (oggetto) shabby.

malanno sm ailment.

malapena : a malapena avv hardly, scarcely.

malato, -a agg ill, sick ♦ sm, f sick person, patient; **essere ~ di cuore** to have a bad heart.

malattia sf illness, disease; **essere in ~** to be on sick leave.

malavita sf underworld.

malconcio, -a, -ci, -ce agg in a sorry state.

maldestro, -a agg (poco abile) inept; (impacciato, goffo) clumsy.

maldicenza sf malicious gossip.

male sm (ingiustizia) evil; (dolore) pain; (malattia) complaint ♦ avv badly; **ti fa ~?** does it hurt?; **mi fanno ~ i piedi** my feet hurt; **fare del ~ a qn** to hurt sb; **non c'è ~!** not bad!; **mal d'aereo** airsickness; **mal d'auto** carsickness; **mal di gola** sore throat; **mal di mare** seasickness; **mal di stomaco** stomachache; **mal di testa** headache; **andare a ~** to go off; **restarci o rimanerci ~** to be disappointed; **sentirsi ~** to feel ill; **di ~ in peggio** from bad to worse.

maledetto, -a pp → **maledire** ♦ agg damned.

maledire vt to curse.

maledizione sf curse.

maleducato, -a agg rude.

maleducazione sf rudeness.

maleodorante agg smelly.

malessere sm (fisico) ailment; (mentale) uneasiness.

malfamato, -a agg notorious.

malfattore, -trice sm, f wrongdoer.

malfermo

malfermo, -a *agg* unsteady.

malformazione *sf* malformation, deformity.

malgrado *prep* in spite of ♦ *cong* although; **mio ~** against my will.

malignità *sf inv* (*d'animo*) malice; (*insinuazione*) spiteful remark.

maligno, -a *agg* (*persona, commento*) malicious; (*MED*) malignant.

malinconia *sf* melancholy.

malinconico, -a, -ci, -che *agg* gloomy.

malincuore : **a malincuore** *avv* reluctantly.

malintenzionato, -a *agg* ill-intentioned.

malinteso *sm* misunderstanding.

malizia *sf* cunning, malice.

malizioso, -a *agg* malicious.

malleabile *agg* malleable.

malmenare *vt* to beat up.

malnutrizione *sf* malnutrition.

malore *sm*: **ho avuto un ~** I suddenly felt ill.

malridotto, -a *agg* in a bad state.

malsano, -a *agg* unhealthy.

Malta *sf* Malta.

maltagliati *smpl* soup pasta, cut into irregular shapes.

maltempo *sm* bad weather.

malto *sm* malt.

maltrattare *vt* to ill-treat.

malumore *sm* bad temper; **essere di ~** to be in a bad mood.

malvagio, -a, -gi, -gie *agg* wicked.

malvolentieri *avv* unwillingly.

mamma *sf* mum (*Br*), mom (*Am*); **~ mia!** my goodness!

mammella *sf* (*di donna*) breast; (*di animale*) udder.

mammifero *sm* mammal.

manager ['mɛnadʒer] *smf inv* manager (*f* manageress).

manata *sf* slap.

mancanza *sf* (*scarsità, assenza*) lack; (*colpa*) fault; **sentire la ~ di qn** to miss sb; **in ~ di** for lack of.

mancare *vi* (*non esserci*) to be missing; (*essere lontano*) to be away; (*form: morire*) to pass away ♦ *vt* (*colpo, bersaglio*) to miss; **è mancata la luce per due ore** the electricity was off for two hours; **mi manchi molto** I miss you a lot; **manca il latte** there's no milk; **mi manca il tempo** I haven't got the time; **mi mancano mille lire** I still need a thousand lire; **ci è mancato poco che cadesse** it nearly fell; **manca un quarto alle quattro** it's quarter to four □ **mancare a** *v + prep* (*promessa*) to fail to keep; **mancare di** *v + prep* to lack.

mancia, -ce *sf* tip; **dare la ~ (a qn)** to tip (sb).

manciata *sf* handful.

mancino, -a *agg* left-handed.

manco *avv* (*fam*) not even; **~ per sogno** ○ **per idea** I wouldn't dream of it.

mandarancio *sm* clementine.

mandare *vt* to send; (*grido*) to give; **~ a chiamare qn** to send for sb; **~ via qn** to send sb away; **~ avanti qn** to send sb on ahead;

manomettere

avanti qc to provide for sthg; ~ **giù** to swallow.

mandarino sm mandarin (orange), tangerine.

mandata sf (di chiave) turn; **chiudere a doppia ~** to double-lock.

mandato sm (DIR) warrant; ~ **d'arresto** arrest warrant.

mandibola sf jaw.

mandolino sm mandolin.

mandorla sf almond.

maneggiare vt (strumenti, attrezzi) to handle; (denaro) to manage, to deal with.

maneggio sm riding school.

manetta sf handle ❑ **manette** sfpl handcuffs.

mangereccio agg m → fungo.

mangiare vt (cibo) to eat; (fig: patrimonio) to squander; (negli scacchi) to take ◆ vi to eat; **far da ~** to do the cooking; **mangiarsi le parole** to mumble.

mangiasoldi agg inv → macchinetta.

mangime sm fodder.

mangione, -a sm, f glutton.

mania sf (fissazione) obsession; **avere la ~ di fare qc** to have a habit of doing sthg.

maniaco, -a, -ci, -che agg manic ◆ sm, f maniac.

manica, -che sleeve; **a maniche corte** ○ **a mezze maniche** short-sleeved ❑ **Manica** sf: **la Manica, il Canale della Manica** the (English) Channel.

manicaretto sm delicacy.

manichino sm (di negozio) dummy; (per artisti) model.

manico, -ci sm handle.

manicomio sm (ospedale) mental hospital; (fig: confusione) madhouse.

manicure sf inv (persona) manicurist; (trattamento) manicure.

maniera sf way; in ~ **che** so that; in ~ **da fare qc** so as to do sthg; **in tutte le maniere** at all costs.

manifestare vt to show ◆ vi to demonstrate ❑ **manifestarsi** vr to appear.

manifestazione sf (corteo) demonstration; (di sentimento) show; (di malattia) symptom; (spettacolo) event.

manifesto sm (cartellone) poster.

maniglia sf (di porta) handle; (di autobus) strap.

manipolare vt (con le mani) to handle; (fig: alterare) to manipulate.

mano, -i sf hand; (di vernice) coat; **dare una ~ a qn** to give sb a hand; **darsi la ~** to shake hands; **fatto a ~** handmade; **di seconda ~** second-hand; **man ~** gradually; **andare contro ~** to drive on the wrong side of the road; **essere alla ~** to be easygoing; **fare man bassa** to take everything; **fuori ~** out of the way; **stare con le mani in ~** to twiddle one's thumbs.

manodopera sf (lavoratori) workforce; (costo) labour.

manomesso, -a pp → manomettere.

manomettere vt (serratura) to

force.

manopola sf knob, control.

manovale sm labourer.

manovella sf handle.

manovra sf manoeuvre.

manovrare vt (congegno) to operate; (fig: persona) to manipulate ♦ vi (Mil) to manoeuvre; (fig: tramare) to plot.

manrovescio sm slap.

mansarda sf attic.

mansione sf task, job.

mantella sf cape.

mantello sm (di animale) coat; (indumento) cloak.

mantenere vt to keep; (sostentare) to support ☐ **mantenersi** vr (pagarsi da vivere) to support o.s.; (conservarsi) to stay, to keep.

mantenimento sm maintenance.

manuale agg & sm manual.

manubrio sm (di bicicletta, moto) handlebars (pl); (di congegno) handle.

manutenzione sf maintenance.

manzo sm (carne) beef.

mappa sf map.

mappamondo sm (globo) globe; (su carta) map of the world.

maraschino sm maraschino (cherry liqueur).

maratona sf marathon.

marca, -che sf (di prodotto) brand; (scontrino) ticket; ~ **da bollo** revenue stamp; **prodotto di ~** quality product.

marcare vt to mark; (goal) to score.

marchio sm mark; (di bestiame) brand; ~ **di fabbrica** trademark; ~ **registrato** registered trademark.

marcia, -ce sf march; (di auto) gear; (sport) walking; **fare ~ indietro** to reverse; **mettersi in ~** to start off.

marciapiede sm pavement (Br), sidewalk (Am); (di stazione) platform.

marciare vi to march.

marcio, -a, -ci, -ce agg rotten.

marcire vi (cibo) to rot; (ferita) to fester.

marco, -chi sm mark.

mare sm sea; **andare al ~** to go to the seaside; **il Mare del Nord** the North Sea.

marea sf tide; **alta ~** high tide; **bassa ~** low tide.

mareggiata sf stormy sea.

maresciallo sm ≃ warrant officer.

margarina sf margarine.

margherita sf daisy.

margine sm (di pagina) margin; (di strada, bosco) edge.

marina sf navy.

marinaio sm sailor.

marinare vt to marinate; ~ **la scuola** to play truant.

marinaro, -a agg (popoli, tradizioni) seafaring; **alla marinara** cooked with seafood.

marinata sf marinade.

marino, -a agg sea (dav s).

marionetta sf marionette.

marito sm husband.

maritozzo sm type of sweet

bread containing sultanas, pine kernels and candied peel (a speciality of Lazio).

marittima, **-a** agg (clima) maritime; (scalo) coastal; **località marittima** seaside resort.

marmellata sf jam; (di arance) marmalade.

marmitta sf (di auto, moto) silencer; (pentola) large cooking pot.

marmo sm marble.

marocchino, **-a** agg & sm, f Moroccan.

Marocco sm: il ~ Morocco.

marrone agg inv brown ♦ sm (colore) brown; (frutto) chestnut.

marron glacé [mar'ron gla'se] sm inv marron glacé (crystallized chestnut).

marsala sm inv Marsala (sweet fortified wine).

marsupio sm (borsello) bum bag (Br), fanny pack (Am); (di animale) pouch.

martedì sm inv Tuesday, → **sabato**.

martellare vt to hammer ♦ vi to throb.

martello sm hammer.

martini® sm inv (vermut) Martini; (cocktail) Martini cocktail.

martire smf martyr.

marzapane sm marzipan.

marziale agg martial.

marziano, **-a** sm, f Martian.

marzo sm March, → **settembre**.

mascalzone sm scoundrel.

mascara sm inv mascara.

mascarpone sm mascarpone (type of cream cheese).

mascella sf jaw.

maschera sf mask; (costume) fancy dress; (di bellezza) face pack; (di cinema, teatro) usher (f usherette).

mascherare vt (volto) to mask; (emozioni) to conceal □ **mascherarsi** vr: **mascherarsi (da)** to dress up (as).

maschile agg (GRAMM) masculine; (sesso, anatomia) male; (abiti) men's (dav s); (per ragazzi) boy's (dav s).

maschio, **-a** agg male ♦ sm (animale, individuo) male; (ragazzo, figlio, neonato) boy; **figlio** ~ son.

mascolino, **-a** agg masculine.

mascotte [ma'skɔt] sf inv mascot.

masochista, **-i**, **-e** smf masochist.

massa sf mass; **una** ~ **di** (errori, gente) loads of; (mattoni, legna) a pile of; **la** ~ **the masses** (pl); **di** ~ mass (dav s); **in** ~ en masse.

massacro sm massacre.

massaggiare vt to massage.

massaggiatore, **-trice** sm, f masseur (f masseuse).

massaggio sm massage.

massaia sf housewife.

massiccio, **-a**, **-ci**, **-ce** agg (corporatura) stout, big; (edificio) solid; **oro** ~ solid gold ♦ sm massif.

massima sf (detto) maxim; (temperatura) maximum temperature; **in linea di** ~ generally speaking.

massimo, -a *agg & sm* maximum; **al ~** at most.

mass media *smpl* mass media.

masso *sm* rock.

masticare *vt* to chew.

mastice *sm* putty.

mastino *sm* mastiff.

matassa *sf* skein.

matematica *sf* mathematics (*sg*).

matematico, -a, -ci, -che *agg* mathematical; (*sicuro*) certain.

materassino *sm* air bed; (*da ginnastica*) mat.

materasso *sm* mattress.

materia *sf* (*in fisica*) matter; (*materiale*) material; (*disciplina, argomento*) subject; **materie prime** raw materials.

materiale *agg* material ◆ *sm* material; (*attrezzatura*) equipment; **beni ~** worldly goods; **~ sintetico** man-made material.

maternità *sf inv* (*condizione*) motherhood; (*di ospedale*) maternity ward; **essere in ~** to be on maternity leave.

materno, -a *agg* maternal; (*paese, lingua*) mother (*dav s*).

matita *sf* pencil.

matrigna *sf* stepmother.

matrimoniale *agg* matrimonial.

matrimonio *sm* marriage; (*cerimonia*) wedding.

mattatoio *sm* slaughterhouse.

mattina *sf* morning; **di ~** in the morning.

mattinata *sf* morning.

mattiniero, -a *agg*: **essere ~**

to be an early riser.

mattino *sm* morning.

matto, -a *agg* mad ◆ *sm*, *f* madman (*f* madwoman); **andare ~ per** to be crazy about.

mattone *sm* brick.

mattonella *sf* tile.

maturare *vi & vt* (*frutta, grano*) to ripen; (*persona*) to mature.

maturità *sf* (*diploma, esame*) = A levels (*pl*) (*Br*), = SATs (*pl*) (*Am*).

---

i MATURITÀ

The "maturità" examination is sat by students aged 18 to 19 in the final year of "scuola superiore". Depending on the type of school, the "maturità" is classed as either classical, scientific, technical or artistic, and a pass allows the student to go on to university. The exam consists of two written and two oral parts: the same written paper in Italian is sat at all schools. The final mark out of 60 covers all subjects, and is based on both the exam results and on continuous assessment over the previous three years.

---

maturo, -a *agg* (*frutto*) ripe; (*persona*) mature.

mazza *sf* (*bastone*) club; (*da baseball, cricket*) bat; **~ da golf** golf club.

mazzo *sm* (*di fiori, chiavi*) bunch; (*di carte*) pack.

me *pron* me, → **mi**.

MEC *abbr* = Mercato Comune Europeo.

meccanica *sf* (*scienza*) mechanics (*sg*), → **meccanico**.

meccanico, -a, -ci, -che *agg*

mechanical ♦ *sm* mechanic.

meccanismo *sm* mechanism.

mèche [mɛʃ] *sfpl* streaks.

medaglia *sf* medal.

medaglione *sm* (*gioiello*) locket; ~ **di vitello** veal medallion.

medesimo, -a *agg* same.

media *sf* (*valore intermedio*) average; (*di voti*) average mark (*Br*), average grade (*Am*); **in** ~ on average; **le (scuole) medie** = secondary school (*sg*) (*Br*), junior high school (*sg*) (*Am*).

mediante *prep* by means of.

mediatore, -trice *sm, f* mediator; (*COMM*) middleman.

medicare *vt* to dress.

medicina *sf* medicine.

medicinale *sm* medicine, drug.

medico, -a, -ci, -che *agg* medical ♦ *sm* doctor; ~ **di guardia** doctor on call.

medievale *agg* medieval.

medio, -a *agg* average; (*di mezzo*) middle ♦ *sm*: (**dito**) ~ middle finger.

mediocre *agg* mediocre.

medioevale = **medievale**.

medioevo *sm* Middle Ages (*pl*).

meditare *vt* to plan ♦ *vi* to meditate.

mediterraneo, -a *agg* Mediterranean ❑ **Mediterraneo** *sm*: **il (mar) Mediterraneo** the Mediterranean (Sea).

medusa *sf* jellyfish.

megafono *sm* megaphone.

meglio *avv* 1. (*comparativo*) better; **mi sento** ~ **di ieri** I feel better than I did yesterday; **andare** ~ to get better; **così va** ~ that's better; **per** ~ **dire** or rather.

2. (*superlativo*) best; **è la cosa che mi riesce** ~ it's the thing I do best; **le persone** ~ **vestite** the best-dressed people.

♦ *agg inv* 1. (*migliore*) better; **la tua macchina è** ~ **della mia** your car is better than mine.

2. (*in costruzioni impersonali*) better; **è** ~ **rimanere qui** it would be better to stay here; **è** ~ **che te lo dica** I'd better tell you.

♦ *sm*: **fare del proprio** ~ to do one's best; **agire per il** ~ to do the right thing.

♦ *sf*: **avere la** ~ **su qn** to get the better of sb.

mela *sf* apple.

melagrana *sf* pomegranate.

melanzana *sf* aubergine (*Br*), eggplant (*Am*); **melanzane alla parmigiana** *fried aubergine slices covered in tomato and Parmesan cheese.*

melenso, -a *agg* dull.

melma *sf* mud.

melo *sm* apple tree.

melodia *sf* melody.

melodramma, -i *sm* melodrama.

melone *sm* melon.

membro, -i *sm* (*di club, associazione*) member.

memorabile *agg* memorable.

memoria *sf* memory; **sapere qc a** ~ to know sthg by heart.

mendicante *smf* beggar.

meno *avv* 1. (*in comparativi*) less; ~ **di** less than; ~ **vecchio** (*di*) younger (than); **camminate** ~ **in fretta** don't walk so fast; **ne voglio**

(di) ~ I want less; ~ **lo vedo meglio sto** the less I see him, the better I feel.

2. *(in superlativi)* least; **la camera ~ cara** the cheapest room; **il ~ interessante** the least interesting; **fare il ~ possibile** to do as little as possible; **la macchina che costa ~ (di tutte)** the least expensive car (of all); **è Luca che mi preoccupa** ~ Luca worries me the least.

3. *(no)*: **non so se accettare o ~** I don't know whether to accept or not.

4. *(nelle ore)*: **le nove ~ un quarto** a quarter to nine *(Br)*, a quarter of nine *(Am)*.

5. *(nelle sottrazioni, nelle temperature)* minus.

6. *(in espressioni)*: **non essere da ~ (di qn)** to be just as good (as sb); **fare a ~ di** to do without; ~ **male (che) c'eri tu!** thank goodness you were there!; **venir** ~ a *(promessa)* to break; *(impegno)* not to fulfil; **non poteva fare a ~ di urlare** he couldn't help screaming.

♦ *prep* except (for); **c'erano tutti ~ (che) lei** they were all there except (for) her; **pensa a tutto ~ che a divertirsi** enjoying himself is the last thing on his mind.

♦ *agg inv* less; **oggi c'è ~ gente** there are fewer people today. □ **a meno che** *cong* unless; **vengo a ~ che non piova** I'm coming unless it rains.

menopausa *sf* menopause.

mensa *sf* canteen.

mensile *agg & sm* monthly.

mensola *sf* shelf.

menta *sf* mint; *(bibita)* peppermint cordial.

mentale *agg* mental.

mentalmente *avv* mentally.

mente *sf* mind; **avere in ~ di fare qc** to be thinking of doing sthg; **imparare/sapere qc a ~ to** learn/know sthg by heart; **sfuggire** O **passare di ~ a qn** to slip sb's mind; **tenere a ~ qc** to bear sthg in mind.

mentire *vi* to lie.

mento *sm* chin.

mentre *cong (temporale)* while; *(avversativa)* while, whereas.

menu *sm inv* menu.

menziona re *vt* to mention.

menzogna *sf* lie.

meraviglia *sf (stupore)* amazement; *(cosa, persona)* marvel; **a ~** perfectly.

meravigliare *vt* to amaze □ **meravigliarsi di** *vr + prep* to be amazed at.

meraviglioso, -a *agg* wonderful.

mercante *sm* trader.

mercantile *agg* merchant *(dav s)* ♦ *sm (nave)* merchant ship.

mercanzia *sf* goods *(pl)*, merchandise.

mercatino *sm* local market.

mercato *sm* market; ~ **dei cambi** foreign exchange market; ~ **nero** black market; **a buon** ~ cheap; **Mercato Comune Europeo** Common Market.

i **MERCATO**

Almost every Italian town has an indoor or outdoor market selling food, flowers and plants. Once or twice a week there will also be a general market with stalls selling clothes, shoes and household items among other things. Prices are generally lower than in shops, and shoppers and stallholders often haggle.

merce *sf* goods *(pl)*, merchandise.

merceria *sf* haberdasher's *(Br)*, notions store *(Am)*.

mercoledì *sm inv* Wednesday, → **sabato**.

mercurio *sm* mercury.

merda *sf & esclam (volg)* shit.

merenda *sf* afternoon snack.

meridionale *agg* southern ◆ *smf* southerner.

Meridione *sm*: **il ~** the South of Italy.

meringa, -ghe *sf* meringue.

meritare *vt* to deserve ◆ *vi* to be good; **meritarsi qc** to deserve sthg.

merito *sm (qualità)* merit; *(riconoscimento)* credit; **per ~ di qn** thanks to sb; **finire a pari ~** to tie.

merlo *sm (uccello)* blackbird; *(di mura)* battlement.

merluzzo *sm* cod.

meschino, -a *agg (spregevole)* mean.

mescolare *vt (mischiare)* to mix; *(insalata)* to toss; *(caffè)* to stir; *(mettere in disordine)* to mix up* ❏ **mescolarsi** *vr (confondersi)* to mingle.

mese *sm* month.

messa *sf* mass.

messaggio *sm* message.

Messico *sm*: **il ~** Mexico.

messinscena *sf (teatrale)* production; *(finzione)* act.

messo, -a *pp* → **mettere**.

mestiere *sm (professione)* job; *(artigianale)* craft; *(manuale)* trade.

mestolo *sm* ladle.

mestruazioni *sfpl* period *(sg)*.

meta *sf (destinazione)* destination; *(scopo)* aim, goal.

metà *sf inv (parte)* half; *(punto di mezzo)* middle; **dividere qc a ~** to divide sthg in half; **essere a ~ strada** to be halfway; **fare a ~ (con qn)** to go halves (with sb).

metabolismo *sm* metabolism.

metafora *sf* metaphor.

metallico, -a, -ci, -che *agg (di metallo)* metal *(dav s)*; *(rumore, voce)* metallic.

metallo *sm* metal.

metano *sm* methane.

meteorologico, -a, -ci, -che *agg* meteorological, weather *(dav s)*.

meticoloso, -a *agg* meticulous.

metodico, -a, -ci, -che *agg* methodical.

metodo *sm* method.

metrico, -a, -ci, -che *agg* metric.

metro *sm (unità di misura)* metre; *(nastro)* tape measure; *(a stecche)* rule; **~ cubo** cubic metre; **~ quadrato** square metre.

metronotte *sm inv* night security guard.

metropoli *sf inv* metropolis.

metropolitana *sf* underground (Br), subway (Am).

mettere *vt* 1. *(collocare)* to put; ~ **un annuncio** to place an advert; ~ **i piatti in tavola** to set the table; ~ **qn alla prova** to put sb to the test; ~ **i libri in ordine** to tidy (up) the books; ~ **l'antenna dritta** to put the aerial straight.

2. *(indossare)*: **mettersi qc** to put sthg on; **mettersi una sciarpa** to put a scarf on, to wear a scarf; **cosa mi metto oggi?** what shall I wear today?

3. *(tempo)*: **metterci**: **ci si mette un'ora per andare** it takes an hour to get there.

4. *(dedicare)*: ~ **attenzione in qc** to do sthg with care; **mettercela tutta** to do one's best.

5. *(far funzionare)* to put on; ~ **gli abbaglianti** to put one's headlights on full beam.

6. *(suscitare)*: ~ **appetito a qn** to make sb hungry; ~ **paura a qn** to scare sb.

7. *(supporre)*: **mettiamo che non venga** let's suppose he doesn't come.

8. *(in espressioni)*: ~ **avanti/indietro l'orologio** to put the clock forward/back; ~ **in chiaro qc** to clear sthg up; ~ **in dubbio qc** to cast doubt on sthg; **mettersi in testa di fare qc** to get it into one's head to do sthg; ~ **insieme** to put together. ❑ **mettersi** *vr* 1. *(porsi)*: **mettiti a sedere qui** sit here; **mettersi a tavola** to sit down to eat; **mettersi nei guai** to get into trouble.

2. *(vestirsi)*: **mettersi in pigiama** to put one's pyjamas on.

3. *(cominciare)*: **mettersi a fare qc** to start doing sthg; **s'è messo a gridare** he started screaming; **mettersi in viaggio** to set off.

4. *(in espressioni)*: **mettersi d'accordo** to agree; **mettersi bene/male** to turn out well/badly; **mettersi con qn** *(in società)* to go into partnership with sb; *(in coppia)* to go out with sb.

mezza *sf*: **la** ~ *(mezzogiorno e mezzo)* half-past twelve.

mezzaluna *(pl* **mezzelune***) sf (parte di luna)* half moon; *(coltello)* chopping blade; *(islamica)* crescent.

mezzanino *sm* mezzanine floor.

mezzanotte *sf* midnight.

mezzo, -a *agg* half ♦ *sm (metà)* half; *(parte centrale)* middle; *(strumento, procedimento)* means; *(veicolo)* vehicle ♦ *avv*: ~ **pieno** half-full; ~ **chilo** half a kilo; ~ **litro** half a litre; **mezza pensione** half board; **abiti di mezza stagione** spring/autumn clothes; **a mezze maniche** short-sleeved; **di mezza età** middle-aged; **quello di** ~ the one in the middle, the middle one; **per** ~ **di** by means of; **le cinque e mezza** ○ ~ half-past five; **non vuole andarci di** ~ he doesn't want to get involved; **fare a** ~ **(con qn)** to share (with sb); **levarsi** ○ **togliersi di** ~ to get out of the way; **mezzi di comunicazione (di massa)** (mass) media; **mezzi pubblici** public transport *(sg)*; **mezzi di trasporto** means of transport ❑ **mezzi** *smpl (eco-*

nomici) means.

mezzogiorno *sm (ora)* midday, noon ❑ **Mezzogiorno** *sm:* il Mezzogiorno Southern Italy.

---

i **MEZZOGIORNO**

The south of Italy, including Sicily and Sardinia, is called "il Mezzogiorno". This area is less industrial than the rest of the country, but is rich in art and culture and is blessed with spectacular scenery.

---

mezzora *sf* half an hour.

mi *(diventa* **me** *se precede* lo, la, li, le, ne) *pron (complemento oggetto)* me; *(complemento di termine)* (to) me; *(riflessivo)* myself; **me li dai?** will you give them to me?

miagolare *vi* to miaow.

mica *avv (fam):* **non ci avrai ~ creduto?** you didn't believe it, did you?; **non sono ~ scemo!** I'm not stupid, am I!; **~ male** not bad (at all).

miccia, -ce *sf* fuse.

micidiale *agg (mortale)* deadly; *(dannoso)* murderous; *(insopportabile)* unbearable.

micosi *sf inv (MED)* fungus.

microfono *sm* microphone.

microscopio *sm* microscope.

midolla *sf (mollica)* crumb.

midollo *(pl f* **midolla)** *sm* marrow.

mie → **mio.**

miei → **mio.**

miele *sm* honey.

migliaio *(pl f* **migliaia)** *sm* thousand; **un ~ (di persone)** about a thousand (people); **a migliaia** by the thousand.

miglio *sm (unità di misura: pl f* **miglia)** mile; *(pianta)* millet.

miglioramento *sm* improvement.

migliorare *vt* to improve ◆ *vi (tempo, situazione)* to improve; *(malato)* to get better.

migliore *agg (comparativo)* better; **il/la ~** *(superlativo)* the best.

mignolo *sm* little finger *(Br)*, pinkie *(Am)*; *(del piede)* little toe.

mila *pl* → **mille.**

milanese *agg* Milanese ◆ *smf* person from Milan.

Milano *sf* Milan.

miliardo *sm* thousand million *(Br)*, billion *(Am)*.

milione *sm* million.

militare *agg* military ◆ *sm* serviceman; **fare il ~** to do one's military service.

mille *(pl* **mila)** *num* a o one thousand, → **sei.**

millefoglie *sm inv* millefeuille *(Br)*, napoleon *(Am)*.

millennio *sm* millennium.

millepiedi *sm inv* millipede.

millesimo, -a *num* thousandth, → **sesto.**

millimetro *sm* millimetre.

milza *sf* spleen.

mimare *vt* to mime.

mimetizzare *vt* to camouflage ❑ **mimetizzarsi** *vr (animali, piante)* to camouflage o.s.

mimo *sm* mime.

mimosa *sf* mimosa.

min. *(abbr di* minimo, *di* minuto) min.

mina sf (esplosiva) mine; (di matita) lead.

minaccia, -ce sf threat.

minacciare vt to threaten; ~ **di fare qc** to threaten to do sthg.

minaccioso, -a agg threatening, menacing.

minatore sm miner.

minerale agg & sm mineral.

minestra sf soup; ~ **in brodo** noodle broth; ~ **di verdure** vegetable soup.

minestrone sm minestrone.

miniatura sf miniature.

miniera sf mine.

minigolf sm minigolf.

minigonna sf miniskirt.

minima sf minimum temperature.

minimizzare vt to minimize.

minimo, -a agg (il più piccolo) slightest, least; (il più basso) lowest; (molto piccolo) very small, slight ♦ sm (parte più piccola) minimum; (di motore) idling speed; **come** ~ **at** the very least.

ministero sm (settore amministrativo) ministry.

ministro sm minister; ~ **degli Esteri** Foreign Secretary (Br), Secretary of State (Am).

minoranza sf minority; **essere in** ~ to be in a minority.

minore agg (comparativo: di età) younger; (di grandezza) smaller; (di importanza) minor; (numero) lower; (grado) lesser; (superlativo: di età) youngest; (di grandezza) smallest; (di importanza) least important; (di

numero) lowest ♦ smf (minorenne) minor.

minorenne smf minor.

minuscola sf small letter.

minuscolo, -a agg (scrittura) small; (molto piccolo) tiny.

minuto, -a agg (persona, corpo) small; (piccolo) tiny, minute; (fine) fine ♦ sm (unità) minute.

mio (f mia, mpl miei, fpl mie) agg: **il** ~ **(la mia)** my ♦ pron: **il** ~ **(la mia)** mine; ~ **padre** my father; **un** ~ **amico** a friend of mine; **questa bici è mia** this bike is mine.

miope agg short-sighted.

mira sf aim; **prendere la** ~ to take aim; **prendere di** ~ **qc** (fig) to pick on sb.

miracolo sm miracle.

miraggio sm mirage.

mirare vi: ~ **a** to aim at.

miriade sf multitude; **una** ~ **di a** multitude of.

mirtillo sm blueberry.

miscela sf (miscuglio) mixture; (di caffè) blend; (benzina) petrol and oil mixture.

mischia sf brawl; (nel rugby) scrum.

mischiare vt to mix; ~ **le carte** to shuffle the cards ❑ **mischiarsi** vr to mix.

miseria sf (estrema) poverty; (quantità insufficiente): **è costato una** ~ it cost next to nothing; **porca** ~ (volg: accidenti) damn!, bloody hell!

misericordia sf mercy.

misero, -a agg (povero) poor, poverty-stricken; (infelice) wretched, miserable; (insufficiente) miserable.

missile *sm* missile.

missionario, -a *sm, f* missionary.

missione *sf* mission.

misterioso, -a *agg* mysterious.

mistero *sm* mystery.

misto, -a *agg* mixed ◆ *sm* mixture; **insalata mista** mixed salad; **~ lana** woollen blend; **~ cotone** cotton blend.

misura *sf* (*unità, provvedimento*) measure; (*dimensione*) measurement; (*taglia*) size; (*moderazione*) moderation; **prendere le misure di qc** to measure sthg; **su ~** made-to-measure.

misurare *vt* to measure; (*abito*) to try on; (*vista*) to test ◆ *vi* to measure ▢ **misurarsi con** *vr* + *prep* to compete with.

misurino *sm* measure.

mite *agg* mild.

mito *sm* myth.

mitra *sm inv* submachine gun.

mitragliatrice *sf* machine gun.

mittente *smf* sender.

mobile *agg* movable ◆ *sm* piece of furniture; **mobili** (*mobilia*) furniture (*sg*).

mobilia *sf* furniture.

mobilitare *vt* to mobilize.

moca *sf inv* coffee machine.

mocassino *sm* mocassin.

moda *sf* fashion; **essere ○ andare di ~** to be in fashion; **passare di ~** to go out of fashion; **alla ~** fashionable; **di ~** fashionable.

modellare *vt* to model.

modellino *sm* model.

modello, -a *sm, f* model ◆ *sm* model; (*per sarta*) pattern; (*modulo*) form.

moderare *vt* to moderate.

moderato, -a *agg* moderate.

moderno, -a *agg* modern.

modestia *sf* modesty.

modesto, -a *agg* modest.

modico, -a, -ci, -che *agg* low.

modifica, -che *sf* alteration.

modo *sm* way; (*opportunità*) chance; (GRAMM: *verbale*) mood; **a ~ mio** in my way; **in ~ da fare qc** so as to do sthg; **di dire** expression; **di ~ che** so that; **in nessun ~** in no way; **in ogni ~** anyway; **in qualche ~** in some way; **in tutti i modi** in every way.

modulazione *sf*: **~ di frequenza** frequency modulation.

modulo *sm* form.

moglie, -gli *sf* wife.

mole *sf* (*dimensione*) massive shape; (*quantità*) **una ~ di lavoro** masses of work.

molestare *vt* to annoy.

molesto, -a *agg* annoying.

molla *sf* (*meccanica*) spring ◆ **molle** *sfpl* (*per camino, ghiaccio*) tongs.

mollare *vt* (*allentare*) to slacken; (*lasciar andare*) to let go; (*fam: fidanzato*) to ditch ◆ *vi* (*desistere*) to give in; **~ un ceffone a qn** (*fam: dare uno schiaffo*) to slap sb.

molle *agg* (*morbido*) soft; (*fig: persona*) weak.

molletta *sf (per capelli)* hair grip; *(per panni)* clothes peg.

mollica, -che *sf* crumb.

molo *sm (di porto)* jetty.

molteplice *agg (complesso)* complex □ **molteplici** *agg pl (numerosi)* numerous, various.

moltiplicare *vt* to multiply.

moltiplicazione *sf (MAT)* multiplication; *(accrescimento)* increase.

moltitudine *sf* multitude.

molto, -a *agg* 1. *(in grande quantità)* a lot of, much; **non ho ~ tempo** I don't have (very) much time; **hai molta fame?** are you very hungry?

2. *(di numero elevato)*: **molti(-e)** a lot of, many; **ci sono molti turisti** there are a lot of tourists.

♦ *pron* a lot, much; **molti** *(molta gente)* many *(people)*; **molti di noi** many of us.

♦ *avv* 1. *(con verbi)* a lot, (very) much; **mi piace ~** I like it a lot o very much.

2. *(con aggettivi, avverbi)* very; *(con participio passato)* much; **è ~ simpatica** she's very nice; **è ~ meglio così** it's much better like this; **è ~ presto/tardi** it's very early/late; **~ volentieri!** certainly!.

momentaneamente *avv* at the moment.

momentaneo, -a *agg* momentary.

momento *sm* moment; *(circostanza)* time; **all'ultimo ~** at the last moment; **da un ~ all'altro** *(tra poco)* (at) any moment; **da ~ che** since; **per il ~** for the time being; **a**

momenti *(tra poco)* soon; *(quasi)* nearly.

monaca, -che *sf* nun.

monaco, -ci *sm* monk.

monarchia *sf* monarchy.

monastero *sm (di monaci)* monastery; *(di monache)* convent.

mondano, -a *agg (di società)* society *(dav s)*; *(terreno)* earthly.

mondiale *agg* world *(dav s)*.

mondo *sm* world.

moneta *sf (di metallo)* coin; *(valuta)* currency; **~ spicciola** change.

monetario, -a *agg* monetary.

monolocale *sm* studio flat *(Br)*, studio apartment *(Am)*.

monopattino *sm* scooter.

monopolio *sm* monopoly.

monosci *sm inv* monoski.

monotono, -a *agg (ripetitivo)* monotonous; *(noioso)* dull.

montacarichi *sm inv* goods lift.

montagna *sf* mountain; *(zona)* the mountains *(pl)*; **andare in ~** to go to the mountains; **montagne russe** roller coaster *(sg)*.

montanaro, -a *sm, f* mountain dweller.

montano, -a *agg* mountain *(dav s)*.

montare *vi (salire)* to go up; *(cavalcare)* to ride ♦ *vt (congegno)* to assemble; *(cavallo, pietra preziosa)* to mount; *(panna)* to whip; *(albumi)* to whisk; *(fecondare)* to cover; **~ in macchina** to get into a car; **~ in treno** to get on a train; **montarsi la testa** to become bigheaded.

montatura *sf (di occhiali*

frames (pl); (di gioiello) setting.

monte sm mountain; andare a ~ to come to nothing; mandare a ~ qc to upset sthg; ~ premi prize money; **il Monte Bianco** Mont Blanc.

montone sm (animale) ram; (carne) mutton; (giaccone) sheepskin jacket.

montuoso, -a agg mountainous.

monumento sm monument.

mora sf (commestibile) blackberry; (del gelso) mulberry; (DIR) default.

morale agg moral ◆ sf morals (pl); (insegnamento) moral ◆ sm morale; essere giù di ~ to be feeling down.

morbido, -a agg soft.

morbillo sm measles (sg).

morbo sm disease.

morboso, -a agg morbid.

mordere vt to bite.

morfina sf morphine.

moribondo, -a agg dying.

morire vi to die; (estinguersi) to die out; ~ di fame to die of hunger; ~ di noia to die of boredom; ~ dal ridere to kill o.s. laughing; bello da ~ stunning.

mormorare vi (bisbigliare) to whisper; (sparlare) to gossip ◆ vt to murmur.

moro, -a agg dark.

morso, -a pp → mordere ◆ sm bite; (di briglia) bit.

mortadella sf Mortadella (large pork sausage served cold in thin slices).

mortale agg mortal; (letale)

deadly ◆ sm mortal.

mortalità sf mortality.

morte sf death; avercela a ~ con qn to have it in for sb.

mortificare vt to mortify.

morto, -a pp → morire ◆ agg dead ◆ sm, f dead man (f dead woman); fare il ~ (nell'acqua) to float on one's back.

mosaico, -ci sm mosaic.

mosca, -sche sf fly; ~ cieca blind man's buff.

Mosca sf Moscow.

moscato sm muscatel (sweet wine).

moscerino sm gnat.

moschettone sm spring clip.

moscone sm (insetto) bluebottle; (imbarcazione) pedalo.

mossa sf movement; (negli scacchi) move.

mosso, -a pp → muovere ◆ agg (mare) rough; (capelli) wavy; (fotografia) blurred.

mostarda sf mustard.

mostra sf exhibition; mettersi in ~ to draw attention to o.s.; in ~ on show; **la Mostra del cinema di Venezia** Venice Film Festival.

ⓘ LA MOSTRA DEL CINEMA DI VENEZIA

The Venice Film Festival, or the "Mostra internazionale d'arte cinematografica di Venezia", has been held every year since 1938 during the last week in August and the first week in September. Film fans flock to the Palazzo del Cinema in Lido di Venezia to see the celeb-

mostrare

rities, to watch important new films and retrospectives, and to attend premières. The festival concludes with the awarding of prizes, including the prestigious "Leone d'oro" (golden lion).

---

mostrare *vt* to show ☐

mostrarsi *vr* to look; **mostrarsi in pubblico** to appear in public.

mostro *sm* monster.

mostruoso, -a *agg (orrendo)* monstrous; *(feroce)* ferocious; *(smisurato)* incredible.

motel *sm inv* motel.

motivo *sm (causa)* reason; *(di stoffa)* pattern; *(musicale)* tune; **per quale ~?** for what reason?; **senza ~** without a reason.

moto *sm (in fisica)* motion; *(movimento)* movement; *(esercizio fisico)* exercise ♦ *sf inv* motorbike; **mettere in ~** *(AUTO)* to start.

motocicletta *sf* motorcycle.

motocross *sm* motocross.

motore *sm* motor, engine; **a ~** motor *(dav s)*.

motorino *sm* moped; **~ d'avviamento** starter.

motoscafo *sm* motorboat.

motto *sm* maxim.

mousse [mus] *sf inv* mousse.

movimentare *vt* to liven up.

movimento *sm (attività)* activity.

mozzafiato *agg inv* breathtaking.

mozzare *vt* to cut off; **~ il fiato a qn** to take sb's breath away.

mozzarella *sf* mozzarella *(a round fresh cheese from Naples made*

from cow's or buffalo's milk)*; **~ in carrozza** mozzarella sandwiched between two slices of bread, then dipped in egg and fried.

mozzicone *sm* stub.

mozzo, -a *agg* cut off ♦ *sm* ship's boy.

mucca, -che *sf* cow.

mucchio *sm (cumulo)* heap; **un ~ di** *(fig: grande quantità)* loads of.

muffa *sf* mould.

muffole *sfpl* mittens.

mugolare *vi* to whine.

mulattiera *sf* mule track.

mulatto, -a *agg & sm, f* mulatto.

mulinello *sm (vortice)* whirl; *(da pesca)* reel.

mulino *sm* mill; **~ a vento** windmill.

mulo *sm* mule.

multa *sf* fine.

multare *vt* to fine.

multiplo, -a *agg & sm* multiple.

multiproprietà *sf inv* timeshare.

mungere *vt* to milk.

municipale *agg* municipal.

municipio *sm* town hall.

munire *vt*: **~ qn/qc di qc** to equip sb/sthg with sthg ☐ **munirsi di** *vr + prep* to equip o.s. with.

muovere *vt* to move; *(critica, accusa)* to make ☐ **muoversi** *vr* to move; *(fam: sbrigarsi)* to hurry up, to get a move on.

mura *sfpl* walls.

murare *vt* to wall up.

muratore *sm* bricklayer.

murena *sf* moray eel.

muro *sm* wall.

muscolare *agg* muscular, muscle *(dav s)*.

muscolo *sm* muscle; **muscoli** *(forza)* brawn *(sg)*.

muscoloso, -a *agg* muscular.

museo *sm* museum.

museruola *sf* muzzle.

musica *sf* music; ~ **classica** classical music; ~ **leggera** light music.

musicale *agg* musical.

musicista, -i, -e *smf* musician.

muso *sm (di animale)* muzzle; *(fam & spreg: di persona)* mug; *(di auto)* front end; *(aereo)* nose; **tenere il ~** to sulk.

muta *sf (da sub)* wet suit; *(di cani)* pack.

mutamento *sm* change.

mutande *sfpl* pants.

mutandine *sfpl* knickers.

mutare *vt & vi* to change.

mutazione *sf* change; *(genetica)* mutation.

mutilato, -a *sm, f* person who has lost a limb; ~ **di guerra** disabled ex-serviceman *(Br)*, disabled war veteran *(Am)*.

muto, -a *agg* dumb; *(silenzioso)* silent; *(cinema, consonante)* silent.

mutua *sf* = National Health Service.

mutuo, -a *agg* mutual ♦ *sm* loan; *(per casa)* mortgage.

N *(abbr di nord)* N.

nafta *sf (olio combustibile)* fuel oil; *(gasolio)* diesel oil.

naftalina *sf* mothballs *(pl)*.

nailon® *sm* nylon.

nanna *sf (fam)*: **andare a ~** to go to beddy-byes.

nano, -a *agg & sm, f* dwarf.

napoletana *sf a type of coffee percolator.*

napoletano, -a *agg & sm, f* Neapolitan.

Napoli *sf* Naples.

narice *sf* nostril.

narrare *vt* to tell.

narrativa *sf* fiction.

nasale *agg* nasal.

nascere *vi* to be born; *(pianta)* to come up; *(sole)* to rise; *(fiume)* to have its source; *(dente)* to come through; *(attività, impresa)* to start up; **sono nata il 31 luglio del 1965** I was born on the 31st of July 1965 ❑ **nascere da** *v + prep* to arise from.

nascita *sf (di bambino, animale)* birth; *(di attività, movimento)* birth; **data di ~** date of birth; **luogo di ~** place of birth.

nascondere *vt* to hide; *(dissimulare)* to hide, to conceal ❑ **nascondersi** *vr* to hide.

nascondino *sm* hide and seek.

nascosto, -a *pp* → **nascon-**

dere ♦ *agg* hidden; **di ~** secretly.

naso *sm* nose; **ficcare il ~ in qc** to poke one's nose into sthg.

nastro *sm* ribbon; **~ adesivo** adhesive tape; **~ trasportatore** conveyor belt.

Natale *sm* Christmas.

---

i NATALE

Italian Christmas celebrations begin on Christmas Eve with a dinner at which special regional dishes are served. The rest of the evening is normally spent playing "tombola" (line bingo) or cards, and in some families the gifts which were placed under the Christmas tree or by the "presepe" (crib) are exchanged now rather than on the 25th. Churchgoers then attend midnight mass. Christmas Day itself is usually spent with the family. Lunch is traditionally rounded off with a "panettone", a domed cake containing raisins and candied fruit.

natalità *sf* birth rate.

natante *sm* craft.

nato, -a *pp* ♦ **nascere** ♦ *agg* (*fig: per natura*) born; **nata Mattei** (*da nubile*) née Mattei.

NATO *sf* NATO.

natura *sf* nature; **~ morta** still life.

naturale *agg* natural.

naturalmente *avv* naturally; (*certamente sì*) naturally, of course.

naufragare *vi* (*nave*) to be wrecked; (*persona*) to be shipwrecked.

naufragio *sm* shipwreck.

naufrago, -a, -ghi, -ghe *sm, f* shipwrecked person.

nausea *sf* nausea.

nauseante *agg* nauseating.

nauseare *vt* to make sick.

nautico, -a, -ci, -che *agg* nautical.

navale *agg* naval.

navata *sf* nave.

nave *sf* ship; **~ passeggeri** passenger ship; **~ traghetto** ferry.

navetta *sf* shuttle; **~ (spaziale)** space shuttle.

navigabile *agg* navigable.

navigare *vi* (*nave*) to sail; (*persona*) to navigate.

navigazione *sf* navigation.

naviglio *sm* (*nave*) vessel; (*canale*) canal.

nazionale *agg* national ♦ *sf* (*squadra*) national team.

nazionalità *sf inv* nationality.

nazione *sf* nation.

ne *pron* 1. (*di lui*) of/about him; (*di lei*) of/about her; (*di loro*) of/about them; **~ apprezzo l'onestà** I value his honesty.
2. (*di un insieme*) of it, of them; **ha dei panini? - ~ vorrei due** have you got any rolls? - I'd like two (of them).
3. (*di ciò*) about it; **non parliamone più** let's not talk about it any more; **non ~ ho idea** I've no idea.
4. (*da ciò*) **~ deriva che ...** it follows that ...
♦ *avv* (*di là*) from there; **~ veniamo proprio ora** we've just come from there.

né *cong*: **né ... né** neither ... nor; **l'uno ~ l'altro sono italiani** neither of them are Italian; **non si è fatto ~ sentire ~ vedere** I haven't heard from him or seen him; **non voglio ~ il primo ~ il secondo** I don't want either the first one or the second.

neanche *cong & avv* not even; **non … ~** not even …; **~ io lo conosco** I don't know him either; **non ho mangiato ~ ~ io** I haven't eaten – neither have I o I haven't either; **~ per sogno** o **per idea!** not on your life!

nebbia *sf* fog.

nebulizzatore *sm* spray.

necessariamente *avv* necessarily.

necessario, -a *agg* necessary ♦ *sm* necessities (*pl*); **è ~ farlo** it must be done; **~ per toeletta** toiletries (*pl*).

necessità *sf inv (bisogno)* necessity.

necessitare : necessitare di *v* + *prep* to need, to require.

necrologio *sm (annuncio)* obituary.

negare *vt* to deny; *(rifiutare)*: **~ qc (a qn)** to refuse (sb) sthg; **~ di aver fatto qc** to deny having done sthg.

negativo, -a *agg & sm* negative.

negato, -a *agg*: **essere ~ per qc** to be hopeless at sthg.

negli = in + gli, → in.

negligente *agg* negligent.

negoziante *smf* shopkeeper.

negozio *sm* shop; **~ di giocattoli** toy shop.

negro, -a *agg & sm, f* black.

nei = in + i, → in.

nel = in + il, → in.

nell' = in + l', → in.

nella = in + la, → in.

nelle = in + le, → in.

nello = in + lo, → in.

nemico, -a, -ci, -che *agg (esercito, stato)* enemy *(dav s)*; *(ostile)* hostile ♦ *sm, f* enemy.

nemmeno = neanche.

neo *sm* mole.

neofascismo *sm* neofascism.

neon *sm* neon.

neonato, -a *sm, f* newborn baby.

neozelandese *agg* New Zealand *(dav s)* ♦ *smf* New Zealander.

neppure = neanche.

nero, -a *agg (colore)* black; *(scuro)* dark; *(pane)* wholemeal ♦ *sm* black.

nervo *sm* nerve; **dare ai** o **sui nervi a qc** to get on sb's nerves.

nervosismo *sm* nervousness.

nervoso, -a *agg* nervous ♦ *sm*: **avere il ~** to be on edge.

nespola *sf* medlar.

nessuno, -a *agg* no ♦ *pron (non una persona)* nobody, no one; *(non una cosa)* none; *(qualcuno)*: **c'è ~?** is anybody in?; **nessuna città è bella quanto Roma** there's no city more beautiful than Rome; **c'è nessun posto libero** there aren't any free seats; **da nessuna parte** nowhere; **~ lo sa** nobody knows; **non ho visto ~** I didn't see anybody; **~ di noi** none of us; **~ dei due** neither of them; **non me ne piace ~** I don't like any of them.

nettezza sf: ~ urbana refuse department.

netto, -a agg (preciso) clear; (deciso) definite; (peso, stipendio) net.

netturbino sm dustman.

neutrale agg neutral.

neutralizzare vt to neutralize.

neutro, -a agg neutral; essere ~ (imparziale) to be neutral ♦ sm (in linguistica) neuter.

neve sf snow.

nevicare v impers to snow; nevica it's snowing.

nevicata sf snowfall.

nevischio sm sleet.

nevralgia sf neuralgia.

nevrotico, -a, -ci, -che agg neurotic.

nicchia sf niche.

nicotina sf nicotine.

nido sm nest.

niente pron 1. (nessuna cosa) nothing; non ... ~ nothing; non faccio ~ la domenica I do nothing on Sundays, I don't do anything on Sundays; ~ di ~ nothing at all; grazie! – di ~! thank you – not at all.

2. (qualcosa) anything; le serve ~? do you need anything?; non per ~, ma ... not that it matters, but ...

3. (poco): da ~ (cosa) not important; (persona) worthless.

♦ agg inv (fam: nessuno): non ha buon senso he has no common sense; ~ paura! never fear!

♦ avv: non ... ~ not ... at all; non me ne importa ~ I couldn't care less; questo non c'entra ~ this doesn't come into it at all; non fa ~ it doesn't matter; ti piace? – per ~! do you like it? – not at all!

♦ sm: basta un ~ per farlo contento the slightest thing makes him happy; un bel ~ nothing at all.

nientemeno avv no less, actually ♦ esclam you don't say!

night(-club) ['nait(-'klab)] sm inv nightclub.

Nilo sm: il ~ the Nile.

ninnananna sf lullaby.

ninnolo sm knick-knack.

nipote smf (di zii) nephew (f niece); (di nonni) grandson (f granddaughter).

nitido, -a agg well-defined.

nitrire vi to neigh.

no avv no; c'eri anche tu, ~? you were there too, weren't you?; lo sai, ~, com'è fatto you know, don't you, what he's like?; le vuoi o ~? do you want it or not?; ~ di certo certainly not; perché ~! why not?

nobile agg & smf noble.

nobiltà sf (aristocrazia) nobility; (di animo, azione) nobleness.

nocciola sf hazelnut ♦ agg inv hazel.

nocciolina sf: ~ (americana) peanut.

nocciolo¹ sm (di frutto) stone.

nocciolo² sm (albero) hazel.

noce sf & sm walnut; ~ di cocco coconut; ~ moscata nutmeg.

nocivo, -a agg harmful.

nodo sm knot; avere un ~ alla gola to have a lump in one's throat.

noi pron (soggetto) we; (complemento oggetto, con preposizione) us; **da ~** (nel nostro paese) in our country; **~ stessi** we ourselves.

noia sf (tedio) boredom; (fastidio) nuisance; **gli è venuto a ~** he's tired of it; **dar ~ a qn** to annoy sb; **avere delle noie con** to have trouble with.

noioso, -a agg (monotono) boring; (fastidioso) annoying.

noleggiare vt (prendere a nolo) to hire; (dare a nolo) to hire out.

noleggio sm hire (Br), rental; **prendere qc a ~** to hire sthg.

nolo = **noleggio**.

nome sm name; (GRAMM) noun; **conoscere qn di ~** to know sb by name; **a ~ di qn** on behalf of sb; **~ di battesimo** Christian name; **~ da ragazza** maiden name.

nominare vt (menzionare) to mention; (eleggere) to appoint.

non avv not, → **affatto, ancora** ecc.

nonché cong (e anche) as well as; (tanto meno) let alone.

noncurante agg: **~ (di)** indifferent (to).

nondimeno cong nevertheless, however.

nonno, -a sm, f grandfather (f grandmother).

nonnulla sm inv: **un ~** a trifle.

nono, -a num ninth, → **sesto**.

nonostante prep in spite of ♦ cong although.

non vedente smf blind person.

nord sm north ♦ agg inv north, northern; **a ~ (di)** north (of); **nel ~** in the north.

nordest sm northeast.

nordico, -a, -ci, -che agg Nordic.

nordovest sm northwest.

norma sf rule; **di ~ as a rule**; **a ~ di legge** according to the law.

normale agg normal.

normalità sf normality.

normanno, -a agg Norman.

norvegese agg, smf & sm Norwegian.

Norvegia sf: **la ~** Norway.

nostalgia sf nostalgia; **avere ~ di casa** O **di paese** to be homesick.

nostro, -a agg: **il ~ (la nostra)** our ♦ pron: **il ~ (la nostra)** ours; **~ padre** our father; **un ~ amico** a friend of ours; **questa casa è nostra** it's our house.

nota sf note; (conto) bill; (elenco) list; **prendere ~ (di qc)** to make a note (of sthg).

notaio sm notary public.

notare vt (osservare, accorgersi di) to notice; (annotare) to note down; **farsi ~** to get o.s. noticed.

notevole agg (differenza, prezzo) considerable; (persona) remarkable.

notificare vt (form) to notify.

notizia sf (informazione) news (sg), piece of news; **le ultime notizie** the latest news; **avere notizie di qn** to hear from sb.

notiziario sm news (sg).

noto, -a agg well-known; **rendere ~ qc a qn** to make sthg known to sb.

nottambulo, -a sm, f night bird.

notte

notte *sf* night; **di ~** at night; **una ~ in bianco** a sleepless night.

notturno, -a *agg* night *(dav s)*; **animale ~** nocturnal animal.

novanta *num* ninety, → **sei**.

novantesimo, -a *num* nineti-eth, → **sesto**.

nove *num* nine, → **sei**.

novecento *num* nine hundred, → **sei** ❑ **Novecento** *sm*: **il Novecento** the twentieth century.

novella *sf* short story.

novembre *sm* November, → **settembre**.

novità *sf inv (cosa nuova)* something new; *(fatto, notizia recente)* (piece of) news *(sg)*; **le ~ musicali** the latest releases.

nozione *sf* notion, idea; **nozioni** *(di matematica, francese)* rudiments.

nozze *sfpl* wedding *(sg)*; **~ d'oro** golden wedding.

nube *sf* cloud.

nubifragio *sm* rainstorm.

nubile *agg* single.

nuca, -che *sf* nape of the neck.

nucleare *agg* nuclear.

nucleo *sm (di cellula, atomo)* nucleus; *(di persone)* group; *(di soldati, polizia)* squad; **~ familiare** family unit.

nudismo *sm* nudism.

nudista, -i, -e *smf* nudist.

nudo, -a *agg (persona)* naked; *(parete)* bare; **mettere a ~ qc** to lay sthg bare ◆ *sm (ARTE)* nude.

nugolo *sm*: **un ~ di** a host of.

nulla = **niente**.

nullità *sf inv (di ragionamento, documento)* nullity; *(persona)*

nobody.

nullo, -a *agg (non valido)* (null and) void; *(SPORT)* drawn.

numerale *agg & sm* numeral.

numerare *vt* to number.

numero *sm (MAT: quantità)* number; *(segno, cifra)* numeral; *(di scarpe)* size; *(di rivista)* issue; **~ civico** house number; **~ chiuso** selective entry system; **~ di conto** account number; **~ di targa** numberplate; **~ di telefono** telephone number; **~ verde** = freefone number *(Br)*, = toll-free number *(Am)*; **dare i numeri** *(fig)* to be off one's head.

numeroso, -a *agg (molteplice)* numerous; *(grande)* large.

numismatica *sf* numismatics *(sg)*.

nuocere : nuocere a *v + prep* to harm.

nuora *sf* daughter-in-law.

nuotare *vi* to swim.

nuoto *sm* swimming.

nuovamente *avv* again.

Nuova Zelanda *sf*: **la ~** New Zealand.

nuovo, -a *agg* new; **di ~** again; **~ di zecca** brand-new.

nuraghe, -ghi *sm* prehistoric stone monument in Sardinia.

nutriente *agg* nutritious.

nutrimento *sm* nourishment.

nutrire *vt (con cibo)* to feed; *(fig: sentimento)* to feel ❑ **nutrirsi di** *vr + prep* to feed on.

nuvola *sf* cloud; **cascare dalle nuvole** to be flabbergasted.

nuvoloso, -a *agg* cloudy.

O *cong* or; **~ ... ~** either ... or.

O *(abbr di ovest)* W.

oasi *sf inv* oasis.

obbediente = ubbidiente.

obbedire = ubbidire.

obbligare *vt*: **~ qn a fare qc** to force sb to do sthg.

obbligato, -a *agg (percorso, passaggio)* fixed; *(costretto)*: **~ a fare qc** obliged to do sthg.

obbligatorio, -a *agg* compulsory.

obbligo, -ghi *sm* obligation; **avere l'~ di fare qc** to be obliged to do sthg.

obelisco, -schi *sm* obelisk.

obeso, -a *agg* obese.

obiettare *vt* to object.

obiettivo, -a *agg* objective ♦ *sm (fotografico)* lens; *(bersaglio, scopo)* objective.

obiettore *sm* objector; **~ di coscienza** conscientious objector.

obiezione *sf* objection.

obitorio *sm* mortuary.

obliquo, -a *agg* slanting.

obliterare *vt* to stamp.

oblò *sm inv* porthole.

obsoleto, -a *agg* obsolete.

oca *(pl* **oche)** *sf* goose.

occasione *sf (momento favorevole)* opportunity; *(affare)* bargain; *(causa, circostanza)* occasion; **avere ~ di fare qc** to have the chance to

do sthg; **cogliere l'~ per fare qc** to take the opportunity to do sthg; **d'~** second-hand.

occhiaie *sfpl* bags, rings.

occhiali *smpl*: **~ (da vista)** glasses; **~ da sole** sunglasses.

occhiata *sf*: **dare un'~ a** to have a look at.

occhiello *sm* buttonhole.

occhio *sm* eye; **a ~ nudo** with the naked eye; **tenere O non perdere d'~ qn/qc** to keep an eye on sb/sthg; **a ~ e croce** roughly; **costare un ~ della testa** to cost a fortune; **saltare O balzare all'~** to be obvious; **a quattr'occhi** in private; **sognare a occhi aperti** to daydream.

occhiolino *sm*: **fare l'~ (a qn)** to wink (at sb).

occidentale *agg (zona)* west, western; *(cultura, società)* Western.

occidente *sm* west ❑ **Occidente** *sm*: **l'Occidente** the West.

occorrente *sm* everything necessary.

occorrenza *sf*: **all'~** if need be.

occorrere *vi* to be necessary; **occorre aspettare** you/we have to wait; **mi occorre tempo** I need time.

occorso, -a *pp* → occorrere.

occulto, -a *agg* occult.

occupare *vt (ingombrare)* to take up; *(paese, università)* to occupy; *(impegnare)* to keep busy ❑ **occuparsi di** *vr* + *prep (prendersi cura di)* to take care of, to look after; *(impicciarsi in)* to interfere in; *(interessarsi di)*: **si occupa di politica** he's in politics; **occupati dei fatti tuoi!**

mind your own business!

occupato, -a *agg (sedia, posto)* taken; *(telefono, bagno)* engaged; *(impegnato)* busy.

occupazione *sf (impiego)* occupation; *(in economia)* employment.

Oceania *sf:* l'~ Oceania.

oceano *sm* ocean.

oculista, -i, -e *smf* eye specialist.

odiare *vt* to hate.

odio *sm* hatred.

odioso, -a *agg* hateful, odious.

odorare *vt* to smell □ **odorare di** *v + prep* to smell of.

odorato *sm* (sense of) smell.

odore *sm* smell □ **odori** *(da cucina) smpl* herbs.

offendere *vt* to offend □ **offendersi** *vr* to take offence.

offensivo, -a *agg* offensive.

offerto, -a *pp* → **offrire** ♦ *smf (proposta)* offer; *(donazione)* donation; *(FIN)* supply; ~ **speciale** special offer.

offesa *sf* offence.

offeso, -a *pp* → **offendere** ♦ *agg* offended.

officina *sf (di fabbrica)* workshop; *(per auto)* garage.

offrire *vt* to offer; *(cena, caffè)* to pay for; ~ **da bere a qn** to buy sb a drink □ **offrirsi di** *vr + prep:* **offrirsi di fare qc** to offer to do sthg.

offuscare *vt (luce)* to darken; *(vista, mente, memoria)* to dim □ **offuscarsi** *vr (vista)* to dim.

oggettivo, -a *agg* objective.

oggetto *sm* object; *(ufficio)*

oggetti smarriti lost property (office) *(Br)*, lost-and-found office *(Am)*.

oggi *avv* today; *(attualmente)* nowadays; ~ **pomeriggio** this afternoon; **il giornale di** ~ today's newspaper; **dall'~ al domani** from one day to the next.

oggigiorno *avv* nowadays.

ogni *agg inv (tutti)* every, each; *(distributivo)* every; **gente di** ~ **tipo** all sorts of people; ~ **giorno/ mese/anno** every day/month/year; ~ **tre giorni** every three days; **in** ~ **caso** in any case; **ad** ~ **modo** anyway; ~ **tanto** every so often; ~ **volta che** whenever.

Ognissanti *sm* All Saints' Day.

ognuno, -a *pron* everyone, everybody; ~ **di voi** each of you.

Olanda *sf:* l'~ Holland.

olandese *agg & sm* Dutch ♦ *smf* Dutchman (f Dutchwoman); **gli olandesi** the Dutch.

oleoso, -a *agg* oily.

olfatto *sm* sense of smell.

oliare *vt* to oil.

oliera *sf* oil and vinegar cruet.

olimpiadi *sfpl:* **le** ~ the Olympic Games.

olio *sm* oil; ~ **(extra-vergine) d'oliva** (extra-virgin) olive oil; ~ **di semi** vegetable oil; **sott'**~ in oil.

oliva *sf* olive; **olive farcite all'an-conetana** *olives stuffed with meat and vegetables, then covered in bread-crumbs and fried.*

olivastro, -a *agg (carnagione)* sallow.

olivo *sm* olive tree.

olmo *sm* elm.

oltraggio *sm* (DIR) offence.

oltralpe : d'oltralpe *agg* on the other side of the Alps.

oltranza : a oltranza *avv* to the (bitter) end.

oltre *prep* (di là da) beyond; (più di) over, more than; (in aggiunta a) as well as, besides ♦ *avv* (più in là) further; ~ **a** (all'infuori di) apart from; (in aggiunta a) as well as; **non ~ le cinque** no later than five o'clock.

oltrepassare *vt* to go beyond.

omaggio *sm* (tributo) homage; (regalo) gift; **in ~** (con prodotto) free.

ombelico, -chi *sm* navel.

ombra *sf* (zona) shade; (figura) shadow; **all'~** in the shade.

ombrello *sm* umbrella.

ombrellone *sm* beach umbrella.

ombretto *sm* eye shadow.

omeopatia *sf* homeopathy.

omesso, -a *pp* → **omettere**.

omettere *vt* to omit; ~ **di fare qc** to omit to do sthg.

omicidio *sm* murder.

omissione *sf* omission.

omogeneizzato *sm* baby food.

omogeneo, -a *agg* (uniforme) homogeneous; (armonico) harmonious.

omonimo, -a *sm, f* (persona) namesake.

omosessuale *smf* homosexual.

On. (abbr di onorevole) Hon.

onda *sf* wave; **andare in ~** to go on the air; **mandare in ~ qc** to broadcast sthg; **onde lunghe/medie/corte** long/medium/short wave (sg); **'onde pericolose'** sign warning swimmers to take care.

ondata *sf* wave; **a ondate** in waves.

ondulato, -a *agg* (terreno) undulating; (capelli) wavy; (lamiera, carta) corrugated.

onere *sm* (form) burden; **oneri fiscali** (DIR) taxes.

onestà *sf* honesty.

onesto, -a *agg* honest.

onnipotente *agg* omnipotent.

onomastico *sm* name day.

i ONOMASTICO

Along with their birthdays, Italians also celebrate their "onomastico", or name day, albeit in a minor way. This is the day when the saint after whom they are named is honoured. Relatives and friends send cards, small gifts or simply their best wishes.

onorare *vt* (celebrare) to honour; (fare onore a) to do credit to.

onorario, -a *agg* (cittadinanza, console) honorary ♦ *sm* fee.

onore *sm* honour; **fare ~ a** (pranzo) to do justice to sthg; (scuola, famiglia) to be a credit to sthg; **in ~ di** in honour of; **fare gli onori di casa** to be the host (f hostess); **farsi ~** to distinguish o.s.

onorevole *agg* (parlamentare) Honourable ♦ *smf* = Member of Parliament (Br), = Congressman (f Congresswoman) (Am).

ONU *(abbr di Organizzazione delle Nazioni Unite)* UN.

opaco, -a, -chi, -che *agg (vetro)* opaque; *(colore, metallo)* dull.

opera *sf* work; *(in musica)* opera; **è tutta ~ sua!** it's all his doing!; **mettersi all'~** to get down to work; **~ d'arte** work of art; **opere pubbliche** public works.

operaio, -a *agg* working-class ◆ *sm, f* worker.

operare *vt (realizzare)* to carry out; *(MED)* to operate on ◆ *vi (agire)* to act ❏ **operarsi** *vr (compiersi)* to take place; *(subire un'operazione)* to have an operation.

operatore, -trice *sm, f (di televisione, cinema)* cameraman *(f* camerawoman); **~ turistico** tour operator.

operazione *sf* operation; *(FIN)* transaction.

opinione *sf* opinion; **l'~ pubblica** public opinion.

opporre *vt (argomenti, ragioni)* to put forward; **~ resistenza** to put up some resistance; **~ un rifiuto** to refuse ❏ **opporsi** *vr:* **opporsi (a)** to oppose.

opportunità *sf inv* opportunity.

opportuno, -a *agg* opportune.

opposizione *sf* opposition.

opposto, -a *pp* → **opporre** ◆ *agg (lato, senso)* opposite; *(idee)* opposing ◆ *sm* opposite.

oppressione *sf* oppression.

oppresso, -a *pp* → **opprimere**.

opprimente *agg* oppressive.

opprimere *vt (popolo)* to oppress; *(angosciare)* to weigh down.

oppure *cong (o invece)* or; *(se no)* or else, otherwise.

optare : optare per *v + prep* to opt for.

opuscolo *sm* brochure.

ora *sf* hour; *(momento)* time ◆ *avv* now; **a che ~ parte il treno?** what time does the train leave?; **è ~ di partire** it's time to leave; **che ~ è?, che ore sono?** what's the time?; **e ~?** now what?; **~ come ~** right now; **~ legale** summertime; **~ locale** local time; **~ di punta** rush hour; **50 km all'~** 50 km an hour; **di buon'~** early; **d'~ in poi** o **in avanti** from now on; **fare le ore piccole** to stay up till the small hours.

orale *agg & sm* oral.

oramai → **ormai**.

orario, -a *agg (segnale)* time *(dav s)*; *(velocità)* per hour; *(tariffa)* hourly ◆ *sm (di lavoro, visite)* hours *(pl)*; *(tabella)* timetable; **fuori ~** after hours; **in ~** on time; **~ di arrivo** arrival time; **~ di partenza** departure time; **~ di apertura** opening hours *(pl)*; **~ di chiusura** closing time; **~ d'ufficio** office hours *(pl)*.

orata *sf* sea bream.

orbita *sf (di satellite)* orbit; *(di occhio)* eye socket.

orchestra *sf* orchestra.

ordigno *sm* device.

ordinare *vt (al ristorante, bar)* to order; *(disporre in ordine)* to put in order; *(comandare)*: **~ a qn di fare**

qc to order sb to do sthg.

ordinario, -a agg (normale) ordinary; (mediocre, scadente) poor.

ordinato, -a agg tidy.

ordinazione sf order.

ordine sm order; **essere in ~** (stanza) to be tidy; (documenti) to be in order; **mettere in ~ qc** (stanza) to tidy sthg; (documenti) to put sthg in order; **~ pubblico** public order.

orecchiabile agg catchy.

orecchiette sfpl tiny ear-shaped pasta from Puglia.

orecchino sm earring.

orecchio (pl f **orecchie**) sm ear; **avere ~** to have a good ear (for music).

orecchioni smpl mumps (sg).

oreficeria sf (negozio) jeweller's.

orfano, -a agg & sm, f orphan.

organico, -a, -ci, -che agg organic ◆ sm staff.

organismo sm (essere vivente) organism; (ente) body.

organizzare vt to organize ❏ **organizzarsi** vr to organize o.s.

organizzato, -a agg organized.

organizzatore, -trice sm, f organizer.

organizzazione sf organization.

organo sm organ.

orgasmo sm orgasm.

orgoglio sm pride.

orgoglioso, -a agg proud.

orientale agg (paese, prodotto) eastern; (persona) oriental ◆ smf Oriental.

orientamento sm (posizione) orientation; (fig: indirizzo) leanings (pl); **perdere l'~** to lose one's bearings; **~ professionale** careers guidance.

orientare vt (carta) to orientate ❏ **orientarsi** vr to find one's bearings.

oriente sm east ❏ **Oriente** sm: l'Oriente the East.

origano sm oregano.

originale agg original; (stravagante) eccentric ◆ sm original.

originario, -a agg (iniziale) original; (paese, lingua) native.

origine sf origin; (causa) origin, cause; **avere ~ da qc** to originate from sthg; **dare ~ a qc** to cause sthg; **di ~ italiana** of Italian origin.

origliare vi to eavesdrop.

orina = urina.

oriundo, -a sm, f: **essere ~ italiano** to be of Italian extraction.

orizzontale agg horizontal.

orizzonte sm horizon.

orlo sm (di fosso) edge; (di bicchiere) rim; (di gonna, pantaloni) hem.

orma sf footprint.

ormai avv (a questo punto) by now; (a quel punto) by then; (quasi) almost; **~ è tardi** it's too late now.

ormeggiare vt & vi to moor.

ormeggio sm mooring.

ormone sm hormone.

ornamento sm ornament.

ornare vt to decorate.

oro sm gold; **d'~** gold.

orologio sm clock; (da polso)

watch.

oroscopo sm horoscope.

orrendo, -a agg (spaventoso, atroce) horrendous; (brutto) horrible, awful.

orribile agg horrible.

orrore sm horror.

orsacchiotto sm teddy bear.

orso sm bear.

ortaggio sm vegetable.

ortica, -che sf nettle.

orticaria sf hives (pl).

orto sm vegetable garden.

ortodosso, -a agg orthodox.

ortografia sf spelling.

orzaiolo sm stye.

orzo sm barley.

osare vt: ~ (fare qc) to dare (to do sthg).

osceno, -a agg obscene.

oscillare vi (dondolare) to swing; (fig: variare) to vary.

oscillazione sf (di pendolo) swing; (di prezzi) fluctuation; (di temperatura) variation.

oscurità sf darkness.

oscuro, -a agg dark ♦ sm: essere all'~ di qc to be in the dark about sthg.

ospedale sm hospital.

ospitale agg (persona) hospitable; (paese) friendly.

ospitalità sf hospitality; mi ha dato ~ per una notte he put me up for a night.

ospitare vt to put up.

ospite smf (chi ospita) host (f hostess); (ospitato) guest.

ospizio sm old people's home.

ossa pl → osso.

osseo, -a agg bone (dav s).

osservare vt (guardare) to observe, to watch; (rilevare) to notice; (rispettare, mantenere) to observe; far ~ qc a qn to point sthg out to sb.

osservatorio sm observatory.

osservazione sf (esame) observation; (commento) observation, remark; (rimprovero) criticism.

ossessionare vt to obsess.

ossessione sf obsession.

ossia cong that is.

ossidare vt to oxidize ❑ ossidarsi vr to oxidize.

ossido sm oxide; ~ di carbonio carbon monoxide.

ossigenare vt to oxygenate; (capelli) to bleach.

ossigeno sm oxygen.

osso sm (umano: pl f ossa) bone; (di carne: pl m ossi) bone.

ossobuco (pl ossibuchi) sm veal knuckle cooked on the bone in tomatoes and white wine (a speciality of Milan).

ostacolare vt to obstruct.

ostacolo sm obstacle; (in atletica) hurdle; (in equitazione) fence.

ostaggio sm hostage.

ostello sm: ~ (della gioventù) (youth) hostel.

ostentare vt to flaunt.

osteria sf inn.

ostetrica, -che sf midwife.

ostia sf (RELIG) host.

ostile agg hostile.

ostilità sf hostility ♦ sfpl (MIL) hostilities.

ostinarsi *vr*: ~ **a fare qc** to persist in doing sthg.

ostinato, -a *agg* obstinate.

ostinazione *sf* persistence.

ostrica, -che *sf* oyster.

ostruire *vt* to obstruct, to block.

ottanta *num* eighty, → **sei**.

ottantesimo, -a *num* eightieth, → **sesto**.

ottantina *sf*: **una ~ (di)** about eighty; **essere sull'~** to be in one's eighties.

ottavo, -a *num* eighth, → **sesto**.

ottenere *vt* to get.

ottico, -a, -ci, -che *agg* (*nervo*) optic; (*strumento*) optical ♦ *sm* optician.

ottimale *agg* optimum.

ottimismo *sm* optimism.

ottimista, -i, -e *smf* optimist.

ottimo, -a *agg* excellent, very good.

otto *num* eight, → **sei** ♦ *sm*: ~ **volante** roller coaster.

ottobre *sm* October, → **settembre**.

ottocento *num* eight hundred, → **sei** ❑ **Ottocento** *sm*: **l'Ottocento** the nineteenth century.

ottone *sm* brass.

otturare *vt* to fill.

otturazione *sf* filling.

ottuso, -a *agg* obtuse.

ovale *agg* oval.

ovatta *sf* cotton wool.

overdose *sf inv* overdose.

ovest *sm & agg inv* west; **a ~ (di qc)** west (of sthg).

ovile *sm* sheepfold.

ovino, -a *agg* sheep (*dav s*).

ovovia *sf* ski lift (*with oval cabins*).

ovunque = **dovunque**.

ovvero *cong* or, in other words.

ovviare *vi*: ~ **a qc** to avoid sthg.

ovvio, -a *agg* obvious.

ozio *sm* idleness.

ozono *sm* ozone.

P

pacato, -a *agg* calm.

pacca, -che *sf* pat.

pacchetto *sm* (*di sigarette, caramelle*) packet; (*pacco*) parcel.

pacchiano, -a *agg* garish.

pacco, -chi *sm* parcel.

pace *sf* peace; **in ~** in peace; **fare (la) ~** to make it up.

pacemaker [pei'smɛkər] *sm inv* pacemaker.

pacifico, -a, -ci, -che *agg* peaceful ❑ **Pacifico** *sm*: **il Pacifico** the Pacific.

pacifista, -i, -e *agg & smf* pacifist.

padella *sf* (*da cucina*) frying pan; (*per malati*) bedpan.

padiglione *sm* (*di ospedale, fiera*) pavilion; (*di giardino*) marquee.

Padova *sf* Padua.

padre *sm* father.

padrino *sm* godfather.

padrone, -a *sm, f* owner; **essere ~ di fare qc** to be free to do sthg; **~ di casa** landlord (*f* landlady).

paesaggio *sm* landscape; (*panorama*) scenery.

paese *sm* (*nazione*) country; (*villaggio*) village; **~ di provenienza** country of origin; **mandare qn a quel ~** (*volg*) to tell sb to get lost □ **Paesi Bassi** *smpl*: **i Paesi Bassi** the Netherlands.

paffuto, -a *agg* plump, chubby.

paga, -ghe *sf* pay.

pagamento *sm* payment; **'~ pedaggio'** 'toll to be paid here'.

pagano, -a *agg & sm, f* pagan.

pagare *vt* to pay; (*offrire*) to buy; **quanto l'hai pagato?** how much did you pay for it?; **~ con assegno** to pay by cheque; **~ con carta di credito** to pay by credit card; **~ in contanti** to pay cash.

pagella *sf* (school) report.

pagina *sf* page.

paglia *sf* straw.

pagliaccio *sm* clown.

pagnotta *sf* round loaf.

paio (*pl f* **paia**) *sm* pair; **un ~ di** (*alcuni*) a couple of; **un ~ di scarpe** a pair of shoes.

Pakistan *sm*: **il ~** Pakistan.

pala *sf* (*vanga*) shovel; (*di mulino, elica*) blade.

palato *sm* palate.

palazzo *sm* (*signorile*) palace; (*edificio*) building; (*condominio*) block of flats (*Br*), apartment building (*Am*); **~ di giustizia** law courts (*pl*); **~ dello sport** indoor stadium.

palco, -chi *sm* (*palcoscenico*) stage; (*pedana*) stand; (*a teatro*) box.

palcoscenico, -ci *sm* stage.

Palermo *sf* Palermo.

Palestina *sf*: **la ~** Palestine.

palestra *sf* gymnasium.

paletta *sf* (*giocattolo, per giardiniere*) spade; (*per lo sporco*) dustpan; (*di polizia, capostazione*) signalling disc.

paletto *sm* stake.

palio *sm*: **mettere qc in ~** to offer sthg as a prize □ **Palio** *sm*: **il Palio (di Siena)** the Palio (*traditional horse race held in the centre of Siena*).

---

i IL PALIO DI SIENA

Siena's famous horse race attracts thousands of visitors to Tuscany on July 2 and August 16 every year. Representatives of Siena's 17 "contrade" (districts) parade in Renaissance costumes, and 10 districts enter a horse and rider in the race which follows. The race is very rough, and the walls of the Piazza del Campo are padded to protect the contestants. The winner is awarded a "palio" (painted banner), and is paraded through the town.

---

palla *sf* ball; **che palle!** (*volg*) what a drag!

pallacanestro *sf* basketball.

pallanuoto *sf* water polo.

pallavolo *sf* volleyball.

pallido, -a *agg* pale.

palloncino *sm* balloon.

pallone *sm* (*palla*) ball; (*da calcio*) football; **~ aerostatico** hot air balloon.

pallottola *sf* bullet.

palma *sf* palm tree.

palmo *sm* palm.

palo *sm* (*di legno*) post; (*di telefono*) pole; **~ della luce** lamppost.

palombaro *sm* (deep sea) diver.

palpebra *sf* eyelid.

palude *sf* marsh, swamp.

panca, -che *sf* bench.

pancarrè *sm* sliced bread.

pancetta *sf* bacon.

panchina *sf* (*di parco*) bench; (*di giardino*) garden seat.

pancia, -ce *sf* (*fam*) belly.

panciotto *sm* waistcoat.

panda *sm inv* panda.

pandoro *sm* conical sponge cake eaten at Christmas.

pane *sm* bread; (*pagnotta*) loaf; (*di burro*) block; **~ a** ○ **in cassetta** sliced bread; **~ integrale** wholemeal bread; **~ tostato** toast; **pan dolce** Christmas cake with candied fruit (a speciality of Genoa); **pan di Spagna** sponge cake.

---

i **PANE**

A staple of the Mediterranean diet, bread is eaten with all Italian meals and waiters bring it automatically to the restaurant table. The main varieties are "pane bianco" (white bread), which is either "comune" (plain) or "speciale" (made with oil), and "pane integrale" (wholemeal bread). It is sold in loaves or sticks or as rolls, and its shapes and names differ from region to region and city to city.

---

panetteria *sf* bakery.

panettone *sm* traditional dome-shaped Christmas cake containing raisins and candied fruit.

panforte *sm* very rich round, flat cake made with almonds, hazelnuts, candied fruits and spices (a speciality of Siena).

pangrattato *sm* breadcrumbs (*pl*).

panico *sm* panic.

panificio *sm* baker's.

panino *sm* roll; **~ imbottito** ○ **ripieno** filled roll; **~ al prosciutto** ham roll.

paninoteca, -che *sf* sandwich bar.

panna *sf*: **~ (montata)** whipped cream; **~ cotta** cold dessert made from cream and sugar, eaten with chocolate or fruit sauce; **~ da cucina** cream.

panne : **in panne** *agg inv*: **ho l'auto in ~** my car has broken down.

pannello *sm* panel.

panno *sm* cloth; **mettersi nei panni di qn** to put o.s. in sb's shoes.

pannocchia *sf* cob.

pannolino *sm* nappy (*Br*), diaper (*Am*).

panorama, -i *sm* panorama.

panoramico, -a, -ci, -che *agg* panoramic.

panpepato *sm* = gingerbread.

pantaloni *smpl* trousers *(Br)*, pants *(Am)*.

pantera *sf* panther.

pantofole *sfpl* slippers.

panzanella *sf* Tuscan salad of tomatoes, anchovies, tuna, onion and herbs, whose special ingredient is moistened bread.

panzerotti *smpl* large ravioli stuffed with cheese and tomato, and fried in oil.

paonazzo, -a *agg* purple.

papà *sm inv (fam)* daddy, dad.

papavero *sm* poppy.

papera *sf (errore):* **fare una ~** to make a slip of the tongue, → **papero**.

papero, -a *sm, f* gosling.

papillon [papi'jon] *sm inv* bow tie.

pappa *sf (fam)* baby food.

pappagallo *sm (animale)* parrot; *(per malati)* bedpan.

pappardelle *sfpl* large noodles; **~ alla lepre** *'pappardelle'* served with hare sauce.

paprica *sf* paprika.

para *sf* crepe rubber.

parabola *sf (MAT)* parabola; *(RELIG)* parable.

parabrezza *sm inv* windscreen.

paracadute *sm inv* parachute.

paracarro *sm* post.

paradiso *sm (RELIG)* paradise, heaven.

paradossale *agg* paradoxical.

paradosso *sm* paradox.

parafango, -ghi *sm* mudguard.

parafulmine *sm* lightning conductor.

paraggi *smpl:* **nei ~** in the neighbourhood.

paragonare *vt:* **~ con** to compare with.

paragone *sm* comparison.

paragrafo *sm* paragraph.

paralisi *sf inv* paralysis.

paralizzare *vt* to paralyse.

parallela *sf* parallel □ **parallele** *sfpl (attrezzo)* parallel bars.

parallelo, -a *agg & sm* parallel.

paralume *sm* lampshade.

parapetto *sm* parapet.

parare *vt (colpi)* to parry; *(occhi)* to shield; *(nel calcio)* to save.

parassita, -i *sm* parasite.

parata *sf (militare)* parade; *(nel calcio)* save.

paraurti *sm inv* bumper.

paravento *sm* screen.

parcella *sf* fee.

parcheggiare *vt* to park.

parcheggio *sm (area)* car park *(Br)*, parking lot *(Am)*; *(manovra)* parking; **~ a pagamento** car park where drivers must pay to park; **~ riservato** private car park.

parchimetro *sm* parking meter.

parco, -chi *sm* park; **~ giochi** o **dei divertimenti** swing park.

---

i | **PARCHI NAZIONALI**

Five Italian national parks have been created by the government to protect the environment and preserve the balance of nature in these designated areas. They are areas of great natural beauty, and are well equipped to welcome visitors. In the Alps the Parco del Gran Paradiso shelters the ibex, and the Parco dello Stelvio the chamois. In the central Apennines are the Parco Nazionale d'Abruzzo and the Parco del Circeo, and in the south is the Parco Nazionale della Calabria.

parecchio, -a agg quite a lot of ♦ pron quite a lot ♦ avv (con agg) quite; (con verbo) quite a lot; **è ~ (tempo) che** aspetto I've been waiting for quite a while.

pareggiare vt (capelli, orlo) to make even; (terreno) to level; (bilancio, conti) to balance ♦ vi to draw.

pareggio sm (in partite) draw; (del bilancio) balance.

parente smf relative.

parentela sf (vincolo) relationship; (famiglia) relatives (pl).

parentesi sf inv (segno) bracket; (commento) digression; **tra ~** in brackets.

pareo sm pareo.

parere sm (opinione) opinion ♦ vi (sembrare) to seem; (apparire) to look ♦ v impers: **pare che** it seems that; **che te ne pare?** what do you think?; **fate come vi pare** do as you like; **mi pare di no** I don't think so; **mi pare di sì** I think so; **mi pare (che) vada bene** it seems (to be) all right; **pare (che) sia vero** it seems (to be) true.

parete sf (di stanza) wall; (di montagna) face.

pari agg inv (in partite, giochi,

superficie) level; (numero) even ♦ sm inv equal; **alla ~ (ragazza)** au pair; **ora siamo ~** now we're even; **essere ~ (uguale)** to be the same as, to be equal to; **essere alla ~ to** be even; **mettersi in ~ con qc** to catch up with sthg; **~ ~** word for word.

Parigi sf Paris.

parlamentare agg parliamentary ♦ smf = Member of Parliament (Br), = Congressman (f Congresswoman) (Am).

parlamento sm parliament.

parlantina sf (fam): **avere una buona ~** to have the gift of the gab.

parlare vi to talk, to speak ♦ vt (lingua) to speak; **~ (a qn) di** to talk o to speak (to sb) about; **parla italiano?** do you speak Italian?

Parma sf Parma.

parmigiano sm Parmesan (cheese).

parola sf word; **prendere la ~** to (begin to) speak; **rivolgere la ~ a qn** to talk to sb; **rimangiarsi la ~** to go back on one's word; **~ d'onore** word of honour; **~ d'ordine** password; **parole crociate** crossword (puzzle) (sg); **è una ~!** it's not easy!

parolaccia, -ce sf swearword.

parrocchia sf (chiesa) parish church; (zona) parish.

parroco, -ci sm parish priest.

parrucca, -che sf wig.

parrucchiere, -a sm, f (per signora) hairdresser.

parso, -a pp = parere.

parte sf part; (lato) side; (direzione) way; (quota) share; (DIR)

partecipare 178

party; **fare ~ di qc** to be part of sthg; **mettere da ~ qc** *(risparmiare)* to put sthg aside; **prendere ~ a qc** to take part in sthg; **stare dalla ~ di** to be on the side of; **la maggior ~ di** most of; **la maggior ~ degli italiani** most Italians; **a ~ questo** apart from that; **a ~** *(spese, pacco)* separate; *(pagare, incartare)* separately; **da ~ di qn** from; *(ringraziare)* on sb's behalf; **d'altra ~** on the other hand; **dall'altra ~** the other way; **da nessuna ~** nowhere; **da ogni ~** everywhere; **da qualche ~** somewhere; **da questa ~** this way; **in ~** partly.

partecipare : partecipare a v + prep *(intervenire)* to take part in; *(spese)* to contribute to; *(gioia, dolore)* to share in.

partenza *sf* departure; *(nello sport)* start; **essere in ~ (per Roma)** to be about to leave (for Rome); **'partenze nazionali/internazionali'** 'domestic/international departures'.

participio *sm* participle.

particolare *agg* particular; *(caratteristico)* distinctive ◆ *sm* detail; **niente di ~** nothing special; **in ~** in particular.

particolareggiato, -a *agg* detailed.

partigiano, -a *sm, f* partisan.

partire *vi* (persona) to leave; *(treno, aereo)* to depart; *(nello sport)* to start; *(colpo)* to go off; **a ~ da** from; **parto da Milano alle cinque** I leave Milan at five.

partita *sf* (competizione) match; *(a carte, a tennis)* game; *(di merce)* consignment; **~ IVA** VAT registra-

tion number.

partito *sm* party.

parto *sm* birth.

partorire *vt* to give birth to.

parziale *agg* (limitato) partial; *(ingiusto)* biased.

pascolo *sm* pasture.

Pasqua *sf* Easter.

pasquale *agg* Easter (dav s).

Pasquetta *sf* Easter Monday.

---

i PASQUETTA

In Italy, Easter still retains its religious significance. Holy Week culminates in a Mass celebrated by the Pope from the balcony of St Peter's, and on Easter Sunday families have a special lunch and exchange Easter eggs. In many regions Easter Monday, a national holiday, is called "Pasquetta". It is traditionally celebrated with a picnic in the country or by the sea.

---

passabile *agg* passable.

passaggio *sm* (transito) passage; *(varco)* thoroughfare; *(in macchina)* lift; *(cambiamento)* change; **essere di ~** to be passing through; **~ a livello** level crossing *(Br)*, grade crossing *(Am)*; **~ pedonale** pedestrian crossing.

passamontagna *sm inv* balaclava.

passante *smf* (persona) passerby ◆ *sm* (per cintura) loop.

passaporto *sm* passport.

passare *vi* to go by; *(da un'apertura)* to go through; *(fare una visita)* to call in; *(cessare)* to go away;

(proposta) to be passed ◆ *vt (attraversare)* to cross; *(trascorrere)* to spend; *(cera, vernice)* to apply; *(esame)* to pass; *(oltrepassare)* to go beyond; *(verdure)* to puree; *(porgere)* to pass; **~ la mano è passato di mente!** it slipped my mind!; **ti passo Matteo** *(al telefono)* here's Matteo; **il treno passa da Firenze** the train goes via Florence; **~ l'aspirapolvere** to vacuum; **~ qc a qn** to pass o to give sb sthg; **~ avanti a qn** to push in front of sb; **~ da** o **per scemo** to be taken for a fool; **~ sopra qc** *(fig: tollerare)* to overlook; **passarsela bene** to get on well; **come te la passi?** how are you getting on?

passatempo *sm* pastime.

passato, -a *agg (trascorso)* over ◆ *sm* past; **~ di verdure** thin vegetable soup.

passaverdura *sm inv* vegetable mill.

passeggero, -a *agg* passing ◆ *sm, f* passenger.

passeggiare *vi* to walk.

passeggiata *sf (camminata)* walk; *(strada)* promenade; **fare una ~** to take a walk.

ℹ️ **PASSEGGIATA**

The Italian custom of taking a stroll with friends or family has survived many changes in fashion and still brings different generations together. Courting couples, families and teenagers alike meet up on Sunday morning or in the late afternoon and stroll slowly round the main square or the park, or along the main street or the promenade. They may stop to say hello to friends and acquaintances, to have an aperitif or to buy cakes and pastries for dessert.

passeggino *sm* pushchair.

passeggio *sm*: **andare a ~** to go for a walk.

passerella *sf (passaggio)* footbridge; *(di aereo, nave)* gangway; *(di sfilata)* catwalk.

passerotto *sm* sparrow.

passione *sf* passion.

passivo, -a *agg* passive ◆ *sm (GRAMM)* passive; *(COMM)* liabilities *(pl)*.

passo *sm (movimento)* step; *(andatura)* pace; *(rumore)* footstep; *(valico)* pass; **allungare il ~** to quicken one's pace; **fare il primo ~** *(fig)* to make the first move; **a ~ d'uomo** dead slow; **'~ carraio** o **carrabile** 'keep clear'; **fare due** o **quattro passi** to go for a short walk; **a due passi** a stone's throw away; **di questo ~** at this rate.

pasta *sf* pasta; *(impasto)* dough; *(pasticcino)* pastry; *(di colla)* paste; **~ in brodo** soup with pasta in it; **~ frolla** shortcrust pastry; **~ sfoglia** puff pastry.

ℹ️ **PASTA**

Most Italians eat pasta at least once a day, and an infinite variety of types can be found: "spaghetti", "bucatini" and "tagliatelle" are just a few examples of "pasta lunga" (long pasta), "penne", "rigatoni" and "fusilli" are common types of "pasta corta" (short pasta). The basic dough is just flour and water, but it can be varied by using a different type of flour and by adding different ingredients and flavourings. "Pasta integrale" is wholemeal pasta, "pasta all'uovo" is enriched with egg, and "pasta verde" is flavoured with spinach. The tradition of making one's own pasta ("pasta fatta in casa") still survives in many families.

pastasciutta *sf* pasta.

pastella *sf* batter.

pasticca, -che = pastiglia.

pasticceria *sf* = cake shop.

pasticcino *sm* pastry.

pasticcio *sm* (*vivanda*) pie; (*disordine*) mess; (*guaio*) trouble; **essere nei pasticci** to be in trouble.

pasticcione, -a *sm, f* bungler.

pastiera *sf* Neapolitan Easter tart with a filling of ricotta cheese and candied fruit.

pastiglia *sf* pastille.

pastizzada *sf* horse meat or beef and vegetables marinated in wine, generally served with polenta (a speciality of Veneto).

pasto *sm* meal.

pastore *sm* (*di greggi*) shepherd; (*sacerdote*) minister; ~ **tedesco** German shepherd, Alsatian (*Br*).

pastorizzato, -a *agg* pasteurized.

patata *sf* potato; **patate fritte** chips (*Br*), French fries (*Am*).

patatine *sfpl* crisps (*Br*), chips (*Am*).

pâté *sm inv* pâté.

patente *sf* licence; ~ (**di guida**) driving licence (*Br*), driver's license (*Am*).

paternità *sf* paternity.

paterno, -a *agg* paternal.

patetico, -a, -ci, -che *agg* pathetic.

patire *vt & vi* to suffer.

patria *sf* homeland.

patrigno *sm* stepfather.

patrimonio *sm* (*beni*) property; (*culturale, spirituale*) heritage.

patrono *sm* patron saint.

pattinaggio *sm* skating; ~ **su ghiaccio** ice skating.

pattinare *vi* to skate; ~ **su ghiaccio** to ice-skate.

pattini *smpl*: ~ **a rotelle** roller skates; ~ **da ghiaccio** ice skates.

pattino *sm* pedalo with oars.

patto *sm* (*accordo*) pact; **a** ~ **che** on condition that.

pattuglia *sf* patrol.

pattumiera *sf* dustbin.

paura *sf* fear; **avere** ~ (**di**) to be afraid (of); **avere** ~ **di fare qc** to be afraid of doing sthg; **fare** ~ **a qn** to frighten sb; **per** ~ **di fare qc** for fear of doing sthg; **per** ~ **che** for fear that.

pauroso, -a *agg* (*spaventoso*) frightening; (*timoroso*) fearful.

pausa *sf* (*intervallo*) break; (*MUS*) pause; **fare una** ~ to take a break.

pavimento *sm* floor.

pavone *sm* peacock.

paziente *agg & smf* patient.

pazienza *sf* patience; **perdere la** ~ to lose one's patience; ~! never mind!

pazzamente *avv* madly.

pazzesco, -a, -schi, -sche *agg* crazy.

pazzia *sf* madness; *(azione)* crazy thing.

pazzo, -a *agg (malato)* mad ◆ *sm, f* madman (f madwoman); **andare ~ per qc** to be crazy about sthg; **essere ~ di qn** to be crazy about sb; **darsi alla pazza gioia** to live it up.

peccare *vi* to sin; **~ di qc** to be guilty of sthg.

peccato *sm* sin; **è un ~ che …** it's a pity that …; **(che) ~!** what a pity!

peccatore, -trice *sm, f* sinner.

pecora *sf* sheep.

pecorino *sm* a cheese made from ewe's milk.

pedaggio *sm* toll.

pedalare *vi* to pedal.

pedale *sm* pedal; **a pedali** pedal *(dav s)*.

pedana *sf (poggiapiedi)* footboard; *(in atletica)* springboard; *(nella scherma)* piste.

pedata *sf (impronta)* footmark; *(calcio)* kick.

pediatra, -i, -e *smf* pediatrician.

pedicure *sm* pedicure.

pedina *sf* piece.

pedonale *agg* pedestrian *(dav s)*.

pedone *sm* pedestrian; *(negli scacchi)* pawn.

peggio *avv & agg inv* worse ◆ *smf:* **il/la ~** the worst; **~ per te!** so

---

much the worse for you!; **temere il ~** to fear the worst; **alla ~** if the worst comes to the worst; **~ che mai** worse than ever.

peggioramento *sm* deterioration.

peggiorare *vt & vi* to worsen.

peggiore *agg (comparativo)* worst ◆ *smf:* **il/la ~** the worst.

pelare *vt* to peel.

pelato, -a *agg* bald ❑ **pelati** *smpl* peeled tomatoes.

pelle *sf* skin; *(conciata)* leather; **avere la ~ d'oca** to have goose pimples.

pellegrinaggio *sm* pilgrimage.

pelletteria *sf (prodotti)* leather goods *(pl)*; *(negozio)* leather goods shop.

pelliccia, -ce *sf (di animale)* fur; *(indumento)* fur coat.

pellicola *sf* film; **~ a colori** colour film.

pelo *sm (del corpo, di tessuto)* hair; *(di animale)* fur; **ce l'ho fatta per un ~** I made it by the skin of my teeth; **c'è mancato un ~ che lo investissero** they narrowly missed hitting him.

peloso, -a *agg* hairy.

peltro *sm* pewter.

peluche [pe'luʃ] *sm inv (tessuto)* plush; *(pupazzo)* cuddly toy.

pena *sf (condanna)* sentence; *(cruccio)* anxiety; *(pietà)* pity; *(RELIG)* torment; **mi fanno ~** I feel sorry for them; **(non) vale la ~ di andarci** it's (not) worth going; **~ di morte** death penalty; **a mala ~** hardly.

penalità *sf inv* penalty.

pendente *agg (appeso)* hanging; *(conto)* pending ◆ *sm (ciondolo)* pendant; *(orecchino)* drop earring.

pendenza *sf (inclinazione)* slope; *(di conto)* outstanding account.

pendere *vi (essere appeso)* to hang; *(essere inclinato)* to slope.

pendici *sfpl* slopes.

pendio *sm* slope.

pendola *sf* pendulum clock.

pendolare *smf* commuter.

pene *sm* penis.

penetrare *vi:* ~ **in qc** *(entrare in)* to enter sthg; *(sog: chiodo, liquido)* to penetrate sthg.

penicillina *sf* penicillin.

penisola *sf* peninsula.

penitenza *sf (religiosa)* penitence; *(nei giochi)* forfeit.

penitenziario *sm* prison.

penna *sf* pen; *(di uccello)* feather; ~ **a sfera** ballpoint pen; ~ **stilografica** fountain pen; ❑ **penne** *sfpl* pasta quills; **penne all'arrabbiata** 'penne' in a spicy sauce of tomatoes and chillies.

pennarello *sm* felt-tip pen.

pennello *sm (da pittore)* brush; *(per vernici, tinte)* paintbrush; ~ **da barba** shaving brush; **a** ~ **like a** glove.

penombra *sf* half-light.

penoso, -a *agg* painful.

pensare *vi* to think ◆ *vt (immaginare)* to think; *(escogitare)* to think up; **cosa ne pensi?** what do you think (of it)?; ~ **a** *(riflettere su, ricordare)* to think about; *(occuparsi di)* to see to; **pensa a un numero**

think of a number; ~ **di fare qc** to be thinking of doing sthg; **penso di no** I don't think so; **penso di sì** I think so; **pensarci su** to think it over.

pensiero *sm* thought; *(preoccupazione)* worry; **stare in** ~ **per qn** to be worried about sb.

pensile *agg* hanging ◆ *sm* wall cupboard.

pensilina *sf (di stazione)* platform roof; *(per autobus)* bus shelter.

pensionante *smf* lodger.

pensionato, -a *sm, f (persona)* pensioner ◆ *sm (per studenti)* hostel.

pensione *sf (somma)* pension; *(albergo)* boardinghouse; *(vitto e alloggio)* board and lodging; **andare in** ~ to retire; **essere in** ~ to be retired; ~ **completa** full board; **mezza** ~ half board.

Pentecoste *sf* Whitsun.

pentirsi *vr:* ~ **di qc** to regret sthg; ~ **di aver fatto qc** to regret doing sthg.

pentola *sf* pot; ~ **a pressione** pressure cooker.

penultimo, -a *agg* penultimate.

pepare *vt* to pepper.

pepato, -a *agg* peppery.

pepe *sm* pepper.

peperonata *sf* stewed sliced peppers, tomatoes and onions.

peperoncino *sm* chilli pepper; ~ **rosso** red chilli pepper.

peperone *sm (capsicum)* pepper.

per *prep* 1. *(indica lo scopo, la desti-*

nazione) for; **è ~ te** it's for you; **fare qc ~ i soldi** to do sthg for money; **equipaggiarsi ~ la montagna** to kit o.s. out for the mountains; **fare qc** (in order) to do sthg; **sono venuto ~ vederti** I've come to see you; **è abbastanza grande ~ capire certe cose** he's old enough to understand these things.

2. (*attraverso*) through; **ti ho cercato ~ tutta la città** I've been looking for you all over town.

3. (*moto a luogo*) for, to; **il treno ~ Genova** the Genoa train; **partire ~ Napoli** to leave for Naples.

4. (*indica una durata, una scadenza*) for; **~ tutta la vita** for one's whole life; **sarò di ritorno ~ le cinque** I'll be back by five; **l'ho vista ~ Pasqua** I saw her at Easter; **fare qc ~ tempo** to do sthg in time; **~ sempre** forever.

5. (*indica il mezzo, il modo*) by; **gli ho parlato ~ telefono** I talked to him over the phone; **viaggiare ~ mare** to travel by sea; **fare qc ~ scherzo** to do sthg for a joke; **~ caso** by chance.

6. (*indica la causa*) for; **piangere ~ la rabbia** to cry with rage; **viaggiare ~ lavoro** to travel on business; **~ aver fatto qc** for doing sthg.

7. (*con valore distributivo*) per; **entrare uno ~ volta** to go in one at a time; **uno ~ uno** one by one.

8. (*come*) as; **tenere qc ~ certo** to take sthg for granted.

9. (*indica il prezzo*): **lo ha venduto ~ un milione** he sold it for a million lira.

10. (MAT): **2 ~ 3 fa 6** 2 times 3 makes 6.

11. (*indica la conseguenza*): **è troppo bello ~ essere vero** it's too good to be true.

12. (*indica limitazione*) for; **~ me, vi sbagliate** as far as I'm concerned, you are wrong; **~ questa volta** this time.

pera *sf* pear.

peraltro *avv* what is more.

perbene *agg inv* decent ◆ *avv* properly.

percentuale *sf* percentage.

percepire *vt* (*sentire*) to perceive; (*ricevere*) to receive.

perché *avv* why; **~ corri?** why are you running?; **~ non ci andiamo?** why don't we go?; **spiegami ~ lo hai fatto** tell me why you did it; **~ no?** why not?; **chissà ~** who knows why; **ecco ~** that's why.

◆ *cong* **1.** (*per il fatto che*) because; **vado ~ ho fretta** I'm going because I'm in a hurry; **~ sì/no!** (just) because!

2. (*affinché*) so that; **telefona ~ non stiano in pensiero** phone so that (they) don't worry.

3. (*cosicché*): **è troppo complicato ~ si possa capire** it's too complicated for anyone to understand.

◆ *sm inv* (*ragione*) reason; **senza un ~** for no reason.

perciò *cong* therefore.

percorrere *vt* (*regione*) to travel over; (*distanza*) to cover.

percorso, -a *pp* → **percorrere** ◆ *sm* journey.

percosse *sfpl* blows.

percosso, -a *pp* → **percuotere**.

percuotere *vt (form)* to beat.

perdere *vt* to lose; *(treno, lezione, film)* to miss; *(tempo, denaro)* to waste; *(liquido, gas)* to leak; **~ sangue** to lose blood; **lasciare ~** not to bother; **non avere nulla da ~** to have nothing to lose; **~ la testa** to lose one's head ❑ **perdersi** *vr* to get lost.

perdita *sf* loss; *(di acqua, gas)* leak; **una ~ di tempo** a waste of time; **a ~ d'occhio** as far as the eye can see.

perdonare *vt* to forgive.

perdono *sm (di colpa, peccato)* pardon; *(scusa)* forgiveness.

perdutamente *avv* desperately.

perfettamente *avv* perfectly.

perfetto, -a *agg* perfect.

perfezionare *vt* to perfect.

perfezione *sf* perfection; **alla ~** perfectly.

perfido, -a *agg* treacherous.

perfino *avv* even.

perforare *vt* to pierce.

pergola *sf* pergola.

pericolante *agg* unsafe.

pericolo *sm* danger; **essere fuori ~** to be out of danger; **essere in ~** to be in danger; **'~ (di morte)'** 'danger of death'.

pericoloso, -a *agg* dangerous.

periferia *sf* outskirts *(pl)*.

perimetro *sm* perimeter.

periodico, -a, -ci, -che *agg* periodic ♦ *sm* periodical.

periodo *sm* period.

perito *sm (esperto)* expert; **~ chimico** qualified chemist.

perla *sf* pearl.

perlustrare *vt* to patrol.

permaloso, -a *agg* touchy.

permanente *agg* permanent ♦ *sf* perm; **'permanente'** 'at all times'.

permanenza *sf* continued stay.

permesso, -a *pp →* **permettere** ♦ *sm (autorizzazione)* permission; *(congedo)* leave; *(documento)* permit; **(è) ~?** *(per entrare)* may I come in?; **~!** *(per passare)* excuse me!; **~ di soggiorno** residence permit.

permettere *vt* to allow; **~ a qn di fare qc** to allow sb to do sthg; **potersi ~ qc** *(spesa, acquisto)* to be able to afford sthg; **permettersi di fare qc** *(prendersi la libertà)* to take the liberty of doing sthg; **potersi ~ di fare qc** *(finanziariamente)* to be able to afford to do sthg.

perno *sm* hinge.

pernottamento *sm* overnight stay.

però *cong (ma)* but; *(tuttavia)* however.

perpendicolare *agg* perpendicular.

perplesso, -a *agg* puzzled.

perquisire *vt* to search.

perquisizione *sf* search.

perseguitare *vt* to persecute.

perseverare *vi* to persevere.

persiana *sf* shutter.

persiano, -a *agg* Persian ♦ *sm (pelliccia)* Persian lamb.

persino = **perfino**.

persistente *agg* persistent.

petrolio

perso, -a pp → perdere.

persona sf person; **c'è una ~ che ti aspetta** there's somebody waiting for you; **conoscere qn di ~** to know sb personally; **in ~** in person.

personaggio sm (di libro, film) character; (pubblico, politico) figure.

personale agg personal ♦ sm (dipendenti) personnel, staff; (fisico) build.

personalità sf inv personality.

personalmente avv personally.

persuadere vt to persuade; **~ qn a fare qc** to persuade sb to do sthg; **~ qn di qc** to convince sb of sthg.

persuaso, -a pp → persuadere.

pertanto cong (perciò) therefore.

perturbare vt to upset.

perturbazione sf disturbance.

Perugia sf Perugia.

pesante agg heavy; (fig: persona, film) boring; (scherzo) in bad taste.

pesare vt to weigh ♦ vi to weigh; (essere pesante) to be heavy; (essere spiacevole) to be hard ❑ **pesarsi** vr to weigh o.s.

pesca, -sche sf (frutto) peach; (attività) fishing; **pesche ripiene** peaches stuffed with macaroons and baked in white wine; **andare a ~** to go fishing; **~ di beneficenza** lucky dip; **~ subacquea** underwater fishing.

pescare vt (pesce) to catch; (carta) to draw; (trovare) to find out; **mi piace ~** I like fishing.

pescatore sm fisherman.

pesce sm fish; **~ d'aprile!** April Fool! ❑ **Pesci** smpl Pisces (sg).

ℹ️ PESCE D'APRILE

April 1 is the occasion for tricks and practical jokes in Italy, as it is in Britain, but in Italy it is named after the paper fish which children secretly attach to the backs of their friends and of passers-by. Recently, newspapers have joined in the fun by publishing fake news stories to catch out the unwary.

pescheria sf fishmonger's.

pescivendolo, -a sm, f fishmonger.

peso sm weight; **lancio del ~** shotput; **~ lordo** gross weight; **~ netto** net weight; **essere di ~ a qn** to be a burden on sb.

pessimismo sm pessimism.

pessimista, -i, -e smf pessimist.

pessimo, -a agg dreadful.

pestare vt (calpestare) to tread on; (uva, aglio) to crush; (picchiare) to beat up.

pesto, -a agg: **buio ~** pitch-black; **occhio ~** black eye ♦ sm: **~ (alla genovese)** pesto (sauce made from basil, pine kernels, garlic, olive oil and cheese; a speciality of Genoa).

petalo sm petal.

petardo sm firecracker.

petroliera sf oil tanker.

petrolio sm oil.

pettegolezzi *smpl* gossip *(sg)*.

pettinare *vt* to comb ❑ **pettinarsi** *vr* to comb one's hair.

pettine *sm* comb.

petto *sm* (*torace*) chest; (*seno*) breast; ~ **di pollo** chicken breast; **a doppio** ~ double-breasted.

pezzo *sm* piece; (*di spazio, tempo*) bit; **è un bel** ~ **che ti cerco** I've been looking for you for quite a while; **andare in (mille) pezzi** to be smashed (to smithereens); **cadere a pezzi** to fall to pieces; ~ **di ricambio** spare part; ~ **grosso** (*fig*) big shot.

piacere *sm* pleasure; (*favore*) favour ◆ *vi*: **mi piace** I like it; **mi piacciono i tulipani** I like tulips; **mi ha fatto molto** ~ **vederla** I was delighted to see her; **per** ~ please; ~ **(di conoscerla)!** pleased to meet you!; ~ **mio!** the pleasure is mine!

piacevole *agg* pleasant.

piaga, -ghe *sf* (*lesione*) sore; (*fig*: *flagello*) plague.

pianerottolo *sm* landing.

pianeta, -i *sm* planet.

piangere *vi* to cry, to weep.

pianista, -i, -e *smf* pianist.

piano, -a *agg* (*piatto*) flat; (*MAT*) plane ◆ *avv* (*lentamente*) slowly; (*a bassa voce*) softly ◆ *sm* (*di edificio*) floor, storey; (*GEOG & MAT*) plane; (*livello*) level; (*programma, disegno*) plan; (*pianoforte*) piano; **andarci** ~ to act with caution; **piano piano** (*poco a poco*) little by little; (*lentamente*) very slowly; **abitano al primo** ~ they live on the first floor (*Br*), they live on the second floor (*Am*); **il** ~ **di sopra/di sotto** the floor above/below; **in primo** ~ in the foreground.

piano-bar *sm inv* bar with music provided by pianist.

pianoforte *sm* piano.

pianoterra = **pianterreno**

pianta *sf* plant; (*di piede*) sole; (*di città*) map; (*di casa*) plan; ~ **grassa** succulent.

piantare *vt* (*semi*) to plant; (*conficcare*) to knock in; (*fam*: *abbandonare*) to leave; **piantala!** stop it!

pianterreno *sm* ground floor (*Br*), first floor (*Am*); **al** ~ on the ground floor (*Br*), on the first floor (*Am*).

pianto *pp* → **piangere** ◆ *sm* crying, weeping.

pianura *sf* plain; **la** ~ **padana** the Paduan Plain.

piastrella *sf* tile.

piattaforma *sf* (*superficie piana*) platform; (*galleggiante*) rig.

piattino *sm* saucer.

piatto, -a *agg* (*piano*) flat; (*monotono*) dreary ◆ *sm* (*recipiente*) plate, dish; (*vivanda*) dish; (*portata*) course; ~ **freddo** cold dish; ~ **del giorno** today's special; ~ **tipico** typical dish; **primo** ~ first course; **secondo** ~ second course; **lavare i piatti** to wash the dishes; **piatti pronti** ready meals.

piazza *sf* square; **fare** ~ **pulita di** to make a clean sweep of.

piazzale *sm* large square.

piazzare *vt* (*collocare*) to place; (*vendere*) to sell ❑ **piazzarsi** *vr* (*in gara*) to be placed.

piccante *agg* spicy.

picchetto sm (di tenda) peg; (di scioperanti, soldati) picket.

picchiare vt (dar botte) to beat (up); (testa, pugni) to bang ♦ vi (alla porta, sul tavolo) to thump; (sole) to beat down; ~ **contro il muro** (urtare) to hit the wall □ **picchiarsi** vr to fight.

piccino, -a agg small.

piccione sm pigeon.

picco, -chi sm (vetta) peak; **a ~** vertically; **colare a ~** to sink.

piccolo, -a agg small; (breve) short; (di poco conto) slight.

piccozza sf ice-axe.

picnic [pik'nik] sm inv picnic.

pidocchio sm louse.

piede sm foot; (di mobile) leg; **andare a piedi** to go on foot; **essere a piedi** to be on foot; **in piedi** standing; **prendere ~** to gain ground.

piedistallo sm pedestal.

piega, -ghe sf fold; (di gonna) pleat; (di pantaloni, grinza) crease; **prendere una brutta ~** to take a turn for the worse.

piegare vt to bend; (foglio, tovaglia) to fold; (letto, sedia) to fold up □ **piegarsi** vr (curvarsi) to bend; (letto, sedia) to fold up; **piegarsi a** vr + prep to give in to.

pieghevole agg (flessibile) pliable; (sedia, tavolo) folding.

Piemonte sm: **il ~** Piedmont.

piena sf flood.

pieno, -a agg full ♦ sm (di carburante) full tank; (culmine) peak; **~ di** full of; **~ di sé** full of oneself; **a stomaco ~** on a full stomach; **in ~ inverno** in the middle of winter; **il**

~, per favore fill her up, please.

pietà sf (compassione) pity; **avere ~ di qn** to take pity on sb; **come attore fa ~** as an actor he's useless.

pietanza sf dish, course.

pietoso, -a agg (che sente pietà) compassionate; (che ispira pietà) pitiful.

pietra sf stone; **~ dura** semi-precious stone; **~ preziosa** precious stone.

pigiama, -i sm pyjamas (pl).

pigiare vt to press.

pigliare vt (prendere) to take; (afferrare) to grab.

pigna sf pine cone.

pignolo, -a agg fussy, meticulous.

pignorare vt (DIR) to distrain.

pigrizia sf laziness.

pigro, -a agg lazy.

pila sf (cumulo) pile; (batteria) battery.

pilastro sm pillar.

pillola sf pill.

pilone sm pylon; (di ponte) pier.

pilota, -i, -e sm/f (di aereo, nave) pilot; (di auto) driver.

pinacoteca, -che sf art gallery.

pineta sf pinewood.

ping-pong sm table tennis.

pinguino sm (animale) penguin; (gelato) chocolate-coated ice cream on a stick.

pinna sf (di pesce) fin; (per nuotare) flipper.

pino sm (albero) pine tree; (legno) pine.

pinoccate *sfpl:* ~ **alla perugina** *almond and pine kernel sweets.*

pinolo *sm* pine kernel.

pinzare *vt (con graffette)* to staple; *(sog: granchio)* to nip.

pinze *sfpl (utensile)* pliers.

pinzette *sfpl* tweezers.

pinzimonio *sm* dip of seasoned oil.

pioggia, -ge *sf* rain.

piolo *sm* rung.

piombare *vi (giungere)* to arrive unexpectedly; *(fig: nella disperazione)* to plunge; *(gettarsi)* ~ **su** to fall upon.

piombino *sm (per pacchi)* lead seal; *(da pesca)* sinker.

piombo *sm* lead; **senza** ~ unleaded.

piovere *v impers* to rain ◆ *vi (pietre, proiettili, insulti)* to rain down; *(proteste)* to pour in; **piove** it's raining.

piovigginare *v impers* to drizzle.

piovoso, -a *agg* rainy.

pipa *sf* pipe.

pipì *sf (fam):* **fare (la)** ~ to have a wee.

pipistrello *sm* bat.

pirata, -i *agg & sm* pirate; ~ **della strada** road hog.

Pirenei *smpl:* **i** ~ the Pyrenees.

pirofila *sf* Pyrex® dish.

piromane *smf* pyromaniac.

piroscafo *sm* steamer.

Pisa *sf* Pisa.

pisarei *smpl:* ~ **e fasò** piacentini *'gnocchi' in a sauce of beans, tomatoes and other vegetables.*

pisciare *vi (volg)* to piss.

piscina *sf* swimming pool.

pisello *sm* pea.

pisolino *sm:* **fare un** ~ to take a nap.

pista *sf (traccia)* trail; *(per corse)* track; *(da sci)* run; *(di aeroporto)* runway; ~ **da ballo** dance floor; ~ **ciclabile** cycle lane.

pistacchio *sm* pistachio.

pistola *sf* pistol, gun.

pitta *sf tart made with a yeasted dough and filled with tomatoes, anchovies, tuna and capers or ricotta cheese and boiled eggs.*

pittore, -trice *sm, f* painter.

pittoresco, -a, -schi, -sche *agg* picturesque.

pittura *sf* painting; '~ **fresca**' 'wet paint'.

pitturare *vt* to paint.

più *avv* 1. *(in comparativi):* ~ **(di)** more *(than);* **ho fatto** ~ **tardi del solito** I was later than usual; ~ **triste che mai** sadder than ever; **poco** ~ **di** just over; **di** ~ *(in maggior quantità)* more; **l'ho pagato di** ~ I paid more for it. 2. *(in superlativi):* **la** ~ **bella città** the most beautiful city; **la collina** ~ **alta** the highest hill; **il** ~ **grande** the biggest; ~ **velocemente possibile** as quickly as possible. 3. *(oltre)* any more; **non parlo** ~ I'm not saying any more; **mai** ~ never again. 4. *(in espressioni):* ~ **o meno** more or less; **per di** ~ what's more; **tre di** ○ **in** ~ three more; ~ **ci pensi, peggio è** the more you think about it, the worse it seems.

♦ *prep* **1.** *(con l'aggiunta di)* plus; **siamo in sei ~ gli ospiti** there are six of us plus guests.

2. *(MAT)*: **3 ~ 3 fa 6** 3 plus 3 makes 6.

♦ *agg inv* **1.** *(in quantità, numero maggiore)* more; **ho ~ lavoro del solito** I've got more work than usual; **ho fatto ~ punti di te** I got more points than you; **~ siamo, meglio è** the more of us there are, the better.

2. *(diversi)* several; **l'ho ripetuto ~ volte** I repeated it several times.

♦ *sm inv* **1.** *(la maggior parte)* most; **il ~ delle volte** more often than not; **parlare del ~ e del meno** to talk about this and that.

2. *(la maggioranza)*: **i ~ the** majority.

piuma *sf* feather.

piumino *sm (trapunta)* duvet; *(giaccone)* quilted jacket.

piumone® *sm (trapunta)* duvet.

piuttosto *avv* rather; **~ che** rather than.

pizza *sf* pizza; **~ capricciosa** pizza with cheese, tomato, artichokes and capers; **~ margherita** pizza with cheese and tomato; **~ napoletana** pizza with cheese, tomato, anchovies and capers; **~ quattro stagioni** pizza with a different topping on each quarter.

ⓘ PIZZA

Originally from Naples, pizza is now internationally popular. In Italy it can be bought at the bar or the baker's, either *al taglio* (cut into rectangles) or as *pizzette* (small pizzas), as well as at pizze-rias, which Italians generally go to in the evening. Besides the traditional "margherita" (just cheese and toma-to) and "napoletana" (cheese, toma-to, anchovies and capers), many other varieties can be found. Pizzas with a mixture of vegetables, with mushrooms, with cold meats, and with different cheeses are particularly popular.

---

pizzaiola *sf*: **alla ~** in a tomato, garlic and oregano sauce.

pizzeria *sf* pizzeria, pizza restaurant.

pizzetta *sf* small pizza eaten as a snack.

pizzicagnolo, -a *sm, f* delicatessen owner.

pizzicare *vt (con le dita)* to pinch; *(pungere)* to sting ♦ *vi (prudere)* to itch; *(cibo)* to be spicy.

pizzicheria *sf* delicatessen.

pizzico, -chi *sm* dash; **un ~ di sale** a pinch of salt.

pizzicotto *sm* pinch.

pizzo *sm (merletto)* lace; *(barba)* goatee.

placare *vt (ira)* to pacify; *(fame, sete)* to satisfy □ **placarsi** *vr (vento)* to die down; *(mare)* to become calmer.

placca, -che *sf (targa)* plate; *(dentaria)* plaque.

placcare *vt (rivestire)* to plate; **placcato d'oro** gold-plated.

plagiare *vt (libro, canzone)* to plagiarize; *(persona)* to coerce.

plagio *sm (imitazione)* plagiarism; *(di persona)* coercion.

plancia, -ce *sf* bridge.

planetario, -a *agg* planetary
♦ *sm* planetarium.

plasmare *vt* to mould.

plastica, -che *sf (sostanza)*
plastic; *(MED)* plastic surgery.

plastico, -a, -ci, -che *agg*
plastic ♦ *sm (modello)* model;
(esplosivo) plastic explosive.

plastilina® *sf* Plasticine®.

platano *sm* plane tree.

platea *sf (settore)* stalls *(pl)*; *(pubblico)* audience.

plausibile *agg* plausible.

plico, -chi *sm* parcel.

plurale *agg & sm* plural.

pneumatico, -ci *sm* tyre.

po' = **poco**.

Po *sm*: **il ~** the Po.

poco, -a, -chi, -che *agg* 1. *(in piccola quantità)* little, not much; **ha poca fantasia** he doesn't have much imagination; **a ~ prezzo** cheap.
2. *(in piccolo numero)*: **pochi** few, not many; **in poche parole** in few words.
♦ *sm* little.
♦ *pron* 1. *(una piccola quantità)* (a) little; *(un piccolo numero)* few, not many; **pochi** *(non molta gente)* few (people); **pochi di noi** few of us.
2. *(in espressioni)*: **aver ~ da fare** to have little to do; **ci vuole ~ a capire che ...** it doesn't take much to understand that ...; **siamo tornati da ~** we've just got back; **è una cosa da ~** it's nothing; **per ~** nearly; **tra ~** soon, shortly; **(a) ~ a ~** poco little by little.
♦ *avv* 1. *(con verbo)* little, not

much; **mangia ~** he doesn't eat much.
2. *(con aggettivo, avverbio)* not very;
~ lontano da qui not very far from here; **è ~ simpatica** she's not very nice; **sta poco bene** he's not very well.
3. *(indica tempo)*: **durare ~** not to last long; **~ dopo/prima** shortly afterwards/before ❑ **un po'** *avv* a bit, a little; **restiamo ancora un po'** we'll stay a bit longer; **un po' di** a bit of, a little; **compra un po' di pane** buy some bread.

podere *sm* farm.

poderoso, -a *agg* powerful.

podio *sm* podium.

poesia *sf (ARTE)* poetry; *(componimento)* poem.

poeta, -essa, -i, -esse *sm, f* poet.

poetico, -a, -ci, -che *agg* poetic.

poggiare *vt* to rest ♦ *vi*: **~ su qc** to rest on sthg.

poggiatesta *sm inv* headrest.

poi *avv* then; *(dopo)* later.

poiché *cong* as, since.

polare *agg* polar.

Polaroid® *sf inv* Polaroid®.

polemica, -che *sf* controversy.

polemico, -a, -ci, -che *agg* *(persona, tono)* argumentative; *(discorso)* controversial.

polenta *sf* polenta *(type of savoury porridge made with maize flour)*; **~ concia valdostana** 'polenta' cooked with soft cheeses and served with Parmesan cheese; **~ e osei** 'polenta' served with small birds wrapped in pork loin and flavoured

Pompei

with sage *(a speciality of Lombardy)*; ~ **pasticciata alla veneta** *'polenta' baked in a meat, tomato and sausage sauce.*

poliambulatorio *sm* = health centre.

poliestere *sm* polyester.

polistirolo *sm* polystyrene.

politica, -che *sf (scienza)* politics *(sg); (linea di condotta)* policy,→ **politico.**

politico, -a, -ci, -che *agg* political ♦ *sm, f* politician.

polizia *sf* police; ~ **stradale** traffic police.

poliziesco, -a, -schi, -sche *agg* police *(dav s); (romanzo, film)* detective *(dav s).*

poliziotto, -a *sm, f* policeman *(f policewoman).*

polizza *sf* policy; ~ **di assicurazione** insurance policy.

pollaio *sm* hen house.

pollame *sm* poultry.

pollice *sm* thumb; *(unità di misura)* inch.

polline *sm* pollen.

pollo *sm* chicken; ~ **arrosto** roast chicken; ~ **alla cacciatora** chicken in a sauce of mushrooms, tomatoes, olives, herbs and wine; ~ **alla diavola** chicken cut open and flattened out, marinated in lemon juice.

polmone *sm* lung.

polmonite *sf* pneumonia.

polo *sm* pole ♦ *sf inv* polo shirt; ~ **Nord/Sud** the North/South Pole.

Polonia *sf:* **la** ~ Poland.

polpaccio *sm* calf.

polpastrello *sm* fingertip.

polpetta *sf* meatball.

polpettone *sm* meat loaf.

polpo *sm* octopus.

polsino *sm* cuff.

polso *sm* wrist; *(MED)* pulse.

poltiglia *sf* paste.

poltrona *sf* armchair; *(di teatro)* seat in the stalls.

poltrone, -a *sm, f* lazy person.

polvere *sf* dust; **latte in** ~ powdered milk; **sapone in** ~ soap powder.

polveroso, -a *agg* dusty.

pomata *sf* ointment.

pomeridiano, -a *agg* afternoon *(dav s).*

pomeriggio *sm* afternoon; **di** ~ in the afternoon.

pomice *sf* pumice.

pomo *sm* knob; ~ **d'Adamo** Adam's apple.

pomodoro *sm* tomato; **pomodori ripieni** *tomatoes stuffed with breadcrumbs, parsley, garlic and egg.*

pompa *sf* pump; *(sfarzo)* pomp; **pompe funebri** undertaker's *(sg).*

pompare *vt* to pump.

Pompei *n* Pompei.

ℹ️ POMPEI

One of the world's most famous archaeological sites, the ancient town of Pompei, not far from Naples, was totally buried in 79 AD when Mount Vesuvius erupted. Today it is open to the public, and offers a unique insight into the ancient Roman way of life.

pompelmo sm grapefruit.

pompiere sm fireman.

pomposo, -a agg (sfarzoso) full of pomp; (ostentato) pompous.

ponderare vt & vi to ponder.

ponente sm west.

ponte sm bridge; (di nave) deck; (impalcatura) scaffolding; ~ **levatoio** drawbridge; **fare il ~** to have the day off between a national holiday and a weekend; **il Ponte Vecchio** the Ponte Vecchio.

---

i IL PONTE VECCHIO

One of Italy's most picturesque bridges, the Ponte Vecchio has come to be the symbol of Florence. Built in 1345 and so the oldest bridge in the city (hence its name), it stands at the narrowest point of the Arno and is connected to the Uffizi Gallery and the Pitti Palace by an arcade. The Ponte Vecchio is famous for the goldsmiths and silversmiths which line it on both sides.

---

pontefice sm pontiff.

pony sm inv pony; ~ **express** express courier service.

popcorn sm popcorn.

popolare agg popular; (popolano) working-class (dav s) ♦ vt to populate.

popolarità sf popularity.

popolazione sf population.

popolo sm people (pl).

popone sm melon.

poppa sf (NAUT) stern.

poppare vt to suck (from the breast).

porcellana sf porcelain.

porcellino sm (maialino) piglet; ~ **d'India** guinea pig.

porcino sm cep (edible brown mushroom with nutty flavour).

porco, -ci sm (animale) pig; (carne) pork.

porcospino sm porcupine.

porgere vt (tendere) to hold out; (dare) to give; **porgo distinti saluti** (in lettera) yours sincerely.

pornografico, -a, -ci, -che agg pornographic.

poro sm pore.

porpora agg inv crimson.

porre vt to put; (condizioni, limiti) to set; (riporre) to place; (supporre) **poniamo che ...** let us suppose that ...; ~ **una domanda** to ask a question; ~ **fine a qc** to put an end to sthg.

porro sm (verdura) leek; (MED) wart.

porta sf door; (di città) gate; (nel calcio) goal.

portabagagli sm inv (bagagliaio) boot (Br), trunk (Am); (sul tetto) roof rack.

portacenere sm inv ashtray.

portachiavi sm inv key ring.

portacipria sm inv compact.

portaerei sf inv aircraft carrier.

portafinestra (pl **portefinestre**) sf French window.

portafoglio sm (per denaro) wallet; (FIN & POL) portfolio.

portafortuna sm inv lucky charm.

portagioie sm inv jewel box.

portalettere = **postino**.

portamento *sm* bearing.

portamonete *sm inv* purse.

portapacchi *sm inv* luggage rack.

portare *vt* (*trasportare*) to carry; (*condurre, prendere*) to take; (*abiti, occhiali*) to wear; (*barba, capelli lunghi*) to have; (*fig: spingere*) to drive; ~ qc a qn (*consegnare*) to take sthg to sb; **portar via** to take; ~ **avanti** to carry on; ~ **fortuna** to bring luck.

portasapone *sm inv* soap dish.

portasigarette *sm inv* cigarette case.

portata *sf* (*piatto*) course; (*di veicolo*) capacity; (*di fiume*) flow; (*importanza*) importance; **essere a ~ di mano** to be within reach; **alla ~ di tutti** within everybody's grasp.

portatile *agg* portable; ~ **di handicap** disabled.

portatore, -trice *sm, f* (*di assegno*) bearer.

portatovagliolo *sm* napkin ring.

portauovo *sm inv* eggcup.

portico *sm* portico.

portiera *sf* door.

portiere *sm* a, f (*portinaio*) concierge, caretaker; (*di albergo*) porter; (*nel calcio*) goalkeeper.

portineria *sf* (*di palazzo*) caretaker's lodge; (*di albergo*) reception.

porto, -a *pp* → porgere ♦ *sm* port; ~ **d'armi** licence to carry firearms.

Portogallo *sm*: **il ~** Portugal.

portoghese *agg, sm & sf* Portuguese.

portone *sm* main entrance.

porzione *sf* portion; (*di cibo*) helping.

posa *sf* pose; **mettersi in ~** to pose.

posacenere *sm inv* ashtray.

posare *vt* to put down ♦ *vi* to pose ❑ **posarsi** *vr* (*uccello*) to perch.

posate *sfpl* cutlery (*sg*).

positivo, -a *agg* positive.

posizione *sf* position.

posologia *sf* dosage.

possedere *vt* (*cose*) to own, to possess; (*qualità*) to have, to possess.

possessivo, -a *agg* possessive.

possesso *sm* possession, ownership; **essere in ~ di qc** to be in possession of sthg.

possibile *agg* possible ♦ *sm*: **fare (tutto) il ~ (per fare qc)** to do everything possible (to do sthg); **ma non è ~!** it can't be true!; **il più presto ~** as soon as possible; **se ~** if possible; **il più ~** (*quantità*) as much as possible; (*numero*) as many as possible.

possibilità *sf inv* (*eventualità*) possibility; (*occasione*) chance; (*capacità*): **avere la ~ di fare qc** to be able to do sthg.

posta *sf* (*negozio*) post office; (*lettere, servizio*) post, mail; **per ~** by post ○ mail; ~ **aerea** air mail.

postale *agg* postal, post (*dav s*).

posteggiare *vt* to park.

posteggiatore, -trice *sm, f*

car park attendant (Br), parking lot attendant (Am).

posteggio sm car park (Br), parking lot (Am); **~ a pagamento** car park where drivers must pay to park.

poster sm inv poster.

posteriore agg (nello spazio) rear, back; (nel tempo) later.

posticipare vt to postpone.

postino, -a sm, f postman (f postwoman).

posto, -a pp → porre ♦ sm place; (spazio) room; (per persona) place, seat; (impiego) job; **mettere a ~** to tidy (up); **~ di blocco** roadblock; **~ letto** bed; **~ di polizia** police station; **al ~ di** in (the) place of.

potabile agg → acqua.

potare vt to prune.

potente agg powerful.

potere vi 1. (essere in grado di) can, to be able; **non ci posso andare** I can't go, I'm not able to go; **puoi farmi un favore?** can you do me a favour?; **non posso farci niente** I can't do anything about it. 2. (avere il permesso di) can, to be able; **non potete parcheggiare qui** you can't park here; **posso entrare?** can o may I come in? 3. (esprime eventualità): **può far freddo** it can get cold; **possono aver perso il treno** they might o could have missed the train; **potrei sbagliarmi** I could be wrong; **può darsi** perhaps; **può darsi che sia partito** he may o might have left. 4. (esprime suggerimento): **puoi provare** you can try.

5. (in espressioni): **non ne posso più!** (sono stufo) I can't take any more!; (sono stanco) I'm exhausted!; **a più non posso** (correre) really fast; (lavorare) really hard; **si può fare** it can be done.

♦ sm 1. (comando) power; **essere al ~** to be in power. 2. (facoltà) power, ability.

povero, -a agg poor ♦ sm, f poor man (f woman); **i poveri** the poor; **~ di qc** lacking in sthg.

pozza sf pool.

pozzanghera sf puddle.

pozzo sm well; **~ petrolifero** oil well.

pranzare vi to have lunch.

pranzo sm (di mezzogiorno) lunch; (banchetto) dinner.

prassi sf usual procedure.

pratica, -che sf practice; (esperienza) practical experience; (documenti) paperwork; **mettere in ~ qc** to put sthg into practice; **in ~** in practice.

praticamente avv (quasi) practically; (concretamente) in a practical way.

pratico, -a, -ci, -che agg practical.

prato sm (distesa d'erba) meadow; (di giardino) lawn.

preavviso sm notice.

precario, -a agg precarious.

precauzione sf precaution.

precedente agg preceding o previous ♦ sm precedent; **precedenti** unprecedented; **precedenti penali** criminal record (sg).

precedenza sf (in auto) right of way; (priorità) priority; **dare la ~**

(a) *(in auto)* to give way (to).

precedere *vt (nello spazio)* to be ahead of; *(nel tempo)* to precede.

precipitàre *vi (cadere)* to fall; *(fig: situazione)* to come to a head ♦ **precipitarsi** *vr* to rush.

precipitazione *sf (atmosferica)* precipitation; *(fretta)* haste.

precipizio *sm* precipice.

precisare *vt* to specify.

precisione *sf (esattezza)* precision; *(accuratezza)* accuracy.

preciso, -a *agg* precise; **sono le due precise** it's exactly two o'clock.

precoce *agg (bambino)* precocious; *(vecchiaia)* premature.

prèda *sf* prey; **essere in ~ a qc** to be prey to sthg.

predetto, -a *pp* → **predire**.

prèdica, -che *sf (RELIG)* sermon; *(fam: ramanzina)* telling-off.

predire *vt* to foretell.

predisporre *vt* to prepare; **~ qn/qc a qc** to predispose sb/sthg to sthg.

predisposizione *sf* tendency.

predominàre *vi* to predominate.

prefabbricato, -a *agg* prefabricated.

preferenza *sf* preference.

preferire *vt* to prefer; **~ qn/qc a qc** to prefer sb/sthg to.

preferito, -a *agg* favourite.

prefiggersi *vr:* **~ uno scopo** to set o.s. a goal.

prefisso, -a *pp* → **prefiggersi** ♦ *sm* code.

pregare *vi* to pray ♦ *vt (Dio)* to

pray to; **~ qn di fare qc** *(supplicare)* to beg sb to do sthg; *(chiedere a)* to ask sb to do sthg; **i passeggeri sono gentilmente pregati di non fumare** passengers are kindly requested not to smoke.

preghiera *sf* prayer.

pregiato, -a *agg* precious.

pregio *sm (qualità)* good quality; *(valore)* value.

pregiudicare *vt* to prejudice.

pregiudicato, -a *sm, f* previous offender.

pregiudizio *sm* prejudice.

prego *esclam (risposta a ringraziamento)* don't mention it!; *(invito a sedersi)* take a seat!; *(invito ad entrare prima)* after you!

preistorico, -a, -ci, -che *agg* prehistoric.

prelavaggio *sm* prewash.

prelevare *vt (soldi)* to withdraw; *(campione, sangue)* to take.

prelievo *sm (in banca)* withdrawal; *(MED)* sample.

preliminare *agg & sm* preliminary.

pre-mamàn *agg inv* maternity *(dav s)*.

prematuro, -a *agg* premature.

premere *vt* to press ♦ *vi:* **~ su** to press on ❑ **premere a** *v + prep:* **~ a qn** to matter to sb.

premiare *vt (dare un premio)* to give a prize to; *(merito, onestà)* to reward.

premiazione *sf* prize-giving.

premio *sm (vincita)* prize; *(ricompensa)* reward; **~ di assicurazione** (insurance) premium.

premunirsi vr: **~ contro qc** to protect o.s. against sthg.

premuroso, -a agg thoughtful.

prendere vt 1. (afferrare) to take.

2. (portare con sé) to take; **prendi l'ombrello** take the umbrella.

3. (mezzi di trasporto, strada) to take; **~ il treno** to take the train; **prenda la prima a destra** take the first on the right.

4. (mangiare, bere) to have; **andiamo a ~ un caffè** let's go for a coffee; **~ qualcosa da bere** to have something to drink; **che cosa prendete?** (da bere) what would you like to drink?

5. (lezioni, voto, stipendio) to get; **~ qc in affitto** to rent sthg.

6. (interpretare) to take; **prenderla bene/male** to take it well/badly.

7. (catturare, sorprendere) to catch; **quanti pesci hai preso?** how many fish have you caught?; **~ qn con le mani nel sacco** to catch sb redhanded.

8. (malattia, stato fisico): **~ freddo** to catch cold; **~ il sole** to sunbathe; **prendersi un raffreddore** to catch a cold.

9. (sottrarre): **~ qc a qn** to take sthg (away) from sb.

10. (scambiare): **~ qn per** to take sb for.

11. (in espressioni) **andare a ~** (persona) to meet; (cosa) to go to get; **prendersi cura di** to look after; **~ fuoco** to catch fire; **~ un impegno** to take on a commitment; **~ le misure di** (oggetto, persona) to measure; **che ti prende?** what's the matter with you?; **prendersela** (offendersi) to get annoyed; (preoccupare) to worry; **prendersela con qn** (arrabbiarsi) to get angry with sb.

◆ vi 1. (colla, cemento) to set; (fuoco) to catch.

2. (cominciare): **~ a fare qc** to start doing sthg.

prendisole sm inv sundress.

prenotare vt to book; **ho prenotato una camera** I've booked a room.

prenotazione sf booking.

preoccupare vt to worry ❑ **preoccuparsi** vr: **preoccuparsi (per)** to worry (about); **preoccuparsi di** vr + prep (occuparsi di) to think about.

preoccupato, -a agg worried.

preoccupazione sf worry.

preparare vt to prepare; (documenti, cose) to get ready; (esame, concorso) to prepare for; **~ da mangiare** to cook ❑ **prepararsi** vr (vestirsi) to get ready; **~ a fare qc** to get ready to do sthg.

preparativi smpl preparations.

preposizione sf preposition.

prepotente agg domineering ◆ smf bully.

presa sf (il prendere) grip; (nello sport, appiglio) hold; (di acqua, gas) supply point; (di sale, pepe) pinch; (di colla, cemento) setting; (di città) capture; (per spina): **~ (di corrente)** socket; **far ~ su** to set; **far ~ su qn** to captivate sb; **~ d'aria** air intake; **essere alle prese con** to be up against.

presbite agg longsighted.

prescindere : **prescindere da** *v* + *prep* to leave aside; **a ~ da** apart from.

prescritto, -a *pp* → **prescrivere**.

prescrivere *vt* to prescribe.

presentare *vt* to present; *(domanda, dimissioni)* to submit; *(persona)*: **~ qn a qn** to introduce sb to sb; **le presento mia moglie** this is my wife □ **presentarsi** *vr* *(farsi conoscere)* to introduce o.s.; *(recarsi)* to present o.s.; *(capitare)* to arise; *(mostrarsi)* to look.

presentatore, -trice *sm, f* presenter.

presentazione *sf* presentation; **fare le presentazioni** to make the introductions.

presente *agg* present ◆ *smf*: **i presenti** those present; **tener ~ che** to bear in mind that; **aver ~** to remember.

presentimento *sm* presentiment.

presenza *sf* presence; **in ~ di tutti** in front of everybody.

presepe = **presepio**.

presepio *sm* Nativity scene, crib.

preservativo *sm* condom.

preside *smf* headteacher *(Br)*, principal *(Am)*.

presidente *smf* president; **~ del Consiglio** Prime Minister; **il ~ della Repubblica** the Italian President.

preso, -a *pp* → **prendere**.

pressappoco *avv* more or less.

pressare *vt* to press.

---

pressione *sf* pressure; **far ~ su qn** to put pressure on sb; **essere sotto ~** to be under pressure.

presso *prep* *(sulle lettere)* c/o; *(vicino a)* near; *(alle dipendenze di)* for, with; **~ qn** *(a casa di)* at sb's home □ **pressi** *smpl*: **nei pressi di Siena** in the vicinity of Siena.

prestare *vt*: **~ qc (a qn)** *(denaro, oggetti)* to lend (sb) sthg, to lend sthg (to sb); **~ aiuto a qn** to lend sb a hand; **~ attenzione a** to pay attention to □ **prestarsi a** *vr* + *prep*: **prestarsi a fare qc** to offer to do sthg.

prestazione *sf* performance □ **prestazioni** *sfpl* services.

prestigiatore, -trice *sm, f* conjurer.

prestito *sm* loan; **dare in ~ qc (a qn)** to lend sthg (to sb); **prendere qc in ~ (da qn)** to borrow sthg (from sb).

presto *avv (fra poco)* soon; *(in fretta)* quickly; *(nella giornata, nel tempo)* early; **fai ~!** hurry up!; **a ~!** see you soon!; **al più ~** as soon as possible.

presumere *vt* to presume.

presunto, -a *pp* → **presumere**.

presuntuoso, -a *agg* conceited.

prete *sm* priest.

pretendere *vt* to claim; *(a torto)* to pretend; **pretende che tutti lo ascoltino** he expects everyone to listen to him; **pretende di essere il migliore** he thinks he's the best.

preteso, -a *pp* → **pretendere**.

pretesto *sm (scusa)* excuse, pretext; *(occasione)* opportunity.

prevalente *agg* prevalent.

prevalere *vi* to prevail.

prevedere *vt* to foresee

prevedere di *v + prep* to expect.

prevenire *vt (anticipare)* to forestall; *(evitare)* to prevent.

preventivo, -a *agg* preventive ♦ *sm* estimate.

prevenzione *sf* prevention.

previdenza *sf* foresight; ~ **sociale** social security *(Br)*, welfare *(Am)*.

previo, -a *agg:* ~ **pagamento** upon payment.

previsione *sf (valutazione)* prediction; *(aspettativa)* expectation; **in ~ di** in anticipation of; **previsioni del tempo** o **meteorologiche** weather forecast.

previsto, -a *pp* → **prevedere** ♦ *agg* expected ♦ *sm:* **più/meno del** ~ more/less than expected.

prezioso, -a *agg* precious, valuable.

prezzemolo *sm* parsley.

prezzo *sm* price; ~ **comprensivo del servizio** price including service charge; **a buon** ~ cheap.

prigione *sf* prison.

prigioniero, -a *agg (rinchiuso)* imprisoned; *(catturato)* captive ♦ *sm, f* prisoner.

prima *avv (in precedenza)* before; *(più presto)* earlier; *(per prima cosa, nello spazio)* first; *(un tempo)* once ♦ *sf (di teatro)* first night; *(marcia)* first gear; *(in treno, aereo)* first class ♦ *cong* before ♦ *prep:* ~ **di** before; **fai** ~ **di qua** it's quicker this way; ~

che arrivi before he arrives; ~ **di fare qc** before doing sthg; ~ **o poi** sooner or later; ~ **d'ora** before now; ~ **di tutto** first of all; **l'anno** ~ the year before.

primario, -a *agg* primary ♦ *sm (MED)* chief physician.

primato *sm (supremazia)* primacy; *(SPORT)* record.

primavera *sf* spring.

primitivo, -a *agg (uomo, civiltà)* primitive; *(originario)* original.

primo, -a *agg* first; *(nel tempo)* early ♦ *sm (portata)* first course; *(giorno)* first; **il** ~ **(di) marzo** the first of March; **di prima qualità** first-class; **ai primi d'ottobre** in early October; **sulle prime** at first, in the beginning.

primogenito, -a *agg & sm, f* firstborn.

principale *agg* main, principal ♦ *smf* manager, boss.

principe *sm* prince.

principessa *sf* princess.

principiante *smf* beginner.

principio *sm (inizio, origine)* beginning; *(concetto, norma)* principle; **in** o **al** ~ at first; **per** ~ on principle.

priorità *sf inv (precedenza)* priority.

privare *vt:* ~ **qn di qc** to deprive sb of sthg □ **privarsi di** *vr + prep* **privarsi di qc** to go without sthg.

privato, -a *agg* private ♦ *sm, (cittadino)* private citizen ♦ *sm:* **in** ~ in private.

privilegiare *vt* to favour.

privo, -a *agg:* ~ **di qc** without sthg, lacking in sthg.

pro *sm inv*: **a che ~?** for what purpose?; **i ~ e i contro** the pros and cons.

probabile *agg* probable; **è ~ che piova** it will probably rain.

probabilità *sf inv* probability.

probabilmente *av* probably.

problema, -i *sm* problem.

proboscide *sf* trunk.

procedere *vi (avanzare, progredire)* to proceed; *(agire)* to behave.

procedimento *sm* procedure.

processare *vt* to try.

processione *sf* procession.

processo *sm* (DIR) trial; *(operazione, metodo)* process.

procinto *sm*: **essere in ~ di fare qc** to be about to do sth.

proclamare *vt* to proclaim.

procurare *vt*: **~ qc a qn** to obtain sth for sb, to get sth for sb; **procurarsi qc** to get sth.

prodotto, -a *pp* → **produrre** ♦ *sm* product.

produrre *vt* to produce; *(provocare)* to cause.

produttore, -trice *sm, f* producer.

produzione *sf* production.

Prof. *(abbr di professore)* Prof.

profano, -a *agg* profane ♦ *sm* layman.

professionale *agg* professional.

professione *sf* profession.

professionista, -i, -e *smf* *(avvocato, medico)* professional person; *(non dilettante)* professional.

professore, -essa *sm, f*

teacher; *(all'università)* professor.

profilo *sm* profile; **di ~** in profile.

profiterole [profite'rɔl] *sm inv* profiteroles *(pl)*.

profitto *sm* profit; **trarre ~ da qc** to take advantage of sth.

profondità *sf inv* depth.

profondo, -a *agg* deep.

Prof.ssa *(abbr di professoressa)* Prof.

profugo, -a, -ghi, -ghe *sm, f* refugee.

profumare *vt* to perfume ♦ *vi* to smell good; **~ di** to smell of.

profumato, -a *agg* scented.

profumeria *sf* perfumery.

profumo *sm (odore)* scent, fragrance; *(cosmetico)* perfume.

progettare *vt* to plan.

progetto *sm* plan.

programma, -i *sm* programme; *(per vacanze, serata)* plan; (SCOL) syllabus; (INFORM) program.

programmare *vt (pianificare)* to plan; (INFORM) to program.

progredire *vi (avanzare)* to advance; *(migliorare)* to progress.

progressivo, -a *agg* progressive.

progresso *sm* progress; **fare progressi** to make progress.

proibire *vt* to forbid; **~ a qn di fare qc** to forbid sb to do sth; **è proibito fumare** smoking is prohibited.

proiettare *vt (film)* to show; *(luce, ombra)* to cast.

proiettile *sm* bullet.

proiezione *sf (di film)* projection, showing.

proletariato sm proletariat.

prolunga, -ghe sf extension.

prolungare vt to prolong □
prolungarsi vr to go on.

promessa sf promise; **mantenere una ~** to keep a promise.

promesso, -a pp → **promettere.**

promettere vt: **~ qc (a qn)** to promise (sb) sthg; **~ (a qn) di fare qc** to promise (sb) to do sthg; **promette bene!** that's a good start!

promontorio sm promontory.

promosso, -a pp → **promuovere.**

promotore, -trice sm, f promoter.

promozione sf promotion; (SCOL): **avere la ~** to go up a class.

promulgare vt to promulgate.

promuovere vt (SCOL) to pass; (impiegato, iniziativa) to promote.

pronome sm pronoun.

pronto, -a agg ready ♦ esclam hello! (on the phone); **essere ~ a fare qc** to be ready to do sthg; **~ soccorso** first aid; **~, chi parla?** hello, who's speaking?

pronuncia, -ce sf pronunciation.

pronunciare vt (parola, lettera) to pronounce; (dire) to say □ **pronunciarsi** vr (parola, lettera) to be pronounced; (dichiararsi) to declare o.s.

pronunzia = **pronuncia.**

proporre vt: **~ qc (a qn)** to propose sthg (to sb); **~ di fare qc** to suggest doing sthg □ **proporsi di**

vr + prep: **proporsi di fare qc** to decide to do sthg.

proporzionato, -a agg well proportioned.

proporzione sf (MAT) ratio; **in ~ a** in proportion to.

proposito sm (progetto) intention; **fare qc di ~** to do sthg on purpose; **a ~, ...** by the way, ...; **capitare a ~** (avvenimento) to happen at the right time.

proposta sf proposal.

proposto, -a pp → **proporre.**

proprietà sf inv property; **'~ privata'** 'private property'.

proprietario, -a sm, f owner.

proprio, -a agg (possessivo) own; (senso) literal, exact; (tipico) characteristic ♦ avv (veramente) really; (precisamente) just; (affatto) at all; **non ne ho ~ idea** I really have no idea; **~ così** that's just it; **non ~** not exactly; **mettersi in ~** to set up on one's own.

prora sf (di nave) prow; (di aereo) nose.

prosa sf prose.

prosciutto sm ham; **~ cotto** (cooked) ham; **~ crudo** Parma ham.

proseguire vt to carry on with, to continue ♦ vi to carry on, to continue.

prospettiva sf (di disegno, punto di vista) perspective; (possibilità) prospect.

prossimità sf: **in ~ di qc** near sthg.

prossimo, -a agg next ♦ sm neighbour.

prostituta sf prostitute.

protagonista, -i, -e *smf* protagonist.

proteggere *vt:* ~ qn/qc (da) to protect sb/sthg (from).

protesta *sf* protest.

protestante *agg & smf* Protestant.

protestare *vi & vt* to protest.

protetto, -a *pp* → **proteggere**.

protezione *sf* protection.

prototipo *sm* prototype.

prova *sf (dimostrazione, conferma)* proof; *(esperimento)* test, trial; *(di spettacolo)* rehearsal; *(esame)* exam; **dar ~ di abilità** to prove to be skilful; **mettere qn alla ~** to put sb to the test; **fino a ~ contraria** until (it's) proved otherwise; **in ~** on trial; **fare le prove** to rehearse.

provare *vt (cibo)* to try; *(vestito)* to try on; *(sentire)* to feel, to experience; *(dimostrare)* to show; *(tentare):* ~ **a fare qc** to try to do sthg; **provarsi qc** to try sthg on □ **provarsi a** *vr + prep:* **provarsi a fare qc** to try to do sthg.

provenienza *sf* origin; **in ~ da** *(treno, aereo)* from.

provenire : provenire da *v + prep* to come from; **proveniente da** *(treno, aereo)* from.

provenuto, -a *pp* → **provenire**.

proverbio *sm* proverb.

provetta *sf* test tube.

provincia, -ce ○ **-cie** *sf (ente)* province; *(opposta a grandi città)* provinces *(pl)*.

provinciale *agg* provincial ◆ *sf* main road.

provino *sm (audizione)* audition; *(fotografico)* screen test.

provocante *agg* provocative.

provocare *vt (causare)* to cause; *(sfidare)* to provoke.

provocazione *sf* provocation.

provolone *sm* a hard cheese made from cow's milk.

provvedere *vi (prendere provvedimenti)* to take measures; *(occuparsi di):* ~ **(a qc)** to provide for (sthg).

provvedimento *sm* measure.

provvisorio, -a *agg* temporary, provisional.

provviste *sfpl* supplies.

prua *sf* prow.

prudente *agg* cautious, prudent.

prudenza *sf* caution, prudence; **'prudenza'** 'caution'.

prudere *vi* to itch; **mi prude una gamba** my leg is itchy.

prugna *sf* plum; ~ **secca** prune.

pruno *sm* prickle, thorn.

prurito *sm* itch.

P.S. *(abbr di postscriptum)* PS ◆ *abbr* = **Pubblica Sicurezza**.

pseudonimo *sm* pseudonym.

psicanalisi *sf* psychoanalysis.

psiche *sf* psyche.

psichiatra, -i, -e *smf* psychiatrist.

psicologia *sf* psychology.

psicologo, -a, -gi, -ghe *sm, f* psychologist.

P.T. *(abbr di poste e telecomunicazioni)* PO.

P.T.P. *(abbr di posto telefonico pub-*

blico) payphone.

pubblicare *vt* to publish.

pubblicazione *sf* publication ❑ **pubblicazioni** *sfpl*: **~ (matrimoniali)** (marriage) banns.

pubblicità *sf inv (annuncio)* advertisement; *(divulgazione)* publicity; *(attività)* advertising.

pubblico, -a, -ci, -che *agg* public; *(statale)* state *(dav s)* ◆ *sm (utenti)* public; *(spettatori)* audience; **in ~** in public; **la Pubblica Sicurezza** the police.

pube *sm* pubis.

pudore *sm* modesty.

pugilato *sm* boxing.

pugile *sm* boxer.

Puglia *sf*: **la ~** Apulia.

pugnalare *vt* to stab.

pugno *sm (mano)* fist; *(colpo)* punch; *(quantità)* handful.

pulce *sf* flea.

Pulcinella *sm* Punch.

pulcino *sm* chick.

puledro, -a *sm, f* colt (*f* filly).

pulire *vt* to clean; **pulirsi il viso/le scarpe** to clean one's face/shoes.

pulita *sf*: **dare una ~** to clean up.

pulito, -a *agg* clean; *(coscienza)* clear.

pulizia *sf (stato)* cleanliness; *(atto)* cleaning; **fare le pulizie** to do the cleaning.

pullman *sm inv* coach.

pullover *sm inv* pullover.

pulmino *sm* minibus.

pulsante *sm* button.

pulsare *vi* to beat.

puma *sm inv* puma.

pungere *vt* to sting.

pungiglione *sm* sting.

punire *vt* to punish.

punizione *sf (castigo)* punishment; *(nel calcio)* free kick.

punta *sf (di matita, spillo, coltello)* point; *(di continente, dita)* tip; **in ~ dei piedi** *(camminare)* on tiptoe.

puntare *vt (arma)* to aim; *(scommettere)* to bet; **~ i piedi** to dig one's heels in.

puntata *sf (episodio)* episode; *(scommessa)* bet; **teleromanzo a puntate** serial.

punteggiatura *sf* punctuation.

punteggio *sm* score.

puntina *sf*: **~ (da disegno)** drawing pin.

puntino *sm* dot; **fare qc a ~** to do sthg properly; **puntini di sospensione** suspension points.

punto, -a *pp →* **pungere** ◆ *sm* point; *(segno grafico)* full stop *(Br)*, period *(Am)*; *(MED, di cucito)* stitch; **~ esclamativo** exclamation mark; **~ interrogativo** question mark; **~ di riferimento** point of reference, landmark; **~ di ritrovo** meeting point; **~ vendita** point of sale; **~ e virgola** semi-colon; **~ di vista** point of view; **due punti** colon; **punti cardinali** points of the compass; **essere sul ~ di fare qc** to be about to do sthg; **essere a buon ~** to be at a good point; **fare il ~ della situazione** to take stock; **mettere a ~ qc** to adjust sthg; **di ~ in bianco** all of a sudden; **a tal ~ che** to such an extent that; **le tre in ~** three o'clock sharp.

puntuale *agg* punctual.

puntualità *sf* punctuality.

puntura *sf* (*di insetto*) sting; (*di spillo*) prick; (*fam: iniezione*) injection.

punzecchiare *vt* (*pungere*) to prick; (*fig: infastidire*) to tease.

pupazzo *sm* puppet.

pupilla *sf* pupil.

purché *cong* provided that.

pure *avv* (*anche*) also, too ♦ *cong* even if; **pur di fare qc** just to do sthg; **faccia ~!** please do!, go ahead!

purè *sm* (*di patate*) mashed potatoes with milk, butter and Parmesan cheese.

purezza *sf* purity.

purga, -ghe *sf* laxative.

purgatorio *sm* Purgatory.

puro, -a *agg* pure; (*verità*) simple.

purosangue *agg inv* thoroughbred.

purtroppo *avv* unfortunately.

pustola *sf* pimple.

putiferio *sm* row.

putrefare *vi* to putrefy, to rot.

putrefatto, -a *pp* → **putrefare** ♦ *agg* rotten.

putrido, -a *agg* putrid.

puttana *sf* (*volg*) whore.

puzza *sf* = **puzzo**.

puzzare *vi* to stink.

puzzo *sm* stink.

puzzola *sf* polecat.

puzzolente *agg* stinking.

qua *avv* here; **al di ~ di** on this side of; **di ~ e di là** here and there; **per di ~** this way.

quaderno *sm* exercise book.

quadrante *sm* (*di orologio*) face; (*di bussola*) quarter.

quadrare *vi* (*bilancia*) to balance; (*coincidere*) to correspond; **non mi quadra** (*fam*) there's something not quite right about it.

quadrato, -a *agg & sm* square; **2 al ~** 2 squared.

quadretto *sm*: **a quadretti** (*tessuto*) checked; (*foglio*) squared.

quadrifoglio *sm* four-leaf clover.

quadrimestre *sm* (*SCOL*) term; (*periodo*) period of four months.

quadro *sm* (*pittura*) painting; (*fig: situazione*) picture; (*TECNOL*) board, panel; (*in azienda*) executive ❑ **quadri** *smpl* (*nelle carte*) diamonds.

quadruplo, -a *agg & sm* quadruple.

quaggiù *avv* down here.

quaglia *sf* quail.

qualche *agg* 1. (*alcuni*) a few, some; **restiamo solo ~ giorno** we are only staying a few days; **~ volta** a few times; **c'è ~ novità?** is there any news?
2. (*indeterminato*) some; **l'ho letto in ~ articolo** I read it in some article; **hai ~ libro da prestarmi?** have

qualcheduno

you any books to lend me?; **in ~ modo** somehow; **da ~ parte** somewhere.

3. *(un certo)* some; **ci siamo frequentati per ~ tempo** we've been seeing each other for some time; **~ cosa** = qualcosa.

qualcheduno, -a = qualcuno.

qualcosa *pron* something; *(nelle interrogative)* anything; **~ di nuovo** something new; **~ da bere** something to drink; **qualcos'altro** something else.

qualcuno, -a *pron (uno)* someone, somebody; *(nelle interrogative)* anyone, anybody; *(alcuni)* some; *(alcuni: nelle interrogative)* any; **qualcun altro** *(persona)* someone else; **~ di voi** some of you; *(nelle interrogative)* any of you.

quale *agg interr* 1. *(persona)* which; **qual è il tuo scrittore preferito?** who is your favourite writer?; **da ~ dentista sei stato?** which dentist have you been to?

2. *(cosa)* which, what; **non so ~ libro scegliere** I don't know which book to choose; **in ~ albergo hai prenotato?** which hotel have you booked?

♦ *agg relativo* such as, like; **alcuni animali quali il cane** some animals such as the dog.

♦ *pron interr* which (one); **~ vuole di questi cappelli?** which of these hats do you want?; **non so ~ scegliere** I don't know which (one) to choose.

♦ *pron relativo* 1. *(soggetto)*: **il/la ~** *(persona)* who; *(cosa)* which, that; **suo fratello, il ~ è un mio amico** his

brother, who is a friend of mine.

2. *(con preposizioni: persona)* who(m); *(cosa)* which, that; **l'albergo nel ~ alloggio** the hotel (that) I'm staying in; **la persona con la ~ parlavo** the person (whom) I was talking to; **l'uomo del ~ conosco il figlio** the man whose son I know.

3. *(in qualità di)* as; **vengo ~ accompagnatore** I'm coming as a tour guide.

qualifica, -che *sf* qualification.

qualificare *vt* to describe, to define ❏ **qualificarsi** *vr* to qualify.

qualificativo, -a *agg* qualifying.

qualità *sf inv* quality; *(varietà)* type; **in ~ di** in one's capacity as.

qualsiasi = qualunque.

qualunque *agg* any; *(quale che)* whatever; **~ cosa** anything; **~ cosa succeda** whatever happens; **~ persona** anyone; **prendine uno ~** take whichever you want.

quando *avv & cong* when; **da ~ sono qui** from when I got here; **da ~ sei qui?** how long have you been here?; **da ~ in qua** since when; **di ~ sono queste foto?** when were these photos taken?

quantità *sf inv* quantity, amount; **una ~ di** a lot ❏ lots of.

quanto, -a *agg interr* 1. *(quantità)* how much; *(numero)* how many; **~ tempo ci vuole?** how long does it take?; **quanti anni hai?** how old are you?

2. *(in frasi esclamative)* what; **quanta fatica sprecata!** what a waste of energy!

◆ agg relativo (quantità) as much as; (numero) as many as; **puoi restare quanti giorni vuoi** you can stay for as many days as you like.
◆ pron interr (quantità) how much; (numero) how many; **prima di comprare il pane guarda ~ ce n'è** before buying the bread see how much there is; **quanti ne vuoi?** how many do you want?; **quanti ne abbiamo oggi?** what's the date today?
◆ pron relativo (quello che: quantità) as much as; (numero) as many as; **dammene ~ ti pare** give me as much as you want; **per ~ ne so** as far as I know.
◆ avv 1. (interrogativo: quantità) how much; (numero) how many; **quant'è?** how much is it?; **~ ti fermi?** how long are you staying?; **~ è alta questa montagna?** how high is this mountain?; **~ mi dispiace!** I'm so sorry!; **~ costa/costano?** how much is it/are they?
2. (relativo) as much as; **mi sforzo ~ posso** I try as hard as I can; **~ prima** as soon as possible.
3. (in espressioni): **in ~** (perché) because; **per ~** however.

quaranta num forty, → **sei**.

quarantena sf quarantine.

quarantesimo, -a num fortieth, → **sesto**.

quarantina sf: **una ~ (di)** about forty; **essere sulla ~** to be in one's forties.

quaresima sf (RELIG): **la ~** Lent.

quarta sf (marcia) fourth gear.

quartetto sm quartet.

quartiere sm area, district; **quartier generale** headquarters (pl).

quarto, -a num fourth ◆ sm (parte) quarter; **un ~ d'ora** a quarter of an hour; **le tre e un ~** quarter past three (Br), quarter after three (Am); **le tre meno un ~** quarter to three (Br), quarter of three (Am); **un ~ di vino** a quarter litre of wine, → **sesto**.

quarzo sm quartz.

quasi avv nearly ◆ cong as if; **~ mai** hardly ever; **~ sempre** almost always; **~ ~ vengo anch'io** I might just come too.

quassù avv up here.

quattordicesimo, -a num fourteenth, → **sesto**.

quattordici num fourteen, → **sei**.

quattrini smpl (fam) money (sg).

quattro num four; **farsi in ~ (per fare qc)** to go out of one's way (to do sthg); **eravamo ~ gatti** (fam) there were only a few of us there; **in ~ e quattr'otto** in less than no time, → **sei**.

quattrocento num four hundred, → **sei** ❑ **Quattrocento** sm: **il Quattrocento** the fifteenth century.

quei → **quello**.

quegli → **quello**.

quello, -a (dav sm **quel** (pl **quei**) + consonante; **quello** (pl **quegli**) + s+consonante, gn, ps, x, z; **quell'** (pl **quegli**) + vocale) agg 1. (indica lontananza) that, those (pl); **quella casa** that house; **quegli alberi** those trees; **quei bambini** those children.

2. (per sottolineare): **spegni quella tv!**

switch that TV off!

3. *(per cosa, persona già nota)* that, those *(pl)*; **non mi piace quella gente** I don't like those people.

♦ **pron 1.** *(indica lontananza)* that (one), those (ones) *(pl)*; **quella è la mia macchina** that one's my car; **prendo ~ in offerta** I'll take the one on special offer; **~ lì** that one (there).

2. *(con pronome relativo)*: **faccio ~ che posso** I'll do what I can; **quelli che potevano si sono fermati** those who could, stopped.

quercia, -ce *sf* oak.

querelare *vt* to bring a legal action against.

quesito *sm* query.

questionario *sm* questionnaire.

questione *sf* question; **è ~ di giorni** it's a matter of days; **in ~** in question.

questo, -a *agg* **1.** *(indica prossimità)* this, these *(pl)*; **questa finestra è aperta** this window is open; **partiamo ~ giovedì** we're leaving this Thursday.

2. *(simile)* such; **non uscire con questa pioggia** don't go out in rain like this.

3. *(il seguente/precedente)* this, these *(pl)*; **~ è il mio consiglio** this is my advice.

♦ **pron 1.** *(indica prossimità)* this (one), these (ones) *(pl)*; **~ è Franco** this is Franco; **~ qui** O **qua** this one (here).

2. *(per riassumere)* that; **~ è tutto** that's all; **questa è bella!** that's rich!

questura *sf* *(organo)* police headquarters *(pl)*.

qui *avv* here; **da ~ in avanti** from now on; **di** O **da ~** from here; **di ~ a un anno** in a year's time; **di ~ a poco** in a little while.

quiete *sf* quiet.

quindi *cong* so, therefore.

quindicesimo, -a *num* fifteenth, → **sesto**.

quindici *num* fifteen; **~ giorni** a fortnight, → **sei**.

quindicina *sf* about fifteen; **una ~ di giorni** about a fortnight.

quinta *(marcia)* fifth gear ❑
quinte *sfpl* *(di teatro)* wings.

quintale *sm* = 100 kilograms.

quinto, -a *num* fifth, → **sesto**.

quintuplo *sm*: **il ~ del prezzo normale** five times the normal price.

Quirinale *nm*: **il ~** official residence of the President of Italy.

---

i IL QUIRINALE

The "Palazzo del Quirinale" has been the official residence of the president of the Italian republic since 1947. It overlooks the square of the same name in Rome and is guarded by armed policemen in full dress uniform. It is here that the president receives foreign heads of state on official business.

quota *sf* *(altitudine)* altitude; *(di denaro, bene)* share; **perdere ~** to lose height; **prendere ~** to climb; **d'iscrizione** *(a circolo)* membership fee.

quotato, -a *agg* valued.

quotidianamente *avv* daily.

quotidiano, -a *agg* daily ◆ *sm* daily (newspaper).

quoziente *sm* quotient; ~ d'intelligenza IQ.

rabarbaro *sm* rhubarb.

rabbia *sf* (*collera*) anger, rage; (*malattia*) rabies; **far ~ a qn** to drive sb mad.

rabbino *sm* rabbi.

rabbioso, -a *agg* angry; (*MED*) rabid.

rabbonire *vt* to calm down ❏

rabbonirsi *vr* to calm down.

rabbrividire *vi* (*di freddo*) to shiver; (*di paura*) to shudder.

raccapezzarsi *vr*: **non mi ci raccapezzo** I can't make it out.

raccapricciante *agg* horrifying.

raccattapalle *smf inv* ball-boy (*f* ball-girl).

raccattare *vt* to pick up.

racchetta *sf* (*da tennis*) racket; (*da ping-pong*) bat (*Br*), paddle (*Am*); (*da sci*) ski pole.

raccogliere *vt* (*da terra*) to pick up; (*frutti, fiori*) to pick; (*mettere insieme*) to collect; (*voti*) to win ❏ **raccogliersi** *vr* (*radunarsi*) to meet, to gather; (*in meditazione,*

preghiera) to gather one's thoughts.

raccolta *sf* collection; (*agricola*) harvest; **fare la ~ di qc** to collect sthg.

raccolto, -a *pp* → **raccogliere** ◆ *sm* harvest, crop.

raccomandare *vt* to recommend; (*affidare*) to entrust; ~ **a qn di fare qc** to urge sb to do sthg ❏ **raccomandarsi** *vr*: **raccomandarsi a** to appeal to; **mi raccomando, non fare tardi!** don't be late now, will you!

raccomandata *sf* registered letter.

raccomandato, -a *agg* (*lettera*) registered; (*candidato*) recommended.

raccomandazione *sf* (*consiglio*) recommendation.

raccontare *vt* to tell.

racconto *sm* (*esposizione*) account; (*romanzo*) short story.

raccordo *sm* connection, link; (*di autostrada*) slip road (*Br*), entrance/exit ramp (*Am*); ~ **anulare** ring road (*Br*), beltway (*Am*).

racimolare *vt* to scrape together.

rada *sf* harbour.

radar *sm inv* radar.

raddoppiare *vt* (*rendere doppio*) to double; (*aumentare*) to redouble ◆ *vi* to double.

radente *agg* (*tiro, volo*) very low.

radere *vt* to shave; ~ **qc al suolo** to raze sthg to the ground ❏ **radersi** *vr* to shave.

radiare *vt* to strike off.

radiatore *sm* radiator.

radiazione *sf* radiation.

radicale *agg* radical.

radicalmente *avv* radically, completely.

radicchio *sm* chicory.

radice *sf* root; **~ quadrata** square root.

radio *sf inv* radio; *(stazione)* radio station; **alla ~** on the radio.

radioamatore, -trice *sm, f* radio ham.

radioascoltatore, -trice *sm, f* listener.

radioattivo, -a *agg* radioactive.

radiocomandato, -a *agg* remote-controlled.

radiografia *sf* X-ray.

radioso, -a *agg* bright.

radiotaxi *sm inv* minicab.

rado, -a *agg* sparse; **di ~** rarely.

radunare *vt (persone)* to gather; *(cose)* to assemble ❑ **radunarsi** *vr* to gather.

raduno *sm* meeting.

rafano *sm* radish.

raffermo, -a *agg* stale.

raffica, -che *sf (di vento)* gust; *(di mitra)* burst.

raffigurare *vt* to portray.

raffinato, -a *agg* refined; *(stile)* sophisticated.

raffineria *sf* refinery.

rafforzare *vt* to strengthen.

raffreddare *vt* to cool; *(fig: rapporti, interesse)* to cool, to dampen ❑ **raffreddarsi** *vr (bevanda, cibo)* to get cold; *(fig: persona, amicizia)* to cool down; *(ammalarsi)* to catch a cold.

raffreddato, -a *agg:* **essere ~** to have a cold.

raffreddore *sm* cold.

rafia *sf* raffia.

ragazza *sf (giovane donna)* girl; *(fidanzata)* girlfriend; **~ madre** single mother.

ragazzata *sf* childish trick.

ragazzo *sm (giovane)* boy; *(fidanzato)* boyfriend.

raggiante *agg* radiant, beaming.

raggio *sm (di sole, infrarosso)* ray; *(area)* range; *(MAT)* radius; *(di ruota)* spoke.

raggirare *vt* to trick, to cheat.

raggiungere *vt (persona)* to catch up; *(luogo)* to reach; *(fig: fine)* to achieve.

raggiunto, -a *pp* → **raggiungere**.

raggomitolarsi *vr* to curl up.

raggranellare *vt* to scrape together.

raggrinzire *vt & vi* to shrivel up ❑ **raggrinzirsi** *vr* to shrivel.

raggruppare *vt (mettere insieme)* to assemble; *(a gruppi)* to group together ❑ **raggrupparsi** *vr* to assemble.

ragguagli *smpl:* **dare ~** to give details.

ragionamento *sm (riflessione)* reasoning; *(discorso)* argument.

ragionare *vi* to reason ❑ **ragionare di** *v + prep (parlare di)* to argue about.

ragione *sf* reason; **avere ~** to be right; **dare ~ a qn** to side with sb;

a maggior ~ even more so.

ragioneria sf (materia) accountancy; (scuola) commercial school; (reparto) accounts (pl).

ragionevole agg reasonable.

ragioniere, -a sm, f accountant.

ragliare vi to bray.

ragnatela sf cobweb, spider's web.

ragno sm spider.

ragù sm inv sauce of minced beef, tomatoes and onions.

RAI sf Italian broadcasting corporation.

rallegramenti smpl congratulations.

rallentare vt to slow down.

rally ['rɛlli] sm inv rally.

ramaiolo sm ladle.

ramanzina sf telling-off.

rame sm copper.

ramino sm rummy.

rammaricarsi : rammaricarsi di vr + prep to regret.

rammendare vt (stoffa) to mend; (lana) to darn.

rammentare vt to remember; ~ qc a qn to remind sb of sthg ❑ **rammentarsi di** vr + prep to remember.

rammollito, -a agg soft.

ramo sm branch.

ramoscello sm twig.

rampa sf flight (of stairs); ~ **di lancio** launch pad.

rampicante agg climbing.

rampone sm (fiocina) harpoon; (in alpinismo) crampon.

rana sf frog.

rancido, -a agg rancid.

rancore sm rancour.

randagio, -a, -gi, -gie o **-ge** agg stray.

randello sm club.

rango, -ghi sm rank.

rannicchiarsi vr to huddle up.

rannuvolarsi vr to cloud over.

ranocchio sm frog.

rantolo sm death rattle.

rapa sf turnip.

rapace agg predatory ♦ sm bird of prey.

rapare vt to crop.

rapida sf rapids (pl).

rapidamente avv rapidly, fast.

rapidità sf rapidity.

rapido, -a agg (svelto) fast; (breve) quick, rapid ♦ sm express (train).

rapimento sm kidnapping.

rapina sf robbery; ~ **a mano armata** armed robbery.

rapinare vt to rob.

rapinatore, -trice sm, f robber.

rapire vt to kidnap.

rapitore, -trice sm, f kidnapper.

rapporto sm (resoconto) report; (tra persone) relationship; (connessione) connection, relation; (MAT) ratio; **rapporti sessuali** sexual intercourse (sg).

rapprendersi vr to curdle.

rappresentante smf representative.

rappresentare vt to represent; (raffigurare) to depict; (mettere in scena) to stage, to perform.

rappresentazione sf (spettacolo) performance; (raffigurazione) representation.

rappreso, -a pp → **rapprendersi**.

raramente avv rarely.

rarità sf inv (scarsità) rarity; (oggetto) rare thing.

raro, -a agg rare.

rasare vt to shave ◻ **rasarsi** vr to shave.

rasato, -a agg shaven.

raschiare vt to scrape.

rasentare vt (sfiorare) to graze; (muro) to hug, to keep close to; (fig: avvicinarsi a) to border on.

rasente prep close to.

raso, -a pp → **radere** ♦ agg (cucchiaio) level; ~ **terra** close to the ground.

rasoio sm razor; ~ **elettrico** electric razor.

rassegna sf review; (cinematografica, teatrale) season; **passare in** ~ (MIL) to review.

rassegnare vt: ~ **le dimissioni** to hand in one's resignation ◻ **rassegnarsi** vr to resign o.s.

rasserenarsi vr to clear up.

rassettare vt (stanza, capelli) to tidy (up); (vestito) to mend.

rassicurare vt to reassure.

rassodare vt (terreno) to harden; (muscoli) to tone.

rassomigliare : **rassomigliare a** v + prep to resemble.

rastrellare vt (foglie) to rake; (fig: zona) to comb.

rastrello sm rake.

rata sf instalment; **pagare qc a**

rate to pay for sthg in instalments.

rateale agg by o in instalments.

ratificare vt (DIR) to ratify.

ratto sm rat.

rattoppare vt to patch.

rattrappire vt to numb ◻ **rattrappirsi** vr to go numb.

rattristare vt to make sad ◻ **rattristarsi** vr to become sad.

rauco, -a, -chi, -che agg raucous.

ravanello sm radish.

ravioli smpl ravioli.

ravvicinare vt (avvicinare) to bring closer; (rappacificare) to reconcile ◻ **ravvicinarsi** vr to be reconciled.

ravvivare vt to brighten up.

razionale agg rational.

razionalità sf rationality.

razionare vt to ration.

razione sf ration.

razza sf (di persone) race; (di animali) breed; (pesce) ray; **che ~ di domanda è questa?** (fam) what sort of question is that?

razzia sf raid.

razziale agg racial.

razzismo sm racism.

razzista, -i, -e agg & smf racist.

razzo sm rocket.

razzolare vi to scratch about.

re sm inv king.

reagire vi: ~ **(a qc)** to react (to sthg).

reale agg (vero) real; (di re) royal.

realista, -i, -e smf realist.

realizzare vt (progetto) to carry

out; (sogno) to fulfil; (film) to produce; (rendersi conto di) to realize; (COMM) to realize ❑ **realizzarsi** vr (persona) to be fulfilled; (progetto) to be carried out; (sogno) to come true.

realizzazione sf (attuazione) carrying-out.

realmente avv really.

realtà sf inv reality; **in ~** in reality.

reato sm offence, crime.

reattore sm (aereo) jet; (motore) jet engine; (in fisica) reactor.

reazionario, -a agg reactionary.

reazione sf reaction.

rebus sm inv game in which pictures represent the syllables of words.

recapitare vt to deliver.

recapito sm (luogo) address; (consegna) delivery; **~ telefonico** (tele)phone number.

recare vt: **~ disturbo a qn** to disturb sb ❑ **recarsi** vr to go.

recensione sf review.

recente agg recent; **di ~** recently.

recentemente avv recently.

recessione sf recession.

recidere vt to cut off.

recintare vt to fence in.

recinto sm (spazio) enclosure; (recinzione) fence.

recipiente sm container.

reciproco, -a, -ci, -che agg reciprocal.

reciso, -a pp → recidere.

recita sf play.

recitare vt (poesia) to recite;

(ruolo) to play ◆ vi to act.

reclamare vi to complain ◆ vt to claim.

réclame [re'klam] sf inv advertising.

reclamo sm (protesta) complaint.

reclinabile agg reclining.

reclusione sf (DIR) imprisonment.

reclutare vt to recruit.

record sm inv record.

recuperare vt (riprendere) to recover, to get back; (svantaggio, tempo) to make up; (rottami) to salvage.

redatto, -a pp → redigere.

redattore, -trice sm, f editor.

redazione sf (stesura) writing; (ufficio) editorial department; (personale) editorial staff.

redditizio, -a agg profitable.

reddito sm income.

redigere vt (articolo, lettera) to write; (documento, contratto) to draw up.

redini sfpl reins.

referendum sm inv referendum.

referenze sfpl references.

referto sm medical report.

refettorio sm refectory, dining hall.

refrigerare vt to refrigerate.

refurtiva sf stolen goods (pl).

regalare vt (dono) to give (as a present); (dare gratis) to give away.

regalo sm (dono) present, gift.

regata sf regatta.

reggere vt (tenere) to hold; (sostenere) to bear, to support; (sopportare) to bear; (governare) to govern; (GRAMM) to take, to be followed by ♦ vi (durare) to last; (essere logico) to stand up, to hold good; (resistere): ~ **a qc** to withstand sthg ❑ **reggersi** vr: **non mi reggo in piedi** I can't stand up.

reggia, -ge sf palace.

reggicalze sm inv suspender belt.

reggimento sm regiment.

reggipetto = reggiseno.

reggiseno sm bra.

regia sf (di film) direction; (di dramma) production.

regime sm (politico) regime; (alimentare) diet.

regina sf queen.

regionale agg regional.

regione sf region.

ℹ️ REGIONE

For administrative purposes Italy is divided up into 20 regions. Each region is made up of different provinces ("province"), and each province is made up of municipalities known as "comuni". Five of the regions have a special statute granting them a greater degree of autonomy than the others: they are Valle d'Aosta, Friuli-Venezia Giulia, Trentino-Alto Adige, Sicily and Sardinia.

---

regista, -i, -e smf director.

registrare vt to register; (su cassetta) to record; (COMM) to enter.

registratore sm tape recorder; ~ **di cassa** cash register.

registrazione sf (di nascita, morte) registration; (di musica, programma) recording; (COMM) entry.

registro sm register; ~ **di classe** attendance register.

regnare vi to reign.

regno sm kingdom; (fig: ambito) realm ❑ **Regno Unito** sm: **il Regno Unito** the United Kingdom.

regola sf rule; **essere in** ~ to be (all) in order; **fare qc a** ~ **d'arte** to do sthg perfectly.

regolabile agg adjustable.

regolamento sm regulations (pl).

regolare agg regular ♦ vt to regulate; (apparecchio, macchina) to adjust; (questione, conto) to settle ❑ **regolarsi** vr (comportarsi) to behave; (moderarsi) to control o.s.; **regolarsi nel bere/mangiare** to watch what one drinks/eats.

regolarmente avv regularly.

regolo sm ruler; ~ **calcolatore** slide rule.

regredire vi to regress.

reintegrare vt to reinstate.

relativamente avv relatively, comparatively; ~ **a** in relation to, as regards.

relativo, -a agg relative; ~ **a** relating to.

relax sm relaxation.

relazione sf relationship; (amorosa) affair; (resoconto) report.

relegare vt to relegate.

religione sf religion.

religioso, -a agg religious ♦

sm, f monk (*f* nun).

reliquia *sf* relic.

relitto *sm* wreck, piece of wreckage.

remare *vi* to row.

remo *sm* oar.

rendere *vt* (*restituire*) to give back, to return; (*far diventare*) to make; (*produrre*) to yield ♦ *vi* (*persona, azienda*) to do well; (*lavoro*) to pay well; **~ possibile** *qc* to make sthg possible; **~ l'idea** (*persona*) to make o.s. clear ❏ **rendersi** *vr* (*diventare*) to become; **rendersi utile** to make o.s. useful.

rendiconto *sm* (*relazione*) report; (*COMM*) statement of accounts.

rendimento *sm* (*efficienza*) efficiency; (*di scolaro, macchina*) performance.

rendita *sf* unearned income; **vivere di ~** (*fig: studente*) to get by on one's past performance.

rene *sm* kidney.

renitente *agg* reluctant; **è ~ ai consigli** he won't listen to advice; **essere ~ alla leva** *to fail to report for military service.*

renna *sf* reindeer.

Reno *sm*: **il ~** the Rhine.

reparto *sm* (*di negozio*) department; (*d'ospedale*) ward; (*MIL*) unit.

repentaglio *sm*: **mettere a ~ qc** to put sthg at risk.

reperibile *agg* (*merce, persona*) available; (*al lavoro*) on call.

reperto *sm* (*resto*) find; (*resoconto*) report.

repertorio *sm* (*teatrale*) repertoire; (*elenco*) index.

replica, -che *sf* (*in televisione*) repeat; (*a teatro*) repeat performance.

replicare *vt* to reply.

repressione *sf* repression.

represso, -a *pp* → **reprimere**.

reprimere *vt* to repress ❏ **reprimersi** *vr* to restrain o.s.

repubblica, -che *sf* republic.

repubblicano, -a *agg* republican.

repulsione *sf* repulsion.

reputare *vt* to consider.

reputazione *sf* reputation.

requisire *vt* to requisition.

requisito *sm* requisite.

resa *sf* (*l'arrendersi*) surrender; (*restituzione*) return; (*rendimento*) yield; **~ dei conti** (*fig*) day of reckoning.

residence ['rezidens] *sm inv* residential hotel.

residente *agg* resident.

residenza *sf* residence.

residenziale *agg* residential.

residuo, -a *agg* residual, remaining ♦ *sm* (*avanzo*) remainder; (*scoria*) waste.

resina *sf* resin.

resistente *agg* (*robusto*) strong; (*durevole*) durable; **~ al calore** heatproof, heat-resistant.

resistenza *sf* resistance; (*di materiale*) strength; (*a fatica, dolore*) endurance; **~ (elettrica)** (electrical) resistance.

resistere *vi* (*tener duro*) to hold out ❏ **resistere a** *v + prep* (*opporsi*) to resist; (*sopportare*) to withstand.

resistito, -a *pp* → **resistere**.

reso 214

reso, -a *pp* → rendere.

resoconto *sm* account.

respingere *vt* to reject; *(attacco, aggressore)* to repel; *(SCOL)* to fail.

respinto, -a *pp* → respingere.

respirare *vi & vt* to breathe.

respiratore *sm (per immersione)* aqualung; *(MED)* respirator.

respirazione *sf* breathing; ~ **artificiale** artificial respiration.

respiro *sm (respirazione)* breathing; *(movimento)* breath; **tirare un ~ di sollievo** to heave a sigh of relief.

responsabile *agg* responsible ♦ *smf (in azienda, negozio)* person in charge; *(colpevole)* culprit; **essere ~ di qc** *(incaricato di)* to be in charge of sthg; *(colpevole di)* to be responsible for sthg.

responsabilità *sf inv* responsibility; *(colpa)* responsibility, liability.

ressa *sf* crowd.

restare *vi* to stay, to remain; *(avanzare)* to be left, to remain; *(trovarsi)* to be; ~ **a piedi** to remain standing; **mi restano pochi giorni** I only have a few days left.

restaurare *vt* to restore.

restauro *sm* restoration.

restituire *vt* to give back, to return.

resto *sm* rest, remainder; *(di denaro)* change; *(MAT)* remainder; **del ~** moreover, besides ❑ **resti** *smpl (ruderi)* ruins; *(di cibo)* leftovers; *(di persona, animale)* remains.

restringere *vt (dimensioni)* to reduce; *(tessuto)* to shrink; *(limitare)* to limit, to restrict ❑ **restringersi**

vr (strada) to (become) narrow; *(stoffa)* to shrink; *(per numero, estensione)* to reduce.

resurrezione *sf* resurrection.

resuscitare = risuscitare.

rete *sf* net; *(recinzione)* wire fence; *(radiotelevisiva, stradale)* network; *(del letto)* bedsprings *(pl)*; *(nel calcio: punto)* goal.

reticente *agg* reticent.

reticolato *sm (intreccio di linee)* network; *(recinzione)* fencing, wire netting.

retina *sf* (ANAT) retina.

retino *sm* net.

retorico, -a, -ci, -che *agg (spreg)* pompous.

retribuire *vt* to remunerate, to pay.

retribuzione *sf* remuneration, pay.

retro *sm inv* back; **sul ~** at the back; **vedi ~** see over.

retrocedere *vi* to recede; *(SPORT)* to be relegated.

retrocesso, -a *pp* → retrocedere.

retrogrado, -a *agg* retrograde.

retromarcia *sf* reverse.

retroscena *sm inv (antefatti)* background.

retrospettivo, -a *agg* retrospective.

retrovisore *sm* rear-view mirror.

retta *sf (linea)* straight line; *(di pensionato)* charge; **dar ~ a** to pay attention to.

rettangolare *agg* rectangular.

rettangolo *sm* rectangle.

rettificare *vt (form)* to rectify.

rettile *sm* reptile.

rettilineo, -a *agg & sm* straight.

retto, -a *pp* → **reggere** ♦ *agg (diritto)* straight; *(persona, comportamento)* honest; **angolo** ~ right angle.

rettore *sm* rector.

reumatismi *smpl* rheumatism *(sg)*.

reversibile *agg* reversible.

revisionare *vt (apparecchio, macchina)* to service, to overhaul; *(testo)* to revise.

revisione *sf (di apparecchio)* service; *(di conti)* audit(ing); *(di scritto)* revision.

revocare *vt* to revoke.

revolver *sm inv* revolver.

riabilitare *vt* to rehabilitate.

riacquistare *vt* to regain.

riaggiustare *vt* to readjust.

rialzare *vt* to raise ❑ **rialzarsi** *vr* to get up.

rialzo *sm* rise.

rianimazione *sf (reparto)* intensive care.

riaperto, -a *pp* → **riaprire**.

riapertura *sf* reopening; ~ **delle scuole** beginning of the school term.

riaprire *vt & vi* to reopen ❑ **riaprirsi** *vr* to reopen.

riarmo *sm* rearming.

riassetto *sm* reorganization.

riassumere *vt (ricapitolare)* to summarize; *(impiegato)* to reemploy; *(riprendere)* to resume.

riassunto, -a *pp* → **riassumere** ♦ *sm* summary.

riattaccare *vt (attaccare di nuovo)* to re-attach; *(bottone)* to sew back on; *(ricominciare)* to start again; *(al telefono)* to hang up.

riavere *vt (avere di nuovo)* to have again; *(avere indietro)* to get back; *(riacquistare)* to regain, to recover ❑ **riaversi da** *vr + prep* to recover from.

ribadire *vt* to confirm.

ribaltabile *agg* folding.

ribaltare *vt* to overturn.

ribassare *vt* to lower ♦ *vi* to fall.

ribasso *sm* fall, reduction.

ribattere *vt (palla)* to return ♦ *vi (replicare)* to answer back.

ribellarsi *vr* to rebel; ~ **a qn** to rebel against sb.

ribelle *agg* rebellious.

ribellione *sf* rebellion.

ribes *sm inv*: ~ **nero** blackcurrant; ~ **rosso** redcurrant.

ribollire *vi (fig)* to seethe.

ribrezzo *sm* horror; **far** ~ **a qn** to revolt sb.

ricadere *vi (cadere di nuovo)* to fall again; *(in errore, vizio)* to relapse; *(capelli, vestiti)* to hang down ❑ **ricadere su** *v + prep* to fall on.

ricalcare *vt* to trace.

ricamare *vt* to embroider.

ricambiare *vt (sentimento, favore)* to return; *(cambiare di nuovo)* to change again.

ricambio *sm (sostituzione)* exchange, replacement; **in** ~ **in**

return ❏ **ricambi** *smpl* spare parts.

ricamo *sm* embroidery.

ricapitolare *vt* to summarize.

ricaricare *vt* (*macchina fotografica, arma*) to reload; (*batteria*) to recharge; (*orologio*) to wind up.

ricattare *vt* to blackmail.

ricatto *sm* blackmail.

ricavare *vt* (*estrarre*) to extract; (*ottenere*) to obtain.

ricavato *sm* (*guadagno*) proceeds (*pl*).

ricchezza *sf* wealth ❏ **ricchezze** *sfpl* wealth (*sg*); ~ **naturali** natural resources.

ricciarelli *smpl* diamond-shaped sweets made from marzipan (a speciality of Siena).

riccio, -a, -ci, -ce *agg* curly ◆ *sm* (*di capelli*) curl; (*animale*) hedgehog; ~ **di mare** sea urchin.

ricciolo *sm* curl.

ricciuto, -a *agg* curly.

ricco, -a, -chi, -che *agg* rich, wealthy; ~ **di qc** rich in sthg.

ricerca, -che *sf* research; (*di persona, di cosa*) search; **essere alla ~ di** to be in search of.

ricercare *vt* (*cercare di nuovo*) to look for (again); (*ladro*) to look for, to search for.

ricercatezza *sf* refinement.

ricercato, -a *agg* (*elegante*) refined; (*apprezzato*) in demand, sought-after; **essere ~ dalla polizia** to be wanted by the police.

ricercatore, -trice *sm, f* researcher.

ricetta *sf* recipe; ~ **medica** prescription.

ricettazione *sf* receiving (stolen goods).

ricevere *vt* (*lettera, regalo*) to receive, to get; (*schiaffo, palla*) to get; (*accogliere*) to welcome; (*ospite*) to entertain; (*cliente, paziente*) to receive.

ricevimento *sm* reception.

ricevitore *sm* receiver.

ricevuta *sf* receipt; **mi può fare una ~?** may I have a receipt?

ricezione *sf* reception.

richiamare *vt* (*ritelefonare, per far tornare*) to call back; (*attirare*) to attract; (*rimproverare*) to reprimand; ~ **alla mente qc a qn** to remind sb of sthg.

richiamo *sm* (*per far tornare*) call; (*attrazione*) appeal, attraction; (*di vaccinazione*) booster.

richiedere *vt* (*ridomandare*) to ask again; (*aiuto, spiegazioni*) to ask for; (*necessitare di*) to require; **gli ho richiesto le chiavi** (*indietro*) I asked him for my keys back.

richiesta *sf* (*domanda*) request; (*esigenza*) demand; **a ~** on request.

richiesto, -a *pp* → **richiedere** ◆ *agg* in demand, sought-after.

richiudere *vt* to close again.

riciclare *vt* to recycle.

ricollegare *vt* (*centri isolati*) to reconnect; (*fatti, discorsi*) to connect, to relate ❏ **ricollegarsi** *vr*: **ricollegarsi a** (*riferirsi*) to refer to; (*fatto*) to be connected with.

ricominciare *vt & vi* to begin again, to start again; ~ **a fare qc** to begin again, to resume doing sthg.

ricompensa *sf* reward.

ricompensare *vt* to reward.

ricomporre *vt* to reconstruct □ **ricomporsi** *vr* to regain one's composure.

ricomposto, -a *pp* → **ricomporre**.

riconciliare *vt* to reconcile □ **riconciliarsi** *vr* to be reconciled.

ricondotto, -a *pp* → **ricondurre**.

ricondurre *vt* (*in luogo*) to take back, to bring back.

riconferma *sf* (*conferma ulteriore*) reconfirmation; (*dimostrazione*) proof.

riconfermare *vt* to reconfirm.

riconoscente *agg* grateful.

riconoscere *vt* to recognize; (*ammettere*) to admit.

riconquistare *vt* (*territorio*) to reconquer; (*stima, rispetto*) to regain.

riconsegnare *vt* to give back.

ricoperto, -a *pp* → **ricoprire**.

ricopiare *vt* to copy.

ricoprire *vt* (*poltrona, dolce*) to cover; (*carica*) to hold; ~ **qn/qc di qc** to cover sb/sthg with sthg.

ricordare *vt* to remember, to recall; ~ **qc a qn** to remind sb of sthg; **non mi ricordo l'indirizzo** I don't remember the address □ **ricordarsi di** *vr + prep* to remember; **ricordarsi di aver fatto qc** to remember doing o having done sthg; **ricordarsi di fare qc** to remember to do sthg.

ricordo *sm* (*memoria*) memory; (*oggetto*) souvenir.

ricorrente *agg* recurrent.

ricorrenza *sf* anniversary.

ricorrere *vi* (*ripetersi*) to recur □ **ricorrere a** *v + prep* (*rivolgersi a*) to turn to; (*utilizzare*) to resort to.

ricorso, -a *pp* → **ricorrere** ♦ *sm* (DIR) appeal; **far ~ a qc** (*utilizzare*) to resort to sthg.

ricostruire *vt* (*edificio*) to rebuild; (*fatto*) to reconstruct.

ricotta *sf* ricotta (*soft cheese made from milk whey*).

ricoverare *vt*: ~ **qn in ospedale** to admit sb to hospital.

ricreare *vt* (*creare di nuovo*) to recreate.

ricreazione *sf* (*a scuola*) break.

ricredersi *vr* to change one's mind.

ricucire *vt* to mend.

ricuperare = **recuperare**.

ridacchiare *vt* to snigger.

ridare *vt* (*dare di nuovo*) to give again; (*restituire*) to give back.

ridere *vi* to laugh; **morire dal ~** to die laughing □ **ridere di** *v + prep* to laugh at.

ridetto, -a *pp* → **ridire**.

ridicolo, -a *agg* ridiculous.

ridimensionare *vt*: ~ **un problema** to get a problem into perspective.

ridire *vt* (*ripetere*) to repeat; **avere qualcosa da ~** to find fault.

ridondante *agg* redundant.

ridosso *sm*: **a ~ (di qc)** behind (sthg).

ridotto, -a *pp* → **ridurre** ♦ *agg* (*prezzo*) reduced; (*formato*) smaller; ~ **male** in a bad state.

ridurre *vt* to reduce □ **ridursi** *vr* (*diminuire*) to shrink; **ridursi a** *vr*

riduzione 218

+ *prep* to be reduced to.

riduzione *sf* reduction.

rielaborare *vt* to redesign.

riempire *vt* to fill; *(modulo)* to fill in; **~ di** to fill with ❏ **riempirsi di** *vr* + *prep (stadio, cinema)* to fill with; *(fam: mangiare)* to stuff o.s. with.

rientrare *vi (entrare di nuovo)* to go/come back in; *(a casa, in patria)* to return; *(essere compreso)* to be included; *(avere una rientranza)* to curve inwards.

riepilogo, -ghi *sm* summary.

rievocare *vt (ricordare)* to recall; *(far ricordare)* to commemorate.

rifare *vt (fare di nuovo)* to do again; *(ricostruire)* to rebuild; **~ il letto** to make the bed ❏ **rifarsi di** *vr* + *prep (perdita)* to recover; **rifarsi di qc su qn** to get one's own back on sb for sthg.

rifatto, -a *pp* → **rifare**.

riferimento *sm* reference; **fare ~ a** to refer to.

riferire *vt*: **~ qc (a qn)** to report sthg (to sb) ❏ **riferirsi a** *vr* + *prep* to refer to.

rifilare *vt*: **~ qc a qn** *(fam: merce)* to palm sthg off onto sb; *(fam: compito)* to saddle sb with sthg.

rifiniture *sfpl* finishing touches.

rifiorire *vi* to flower again.

rifiutare *vt* to refuse; **~ di fare qc** to refuse to do sthg.

rifiuto *sm* refusal ❏ **rifiuti** *smpl (spazzatura)* rubbish *(sg)* (Br), trash *(sg)* (Am).

riflessione *sf* reflection.

riflessivo, -a *agg* reflexive.

riflesso, -a *pp* → **riflettere** ♦ *sm (luce)* reflection; *(conseguenza)* repercussion; *(MED)* reflex.

riflettere *vt & vi* to reflect; **~ su** to reflect on, to think about ❏ **riflettersi** *vr* to be reflected; **riflettersi su** *vr* + *prep (influire)* to influence, to have repercussions on.

riflettore *sm (di teatro)* spotlight; *(di stadio)* floodlight.

riflusso *sm (flusso contrario)* flow; *(di marea)* ebb.

riforma *sf* reform.

riformare *vt* to reform; *(MIL)* to invalid out.

rifornimento *sm*: **fare ~ di qc** to stock up with sthg ❏ **rifornimenti** *smpl* supplies.

rifornire *vt*: **~ qn/qc di** to supply sb/sthg with ❏ **rifornirsi di** *vr* + *prep* to stock up with.

rifrangere *vt* to refract.

rifratto, -a *pp* → **rifrangere**.

rifugiarsi *vr* to take refuge.

rifugiato, -a *sm, f* refugee.

rifugio *sm (riparo)* shelter, refuge; **~ alpino** mountain hut.

riga, -ghe *sf* line; *(di capelli)* parting; *(righello)* ruler; **mettersi in ~** to get into line; **a righe** *(tessuto)* striped; *(foglio)* lined.

rigare *vt* to scratch ♦ *vi*: **~ diritto** to toe the line.

rigattiere *sm* junk dealer.

rigettare *vt (gettare indietro)* to throw back; *(respingere)* to reject; *(fam: vomitare)* to throw up.

rigetto *sm (MED)* rejection.

rigidità sf (di oggetto) rigidity; (del corpo) stiffness; (di clima) harshness; (di regolamento, persona) strictness.

rigido, -a agg (non elastico) rigid; (membra) stiff; (clima) harsh; (severo) strict.

rigirare vt (voltare) to turn (round); ~ **il discorso** to change the subject ❑ **rigirarsi** vr (voltarsi) to turn round; (nel letto) to turn over.

rigo, -ghi sm line.

rigoglioso, -a agg luxuriant.

rigore sm rigour; (SPORT) penalty; **essere di** ~ to be compulsory.

rigoroso, -a agg rigorous.

rigovernare vt to wash up.

riguardare vt (guardare di nuovo) to look at again; (controllare) to check; (concernere) to concern ❑ **riguardarsi** vr to look after o.s.; **riguardati!** look after yourself!, take care!; **questo non ti riguarda** this has nothing to do with you.

riguardo sm (attenzione) care; (stima) regard, respect; ~ **a** with regard to.

rilanciare vt to relaunch.

rilancio sm relaunch; (economico) recovery.

rilasciare vt (intervista) to give; (ostaggio) to release; (documento, diploma) to issue.

rilassare vt to relax ❑ **rilassarsi** vr to relax.

rilegare vt to bind.

rilento avv: **a** ~ slowly.

rilevante agg relevant.

rilevare vt (notare) to notice; (mettere in evidenza) to point out;

(dati) to collect; (COMM) to take over.

rilievo sm relief; **mettere in** ~ **qc** to emphasize sthg.

riluttante agg reluctant.

rima sf rhyme.

rimandare vt (mandare di nuovo) to send again; (mandare indietro) to send back; (riunione, esame) to postpone; ~ **qn a qc** (in testo) to refer sb to sthg; ~ **qn in italiano** (SCOL) to make sb resit their Italian exam.

rimando sm cross-reference.

rimanente agg remaining ♦ sm remainder.

rimanenza sf remainder.

rimanere vi (in luogo) to stay, to remain; (nel tempo) to last, to remain; (avanzare) to be left; (essere) to be; **mi sono rimaste diecimila lire** I have ten thousand lire left; **siamo rimasti in due** there are (only) two of us left; **sono rimasto solo** I was left on my own; ~ **indietro** (di luogo) to be left behind; (nel lavoro) to fall behind.

rimarginare vt to heal ❑ **rimarginarsi** vr to heal.

rimasto, -a pp → **rimanere**.

rimasuglio sm scrap.

rimbalzare vi (palla) to bounce; (proiettile) to ricochet.

rimbalzo sm (di palla) bounce; (di proiettile) ricochet.

rimbambito, -a agg daft.

rimboccare vt (lenzuola, coperta) to tuck in; (maniche, pantaloni) to turn up; **rimboccarsi le maniche** to roll up one's sleeves.

rimbombare vi to rumble.

rimborsare vt to reimburse, to refund.

rimborso sm refund; **~ spese** refund of expenses.

rimediare vt (fam: procurarsi) to find ♦ vi: **~ a qc** (sbaglio, danno) to make amends for sth.

rimedio sm remedy; **porre ~ a qc** to remedy sth.

rimescolare vt (liquido) to mix well; (carte) to shuffle.

rimessa sf (per veicoli) garage; (per aerei) hangar; (nel calcio) throw-in.

rimesso, -a pp → rimettere.

rimettere vt (mettere di nuovo) to put back; (indossare di nuovo) to put back on; (perdonare) to forgive, to pardon; (vomitare) to vomit; **~ a posto** to tidy up; **rimetterci (qc)** to lose (sth) □ **rimettersi** vr (guarire) to get better, to recover; (tempo) to clear up; **rimettersi a fare qc** to start doing sth again.

rimmel® sm inv mascara.

rimodernare vt to modernize.

rimontare vt to reassemble ♦ vi to catch up.

rimorchiare vt (veicolo) to tow; (fam: ragazza) to pick up.

rimorchiatore sm tug.

rimorchio sm (operazione) towing; (di veicolo) trailer.

rimorso sm remorse.

rimosso, -a pp → rimuovere.

rimozione sf (spostamento) removal; (fig: licenziamento) dismissal; **'~ forzata** O **coatta'** 'tow-away zone'.

rimpatriare vt to repatriate ♦ vi to go home.

rimpiangere vt: **~ di aver fatto qc** to regret doing sth.

rimpianto, -a pp → rimpiangere ♦ sm regret.

rimpiattino sm hide-and-seek.

rimpiazzare vt to replace.

rimpicciolire vt to make smaller ♦ vi to become smaller.

rimpinzarsi : rimpinzarsi di vr + prep to stuff o.s. with.

rimproverare vt to scold.

rimprovero sm scolding.

rimuginare vt to brood over ♦ vi: **~ (su qc)** to ponder (sth).

rimuovere vt (spostare) to remove; (da carica) to dismiss.

Rinascimento sm: il **~** the Renaissance.

rinascita sf (di foglie, capelli) regrowth; (economica, sociale) revival.

rincalzare vt (lenzuola) to tuck in; (muro, scala) to prop up.

rincarare vi to increase in price.

rincasare vi to return home.

rinchiudere vt to confine □ **rinchiudersi in** vr + prep to shut o.s. up in.

rinchiuso, -a pp → rinchiudere.

rincorrere vt to chase.

rincorsa sf run-up.

rincorso, -a pp → rincorrere.

rincrescere vi: **mi rincresce che tu parta** I'm sorry you're leaving; **mi rincresce di non poterti aiutare** I'm sorry I can't help you.

rinculo sm recoil.

rinfacciare *vt*: ~ qc a qn *(colpa, difetto)* to reproach sb with o for sthg; *(favore)* to throw sthg in sb's face.

rinforzare *vt (muscoli, capelli)* to strengthen; *(rendere più solido)* to reinforce.

rinforzo *sm* reinforcement.

rinfrescante *agg* refreshing.

rinfrescare *vt (atmosfera)* to cool ♦ *v impers*: **è rinfrescato** it's got cooler; **~ la memoria a qn** to refresh sb's memory ☐ **rinfrescarsi** *vr (ristorarsi)* to refresh o.s.; *(lavarsi)* to freshen up.

rinfresco, -schi *sm* reception.

rinfusa : alla rinfusa *avv* higgledy-piggledy.

ringhiare *vi* to snarl.

ringhiera *sf (di balcone)* railings *(pl)*; *(di scala)* banisters *(pl)*.

ringiovanire *vt*: ~ qn to make sb look younger ♦ *vi* to look young again, to be rejuvenated.

ringraziamento *sm* thanks *(pl)*.

ringraziare *vt* to thank; ~ qn di qc to thank sb for sthg.

rinnegare *vt (persona)* to disown; *(fede)* to renounce.

rinnovamento *sm (cambiamento)* updating; *(di impianti, locale)* renovation.

rinnovare *vt* to renew; *(locale)* to renovate.

rinnovo *sm (di contratto, guardaroba)* renewal; *(di casa)* renovation.

rinoceronte *sm* rhinoceros.

rinomato, -a *agg* famous.

rinsaldare *vt* to strengthen.

rintocco, -chi *sm (di campana)* toll; *(di orologio)* chime.

rintracciare *vt* to track down.

rintronare *vt* to deafen ♦ *vi* to boom.

rinuncia, -ce *sf* renunciation.

rinunciare : rinunciare a *v + prep (rifiutare)* to renounce; *(privarsi di)* to give up; ~ **a fare qc** to give up doing sthg.

rinunzia = **rinuncia**.

rinunziare = **rinunciare**.

rinvenire *vt (trovare)* to find; *(scoprire)* to find out ♦ *vi* to come round/to, to revive.

rinvenuto, -a *pp* → **rinvenire**.

rinviare *vt* to return; ~ qc (a) *(posporre)* to postpone sthg (until).

rinvio *sm (di lettera, palla)* return; *(di appuntamento, riunione)* postponement; *(a pagina, capitolo)* cross-reference.

rione *sm* quarter.

riordinare *vt (mettere in ordine)* to tidy up; *(cambiare ordine)* to reorganize.

riorganizzare *vt* to reorganize.

riparare *vt (aggiustare)* to repair; *(proteggere)* to protect; *(rimediare)* to make up for ☐ **ripararsi** *vr* to shelter; **ripararsi da qc** to shelter/protect o.s. from sthg.

riparazione *sf* repair.

riparo *sm (protezione)* protection; *(rifugio)* shelter.

ripartire *vt (eredità, guadagno)* to share out; *(compiti, responsabilità)* to allocate ♦ *vi* to leave again.

ripassare vt to go over ♦ vi to go/come back.

ripensare : ripensare a v + prep (riflettere su) to think over; (cambiare idea) to change one's mind about; (ricordare) to recall.

ripercosso, -a pp → **ripercuotersi**.

ripercuotersi : ripercuotersi su vr + prep to influence.

ripercussione sf repercussion.

ripescare vt (dall'acqua) to fish out; (ritrovare) to find.

ripetere vt to repeat □ **ripetersi** vr (persona) to repeat o.s.; (avvenimento) to happen again.

ripetitivo, -a agg repetitive.

ripetizione sf (replica) repetition □ **ripetizioni** sfpl private lessons.

ripiano sm shelf.

ripicca, -che sf: **per ~** out of spite.

ripido, -a agg steep.

ripiegare vt (lenzuola) to fold (up); (piegare di nuovo) to refold ♦ vi (indietreggiare) to retreat □ **ripiegare su** v + prep (rassegnarsi a) to make do with.

ripiego, -ghi sm expedient; **per ~** as a makeshift.

ripieno, -a agg: **~ (di qc)** (casa, cassetto) full (of sthg); (panino) filled (with sthg); (tacchino) stuffed (with sthg) ♦ sm (di panino) filling.

riporre vt (mettere al suo posto) to put back; (mettere via) to put away; **~ la propria fiducia in qn** to place one's trust in sb.

riportare vt (restituire, ricondurre) to take/bring back; (riferire)

to report, to tell; (ottenere) to obtain.

riposare vi (rilassarsi) to rest; (dormire) to sleep ♦ vt to rest □ **riposarsi** vr (rilassarsi) to rest; (dormire) to sleep.

riposo sm rest; (sonno) sleep; **a ~** retired.

ripostiglio sm store room.

riposto, -a pp → **riporre**.

riprendere vt (prendere di nuovo) to take again; (ritirare) to take back; (ricominciare) to resume; (rimproverare) to reproach; (filmare) to shoot, to film ♦ vi: **~ a fare qc** to start doing sthg again □ **riprendersi da** vr + prep to recover from.

ripresa sf (di attività) resumption; (da malattia) recovery; (di motore) acceleration; (cinematografica) shot; **a più riprese** several times.

ripreso, -a pp → **riprendere**.

riprodotto, -a pp → **riprodurre**.

riprodurre vt to reproduce □ **riprodursi** vr to reproduce.

riproduzione sf reproduction.

riprova sf confirmation.

riprovevole agg reprehensible.

ripugnante agg disgusting.

ripugnare vi: **~ a qn** (disgustare qn) to repel o disgust sb.

ripulire vt (pulire) to clean up (rubare) to clean out.

riquadro sm square; (di parete soffitto) panel.

risalire vt to go back up □ **risalire a** v + prep to go back to.

risaltare *vi* to stand out.

risalto *sm* prominence; **mettere in ~ qc** to make sthg stand out.

risaputo, -a *agg*: **è ~ che ...** it is common knowledge that ...

risarcimento *sm* compensation.

risarcire *vt*: **~ qn (di qc)** to compensate sb (for sthg).

risata *sf* laugh.

riscaldamento *sm* heating; **~ centrale** central heating.

riscaldare *vt* (*stanza*) to heat; (*mani*) to warm; (*cibo*) to heat up ❏ **riscaldarsi** *vr* (*persona*) to warm up; (*diventare caldo*) to get warmer.

riscatto *sm* ransom.

rischiarare *vt* to light up ❏ **rischiararsi** *vr* to clear.

rischiare *vt* to risk ◆ *vi*: **rischio di arrivare in ritardo** I'm likely to be late; **ha rischiato di essere investito** he nearly got run over.

rischio *sm* risk; **correre il ~ di fare qc** to run the risk of doing sthg.

rischioso, -a *agg* risky.

risciacquare *vt* to rinse.

riscontrare *vt* to find.

riscontro *sm* (*conferma*) confirmation.

riscosso, -a *pp* → **riscuotere**.

riscuotere *vt* (*somma*) to collect; (*stipendio, pensione*) to receive; (*assegno*) to cash; (*successo, consenso*) to win, to earn.

risentire : risentire di *v + prep* to be affected by ❏ **risentirsi** *vr*: **risentirsi di** o **per qc** to take offence at sthg.

riserva *sf* (*provvista, giocatore*) reserve; (*di caccia, pesca*) preserve; (*restrizione*) reservation; **essere in ~** (*AUTO*) to be low on petrol (*Br*) o gas (*Am*); **di ~** in reserve.

riservare *vt* to save; (*prenotare*) to book, to reserve.

riservato, -a *agg* (*posto, carattere*) reserved; (*informazione, lettera*) confidential.

risi e bisi *smpl* rice and pea soup (a speciality of Veneto).

risiedere *vi* to reside.

riso *pp* → **ridere** ◆ *sm* (*cereale*) rice; (*il ridere: pl f risa*) laughter.

risolto, -a *pp* → **risolvere**.

risoluto, -a *agg* (*deciso*) determined.

risoluzione *sf* (*decisione*) resolution.

risolvere *vt* (*problema, caso*) to solve; (*questione*) to resolve ❏ **risolversi** *vr* (*problema*) to resolve itself; **risolversi a fare qc** to make up one's mind to do sthg; **risolversi in** *vr + prep* (*andare a finire*) to turn out.

risonanza *sf* of resonance; **avere ~ grande ~** (*fatto, notizia*) to arouse a great deal of interest.

risorgere *vi* (*risuscitare*) to revive; (*problema*) to recur.

risorsa *sf* resort ❏ **risorse** *sfpl* resources.

risorto, -a *pp* → **risorgere**.

risotto *sm* risotto; **~ alla boscaiola** risotto with tomatoes, mushrooms and parsley; **~ di mare** seafood risotto; **~ alla milanese** risotto with saffron and lots of

Parmesan cheese; ~ **ai tartufi** *risotto with truffles.*

risparmiare *vi* to save ◆ *vt* (*non consumare*) to save; (*non uccidere*) to spare; (*evitare*): ~ **qc a qn** to spare sb sthg.

risparmio *sm* (*somma*) savings (*pl*); (*di tempo, soldi, fatica*) saving.

rispecchiare *vt* to reflect.

rispettabile *agg* respectable.

rispettare *vt* to respect; **farsi** ~ to command respect.

rispettivamente *avv* respectively.

rispettivo, -a *agg* respective.

rispetto *sm* respect; **mancare di** ~ **(a qn)** to be disrespectful (to sb); ~ **a** (*a paragone di*) compared to; (*in relazione a*) as for.

rispettoso, -a *agg* respectful.

risplendere *vi* to shine.

rispondere *vi* to answer, to reply; (*freni*) to respond ❏ **rispondere a** *v* + *prep* (*corrispondere*) to meet; ~ **a qn** to answer sb; **rispondere di** *v* + *prep* to be responsible for.

risposta *sf* answer; (*azione*) response; **in** ~ **a qc** in reply to sthg.

risposto *pp* → **rispondere**.

rissa *sf* brawl.

ristabilire *vt* to restore ❏ **ristabilirsi** *vr* to recover.

ristagnare *vi* (*acqua*) to become stagnant; (*fig: industria*) to stagnate.

ristampa *sf* (*opera*) reprint.

ristorante *sm* restaurant.

ristoro *sm* refreshment.

ristretto, -a *pp* → **restringere** ◆ *agg* (*numero*) limited; (*brodo*) thick; (*uso*) restricted.

ristrutturare *vt* (*azienda*) to reorganize; (*casa*) to alter.

risucchiare *vt* to suck in.

risultare *vi* to turn out to be; **mi risulta che** ... I understand that ...; **non mi risulta** not as far as I know ❏ **risultare da** *v* + *prep* to result from.

risultato *sm* result.

risuolare *vt* to resole.

risuscitare *vt* to resuscitate.

risvegliare *vt* (*dal sonno*) to wake up; (*memoria, appetito*) to awaken.

risvolto *sm* (*di pantaloni*) turn-up (*Br*), cuff (*Am*); (*di giacca*) lapel; (*fig: conseguenza*) implication.

ritagliare *vt* to cut out.

ritaglio *sm* (*di giornale*) cutting; (*di stoffa*) scrap; **nei ritagli di tempo** in one's spare time.

ritardare *vi* to be late ◆ *vt* (*rimandare*) to delay; (*rallentare*) to slow down.

ritardatario, -a *sm, f* latecomer.

ritardo *sm* (*di treno, pagamento*) delay; **in** ~ late.

ritenere *vt* (*giudicare*) to believe; (*somma*) to deduct.

ritentare *vt* to try again.

ritirare *vt* to withdraw; (*pacco, da lavanderia*) to collect; (*insulto, promessa*) to take back ❏ **ritirarsi** *vr* (*da attività*) to retire; (*restringersi*) to shrink.

ritirata *sf* retreat.

ritiro sm (di pacco) collection; (di patente, passaporto) confiscation; (sportivo, spirituale) retreat; (da attività) retirement.

ritmo sm (MUS) rhythm; (di pulsazioni) beat; (di vita, lavoro) pace.

rito sm rite.

ritornare vi (andare, venire di nuovo) to return, to go/come back; (ricomparire) to recur; (ridiventare): ~ **pulito** to be clean again.

ritornello sm chorus.

ritorno sm return; **essere di** ~ to be back.

ritrarre vt (ritirare) to withdraw; (rappresentare) to portray.

ritratto, -a pp → **ritrarre** ♦ sm portrait.

ritrovare vt (cosa persa) to find; (riacquistare) to regain □ **ritrovarsi** vr (incontrarsi) to meet; (in situazione) to find o.s.

ritrovo sm meeting place.

ritto, -a agg upright.

riunione sf (incontro) meeting; (riconciliazione) reconciliation.

riunire vt to bring together □ **riunirsi** vr to meet again.

riuscire vi (avere esito) to turn out; (aver successo) to succeed; ~ a **fare qc** to manage to do sthg; ~ **in qc** to succeed in sthg.

riva sf (di fiume) bank; (di lago, mare) shore.

rivale agg & smf rival.

rivalutare vt to revalue.

rivedere vt (vedere di nuovo) to see again; (riesaminare) to review; (ripassare) to revise □ **rivedersi** vr to meet again.

rivelare vt to reveal.

rivendicare vt (diritto, bene) to claim; (attentato) to claim responsibility for.

rivendita sf (negozio) dealer.

rivenditore, -trice sm, f retailer; ~ **autorizzato** authorized dealer.

riversare vt (fig: affetto) to lavish; (colpa) to heap □ **riversarsi** vr to pour.

rivestimento sm covering.

rivestire vt (poltrona) to cover; (carica) to hold; (ruolo) to play □ **rivestirsi** vr to get dressed again.

riviera sf coast.

i LA RIVIERA ADRIATICA

The bathing resorts which line the winding Adriatic coast are collectively known as "la Riviera Adriatica". Tourists from the rest of Italy and from abroad flock to famous resorts like Jesolo near Venice and Rimini on the Romagna coast. Renowned for its beautiful beaches and its first-rate amenities, Rimini is the quintessential Italian seaside town, teeming with life 24 hours a day.

rivincita sf (di partita) return match; (rivalsa) revenge.

rivisto, -a pp → **rivedere** ♦ sf (giornale) magazine.

rivolgere vt (parola) to address; (attenzione, occhiata) to direct □ **rivolgersi a** vr + prep to go and speak to.

rivoltante agg revolting.

rivoltare vt (rigirare) to turn over; (disgustare) to disgust □ **rivoltarsi** vr to rebel.

rivoltella sf revolver.

rivolto, -a pp → **rivolgere** ♦ sf revolt.

rivoluzionario, -a agg & sm, f revolutionary.

rivoluzione sf revolution.

rizzare vt to stand on end □ **rizzarsi** vr to stand up.

roastbeef ['rɔzbif] sm inv joint of beef braised or grilled, then served sliced.

roba sf (cose) stuff, things (pl); ~ da mangiare things to eat; ~ da matti! (well I) never!

robiola sf a type of soft rindless cheese.

robot sm inv (automa) robot; (da cucina) food processor.

robusto, -a agg robust, sturdy.

rocca, -che sf fortress.

roccaforte sf stronghold.

rocchetto sm reel, spool.

roccia, -ce sf rock.

roccioso, -a agg rocky.

roco, -a, -chi, -che agg hoarse.

rodaggio sm running-in.

rodere vt to gnaw □ **rodersi di** vr + prep to be consumed with.

rogna sf (malattia) scabies; (fam: guaio) nuisance.

rognone sm kidney; **rognoni alla romana** kidneys fried with garlic, parsley and white wine.

Roma sf Rome.

Romania sf: la ~ Romania.

romanico, -a, -ci, -che agg

Romanesque.

romano, -a agg & sm, f Roman.

romanticismo sm romanticism.

romantico, -a, -ci, -che agg romantic.

romanzo sm (libro) novel.

rombo sm (rumore) roar; (pesce) turbot; **a rombi** (disegno) diamond-patterned.

rompere vt to break; (fidanzamento) to break off; (strappare) to tear ♦ vi (coppia) to break up; **rompersi una gamba** to break one's leg; **smetti di ~!** (fam) lay off! □ **rompersi** vr to break.

rompicapo sm puzzle.

rompiscatole smf inv (fam) pest, pain in the neck.

rondine sf swallow.

ronzare vi to buzz.

ronzio sm (di insetti) buzzing; (rumore) drone.

rosa agg inv (di colore) pink; (sentimentale) sentimental ♦ sf rose ♦ sm (colore) pink.

rosé sm inv rosé.

rosicchiare vt to gnaw, to nibble.

rosmarino sm rosemary.

roso, -a pp → **rodere**.

rosolare vt to brown.

rosolia sf German measles (sg).

rosone sm (di soffitti) ceiling rose; (vetrata) rose window.

rospo sm toad.

rossetto sm lipstick.

rosso, -a agg & sm red; ~ **d'uovo** egg yolk.

rosticceria sf shop selling cooke

food such as roast chicken, lasagna etc.

rosticciana sf grilled or fried pork.

rotaie sfpl rails.

rotazione sf rotation.

rotella sf cog.

rotolare vi (palla, valanga) to roll □ **rotolarsi** vr to roll.

rotolo sm roll; **andare a rotoli** to go to rack and ruin.

rotonda sf circular terrace.

rotondo, -a agg round.

rotta sf route.

rotto, -a pp → **rompere** ♦ agg (spezzato, guasto) broken; (strappato) torn.

rottura sf (azione) breaking; (interruzione) breaking-off; (fam: seccatura) nuisance.

roulette [ru'lɛt] sf roulette.

roulotte [ru'lɔt] sf inv caravan.

routine [ru'tin] sf inv routine.

rovente agg red-hot.

rovescia sf: **alla ~** upside down; (sottosopra) inside out.

rovesciare vt (liquido) to spill; (tavolo, sedia) to overturn; (situazione) to turn upside down □ **rovesciarsi** vr (versarsi) to spill; (capovolgersi) to overturn; (barca) to capsize.

rovescio sm (di vestito, stoffa) wrong side; (pioggia) downpour; (nel tennis) backhand; **al ~** (con l'interno all'esterno) inside out; (con il davanti dietro) back to front.

rovina sf ruin; **andare in ~** to collapse □ **rovine** sfpl ruins.

rovinare vt to ruin □ **rovinarsi**

vr (cosa) to be ruined; (persona) to be ruined.

rovo sm bramble bush.

rozzo, -a agg rough.

ruba sf: **andare a ~** to sell like hot cakes.

rubare vt to steal ♦ vi: **hanno rubato in casa mia** my house has been burgled; **~ qc a qn** to steal sthg from sb.

rubinetto sm tap.

rubino sm ruby.

rubrica, -che sf (di indirizzi) address book; (di giornale) column.

ruderi smpl ruins.

rudimentale agg rudimentary, basic.

ruffiano, -a sm, f creep.

ruga, -ghe sf wrinkle.

rugby ['rɛgbi] sm rugby.

ruggine sf rust.

ruggire vi to roar.

rugiada sf dew.

rullino sm roll of film; **un ~ da 24** a 24-exposure film.

rullo sm (rotolo, arnese) roller; (di tamburo) roll.

rum sm inv rum.

rumore sm noise.

rumoroso, -a agg noisy.

ruolo sm role.

ruota sf wheel; **~ di scorta** spare wheel.

ruotare vi & vt to rotate.

rupe sf cliff.

ruscello sm stream.

ruspa sf excavator.

Russia sf: **la ~** Russia.

russo, -a agg, sm & sf Russian.

rustico, -a, -ci, -che agg rustic.

ruttare vi to belch.

ruvido, -a agg rough.

ruzzolare vi to tumble down.

ruzzolone sm tumble.

S

sabato sm Saturday; **torniamo ~** we'll be back on Saturday; **oggi è ~** it's Saturday today; **~ 6 maggio** Saturday 6 May; **~ pomeriggio** Saturday afternoon; **~ prossimo** next Saturday; **~ scorso** last Saturday; **di ~** on Saturdays; **a ~!** see you Saturday!

sabbia sf sand.

sabotare vt to sabotage.

sacca, -che sf (borsa) bag.

saccarina sf saccharin.

saccente agg conceited.

saccheggiare vt (case, villaggi) to loot; (fig: con acquisti) to buy up.

sacchetto sm bag.

sacco, -chi sm (di carta, nylon®) bag; (di iuta) sack; **un ~ di** a lot of; **~ a pelo** sleeping bag.

sacerdote sm priest.

sacrificare vt to sacrifice ❑

sacrificarsi vr to make sacrifices.

sacrificio sm sacrifice.

sacro, -a agg sacred.

sadico, -a, -ci, -che agg sadistic ◆ sm, f sadist.

safari sm inv safari.

saggezza sf wisdom.

saggio, -a, -gi, -ge agg wise ◆ sm (persona) wise man, sage; (campione) sample; (libro, ricerca) essay.

Sagittario sm Sagittarius.

sagoma sf (profilo, forma) outline; (fam: persona) character.

sagra sf festival, feast.

i **SAGRA**

A "sagra" is a local festival held in celebration of the agricultural produce typical of a particular town or village (wine, truffles, cherries and so on). As well as sampling and buying the local produce, you can eat and drink in the open air and sometimes dance to the music of the local brass band.

sai → sapere.

saint-honoré [sɛ̃ɔnɔ're] sm inv dessert consisting of a puff pastry base topped with cream and surrounded by choux buns.

sala sf (salotto) living room; (di palazzo) hall; **~ d'aspetto** o **d'attesa** waiting room; **~ da gioco** gaming room; **~ operatoria** operating theatre; **~ da pranzo** dining room.

salame sm salami.

salare vt to salt.

salario sm wage.

salatini smpl salted crackers.

salato, -a agg (con sale) salted (con troppo sale) salty; (fam: caro) expensive.

saldare vt (metalli) to weld; (de

bito, conto) to settle.

saldo, -a *agg (resistente, stabile)* firm ◆ *sm* balance ❏ **saldi** *mpl* sales.

sale *sm* salt; ~ **grosso** cooking salt.

salice *sm* willow; ~ **piangente** weeping willow.

saliente *agg* salient.

saliera *sf* saltcellar *(Br)*, salt shaker *(Am)*.

salire *vt (scale)* to go up ◆ *vi* to go up; *(aereo)* to climb; ~ **in** O **su** *(treno, moto)* to get onto; *(auto)* to get into; ~ **su** *(tetto, podio)* to climb onto; ~ **a bordo** to board.

salita *sf* climb; **in** ~ uphill.

saliva *sf* saliva.

salmì *sm* → **lepre**.

salmone *sm* salmon.

salone *sm (sala)* sitting room; *(mostra)* show.

salotto *sm* lounge.

salpare *vi (partire)* to set sail ◆ *vt*: ~ **l'ancora** to weigh anchor.

salsa *sf* sauce; ~ **di pomodoro** tomato sauce.

salsiccia, -ce *sf* sausage.

saltare *vt (scavalcare)* to jump (over); *(omettere)* to skip ◆ *vi* to jump; **fare** ~ **qc** to blow sthg up; ~ **fuori (da qc)** to jump out (from sthg); ~ **giù da qc** to jump down from sthg; ~ **su (qc)** to jump on (sthg).

saltimbocca *sm inv* thin slices of veal rolled up with ham and sage.

salto *sm (balzo)* jump; *(visita)* fare un ~ **in città** to pop into town; ~ **in alto/lungo** high/long

jump; ~ **con l'asta** pole vault.

salumeria *sf* delicatessen.

salumi *smpl* cold meats and salami.

salutare *vt (incontrandosi)* to greet, to say hello to; *(andando via)* to say goodbye to ❏ **salutarsi** *vr (incontrandosi)* to say hello; *(andando via)* to say goodbye; **salutamelo!** say hello to him from me!

salute *sf* health; **bere alla ~ di qn** to drink to sb's health.

saluto *sm (incontrandosi)* greeting; *(andando via)* goodbye; *(col capo)* nod; *(con la mano)* wave.

salvadanaio *sm* moneybox.

salvagente *sm (giubbotto)* life jacket; *(ciambella)* life buoy; *(spartitraffico)* traffic island.

salvaguardare *vt* to safeguard.

salvare *vt (vita, persona)* to survive; *(onore)* to protect ❏ **salvarsi** *vr* to save o.s.

salvataggio *sm* rescue.

salvavita® *sm inv* fuse box.

salve *esclam (fam)* hello!

salvezza *sf* safety.

salvia *sf* sage.

salvietta *sf* wet wipe.

salvo, -a *agg* safe ◆ *prep* except for; **essere in** ~ to be safe; ~ **imprevisti** barring accidents.

san → **santo**.

sandali *smpl* sandals.

sangue *sm* blood; **a ~ freddo** in cold blood.

sanguinare *vi* to bleed.

sanità *sf* health service.

sanitario, -a *agg (sistema,*

servizio) health *(dav s)*; *(condizioni)* sanitary ❑ **sanitari** *smpl* bathroom fittings.

San Marino *sf* San Marino.

ℹ️ SAN MARINO

In central northern Italy, not far from the Adriatic coast, sits San Marino, one of the world's smallest countries. Although it is only 60 kilometres square, it is a fully independent sovereign state, and has its own currency and stamps.

---

sano, -a *agg* healthy; **~ e salvo** safe and sound; **~ come un pesce** as fit as a fiddle.

San Silvestro *sf*: **la notte di ~** New Year's Eve.

ℹ️ SAN SILVESTRO

New Year's Eve is known as "San Silvestro" in Italy. People either spend the evening at home, with family and friends, or go out to a "veglione" (dance) which lasts until the small hours of New Year's Day. A "cenone" (big dinner) is eaten, and on the stroke of midnight bottles of "spumante" (sparkling wine) are uncorked and everyone wishes each other "buon anno" (Happy New Year). Firecrackers are let off and in some areas the tradition of throwing old objects out of the window still survives.

---

santo, -a *agg* holy ♦ *sm, f* saint; Santo Stefano = Boxing Day; **tutto il ~ giorno** all day long.

ℹ️ SANTO

Every village, town and city in Italy has its own patron saint, honoured once a year with a festival combining religious processions and ceremonies with other more secular events. The streets are decorated with illuminations and there is often a funfair and sweet stalls. Schools and businesses are closed for the day.

---

santuario *sm* sanctuary.

sanzione *sf* sanction.

sapere *vt* to know; **mi sa che non viene** I don't think he's coming; **~ fare qc** to know how to do sthg; **sai sciare?** can you ski?; **far ~ qc a qn** to let sb know sthg ❑ **sapere di** *v + prep* to taste of.

sapone *sm* soap; **~ da bucato** = household soap.

saponetta *sf* bar of soap.

sapore *sm* taste, flavour.

saporito, -a *agg* tasty.

saracinesca, -sche *sf* shutter.

sarcastico, -a, -ci, -che *agg* sarcastic.

sarde *sfpl*: **~ e beccaficu** *fried sardines stuffed with breadcrumbs, pecorino cheese and tomatoes.*

Sardegna *sf*: **la ~** Sardinia.

sardina *sf* sardine.

sardo, -a *agg & sm, f* Sardinian.

sarto, -a *sm, f* dressmaker; *(pe azienda)* tailor.

sartù *sm inv*: **~ di riso** *rice moul filled with liver, mushrooms, pea meatballs, mozzarella cheese an* boiled eggs (a speciality of Naples).

sasso sm stone.

sassofono sm saxophone.

satellite sm (naturale, artificiale) satellite; (TV) satellite TV.

satira sf satire.

sauna sf sauna.

savoiardi smpl sponge fingers.

saziare vt to satisfy.

sazietà sf: mangiare a ~ to eat one's fill.

sazio, -a agg full.

sbadato, -a agg careless.

sbadigliare vi to yawn.

sbadiglio sm yawn.

sbafo sm: a ~ at somebody else's expense.

sbagliare vt to get wrong ♦ vi (fare un errore) to make a mistake; (avere torto) to be wrong; ~ mira to miss one's aim; ~ strada to take the wrong road; ho sbagliato a contare I counted wrong ▫

sbagliarsi vr (fare un errore) to make a mistake; (avere torto) to be wrong; sbagliarsi di grosso to be completely wrong.

sbagliato, -a agg wrong.

sbaglio sm mistake; fare uno ~ to make a mistake; fare qc per ~ to do sthg by mistake.

sballottare vt to toss about.

sbalzare vt to throw.

sbalzo sm (di temperatura) sudden change.

sbandare vi to skid.

sbandata sf skid; prendersi una ~ per qn to fall for sb.

sbandierare vt (sventolare) to wave; (ostentare) to show off.

sbando sm: allo ~ adrift.

sbaraglio sm: andare allo ~ to risk everything.

sbarazzare vt to clear up ▫ **sbarazzarsi di** vr + prep to get rid of.

sbarazzino, -a agg cheeky.

sbarcare vt (merce) to unload; (passeggeri) to disembark ♦ vi (da nave) to disembark.

sbarco sm (di merci) unloading; (di passeggeri) disembarkation.

sbarra sf (spranga) bar; (segno grafico) stroke; (di passaggio a livello) barrier.

sbarrare vt (porta, finestra) to bar; (passaggio) to block; ~ gli occhi to open one's eyes wide.

sbarrato, -a agg (strada) blocked; (porta) barred; (casella) crossed; (parola) crossed out; (occhi) wide open.

sbatacchiare vt to bang, to slam.

sbattere vt to beat; (porta) to bang, to slam ♦ vi to bang; ~ contro (muro) to bang against, to knock against; ~ fuori qn to throw sb out ▫ **sbattersene** vr (fam) not to give a damn.

sbattuto, -a agg downcast.

sbavare vi to dribble.

sbellicarsi vr: ~ dal ridere to split one's sides laughing.

sbiadire vt to fade ▫ **sbiadirsi** vr to fade.

sbiadito, -a agg faded.

sbiancare vi to grow pale ♦ vt to bleach.

sbieco, -a, -chi, -che agg: di ~ (obliquamente) at an angle.

sbigottire vt to dismay □ **sbigottirsi** vr to be dismayed.

sbigottito, -a agg dismayed, aghast.

sbilanciare vt to unbalance □ **sbilanciarsi** vr (perdere l'equilibrio) to lose one's balance; (fig: compromettersi) to compromise o.s.

sbirciare vt (con curiosità) to eye; (di sfuggita) to peep at.

sbizzarrirsi vr to satisfy one's whims.

sbloccare vt to unblock; ~ **la situazione** to get things moving □ **sbloccarsi** vr (meccanismo) to become unblocked; (situazione) to return to normal.

sboccare : sboccare in v + prep (fiume) to flow into; (strada) to lead into; (concludersi con) to end in.

sboccato, -a agg foul-mouthed.

sbocciare vi to bloom.

sbocco, -chi sm (di strada) end; (di fiume) mouth; (fig: esito) way out.

sbornia sf (fam) prendersi una ~ to get plastered.

sborsare vt (pagare) to pay out.

sbottare vi (in risata) to burst out; (di rabbia) to explode.

sbottonare vt to unbutton; **sbottonarsi la giacca** to undo one's jacket □ **sbottonarsi** vr (fam: confidarsi) to open up.

sbracciarsi vr to wave one's arms about.

sbracciato, -a agg (vestito) sleeveless; (persona) with bare arms.

sbraitare vi to shout.

sbranare vt to tear to pieces.

sbriciolare vt to crumble □ **sbriciolarsi** vr (pane, muro) to crumble.

sbrigare vt (faccenda) to deal with □ **sbrigarsi** vr to hurry; **sbrigarsi a fare qc** to hurry up and do sthg.

sbrodolare vt to stain.

sbronza sf (fam): **prendersi una ~** to get plastered.

sbronzo, -a agg (fam) plastered.

sbucare vi (uscire) to come out; (saltar fuori) to spring out.

sbucciare vt to peel; **sbucciarsi un ginocchio** to graze one's knee.

sbuffare vi (per fastidio, noia) to snort; (per caldo) to pant.

scabroso, -a agg indecent.

scacchi smpl chess (sg); **a ~** (tessuto) checked.

scacciare vt (persona, animale) to drive away; (preoccupazioni) to dispel.

scadente agg (prodotto) poor-quality; (qualità) poor.

scadenza sf (di cibo) sell-by date; (di documento, contratto) expiry date; (di medicinali) "use-by" date; (per iscrizione, consegna) deadline.

scadere vi to expire; (cibo) to pass its sell-by date.

scaffale sm shelf.

scafo sm hull.

scaglia sf (frammento) flake, chip; (di pesce) scale.

scagliare vt to throw □ **scagliarsi contro** vr + prep (assalire) to hurl o.s. against; (fig *insultare)* to hurl abuse at.

scaglione *sm* echelon; **a scaglioni** in groups.

scala *sf (gradini)* stairs *(pl)*, staircase; *(a pioli)* ladder; *(di valori)* scale; **su larga ~** on a large scale; **~ mobile** escalator; **le scale** the stairs.

scalare *vt (mura, montagna)* to climb; *(somma)* to knock off; *(capelli)* to layer.

scalata *sf* climb.

scalatore, -trice *sm, f* climber.

scalcinato, -a *agg (fig: casa)* shabby.

scaldabagno *sm* water heater.

scaldare *vt* to heat □ **scaldarsi** *vr (al fuoco, al sole)* to warm o.s.; *(fig: accalorarsi)* to get excited.

scaleo *sm* stepladder.

scalfire *vt* to scratch.

scalinata *sf* flight of steps.

scalino *sm* step.

scalmanarsi *vr* to get worked up.

scalo *sm* call; **fare ~ a** *(in aereo)* to make a stopover at; *(in nave)* to call at; **~ merci** goods yard *(Br)*, freight yard *(Am)*.

scaloppina *sf* escalope.

scalpore *sm (risonanza)* stir; **fare o destare ~** to cause a stir.

scaltro, -a *agg* shrewd.

scalzo, -a *agg* barefooted.

scambiare *vt* to exchange, to swap; **~ qn/qc per** *(confondere)* to mistake sb/sthg for; **scambiarsi qc** to exchange sthg.

scambio *sm (di regali, opinioni)* exchange; *(confusione)* mistake;

(COMM) trade; **fare a ~ con qn** to swap with sb.

scampagnata *sf* trip to the country.

scampare *vt* to escape; **scamparla (bella)** to have a narrow escape □ **scampare a** *v + prep* to escape.

scampo *sm*: **non c'è (via di) ~** there is no way out; **trovare ~ in qc** to find safety in sthg □ **scampi** *smpl* scampi *(sg)*.

scampolo *sm* remnant.

scandalizzare *vt* to make a spectacle of o.s. □ **scandalizzarsi** *vr* to be scandalized.

scandalo *sm* scandal; **dare ~** to make a spectacle of o.s.; **fare ~** to cause a scandal.

scandaloso, -a *agg* scandalous.

Scandinavia *sf*: **la ~** Scandinavia.

scandire *vt* to articulate.

scannare *vt (animale)* to butcher; *(persona)* to cut the throat of.

scansafatiche *smf inv* idler, waster.

scansare *vt (spostare)* to shift; *(colpo)* to ward off; *(difficoltà, fatica)* to avoid; *(persona)* to shun □ **scansarsi** *vr* to step aside.

scanso *sm*: **a ~ di equivoci** *(in order)* to avoid any misunderstandings.

scantinato *sm* basement.

scanzonato, -a *agg* easygoing.

scapaccione *sm* slap.

scapestrato, -a *agg* dissolute.

scapito sm: a ~ di to the detriment of.

scapolo sm bachelor.

scappamento sm → tubo.

scappare vi (fuggire) to escape; (da casa) to run away; (andare) to rush; **mi è scappato detto** I let it slip; **mi è scappato di mano** it slipped out of my hands; **mi è scappato di mente** it slipped my mind; **mi è scappato da ridere** I couldn't help laughing; **lasciarsi ~ l'occasione** to miss an opportunity.

scappatella sf casual affair.

scappatoia sf way out.

scarabocchiare vt to scrawl ♦ vi to scribble.

scarafaggio sm cockroach.

scaramanzia sf: **per ~** for luck.

scaraventare vt to hurl ❑ **scaraventarsi** vr to fling o.s.

scarcerare vt to release.

scarica, -che sf (di pugni) hail; (di pistola) volley; **~ elettrica** electrical discharge.

scaricare vt (merci, camion, arma) to unload; (passeggeri) to let off; (batteria) to run down; (fig: colpa) to shift ❑ **scaricarsi** vr (batteria) to go flat; (fig: rilassarsi) to unwind.

scarico, -a, -chi, -che agg (camion, arma) unloaded; (batteria) flat ♦ sm (di merci) unloading; (discarica) dump; **'divieto di ~'** 'no dumping'.

scarlatto, -a agg scarlet.

scarpa sf shoe; **che numero di scarpe porta?** what size shoe do you take?; **scarpe da ginnastica** plimsolls (Br), sneakers (Am).

scarpata sf slope.

scarponi smpl boots; **~ da sci** ski boots.

scarseggiare vi to be scarce ❑

scarseggiare di v + prep to be short of.

scarsità sf inv scarcity, shortage.

scarso, -a agg scarce; **un chilo ~** just under a kilo.

scartare vt (regalo) to unwrap; (eliminare) to reject; (nelle carte) to discard.

scarto sm (scelta) discarding; (cosa scartata) reject; (differenza) gap, difference.

scassinare vt to break open.

scasso sm → furto.

scatenare vt to provoke, to stir up ❑ **scatenarsi** vr (temporale) to break; (persona) to go wild.

scatenato, -a agg (persona, ballo) wild.

scatola sf box; (di latta) tin, can; **in ~** (cibo) tinned, canned; **rompere le scatole a qn** (fam) to get up sb's nose.

scattante agg agile.

scattare vt (foto) to take ♦ vi (balzare) to jump; (molla, congegno) to be released; (allarme) to go off; (manifestare ira) to fly into a rage; **far ~** (molla, congegno) to release; (allarme) to set off.

scatto sm (di congegno) release; (rumore) click; (di foto) shot; (balzo) fit; **di ~** suddenly.

scaturire : **scaturire da** v + prep (sgorgare) to gush from; (fig: derivare) to come from.

scavalcare vt (muro, ostacolo) to climb over; (fig: concorrenti) to overtake.

scavare vt (fossa, terreno) to dig; (render cavo) to hollow out.

scavo sm excavation.

scegliere vt to choose.

scelta sf choice; (raccolta) selection; **non avere ~** to have no choice; **frutta o formaggio a ~** 'choice of fruit or cheese'.

scelto, -a pp → **scegliere ♦** agg (gruppo) select; (frutta) choice.

scemo, -a agg (fam) stupid, silly.

scena sf scene.

scenata sf row, scene.

scendere vi (venir giù) to go/come down; (da treno) to get off; (diminuire) to go down ♦ vt to go/come down; **~ dal treno** to get off the train; **~ dalla macchina** to get out of the car.

sceneggiato sm serial.

sceneggiatura sf screenplay.

scervellarsi vr to rack one's brains.

sceso, -a pp → **scendere**

scettico, -a, -ci, -che agg sceptical.

scheda sf (cartoncino) card; (modulo) form; **~ magnetica** magnetic card.

schedare vt (libro) to catalogue; **è stato schedato dalla polizia** he has a police record.

schedario sm (raccolta) file; (mobile) filing cabinet.

schedina sf = pools coupon.

ℹ **SCHEDINA**

The coupon you fill in to play "totocalcio" (the football pools)

is called a "schedina"; it can be bought at tobacconists and bars. Players must predict the results of 13 games, marking the coupon with 1 for a home win, 2 for an away win, and X for a draw. Winners receive prizes ranging from a few thousand to several billion lire.

scheggia, -ge sf splinter.

scheletro sm skeleton.

schema, -i sm plan.

scherma sf fencing.

schermo sm screen.

scherno sm derision.

scherzare vi to joke.

scherzo sm (battuta, gesto) joke; (brutto tiro) trick; **è uno ~** (cosa facile) it's child's play; **fare qc per ~** to do sthg for a laugh.

scherzoso, -a agg playful.

schiaccianoci sm inv nutcrackers (pl).

schiacciare vt (comprimere) to crush; (noce) to crack; (pulsante) to press; (fig: avversario) to overwhelm; (SPORT) to smash.

schiacciarsi vr to get squashed.

schiacciata sf (focaccia) type of flat salted bread made with olive oil; (SPORT) smash.

schiacciato, -a agg (appiattito) flat; (deformato) squashed.

schiaffo sm slap.

schiamazzi smpl screams.

schiantare vt to break.

schiantarsi vr to break up.

schianto sm (rumore) crash; **è uno ~!** (fam) she's/it's a knockout!

schiarire vt to lighten.

schiarirsi vr (cielo) to clear up; (co-

lore) to become lighter; **schiarirsi la voce** to clear one's throat.

schiavitù *sf* slavery.

schiavo, -a *sm, f* slave ♦ *agg:* ~ **di** a slave to.

schiena *sf* back.

schienale *sm* back.

schiera *sf* group.

schierare *vt (esercito, squadra)* to draw up; *(libri, oggetti)* to line up ☐

schierarsi *vr (mettersi in fila)* to line up; **schierarsi con/contro qn** to side with/oppose sb.

schietto, -a *agg (persona)* frank; *(vino)* not watered-down.

schifezza *sf:* **essere una ~** *(cibo)* to be disgusting; *(film)* to be awful.

schifo *sm* disgust; **mi fa ~ it** makes me sick; **fare ~** *(cibo, insetto)* to be disgusting; *(film)* to be awful.

schifoso, -a *agg (disgustoso)* disgusting; *(pessimo, brutto)* awful.

schioccare *vt (dita)* to snap; *(lingua)* to click.

schiuma *sf (marina)* foam; *(di sapone)* lather; **~ da barba** shaving foam.

schivare *vt* to dodge, to avoid.

schivo, -a *agg* reserved, shy.

schizzare *vt* to splash ♦ *vi (acqua, getto)* to spurt; *(fig: saltar via)* to dart away.

schizzo *sm (spruzzo)* stain, splash; *(disegno)* sketch.

sci *sm inv (attrezzo)* ski; *(attività)* skiing; **~ d'acqua** water skiing; **~ da fondo** cross-country skiing.

scia *sf (di nave)* wake; *(di profumo, fumo)* trail.

sciacquare *vt* to rinse; **sciac-** quarsi la bocca to rinse out one's mouth.

sciacquone *sm* flush; **tirare lo ~** to flush the toilet.

sciagura *sf* disaster.

sciagurato, -a *agg (sfortunato)* unlucky; *(cattivo)* wicked.

scialacquare *vt* to squander.

scialbo, -a *agg (colore)* pale; *(sapore)* bland; *(persona)* dull.

scialle *sm* shawl.

scialuppa *sf (colore)* sloop; **~ di salvataggio** lifeboat.

sciame *sm* swarm.

sciangai *sm (gioco)* pick-up-sticks.

sciare *vi* to ski.

sciarpa *sf* scarf.

sciatore, -trice *sm, f* skier.

sciatto, -a *agg* untidy.

scientifico, -a, -ci, -che *agg* scientific.

scienza *sf (studio della realtà)* science; *(sapere)* knowledge ☐ **scienze** *sfpl* science *(sg)*.

scienziato, -a *sm, f* scientist.

scimmia *sf* monkey.

scimmiottare *vt* to ape.

scindere *vt (dividere)* to divide.

scintilla *sf* spark.

scintillare *vi* to sparkle.

scioccare *vt* to shock.

sciocchezza *sf (cosa stupida)* silly thing; *(cosa poco importante)* trifle.

sciocco, -a, -chi, -che *agg* silly.

sciogliere *vt (nodo)* to untie; *(capelli)* to loosen; *(animale)* to let loose; *(ghiaccio, burro)* to melt;

(*pastiglia, società*) to dissolve; (*mistero*) to solve; (*assemblea*) to close ❑ **sciogliersi** *vr* (*nodo*) to come untied; (*neve, burro*) to melt.

scioglilingua *sm inv* tongue twister.

sciolto, -a *pp* → **sciogliere** ◆ *agg* (*disinvolto*) easy; (*agile*) agile.

sciopero *sm* strike; **essere in ~** to be on strike.

sciovia *sf* ski lift.

scippare *vt*: **~ qn** to snatch sb's bag.

scippo *sm* bagsnatching.

sciroppo *sm* (*medicina*) cough mixture; (*di frutta*) syrup.

scissione *sf* (*separazione*) split.

scisso, -a *pp* → **scindere**.

sciupare *vt* (*vestito, libro*) to spoil, to ruin ❑ **sciuparsi** *vr* (*rovinarsi*) to get spoiled; (*deperire*) to become run down.

scivolare *vi* (*scorrere*) to glide; (*perdere l'equilibrio*) to slip, to slide.

scivolo *sm* (*gioco*) slide.

scivoloso, -a *agg* slippery.

scoccare *vt* (*freccia*) to shoot ◆ *vi* (*ore*) to strike.

scocciare *vt* (*fam*) to annoy ❑ **scocciarsi** *vr* (*fam*) to be annoyed.

scodella *sf* bowl.

scodinzolare *vi* to wag its tail.

scogliera *sf* rocks (*pl*).

scoglio *sm* (*roccia*) rock; (*fig*) stumbling block.

scoiattolo *sm* squirrel.

scolapasta *sm inv* colander.

scolapiatti *sm inv* draining rack.

scolare *vt* to drain.

scolaro, -a *sm, f* schoolboy (*f* schoolgirl).

scolastico, -a, -ci, -che *agg* school (*dav s*).

scollare *vt* (*staccare*) to unstick ❑ **scollarsi** *vr* to come unstuck.

scollato, -a *agg* (*abito*) low-cut.

scollatura *sf* neckline.

scolorire *vt* to fade ❑ **scolorirsi** *vr* to fade.

scolpire *vt* to sculpt; (*legno*) to carve; (*iscrizione*) to engrave.

scombussolare *vt* to upset.

scommessa *sf* bet.

scommesso, -a *pp* → **scommettere**.

scommettere *vt* to bet.

scomodare *vt* to bother ❑ **scomodarsi** *vr* to put o.s. out; **scomodarsi a fare qc** to go to the bother of doing sthg.

scomodo, -a *agg* (*poltrona*) uncomfortable; (*orario*) inconvenient.

scompagnato, -a *agg* (*calzini*) odd.

scomparire *vi* (*sparire*) to disappear.

scomparso, -a *pp* → **scomparire**.

scompartimento *sm* (*di treno*) compartment.

scomparto *sm* compartment.

scompigliare *vt* (*capelli*) to ruffle, to mess up.

scompiglio *sm* confusion.

scomporre *vt* (*mobile, armadio*) to take to pieces ❑ **scomporsi** *vr* (*perdere il controllo*) to lose one's composure.

scomposto, -a *pp* → **scomporre**.

sconcertare *vt* to disconcert.

sconcio, -a, -ci, -ce *agg* (osceno) obscene.

sconfiggere *vt* to defeat.

sconfinare *vi* (uscire dai confini) to cross the border; (fig): ~ **da** to stray from.

sconfinato, -a *agg* boundless.

sconfitta *sf* defeat.

sconfitto, -a *pp* → **sconfiggere**.

sconforto *sm* dejection.

scongelare *vt* to defrost.

scongiurare *vt* (supplicare) to implore; (pericolo, minaccia) to ward off.

sconnesso, -a *agg* (ragionamento) incoherent.

sconosciuto, -a *agg* unknown ♦ *sm, f* stranger.

sconsiderato, -a *agg* thoughtless.

sconsigliare *vt* to advise against; ~ **qc a qn** to advise sb against sthg; ~ **a qn di fare qc** to advise sb against doing sthg.

scontare *vt* (detrarre) to deduct; (pena) to serve; (colpa, errore) to pay for.

scontato, -a *agg* (prezzo) discounted; (previsto) taken for granted; **dare qc per** ~ to take sthg for granted.

scontento, -a *agg:* ~ **(di)** dissatisfied (with).

sconto *sm* discount; **fare uno** ~ to give a discount.

scontrarsi *vr* (urtarsi) to collide;

(combattere, discordare) to clash.

scontrino *sm* receipt; **'munirsi dello scontrino alla cassa'** 'pay at the till and obtain a receipt'.

scontro *sm* (urto) collision; (combattimento, fig) clash.

scontroso, -a *agg* surly.

sconveniente *agg* (indecente) improper.

sconvolgente *agg* disturbing.

sconvolgere *vt* (persona) to disturb, to shake; (ordine, piani) to upset.

sconvolto, -a *pp* → **sconvolgere**.

scopa *sf* (arnese) broom.

scoperta *sf* discovery.

scoperto, -a *pp* → **scoprire** ♦ *agg* uncovered; (capo, braccia) bare.

scopo *sm* purpose, aim; **allo** ~ **di fare qc** in order to do sthg; **a che** ~? for what purpose?

scoppiare *vi* (spaccarsi) to burst; (esplodere) to explode; ~ **dal caldo** (fam) to be boiling (hot); ~ **a piangere** to burst into tears; ~ **a ridere** to burst out laughing.

scoppio *sm* (rumore, di pneumatico) bang; (esplosione) explosion; (di risa) burst; (di guerra) outbreak; **a** ~ **ritardato** delayed-action.

scoprire *vt* to discover; (liberare da copertura) to uncover ▢ **scoprirsi** *vr* (svestirsi) to dress less warmly; (rivelarsi) to give o.s. away.

scoraggiare *vt* to discourage ▢ **scoraggiarsi** *vr* to become discouraged.

scorbutico, -a, -ci, -che *agg* (scontroso) cantankerous.

scorciatoia *sf* short cut; prendere una ~ to take a short cut.

scordare *vt* to forget ❑ **scordarsi di** *vr + prep* to forget; **scordarsi di fare qc** to forget to do sthg.

scorgere *vt* to see, to make out.

scorpacciata *sf*: fare una ~ (di qc) to stuff o.s. (with sthg).

scorpione *sm* scorpion ❑ Scorpione *sm* Scorpio.

scorrazzare *vi* to run around.

scorrere *vi* (*liquido, fiume, traffico*) to flow; (*fune*) to run; (*tempo*) to pass ◆ *vt* (*giornale, libro*) to glance through.

scorretto, -a *agg* (*errato*) incorrect; (*sleale*) unfair.

scorrevole *agg* (*porta*) sliding; (*traffico, stile*) flowing.

scorrimento *sm* (*di traffico*) flow.

scorsa *sf*: dare una ~ a qc to glance through sthg.

scorso, -a *pp* → **scorrere** ◆ *agg* last.

scorta *sf*: fare ~ di qc to stock up with sthg; **di** ~ spare.

scortare *vt* to escort.

scortese *agg* impolite.

scorticare *vt* (*pelle*) to graze; (*animale*) to skin.

scorto, -a *pp* → **scorgere**.

scorza *sf* (*di albero*) bark; (*di frutto*) peel.

scorzanera *sf* *type of bitter-tasting root vegetable.*

scosceso, -a *agg* steep.

scossa *sf* (*movimento*) jolt; (*elettrica*) shock.

scosso, -a *pp* → **scuotere** ◆ *agg* shaken.

scossone *sm* jolt.

scostare *vt* to move aside ❑ **scostarsi** *vr* to move aside.

scotch®¹ [skɔtʃ] *sm inv* (*nastro adesivo*) = Sellotape® (Br), Scotch® tape (Am).

scotch² [skɔtʃ] *sm inv* (*whisky*) Scotch.

scottadito : a scottadito *avv* piping hot.

scottare *vt* (*ustionare*) to burn; (*cuocere*) to scald ◆ *vi* (*bevanda, pietanza*) to be too hot ❑ **scottarsi** *vr* to burn o.s.

scottatura *sf* burn.

scotto, -a *agg* overcooked.

scout ['skaut] *smf inv* scout.

scovare *vt* (*negozio, ristorante*) to discover.

Scozia *sf*: la ~ Scotland.

scozzese *agg* Scottish ◆ *smf* Scotsman (*f* Scotswoman); gli scozzesi the Scots.

screditare *vt* to discredit.

screpolare *vt* to crack ❑ **screpolarsi** *vr* to crack.

screziato, -a *agg* streaked.

screzio *sm* disagreement.

scricchiolare *vi* to creak.

scricchiolio *sm* creaking.

scriminatura *sf* parting.

scritta *sf* inscription.

scritto, -a *pp* → **scrivere** ◆ *agg* written ◆ *sm* (*opera*) work; (*cosa scritta*) letter.

scrittore, -trice *sm, f* writer.

scrittura *sf* writing.

scrivania *sf* writing desk.

scrivere *vt & vi* to write; **~ a qn** to write to sb ❏ **scriversi** *vr (parola):* **come si scrive 'cuore'?** how do you write o spell 'cuore'?

scroccare *vt (fam)* to scrounge.

scrollare *vt (agitare)* to shake; *(spalle)* to shrug; **scrollarsi qc di dosso** to shake sthg off.

scrosciare *vi (pioggia)* to pelt down; *(applausi)* to thunder.

scroscio *sm (d'acqua)* pelting; *(d'applausi)* thunder.

scrostare *vt (intonaco)* to strip off ❏ **scrostarsi** *vr (pareti, tegame)* to peel.

scrupolo *sm (timore)* scruple; *(diligenza)* conscientiousness; **senza scrupoli** unscrupulous.

scrupoloso, -a *agg (persona)* scrupulous; *(resoconto, lavoro)* meticulous.

scrutare *vt* to scrutinize; *(orizzonte)* to search.

scucire *vt (cucitura)* to unpick ❏ **scucirsi** *vr* to come unstitched.

scuderia *sf* stable.

scudetto *sm (SPORT)* championship shield.

scudo *sm* shield.

sculacciare *vt* to spank.

scultore, -trice *sm, f* sculptor.

scultura *sf* sculpture.

scuola *sf* school; **andare a ~** to go to school; **~ elementare** = primary school *(Br)*, grade school *(Am)(for children aged from 6 to 11);* **~ guida** driving school; **~ materna** nursery school *(for children aged from 3 to 5);* **~ media** *first three years of secondary school for children aged*

from 11 to 14; **~ dell'obbligo** compulsory education; **scuole tecniche** schools which prepare their students for practical professions; **scuole serali** evening classes.

scuotere *vt (testa, spalle)* to shrug ❏ **scuotersi** *vr* to shake o.s.

scurire *vt* to darken ◆ *vi* to grow dark ❏ **scurirsi** *vr* to grow dark.

scuro, -a *agg* dark ◆ *sm (buio)* darkness.

scusa *sf* excuse; **chiedere ~ (a qn)** to apologize (to sb).

scusare *vt (perdonare)* to forgive; *(giustificare)* to excuse ❏ **scusarsi** *vr* to apologize; **(mi) scusi, dov'è la stazione?** excuse me, where is the station?; **scusi!** sorry!

sdebitarsi *vr:* **~ con qn di qc** to repay sb for sthg.

sdentato, -a *agg* toothless.

sdolcinato, -a *agg* oversentimental.

sdraia *sf* deckchair.

sdraiarsi *vr* to lie down.

sdraio *sm:* **(sedia a) ~** deckchair.

sdrammatizzare *vt* to play down.

sdrucciolare *vi* to slip.

se *cong* 1. *(nel caso in cui)* if; **rimani ~ vuoi** stay if you want; **~ è possibile** if it's possible; **~ fossi in te** if I were you; **~ non sbaglio ...** if I'm not wrong ...

2. *(dato che)* if; **~ lo dici, sarà vero** if you say so, it must be true.

3. *(in frasi dubitative & interrogative indirette)* whether, if; **vedi ~ puoi venire** see whether o if you can come; **chiedile ~ le piace** ask her if

she likes it.
4. *(esprime un suggerimento)*: **e ~ andassimo al cinema?** how about going to the cinema?
5. *(esprime un augurio)* if; **~ solo potessi!** if only I could!
6. *(in espressioni)*: **anche ~** even if; **~ mai** if, never; **neanche ~** even if; **~ non altro** if nothing else; **~ no** otherwise.
♦ *pron* → **sì**.

sé *pron (per cosa)* itself; *(per persona)* himself/herself/themselves; **tenere qc per ~** to keep sthg for oneself; **pensa solo a se stesso** he only thinks of himself.

sebbene *cong* although.

sec. *(abbr di secolo)* c.

secca, -che *sf (di mare, fiume)* shallows *(pl)*.

seccare *vt* to dry; *(prosciugare)* to dry up; *(infastidire)* to annoy ❏ **seccarsi** *vr* to dry; *(prosciugarsi)* to dry up; *(infastidirsi)* to get annoyed.

seccato, -a *agg (infastidito)* annoyed.

seccatore, -trice *sm, f* nuisance.

seccatura *sf (fastidio)* nuisance.

secchiello *sm (contenitore)* bucket.

secchio *sm* bucket.

secchione, -a *sm, f (fam)* swot.

secco, -a, -chi, -che *agg* dry; *(funghi, prugne)* dried; *(brusco)* curt ♦ *sm*: **essere a ~ di qc** *(fig: non avere)* to be without sthg; **tirare in ~ una barca** to beach a boat; **lavare a ~** to dry-clean.

secolare *agg (vecchio di secoli)* age-old.

secolo *sm* century; *(periodo lungo)*: **non lo vedo da secoli** I haven't seen him for ages.

seconda *sf (marcia)* second gear; **viaggiare in ~** to travel second-class; **a ~ di** according to.

secondario, -a *agg* secondary; **scuola secondaria** secondary school.

secondo, -a *num* second ♦ *agg (altro)* second ♦ *sm (tempo)* second; *(portata)* main course ♦ *prep* according to; **~ me** in my opinion; **di seconda mano** second-hand, → **sesto**.

sedano *sm* celery.

sedativo *sm* sedative.

sede *sf (di organizzazione)* headquarters *(pl)*; *(di azienda)* head office.

sedentario, -a *agg* sedentary.

sedere *sm (parte del corpo)* bottom ♦ *vi*: **mettersi a ~** to sit down ❏ **sedersi** *vr* to sit down.

sedia *sf* chair.

sedicesimo, -a *num* sixteenth, → **sesto**.

sedici *num* sixteen, → **sei**.

sedile *sm (di veicolo)* seat.

sedotto, -a *pp* → **sedurre**.

seducente *agg* seductive.

sedurre *vt (uomo, donna)* to seduce; *(sog: idea, proposta)* to appeal to.

seduta *sf* session.

sega, -ghe *sf* saw.

segale *sf* rye.

segare *vt* to saw.

seggio *sm* seat; **~ elettorale**

seggiola 242

polling station.

seggiola *sf* chair.

seggiolino *sm (sedia pieghevole)* folding chair.

seggiolone *sm (per bambini)* high chair.

seggiovia *sf* chair lift.

segnalare *vt (comunicare)* to point out; *(indicare)* to indicate.

segnalazione *sf (indicazione)* indication; *(raccomandazione)* recommendation.

segnale *sm (indicazione)* signal; *(stradale)* sign; ~ **acustico** sound signal; ~ **d'allarme** alarm; ~ **orario** time signal.

segnaletica *sf (stradale)* road signs *(pl)*.

segnalibro *sm* bookmark.

segnaposto *sm* place card.

segnare *vt (mettere un segno)* to mark; *(indicare)* to indicate; *(SPORT)* to score; **segnarsi qc** to make a note of sthg.

segno *sm* sign; *(lettera, numero)* symbol; *(contrassegno, traccia)* mark; **fare** ~ **a qn di fare qc** to signal sb to do sthg; **fare** ~ **di no** to shake one's head; **fare** ~ **di sì** to nod one's head; **perdere il** ~ to lose one's place; **cogliere** o **colpire nel** ~ *(fig)* to hit the mark.

segretario, -a *sm, f* secretary.

segreteria *sf (di azienda, scuola)* secretary's office; *(di partito)* position of Secretary □ **segreteria telefonica** *sf* answering machine.

segreto, -a *agg & sm* secret.

seguente *agg* following, next.

seguire *vt* to follow ◆ *vi* to follow; *(continuare)*: **segue a pag. 70**

continued on page 70.

seguito *sm (proseguimento)* continuation; *(risultato)* result; *(scorta)* retinue; *(favore)* following; **in** ~ **a** following; **di** ~ at a stretch, on end; **in** ~ subsequently.

sei¹ → **essere**.

sei² *agg num* six; **ha** ~ **anni** he/she is six (years old); **sono le** ~ it's six o'clock; **il** ~ **gennaio** the sixth of January; **pagina** ~ page six; **il** ~ **di picche** the six of spades; **erano in** ~ there were six of them.

seicento *num* six hundred, → **sei** □ **Seicento** *sm*: **il Seicento** the seventeenth century.

selciato *sm* cobbles *(pl)*, cobbled surface.

selettivo, -a *agg* selective.

selezionare *vt* to select.

selezione *sf* selection.

self-service ['sɛl 'sɜːvɪs] *agg inv & sm inv* self-service.

sella *sf* saddle.

selvaggina *sf* game.

selvaggio, -a, -gi, -ge *agg* wild; *(tribù)* savage; *(delitto)* brutal ◆ *sm, f* savage.

selvatico, -a, -ci, -che *agg* wild.

semaforo *sm (apparecchio)* traffic lights *(pl)*.

sembrare *vi* to seem ◆ *v impers*: **sembra che** it seems that; **mi sembra di conoscerlo** I think I know him; **sembra che stia per piovere** it looks like it's going to rain.

seme *sm* seed; *(nocciolo)* stone; *(di carte da gioco)* suit.

semestre *sm* six-month period; *(SCOL)* semester.

semifinale *sf* semifinal.

semifreddo *sm dessert similar to ice cream.*

seminare *vt* to sow.

seminario *sm* seminar; *(RELIG)* seminary.

seminterrato *sm* basement.

semmai *cong* if (ever) ◆ *avv* if anything.

semolino *sm* semolina.

semplice *agg* simple; *(filo, consonante)* single; **è una ~ proposta** it's just a suggestion.

semplicemente *avv* simply.

semplicità *sf* simplicity.

semplificare *vt* to simplify.

sempre *avv* always; *(ancora)* still; **va ~ meglio/peggio** things are getting better and better/worse and worse; **~ che ci riesca** provided he manages it; **da ~** always; **di ~** usual; **per ~** forever.

senape *sf* mustard.

senato *sm* senate.

senatore, -trice *sm, f* senator.

sennò *avv (altrimenti)* otherwise.

seno *sm (petto)* breast.

sensazionale *agg* sensational.

sensazione *sf* sensation, feeling; **fare ~** to cause a sensation.

sensibile *agg* sensitive; *(notevole)* noticeable; **~ a (caldo, freddo)** sensitive to; *(complimenti)* susceptible to.

sensibilità *sf* sensitivity.

senso *sm (facoltà, coscienza)* sense; *(sentimento, impressione)* feeling; *(significato)* meaning, sense; *(direzione)* direction; **non avere ~ to**

make no sense; **a ~ unico** one-way; **in ~ orario** clockwise; **perdere i sensi** to lose consciousness.

sentenza *sf (di processo)* sentence; *(massima)* maxim.

sentiero *sm* path.

sentimentale *agg* sentimental.

sentimento *sm* feeling.

sentire *vt (udire)* to hear; *(percepire, con il tatto)* to feel; *(odore)* to smell; *(sapore)* to taste; **senti!** listen! □ **sentirsi** *vr (bene, stanco, allegro)* to feel; **sentirsi di fare qc** to feel like doing sthg; **sentirsi bene/male** to feel well/ill; *(telefonarsi)*: **ci sentiamo domani** speak to you tomorrow.

senza *prep & cong* without; **~ di me** without me; **senz'altro** certainly, of course; **~ dubbio** undoubtedly; **~ che tu te ne accorga** without you noticing it.

senzatetto *smf inv* homeless person.

separare *vt* to separate □ **separarsi** *vr (coniugi)* to separate; *(gruppo)* to split up; **separarsi da** *vr + prep (coniuge)* to separate from.

separato, -a *agg (disgiunto)* separate; *(coniuge)* separated.

separazione *sf* separation.

sepolto, -a *pp* → **seppellire**.

seppellire *vt* to bury.

seppia *sf* cuttlefish.

sequenza *sf* sequence.

sequestrare *vt (DIR)* to sequestrate; *(persona)* to kidnap.

sequestro *sm (DIR)* sequestration; *(rapimento)* kidnapping.

sera *sf* evening; **di ~** in the evening.

serale *agg* evening *(dav s).*

serata *sf* evening; *(ricevimento)* party.

serbare *vt* to put aside, to keep; **~ rancore a qn** to bear sb a grudge.

serbatoio *sm (di veicolo)* tank.

serbo *sm:* **avere qc in ~** to have sthg in store; **tenere qc in ~** to put sthg aside.

serenata *sf* serenade.

sereno, -a *agg (tempo, cielo)* clear; *(persona)* calm ♦ *sm (bel tempo)* fine weather.

serie *sf inv (successione)* series *(inv);* *(insieme)* set; *(SPORT)* division; **produzione in ~** mass production.

serietà *sf* seriousness; *(coscienziosità)* reliability.

serio, -a *agg* serious; *(coscienzioso)* reliable ♦ *sm:* **sul ~** *(davvero)* seriously; **prendere qn/qc sul ~** to take sb/sthg seriously.

serpente *sm* snake; *(pelle)* snakeskin.

serra *sf (per piante)* greenhouse.

serranda *sf* rolling shutter.

serrare *vt (chiudere)* to close; *(stringere)* to shut tightly.

serratura *sf* lock.

servire *vt* to serve ♦ *vi (in tennis, pallavolo)* to serve; *(essere utile)* to be of use; **~ a fare qc** to be used for doing sthg; **~ a qn** to be of use to sb; **mi serve un martello** I need a hammer; **~ da** to be used as ❑ **servirsi** *vr (prendere da mangiare/bere)* to help o.s.; **servirsi da** to shop at; **servirsi di** *vr + prep (utilizzare)* to use.

servitù *sf (condizione)* slavery; *(personale)* domestic staff.

servizio *sm* service; *(di piatti, bicchieri)* set; *(giornalistico)* report; **essere di ~** to be on duty; **'~ compreso'** 'service included'; **~ militare** military service ❑ **servizi** *smpl (di abitazione)* kitchen and bathroom.

sessanta *num* sixty, → **sei**.

sessantesimo, -a *num* sixtieth, → **sesto**.

sessantina *sf:* **una ~ (di)** about sixty; **essere sulla ~** to be in one's sixties.

sesso *sm* sex.

sessuale *agg* sexual.

sesto, -a *agg num & pron num* sixth ♦ *sm (frazione)* sixth; **rimettersi in ~** to recover.

seta *sf* silk.

setacciare *vt (separare)* to sieve.

sete *sf* thirst; **avere ~** to be thirsty.

settanta *num* seventy, → **sei**.

settantesimo, -a *num* seventieth, → **sesto**.

settantina *sf:* **una ~ (di)** about seventy; **essere sulla ~** to be in one's seventies.

sette *num* seven, → **sei**.

settecento *num* seven hundred, → **sei** ❑ **Settecento** *sm:* **il Settecento** the eighteenth century.

settembre *sm* September; **a ~, in ~** in September; **lo scorso ~** last September; **il prossimo ~** next September; **all'inizio di ~** at the beginning of September; **alla fine di ~** at the end of September; **è**

due ~ the second of September.

settentrionale *agg* northern.

settentrione *sm* north.

setter *sm inv* setter.

settimana *sf* week.

settimanale *agg* weekly ◆ *sm* weekly publication.

settimo, -a *num* seventh, = sesto.

settore *sm* sector.

severamente *avv*: 'è ~ vietato attraversare i binari' 'crossing the track is strictly forbidden'.

severo, -a *agg* strict, severe.

sevizie *sfpl* torture (*sg*).

sexy *agg inv* sexy.

sezione *sf* section; (*MED*) dissection.

sfaccendato, -a *agg* lazy.

sfacchinata *sf* hard work.

sfacciato, -a *agg* (*persona*) cheeky.

sfacelo *sm* (*rovina*) ruin.

sfamare *vt* to feed ❑ **sfamarsi** *vr* to satisfy one's hunger.

sfare *vt* to undo.

sfarzo *sm* pomp, magnificence.

sfasciare *vt* (*sbendare*) to unbandage; (*rompere*) to smash ❑ **sfasciarsi** *vr* (*rompersi*) to fall to pieces.

sfaticato, -a *agg* lazy.

sfatto, -a *pp* = sfare.

sfavorevole *agg* unfavourable.

sfera *sf* sphere.

sferrare *vt* (*attacco*) to launch; ~ **un colpo contro qn** to lash out at sb.

sfibrare *vt* to exhaust.

sfida *sf* challenge.

sfidare *vt* to challenge; (*pericolo, morte*) to defy; ~ **qn a fare qc** to challenge sb to do sthg.

sfiducia *sf* distrust.

sfigurare *vt* to disfigure ◆ *vi* to make a bad impression.

sfilare *vt* (*togliere*) to take off ◆ *vi* (*marciare*) to parade; **sfilarsi le scarpe** to slip off one's shoes ❑ **sfilarsi** *vr* (*calze*) to ladder.

sfilata *sf* (*corteo*) march; (*di moda*) fashion show.

sfinire *vt* to exhaust.

sfiorare *vt* to skim (over).

sfiorire *vi* to wither.

sfitto, -a *agg* vacant.

sfizioso, -a *agg* enticing.

sfocato, -a = sfuocato.

sfociare *vt*: **sfociare in** *v + prep* (*fiume*) to flow into.

sfoderare *vt* (*giacca*) to remove the lining from; (*spada*) to draw; (*fig*) to show off.

sfoderato, -a *agg* unlined.

sfogare *vt* to give vent to ❑ **sfogarsi** *vr* (*aprirsi*) to pour out one's feelings; **sfogarsi su qn** (*scaricare la collera*) to vent one's anger on sb.

sfoggiare *vt* to show off.

sfogliare *vt* (*giornale*) to leaf through.

sfogliatelle *sfpl* puff pastries filled with spiced ricotta cheese and candied fruit.

sfogo, -ghi *sm* (*passaggio*) outlet; (*di sentimenti*) outburst; (*eruzione cutanea*) rash; **dare ~ a qc** to give vent to sthg.

sfoltire vt to thin.

sfondare vt (contenitore) to break the bottom of; (porta) to break down ◻ **sfondarsi** vr (contenitore) to burst at the bottom.

sfondo sm background.

sformato sm savoury pudding made with vegetables and cheese or sometimes with meat, baked in a mould and then turned out.

sfornare vt (pane, dolci) to take out of the oven.

sfortuna sf misfortune; **portare ~** to bring bad luck.

sfortunatamente avv unfortunately.

sfortunato, -a agg unlucky.

sforzare vt to force; (occhi, voce, motore) to strain ◻ **sforzarsi** vr to make an effort.

sforzo sm effort; **fare uno ~** to make an effort.

sfottere vt (fam) to tease.

sfratto sm eviction.

sfrecciare vi to shoot past.

sfregare vt (strofinare) to rub.

sfregio sm (taglio) gash.

sfrenato, -a agg unrestrained.

sfrontato, -a agg impudent.

sfruttamento sm exploitation.

sfruttare vt to exploit.

sfuggire vi (scappare) to escape ◻ **sfuggire a** v + prep (sottrarsi a) to escape from; **~ di mano a qn** to slip out of sb's hands; **~ di mente a qn** to slip sb's mind; **non gli sfugge nulla** he misses nothing.

sfuggita : **di sfuggita** avv in passing.

sfumare vt (colore) to shade off; (capelli) to taper ◆ vi (colore) to shade off; (svanire) to vanish.

sfumato, -a agg (colore) soft.

sfumatura sf (tonalità) shade; (fig: piccola differenza) touch, hint; (di capelli) tapering.

sfuocato, -a agg blurred, out of focus.

sfuriata sf (sfogo violento) outburst of anger; (rimprovero) telling off.

sgabello sm stool.

sgabuzzino sm storage room.

sgambetto sm: **fare lo ~ a qn** to trip sb up.

sganciare vt (vestito, allacciatura) to unfasten; (rimorchio, vagone) to uncouple; (bombe) to drop; (fam: soldi) to fork out ◻ **sganciarsi** vr (staccarsi) to come undone.

sgarbato, -a agg impolite.

sghignazzare vi to laugh scornfully.

sgobbare vi (fam) to slog.

sgocciolare vt (bottiglia) to drain ◆ vi to drip.

sgolarsi vr to make o.s. hoarse.

sgomb(e)rare vt (strada, soffitta) to clear.

sgombero, -a = sgombro.

sgombro, -a agg clear ◆ sm (evacuazione) evacuation; (pesce) mackerel.

sgomentare vt to dismay ◻ **sgomentarsi** vr to be dismayed.

sgominare vt to rout.

sgonfiare vt to deflate ◻ **sgonfiarsi** vr (canotto) to deflate; (caviglia) to go down.

sgorbio *sm (scarabocchio)* scribble; *(fig: persona)* fright.

sgradevole *agg* unpleasant.

sgradito, -a *agg* unwelcome.

sgranare *vt (fagioli)* to shell.

sgranchirsi *vr:* ~ **le gambe** to stretch one's legs.

sgranocchiare *vt* to munch.

sgraziato, -a *agg* graceless.

sgretolare *vt (frantumare)* to cause to crumble □ **sgretolarsi** *vr* to crumble.

sgridare *vt* to scold.

sguaiato, -a *agg* coarse.

sgualcire *vt* to crumple □ **sgualcirsi** *vr* to become crumpled.

sguardo *sm (occhiata)* look; *(espressione)* expression.

sguinzagliare *vt (cane)* to take off the lead.

sgusciare *vt (fagioli)* to shell ♦ *vi (sfuggire)* to slip away.

shampoo ['ʃampo] *sm inv* shampoo.

shock [ʃɔk] *sm inv* shock.

si *(diventa* **se** *quando precede* **lo, la, li, le, ne)** *pron* 1. *(riflessivo: persona)* himself *(f* herself*)*, themselves *(pl)*; *(impersonale)* oneself; *(cosa, animale)* itself, themselves *(pl)*; **lavarsi** to wash (oneself); ~ **stanno preparando** they are getting ready. 2. *(con verbo transitivo)*: **lavarsi i denti** to brush one's teeth; ~ **è comprato un vestito** he bought himself a suit. 3. *(reciproco)* each other, one another; ~ **sono conosciuti a Roma** they met in Rome. 4. *(impersonale)*: ~ **può sempre**

provare one O you can always try; ~ **dice che ...** they say that ..., it is said that ...; ~ **vede che è stanco** one O you can see he's tired; ~ **prega di non fumare'** 'please do not smoke'; **non** ~ **sa mai** you never know. 5. *(passivo)*: **questi prodotti** ~ **trovano dappertutto** these products are found everywhere.

sì *avv & sm inv* yes; **dire di** ~ to say yes; **uno** ~ **e uno no** every other one.

sia[1] → **essere**.

sia[2] *cong*: ~ **... che, ~ ... ~** both ... and; ~ **che ... ~ che** whether ... or; ~ **che tu venga, ~ che tu non venga** whether you come or not.

siamo → **essere**.

sicché *cong (e quindi)* and so.

siccità *sf inv* drought.

siccome *cong* as, since.

Sicilia *sf:* **la** ~ Sicily.

siciliano, -a *agg & sm, f* Sicilian.

sicura *sf (di auto)* safety lock; *(di arma)* safety catch.

sicurezza *sf (mancanza di pericolo)* safety, security; *(certezza)* certainty; **di** ~ safety *(dav s)*, security *(dav s)*.

sicuro, -a *agg* safe; *(amico, informazione)* reliable; *(fiducioso)* confident; *(certo)* certain ♦ *avv* certainly; **di** ~ certainly; **andare sul** ~ to play safe; **essere** ~ **di sé** to be sure of o.s.; **al** ~ in a safe place.

Siena *sf* Siena.

siepe *sf* hedge.

sieropositivo, -a *agg* HIV-positive.

siete → essere.

Sig. *(abbr di signor)* Mr.

Sig.a *(abbr di signora)* Ms.

sigaretta *sf* cigarette.

sigaro *sm* cigar.

Sigg. *abbr* Messrs.

sigla *sf (abbreviazione)* acronym; *(musicale)* signature tune; ~ **auto-mobilistica** *two-letter abbreviation of province on a vehicle's number plate.*

Sig.na *(abbr di signorina)* Miss.

significare *vt* to mean; **che cosa significa?** what does it mean?

significativo, -a *agg (discorso)* significant; *(sguardo)* meaningful.

significato *sm* meaning.

signor *sm* → signore.

signora *sf (donna)* lady; *(moglie)* wife; **buon giorno ~** good morning (Madam); **Gentile Signora** *(in una lettera)* Dear Madam; **la ~ Poli** Mrs Poli; **signore e signori** ladies and gentlemen.

signore *sm (uomo)* gentleman; **buon giorno ~** good morning (Sir); **il ~ desidera?** what can I do for you, sir?; **Gentile Signore** *(in una lettera)* Dear Sir; **i Signori Rossi** *(marito e moglie)* Mr and Mrs Rossi; **il Signor Martini** Mr Martini.

signorina *sf (ragazza)* young lady; **buon giorno ~** good morning (Madam); **la ~ Logi** Miss Logi.

Sig.ra *abbr* Mrs.

silenzio *sm* silence; **fare ~** to be quiet.

silenzioso, -a *agg* quiet, silent.

sillaba *sf* syllable.

simbolico, -a, -ci, -che *agg* symbolic.

simbolo *sm* symbol.

simile *agg (analogo)* similar; *(tale)*: **una persona ~** such a person; **~ a** similar to.

simmetrico, -a, -ci, -che *agg* symmetric(al).

simpatia *sf (inclinazione)* liking; *(qualità)* pleasantness.

simpatico, -a, -ci, -che *agg* nice.

simulare *vt (fingere)* to feign; *(imitare)* to simulate.

simultaneo, -a *agg* simultaneous.

sin = sino.

sinagoga, -ghe *sf* synagogue.

sincero, -a *agg (persona)* sincere; *(dolore, gioia)* genuine, heartfelt.

sindacalista, -i, -e *smf* trade unionist.

sindacato *sm (di lavoratori)* trade union.

sindaco, -ci *sm* mayor.

sinfonia *sf* symphony.

singhiozzo *sm* hiccups *(pl)* ❑ **singhiozzi** *smpl* sobs; **a singhiozzi** *(fig)* by fits and starts.

singolare *agg (originale)* unusual; *(GRAMM)* singular ◆ *sm (GRAMM)* singular.

singolo, -a *agg* single.

sinistra *sf*: **la ~** the left; *(POL)* the left (wing); **scrivere con la ~** to write with one's left hand; **a ~** left; **a ~ di** to the left of.

sinistro, -a *agg* left; *(minaccioso)* sinister ◆ *sm* accident.

sino ◆ = fino.

sinonimo *sm* synonym.

sintesi *sf inv* (*riassunto*) summary.

sintetico, -a, -ci, -che *agg* (*artificiale*) synthetic; (*succinto*) brief.

sintetizzare *vt* (*riassumere*) to summarize.

sintomo *sm* symptom.

sintonizzare *vt* to tune in □ **sintonizzarsi su** *vr + prep* to tune in to.

sipario *sm* curtain.

sirena *sf* (*apparecchio*) siren; (*nella mitologia*) mermaid.

siringa, -ghe *sf* (*per iniezioni*) syringe; (*da cucina*) ≃ piping bag.

sistema, -i *sm* system.

sistemare *vt* (*ordinare*) to tidy up; (*risolvere*) to sort out, to settle; (*alloggiare*) to find accommodation (*Br*) o accommodations (*Am*) for; (*procurare un lavoro a*) to find a job for; (*maritare*) to marry o □ **sistemarsi** *vr* (*risolversi*) to be settled; (*trovare alloggio*) to find accommodation (*Br*) o accommodations (*Am*); (*trovare lavoro*) to find work; (*sposarsi*) to marry.

sistematico, -a, -ci, -che *agg* systematic.

sistemazione *sf* (*disposizione*) arrangement; (*alloggio*) accommodation (*Br*), accommodations (*Am*); (*lavoro*) employment.

situare *vt* to situate, to locate.

situazione *sf* situation.

skate-board [ˈskeɪt ˈbɔːd] *sm inv* skateboard.

ski-lift [skiˈlift] *sm inv* ski lift.

ski-pass [skiˈpas] *sm inv* ski pass.

slacciare *vt* to undo.

slanciato, -a *agg* slender.

slancio *sm* (*balzo*) dash; (*fig*) burst.

slavina *sf* snowslide.

slavo, -a *agg* Slavonic, Slav.

sleale *agg* (*persona*) disloyal; (*azione*) treacherous.

slegare *vt* to untie.

slip *sm inv* briefs (*pl*).

slitta *sf* sledge.

slittare *vi* to slide; (*automobile*) to skid.

slogan *sm inv* slogan.

slogare *vt* to dislocate.

slogatura *sf* dislocation.

smacchiatore *sm* stain remover.

smagliante *agg* dazzling.

smagliare *vt* (*collant, calze*) to ladder.

smagliatura *sf* (*di calze*) ladder; (*della pelle*) stretch mark.

smaltire *vt* (*merce*) to sell off; (*rifiuti*) to discharge; (*cibo*) to digest; ~ **la sbornia** to get over one's hangover.

smalto *sm* (*per metalli, di denti*) enamel; (*per ceramica*) glaze; (*per unghie*) nail varnish.

smania *sf* (*agitazione*) restlessness; (*desiderio*) craving; **aver la ~ di qc** to have a craving for sthg.

smarrire *vt* to lose □ **smarrirsi** *vr* to get lost.

smarrito, -a *agg* lost; (*sbigottito*) bewildered.

smascherare *vt* to unmask.

smemorato, -a *agg* absentminded.

smentire vt (notizia) to deny; (testimonianza) to refute.

smentita sf (di notizia) denial.

smeraldo sm emerald.

smesso, -a pp → **smettere**.

smettere vt to stop; (abito) to stop wearing; **smettere di fare qc** to stop doing sthg; **smettila!** stop it!

smidollato, -a agg spineless.

sminuire vt to belittle.

sminuzzare vt to crumble.

smistamento sm (di posta, pacchi) sorting; (di treni) shunting.

smistare vt (posta) to sort; (treni) to shunt.

smisurato, -a agg enormous, huge.

smodato, -a agg excessive.

smog sm inv smog.

smoking sm inv dinner jacket (Br), tuxedo (Am).

smontabile agg that can be dismantled.

smontare vt (macchina, libreria) to take to pieces; (fig: far perdere l'entusiasmo a) to discourage ◆ vi (da cavallo) to dismount; (da turno di lavoro) to finish (work).

smorfia sf grimace.

smorfioso, -a agg simpering.

smorzare vt (suoni) to muffle; (colore) to tone down; (entusiasmo) to dampen.

smosso, -a pp → **smuovere**.

smottamento sm landslide.

smunto, -a agg pinched.

smuovere vt (spostare) to shift; (da proposito, intenzione) to deter.

smussare vt (spigolo) to round off.

snack-bar sm inv snack bar.

snaturato, -a agg inhuman.

snello, -a agg slim, slender.

snervante agg exhausting.

snidare vt to flush out.

snobismo sm snobbery.

snodare vt (slegare) to untie; (arti) to loosen up ❑ **snodarsi** vr (slegarsi) to come loose.

sobbalzare vi (balzare) to jolt; (trasalire) to jump.

sobborgo, -ghi sm suburb.

sobrio, -a agg sober.

socchiudere vt (porta) to leave ajar; (occhi) to half-close.

socchiuso, -a pp → **socchiudere**.

soccorrere vt to help.

soccorso, -a pp → **soccorrere** ◆ sm help, aid; ~ **stradale** breakdown service.

sociale agg social.

socialista, -i, -e agg socialist.

socializzare vi to socialize.

società sf inv (gruppo umano) society; (associazione) association, club; (COMM) company; ~ **per azioni** limited company (Br), incorporated company (Am).

socievole agg sociable.

socio, -a, -ci, cie sm, f (di circolo) member; (COMM) partner.

soda®[1] sf soda.

soda[2] sf (bevanda) soda water.

soddisfacente agg satisfactory.

soddisfare vt to satisfy.

soddisfatto, -a agg satisfied; **essere ~ di** (contento) to be satisfied with.

soddisfazione — sollecitare

soddisfazione *sf* satisfaction.

sodo, -a *agg* hard, firm.

sofà *sm inv* sofa.

sofferente *agg* suffering.

sofferto, -a *pp* → **soffrire**

soffiare *vi* to blow ♦ *vt* to blow; ~ **qn/qc a qn** to pinch sb/sthg from sb; **soffiarsi il naso** to blow one's nose.

soffiata *sf (fam)* tip-off.

soffice *agg* soft.

soffio *sm (di fiato, vento)* breath; ~ **al cuore** heart murmur.

soffitta *sf* attic.

soffitto *sm* ceiling.

soffocante *agg* suffocating, stifling.

soffocare *vt* to suffocate ♦ *vi* to suffocate.

soffriggere *vt & vi* to fry lightly.

soffrire *vt (patire)* to suffer; *(sopportare)* to bear ♦ *vi* to suffer □ **soffrire di** *v + prep* to suffer from.

soffritto *sm* lightly fried onions and herbs.

sofisticato, -a *agg* sophisticated.

software ['softwer] *sm* software.

soggetto, -a *agg:* **essere ~ a** to be subject to ♦ *sm* subject.

soggezione *sf (sottomissione)* subjection; *(imbarazzo)* uneasiness; **dare ~ a qn** to make sb ill at ease.

soggiorno *sm (permanenza)* stay; *(stanza)* living room.

soglia *sf* threshold.

sogliola *sf* sole.

sognare *vt* to dream of o about

♦ *vi* to dream; ~ **ad occhi aperti** to daydream.

sogno *sm* dream; **fare un brutto** ~ to have a bad dream.

soia *sf* soya.

solaio *sm* attic.

solamente *avv* only, just.

solare *agg* solar, sun *(dav s)*.

solarium *sm inv* solarium.

solco, -chi *sm (in terreno)* furrow; *(incisione)* groove; *(scia)* wake.

soldato *sm* soldier; ~ **semplice** private.

soldo *sm:* **non avere un** ~ to be penniless □ **soldi** *smpl (denaro)* money *(sg)*.

sole *sm* sun; **prendere il** ~ to sunbathe.

soleggiato, -a *agg* sunny.

solenne *agg* solemn.

solere *v impers:* **come si suol dire** as they say.

soletta *sf (suola)* insole.

solfo = **zolfo**.

solidale *agg:* **essere ~ con qn** to be in agreement with sb.

solidarietà *sf* solidarity.

solido, -a *agg & sm* solid.

solista, -i, -e *smf* soloist.

solitario, -a *agg (persona)* lonely, solitary; *(luogo)* lonely ♦ *sm (di carte)* patience *(Br)*, solitaire *(Am)*; *(brillante)* solitaire.

solito, -a *agg* usual; **essere ~ fare qc** to be in the habit of doing sthg; **(come) al** ~ as usual; **di** ~ usually.

solitudine *sf* solitude.

sollecitare *vt (risposta, pagamento)* to press for.

solleone

252

solleone sm (caldo) summer heat; (periodo) dog days (pl).

solletico sm tickling; **soffrire il ~** to be ticklish.

sollevamento sm lifting; **~ pesi** (SPORT) weight lifting.

sollevare vt (tirare su) to lift, to raise; (problema, questione) to raise; (fare insorgere) to stir up ❑ **sollevarsi** vr (da terra) to get up; (insorgere) to rise up.

sollevato, -a agg (confortato) relieved.

sollievo sm relief.

solo, -a agg (senza compagnia) alone; (isolato) lonely; (unico) only ♦ avv (soltanto) only, just; **c'è un ~ posto a sedere** there's only one seat; **da ~** by oneself; **ho ~ 5 000 lire** I only have 5,000 lire; **non ~ ... ma anche** not only ... but also; **a ~** (MUS) solo.

soltanto avv only.

solubile agg soluble; **caffè ~** instant coffee.

soluzione sf solution.

Somalia sf: **la ~** Somalia.

somaro, -a sm, f (asino) donkey, ass; (fig: a scuola) dunce.

somiglianza sf resemblance.

somigliare : **somigliare a** v + prep (nell'aspetto) to look like; (nel modo di essere) to be like ❑ **somigliarsi** vr to be alike.

somma sf sum.

sommare vt (MAT) to add up.

sommario, -a agg brief ♦ sm (di libro) brief.

sommergere vt to submerge; **~ di** (fig) to overwhelm with.

sommergibile sm submarine.

sommerso, -a pp → **sommergere** ♦ agg (isola, città) underwater.

somministrare vt to administer.

sommità sf inv (cima) summit.

sommo, -a agg highest; (eccellente) outstanding, excellent; **per sommi capi** in short, in brief.

sommossa sf uprising.

sommozzatore, -trice sm, f (deep-sea) diver.

sonda sf (spaziale, MED) probe.

sondaggio sm (indagine) survey.

sondare vt (fondo marino) to sound; (intenzioni, opinioni) to sound out.

sonnambulo, -a agg: **essere ~** to sleepwalk.

sonnellino sm nap.

sonnifero sm sleeping pill.

sonno sm sleep; **avere ~** to be sleepy; **prendere ~** to fall asleep.

sono → **essere**.

sonoro, -a agg (onde, di film) sound (dav s); (voce, risata, schiaffo) ringing ♦ sm (di film) soundtrack.

sontuoso, -a agg sumptuous.

soppiatto : **di soppiatto** avv secretly.

sopportare vt (peso) to support, to bear; (umiliazione, dolore) to bear; (tollerare) to put up with.

soppresso, -a pp → **sopprimere**.

sopprimere vt (legge) to abolish; (servizio, treno) to withdraw, to do away with; (parola) to delete.

sopra prep (su) on; (al di sopra di)

above; *(al di là di)* over; *(riguardo a)* about, on ♦ *avv (in alto)* above; *(in lettera, scritto):* **come precisato ~** as detailed above; **al di ~ di** above; **di ~** upstairs.

soprabito *sm* overcoat.

sopracciglio *(pl f* **sopracciglia)** *sm* eyebrow.

sopraffare *vt* to overcome.

sopraffatto, -a *pp →* **sopraffare.**

sopraggiungere *vi (giungere all'improvviso)* to arrive (unexpectedly); *(accadere)* to occur (unexpectedly).

sopraggiunto, -a *pp →* **sopraggiungere.**

sopralluogo, -ghi *sm (di polizia)* on-the-spot investigation; *(visita)* inspection.

soprammobile *sm* ornament.

soprannaturale *agg* supernatural.

soprannome *sm* nickname.

soprano *sm* soprano.

soprassalto : di soprassalto *avv* with a start.

soprattutto *avv* above all, especially.

sopravvalutare *vt* to overestimate.

sopravvento *sm:* **avere il ~ su** to have the upper hand over.

sopravvissuto, -a *pp →* **sopravvivere** ♦ *sm,f* survivor.

sopravvivere *vi* to survive ❑ **sopravvivere a** *v + prep* to survive.

soprelevata *sf* elevated section.

soprintendente *smf (a attività, lavoro)* superintendent, supervisor.

soprintendenza *sf (attività)* supervision; *(ufficio)* superintendency.

sopruso *sm* abuse of power.

soqquadro *sm:* **mettere qc a ~** to turn sthg upside down.

sorbetto *sm* sorbet.

sorbire *vt* to sip; **sorbirsi qn/qc** *(fig)* to put up with sb/sthg.

sorcio *sm* mouse.

sordido, -a *agg* sordid, squalid.

sordina *sf:* **in ~** softly.

sordo, -a *agg (non udente)* deaf; *(rumore, tonfo)* muffled, dull ♦ *sm, f* deaf person.

sordomuto, -a *agg* deaf and dumb ♦ *sm, f* deaf and dumb person.

sorella *sf* sister.

sorellastra *sf* stepsister.

sorgente *sf (d'acqua)* spring; *(di fiume, elettricità, calore)* source.

sorgere *vi* to rise; *(sospetto, dubbio)* to arise.

sorpassare *vt (AUTO)* to overtake; *(superare)* to exceed.

sorpassato, -a *agg* old-fashioned.

sorpasso *sm (di veicolo)* overtaking; **fare un ~** to overtake.

sorprendere *vt (cogliere)* to catch; *(stupire)* to surprise ❑ **sorprendersi di** *vr + prep* to be surprised at.

sorpresa *sf* surprise; **fare una ~ a qn** to give sb a surprise; **di ~** by surprise.

sorpreso, -a *pp* → **sorprendere**.

sorreggere *vt* to support.

sorretto, -a *pp* → **sorreggere**.

sorridente *agg* smiling.

sorridere *vi* to smile.

sorriso, -a *pp* → **sorridere** ♦ *sm* smile.

sorsata *sf* gulp.

sorso *sm* (*sorsata*) gulp; (*piccola quantità*) sip.

sorta *sf* kind, sort.

sorte *sf* fate; **tirare a ~** to draw lots.

sorteggio *sm* draw.

sortilegio *sm* spell.

sorveglianza *sf* supervision; (*POLIZIA*) surveillance.

sorvegliare *vt* to watch.

sorvolare *vt* (*territorio*) to fly over ♦ *vi*: **~ su** (*territorio*) to fly over; (*fig*) to pass over.

S.O.S. *sm* SOS; **lanciare un ~** to send out an SOS.

sosia *smf inv* double.

sospendere *vt* (*attaccare*) to hang; (*attività, pagamenti, funzionario*) to suspend.

sospensione *sf* suspension.

sospeso, -a *pp* → **sospendere** ♦ *agg* (*interrotto*) suspended; **lasciare qc in ~** to leave sthg unfinished; **tenere qn in ~** to keep sb in suspense.

sospettare *vt* to suspect ♦ *vi*: **~ di qn** (*avere sospetti su*) to suspect sb; (*diffidare di*) to be suspicious of sb.

sospetto, -a *agg* suspicious ♦

sm, f suspect ♦ *sm* suspicion.

sospirare *vi* to sigh; **farsi ~** to keep sb waiting.

sospiro *sm* sigh; **tirare un ~ di sollievo** to heave a sigh of relief.

sosta *sf* (*in luogo*) stop; (*pausa*) break; **fare ~ a/in** to make a stop at/in; **'divieto di ~'** 'no waiting'; **senza ~** nonstop; **'~ consentita solo per carico e scarico'** 'no waiting except for loading and unloading'.

sostantivo *sm* noun.

sostanza *sf* substance.

sostanzioso, -a *agg* (*cibo*) nourishing; (*notevole*) substantial.

sostare *vi* (*fermarsi*) to stop.

sostegno *sm* support.

sostenere *vt* to support; **~ che** to maintain (that); **~ gli esami** to sit exams ❑ **sostenersi** *vr* (*tenersi dritto*) to hold o.s. up.

sostenitore, -trice *sm, f* supporter.

sostentamento *sm* maintenance.

sostenuto, -a *agg* (*tono, stile*) elevated; (*ritmo, passo*) sustained.

sostituire *vt* (*rimpiazzare*) to replace; (*prendere il posto di*) to take over from; **~ qn/qc con** to substitute sb/sthg with; **~ qn/qc a** to substitute sb/sthg for.

sostituto, -a *sm, f* substitute.

sostituzione *sf* substitution.

sottaceti *smpl* pickles.

sottana *sf* (*gonna*) skirt; (*di prete*) cassock.

sotterfugio *sm* subterfuge.

sotterraneo, -a *agg* underground; *(fig)* clandestine, secret ♦ *sm* cellar.

sottigliezza *sf (di spessore)* thinness; *(fig)* subtlety; *(dettaglio)* quibble.

sottile *agg (non spesso)* thin; *(capelli)* fine; *(slanciato)* slim; *(vista, odorato, ingegno)* sharp, keen; **non andare per il** ~ not to mince matters.

sottintendere *vt* to imply.

sottinteso, -a *pp* → **sottintendere** ♦ *sm* allusion.

sotto *prep* under; *(più in basso di)* below ♦ *avv (in posizione inferiore)* underneath; *(più in basso, in scritto)* below; **al di ~ di** under, below; **sott'olio** in oil; **di ~** *(al piano inferiore)* downstairs.

sottobanco *avv (comprare)* under the counter.

sottobicchiere *sm* coaster.

sottobosco *sm* undergrowth.

sottobraccio *avv (prendere)* by the arm; *(camminare)* arm in arm.

sottofondo *sm (MUS)* background music.

sottolineare *vt* to underline; *(dare risalto a)* to emphasize.

sottolio → **sotto**.

sottomarino, -a *agg* underwater *(dav s)* ♦ *sm* submarine.

sottomesso, -a *pp* → **sottomettere** ♦ *agg* submissive.

sottomettere *vt (al proprio dominio)* to subdue □ **sottomettersi a** *vr + prep* to submit to.

sottopassaggio *sm (per auto)* underpass; *(per pedoni, in stazione)* subway, underpass; **'servirsi del ~'** 'please use the subway'.

sottoporre *vt:* ~ **qn a qc** to subject sb to sthg; ~ **qc a qn** to submit sthg to sb □ **sottoporsi a** *vr + prep (subire)* to undergo.

sottoposto, -a *pp* → **sottoporre**.

sottoscala *sm inv* cupboard under the stairs.

sottoscritto, -a *pp* → **sottoscrivere** ♦ *sm, f* undersigned.

sottoscrivere *vt* to sign □ **sottoscrivere a** *v + prep* to subscribe to.

sottosopra *avv* upside down.

sottostante *agg* lower.

sottosuolo *sm (di terreno)* subsoil; *(locale)* basement.

sottosviluppato, -a *agg* underdeveloped.

sottoterra *avv* underground.

sottotitoli *smpl* subtitles.

sottovalutare *vt* to underestimate.

sottoveste *sf* underskirt.

sottovoce *avv* in a low voice.

sottovuoto *avv* vacuum-packed.

sottrarre *vt (MAT)* to subtract; *(fondi)* to take away, to remove; ~ **qc a qn** *(rubare)* to steal sthg from sb □ **sottrarsi a** *vr + prep* to escape, to avoid.

sottratto, -a *pp* → **sottrarre**.

sottrazione *sf (MAT)* subtraction; *(furto)* removal.

souvenir [suve'nir] *sm inv* souvenir.

sovietico, -a, -ci, -che *agg* soviet.

sovraccaricare vt to overload.

sovrano, -a agg & sm, f sovereign.

sovrapporre vt to put on top of.

sovrapposto, -a pp → sovrapporre.

sovrastare vt (valle, paese) to overhang.

sovrumano, -a agg superhuman.

sovvenzionare vt to subsidize.

sovversivo, -a agg subversive.

sozzo, -a agg filthy.

S.p.A. (abbr di società per azioni) = Ltd (Br), = Inc. (Am).

spaccare vt to break, to split ❑ **spaccarsi** vr to break, to split.

spaccatura sf split.

spacciare (droga) to push ❑ **spacciarsi per** vr + prep to pass o.s. off as.

spacciatore, -trice sm, f (di droga) pusher.

spacco, -chi sm split; (di gonna) slit.

spaccone, -a sm, f boaster.

spada sf sword.

spaesato, -a agg disorientated.

spaghetteria sf restaurant specializing in pasta dishes.

spaghetti smpl spaghetti (sg); ~ aglio, olio e peperoncino spaghetti with garlic, chilli and olive oil; ~ alla carbonara spaghetti in an egg, bacon and cheese sauce; ~ pomodoro e basilico spaghetti in a fresh tomato and basil sauce; ~ alla puttanesca spaghetti in a sauce of tomatoes, anchovies, olives and capers; ~ alle vongole spaghetti in a clam sauce.

Spagna sf: la ~ Spain.

spagnolo, -a agg Spanish ♦ sm, f Spaniard ♦ sm (lingua) Spanish.

spago, -ghi sm string.

spaiato, -a agg odd.

spalancare vt to open wide.

spalla sf shoulder; voltare le spalle a qn to turn one's back on sb; di spalle from behind.

spalliera sf (di letto) head; (SPORT) wall bars (pl).

spallina sf (di reggiseno, sottoveste) strap; (imbottitura) shoulder pad.

spalmare vt to spread.

spalti smpl (di stadio) terraces.

spandere vt (versare) to pour; (spargere) to spread ❑ **spandersi** vr to spread.

spappolare vt to pulp ❑ **spappolarsi** vr to get mushy.

sparare vi to fire ♦ vt (colpo, fucilata) to fire.

sparecchiare vi to clear the table ♦ vt: ~ la tavola to clear the table.

spareggio sm (SPORT) play-off.

spargere vt (sparpagliare) to scatter; (versare) to spill; (divulgare) to spread ❑ **spargersi** vr (sparpagliarsi) to scatter; (divulgarsi) to spread.

sparire vi to disappear.

sparlare : sparlare di v + prep to run down.

sparo sm shot.

sparpagliare vt to scatter

sparpagliarsi *vr* to scatter.

sparso, -a *pp* → **spargere** ♦ *agg* scattered.

spartire *vt (dividere)* to share out.

spartitraffico *sm inv* central reservation *(Br)*, median strip *(Am)*.

spasmo *sm* spasm.

spassarsela *vr* to have a good time.

spasso *sm (film, scena)* amusement, fun; *(persona)* laugh, scream; *(passeggiata)*: **andare a ~** to go for a walk; **essere a ~** *(fig)* to be out of work.

spauracchio *sm* scarecrow.

spaventapasseri *sm inv* scarecrow.

spaventare *vt* to frighten ❑ **spaventarsi** *vr* to become frightened.

spavento *sm (paura)* fear, fright; **far ~ a qn** to give sb a fright.

spaventoso, -a *agg* frightening.

spazientirsi *vr* to lose one's patience.

spazio *sm* space.

spazioso, -a *agg* spacious.

spazzaneve *sm inv* snowplough.

spazzare *vt (pavimento)* to sweep; *(sporco, foglie)* to sweep up.

spazzatura *sf (rifiuti)* rubbish.

spazzino, -a *sm, f* road sweeper.

spazzola *sf (per capelli)* hairbrush; *(per abiti)* clothes brush; **~ da scarpe** shoe brush.

spazzolare *vt* to brush.

spazzolino *sm*: **~ (da denti)** toothbrush.

spazzolone *sm* scrubbing brush.

specchiarsi *vr* to look at o.s. (in a mirror).

specchietto *sm (da borsetta)* pocket mirror; *(prospetto)* scheme, table; **~ (retrovisore)** rear-view mirror.

specchio *sm* mirror.

speciale *agg* special.

specialista, -i, -e *sm, f* specialist.

specialità *sf inv* speciality; **~ della casa** speciality of the house.

specialmente *avv* especially.

specie *sf inv (di piante, animali)* species *(inv)*; *(sorta)* kind ♦ *avv* especially; **una ~ di** a kind of.

specificare *vt* to specify.

specifico, -a, -ci, -che *agg* specific.

speculare *vi* to speculate.

speculazione *sf* speculation.

spedire *vt* to send.

spedizione *sf (di lettera, merci)* sending; *(viaggio)* expedition.

spegnere *vt (fuoco, sigaretta)* to put out; *(luce, TV, gas)* to turn off.

spellare *vt (coniglio)* to skin ❑ **spellarsi** *vr* to peel.

spendere *vt & vi* to spend.

spensierato, -a *agg* carefree.

spento, -a *pp* → **spegnere** ♦ *agg (colore)* dull; *(sguardo)* lifeless.

speranza *sf* hope.

sperare *vt* to hope for; **spero che venga** I hope he'll come; **spero**

sperduto

258

di sì I hope so; **~ di fare qc** to hope to do sthg ❑ **sperare in** v + prep to trust in.

sperduto, -a agg (luogo) out-of-the-way; (persona) lost.

spericolato, -a agg fearless.

sperimentale agg experimental.

sperimentare vt (sottoporre a esperimento, fig) to test; (fare esperienza di) to experience.

sperma sm sperm.

sperperare vt to squander.

spesa sf (somma) expense; (acquisti) shopping; **fare la ~** to do the shopping; **fare spese** (acquisti) to go shopping ❑ **spese** sfpl (uscite) expenses; **spese postali** postage (sg); **spese di viaggio** travel expenses; **a spese di** at the expense of.

spesso, -a agg thick ◆ avv often.

spessore sm thickness.

Spett. abbr = spettabile.

spettabile agg (nelle lettere): **~ ditta** Messrs ... & Co.

spettacolo sm (rappresentazione) show; (vista) sight.

spettare : **spettare a** v + prep to be up to; **spetta a te dirglielo** it's up to you to tell him.

spettatore, -trice sm, f (di spettacolo) member of the audience; (di avvenimento) onlooker.

spettinare vt: **~ qn** to ruffle sb's hair ❑ **spettinarsi** vr to get one's hair messed up.

spettro sm (fantasma) spectre.

spezia sf spice.

spezzare vt (rompere) to break; (viaggio, giornata) to break (up) ❑ **spezzarsi** vr to break.

spezzatino sm stew.

spezzato, -a agg (diviso) broken ◆ sm (vestito) jacket and trousers.

spezzettare vt to break into small pieces.

spia sf (di polizia) informer; (agente) spy; (luminosa) warning light; (indizio) indication, sign; **fare la ~** to be a sneak.

spiacente agg: **essere ~ (fare qc)** to be sorry (for doing sthg).

spiacevole agg unpleasant.

spiaggia, -ge sf beach; **~ privata** private beach.

spianare vt (terreno) to level; (pasta) to roll out; **~ il terreno** (fig) to prepare the ground.

spiare vt to spy on.

spiazzo sm open space.

spiccare vi (risaltare) to stand out ◆ vt: **~ un balzo** to jump; **~ il volo** to fly off.

spiccato, -a agg marked, strong.

spicchio sm (d'arancia) segment; (di mela, pera) slice; **~ d'aglio** clove of garlic.

spicciarsi vr to hurry up.

spicciolo, -a agg: **moneta spicciola** small change ❑ **spiccioli** smpl small change.

spiedino sm (pietanza) kebab.

spiedo sm spit; **allo ~** spit roasted.

spiegare vt (far capire) to explain; (vele) to unfurl; (lenzuola) t unfold; ~ **qc a qn** to explain sthg to sb ◻ **spiegarsi** *vr (farsi capire)* to make o.s. clear; *(diventare chiaro)* to become clear; **spieghiamoci!** let's get things straight!

spiegazione *sf* explanation.

spietato, -a *agg* ruthless.

spiga, -ghe *sf (di grano)* ear.

spigolo *sm (di mobile, muro)* corner.

spilla *sf* brooch; ~ **da balia** safety pin.

spillare *vt (soldi):* ~ **qc a qn** to tap sb for sthg.

spillo *sm (da sarto)* pin.

spilorcio, -a, -ci, -ce *agg* mean, stingy.

spina *sf (di pianta)* thorn; *(di riccio)* spine; *(lisca)* bone; *(elettrica)* plug; **birra alla** ~ draught beer; ~ **dorsale** backbone.

spinaci *smpl* spinach (sg).

spinello *sm (fam: sigaretta)* joint.

spingere *vt & vi* to push; ~ **qn a fare qc** to press sb to do sthg ◻ **spingersi** *vr* to push on.

spinoso, -a *agg* prickly, thorny.

spinta *sf (pressione, urto)* push; *(incoraggiamento)* incentive, spur; *(raccomandazione):* **dare una** ~ **a qn** to pull strings for sb.

spinto, -a *pp →* **spingere** ♦ *agg (scabroso)* risqué.

spintone *sm* push, shove.

spionaggio *sm* espionage.

spioncino *sm* peephole, spy ~ole.

~piraglio *sm (fessura)* chink; *(di ~ce)* gleam, glimmer.

pirale *sf* spiral; *(anticoncezio-*

nale) coil.

spirito *sm (intelletto)* mind; *(fantasma, disposizione d'animo,* RELIG) spirit; *(vivacità d'ingegno)* wit; *(senso dell'umorismo)* humour; *(alcol):* **ciliegie sotto** ~ cherries preserved in alcohol.

spiritoso, -a *agg* witty.

spirituale *agg* spiritual.

splendente *agg* shining.

splendere *vi* to shine.

splendido, -a *agg (bellissimo)* magnificent.

splendore *sm* splendour; *(luce)* brilliance.

spogliare *vt (svestire)* to undress; ~ **qn di qc** *(derubare, privare)* to strip sb of sthg ◻ **spogliarsi** *vr* to undress.

spogliarello *sm* striptease.

spogliatoio *sm (di palestra, piscina)* changing room; *(di abitazione)* dressing room.

spoglio *sm (di schede elettorali)* counting.

spola *sf (bobina)* spool; **fare la** ~ **(tra)** to go to and fro (between).

spolpare *vt* to strip the flesh off.

spolverare *vt & vi* to dust.

sponda *sf (di fiume)* bank; *(di lago)* shore; *(di letto)* edge; *(di biliardo)* cushion.

sponsorizzare *vt* sponsor.

spontaneo, -a *agg* spontaneous; *(non artificioso)* natural.

spopolare *vt* to depopulate ♦ *vi* to draw the crowds ◻ **spopolarsi** *vr* to become depopulated.

sporadico, -a, -ci, -che *agg*

sporadic.

sporcare vt to dirty; **sporcarsi le mani** to get one's hands dirty ❑ **sporcarsi** vr to get dirty.

sporcizia sf (l'esser sporco) dirtiness; (cosa sporca) dirt.

sporco, -a, -chi, -che agg dirty ♦ sm dirt.

sporgente agg protruding; (occhi) bulging.

sporgere vt to put out ♦ vi to stick out ❑ **sporgersi** vr to lean out.

sport sm inv sport.

sporta sf shopping bag.

sportello sm (di mobile, treno) door; (di banca, posta) window, counter; ~ **automatico** cash dispenser.

sportivo, -a agg (programma, campo) sports (dav s); (persona) sporty; (abbigliamento) casual; (comportamento, spirito) sporting ♦ sm, f sportsman (f sportswoman).

sporto, -a pp → sporgere.

sposare vt to marry ❑ **sposarsi** vr to get married; **sposarsi con** vr + prep to marry.

sposato, -a agg married.

sposo, -a sm, f bridegroom (f bride); **gli sposi** the newlyweds.

spossante agg exhausting.

spostare vt to move; (cambiare) to change ❑ **spostarsi** vr to move.

spot sm inv (faretto) spotlight; (pubblicità) advert.

spranga, -ghe sf bar.

spray sm inv spray.

sprecare vt to waste.

spreco, -chi sm waste.

spregiudicato, -a agg (senza scrupoli) unscrupulous.

spremere vt (arancia, limone) to squeeze.

spremiagrumi sm inv lemon squeezer.

spremuta sf fresh fruit juice; ~ **di arancia** freshly-squeezed orange juice.

sprezzante agg scornful.

sprigionare vt to emit ❑ **sprigionarsi** vr to emanate.

sprizzare vi to spurt.

sprofondare vi (crollare) to collapse; (affondare) to sink.

sproporzionato, -a agg out of all proportion.

sproposito sm blunder; (somma esagerata): **costa uno** ~ it costs a fortune; **parlare a** ~ to talk out of turn.

sprovveduto, -a agg inexperienced.

sprovvisto, -a agg: ~ **di** lacking in; **cogliere qn alla sprovvista** to catch sb unawares.

spruzzare vt (profumo) to spray; (acqua) to sprinkle; (persona) to splash.

spruzzatore sm spray.

spruzzo sm spray.

spugna sf (da bagno) sponge; (tessuto) towelling.

spuma sf (schiuma) foam, froth.

spumante sm sparkling wine.

_i_ SPUMANTE

The sparkling wine calle₀
"spumante" can be drunk as a₀

aperitif or as a dessert wine, and comes in sweet, dry or muscat versions, the latter being named after the grape variety. This Italian answer to champagne gets its name from the fact that it releases lots of bubbles, or foam ("spuma"), when uncorked. No birthday or wedding is complete without "spumante", and it is also traditional to open a bottle at midnight on New Year's Eve.

---

spumone *sm (dolce)* a foamy dessert made from whisked egg white, milk and sugar.

spuntare *vi (apparire)* to appear ◆ *vt (tagliare la punta di)* to break the point of; **spuntarsi i capelli** to trim one's hair; **spuntarla** *(fig)* to make it.

spuntino *sm* snack.

spunto *sm (punto di partenza)* starting point.

sputare *vt* to spit out ◆ *vi* to spit.

sputo *sm* spit.

squadra *sf (di operai, SPORT)* squad, team; *(strumento)* set square.

squadrare *vt (scrutare)* to look at closely; *(foglio, blocco)* to square.

squagliare *vt* to melt; **squagliarsela** *(fam)* to clear off ▫ **squagliarsi** *vr* to melt.

squalificare *vt* to disqualify.

squallido, -a *agg* wretched, miserable.

squallore *sm* wretchedness, misery.

squalo *sm* shark.

squama *sf* scale.

squamarsi *vr* to flake off.

squarciagola : a squarciagola *avv* at the top of one's voice.

squarciare *vt* to rip.

squartare *vt* to quarter.

squattrinato, -a *agg* penniless.

squilibrato, -a *agg* unbalanced.

squilibrio *sm (fisico)* disequilibrium; *(psichico)* derangement; *(disparità)* imbalance.

squillo *sm (di telefono, campanello)* ring; *(di tromba)* blare.

squisito, -a *agg (cibo)* delicious; *(raffinato)* exquisite; *(persona)* delightful.

sradicare *vt (albero)* to uproot.

srotolare *vt* to unroll.

stabile *agg* stable; *(lavoro, occupazione)* steady ◆ *sm (edificio)* building.

stabilimento *sm (complesso)* factory, plant; **~ balneare** bathing establishment.

ℹ STABILIMENTI BALNEARI

Many Italian seaside resorts have their "stabilimenti balneari", bathing clubs on the beach which provide a bar, showers and changing huts, and hire out beach umbrellas, deckchairs and pedalos. Some even organize volleyball tournaments, treasure hunts and dances.

---

stabilire *vt* to establish; *(fissare)* to fix; **~ che** *(decidere)* to decide (that) ▫ **stabilirsi** *vr* to settle.

stabilità

stabilità *sf* stability.

staccare *vt (separare)* to detach, to separate; *(SPORT)* to leave behind ◆ *vi (risaltare)* to stand out; *(fam: finire il lavoro)* to knock off ❑ **staccarsi** *vr (bottone, cerotto)* to come off; **staccarsi da** *(venir via da)* to come off; *(fig: allontanarsi)* to move away from.

staccionata *sf (recinzione)* fence; *(SPORT)* hurdle.

stadio *sm (SPORT)* stadium; *(fase)* stage.

staffa *sf (di sella, pantaloni)* stirrup; **perdere le staffe** *(fig)* to fly off the handle.

staffetta *sf (SPORT)* relay race.

stagionale *agg* seasonal ◆ *smf* seasonal worker.

stagionato, -a *agg* seasoned.

stagione *sf* season; **alta/bassa ~** high/low season; **vestiti di mezza ~** clothes for spring and autumn.

stagno, -a *agg (a tenuta d'acqua)* watertight; *(a tenuta d'aria)* airtight ◆ *sm (laghetto)* pond; *(metallo)* tin.

stagnola *sf* tinfoil.

stalla *sf (per cavalli)* stable; *(per bovini)* cowshed.

stamattina *avv* this morning.

stambecco, -chi *sm* ibex.

stampa *sf (tecnica)* printing; *(con stampante, opera)* print; *(giornalisti)*: **la ~** the press; **'stampe'** 'printed matter'.

stampante *sf (INFORM)* printer.

stampare *vt* to print; *(pubblicare)* to publish; *(nella memoria)* to impress.

stampatello *sm* block letters *(pl)*.

stampella *sf* crutch.

stampo *sm* mould; *(fig: sorta)* type.

stancare *vt (affaticare)* to tire; *(stufare)* to bore ❑ **stancarsi** *vr* to get tired; **stancarsi di** *(stufarsi di)* to grow tired of.

stanchezza *sf* tiredness.

stanco, -a, -chi, -che *agg* tired; *(stufo)*: **~ di** fed up with; **~ morto** dead tired.

stanghetta *sf (di occhiali)* leg.

stanotte *avv* tonight; *(nella notte appena passata)* last night.

stante *agg*: **a sé ~** separate, independent.

stantio, -a *agg (cibo)* stale.

stanza *sf (camera)* room; **~ da bagno** bathroom; **~ da letto** bedroom.

stanziare *vt* to allocate.

stare *vi (rimanere)* to stay; *(abitare)* to live; *(con gerundio)*: **sto leggendo** I'm reading; **come sta?** how are you?; **ti sta bene!** (it) serves you right!; **ci stai?** is that OK with you?; **sta a voi decidere** it's up to you to decide; **queste scarpe mi stanno strette** these shoes are tight; **~ per fare qc** to be about to do sthg; **~ bene/male** to be well/not very well; **~ a guardare** to watch; **~ in piedi** to stand (up); **~ seduto** to be sitting; **~ simpatico a qn** to like sb; **~ zitto** to shut up; **starci** to fit.

starnutire *vi* to sneeze.

starnuto *sm* sneeze.

stasera *avv* this evening, tonight.

statale *agg* state *(dav s)*, government (dav s) ♦ smf civil servant ♦ sf main road.

statistica, -che sf (disciplina) statistics (pl); (dati) statistic.

stato pp → essere, stare ♦ sm (condizione) state, condition; (nazione) state; **essere in ~ interessante** to be pregnant; **~ d'animo** state of mind; **~ civile** marital status; **gli Stati Uniti (d'America)** the United States (of America).

statua sf statue.

statunitense agg United States (dav s), of the United States.

statura sf (fisica) height.

statuto sm statute.

stazionario, -a agg (immutato) unchanged.

stazione sf station; **~ degli autobus** bus station; **~ balneare** seaside resort; **~ centrale** central station; **~ ferroviaria** railway station (Br), railroad station (Am); **~ di polizia** police station; **~ sciistica** ski resort; **~ di servizio** petrol station (Br), gas station (Am); **~ termale** spa.

stecca, -che sf (asticella) stick; (di sigarette) carton; (da biliardo) cue.

steccato sm fence.

stella sf star; **stelle filanti** shooting stars; **albergo a tre stelle** three-star hotel.

stellato, -a agg starry.

stelo sm (di fiore) stem.

stemma, -i sm coat of arms.

stendere vt (allungare) to stretch (out); (panni, vele) to spread (out); (bucato) to hang out ❏ **stendersi** vr (sdraiarsi) to lie down.

stenografare vt to take down in shorthand.

stentare vi: **~ a fare qc** to find it hard to do sthg.

stento sm: **a ~** with difficulty ❏ **stenti** smpl (privazioni) hardship (sg).

sterco, -chi sm dung.

stereo sm inv stereo.

stereotipo sm stereotype.

sterile agg (uomo, donna) sterile.

sterilizzare vt to sterilize.

sterlina sf pound (sterling).

sterminare vt to exterminate.

sterminato, -a agg immense.

sterminio sm extermination.

sterzare vi to steer.

sterzo sm steering.

steso, -a pp → stendere.

stesso, -a agg same; (in persona, proprio): **il presidente ~** the president himself in person ♦ pron: **lo ~/la stessa** the same (one); **io ~** I myself; **lei stessa** she herself; **lo faccio per me ~** I'm doing it for myself; **fare qc lo ~** to do sthg just the same; **fa ○ è lo ~** it doesn't matter; **per me è lo ~** it's all the same to me.

stesura sf (atto) drafting; (documento) draft.

stile sm style; **~ libero** freestyle.

stilista, -i, -e smf designer.

stilografica, -che sf fountain pen.

stima sf (valutazione) valuation; (apprezzamento) esteem; **fare la ~ di qc** to estimate the value of sthg; **avere ~ di qn** to have a high opinion of sb.

stimare vt (valutare) to value; (ritenere) to consider; (apprezzare) to respect.

stimolare vt to stimulate; ~ **qn a fare qc** to spur sb on to do sthg.

stimolo sm stimulus.

stingere vi to fade ☐ **stingersi** vr to fade.

stinto, -a pp → **stingere**.

stipendio sm salary.

stipite sm (di porta, finestra) jamb.

stipulare vt to draw up.

stirare vt (con il ferro) to iron.

stiro sm → **asse, ferro**.

stirpe sf stock, birth.

stitichezza sf constipation.

stivale sm boot.

stivaletto sm ankle boot.

stizza sf anger.

stizzirsi vr to get irritated.

stoccafisso sm wind-dried cod, stockfish.

stoffa sf material, fabric; **avere la ~ di** to have the makings of.

stola sf stole.

stolto, -a agg stupid.

stomaco, -chi o **-ci** sm stomach.

stonato, -a agg (MUS) off key.

stop sm inv (AUTO: segnale) stop sign; (AUTO: luce) brake light (Br), stoplight ♦ esclam stop!; **'stop con segnale rosso'** 'stop when light is on red'.

storcere vt to twist; ~ **il naso** to turn up one's nose; **storcersi una caviglia** to twist one's ankle ☐ **storcersi** vr to twist.

stordire vt to stun.

stordito, -a agg stunned.

storia sf (avvenimenti umani, materia, opera) history; (vicenda, invenzione) story; (faccenda) business (no pl); (scusa) excuse.

storico, -a, -ci, -che agg historic(al) ♦ sm, f historian.

stormo sm (di uccelli) flock.

storpiare vt (rendere storpio) to cripple; (parola) to mangle; (concetto) to twist.

storta sf: **prendere una ~ al piede** to sprain one's foot.

storto, -a pp → **storcere** ♦ agg (chiodo) twisted, bent; (gambe, quadro) crooked; **andare ~** to go wrong.

stoviglie sfpl dishes.

strabico, -a, -ci, -che agg (persona) squint-eyed; (occhi) squint.

straccadenti smpl type of very hard biscuit.

stracchino sm a creamy cow's milk cheese from Lombardy.

stracciare vt (vestito, foglio) to tear.

stracciatella sf (gelato) chocolate-chip ice cream; (minestra) broth enriched with eggs, semolina and Parmesan cheese.

straccio sm rag; (per pulizie) duster, cloth.

straccione, -a sm, f ragamuffin.

strada sf road; (urbana) street; (percorso) way; **facendo** on the way; **tagliare la ~ a qn** to cut across sb; ~ **panoramica** scenic route; ~ **senza uscita** dead end; '~ **deformata'** 'uneven road surface';

stringa

'~ **privata'** 'private road'; '~ **transitabile con catene'** 'road negotiable with chains'.

stradale *agg* road (*dav s*) ♦ *sf* traffic police.

strafalcione *sm* (*sproposito*) howler.

straforo : di straforo *avv* on the sly.

strafottente *agg* arrogant.

strage *sf* massacre.

stralunato, -a *agg* (*occhi*) rolling; (*persona*) dazed.

stramazzare *vi* to fall heavily.

strangolare *vt* to strangle.

straniero, -a *agg* foreign ♦ *sm, f* foreigner.

strano, -a *agg* strange.

straordinario, -a *agg* extraordinary; (*treno*) special ♦ *sm* (*lavoro*) overtime.

strapazzare *vt* to ill-treat ❏ **strapazzarsi** *vr* to tire o.s. out.

strappo *sm* (*in tessuto, MED*) tear; (*fam: passaggio*) lift (*Brit*), ride (*Am*); **fare uno ~ alla regola** to make an exception to the rule.

straripare *vi* to overflow.

strascico, -chi *sm* (*di abito*) train; (*fig: conseguenza*) aftereffect.

strascinati *smpl* squares of pasta in a tomato and minced meat sauce (*a speciality of Calabria*).

stratagemma, -i *sm* stratagem.

strategia *sf* strategy.

strato *sm* (*di polvere, di crema*) layer; (*di vernice, smalto*) coat.

stravagante *agg* eccentric.

stravedere : stravedere per *v*

+ *prep* to be crazy about.

stravisto *pp* → **stravedere**.

stravolgere *vt* to distort.

stravolto, -a *pp* → **stravolgere**.

strazio *sm*: **essere uno ~** (*libro, film*) to be awful; (*persona*) to be a pain.

strega, -ghe *sf* witch.

stregone *sm* (*mago*) sorcerer; (*di tribù*) witchdoctor.

stremare *vt* to exhaust.

stremo *sm*: **essere allo ~ delle forze** to be at the end of one's tether.

strepitoso, -a *agg* resounding.

stress *sm* stress.

stressante *agg* stressful.

stretta, -e *sf* grip; **~ di mano** handshake; **mettere alle strette qn** to put sb in a tight corner.

strettamente *avv* (*serratamente*) tightly; (*rigorosamente*) strictly.

stretto, -a *pp* → **stringere** ♦ *agg* (*strada, stanza*) narrow; (*vestito, scarpe*) tight; (*rigoroso, preciso*) strict ♦ *sm* strait; **parenti stretti** close family (*sg*).

strettoia *sf* bottleneck.

striato, -a *agg* streaked.

stridere *vi* (*freni*) to creak; (*cicale, grilli*) to chirr; (*colori*) to clash.

strillare *vi & vt* to scream.

strillo *sm* scream.

striminzito, -a *agg* (*vestito*) shabby; (*persona*) skinny.

stringa, -ghe *sf* lace.

stringato

stringato, -a agg concise.

stringere vt (vite, nodo) to tighten; (denti, pugno) to clench; (labbra) to press; (tenere stretto) to grip; (abito) to take in; (patto, accordo) to conclude ♦ vi to be tight; ~ qn tra le braccia to hug sb; ~ la mano a qn to shake hands with sb; ~ i tempi to get a move on; **il tempo stringe** time is short □ **stringersi** vr to squeeze up.

striscia, -sce sf (nastro) strip; (riga) stripe; **strisce (pedonali)** zebra crossing (sg).

strisciare vi (serpente) to slither; (passare rasente) to scrape ♦ vt (macchina) to scrape; (piedi) to drag.

striscione sm banner.

stritolare vt to crush.

strizzare vt to wring out; ~ **l'occhio** to wink.

strofinaccio sm cloth.

strofinare vt to rub.

stroncare vt to break off; (rivolta) to put down; (libro, film) to pan.

stropicciare vt (braccio, occhi) to rub; (vestito) to crease.

strozzapreti smpl 'gnocchi' either in a meat sauce, or made with eggs and spinach and served with butter and cheese.

strozzare vt (strangolare) to strangle; (sog: cibo) to choke □ **strozzarsi** vr to choke.

strudel sm inv apple strudel.

strumento sm (musicale, di precisione) instrument; (di fabbro, meccanico) tool.

strusciare vt to rub □ **strusciarsi** vr to rub o.s.

strutto sm lard.

struttura sf structure.

struzzo sm ostrich.

stuccare vt (buco) to plaster; (vetro) to putty.

stucco, -chi sm (malta) plaster; (decorazione) stucco; **rimanere di** ~ to be dumbfounded.

studente, -essa sm, f student; (di liceo) pupil.

studentesco, -a, -schi, -sche agg student (dav s).

studentessa → studente.

studiare vt & vi to study.

studio sm (attività) studying; (ricerca, stanza) study; (di professionista) office; (di televisione, radio) studio; ~ **medico** surgery (Br), office (Am); **gli studi** (scuola, università) studies.

studioso, -a agg studious ♦ sm, f scholar.

stufa sf stove; ~ **elettrica** heater.

stufare vt (seccare): **mi hai stufato con le tue chiacchiere!** I'm sick and tired of you talking! □ **stufarsi** vr: **stufarsi (di)** (fam) to get fed up (with).

stufato sm stew.

stufo, -a agg (fam): **essere** ~ **(di)** to be fed up (with).

stuoia sf straw mat.

stupefacente agg amazing ♦ sm drug.

stupendo, -a agg marvellous.

stupidaggine sf stupid thing.

stupido, -a agg stupid.

stupire vt to amaze □ **stupirsi di** vr + prep to be amazed by.

stupore sm astonishment.

stupro *sm* rape.

sturare *vt* to unblock.

stuzzicadenti *sm inv* toothpick.

stuzzicare *vt (irritare)* to tease; ~ **l'appetito** to whet one's appetite.

su *prep* 1. *(stato in luogo)* on; **le chiavi sono sul tavolo** the keys are on the desk; **a 2 000 metri sul livello del mare** at 2,000 metres above sea level; **una casa sul mare** a house by the sea.

2. *(moto a luogo)* on, onto; **venite sulla terrazza** come onto the terrace.

3. *(argomento)* about, on; **un libro sulla vita di Napoleone** a book about Napoleon's life.

4. *(tempo)* around; **vengo sul tardo pomeriggio** I'll come in the late afternoon; **sul momento** at that moment; **sul presto** fairly early.

5. *(prezzo e misura)* about; **costerà sulle 200 000 lire** it will cost about 200,000 lire; **peserà sui tre chili** he weighs about three kilos; **un uomo sulla quarantina** a man about forty years old.

6. *(modo)*: **facciamo dolci solo ~ ordinazione** we only make cakes to order; **~ appuntamento** by appointment; **vestito ~ misura** made-to-measure suit; **parlare sul serio** to be serious; **nove volte ~ dieci** nine times out of ten.

♦ *avv* 1. *(in alto)* up; *(al piano di sopra)* upstairs; **in ~** *(verso l'alto)* up(wards); *(in poi)* onwards; **dai 18 anni in ~** from the age of 18 onwards.

2. *(per esortare)* come on; ~, **sbri-**

gatevi! come on, hurry up!; ~ **con la vita!** cheer up!

sub *smf inv* diver.

subacqueo, -a *agg* underwater ♦ *sm, f* diver.

subbuglio *sm* turmoil; **essere in ~** to be in a turmoil.

subdolo, -a *agg* sly.

subentrare *vi*: ~ **a qn** to take sb's place.

subire *vt (ingiustizia, conseguenze)* to suffer; *(operazione)* to undergo; ~ **un torto** to be wronged.

subissare *vt*: ~ **qn di qc** to shower sb with sthg.

subito *avv (immediatamente)* straightaway, immediately, at once; **torno ~** I'll be right back.

sublime *agg* sublime.

subordinato, -a *agg*: ~ **a** *(dipendente da)* dependent on.

suburbano, -a *agg* suburban.

succedere *vi (accadere)* to happen; ~ **a qn** *(subentrare)* to succeed sb; **che cos'è successo?** what happened? ❑ **succedersi** *vr* to follow one another.

successivamente *avv* afterwards.

successivo, -a *agg* following.

successo, -a *pp* → **succedere** ♦ *sm* success; **di ~** successful.

successore *sm* successor.

succhiare *vt* to suck.

succhiotto *sm* dummy.

succinto, -a *agg (conciso)* succinct; *(abito)* scanty.

succo, -chi *sm* juice; ~ **di frutta** fruit juice; ~ **di pomodoro** tomato juice.

sud *sm* south ◆ *agg inv* south; **a ~** (di qc) south (of sthg); **nel ~** in the south.

Sudafrica *sm*: **il ~** South Africa.

Sudamerica *sm*: **il ~** South America.

sudare *vi* to sweat.

suddetto, -a *agg* abovementioned.

suddividere *vt* to subdivide.

sudest *sm* southeast.

sudicio, -a, -ci, -ce o **-cie** *agg* dirty.

sudore *sm* sweat.

sudovest *sm* southwest.

sue → suo.

sufficiente *agg* (che basta) enough, sufficient; (tono, atteggiamento) arrogant ◆ *sm* (SCOL) pass.

sufficienza *sf*: **a ~** enough.

suffragio *sm* (voto) vote; **~ universale** universal suffrage.

suggerimento *sm* suggestion.

suggerire *vt* (consigliare) to suggest; (risposta) to tell.

suggestionare *vt* to influence.

suggestivo, -a *agg* evocative.

sughero *sm* cork.

sugli = su + gli, → su.

sugo, -ghi *sm* (condimento) sauce; (di arrosto) juices (pl); (succo) juice; **~ di pomodoro** tomato sauce.

sui = su + i, → su.

suicidarsi *vr* to commit suicide.

suicidio *sm* suicide.

suino, -a *agg* pork (dav s) ◆ *sm* pig.

sul = su + il, → su.

sull' = su + l', → su.

sulla = su + la, → su.

sulle = su + le, → su.

sullo = su + lo, → su.

suo (f **sua**, mpl **suoi**, fpl **sue**) *agg* (di lui) his; (di lei) her; (di esso, essa) its; (forma di cortesia) your; (proprio) one's ◆ *pron* (di lui) his; (di lei) hers; (di esso, essa) its; (forma di cortesia) yours; (proprio) one's; **i suoi** his family; (di lei) her family.

suocero, -a *sm, f* father-in-law (f mother-in-law) ❑ **suoceri** *smpl* in-laws.

suoi → suo.

suola *sf* sole.

suolo *sm* (terra) ground; (terreno) soil.

suonare *vt* (strumento) to play; (campanello) to ring; (clacson) to sound; (allarme) to set off; (ore) to strike ◆ *vi* (musicista) to play; (telefono, campana) to ring; (allarme, sveglia) to go off; (fig: parole) to sound.

suono *sm* sound.

suora *sf* nun.

super *sf inv* four-star (petrol) (Br), premium (Am).

superare *vt* (confine, traguardo, fiume) to cross; (limite) to exceed; (veicolo) to overtake; (esame, concorso, prova) to pass; (ostacolo) to overcome; (essere migliore di) to beat; **ha superato la trentina** he's over 30.

superbo, -a *agg* (arrogante) haughty; (grandioso) superb.

superficiale *agg* superficial.

superficie, -ci *sf* surface; (MAT) area.

superfluo, -a agg superfluous.

superiore sm, f superior ♦ agg (di sopra) upper; (quantità, numero) larger, greater; (prezzo) higher; (qualità) superior; **di età ~ ai 26 anni** above 26.

superlativo sm superlative.

supermercato sm supermarket.

superstrada sf = (toll-free) motorway (Br), = (toll-free) expressway (Am).

suppergiù avv more or less.

supplementare agg extra.

supplemento sm supplement; (di prezzo) extra charge; **~ rapido** additional charge for fast train.

supplente smf (SCOL) supply teacher.

supporre vt to suppose.

supposta sf suppository.

supposto, -a pp → **supporre**.

surriscaldare vt to overheat.

suscitare vt to arouse.

susina sf plum.

susseguire vt to follow ❑ **susseguirsi** vr to follow one another.

sussidio sm subsidy.

sussulto sm (sobbalzo) start.

sussurrare vt to whisper.

svagarsi vr (divertirsi) to enjoy o.s.; (distrarsi) to take one's mind off things.

svago, -ghi sm (divertimento) fun; (passatempo) pastime.

svaligiare vt to burgle.

svalutare vt to devalue.

svanire vi to disappear, to vanish.

svantaggio sm (aspetto negativo) disadvantage; **essere in ~** (SPORT) to be behind.

svariato, -a agg (vario) varied; (numeroso) various.

svedese agg & sm Swedish ♦ smf Swede.

sveglia sf (orologio) alarm clock; **la ~ è alle sei** we have to get up at six.

svegliare vt to wake (up) ❑ **svegliarsi** vr to wake up.

sveglio, -a agg (desto) awake; (intelligente) smart.

svelare vt to reveal.

svelto, -a agg quick; **alla svelta** quickly.

svendita sf sale.

svenire vi to faint.

sventare vt to foil.

sventolare vt to wave ♦ vi to flutter.

sventura sf (sfortuna) bad luck, misfortune; (disgrazia) disaster.

svenuto, -a pp → **svenire**.

svestire vt to undress ❑ **svestirsi** vr to get undressed.

Svezia sf: **la ~** Sweden.

sviare vt to distract; **~ il discorso** to change the subject.

svignarsela vr (fam) to sneak off.

sviluppare vt to develop ❑ **svilupparsi** vr (ragazzo) to grow; (industria, attività) to expand, to grow; (incendio, infezione) to spread.

sviluppo sm development; **età dello ~** puberty.

svincolo sm (stradale) motor-

svitare

way junction.

svitare vt to unscrew.

Svizzera sf: la ~ Switzerland.

svizzero, -a agg & sm, f Swiss.

svogliato, -a agg listless.

svolgere vt (attività, lavoro) to carry out; (srotolare) to unroll, to unwind; (tema) to write ❑ **svolgersi** vr (fatto, film) to take place; (srotolarsi) to unwind.

svolta sf turn; (mutamento) turning point.

svoltare vi to turn; ~ a sinistra to turn left.

svolto, -a pp → svolgere.

svuotare vt to empty.

tabaccaio, -a sm, f tobacconist.

tabaccheria sf tobacconist's.

tabacco, -chi sm tobacco.

tabella sf (cartellone) board; (prospetto) table; ~ **oraria** timetable.

tabellone sm (con orari) timetable (board); (per affissioni) billboard.

tabù sm inv taboo.

tacca, -che sf notch.

taccagno, -a agg mean.

tacchino sm turkey.

tacciare vt: ~ qn di qc to accuse sb of sthg.

tacco, -chi sm heel; **tacchi a spillo** stilettos.

taccuino sm notebook.

tacere vi to be quiet ◆ vt to keep quiet about.

taciturno, -a agg taciturn.

tafano sm horsefly.

tafferuglio sm brawl.

taglia sf (misura) size; (corporatura) build; ~ **unica** one size.

tagliacarte sm inv paper knife.

taglialegna sm inv woodcutter.

tagliando sm coupon.

tagliare vt to cut; (affettare) to slice; (carne) to carve; (legna) to chop; (recidere) to cut off; (ritagliare) to cut out; (intersecare) to cut across; (vino) to mix; ~ **corto** to cut short; ~ **la strada a qn** to cut in front of sb; **tagliarsi i capelli** to have one's hair cut ❑ **tagliarsi** vr to cut o.s.

tagliatelle sfpl tagliatelle (sg).

tagliaunghie sm inv nail clippers (pl).

tagliente agg sharp.

tagliere sm chopping board.

taglio sm cut; (di stoffa) length; (parte tagliente) edge; ~ **cesareo** (MED) caesarean section; **banconote di piccolo/grosso taglio** small/large denomination bank notes.

tagliuzzare vt to cut into small pieces.

tailleur [ta'jœr] sm inv suit (for women).

Taiwan sm: **il** ~ Taiwan.

talco sm talcum powder.

tale agg dimostrativo **1.** (di questo

tipo) such; **non ammetto tali atteggiamenti** I won't allow such behaviour.

2. (*così grande*): **mi hai fatto una ~ paura!** you gave me such a fright!; **è un ~ disordinato!** he's so untidy!; **fa un ~ freddo!** it's so cold!; **è di una gentilezza ~ che non si può dirgli di no** he's so nice (that) you can't say no to him; **fa un rumore ~ da farti venire il mal di testa** it makes so much noise (that) it gives you a headache.

3. (*in paragoni*): **~ ...** ~ like ... like; **~ madre ~ figlia** like mother like daughter; **~ quale** just like; **è ~ quale lo ricordavo** he's just like I remembered.

♦ *agg indefinito* (*non precisato*): **ti cerca un tal signor Marchi** someone called Mr Marchi is looking for you; **il giorno ~ all'ora ~** on such and such a day at such and such a time.

♦ *pron indefinito* (*persona non precisata*): **un ~ mi ha chiesto di te** some man asked me about you; **quel ~** that person.

taleggio *sm* a type of soft cheese from Lombardy.

talento *sm* talent.

talloncino *sm* counterfoil.

tallone *sm* heel.

talmente *avv* so.

talora *avv* sometimes.

talpa *sf* mole.

talvolta *avv* sometimes.

tamburellare *vi* to drum.

tamburello *sm* (*strumento*) tambourine; (*gioco*) ball game played with a round bat.

tamburo *sm* drum.

Tamigi *sm*: **il ~** the Thames.

tamponamento *sm* collision; **~ a catena** pileup.

tamponare *vt* (*AUTO*) to bump into; (*ferita*) to plug.

tampone *sm* (*MED*) wad; (*assorbente interno*) tampon.

tana *sf* den.

tandem *sm inv* tandem.

tanfo *sm* stench.

tanga *sm inv* tanga.

tangente *sf* (*MAT*) tangent; (*quota*) share.

tangenziale *sf* bypass.

tango, -ghi *sm* tango.

tanica, -che *sf* (*recipiente*) (jerry) can.

tantino : **un tantino** *avv* a little, a bit.

tanto, -a *agg* **1.** (*in grande quantità*) a lot of, much; (*così tanto*) such a lot of, so much; **abbiamo ancora ~ tempo** we've still got a lot of time; **lo conosco da ~ tempo** I've known him for a long time.

2. (*in numero elevato*): **tanti(-e)** a lot of, many; (*così tanti*) such a lot of, so many; **ho tanti amici** I've got a lot of o many friends; **tanti auguri!** all the best!; (*di compleanno*) happy birthday!

3. (*in paragoni*): **~ ... quanto** (*quantità*) as much ... as; (*numero*) as many ... as; **non ho tanta immaginazione quanta ne hai tu** I haven't got as much imagination as you; **ha tanti fratelli quante sorelle** he's got as many brothers as sisters.

♦ *pron* **1.** (*una grande quantità*) a lot, much; (*così tanto*) such a lot, so

tappa

much; **mi piace il cioccolato e ne mangio** ~ I like chocolate and eat a lot of it; **c'è ~ da fare** there's a lot o plenty to do.

2. (un grande numero): **tanti(-e)** many, a lot; (così tanti) so many, such a lot; **è una ragazza come tante** she's just an ordinary girl; **l'hanno visto in tanti** many people saw it.

3. (una quantità indeterminata): **di questi soldi tanti sono per la casa, tanti per le tue spese** so much of this money is for the house and so much for your expenses; **pago un ~ al mese** I pay so much per month.

4. (in paragoni): ~ **quanto** as much as; **tanti quanti** as many as.

5. (in espressioni): ~ **vale che tu stia a casa** you may as well stay at home; **di ~ in ~** from time to time.

♦ avv **1.** (molto) very; **ti ringrazio ~** thank you very much; **non ~** (poco) not much; ~ **meglio!** so much the better!

2. (così) so; **è ~ sciocco da crederci** he's silly enough to believe it; **è ~ grasso che non ci passa** he's so fat that he can't get through; **non pensavo piovesse ~** I didn't think it rained so much.

3. (in paragoni): ~ ... **quanto** as ... as; **non studia ~ quanto potrebbe** he doesn't study as much as he could.

4. (soltanto): **per divertirsi/parlare** just for enjoyment/for the sake of talking; ~ **per cambiare** just for a change; **una volta ~** for once.

♦ cong after all.

tappa sf (fermata) stop; (parte di tragitto, nel ciclismo) stage.

tappare vt (buco, falla) to plug; (bottiglia) to cork; **tapparsi le orecchie** to turn a deaf ear.

tapparella sf store.

tappeto sm (da pavimento) carpet; (più piccolo) rug; **mandare qn al ~** (SPORT) to floor sb.

tappezzare vt (pareti) to paper; (poltrona) to cover.

tappezzeria sf (tessuto) soft furnishings (pl); (carta da parati) wallpaper.

tappo sm (di plastica, metallo) top; (di sughero) cork; (fam: spreg: persona bassa) shorty.

taralli smpl ring-shaped biscuits flavoured with aniseed and pepper (a speciality of southern Italy).

tarantella sf tarantella (a folk dance from the South of Italy).

tarantola sf tarantula.

tarchiato, -a agg stocky.

tardare vi (arrivare tardi) to be late ♦ vt (ritardare) to delay; ~ **a fare qc** to be late in doing sthg.

tardi avv late; **fare** ~ to be late; **più** ~ later; **al più** ~ at the latest; **sul** ~ late in the day.

targa, -ghe sf (di auto) number-plate; (con indicazione) plate.

targhetta sf (su campanello) nameplate; (piccola targa) plate.

tariffa sf rate; (di trasporti) fare; ~ **ridotta** reduced fare; ~ **unica** flat rate.

tarlo sm woodworm.

tarma sf moth.

tarocchi smpl tarot cards.

tartagliare vi to stammer, to

stutter.

tartaro sm tartar.

tartaruga, -ghe sf (di terra) tortoise; (di mare) turtle; (materiale) tortoiseshell.

tartina sf canapé.

tartufo sm (fungo) truffle; (gelato) type of chocolate ice cream.

tasca, -sche sf (di giacca, pantaloni) pocket.

tascabile agg pocket (dav s) ♦ sm paperback.

taschino sm breast pocket.

tassa sf (imposta) tax; (per servizio) fee; ~ **di iscrizione** membership fee.

tassametro sm taximeter.

tassare vt to tax.

tassativo, -a agg peremptory.

tassello sm plug.

tassì = taxi.

tassista, -i, -e smf taxi driver.

tasso sm (indice) rate; (percentuale) percentage; (animale) badger; ~ **di cambio** exchange rate.

tastare vt (polso) to take; ~ **il terreno** (fig) to see how the land lies.

tastiera sf keyboard.

tasto sm (di pianoforte, computer) key; (di TV, radio) button.

tastoni avv: **procedere (a)** ~ to feel one's way.

tattico, -a, -ci, -che agg tactical.

tatto sm (senso) touch; (fig: accortezza) tact.

tatuaggio sm tattoo.

tatuare vt to tattoo.

tavola sf (MAT: mobile) table;

(asse) plank; **mettersi** o **andare a** ~ to sit down to eat; ~ **calda** snack bar.

tavoletta sf bar.

tavolino sm (da salotto) small table; (di bar) table; (scrivania) writing desk.

tavolo sm table.

taxi sm inv taxi.

tazza sf cup; (del water) toilet bowl; **una** ~ **di caffè** a cup of coffee.

tazzina sf coffee cup.

T.C.I. (abbr di Touring Club Italiano) ≈ AA, ≈ RAC.

te pron you, → **ti**.

tè sm inv tea.

teatrale agg theatrical.

teatrino sm puppet theatre.

teatro sm theatre; ~ **tenda** marquee used for public performances.

tecnica, -che sf technique; (tecnologia) technology, → **tecnico**.

tecnico, -a, -ci, -che agg technical ♦ sm, f technician.

tecnologia sf technology.

tecnologico, -a, -ci, -che agg technological.

tedesco, -a, -schi, -sche agg, sm & sf German.

tegame sm pan.

teglia sf baking tin.

tegola sf tile.

teiera sf teapot.

tel. (abbr di telefono) tel.

tela sf (tessuto) cloth; (quadro) canvas; ~ **cerata** oilcloth.

telaio sm (per tessere) loom; (di macchina) chassis; (di finestra, letto) frame.

telecamera *sf* television camera.

telecomando *sm* remote control.

telecronaca, -che *sf* television report.

teleferica, -che *sf* cableway.

telefilm *sm inv* TV film *(Br)*, TV movie *(Am)*.

telefonare *vi & vt* to (tele)phone; ~ **a qn** to (tele)phone sb.

telefonata *sf* (tele)phone call; ~ **a carico (del destinatario)** reverse charge call.

telefonico, -a, -ci, -che *agg* (tele)phone *(dav s)*.

telefonino *sm* mobile phone.

telefonista, -i, -e *smf* switchboard operator.

telefono *sm* telephone; ~ **cellulare** mobile phone; ~ **a gettoni** payphone; ~ **pubblico** public phone; *(cabina)* call box; ~ **a scatti** metered phone; ~ **a scheda (magnetica)** cardphone; **al ~** on the phone; **per ~** by phone.

telegiornale *sm* television news *(sg)*.

telegrafare *vt & vi* to cable, to telegraph.

telegramma, -i *sm* telegram.

teleobiettivo *sm* telephoto lens.

Telepass® *sm inv* motorway toll card.

teleromanzo *sm* serial.

teleschermo *sm* television screen.

telescopio *sm* telescope.

teleselezione *sf* direct dialling.

televisione *sf* television; **alla ~** on television.

televisivo, -a *agg* television *(dav s)*.

televisore *sm* television (set); ~ **in bianco e nero** black-and-white television; ~ **a colori** colour television.

telex *sm inv* telex.

telo *sm* cloth.

tema, -i *sm (argomento, soggetto)* topic, subject; *(SCOL)* essay; *(MUS)* theme.

temere *vt* to fear, to be afraid of ◆ *vi* to be afraid; **temo che non venga** I'm afraid he won't come; **temo di no** I'm afraid not; **temo di sì** I'm afraid so; **temo di non farcela** I'm afraid I can't make it ❑ **temere per** *v + prep* to fear for.

tempera *sf* tempera.

temperamatite *sm inv* pencil sharpener.

temperamento *sm (carattere)* temperament; *(carattere forte)* strong character.

temperato, -a *agg (clima, stagione)* temperate.

temperatura *sf* temperature.

temperino *sm (coltello)* penknife; *(temperamatite)* pencil sharpener.

tempesta *sf* storm; ~ **di neve** blizzard.

tempestare *vt*: ~ **qn di domande** to bombard sb with questions.

tempestivo, -a *agg* timely.

tempestoso, -a *agg* stormy.

tempia sf temple (ANAT).

tempio sm temple (building).

tempo sm (cronologico, ritmo) time; (meteorologico) weather; (GRAMM) tense; (di partita) half; (di film) part; **quanto ~ ci vuole?** how long does it take?; **avere il ~ di ~ per fare qc** to have the time to do sthg; **fare qc per ~** to do sthg in time; **perdere ~** to waste time; **~ di cottura** cooking time; **~ libero** free time; **~ fa** some time ago; **in ~** in time; **allo stesso ~** at the same time.

temporale agg (GRAMM) of time ◆ sm (thunder)storm.

temporaneo, -a agg temporary.

temporeggiare vi to play for time.

tenace agg (persona, carattere) tenacious.

tenacia sf tenacity.

tenaglie sfpl pliers.

tenda sf (di finestra) curtain; (da campeggio) tent; **~ canadese** ridge tent.

tendenza sf tendency.

tendere vt (elastico, muscoli) to stretch; (corda) to tighten; (mano) to hold out ❏ **tendere a** v + prep: **~ a qc** (propendere per) to be inclined to sthg; (essere simile a) to verge on sthg; **~ a fare qc** to tend to do sthg.

tendine sm tendon.

tenebre sfpl darkness (sg).

tenente sm lieutenant.

tenere vt 1. (reggere) to hold; **~ qc in mano** to hold sthg (in one's hand); **~ qn per mano** to hold sb by the hand.

2. (mantenere) to keep; **~ la finestra aperta** to keep the window open; **~ le mani in tasca** to keep one's hands in one's pockets; **~ qc a mente** to remember sthg; **~ il posto a qn** to keep a seat for sb; **~ qn occupato** to keep sb busy; **tenga pure il resto** keep the change.

3. (promessa, segreto) to keep.

4. (conferenza, riunione) to hold; **~ un discorso** to make a speech.

5. (non allontanarsi da): **~ la destra/sinistra** to keep right/left; **~ la strada** to hold the road.

6. (in espressioni): **tieni!** (dando qc) here!; **la lana tiene caldo** wool is warm; **~ compagnia a qn** to keep sb company; **~ conto di qc** to take sthg into account; **~ d'occhio qn** to keep an eye on sb.

◆ vi (corda, diga) to hold; **questa colla non tiene** this glue isn't sticking; **~ duro** to hold out ❏ **tenere a** v + prep (dare importanza a) to care about; **~ a fare qc** to be keen to do sthg; **tenere per** v + prep (fare il tifo per) to support; **per che squadra tieni?** which team do you support?; **tenersi** vr 1. (reggersi): **tenersi (a)** to hold on (to); **tieni forte!** hold on!

2. (restare): **tieniti pronto** be ready; **tenersi in disparte** to stand apart; **tenersi a disposizione di qn** to be at sb's disposal; **tenersi a distanza** to keep one's distance.

3. (aver luogo) to be held.

tenerezza sf tenderness.

tenero, -a agg (cibo) tender; (materia) soft.

tenia *sf* tapeworm.

tennis *sm* tennis; ~ **da tavolo** table tennis.

tennista, -i, -e *smf* tennis player.

tenore *sm (tono)* tone; *(MUS)* tenor; ~ **di vita** standard of living.

tensione *sf* tension; **alta** ~ high voltage.

tentacolo *sm* tentacle.

tentare *vt (sperimentare)* to try; *(allettare)* to tempt; ~ **di fare qc** to try o to attempt to do sthg.

tentativo *sm* attempt.

tentazione *sf* temptation.

tentennare *vi (oscillare)* to wobble; *(esitare)* to hesitate.

tentoni *avv*: **andare (a)** ~ to feel one's way.

tenuta *sf (abbigliamento)* clothes *(pl)*; *(di liquidi, gas)* capacity; *(podere)* estate; **a** ~ **d'aria** airtight; ~ **di strada** roadholding.

teoria *sf* theory; **in** ~ in theory.

teoricamente *avv* theoretically.

teorico, -a, -ci, -che *agg* theoretical.

tepore *sm* warmth.

teppista, -i, -e *smf* hooligan.

tequila [te'kila] *sf inv* tequila.

terapeutico, -a, -ci, -che *agg* therapeutic.

terapia *sf* therapy.

tergicristallo *sm* windscreen wiper.

tergiversare *vi* to avoid the issue.

tergo *sm*: **a** ~ overleaf.

terital® *sm* Terylene®.

termale *agg* thermal.

terme *sfpl (stabilimento)* spa *(sg)*; *(nell'antica Roma)* baths.

termico, -a, -ci, -che *agg (di temperatura)* thermal.

terminal *sm inv* (air) terminal.

terminale *agg* final ♦ *sm* terminal.

terminare *vt* to finish ♦ *vi* to end.

termine *sm (fine)* end; *(scadenza)* deadline; *(parola)* term; **portare** o **condurre a** ~ **qc** to bring sthg to a conclusion; **a breve/lungo** ~ short-/long-term; **senza mezzi termini** without beating about the bush ❑ **termini** *smpl* terms.

termite *sf* termite.

termometro *sm* thermometer.

termos = thermos.

termosifone *sm* radiator.

termostato *sm* thermostat.

terra *sf (pianeta)* Earth; *(terraferma, territorio)* land; *(suolo)* ground; *(sostanza)* soil; ~ **battuta** *(SPORT)* clay; **a** o **per** ~ *(sedere)* on the ground; *(cadere)* to the ground; **essere a** ~ to feel low; **essere** ~ ~ to be down to earth.

terracotta *sf* terracotta.

terraferma *sf* dry land.

terrapieno *sm* embankment.

terrazza *sf* terrace.

terrazzo *sm (balcone)* balcony; *(di terreno)* terrace.

terremoto *sm* earthquake.

terreno, -a *agg (vita)* earthly *(beni)* worldly ♦ *sm (suolo)* land *(appezzamento)* plot of land.

terreo, -a *agg* wan.

terrestre *agg (del pianeta)* of the Earth; *(di terraferma)* land *(dav s)*.

terribile *agg* terrible; *(irrequieto)* wild.

terrificante *agg* terrifying.

terrina *sf* tureen.

territoriale *agg* territorial.

territorio *sm (nazionale, straniero)* territory; *(montuoso, desertico)* region.

terrore *sm* terror.

terrorismo *sm* terrorism.

terrorista, -i, -e *smf* terrorist.

terrorizzare *vt* to terrorize.

terso, -a *agg* clear.

terza *sf (marcia)* third gear.

terzetto *sm* trio.

terzino *sm* fullback.

terzo, -a *num* third; **la terza età** old age ☐ **terzi** *smpl (altri)* others, → **sesto**.

terzultimo, -a *sm, f* third from last.

tesa *sf* brim.

teschio *sm* skull.

tesi *sf inv* theory; ~ **(di laurea)** thesis.

teso, -a *pp* → **tendere** ◆ *agg (corda)* taut; *(faccia, situazione)* tense; *(rapporti)* strained.

tesoreria *sf* treasury.

tesoro *sm (oggetti preziosi, denaro)* treasure; *(naturale)* resources *(pl)*; *(fam: appellativo)* darling; **ministro del Tesoro** Chancellor of the Exchequer *(Br)*, Secretary of the Treasury *(Am)*.

tessera *sf* membership card; ~ **magnetica** magnetic card.

tessere *vt* to weave.

tessile *agg* textile *(dav s)*.

tessitura *sf* weaving.

tessuto *sm (stoffa)* material; *(muscolare, osseo)* tissue.

test *sm inv* test; ~ **di gravidanza** pregnancy test.

testa *sf* head; **di** ~ *(vagone)* front; **mettersi in** ~ **di fare qc** to set one's mind on doing sthg; **dalla** ~ **ai piedi** from head to foot; **essere in** ~ **(a qc)** to be in the lead (in sthg); **fare qc di** ~ **propria** to do sthg off one's own bat; **montarsi la** ~ to become bigheaded; **perdere la** ~ to lose one's head; **dare alla** ~ **a qn** to go to sb's head; **essere fuori di** ~ to be out of one's mind; **fare a** ~ **o croce** to toss up; **a** ~ each.

testamento *sm* will.

testardo, -a *agg* stubborn.

testaroli *smpl* broad pasta in a 'pesto' sauce *(a speciality of La Spezia)*.

teste *smf* witness.

testicolo *sm* testicle.

testimone *smf* witness.

testimoniare *vt (il vero, falso)* to testify; *(provare)* to prove ◆ *vi* to testify.

testina *sf* head.

testo *sm* text.

testone, -a *sm, f* stubborn person.

testuggine *sf* tortoise.

tetano *sm* tetanus.

tetro, -a *agg* gloomy.

tettarella *sf* teat.

tette *sfpl (fam)* boobs.

tetto *sm* roof; **i senza ~ the** homeless.

tettoia *sf* canopy.

Tevere *sm*: **il ~ the** Tiber.

TG *sm inv* TV news *(sg)*.

thermos *sm inv* Thermos flask®.

thriller *sm inv* thriller.

ti *(diventa* **te** *se precede* lo, la, li, le, ne) *pron (complemento oggetto)* you; *(complemento di termine)* (to) you; *(riflessivo)* yourself; **te li do** I'll give them to you.

tibia *sf* tibia.

tic *sm inv (nervoso)* tic; *(rumore)* tick.

ticchettio *sm* ticking.

ticket *sm inv (MED)* prescription charge.

tiepido, -a *agg* lukewarm.

tifare: **tifare per** *v + prep* to support.

tifo *sm (SPORT)*: **fare il ~ per** to be a fan of.

tifone *sm* typhoon.

tifoso, -a *sm, f* supporter, fan.

tiglio *sm* lime.

tigrato, -a *agg* striped.

tigre *sm o f* tiger.

tilt *sm*: **andare in ~ to** stop functioning.

timballo *sm* pie.

timbrare *vt* to stamp.

timbro *sm (arnese, marchio)* stamp; *(di voce)* timbre.

timer ['taimer] *sm inv* timer.

timidezza *sf* shyness.

timido, -a *agg (persona, sguardo)* shy, timid; *(tentativo, accenno)* bashful.

timo *sm* thyme.

timone *sm* rudder.

timore *sm* fear.

timpano *sm* eardrum.

tinello *sm* small dining room.

tingere *vt* to dye; **tingersi i capelli** to dye one's hair.

tinozza *sf* tub.

tinta *sf (materiale)* paint; *(colore)* colour; **farsi la ~** *(dal parrucchiere)* to have one's hair dyed; **in ~ unita** in one colour.

tintarella *sf (fam)* suntan.

tintinnare *vi* to tinkle.

tinto, -a *pp* → **tingere** ♦ *agg* dyed.

tintoria *sf* dry cleaner's.

tintura *sf*: **~ di iodio** iodine.

tipa *sf (fam) (donna)* woman; *(ragazza)* girl.

tipico, -a, -ci, -che *agg* typical.

tipo *sm (specie)* type, kind; *(modello)* type; *(fam: individuo)* bloke *(Br)*, guy *(Am)*.

tipografia *sf (stabilimento)* printing works *(sg)*.

tipografo, -a *sm, f* printer.

TIR *sm inv (abbr di Transports Internationaux Routiers)* HGV.

tiramisù *sm inv* dessert made from sponge soaked in coffee and covered with sweetened cream cheese and cocoa.

tiranno, -a *sm, f* tyrant.

tirare *vt* to pull; *(lanciare)* to throw; *(riga, tende)* to draw; *(sparare)* to fire ♦ *vi* to be tight; **tira vento** it's windy; **~ calci contro q**

to kick sthg; **~ diritto** to go straight on; **~ fuori** to pull out; **~ a indovinare** to guess; **~ a sorte** to draw lots; **~ su** to lift; **tirarsi indietro** (*rinunciare*) to draw back; **'tirare'** (*su porta*) 'pull'.

tiratore *sm* shot.

tiratura *sf* (*di giornale*) circulation.

tirchio, -a *agg* (*fam*) mean.

tiro *sm* (*d'arma*) shooting; (*SPORT*) shot; (*traino*) draught; **~ con l'arco** archery; **giocare un brutto ~ a qn** to play a nasty trick on sb.

tirocinio *sm* apprenticeship.

tiroide *sf* thyroid.

tirrenico, -a, -ci, -che *agg* Tyrrhenian.

Tirreno *sm*: **il (mar) ~** the Tyrrhenian Sea.

tisana *sf* herb tea.

titolare *smf* owner.

titolo *sm* title; **~ di studio** academic qualification; **titoli di credito** instruments of credit.

titubante *agg* hesitant.

tivù *sf inv* (*fam*) TV, telly (*Br*).

tizio, -a *sm*, *f* person.

tizzone *sm* ember.

toast [tɔst] *sm inv* toasted sandwich.

toccare *vt* to touch; (*tastare*) to feel; (*argomento*) to touch on; (*riguardare*) to concern ♦ *vi* to touch the bottom; **'vietato ~'** 'do not touch' ♦ **toccare a** *v + prep* (*spettare*) to be up to; (*capitare*) to happen to; **a chi tocca?** whose turn is it?; **mi tocca ricomprarlo** I have to buy it back.

tocco, -chi *sm* touch.

toga, -ghe *sf* (*di magistrato*) robe.

togliere *vt* (*rimuovere*) to take off; (*privare di*) to take away; (*liberare*) to get out; **~ qc a qn** to take sthg (away) from sb; **ciò non toglie che ...** this doesn't mean that ...; **togliersi gli occhiali** to take one's glasses off; **~ l'appetito a qn** to put sb off his food.

toilette [twa'lɛt] *sf inv* toilet.

tollerabile *agg* tolerable.

tollerante *agg* tolerant.

tollerare *vt* to tolerate.

tolto, -a *pp* → **togliere**.

tomba *sf* grave.

tombino *sm* manhole.

tombola *sf* ≃ bingo.

tonaca, -che *sf* habit.

tonalità *sf inv* (*di colore*) shade; (*MUS*) key.

tondo, -a *agg* (*circolare*) round.

tonfo *sm* (*rumore*) thud; (*caduta*) fall.

tonico, -a, -ci, -che *agg & sm* tonic.

tonificare *vt* to tone up.

tonnellata *sf* ton.

tonno *sm* tuna fish; **~ in scatola** tinned tuna fish.

tono *sm* tone; **essere giù di ~** to be under the weather.

tonsille *sfpl* tonsils.

tonto, -a *agg* stupid; **fare il finto ~** to pretend not to understand.

top *sm inv* top.

topaia *sf* dump.

topazio *sm* topaz.

topless *sm inv:* essere in ~ to be topless.

topo *sm* mouse.

toppa *sf (di stoffa)* patch; *(di serratura)* keyhole.

torace, -ci *sm* thorax, chest.

torbido, -a *agg* cloudy.

torcere *vt (panni)* to wring; *(piegare)* to twist ❑ **torcersi** *vr* to double up.

torchio *sm* press.

torcia, -ce *sf* torch.

torcicollo *sm* stiff neck.

torero *sm* bullfighter.

Torino *sf* Turin.

tormenta *sf* blizzard.

tormentare *vt (procurare fastidio)* to annoy ❑ **tormentarsi** *vr* to fret.

tormento *sm (angoscia)* torment; *(fastidio)* nuisance.

tornaconto *sm* advantage.

tornante *sm* hairpin bend.

tornare *vi* to go/come back; *(ridiventare)* to become again; *(riuscire giusto)* to be correct; ~ **utile** to come in handy; ~ **a casa** to go/come home.

torneo *sm* tournament.

toro *sm* bull ❑ **Toro** *sm* Taurus.

torre *sf (edificio)* tower; *(negli scacchi)* rook; ~ **di controllo** control tower; **la** ~ **di Pisa** the Leaning Tower of Pisa.

---

i **TORRE DI PISA**

The famous bell tower of Pisa cathedral, known as the "Torre Pendente" (Leaning Tower), stands in the magnificent Campo dei Miracoli. The building dates back to the late XIIth century but is now closed to the public. A total of 294 steps lead up the spiral staircase to the bell chamber above. It was from here that Galileo conducted his famous experiments regarding the laws of gravity.

---

torrefazione *sf (negozio)* shop where coffee is roasted and sold.

torrente *sm* torrent.

torrido, -a *agg* torrid.

torrione *sm* keep.

torrone *sm* nougat.

torsione *sf* twisting.

torso *sm* torso; **a** ~ **nudo** barechested.

torsolo *sm* core.

torta *sf (dolce)* cake; ~ **gelato** ice-cream gâteau; ~ **di mele** apple tart; ~ **pasqualina** puff-pastry tart filled with spinach, ricotta cheese, Parmesan cheese and eggs (a speciality of Genoa); ~ **salata** flan.

tortellini *smpl* tortellini; ~ **all'emiliana** 'tortellini' filled with pork, ham, Parmesan cheese and spices, generally served in broth.

tortiera *sf* cake tin.

tortino *sm* pie.

torto, -a *pp* → **torcere** ♦ *sm (ingiustizia)* wrong; *(colpa):* **avere** ~ to be wrong; **a** ~ wrongly.

tortora *sf* turtledove.

tortuoso, -a *agg* winding.

tortura *sf* torture.

torturare *vt* to torture.

tosaerba *sm inv o sf inv* lawnmower.

tosare *vt (pecora)* to shear; *(siepe)* to clip.

Toscana *sf*: la ~ Tuscany.

toscano, -a *agg* Tuscan.

tosse *sf* cough.

tossico, -a, -ci, -che *agg* toxic.

tossicomane *smf* drug addict.

tossire *vi* to cough.

tosta *agg f* → **faccia**.

tostapane *sm inv* toaster.

tostare *vt* to toast.

tot *agg inv & pron inv (quantità)* so much; *(numero)* so many *(pl)*.

totale *agg & sm* total; **in ~** in total.

totalità *sf*: la ~ **di** all of.

totalizzare *vt* to score.

totano *sm* squid.

totip *sm* betting game based on horse racing similar to the pools.

totocalcio *sm* pools *(pl)*.

toupet [tu'pe] *sm inv* toupee.

tournée [tur'ne] *sf inv* tour.

tovaglia *sf* tablecloth.

tovagliolo *sm* napkin.

tozzo, -a *agg* squat ♦ *sm*: un ~ **di** pane a crust of bread.

tra *prep (in mezzo a due)* between; *(in mezzo a molti)* among(st); *(di tempo, distanza)* in; **tenere qn ~ le braccia** to hold sb in one's arms; **quale preferisci ~ questi?** which one of these do you like best?; **detto ~ (di) noi** between me and you; **~ sé e sé** to oneself.

traballare *vi* to stagger.

trabiccolo *sm (fam)* car.

traboccare *vi* to overflow.

trabocchetto *sm* trap.

tracannare *vt* to gulp down.

traccia, -ce *sf (segno)* mark; *(indizio)* trace.

tracciare *vt (solco)* to trace; *(disegnare)* to draw.

tracciato *sm (percorso)* route; *(grafico)* graph.

trachea *sf* windpipe.

tracolla *sf* shoulder bag; **a ~** over one's shoulder.

tradimento *sm (slealtà)* treachery; *(adulterio)* infidelity; **a ~** by surprise.

tradire *vt* to betray; *(coniuge)* to be unfaithful to □ **tradirsi** *vr* to give o.s. away.

traditore, -trice *sm, f* traitor.

tradizionale *agg* traditional.

tradizione *sf* tradition.

tradotto, -a *pp* → **tradurre**.

tradurre *vt* to translate.

traduttore, -trice *sm, f* translator.

traduzione *sf* translation.

trafelato, -a *agg* breathless.

trafficare *vt* to deal in ♦ *vi* to busy o.s.

traffico, -ci *sm (di veicoli)* traffic; *(di droga, armi)* dealing.

trafiggere *vt* to pierce.

trafiletto *sm* short article.

trafitto, -a *pp* → **trafiggere**.

traforo *sm* tunnel.

tragedia *sf* tragedy.

traghetto *sm* ferry.

tragico, -a, -ci, -che *agg* tragic.

tragitto *sm* journey.

traguardo sm finishing line.

traiettoria sf trajectory.

trainare vt (tirare) to tow.

traino sm (operazione) pulling; (di auto) towing.

tralasciare vt to leave out.

traliccio sm (per elettricità) pylon.

tram sm inv tram.

trama sf plot.

tramandare vt to pass on.

trambusto sm turmoil.

tramezzino sm sandwich.

tramite prep through.

tramontana sf north wind.

tramonto sm sunset.

tramortire vt to stun.

trampolino sm (per tuffi) springboard, divingboard; (sci) ski jump.

tramutare vt: ~ qn/qc in to change sb/sthg into ❑ **tramutarsi in** vr + prep to turn into.

trancio sm slice.

tranello sm trap.

trangugiare vt to gulp down.

tranne prep except (for); ~ che unless.

tranquillante sm tranquillizer.

tranquillità sf (stato d'animo) calm; (di luogo) peacefulness; (sicurezza) peace of mind.

tranquillizzare vt to reassure ❑ **tranquillizzarsi** vr to calm down.

tranquillo, -a agg quiet; (non preoccupato) calm; **stai** ~ don't worry.

transalpino, -a agg transalpine.

transatlantico, -a, -ci, -che agg transatlantic ◆ sm ocean liner.

transatto pp → transigere.

transazione sf transaction.

transenna sf barrier.

transigere vi: in fatto di puntualità non transige she won't stand for people being late.

transistor sm inv transistor.

transitabile agg passable.

transitare vi to pass.

transitivo, -a agg (GRAMM) transitive.

transito sm transit; '**divieto di** ~' 'no entry'.

transizione sf transition.

trapano sm drill.

trapassare vt to pierce.

trapelare vi to leak out.

trapezio sm (di circo) trapeze.

trapezista, -i, -e smf trapeze artist.

trapiantare vt to transplant.

trapianto sm transplant.

trappola sf trap.

trapunta sf quilt.

trarre vt: ~ **in inganno** qn to deceive sb; ~ **origine da** qc to come from sthg; ~ **in salvo** qn to rescue sb; ~ **vantaggio da** qc to benefit from sthg.

trasalire vi to jump.

trasandato, -a agg shabby.

trasbordare vt to transfer ◆ vi to change ship/plane/train.

trascinare vt to drag ❑ **trascinarsi** vr (strisciare) to drag o.s. along; (nel tempo) to drag on.

trascorrere *vt* to spend ♦ *vi* to pass.

trascorso, -a *pp* → **trascorrere**.

trascritto, -a *pp* → **trascrivere**.

trascrivere *vt* to transcribe.

trascurabile *agg* negligible.

trascurare *vt* (*lavoro, persona*) to neglect; (*dettagli*) to disregard.

trascurato, -a *agg* neglected.

trasferibile *agg* (*biglietto*) transferable ♦ *sm* transfer.

trasferimento *sm* transfer.

trasferire *vt* (*impiegato*) to transfer; (*negozio, sede*) to move □ **trasferirsi** *vr* to move.

trasferta *sf* (*viaggio*) transfer; (*indennità*) travelling expenses (*pl*); (*SPORT*) away game.

trasformare *vt* to transform; ~ **qc in qc** to turn sthg into sthg; (*edificio, stanza*) to convert sthg into sthg □ **trasformarsi** *vr* to change completely; **trasformarsi in** to turn into.

trasformatore *sm* transformer.

trasformazione *sf* transformation.

trasfusione *sf* transfusion.

trasgredire *vt* to disobey.

traslocare *vi* to move.

trasloco, -chi *sm* (*di mobili*) removal; (*trasferimento*) move.

trasmesso, -a *pp* → **trasmettere**.

trasmettere *vt* (*RADIO, TV*) to broadcast; (*malattia*) to pass on; (*far pervenire*) to send.

trasmissione *sf* (*programma*) programme; (*TECNOL*) transmission.

trasparente *agg* (*acqua*) transparent; (*vestito*) see-through.

trasparenza *sf* transparency.

traspirazione *sf* perspiration.

trasportare *vt* to transport.

trasporto *sm* transport.

trastullarsi *vr* (*divertirsi*) to amuse o.s.; (*perdere tempo*) to waste time.

trasversale *agg* (*obliquo*) cross (*dav s*); (*via*) side (*dav s*).

trattamento *sm* treatment.

trattare *vt* (*persona*) to treat; (*argomento*) to discuss; (*negoziare*) to negotiate; (*commerciare*) to deal in □ **trattare di** *v + prep* to deal with; **trattarsi** *vr*: **di cosa si tratta?** what is it about?

trattative *sfpl* negotiations.

trattato *sm* (*patto*) treaty; (*testo*) treatise.

trattenere *vt* (*far rimanere*) to detain; (*lacrime, risa*) to hold back; (*somma*) to deduct; ~ **qn dal fare qc** to stop sb doing sthg □ **trattenersi** *vr* to stay; **quanto si trattiene?** how long are you staying?; **trattenersi dal fare qc** to stop o.s. doing sthg.

trattenuta *sf* deduction.

trattino *sm* (*tra parole*) hyphen; (*per discorso diretto*) dash.

tratto, -a *pp* → **trarre** ♦ *sm* (*di penna*) stroke; (*di strada, mare*) stretch; **ad un ~, d'un ~** suddenly □ **tratti** *smpl* features.

trattore *sm* tractor.

trattoria

trattoria *sf* restaurant specializing in local cuisine.

ℹ️ TRATTORIA

In the past the term "trattoria" was used to describe an inexpensive family-run restaurant, but today "trattorie" can be very expensive. They serve traditional Italian food typical of the region in rustic-looking but often upmarket surroundings.

trauma, -i *sm* (*shock*) shock; (*MED*) trauma.

travagliato, -a *agg* troubled.

travaglio *sm* labour.

travasare *vt* to decant.

trave *sf* beam.

traveggole *sfpl*: **avere le ~** to be seeing things.

traveller's cheque ['travelər 'tʃɛk] *sm inv* traveller's cheque.

traversa *sf* (*via*) side street; (*SPORT*) crossbar.

traversare *vt* to cross.

traversata *sf* (*marittima*) crossing; (*aerea*) flight.

traverso, -a *agg* side (*dav s*) ♦ *avv*: **di ~** crosswise.

travestimento *sm* disguise.

travestire *vt* to dress up ◇ **travestirsi da** *vr + prep* to dress up as.

travisare *vt* to misinterpret.

travolgere *vt* to sweep away.

travolto, -a *pp → travolgere*.

tre *num* three, → **sei**.

treccia, -ce *sf* plait.

trecento *num* three hundred, → **sei** □ **Trecento** *sm*: **il ~** the fourteenth century.

tredicesima *sf* Christmas bonus.

tredicesimo, -a *num* thirteenth, → **sesto**.

tredici *num* thirteen, → **sei**.

tregua *sf* (*armistizio*) truce; (*sosta*) rest.

trekking *sm* trekking.

tremare *vi*: **~ (di)** (*paura*) to shake ○ tremble (with); (*freddo*) to shiver ○ tremble (with).

tremarella *sf* (*fam*) shivers (*pl*).

tremendo, -a *agg* terrible, awful.

trementina *sf* turpentine.

tremila *num* three thousand, → **sei**.

Tremiti *sfpl*: **le (isole) ~** the Tremiti Islands.

tremito *sm* shudder.

trenino *sm* toy train.

treno *sm* train; **~ diretto** fast train; **~ espresso** express train; **~ intercity** Intercity train®; **~ interregionale** long-distance train; **~ merci** goods train (*Br*), freight train (*Am*); **~ regionale** local train; **'treni in arrivo'** 'arrivals'; **'treni in partenza'** 'departures'.

trenta *num* thirty, → **sei**.

trentesimo, -a *num* thirtieth, → **sesto**.

trentina *sf*: **una ~ (di)** about thirty; **essere sulla ~** to be in one's thirties.

Trentino *sm*: **il ~-Alto Adige** Trentino-Alto Adige.

tresca, -sche sf intrigue.

triangolare agg triangular.

triangolo sm triangle.

tribolare vi to suffer.

tribù sf inv tribe.

tribuna sf stand.

tribunale sm court.

tributo sm tax.

tricheco, -chi sm walrus.

triciclo sm tricycle.

tricolore agg three-coloured.

tridimensionale agg three-dimensional.

triennio sm three-year period.

Trieste sf Trieste.

trifoglio sm clover.

trifolato, -a agg (verdura, carne) cooked in oil, garlic and parsley.

triglia sf red mullet.

trimestre sm (tre mesi) quarter; (SCOL) term.

trincea sf trench.

trinciapollo sm inv poultry shears (pl).

trio sm trio.

trionfale agg triumphal.

trionfare vi (vincere) to triumph.

trionfo sm triumph.

triplicare vt to triple.

triplice agg triple.

triplo, -a agg triple ♦ sm: il ~ three times as much.

trippa sf tripe.

triste agg sad; (luogo) gloomy.

tristezza sf (afflizione) sadness; (squallore) dreariness.

tritacarne sm inv mincer (Br),

grinder (Am).

tritaghiaccio sm inv ice crusher.

tritare vt to chop; (carne) to mince (Br), to grind (Am).

trito, -a agg chopped ♦ sm chopped ingredients (pl); ~ e ritrito (fig) trite.

triturare vt to mince (Br), to grind (Am).

trivellare vt to drill.

triviale agg crude.

trofeo sm trophy.

tromba sf trumpet; ~ d'aria whirlwind; ~ delle scale stairwell.

trombone sm trombone.

troncare vt to cut off.

tronco, -chi sm trunk.

trono sm throne.

tropicale agg tropical.

tropico sm tropic; i tropici the tropics.

troppo, -a agg 1. (in quantità eccessiva) too much; c'è troppa acqua there's too much water. 2. (in numero eccessivo): troppi(-e) too many; ho mangiato troppi biscotti I've eaten too many biscuits.
♦ pron 1. (una quantità eccessiva) too much; ho poco tempo libero, tu ~ I have little free time, you have too much.
2. (un numero eccessivo): troppi(-e) too many; non voglio altri problemi, ne ho fin troppi I don't want any more problems, I've got too many already; lo sanno in troppi too many people know.
♦ avv 1. (in misura eccessiva) too; sei ~ stanco you are too tired; parla

troppo *(running head, right)*

velocemente he speaks too quickly; **spendo** ~ I spend too much; **ho bevuto un bicchiere di** ~ I've had one drink too many; **essere di** ~ to be in the way.

2. *(molto)*: **non mi sento** ~ **bene** I'm not feeling too good.

trota *sf* trout.

trottare *vi* to trot.

trotto *sm* trot.

trottola *sf* spinning top.

troupe [trup] *sf inv* troupe.

trovare *vt* to find; *(per caso)* to come across; **andare a** ~ **qn** to go and see sb ❑ **trovarsi** *vr (essere, stare)* to be; *(incontrarsi)* to meet.

trovata *sf* good idea.

truccare *vt (attore)* to make up; *(motore)* to soup up; *(risultato, partita)* to fix ❑ **truccarsi** *vr* to make o.s. up.

trucco, -chi *sm (artificio, inganno)* trick; *(cosmetico)* make-up; *(operazione)* making-up.

truce *agg* fierce.

trucidare *vt* to slaughter.

truciolo *sm* shaving.

truffa *sf* fraud.

truffare *vt* to swindle.

truffatore, -trice *sm, f* swindler.

truppa *sf* troop.

tu *pron* you ♦ *sm*: **a** ~ **per** ~ face to face; ~ **stesso** you yourself; **se lo dici** ~! if you say so!

tubare *vi* to coo.

tubatura *sf* piping, pipes *(pl)*.

tubercolosi *sf* tuberculosis.

tubero *sm* tuber.

tubetto *sm* tube.

tubo *sm* pipe; ~ **di scappamento** exhaust (pipe).

tue → **tuo**.

tuffarsi *vr (in acqua)* to dive.

tuffo *sm* dive.

tulipano *sm* tulip.

tumbada *sf* baked egg custard with crushed macaroons.

tumore *sm* tumour.

tunica, -che *sf* tunic.

Tunisia *sf*: **la** ~ Tunisia.

tunnel *sm inv* tunnel.

tuo (*f* **tua**, *mpl* **tuoi**, *fpl* **tue**) *agg*: **il** ~ **(la tua)** your ♦ *pron*: **il** ~ **(la tua)** yours; ~ **padre** your father; **un** ~ **amico** a friend of yours; **questi soldi sono tuoi** this is your money.

tuoi → **tuo**.

tuonare *v impers*: **tuona** it's thundering.

tuono *sm (di lampo)* thunder.

tuorlo *sm*: ~ **(d'uovo)** yolk.

turacciolo *sm (di sughero)* cork; *(di plastica)* top.

turare *vt (buco)* to plug; *(orecchie, naso)* to block ❑ **turarsi** *vr*: ~ **il naso** to hold one's nose.

turbamento *sm (sconcerto)* anxiety.

turbante *sm (copricapo)* turban.

turbare *vt (sconcertare)* to trouble.

turbolento, -a *agg (persona)* boisterous.

turchese *agg & sm* turquoise.

Turchia *sf*: **la** ~ Turkey.

turismo *sm* tourism.

turista, -i, -e *smf* tourist.

turistico, -a, -ci, -che *a*

tourist *(dav s)*.

turno *sm (di lavoro)* shift; *(di gioco)* turn; **è il tuo ~** it's your turn; **fare a ~ (a fare qc)** to take turns (to do sthg); **essere di ~** to be on duty.

tuta *sf (da lavoro)* overalls *(pl)*; *(sportiva)* tracksuit.

tutela *sf* protection.

tutelare *vt* to protect ❏ **tutelarsi** *vr* to protect o.s.

tutina *sf* romper suit.

tuttavia *cong* yet, nevertheless.

tutto, -a *agg* **1.** *(la totalità di)* all (of), the whole (of); **~ il vino** all the wine; **~ il giorno** all day, the whole day; **in tutta Europa** all over Europe; **tutti i presenti** everyone present; **tutte le piante** all the plants; **tutti e cinque** all five of us/you/them; **tutti e due** both of us/you/them; **tutta una pizza** a whole pizza.

2. *(ogni)* **tutti(-e)** every; **telefona tutti i giorni** he phones every day; **in tutti i casi** in every case; **tutte le volte che** every time (that).

3. *(esclusivamente)* all; **è tutta colpa tua** it's all your fault; **è ~ casa e chiesa** he's a family man and a regular churchgoer.

4. *(molto)* very; **è tutta contenta** she's very happy; **sei ~ sporco** you're all dirty.

◆ *pron* **1.** *(la totalità)* all; **bevilo ~** drink all of it; **li ho visti tutti** I've seen all of them; **in ~** *(nel complesso)* in all; **in ~ fanno 300 000 lire** that's 300,000 lira in all.

2. *(la totalità della gente)*: **tutti** everyone, all; **verremo tutti** *(quan-*

ti*)* we will all come, everybody will come; **tutti voi** all of you.

3. *(ogni cosa)* everything; **mi ha raccontato ~** he told me everything; **non è ~** that's not everything; **vende di ~** it sells all sorts of things; **mangio un po' di ~** I eat a bit of everything; **in ~ e per ~** completely; **~ compreso** all in; **~ esaurito** sold out; **~ sommato** all things considered.

4. *(qualunque cosa)* anything; **è capace di ~** he's capable of anything.

◆ *avv (interamente)* completely; **tutt'altro** anything but; **~ il contrario** quite the opposite; **del ~** completely; **tutt'al più** at the most.

◆ *sm*: **il ~** the lot; **il ~ per ~** everything.

tuttora *avv* still.

tutù *sm inv* tutu.

T.V. *sf inv* TV.

tweed [twid] *sm* tweed.

U

ubbidiente *agg* obedient.

ubbidire *vi* to obey.

ubriacare *vt*: **~ qn** to get sb drunk ❏ **ubriacarsi** *vr* to get drunk.

ubriaco, -a, -chi, -che *agg & sm, f* drunk.

uccello *sm* bird.

uccidere vt to kill ◻ **uccidersi**
vt to kill o.s.

udienza sf (colloquio) audience;
(DIR) hearing.

udire vt to hear.

udito sm hearing.

uffa esclam tut!

ufficiale agg official ♦ sm (MIL)
officer; (funzionario): ~ **giudiziario**
clerk of the court.

ufficialmente avv officially.

ufficio sm office; ~ **cambi**
bureau de change; ~ **di collocamento** employment office; ~ **informazioni** information bureau; ~
oggetti smarriti lost property
office (Brit), lost-and-found office
(Am); ~ **postale** post office; ~ **turistico** tourist office.

Uffizi mpl: **gli ~** the Uffizi (art
gallery in Florence).

ⓘ GLI UFFIZI

Situated by the Arno river in
Florence, the Galleria degli Uffizi
is one of the world's most important
museums. It is called the "Uffizi"
because it was originally built in the
XVIth century to house government
offices. Although it specializes in
masterpieces from the Italian
Renaissance, the U-shaped gallery
also contains countless works of art
from other periods and by non-
Italian artists.

Ufo sm inv UFO.

uggioso, -a agg dull.

uguaglianza sf equality.

uguagliare vt to equal.

uguale agg (identico) the same;
(pari) equal ♦ avv: **costano ~** they
cost the same; **essere ~ a** (identico)
to be the same as; (pari) to be
equal to; (MAT) to equal.

ugualmente avv (in modo
uguale) equally; (lo stesso) all the
same.

ulcera sf ulcer.

uliva = oliva.

ulivo = olivo.

ulteriore agg further.

ultimare vt to finish.

ultimatum sm inv ultimatum.

ultimo, -a agg last; (più recente)
latest ♦ sm, f last (one); **da ~** in the
end; **fino all'~** till the end; **per ~**
last; **l'~ piano** the top floor.

ultravioletto, -a agg ultraviolet.

umanità sf humanity.

umano, -a agg human; (benevolo) humane.

umidità sf (di clima) humidity;
(di stanza, muro) dampness.

umido, -a agg (bagnato) damp;
(clima) humid ♦ sm: **in ~** stewed.

umile agg humble.

umiliante agg humiliating.

umiliare vt to humiliate ◻
umiliarsi vr to humble o.s.

umiliazione sf humiliation.

umore sm mood; **essere di
buon/cattivo ~** to be in a good/bad
mood.

umorismo sm humour.

umoristico, -a, -ci, -che
agg humorous.

un → uno.

un' → uno.

unanime *agg* unanimous.

unanimità *sf* unanimity; **all'~** unanimously.

uncinetto *sm* crochet hook.

undicesimo, -a *num* eleventh, → **sesto**.

undici *num* eleven, → **sei**.

ungere *vt (padella, teglia)* to grease; *(macchiare)* to get greasy ❑ **ungersi** *vr (macchiarsi)* to get covered in grease; **ungersi di crema solare** to put suntan lotion on.

Ungheria *sf:* **l'~** Hungary.

unghia *sf* nail.

unicamente *avv* only.

unico, -a, -ci, -che *agg (singolo)* only; *(incomparabile)* unique.

unifamiliare *agg* one-family *(dav s)*.

uniformare *vt (adeguare)* to adapt; *(superficie)* to level ❑ **uniformarsi** *a vr + prep* to comply with.

uniforme *agg & sf* uniform.

unione *sf* union; **l'Unione Sovietica** the Soviet Union.

unire *vt (mettere insieme)* to join; *(persone)* to unite; *(collegare)* to link; *(mescolare)* to combine ❑ **unirsi** *vr (associarsi)* to join together; *(strade)* to meet.

unità *sf inv* unit; *(unione)* unity; **~ di misura** unit of measurement.

unito, -a *agg (amici, parenti)* close; *(da uno scopo)* united; *(oggetti)* joined.

universale *agg* universal.

università *sf inv* university.

universitario, -a *agg* university *(dav s)*.

universo *sm* universe.

uno, -a *(dav sm un + consonante o vocale,* **uno** *+ s+consonante, gn, ps, x, z; dav sf un + vocale,* **una** *+ consonante)* *art indeterminativo* a, an; **~ studente** a student; **una donna** a woman; **un albero** a tree; **un'arancia** an orange; **un giorno ci andrò** one day I'll go; **ho avuto una fortuna!** it was such a stroke of luck!

◆ *pron* 1. *(uno qualunque)* one; **me ne dai ~?** can you give me one (of them)?; **~ dei miei libri/dei migliori** one of my books/of the best; **l'un l'altro** each other, one another; **sanno tutto l'~ dell'altro** they know everything about each other; **l'~ o l'altro** either (of you/them/us); **né l'~ né l'altro** neither (of you/them/us); **l'~ e l'altro** both (of you/them/us).

2. *(un tale)* someone, somebody; **sta parlando con una** he's talking to some woman.

3. *(uso impersonale)* one, you; **se ~ può** if one o you can.

◆ *num* one, → **sei**.

unto, -a *pp* → **ungere** ◆ *sm* grease.

untuoso, -a *agg* greasy.

uomo *(pl* **uomini)** *sm* man; **~ d'affari** businessman; **da ~** men's.

uovo *(pl f* **uova)** *sm* egg; **~ in camicia** poached egg; **~ alla coque** boiled egg; **~ di Pasqua** Easter egg; **~ sodo** hard-boiled egg; **~ al tegamino** fried egg; **uova strapazzate** scrambled eggs.

uragano *sm* hurricane.

urbano, -a *agg* urban.

urgente *agg* urgent.

urgenza sf (necessità) urgency; (MED) emergency; **essere operato d'~** to have emergency surgery.

urgere vi to be needed urgently.

urina sf urine.

urlare vi (persona) to scream; (animale) to howl ♦ vt to yell.

urlo sm (di persona: pl f **urla**) scream; (di animale: pl m **urli**) howl.

urna sf: **andare alle urne** to go to the polls.

urrà esclam hurrah!

URSS sf: **l'(ex) ~** the former USSR.

urtare vt (scontrare) to bump into; (irritare) to annoy ♦ vi: **~ contro o in qc** to bump into sthg ▫ **urtarsi** vr (scontrarsi) to collide; (irritarsi) to get annoyed.

urto sm crash.

USA smpl: **gli ~** the USA (sg).

usanza sf custom.

usare vt to use; **~ fare qc** to be in the habit of doing sthg; **qui usa così** it's the custom here.

usato, -a agg (consumato) worn; (di seconda mano) used ♦ sm second-hand goods (pl).

usciere, -a sm, f usher.

uscio sm door.

uscire vi to go out; (libro, numero) to come out; **~ di strada** to go off the road.

uscita sf (porta) exit, way out; (al cinema, ristorante) evening out; (di autostrada) junction; (di libro) publication; (di film) release; (COMM) expenditure; **ci vediamo all'~ da scuola** I'll meet you after school; **~ di sicurezza o emergenza** emergency exit.

usignolo sm nightingale.

uso sm (impiego) use; (abitudine) custom; **fuori ~** out of use; **'per ~ esterno'** 'for external use'.

USSL (abbr di Unità Socio-Sanitaria Locale) local health and social centre.

ustionare vt to burn; **ustionarsi un braccio** to burn one's arm.

ustione sf burn.

usuale agg common.

usufruire : **usufruire di** v + prep to make use of.

usuraio, -a sm, f moneylender.

utensile sm tool; **utensili da cucina** kitchen utensils.

utente smf user.

utero sm uterus.

utile agg useful ♦ sm (COMM) profit; **rendersi ~** to be helpful; **posso esserle ~?** can I help you?

utilità sf usefulness; **essere di grande ~** to be of great use.

utilitaria sf economy car.

utilizzare vt to use, to make use of.

uva sf grapes (pl).

uvetta sf raisins (pl).

va → **andare**.

vacanza sf holiday (Br), vacation (Am); **andare/essere in ~** to go/be on holiday (Br), to go/be on vacation (Am).

vacca, -che sf cow.

vaccinare *vt* to vaccinate.

vaccinazione *sf* vaccination.

vacillare *vi* *(barcollare)* to sway; *(fig: memoria, coraggio)* to be failing.

vado → **andare**.

vagabondo, -a *sm, f (senza dimora fissa)* tramp; *(fannullone)* loafer.

vagare *vi* to wander.

vagina *sf* vagina.

vagito *sm* wailing.

vaglia *sm inv* money order; **~ postale** postal order.

vagliare *vt (valutare)* to weigh up.

vago, -a, -ghi, -ghe *agg* vague.

vagone *sm* carriage *(Br)*, car *(Am)*; **~ letto** sleeper; **~ ristorante** restaurant car.

vai → **andare**.

valanga, -ghe *sf* avalanche.

Val d'Aosta = **Valle d'Aosta**.

valere *vi (biglietto)* to be valid; *(regola)* to apply; *(avere valore)* to be worth ♦ *vt (avere un valore di)* to be worth; *(equivalere a)* to be equal to; **~ la pena di fare qc** to be worth doing sthg; **far ~ qc** to assert sthg; **vale a dire** that is to say ❏ **valersi di** *vr + prep* to take advantage of.

valevole *agg* valid.

valico, -chi *sm* pass.

validità *sf* validity.

valido, -a *agg (valevole)* valid; *(efficace)* effective; *(abile)* capable.

valigia, -gie o **-ge** *sf* suitcase; **fare le valigie** to pack.

vallata *sf* valley.

valle *sf* valley ❏ **Valle d'Aosta**

sf: **la Valle d'Aosta** Valle d'Aosta.

valore *sm* value; *(validità)* validity; *(talento)* merit ❏ **valori** *smpl (gioielli)* valuables; *(ideali)* values.

valorizzare *vt* to bring out.

valoroso, -a *agg* courageous.

valso, -a *pp* → **valere**.

valuta *sf* currency.

valutare *vt (quadro, persona)* to value; *(valore, peso)* to estimate.

valutazione *sf (di un bene)* valuation; *(calcolo sommario)* estimate; *(SCOL)* assessment.

valvola *sf (in meccanica)* valve; *(in elettrotecnica)* fuse.

vampata *sf* blaze.

vampiro *sm* vampire.

vandalismo *sm* vandalism.

vandalo, -a *sm, f* vandal.

vanga, -ghe *sf* spade.

vangelo *sm* gospel.

vanificare *vt* to nullify.

vaniglia *sf* vanilla.

vanità *sf* vanity.

vanitoso, -a *agg* vain.

vanno → **andare**.

vano, -a *agg* vain ♦ *sm (stanza)* room; *(apertura)* space.

vantaggio *sm* advantage; *(in competizioni)* lead; **trarre ~ da qc** to benefit from sthg; **essere in ~** to be in the lead.

vantaggioso, -a *agg* favourable.

vantarsi *vr* to boast; **~ di fare qc** to boast about doing sthg.

vanvera *sf*: **parlare a ~** to talk nonsense.

vapore *sm*: **~ (acqueo)** steam; **cuocere a ~** to steam.

vaporetto *sm* steamer.

vaporizzatore *sm* spray.

vaporoso, -a *agg (abito)* floaty.

varare *vt (legge)* to pass; *(nave)* to launch.

varcare *vt* to cross.

varco, -chi *sm* passage.

variabile *agg* variable.

variante *sf* variation.

variare *vt* to vary ♦ *vi (modificarsi)* to vary; *(essere diverso)* to fluctuate.

variazione *sf* variation.

varice *sf* varicose vein.

varicella *sf* chickenpox.

variegato, -a *agg* variegated.

varietà *sf inv* variety ♦ *sm inv* variety show.

vario, -a *agg (svariato)* varied; *(numeroso, diverso)* various.

variopinto, -a *agg* multicoloured.

vasca, -sche *sf (contenitore)* tank; *(di fontana)* basin; *(nel nuoto)* length; **~ (da bagno)** bath.

vaschetta *sf* basin.

vasellame *sm* crockery.

vasetto *sm (di yogurt)* pot; *(di marmellata)* jar.

vaso *sm* vase; *(per piante)* pot.

vassoio *sm* tray.

vasto, -a *agg (superficie)* vast.

Vaticano *sm*: **il ~** the Vatican.

---

i IL VATICANO

The Vatican City, situated on the right bank of the Tiber in Rome, is the Pope's official residence. The Basilica of Saint Peter,

one of the most magnificent Catholic churches in the world, stands here. The Vatican is an independent country, with its own currency and stamps, and the Pope is the head of state. The vast number of works of art concentrated here make it one of Italy's most important cultural centres.

---

ve → vi.

vecchiaia *sf* old age.

vecchio, -a *agg* old; *(sorpassato)* old-fashioned ♦ *sm, f* old man *(f* old woman).

vece *sf*: **fare le veci di qn** to take sb's place.

vedere *vt & vi* to see; **vedrò di fare qualcosa** I'll see what I can do; **questo non ha niente a che ~ con me** this has nothing to do with me; **non la posso ~** *(fig)* I can't stand her; **non vedo l'ora di arrivare** I can't wait to get there; **farsi ~ da uno specialista** to see a specialist; **da qui si vede il mare** you can see the sea from there ❏ **vedersi** *vr (guardarsi)* to see o.s.; *(incontrarsi)* to meet; **ci vediamo!** see you!

vedovo, -a *sm, f* widower *(f* widow).

veduta *sf* view.

vegetale *agg* vegetable *(dav s)* ♦ *sm* plant.

vegetariano, -a *agg* vegetarian.

vegetazione *sf* vegetation.

veglia *sf* wakefulness.

veglione *sm* ball.

veicolo *sm* vehicle; **'veicoli lenti**

'slow lane'.

vela *sf (tela)* sail; *(sport)* sailing.

velare *vt* to veil.

veleno *sm* poison.

velenoso, -a *agg (sostanza)* poisonous.

velina *sf* tissue paper.

vellutato, -a *agg* velvety.

velluto *sm* velvet; **~ a coste** cord.

velo *sm (indumento)* veil.

veloce *agg* fast.

velocemente *avv* quickly.

velocità *sf* speed; **'~ max 15 kmh'** = 'maximum speed 10 mph'.

vena *sf* vein; **non essere in ~ di qc** not to be in the mood for sthg.

vendemmia *sf* grape harvest.

vendemmiare *vi* to harvest the grapes.

vendere *vt* to sell; **'vendesi'** 'for sale'.

vendetta *sf* revenge.

vendicare *vt* to avenge ❑ **vendicarsi** *vr* to avenge o.s.; **vendicarsi di** to take one's revenge for; **vendicarsi su qn** to take one's revenge on sb.

vendita *sf* sale; **essere in ~** to be on sale; **'in ~ qui'** 'on sale here'.

venditore, -trice *sm, f* seller; **~ ambulante** pedlar.

venerdì *sm inv* Friday, → **sabato**.

Venezia *sf* Venice.

veneziana *sf* venetian blind, → **veneziano**.

veneziano, -a *agg & sm, f* Venetian.

venire *vi* to come; **mi viene da piangere** I feel like crying; **quanto vengono le mele?** how much are the apples?; **~ bene/male** to turn out well/badly; **~ giù** to come down; **~ via** *(persona)* to leave; *(macchia)* to come out; *(etichetta)* to come off; **~ a sapere qc** to learn sthg.

ventata *sf* gust.

ventesimo, -a *num* twentieth, → **sesto**.

venti *num* twenty, → **sei**.

ventilare *vt* to ventilate.

ventilatore *sm* ventilator.

ventina *sf*: **una ~ (di)** about twenty; **essere sulla ~** to be in one's twenties.

vento *sm* wind; **'forte ~ laterale'** 'strong side wind'.

ventosa *sf (di gomma)* suction pad.

ventoso, -a *agg* windy.

ventre *sm* stomach.

venturo, -a *agg* next.

venuto, -a → **venire**.

veramente *avv* really.

veranda *sf* veranda.

verbale *sm* minutes *(pl)*.

verbo *sm* verb.

verde *agg* green ♦ *sm (colore)* green; *(vegetazione)* greenery.

verdetto *sm* verdict.

verdura *sf* vegetables *(pl)*.

verduraio, -a *sm, f* greengrocer.

vergine *agg* virgin; *(cassetta)* blank ♦ **Vergine** *sf* Virgo.

vergogna *sf (pentimento, scandalo)* shame; *(timidezza)* shyness;

(*imbarazzo*) embarrassment.

vergognarsi *vr*: ~ **(di)** (*per disonore*) to be ashamed (of); (*per timidezza*) to be embarrassed (about).

vergognoso, -a *agg* (*scandaloso*) shameful; (*timido*) shy.

verifica, -che *sf* check.

verificare *vt* to check ❑ **verificarsi** *vr* to happen.

verità *sf* truth; **dire la ~** to tell the truth.

verme *sm* worm.

vermicelli *smpl* vermicelli (*sg*).

vermut *sm inv* vermouth.

vernice *sf* (*sostanza*) paint; (*pelle*) patent leather; '~ **fresca**' 'wet paint'.

verniciare *vt* to paint.

vero, -a *agg* (*reale*) true; (*autentico*) real, genuine ♦ *sm* truth.

verosimile *agg* likely, probable.

verruca, -che *sf* wart.

versamento *sm* deposit.

versante *sm* slopes (*pl*).

versare *vt* (*in recipiente*) to pour; (*rovesciare*) to spill; (*pagare*) to pay; (*depositare*) to deposit ❑ **versarsi** *vr* to spill.

versatile *agg* versatile.

versione *sf* version; (*traduzione*) translation.

verso *sm* (*di poesia*) line; (*di animale*) cry; (*direzione*) direction ♦ *prep* (*in direzione di, nei confronti di*) towards; (*in prossimità di*) near; (*di tempo, età*) around, about; **non c'è ~ di convincerlo** there's no way of convincing him; **fare il ~ a qn** to

mimic sb.

vertebra *sf* vertebra.

verticale *agg & sf* vertical.

vertice *sm* peak; (MAT) vertex.

vertigine *sf* dizziness; **soffrire di vertigini** to be afraid of heights.

vescovo *sm* bishop.

vespa *sf* wasp.

vestaglia *sf* dressing gown.

veste *sf*: **in ~ di** as.

vestiario *sm* wardrobe, clothes (*pl*).

vestire *vt & vi* to dress.

vestirsi *vr* to get dressed.

vestito *sm* (*da uomo*) suit; (*da donna*) dress ❑ **vestiti** *smpl* (*indumenti*) clothes.

Vesuvio *sm*: **il ~** Vesuvius.

veterinario, -a *sm, f* vet(erinary surgeon) (Br), veterinarian (Am).

vetrata *sf* (*di casa*) glass door/window; (*di chiesa*) stained glass window.

vetrina *sf* (*di negozio*) shop window.

vetro *sm* (*materiale*) glass; (*frammento*) piece of glass; (*di finestra*) windowpane; (*di auto*) window.

vetta *sf* top.

vettovaglie *sfpl* supplies.

vettura *sf* (*automobile*) car; (*di treno*) carriage (Br), car (Am).

vezzeggiativo *sm* term of endearment.

vezzo *sm* habit.

vi (*diventa* **ve** *se precede* lo, la, li, le, ne) *pron* (*complemento oggetto*) you; (*complemento di termine*) (to) you; (*riflessivo*) yourselves; (*reciproco*) each other ◆ *avv* = **ci**; **ve li do** I'll give them to you.

via *sf* way; (*strada*) street, road ◆ *avv away* ◆ *prep* **via** ◆ esclam (*per scacciare*) go away!; (*in gara, gioco*) go! ◆ *sm inv*: **dare il ~** (SPORT) to give the starting signal; **dare il ~ a qc** (*progetto*) to give the green light to sthg; **~ aerea** (*posta*) by airmail; **~ mare** by sea; **~ terra** overland; **in ~ eccezionale** as an exception; **per ~ di** (*a causa di*) because of; **in ~ di guarigione** on the road to recovery; **una ~ di mezzo** a middle course; **e così ~** and so on.

viabilità *sf* practicability.

Viacard® *sf inv* credit card for motorway tolls.

viaggiare *vi* to travel.

viaggiatore, -trice *sm, f* passenger.

viaggio *sm* travel; (*tragitto*) journey; (*gita*) trip; **buon ~!** have a good trip!; **essere in ~** to be away; **fare un ~** to go on a trip; **~ d'affari** business trip; **~ di nozze** honeymoon; **~ organizzato** package tour.

viale *sm* (*corso*) avenue; (*in un parco*) path.

viavai *sm* coming and going.

vibrare *vi* to vibrate.

vibrazione *sf* vibration.

vice *smf inv* deputy.

vicenda *sf* event □ **a vicenda** *avv* in turn.

viceversa *avv* vice versa.

vicinanza *sf* proximity; **nelle vicinanze (di qc)** in the vicinity (of sthg).

vicinato *sm* (*zona*) neighbourhood; (*vicini*) neighbours (*pl*).

vicino, -a *agg* (*nello spazio*) near, nearby; (*nel tempo*) close at hand ◆ *sm, f* neighbour ◆ *avv* nearby ◆ *prep*: **~ a** (*accanto a*) next to; (*nei pressi di*) near; **~ di casa** neighbour; **da ~** close up.

vicolo *sm* alley; **~ cieco** blind alley.

video *sm inv* (*musicale*) video; (*schermo*) screen.

videocassetta *sf* video(cassette).

videocitofono *sm* entryphone with closed circuit TV.

videogame [videogeim] = **videogioco**.

videogioco, -chi *sm* video game.

videoregistratore *sm* video(recorder) (*Br*), VCR (*Am*).

Videotel® *sm* = Viewdata™.

vietare *vt* to forbid; **~ a qn di fare qc** to forbid sb to do sthg; **~ qc a qn** to forbid sthg to sb.

vietato, -a *agg* forbidden; **'~ l'accesso'** 'no entry'; **'~ l'accesso ai mezzi non autorizzati'** 'no entry for unauthorized vehicles'; **'è fare il bagno nelle ore notturne'** 'no swimming at night'; **'~ fumare'** 'no smoking'; **'~ ai minori'** 'adults only'.

Vietnam *sm*: **il ~** Vietnam.

vigilare *vt* to watch over.

vigile *agg* watchful ◆ *smf*: **~ (urbano)** local police officer who deals mainly with traffic offences; **i vigili del fuoco** the fire brigade.

vigilia *sf* eve; **~ di Natale** Christmas Eve.

vigliacco, -a, -chi, -che *agg*
cowardly ♦ *sm, f* coward.

vigna *sf* vines (*pl*).

vigore *sm* vigour; **in ~** (*DIR*) in
force.

vile *agg* cowardly.

villa *sf* villa.

villaggio *sm* village; **~ turistico**
holiday village.

villano, -a *agg* rude ♦ *sm, f*
boor.

villeggiatura *sf* holiday (*Br*),
vacation (*Am*).

villetta *sf* cottage.

vimini *smpl* wicker (*sg*).

vinavil® *sm* glue.

vincere *vt* (*gioco, partita,
battaglia*) to win; (*avversario*) to
beat ♦ *vi* to win.

vincita *sf* (*vittoria*) win; (*premio*)
winnings (*pl*).

vincitore, -trice *sm, f* winner.

vincolo *sm* (*legame*) tie; (*obbligo*)
obligation.

vino *sm* wine; **~ bianco** white
wine; **~ rosso** red wine.

---

i VINO

Wines are produced in every
Italian region, and their
names reflect either the area where
they are produced (like "Chianti") or
the grape varieties they are made
from ("moscato"). "Vino da tavola"
on a label indicates an inexpensive
table wine, while DOC ("denominazione d'origine controllata"),
DOCG ("denominazione d'origine
controllata e garantita"), and VQPRD

("vino di qualità prodotto in regioni
delimitate") all indicate that the wine
is of superior quality.

---

vinto, -a *pp* → **vincere** ♦ *agg*
(*partita*) won; (*concorrente*) beaten;
darla vinta a qn to let sb have their
way; **non darsi per ~** not to give
up.

viola *agg inv & sm inv* purple ♦ *sf*
(*fiore*) violet.

violare *vt* to violate.

violentare *vt* to rape.

violento, -a *agg* violent.

violenza *sf* violence.

violino *sm* violin.

viottolo *sm* track.

vipera *sf* viper.

virare *vi* (*NAUT*) to come about;
(*aereo*) to turn.

virgola *sf* (*GRAMM*) comma;
(*MAT*) point.

virgolette *sfpl* quotation
marks.

virile *agg* manly.

virtù *sf inv* virtue.

virus *sm inv* virus.

viscere *sfpl* entrails.

viscido, -a *agg* slimy.

viscosa *sf* viscose.

visibile *agg* (*che si vede*) visible;
(*chiaro*) evident.

visibilità *sf* visibility.

visiera *sf* peak.

visionare *vt* to examine.

visione *sf* (*vista*) sight; (*modo di
vedere*) view; (*apparizione*) vision;
prendere ~ di qc to look over sthg;
prima ~ TV premiere.

visita *sf* (*di amico*) visit; (*di medico*)

examination; **fare ~ a qn** to pay sb a visit; **~ medica** medical examination.

visitare *vt* to visit; *(sog: medico)* to examine.

viso *sm* face.

vispo, -a *agg* lively.

vissuto, -a *pp* → **vivere**.

vista *sf (facoltà)* (eye)sight; *(possibilità di vedere)* sight; *(panorama)* view; **conoscere qn di ~** to know sb by sight; **a prima ~** at first sight.

visto, -a *pp* → **vedere** ◆ *sm* visa.

vistoso, -a *agg* gaudy.

vita *sf* life; *(ANAT)* waist.

vitale *agg* vital.

vitamina *sf* vitamin.

vite *sf (pianta)* vine; *(utensile)* screw.

vitello *sm (animale)* calf; *(carne)* veal; *(pelle)* calfskin; **~ tonnato** boiled veal served cold with tuna mayonnaise.

vittima *sf* victim.

vitto *sm* food; **~ e alloggio** board and lodging.

vittoria *sf* victory.

viva *esclam*: **~ le vacanze!** hurray for the holidays!

vivace *agg (persona)* lively; *(colore)* bright.

vivacità *sf* vivacity.

vivaio *sm (di piante)* nursery; *(di pesci)* hatchery.

vivanda *sf* food.

vivente *agg* → **essere**.

vivere *vi* to live ◆ *vt (vita)* to live; *(passare)* to live through.

viveri *smpl* food *(sg)*.

vivo, -a *agg (vivente)* alive, living; *(persona)* lively; *(colore)* bright; **dal ~** from life; **farsi ~ (con qn)** to get in touch (with sb).

viziare *vt* to spoil.

viziato, -a *agg (bambino)* spoilt; *(aria)* stale.

vizio *sm (cattiva abitudine)* bad habit; *(morale)* vice; *(difetto)* defect.

V.le *(abbr di viale)* Ave.

vocabolario *sm (dizionario)* dictionary; *(lessico)* vocabulary.

vocabolo *sm* word.

vocale *agg* vocal ◆ *sf* vowel.

vocazione *sf (inclinazione)* natural bent.

voce *sf (suono)* voice; *(diceria)* rumour; *(di elenco)* entry; **a bassa/alta ~** in a low/loud voice; **sotto ~** in a whisper.

voga *sf*: **essere in ~** to be in fashion.

vogatore, -trice *sm, f* oarsman *(f* oarswoman) ◆ *sm* rowing machine.

voglia *sf (desiderio)* desire; *(sulla pelle)* birthmark; **avere ~ di fare qc** to feel like doing sthg; **avere ~ di qc** to feel like sthg; **levarsi la ~ di qc** to satisfy one's desire for sthg; **contro ~** unwillingly.

voi *pron* you; **~ stessi** you yourselves.

volano *sm* shuttlecock.

volante *agg* flying ◆ *sm (di veicolo)* steering wheel ◆ *sf (polizia)* flying squad.

volantino *sm* leaflet.

volare *vi* to fly.

volatile *sm* bird.

vol-au-vent [volo'van] *sm inv* vol-au-vent.

volenteroso, -a *agg* willing.

volentieri *avv (con piacere)* willingly; *(come risposta)* with pleasure.

volere *vt* 1. *(desiderare, esigere)* to want; **cosa vuoi?** what do you want?; **voglio delle spiegazioni** I want some explanations; **~ fare qc** to want to do sthg; **voglio che tu venga** I want you to come; **cosa volete fare stasera?** what do you want to do tonight?; **ti vogliono al telefono** you're wanted on the phone; **come vuoi** as you like; **vorrei un cappuccino** I'd like a cappuccino; **vorrei andare** I'd like to go; **senza volerlo** unintentionally; **se vuole accomodarsi?** if you would care to take a seat! 2. *(consentire a):* **se tua madre vuole, ti porto al cinema** if your mother agrees, I'll take you to the cinema; **vogliamo andare?** shall we go? 3. *(soldi):* **quanto vuole per questo orologio?** how much do you want for this watch? 4. *(credere)* to think; **la leggenda vuole che ...** legend has it that ... 5. *(decidersi a):* **la macchina non vuole partire** the car won't start. 6. *(necessitare di)* to need; **volerci** *(coraggio, materiale)* to need; *(tempo)* to take; **ci vuole pazienza** you must be patient; **ci vogliono ancora dieci minuti per finire** it'll take another ten minutes to finish. 7. *(in espressioni)*: **voler bene a qn** *(affetto)* to be fond of sb; *(amare)* to love sb; **voler dire** to mean; **volerne a qn** to have a grudge against sb.

◆ *sm* will, wish; **contro il ~ di qn** against sb's wishes.

volgare *agg* vulgar.

volgere *vt* to turn; **il tempo volge al bello** the weather's getting better; **~ al termine** to draw to an end.

volo *sm* flight; **~ charter** charter flight; **~ di linea** scheduled flight; **capire qc al ~** to understand sthg straightaway.

volontà *sf inv* will; **buona ~** goodwill; **a ~** as much as one likes.

volontario, -a *agg* voluntary ◆ *sm, f* volunteer.

volpe *sf* fox.

volt *sm inv* volt.

volta *sf (circostanza)* time; *(di edificio)* vault; **a sua ~** in his/her turn; **di ~ in ~** from time to time; **una ~** once; **due volte** twice; **tre volte** three times; **una ~ che** once; **una ~ tanto** just for once; **uno per ~** alla ~ one at a time; **a volte** sometimes.

voltafaccia *sm inv* about-turn.

voltare *vt & vi* to turn; **~ l'angolo** to turn the corner; **~ pagina** to turn over a new leaf ❑ **voltarsi** *vr* to turn.

voltastomaco *sm* nausea; **dare il ~ a qn** to make sb feel sick.

volto, -a *pp* → **volgere** ◆ *sm* face.

volubile *agg* fickle.

volume *sm* volume.

voluminoso, -a *agg* voluminous, bulky.

vomitare *vt & vi* to vomit, to throw up.

vomito *sm* vomit.

vongola *sf* clam.

vorace *agg (animale)* voracious; *(persona)* greedy.

voragine *sf* abyss.

vortice *sm* whirl.

vostro, -a *agg:* **il ~ (la vostra)** your ♦ *pron:* **il ~ (la vostra)** yours; **~ padre** your father; **un ~ amico** a friend of yours; **sono vostri questi bagagli?** is this your luggage?

votare *vt* to vote on ♦ *vi* to vote.

votazione *sf (procedimento)* vote; *(SCOL)* marks *(pl)*.

voto *sm (DIR)* vote; *(SCOL)* marks *(pl)*.

vulcanico, -a, -ci, -che *agg* volcanic.

vulcano *sm* volcano.

vulnerabile *agg* vulnerable.

vuotare *vt* to empty ❑ **vuotarsi** *vr* to empty.

vuoto, -a *agg* empty; *(pagina)* blank ♦ *sm (spazio vuoto)* empty space; *(bottiglia)* empty (bottle); *(in fisica)* vacuum; **andare a ~** to fail; **parlare a ~** to waste one's breath.

watt [vat] *sm inv* watt.

wc *(abbr di water closet)* WC.

week-end [wi'kend] *sm inv* weekend.

western ['westərn] *agg inv:* **film ~** western.

whisky [wiski] *sm inv* whisky.

windsurf [windsərf] *sm inv (tavola)* windsurf board; *(sport)* windsurfing.

würstel ['vurstel] *sm inv* frankfurter.

xenofobia *sf* xenophobia.

xilofono *sm* xylophone.

yacht [jɔt] *sm inv* yacht.

yoga *sm* yoga.

yogurt *sm inv* yoghurt.

zabaione *sm* cream dessert made from egg yolks whipped with sugar and Marsala.

zafferano *sm* saffron.

zaino *sm* rucksack.

zampa *sf* paw; **a quattro zampe** on all fours.

zampillo *sm* spurt.

zampirone *sm* mosquito repellent.

zampone *sm* boiled pig's trotter stuffed with minced meat and spices.

zanna *sf (di elefante)* tusk; *(di car-*

wafer ['vafer] *sm inv* wafer.

Walkman® *sm inv* Walkman®, personal stereo.

water (closet) [vater ('klɔz)] *sm inv* toilet.

nivori) fang.

zanzara *sf* mosquito.

zanzariera *sf* mosquito net.

zappa *sf* hoe.

zappare *vt* to hoe.

zattera *sf* raft.

zavorra *sf* ballast.

zazzera *sf* fringe.

zebra *sf* zebra ▫ **zebre** *sfpl (fam)* zebra crossing *(sg) (Br)*, crosswalk *(sg) (Am)*.

zecca, -che *sf (insetto)* tick; *(officina di monete)* mint.

zelante *agg* zealous.

zelo *sm* zeal.

zenzero *sm* ginger.

zeppo, -a *agg* crammed.

zeppole *sfpl* type of ring doughnut *eaten at carnival time in the south of Italy.*

zerbino *sm* doormat.

zero *sm* zero; *(SPORT)* nil; **sotto ~** subzero.

zigomo *sm* cheekbone.

zigzag *sm inv* zigzag.

zimbello *sm* laughingstock.

zingaro, -a *sm, f* gipsy.

zio, -a *sm, f* uncle *(f* aunt*)*.

zip *sm inv* zip.

zitella *sf (spreg)* spinster.

zitto, -a *agg* silent; **state zitti!** be quiet!

zoccolo *sm (calzatura)* clog; *(di cavallo)* hoof.

zodiaco *sm* zodiac.

zolfo *sm* sulphur.

zolla *sf* clod.

zolletta *sf* lump.

zona *sf* area; **~ blu ○ verde** *zone where traffic is restricted;* **~ disco** *parking meter zone;* **~ industriale** industrial estate; **'~ militare'** *'army property';* **~ pedonale** pedestrian precinct *(Br)*, pedestrian zone *(Am)*.

zonzo : a zonzo *avv:* **andare a ~** to wander about.

zoo *sm inv* zoo.

zoom [dzum] *sm inv* zoom.

zoppicare *vi* to limp.

zoppo, -a *agg* lame.

zucca, -che *sf* pumpkin.

zuccherato, -a *agg* sweetened.

zuccheriera *sf* sugar bowl.

zucchero *sm* sugar; **~ filato** candyfloss; **~ vanigliato** vanilla sugar; **~ a velo** icing sugar *(Br)*, confectioner's sugar *(Am)*.

zuccheroso, -a *agg* sugary.

zucchina *sf* courgette; **zucchine ripiene** *courgettes stuffed with minced meat, breadcrumbs, eggs and spices.*

zucchino = **zucchina**.

zuccone, -a *sm, f (sciocco)* blockhead; *(testardo)* stubborn person.

zuccotto *sm* ice-cream sponge.

zuffa *sf* brawl.

zuppa *sf* soup; **~ inglese** ≈ trifle *(Br)*, *dessert made from sponge soaked in liqueur, with custard and chocolate.*

zuppiera *sf* tureen.

zuppo, -a *agg:* **~ (di)** soaked (with).

Zurigo *sf* Zurich.

ENGLISH-ITALIAN
INGLESE-ITALIANO

a [*stressed* eɪ, *unstressed* ə] (*an before vowel or silent 'h'*) *indefinite article* **1.** un/uno (una/un'); **a restaurant** un ristorante; **a brush** uno spazzolino; **a chair** una sedia; **an island** un'isola; **a friend** un amico (un'amica); **to be a doctor** essere medico, fare il medico.

2. (*instead of the number one*) un/uno (una/un'); **a month ago** un mese fa; **a hundred and twenty pounds** centoventi sterline; **a thousand** mille; **four and a half** quattro e mezzo.

3. (*in prices, ratios*) a; **£2 a kilo** 2 sterline al chilo; **three times a week** tre volte alla settimana.

AA *n* (*Br: abbr of Automobile Association*) ≈ ACI *m*.

aback [əˈbæk] *adv*: **to be taken ~** restare sbalordito(-a).

abandon [əˈbændən] *vt* abbandonare.

abattoir [ˈæbətwɑːʳ] *n* mattatoio *m*.

abbey [ˈæbɪ] *n* abbazia *f*.

abbreviation [əˌbriːvɪˈeɪʃn] *n* abbreviazione *f*.

abdomen [ˈæbdəmən] *n* addome *m*.

abide [əˈbaɪd] *vt*: **I can't ~ him** non lo sopporto □ **abide by** *vt fus* rispettare.

ability [əˈbɪlɪtɪ] *n* capacità *f inv*.

able [ˈeɪbl] *adj* capace; **to be ~ to do sthg** essere capace di fare qc, poter fare qc.

abnormal [æbˈnɔːml] *adj* anormale.

aboard [əˈbɔːd] *adv* a bordo ◆ *prep* a bordo di, su.

abolish [əˈbɒlɪʃ] *vt* abolire.

aborigine [ˌæbəˈrɪdʒənɪ] *n* aborigeno *m* (-a *f*).

abort [əˈbɔːt] *vt* (*call off*) sospendere.

abortion [əˈbɔːʃn] *n* aborto *m*; **to have an ~** abortire.

about [əˈbaʊt] *adv* **1.** (*approximately*) circa, più o meno; **~ 50 people** una cinquantina di persone; **~ a thousand** un migliaio; **at ~ six o'clock** verso le sei.

2. (*referring to place*) qua e là; **to walk ~** camminare.

3. (*on the point of*): **to be ~ to do sthg** stare per fare qc.

◆ *prep* **1.** (*concerning*) su, a proposito di; **a book ~ Scotland** un libro sulla Scozia; **what's it ~?** di che cosa si tratta?; **I'll talk to you ~ it** te ne parlerò; **what ~ a coffee?** cosa ne diresti di un caffè?

2. (*referring to place*) per, in giro per;

there are lots of hotels ~ the town ci sono molti alberghi nella città.

above [ə'bʌv] *prep* sopra ◆ *adv (higher)* (di) sopra; *(more)* oltre; ~ **all** soprattutto.

abroad [ə'brɔːd] *adv* all'estero.

abrupt [ə'brʌpt] *adj (sudden)* improvviso(-a).

abscess ['æbses] *n* ascesso *m*.

absence ['æbsəns] *n* assenza *f*.

absent ['æbsənt] *adj* assente.

absent-minded [-'maɪndɪd] *adj* distratto(-a).

absolute ['æbsəluːt] *adj* assoluto(-a).

absolutely [*adv* 'æbsəluːtlɪ, *excl* æbsə'luːtlɪ] *adv (completely)* assolutamente ◆ *excl* assolutamente!

absorb [əb'sɔːb] *vt* assorbire.

absorbed [əb'sɔːbd] *adj*: **to be ~ in sthg** essere assorto(-a) in qc.

absorbent [əb'sɔːbənt] *adj* assorbente.

abstain [əb'steɪn] *vi*: **to ~ (from)** astenersi (da).

absurd [əb'sɜːd] *adj* assurdo(-a).

ABTA ['æbtə] *n* associazione *f* delle agenzie di viaggio britanniche.

abuse [*n* ə'bjuːs, *vb* ə'bjuːz] *n (insults)* insulti *mpl*; *(wrong use)* abuso *m*; *(maltreatment)* maltrattamento *m* ◆ *vt (insult)* insultare; *(use wrongly)* abusare di; *(maltreat)* maltrattare.

abusive [ə'bjuːsɪv] *adj* offensivo(-a).

AC *(abbr of alternating current)* c.a.

academic [ækə'demɪk] *adj (educational)* accademico(-a) ◆ *n* professore *m* universitario (professoressa *f* universitaria).

academy [ə'kædəmɪ] *n* acca-

demia *f*.

accelerate [ək'seləreɪt] *vi* accelerare.

accelerator [ək'seləreɪtə] *n* acceleratore *m*.

accent ['æksent] *n* accento *m*.

accept [ək'sept] *vt* accettare.

acceptable [ək'septəbl] *adj* accettabile.

access ['ækses] *n* accesso *m*.

accessible [ək'sesəbl] *adj (place)* accessibile.

accessories [ək'sesərɪz] *npl* accessori *mpl*.

access road *n* strada *f* d'accesso.

accident ['æksɪdənt] *n* incidente *m*; **by ~** per caso.

accidental [æksɪ'dentl] *adj* accidentale.

accident insurance *n* assicurazione *f* contro gli infortuni.

accident-prone *adj* soggetto(-a) a frequenti infortuni.

acclimatize [ə'klaɪmətaɪz] *vi* acclimatarsi.

accommodate [ə'kɒmədeɪt] *vt* alloggiare.

accommodation [ə,kɒmə'deɪʃn] *n* alloggio *m*.

accommodations [ə,kɒmə'deɪnz] *npl (Am)* = **accommodation**.

accompany [ə'kʌmpənɪ] *vt* accompagnare.

accomplish [ə'kʌmplɪʃ] *vt* realizzare.

accord [ə'kɔːd] *n*: **of one's own ~** di propria iniziativa.

accordance [ə'kɔːdəns] *n*: **in ~ with** in conformità a.

according [ə'kɔːdɪŋ]: **according**

to *prep* secondo.

accordion [əˈkɔːdɪən] *n* fisarmonica *f.*

account [əˈkaʊnt] *n (at bank, shop)* conto *m; (report)* resoconto *m;* **to take into ~** tener conto di; **on no ~** in nessun caso; **on ~ of** a causa di ◆ **account for** *vt fus (explain)* spiegare; *(constitute)* rappresentare.

accountant [əˈkaʊntənt] *n* ragioniere *m (-a f).*

account number *n* numero *m* di conto.

accumulate [əˈkjuːmjʊleɪt] *vt* accumulare.

accurate [ˈækjʊrət] *adj* preciso(-a).

accuse [əˈkjuːz] *vt:* **to ~ sb of sthg** accusare qn di qc.

accused [əˈkjuːzd] *n:* **the ~** l'imputato *m (-a f).*

ace [eɪs] *n (card)* asso *m.*

ache [eɪk] *n* dolore *m* ◆ *vi:* **my head ~s** mi fa male la testa.

achieve [əˈtʃiːv] *vt* ottenere.

acid [ˈæsɪd] *adj* acido(-a) ◆ *n* acido *m.*

acid rain *n* pioggia *f* acida.

acknowledge [əkˈnɒlɪdʒ] *vt (accept)* riconoscere; *(letter)* accusare ricevuta di.

acne [ˈæknɪ] *n* acne *f.*

acorn [ˈeɪkɔːn] *n* ghianda *f.*

acoustic [əˈkuːstɪk] *adj* acustico(-a).

acquaintance [əˈkweɪntəns] *n (person)* conoscente *mf.*

acquire [əˈkwaɪə*] *vt* acquisire.

acre [ˈeɪkə*] *n* = 4 046,9 m², acro *m.*

acrobat [ˈækrəbæt] *n* acrobata *mf.*

across [əˈkrɒs] *prep (to, on one side of)* dall'altra parte di; *(from one side to the other of)* attraverso, da una parte all'altra di ◆ *adv (to other side)* dall'altra parte; **to walk ~ sthg** attraversare qc (a piedi); **to drive ~ sthg** attraversare qc (in macchina); **10 miles ~** largo 10 miglia; **~ from** di fronte a.

acrylic [əˈkrɪlɪk] *n* acrilico *m.*

act [ækt] *vi* agire; *(behave)* comportarsi; *(in play, film)* recitare ◆ *n* atto *m; (POL)* legge *f; (performance)* numero *m;* **to ~ as** *(serve as)* fare da.

action [ˈækʃn] *n* azione *f;* **to take ~** agire; **to put sthg into ~** mettere in pratica qc; **out of ~** *(machine)* fuori uso; *(person)* fuori combattimento.

active [ˈæktɪv] *adj (busy)* attivo(-a).

activity [ækˈtɪvətɪ] *n* attività *f inv.*

activity holiday *n* vacanza organizzata per ragazzi con attività ricreative di vario genere.

act of God *n* causa *f* di forza maggiore.

actor [ˈæktə*] *n* attore *m.*

actress [ˈæktrɪs] *n* attrice *f.*

actual [ˈæktʃʊəl] *adj (real)* effettivo(-a), reale; *(itself)* in sé.

actually [ˈæktʃʊəlɪ] *adv (really)* veramente; *(in fact)* in effetti.

acupuncture [ˈækjʊpʌŋktʃə*] *n* agopuntura *f.*

acute [əˈkjuːt] *adj* acuto(-a).

ad [æd] *n (inf) (for product)* pubblicità *f inv; (for job)* annuncio *m.*

AD *(abbr of Anno Domini)* d.C.

adapt [ə'dæpt] vt adattare ◆ vi adattarsi.

adapter [ə'dæptə'] n (for foreign plug) adattatore m; (for several plugs) presa f multipla.

add [æd] vt (put, say in addition) aggiungere; (numbers, prices) sommare ❑ **add up** vt sep sommare; **add up to** vt fus (total) ammontare a.

adder [ædə'] n vipera f.

addict [ædɪkt] n tossicodipendente mf.

addicted [ə'dɪktɪd] adj: **to be ~ to** sthg essere assuefatto(-a) a qc.

addiction [ə'dɪkʃn] n dipendenza f.

addition [ə'dɪʃn] n (added thing) aggiunta f; (in maths) addizione f; **in ~** inoltre; **in ~ to** oltre a.

additional [ə'dɪʃənl] adj supplementare.

additive [ædɪtɪv] n additivo m.

address [ə'dres] n (on letter) indirizzo m ◆ vt (speak to) rivolgersi a; (letter) indirizzare.

address book n rubrica f.

addressee [ædre'si:] n destinatario m (-a f).

adequate [ædɪkwət] adj adeguato(-a).

adhere [əd'hɪə'] vi: **to ~ to** (stick to) aderire a; (obey) rispettare.

adhesive [əd'hi:sɪv] adj adesivo(-a) ◆ n adesivo m.

adjacent [ə'dʒeɪsənt] adj adiacente.

adjective [ædʒɪktɪv] n aggettivo m.

adjoining [ə'dʒɔɪnɪŋ] adj contiguo(-a).

adjust [ə'dʒʌst] vt aggiustare ◆

vi: **to ~ to** adattarsi a.

adjustable [ə'dʒʌstəbl] adj regolabile.

adjustment [ə'dʒʌstmənt] n (of machine) regolazione f; (of plan) modifica f.

administration [əd,mɪnɪ'streɪʃn] n amministrazione f.

administrator [əd'mɪnɪstreɪtə'] n amministratore m (-trice f).

admiral [ædmərəl] n ammiraglio m.

admire [əd'maɪə'] vt ammirare.

admission [əd'mɪʃn] n (permission to enter, entrance cost) ingresso m.

admission charge n ingresso m.

admit [əd'mɪt] vt (confess) ammettere; (allow to enter) far entrare; **to ~ to** sthg ammettere qc; **'~s one'** (on ticket) 'valido per una sola persona'.

adolescent [ædə'lesnt] n adolescente mf.

adopt [ə'dɒpt] vt adottare.

adopted [ə'dɒptɪd] adj adottivo(-a).

adorable [ə'dɔ:rəbl] adj adorabile.

adore [ə'dɔ:'] vt adorare.

Adriatic [eɪdrɪ'ætɪk] n: **the ~ (Sea)** l'Adriatico m, il mar Adriatico.

adult [ædʌlt] n adulto m (-a f) ◆ adj (entertainment, films) per adulti; (animal) adulto(-a).

adult education n = educazione f permanente.

adultery [ə'dʌltərɪ] n adulterio m.

advance [əd'vɑːns] n (money) anticipo m; (movement) avanzamento m ♦ adj (payment) anticipato(-a) ♦ vt anticipare ♦ vi (move forward) avanzare; (improve) fare progressi; **~ warning** preavviso m.

advance booking n prenotazione f anticipata.

advanced [əd'vɑːnst] adj (student) di livello avanzato; (level) avanzato(-a).

advantage [əd'vɑːntɪdʒ] n vantaggio m; **to take ~ of** approfittare di.

adventure [əd'ventʃəʳ] n avventura f.

adventurous [əd'ventʃərəs] adj avventuroso(-a).

adverb [ædvɜːb] n avverbio m.

adverse ['ædvɜːs] adj avverso(-a).

advert ['ædvɜːt] = **advertisement**.

advertise ['ædvətaɪz] vt (product, event) fare pubblicità a.

advertisement [əd'vɜːtɪsmənt] n (for product) pubblicità f inv; (for job) annuncio m.

advice [əd'vaɪs] n consigli mpl; **a piece of ~** un consiglio; **to ask for sb's ~** chiedere consiglio a qn.

advisable [əd'vaɪzəbl] adj consigliabile.

advise [əd'vaɪz] vt consigliare; **to ~ sb to do sthg** consigliare a qn di fare qc; **to ~ sb against doing sthg** sconsigliare a qn di fare qc.

advocate [n 'ædvəkət, vb 'ædvəkeɪt] n (JUR) avvocato m (difensore) ♦ vt sostenere.

aerial ['eərɪəl] n antenna f.

aerobics [eə'rəubɪks] n aerobica f.

aerodynamic [ˌeərəudaɪ'næmɪk] adj aerodinamico(-a).

aeroplane ['eərəpleɪn] n aeroplano m.

aerosol ['eərəsɒl] n aerosol m.

affair [ə'feəʳ] n (event) affare m; (love affair) relazione f.

affect [ə'fekt] vt (influence) incidere su.

affection [ə'fekʃn] n affetto m.

affectionate [ə'fekʃnət] adj affettuoso(-a).

affluent ['æfluənt] adj ricco(-a).

afford [ə'fɔːd] vt: **to be able to ~ sthg** potersi permettere qc; **I can't ~ it** non me lo posso permettere; **I can't ~ the time** non ho tempo.

affordable [ə'fɔːdəbl] adj accessibile.

afloat [ə'fləut] adj a galla.

afraid [ə'freɪd] adj spaventato(-a); **to be ~ of** aver paura di; **I'm ~ so/not** temo di sì/di no.

Africa ['æfrɪkə] n l'Africa f.

African ['æfrɪkən] adj africano(-a) ♦ n africano m (-a f).

after ['ɑːftəʳ] prep & adv dopo ♦ conj dopo che; **he arrived ~ me** arrivò dopo di me; **a quarter ~ ten** (Am) le dieci e un quarto; **to be ~ sb/sthg** (in search of) cercare qn/qc; **~ all** dopo tutto ❑ **afters** npl dessert m.

aftercare ['ɑːftəkeəʳ] n assistenza f postospedaliera.

aftereffects ['ɑːftərɪˌfekts] npl conseguenze fpl; (of illness) postumi mpl.

afternoon [ˌɑːftə'nuːn] n pomeriggio m; **good ~!** buon giorno! (il pomeriggio).

afternoon tea n spuntino

pomeridiano a base di tramezzini, dolci, tè o caffè.

aftershave [ˈɑːftəʃeɪv] *n* dopo-barba *m*.

aftersun [ˈɑːftəsʌn] *n* doposole *m*.

afterwards [ˈɑːftəwədz] *adv* dopo.

again [əˈgen] *adv* ancora, di nuovo; **~ and ~** più volte; **never ... ~** non ... mai più.

against [əˈgenst] *prep* contro; **to lean ~ sth** appoggiarsi a qc; **~ the law** contro la legge.

age [eɪdʒ] *n* età *f*; **under ~** minorenne; **I haven't seen him for ~s** (*inf*) non lo vedo da secoli.

aged [eɪdʒd] *adj*: **~ eight** di otto anni.

age group *n* fascia *f* d'età.

age limit *n* limite *m* d'età.

agency [ˈeɪdʒənsɪ] *n* agenzia *f*.

agenda [əˈdʒendə] *n* ordine *m* del giorno.

agent [ˈeɪdʒənt] *n* agente *mf*.

aggression [əˈgreʃn] *n* aggressività *f*; **act of ~** aggressione *f*.

aggressive [əˈgresɪv] *adj* aggressivo(-a).

agile [*Br* ˈædʒaɪl, *Am* ˈædʒəl] *adj* agile.

agility [əˈdʒɪlɪtɪ] *n* agilità *f*.

agitated [ˈædʒɪteɪtɪd] *adj* agitato(-a).

ago [əˈgəʊ] *adv*: **a month ~** un mese fa; **how long ~?** quanto tempo fa?

agonizing [ˈægənaɪzɪŋ] *adj* (*pain*) atroce; (*decision*) straziante.

agony [ˈægənɪ] *n* (*physical*) dolore *m* atroce; (*mental*) agonia *f*.

agree [əˈgriː] *vi* (*be in agreement*) essere d'accordo; (*consent*) acconsentire; (*correspond*) concordare; **it doesn't ~ with me** (*food*) mi fa male; **to ~ to sth** accettare qc; **to ~ to do sth** accettare di fare qc ❑

agree on *vt fus* (*time, price*) concordare, mettersi d'accordo su.

agreed [əˈgriːd] *adj* stabilito(-a); **to be ~** (*person*) essere d'accordo.

agreement [əˈgriːmənt] *n* accordo *m*; **in ~ with** d'accordo con.

agriculture [ˈægrɪkʌltʃəʳ] *n* agricoltura *f*.

ahead [əˈhed] *adv* (*in front*) davanti; (*forwards*) avanti; **the months ~** i prossimi mesi; **to be ~** (*winning*) condurre; **~ of** (*in front of*) davanti a; (*in better position than*) in vantaggio su; (*in time*) in anticipo su.

aid [eɪd] *n* aiuto *m* ◆ *vt* aiutare; **in ~ of** a favore di; **with the ~ of** con l'aiuto di.

AIDS [eɪdz] *n* AIDS *m*.

ailment [ˈeɪlmənt] *n* (*fml*) acciacco *m*.

aim [eɪm] *n* (*purpose*) scopo *m* ◆ *vt* (*gun, camera, hose*) puntare ◆ *vi*: **to ~ (at)** mirare (a); **to ~ to do sth** avere l'intenzione di fare qc.

air [eəʳ] *n* aria *f* ◆ *vt* (*room*) arieggiare ◆ *adj* aereo(-a); (*travel*) in aereo; **by ~** (*travel*) in aereo; (*send*) via aerea.

airbed [ˈeəbed] *n* materassino *m*.

airborne [ˈeəbɔːn] *adj* in volo.

air-conditioned [-kənˈdɪʃnd] *adj* con aria condizionata.

air-conditioning [-kənˈdɪʃnɪŋ] *n* aria *f* condizionata.

aircraft [ˈeəkrɑːft] (*pl inv*) *n* aeromobile *m*.

aircraft carrier [-ˌkærɪəʳ] *n*

portaerei f inv.

airfield ['eəfi:ld] n campo m d'aviazione.

airforce ['eəfɔ:s] n aeronautica f militare.

air freshener [-'freʃnə'] n deodorante m per ambienti.

airhostess ['eəhəʊstɪs] n hostess f inv.

airing cupboard ['eərɪŋ-] n sgabuzzino della caldaia dove viene riposta la biancheria ad asciugare.

airletter ['eə,letə'] n aerogramma m.

airline ['eəlaɪn] n compagnia f aerea.

airliner ['eə,laɪnə'] n aereo m di linea.

airmail ['eəmeɪl] n posta f aerea; **by** ~ per via aerea.

airplane ['eəpleɪn] n (Am) aeroplano m.

airport ['eəpɔ:t] n aeroporto m.

air raid n incursione f aerea.

airsick ['eəsɪk] adj: **to be** ~ soffrire di mal d'aria.

air steward n assistente m di volo.

air stewardess n assistente f di volo.

air traffic control n (people) controllori mpl di volo.

airy ['eərɪ] adj arioso(-a).

aisle [aɪl] n (in church) navata f; (in plane, cinema) corridoio m; (in supermarket) corsia f.

aisle seat n posto m corridoio.

ajar [ə'dʒɑ:'] adj socchiuso(-a).

alarm [ə'lɑ:m] n allarme m ◆ vt allarmare.

alarm clock n sveglia f.

alarmed [ə'lɑ:md] adj (door, car)

dotato(-a) di allarme.

alarming [ə'lɑ:mɪŋ] adj allarmante.

Albert Hall ['ælbət-] n: **the** ~ l'Albert Hall f (sala concerti di Londra).

---

i THE ALBERT HALL

Grande sala di concerti di Londra, l'Albert Hall fu così chiamata in onore del principe Alberto, consorte della regina Vittoria. Oltre a concerti, ospita manifestazioni varie, incluse quelle sportive.

---

album ['ælbəm] n album m inv.

alcohol ['ælkəhɒl] n alcool m.

alcohol-free adj analcolico(-a).

alcoholic [,ælkə'hɒlɪk] adj alcolico(-a) ◆ n alcolizzato m (-a f).

alcoholism ['ælkəhɒlɪzm] n alcolismo m.

alcove ['ælkəʊv] n rientranza f.

ale [eɪl] n birra f.

alert [ə'lɜ:t] adj vigile ◆ vt allertare.

A levels npl ≃ esami mpl di maturità.

---

i A LEVELS

All'età di 18 anni, gli studenti che hanno deciso di frequentare gli ultimi due anni facoltativi della scuola superiore devono superare questi esami. La maggior parte degli studenti sostiene esami in tre, al massimo quattro, discipline. Le università hanno la facoltà di accettare o respingere le domande di iscrizione sulla base della votazione finale, che risulta pertanto estremamente importante.

---

algebra ['ældʒɪbrə] n algebra f.

alias ['eɪlɪəs] adv alias.

alibi ['ælɪbaɪ] n alibi m inv.

alien ['eɪlɪən] n (foreigner) straniero m (-a f); (from outer space) alieno m (-a f).

alight [ə'laɪt] adj in fiamme ◆ vi (fml: from train, bus): to ~ (from) scendere (da).

align [ə'laɪn] vt allineare.

alike [ə'laɪk] adj simile ◆ adv allo stesso modo; to look ~ assomigliarsi.

alive [ə'laɪv] adj (living) vivo(-a).

all [ɔːl] adj (of) tutto(-a); ~ the food tutto il cibo; ~ the money tutti i soldi; ~ the houses tutte le case; ~ trains stop at Tonbridge tutti i treni fermano a Tonbridge; ~ the time sempre; ~ day tutto il giorno.
◆ adv 1. (completely) completamente, interamente; ~ alone tutto solo (tutta sola).
2. (in scores): it's two ~ sono due pari.
3. (in phrases): ~ but empty quasi vuoto; ~ over (finished) finito.
◆ pron 1. (the whole amount) tutto(-a); ~ of the work tutto il lavoro; is that ~? (in shop) basta così?
2. (everybody, everything) tutti(-e); ~ of the girls/rooms tutte le ragazze/camere; ~ of us went ci siamo andati tutti.
3. (with superlative): the best of ~ il migliore di tutti.
4. (in phrases): in ~ (in total) in tutto; (in summary) nel complesso;

can I help you at ~? posso esserle di aiuto?

Allah ['ælə] n Allah m.

allege [ə'ledʒ] vt asserire.

allergic [ə'lɜːdʒɪk] adj: to be ~ to essere allergico(-a).

allergy ['ælədʒɪ] n allergia f.

alleviate [ə'liːvɪeɪt] vt alleviare.

alley ['ælɪ] n (narrow street) vicolo m.

alligator ['ælɪgeɪtə'] n alligatore m.

all-in adj (Br: inclusive) tutto compreso (inv).

all-night adj (bar, petrol station) aperto(-a) tutta la notte.

allocate ['æləkeɪt] vt (money, task) assegnare.

allotment [ə'lɒtmənt] n (Br: for vegetables) piccolo lotto di terra preso in affitto per coltivarvi ortaggi.

allow [ə'laʊ] vt (permit) permettere; (time, money) calcolare; to ~ sb to do sthg permettere a qn di fare qc; to be ~ed to do sthg avere il permesso di fare qc, poter fare qc.
❏ **allow for** vt fus tener conto di.

allowance [ə'laʊəns] n (state benefit) assegno m; (for expenses) indennità f inv; (Am: pocket money) paghetta f.

all right adv (satisfactorily) bene; (yes, okay) va bene ◆ adj: is everything ~? va tutto bene?; is it ~ if I smoke? Le dispiace se fumo?; are you ~? ti senti bene?; how was the film? – it was ~ com'era il film? – niente di speciale; how are you? – I'm ~ come stai? – non c'è male.

ally ['ælaɪ] n alleato m (-a f).

almond ['ɑːmənd] n mandorla f.

almost ['ɔːlməʊst] adv quasi.

alone [ə'ləʊn] adj solo(-a) ◆ adv

da solo(-a); **to leave sb ~** lasciare qn in pace; **to leave sthg ~** lasciar stare qc.

along [ə'lɒŋ] *prep* lungo ♦ *adv*: **to walk ~** camminare; **to bring sthg ~** portare qc; **all ~** sempre; **~ with** insieme a.

alongside [ə,lɒŋ'saɪd] *prep* accanto a ♦ *adv*: **to come ~** accostare.

aloof [ə'lu:f] *adj* distaccato(-a).

aloud [ə'laud] *adv* a voce alta.

alphabet ['ælfəbet] *n* alfabeto *m*.

Alps [ælps] *npl*: **the ~** le Alpi.

already [ɔ:l'redɪ] *adv* già.

also ['ɔ:lsəu] *adv* anche.

altar ['ɔ:ltə^r] *n* altare *m*.

alter ['ɔ:ltə^r] *vt* cambiare.

alteration [,ɔ:ltə'reɪʃn] *n* modifica *f*.

alternate [*Br* ɔ:l'tɜ:nət, *Am* 'ɔ:ltərnət] *adj* alterni(-e).

alternating current [,ɔ:ltə-nettɪŋ-] *n* corrente *f* alternata.

alternative [ɔ:l'tɜ:nətɪv] *adj* alternativo(-a) ♦ *n* alternativa *f*.

alternatively [ɔ:l'tɜ:nətɪvlɪ] *adv* in alternativa.

alternator ['ɔ:ltəneɪtə^r] *n* alternatore *m*.

although [ɔ:l'ðəu] *conj* sebbene, benché.

altitude ['æltɪtju:d] *n* altitudine *f*.

altogether [,ɔ:ltə'geðə^r] *adv* (*completely*) del tutto; (*in total*) in tutto.

aluminium [,æljʊ'mɪnɪəm] *n* (*Br*) alluminio *m*.

aluminum [ə'lu:mɪnəm] (*Am*) = **aluminium**.

always ['ɔ:lweɪz] *adv* sempre.

am [æm] → **be**.

a.m. (*abbr of ante meridiem*): **at two ~** alle due di notte; **at ten ~** alle dieci di mattina.

amateur ['æmətə^r] *n* dilettante *mf*.

amazed [ə'meɪzd] *adj* stupito(-a).

amazing [ə'meɪzɪŋ] *adj* incredibile.

Amazon ['æməzn] *n* (*river*): **the ~** il Rio delle Amazzoni.

ambassador [æm'bæsədə^r] *n* ambasciatore *m* (-trice *f*).

amber ['æmbə^r] *adj* (*traffic lights*) giallo(-a); (*jewellery*) d'ambra.

ambiguous [æm'bɪgjʊəs] *adj* ambiguo(-a).

ambition [æm'bɪʃn] *n* ambizione *f*.

ambitious [æm'bɪʃəs] *adj* ambizioso(-a).

ambulance ['æmbjʊləns] *n* ambulanza *f*.

ambush ['æmbʊʃ] *n* imboscata *f*.

amenities [ə'mi:nətɪz] *npl* (*in hotel*) comfort *m inv*; (*in town*) strutture *fpl* (sportive, ricreative ecc.).

America [ə'merɪkə] *n* l'America *f*.

American [ə'merɪkən] *adj* americano(-a) ♦ *n* (*person*) americano *m* (-a *f*).

amiable ['eɪmɪəbl] *adj* amabile.

ammunition [,æmjʊ'nɪʃn] *n* munizioni *fpl*.

amnesia [æm'ni:zɪə] *n* amnesia *f*.

among(st) [ə'mʌŋ(st)] *prep* tra, fra.

amount [ə'maunt] *n* (*quantity*) quantità *f inv*; (*sum*) somma *f*.

amount to *vt fus (total)* ammontare a.

amp [æmp] *n* ampere *m inv*; a 13-~ **plug** una spina con fusibile da 13 ampere.

ample [ˈæmpl] *adj* più che sufficiente.

amplifier [ˈæmplɪfaɪəʳ] *n* amplificatore *m*.

amputate [ˈæmpjʊteɪt] *vt* amputare.

Amtrak [ˈæmtræk] *n compagnia ferroviaria statunitense.*

amuse [əˈmjuːz] *vt* divertire.

amusement arcade [əˈmjuːzmənt-] *n* sala *f* giochi.

amusement park *n* luna park *m inv*.

amusements [əˈmjuːzmənts] *npl* giostre e giochi al luna park.

amusing [əˈmjuːzɪŋ] *adj* divertente.

an [stressed æn, unstressed ən] → **a**.

anaemic [əˈniːmɪk] *adj (Br: person)* anemico(-a).

anaesthetic [ˌænɪsˈθetɪk] *n (Br)* anestetico *m*.

analgesic [ˌænælˈdʒiːsɪk] *n* analgesico *m*.

analyse [ˈænəlaɪz] *vt* analizzare.

analyst [ˈænəlɪst] *n* analista *mf*.

analyze [ˈænəlaɪz] *(Am)* = **analyse**.

anarchy [ˈænəkɪ] *n* anarchia *f*.

anatomy [əˈnætəmɪ] *n (science)* anatomia *f*; *(of animal)* struttura *f*; *(of person)* corpo *m*.

ancestor [ˈænsestəʳ] *n* antenato *m* (-a *f*).

anchor [ˈæŋkəʳ] *n* àncora *f*.

anchovy [ˈæntʃəvɪ] *n* acciuga *f*.

ancient [ˈeɪnʃənt] *adj (customs,* monument*)* antico(-a).

and [strong form ænd, weak form ənd, ən] *conj* e, ed *(before vowel)*; **more ~ more** sempre più; **~ you?** e tu?; **a hundred ~ one** centouno; **to try ~ do sthg** cercare di fare qc; **to go ~ see** andare a vedere.

Andes [ˈændiːz] *npl*: **the ~** le Ande.

anecdote [ˈænɪkdəʊt] *n* aneddoto *m*.

anemic [əˈniːmɪk] *(Am)* = **anaemic.**

anesthetic [ˌænɪsˈθetɪk] *(Am)* = **anaesthetic.**

angel [ˈeɪndʒl] *n* angelo *m*.

anger [ˈæŋgəʳ] *n* rabbia *f*.

angina [ænˈdʒaɪnə] *n* angina *f* pectoris.

angle [ˈæŋgl] *n* angolo *m*; **at an ~** storto(-a).

angler [ˈæŋgləʳ] *n* pescatore *m* (-trice *f*).

angling [ˈæŋglɪŋ] *n* pesca *f*.

angry [ˈæŋgrɪ] *adj (person)* arrabbiato(-a); *(words)* pieno(-a) di rabbia; **to get ~ (with sb)** arrabbiarsi (con qn).

animal [ˈænɪml] *n* animale *m*.

aniseed [ˈænɪsiːd] *n* semi *mpl* d'anice.

ankle [ˈæŋkl] *n* caviglia *f*.

annex [ˈæneks] *n (building)* edificio *m* annesso.

annihilate [əˈnaɪəleɪt] *vt* annientare.

anniversary [ˌænɪˈvɜːsərɪ] *n* anniversario *m*.

announce [əˈnaʊns] *vt* annunciare.

announcement [əˈnaʊnsmənt] *n* annuncio *m*.

any

announcer [əˈnaʊnsər] *n* annunciatore *m* (-trice *f*).

annoy [əˈnɔɪ] *vt* dare fastidio a.

annoyed [əˈnɔɪd] *adj* seccato(-a); **to get ~ (with sb)** arrabbiarsi (con qn).

annoying [əˈnɔɪɪŋ] *adj* seccante, irritante.

annual [ˈænjʊəl] *adj* annuale.

anonymous [əˈnɒnɪməs] *adj* anonimo(-a).

anorak [ˈænəræk] *n* giacca *f* a vento.

another [əˈnʌðər] *adj* un altro (un'altra) ♦ *pron* un'altro (un'altra *f*); **can I have ~ (one)?** posso prenderne un altro?; **in ~ two weeks** fra altre due settimane; **one ~** l'un l'altro (l'un l'altra); **to help one ~** aiutarsi (l'un l'altro); **to talk to one ~** parlarsi; **one after ~** uno dopo l'altro (una dopo l'altra).

answer [ˈɑːnsər] *n* risposta *f* ♦ *vt* rispondere a ♦ *vi* rispondere; **to ~ the door** andare ad aprire (la porta); **to ~ the phone** rispondere al telefono ❑ **answer back** *vi* rispondere male.

answering machine [ˈɑːnsərɪŋ-] = **answerphone**.

answerphone [ˈɑːnsəfəʊn] *n* segreteria *f* telefonica.

ant [ænt] *n* formica *f*.

Antarctic [ænˈtɑːktɪk] *n*: **the ~** l'Antartide *f*.

antenna [ænˈtenə] *n* (*Am: aerial*) antenna *f*.

anthem [ˈænθəm] *n* inno *m*.

antibiotics [ˌæntɪbaɪˈɒtɪks] *npl* antibiotici *mpl*.

anticipate [ænˈtɪsɪpeɪt] *vt* (*expect*) aspettarsi; (*guess correctly*)

prevedere.

anticlimax [ˌæntɪˈklaɪmæks] *n* delusione *f*.

anticlockwise [ˌæntɪˈklɒkwaɪz] *adv* (*Br*) in senso antiorario.

antidote [ˈæntɪdəʊt] *n* antidoto *m*.

antifreeze [ˈæntɪfriːz] *n* antigelo *m*.

antihistamine [ˌæntɪˈhɪstəmɪn] *n* antistaminico *m*.

antiperspirant [ˌæntɪˈpɜːspərənt] *n* deodorante *m* (ad azione antitraspirante).

antiquarian bookshop [ˌæntɪˈkweərɪən-] *n* libreria *f* antiquaria.

antique [ænˈtiːk] *n* pezzo *m* d'antiquariato.

antique shop *n* negozio *m* d'antiquariato.

antiseptic [ˌæntɪˈseptɪk] *n* antisettico *m*.

antisocial [ˌæntɪˈsəʊʃl] *adj* (*person*) asociale; (*behaviour*) incivile.

antlers [ˈæntləz] *npl* palchi *mpl*.

anxiety [æŋˈzaɪətɪ] *n* ansia *f*.

anxious [ˈæŋkʃəs] *adj* (*worried*) preoccupato(-a); (*eager*) ansioso(-a).

any [ˈenɪ] *adj* **1.** (*in questions*): **have you got ~ money?** hai (dei) soldi?; **have you got ~ postcards?** ha delle cartoline?; **is there ~ coffee left?** c'è ancora del caffè?

2. (*in negatives*): **I haven't got ~ money** non ho soldi; **I haven't got ~ Italian stamps** non ho nessun francobollo italiano; **we don't have ~ rooms** non abbiamo camere libere.

3. (*no matter which*) qualunque, qualsiasi; **take ~ one you like** pren-

di quello che preferisci.
◆ *pron* 1. *(in questions)* ne; **I'm looking for a hotel – are there ~ nearby?** sto cercando un albergo – ce ne sono da queste parti? 2. *(in negatives)* ne; **I don't want ~ (of them)** non ne voglio. 3. *(no matter which one)*: **you can sit at ~ of the tables** potete sedere a qualsiasi tavolo.
◆ *adv* 1. *(in questions)*: **is that ~ better?** così va un po' meglio?; **is there ~ more ice cream?** c'è ancora un po' di gelato?; **~ other questions?** altre domande? 2. *(in negatives)*: **he's not ~ better** non c'è nessun miglioramento; **we can't wait ~ longer** non possiamo più aspettare.

anybody ['enɪˌbɒdɪ] = anyone.

anyhow ['enɪhau] *adv* comunque; *(carelessly)* alla rinfusa.

anyone ['enɪwʌn] *pron (someone)* qualcuno; *(any person)* chiunque; **is ~ there?** c'è nessuno?; **there wasn't ~ in** non c'era nessuno.

anything ['enɪθɪŋ] *pron (something)* qualcosa; *(no matter what)* qualunque cosa, qualsiasi cosa; **have you ~ bigger?** ha niente di più grande?; **I don't want ~ to eat** non voglio mangiare niente.

anyway ['enɪweɪ] *adv* comunque.

anywhere ['enɪweəʳ] *adv (in questions)* da qualche parte; *(with negative)* da nessuna parte; *(any place)* dovunque, da qualunque OR qualsiasi parte; **did you go ~ else?** siete andati da qualche altra parte?; **~ you like** dove vuoi.

apart [ə'pɑːt] *adv (separated)*: **the towns are 5 miles ~** le due città distano 8 km l'una dall'altra; **we live ~** non viviamo insieme; **to**

come ~ andare in pezzi; **~ from** *(except for)* a parte; *(as well as)* oltre a.

apartheid [ə'pɑːtheɪt] *n* apartheid *f*.

apartment [ə'pɑːtmənt] *n (Am)* appartamento *m*.

apathetic [ˌæpə'θetɪk] *adj* apatico(-a).

ape [eɪp] *n* scimmia *f*.

aperitif [əˌperə'tiːf] *n* aperitivo *m*.

aperture ['æpətʃəʳ] *n (of camera)* apertura *f*.

APEX ['eɪpeks] *n (plane ticket)* biglietto *m* APEX; *(Br: train ticket)* biglietto ferroviario con data prefissata e dal prezzo ridotto comprato due settimane prima della partenza.

apiece [ə'piːs] *adv (for each item)* l'uno (l'una); *(to, for each person)* ciascuno(-a).

apologetic [əˌpɒlə'dʒetɪk] *adj*: **to be ~** scusarsi.

apologize [ə'pɒlədʒaɪz] *vi*: **to ~ (to sb for sthg)** scusarsi (con qn per qc).

apology [ə'pɒlədʒɪ] *n* scuse *fpl*.

apostrophe [ə'pɒstrəfɪ] *n* apostrofo *m*.

appal [ə'pɔːl] *vt (Br)* sconvolgere.

appall [ə'pɔːl] *(Am)* = appal.

appalling [ə'pɔːlɪŋ] *adj* spaventoso(-a).

apparatus [ˌæpə'reɪtəs] *n (device)* apparecchio *m*; *(in gym)* attrezzatura *f*.

apparently [ə'pærəntlɪ] *adv (it seems)* a quanto pare; *(evidently)* evidentemente.

appeal [ə'piːl] *n (JUR)* appello *m*; *(fundraising campaign)* raccolta *f* di fondi ♦ vi (JUR) fare appello; **to ~ to sb for help** chiedere aiuto a qn; **it doesn't ~ to me** non mi attira.

appear [ə'pɪəʳ] vi apparire; (seem) sembrare; (before court) comparire; **it ~s that** sembra che.

appearance [ə'pɪərəns] n (arrival) comparsa f; (look) aspetto m.

appendices [ə'pendɪsi:z] pl → appendix.

appendicitis [ə,pendɪ'saɪtɪs] n appendicite f.

appendix [ə'pendɪks] (pl -dices) n appendice f.

appetite ['æpɪtaɪt] n appetito m.

appetizer ['æpɪtaɪzəʳ] n stuzzichino m.

appetizing ['æpɪtaɪzɪŋ] adj appetitoso(-a).

applaud [ə'plɔ:d] vt & vi applaudire.

applause [ə'plɔ:z] n applauso m.

apple ['æpl] n mela f.

apple charlotte [-'ʃɑ:lət] n dolce di pane o pan di Spagna, ripieno di mele e pane sbriciolato e cotto in forno.

apple crumble n mele cotte ricoperte da uno strato di pasta frolla sbriciolata.

apple juice n succo m di mela.

apple pie n torta f di mele ricoperta di pasta.

apple sauce n mele fpl grattugiate.

apple tart n crostata f di mele.

apple turnover [-'tɜ:n,əʊvəʳ] n sfogliatella f di mele.

appliance [ə'plaɪəns] n apparecchio m; **electrical/domestic ~** elettrodomestico m.

applicable [ə'plɪkəbl] adj: **to be ~ (to)** essere applicabile (a); **if ~** se pertinente.

applicant ['æplɪkənt] n candidato m (-a f).

application [,æplɪ'keɪʃn] n (for job, membership) domanda f.

application form n modulo m di domanda.

apply [ə'plaɪ] vt (lotion, paint) dare; (brakes) azionare ♦ vi: **to ~ (to sb for sthg)** (make request) fare domanda (per qc presso qn); **to ~ (to sb)** (be applicable) essere valido (per qn); **to ~ for a job** fare domanda di lavoro.

appointment [ə'pɔɪntmənt] n (with doctor, hairdresser, businessman) appuntamento m; **to have/make an ~ (with)** avere/prendere un appuntamento (con); **by ~** per OR su appuntamento.

appreciable [ə'pri:ʃəbl] adj apprezzabile.

appreciate [ə'pri:ʃɪeɪt] vt apprezzare; (understand) rendersi conto di.

apprehensive [,æprɪ'hensɪv] adj preoccupato(-a).

apprentice [ə'prentɪs] n apprendista mf.

apprenticeship [ə'prentɪʃɪp] n apprendistato m.

approach [ə'prəʊtʃ] n (road) accesso m; (to problem, situation) approccio m ♦ vt (come nearer to) avvicinare; (problem, situation) affrontare ♦ vi avvicinarsi.

appropriate [ə'prəʊprɪət] adj adatto(-a).

approval [ə'pru:vl] n approvazione f.

approve [ə'pru:v] vi: **to ~ (of sb/sthg)** approvare (qn/qc).

approximate [əˈprɒksɪmət] *adj* approssimativo(-a).

approximately [əˈprɒksɪmətlɪ] *adv* circa.

Apr. *(abbr of April)* apr.

apricot [ˈeɪprɪkɒt] *n* albicocca *f*.

April [ˈeɪprəl] *n* aprile *m*, → September.

April Fools' Day *n* il primo aprile, giorno in cui si fanno i 'pesci d'aprile'.

---

i APRIL FOOLS' DAY

Come in Italia, anche in Gran Bretagna il primo aprile è occasione di scherzi e burle di ogni genere. A differenza dell'Italia, però, non è consentito fare scherzi dopo mezzogiorno e non esiste la tradizione del pesce di carta.

---

apron [ˈeɪprən] *n* grembiule *m* (da cucina).

apt [æpt] *adj (appropriate)* appropriato(-a); **to be ~ to do sthg** avere tendenza a fare qc.

aquarium [əˈkweərɪəm] *(pl* **-ria** [-rɪə]*) n* acquario *m*.

Aquarius [əˈkweərɪəs] *n* Acquario *m*.

aqueduct [ˈækwɪdʌkt] *n* acquedotto *m*.

Arab [ˈærəb] *adj* arabo(-a) ◆ *n (person)* arabo *m* (-a *f*).

Arabic [ˈærəbɪk] *adj* arabo(-a) ◆ *n (language)* arabo *m*.

arbitrary [ˈɑːbɪtrərɪ] *adj* arbitrario(-a).

arc [ɑːk] *n* arco *m*.

arcade [ɑːˈkeɪd] *n (for shopping)* galleria *f*; *(of video games)* sala *f*

giochi.

arch [ɑːtʃ] *n* arco *m*.

archaeology [ˌɑːkɪˈɒlədʒɪ] *n* archeologia *f*.

archbishop [ˌɑːtʃˈbɪʃəp] *n* arcivescovo *m*.

archery [ˈɑːtʃərɪ] *n* tiro *m* con l'arco.

archipelago [ˌɑːkɪˈpeləgəʊ] *n* arcipelago *m*.

architect [ˈɑːkɪtekt] *n* architetto *mf*.

architecture [ˈɑːkɪtektʃəˈ] *n* architettura *f*.

archives [ˈɑːkaɪvz] *npl* archivi *mpl*.

Arctic [ˈɑːktɪk] *n*: **the ~** l'Artide *f*.

are [weak form əˈ, strong form ɑːˈ] → be.

area [ˈeərɪə] *n (region)* zona *f*; *(space, zone)* area *f*; *(surface size)* superficie *f*; **dining ~** zona pranzo.

area code *n (Am)* prefisso *m*.

arena [əˈriːnə] *n (at circus)* pista *f*; *(sports ground)* campo *m*.

aren't = are not.

Argentina [ˌɑːdʒənˈtiːnə] *n* l'Argentina *f*.

argue [ˈɑːgjuː] *vi (quarrel)*: **to ~ (with sb about sthg)** litigare (con qn per qc) ◆ *vt*: **to ~ (that)** ... sostenere (che) ...

argument [ˈɑːgjʊmənt] *n (quarrel)* discussione *f*; *(reason)* argomento *m*.

arid [ˈærɪd] *adj* arido(-a).

Aries [ˈeəriːz] *n* Ariete *m*.

arise [əˈraɪz] *(pt* arose, *pp* arisen [əˈrɪzn]*) vi (problem, opportunity)* presentarsi; **to ~ from** derivare da.

aristocracy [ˌærɪˈstɒkrəsɪ] *n* aristocrazia *f*.

arithmetic [əˈrɪθmətɪk] n aritmetica f.

arm [ɑːm] n (of person) braccio m; (of chair) bracciolo m; (of garment) manica f.

armbands [ˈɑːmbændz] npl (for swimming) braccioli mpl.

armchair [ˈɑːmtʃeəʳ] n poltrona f.

armed [ɑːmd] adj armato(-a).

armed forces npl: the ~ le forze armate.

armor (Am) = **armour**.

armour [ˈɑːməʳ] n (Br) armatura f.

armpit [ˈɑːmpɪt] n ascella f.

arms [ɑːmz] npl (weapons) armi fpl.

army [ˈɑːmɪ] n esercito m.

A road n (Br) strada f statale.

aroma [əˈrəʊmə] n aroma m.

aromatic [ˌærəˈmætɪk] adj aromatico(-a).

arose [əˈrəʊz] pt → **arise**.

around [əˈraʊnd] adv in giro ◆ prep (surrounding) intorno a; (to the other side of) dall'altra parte di; (near) vicino a; (all over) per; (approximately) circa; ~ **here** (in the area) da queste parti; ~ **the corner** dietro l'angolo; **to turn** ~ girarsi; **to look** ~ (turn head) guardarsi intorno; (in shop, city) dare un'occhiata in giro; **at** ~ **two o'clock** verso le due; **is Paul** ~? c'è Paul?

arouse [əˈraʊz] vt destare.

arrange [əˈreɪndʒ] vt (flowers, books) sistemare; (meeting, event) organizzare; **to ~ to do sthg (with sb)** mettersi d'accordo (con qn) per fare qc.

arrangement [əˈreɪndʒmənt] n (agreement) accordo m; (layout) disposizione f; **by** ~ su richiesta; **to make ~s (to do sthg)** fare il necessario (per fare qc).

arrest [əˈrest] n arresto m ◆ vt arrestare; **under** ~ in arresto.

arrival [əˈraɪvl] n arrivo m; **on** ~ all'arrivo; **new** ~ (person) nuovo arrivato m (nuova arrivata f).

arrive [əˈraɪv] vi arrivare; **to** ~ (at place) arrivare in/a.

arrogant [ˈærəgənt] adj arrogante.

arrow [ˈærəʊ] n freccia f.

arson [ˈɑːsn] n incendio m doloso.

art [ɑːt] n arte f □ **arts** npl (humanities) discipline fpl umanistiche; **the ~s** (fine arts) l'arte f.

artefact [ˈɑːtɪfækt] n manufatto m.

artery [ˈɑːtərɪ] n arteria f.

art gallery n galleria f d'arte.

arthritis [ɑːˈθraɪtɪs] n artrite f.

artichoke [ˈɑːtɪtʃəʊk] n carciofo m.

article [ˈɑːtɪkl] n articolo m.

articulate [ɑːˈtɪkjʊlət] adj chiaro(-a).

artificial [ˌɑːtɪˈfɪʃl] adj artificiale.

artist [ˈɑːtɪst] n artista mf.

artistic [ɑːˈtɪstɪk] adj (design) artistico(-a); (person) dotato(-a) di senso artistico.

arts centre n centro m artistico.

as [unstressed əz, stressed æz] adv (in comparisons): ~ ... ~ (così) ... come; ~ **white** ~ **snow** bianco come la neve; **he's** ~ **tall** ~ **I am** è alto quanto me; ~ **many** ~ tanti ...

quanti (tante ... quante); ~ **much** ~ **tanto** ... quanto (tanta ... quanta); **twice** ~ **big** due volte più grande.

♦ *conj* **1.** *(referring to time)* mentre, nel momento in cui; ~ **the plane was coming in to land** nel momento in cui l'aereo si preparava ad atterrare.

2. *(referring to manner)* come; ~ **expected** ... come previsto ...; **do** ~ **you like** fa' come vuoi.

3. *(introducing a statement)* come; ~ **you know** ... come sai ...

4. *(because)* poiché, dato che.

5. *(in phrases):* ~ **for** quanto a; ~ **from** (a partire) da; ~ **if** come se; **it looks** ~ **if it will rain** sembra che stia per piovere.

♦ *prep (referring to function, job)* come; **to work** ~ **a teacher** fare l'insegnante.

asap *(abbr of as soon as possible)* il più presto possibile.

ascent [ə'sent] *n (climb)* scalata *f.*

ascribe [ə'skraɪb] *vt:* **to** ~ **sthg to** attribuire qc a.

ash [æʃ] *n (from cigarette, fire)* cenere *f; (tree)* frassino *m.*

ashore [ə'ʃɔː] *adv* a riva.

ashtray [ˈæʃtreɪ] *n* portacenere *m inv.*

Asia [Br 'eɪʃə, Am 'eɪʒə] *n* l'Asia *f.*

Asian [Br 'eɪʃn, Am 'eɪʒn] *adj* asiatico(-a) ♦ *n* asiatico *m* (-a *f*).

aside [ə'saɪd] *adv (to one side)* da lato; **to move** ~ spostarsi.

ask [ɑːsk] *vt (person)* chiedere a; *(request)* chiedere; *(invite)* invitare ♦ *vi:* **to** ~ **about** sthg chiedere informazioni su qc; **to** ~ **sb sthg** chiedere qc a qn; **to** ~ **sb about sthg** chiedere a qn di qc; **to** ~ **sb to**

do sthg chiedere a qn di fare qc; **to** ~ **sb for sthg** chiedere qc a qn; **to** ~ **a question** fare una domanda; **can I** ~ **you about this translation?** posso farti qualche domanda su questa traduzione? ❑ **ask for** *vt fus (ask to talk to)* chiedere di; *(request)* chiedere.

asleep [ə'sliːp] *adj* addormentato(-a); **to be** ~ dormire; **to fall** ~ addormentarsi.

asparagus [ə'spærəgəs] *n* asparagi *mpl.*

asparagus tips *npl* punte *fpl* d'asparagi.

aspect ['æspekt] *n* aspetto *m.*

aspirin ['æsprɪn] *n* aspirina® *f.*

ass [æs] *n (animal)* asino *m.*

assassinate [ə'sæsɪneɪt] *vt* assassinare.

assault [ə'sɔːlt] *n* aggressione *f* ♦ *vt* aggredire.

assemble [ə'sembl] *vt (bookcase, model)* montare ♦ *vi* riunirsi.

assembly [ə'semblɪ] *n (at school)* riunione quotidiana di alunni e professori.

assembly hall *n (at school)* locale di una scuola dove alunni e professori si riuniscono ogni giorno prima delle lezioni.

assembly point *n* punto di raduno in caso di emergenza.

assert [ə'sɜːt] *vt (fact, innocence)* sostenere; *(authority)* far valere; **to** ~ **o.s.** farsi valere.

assess [ə'ses] *vt (person, situation, effect)* valutare; *(value, damage, cost)* stimare.

assessment [ə'sesmənt] *n (of person, situation, effect)* valutazione *f; (of value, damage, cost)* stima *f.*

asset ['æset] *n (valuable person,*

thing) punto *m* di forza.

assign [ə'saɪn] *vt*: to ~ sthg to sb *(give)* assegnare qc a qn; to ~ sb to do sthg *(designate)* incaricare qn di fare qc.

assignment [ə'saɪnmənt] *n (task)* incarico *m*; (SCH) ricerca *f*.

assist [ə'sɪst] *vt* aiutare.

assistance [ə'sɪstəns] *n* aiuto *m*; to be of ~ (to sb) essere d'aiuto (a qn).

assistant [ə'sɪstənt] *n* assistente *mf*.

associate [*n* ə'səʊʃɪət, *vb* ə'səʊʃɪeɪt] *n (partner)* socio *m* (-a *f*); *(colleague)* collega *mf* ♦ *vt*: to ~ sb/sthg with associare qn/qc a; to be ~d with venire associato a.

association [ə,səʊsɪ'eɪʃn] *n* associazione *f*.

assorted [ə'sɔːtɪd] *adj* assortito(-a).

assortment [ə'sɔːtmənt] *n* assortimento *m*.

assume [ə'sjuːm] *vt (suppose)* supporre; *(control)* assumere; *(responsibility)* assumersi.

assurance [ə'ʃʊərəns] *n (promise)* promessa *f*; *(insurance)* assicurazione *f*.

assure [ə'ʃʊər] *vt* assicurare; to ~ sb (that) ... assicurare a qn che ...

asterisk [æstərɪsk] *n* asterisco *m*.

asthma [æsmə] *n* asma *f*.

asthmatic [æs'mætɪk] *adj* asmatico(-a).

astonished [ə'stɒnɪʃt] *adj* stupito(-a).

astonishing [ə'stɒnɪʃɪŋ] *adj* incredibile.

astound [ə'staʊnd] *vt* sbalordire.

astray [ə'streɪ] *adv*: to go ~ smarrirsi.

astrology [ə'strɒlədʒɪ] *n* astrologia *f*.

astronomy [ə'strɒnəmɪ] *n* astronomia *f*.

asylum [ə'saɪləm] *n (mental hospital)* manicomio *m*.

at [unstressed ət, stressed æt] *prep* **1.** *(indicating place, position)* a; ~ school a scuola; ~ the hotel in OR all'albergo; ~ home a casa; ~ my mother's da mia madre.
2. *(indicating direction)*: to throw sthg ~ qn/qc contro; to look ~ sb/sthg guardare qn/qc; to smile ~ sb sorridere a qn.
3. *(indicating time)* a; ~ nine o'clock alle nove; ~ night di notte.
4. *(indicating rate, level, speed)* a; it works out ~ £5 each viene 5 sterline a testa; ~ 60 km/h a 60km/h.
5. *(indicating activity)*: she's ~ lunch sta pranzando; to be good/bad ~ sthg essere/non essere bravo in qc.
6. *(indicating cause)*: shocked ~ sthg scioccato da qc; angry ~ sb arrabbiato con qn; delighted ~ sthg contentissimo di qc.

ate [Br et, Am et] *pt* → **eat**.

atheist [ˈeɪθɪɪst] *n* ateo *m* (-a *f*).

athlete [æθliːt] *n* atleta *mf*.

athletics [æθ'letɪks] *n* atletica *f*.

Atlantic [ət'læntɪk] *n*: the ~ (Ocean) l'Atlantico *m*, l'Oceano *m* Atlantico.

atlas [ætləs] *n* atlante *m*.

atmosphere [ætməsfɪə*r*] *n* atmosfera *f*; *(air in room)* aria *f*.

atom [ætəm] *n* atomo *m*.

A to Z *n (map)* stradario *m*.

atrocious [əˈtrəʊʃəs] *adj* (*very bad*) orrendo(-a).

attach [əˈtætʃ] *vt* attaccare; **to ~ sthg to sthg** attaccare qc a qc.

attachment [əˈtætʃmənt] *n* (*device*) accessorio *m*.

attack [əˈtæk] *n* attacco *m* ◆ *vt* aggredire.

attacker [əˈtækə*ʳ*] *n* aggressore *m*.

attain [əˈteɪn] *vt* (*fml*) conseguire.

attempt [əˈtempt] *n* tentativo *m* ◆ *vt* tentare; **to ~ to do sthg** tentare di fare qc.

attend [əˈtend] *vt* (*meeting*) partecipare a; (*school*) frequentare; (*mass*) ascoltare ☐ **attend to** *vt fus* (*deal with*) occuparsi di.

attendance [əˈtendəns] *n* (*people at concert, match*) affluenza *f*; (*at school*) frequenza *f*.

attendant [əˈtendənt] *n* (*at public toilets, cloakroom*) addetto *m* (-a *f*); (*at museum*) custode *mf*.

attention [əˈtenʃn] *n* attenzione *f*; **to pay ~ (to)** fare attenzione (a).

attic [ˈætɪk] *n* soffitta *f*.

attitude [ˈætɪtjuːd] *n* atteggiamento *m*.

attorney [əˈtɜːnɪ] *n* (*Am*) avvocato *m*.

attract [əˈtrækt] *vt* attirare.

attraction [əˈtrækʃn] *n* (*liking*) attrazione *f*; (*attractive feature*) attrattiva *f*.

attractive [əˈtræktɪv] *adj* attraente.

attribute [əˈtrɪbjuːt] *vt*: **to ~ sthg to** attribuire qc a.

aubergine [ˈəʊbəʒiːn] *n* (*Br*) melanzana *f*.

auburn [ˈɔːbən] *adj* castano ramato (*inv*).

auction [ˈɔːkʃn] *n* asta *f*.

audience [ˈɔːdɪəns] *n* (*of play, concert, film*) pubblico *m*; (*of TV*) telespettatori *mpl*; (*of radio*) ascoltatori *mpl*.

audio [ˈɔːdɪəʊ] *adj* audio (*inv*).

audio-visual [-ˈvɪʒʊəl] *adj* audiovisivo(-a).

auditorium [ˌɔːdɪˈtɔːrɪəm] *n* sala *f*.

Aug. (*abbr of August*) ago.

August [ˈɔːgəst] *n* agosto *m*, → **September.**

aunt [ɑːnt] *n* zia *f*.

au pair [ˌəʊˈpeəʳ] *n* ragazza *f* alla pari.

aural [ˈɔːrəl] *adj* uditivo(-a).

Australia [ɒˈstreɪlɪə] *n* l'Australia *f*.

Australian [ɒˈstreɪlɪən] *adj* australiano(-a) ◆ *n* australiano *m* (-a *f*).

Austria [ˈɒstrɪə] *n* l'Austria *f*.

Austrian [ˈɒstrɪən] *adj* austriaco(-a) ◆ *n* austriaco *m* (-a *f*).

authentic [ɔːˈθentɪk] *adj* autentico(-a).

author [ˈɔːθəʳ] *n* (*of book, article*) autore *m* (-trice *f*); (*by profession*) scrittore *m* (-trice *f*).

authority [ɔːˈθɒrətɪ] *n* autorità *inv*; **the authorities** le autorità.

authorization [ˌɔːθəraɪˈzeɪʃn] *n* autorizzazione *f*.

authorize [ˈɔːθəraɪz] *vt* autorizzare; **to ~ sb to do sthg** autorizzare qn a fare qc.

autobiography [ˌɔːtəbaˈɒgrəfɪ] *n* autobiografia *f*.

autograph [ˈɔːtəgrɑːf] *n* autografo *m*.

grafo m.

automatic [ɔːtəˈmætɪk] adj automatico(-a) ♦ n (car) automobile f con cambio automatico.

automatically [ɔːtəˈmætɪklɪ] adv automaticamente.

automobile [ˈɔːtəməbiːl] n (Am) automobile f.

autumn [ˈɔːtəm] n autunno m; in (the) ~ in autunno.

auxiliary (verb) [ɔːgˈzɪljərɪ] n ausiliare m.

available [əˈveɪləbl] adj disponibile.

avalanche [ˈævəlɑːnʃ] n valanga f.

Ave. (abbr of avenue) V.le.

avenue [ˈævənjuː] n viale m.

average [ˈævərɪdʒ] adj medio(-a); (not very good) mediocre ♦ n media f; on ~ in media.

aversion [əˈvɜːʃn] n avversione f.

aviation [ˌeɪvɪˈeɪʃn] n aviazione f.

avid [ˈævɪd] adj avido(-a).

avocado [ˌævəˈkɑːdəʊ] (pl -s OR -es) n: ~ (pear) avocado m inv.

avoid [əˈvɔɪd] vt evitare; to ~ doing sthg evitare di fare qc.

await [əˈweɪt] vt attendere.

awake [əˈweɪk] (pt awoke, pp awoken) adj sveglio(-a) ♦ vi svegliarsi.

award [əˈwɔːd] n premio m ♦ vt: to ~ sb sthg (prize) assegnare qc a qn; (damages, compensation) accordare qc a qn.

aware [əˈweə] adj consapevole; to be ~ of rendersi conto di.

away [əˈweɪ] adv via; (look, turn) da un'altra parte; **to drive** ~ allontanarsi; **to walk** ~ allontanarsi; to

go ~ **on holiday** partire per le vacanze; **to put** sthg ~ mettere a posto qc; **to take** sthg ~ **(from sb)** portare via qc (a qn), prendere qc (a qn); **far** ~ molto lontano; **it's 10 miles** ~ **(from here)** è a 10 miglia (da qui); **the festival is two weeks** ~ mancano due settimane al festival.

awesome [ˈɔːsəm] adj (impressive) imponente; (inf: excellent) fantastico(-a).

awful [ˈɔːfəl] adj orribile; **I feel** ~ sto malissimo; **an** ~ **lot of** un mucchio di.

awfully [ˈɔːflɪ] adv (very) molto, terribilmente.

awkward [ˈɔːkwəd] adj (movement) sgraziato(-a); (position) goffo(-a); (shape, size) poco maneggevole; (situation, question) imbarazzante; (task, time) difficile.

awning [ˈɔːnɪŋ] n tenda f.

awoke [əˈwəʊk] pt → awake.

awoken [əˈwəʊkən] pp → awake.

axe [æks] n scure f.

axle [ˈæksl] n asse m.

B

BA (abbr of Bachelor of Arts) (degree) laurea f in materie umanistiche; (person) laureato m (-a f) in materie umanistiche.

babble [ˈbæbl] vi balbettare.

baby [ˈbeɪbɪ] n bambino m (-a f); **to have a** ~ avere un bambino;

sweetcorn piccole spighe di mais.

baby carriage n (Am) carrozzina f.

baby food n alimenti mpl per l'infanzia.

baby-sit vi fare da baby-sitter.

baby wipe n salvietta f umidificata (per bambini).

back [bæk] adv indietro ◆ n (of person) schiena f; (of chair) schienale m; (of car, book, bank note) retro m; (of room) fondo m; (of hand) dorso m ◆ adj (seat, wheels) posteriore ◆ vi (car, driver) fare retromarcia ◆ vt (support) appoggiare; **to put sthg ~** rimettere qc (a posto); **to arrive ~** ritornare; **to give sthg ~** restituire OR dare indietro qc; **to write ~** rispondere a qn; **at the ~ of** sul retro di, dietro; **in ~ of** (Am) sul retro di, dietro; **~ to front** davanti di dietro ❑ **back up** vt sep (support) appoggiare ◆ vi (car, driver) fare retromarcia.

backache ['bækeɪk] n mal m di schiena.

backbone ['bækbəʊn] n spina f dorsale.

back door n porta f posteriore.

backfire [,bæk'faɪə*] vi (car) fare un'autoaccensione.

background ['bækgraʊnd] n sfondo m; (of person) background m inv.

backlog ['bæklɒg] n cumulo m; **a ~ of work** del lavoro arretrato.

backpack ['bækpæk] n zaino m.

backpacker ['bækpækə*] n persona che viaggia con zaino e sacco a pelo.

back seat n sedile m posteriore.

backside [,bæk'saɪd] n (inf) sedere m.

back street n viuzza f.

backstroke ['bækstrəʊk] n dorso m (nel nuoto).

backwards ['bækwədz] adv (look) indietro; (fall, move) all'indietro; (wrong way round) al contrario.

bacon ['beɪkən] n pancetta f, bacon m; **~ and eggs** uova fpl e pancetta.

bacteria [bæk'tɪərɪə] npl batteri mpl.

bad [bæd] (compar **worse**, superl **worst**) adj cattivo(-a); (harmful) dannoso(-a); (accident, wound) brutto(-a); (eyesight, heart) debole; (arm, leg) malandato(-a); **drinking is ~ for you** bere ti fa male; **to go ~** (milk, yoghurt) andare a male; **not ~** (film, food, journey) niente male; **how are you? – not ~** come stai? – non c'è male.

badge [bædʒ] n distintivo m.

badger ['bædʒə*] n tasso m.

badly ['bædlɪ] (compar **worse**, superl **worst**) adv male; (injured) gravemente; (affected) profondamente; (very much) tanto.

badly paid [-'peɪd] adj mal pagato(-a).

badminton ['bædmɪntən] n badminton m.

bad-tempered [-'tempəd] adj irascibile.

bag [bæg] n sacchetto m; (handbag) borsa f; (piece of luggage) borsone m; **a ~ of crisps** un sacchetto di patatine.

bagel ['beɪgl] n panino a forma di ciambella.

baggage ['bægɪdʒ] n bagagli mpl.

baggage allowance n franchigia f bagaglio.

baggage reclaim n ritiro m bagagli.

baggy ['bægɪ] adj largo(-a).

bagpipes ['bægpaɪps] npl cornamusa f.

bail [beɪl] n cauzione f.

bait [beɪt] n esca f.

bake [beɪk] vt cuocere (al forno) ♦ n: **vegetable ~** verdure fpl al forno.

baked [beɪkt] adj cotto(-a) al forno.

baked Alaska [-ə'læskə] n meringata f.

baked beans npl fagioli mpl al sugo di pomodoro.

baked potato n patata f cotta al forno con la buccia.

baker ['beɪkə'] n fornaio m (-a f); **~'s (shop)** panificio m, panetteria f.

Bakewell tart ['beɪkwel-] n torta con una base di pasta frolla, uno strato di marmellata e uno di pan di Spagna alle mandorle, ricoperta da una glassa dal caratteristico aspetto a onde.

balance ['bæləns] n (of person) equilibrio m; (of bank account, remainder) saldo m ♦ vt (object) tenere in equilibrio.

balcony ['bælkənɪ] n balcone m.

bald [bɔːld] adj calvo(-a).

bale [beɪl] n balla f.

ball [bɔːl] n (SPORT) palla f; (in football, rugby) pallone m; (in golf, table tennis) pallina f; (of wool, string) gomitolo m; (dance) ballo m; **on the ~** (fig) in gamba.

ballad ['bæləd] n ballata f.

ballerina [,bælə'riːnə] n ballerina f.

ballet ['bæleɪ] n balletto m.

ballet dancer n ballerino m classico (ballerina classica f).

balloon [bə'luːn] n (at party etc) palloncino m.

ballot ['bælət] n (vote) votazione f a scrutinio segreto.

ballpoint pen ['bɔːlpɔɪnt-] n penna f a sfera.

ballroom ['bɔːlrʊm] n sala f da ballo.

ballroom dancing n ballo m liscio.

bamboo [bæm'buː] n bambù m.

bamboo shoots npl germogli mpl di bambù.

ban [bæn] n divieto m ♦ vt vietare; **to ~ sb from doing sthg** vietare a qn di fare qc.

banana [bə'nɑːnə] n banana f.

banana split n banana split f inv.

band [bænd] n (musical group) banda f; (for rock, jazz) complesso m, gruppo m; (strip of paper, rubber) striscia f.

bandage ['bændɪdʒ] n benda f ♦ vt fasciare.

B and B abbr = bed and breakfast.

bandstand ['bændstænd] n palco m dell'orchestra.

bang [bæŋ] n (of gun, explosion) scoppio m ♦ vt sbattere.

banger ['bæŋə'] n (Br: inf: sausage) salsiccia f; **~s and mash** salsicce e purè di patate.

bangle ['bæŋgl] n braccialetto m.

bangs [bæŋz] npl (Am) frangia f.

banister ['bænɪstə'] n ringhiera f.

banjo ['bændʒəʊ] n (pl -s OR -es) n banjo m inv.

bank [bæŋk] n (for money) banca f; (of river, lake) riva f; (slope) scarpata f.

bank account n conto m bancario.

bank book n libretto m di banca.

bank charges npl commissioni fpl bancarie.

bank clerk n impiegato m (-a f) di banca.

bank draft n assegno m circolare.

banker [bæŋkər] n banchiere m.

banker's card n carta f assegni.

bank holiday n (Br) giorno m festivo.

bank manager n direttore m (-trice f) di banca.

bank note n banconota f.

bankrupt [bæŋkrʌpt] adj fallito(-a).

bank statement n estratto m conto.

banner [bænər] n striscione m.

bannister [bænistər] = **banister**.

banquet [bæŋkwɪt] n (formal dinner) banchetto m; (at Indian restaurant etc) menu per più persone.

bap [bæp] n (Br) panino m.

baptize [Br bæp'taɪz, Am 'bæptaɪz] vt battezzare.

bar [ba:r] n (pub, in hotel) bar m inv; (counter in pub) banco m; (of metal, wood) sbarra f; (of chocolate) tavoletta f ♦ vt (obstruct) sbarrare; **a ~ of soap** una saponetta.

barbecue [ba:bɪkju:] n barbecue m inv ♦ vt arrostire alla griglia.

barbecue sauce n salsa pic-

cante usata per condire carne o pesce alla griglia.

barbed wire [ba:bd-] n filo m spinato.

barber [ba:bər] n barbiere m; ~**'s** (shop) barbiere m.

bar code n codice m a barre.

bare [beər] adj (feet, arms) nudo(-a); (head) scoperto(-a); (room, cupboard) vuoto(-a); **the ~ minimum** il minimo indispensabile.

barefoot [beəfʊt] adv a piedi nudi.

barely [beəlɪ] adv (hardly) appena; (with difficulty) a malapena.

bargain [ba:gɪn] n (agreement) accordo m; (cheap buy) occasione f ♦ vi (haggle) contrattare sul prezzo □ **bargain for** vt fus aspettarsi.

bargain basement n reparto m occasioni.

barge [ba:dʒ] n chiatta f □ **barge in** vi fare irruzione; **to ~ in on sb** interrompere qn.

bark [ba:k] n (of tree) corteccia f ♦ vi abbaiare.

barley [ba:lɪ] n orzo m.

barmaid [ba:meɪd] n barista f.

barman [ba:mən] (pl -men [-mən]) n barista m.

bar meal n pasto leggero servito in un bar o un pub.

barn [ba:n] n granaio m.

barometer [bə'rɒmɪtər] n barometro m.

baron [bærən] n barone m.

baroque [bə'rɒk] adj barocco(-a).

barracks [bærəks] npl caserma f.

barrage [bæra:ʒ] n (of questions)

raffica f; *(of criticism)* ondata f.

barrel ['bærəl] n *(of beer, wine, oil)* barile m; *(of gun)* canna f.

barren ['bærən] adj *(land, soil)* sterile.

barricade [,bærɪ'keɪd] n barricata f.

barrier ['bærɪə'] n barriera f.

barrister ['bærɪstə'] n *(Br)* avvocato m.

bartender ['bɑ:tendə'] n *(Am)* barista m.

barter ['bɑ:tə'] vi barattare.

base [beɪs] n base f ♦ vt: **to ~ sthg on** basare qc su; **I'm ~d in London** ho base a Londra.

baseball ['beɪsbɔ:l] n baseball m.

baseball cap n cappellino m da baseball.

basement ['beɪsmənt] n seminterrato m.

bases ['beɪsi:z] pl → **basis**.

bash [bæʃ] vt *(inf)* sbattere.

basic ['beɪsɪk] adj *(fundamental)* fondamentale; *(accommodation, meal)* semplice ❑ **basics** npl: **the ~s** i rudimenti.

basically ['beɪsɪkli] adv *(in conversation)* in sostanza; *(fundamentally)* fondamentalmente.

basil ['bæzl] n basilico m.

basin ['beɪsn] n *(washbasin)* lavabo m; *(bowl)* terrina f.

basis ['beɪsɪs] n *(pl* -ses*)* n base f; **on a weekly ~** settimanalmente; **on the ~ of** sulla base di.

basket ['bɑ:skɪt] n cesto m.

basketball ['bɑ:skɪtbɔ:l] n *(game)* pallacanestro f.

basmati rice [bəz'mæti-] n tipo di riso aromatico utilizzato nella cucina indiana.

bass¹ [beɪs] n *(singer)* basso m ♦ adj: **~ guitar** basso m.

bass² [bæs] n *(freshwater fish)* pesce m persico; *(sea fish)* spigola f, branzino m.

bassoon [bə'su:n] n fagotto m.

bastard ['bɑ:stəd] n *(vulg)* stronzo m *(-a* f*)*.

bat [bæt] n *(in cricket, baseball)* mazza f; *(in table tennis)* racchetta f; *(animal)* pipistrello m.

batch [bætʃ] n *(of goods)* lotto m; *(of people)* scaglione m.

bath [bɑ:θ] n bagno m; *(tub)* vasca f *(da bagno)* ♦ vt fare il bagno a; **to have a ~** fare il OR un bagno ❑ **baths** npl *(Br: public swimming pool)* piscina f.

bathe [beɪð] vi fare il bagno.

bathing ['beɪðɪŋ] n *(Br)* balneazione f.

bathrobe ['bɑ:θrəʊb] n *(for bathroom, swimming pool)* accappatoio m; *(dressing gown)* vestaglia f.

bathroom ['bɑ:θrʊm] n bagno m.

bathroom cabinet n armadietto m del bagno.

bathtub ['bɑ:θtʌb] n vasca f da bagno.

baton ['bætən] n *(of conductor)* bacchetta f; *(truncheon)* manganello m.

batter ['bætə'] n *(CULIN)* pastella f ♦ vt *(wife, child)* picchiare.

battered ['bætəd] adj *(CULIN)* ricoperto di pastella e fritto.

battery ['bætəri] n *(for radio)* pila f; *(for car)* batteria f.

battery charger [-,tʃɑ:dʒə'] n caricabatteria m inv.

battle ['bætl] n battaglia f.

battlefield ['bætlfi:ld] n campo

battlements

m di battaglia.

battlements ['bætlmənts] *npl*
parapetto *m*.

battleship ['bætlʃɪp] *n* corazzata *f*.

bay [beɪ] *n* (on coast) baia *f*; (for parking) posto *m* macchina.

bay leaf *n* foglia *f* d'alloro.

bay window *n* bow-window
m inv.

B & B *abbr* = **bed and breakfast**.

BC (abbr of before Christ) a.C.

be [bi:] (pt **was, were,** pp **been**) vi
1. (exist) essere; **there is c'è; there
are** ci sono; **are there any shops
near here?** ci sono dei negozi qui
vicino?

2. (referring to location) essere; **the
hotel is near the airport** l'albergo è
OR si trova vicino all'aeroporto.

3. (referring to movement): **has the
postman been?** è venuto il postino?; **have you ever been to Ireland?**
sei mai stato in Irlanda?; **I'll ~
there in ten minutes** sarò lì tra
dieci minuti.

4. (occur) essere; **my birthday is in
November** il mio compleanno è in
novembre.

5. (identifying, describing) essere;
he's a doctor è medico; **I'm Italian**
sono italiano; **I'm hot/cold** ho
caldo/freddo.

6. (referring to health) stare; **how are
you?** come sta?; **I'm fine** sto bene;
she's ill è malata.

7. (referring to age): **how old are you?**
quanti anni hai?; **I'm 14 (years old)**
ho 14 anni.

8. (referring to cost) costare; **how
much is it?** (item) quanto costa?;
(meal, shopping) quant'è?; **it's £10**

(item) costa 10 sterline; (meal, shopping) sono 10 sterline.

9. (referring to time, dates) essere;
what time is it? che ore sono?; **it's
ten o'clock** sono le dieci; **it's the
9th of April** è il 9 aprile.

10. (referring to measurement) essere;
it's 2 m wide/long è largo/lungo
2 m; **I'm 6 feet tall** sono alto
1 metro e 80; **I'm 8 stone** peso 50
chili.

11. (referring to weather) fare; **it's
hot/cold** fa caldo/freddo; **it's sunny**
c'è il sole; **it's windy** c'è vento; **it's
going to be nice today** oggi farà
bello.

◆ *aux vb* 1. (forming continuous
tense): **I'm learning Italian** sto
imparando l'italiano; **what are you
reading?** cosa stai leggendo?; cosa
leggi?; **he's arriving tomorrow** arriva domani, arriverà domani; **we've
been visiting the museum** abbiamo
visitato il museo.

2. (forming passive) essere; **the
flight was delayed** il volo è stato
ritardato.

3. (with infinitive to express order): **all
rooms are to ~ vacated by 10 a.m.**
tutte le camere devono essere lasciate libere per le 10.

4. (with infinitive to express future
tense): **the race is to start at noon**
la corsa è prevista per mezzogiorno.

5. (in tag questions): **it's cold, isn't
it?** fa freddo, (non è) vero?

beach [bi:tʃ] *n* spiaggia *f*.

bead [bi:d] *n* (of glass, wood etc)
grano *m*.

beak [bi:k] *n* becco *m*.

beaker ['bi:kəʳ] *n* bicchiere *m*.

beam [bi:m] *n* (of light) raggio *m*;
(of wood, concrete) trave *f* ◆ vi (smile)

sorridere.

bean [biːn] n fagiolo m; (of coffee) chicco m.

bean curd [-kɑːd] n tofu m.

beansprouts [ˈbiːnsprauts] npl germogli mpl di soia.

bear [beəˀ] (pt **bore**, pp **borne**) n (animal) orso m ◆ vt (support) reggere; (endure) sopportare; **to ~ left/right** tenersi sulla sinistra/destra.

bearable [ˈbeərəbl] adj sopportabile.

beard [biəd] n barba f.

bearer [ˈbeərəˀ] n (of cheque) portatore m; (of passport) titolare mf.

bearing [ˈbeərɪŋ] n (relevance) attinenza f; **to get one's ~s** orizzontarsi.

beast [biːst] n bestia f.

beat [biːt] (pt **beat**, pp **beaten** [biːtn]) n (of heart, pulse) battito m; (MUS) tempo m ◆ vt battere; (eggs, cream) sbattere ❑ **beat down** vi (sun, rain) battere ◆ vt sep: I ~ **him down to £20** gli ho fatto abbassare il prezzo a 20 sterline; **beat up** vt sep pestare.

beautiful [ˈbjuːtɪful] adj bello(-a).

beauty [ˈbjuːtɪ] n bellezza f.

beauty parlour n istituto m di bellezza.

beauty spot n (place) bellezza f naturale.

beaver [ˈbiːvəˀ] n castoro m.

became [bɪˈkeɪm] pt → become.

because [bɪˈkɒz] conj perché; **~ of** a causa di.

beckon [ˈbekən] vi: **to ~ (to)** fare cenno (a).

become [bɪˈkʌm] (pt **became**, pp become) vi diventare; **what became of him?** cosa ne è stato di lui?

bed [bed] n letto m; (of sea) fondo m; (CULIN) strato m; **in ~** a letto; **to get out of ~** alzarsi; **to go to ~** andare a letto; **to go to ~ with sb** andare a letto con qn; **to make the ~** fare il letto.

bed and breakfast n (Br) = pensione f.

<table><tr><td>*i*</td><td>**BED AND BREAKFAST**</td></tr></table>

I **"B & B"**, anche detti "guest houses", sono delle abitazioni private che hanno una o più camere riservate ad ospiti paganti. Si trovano in tutte le città e principali località turistiche e sono di solito meno care degli alberghi. Nel prezzo della camera è inclusa la tipica colazione all'inglese, a base di uova e pancetta, salsicce, pane tostato, tè o caffè.

---

bedclothes [ˈbedkləuðz] npl lenzuola fpl e coperte fpl.

bedding [ˈbedɪŋ] n biancheria f da letto.

bed linen n lenzuola fpl (e federe fpl).

bedroom [ˈbedrum] n camera f da letto.

bedside table [ˈbedsaɪd-] n comodino m.

bedsit [ˈbedˌsɪt] n (Br) camera f ammobiliata.

bedspread [ˈbedspred] n copriletto m inv.

bedtime [ˈbedtaɪm] n ora f di andare a letto.

bee [biː] n ape f.

beech [biːtʃ] n faggio m.

beef [bi:f] *n* manzo *m*; ~ Wellington pasticcio *m* di manzo.
beefburger ['bi:f,bə:gə^r] *n* hamburger *m inv*.
beehive ['bi:haɪv] *n* alveare *m*.
been [bi:n] *pp* → **be**.
beer [bɪə^r] *n* birra *f*.

---

i BEER

L a birra è di granluoga la bevanda alcolica più diffusa in Gran Bretagna. Qui, le birre si dividono in due categorie principali: "bitter" e "lager". La "bitter", conosciuta in Scozia come "heavy", è birra scura e ha un sapore amarognolo, mentre la "lager" è la birra chiara diffusa anche nel resto d'Europa. La "real ale" è un particolare tipo di birra scura, prodotto da piccole birrerie con metodi tradizionali e generalmente è più cara. Negli Stati Uniti la birra è prevalentemente birra chiara.

---

beer garden *n* giardino per i clienti di un *pub*.
beer mat *n* sottobicchiere *m*.
beetle ['bi:tl] *n* scarabeo *m*.
beetroot ['bi:tru:t] *n* barbabietola *f*.
before [bɪ'fɔ:^r] *adv* prima ◆ *prep* prima di; *(fml: in front of)* davanti a ◆ *conj*: ~ **it gets too late** prima che sia troppo tardi; **I've been there** ~ ci sono già stato; ~ **doing sthg** prima di fare qc; ~ **you leave** prima di partire; **the day** ~ il giorno prima; **the week** ~ **last** due settimane fa.
beforehand [bɪ'fɔ:hænd] *adv* in anticipo.

befriend [bɪ'frend] *vt* trattare da amico.
beg [beg] *vi* elemosinare ◆ *vt*: to ~ **sb to do sthg** supplicare qn di fare qc; to ~ **for sthg** elemosinare qc.
began [bɪ'gæn] *pt* → **begin**.
beggar ['begə^r] *n* mendicante *mf*.
begin [bɪ'gɪn] *(pt* **began**, *pp* **begun**) *vt & vi* cominciare, iniziare; to ~ **doing** OR **to do sthg** cominciare a fare qc; to ~ **by doing sthg** cominciare col fare qc; to ~ **with** *(at the start)* all'inizio; *(firstly)* per prima cosa.
beginner [bɪ'gɪnə^r] *n* principiante *mf*.
beginning [bɪ'gɪnɪŋ] *n* inizio *m*.
begun [bɪ'gʌn] *pp* → **begin**.
behalf [bɪ'hɑ:f] *n*: **on ~ of** a nome di.
behave [bɪ'heɪv] *vi* comportarsi; to ~ **(o.s.)** *(be good)* comportarsi bene.
behavior [bɪ'heɪvjə^r] *(Am)* = **behaviour**.
behaviour [bɪ'heɪvjə^r] *n* comportamento *m*.
behind [bɪ'haɪnd] *adv (at the back)* dietro; *(late)* indietro ◆ *prep (at the back of)* dietro ◆ *n (inf)* dietro *m*; **to leave sthg** ~ dimenticare qc; **to stay** ~ restare indietro; **we're all** ~ **you** *(supporting)* siamo tutti con te.
beige [beɪʒ] *adj* beige (*inv*).
being [bi:ɪŋ] *n* essere *m*; **to come into** ~ nascere.
belated [bɪ'leɪtɪd] *adj* tardivo(-a).
belch [beltʃ] *vi* ruttare.
Belgian ['beldʒən] *adj* belga ◆ *n* belga *mf*.
Belgian waffle *n (Am)* ciald

dalla caratteristica superficie a quadretti che si mangia con sciroppo d'acero, panna o frutta.

Belgium ['beldʒəm] n il Belgio.

belief [bɪ'li:f] n (faith) fede f; (opinion) convinzione f.

believe [bɪ'li:v] vt credere ♦ vi: to ~ in (God) credere in; to ~ in doing sthg credere che sia giusto fare qc.

believer [bɪ'li:vər] n credente mf.

bell [bel] n (of church) campana f; (of phone) suoneria f; (of door) campanello m.

bellboy ['belbɔɪ] n fattorino m d'albergo.

bellow ['beləʊ] vi muggire.

belly ['belɪ] n (inf) pancia f.

belly button n (inf) ombelico m.

belong [bɪ'lɒŋ] vi (be in right place) essere al suo posto; to ~ to (property) appartenere a; (to club, party) far parte di; **where does this ~?** dove sta questo?

belongings [bɪ'lɒŋɪŋz] npl effetti mpl personali.

below [bɪ'ləʊ] adv sotto; (downstairs) di sotto; (in text) qui sotto ♦ prep sotto.

belt [belt] n (for clothes) cintura f; (TECH) cinghia f.

beltway ['beltweɪ] n (Am) raccordo m anulare.

bench [bentʃ] n panchina f.

bend [bend] (pt & pp bent) n (in road) curva f; (in river) ansa f; (in pipe) gomito m ♦ vt piegare ♦ vi (road, river, pipe) fare una curva ♦ **bend down** vi abbassarsi; **bend over** vi chinarsi.

beneath [bɪ'ni:θ] adv & prep sotto.

beneficial [,benɪ'fɪʃl] adj benefico(-a).

benefit ['benɪfɪt] n (advantage) beneficio m; (money) indennità f inv ♦ vt giovare a ♦ vi: to ~ (from) beneficiare (di); for the ~ of per.

benign [bɪ'naɪn] adj (MED) benigno(-a).

bent [bent] pt & pp → bend.

bereaved [bɪ'ri:vd] adj (family) del defunto.

beret ['bereɪ] n basco m.

Bermuda shorts [bə'mju:də-] npl bermuda mpl.

berry ['berɪ] n bacca f.

berserk [bə'zɜ:k] adj: to go ~ andare su tutte le furie.

berth [bɜ:θ] n (for ship) ormeggio m; (in ship, train) cuccetta f.

beside [bɪ'saɪd] prep (next to) accanto a; that's ~ the point questo non c'entra.

besides [bɪ'saɪdz] adv inoltre ♦ prep oltre a.

best [best] adj migliore ♦ adv meglio ♦ n: the ~ il migliore (la migliore); **a pint of ~** (beer) = un boccale di birra scura; **I like this one ~** questo mi piace più di tutti; **she played ~** ha giocato meglio di tutti; **the ~ thing to do is ...** la miglior cosa da fare è ...; to **make the ~ of sthg** accontentarsi di qc; to **do one's ~** fare del proprio meglio; **'~ before ...'** 'da consumarsi preferibilmente entro ...'; at ~ per bene che vada; **all the ~!** auguri!

best man n testimone m (di nozze).

best-seller [-'selər] n (book) best seller m inv.

bet [bet] (pt & pp bet) n scom-

betray

messa *f* ♦ *vt* scommettere ♦ *vi*: to ~ (on) scommettere (su); I ~ (that) you can't do it scommetto che non sei capace di farlo.

betray [bɪ'treɪ] *vt* tradire.

better ['betə'] *adj* migliore ♦ *adv* meglio; **she's ~ at tennis than me** è più brava di me a tennis; **are you ~ now?** stai meglio adesso?; **you had ~ ... faresti meglio a ...; to get ~** migliorare.

betting ['betɪŋ] *n* scommesse *fpl.*

betting shop *n* (Br) = sala *f* scommesse.

between [bɪ'twiːn] *prep* tra, fra ♦ *adv* (in time) nel frattempo; **in ~** (in space) in mezzo; (in time) nel frattempo.

beverage ['bevərɪdʒ] *n* (fml) bevanda *f.*

beware [bɪ'weə'] *vi*: to ~ of stare attento a; '~ of the dog' 'attenti al cane'.

bewildered [bɪ'wɪldəd] *adj* sconcertato(-a).

beyond [bɪ'jɒnd] *prep* oltre ♦ *adv* più avanti; ~ doubt senza dubbio; ~ reach irraggiungibile.

biased ['baɪəst] *adj* di parte.

bib [bɪb] *n* (for baby) bavaglino *m.*

bible ['baɪbl] *n* bibbia *f.*

biceps ['baɪseps] *n* bicipite *m.*

bicycle ['baɪsɪkl] *n* bicicletta *f.*

bicycle path *n* pista *f* ciclabile.

bicycle pump *n* pompa *f* per la bicicletta.

bid [bɪd] (pt & pp bid) *n* (at auction) offerta *f*; (attempt) tentativo *m* ♦ *vt* (money) fare un'offerta di ♦ *vi*: to ~ (for) fare un'offerta (per).

bidet ['biːdeɪ] *n* bidè *m inv.*

big [bɪg] *adj* grande; (problem, mistake, risk) grosso(-a); **my ~ brother** mio fratello maggiore; **how ~ is it?** quanto è grande?

bike [baɪk] *n* (inf) (bicycle) bici *f inv*; (motorcycle) moto *f inv.*

biking ['baɪkɪŋ] *n*: to go ~ (on bicycle) andare in bicicletta; (on motorcycle) andare in moto.

bikini [bɪ'kiːnɪ] *n* bikini® *m inv.*

bikini bottom *n* pezzo *m* di sotto del bikini®.

bikini top *n* pezzo *m* di sopra del bikini®.

bilingual [baɪ'lɪŋgwəl] *adj* bilingue.

bill [bɪl] *n* (for meal, hotel room) conto *m*; (for electricity etc) bolletta *f*; (Am: bank note) banconota *f*; (at cinema, theatre) programma *m*; (POL) proposta *f* di legge; **can I have the ~, please?** il conto, per favore.

billboard ['bɪlbɔːd] *n* tabellone *m.*

billfold ['bɪlfəʊld] *n* (Am) portafoglio *m.*

billiards ['bɪljədz] *n* biliardo *m.*

billion ['bɪljən] *n* (thousand million) miliardo *m*; (Br: million million) mille miliardi.

bin [bɪn] *n* (rubbish bin) pattumiera *f*; (wastepaper bin) cestino *m*; (for flour) barattolo *m*; (on plane) armadietto *m* in alto; **bread ~** portapane *m inv.*

bind [baɪnd] (pt & pp bound) *vt* (tie up) legare.

binding ['baɪndɪŋ] *n* (of book) rilegatura *f*; (for ski) attacco *m.*

bingo ['bɪŋgəʊ] *n* = tombola *f.*

i   BINGO

Questo gioco, simile alla tombola, è molto popolare in Gran Bretagna. I giocatori comprano delle cartelle con dei numeri, da contrassegnare man mano che vengono estratti. Vince chi completa per primo una fila di numeri o l'intera cartella. Si gioca in grandi sale, spesso ex cinema ristrutturati, e si vincono premi, talvolta in denaro.

binoculars [bɪˈnɒkjʊləz] *npl* binocolo *m*.

biodegradable [ˌbaɪəʊdɪˈgreɪdəbl] *adj* biodegradabile.

biography [baɪˈɒgrəfɪ] *n* biografia *f*.

biological [ˌbaɪəˈlɒdʒɪkl] *adj* biologico(-a).

biology [baɪˈɒlədʒɪ] *n* biologia *f*.

birch [bɜ:tʃ] *n* betulla *f*.

bird [bɜ:d] *n* uccello *m*; (*Br: inf: woman*) pollastrella *f*.

bird-watching [-ˌwɒtʃɪŋ] *n* osservazione *f* degli uccelli.

Biro® [ˈbaɪərəʊ] (*pl* -s) *n* biro® *f inv*.

birth [bɜ:θ] *n* nascita *f*; **by** ~ di nascita; **to give** ~ **to** dare alla luce, partorire.

birth certificate *n* certificato *m* di nascita.

birth control *n* controllo *m* delle nascite.

birthday [ˈbɜ:θdeɪ] *n* compleanno *m*; **happy** ~! buon compleanno!

birthday card *n* biglietto *m* d'auguri di compleanno.

birthday party *n* festa *f* di compleanno.

birthplace [ˈbɜ:θpleɪs] *n* luogo *m* di nascita.

biscuit [ˈbɪskɪt] *n* (*Br*) biscotto *m*; (*Am: scone*) focaccina di pasta non lievitata da mangiare con burro e marmellata o insieme a piatti salati.

bishop [ˈbɪʃəp] *n* (RELIG) vescovo *m*; (*in chess*) alfiere *m*.

bistro [ˈbi:strəʊ] (*pl* -s) *n* ristorantino *m*.

bit [bɪt] *pt* → **bite** ♦ *n* (*piece*) pezzetto *m*; (*of drill*) punta *f*; (*of bridle*) morso *m*; (*amount*): **a** ~ **of** money un po' di soldi; **to do a** ~ **of reading** leggere un po'; **a** ~ per niente; ~ **by** ~ a poco a poco.

bitch [bɪtʃ] *n* (*vulg: woman*) stronza *f*; (*dog*) cagna *f*.

bite [baɪt] (*pt* **bit**, *pp* **bitten**) *n* morso *m*; (*from insect*) puntura *f* ♦ *vt* mordere; (*subj: insect*) pungere; **to have a** ~ **to eat** mangiare un boccone.

bitter [ˈbɪtəʳ] *adj* (*taste, food*) amaro(-a); (*weather, wind*) pungente; (*person*) amareggiato(-a); (*argument, conflict*) aspro(-a) ♦ *n* (*Br: beer*) tipo di birra amarognola.

bitter lemon *n* limonata *f* amara.

bizarre [bɪˈzɑ:ʳ] *adj* bizzarro(-a).

black [blæk] *adj* nero(-a) ♦ *n* (*colour*) nero *m*; (*person*) negro *m* (a *f*) ❑ **black out** *vi* perdere conoscenza.

black and white *adj* in bianco e nero.

blackberry [ˈblækbrɪ] *n* mora *f*.

blackbird [ˈblækbɜ:d] *n* merlo *m*.

blackboard [ˈblækbɔ:d] *n* lavagna *f*.

black cherry n ciliegia f nera.

blackcurrant ['blæk'kʌrənt] n ribes m inv nero.

black eye n occhio m nero.

Black Forest gâteau n torta f di cioccolato e panna.

black ice n strato m di ghiaccio invisibile.

blackmail ['blækmeɪl] n ricatto m ♦ vt ricattare.

blackout ['blækaʊt] n (power cut) black-out m inv.

black pepper n pepe m nero.

black pudding n (Br) sanguinaccio m.

blacksmith ['blæksmɪθ] n fabbro m.

bladder ['blædər] n vescica f.

blade [bleɪd] n (of knife, saw) lama f; (of propeller, oar) pala f; (of grass) filo m.

blame [bleɪm] n colpa f ♦ vt incolpare; to ~ sb for sthg incolpare qn di qc; to ~ sthg on sb dare a qn la colpa di qc.

bland [blænd] adj (food) insipido(-a).

blank [blæŋk] adj (space, cassette) vuoto(-a); (page) bianco(-a); (expression) assente ♦ n (empty space) spazio m (in) bianco.

blank cheque n assegno m in bianco.

blanket ['blæŋkɪt] n coperta f.

blast [blɑːst] n (explosion) esplosione f; (of wind) raffica f; (of air) folata f ♦ excl (inf) maledizione!; at full ~ a tutto volume.

blaze [bleɪz] n (fire) incendio m ♦ vi (fire) ardere; (sun, light) risplendere.

blazer ['bleɪzər] n blazer m inv.

bleach [bliːtʃ] n candeggina f ♦ vt (clothes) candeggiare; (hair) decolorare.

bleak [bliːk] adj triste.

bleed [bliːd] (pt & pp **bled** [bled]) vi sanguinare.

blend [blend] n (of coffee, whisky) miscela f ♦ vt mescolare.

blender ['blendər] n frullatore m.

bless [bles] vt benedire; ~ you! (said after sneeze) salute!

blessing ['blesɪŋ] n benedizione f.

blew [bluː] pt → **blow.**

blind [blaɪnd] adj cieco(-a) ♦ n (for window) tendina f avvolgibile ♦ npl: the ~ i non vedenti.

blind corner n svolta f senza visibilità.

blindfold ['blaɪndfəʊld] n benda f ♦ vt bendare.

blind spot n (AUT) punto m senza visibilità.

blink [blɪŋk] vi battere le palpebre.

blinkers ['blɪŋkəz] npl (Br) paraocchi mpl.

bliss [blɪs] n estasi f.

blister ['blɪstər] n vescica f.

blizzard ['blɪzəd] n bufera f di neve.

bloated ['bləʊtɪd] adj (after eating) strapieno(-a).

blob [blɒb] n (of paint) chiazza f.

block [blɒk] n (of stone, wood, ice) blocco m; (building) palazzo m; (Am: in town, city) isolato m ♦ vt (obstruct) bloccare; to have a ~ed (up) nose avere il naso chiuso ☐ **block up** vt sep ostruire.

blockage ['blɒkɪdʒ] n ostruzione f.

board

block capitals *npl* stampatello *m* maiuscolo.

block of flats *n* condominio *m*.

bloke [bləʊk] *n* (*Br: inf*) tipo *m*, tizio *m*.

blond [blɒnd] *adj* biondo(-a) ♦ biondo *m*.

blonde [blɒnd] *adj* biondo(-a) ♦ *n* bionda *f*.

blood [blʌd] *n* sangue *m*.

blood donor *n* donatore *m* (-trice *f*) di sangue.

blood group *n* gruppo *m* sanguigno.

blood poisoning *n* setticemia *f*.

blood pressure *n* pressione *f* sanguigna; **to have high ~** avere la pressione alta; **to have low ~** avere la pressione bassa.

bloodshot [ˈblʌdʃɒt] *adj* arrossato(-a).

blood test *n* analisi *f inv* del sangue.

blood transfusion *n* trasfusione *f* di sangue.

bloody [ˈblʌdɪ] *adj* (*hands, handkerchief*) insanguinato(-a); (*Br: vulg: damn*) maledetto(-a) ♦ *adv* (*Br: vulg*) veramente.

bloody mary [-ˈmeərɪ] *n* Bloody Mary *m inv*.

bloom [bluːm] *n* fiore *m* ♦ *vi* fiorire; **in ~** in fiore.

blossom [ˈblɒsəm] *n* fiori *mpl*.

blot [blɒt] *n* macchia *f*.

blotch [blɒtʃ] *n* chiazza *f*.

blotting paper [ˈblɒtɪŋ-] *n* carta *f* assorbente.

blouse [blaʊz] *n* camicetta *f*.

blow [bləʊ] (*pt* blew, *pp* blown) *vt* (*subj: wind*) soffiare; (*whistle, trumpet*) suonare; (*bubbles*) fare ♦ *vi* soffiare; (*fuse*) saltare ♦ *n* colpo *m*; **to ~ one's nose** soffiarsi il naso ☐ **blow up** *vt sep* (*cause to explode*) far saltare in aria; (*inflate*) gonfiare ♦ *vi* (*explode*) saltare in aria.

blow-dry *n* piega *f* föhn ♦ *vt* fonare.

blown [bləʊn] *pp* → **blow**.

BLT *n* panino imbottito con pancetta, lattuga e pomodoro.

blue [bluː] *adj* azzurro(-a); (*film*) spinto(-a) ♦ *n* azzurro *m* ☐ **blues** *n* (*MUS*) blues *m*.

bluebell [ˈbluːbel] *n* campanula *f*.

blueberry [ˈbluːbərɪ] *n* mirtillo *m*.

bluebottle [ˈbluːbɒtl] *n* moscone *m*.

blue cheese *n* formaggio con muffa di stagionatura.

bluff [blʌf] *n* (*cliff*) promontorio *m* ♦ *vi* bleffare.

blunder [ˈblʌndəʳ] *n* cantonata *f*.

blunt [blʌnt] *adj* (*pencil*) spuntato(-a); (*knife*) non affilato(-a); (*fig: person*) brusco(-a).

blurred [blɜːd] *adj* (*photo*) sfocato(-a); (*vision*) offuscato(-a).

blush [blʌʃ] *vi* arrossire.

blusher [ˈblʌʃəʳ] *n* fard *m inv*.

blustery [ˈblʌstərɪ] *adj* burrascoso(-a).

board [bɔːd] *n* (*plank*) tavola *f*; (*notice board, for games*) tabellone *m*; (*for chess*) scacchiera *f*; (*blackboard*) lavagna *f*; (*of company*) consiglio *m* d'amministrazione ♦ *vt* (*plane, ship*) imbarcarsi su; (*bus*) salire su; **~ and lodging** vitto e alloggio; **full ~** pensione *f* comple-

board game

ta; **half ~** mezza pensione; **on ~** *adv* a bordo ♦ *prep* su.

board game *n* gioco *m* di società.

boarding ['bɔːdɪŋ] *n* imbarco *m*.

boarding card *n* carta *f* d'imbarco.

boardinghouse ['bɔːdɪŋhaʊs], *pl* -**hauzɪz**] *n* pensione *f*.

boarding school *n* collegio *m*.

board of directors *n* consiglio *m* d'amministrazione.

boast [bəʊst] *vi*: **to ~ (about sthg)** vantarsi (di qc).

boat [bəʊt] *n* (*small*) barca *f*; (*large*) nave *f*; **by ~** in barca.

bob [bɒb] *n* (*hairstyle*) carré *m inv*.

bobby pin ['bɒbɪ-] *n* (*Am*) forcina *f*.

bodice ['bɒdɪs] *n* corpino *m*.

body ['bɒdɪ] *n* corpo *m*; (*of car*) carrozzeria *f*; (*organization*) organismo *m*.

bodyguard ['bɒdɪgɑːd] *n* (*person*) guardia *f* del corpo.

bodywork ['bɒdɪwɜːk] *n* carrozzeria *f*.

bog [bɒg] *n* pantano *m*.

bogus ['bəʊgəs] *adj* falso(-a).

boil [bɔɪl] *vt* (*water*) bollire, far bollire; (*kettle*) mettere a bollire; (*food*) lessare ♦ *vi* bollire ♦ *n* (*on skin*) foruncolo *m*.

boiled egg [bɔɪld-] *n* uovo *m* alla coque.

boiled potatoes [bɔɪld-] *npl* patate *fpl* lesse.

boiler ['bɔɪlə˚] *n* caldaia *f*.

boiling (hot) ['bɔɪlɪŋ-] *adj* (*inf*) (*water*) bollente; **I'm ~** sto morendo di caldo; **it's ~** si scoppia dal caldo.

bold [bəʊld] *adj* (*brave*) audace.

bollard ['bɒlɑːd] *n* (*Br: on road*) colonnina *f* spartitraffico.

bolt [bəʊlt] *n* (*on door, window*) chiavistello *m*; (*screw*) bullone *m* ♦ *vt* (*door, window*) sprangare.

bomb [bɒm] *n* bomba *f* ♦ *vt* bombardare.

bombard [bɒm'bɑːd] *vt* bombardare.

bomb scare *n* allarme causato dalla presunta presenza di una bomba.

bomb shelter *n* rifugio *m* antiaereo.

bond [bɒnd] *n* (*tie, connection*) legame *m*.

bone [bəʊn] *n* (*of person, animal*) osso *m*; (*of fish*) lisca *f*.

boned [bəʊnd] *adj* (*chicken*) disossato(-a); (*fish*) senza lische.

boneless ['bəʊnləs] *adj* (*chicken, pork*) disossato(-a).

bonfire ['bɒn,faɪə˚] *n* falò *m inv*.

bonnet ['bɒnɪt] *n* (*Br: of car*) cofano *m*.

bonus ['bəʊnəs] (*pl* -**es**) *n* (*extra money*) gratifica *f*; (*additional advantage*) extra *m inv*.

bony ['bəʊnɪ] *adj* (*fish*) pieno(-a) di spine; (*chicken*) pieno di ossi.

boo [buː] *vi* fischiare.

boogie ['buːgɪ] *vi* (*inf*) ballare.

book [bʊk] *n* libro *m*; (*for writing in*) quaderno *m*; (*of tickets, stamps*) blocchetto *m*; (*of matches*) pacchetto *m* ♦ *vt* (*reserve*) prenotare □ **book in** *vi* (*at hotel*) registrarsi.

bookable ['bʊkəbl] *adj* (*seats, flight*) prenotabile.

bookcase ['bʊkkeɪs] *n* libreria *f*

booking ['bʊkɪŋ] n (reservation) prenotazione f.

booking office n (at theatre) botteghino m; (at station) ufficio m prenotazioni.

bookkeeping ['bʊk,ki:pɪŋ] n contabilità f.

booklet ['bʊklɪt] n opuscolo m.

bookmaker's ['bʊk,meɪkəz] n ≃ sala f scommesse.

bookmark ['bʊkma:k] n segnalibro m.

bookshelf ['bʊkʃelf] (pl -shelves [-ʃelvz]) n scaffale m.

bookshop ['bʊkʃɒp] n libreria f.

bookstall ['bʊkstɔ:l] n bancarella f di libri.

bookstore ['bʊkstɔ:ʳ] = bookshop.

book token n buono m libri.

boom [bu:m] n (sudden growth) boom m inv ◆ vi (voice, guns) tuonare.

boost [bu:st] vt (profits, production) incrementare; (confidence) aumentare; (spirits) sollevare.

booster ['bu:stəʳ] n (injection) richiamo m.

boot [bu:t] n (shoe) stivale m; (for walking) scarpone m; (for football) scarpetta f; (Br: of car) bagagliaio m.

booth [bu:ð] n (for telephone) cabina f; (at fairground) baraccone m.

booze [bu:z] n (inf) alcool m ◆ vi (inf) sbevazzare.

bop [bɒp] n (inf: dance): to have a ~ ballare.

border ['bɔ:dəʳ] n (of country) frontiera f; (edge) orlo m; the **Borders** zona di confine fra Inghilterra

e Scozia.

bore [bɔ:ʳ] pt → bear ◆ n (inf) noia f ◆ vt (person) annoiare; (hole) praticare.

bored [bɔ:d] adj annoiato(-a).

boredom ['bɔ:dəm] n noia f.

boring ['bɔ:rɪŋ] adj noioso(-a).

born [bɔ:n] adj: to be ~ nascere.

borne [bɔ:n] pp → bear.

borough ['bʌrə] n ≃ comune m.

borrow ['bɒrəʊ] vt: to ~ sthg (from sb) prendere in prestito qc (da qn).

bosom ['bʊzəm] n seno m.

boss [bɒs] n capo m ❑ **boss around** vt sep dare ordini a.

bossy ['bɒsɪ] adj autoritario(-a).

botanical garden [bə'tænɪkl-] n giardino m botanico.

both [bəʊθ] adj & pron tutti(-e) e due, entrambi(-e) ◆ adv: ~ ... and sia ... sia ... che; it is ~ **stupid and dangerous** è stupido e pericoloso insieme; ~ **of them** entrambi, tutti e due; ~ **of us** entrambi, tutti e due.

bother ['bɒðəʳ] vt (worry) preoccupare; (annoy, pester) disturbare ◆ vi preoccuparsi ◆ n (trouble) fatica f; I can't be ~ed non ne ho voglia; don't ~, I'll go! non ti scomodare, vado io!; it's no ~! non c'è problema!

bottle ['bɒtl] n bottiglia f; (for baby) biberon m inv.

bottle bank n campana f per la raccolta del vetro.

bottled ['bɒtld] adj imbottigliato(-a); ~ **beer** birra in bottiglia; ~ **water** acqua minerale.

bottle opener [-,əʊpnəʳ] n apribottiglie m inv.

bottom ['bɒtəm] *adj* (lowest, last) ultimo(-a); (worst) più basso(-a) ◆ *n* fondo *m*; (of hill) piedi *mpl*; (buttocks) sedere *m*; **the ~ shelf** l'ultimo scaffale in basso; **~ gear** prima *f*.

bought [bɔːt] *pt & pp* → **buy**.

boulder ['bəʊldə'] *n* masso *m*.

bounce [baʊns] *vi* (rebound) rimbalzare; (jump) saltare; (cheque) essere scoperto.

bouncer ['baʊnsə'] *n* (inf) buttafuori *m inv*.

bouncy ['baʊnsı] *adj* (person) pimpante.

bound [baʊnd] *pt & pp* → **bind** ◆ *vi* saltellare ◆ *adj*: **it's ~ to rain** pioverà di sicuro; **to be ~ for** essere diretto(-a) a; **it's out of ~s** l'accesso è vietato.

boundary ['baʊndrı] *n* confine *m*.

bouquet [bʊ'keı] *n* bouquet *m inv*; (big bunch of flowers) mazzo *m* di fiori.

bourbon ['bɜːbən] *n* bourbon *m inv*.

bout [baʊt] *n* (of illness) attacco *m*; (of activity) periodo *m*.

boutique [buːˈtiːk] *n* boutique *f inv*.

bow¹ [baʊ] *n* (of head) inchino *m*; (of ship) prua *f* ◆ *vi* inchinarsi.

bow² [bəʊ] *n* (knot) fiocco *m*; (weapon) arco *m*; (MUS) archetto *m*.

bowels ['baʊəlz] *npl* (ANAT) intestino *m*.

bowl [bəʊl] *n* ciotola *f*; (for washing) bacinella *f*; (of toilet) tazza *f*; **fruit ~** fruttiera *f*; **salad ~** insalatiera *f*; **sugar ~** zuccheriera *f* ❑ **bowls** *npl* bocce *fpl*.

bowling alley ['bəʊlıŋ-] *n* (building) bowling *m inv*.

bowling green ['bəʊlıŋ-] *n* campo *m* di bocce.

bow tie [,bəʊ-] *n* farfalla *f*.

box [bɒks] *n* scatola *f*; (on form) casella *f*; (in theatre) palco *m* ◆ *vi* fare del pugilato; **a ~ of chocolates** una scatola di cioccolatini; **jewellery ~** portagioie *m inv*; **tool ~** cassetta *f* degli attrezzi.

boxer ['bɒksə'] *n* (fighter) pugile *m*.

boxer shorts *npl* boxer *mpl*.

boxing ['bɒksıŋ] *n* pugilato *m*.

Boxing Day *n* Santo Stefano *m*.

BOXING DAY

Giorno festivo in tutta la Gran Bretagna, il 26 dicembre era in passato il giorno in cui i garzoni di bottega e i servitori ricevevano in dono somme extra di denaro dette "Christmas boxes". Oggi la tradizione sopravvive sotto forma di mance elargite ai lattai, agli spazzini e ai ragazzi che consegnano i giornali.

boxing gloves *npl* guantoni *mpl*.

boxing ring *n* ring *m inv*.

box office *n* botteghino *m*.

boy [bɔı] *n* ragazzo *m*; (son) figlio *m* ◆ *excl* (inf): **(oh) ~!** accidenti!

boycott ['bɔıkɒt] *vt* boicottare.

boyfriend ['bɔıfrend] *n* ragazzo *m*.

boy scout *n* boy-scout *m inv*.

BR *abbr* = **British Rail**.

bra [brɑː] *n* reggiseno *m*.

brace [breıs] *n* (for teeth) apparecchio *m* (per i denti) ❑ **braces** *npl*

(Br) bretelle *fpl.*

bracelet [ˈbreɪslɪt] *n* braccialetto *m.*

bracken [ˈbrækn] *n* felce *f.*

bracket [ˈbrækɪt] *n (written symbol)* parentesi *f inv; (support)* reggimensola *m inv.*

brag [bræg] *vi* vantarsi.

braid [breɪd] *n (hairstyle)* treccia *f; (on clothes)* passamano *m.*

brain [breɪn] *n* cervello *m.*

brainy [ˈbreɪnɪ] *adj (inf)* sveglio(-a).

braised [breɪzd] *adj* brasato(-a).

brake [breɪk] *n* freno *m* ♦ *vi* frenare.

brake block *n* freno *m.*

brake fluid *n* fluido *m* dei freni.

brake light *n* stop *m inv.*

brake pad *n* pastiglia *f (del freno).*

brake pedal *n (*pedale *m* del) freno *m.*

bran [bræn] *n* crusca *f.*

branch [brɑːntʃ] *n* ramo *m; (of bank, company)* filiale *f* ❑ **branch off** *vi* diramarsi.

branch line *n* diramazione *f.*

brand [brænd] *n* marca *f* ♦ *vt:* **to ~ sb (as)** bollare qn (come).

brand-new *adj* nuovo(-a) di zecca.

brandy [ˈbrændɪ] *n* brandy *m inv.*

brash [bræʃ] *adj (pej)* sfrontato(-a).

brass [brɑːs] *n* ottone *m.*

brass band *n* fanfara *f.*

brasserie [ˈbræsərɪ] *n* = trattoria *f.*

brassiere [*Br* ˈbræsɪəʳ, *Am* brəˈzɪr] *n* reggiseno *m.*

brat [bræt] *n (inf)* discolo *m (-a f).*

brave [breɪv] *adj* coraggioso(-a).

bravery [ˈbreɪvərɪ] *n* coraggio *m.*

bravo [ˌbrɑːˈvəʊ] *excl* bravo(-a)!

brawl [brɔːl] *n* rissa *f.*

Brazil [brəˈzɪl] *n* il Brasile.

brazil nut *n* noce *f* del Brasile.

breach [briːtʃ] *vt (contract)* rompere; *(confidence)* tradire.

bread [bred] *n* pane *m;* **~ and butter** pane *m* imburrato.

bread bin *n (Br)* portapane *m inv.*

breadboard [ˈbredbɔːd] *n* tagliere *m (per il pane).*

bread box *(Am)* = **bread bin**.

breadcrumbs [ˈbredkrʌmz] *npl* pangrattato *m.*

breaded [ˈbredɪd] *adj* impanato(-a).

bread knife *n* coltello *m* da pane.

bread roll *n* panino *m.*

breadth [bretθ] *n* larghezza *f,* ampiezza *f.*

break [breɪk] *(vt* broke, *pp* broken) *n (interruption)* interruzione *f; (rest, pause)* pausa *f; (SCH)* ricreazione *f* ♦ *vt* rompere; *(law, rule)* infrangere; *(promise, contract)* non rispettare; *(a record)* battere ♦ *vi* rompersi; *(dawn)* spuntare; *(voice)* cambiare; **without a ~** senza sosta; **a lucky ~** un colpo di fortuna; **to ~ one's leg** rompersi la gamba; **to ~ the news to sb** dare una notizia a qn; **to ~ one's journey** fare una sosta ❑ **break down** *vi (car, machine)* guastarsi ♦ *vt (door, barrier)* abbattere; **break in** *vi (enter by force)* fare irruzione;

break off vt (detach) staccare; (holiday) interrompere ♦ vi (stop suddenly) interrompersi; **break out** vi (fire, war, panic) scoppiare; **he broke out in a rash** gli è venuto uno sfogo; **break up** vi (with spouse, partner) lasciarsi; (meeting, marriage, school) finire.

breakage ['breɪkɪdʒ] n danni mpl.

breakdown ['breɪkdaʊn] n (of car) guasto m; (in communications, negotiation) interruzione f; (mental) esaurimento m nervoso.

breakdown truck n carro m attrezzi.

breakfast ['brekfəst] n colazione f; **to have ~** fare colazione; **to have sthg for ~** mangiare qc a colazione.

breakfast cereal n cereali mpl.

break-in n scasso m.

breakwater ['breɪk,wɔːtər] n frangiflutti m inv.

breast [brest] n (of woman) seno m; (of chicken, duck) petto m.

breastbone ['brestbəʊn] n sterno m.

breast-feed vt allattare (al seno).

breaststroke ['breststrəʊk] n nuoto m a rana.

breath [breθ] n (of person) alito m; (air inhaled) respiro m; **out of ~** senza fiato; **to go for a ~ of fresh air** andare a prendere una boccata d'aria.

Breathalyser® ['breθəlaɪzər] n (Br) etilometro m.

Breathalyzer® ['breθəlaɪzər] (Am) = **Breathalyser®**.

breathe [briːð] vi respirare ❑

breathe in vi inspirare; **breathe out** vi espirare.

breathtaking ['breθ,teɪkɪŋ] adj mozzafiato (inv).

breed [briːd] (pt & pp bred [bred]) n (of animal) razza f; (of plant) varietà f inv ♦ vt (animals) allevare ♦ vi riprodursi.

breeze [briːz] n brezza f.

breezy ['briːzɪ] adj (weather, day) ventilato(-a).

brew [bruː] vt (tea) fare ♦ vi: **the tea/coffee is ~ed** il tè/caffè è pronto.

brewery ['brʊərɪ] n fabbrica f di birra.

bribe [braɪb] n bustarella f, tangente f ♦ vt corrompere.

bric-a-brac ['brɪkəbræk] n cianfrusaglie fpl.

brick [brɪk] n mattone m.

bricklayer ['brɪk,leɪər] n muratore m.

brickwork ['brɪkwɜːk] n muratura f di mattoni.

bride [braɪd] n sposa f.

bridegroom ['braɪdgrʊm] n sposo m.

bridesmaid ['braɪdzmeɪd] n damigella f d'onore.

bridge [brɪdʒ] n ponte m; (card game) bridge m.

bridle ['braɪdl] n briglia f.

bridle path n sentiero m (per cavalli).

brief [briːf] adj breve ♦ vt mettere al corrente; **in ~** in breve ❑ **briefs** npl mutande fpl.

briefcase ['briːfkeɪs] n (hard) ventiquatt'ore f inv; (soft) cartella f.

briefly ['briːflɪ] adv brevemente.

brigade [brɪˈɡeɪd] *n* brigata *f*.

bright [braɪt] *adj* (*light, sun*) vivido(-a); (*weather, room, idea*) luminoso(-a); (*clever*) sveglio(-a); (*lively, cheerful, in colour*) vivace.

brilliant [ˈbrɪljənt] *adj* brillante; (*inf: wonderful*) stupendo(-a).

brim [brɪm] *n* (*of hat*) tesa *f*; **it's full to the ~** è pieno fino all'orlo.

brine [braɪn] *n* salamoia *f*.

bring [brɪŋ] (*pt & pp* **brought**) *vt* portare ❏ **bring along** *vt sep* portare; **bring back** *vt sep* riportare; **bring in** *vt sep* (*introduce*) introdurre; (*earn*) rendere; **bring out** *vt sep* (*new product*) far uscire; **bring up** *vt sep* (*child*) allevare; (*subject*) sollevare; (*food*) vomitare.

brink [brɪŋk] *n*: **on the ~ of sthg** sull'orlo di qc; **on the ~ of doing sthg** sul punto di fare qc.

brisk [brɪsk] *adj* (*quick*) rapido(-a); (*efficient*) energico(-a); (*wind*) pungente.

bristle [ˈbrɪsl] *n* (*of brush*) setola *f*; (*on chin*) pelo *m* ispido.

Britain [ˈbrɪtn] *n* la Gran Bretagna.

British [ˈbrɪtɪʃ] *adj* britannico(-a) ◆ *npl*: **the ~** i Britannici.

British Rail *n* = le Ferrovie dello Stato.

British Telecom [-ˈtelɪkɒm] *n* = la Telecom Italia.

Briton [ˈbrɪtn] *n* britannico *m* (-a *f*).

brittle [ˈbrɪtl] *adj* friabile.

broad [brɔːd] *adj* ampio(-a); (*accent*) marcato(-a).

B road *n* (*Br*) = strada *f* provinciale.

broad bean *n* fava *f*.

broadcast [ˈbrɔːdkɑːst] (*pt & pp* **broadcast**) *n* trasmissione *f* ◆ *vt* trasmettere.

broadly [ˈbrɔːdlɪ] *adv* (*in general*) grossomodo; **~ speaking** in linea di massima.

broccoli [ˈbrɒkəlɪ] *n* broccoli *mpl*.

brochure [ˈbrəʊʃə[r]] *n* opuscolo *m*.

broiled [brɔɪld] *adj* (*Am*) alla griglia.

broke [brəʊk] *pt* → **break** ◆ *adj* (*inf*) al verde.

broken [ˈbrəʊkn] *pp* → **break** ◆ *adj* rotto(-a); (*English, Italian*) stentato(-a).

bronchitis [brɒŋˈkaɪtɪs] *n* bronchite *f*.

bronze [brɒnz] *n* bronzo *m*.

brooch [brəʊtʃ] *n* spilla *f*.

brook [brʊk] *n* ruscello *m*.

broom [bruːm] *n* scopa *f*.

broomstick [ˈbruːmstɪk] *n* manico *m* di scopa.

broth [brɒθ] *n* brodo *m*.

brother [ˈbrʌðə[r]] *n* fratello *m*.

brother-in-law *n* cognato *m*.

brought [brɔːt] *pt & pp* → **bring**.

brow [braʊ] *n* (*forehead*) fronte *f*; (*eyebrow*) sopracciglio *m*.

brown [braʊn] *adj* (*tanned*) abbronzato(-a); (*eyes, hair*) castano(-a) ◆ *n* marrone *m*.

brown bread *n* pane *m* integrale.

brownie [ˈbraʊnɪ] *n* (*CULIN*) biscotto con noci e cioccolato.

Brownie [ˈbraʊnɪ] *n* giovane esploratrice *f*, coccinella *f*.

brown rice *n* riso *m* integrale.

brown sauce n (Br) salsa piccante, usata con la carne e i salumi.

brown sugar n zucchero m di canna.

browse [braʊz] vi (in shop) dare un'occhiata; **to ~ through** (book, paper) sfogliare.

browser ['braʊzəʳ] n: **'~s welcome'** 'entrata libera'.

bruise [bru:z] n livido m.

brunch [brʌntʃ] n brunch m inv.

brunette [bru:'net] n bruna f.

brush [brʌʃ] n (for hair) spazzola f; (for teeth) spazzolino m; (for painting) pennello m ♦ vt spazzolare; (clean, tidy) spazzare; (move with hand) scostare; **to ~ one's hair** spazzolarsi i capelli; **to ~ one's teeth** lavarsi i denti.

Brussels ['brʌslz] n Bruxelles f.

brussels sprouts npl cavoletti mpl di Bruxelles.

brutal ['bru:tl] adj brutale.

BSc n (abbr of Bachelor of Science) (titolare di una) laurea in discipline scientifiche.

BT abbr = British Telecom.

bubble ['bʌbl] n bolla f.

bubble bath n bagnoschiuma m inv.

bubble gum n gomma f da masticare (con cui si può fare le bolle).

bubbly ['bʌblɪ] n (inf) spumante m.

buck [bʌk] n (Am: inf: dollar) dollaro m; (male animal) maschio m.

bucket ['bʌkɪt] n secchio m.

Buckingham Palace ['bʌkɪŋəm-] n il Palazzo di Buckingham (residenza della famiglia reale britannica).

Situato alla fine del Mall, fra Green Park e St James's Park, il Palazzo di Buckingham è la residenza ufficiale del sovrano britannico a Londra. Fu costruito nel 1703 dal Duca di Buckingham. Nel cortile antistante si svolge ogni giorno la cerimonia del cambio della Guardia.

buckle ['bʌkl] n fibbia f ♦ vt (fasten) allacciare ♦ vi (warp) piegarsi.

buck's fizz [,bʌks'fɪz] n bibita a base di champagne e succo d'arancia.

bud [bʌd] n germoglio m ♦ vi germogliare.

Buddhist ['bʊdɪst] n buddista mf.

buddy ['bʌdɪ] n (inf) amico m.

budge [bʌdʒ] vi spostarsi.

budgerigar ['bʌdʒərɪgɑːʳ] n pappagallino m.

budget ['bʌdʒɪt] adj (holiday, travel) a basso prezzo ♦ n bilancio m preventivo; **the Budget** (Br) la Legge finanziaria ❏ **budget for** vt fus: **to ~ for sthg** preventivare la spesa di qc.

budgie ['bʌdʒɪ] n (inf) pappagallino m.

buff [bʌf] n (inf) patito m (-a f).

buffalo ['bʌfələʊ] (pl -s OR -es) n bufalo m.

buffalo wings npl (Am) ali fpl di pollo fritte.

buffer ['bʌfəʳ] n (on train) respingente m.

buffet [Br 'bʊfeɪ, Am bə'feɪ] n buffet m inv.

buffet car n vagone m ristorante.

bug [bʌg] n (insect) insetto m; (inf: mild illness) virus m inv ♦ vt (inf: annoy) dare fastidio a.

buggy [bʌgɪ] n (pushchair) passeggino m; (Am: pram) carrozzina f.

bugle [bjuːgl] n tromba f.

build [bɪld] (pt & pp **built**) n corporatura f ♦ vt costruire ❑ **build up** vt sep aumentare ♦ vi accumularsi.

builder [bɪldəʳ] n costruttore m (-trice f).

building [bɪldɪŋ] n edificio m.

building site n cantiere m edile.

building society n (Br) = istituto m di credito edilizio.

built [bɪlt] pt & pp → build.

built-in adj incorporato(-a).

built-up area n agglomerato m urbano.

bulb [bʌlb] n (for lamp) lampadina f; (of plant) bulbo m.

Bulgaria [bʌlˈgeərɪə] n la Bulgaria.

bulge [bʌldʒ] vi essere rigonfio(-a).

bulk [bʌlk] n: the ~ of la maggior parte di; **in** ~ all'ingrosso.

bulky [bʌlkɪ] adj ingombrante.

bull [bʊl] n toro m.

bulldog [bʊldɒg] n bulldog m inv.

bulldozer [bʊldəʊzəʳ] n bulldozer m inv.

bullet [bʊlɪt] n proiettile m, pallottola f.

bulletin [bʊlətɪn] n (on radio, TV) notiziario m; (publication) bollettino m.

bullfight [bʊlfaɪt] n corrida f.

bull's-eye n centro m (del bersaglio).

bully [bʊlɪ] n prepotente mf ♦ vt fare il prepotente con.

bum [bʌm] n (inf: bottom) sedere m; (Am: inf: tramp) barbone m (-a f).

bum bag n marsupio m.

bumblebee [bʌmblbiː] n bombo m.

bump [bʌmp] n (on knee, leg) rigonfiamento m; (on head) bernoccolo m; (on road) cunetta f; (sound) tonfo m; (minor accident) scontro m leggero ♦ vt (head, leg) sbattere ❑ **bump into** vt fus (hit) sbattere contro; (meet) imbattersi in.

bumper [bʌmpəʳ] n (on car) paraurti m inv; (Am: on train) respingente m.

bumpy [bʌmpɪ] adj (road) dissestato(-a); **the flight was ~** c'è stata un po' di turbolenza durante il volo.

bun [bʌn] n (cake) focaccina f; (bread roll) panino m; (hairstyle) crocchia f.

bunch [bʌntʃ] n (of people) gruppo m; (of flowers, keys) mazzo m; (of grapes) grappolo m; (of bananas) casco m.

bundle [bʌndl] n fascio m.

bung [bʌŋ] n tappo m.

bungalow [bʌŋgələʊ] n casa f un solo piano.

bunion [bʌnjən] n rigonfiamento m dell'alluce.

bunk [bʌŋk] n (bed) cuccetta f.

bunk bed n letto m a castello.

bunker [bʌŋkəʳ] n bunker m inv; (for coal) carbonaia f.

bunny [ˈbʌnɪ] n coniglietto m.

buoy [Br bɔɪ, Am ˈbuːɪ] n boa f.

buoyant [ˈbɔɪənt] adj galleggiante.

BUPA [ˈbuːpə] n compagnia d'assicurazione britannica per assistenza medica privata.

burden [ˈbɜːdn] n (load) carico m; (responsibility) peso m.

bureaucracy [bjʊəˈrɒkrəsɪ] n burocrazia f.

bureau de change [ˌbjʊərəʊdəˈʃɒndʒ] n agenzia f di cambio.

burger [ˈbɜːgəʳ] n hamburger m inv; (made with nuts, vegetables etc) hamburger vegetariano.

burglar [ˈbɜːgləʳ] n scassinatore m (-trice f).

burglar alarm n allarme m antifurto.

burglarize [ˈbɜːgləraɪz] (Am) = burgle.

burglary [ˈbɜːglərɪ] n furto m con scasso.

burgle [ˈbɜːgl] vt scassinare.

burial [ˈberɪəl] n sepoltura f.

burn [bɜːn] (pt & pp burnt OR burned) n bruciatura f ◆ vt & vi bruciare ❑ **burn down** vt sep incendiare ◆ vi: **the building was ~ed down** l'edificio è stato interamente distrutto dalle fiamme.

burning (hot) [ˈbɜːnɪŋ-] adj rovente.

Burns' Night [bɜːnz-] n festa celebrata in onore del poeta scozzese Robert Burns il 25 gennaio.

---

i BURNS' NIGHT

Il 25 gennaio gli scozzesi commemorano la nascita del poeta Robert Burns (1759–96). La tradizione vuole che in occasione di questa ricorrenza si allestiscano le cosiddette "Burns' Suppers", cene a base di piatti tradizionali scozzesi, come l'haggis, accompagnate da whisky. Durante queste cene i commensali recitano a turno versi delle poesie di Burns.

---

burnt [bɜːnt] pt & pp → burn.

burp [bɜːp] vi (inf) ruttare.

burrow [ˈbʌrəʊ] n tana f.

burst [bɜːst] (pt & pp burst) n scoppio m ◆ vt far scoppiare ◆ vi scoppiare; **he ~ into the room** irruppe nella stanza; **to ~ into tears** scoppiare in lacrime; **to ~ open** (door) spalancarsi.

bury [ˈberɪ] vt seppellire.

bus [bʌs] n autobus m inv; **by ~** in autobus.

bus conductor [-ˌkənˈdʌktəʳ] n bigliettaio m (-a f).

bus driver n conducente mf.

bush [bʊʃ] n cespuglio m.

business [ˈbɪznɪs] n affari mpl; (shop, firm) impresa f; (affair) faccenda f; **mind your own ~!** fatti gli affari tuoi!; **'~ as usual'** 'aperto (regolarmente)'.

business card n biglietto f da visita.

business class n business class f inv.

business hours npl orario m di apertura.

by

businessman ['bɪznɪsmæn] (*pl* **-men** [-men]) *n* uomo *m* d'affari.

business studies *npl* ≈ amministrazione *f* aziendale.

businesswoman ['bɪznɪs,wʊmən] (*pl* **-women** [-wɪmɪn]) *n* donna *f* d'affari.

busker ['bʌskəʳ] *n* (*Br*) musicista *mf* ambulante.

bus lane *n* corsia *f* preferenziale (per autobus).

bus pass *n* abbonamento *m* all'autobus.

bus shelter *n* pensilina *f*.

bus station *n* stazione *f* degli autobus.

bus stop *n* fermata *f* dell'autobus.

bust [bʌst] *n* (*of woman*) seno *m* ♦ *adj*: **to go ~** (*inf*) fallire.

bustle ['bʌsl] *n* (*activity*) trambusto *m*.

bus tour *n* gita *f* in autobus.

busy ['bɪzɪ] *adj* occupato(-a); (*day, schedule*) pieno(-a); (*street, office*) affollato(-a); **to be ~ doing sthg** essere occupato a fare qc.

busy signal *n* (*Am*) segnale *m* di occupato.

but [bʌt] *conj* ma, però ♦ *prep* tranne; **the last ~ one** il penultimo (la penultima); **~ for** a parte.

butcher ['bʊtʃəʳ] *n* macellaio *m* (-a *f*); **~'s** (*shop*) macelleria *f*.

butt [bʌt] *n* (*of rifle*) calcio *m*; (*of cigarette, cigar*) mozzicone *m*.

butter ['bʌtəʳ] *n* burro *m* ♦ *vt* imburrare.

butter bean *n* fagiolo *m* bianco.

buttercup ['bʌtəkʌp] *n* ranuncolo *m*.

butterfly ['bʌtəflaɪ] *n* farfalla *f*.

butterscotch ['bʌtəskɒtʃ] *n* caramella dura di zucchero e burro.

buttocks ['bʌtəks] *npl* natiche *fpl*.

button ['bʌtn] *n* bottone *m*; (*Am: badge*) distintivo *m*.

buttonhole ['bʌtnhəʊl] *n* (*hole*) occhiello *m*.

button mushroom *n* champignon *m inv*.

buttress ['bʌtrɪs] *n* contrafforte *m*.

buy [baɪ] (*pt & pp* **bought**) *vt* comprare ♦ *n*: **a good ~** un buon acquisto; **to ~ sthg for sb, to ~ sb sthg** comprare qc per qn, comprare qc a qn.

buzz [bʌz] *vi* ronzare ♦ *n*: (*inf: phone call*): **to give sb a ~** dare un colpo di telefono a qn.

buzzer ['bʌzəʳ] *n* cicalino *m*.

by [baɪ] *prep* **1.** (*expressing cause, agent*) da; **he was hit ~ a car** è stato investito da un'automobile; **funded ~ the government** finanziato dal governo; **a book ~ Joyce** un libro di Joyce.

2. (*expressing method, means*): **~ car/train/plane** in macchina/treno/aereo; **~ post/phone** per posta/telefono; **to pay ~ credit card** pagare con la carta di credito; **to win ~ cheating** vincere con l'imbroglio.

3. (*near to, beside*) vicino a, accanto a; **~ the sea** (*holiday*) al mare; (*town*) sul mare.

4. (*past*) davanti a; **a car went ~ the house** un'automobile è passata davanti alla casa.

5. (*via*) da; **go out ~ the door on the left** uscite dalla porta sulla sinistra.

6. *(with time)*: **be there ~ nine** trovati lì per le nove; **~ day/night** di giorno/notte; **~ now** ormai.

7. *(expressing quantity)*: **sold ~ the dozen/thousand** venduti a dozzine/migliaia; **prices fell ~ 20%** i prezzi sono diminuiti del 20%; **we charge ~ the hour** facciamo pagare a ore.

8. *(expressing meaning)*: **what do you mean ~ that?** cosa intendi dire con questo?

9. *(in sums, measurements)* per; **two metres ~ five** due metri per cinque.

10. *(according to)* per, secondo; **~ law** per legge; **it's fine ~ me** per me va bene.

11. *(expressing gradual process)*: **bit ~ bit** (a) poco a poco; **one ~ one** uno per uno; **year ~ year** di anno in anno.

12. *(in phrases)*: **~ mistake** per errore; **~ oneself** *(alone)* (da) solo; *(unaided)* da solo; **he's a lawyer ~ profession** è avvocato di professione.

♦ *adv (past)*: **to go ~** passare.

bye(-bye) [baɪ(baɪ)] *excl (inf)* ciao!

bypass ['baɪpɑːs] *n (road)* circonvallazione *f*.

C

C *(abbr of Celsius, centigrade)* C.

cab [kæb] *n (taxi)* taxi *m inv*; *(of lorry)* cabina *f*.

cabaret ['kæbəreɪ] *n* spettacolo

m di cabaret.

cabbage ['kæbɪdʒ] *n* cavolo *m*.

cabin ['kæbɪn] *n* cabina *f*; *(wooden house)* capanna *f*.

cabin crew *n* personale *m* di bordo.

cabinet ['kæbɪnɪt] *n (cupboard)* armadietto *m*; *(POL)* consiglio *m* di gabinetto.

cable ['keɪbl] *n* cavo *m*.

cable car *n* funivia *f*.

cable television *n* televisione *f* via cavo.

cactus ['kæktəs] *(pl* **-tuses** OR **-ti** [-taɪ]) *n* cactus *m inv*.

Caesar salad [ˌsiːzə-] *n* insalata di lattuga, acciughe, olive, crostini e parmigiano.

cafe ['kæfeɪ] *n* caffè *m*.

cafeteria [ˌkæfɪˈtɪərɪə] *n* ristorante *m* self-service.

cafetière [kæfˈtjeəʳ] *n* tipo di caffettiera con pressa che separa la polvere dal caffè ottenuto.

caffeine ['kæfiːn] *n* caffeina *f*.

cage [keɪdʒ] *n* gabbia *f*.

cagoule [kəˈguːl] *n (Br)* K-way® *m inv*.

Cajun ['keɪdʒən] *adj* tipico della popolazione di origine francese della Louisiana.

 CAJUN

Coloni di origine francese, i "Cajuns" si stabilirono inizialmente nella Nuova Scozia da dove, nel diciottesimo secolo, furono deportati in Louisiana. Lì svilupparono una lingua ed una cultura proprie ed oggi sono conosciuti per la loro cucina, caratterizzata dall'uso di spezie piccanti, e per la loro musica folkloristica, in cui predominano il violino e la fisarmonica.

cake [keɪk] *n (large)* torta *f*; *(small)* pasta *f*; *(of soap)* pezzo *m*.

calculate [ˈkælkjʊleɪt] *vt* calcolare.

calculator [ˈkælkjʊleɪtəʳ] *n* calcolatrice *f*.

calendar [ˈkælɪndəʳ] *n* calendario *m*.

calf [kɑːf] *(pl* calves) *n (of cow)* vitello *m*; *(part of leg)* polpaccio *m*.

call [kɔːl] *n (visit)* visita *f*; *(phone call)* telefonata *f*; *(of bird)* richiamo *m*; *(at airport)* chiamata *f*; *(at hotel)* sveglia *f* ♦ *vt* chiamare; *(meeting)* convocare; *(elections, strike)* indire ♦ *vi (visit)* passare; *(phone)* chiamare; **on ~** *(nurse, doctor)* reperibile; **to pay sb a ~** fare una visita a qn; **to be ~ed** chiamarsi; **what is he ~ed?** come si chiama?; **to ~ sb a liar** dare del bugiardo a qn; **to ~ sb's name** chiamare qn; **this train ~s at ...** questo treno ferma a ...; **who's ~ing?** chi parla? ❑ **call back** *vt sep* richiamare ♦ *vi (phone again)* richiamare; *(visit again)* ripassare; **call for** *vt fus (come to fetch)* passare a prendere; *(demand)* chiedere; *(require)* richiedere; **call in** *vt (visit)* fare visita a; **to ~ on sb to do sthg** chiedere a qn di fare qc; **call out** *vt sep (name, winner)* annunciare; *(doctor, fire brigade)* chiamare ♦ *vi* gridare; **call up** *vt sep (MIL)* chiamare alle armi; *(telephone)* chiamare.

call box *n* cabina *f* telefonica.

caller [ˈkɔːləʳ] *n (visitor)* visitatore *m (-trice f)*; *(on phone)* persona che chiama.

calm [kɑːm] *adj* calmo(-a) ♦ *vt*

calmare. ❑ **calm down** *vt sep* calmare ♦ *vi* calmarsi.

Calor gas® [ˈkælə-] *n* butano *m*.

calorie [ˈkælərɪ] *n* caloria *f*.

calves [kɑːvz] *pl* → **calf**.

camcorder [ˈkæm,kɔːdəʳ] *n* videocamera *f*.

came [keɪm] *pt* → **come**.

camel [ˈkæml] *n* cammello *m*.

camembert [ˈkæməmbeəʳ] *n* camembert *m inv*.

camera [ˈkæmərə] *n (for photographs)* macchina *f* fotografica; *(for filming)* macchina da presa.

cameraman [ˈkæmərəmæn] *(pl* -men [-men]) *n* cameraman *m inv*.

camera shop *n* fotografo *m*.

camisole [ˈkæmɪsəʊl] *n* canottiera *f*.

camp [kæmp] *n (for holiday-makers)* campeggio *m*, camping *m inv*; *(for soldiers, prisoners)* campo *m* ♦ *vi* accamparsi.

campaign [kæmˈpeɪn] *n* campagna *f* ♦ *vi*: **to ~ (for/against)** fare una campagna (per/contro).

camp bed *n* branda *f*.

camper [ˈkæmpəʳ] *n (person)* campeggiatore *m (-trice f)*; *(van)* camper *m inv*.

camping [ˈkæmpɪŋ] *n*: **to go ~** andare in campeggio.

camping stove *n* fornello *m* da campeggio.

campsite [ˈkæmpsaɪt] *n* campeggio *m*, camping *m inv*.

campus [ˈkæmpəs] *(pl* -es) *n* campus *m inv*.

can¹ [kæn] *n (of food)* scatola *f*; *(of drink)* lattina *f*; *(of paint)* barattolo *m*; *(of oil)* latta *f*.

can² [*weak form* kən, *strong form*

kæn] (*pt & conditional* could) *aux vb*
1. (*be able to*) potere; ~ **you help
me?** puoi aiutarmi?; **I ~ see you** ti
vedo.
2. (*know how to*) sapere; ~ **you
drive?** sai guidare?; **I ~ speak
Italian** parlo (l')italiano.
3. (*be allowed to*) potere; **you can't
smoke here** è proibito fumare qui.
4. (*in polite requests*) potere; ~ **you
tell me the time?** mi può dire
l'ora?, mi sa dire l'ora?; ~ **I speak
to the manager?** posso parlare al
direttore?
5. (*expressing occasional occurrence*):
it ~ get cold at night può fare freddo la notte.
6. (*expressing possibility*) potere;
they could be lost si potrebbero
essere persi.
Canada ['kænədə] *n* il Canada.
Canadian [kə'neɪdɪən] *adj* canadese ♦ *n* canadese *mf*.
canal [kə'næl] *n* canale *m*.
canapé ['kænəpeɪ] *n* tartina *f*.
cancel ['kænsl] *vt* annullare.
cancellation [ˌkænsə'leɪʃn] *n*
annullamento *m*.
cancer ['kænsə'] *n* cancro *m*.
Cancer ['kænsə'] *n* Cancro *m*.
candidate ['kændɪdət] *n* candidato *m* (-a *f*).
candle ['kændl] *n* candela *f*.
candlelit dinner ['kændllɪt-] *n*
cena *f* a lume di candela.
candy ['kændɪ] *n* (*Am*) (*confectionery*) dolciumi *mpl*; (*sweet*) caramella *f*.
candyfloss ['kændɪflɒs] *n* (*Br*)
zucchero *m* filato.
cane [keɪn] *n* (*for walking*) bastone *m*; (*for punishment*) bacchetta *f*;
(*for furniture, baskets*) vimini *mpl*.

canister ['kænɪstə'] *n* (*for tea*)
barattolo *m*; (*for gas*) bombola *f*.
cannabis ['kænəbɪs] *n* cannabis
f.
canned [kænd] *adj* (*food*) in scatola; (*drink*) in lattina.
cannon ['kænən] *n* cannone *m*.
cannot ['kænɒt] = **can not**.
canoe [kə'nuː] *n* canoa *f*.
canoeing [kə'nuːɪŋ] *n* canottaggio *m*.
canopy ['kænəpɪ] *n* (*over bed etc*)
baldacchino *m*.
can't [kɑːnt] = **cannot**.
cantaloup(e) ['kæntəluːp] *n*
melone *m* (cantalupo).
canteen [kæn'tiːn] *n* mensa *f*.
canvas ['kænvəs] *n* (*for tent, bag*)
tela *f*.
cap [kæp] *n* (*hat*) berretto *m*; (*of
pen, bottle*) tappo *m*; (*contraceptive*)
diaframma *m*.
capable ['keɪpəbl] *adj* (*competent*)
capace; **to be ~ of doing sthg** essere capace di fare qc.
capacity [kə'pæsɪtɪ] *n* (*ability*)
capacità *f inv*; (*of stadium, theatre*)
capienza *f*.
cape [keɪp] *n* (*of land*) capo *m*;
(*cloak*) cappa *f*.
capers ['keɪpəz] *npl* capperi *mpl*.
capital ['kæpɪtl] *n* (*of country*)
capitale *f*; (*money*) capitale *m*; (*letter*) maiuscola *f*.
capital punishment *n* pena
f capitale.
cappuccino [ˌkæpʊ'tʃiːnəʊ] (*pl
-s*) *n* cappuccino *m*.
Capricorn *n* Capricorno *m*.
capsicum ['kæpsɪkəm] *n* peperone *m*.
capsize [kæp'saɪz] *vi* rovesciarsi.

capsule ['kæpsju:l] *n (for medicine)* capsula *f.*

captain ['kæptɪn] *n* capitano *m.*

caption ['kæpʃn] *n* didascalia *f.*

capture ['kæptʃəʳ] *vt (person, animal)* catturare; *(town, castle)* conquistare.

car [ka:ʳ] *n (motorcar)* automobile *f,* macchina *f; (railway wagon)* vagone *m.*

carafe [kəˈræf] *n* caraffa *f.*

caramel ['kærəmel] *n (sweet)* caramella *f* mou®; *(burnt sugar)* caramello *m.*

carat ['kærət] *n* carato *m;* **24-~ gold** oro a 24 carati.

caravan ['kærəvæn] *n (Br)* roulotte *f inv.*

caravanning ['kærəvænɪŋ] *n (Br):* **to go ~** andare in vacanza in roulotte.

caravan site *n (Br)* campeggio *m* per roulotte.

carbohydrate [ˌka:bəʊˈhaɪdreɪt] *n (in foods)* carboidrato *m.*

carbon ['ka:bən] *n* carbone *m.*

carbon copy *n* copia *f* fatta con carta carbone.

carbon dioxide [-daɪˈɒksaɪd] *n* anidride *f* carbonica.

carbon monoxide [-mɒˈnɒksaɪd] *n* monossido *m* di carbonio.

car boot sale *n (Br)* mercatino di oggetti usati esposti nei bagagliai aperti delle automobili dei venditori.

carburetor [ˌka:bəˈretəʳ] *(Am)* = **carburettor.**

carburettor [ˌka:bəˈretəʳ] *n (Br)* carburatore *m.*

car crash *n* incidente *m* automobilistico.

card [ka:d] *n (for filing, notes)* scheda *f; (for greetings)* biglietto *m; (showing membership)* tessera *f; (of businessperson)* biglietto da visita; *(postcard)* cartolina *f; (playing card)* carta *f; (cardboard)* cartoncino *m;* **~s** *(game)* carte *fpl.*

cardboard ['ka:dbɔ:d] *n* cartone *m.*

car deck *n* ponte *m* auto.

cardiac arrest [ˌka:dɪæk-] *n* arresto *m* cardiaco.

cardigan ['ka:dɪgən] *n* cardigan *m inv.*

care [keəʳ] *n* cura *f* ◆ *vi:* **I don't ~** non me ne importa; **to take ~ of** *(look after)* prendersi cura di; *(deal with)* occuparsi di; **would you ~ to ...?** *(fml)* se vuole ...?; **to take ~ to do sthg** stare attento a fare qc; **take ~!** *(goodbye)* stammi bene!; **with ~** con cura; **to ~ about** *(think important)* avere a cuore; *(person)* voler bene a.

career [kəˈrɪəʳ] *n* carriera *f.*

carefree ['keəfri:] *adj* spensierato(-a).

careful ['keəful] *adj (cautious)* attento(-a); *(driver)* prudente; *(thorough)* accurato(-a); **be ~!** attento(-a)!

carefully ['keəflɪ] *adv (cautiously)* con cautela; *(thoroughly)* attentamente.

careless ['keələs] *adj (inattentive)* sbadato(-a); *(unconcerned)* spensierato(-a).

caretaker ['keəˌteɪkəʳ] *n (Br)* custode *mf.*

car ferry *n* traghetto *m.*

cargo ['ka:gəʊ] *(pl* **-es** OR **-s)** *n* carico *m.*

car hire *n (Br)* autonoleggio *m.*

Caribbean [Br ˌkærɪˈbiːən, Am kəˈrɪbɪən] n: **the ~** (area) i Caraibi.

caring [ˈkeərɪŋ] adj premuroso(-a).

carnation [kɑːˈneɪʃn] n garofano m.

carnival [ˈkɑːnɪvl] n carnevale m.

carousel [ˌkærəˈsel] n (for luggage) nastro m trasportatore; (Am: merry-go-round) giostra f.

carp [kɑːp] n carpa f.

car park n (Br) parcheggio m.

carpenter [ˈkɑːpəntəʳ] n falegname m.

carpentry [ˈkɑːpəntrɪ] n falegnameria f.

carpet [ˈkɑːpɪt] n (rug) tappeto m; (wall-to-wall) moquette f inv.

car rental n (Am) autonoleggio m.

carriage [ˈkærɪdʒ] n carrozza f.

carriageway [ˈkærɪdʒweɪ] n (Br) carreggiata f.

carrier (bag) [ˈkærɪəʳ-] n sacchetto m.

carrot [ˈkærət] n carota f.

carrot cake n torta f di carote.

carry [ˈkærɪ] vt portare; (disease) essere portatore di ◆ vi (voice, sound) arrivare ❑ **carry on** vi continuare ◆ vt fus (continue) continuare; (conduct) compiere; **to ~ on doing sthg** continuare a fare qc; **carry out** vt sep (work, repairs, investigation) effettuare; (plan) portare a compimento; (order) eseguire; (promise) adempiere.

carrycot [ˈkærɪkɒt] n (Br) culla f portatile.

carryout [ˈkærɪaʊt] n (Am & Scot: meal) cibo m da asporto.

carsick [ˈkɑːˌsɪk] adj: **to be ~** soffrire il mal d'auto.

cart [kɑːt] n (for transport) carro m; (inf: video game cartridge) cartuccia f; (Am: in supermarket) carrello m.

carton [ˈkɑːtn] n (of milk, juice) cartone m; (box) scatola f.

cartoon [kɑːˈtuːn] n (drawing) vignetta f; (comic strip) fumetto m; (film) cartone m animato.

cartridge [ˈkɑːtrɪdʒ] n cartuccia f.

carve [kɑːv] vt (wood, stone) intagliare; (meat) tagliare.

carvery [ˈkɑːvərɪ] n ristorante dove si mangia carne arrosto, tagliata appositamente al banco per il cliente.

car wash n autolavaggio m.

case [keɪs] n (Br: suitcase) valigia f; (container) custodia f; (instance, patient) caso m; (JUR: trial) causa f; **in any ~** in ogni caso; **in ~** it rains nel caso che piova; **in ~ of** in caso di; (just) **in ~** in caso di necessità; **in that ~** allora.

cash [kæʃ] n (coins, notes) contanti mpl; (money in general) soldi mpl ◆ vt: **to ~ a cheque** incassare un assegno; **to pay ~** pagare in contanti.

cash desk n cassa f.

cash dispenser [-ˌdɪˈspensəʳ] n cassa f automatica.

cashew (nut) [ˈkæʃuː-] n noce f di acagiù.

cashier [kæˈʃɪəʳ] n cassiere m (-a f).

cashmere [kæʃˈmɪəʳ] n cachemire m.

cashpoint [ˈkæʃpɔɪnt] n (Br) cassa f automatica.

cash register n registratore m di cassa.

casino [kə'si:nəu] n casinò m inv.

cask [ka:sk] n barile m.

cask-conditioned [-.kən'dɪʃnd] adj fermentato(-a) in barili.

casserole ['kæsərəul] n (stew) stufato m; ~ **(dish)** casseruola f.

cassette [kə'set] n cassetta f.

cassette recorder n registratore m (a cassette).

cast [ka:st] (pt & pp cast) n (actors) cast m (for broken bone) ingessatura f ◆ vt (shadow, light, look) gettare; **to ~ doubt on** mettere in dubbio; **to ~ one's vote** votare □ **cast off** vi (boat, ship) salpare.

caster [ka:stə'] n rotella f.

caster sugar n (Br) zucchero m semolato.

castle ['ka:sl] n (building) castello m; (in chess) torre f.

casual ['kæʒuəl] adj (relaxed) disinvolto(-a); (offhand) noncurante; (clothes) casual (inv); ~ **work** lavoro m occasionale.

casualty ['kæʒjuəltɪ] n (injured person) ferito m (-a f); (dead person) morto m (-a f); ~ **(ward)** pronto soccorso m.

cat [kæt] n gatto m.

catalog ['kætəlɒg] (Am) = **catalogue**.

catalogue ['kætəlɒg] n catalogo m.

catapult ['kætəpʌlt] n fionda f.

cataract ['kætərækt] n (in eye) cateratta f.

catarrh [kə'ta:'] n catarro m.

catastrophe [kə'tæstrəfɪ] n catastrofe f.

catch [kætʃ] (pt & pp caught) vt prendere; (surprise, hear) cogliere; (attention) attirare ◆ vi (become hooked) impigliarsi ◆ n (of window, door) fermo m; (snag) intoppo m □ **catch up** vt sep raggiungere ◆ vi: **to ~ up (with sthg)** (sleep, work) recuperare (qc); **to ~ up with sb** raggiungere qn.

catching ['kætʃɪŋ] adj (inf) contagioso(-a).

category ['kætəgərɪ] n categoria f.

cater ['keɪtə']: **cater for** vt fus (Br) (needs) provvedere a; (anticipate) tenere conto di; (tastes) soddisfare.

caterpillar ['kætəpɪlə'] n bruco m.

cathedral [kə'θi:drəl] n cattedrale f, duomo m.

Catholic ['kæθlɪk] adj cattolico(-a) ◆ n cattolico m (-a f).

Catseyes® ['kætsaɪz] npl (Br) catarifrangenti mpl.

cattle ['kætl] npl bestiame m.

cattle grid n griglia metallica posta sul suolo stradale per impedire il passaggio di pecore, mucche ecc.

caught [kɔ:t] pt & pp → **catch**.

cauliflower ['kɒlɪˌflauə'] n cavolfiore m.

cauliflower cheese n cavolfiore gratinato con besciamella.

cause [kɔ:z] n causa f; (justification) ragione f ◆ vt causare; **to ~ sb to make a mistake** far fare un errore a qn.

causeway ['kɔ:zweɪ] n strada f rialzata.

caustic soda [,kɔ:stɪk-] n soda f caustica.

caution ['kɔ:ʃn] n (care) cautela f; (warning) avvertimento m.

cautious [ˈkɔːʃəs] *adj* cauto(-a).

cave [keɪv] *n* grotta *f* □ **cave in** *vi* crollare.

caviar(e) [ˈkævɪɑːʳ] *n* caviale *m*.

cavity [ˈkævətɪ] *n* (in tooth) carie *f inv*.

CD *n* (abbr of compact disc) CD *m inv*.

CDI *n* (abbr of compact disc interactive) CDI *m inv*.

CD player *n* lettore *m* di compact disc.

CDW *n* (abbr of collision damage waiver) franchigia *f*.

cease [siːs] *vt & vi* (fml) cessare.

ceasefire [ˈsiːsˌfaɪəʳ] *n* cessate il fuoco *m inv*.

ceilidh [ˈkeɪlɪ] *n* festa scozzese o irlandese con danze folcloristiche.

---

i **CEILIDH**

Il "ceilidh" è una tradizionale forma di intrattenimento scozzese o irlandese con musica, canti e balli. In passato i "ceilidh" erano serate organizzate da un numero ristretto di parenti e amici, mentre i "ceilidh" moderni sono spesso grandi feste danzanti aperte al pubblico.

---

ceiling [ˈsiːlɪŋ] *n* soffitto *m*.

celebrate [ˈselɪbreɪt] *vt* (win, birthday) festeggiare; (Mass) celebrare ♦ *vi* festeggiare.

celebration [ˌselɪˈbreɪʃn] *n* (event) festa *f* □ **celebrations** *npl* (festivities) festeggiamenti *mpl*.

celebrity [sɪˈlebrətɪ] *n* (person) celebrità *f inv*.

celeriac [sɪˈlerɪæk] *n* sedano *m* rapa.

celery [ˈselərɪ] *n* sedano *m*.

cell [sel] *n* (of plant, body) cellula *f*; (in prison) cella *f*.

cellar [ˈseləʳ] *n* cantina *f*.

cello [ˈtʃeləʊ] (pl **-s**) *n* violoncello *m*.

Cellophane® [ˈseləfeɪn] *n* cellophane® *m*.

Celsius [ˈselsɪəs] *adj* Celsius (inv).

cement [sɪˈment] *n* cemento *m*.

cement mixer *n* betoniera *f*.

cemetery [ˈsemɪtrɪ] *n* cimitero *m*.

cent [sent] *n* (Am) cent *m inv*.

center [ˈsentəʳ] (Am) = **centre**.

centigrade [ˈsentɪɡreɪd] *adj* centigrado(-a).

centimetre [ˈsentɪˌmiːtəʳ] *n* centimetro *m*.

centipede [ˈsentɪpiːd] *n* centopiedi *m inv*.

central [ˈsentrəl] *adj* centrale.

central heating *n* riscaldamento *m* autonomo.

central locking [-ˈlɒkɪŋ] *n* chiusura *f* delle porte centralizzata.

central reservation *n* (Br) zona *f* spartitraffico.

centre [ˈsentəʳ] *n* (Br) centro *m* ♦ *adj* (Br) centrale; **the ~ of attention** il centro dell'attenzione.

century [ˈsentʃʊrɪ] *n* secolo *m*.

ceramic [sɪˈræmɪk] *adj* di ceramica □ **ceramics** *npl* oggetti *mpl* di ceramica.

cereal [ˈsɪərɪəl] *n* (breakfast food) cereali *mpl*.

ceremony [ˈserɪmənɪ] *n* cerimonia *f*.

certain [ˈsɜːtn] *adj* certo(-a);

she's ~ to be late farà tardi di sicuro; to be ~ of sthg essere certo di qc; to make ~ (that) assicurarsi che.

certainly ['sɜːtnlɪ] adv certamente, certo.

certificate [sə'tɪfɪkət] n certificato m.

certify ['sɜːtɪfaɪ] vt (declare true) attestare.

chain [tʃeɪn] n catena f; (of islands) arcipelago m ◆ vt: to ~ sthg to sthg incatenare qc a qc.

chain store n negozio che fa parte di una catena.

chair [tʃeə^r] n sedia f.

chair lift n seggiovia f.

chairman ['tʃeəmən] (pl -men [-mən]) n presidente m.

chairperson ['tʃeə,pɜːsn] (pl -s) n presidente m (-essa f).

chairwoman ['tʃeə,wʊmən] (pl -women [-,wɪmɪn]) n presidentessa f.

chalet ['ʃæleɪ] n chalet m inv; (at holiday camp) bungalow m inv.

chalk [tʃɔːk] n gesso m; a piece of ~ un gesso.

chalkboard ['tʃɔːkbɔːd] n (Am) lavagna f.

challenge ['tʃælɪndʒ] n sfida f ◆ vt (question) mettere in discussione; to ~ sb (to sthg) sfidare qn (a qc).

chamber ['tʃeɪmbə^r] n (room) sala f.

chambermaid ['tʃeɪmbəmeɪd] n cameriera f (d'albergo).

champagne [,ʃæm'peɪn] n champagne m inv.

champion ['tʃæmpjən] n campione m (-essa f).

championship ['tʃæmpjənʃɪp] n campionato m.

chance [tʃɑːns] n (luck) caso m; (possibility) probabilità f inv; (opportunity) possibilità f inv, occasione f ◆ vt: to ~ it (inf) provarci. to take a ~ rischiare; by ~ per caso; I came on the off ~ you'd be here sono venuto per vedere se per caso ci fossi.

Chancellor of the Exchequer [tʃɑːnsələrəvðəɪks'tʃekə^r] n (Br) = ministro m del Tesoro.

chandelier [,ʃændə'lɪə^r] n lampadario m.

change [tʃeɪndʒ] n (alteration) cambiamento m; (money received back) resto m; (coins) spiccioli mpl ◆ vt cambiare ◆ vi cambiare; (change clothes) cambiarsi; a ~ of clothes vestiti mpl di ricambio; do you have ~ for a pound? mi può cambiare una sterlina?; for a ~ per cambiare; to get ~d cambiarsi; to ~ money cambiare i soldi; to ~ a nappy cambiare un pannolino; to ~ a wheel cambiare una ruota; to ~ trains/planes cambiare treno/aereo; all ~! (on train) per tutte le altre stazioni si cambia!

changeable ['tʃeɪndʒəbl] adj (weather) variabile.

change machine n distributore automatico di monete.

changing room ['tʃeɪndʒɪŋ-] n (for sport) spogliatoio m; (in shop) camerino m.

channel ['tʃænl] n canale m; the (English) Channel la Manica.

Channel Islands npl: the ~ le Isole della Manica.

Channel Tunnel n: the ~ il

tunnel sotto la Manica.

i **CHANNEL TUNNEL**

Chiamato anche Eurotunnel, il "Channel Tunnel" è il collegamento ferroviario costruito sotto la Manica tra Cheriton, vicino a Folkestone, e Coquelles, nei pressi di Calais. Inaugurato nel 1994, consente il trasporto di automezzi su un treno chiamato "Le Shuttle". Treni passeggeri piuttosto frequenti collegano direttamente Londra a Parigi e ad altre capitali europee.

chant [tʃɑːnt] vt (RELIG) cantare; (words, slogan) scandire.

chaos [ˈkeɪɒs] n caos m.

chaotic [keɪˈɒtɪk] adj caotico(-a).

chap [tʃæp] n (Br: inf) tipo m.

chapatti [tʃəˈpætɪ] n pane m azzimo indiano.

chapel [ˈtʃæpl] n cappella f.

chapped [tʃæpt] adj screpolato(-a).

chapter [ˈtʃæptə*] n capitolo m.

character [ˈkærəktə*] n carattere m; (in film, book, play) personaggio m; (inf: person, individual) tipo m.

characteristic [ˌkærəktəˈrɪstɪk] adj caratteristico(-a) ◆ n caratteristica f.

charcoal [ˈtʃɑːkəʊl] n (for barbecue) carbone m di legna.

charge [tʃɑːdʒ] n (price) spesa f; (JUR) accusa f ◆ vt (customer) far pagare; (money) chiedere; (JUR) accusare; (battery) ricaricare ◆ vi (sb: money) far pagare; (rush) precipitarsi; **to be in ~ (of)** essere re-

sponsabile (di); **to take ~ (of)** assumere la responsabilità (di); **free of ~** gratis; **extra ~** supplemento m; **there is no ~ for service** il servizio è gratuito.

char-grilled [ˈtʃɑːgrɪld] adj alla brace.

charity [ˈtʃærɪtɪ] n (organization) ente m di beneficenza; **to give to ~** dare soldi in beneficenza.

charity shop n negozio che vende articoli vari, il cui ricavato è destinato ad un ente di beneficenza.

charm [tʃɑːm] n (attractiveness) fascino m ◆ vt affascinare.

charming [ˈtʃɑːmɪŋ] adj affascinante.

chart [tʃɑːt] n (diagram) grafico m; (map) carta f; **the ~s** l'hit-parade f inv.

chartered accountant [ˌtʃɑːtəd-] n esperto m (-a f) contabile.

charter flight [ˈtʃɑːtə-] n volo m charter.

chase [tʃeɪs] n inseguimento m ◆ vt inseguire.

chat [tʃæt] n chiacchierata f ◆ vi chiacchierare; **to have a ~ (with)** fare quattro chiacchiere (con) ❑ **chat up** vt sep (Br: inf) agganciare.

château [ˈʃætəʊ] n castello m.

chat show n (Br) talk show m inv.

chatty [ˈtʃætɪ] adj (person) chiacchierone(-a); (letter) pieno di pettegolezzi.

chauffeur [ˈʃəʊfə*] n autista m.

cheap [tʃiːp] adj a buon mercato; (pej: low-quality) dozzinale.

cheap day return n biglietto di andata e ritorno a prezzo ridotto, valido per un solo giorno e soggetto a *restrizioni di orario.*

cheaply ['tʃi:plɪ] *adv* a basso prezzo.

cheat [tʃi:t] *n* imbroglione *m* (-a *f*) ♦ *vi* imbrogliare ♦ *vt*: **to ~ sb out of sthg** sottrarre qc a qn con l'inganno.

check [tʃek] *n* (*inspection*) controllo *m*; (*Am: bill*) conto *m*; (*Am: tick*) segno *m*; (*Am*) = **cheque** ♦ *vt* controllare; (*Am: tick*) spuntare ♦ *vi* verificare; **to ~ for sthg** controllare qc; **to ~ on sthg** controllare qc ❏ **check in** *vt sep* (*luggage*) far passare al check-in ♦ *vi* (*at hotel*) farsi registrare; (*at airport*) fare il check-in; **check off** *vt sep* spuntare; **check out** *vi* saldare il conto e andarsene; **check up** *vi*: **to ~ up (on)** fare delle indagini (su).

checked [tʃekt] *adj* a quadri.

checkers ['tʃekəz] *n* (*Am*) dama *f*.

check-in desk *n* banco *m* dell'accettazione bagagli OR del check-in.

checkout ['tʃekaʊt] *n* cassa *f*.

checkpoint ['tʃekpɔɪnt] *n* posto *m* di blocco.

checkroom ['tʃekrʊm] *n* (*Am*) deposito *m* bagagli.

checkup ['tʃekʌp] *n* check-up *m inv*.

cheddar (cheese) ['tʃedəᵊ-] *n* tipo di formaggio semi-stagionato.

cheek [tʃi:k] *n* guancia *f*; **what a ~!** che faccia tosta!

cheeky ['tʃi:kɪ] *adj* sfacciato(-a).

cheer [tʃɪəʳ] *n* acclamazione *f* ♦ *vi* acclamare.

cheerful ['tʃɪəfʊl] *adj* allegro(-a); (*colour*) vivace.

cheerio [tʃɪərɪ'əʊ] *excl* (*Br: inf*)

ciao!

cheers [tʃɪəz] *excl* (*when drinking*) cincin!; (*Br: inf: thank you*) grazie!

cheese [tʃi:z] *n* formaggio *m*.

cheeseboard ['tʃi:zbɔ:d] *n* (*cheese and biscuits*) piatto *m* di formaggi.

cheeseburger ['tʃi:z,bɜ:gəʳ] *n* cheeseburger *m inv* (*panino con hamburger e formaggio fuso*).

cheesecake ['tʃi:zkeɪk] *n* dolce a base di biscotti, formaggio fresco e panna.

chef [ʃef] *n* chef *m inv*.

chef's special *n* specialità *f inv* della casa.

chemical ['kemɪkl] *adj* chimico(-a) ♦ *n* sostanza *f* chimica.

chemist ['kemɪst] *n* (*Br: pharmacist*) farmacista *mf*; (*scientist*) chimico *m* (-a *f*); **~'s** (*Br: shop*) farmacia *f*.

chemistry ['kemɪstrɪ] *n* chimica *f*.

cheque [tʃek] *n* (*Br*) assegno *m*; **to pay by ~** pagare con un assegno.

chequebook ['tʃekbʊk] *n* libretto *m* degli assegni.

cheque card *n* carta *f* assegni.

cherry ['tʃerɪ] *n* ciliegia *f*.

chess [tʃes] *n* scacchi *mpl*.

chest [tʃest] *n* (*of body*) torace *m*; (*box*) cassa *f*.

chestnut ['tʃesnʌt] *n* castagna *f* ♦ *adj* (*colour*) castano(-a).

chest of drawers *n* cassettone *m*.

chew [tʃu:] *vt* masticare ♦ *n* (*sweet*) caramella *f* (morbida).

chewing gum ['tʃu:ɪŋ-] *n* gomma *f* da masticare.

chic [ʃiːk] *adj* alla moda, chic *(inv)*.

chicken ['tʃɪkɪn] *n (bird)* gallina *f*; *(meat)* pollo *m*.

chicken breast *n* petto *m* di pollo.

chicken Kiev [-'kiːev] *n* filetto di pollo farcito con burro all'aglio, impanato e fritto.

chicken pox [-pɒks] *n* varicella *f*.

chickpea ['tʃɪkpiː] *n* cece *m*.

chicory ['tʃɪkərɪ] *n* cicoria *f*.

chief [tʃiːf] *adj (highest-ranking)* capo *(inv)*; *(main)* principale ◆ *n* capo *m*.

chiefly ['tʃiːflɪ] *adv (mainly)* principalmente; *(especially)* soprattutto.

child [tʃaɪld] *(pl* **children**) *n (young boy, girl)* bambino *m* (-a *f*); *(son, daughter)* figlio *m* (-a *f*).

child abuse *n* maltrattamento *m* di minori.

child benefit *n (Br)* = assegno *m* di famiglia.

childhood ['tʃaɪldhʊd] *n* infanzia *f*.

childish ['tʃaɪldɪʃ] *adj (pej)* infantile.

childminder ['tʃaɪld,maɪndə*r*] *n (Br)* bambinaia *f*.

children ['tʃɪldrən] *pl* → **child**.

childrenswear ['tʃɪldrənzweə*r*] *n* abbigliamento *m* per bambini.

child seat *n (in car)* seggiolino *m* per bambini.

Chile ['tʃɪlɪ] *n* il Cile.

chill [tʃɪl] *n (illness)* infreddatura *f* ◆ *vt* raffreddare; **there's a ~ in the air** l'aria è fredda.

chilled [tʃɪld] *adj* freddo(-a); **'serve ~'** 'servire fresco'.

chilli ['tʃɪlɪ] *(pl* **-ies**) *n (vegetable)* peperoncino *m* piccante; *(dish)* = **chilli con carne**.

chilli con carne ['tʃɪlɪkɒn-'kɑːnɪ] *n* piatto messicano a base di carne e fagioli rossi cotti in spezie e salsa piccante.

chilly ['tʃɪlɪ] *adj* freddo(-a).

chimney ['tʃɪmnɪ] *n* camino *m*.

chimneypot ['tʃɪmnɪpɒt] *n* comignolo *m*.

chimpanzee [,tʃɪmpən'ziː] *n* scimpanzé *m inv*.

chin [tʃɪn] *n* mento *m*.

china ['tʃaɪnə] *n (material)* porcellana *f*.

China ['tʃaɪnə] *n* la Cina.

Chinese [,tʃaɪ'niːz] *adj* cinese ◆ *n (language)* cinese *m* ◆ *npl*: **the ~ i** cinesi; **a ~ restaurant** un ristorante cinese.

chip [tʃɪp] *n (small piece)* scheggia *f*; *(mark)* scheggiatura *f*; *(counter)* fiche *f inv*; *(COMPUT)* chip *m inv* ◆ *vt* scheggiare ❑ **chips** *npl (Br:* French fries) patate *fpl* fritte; *(Am: crisps)* patatine *fpl*.

chiropodist [kɪ'rɒpədɪst] *n* callista *mf*.

chisel ['tʃɪzl] *n* cesello *m*.

chives [tʃaɪvz] *npl* erba *f* cipollina.

chlorine ['klɔːriːn] *n* cloro *m*.

choc-ice ['tʃɒkaɪs] *n (Br)* blocco di gelato ricoperto di cioccolato.

chocolate ['tʃɒkələt] *n (food)* cioccolato *m*, cioccolata *f*; *(sweet)* cioccolatino *m*; *(drink)* cioccolata ◆ *adj* al cioccolato.

chocolate biscuit *n* biscotto *m* al cioccolato.

choice [tʃɔɪs] *n* scelta *f* ◆ *adj*

(meat, ingredients) di prima qualità; **the dressing of your ~** il condimento di vostra scelta.

choir ['kwaɪəʳ] *n* coro *m*.

choke [tʃəʊk] *n (AUT)* (valvola *f* dell')aria *f inv* ◆ *vt* soffocare ◆ *vi (on fishbone etc)* strozzarsi; *(to death)* soffocare.

cholera ['kɒlərə] *n* colera *m*.

choose [tʃuːz] *(pt chose, pp chosen) vt & vi* scegliere; **to ~ to do sthg** scegliere di fare qc.

chop [tʃɒp] *n (of meat)* braciola *f* ◆ *vt* tagliare ❑ **chop down** *vt sep* abbattere; **chop up** *vt sep* tagliare a pezzetti.

chopper ['tʃɒpəʳ] *n (inf: helicopter)* elicottero *m*.

chopping board ['tʃɒpɪŋ-] *n* tagliere *m*.

choppy ['tʃɒpɪ] *adj* increspato(-a).

chopsticks ['tʃɒpstɪks] *npl* bastoncini *mpl* cinesi.

chop suey [,tʃɒp'suːɪ] *n* piatto cinese a base di riso, striscioline di maiale o pollo, verdura e germogli di soia.

chord [kɔːd] *n* accordo *m*.

chore [tʃɔːʳ] *n* faccenda *f*.

chorus [ˈkɔːrəs] *n (part of song)* ritornello *m*; *(group of singers, dancers)* coro *m*.

chose [tʃəʊz] *pt* → **choose**.

chosen [ˈtʃəʊzn] *pp* → **choose**.

choux pastry [ʃuː-] *n* pasta *f* per bignè.

chowder ['tʃaʊdəʳ] *n* zuppa di pesce o frutti di mare.

chow mein [,tʃaʊ'meɪn] *n* piatto cinese di tagliolini fritti con verdure, carne o frutti di mare.

Christ [kraɪst] *n* Cristo *m*.

christen [ˈkrɪsn] *vt (baby)* battezzare.

Christian [ˈkrɪstʃən] *adj* cristiano(-a) ◆ *n* cristiano *m* (-a *f*).

Christian name *n* nome *m* di battesimo.

Christmas [ˈkrɪsməs] *n* Natale *m*; **Happy ~!** Buon Natale!

Christmas card *n* biglietto *m* d'auguri di Natale.

Christmas carol [-ˈkærəl] *n* canto *m* di Natale.

Christmas Day *n* il giorno di Natale.

Christmas Eve *n* la vigilia di Natale.

Christmas pudding *n* dolce tradizionale natalizio a base di uva passa e frutta candita.

Christmas tree *n* albero *m* di Natale.

chrome [krəʊm] *n* cromo *m*.

chuck [tʃʌk] *vt (inf) (throw)* buttare; *(boyfriend, girlfriend)* mollare ❑ **chuck away** *vt sep* buttare via.

chunk [tʃʌŋk] *n* pezzo *m*.

church [tʃɜːtʃ] *n* chiesa *f*; **to go to ~** andare in chiesa.

churchyard [ˈtʃɜːtʃjɑːd] *n* cimitero *m*.

chute [ʃuːt] *n* scivolo *m*.

chutney [ˈtʃʌtnɪ] *n* salsa piccante agrodolce a base di frutta e spezie.

cider [ˈsaɪdəʳ] *n* sidro *m*.

cigar [sɪˈɡɑːʳ] *n* sigaro *m*.

cigarette [,sɪɡəˈret] *n* sigaretta *f*.

cigarette lighter *n* accendino *m*.

cinema [ˈsɪnəmə] *n* cinema *m inv*.

cinnamon [ˈsɪnəmən] *n* cannella *f*.

circle ['sɜːkl] n (shape, ring) cerchio m; (in theatre) galleria f ◆ vt (draw circle around) cerchiare; (move round) girare intorno a ◆ vi (plane) girare in circolo.

circuit ['sɜːkɪt] n (track) circuito m; (lap) giro m.

circular ['sɜːkjʊləʳ] adj circolare ◆ n circolare f.

circulation [ˌsɜːkjʊ'leɪʃn] n (of blood) circolazione f; (of newspaper, magazine) tiratura f.

circumstances ['sɜːkəmstənsɪz] npl circostanze fpl; **in** OR **under the** ~ date le circostanze.

circus ['sɜːkəs] n circo m.

cistern ['sɪstən] n (of toilet) serbatoio m dell'acqua.

citizen ['sɪtɪzn] n cittadino m (-a f).

city ['sɪtɪ] n città f inv; **the City** la City (il centro finanziario di Londra).

city centre n centro m (della) città.

city hall n (Am) municipio m.

civilian [sɪ'vɪljən] n civile m.

civilized ['sɪvɪlaɪzd] adj (society) civilizzato(-a); (person, evening) cortese.

civil rights [ˌsɪvl-] npl diritti mpl civili.

civil servant [ˌsɪvl-] n impiegato m (-a f) statale.

civil service [ˌsɪvl-] n amministrazione f pubblica.

civil war [ˌsɪvl-] n guerra f civile.

cl (abbr of centilitre) cl.

claim [kleɪm] n (assertion) affermazione f; (demand) richiesta f, domanda f; (for insurance) domanda di indennizzo ◆ vt (allege) affer-

mare, sostenere; (demand) richiedere; (credit, responsibility) rivendicare ◆ vi (on insurance) richiedere l'indennizzo.

claimant ['kleɪmənt] n (of benefit) richiedente mf.

claim form n modulo m per il rimborso.

clam [klæm] n vongola f.

clamp [klæmp] n (for car) ganascia f (bloccaruota) ◆ vt (car) bloccare con ganasce.

clap [klæp] vi applaudire.

claret ['klærət] n vino rosso di Bordeaux.

clarinet [ˌklærə'net] n clarinetto m.

clash [klæʃ] n (noise) rumore m metallico; (confrontation) scontro m ◆ vi (colours) stonare; (event, date) coincidere.

clasp [klɑːsp] n (fastener) fermaglio m ◆ vt stringere.

class [klɑːs] n classe f; (teaching period) lezione f ◆ vt: **to** ~ **sb/sthg** (**as**) classificare qn/qc (come).

classic ['klæsɪk] adj classico(-a) ◆ n classico m.

classical ['klæsɪkl] adj classico(-a).

classical music n musica f classica.

classification [ˌklæsɪfɪ'keɪʃn] n classificazione f.

classified ads [ˌklæsɪfaɪd-] npl piccoli annunci mpl.

classroom ['klɑːsrʊm] n aula f.

claustrophobic [ˌklɔːstrə'fəʊbɪk] adj (person) claustrofobo(-a); (place, situation) claustrofobico(-a).

claw [klɔː] n (of bird, cat, dog) artiglio m; (of crab, lobster) pinza f.

clay [kleɪ] n argilla f.

clean [kliːn] vt pulire ♦ adj pulito(-a); **to ~ one's teeth** lavarsi i denti; **I have a ~ driving licence** non sono mai stato multato per infrazioni gravi.

cleaner ['kliːnəʳ] n (person) addetto m (-a f) alle pulizie; (substance) detergente m.

cleanse [klenz] vt pulire.

cleanser ['klenzəʳ] n detergente m.

clear [klɪəʳ] adj chiaro(-a); (transparent) trasparente; (unobstructed) libero(-a); (view) sgombro(-a); (day, sky) sereno(-a) ♦ vt (road, path) sgombrare; (pond) ripulire; (jump over) saltare; (declare not guilty) scagionare; (authorize) autorizzare; (cheque) autorizzare l'accreditamento di ♦ vi (weather) schiarirsi; (fog) levarsi; **to ~ (about sthg)** avere capito esattamente (qc); **to be ~ of sthg** (not touching) essere staccato da qc; **to ~ one's throat** schiarirsi la voce; **to ~ the table** sparecchiare ❑ **clear up** vt sep (room, toys) mettere a posto; (problem, confusion) chiarire ♦ vi (weather) schiarirsi; (tidy up) mettere a posto.

clearance ['klɪərəns] n (authorization) autorizzazione f; (free distance) distanza f; (for takeoff) autorizzazione (al decollo).

clearance sale n liquidazione f totale della merce.

clearing ['klɪərɪŋ] n radura f.

clearly ['klɪəlɪ] adv chiaramente.

clearway ['klɪəweɪ] n (Br) strada f con divieto di fermata.

clementine ['kleməntaɪn] n mandarancio m.

clerk [Br klɑːk, Am klɜːrk] n (in office) impiegato m (-a f); (Am: in shop) commesso m (-a f).

clever ['klevəʳ] adj (person) intelligente; (idea, device) ingegnoso(-a).

click [klɪk] n scatto m ♦ vi (make sound) schioccare.

client ['klaɪənt] n cliente mf.

cliff [klɪf] n (by the sea) scoglio m; (inland) rupe f.

climate ['klaɪmət] n clima m.

climax ['klaɪmæks] n culmine m.

climb [klaɪm] vt salire su; (tree) arrampicarsi su; (mountain) scalare ♦ vi salire; (plane) prendere quota ❑ **climb down** vt fus scendere da ♦ vi scendere; **climb up** vt fus salire su.

climber ['klaɪməʳ] n (person) scalatore m (-trice f).

climbing ['klaɪmɪŋ] n alpinismo m; **to go ~** fare alpinismo.

climbing frame n (Br) castello m (gioco per bambini).

clingfilm ['klɪŋfɪlm] n (Br) pellicola f (per alimenti).

clinic ['klɪnɪk] n clinica f.

clip [klɪp] n (fastener) fermaglio m; (for paper) graffetta f; (of film, programme) sequenza f ♦ vt (fasten) fermare insieme; (cut) tagliare; (tickets) forare.

cloak [kləʊk] n mantello m.

cloakroom ['kləʊkrʊm] n (for coats) guardaroba m inv; (Br: toilet) toilettes fpl.

clock [klɒk] n orologio m; (mileometer) contachilometri m inv; **round the ~** 24 ore su 24.

clockwise ['klɒkwaɪz] adv in senso orario.

clog [klɒg] n zoccolo m ♦ vt n

tasare.

close[1] [kləus] *adj* vicino(-a); *(relation, contact, resemblance)* stretto(-a); *(friend)* intimo(-a); *(examination)* attento(-a); *(race, contest)* combattuto(-a) ♦ *adv* vicino; **~ by** vicino; **~ to** *(near)* vicino a; *(on the verge of)* sull'orlo di.

close[2] [kləuz] *vt* chiudere ♦ *vi (door, jar, eyes)* chiudersi; *(shop, office)* chiudere; *(deadline, offer, meeting)* finire ◻ **close down** *vt sep & vi* chiudere (definitivamente).

closed [kləuzd] *adj* chiuso(-a).

closely ['kləuslı] *adv (related, involved)* strettamente; *(follow, examine)* da vicino, attentamente.

closet ['klɒzɪt] *n (Am)* armadio *m*.

close-up ['kləus-] *n* primo piano *m*.

closing time ['kləuzɪŋ-] *n* orario *m* di chiusura.

clot [klɒt] *n (of blood)* grumo *m*.

cloth [klɒθ] *n (fabric)* stoffa *f*, tessuto *m*; *(piece of cloth)* strofinaccio *m*, panno *m*.

clothes [kləuðz] *npl* vestiti *mpl*, abiti *mpl*.

clothesline ['kləuðzlaın] *n* filo *m* della biancheria.

clothes peg *n (Br)* molletta *f*.

clothespin ['kləuðzpın] *(Am)* = clothes peg.

clothes shop *n* negozio *m* di abbigliamento.

clothing ['kləuðıŋ] *n* abbigliamento *m*.

clotted cream [klɒtıd-] *n panna molto densa tipica della Cornovaglia*.

cloud [klaud] *n* nuvola *f*.

cloudy ['klaudı] *adj (sky, day)* nuvoloso(-a); *(liquid)* torbido(-a).

clove [kləuv] *n (of garlic)* spicchio *m* ◻ **cloves** *npl (spice)* chiodi *mpl* di garofano.

clown [klaun] *n* pagliaccio *m*.

club [klʌb] *n (organization)* club *m inv*, circolo *m*; *(nightclub)* locale *m* notturno; *(stick)* mazza *f* ◻ **clubs** *npl (in cards)* fiori *mpl*.

clubbing ['klʌbıŋ] *n*: **to go ~** *(inf)* andare in discoteca.

club class *n* club class *f inv*.

club sandwich *n (Am)* sandwich *a due o più strati*.

club soda *n (Am)* acqua *f* di seltz.

clue [klu:] *n (information)* indizio *m*; *(in crossword)* definizione *f*; **I haven't got a ~** non ho la minima idea.

clumsy ['klʌmzı] *adj (person)* goffo(-a).

clutch [klʌtʃ] *n* frizione *f* ♦ *vt* tenere stretto, afferrare.

cm *(abbr of centimetre)* cm.

c/o *(abbr of care of)* c/o.

Co. *(abbr of company)* C.ia.

coach [kəutʃ] *n (bus)* pullman *m inv*, autobus *m inv*; *(of train)* carrozza *f*; *(SPORT)* allenatore *m* (-trice *f*).

coach party *n (Br)* gruppo *m in viaggio organizzato in pullman*.

coach station *n* stazione *f* dei pullman.

coach trip *n (Br)* escursione *f in pullman*.

coal [kəul] *n* carbone *m*.

coal mine *n* miniera *f* di carbone.

coarse [kɔ:s] *adj (rough)* ruvido(-a); *(vulgar)* rozzo(-a).

coast [kəust] *n* costa *f*.

coaster ['kəʊstə'] n (for glass) sottobicchiere m.

coastguard ['kəʊstgɑːd] n guardia f costiera.

coastline ['kəʊstlaɪn] n costa f.

coat [kəʊt] n cappotto m; (of animal) pelo m ♦ vt: **to ~ sthg (with)** ricoprire qc (con OR di).

coat hanger n gruccia f (per abiti).

coating ['kəʊtɪŋ] n rivestimento m.

cobbled street ['kɒbld-] n strada f in acciottolato.

cobbles ['kɒblz] npl ciottoli mpl.

cobweb ['kɒbweb] n ragnatela f.

Coca-Cola® [,kəʊkə'kəʊlə] n Coca-Cola® f.

cocaine [kəʊ'keɪn] n cocaina f.

cock [kɒk] n (male chicken) gallo m.

cock-a-leekie [,kɒkə'liːkɪ] n zuppa f di porri e pollo.

cockerel ['kɒkərəl] n galletto m.

cockles ['kɒklz] npl cardii mpl.

cockpit ['kɒkpɪt] n cabina f di pilotaggio.

cockroach ['kɒkrəʊtʃ] n scarafaggio m.

cocktail ['kɒkteɪl] n cocktail m inv.

cocktail party n cocktail m inv.

cock-up n (Br: vulg) casino m.

cocoa ['kəʊkəʊ] n (drink) cacao m.

coconut ['kəʊkənʌt] n noce f di cocco.

cod [kɒd] (pl inv) n merluzzo m.

code [kəʊd] n codice m; (dialling code) prefisso m.

cod-liver oil n olio m di fegato di merluzzo.

coeducational [,kəʊedju:'keɪʃənl] adj misto(-a).

coffee ['kɒfɪ] n caffè m inv; **black/white ~** caffè nero/macchiato; **ground/instant ~** caffè macinato/istantaneo.

coffee bar n (Br) caffè m inv.

coffee break n pausa f per il caffè.

coffeepot ['kɒfɪpɒt] n caffettiera f.

coffee shop n (cafe) caffè m inv, bar m inv; (in store etc) caffetteria f.

coffee table n tavolino m (basso).

coffin ['kɒfɪn] n bara f.

cog(wheel) ['kɒg(wiːl)] n ingranaggio m.

coil [kɔɪl] n (of rope) rotolo m; (Br: contraceptive) spirale f ♦ vt avvolgere, arrotolare.

coin [kɔɪn] n moneta f.

coinbox ['kɔɪnbɒks] n (Br) telefono m a monete.

coincide [,kəʊɪn'saɪd] vi: **to ~ (with)** coincidere (con).

coincidence [kəʊ'ɪnsɪdəns] n coincidenza f.

Coke® [kəʊk] n coca® f.

colander ['kʌləndə'] n colino m.

cold [kəʊld] adj freddo(-a) ♦ n (illness) raffreddore m; (low temperature) freddo m; **I'm ~** ho freddo; **it's ~** fa freddo; **to get ~** (food, drink) raffreddarsi; (person) avere freddo; (weather) venire freddo; **to catch ~** prendere freddo; **to catch a ~** prendere il raffreddore.

cold cuts (Am) = **cold meats**.

cold meats npl affettati mpl.

coleslaw ['kəʊlslɔː] n insalata di

cavolo, carote, cipolle e maionese.

colic ['kɒlɪk] *n* colica *f*.

collaborate [kə'læbəreɪt] *vi* collaborare.

collapse [kə'læps] *vi (building, tent)* crollare; *(person)* avere un collasso.

collar ['kɒlə*r*] *n (of shirt, coat)* colletto *m*; *(of dog, cat)* collare *m*.

collarbone ['kɒləbəʊn] *n* clavicola *f*.

colleague ['kɒliːg] *n* collega *mf*.

collect [kə'lekt] *vt* raccogliere; *(as a hobby)* collezionare; *(go and get)* andare a prendere ◆ *vi (dust, leaves, crowd)* raccogliersi ◆ *adv (Am):* **to call ~** fare una telefonata a carico del destinatario.

collection [kə'lekʃn] *n (of stamps, coins etc)* collezione *f*, raccolta *f*; *(of stories, poems)* raccolta; *(of money)* colletta *f*; *(of mail)* levata *f*.

collector [kə'lektə*r*] *n (as a hobby)* collezionista *mf*.

college ['kɒlɪdʒ] *n (school)* istituto *m* superiore; *(Br: of university)* tipo di organizzazione indipendente di studenti e professori in cui si dividono certe università; *(Am: university)* università *f inv*.

collide [kə'laɪd] *vi:* **to ~ (with)** scontrarsi (con).

collision [kə'lɪʒn] *n* collisione *f*.

cologne [kə'ləʊn] *n (acqua f di)* colonia *f*.

colon ['kəʊlən] *n (GRAMM)* due punti *mpl*.

colonel ['kɜːnl] *n* colonnello *m*.

colony ['kɒlənɪ] *n* colonia *f*.

color ['kʌlə*r*] *(Am)* = **colour.**

colour ['kʌlə*r*] *n* colore *m* ◆ *adj*

(photograph, film) a colori ◆ *vt (hair)* tingere; *(food)* colorare □ **colour in** *vt sep* colorare.

colour-blind *adj* daltonico(-a).

colourful ['kʌləful] *adj* vivace.

colouring ['kʌlərɪŋ] *n (of food)* colorante *m*; *(complexion)* colorito *m*.

colouring book *n* album *m inv* da colorare.

colour supplement *n* supplemento *m* a colori.

colour television *n* televisione *f* a colori.

column ['kɒləm] *n* colonna *f*; *(newspaper article)* rubrica *f*.

coma ['kəʊmə] *n* coma *m inv*.

comb [kəʊm] *n* pettine *m* ◆ *vt:* **to ~ one's hair** pettinarsi.

combination [ˌkɒmbɪ'neɪʃn] *n* combinazione *f*.

combine [kəm'baɪn] *vt:* **to ~ sthg (with)** combinare qc (con).

combine harvester [ˌkɒmbaɪn-'hɑːvɪstə*r*] *n* mietitrebbia *f*.

come [kʌm] *(pt* came, *pp* come) *vi* 1. *(move)* venire; **we came by taxi** siamo venuti in taxi; **~ and see!** vieni a vedere!; **~ here!** vieni qui!

2. *(arrive)* arrivare; **they still haven't ~** non sono ancora arrivati; **to ~ home** tornare a casa; **'coming soon'** 'prossimamente'.

3. *(in order):* **to ~ first** *(in sequence)* venire per primo; *(in competition)* arrivare primo; **to ~ last** *(in sequence)* venire per ultimo; *(in competition)* arrivare ultimo.

4. *(reach):* **to ~ up/down to** arrivare a.

5. *(become):* **to ~ undone** slacciarsi; **to ~ true** realizzarsi.

6. *(be sold):* **they ~ in packs of six** si

vendono in confezioni da sei.
❑ **come across** vt fus (person) imbattersi in; (thing) trovare (per caso); **come along** vi (progress) procedere; (arrive) arrivare; **~ along!** (as encouragement) forza!; (hurry up) sbrigati!; **come apart** vi cadere a pezzi; **come back** vi tornare; **come down** vi (price) calare; **come down with** vt fus (illness) buscarsi; **come from** vt fus venire da; **come in** vi (enter) entrare; (arrive) arrivare; (tide) salire; **~ in!** avanti!; **come off** vi (become detached) staccarsi, venir via; (succeed) riuscire; **come on** vi (project) procedere; (student) fare progressi; **~ on!** (as encouragement) forza!; (hurry up) sbrigati!; **come out** vi uscire; (photo) venire, riuscire; (stain) scomparire; (sun, moon) apparire; **come over** vi (visit) venire; **come round** vi (visit) venire; (regain consciousness) riprendere conoscenza; **come to** vt fus (subj: bill): **it ~s to £10** viene 10 sterline; **come up** vi (go upstairs) salire; (be mentioned) essere sollevato(-a); (happen, arise) presentarsi; (sun, moon) sorgere; **come up with** vt fus (idea) proporre.

comedian [kəˈmiːdjən] n comico m (-a f).

comedy [ˈkɒmədi] n commedia f; (humour) humour m.

comfort [ˈkʌmfət] n (ease) benessere m; (luxury) comfort m inv, comodità f inv; (consolation) conforto m ◆ vt confortare, consolare.

comfortable [ˈkʌmfətbl] adj comodo(-a); (after operation) in condizioni stazionarie; (financially) agiato(-a); **I don't feel ~ here** non

mi sento a mio agio qui.

comic [ˈkɒmɪk] adj comico(-a) ◆ n (person) comico m (-a f); (magazine) giornalino m.

command [kəˈmɑːnd] n (order) comando m, ordine m; (mastery) padronanza f ◆ vt (order) ordinare a; (be in charge of) comandare.

commander [kəˈmɑːndər] n comandante m.

commemorate [kəˈmeməreɪt] vt commemorare.

commence [kəˈmens] vi (fml) cominciare.

comment [ˈkɒment] n commento m ◆ vi commentare.

commentary [ˈkɒməntri] n (on TV) telecronaca f; (on radio) radiocronaca f.

commentator [ˈkɒmənteɪtər] n (on TV) telecronista mf; (on radio) radiocronista mf.

commerce [ˈkɒmɜːs] n commercio m.

commercial [kəˈmɜːʃl] adj commerciale ◆ n pubblicità f inv.

commercial break n intervallo m pubblicitario.

commission [kəˈmɪʃn] n commissione f.

commit [kəˈmɪt] vt (crime, sin) commettere; **to ~ o.s. (to doing sthg)** impegnarsi (a fare qc); **to ~ suicide** suicidarsi.

committee [kəˈmɪti] n comitato m.

commodity [kəˈmɒdəti] n merce f, articolo m.

common ['kɒmən] *adj* comune; *(pej: vulgar)* volgare ♦ *n (Br: land)* prato *m* pubblico; **in ~** *(shared)* in comune.

commonly ['kɒmənlɪ] *adv (generally)* comunemente.

Common Market *n* Mercato *m* comune.

common room *n (for teachers)* sala *f* professori; *(for students)* sala di ritrovo.

common sense *n* buon senso *m*.

Commonwealth ['kɒmən-welθ] *n*: **the ~** il Commonwealth.

communal ['kɒmjunl] *adj (bath-room, kitchen)* in comune.

communicate [kə'mjuːnɪkeɪt] *vi*: **to ~ (with)** comunicare (con).

communication [kə,mjuːnɪ-'keɪʃn] *n* comunicazione *f*.

communication cord *n (Br)* freno *m* di emergenza.

communist ['kɒmjunɪst] *n* comunista *mf*.

community [kə'mjuːnətɪ] *n* comunità *f inv*.

community centre *n* centro *m* sociale.

commute [kə'mjuːt] *vi* fare il pendolare.

commuter [kə'mjuːtə'] *n* pendolare *mf*.

compact [*adj* kəm'pækt, *n* 'kɒmpækt] *adj* compatto(-a) ♦ *n (for make-up)* portacipria *m inv*; *(Am: car)* utilitaria *f*.

compact disc [,kɒmpækt-] *n* compact disc *m inv*.

compact disc player *n* lettore *m* di compact disc.

company ['kʌmpənɪ] *n (business)*

società *f inv*, compagnia *f*; *(companionship, guests)* compagnia; **to keep sb ~** fare OR tenere compagnia a qn.

company car *n* auto *f* della ditta.

comparatively [kəm'pærətɪvlɪ] *adv* relativamente.

compare [kəm'peə'] *vt*: **to ~ sthg (with)** confrontare qc (con); **~d with** paragonato a.

comparison [kəm'pærɪsn] *n* confronto *m*, paragone *m*; **in ~ with** in confronto a.

compartment [kəm'pɑːtmənt] *n (of train)* scompartimento *m*; *(section)* compartimento *m*.

compass ['kʌmpəs] *n (magnetic)* bussola *f*; **(a pair of) ~es** un compasso.

compatible [kəm'pætəbl] *adj* compatibile.

compensate ['kɒmpenseɪt] *vt* risarcire ♦ *vi*: **to ~ (for sthg)** compensare (qc); **to ~ sb for sthg** compensare qn di OR per qc.

compensation [,kɒmpen'seɪʃn] *n (money)* risarcimento *m*.

compete [kəm'piːt] *vi (take part)* gareggiare, concorrere; **to ~ with sb for sthg** competere con qn per qc.

competent ['kɒmpɪtənt] *adj* competente.

competition [,kɒmpɪ'tɪʃn] *n (race, contest)* gara *f*, competizione *f*; *(rivalry)* concorrenza *f*; **the ~** *(rivals)* la concorrenza.

competitive [kəm'petətɪv] *adj (price)* competitivo(-a); *(person)* che ha spirito di competizione.

competitor [kəm'petɪtə'] *n* concorrente *mf*.

complain [kəm'pleɪn] *vi*: **to ~ (about)** lamentarsi (di).

complaint [kəm'pleɪnt] *n (statement)* lamentela *f*, reclamo *m*; *(illness)* malattia *f*.

complement ['kɒmplɪˌment] *vt* completare.

complete [kəm'pliːt] *adj* completo(-a) ♦ *vt* completare; *(a form)* riempire; **~ with** completo di.

completely [kəm'pliːtlɪ] *adv* completamente.

complex ['kɒmpleks] *adj* complesso(-a) ♦ *n* complesso *m*.

complexion [kəm'plekʃn] *n (of skin)* carnagione *f*.

complicated ['kɒmplɪkeɪtɪd] *adj* complicato(-a).

compliment [*n* 'kɒmplɪmənt, *vb* 'kɒmplɪment] *n* complimento *m* ♦ *vt* fare i complimenti a.

complimentary [ˌkɒmplɪ'mentərɪ] *adj (seat, ticket)* (in) omaggio *(inv)*; *(words, person)* lusinghiero(-a).

compose [kəm'pəʊz] *vt* comporre; **to be ~d of** essere composto da OR di.

composed [kəm'pəʊzd] *adj* composto(-a), calmo(-a).

composer [kəm'pəʊzəʳ] *n* compositore *m* (-trice *f*).

composition [ˌkɒmpə'zɪʃn] *n (essay)* composizione *f*.

compound ['kɒmpaʊnd] *n (substance)* composto *m*; *(word)* parola *f* composta.

comprehensive [ˌkɒmprɪ'hensɪv] *adj* esauriente, completo(-a).

comprehensive (school) *n (Br)* scuola secondaria ad ammissione non selettiva.

compressed air [kəm'prest-] *n* aria *f* compressa.

comprise [kəm'praɪz] *vt* comprendere.

compromise ['kɒmprəmaɪz] *n* compromesso *m*.

compulsory [kəm'pʌlsərɪ] *adj* obbligatorio(-a).

computer [kəm'pjuːtəʳ] *n* computer *m inv*.

computer game *n* gioco *m* su computer.

computerized [kəm'pjuːtə-raɪzd] *adj* computerizzato(-a).

computer operator *n* operatore *m* (-trice *f*) di computer.

computer programmer [-'prəʊgræməʳ] *n* programmatore *m* (-trice *f*).

computing [kəm'pjuːtɪŋ] *n* informatica *f*.

con [kɒn] *n (inf: trick)* truffa *f*; **all mod ~s** tutti i comfort.

conceal [kən'siːl] *vt* nascondere.

conceited [kən'siːtɪd] *adj (pej)* presuntuoso(-a).

concentrate ['kɒnsəntreɪt] *vi* concentrarsi ♦ *vt*: **to be ~d** *(in one place)* essere concentrato; **to ~ on** sthg concentrarsi su qc.

concentrated ['kɒnsəntreɪtɪd] *adj (juice, soup, baby food)* concentrato(-a).

concentration [ˌkɒnsən'treɪʃn] *n* concentrazione *f*.

concern [kən'sɜːn] *n (worry)* preoccupazione *f*; *(matter of interest)* affare *m*; *(COMM)* azienda *f* ♦ *vt (be about)* trattare di; *(worry)* preoccupare; *(involve)* riguardare; **to be ~ed about** essere preoccupato per; **to be ~ed with** riguardare; **to ~ o.s. with sthg** preoccuparsi di qc.

as far as I'm ~ed per quanto mi riguarda.

concerned [kən'sɜːnd] *adj (worried)* preoccupato(-a).

concerning [kən'sɜːnɪŋ] *prep* riguardo a, circa.

concert ['kɒnsət] *n* concerto *m*.

concession [kən'sɛʃn] *n (reduced price)* riduzione *f*.

concise [kən'saɪs] *adj* conciso(-a).

conclude [kən'kluːd] *vt* concludere ♦ *vi (fml: end)* concludersi.

conclusion [kən'kluːʒn] *n* conclusione *f*.

concrete ['kɒŋkriːt] *adj (building, path)* di cemento; *(idea, plan)* concreto(-a) ♦ *n* calcestruzzo *m*, cemento *m* armato.

concussion [kən'kʌʃn] *n* commozione *f* cerebrale.

condensation [ˌkɒndenˈseɪʃn] *n* condensazione *f*.

condensed milk [kən'denst-] *n* latte *m* condensato.

condition [kən'dɪʃn] *n* condizione *f*; *(illness)* malattia *f*; **to be out of ~** non essere in forma; **on ~ that** a condizione che (+ *subjunctive)*.

conditioner [kən'dɪʃnər] *n (for hair)* balsamo *m*; *(for clothes)* ammorbidente *m*.

condo ['kɒndəʊ] *(Am: inf)* = **condominium**.

condom ['kɒndəm] *n* preservativo *m*.

condominium [ˌkɒndə'mɪnɪəm] *n (Am) (block of flats)* condominio *m*; *(flat)* appartamento *m* in un condominio.

conduct [*vb* kən'dʌkt, *n* 'kɒndʌkt] *vt (investigation, business)* dirigere, condurre; *(MUS)* dirigere ♦ *n (fml: behaviour)* condotta *f*; **to ~ o.s.** *(fml)* comportarsi.

conductor [kən'dʌktər] *n (MUS)* direttore *m* (-trice *f*) d'orchestra; *(on bus)* bigliettaio *m* (-a *f*); *(Am: on train)* capotreno *mf*.

cone [kəʊn] *n* cono *m*; *(on roads)* cono spartitraffico.

confectioner's [kən'fekʃnəz] *n (shop)* negozio *m* di dolciumi.

confectionery [kən'fekʃnərɪ] *n* dolciumi *mpl*.

conference ['kɒnfərəns] *n* conferenza *f*.

confess [kən'fes] *vi*: **to ~ (to sthg)** confessare (qc).

confession [kən'feʃn] *n* confessione *f*.

confidence ['kɒnfɪdəns] *n (self-assurance)* sicurezza *f* di sé; *(trust)* fiducia *f*; **to have ~ in** avere fiducia in.

confident ['kɒnfɪdənt] *adj (self-assured)* sicuro(-a) di sé; *(certain)* sicuro.

confined [kən'faɪnd] *adj* ristretto(-a).

confirm [kən'fɜːm] *vt* confermare.

confirmation [ˌkɒnfə'meɪʃn] *n* conferma *f*; *(RELIG)* cresima *f*.

conflict [*n* 'kɒnflɪkt, *vb* kən'flɪkt] *n* conflitto *m* ♦ *vi*: **to ~ (with)** essere in conflitto (con).

conform [kən'fɔːm] *vi*: **to ~ (to)** conformarsi a.

confuse [kən'fjuːz] *vt* confondere; **to ~ sthg with sthg** confondere qc con qc.

confused [kən'fjuːzd] *adj* confuso(-a).

confusing [kən'fju:zɪŋ] *adj* (explanation, plot) confuso(-a).

confusion [kən'fju:ʒn] *n* confusione *f*.

congested [kən'dʒestɪd] *adj* (street) congestionato(-a).

congestion [kən'dʒestʃn] *n* (traffic) congestione *f*.

congratulate [kən'grætʃʊleɪt] *vt*: to ~ sb (on sthg) congratularsi con qn (per OR di qc).

congratulations [kən‚grætʃʊ'leɪʃənz] *excl* congratulazioni!

congregate ['kɒŋgrɪgeɪt] *vi* riunirsi.

Congress ['kɒŋgres] *n* (Am) il Congresso.

conifer ['kɒnɪfə'] *n* conifera *f*.

conjunction [kən'dʒʌŋkʃn] *n* (GRAMM) congiunzione *f*.

conjurer ['kʌndʒərə'] *n* prestigiatore *m* (-trice *f*).

connect [kə'nekt] *vt* collegare, connettere; (telephone, machine) collegare; (caller on phone) mettere in comunicazione ♦ *vi*: to ~ with (train, plane) avere la coincidenza con; to ~ sthg with sthg (associate) collegare qc con OR a qc.

connecting flight [kə'nektɪŋ-] *n* volo *m* di coincidenza.

connection [kə'nekʃn] *n* (link) collegamento *m*; (train, plane) coincidenza *f*; a bad ~ (on phone) la linea è disturbata; a loose ~ (in machine) un contatto difettoso; in ~ with riguardo a, a proposito di.

conquer ['kɒŋkə'] *vt* (country) conquistare.

conscience ['kɒnʃəns] *n* coscienza *f*.

conscientious [‚kɒnʃɪ'enʃəs] *adj* coscienzioso(-a).

conscious ['kɒnʃəs] *adj* (awake) cosciente; (deliberate) consapevole; to be ~ of (aware) essere consapevole di.

consent [kən'sent] *n* consenso *m*.

consequence ['kɒnsɪkwəns] *n* (result) conseguenza *f*.

consequently ['kɒnsɪkwəntlɪ] *adv* di conseguenza.

conservation [‚kɒnsə'veɪʃn] *n* tutela *f* dell'ambiente.

conservative [kən'sɜ:vətɪv] *adj* conservatore(-trice) □ **Conservative** *adj* conservatore(-trice) ♦ *n* conservatore *m* (-trice *f*).

conservatory [kən'sɜ:vətrɪ] *n* veranda *f* vetrata.

consider [kən'sɪdə'] *vt* considerare; to ~ doing sthg pensare di fare qc.

considerable [kən'sɪdrəbl] *adj* considerevole.

consideration [kən‚sɪdə'reɪʃn] *n* considerazione *f*; to take sthg into ~ prendere qc in considerazione.

considering [kən'sɪdərɪŋ] *prep* considerando.

consist [kən'sɪst] : **consist in** *vt fus* consistere in; to ~ in doing sthg consistere nel fare qc □ **consist of** *vt fus* essere composto OR da.

consistent [kən'sɪstənt] *adj* (coherent) coerente; (worker, performance) costante.

consolation [‚kɒnsə'leɪʃn] *n* consolazione *f*.

console ['kɒnsəʊl] *n* console *f inv*.

consonant ['kɒnsənənt] *n* consonante *f*.

conspicuous [kən'spɪkjʊəs] *adj*

constable 64

cospicuo(-a).

constable ['kʌnstəbl] n (Br) agente m di polizia.

constant ['kɒnstənt] adj (unchanging) costante; (continuous) continuo(-a).

constantly ['kɒnstəntlɪ] adv (all the time) continuamente.

constipated ['kɒnstɪpeɪtɪd] adj stitico(-a).

constitution [ˌkɒnstɪ'tjuːʃn] n costituzione f.

construct [kən'strʌkt] vt costruire.

construction [kən'strʌkʃn] n costruzione f; **under ~** in costruzione.

consul ['kɒnsəl] n console m.

consulate ['kɒnsjulət] n consolato m.

consult [kən'sʌlt] vt consultare.

consultant [kən'sʌltənt] n (Br: doctor) specialista mf.

consume [kən'sjuːm] vt consumare.

consumer [kən'sjuːmər] n consumatore m (-trice f).

contact ['kɒntækt] n (communication) contatto m; (person) conoscenza f ♦ vt mettersi in contatto con; **in ~ with** (in communication with) in contatto con; (touching) a contatto con.

contact lens n lente f a contatto.

contagious [kən'teɪdʒəs] adj contagioso(-a).

contain [kən'teɪn] vt contenere.

container [kən'teɪnər] n (box etc) contenitore m, recipiente m.

contaminate [kən'tæmɪneɪt] vt contaminare.

contemporary [kən'tempərərɪ] adj contemporaneo(-a) ♦ n contemporaneo m (-a f).

contend [kən'tend] : **contend with** vt fus affrontare.

content [adj kən'tent, n 'kɒntent] adj contento(-a) ♦ n (of vitamins, fibre etc) contenuto m ❏ **contents** npl (things inside) contenuto m; (at beginning of book) indice m.

contest [n 'kɒntest, vb kən'test] n (competition) gara f, concorso m; (struggle) lotta f ♦ vt (election, seat) candidarsi per; (decision, will) contestare.

context ['kɒntekst] n contesto m.

continent ['kɒntɪnənt] n continente m; **the Continent** (Br) l'Europa f continentale.

continental [ˌkɒntɪ'nentl] adj (Br: European) (dell'Europa) continentale.

continental breakfast n colazione f continentale.

continental quilt n (Br) piumone® m.

continual [kən'tɪnjuəl] adj continuo(-a).

continually [kən'tɪnjuəlɪ] adv continuamente, di continuo.

continue [kən'tɪnjuː] vt & vi continuare; **to ~ doing sthg** continuare a fare qc; **to ~ with sthg** continuare con qc.

continuous [kən'tɪnjuəs] adj continuo(-a).

continuously [kən'tɪnjuəslɪ] adv continuamente, senza interruzione.

contraception [ˌkɒntrə'sepʃn] n contraccezione f.

contraceptive [ˌkɒntrə'septɪv] n contraccettivo m.

contract [n 'kɒntrækt, vb kən'trækt] n contratto m ◆ vt (fml: illness) contrarre.

contradict [ˌkɒntrə'dɪkt] vt contraddire.

contraflow ['kɒntrəfləʊ] n (Br) sistema che permette il traffico nei due sensi su una stessa carreggiata dell'autostrada per lavori in corso o per un incidente.

contrary ['kɒntrərɪ] n: on the ~ al contrario.

contrast [n 'kɒntrɑːst, vb kən'trɑːst] n contrasto m ◆ vt mettere in contrasto; in ~ to contrariamente a.

contribute [kən'trɪbjuːt] vt (help, money) dare (come contributo) ◆ vi: to ~ to contribuire a.

contribution [ˌkɒntrɪ'bjuːʃn] n contributo m.

control [kən'trəʊl] n controllo m; (operating device) comando m ◆ vt controllare; (machine) regolare; to be in ~ avere la situazione sotto controllo; to get out of ~ (situation) sfuggire di mano; to go out of ~ (car, plane) non rispondere ai comandi; under ~ sotto controllo ❑ controls npl comandi mpl.

control tower n torre f di controllo.

controversial [ˌkɒntrə'vɜːʃl] adj controverso(-a); (person) polemico(-a).

convenience [kən'viːnjəns] n comodità f inv; at your ~ quando Le è più comodo.

convenient [kən'viːnjənt] adj comodo(-a); would tomorrow be ~? domani andrebbe bene?

convent ['kɒnvənt] n convento m.

conventional [kən'venʃənl] adj convenzionale.

conversation [ˌkɒnvə'seɪʃn] n conversazione f.

conversion [kən'vɜːʃn] n (change) trasformazione f; (of currency) conversione f; (to building) ristrutturazione f.

convert [kən'vɜːt] vt (change) trasformare; (currency, person) convertire; to ~ sthg into trasformare qc in.

converted [kən'vɜːtɪd] adj (barn, loft) ristrutturato(-a).

convertible [kən'vɜːtəbl] n cabriolet m inv.

convey [kən'veɪ] vt (fml: transport) trasportare; (idea, impression) dare.

convict [n 'kɒnvɪkt, vb kən'vɪkt] n carcerato m (-a f) ◆ vt: to ~ sb (of) giudicare qn colpevole (di).

convince [kən'vɪns] vt: to ~ sb (of sthg) convincere qn (di qc); to ~ sb to do sthg convincere qn a fare qc.

convoy ['kɒnvɔɪ] n convoglio m.

cook [kʊk] n cuoco m (-a f) ◆ vt (meal) cucinare; (food) cuocere ◆ vi (person) cucinare; (food) cuocere.

cookbook ['kʊkbʊk] = **cookery book**.

cooker ['kʊkə'] n cucina f (elettrodomestico).

cookery ['kʊkərɪ] n cucina f.

cookery book n libro m di cucina.

cookie ['kʊkɪ] n (Am) biscotto m.

cooking ['kʊkɪŋ] n cucina f.

cooking apple n mela f da cuocere.

cooking oil n olio m per cucinare.

cool [kuːl] *adj (temperature)* fresco(-a); *(calm)* calmo(-a); *(unfriendly)* freddo(-a); *(inf: great)* fantastico (-a) ♦ *vt* raffreddare ❑ **cool down** *vi (become colder)* raffreddarsi; *(become calmer)* calmarsi.

cooperate [kəʊˈɒpəreɪt] *vi* collaborare, cooperare.

cooperation [kəʊɒpəˈreɪʃn] *n* collaborazione f.

cooperative [kəʊˈɒpərətɪv] *adj (helpful)* disposto(-a) a collaborare.

coordinates [kəʊˈɔːdɪnəts] *npl (clothes)* coordinati *mpl*.

cope [kəʊp] *vi*: **to ~ with** far fronte a; **I can't ~!** non ce la faccio!

copilot [ˈkəʊpaɪlət] *n* secondo pilota *m*.

copper [ˈkɒpəʳ] *n (metal)* rame m; *(Br: inf: coin)* moneta in rame da uno e due penny.

copy [ˈkɒpɪ] *n* copia f ♦ *vt* copiare.

cord(uroy) [ˈkɔːd(ərɔɪ)] *n* velluto m a coste.

core [kɔːʳ] *n (of fruit)* torsolo m.

coriander [ˌkɒrɪˈændəʳ] *n* coriandolo m *(spezia)*.

cork [kɔːk] *n (in bottle)* tappo m (di sughero).

corkscrew [ˈkɔːkskruː] *n* cavatappi m *inv*.

corn [kɔːn] *n (Br: crop)* cereali *mpl*; *(Am: maize)* granturco m; *(on foot)* callo m.

corned beef [ˌkɔːnd-] *n* carne f di manzo in scatola.

corner [ˈkɔːnəʳ] *n* angolo m; *(bend in road)* curva f; *(in football)* calcio m d'angolo; **it's just around the ~** è qui dietro l'angolo.

corner shop *n (Br)* negozietto m *(di alimentari e prodotti per la casa)*.

cornet [ˈkɔːnɪt] *n (Br: ice-cream cone)* cornetto m.

cornflakes [ˈkɔːnfleɪks] *npl* corn-flakes *mpl*.

corn-on-the-cob *n* pannocchia f bollita.

Cornwall [ˈkɔːnwɔːl] *n* la Cornovaglia.

corporal [ˈkɔːpərəl] *n* caporale m.

corpse [kɔːps] *n* cadavere m.

correct [kəˈrekt] *adj* giusto(-a) ♦ *vt* correggere.

correction [kəˈrekʃn] *n* correzione f.

correspond [ˌkɒrɪˈspɒnd] *vi*: **to ~ (to)** *(match)* corrispondere (a); **to ~ (with)** *(exchange letters)* essere in corrispondenza (con).

corresponding [ˌkɒrɪˈspɒndɪŋ] *adj* corrispondente.

corridor [ˈkɒrɪdɔːʳ] *n* corridoio m.

corrugated iron [ˈkɒrəgeɪtɪd-] *n* lamiera f ondulata.

corrupt [kəˈrʌpt] *adj* corrotto(-a).

cosmetics [kɒzˈmetɪks] *npl* cosmetici *mpl*.

cost [kɒst] *(pt & pp* **cost)** *n* costo m; *(fig: loss)* prezzo m ♦ *vt* costare; **how much does it ~?** quanto costa?

costly [ˈkɒstlɪ] *adj (expensive)* costoso(-a).

costume [ˈkɒstjuːm] *n* costume m.

cosy [ˈkəʊzɪ] *adj (Br: room, house)* accogliente.

cot [kɒt] *n (Br: for baby)* lettino m *(per bambini)*; *(Am: camp bed* brandina f.

cottage [ˈkɒtɪdʒ] n cottage m inv.

cottage cheese n formaggio m magro in fiocchi.

cottage pie n (Br) pasticcio a base di carne macinata e purè di patate.

cotton [ˈkɒtn] adj di cotone ◆ n cotone m.

cotton candy n (Am) zucchero m filato.

cotton wool n cotone m idrofilo.

couch [kautʃ] n divano m; (at doctor's) lettino m.

couchette [kuːˈʃet] n cuccetta f.

cough [kɒf] n tosse f ◆ vi tossire; **to have a ~** avere la tosse.

cough mixture n sciroppo m per la tosse.

could [kʊd] pt → **can**.

couldn't [ˈkʊdnt] = could not.

could've [ˈkʊdəv] = could have.

council [ˈkaunsl] n (Br: of town) comune m; (Br: of county) = regione f; (organization) consiglio m.

council house n (Br) casa f popolare.

councillor [ˈkaunsələr] n (Br: of town, county) consigliere m (-a f).

council tax n (Br) = tassa f comunale.

count [kaunt] vt & vi contare ◆ n (nobleman) conte m ❑ **count on** vt fus contare su.

counter [ˈkauntər] n (in shop) banco m; (in bank) sportello m; (in board game) fiche f inv.

counterclockwise [ˌkauntəˈklɒkwaɪz] adv (Am) in senso antiorario.

counterfoil [ˈkauntəfɔɪl] n matrice f.

countess [ˈkauntɪs] n contessa f.

country [ˈkʌntrɪ] n paese m; (countryside) campagna f ◆ adj di campagna.

country and western n (musica f) country m.

country house n villa f di campagna.

country road n strada f di campagna.

countryside [ˈkʌntrɪsaɪd] n campagna f.

county [ˈkauntɪ] n contea f.

couple [ˈkʌpl] n coppia f; **a ~ (of)** un paio (di).

coupon [ˈkuːpɒn] n (for discount etc) buono m; (for orders, enquiries) tagliando m.

courage [ˈkʌrɪdʒ] n coraggio m.

courgette [kɔːˈʒet] n (Br) zucchino m.

courier [ˈkurɪər] n (for holidaymakers) accompagnatore m (-trice f); (for delivering letters) corriere m.

course [kɔːs] n corso m; (of meal) portata f; (of treatment, injections) ciclo m; (of ship, plane) rotta f; (of golf) campo m; **of ~** (certainly) certo; (evidently) naturalmente; **of ~ not** certo che no; **in the ~ of** nel corso di, durante.

court [kɔːt] n (JUR: building, room) tribunale m; (SPORT) campo m; (of king, queen) corte f.

courtesy coach [ˈkɜːtɪsɪ-] n pullman m inv gratuito (di hotel, aeroporto, ecc.).

court shoes npl scarpe fpl décolleté.

courtyard [ˈkɔːtjɑːd] n cortile m.

cousin ['kʌzn] *n* cugino *m* (-a *f*).

cover ['kʌvə'] *n* (covering) fodera *f*; (lid) coperchio *m*; (of book, magazine) copertina *f*; (blanket) coperta *f*; (insurance) copertura *f* ♦ *vt* coprire; (apply to) comprendere; (discuss) trattare; (report) fare un servizio su; **to be ~ed in** essere ricoperto di OR da; **to ~ sthg with sthg** coprire qc con qc; **to take ~** mettersi al riparo □ **cover up** *vt sep* (put on) coprire; (facts, truth) nascondere.

cover charge *n* coperto *m*.

cover note *n* (Br) polizza *f* di assicurazione provvisoria.

cow [kaʊ] *n* vacca *f*.

coward ['kaʊəd] *n* vigliacco *m* (-a *f*).

cowboy ['kaʊbɔɪ] *n* cow-boy *m inv*.

crab [kræb] *n* granchio *m*.

crack [kræk] *n* (in cup, glass) incrinatura *f*, crepa *f*; (gap) fessura *f* ♦ *vt* (cup, glass, wood) incrinare; (nut) schiacciare; (egg) rompere; (whip) schioccare ♦ *vi* (cup, glass, wood) incrinarsi; **to ~ a joke** (inf) fare una battuta.

cracker ['krækə'] *n* (biscuit) cracker *m inv*; (for Christmas) tubo di cartone rivestito di carta da regalo che quando viene aperto produce uno scoppio e rilascia una sorpresa. Tipico delle feste natalizie.

cradle ['kreɪdl] *n* culla *f*.

craft [krɑːft] *n* (skill) arte *f*; (trade) artigianato *m*; (boat: pl inv) imbarcazione *f*.

craftsman ['krɑːftsmən] (pl -men [-mən]) *n* artigiano *m*.

cram [kræm] *vt*: **to ~ sthg into** stipare qc in; **to be crammed with**

essere stipato di.

cramp [kræmp] *n* crampo *m*; **stomach ~s** crampi allo stomaco.

cranberry ['krænbərɪ] *n* mirtillo *m*.

cranberry sauce *n* salsa *f* di mirtilli.

crane [kreɪn] *n* (machine) gru *f inv*.

crap [kræp] *adj* (vulg) di merda ♦ *n* (vulg) merda *f*.

crash [kræʃ] *n* (accident) incidente *m*; (noise) schianto *m* ♦ *vt* (car) sfasciare ♦ *vi* (car, train) schiantarsi; (plane) precipitare □ **crash into** *vt fus* schiantarsi contro.

crash helmet *n* casco *m*.

crash landing *n* atterraggio *m* di fortuna.

crate [kreɪt] *n* cassa *f*.

crawl [krɔːl] *vi* (baby) andare carponi; (person) strisciare; (insect) muoversi lentamente; (traffic) andare a passo d'uomo ♦ *n* (swimming stroke) stile *m* libero.

crawler lane ['krɔːlə'-] *n* (Br) corsia *f* per veicoli lenti.

crayfish ['kreɪfɪʃ] (pl inv) *n* gambero *m* di fiume.

crayon ['kreɪɒn] *n* matita *f* colorata.

craze [kreɪz] *n* mania *f*.

crazy ['kreɪzɪ] *adj* matto(-a), pazzo(-a); **to be ~ about** andare pazzo per.

crazy golf *n* minigolf *m*.

cream [kriːm] *n* crema *f*; (fresh) panna *f* ♦ *adj* (in colour) color crema (inv).

cream cake *n* (Br) torta *f* alla panna.

cream cheese *n* formaggio *m* cremoso.

cream sherry n sherry m inv dolce.

cream tea n (Br) merenda a base di tè e 'scones', serviti con marmellata e panna.

creamy ['kri:mɪ] adj (food) alla panna; (texture) cremoso(-a).

crease [kri:s] n grinza f.

creased [kri:st] adj sgualcito(-a).

create [kri:'eɪt] vt creare.

creative [kri:'eɪtɪv] adj creativo(-a).

creature ['kri:tʃəʳ] n creatura f.

crèche [kreʃ] n (Br) nursery f inv.

credit ['kredɪt] n (praise) merito m; (money) credito m; (part of school, university course) sezione completata di un corso di studio; **to be in ~** essere in attivo ❑ **credits** npl (of film) titoli mpl.

credit card n carta f di credito; **to pay by ~** pagare con la carta di credito; **'all major ~s accepted'** 'si accettano tutte le maggiori carte di credito'.

creek [kri:k] n (inlet) insenatura f; (Am: river) ruscello m.

creep [kri:p] (pt & pp **crept**) vi (crawl) strisciare; (walk) muoversi furtivamente ◆ n (inf: groveller) leccapiedi mf inv.

cremate [krɪ'meɪt] vt cremare.

crematorium [ˌkreməˈtɔːrɪəm] n crematorio m.

crepe [kreɪp] n (thin pancake) crêpe f inv.

crept [krept] pt & pp → **creep**.

cress [kres] n crescione m.

crest [krest] n cresta f; (emblem) stemma m.

crew [kru:] n (of ship, plane) equipaggio m.

crew neck n girocollo m.

crib [krɪb] n (Am: cot) lettino m (per bambini).

cricket ['krɪkɪt] n (game) cricket m; (insect) grillo m.

crime [kraɪm] n crimine m.

criminal ['krɪmɪnl] adj criminale ◆ n criminale mf.

cripple ['krɪpl] n storpio m (-a f) ◆ vt (subj: disease, accident) storpiare.

crisis ['kraɪsɪs] (pl **crises** ['kraɪsi:z]) n crisi f inv.

crisp [krɪsp] adj (bacon, pastry) croccante; (fruit, vegetable) sodo(-a) ❑ **crisps** npl (Br) patatine fpl.

crispy ['krɪspɪ] adj croccante.

critic ['krɪtɪk] n critico m (-a f).

critical ['krɪtɪkl] adj critico(-a).

criticize ['krɪtɪsaɪz] vt criticare.

crockery ['krɒkərɪ] n stoviglie fpl.

crocodile ['krɒkədaɪl] n coccodrillo m.

crocus ['krəʊkəs] (pl -es) n croco m.

crooked ['krʊkɪd] adj (bent, twisted) storto(-a).

crop [krɒp] n (kind of plant) coltivazione f; (harvest) raccolto m ❑ **crop up** vi saltare fuori.

cross [krɒs] adj arrabbiato(-a) ◆ n croce f; (mixture) incrocio m ◆ vt (road, river, ocean) attraversare; (arms, legs) incrociare; (Br: cheque) sbarrare ◆ vi (intersect) incrociarsi ❑ **cross out** vt sbarrare; **cross over** vt fus (road) attraversare.

crossbar ['krɒsbɑːʳ] n (of goal) traversa f; (of bicycle) canna f.

cross-Channel ferry n traghetto m di servizio sulla Manica.

cross-country (running) n corsa f campestre.

crossing ['krɒsɪŋ] n (on road) attraversamento m; (sea journey) traversata f.

crossroads ['krɒsrəʊdz] (pl inv) n incrocio m.

crosswalk ['krɒswɔːk] n (Am) passaggio m pedonale.

crossword (puzzle) ['krɒswɜːd-] n cruciverba m inv.

crotch [krɒtʃ] n (of person) inforcatura f.

crouton ['kruːtɒn] n crostino m.

crow [krəʊ] n cornacchia f.

crowbar ['krəʊbɑːʳ] n piede m di porco.

crowd [kraʊd] n folla f; (at match) spettatori mpl.

crowded ['kraʊdɪd] adj affollato(-a).

crown [kraʊn] n (of king, queen, on tooth) corona f; (of head) sommità f inv.

Crown Jewels npl: the ~ i gioielli della Corona.

---

i **CROWN JEWELS**

Indossati dal sovrano in occasione di cerimonie importanti, i gioielli della Corona britannica sono esposti nella Torre di Londra. I gioielli dell'antica corona di Scozia sono invece esposti al castello di Edimburgo.

---

crucial ['kruːʃl] adj cruciale.

crude [kruːd] adj (drawing) abbozzato(-a); (estimate) approssimativo(-a); (rude) rozzo(-a).

cruel [krʊəl] adj crudele.

cruelty ['krʊəltɪ] n crudeltà f.

cruet (set) ['kruːɪt-] n ampolliera f.

cruise [kruːz] n crociera f ♦ vi (car, plane, ship) andare a velocità di crociera.

cruiser ['kruːzəʳ] n (pleasure boat) cabinato m.

crumb [krʌm] n briciola f.

crumble ['krʌmbl] n frutta cotta ricoperta da uno strato di pasta frolla sbriciolata ♦ vi (building, cliff) sgretolarsi; (pastry, cake, cheese) sbriciolarsi.

crumpet ['krʌmpɪt] n tipo di focaccia da mangiarsi calda con burro, marmellata, ecc.

crunchy ['krʌntʃɪ] adj croccante.

crush [krʌʃ] n (drink) spremuta f ♦ vt schiacciare; (ice) frantumare.

crust [krʌst] n crosta f.

crusty ['krʌstɪ] adj croccante.

crutch [krʌtʃ] n (stick) stampella f; (between legs) = **crotch**.

cry [kraɪ] n urlo m, grido m; (of bird) verso m ♦ vi (weep) piangere; (shout) urlare, gridare ❑ **cry out** vi urlare, gridare.

crystal ['krɪstl] n (in jewellery etc) cristallo m; (glass) cristallo m.

cub [kʌb] n (animal) cucciolo m.

Cub [kʌb] n lupetto m.

cube [kjuːb] n cubo m; (of sugar, ice) cubetto m.

cubicle ['kjuːbɪkl] n cabina f.

Cub Scout = **Cub**.

cuckoo ['kʊkuː] n cuculo m.

cucumber ['kjuːkʌmbəʳ] n cetriolo m.

cuddle ['kʌdl] n coccola f.

cuddly toy ['kʌdlɪ-] n pupazzo

m di peluche.

cue [kju:] *n* (*in snooker, pool*) stecca *f.*

cuff [kʌf] *n* (*of sleeve*) polsino *m*; (*Am: of trousers*) risvolto *m.*

cuff links *npl* gemelli *mpl.*

cuisine [kwi'zi:n] *n* cucina *f.*

cul-de-sac ['kʌldəsæk] *n* vicolo *m* cieco.

cult [kʌlt] *n* (RELIG) culto *m* ◆ *adj* di culto.

cultivate ['kʌltɪveɪt] *vt* (*grow*) coltivare.

cultivated ['kʌltɪveɪtɪd] *adj* (*person*) raffinato(-a).

cultural ['kʌltʃərəl] *adj* culturale.

culture ['kʌltʃəʳ] *n* cultura *f.*

cumbersome ['kʌmbəsəm] *adj* ingombrante.

cumin ['kju:mɪn] *n* cumino *m.*

cunning ['kʌnɪŋ] *adj* furbo(-a).

cup [kʌp] *n* tazza *f*; (*trophy, competition, of bra*) coppa *f.*

cupboard ['kʌbəd] *n* (*for food, dishes*) credenza *f*; (*for clothes*) armadio *m.*

curator [kjʊə'reɪtəʳ] *n* conservatore *m* (*di museo*).

curb [kɜ:b] (*Am*) = **kerb**.

curd cheese [kɜ:d-] *n* cagliata *f.*

cure [kjʊəʳ] *n* (*for illness*) cura *f* ◆ *vt* (*illness, person*) curare; (*food*) trattare.

curious ['kjʊərɪəs] *adj* curioso(-a).

curl [kɜ:l] *n* (*of hair*) riccio *m* ◆ *vt* (*hair*) arricciare.

curler ['kɜ:ləʳ] *n* bigodino *m.*

curly ['kɜ:lɪ] *adj* riccio(-a).

currant ['kʌrənt] *n* uvetta *f.*

currency ['kʌrənsɪ] *n* (*money*) moneta *f.*

current ['kʌrənt] *adj* attuale ◆ *n* corrente *f.*

current account *n* (*Br*) conto *m* corrente.

current affairs *npl* attualità *f.*

currently ['kʌrəntlɪ] *adv* attualmente.

curriculum [kə'rɪkjələm] *n* curricolo *m.*

curriculum vitae [-'vi:taɪ] *n* (*Br*) curriculum vitae *m inv.*

curried ['kʌrɪd] *adj* al curry.

curry ['kʌrɪ] *n* piatto *m* al curry.

curse [kɜ:s] *vi* bestemmiare.

cursor ['kɜ:səʳ] *n* cursore *m.*

curtain ['kɜ:tn] *n* (*in house*) tenda *f*; (*in theatre*) sipario *m.*

curve [kɜ:v] *n* curva *f* ◆ *vi* curvare.

curved [kɜ:vd] *adj* curvo(-a).

cushion ['kʊʃn] *n* (*for sitting on*) cuscino *m.*

custard ['kʌstəd] *n* crema *f* gialla.

custom ['kʌstəm] *n* (*tradition*) usanza *f*; '**thank you for your ~** 'arrivederci e grazie'.

customary ['kʌstəmrɪ] *adj* abituale.

customer ['kʌstəməʳ] *n* (*of shop*) cliente *mf.*

customer services *n* (*department*) servizio *m* clienti.

customs ['kʌstəmz] *n* dogana *f*; **to go through ~** passare la dogana.

customs duty *n* dazio *m* doganale.

customs officer *n* doganiere *m.*

cut [kʌt] (*vt & pp* **cut**) *n* taglio *m*; (*in taxes*) riduzione *f* ◆ *vt & vi* tagliare; **~ and blow-dry** taglio e piega föhn; **to ~ o.s.** tagliarsi; **to ~ one's finger** tagliarsi un dito; **to have one's hair ~** tagliarsi i capelli; **to ~ the grass** tagliare l'erba; **to ~ sthg open** aprire qc ❑ **cut back** vi: **to ~ back on sthg** ridurre qc; **cut down** vt sep (tree) tagliare; **cut down on** vt fus ridurre; **cut off** vt sep (supply) sospendere; **I've been ~ off** (on phone) è caduta la linea; **to be ~ off** (isolated) rimanere isolato; **cut out** vt sep (newspaper article, photo) ritagliare ♦ vi (engine) spegnersi; **to ~ out smoking** smettere di fumare; **~ it out!** (inf) dacci un taglio!; **cut up** vt sep tagliare a pezzetti.

cute [kju:t] adj carino(-a).

cut-glass adj in vetro intagliato.

cutlery ['kʌtləri] n posate fpl.

cutlet ['kʌtlɪt] n (of meat) costoletta f; (of nuts, vegetables) crocchetta f.

cut-price adj a prezzo scontato.

cutting ['kʌtɪŋ] n (from newspaper) ritaglio m.

CV n (Br: abbr of curriculum vitae) curriculum m inv.

cwt abbr = hundredweight.

cycle ['saɪkl] n (bicycle) bicicletta f; (series) ciclo m ♦ vi andare in bicicletta.

cycle hire n noleggio m biciclette.

cycle lane n pista f ciclabile.

cycle path n pista f ciclabile.

cycling ['saɪklɪŋ] n ciclismo m; **to go ~** andare in bicicletta.

cycling shorts npl pantaloncini mpl da ciclista.

cyclist ['saɪklɪst] n ciclista mf.

cylinder ['sɪlɪndəʳ] n (of gas) bombola f; (in engine) cilindro m.

cynical ['sɪnɪkl] adj cinico(-a).

Czech [tʃek] adj ceco(-a) ♦ n (person) ceco m (-a f); (language) ceco m.

Czechoslovakia [ˌtʃekəsləˈvækɪə] n la Cecoslovacchia.

Czech Republic n: **the ~** la Repubblica Ceca.

D

dab [dæb] vt (wound) tamponare.

dad [dæd] n (inf) papà m inv, babbo m.

daddy ['dædɪ] n (inf) papà m inv, babbo m.

daddy longlegs [-'lɒŋlegz] (pl inv) n tipula f.

daffodil ['dæfədɪl] n giunchiglia f.

daft [dɑ:ft] adj (Br: inf) stupido(-a).

daily ['deɪlɪ] adj quotidiano(-a) ♦ adv quotidianamente ♦ n: **a ~** (newspaper) un quotidiano.

dairy ['deərɪ] n (on farm) caseificio m; (shop) latteria f.

dairy product n latticino m.

daisy ['deɪzɪ] n margherita f.

dam [dæm] n diga f.

damage ['dæmɪdʒ] n danno m ♦ vt danneggiare; (back, leg) lesionare.

damn [dæm] excl (inf) accidenti ♦ adj (inf) maledetto(-a); **I don't**

give a ~ non me ne importa un accidente.

damp [dæmp] *adj* umido(-a) ♦ *n* umidità *f*.

damson ['dæmzn] *n* susina *f* damaschina.

dance [dɑːns] *n* danza *f*; *(social event)* ballo *m* ♦ *vi* ballare; **to have a ~ ballare.**

dance floor *n (in club)* pista *f* da ballo.

dancer ['dɑːnsəʳ] *n* ballerino *m* (-a *f*).

dancing ['dɑːnsɪŋ] *n* danza *f*; **to go ~** andare a ballare.

dandelion ['dændɪlaɪən] *n* dente *m* di leone.

dandruff ['dændrʌf] *n* forfora *f*.

Dane [deɪn] *n* danese *mf*.

danger ['deɪndʒəʳ] *n* pericolo *m*; **in ~** in pericolo.

dangerous ['deɪndʒərəs] *adj* pericoloso(-a).

Danish ['deɪnɪʃ] *adj* danese ♦ *n (language)* danese *m*.

Danish pastry *n* sfoglia *f* alla frutta.

dare [deəʳ] *vt*: **to ~ to do sthg** osare fare qc; **to ~ sb to do sthg** sfidare qn a fare qc; **how ~ you!** come ti permetti!

daring ['deərɪŋ] *adj* audace.

dark [dɑːk] *adj (room, night)* buio(-a); *(colour, skin)* scuro(-a); *(person)* bruno(-a) ♦ *n*: **after ~** col buio; **the ~** il buio.

dark chocolate *n* cioccolata *f* fondente.

dark glasses *npl* occhiali *mpl* curi.

darkness ['dɑːknɪs] *n* oscurità *f*.

darling ['dɑːlɪŋ] *n (term of affec-*

tion) caro *m* (-a *f*).

dart [dɑːt] *n* freccia *f* ❏ **darts** *n (game)* freccette *fpl*.

dartboard ['dɑːtbɔːd] *n* bersaglio *m* per freccette.

dash [dæʃ] *n (of liquid)* goccio *m*; *(in writing)* trattino *m* ♦ *vi* precipitarsi.

dashboard ['dæʃbɔːd] *n* cruscotto *m*.

data ['deɪtə] *n* dati *mpl*.

database ['deɪtəbeɪs] *n* data base *m inv*.

date [deɪt] *n (day)* data *f*; *(meeting)* appuntamento *m*; *(Am: person)* ragazzo *m* (-a *f*); *(fruit)* dattero *m* ♦ *vt (cheque, letter)* datare; *(person)* uscire con ♦ *vi (become unfashionable)* passare di moda; **what's the ~?** quanti ne abbiamo oggi?; **to have a ~ with sb** avere (un) appuntamento con qn.

date of birth *n* data *f* di nascita.

daughter ['dɔːtəʳ] *n* figlia *f*.

daughter-in-law *n* nuora *f*.

dawn [dɔːn] *n* alba *f*.

day [deɪ] *n (of week)* giorno *m*; *(period, working day)* giornata *f*; **what ~ is it today?** che giorno è oggi?; **what a lovely ~!** che bella giornata!; **to have a ~ off** avere un giorno libero; **to have a ~ out** trascorrere una giornata fuori; **by ~** *(travel)* di giorno; **the ~ after tomorrow** dopodomani; **the ~ before** il giorno prima; **the ~ before yesterday** l'altro ieri, ieri l'altro; **the following ~** il giorno dopo; **have a nice ~!** buona giornata!

daylight ['deɪlaɪt] *n (light)* luce *f* (del giorno); *(dawn)* alba *f*.

day return *n (Br: railway ticket)*

biglietto di andata e ritorno valido per un giorno.

dayshift ['deɪʃɪft] n turno m di giorno.

daytime ['deɪtaɪm] n giorno m.

day-to-day adj (everyday) quotidiano(-a).

day trip n gita f (di un giorno).

dazzle ['dæzl] vt abbagliare.

DC (abbr of direct current) c.c.

dead [ded] adj morto(-a); (battery) scarico(-a) ♦ adv proprio; **the line has gone ~** è caduta la linea; **~ on time** in perfetto orario; **it's ~ ahead** è proprio a diritto; **'~ 'slow'** 'a passo d'uomo'.

dead end n (street) strada f senza uscita.

deadline ['dedlaɪn] n termine m ultimo, scadenza f.

deaf [def] adj sordo(-a) ♦ npl: **the ~** i non udenti.

deal [di:l] (pt & pp dealt) n (agreement) accordo m ♦ vt (cards) dare; **a good/bad ~** un buon/cattivo affare; **a great ~ of** una gran quantità di; **it's a ~!** affare fatto! ◻ **deal in** vt fus commerciare in; **deal with** vt fus (handle) affrontare; (be about) trattare di.

dealer ['di:lə*] n (COMM) commerciante mf; (in drugs) spacciatore m (-trice f).

dealt [delt] pt & pp → deal.

dear [dɪə*] adj caro(-a) ♦ n: **my ~** mio caro (mia cara); **Dear Sir** Gentile Signore; **Dear Madam** Gentile Signora; **Dear John** Caro John; **oh ~!** oh Dio!

death [deθ] n morte f.

debate [dɪ'beɪt] n dibattito m ♦ vt (wonder) riflettere su.

debit ['debɪt] n debito m ♦ vt (account) addebitare su.

debt [det] n (money owed) debito m; **to be in ~** essere indebitato.

Dec. (abbr of December) dic.

decaff ['di:kæf] n (inf) caffè m inv decaffeinato.

decaffeinated [dɪ'kæfɪneɪtɪd] adj decaffeinato(-a).

decanter [dɪ'kæntə*] n bottiglia f da liquore.

decay [dɪ'keɪ] n (of wood) disfacimento m; (of building) rovina f; (of tooth) carie f ♦ vi (rot) putrefarsi.

deceive [dɪ'si:v] vt ingannare.

decelerate [,di:'selərent] vi decelerare.

December [dɪ'sembə*] n dicembre m, → September.

decent ['di:snt] adj (adequate, respectable) decente; (kind) carino(-a); (people) perbene inv.

decide [dɪ'saɪd] vt & vi decidere; **to ~ to do sthg** decidere di fare qc ◻ **decide on** vt fus scegliere.

decimal ['desɪml] adj decimale.

decimal point n = virgola f.

decision [dɪ'sɪʒn] n decisione f; **to make a ~** prendere una decisione.

decisive [dɪ'saɪsɪv] adj (person) deciso(-a); (event, factor) decisivo(-a).

deck [dek] n (level of ship) ponte m; (exposed part of ship) coperta f; (of bus) piano m; (of cards) mazzo m.

deckchair ['dektʃeə*] n sedia f a sdraio.

declare [dɪ'kleə*] vt dichiarare ♦ **to ~ (that)** dichiarare che; **'goods to ~'** 'articoli da dichiarare'; **'nothi-**

ing to ~' 'nulla da dichiarare'.

decline [dɪ'klaɪn] n calo m; (of country) declino m ♦ vi (get worse) peggiorare; (refuse) decorare.

decorate ['dekəreɪt] vt (with wall-paper) tappezzare; (with paint) pitturare; (make attractive) decorare.

decoration [dekə'reɪʃn] n (decorative object) decorazione f.

decorator ['dekəreɪtə^r] n imbianchino m.

decrease [n 'di:kri:s, vb di:'kri:s] n diminuzione f ♦ vi diminuire.

dedicated ['dedɪkeɪtɪd] adj (committed) devoto(-a).

deduce [dɪ'dju:s] vt dedurre.

deduct [dɪ'dʌkt] vt dedurre.

deduction [dɪ'dʌkʃn] n deduzione f.

deep [di:p] adj profondo(-a); (colour) intenso(-a) ♦ adv in profondità; **the pool is 2 metres ~** la piscina è profonda 2 metri.

deep end n (of swimming pool) parte dove l'acqua è più alta.

deep freeze n congelatore m.

deep-fried [-'fraɪd] adj fritto(-a).

deep-pan adj: ~ **pizza** pizza a pasta alta e soffice.

deer [dɪə^r] (pl inv) n cervo m.

defeat [dɪ'fi:t] n sconfitta f ♦ vt (team, army, government) sconfiggere.

defect ['di:fekt] n difetto m.

defective [dɪ'fektɪv] adj difettoso(-a).

defence [dɪ'fens] n difesa f.

defend [dɪ'fend] vt difendere.

defense [dɪ'fens] (Am) = defence.

deficiency [dɪ'fɪʃnsɪ] n (lack)

carenza f.

deficit ['defɪsɪt] n deficit m inv.

define [dɪ'faɪn] vt definire.

definite ['defɪnɪt] adj (clear) preciso(-a); (certain) sicuro(-a); (improvement) deciso(-a).

definite article n articolo m determinativo.

definitely ['defɪnɪtlɪ] adv (certainly) senz'altro.

definition [defɪ'nɪʃn] n (of word) definizione f.

deflate [dɪ'fleɪt] vt (tyre) sgonfiare.

deflect [dɪ'flekt] vt (ball) deviare.

defogger [ˌdi:'fɒgə^r] n (Am) demidificatore m.

deformed [dɪ'fɔ:md] adj deformato(-a).

defrost [ˌdi:'frɒst] vt (food) scongelare; (fridge) sbrinare; (Am: demist) disappannare.

degree [dɪ'gri:] n (unit of measurement, amount) grado m; (qualification) = laurea f; **to have a ~ in sthg** avere una laurea in qc.

dehydrated [ˌdi:haɪ'dreɪtɪd] adj (food) liofilizzato(-a); (person) disidratato(-a).

de-ice [ˌdi:'aɪs] vt togliere il ghiaccio da.

de-icer [ˌdi:'aɪsə^r] n antighiaccio m.

dejected [dɪ'dʒektɪd] adj sconsolato(-a).

delay [dɪ'leɪ] n ritardo m ♦ vt (flight, departure) ritardare; (person) trattenere ♦ vi indugiare; **without ~** senza indugio.

delayed [dɪ'leɪd] adj (train, flight) in ritardo.

delegate [n 'delɪgət, vb 'delɪgeɪt]

delegato m (-a f) ♦ vt (person) delegare.

delete [dɪ'liːt] vt cancellare.

deli ['delɪ] n (inf: abbr of delicatessen) negozio m di specialità gastronomiche.

deliberate [dɪ'lɪbərət] adj (intentional) intenzionale.

deliberately [dɪ'lɪbərətlɪ] adv (intentionally) deliberatamente.

delicacy ['delɪkəsɪ] n (food) leccornia f.

delicate ['delɪkət] adj delicato(-a).

delicatessen [ˌdelɪkə'tesn] n negozio m di specialità gastronomiche.

delicious [dɪ'lɪʃəs] adj squisito(-a).

delight [dɪ'laɪt] n (feeling) gioia f ♦ vt deliziare; **to take (a) ~ in doing sthg** provare piacere a fare qc.

delighted [dɪ'laɪtɪd] adj felicissimo(-a).

delightful [dɪ'laɪtful] adj delizioso(-a).

deliver [dɪ'lɪvər] vt (goods, letters, newspaper) consegnare; (speech, lecture) tenere; (baby) far nascere.

delivery [dɪ'lɪvərɪ] n (of goods, letters) consegna f; (birth) parto m.

delude [dɪ'luːd] vt illudere.

de luxe [də'lʌks] adj di lusso.

demand [dɪ'mɑːnd] n (request) richiesta f; (claim) rivendicazione f; (COMM) domanda f; (requirement) esigenza f ♦ vt (request forcefully) pretendere; (require) richiedere; **to ~ to do sthg** esigere di fare qc; **in ~** richiesto.

demanding [dɪ'mɑːndɪŋ] adj esigente.

demerara sugar [deməˈreərə] n zucchero m di canna.

demist [ˌdiː'mɪst] vt (Br) disappannare.

demister [ˌdiː'mɪstər] n (Br) deumidificatore m.

democracy [dɪ'mɒkrəsɪ] n democrazia f.

Democrat ['deməkræt] n (Am) democratico m (-a f).

democratic [deməˈkrætɪk] adj democratico(-a).

demolish [dɪ'mɒlɪʃ] vt (building) demolire.

demonstrate ['demənstreɪt] vt (prove) dimostrare; (machine, appliance) mostrare il funzionamento di ♦ vi dimostrare.

demonstration [demənˈstreɪʃn] n dimostrazione f.

denial [dɪ'naɪəl] n (refusal) rifiuto m; (statement) smentita f.

denim ['denɪm] n denim m ❑ **denims** npl jeans mpl.

denim jacket n giubbotto m di jeans.

Denmark ['denmɑːk] n la Danimarca.

dense [dens] adj (crowd, forest) fitto(-a); (smoke) denso(-a).

dent [dent] n ammaccatura f.

dental ['dentl] adj dentale.

dental floss [-flɒs] n filo m interdentale.

dental surgeon n dentista m.

dental surgery n (place) studio m dentistico.

dentist ['dentɪst] n dentista mf; **to go to the ~'s** andare dal dentista.

dentures ['dentʃəz] npl dentiera f.

deny [dɪ'naɪ] *vt* negare.

deodorant [di:'əʊdərənt] *n* deodorante *m*.

depart [dɪ'pɑ:t] *vi* partire.

department [dɪ'pɑ:tmənt] *n (of business, shop)* reparto *m*; *(of government)* ministero *m*; *(of school, university)* dipartimento *m*.

department store *n* grandi magazzini *mpl*.

departure [dɪ'pɑ:tʃə'] *n* partenza *f*; **'~'s** *(at airport)* 'partenze'.

departure lounge *n* sala *f* partenze.

depend [dɪ'pend] *vi*: **it ~s** dipende □ **depend on** *vt fus* dipendere da; **~ing on** a seconda di.

dependable [dɪ'pendəbl] *adj* affidabile.

deplorable [dɪ'plɔ:rəbl] *adj* deplorevole.

deport [dɪ'pɔ:t] *vt* espellere.

deposit [dɪ'pɒzɪt] *n* deposito *m* ♦ *vt* depositare.

deposit account *n (Br)* conto *m* vincolato.

depot ['di:pəʊ] *n (Am: for buses, trains)* stazione *f*.

depressed [dɪ'prest] *adj* depresso(-a).

depressing [dɪ'presɪŋ] *adj* deprimente.

depression [dɪ'preʃn] *n* depressione *f*.

deprive [dɪ'praɪv] *vt*: **to ~ sb of sthg** privare qn di qc.

depth [depθ] *n (distance down)* profondità *f inv*; **out of one's ~** *(when swimming)* dove non si tocca; *(fig: unable to cope)* non all'altezza; **~ of field** *(in photography)* profondità di campo.

deputy ['depjʊtɪ] *adj* vice *(inv)*.

derailleur [də'reɪljə'] *n* deragliatore *m*.

derailment [dɪ'reɪlmənt] *n* deragliamento *m*.

derelict ['derəlɪkt] *adj* abbandonato(-a).

derv [dɜ:v] *n (Br)* benzina *f* diesel.

descend [dɪ'send] *vt* & *vi* scendere.

descendant [dɪ'sendənt] *n* discendente *mf*.

descent [dɪ'sent] *n* discesa *f*.

describe [dɪ'skraɪb] *vt* descrivere.

description [dɪ'skrɪpʃn] *n* descrizione *f*.

desert [*n* 'dezət, *vb* dɪ'zɜ:t] *n* deserto *m* ♦ *vt* abbandonare.

deserted [dɪ'zɜ:tɪd] *adj* deserto(-a).

deserve [dɪ'zɜ:v] *vt* meritare.

design [dɪ'zaɪn] *n (pattern)* disegno *m*; *(art)* design *m*; *(of machine, building)* progetto *m* ♦ *vt (dress)* disegnare; *(machine, building)* progettare; **to be ~ed for** essere concepito per.

designer [dɪ'zaɪnə'] *n (of clothes)* stilista *mf*; *(of building)* architetto *m*; *(of product)* designer *mf inv* ♦ *adj (clothes, sunglasses)* firmato(-a).

desirable [dɪ'zaɪərəbl] *adj* desiderabile.

desire [dɪ'zaɪə'] *n* desiderio *m* ♦ *vt* desiderare; **it leaves a lot to be ~d** lascia molto a desiderare.

desk [desk] *n (in home, office)* scrivania *f*; *(at airport, station, of pupil)* banco *m*; *(at hotel)* portineria *f*.

desktop publishing ['desk-
ˌtɒp-] n desktop publishing m.

despair [dɪ'speə'] n disperazione
f.

despatch [dɪ'spætʃ] = dispatch.

desperate ['desprət] adj dispe-
rato(-a); **to be ~ for** sthg avere un
disperato bisogno di qc.

despicable [dɪ'spɪkəbl] adj spregevole.

despise [dɪ'spaɪz] vt disprezzare.

despite [dɪ'spaɪt] prep nonostante.

dessert [dɪ'zɜːt] n dessert m inv.

dessertspoon [dɪ'zɜːtspuːn] n
cucchiaino m.

destination [ˌdestɪ'neɪʃn] n destinazione f.

destroy [dɪ'strɔɪ] vt distruggere.

destruction [dɪ'strʌkʃn] n distruzione f.

detach [dɪ'tætʃ] vt staccare.

detached house [dɪ'tætʃt-] n
villetta f unifamiliare.

detail ['diːteɪl] n dettaglio m; **in ~**
dettagliatamente ❑ **details** npl
(facts) informazioni fpl.

detailed ['diːteɪld] adj dettaglia-
to(-a).

detect [dɪ'tekt] vt (sense) avvertire; (find) scoprire.

detective [dɪ'tektɪv] n detective
mf inv; **a ~ story** un racconto poliziesco.

detention [dɪ'tenʃn] n (SCH)
punizione che consiste nel trattenere un
alunno a scuola oltre l'orario scolastico.

detergent [dɪ'tɜːdʒənt] n detersivo m.

deteriorate [dɪ'tɪərɪəreɪt] vi
deteriorarsi.

determination [dɪˌtɜːmɪ'neɪʃn]
n determinazione f.

determine [dɪ'tɜːmɪn] vt (control)
determinare; (find out) accertare.

determined [dɪ'tɜːmɪnd] adj
risoluto(-a); **to be ~ to do** sthg
essere determinato a fare qc.

deterrent [dɪ'terənt] n deter-
rente m.

detest [dɪ'test] vt detestare.

detour ['diːˌtuə'] n deviazione f.

detrain [ˌdiː'treɪn] vi (fml) scendere dal treno.

deuce [djuːs] n (in tennis) parità f.

devastate ['devəsteɪt] vt deva-
stare.

develop [dɪ'veləp] vt sviluppare;
(machine, method) perfezionare; (illness, habit) contrarre ◆ vi (evolve)
svilupparsi.

developing country [dɪ-
'veləpɪŋ-] n paese m in via di sviluppo.

development [dɪ'veləpmənt] n
sviluppo m; **a housing ~** un complesso residenziale.

device [dɪ'vaɪs] n congegno m.

devil ['devl] n diavolo m; **what
the ~ ...?** (inf) che diavolo ...?

devise [dɪ'vaɪz] vt escogitare.

devoted [dɪ'vəʊtɪd] adj (person)
affezionato(-a).

dew [djuː] n rugiada f.

diabetes [ˌdaɪə'biːtiːz] n diabete
m.

diabetic [ˌdaɪə'betɪk] adj (person)
diabetico(-a); (chocolate) per diabe-
tici ◆ n diabetico m (-a f).

diagnosis [ˌdaɪəg'nəʊsɪs] (pl -oses
[-əʊsiːz]) n diagnosi f inv.

diagonal [daɪ'ægənl] adj diagonale.

diagram ['daɪəgræm] *n* diagramma *m*.

dial ['daɪəl] *n (of telephone)* disco *m* combinatore; *(of clock)* quadrante *m; (of radio)* scala *f* ◆ *vt (number)* comporre.

dialling code ['daɪəlɪŋ-] *n (Br)* prefisso *m* telefonico.

dialling tone ['daɪəlɪŋ-] *n (Br)* segnale *m* di libero.

dial tone *(Am)* = **dialling tone**.

diameter [daɪˈæmɪtəʳ] *n* diametro *m*.

diamond ['daɪəmənd] *n (gem)* diamante *m* ❑ **diamonds** *npl (in cards)* quadri *mpl*.

diaper ['daɪpəʳ] *n (Am)* pannolino *m*.

diarrhoea [ˌdaɪəˈrɪə] *n* diarrea *f*.

diary ['daɪərɪ] *n (for appointments)* agenda *f; (journal)* diario *m*.

dice [daɪs] *(pl inv)* *n* dado *m*.

diced [daɪst] *adj* a dadini.

dictate [dɪkˈteɪt] *vt* dettare.

dictation [dɪkˈteɪʃn] *n* dettato *m*.

dictator [dɪkˈteɪtəʳ] *n* dittatore *m* (-trice *f*).

dictionary ['dɪkʃənrɪ] *n* dizionario *m*.

did [dɪd] *pt* → **do**.

die [daɪ] *(pt & pp died, cont dying* ['daɪŋ]) *vi* morire; **to be dying for sthg** *(inf)* morire dalla voglia di qc; **to be dying to do sthg** *(inf)* morire dalla voglia di fare qc ❑ **die away** *vi* spegnersi; **die out** *vi* scomparire.

diesel ['diːzl] *n (fuel)* gasolio *m; (car)* diesel *m inv*.

diet ['daɪət] *n (for slimming, health)* dieta *f; (food eaten)* alimentazione *f*

◆ *vi* essere a dieta ◆ *adj* dietetico(-a).

diet Coke® *n* coca *f* light®.

differ ['dɪfəʳ] *vi:* **to ~ (from)** *(disagree)* non essere d'accordo (con); *(be dissimilar)* essere diverso (da).

difference ['dɪfrəns] *n* differenza *f*; **it makes no ~** è lo stesso; **a ~ of opinion** una divergenza di opinioni.

different ['dɪfrənt] *adj* diverso(-a); **to be ~ (from)** essere diverso (da); **a ~ route** un'altra strada.

differently ['dɪfrəntlɪ] *adv* in modo diverso.

difficult ['dɪfɪkəlt] *adj* difficile.

difficulty ['dɪfɪkəltɪ] *n* difficoltà *f inv*.

dig [dɪg] *(pt & pp dug)* *vt & vi* scavare ❑ **dig out** *vt sep (rescue)* estrarre; *(find)* scovare; **dig up** *vt sep (from ground)* dissotterrare.

digest [dɪˈdʒest] *vt* digerire.

digestion [dɪˈdʒestʃn] *n* digestione *f*.

digestive (biscuit) [dɪˈdʒestɪv-] *n (Br)* biscotto *m* di frumento con farina integrale.

digit ['dɪdʒɪt] *n (figure)* cifra *f; (finger, toe)* dito *m*.

digital ['dɪdʒɪtl] *adj* digitale.

dill [dɪl] *n* aneto *m*.

dilute [daɪˈluːt] *vt (liquid)* diluire.

dim [dɪm] *adj (light)* debole; *(room)* buio(-a); *(inf: stupid)* ottuso(-a) ◆ *vt (light)* abbassare.

dime [daɪm] *n (Am)* moneta *f* da dieci centesimi di dollaro.

dimensions [dɪˈmenʃnz] *npl* dimensioni *fpl*.

din [dɪn] *n* baccano *m*.

dine [daɪn] *vi* cenare ❑ **dine out**

diner

vi cenare fuori.

diner ['daɪnə^r] *n* (*Am*: *restaurant*) = tavola *f* calda; (*person*) cliente *mf*.

ℹ️ DINER

Piccoli ristoranti senza grandi pretese, i "diners" sono situati principalmente lungo autostrade e strade statali, ma si trovano anche in città. Servono pasti leggeri e sono frequentati soprattutto da camionisti e automobilisti di passaggio. A volte hanno il caratteristico aspetto di vecchi vagoni ferroviari.

---

dinghy ['dɪŋɡɪ] *n* (*with sail, oars*) barca *f*; (*for racing*) dinghy *m inv*; (*made of rubber*) canotto *m*.

dingy ['dɪndʒɪ] *adj* (*clothes*) sporco(-a); (*town, hotel*) squallido(-a).

dining car ['daɪnɪŋ-] *n* carrozza *f* ristorante.

dining hall ['daɪnɪŋ-] *n* refettorio *m*.

dining room ['daɪnɪŋ-] *n* sala *f* da pranzo.

dinner ['dɪnə^r] *n* (*at lunchtime*) pranzo *m*; (*in evening*) cena *f*; **to have ~** (*at lunchtime*) pranzare; (*in evening*) cenare.

dinner jacket *n* giacca *f* dello smoking.

dinner party *n* cena *f*.

dinner set *n* servizio *m* da tavola.

dinner suit *n* smoking *m inv*.

dinnertime ['dɪnətaɪm] *n* (*at lunchtime*) ora *f* di pranzo; (*in evening*) ora di cena.

dinosaur ['daɪnəsɔ:^r] *n* dino-

sauro *m*.

dip [dɪp] *n* (*in road, land*) avvallamento *m*; (*food*) salsetta cremosa in cui intingere patatine o verdure crude ♦ *vt* (*into liquid*) immergere ♦ *vi* (*road, land*) digradare; **to have a ~** (*swim*) fare una nuotatina; **to ~ one's headlights** (*Br*) spegnere gli abbaglianti.

diploma [dɪ'pləʊmə] *n* diploma *m*.

dipstick ['dɪpstɪk] *n* asta *f* di livello.

direct [dɪ'rekt] *adj* diretto(-a) ♦ *adv* (*go*) direttamente; (*travel*) senza fermarsi ♦ *vt*: **can you ~ me to the railway station?** mi può indicare la strada per la stazione?

direct current *n* corrente *f* continua.

direction [dɪ'rekʃn] *n* (*of movement*) direzione *f*; **to ask for ~s** chiedere indicazioni ❑ **directions** *npl* (*instructions*) istruzioni *fpl*.

directly [dɪ'rektlɪ] *adv* (*exactly*) proprio; (*soon*) subito.

director [dɪ'rektə^r] *n* (*of company*) amministratore *m* (-trice *f*); (*of film, play, TV programme*) regista *mf*; (*organizer*) direttore *m* (-trice *f*).

directory [dɪ'rektərɪ] *n* elenco *m*.

directory enquiries *n* (*Br*) informazioni *fpl* elenco abbonati.

dirt [dɜ:t] *n* sporcizia *f*; (*earth*) terra *f*.

dirty ['dɜ:tɪ] *adj* sporco(-a).

disability [ˌdɪsə'bɪlətɪ] *n* handicap *m inv*; (*through old age, illness*) invalidità *f inv*.

disabled [dɪs'eɪbld] *adj* disabile ♦ *npl*: **the ~** i portatori di handicap; '**~ toilet**' 'toilette per portatori di handicap'.

disadvantage [ˌdɪsəd'vɑːntɪdʒ] n svantaggio m.

disagree [ˌdɪsə'griː] vi non essere d'accordo; **to ~ with sb (about)** non essere d'accordo con qn (su); **those mussels ~d with me** quelle cozze mi hanno fatto male.

disagreement [ˌdɪsə'griːmənt] n (argument) discussione f; (dissimilarity) disaccordo m.

disappear [ˌdɪsə'pɪəʳ] vi sparire.

disappearance [ˌdɪsə'pɪərəns] n scomparsa f.

disappoint [ˌdɪsə'pɔɪnt] vt deludere.

disappointed [ˌdɪsə'pɔɪntɪd] adj deluso(-a).

disappointing [ˌdɪsə'pɔɪntɪŋ] adj deludente.

disappointment [ˌdɪsə'pɔɪntmənt] n delusione f.

disapprove [ˌdɪsə'pruːv] vi: **to ~ of** disapprovare.

disarmament [dɪs'ɑːməmənt] n disarmo m.

disaster [dɪ'zɑːstəʳ] n disastro m.

disastrous [dɪ'zɑːstrəs] adj disastroso(-a).

disc [dɪsk] n (Br) disco m; (Br: CD) compact disc m inv; **I slipped a ~** mi è venuta l'ernia al disco.

discard [dɪ'skɑːd] vt scartare.

discharge [dɪs'tʃɑːdʒ] vt (prisoner) rilasciare; (patient) dimettere; (soldier) congedare; (smoke, gas) emettere; (liquid) scaricare.

discipline ['dɪsɪplɪn] n disciplina f.

disc jockey n disc-jockey mf inv.

disco ['dɪskəʊ] (pl -s) n (place) discoteca f; (event) festa f.

discoloured [dɪs'kʌləd] adj scolorito(-a).

discomfort [dɪs'kʌmfət] n fastidio m.

disconnect [ˌdɪskə'nekt] vt staccare; (gas supply) chiudere; (pipe) scollegare.

discontinued [ˌdɪskən'tɪnjuːd] adj (product) di fine serie.

discotheque ['dɪskəʊtek] n (place) discoteca f; (event) festa f.

discount ['dɪskaʊnt] n sconto m.

discover [dɪ'skʌvəʳ] vt scoprire.

discovery [dɪ'skʌvərɪ] n scoperta f.

discreet [dɪ'skriːt] adj discreto(-a).

discrepancy [dɪ'skrepənsɪ] n discrepanza f.

discriminate [dɪ'skrɪmɪneɪt] vi: **to ~ against sb** discriminare contro qn.

discrimination [dɪˌskrɪmɪ'neɪʃn] n (unfair treatment) discriminazione f.

discuss [dɪ'skʌs] vt discutere.

discussion [dɪ'skʌʃn] n discussione f.

disease [dɪ'ziːz] n malattia f.

disembark [ˌdɪsɪm'bɑːk] vi sbarcare.

disgrace [dɪs'greɪs] n (shame) vergogna f; **it's a ~** è una vergogna.

disgraceful [dɪs'greɪsfʊl] adj vergognoso(-a).

disguise [dɪs'gaɪz] n travestimento m ♦ vt travestire; **in ~** travestito.

disgust [dɪs'gʌst] n disgusto m ♦ vt disgustare.

disgusting [dɪs'gʌstɪŋ] adj

sgustoso(-a).

dish [dɪʃ] n piatto m; **to do the ~es** fare i piatti; **'~ of the day'** 'piatto del giorno □ **dish up** vt sep servire.

dishcloth ['dɪʃklɒθ] n strofinaccio m.

disheveled [dɪ'ʃevəld] (Am) = **dishevelled**.

dishevelled [dɪ'ʃevəld] adj (Br: hair) arruffato(-a); (appearance) trasandato(-a).

dishonest [dɪs'ɒnɪst] adj disonesto(-a).

dish towel n (Am) strofinaccio m.

dishwasher ['dɪʃ,wɒʃər] n (machine) lavastoviglie f inv.

disinfectant [,dɪsɪn'fektənt] n disinfettante m.

disintegrate [dɪs'ɪntɪgreɪt] vi disintegrarsi.

disk [dɪsk] n (Am) = **disc**; (COMPUT) dischetto m.

disk drive n drive m inv.

dislike [dɪs'laɪk] n (poor opinion) antipatia f ♦ vt: **I ~ them** non mi piacciono; **to take a ~ to** prendere in antipatia.

dislocate ['dɪsləkeɪt] vt: **to ~ one's shoulder** slogarsi la spalla.

dismal ['dɪzml] adj (weather, place) deprimente; (terrible) pessimo(-a).

dismantle [dɪs'mæntl] vt smontare.

dismay [dɪs'meɪ] n sgomento m.

dismiss [dɪs'mɪs] vt (not consider) ignorare; (from job) licenziare; (from classroom) congedare.

disobedient [,dɪsə'biːdjənt] adj disubbidiente.

disobey [,dɪsə'beɪ] vt disubbidire.

disorder [dɪs'ɔːdər] n (confusion) disordine m; (illness) disturbo m.

disorganized [dɪs'ɔːgənaɪzd] adj disorganizzato(-a).

dispatch [dɪ'spætʃ] vt inviare.

dispense [dɪ'spens]: **dispense with** vt fus fare a meno di.

dispenser [dɪ'spensər] n (device) distributore m.

dispensing chemist [dɪ-'spensɪŋ-] n (Br: shop) farmacia f.

disperse [dɪ'spɜːs] vt disperdere ♦ vi disperdersi.

display [dɪ'spleɪ] n (of goods) esposizione f; (public event) spettacolo m; (readout) schermo m ♦ vt (goods, information) esporre; (feeling, quality) manifestare; **on ~** in mostra.

displeased [dɪs'pliːzd] adj contrariato(-a).

disposable [dɪ'spəuzəbl] adj usa e getta (inv).

dispute [dɪ'spjuːt] n (argument) controversia f; (industrial) vertenza f ♦ vt mettere in discussione.

disqualify [,dɪs'kwɒlɪfaɪ] vt squalificare; **he is disqualified from driving** (Br) gli hanno ritirato la patente.

disregard [,dɪsrɪ'gɑːd] vt ignorare.

disrupt [dɪs'rʌpt] vt disturbare.

disruption [dɪs'rʌpʃn] n disordine m.

dissatisfied [,dɪs'sætɪsfaɪd] adj insoddisfatto(-a).

dissolve [dɪ'zɒlv] vt sciogliere ♦ vi sciogliersi.

dissuade [dɪ'sweɪd] vt: **to ~ sb from doing sthg** dissuadere qn da fare qc.

distance ['dɪstəns] n distanza f; **from a ~** da lontano; **in the ~** in lontananza.

distant ['dɪstənt] adj distante; (in time) lontano(-a).

distilled water [dɪ'stɪld-] n acqua f distillata.

distillery [dɪ'stɪlərɪ] n distilleria f.

distinct [dɪ'stɪŋkt] adj (separate) distinto(-a); (noticeable) chiaro(-a).

distinction [dɪ'stɪŋkʃn] n (difference) distinzione f; (mark in exam) lode f.

distinctive [dɪ'stɪŋktɪv] adj inconfondibile.

distinguish [dɪ'stɪŋgwɪʃ] vt (perceive) distinguere; **to ~ sthg from sthg** distinguere qc da qc.

distorted [dɪ'stɔːtɪd] adj distorto(-a).

distract [dɪ'strækt] vt distrarre.

distraction [dɪ'strækʃn] n distrazione f.

distress [dɪ'stres] n (pain) sofferenza f; (anxiety) angoscia f.

distressing [dɪ'stresɪŋ] adj doloroso(-a).

distribute [dɪ'strɪbjuːt] vt distribuire.

distributor [dɪ'strɪbjʊtər] n (COMM) distributore m; (AUT) spinterogeno m.

district ['dɪstrɪkt] n regione f; (of town) quartiere m.

district attorney n (Am) = procuratore m della Repubblica.

disturb [dɪ'stɜːb] vt (interrupt) disturbare; (worry) turbare; (move) muovere; **'do not ~'** 'non disturbare'.

disturbance [dɪ'stɜːbəns] n (violence) disordini mpl.

ditch [dɪtʃ] n fossato m.

ditto ['dɪtəʊ] adv idem.

divan [dɪ'væn] n divano m.

dive [daɪv] (pt Am **-d** OR **dove**, pt Br **-d**) n (of swimmer) tuffo m ♦ vi tuffarsi; (under sea) immergersi.

diver ['daɪvər] n (from divingboard, rock) tuffatore m (-trice f); (under sea) sommozzatore m (-trice f).

diversion [daɪ'vɜːʃn] n (of traffic) deviazione f; (amusement) diversivo m.

divert [daɪ'vɜːt] vt (traffic, river) deviare; (attention) distrarre.

divide [dɪ'vaɪd] vt dividere ♦ vi dividersi.

divide up vt sep dividere.

diving ['daɪvɪŋ] n (from divingboard, rock) tuffi mpl; (under sea) immersioni fpl; **to go ~** fare sub.

divingboard ['daɪvɪŋbɔːd] n trampolino m.

division [dɪ'vɪʒn] n divisione f; (in football league) serie f.

divorce [dɪ'vɔːs] n divorzio m ♦ vt divorziare da.

divorced [dɪ'vɔːst] adj divorziato(-a).

DIY n (abbr of do-it-yourself) il fai da te.

dizzy ['dɪzɪ] adj: **I feel ~** mi gira la testa.

DJ n (abbr of disc jockey) discjockey mf inv.

do [duː] (pt **did**, pp **done**, pl **dos**) aux vb **1.** (in negatives): **don't ~ that!** non farlo!; **she didn't listen** non ha ascoltato.
2. (in questions): **~ you like it?** ti piace?; **how ~ you do it?** come si fa?

dock

3. (referring to previous verb): **I eat more than you** ~ io mangio più di te; **you made a mistake – no I didn't!** ti sei sbagliato – non è vero!; **so** ~ **I** anch'io.

4. (in question tags) vero?, non è vero?; **so, you like Scotland,** ~ **you?** e così ti piace la Scozia, non è vero?

5. (for emphasis): **I** ~ **like this bedroom** questa camera mi piace proprio; ~ **come in!** si accomodi!

◆ vt 1. (perform) fare; **to** ~ **one's homework** fare i compiti; **what is she doing?** cosa sta facendo?; **what can I** ~ **for you?** in cosa posso esserle utile?

2. (attend to): **to** ~ **one's hair** pettinarsi; **to** ~ **one's make-up** truccarsi; **to** ~ **one's teeth** lavarsi i denti.

3. (cause) fare; **to** ~ **damage** danneggiare; **to** ~ **sb good** fare bene a qn.

4. (have as job): **what do you** ~? che lavoro fai?

5. (provide, offer) fare; **we** ~ **pizzas for under £4** facciamo pizze a meno di 4 sterline.

6. (study) fare.

7. (subj: vehicle) fare; **the car was doing 50 mph** la macchina andava a 80 all'ora.

8. (inf: visit) fare; **we're doing Scotland next week** la settimana prossima facciamo la Scozia.

◆ vi 1. (behave, act) fare; ~ **as I say** fai come ti dico.

2. (progress, get on) andare; **to** ~ **badly** andare male; **to** ~ **well** andare bene.

3. (be sufficient) bastare; **will £5** ~? bastano 5 sterline?

4. (in phrases): **how do you** ~? piacere!; **what has that got to** ~ **with**

it? e questo che c'entra?

◆ n (party) festa f; **the** ~**s and don'ts** le cose da fare e da non fare.

❏ **do out of** vt sep (inf): **to** ~ **sb out of sthg** fregare qc a qn; **do up** vt sep (fasten) allacciare; (decorate) rinnovare; (wrap up) impacchettare; **do with** vt fus (need): **I could** ~ **with a drink** mi ci vuole proprio un bicchierino; **do without** vt fus fare a meno di.

dock [dɒk] n (for ships) molo m; (JUR) banco m degli imputati ◆ vi attraccare.

doctor ['dɒktər] n dottore m (-essa f); **to go to the** ~'**s** andare dal dottore.

document ['dɒkjumənt] n documento m.

documentary [ˌdɒkjuˈmentəri] n documentario m.

Dodgems® ['dɒdʒəmz] npl (Br) autoscontri mpl.

dodgy ['dɒdʒi] adj (Br: inf: plan) rischioso(-a); (car) poco sicuro(-a).

does [weak form dəz, strong form dʌz] → **do**.

doesn't ['dʌznt] = does not.

dog [dɒg] n cane m.

dog food n cibo m per cani.

doggy bag ['dɒgɪ-] n sacchetto per portar via gli avanzi di un pasto consumato al ristorante.

do-it-yourself n il fai da te.

dole [dəʊl] n: **to be on the** ~ (Br) prendere il sussidio di disoccupazione.

doll [dɒl] n bambola f.

dollar ['dɒlər] n dollaro m.

Dolomites ['dɒləmaɪts] npl: **the** ~ le Dolomiti.

dolphin ['dɒlfɪn] *n* delfino *m*.

dome [dəʊm] *n* cupola *f*.

domestic [də'mestɪk] *adj (of house, family)* domestico(-a); *(of country)* nazionale, interno(-a).

domestic appliance *n* elettrodomestico *m*.

domestic flight *n* volo *m* nazionale.

domestic science *n* economia *f* domestica.

dominate ['dɒmɪneɪt] *vt* dominare.

dominoes ['dɒmɪnəʊz] *n* domino *m*.

donate [də'neɪt] *vt* donare.

donation [də'neɪʃn] *n* donazione *f*.

done [dʌn] *pp* → **do** ◆ *adj (finished)* finito(-a); *(cooked)* cotto(-a).

donkey ['dɒŋkɪ] *n* asino *m*.

don't [dəʊnt] = **do not**.

door [dɔːʳ] *n (of building)* porta *f*; *(of vehicle, cupboard)* sportello *m*.

doorbell ['dɔːbel] *n* campanello *m*.

doorknob ['dɔːnɒb] *n* pomello *m*.

doorman ['dɔːmən] *(pl* **-men)** *n* portiere *m*.

doormat ['dɔːmæt] *n* zerbino *m*.

doormen ['dɔːmən] *pl* → **doorman**.

doorstep ['dɔːstep] *n* gradino *m* della porta; *(Br: inf: piece of bread)* grossa fetta *f* di pane.

doorway ['dɔːweɪ] *n* porta *f*.

dope [dəʊp] *n (inf: any illegal drug)* roba *f*; *(marijuana)* erba *f*.

dormitory ['dɔːmtrɪ] *n* dormitorio *m*.

Dormobile® ['dɔːməbiːl] *n* camper *m inv*.

dosage ['dəʊsɪdʒ] *n* dosaggio *m*.

dose [dəʊs] *n (amount)* dose *f*; *(of illness)* attacco *m*.

dot [dɒt] *n* punto *m*; **on the ~** *(fig)* in punto.

dotted line [dɒtd-] *n* linea *f* punteggiata.

double ['dʌbl] *adj* doppio(-a) ◆ *adv (twice)* due volte ◆ *n (twice the amount)* doppio *m*; *(alcohol)* dose *f* doppia ◆ *vt & vi* raddoppiare; ~ **three, two, eight** trentatré, ventotto; **a ~ whisky** un doppio whisky; **to bend sthg ~** piegare qc in due ❑ **doubles** *n (in tennis)* doppio *m*.

double bed *n* letto *m* matrimoniale.

double-breasted [-'brestɪd] *adj* a doppio petto.

double cream *n (Br)* panna molto densa ad alto contenuto di grassi.

double-decker (bus) [-'dekəʳ-] *n* autobus *m inv* a due piani.

double doors *npl* porte *fpl* a due battenti.

double-glazing ['gleɪzɪŋ] *n* doppi vetri *mpl*.

double room *n* camera *f* per due.

doubt [daʊt] *n* dubbio *m* ◆ *vt* dubitare di; **I ~ it** ne dubito; **I ~ she'll be there** dubito che ci sarà; **in ~** in dubbio; **no ~** *(almost certainly)* senza dubbio.

doubtful ['daʊtfʊl] *adj (uncertain)* incerto(-a); **it's ~ that ...** è improbabile che ... (+ *subjunctive*).

dough [dəʊ] *n* pasta *f*, impasto *m* (*per pane, dolci*).

doughnut ['dəʊnʌt] *n* bom-

dove

bolone *m*.

dove[1] [dʌv] *n* (*bird*) colomba *f*.

dove[2] [dəʊv] *pt* (*Am*) → **dive**.

Dover ['dəʊvə'] *n* Dover.

Dover sole *n* sogliola *f* di Dover.

down [daʊn] *adv* **1.** (*towards the bottom*) giù; ~ **here** quaggiù; ~ **there** laggiù; **to fall** ~ cadere. **2.** (*along*): **I'm going** ~ **to the shops** vado ai negozi. **3.** (*downstairs*): **I'll come** ~ **later** scenderò più tardi. **4.** (*southwards*): **we're going** ~ **to London** andiamo a Londra. **5.** (*in writing*): **to write sthg** ~ scrivere qc.
♦ *prep* **1.** (*towards the bottom of*): **they ran** ~ **the hill** corsero giù per la collina. **2.** (*along*) lungo; **I was walking** ~ **the street** camminavo lungo la strada.
♦ *adj* (*inf: depressed*) giù (*inv*).
♦ *n* (*feathers*) piumino *m*.
❑ **downs** *npl* (*Br*) colline *fpl*.

downhill [,daʊn'hɪl] *adv* in discesa.

Downing Street ['daʊnɪŋ-] *n* Downing Street *f* (*strada che indica dove si trova la residenza del primo ministro*).

---

i DOWNING STREET

Questa strada di Londra è divenuta famosa in quanto ospita al numero 10 la residenza ufficiale del primo ministro e al numero 11 quella del Cancelliere dello Scacchiere (ministro delle Finanze). L'espressione "Downing Street" designa, per estensione, il primo ministro stesso e i suoi collaboratori.

---

downpour ['daʊnpɔ:'] *n* acquazzone *m*.

downstairs [,daʊn'steəz] *adj* di sotto ♦ *adv* al piano di sotto; **to go** ~ scendere giù.

downtown [,daʊn'taʊn] *adj* (*hotel*) del centro; (*train*) per il centro ♦ *adv* in centro; ~ **New York** il centro di New York.

down under *adv* (*Br: inf: in Australia*) in Australia.

downwards ['daʊnwədz] *adv* verso il basso.

doz. *abbr* = **dozen**.

doze [dəʊz] *vi* fare un pisolino.

dozen ['dʌzn] *n* dozzina *f*; **a** ~ **eggs** una dozzina di uova.

Dr (*abbr of doctor*) Dott. *m* (Dott.ssa *f*).

drab [dræb] *adj* grigio(-a).

draft [drɑ:ft] *n* (*early version*) bozza *f*; (*money order*) tratta *f*; (*Am*) = **draught**.

drag [dræg] *vt* (*pull along*) trascinare ♦ *vi* (*along ground*) strascicare; **what a** ~! (*inf*) che seccatura! ❑ **drag on** *vi* trascinarsi.

dragonfly ['drægnflaɪ] *n* libellula *f*.

drain [dreɪn] *n* (*sewer*) fogna *f*; (*grating in street*) tombino *m* ♦ *vt* (*tank, radiator*) svuotare ♦ *vi* (*vegetables, washing-up*) scolare.

draining board ['dreɪnɪŋ-] *n* scolatoio *m*.

drainpipe ['dreɪnpaɪp] *n* tubo *m* di scarico.

drama ['drɑ:mə] *n* (*play, exciting event*) dramma *m*; (*art*) teatro *m* (*excitement*) emozioni *fpl*.

dramatic [drə'mætɪk] *adj (impressive)* sensazionale.

drank [dræŋk] *pt* → **drink**.

drapes [dreɪps] *npl (Am)* tende *fpl*.

drastic ['dræstɪk] *adj* drastico(-a); *(improvement)* netto(-a).

drastically ['dræstɪklɪ] *adv* sensibilmente.

draught [drɑ:ft] *n (Br: of air)* corrente *f* d'aria.

draught beer *n* birra *f* alla spina.

draughts [drɑ:fts] *n (Br)* dama *f*.

draughty [drɑ:ftɪ] *adj* pieno(-a) di correnti d'aria.

draw [drɔ:] *(pt* drew, *pp* drawn) *vt (with pen, pencil)* disegnare; *(line)* tracciare; *(pull)* tirare; *(attract)* attirare; *(conclusion)* trarre; *(comparison)* fare ◆ *vi (with pen, pencil)* disegnare; *(SPORT)* pareggiare ◆ *n (SPORT: result)* pareggio *m; (lottery)* estrazione *f;* **to ~ the curtains** tirare le tende ❑ **draw out** *vt sep (money)* prelevare; **draw up** *vt sep (list, plan)* stendere ◆ *vi (car, bus)* accostarsi.

drawback ['drɔ:bæk] *n* inconveniente *m*.

drawer [drɔ:ʳ] *n* cassetto *m*.

drawing ['drɔ:ɪŋ] *n* disegno *m*.

drawing pin *n (Br)* puntina *f* da disegno.

drawing room *n* salotto *m*.

drawn [drɔ:n] *pp* → **draw**.

dreadful ['dredful] *adj* terribile.

dream [dri:m] *n* sogno *m* ◆ *vt* sognare ◆ *vi:* **to ~ (of)** sognare (di); **a ~ house** una casa di sogno.

dress [dres] *n* vestito *m; (clothes)* abbigliamento *m* ◆ *vt* vestire;

(wound) fasciare; *(salad)* condire ◆ *vi (get dressed)* vestirsi; *(in particular way)* vestire; **to be ~ed in** essere vestito di; **to get ~ed** vestirsi ❑ **dress up** *vi* mettersi in ghingheri.

dress circle *n* prima galleria *f*.

dresser ['dresəʳ] *n (Br: for crockery)* credenza *f; (Am: chest of drawers)* comò *m inv*.

dressing ['dresɪŋ] *n (for salad)* condimento *m; (for wound)* fasciatura *f*.

dressing gown *n* vestaglia *f*.

dressing room *n* camerino *m*.

dressing table *n* toilette *f inv*.

dressmaker ['dres,meɪkəʳ] *n* sarta *f*.

dress rehearsal *n* prova *f* generale.

drew [dru:] *pt* → **draw**.

dribble ['drɪbl] *vi (liquid)* gocciolare; *(baby)* sbavare.

drier ['draɪəʳ] = **dryer**.

drift [drɪft] *n (of snow)* cumulo *m* ◆ *vi (in wind)* essere spinto dal vento; *(in water)* essere spinto dalla corrente.

drill [drɪl] *n* trapano *m* ◆ *vt (hole)* fare.

drink [drɪŋk] *(pt* drank, *pp* drunk) *n* bevanda *f; (alcoholic)* bicchierino *m* ◆ *vt & vi* bere; **would you like a ~?** vuoi qualcosa da bere?; **to have a ~** *(alcoholic)* bere un bicchierino.

drinkable ['drɪŋkəbl] *adj (safe to drink)* potabile; *(wine)* bevibile.

drinking water ['drɪŋkɪŋ-] *n* acqua *f* potabile.

drip [drɪp] *n (drop)* goccia *f; (MED)* flebo *f inv* ◆ *vi* gocciolare.

drip-dry *adj* che non si stira.

dripping (wet) ['drɪpɪŋ-] *adj* fradicio(-a).

drive [draɪv] (*pt* **drove**, *pp* **driven** ['drɪvn]) *n* (*journey*) viaggio *m* (in macchina); (*in front of house*) viale *m* d'accesso ♦ *vi* (*drive car*) guidare; (*travel in car*) andare in macchina ♦ *vt* (*car, bus, train*) guidare; (*take in car*) portare (in macchina); (*operate, power*): **it's driven by electricity** funziona a elettricità; **it's two hours' ~ from here** è a due ore di macchina da qui; **to go for a ~** andare a fare un giro in macchina; **to ~ sb to do sthg** spingere qn a fare qc; **to ~ sb mad** far diventare matto qn; **can you ~ me to the station?** mi accompagni alla stazione?

drivel ['drɪvl] *n* scemenze *fpl*.

driven *pp* → **drive**.

driver ['draɪvəʳ] *n* (*of car, bus*) conducente *mf*; (*of train*) macchinista *mf*; (*of taxi*) tassista *mf*.

driver's license (*Am*) = **driving licence**.

driveshaft ['draɪvʃɑːft] *n* albero *m* motore.

driveway ['draɪvweɪ] *n* vialetto *m* d'accesso.

driving lesson ['draɪvɪŋ-] *n* lezione *f* di guida.

driving licence ['draɪvɪŋ-] *n* (*Br*) patente *f* di guida.

driving test ['draɪvɪŋ-] *n* esame *m* di guida.

drizzle ['drɪzl] *n* pioggerellina *f*.

drop [drɒp] *n* (*drip*) goccia *f*; (*small amount*) goccio *m*; (*distance down*) salto *m*; (*decrease*) calo *m*; (*in wages*) riduzione *f* ♦ *vt* lasciar cadere; (*reduce*) ridurre; (*from vehicle*) far scendere; (*omit*) saltare ♦ *vi* (*fall*) cadere; (*decrease*) diminuire;

to ~ a hint that far capire che; **to ~ sb a line** scrivere due righe a qn □ **drop in** *vi* (*inf*) fare un salto; **drop off** *vt sep* (*from vehicle*) far scendere ♦ *vi* (*fall asleep*) addormentarsi; (*fall off*) staccarsi; **drop out** *vi* (*of college, race*) ritirarsi.

drought [draʊt] *n* siccità *f inv*.

drove [drəʊv] *pt* → **drive**.

drown [draʊn] *vi* annegare.

drug [drʌg] *n* (*MED*) farmaco *m*; (*stimulant*) droga *f* ♦ *vt* drogare.

drug addict *n* tossicodipendente *mf*.

druggist ['drʌgɪst] *n* (*Am*) farmacista *mf*.

drum [drʌm] *n* (*MUS*) tamburo *m*; (*container*) fusto *m* □ **drums** *npl* batteria *f*.

drummer ['drʌməʳ] *n* batterista *mf*.

drumstick ['drʌmstɪk] *n* (*of chicken*) coscia *f* (di pollo).

drunk [drʌŋk] *pp* → **drink** ♦ *adj* ubriaco(-a) ♦ *n* ubriaco *m* (-a *f*); **to get ~** ubriacarsi.

dry [draɪ] *adj* secco(-a); (*weather, day*) asciutto(-a) ♦ *vt* asciugare ♦ *vi* asciugarsi; **to ~** *vi* asciugarsi; **to ~ one's hair** asciugarsi i capelli □ **dry up** *vi* (*become dry*) seccarsi; (*dry the dishes*) asciugare i piatti.

dry-clean *vt* pulire a secco.

dry cleaner's *n* lavanderia *f* (a secco).

dryer ['draɪəʳ] *n* (*for clothes*) asciugabiancheria *m inv*; (*for hair*) asciugacapelli *m inv*.

dry-roasted peanuts ['-rəʊstɪd-] *npl* arachidi *fpl* tostate.

DSS *n* (*Br*) ministero britannico per la previdenza sociale.

DTP *n* (*abbr of desktop publishing*) desktop publishing *m.*

dual carriageway ['dju:əl-] *n* (*Br*) strada *f* a doppia carreggiata.

dubbed [dʌbd] *adj* (*film*) doppiato(-a).

dubious ['dju:bjəs] *adj* (*suspect*) dubbio(-a).

duchess ['dʌtʃɪs] *n* duchessa *f.*

duck [dʌk] *n* anatra *f* ♦ *vi* abbassarsi.

due [dju:] *adj* (*expected*) atteso(-a); (*owed*) dovuto(-a); **to be ~** (*bill, rent*) scadere; **in ~ course** a tempo debito; **~ to** a causa di.

duet [dju:'et] *n* duetto *m.*

duffel bag ['dʌfl-] *n* sacca *f* da viaggio.

duffel coat ['dʌfl-] *n* montgomery *m inv.*

dug [dʌg] *pt & pp → dig.*

duke [dju:k] *n* duca *m.*

dull [dʌl] *adj* (*boring*) noioso(-a); (*not bright*) spento(-a); (*weather*) coperto(-a); (*pain*) sordo(-a).

dumb [dʌm] *adj* (*inf: stupid*) stupido(-a); (*unable to speak*) muto(-a).

dummy ['dʌmɪ] *n* (*Br: for baby*) ciuccio *m*; (*for clothes*) manichino *m.*

dump [dʌmp] *n* (*for rubbish*) discarica *f*; (*inf: place*) porcile *m* ♦ *vt* (*drop carelessly*) gettare; (*get rid of*) scaricare.

dumpling ['dʌmplɪŋ] *n* gnocco di pasta cotto al vapore e servito insieme agli stufati.

dune [dju:n] *n* duna *f.*

dungarees [ˌdʌŋgə'ri:z] *npl* (*for work*) tuta *f*; (*Br: fashion item*) salopette *f inv.*

dungeon ['dʌndʒən] *n* segreta *f.*

duplicate ['dju:plɪkət] *n* duplicato *m.*

during ['djuərɪŋ] *prep* durante.

dusk [dʌsk] *n* crepuscolo *m.*

dust [dʌst] *n* polvere *f* ♦ *vt* spolverare.

dustbin ['dʌstbɪn] *n* (*Br*) pattumiera *f.*

dustcart ['dʌstkɑ:t] *n* (*Br*) camion *m inv* delle immondizie.

duster ['dʌstə[r]] *n* straccio *m* (*per spolverare*).

dustman ['dʌstmən] (*pl* -men [-mən]) *n* (*Br*) netturbino *m.*

dustpan ['dʌstpæn] *n* paletta *f* (*per la spazzatura*).

dusty ['dʌstɪ] *adj* polveroso(-a).

Dutch [dʌtʃ] *adj* olandese ♦ *n* (*language*) olandese *m* ♦ *npl*: **the ~** gli olandesi.

Dutchman ['dʌtʃmən] (*pl* -men [-mən]) *n* olandese *m.*

Dutchwoman ['dʌtʃˌwumən] (*pl* -women [-ˌwɪmɪn]) *n* olandese *f.*

duty ['dju:tɪ] *n* (*moral obligation*) dovere *m*; (*tax*) dazio *m*, tassa *f*; **to be on ~** essere in OR di servizio; **to be off ~** essere fuori servizio, essere libero ❑ **duties** *npl* (*job*) mansioni *fpl.*

duty chemist's *n* farmacia *f* di turno.

duty-free *adj* esente da dazio ♦ *n* duty free *m inv.*

duty-free shop *n* duty free shop *m inv.*

duvet ['dju:veɪ] *n* piumone®.

dwarf [dwɔ:f] (*pl* dwarves [dwɔ:vz]) *n* nano *m* (-a *f*).

dwelling ['dwelɪŋ] *n* (*fml*) abitazione *f.*

dye [daɪ] *n* tinta *f* ♦ *vt* tingere.

dynamite ['daɪnəmaɪt] n dinamite f.

dynamo ['daɪnəməʊ] (pl -s) n (on bike) dinamo f inv.

dyslexic [dɪs'leksɪk] adj dislessico(-a).

E

E (abbr of east) E.

E111 E111 m.

each [iːtʃ] adj ogni (inv), ciascuno(-a) ◆ pron ogni uno, ciascuno(-a); ognuno m (-a f); ~ one ognuno; ~ of them ognuno di loro; one ~ uno ciascuno; one of ~ uno di ciascuno; they know ~ other si conoscono.

eager ['iːgəʳ] adj (pupil, expression) entusiasta; to be ~ to do sthg essere impaziente di fare qc.

eagle ['iːgl] n (bird) aquila f.

ear [ɪəʳ] n orecchio m; (of corn) spiga f.

earache ['ɪəreɪk] n: to have ~ avere mal m d'orecchi.

earl [ɜːl] n conte m.

early ['ɜːlɪ] adj (childhood) primo(-a); (train) di buon'ora; (before usual or arranged time) anticipato(-a), precoce ◆ adv presto; in the ~ morning di primo mattino; in the ~ 20th century all'inizio del XX secolo; at the earliest al più presto; ~ on presto; to have an ~ night andare a letto presto.

earn [ɜːn] vt (money) guadagnare; (praise, success) guadagnarsi; to ~ a living guadagnarsi da vivere.

earnings ['ɜːnɪŋz] npl guadagni mpl.

earphones ['ɪəfəʊnz] npl cuffie fpl.

earplugs ['ɪəplʌgz] npl tappi mpl per le orecchie.

earrings ['ɪərɪŋz] npl orecchini mpl.

earth [ɜːθ] n terra f ◆ vt (Br: appliance) mettere a terra; how on ~ ...? come diavolo ...?

earthenware ['ɜːθnweəʳ] adj di terracotta.

earthquake ['ɜːθkweɪk] n terremoto m.

ease [iːz] n (lack of difficulty) facilità f ◆ vt (pain, problem) alleviare; at ~ a proprio agio; with ~ con facilità □ **ease off** vi (pain, rain) attenuarsi.

easily ['iːzɪlɪ] adv facilmente; (by far) senza dubbio.

east [iːst] n est m ◆ adj dell'est ◆ adv a est; in the ~ of England nell'Inghilterra orientale; the East (Asia) l'Oriente m.

eastbound ['iːstbaʊnd] adj diretto(-a) a est.

Easter ['iːstəʳ] n Pasqua f.

eastern ['iːstən] adj orientale, dell'est □ **Eastern** adj (Asian) orientale.

Eastern Europe n l'Europa f dell'Est.

eastwards ['iːstwədz] adv verso est.

easy ['iːzɪ] adj facile; (without problems) tranquillo(-a); to take it ~ prendersela con calma.

easygoing [ˌiːzɪ'gəʊɪŋ] adj rilassato(-a).

eat [iːt] (pt ate, pp eaten ['iːtn]) vt

& vi mangiare ❑ **eat out** *vi* mangiare fuori.

eating apple ['iːtɪŋ-] *n* mela *f* (da mangiare cruda).

ebony ['ebənɪ] *n* ebano *m*.

EC *n (abbr of European Community)* CE *f*.

eccentric [ɪk'sentrɪk] *adj* eccentrico(-a).

echo ['ekəʊ] *(pl -es) n* eco *f* ◆ *vi* fare eco.

ecology [ɪ'kɒlədʒɪ] *n* ecologia *f*.

economic [ˌiːkə'nɒmɪk] *adj* economico(-a) ❑ **economics** *n* economia *f*.

economical [ˌiːkə'nɒmɪkl] *adj (car, system)* economico(-a); *(person)* parsimonioso(-a).

economize [ɪ'kɒnəmaɪz] *vi* economizzare, risparmiare.

economy [ɪ'kɒnəmɪ] *n* economia *f*.

economy class *n* classe *f* economica.

economy size *adj* in confezione economica.

ecstasy ['ekstəsɪ] *n* estasi *f inv.*

ECU ['ekjuː] *n* ECU *m inv.*

eczema ['eksɪmə] *n* eczema *m.*

edge [edʒ] *n* bordo *m*; *(of knife)* taglio *m.*

edible ['edɪbl] *adj* commestibile.

Edinburgh ['edɪnbrə] *n* Edimburgo *f.*

Edinburgh Festival *n:* the ~ il festival di Edimburgo.

i **EDINBURGH FESTIVAL**

La capitale scozzese ospita ogni anno, nel mese di agosto, un festival internazionale di musica, teatro e danza di altissima qualità. Parallelamente alle rappresentazioni più classiche del programma ufficiale, la sezione "Fringe" del festival propone centinaia di produzioni indipendenti, messe in scena in piccoli locali sparsi un po' in tutta la città.

edition [ɪ'dɪʃn] *n* edizione *f*; *(of TV programme)* puntata *f.*

editor ['edɪtə*r*] *n (of newspaper, magazine)* direttore *m* (-trice *f*); *(of book)* curatore *m* (-trice *f*); *(of film, TV programme)* tecnico *m* (-a *f*) del montaggio.

editorial [ˌedɪ'tɔːrɪəl] *n* editoriale *m.*

educate ['edʒʊkeɪt] *vt* istruire.

education [ˌedʒʊ'keɪʃn] *n* istruzione *f.*

EEC *n* C.E.E. *f.*

eel [iːl] *n* anguilla *f.*

effect [ɪ'fekt] *n* effetto *m*; **to put sthg into** ~ mettere qc in atto; **to take** ~ *(drug)* fare effetto; *(law)* entrare in vigore.

effective [ɪ'fektɪv] *adj (successful)* efficace; *(law, system)* effettivo(-a).

effectively [ɪ'fektɪvlɪ] *adv (successfully)* efficacemente; *(in fact)* effettivamente.

efficient [ɪ'fɪʃənt] *adj* efficiente.

effort ['efət] *n* sforzo *m*; **to make an** ~ **to do sthg** fare uno sforzo per fare qc; **it's not worth the** ~ non ne vale la pena.

e.g. *adv* ad es.

egg [eg] *n* uovo *m.*

egg cup *n* portauovo *m inv.*

egg mayonnaise *n* uova *fpl* sode in maionese.

eggplant ['egplɑːnt] n (Am) melanzana f.

egg white n albume m.

egg yolk n tuorlo m.

Egypt ['iːdʒɪpt] n l'Egitto m.

eiderdown ['aɪdədaʊn] n piumone® m.

eight [eɪt] num otto, → **six**.

eighteen [ˌeɪ'tiːn] num diciotto, → **six**.

eighteenth [ˌeɪ'tiːnθ] num diciottesimo(-a), → **sixth**.

eighth [eɪtθ] num ottavo(-a), → **sixth**.

eightieth ['eɪtɪɪθ] num ottantesimo(-a), → **sixth**.

eighty ['eɪtɪ] num ottanta, → **six**.

Eire ['eərə] n la Repubblica d'Irlanda.

Eisteddfod [aɪ'stedfəd] n festival culturale gallese.

---

i EISTEDDFOD

Questo festival si tiene ogni anno in Galles, nel mese di agosto, per celebrare la lingua e la cultura della regione. Nel corso della manifestazione, le cui origini risalgono al dodicesimo secolo, si svolgono gare di musica, poesia e teatro.

---

either adj: ~ book will do va bene sia l'uno che l'altro libro ♦ pron: **I'll take** ~ **(of them)** prendo o l'uno(-a) o l'altro(-a); **I don't like** ~ **(of them)** non mi piace né l'uno(-a) né l'altro(-a) ♦ adv: **I can't** ~ non posso neanch'io; ~ ... **or** o ... o; **on** ~ **side** su entrambi i lati.

eject [r'dʒekt] vt (cassette) espellere.

elaborate [r'læbrət] adj (needlework, design) elaborato(-a).

elastic [r'læstɪk] n elastico m.

elastic band n (Br) elastico m.

elbow ['elbəʊ] n (of person) gomito m.

elder ['eldə'] adj più vecchio(-a), maggiore.

elderly ['eldəlɪ] adj anziano(-a) ♦ npl: **the** ~ gli anziani.

eldest ['eldɪst] adj: **the** ~ **son/daughter** il figlio/la figlia maggiore.

elect [r'lekt] vt eleggere; **to** ~ **to do sthg** (fml: choose) scegliere di fare qc.

election [r'lekʃn] n elezione f.

electric [r'lektrɪk] adj elettrico(-a).

electrical goods [r'lektrɪkl-] npl apparecchi mpl elettrici.

electric blanket n coperta f elettrica.

electric drill n trapano m elettrico.

electric fence n recinto m elettrificato.

electrician [ˌɪlek'trɪʃn] n elettricista mf.

electricity [ˌɪlek'trɪsətɪ] n elettricità f.

electric shock n scossa f elettrica.

electrocute [r'lektrəkjuːt] vt fulminare.

electronic [ˌɪlek'trɒnɪk] adj elettronico(-a).

elegant ['elɪgənt] adj elegante.

element ['elɪmənt] n elemento m; (of fire, kettle) resistenza f; **the**

~**s** *(weather)* gli elementi.

elementary [ˌelɪˈmentərɪ] *adj* elementare.

elephant [ˈelɪfənt] *n* elefante *m*.

elevator [ˈelɪveɪtər] *n (Am)* ascensore *m*.

eleven [ɪˈlevn] *num* undici, → **six**.

eleventh [ɪˈlevnθ] *num* undicesimo(-a), → **sixth**.

eligible [ˈelɪdʒəbl] *adj* che ha i requisiti.

eliminate [ɪˈlɪmɪneɪt] *vt* eliminare.

Elizabethan [ɪˌlɪzəˈbiːθn] *adj* elisabettiano(-a) *(seconda metà del XVI sec.)*.

elm [elm] *n* olmo *m*.

else [els] *adv*: **I don't want anything ~** non voglio nient'altro; **anything ~?** altro?; **everyone ~** tutti gli altri; **nobody ~** nessun altro; **nothing ~** nient'altro; **somebody ~** qualcun altro; **something ~** qualcos'altro; **somewhere ~** da qualche altra parte; **what ~?** che altro?; **who ~?** chi altri?; **or ~** altrimenti.

elsewhere [elsˈweər] *adv* altrove.

embankment [ɪmˈbæŋkmənt] *n (next to river)* argine *m*; *(next to road, railway)* terrapieno *m*.

embark [ɪmˈbɑːk] *vi (board ship)* imbarcarsi.

embarkation card [ˌembɑːˈkeɪʃn-] *n* carta *f* d'imbarco.

embarrass [ɪmˈbærəs] *vt* imbarazzare.

embarrassed [ɪmˈbærəst] *adj* imbarazzato(-a).

embarrassing [ɪmˈbærəsɪŋ] *adj* imbarazzante.

embarrassment [ɪmˈbærəs-mənt] *n* imbarazzo *m*.

embassy [ˈembəsɪ] *n* ambasciata *f*.

emblem [ˈembləm] *n* emblema *m*.

embrace [ɪmˈbreɪs] *vt* abbracciare.

embroidered [ɪmˈbrɔɪdəd] *adj* ricamato(-a).

embroidery [ɪmˈbrɔɪdərɪ] *n* ricamo *m*.

emerald [ˈemərəld] *n* smeraldo *m*.

emerge [ɪˈmɜːdʒ] *vi* emergere.

emergency [ɪˈmɜːdʒənsɪ] *n* emergenza ♦ *adj* di emergenza; **in an ~** in caso di emergenza.

emergency exit *n* uscita *f* di sicurezza.

emergency landing *n* atterraggio *m* di emergenza.

emergency services *npl* servizi *mpl* di pronto intervento.

emigrate [ˈemɪɡreɪt] *vi* emigrare.

emit [ɪˈmɪt] *vt* emettere.

emotion [ɪˈməʊʃn] *n* emozione *f*.

emotional [ɪˈməʊʃənl] *adj* emotivo(-a).

emphasis [ˈemfəsɪs] *n (pl* -ases [-əsiːz]*)* enfasi *f*; **to put the ~ on** sthg dare importanza a qc.

emphasize [ˈemfəsaɪz] *vt* sottolineare.

empire [ˈempaɪər] *n* impero *m*.

employ [ɪmˈplɔɪ] *vt* impiegare.

employed [ɪmˈplɔɪd] *adj* impiegato(-a).

employee [ɪmˈplɔɪiː] *n* dipendente *mf*.

employer [ɪmˈplɔɪər] *n* datore *m* (-trice *f*) di lavoro.

employment [ɪmˈplɔɪmənt] *n* impiego *m*.

employment agency *n* agenzia *f* di collocamento.

empty [ˈemptɪ] *adj* vuoto(-a); *(threat, promise)* vano(-a) ♦ *vt* vuotare.

EMU *n (abbr of Economic Monetary Union)* unione *f* economica e monetaria.

emulsion (paint) [ɪˈmʌlʃn-] *n* pittura *f* a emulsione.

enable [ɪˈneɪbl] *vt*: **to ~ sb to do sthg** permettere a qn di fare qc.

enamel [ɪˈnæml] *n* smalto *m*.

enclose [ɪnˈkləʊz] *vt (surround)* cingere, circondare; *(with letter)* allegare.

enclosed [ɪnˈkləʊzd] *adj (space)* contenuto(-a), limitato(-a).

encounter [ɪnˈkaʊntəʳ] *vt* incontrare.

encourage [ɪnˈkʌrɪdʒ] *vt* incoraggiare; **to ~ sb to do sthg** incoraggiare qn a fare qc.

encouragement [ɪnˈkʌrɪdʒmənt] *n* incoraggiamento *m*.

encyclopedia [ɪnˌsaɪkləˈpiːdjə] *n* enciclopedia *f*.

end [end] *n* fine *f*; *(purpose)* fine *m* ♦ *vt (story, evening, holiday)* finire; *(war, practice)* finire, mettere fine a ♦ *vi* finire; **to come to an ~** finire, giungere alla fine; **to put an ~ to sthg** mettere fine a qc; **for days on ~** per giorni e giorni; **in the ~** alla fine; **to make ~s meet** sbarcare il lunario ❑ **end up** *vi* finire; **to ~ up doing sthg** finire con il fare qc.

endangered species [ɪnˈdeɪndʒəd-] *n* specie *f inv* in via d'estinzione.

ending [ˈendɪŋ] *n (of story, film,* book) fine *f*; *(GRAMM)* desinenza *f*.

endive [ˈendaɪv] *n (curly)* indivia *f* (riccia); *(chicory)* cicoria *f*.

endless [ˈendlɪs] *adj* interminabile, senza fine.

endorsement [ɪnˈdɔːsmənt] *n (of driving licence)* infrazione registrata sulla patente.

endurance [ɪnˈdjʊərəns] *n* resistenza *f*, sopportazione *f*.

endure [ɪnˈdjʊəʳ] *vt* sopportare.

enemy [ˈenɪmɪ] *n* nemico *m* (-a *f*).

energy [ˈenədʒɪ] *n* energia *f*.

enforce [ɪnˈfɔːs] *vt (law)* applicare, far rispettare.

engaged [ɪnˈgeɪdʒd] *adj (to be married)* fidanzato(-a); *(Br: phone)* occupato(-a); *(toilet)* occupato(-a); **to get ~** fidanzarsi.

engaged tone *n (Br)* segnale *m* di occupato.

engagement [ɪnˈgeɪdʒmənt] *n (to marry)* fidanzamento *m*; *(appointment)* appuntamento *m*.

engagement ring *n* anello *m* di fidanzamento.

engine [ˈendʒɪn] *n (of vehicle)* motore *m*; *(of train)* locomotiva *f*.

engineer [ˌendʒɪˈnɪəʳ] *n (of roads, machinery)* ingegnere *m*; *(to do repairs)* tecnico *m* (-a *f*).

engineering [ˌendʒɪˈnɪərɪŋ] *n* ingegneria *f*.

engineering works *npl (on railway line)* lavori *mpl* in corso.

England [ˈɪŋglənd] *n* l'Inghilterra *f*.

English [ˈɪŋglɪʃ] *adj* inglese ♦ *n (language)* inglese *m* ♦ *npl*: **the ~** gli inglesi.

English breakfast *n* colazio *f*.

ne *f* all'inglese.

English Channel *n*: the ~ la Manica.

Englishman ['ɪŋglɪʃmən] (*pl* **-men** [-mən]) *n* inglese *m*.

Englishwoman ['ɪŋglɪʃˌwʊmən] (*pl* **-women** [-ˌwɪmɪn]) *n* inglese *f*.

engrave [ɪn'greɪv] *vt* incidere.

engraving [ɪn'greɪvɪŋ] *n* incisione *f*.

enjoy [ɪn'dʒɔɪ] *vt* godersi; **to ~ doing sthg** divertirsi a fare qc; **I ~ swimming** mi piace nuotare; **to ~ o.s.** divertirsi; **~ your meal!** buon appetito!

enjoyable [ɪn'dʒɔɪəbl] *adj* piacevole.

enjoyment [ɪn'dʒɔɪmənt] *n* piacere *m*.

enlargement [ɪn'lɑːdʒmənt] *n* (*of photo*) ingrandimento *m*.

enormous [ɪ'nɔːməs] *adj* enorme.

enough [ɪ'nʌf] *adj* abbastanza (*inv*), sufficiente ♦ *pron & adv* abbastanza; **~ time** abbastanza tempo; **is that ~?** è abbastanza?, basta?; **it's not big ~** non è abbastanza grande; **to have had ~ (of)** averne abbastanza (di).

enquire [ɪn'kwaɪə^r] *vi* informarsi.

enquiry [ɪn'kwaɪərɪ] *n* (*question*) domanda *f*; (*investigation*) indagine *f*, inchiesta *f*; **'Enquiries'** 'Informazioni'.

enquiry desk *n* banco *m* informazioni.

enrol [ɪn'rəʊl] *vi* (*Br*) iscriversi.

enroll [ɪn'rəʊl] (*Am*) = **enrol**.

en suite bathroom [ɒn'swiːt] *n* bagno *m* privato.

ensure [ɪn'ʃʊə^r] *vt* garantire, assicurare.

entail [ɪn'teɪl] *vt* comportare.

enter ['entə^r] *vt* entrare in; (*college, competition*) iscriversi a; (*on form*) scrivere ♦ *vi* entrare; (*in competition*) iscriversi.

enterprise ['entəpraɪz] *n* (*company*) impresa *f*; (*plan*) iniziativa *f*.

entertain [ˌentə'teɪn] *vt* (*amuse*) divertire.

entertainer [ˌentə'teɪnə^r] *n* intrattenitore *m* (*-trice f*).

entertaining [ˌentə'teɪnɪŋ] *adj* divertente.

entertainment [ˌentə'teɪnmənt] *n* (*amusement*) divertimento *m*; (*show*) spettacolo *m*.

enthusiasm [ɪn'θjuːzɪæzm] *n* entusiasmo *m*.

enthusiast [ɪn'θjuːzɪæst] *n* appassionato *m* (*-a f*).

enthusiastic [ɪnˌθjuːzɪ'æstɪk] *adj* entusiasta.

entire [ɪn'taɪə^r] *adj* intero(-a).

entirely [ɪn'taɪəlɪ] *adv* completamente.

entitle [ɪn'taɪtl] *vt*: **to ~ sb to sthg** dare a qn diritto a qc; **to ~ sb to do sthg** dare diritto a qn di fare qc.

entrance ['entrəns] *n* entrata *f*, ingresso *m*.

entrance fee *n* biglietto *m* d'ingresso.

entry ['entrɪ] *n* (*door, gate, admission*) entrata *f*, ingresso *m*; (*in dictionary*) voce *f*; (*piece in competition*) cosa *f* presentata; **'no ~'** (*on door*) 'ingresso vietato'; (*road sign*) 'divieto d'accesso'.

envelope ['envələʊp] *n* busta *f*.

envious ['envɪəs] *adj* invidioso(-a).

environment [ɪn'vaɪərənmənt] *n* ambiente *m*; **the ~** l'ambiente (naturale).

environmental [ɪn,vaɪərən'mentl] *adj* ambientale.

environmentally friendly [ɪn,vaɪrən'mentəlɪ-] *adj* che rispetta l'ambiente, ecologico(-a).

envy ['envɪ] *vt* invidiare.

epic ['epɪk] *n* epopea *f*.

epidemic [,epɪ'demɪk] *n* epidemia *f*.

epileptic [,epɪ'leptɪk] *adj* epilettico(-a).

episode ['epɪsəʊd] *n* episodio *m*.

equal ['iːkwəl] *adj (of same amount)* uguale; *(with equal rights)* uguale, pari *(inv)* ♦ *vt (number)* fare; **to be ~ to** *(number)* essere uguale a.

equality [ɪ'kwɒlɪtɪ] *n* uguaglianza *f*.

equalize ['iːkwəlaɪz] *vi* pareggiare.

equally ['iːkwəlɪ] *adv (bad, good, matched)* ugualmente; *(pay, treat, share)* equamente; *(at the same time)* allo stesso modo.

equation [ɪ'kweɪʒn] *n* equazione *f*.

equator [ɪ'kweɪtər] *n*: **the ~** l'equatore *m*.

equip [ɪ'kwɪp] *vt*: **to ~ sb/sthg with** fornire qn/qc di.

equipment [ɪ'kwɪpmənt] *n* attrezzatura *f*.

equipped [ɪ'kwɪpt] *adj*: **to be ~ with** essere fornito(-a) di.

equivalent [ɪ'kwɪvələnt] *adj* equivalente ♦ *n* equivalente *m*.

erase [ɪ'reɪz] *vt (letter, word)* cancellare.

eraser [ɪ'reɪzər] *n* gomma *f*.

erect [ɪ'rekt] *adj (person, posture)* eretto(-a) ♦ *vt (tent)* montare; *(monument)* erigere.

ERM *n* meccanismo *m* di cambio (dello SME).

erotic [ɪ'rɒtɪk] *adj* erotico(-a).

errand ['erənd] *n* commissione *f*.

erratic [ɪ'rætɪk] *adj* irregolare, incostante.

error ['erər] *n* errore *m*.

escalator ['eskəleɪtər] *n* scala *f* mobile.

escalope ['eskələp] *n* cotoletta *f* alla milanese.

escape [ɪ'skeɪp] *n* fuga *f* ♦ *vi*: **to ~ (from)** *(from prison)* evadere (da); *(from danger)* fuggire (da); *(leak)* fuoriuscire (da).

escort [*n* 'eskɔːt, *vb* ɪ'skɔːt] *n (guard)* scorta *f* ♦ *vt* accompagnare.

espadrilles ['espə,drɪlz] *npl* espadrillas *fpl*.

especially [ɪ'speʃəlɪ] *adv (in particular)* specialmente, soprattutto; *(on purpose)* apposta; *(very)* particolarmente.

esplanade [,esplə'neɪd] *n* passeggiata *f* (a mare).

essay ['eseɪ] *n (at school, university)* composizione *f*, tema *m*.

essential [ɪ'senʃl] *adj (indispensable)* essenziale □ **essentials** *npl*: **the ~s** l'essenziale *m*; **the bare ~s** il minimo indispensabile.

essentially [ɪ'senʃəlɪ] *adv* essenzialmente.

establish [ɪ'stæblɪʃ] *vt (set up, create)* fondare; *(fact, truth)* stabilire.

establishment [rˈstæblɪʃmənt]
n (business) azienda f.

estate [ɪˈsteɪt] n (land in country)
proprietà f inv; (for housing) complesso m residenziale; (Br: car) =
estate car.

estate agent n (Br) agente mf
immobiliare.

estate car n (Br) station wagon
f inv.

estimate [n ˈestɪmət, vb ˈestɪmeɪt]
n (guess) stima f; (from builder,
plumber) preventivo m ♦ vt stimare, valutare.

estuary [ˈestjʊərɪ] n estuario m.

ethnic minority [ˈeθnɪk-] n
minoranza f etnica.

EU n (abbr of European Union) U.E.

Eurocheque [ˈjʊərəʊtʃek] n
eurochèque m inv.

Europe [ˈjʊərəp] n l'Europa f.

European [ˌjʊərəˈpɪən] adj euro-
peo(-a) ♦ n europeo m (-a f).

European Community n
Comunità f Europea.

evacuate [ɪˈvækjʊeɪt] vt evacuare.

evade [ɪˈveɪd] vt (person, issue)
evitare; (responsibility) sottrarsi a.

evaporated milk [ɪˈvæpəreɪ-
tɪd-] n latte m concentrato.

eve [iːv] n: on the ~ of alla vigilia
di.

even [ˈiːvn] adj (uniform, equal)
regolare, uniforme; (level, flat) li-
scio(-a), piano(-a); (contest) alla
pari; (number) pari (inv) ♦ adv perfino, anche; to break ~ fare pari;
not ~ nemmeno; ~ so ciò nonostante; ~ though anche se.

evening [ˈiːvnɪŋ] n sera f; (event,
period) serata f; good ~! buona
sera!; in the ~ di OR la sera.

evening classes npl corsi mpl
serali.

evening dress n (formal clothes)
abito m da sera; (woman's garment)
vestito m da sera.

evening meal n cena f.

event [ɪˈvent] n (occurrence) evento m, avvenimento m; (SPORT)
prova f; in the ~ of (fml) in caso di.

eventual [ɪˈventʃʊəl] adj finale.

eventually [ɪˈventʃʊəlɪ] adv alla
fine.

ever [ˈevər] adv mai; it's the worst
~ è il peggiore che sia mai esistito;
he was ~ so angry era veramente
arrabbiato; for ~ (eternally) per
sempre; we've been waiting for ~
aspettiamo da tantissimo; hardly
~ quasi mai □ ever since adv fin
da allora ♦ prep da ... in poi ♦ conj
fin da quando.

every [ˈevrɪ] adj ogni (inv); ~ day
ogni giorno, tutti i giorni; ~ other
day ogni due giorni; one in ~ ten
uno su dieci; we make ~ effort ...
facciamo ogni sforzo ...; ~ so
often ogni tanto.

everybody [ˈevrɪˌbɒdɪ] = everyone.

everyday [ˈevrɪdeɪ] adj di ogni
giorno, quotidiano(-a).

everyone [ˈevrɪwʌn] pron ognuno m (-a f), tutti mpl (-e fpl).

everyplace [ˈevrɪˌpleɪs] (Am) =
everywhere.

everything [ˈevrɪθɪŋ] pron tutto,
ogni cosa.

everywhere [ˈevrɪweər] adv
dappertutto; (wherever) dovunque.

evidence [ˈevɪdəns] n (proof)

prova f; *(legal statement)* testimonianza f.

evident ['evidənt] *adj* evidente.

evidently ['evidəntli] *adv* evidentemente.

evil ['i:vl] *adj* cattivo(-a), malvagio(-a) ♦ *n* male *m*.

ex [eks] *n (inf: wife, husband, partner)* ex *mf*.

exact [ıg'zækt] *adj* esatto(-a); '~ fare ready please' 'si prega di munirsi dell'esatta somma per il biglietto'.

exactly [ıg'zæktlı] *adv & excl* esattamente.

exaggerate [ıg'zædʒəreıt] *vt & vi* esagerare.

exaggeration [ıg,zædʒə'reıʃn] *n* esagerazione f.

exam [ıg'zæm] *n* esame *m*; **to take an ~** fare un esame.

examination [ıg,zæmı'neıʃn] *n* esame *m*; *(MED)* visita f.

examine [ıg'zæmın] *vt* esaminare; *(MED)* visitare.

example [ıg'zɑ:mpl] *n* esempio *m*; **for ~** per esempio.

exceed [ık'si:d] *vt (be greater than)* superare; *(go beyond)* oltrepassare.

excellent ['eksələnt] *adj* eccellente.

except [ık'sept] *prep & conj* eccetto, tranne; **~ for** a parte, all'infuori di; **'~ for access'** 'escluso residenti'; **'~ for loading'** 'escluso (per le operazioni di) carico'.

exception [ık'sepʃn] *n (thing excepted)* eccezione f.

exceptional [ık'sepʃnəl] *adj* eccezionale.

excerpt ['eksɜ:pt] *n* estratto *m*.

excess [ık'ses, *before nouns* 'ekses]

adj in eccesso ♦ *n* eccesso *m*.

excess baggage *n* bagaglio *m* in eccedenza.

excess fare *n (Br)* supplemento *m*.

excessive [ık'sesıv] *adj* eccessivo(-a).

exchange [ıks'tʃeındʒ] *n (of telephones)* centralino *m*; *(of students)* scambio *m* ♦ *vt* scambiare; **to ~ sthg for sthg** scambiare qc con qc; **we're here on an ~** siamo qui con uno scambio.

exchange rate *n* tasso *m* di cambio.

excited [ık'saıtıd] *adj* eccitato(-a).

excitement [ık'saıtmənt] *n* eccitazione f; *(exciting thing)* cosa f eccitante.

exciting [ık'saıtıŋ] *adj* eccitante, emozionante.

exclamation mark [,eksklə'meıʃn-] *n (Br)* punto *m* esclamativo.

exclamation point [,eksklə'meıʃn-] *(Am)* = **exclamation mark**.

exclude [ık'sklu:d] *vt* escludere.

excluding [ık'sklu:dıŋ] *prep* escluso(-a).

exclusive [ık'sklu:sıv] *adj* esclusivo(-a) ♦ *n* esclusiva f; **~ of** escluso(-a).

excursion [ık'skɜ:ʃn] *n* escursione f.

excuse [*n* ık'skju:s, *vb* ık'skju:z] *n* scusa f ♦ *vt (forgive)* scusare; *(let off)* dispensare; **~ me!** mi scusi!

ex-directory *adj (Br)* fuori elenco.

execute ['eksıkju:t] *vt (kill)* giustiziare.

executive [ɪgˈzekjʊtɪv] adj (room) per dirigenti ♦ n (person) dirigente mf.

exempt [ɪgˈzempt] adj: ~ (from) esente (da).

exemption [ɪgˈzempʃn] n esenzione f.

exercise [ˈeksəsaɪz] n esercizio m ♦ vi fare esercizio OR del moto; **to do** ~s fare degli esercizi.

exercise book n quaderno m.

exert [ɪgˈzɜːt] vt esercitare.

exhaust [ɪgˈzɔːst] vt esaurire ♦ n: ~ (pipe) tubo m di scappamento.

exhausted [ɪgˈzɔːstɪd] adj esausto(-a).

exhibit [ɪgˈzɪbɪt] n (in museum, gallery) oggetto m esposto ♦ vt (in exhibition) esporre.

exhibition [ˌeksɪˈbɪʃn] n (of art) esposizione f, mostra f.

exist [ɪgˈzɪst] vi esistere.

existence [ɪgˈzɪstəns] n esistenza f; **to be in** ~ esistere.

existing [ɪgˈzɪstɪŋ] adj esistente.

exit [ˈeksɪt] n uscita f ♦ vi uscire.

exotic [ɪgˈzɒtɪk] adj esotico(-a).

expand [ɪkˈspænd] vi (in size) espandersi; (in number) aumentare.

expect [ɪkˈspekt] vt (believe likely) aspettarsi, prevedere; (await) aspettare; **to** ~ **to do sthg** prevedere di fare qc; **to** ~ **sb to do sthg** (require) aspettarsi che qn faccia qc; **to be** ~**ing** (be pregnant) aspettare un bambino.

expedition [ˌekspɪˈdɪʃn] n spedizione f; (short outing) gita f.

expel [ɪkˈspel] vt (from school) espellere.

expense [ɪkˈspens] n spesa f,

costo m; **at the** ~ **of** (fig) a spese di ❏ **expenses** npl (of business trip) spese fpl.

expensive [ɪkˈspensɪv] adj costoso(-a), caro(-a).

experience [ɪkˈspɪərɪəns] n esperienza f ♦ vt provare.

experienced [ɪkˈspɪərɪənst] adj esperto(-a).

experiment [ɪkˈsperɪmənt] n esperimento m ♦ vi fare esperimenti.

expert [ˈekspɜːt] adj (advice) esperto(-a); (treatment) apposito(-a) ♦ n esperto m (-a f).

expire [ɪkˈspaɪəʳ] vi scadere.

expiry date [ɪkˈspaɪərɪ-] n data f di scadenza.

explain [ɪkˈspleɪn] vt spiegare.

explanation [ˌekspləˈneɪʃn] n spiegazione f.

explode [ɪkˈspləʊd] vi (bomb) esplodere.

exploit [ɪkˈsplɔɪt] vt (person) sfruttare.

explore [ɪkˈsplɔːʳ] vt (place) esplorare.

explosion [ɪkˈspləʊʒn] n (of bomb etc) esplosione f.

explosive [ɪkˈspləʊsɪv] n esplosivo m.

export [n ˈekspɔːt, vb ɪkˈspɔːt] n (of goods) esportazione f; (goods themselves) merce f d'esportazione ♦ vt esportare.

exposed [ɪkˈspəʊzd] adj (place) non riparato(-a).

exposure [ɪkˈspəʊʒəʳ] n (photograph) foto f inv; (MED) assideramento m; (to heat, radiation) esposizione f.

express [ɪkˈspres] adj (letter, deliv-

ery, train) espresso(-a) ◆ n (train)
espresso m ◆ vt esprimere ◆ adv
per espresso.

expression [ɪkˈspreʃn] n espressione f.

espresso [ɪkˈspresəʊ] (pl -s) n
espresso m.

expressway [ɪkˈspresweɪ] n (Am)
autostrada f (urbana).

extend [ɪkˈstend] vt prolungare;
(hand) offrire ◆ vi estendersi.

extension [ɪkˈstenʃn] n (of building) sala f annessa; (for phone at
work) interno m; (for phone in private house) apparecchio m supplementare; (for permit, essay) proroga
f.

extension lead n prolunga f.

extensive [ɪkˈstensɪv] adj (area)
esteso(-a), ampio(-a); (damage)
grave; (selection) ampio.

extent [ɪkˈstent] n (of damage,
knowledge) estensione f; **to a certain** ~ fino ad un certo punto; **to
what** ~ ...? fino a che punto ...?

exterior [ɪkˈstɪərɪəʳ] adj esterno(-a) ◆ n (of car, building) esterno
m.

external [ɪkˈstɜːnl] adj esterno(-a).

extinct [ɪkˈstɪŋkt] adj estinto(-a).

extinction [ɪkˈstɪŋkʃn] n estinzione f.

extinguish [ɪkˈstɪŋgwɪʃ] vt (fire,
cigarette) spegnere.

extinguisher [ɪkˈstɪŋgwɪʃəʳ] n
estintore m.

extortionate [ɪkˈstɔːʃnət] adj
esorbitante.

extra [ˈekstrə] adj (additional)
extra (inv), supplementare; (spare)
altro(-a), in più ◆ n extra m inv ◆
adv (especially) eccezionalmente;

(more) di più; ~ **charge** supplemento m; ~ **large** extra-large (inv) □
extras npl (in price) spese fpl supplementari.

extract [n ˈekstrækt, vb ɪkˈstrækt]
n (of yeast, malt etc) estratto m; (from
book, opera) brano m ◆ vt (tooth)
estrarre.

extractor fan [ɪkˈstræktə-] n
(Br) aspiratore m.

extraordinary [ɪkˈstrɔːdnrɪ] adj
straordinario(-a).

extravagant [ɪkˈstrævəgənt] adj
dispendioso(-a).

extreme [ɪkˈstriːm] adj estremo(-a) ◆ n estremo m.

extremely [ɪkˈstriːmlɪ] adv
estremamente.

extrovert [ˈekstrəvɜːt] n estroverso m (-a f).

eye [aɪ] n occhio m; (of needle)
cruna f ◆ vt osservare attentamente; **to keep an** ~ **on** tenere d'occhio.

eyebrow [ˈaɪbraʊ] n sopracciglio
m.

eye drops npl collirio m, gocce
fpl per gli occhi.

eyeglasses [ˈaɪglɑːsɪz] npl (Am)
occhiali mpl.

eyelash [ˈaɪlæʃ] n ciglio m.

eyelid [ˈaɪlɪd] n palpebra f.

eyeliner [ˈaɪlaɪnəʳ] n eye-liner m
inv.

eye shadow n ombretto m.

eyesight [ˈaɪsaɪt] n vista f.

eye test n esame m oculistico.

eyewitness [ˌaɪˈwɪtnɪs] n testimone mf oculare.

F *(abbr of Fahrenheit)* F.

fabric ['fæbrɪk] *n (cloth)* stoffa *f*, tessuto *m*.

fabulous ['fæbjʊləs] *adj* favoloso(-a).

facade [fə'sɑ:d] *n* facciata *f*.

face [feɪs] *n* faccia *f*; *(of cliff, mountain)* parete *f*; *(of clock, watch)* quadrante *m* ◆ *vt* essere di fronte a; *(accept, cope with)* affrontare; **to be ~d with** avere di fronte ❑ **face up to** *vt fus* affrontare.

facecloth ['feɪsklɒθ] *n (Br)* panno *m* di spugna.

facial ['feɪʃl] *n* trattamento *m* del viso.

facilitate [fə'sɪlɪteɪt] *vt (fml)* facilitare.

facilities [fə'sɪlɪti:z] *npl* attrezzature *fpl*.

facsimile [fæk'sɪmɪlɪ] *n* facsimile *m inv*.

fact [fækt] *n* fatto *m*; **in ~** in effetti.

factor ['fæktər] *n* fattore *m*; **~ ten suntan lotion** crema *f* abbronzante a fattore di protezione dieci.

factory ['fæktərɪ] *n* fabbrica *f*.

faculty ['fækltɪ] *n* facoltà *f inv*.

FA Cup *n* = coppa *f* Italia *(di calcio)*.

fade [feɪd] *vi (light, sound)* affievolirsi; *(flower)* appassire; *(jeans, wallpaper)* sbiadire, sbiadirsi.

faded ['feɪdɪd] *adj (jeans)* sbiadito(-a).

fag [fæg] *n (Br: inf: cigarette)* siga-

---

retta *f*.

Fahrenheit ['færənhaɪt] *adj* Fahrenheit *(inv)*.

fail [feɪl] *vt (exam)* non superare ◆ *vi* fallire; *(in exam)* essere bocciato; *(engine)* guastarsi; **to ~ to do sthg** *(not do)* non fare qc.

failing ['feɪlɪŋ] *n* difetto *m* ◆ *prep*: **~ that** se no.

failure ['feɪljər] *n* fallimento *m*; *(unsuccessful person)* fallito *m (-a f)*; *(act of neglecting)* mancanza *f*.

faint [feɪnt] *vi* svenire ◆ *adj* debole; *(outline)* indistinto(-a). **I haven't the ~est idea** non ho la più pallida idea.

fair [feər] *adj (just)* giusto(-a), equo(-a); *(quite large, quite good)* discreto(-a); *(hair, person)* biondo(-a); *(skin)* chiaro(-a); *(weather)* bello(-a) ◆ *n (funfair)* luna park *m inv*; *(trade fair)* fiera *f*; **~ enough!** mi sembra giusto!

fairground ['feəgraʊnd] *n* luna park *m inv*.

fair-haired [-'heəd] *adj* biondo(-a).

fairly ['feəlɪ] *adv (quite)* abbastanza.

fairy ['feərɪ] *n* fata *f*.

fairy tale *n* fiaba *f*.

faith [feɪθ] *n* fede *f*.

faithfully ['feɪθfʊlɪ] *adv*: **Yours ~** Distinti saluti.

fake [feɪk] *n (painting etc)* falso *m* ◆ *vt (signature, painting)* falsificare.

fall [fɔ:l] *(pt fell, pp fallen ['fɔ:ln])* *vi* cadere; *(number, pound, night)* scendere ◆ *n* caduta *f*; *(decrease)* abbassamento *m*; *(Am: autumn)* autunno *m*; **to ~ asleep** addormentarsi; **to ~ ill** ammalarsi; **to ~ in love** innamorarsi ❑ **falls** *npl (water-*

fall) cascate *fpl;* **fall behind** *vi (with work, rent)* rimanere indietro; **fall down** *vi (lose balance)* cadere; **fall off** *vi* cadere; **fall out** *vi (hair, teeth)* cadere; *(argue)* litigare; **fall over** *vi* cadere per terra; **fall through** *vi* fallire.

false [fɔːls] *adj* falso(-a).

false alarm *n* falso allarme *m.*

false teeth *npl* dentiera *f.*

fame [feɪm] *n* fama *f.*

familiar [fəˈmɪljəʳ] *adj (known)* familiare; *(informal)* (troppo) confidenziale; **to be ~ with** *(know)* conoscere.

family [ˈfæmlɪ] *n* famiglia *f* ◆ *adj (size)* familiare, da famiglia; *(film, holiday)* per famiglie.

family planning clinic [-ˈplænɪŋ-] *n* = consultorio *m* familiare.

family room *n (at hotel)* camera *f* familiare; *(at pub, airport)* sala *f* per famiglie con bambini.

famine [ˈfæmɪn] *n* carestia *f.*

famished [ˈfæmɪʃt] *adj (inf)* molto affamato(-a).

famous [ˈfeɪməs] *adj* famoso(-a).

fan [fæn] *n (held in hand)* ventaglio *m;* *(electric)* ventilatore *m;* *(enthusiast)* ammiratore *m* (-trice *f*); *(supporter)* tifoso *m* (-a *f*).

fan belt *n* cinghia *f* del ventilatore.

fancy [ˈfænsɪ] *vt (inf: feel like)* avere voglia di ◆ *adj (elaborate)* ricercato(-a); **I ~ her** *(inf)* mi piace; **~ (that)!** pensa un po'!

fancy dress *n* costume *m* (per maschera).

fan heater *n* stufa *f* elettrica con ventilatore.

fanlight [ˈfænlaɪt] *n (Br)* lunetta *f.*

fantastic [fænˈtæstɪk] *adj* fantastico(-a).

fantasy [ˈfæntəsɪ] *n (imagined thing)* fantasia *f.*

far [fɑːʳ] *(compar* **further** OR **farther***, superl* **furthest** OR **farthest***) adv* lontano; *(in degree)* molto, assai ◆ *adj* **at the ~ end (of)** in fondo (a); **how ~ is it (to London)?** quanto è lontano (da Londra)?; **as ~ as** *(place)* fino a; **as ~ as I'm concerned** per quanto mi riguarda; **as ~ as I know** per quel che ne so; **~ better** assai migliore; **by ~** di gran lunga; **so ~** *(until now)* finora; **to go too ~** *(behave unacceptably)* oltrepassare i limiti.

farce [fɑːs] *n (ridiculous situation)* farsa *f.*

fare [feəʳ] *n (on bus, train etc)* tariffa *f;* *(fml: food)* cibo *m* ◆ *vi* passarsela.

Far East *n:* **the ~** l'Estremo Oriente *m.*

fare stage *n (Br)* fermata di autobus dove il prezzo del biglietto cambia.

farm [fɑːm] *n* fattoria *f.*

farmer [ˈfɑːməʳ] *n* agricoltore *m.*

farmhouse [ˈfɑːmhaus, *pl* -hauzɪz] *n* casa *f* colonica.

farming [ˈfɑːmɪŋ] *n* agricoltura *f;* *(of animals)* allevamento *m.*

farmland [ˈfɑːmlænd] *n* terreno *m* coltivabile.

farmyard [ˈfɑːmjɑːd] *n* aia *f.*

farther [ˈfɑːðəʳ] → **far.**

farthest [ˈfɑːðəst] → **far.**

fascinating [ˈfæsɪneɪtɪŋ] *adj* affascinante.

fascination [ˌfæsɪˈneɪʃn] *n* fascino m.

fashion ['fæʃn] n moda f; (manner) modo m, maniera f; **to be in ~** essere di moda; **to be out of ~** essere fuori moda.

fashionable ['fæʃnəbl] adj di moda, alla moda.

fashion show n sfilata f di moda.

fast [fɑːst] adv (quickly) velocemente, rapidamente; (securely) saldamente ♦ adj veloce, rapido(-a); **to be ~** (clock) andare avanti; **~ asleep** profondamente addormentato; **a ~ train** un treno diretto.

fasten ['fɑːsn] vt (belt) allacciare; (coat) abbottonare; (two things) fissare.

fastener ['fɑːsnər] n chiusura f, fermaglio m.

fast food n: **~ outlet** fast food m inv.

fat [fæt] adj grasso (-a) ♦ n grasso m.

fatal ['feɪtl] adj (accident, disease) mortale.

father ['fɑːðər] n padre m.

Father Christmas n (Br) Babbo m Natale.

father-in-law n suocero m.

fattening ['fætnɪŋ] adj che fa ingrassare.

fatty ['fætɪ] adj grasso (-a).

faucet ['fɔːsɪt] n (Am) rubinetto m.

fault [fɔːlt] n (responsibility) colpa f; (flaw) difetto m; (in machine) guasto m; **it's your ~** è colpa tua.

faulty ['fɔːltɪ] adj difettoso m.

favor ['feɪvər] (Am) = **favour**.

favour ['feɪvər] n (Br: kind act) favore m ♦ vt (prefer) preferire; **to

be in ~ of** essere in favore di; **to do sb a ~** fare un favore a qn.

favourable ['feɪvrəbl] adj favorevole.

favourite ['feɪvrɪt] adj favorito(-a) ♦ n favorito m (-a f).

fax [fæks] n fax m inv ♦ vt (document) inviare per fax, faxare; (person) inviare un fax a.

fear [fɪər] n paura f ♦ vt (be afraid of) aver paura di, temere; **for ~ of** per paura di.

feast [fiːst] n (meal) banchetto m.

feather ['feðər] n penna f, piuma f.

feature ['fiːtʃər] n (characteristic) caratteristica f; (in newspaper, on radio, TV) servizio m (speciale) ♦ vt (subj: film) avere come protagonista; **~s** (of face) lineamenti mpl.

feature film n lungometraggio m.

Feb. (abbr of February) feb.

February ['februərɪ] n febbraio m, → **September**.

fed [fed] pp → **feed**.

fed up adj stufo(-a); **to be ~ with** essere stufo di.

fee [fiː] n pagamento m; (of doctor, lawyer) onorario m.

feeble ['fiːbl] adj debole.

feed [fiːd] (pt & pp fed) vt (person, animal) dare da mangiare a; (baby) allattare; (insert) immettere.

feel [fiːl] (pt & pp felt) vt (touch) tastare, toccare; (experience) sentire; (think) credere, pensare ♦ vi sentirsi; (seem) essere ♦ n (of material): **I like the ~ of it** è piacevole al tatto; **to ~ cold/hungry** avere freddo/fame; **to ~ like** (fancy) avere voglia di; **to ~ up to doing sth** sentirsela di fare qc.

feeling ['fiːlɪŋ] n *(emotion)* sentimento m; *(sensation)* sensazione f; *(belief)* opinione f; **to hurt sb's ~s** ferire i sentimenti di qn.

feet [fiːt] → **foot**.

fell [fel] pt → **fall** ♦ vt *(tree)* abbattere.

fellow ['feləʊ] n *(man)* tipo m, individuo m ♦ adj: **my ~ students** i miei compagni di classe.

felt [felt] pt & pp → **feel** ♦ n feltro m.

felt-tip pen n pennarello m.

female ['fiːmeɪl] adj femminile; *(child, animal)* femmina ♦ n *(animal)* femmina f.

feminine ['femɪnɪn] adj femminile.

feminist ['femɪnɪst] n femminista mf.

fence [fens] n recinto m.

fencing ['fensɪŋ] n *(SPORT)* scherma f.

fend [fend] vi: **to ~ for o.s.** provvedere a se stesso.

fender ['fendər] n *(for fireplace)* parafuoco m; *(Am: on car)* parafango m.

fennel ['fenl] n finocchio m.

fern [fɜːn] n felce f.

ferocious [fəˈrəʊʃəs] adj feroce.

ferry ['ferɪ] n traghetto m.

fertile ['fɜːtaɪl] adj *(land)* fertile.

fertilizer ['fɜːtɪlaɪzər] n fertilizzante m.

festival ['festɪvl] n *(of music, arts etc)* festival m inv; *(holiday)* festa f.

feta cheese ['fetə-] n formaggio bianco di latte di pecora di origine greca.

fetch [fetʃ] vt andare a prendere; *(be sold for)* essere venduto per.

fete [feɪt] n festa f all'aperto *(a scopo di beneficenza)*.

i **FETE**

Vengono così chiamate le feste all'aperto organizzate, soprattutto nei mesi estivi, per raccogliere soldi da destinare ad opere di beneficenza o al finanziamento di iniziative e progetti per il quartiere. Comprendono gare, forme varie di intrattenimento e la vendita di prodotti fatti in casa.

fever ['fiːvər] n *(MED)* febbre f; **to have a ~** avere la febbre.

feverish ['fiːvərɪʃ] adj *(having a fever)* febbricitante.

few [fjuː] adj pochi(-e); ♦ pron pochi mpl (-e fpl) ❑ **a few** adj qualche *(inv)* ♦ pron alcuni mpl (-e fpl); **quite a ~** parecchi.

fewer ['fjuːər] adj & pron meno *(inv)*.

fiancé [fɪˈɒnseɪ] n fidanzato m.

fiancée [fɪˈɒnseɪ] n fidanzata f.

fib [fɪb] n *(inf)* (piccola) bugia f.

fiber ['faɪbər] *(Am)* = **fibre**.

fibre ['faɪbər] n fibra f.

fibreglass ['faɪbəɡlɑːs] n fibra f di vetro.

fickle ['fɪkl] adj incostante, volubile.

fiction ['fɪkʃn] n narrativa f.

fiddle ['fɪdl] n *(violin)* violino m ♦ vi: **to ~ with sthg** giocherellare con qc.

fidget ['fɪdʒɪt] vi agitarsi.

field [fiːld] *n* campo *m*.

field glasses *npl* binocolo *m*.

fierce [fɪəs] *adj* feroce; *(storm, heat)* violento(-a).

fifteen [fɪfˈtiːn] *num* quindici, → **six**.

fifteenth [fɪfˈtiːnθ] *num* quindicesimo(-a), → **sixth**.

fifth [fɪfθ] *num* quinto(-a), → **sixth**.

fiftieth [ˈfɪftɪəθ] *num* cinquantesimo(-a), → **sixth**.

fifty [ˈfɪftɪ] *num* cinquanta, → **six**.

fig [fɪg] *n* fico *m*.

fight [faɪt] (*pt & pp* **fought**) *n* rissa *f*; *(argument)* lite *f*; *(struggle)* lotta *f* ♦ *vt* combattere; *(person)* azzuffarsi con ♦ *vi* (physically) combattere; *(quarrel)* litigare; *(struggle)* lottare; **to have a ~ with sb** fare a pugni con qn ◻ **fight back** *vi* difendersi; **fight off** *vt sep* (attacker) respingere; *(illness)* vincere.

fighting [ˈfaɪtɪŋ] *n* combattimento *m*.

figure [Br ˈfɪgəʳ, Am ˈfɪgjər] *n* figura *f*; *(number, statistic)* cifra *f* ◻ **figure out** *vt sep* riuscire a capire.

file [faɪl] *n* (folder) cartella *f*; *(information on person)* schedario *m*; *(COMPUT)* file *m inv*; *(tool)* lima *f* ♦ *vt* (complaint, petition) presentare; *(nails)* limare; **in single ~** in fila indiana.

filing cabinet [ˈfaɪlɪŋ-] *n* schedario *m*.

fill [fɪl] *vt* riempire; *(role)* ricoprire; *(tooth)* otturare ◻ **fill in** *vt sep* (form) riempire; **fill up** *vt sep* riempire; **~ her up!** (with petrol) il pieno, per favore!

filled roll [fɪld-] *n* panino *m* im-

bottito.

fillet [ˈfɪlɪt] *n* filetto *m*.

fillet steak *n* bistecca *f* di filetto.

filling [ˈfɪlɪŋ] *n* (of cake, sandwich) ripieno *m*; *(in tooth)* otturazione *f* ♦ *adj*: **it's very ~** sazia molto.

filling station *n* stazione *f* di servizio.

film [fɪlm] *n* (at cinema) film *m inv*; *(for camera)* pellicola *f* ♦ *vt* filmare.

film star *n* divo *m* (-a *f*) del cinema.

filter [ˈfɪltəʳ] *n* filtro *m*.

filthy [ˈfɪlθɪ] *adj* sudicio(-a).

fin [fɪn] *n* pinna *f*.

final [ˈfaɪnl] *adj* ultimo(-a); *(decision)* definitivo(-a) ♦ *n* finale *f*.

finalist [ˈfaɪnəlɪst] *n* finalista *mf*.

finally [ˈfaɪnəlɪ] *adv* (at last) finalmente; *(lastly)* infine.

finance [*n* ˈfaɪnæns, *vb* faɪˈnæns] *n* (money) finanziamento *m*; *(profession)* finanza *f* ♦ *vt* finanziare ◻ **finances** *npl* finanze *fpl*.

financial [fɪˈnænʃl] *adj* finanziario(-a).

find [faɪnd] (*pt & pp* **found**) *vt* trovare; *(find out)* scoprire ♦ *n* scoperta *f*; **to ~ the time to do sthg** trovare il tempo di fare qc ◻ **find out** *vt sep* (fact, truth) scoprire ♦ *vi*: **to ~ out (about sthg)** (learn) scoprire (qc); *(get information)* informarsi (su qc).

fine [faɪn] *adv* (thinly) finemente; *(well)* bene ♦ *n* multa *f* ♦ *vt* multare ♦ *adj* (good) buono(-a); *(weather, day)* bello(-a); *(thin)* sottile; **it's ~** (satisfactory) va bene; **I'm ~** (in health) sto bene.

fine art *n* belle arti *fpl*.

finger ['fɪŋgə^r] n dito m.

fingernail ['fɪŋgəneɪl] n unghia f.

fingertip ['fɪŋgətɪp] n polpastrello m.

finish ['fɪnɪʃ] n fine f; (on furniture) finitura f ♦ vt & vi finire; **to ~ doing sthg** finire di fare qc ❑ **finish off** vt sep finire; **finish up** vi finire; **to ~ up doing sthg** finire a fare qc.

Finland ['fɪnlənd] n la Finlandia.

Finn [fɪn] n finlandese mf.

Finnan haddock ['fɪnən-] n (Scot) eglefino m affumicato (tipico della Scozia).

Finnish ['fɪnɪʃ] adj finlandese ♦ n (language) finlandese m.

fir [fɜ:^r] n abete m.

fire ['faɪə^r] n fuoco m; (uncontrolled) incendio m; (device) stufa f ♦ vt (from job) licenziare; **to ~ a gun** sparare; **on ~** in fiamme; **to catch ~** prendere fuoco; **to make a ~** accendere un fuoco.

fire alarm n allarme m antincendio.

fire brigade n (Br) vigili mpl del fuoco.

fire department (Am) = **fire brigade**.

fire engine n autopompa f.

fire escape n scala f antincendio.

fire exit n uscita f di sicurezza.

fire extinguisher n estintore m.

fire hazard n: **it's a ~** rappresenta un pericolo di incendio.

fireman ['faɪəmən] (pl -men [-mən]) n vigile m del fuoco.

fireplace ['faɪəpleɪs] n caminetto m.

fire regulations npl norme fpl antincendio.

fire station n caserma f dei vigili del fuoco.

firewood ['faɪəwʊd] n legna f da ardere.

firework display ['faɪəwɜ:k-] n fuochi mpl d'artificio.

fireworks ['faɪəwɜ:ks] npl (rockets) fuochi mpl d'artificio.

firm [fɜ:m] adj (fruit) sodo(-a); (mattress) duro(-a); (structure) solido(-a); (grip) saldo(-a); (decision, belief) fermo(-a) ♦ n ditta f.

first [fɜ:st] adj primo(-a) ♦ adv prima; (for the first time) per la prima volta ♦ n (event) novità f inv ♦ pron: **the ~** il primo (la prima); **(gear)** prima f; **~ thing (in the morning)** per prima cosa; **for the ~ time** per la prima volta; **the ~ of January** il primo gennaio; **at ~** dapprima; **~ of all** prima di tutto.

first aid n pronto soccorso m.

first-aid kit n cassetta f del pronto soccorso.

first class n (mail) posta celere, di solito consegnata entro uno o due giorni; (on train, plane, ship) prima classe f.

first-class adj (stamp) per consegna celere; (ticket) di prima (classe); (very good) di prima qualità.

first floor n (Br: floor above ground floor) primo piano m; (Am: ground floor) pianterreno m.

firstly ['fɜ:stlɪ] adv in primo luogo.

First World War n: **the ~** l prima guerra mondiale.

fish [fɪʃ] (pl inv) n pesce m ♦ vi pescare.

fish and chips n pesce m e patate fritti.

ℹ️ FISH AND CHIPS

È il piatto da asporto inglese per eccellenza. Il pesce viene fritto in una pastella a base di farina, latte e uova e viene servito, insieme alle patate fritte, avvolto in carta di pacchi prima e quindi in carta di giornale. Spesso è consumato direttamente per strada. I negozi di "fish and chips", molto diffusi in tutta la Gran Bretagna, vendono altri cibi fritti, come ad esempio salsicce, pollo, salsicce di sanguinaccio, e spesso anche tortine di carne.

fishcake ['fɪʃkeɪk] n crocchetta f di pesce.

fisherman ['fɪʃəmən] (pl -men [-mən]) n pescatore m.

fish farm n vivaio m.

fish fingers npl (Br) bastoncini mpl di pesce.

fishing ['fɪʃɪŋ] n pesca f; **to go** ~ andare a pesca.

fishing boat n barca f da pesca.

fishing rod n canna f da pesca.

fishmonger's ['fɪʃ,mʌŋgəz] n (shop) pescheria f.

fish sticks (Am) = **fish fingers**.

fish supper n (Scot) pesce m e patate fritti.

fist [fɪst] n pugno m.

fit [fɪt] adj (healthy) in forma ◆ vt (be right size for) andare (bene) a; (kitchen, bath) installare; (a lock) mettere; (insert) inserire ◆ vi (be right size) andare bene ◆ n (of coughing, anger) attacco m; (epileptic) crisi f inv epilettica; **they're a good** ~ (clothes, shoes) sono della misura giusta.

be ~ **for sthg** (suitable) essere adatto(-a) a qc; ~ **to eat** buono(-a) da mangiare; **it doesn't** ~ (object) non c'entra; **it doesn't** ~ **me** (jacket, skirt) non mi sta OR va; **to get** ~ rimettersi in forma; **to keep** ~ tenersi in forma ◆ **fit in** vt sep (find time to do) trovare il tempo per ◆ vi (belong) inserirsi.

fitness ['fɪtnɪs] n (health) forma f.

fitted carpet [,fɪtəd-] n moquette f inv.

fitted sheet [,fɪtəd-] n lenzuolo m con gli angoli.

fitting room ['fɪtɪŋ-] n camerino m.

five [faɪv] num cinque, → **six**.

fiver ['faɪvə] n (Br: inf) cinque sterline fpl; (note) banconota f da cinque sterline.

fix [fɪks] vt (attach, decide on) fissare; (mend) riparare; (drink, food) preparare; (arrange) organizzare ◆ **fix up** vt sep: **to** ~ **sb up with sthg** procurare qc a qn.

fixture ['fɪkstʃə] n (SPORT) incontro m; ~s **and fittings** installazioni fpl.

fizzy ['fɪzɪ] adj frizzante.

flag [flæg] n bandiera f.

flake [fleɪk] n (of snow) fiocco m ◆ vi sfaldarsi.

flame [fleɪm] n fiamma f.

flammable ['flæməbl] adj infiammabile.

flan [flæn] n flan m inv.

flannel ['flænl] n (material) flanella f; (Br: for washing face) panno m di spugna ◆ **flannels** npl pantaloni mpl di flanella.

flap [flæp] n (of envelope) linguetta f; (of pocket) risvolto m ◆ vt (wings) battere.

flapjack [ˈflæpdʒæk] *n (Br)* biscotto *m* di avena.

flare [fleəʳ] *n (signal)* razzo *m*.

flared [fleəd] *adj (trousers)* a zampa d'elefante; *(skirt)* scampanato(-a).

flash [flæʃ] *n (of light)* lampo *m; (for camera)* flash *m inv* ◆ *vi (light)* lampeggiare; **a ~ of lightning** un lampo; **to ~ one's headlights** lampeggiare.

flashlight [ˈflæʃlaɪt] *n* torcia *f* elettrica.

flask [flɑːsk] *n (Thermos)* thermos® *m inv; (hip flask)* borraccia *f*.

flat [flæt] *adj* piatto(-a); *(battery)* scarico(-a); *(drink)* sgasato(-a); *(rate, fee)* unico(-a) ◆ *adv (level)* in piano ◆ *n (Br: apartment)* appartamento *m*; **a ~ (tyre)** una gomma a terra; **~ out** a più non posso.

flatter [ˈflætəʳ] *vt* adulare.

flavor [ˈfleɪvəʳ] *(Am)* = **flavour**.

flavour [ˈfleɪvəʳ] *n (Br: taste)* sapore *m; (of ice cream)* gusto *m*.

flavoured [ˈfleɪvəd] *adj:* **lemon-~** al gusto di limone.

flavouring [ˈfleɪvərɪŋ] *n* aroma *m*.

flaw [flɔː] *n* difetto *m*.

flea [fliː] *n* pulce *f*.

flea market *n* mercato *m* delle pulci.

fleece [fliːs] *n (downy material)* vello *m*.

fleet [fliːt] *n (of ships)* flotta *f*.

Flemish [ˈflemɪʃ] *adj* fiammingo(-a) ◆ *n (language)* fiammingo *m*.

flesh [fleʃ] *n (of person, animal)* carne *f; (of fruit, vegetable)* polpa *f*.

flew [fluː] *pt* → **fly**.

flex [fleks] *n* cavetto *m*.

flexible [ˈfleksəbl] *adj* flessibile.

flick [flɪk] *vt (a switch)* premere; *(with finger)* colpire con il dito ❑ **flick through** *vt fus* sfogliare.

flies [flaɪz] *npl (of trousers)* patta *f*.

flight [flaɪt] *n* volo *m*; **a ~ (of stairs)** una rampa (di scale).

flight attendant *n* assistente *mf* di volo.

flimsy [ˈflɪmzɪ] *adj (object)* poco consistente; *(clothes)* leggero(-a).

fling [flɪŋ] *(pt & pp* **flung**) *vt* lanciare.

flint [flɪnt] *n (of lighter)* pietrina *f*.

flip-flop [flɪp-] *n (Br: shoe)* infradito *m inv or f inv*.

flipper [ˈflɪpəʳ] *n (Br: of swimmer)* pinna *f*.

flirt [flɜːt] *vi:* **to ~ (with sb)** flirtare (con qn).

float [fləʊt] *n (for swimming)* tavoletta *f; (for fishing)* galleggiante *m; (in procession)* carro *m; (drink)* bevanda con del gelato aggiunto ◆ *vi* galleggiare.

flock [flɒk] *n (of birds)* stormo *m; (of sheep)* gregge *m* ◆ *vi (people)* accalcarsi.

flood [flʌd] *n* alluvione *f* ◆ *vt* inondare ◆ *vi* straripare.

floodlight [ˈflʌdlaɪt] *n* riflettore *m*.

floor [flɔːʳ] *n (of room)* pavimento *m; (storey)* piano *m; (of nightclub)* pista *f*.

floorboard [ˈflɔːbɔːd] *n* asse *f* del pavimento.

floor show *n* varietà *m inv*.

flop [flɒp] *n (inf)* fiasco *m*.

floppy disk [ˈflɒpɪ-] *n* floppy disk *m inv*.

floral [ˈflɔːrəl] *adj (pattern)* floreale.

Florence ['flɒrəns] n Firenze f.

Florida Keys ['flɒrɪdə-] npl: **the ~** l'arcipelago m Keys.

---

i FLORIDA KEYS

Gruppo di piccole isole che si estende per oltre 150 chilometri al largo della costa meridionale della Florida, le "Florida Keys" comprendono le famose località di Key West e Key Largo. Una rete di strade e ponti, la "Overseas Highway", collega le isole fra di loro.

---

florist's ['flɒrɪsts] n (shop) fioraio m.

flour ['flaʊə'] n farina f.

flow [fləʊ] n (of river, blood) flusso m ♦ vi (river, blood) scorrere.

flower ['flaʊə'] n fiore m.

flowerbed ['flaʊəbed] n aiuola f.

flowerpot ['flaʊəpɒt] n vaso m da fiori.

flown [fləʊn] pp → **fly**.

fl oz abbr = **fluid ounce**.

flu [fluː] n influenza f.

fluent ['fluːənt] adj: **to be ~ in Italian**, **to speak ~ Italian** parlare italiano correntemente.

fluff [flʌf] n (on clothes) pelucchi mpl.

fluid ounce ['fluːɪd-] n = 0,03 l.

flume [fluːm] n canale m.

flung [flʌŋ] pp → **fling**.

flunk [flʌŋk] vt (Am: inf: exam) essere bocciato(-a) a.

fluorescent [fluə'resənt] adj fluorescente.

flush [flʌʃ] vi (toilet) funzionare ♦

vt: **to ~ the toilet** tirare lo sciacquone.

flute [fluːt] n flauto m traverso.

fly [flaɪ] (pt **flew**, pp **flown**) n (insect) mosca f; (of trousers) patta f ♦ vt (plane, helicopter) pilotare; (airline) volare con; (transport) trasportare in aereo ♦ vi volare; (passenger) andare in aereo; (pilot a plane) pilotare un aereo; (flag) sventolare.

fly-drive n fly and drive m inv.

flying ['flaɪɪŋ] n: **I'm frightened of ~** ho paura di volare.

flyover ['flaɪ,əʊvə'] n (Br) cavalcavia m inv.

flypaper ['flaɪ,peɪpə'] n carta f moschicida.

flysheet ['flaɪʃiːt] n telo m protettivo.

FM n FM f.

foal [fəʊl] n puledro m.

foam [fəʊm] n (bubbles) schiuma f; (foam rubber) gommapiuma® f.

focus ['fəʊkəs] n (of camera) fuoco m ♦ vi (with camera, binoculars) mettere a fuoco; **in ~** a fuoco; **out of ~** sfocato.

fog [fɒg] n nebbia f.

fogbound ['fɒgbaʊnd] adj bloccato(-a) dalla nebbia.

foggy ['fɒgɪ] adj nebbioso(-a).

fog lamp n antinebbia m inv.

foil [fɔɪl] n (thin metal) carta f di alluminio.

fold [fəʊld] n (in paper, material) piega f ♦ vt piegare; (wrap) avvolgere; **to ~ one's arms** incrociare le braccia ❑ **fold up** vi (chair, bed, bicycle) piegarsi.

folder ['fəʊldə'] n cartella f.

foliage ['fəʊlɪdʒ] n fogliame m.

folk [fəʊk] *npl (people)* gente *f* ♦ *n*: ~ **(music)** folk *m* ❏ **folks** *npl (inf: relatives)*: **my** ~**s** i miei.

follow [ˈfɒləʊ] *vt* seguire; *(in order, time)* seguire a ♦ *vi* seguire; ~**ed by** *(in time)* seguito da; **as** ~**s** come segue ❏ **follow on** *vi (come later)* seguire.

following [ˈfɒləʊɪŋ] *adj (next)* successivo(-a); *(mentioned below)* seguente ♦ *prep* dopo.

follow on call *n* chiamata *f* successiva.

fond [fɒnd] *adj*: **to be** ~ **of** amare.

fondue [ˈfɒnduː] *n* fonduta *f*.

food [fuːd] *n* cibo *m*.

food poisoning [-ˈpɔɪznɪŋ] *n* avvelenamento *m* da cibo.

food processor [-ˈprəʊsesəʳ] *n* tritatutto-frullatore *m inv* elettrico.

foodstuffs [ˈfuːdstʌfs] *npl* generi *mpl* alimentari.

fool [fuːl] *n (idiot)* stupido *m* (-a *f*); *(pudding)* mousse *f inv* di frutta ♦ *vt* ingannare.

foolish [ˈfuːlɪʃ] *adj* stupido(-a).

foot [fʊt] *(pl* **feet***) n (of person)* piede *m*; *(of animal)* zampa *f*; *(measurement)* = 30,48 cm, piede; *(of hill, cliff, bed)* piedi *mpl*; *(of wardrobe, tripod, stairs)* base *f*; **by** ~ a piedi; **on** ~ a piedi.

football [ˈfʊtbɔːl] *n (Br: soccer)* calcio *m*; *(Am: American football)* football *m* americano; *(ball)* pallone *m*.

footballer [ˈfʊtbɔːləʳ] *n (Br)* calciatore *m* (-trice *f*).

football pitch *n (Br)* campo di calcio.

footbridge [ˈfʊtbrɪdʒ] *n* sovrappassaggio *m*.

footpath [ˈfʊtpɑːθ, *pl* -pɑːðz] *n* sentiero *m*.

footprint [ˈfʊtprɪnt] *n* orma *f*.

footstep [ˈfʊtstep] *n* passo *m*.

footwear [ˈfʊtweəʳ] *n* calzature *fpl*.

for [fɔːʳ] *prep* **1.** *(expressing intention, purpose, reason)* per; **this book is** ~ **you** questo libro è per te; **what did you do that** ~? perché l'hai fatto?; **what's it** ~? a cosa serve?; **a town famous** ~ **its wine** una città famosa per il suo vino; ~ **this reason** per questo motivo; **to go** ~ **a walk** andare a fare una passeggiata; '~ **sale**' 'vendesi'.

2. *(during)*: **I've lived here** ~ **ten years** abito qui da dieci anni, sono dieci anni che abito qui; **we talked** ~ **hours** abbiamo chiacchierato per ore.

3. *(by, before)* per; **be there** ~ **eight p.m.** trovati lì per le otto di sera; **I'll do it** ~ **tomorrow** lo farò per domani.

4. *(on the occasion of)* per; **I got socks** ~ **Christmas** ho avuto dei calzini per Natale; **what's** ~ **dinner?** cosa c'è per cena?

5. *(on behalf of)* per; **to do sthg** ~ **sb** fare qc per qn.

6. *(with time and space)* per; **there's no room** ~ **your suitcase** non c'è posto per la tua valigia; **have you got time** ~ **a coffee?** hai tempo per un caffè?; **it's time** ~ **dinner** è ora di cena.

7. *(expressing distance)* per; '**roadworks** ~ **20 miles**' 'lavori in corso per 32 chilometri'.

8. *(expressing destination)* per; **a ticket** ~ **Edinburgh** un biglietto per Edimburgo; **this train is** ~ **London only** questo treno ferma solo

Londra.

9. *(expressing price)*: **I bought it ~ £5** l'ho comprato per 5 sterline, l'ho pagato 5 sterline.

10. *(expressing meaning)* per; **what's the Italian ~ 'boy'?** come si dice 'boy' in italiano?

11. *(with regard to)* per; **it's warm ~ November** fa caldo per essere novembre; **it's easy ~ you** è facile per te; **it's too far ~ us to walk** è troppo lontano per andarci a piedi.

forbid [fə'bɪd] *(pt* **-bade** [-'beɪd], *pp* **-bidden)** *vt* proibire, vietare; **to ~ sb to do sthg** proibire OR vietare a qn di fare qc.

forbidden [fə'bɪdn] *adj* proibito(-a).

force [fɔːs] *n* forza *f* ◆ *vt* forzare; **to ~ sb to do sthg** costringere qn a fare qc; **to ~ one's way through** farsi strada con la forza; **the ~s** le forze armate.

ford [fɔːd] *n* guado *m*.

forecast ['fɔːkɑːst] *n* previsione *f*.

forecourt ['fɔːkɔːt] *n* spiazzo *m*.

forefinger ['fɔːˌfɪŋɡəʳ] *n* indice *m*.

foreground ['fɔːɡraund] *n* primo piano *m*.

forehead ['fɔːhed] *n* fronte *f*.

foreign ['fɒrən] *adj* straniero(-a); *(travel)* all'estero.

foreign currency *n* valuta *f* estera.

foreigner ['fɒrənəʳ] *n* straniero *s* (-a *f*).

foreign exchange *n* cambio *m*.

Foreign Secretary *n* (Br) ministro *m* degli Esteri.

foreman ['fɔːmən] *(pl* **-men** [-mən]) *n (of workers)* capo operaio *m*.

forename ['fɔːneɪm] *n (fml)* nome *m* (di battesimo).

foresee [fɔː'siː] *(pt* **-saw** [-'sɔː], *pp* **-seen** [-'siːn]) *vt* prevedere.

forest ['fɒrɪst] *n* foresta *f*.

forever [fə'revəʳ] *adv (eternally)* per sempre; *(continually)* in continuazione.

forgave [fə'ɡeɪv] *pt* → **forgive**.

forge [fɔːdʒ] *vt (copy)* falsificare.

forgery ['fɔːdʒərɪ] *n (copy)* falso *m*.

forget [fə'ɡet] *(pt* **-got**, *pp* **-gotten)** *vt* dimenticare; *(give up)* lasciar perdere ◆ *vi* dimenticarsi; **to ~ about sthg** dimenticarsi di qc; **to ~ how to do sthg** dimenticare come si fa qc; **to ~ to do sthg** dimenticare di fare qc; **~ it!** lascia perdere!

forgetful [fə'ɡetful] *adj* smemorato(-a).

forgive [fə'ɡɪv] *(pt* **-gave**, *pp* **-given** [-'ɡɪvn]) *vt* perdonare.

forgot [fə'ɡɒt] *pt* → **forget**.

forgotten [fə'ɡɒtn] *pp* → **forget**.

fork [fɔːk] *n (for eating with)* forchetta *f*; *(for gardening)* forca *f*; *(of road, path)* bivio *m* □ **forks** *npl (of bike, motorbike)* forcelle *fpl*.

form [fɔːm] *n (type, shape)* forma *f*; *(piece of paper)* modulo *m*; *(SCH)* classe *f* ◆ *vt* formare; *(constitute)* costituire; *(produce)* creare ◆ *vi* formarsi; **off ~** giù di forma; **on ~** in forma; **to ~ part of** fare parte di.

formal ['fɔːml] *adj* formale.

formality [fɔː'mælətɪ] *n* formalità *f inv*; **it's just a ~** è solo una formalità.

format [fɔ:mæt] n formato m.

former [fɔ:mə*] adj (previous) precedente; (first) primo(-a) ◆ pron: **the ~** il primo; **the ~ President** l'ex Presidente.

formerly [fɔ:məlɪ] adv precedentemente.

formula [fɔ:mjulə] (pl **-as** OR **-ae** [i:]) n formula f.

fort [fɔ:t] n forte m.

forthcoming [fɔ:θkʌmɪŋ] adj (future) prossimo(-a).

fortieth [fɔ:tɪɪθ] num quarantesimo(-a), → **sixth**.

fortnight [fɔ:tnaɪt] n (Br) quindici giorni mpl.

fortunate [fɔ:tʃnət] adj fortunato(-a).

fortunately [fɔ:tʃnətlɪ] adv fortunatamente.

fortune [fɔ:tʃu:n] n fortuna f; **it costs a ~** (inf) costa una fortuna.

forty [fɔ:tɪ] num quaranta, → **six**.

forward [fɔ:wəd] adv (move, lean) in avanti ◆ n (SPORT) attaccante mf ◆ vt spedire; **to look ~ to doing sthg** non vedere l'ora di fare qc.

forwarding address [fɔ:wədɪŋ-] n recapito m nuovo.

fought [fɔ:t] pp → **fight**.

foul [faul] adj (unpleasant) disgustoso(-a) ◆ n fallo m.

found [faund] pp → **find** ◆ vt fondare.

foundation (cream) [faundeɪʃn-] n fondotinta m inv.

foundations [faundeɪʃnz] npl fondamenta fpl.

fountain [fauntin] n fontana f.

fountain pen n penna f stilografica.

four [fɔ:*] num quattro, → **six**.

four-star (petrol) n super f inv.

fourteen [fɔ:ti:n] num quattordici, → **six**.

fourteenth [fɔ:ti:nθ] num quattordicesimo(-a), → **sixth**.

fourth [fɔ:θ] num quarto(-a), → **sixth**.

four-wheel drive n (car) veicolo m a quattro ruote motrici.

fowl [faul] (pl inv) n volatile m.

fox [fɒks] n volpe f.

foyer [fɔɪeɪ] n (of hotel) hall f inv; (of theatre) foyer m inv.

fraction [frækʃn] n frazione f.

fracture [fræktʃə*] n frattura f ◆ vt fratturare.

fragile [frædʒaɪl] adj fragile.

fragment [frægmənt] n frammento m.

fragrance [freɪgrəns] n profumo m.

frail [freɪl] adj debole.

frame [freɪm] n (of window, tent, bicycle) telaio m; (of picture, photo) cornice f; (of glasses) montatura f ◆ vt (photo, picture) incorniciare.

France [frɑ:ns] n la Francia.

frank [fræŋk] adj franco(-a).

frankfurter [fræŋkfɜ:tə*] n würstel m inv.

frankly [fræŋklɪ] adv francamente.

frantic [fræntɪk] adj frenetico(-a).

fraud [frɔ:d] n (crime) frode f.

freak [fri:k] adj strano(-a) ◆ n (inf: fanatic) fanatico m (-a f).

freckles [freklz] npl lentiggini fpl.

free [fri:] *adj* libero(-a); *(costing nothing)* gratuito(-a) ◆ *adv* gratis; **for ~** gratis; **~ of charge** gratis; **to be ~ to do sthg** essere libero di fare qc.

freedom ['fri:dəm] *n* libertà *f*.

freefone ['fri:fəun] *n* (*Br*) = numero *m* verde.

free gift *n* omaggio *m*.

free house *n* (*Br*) pub *m inv* (*che può vendere qualsiasi birra, non appartenecha a nessuna ditta*).

free kick *n* calcio *m* di punizione.

freelance ['fri:lɑ:ns] *adj* freelance *(inv)*.

freely ['fri:li] *adv* liberamente; *(available)* facilmente.

free period *n* (*SCH*) ora *f* di buco.

freepost ['fri:pəust] *n* affrancatura *f* a carico del destinatario.

free-range *adj* (*chicken*) ruspante; (*eggs*) di galline ruspanti.

free time *n* tempo *m* libero.

freeway ['fri:wei] *n* (*Am*) superstrada *f*.

freeze [fri:z] (*pt* froze, *pp* frozen) *vt* congelare ◆ *vi* gelare ◆ *v impers*: **it's freezing** fa un freddo polare.

freezer ['fri:zər] *n* (*deep freeze*) congelatore *m*; (*part of fridge*) freezer *m inv*.

freezing ['fri:zɪŋ] *adj* gelato(-a); *(temperatures)* sotto zero.

freezing point *n* temperatura *f* di congelamento.

freight [freit] *n* (*goods*) carico *m*.

French [frentʃ] *adj* francese ◆ *n* (*language*) francese *m* ◆ *npl*: **the ~** i francesi.

French bean *n* fagiolino *m*.

French bread *n* baguette *f inv*.

French dressing *n* (*in UK*) *condimento per insalata a base di olio e aceto*; (*in US*) *condimento per insalata a base di maionese e ketchup*.

French fries *npl* patatine *fpl* fritte.

Frenchman ['frentʃmən] (*pl* -men [-mən]) *n* francese *m*.

French toast *n* (*fried bread*) *fetta di pane passata nell'uovo e fritta*.

French windows *npl* portafinestra *f*.

Frenchwoman ['frentʃˌwumən] (*pl* -women [-ˌwimin]) *n* francese *f*.

frequency ['fri:kwənsi] *n* frequenza *f*.

frequent ['fri:kwənt] *adj* frequente.

frequently ['fri:kwəntli] *adv* frequentemente.

fresh [freʃ] *adj* fresco(-a); (*water*) dolce; (*new*) nuovo(-a); **to get some ~ air** prendere un po' d'aria fresca.

fresh cream *n* panna *f* fresca.

freshen ['freʃn]: **freshen up** *vi* rinfrescarsi.

freshly ['freʃli] *adv* appena.

fresh orange (juice) *n* spremuta *f* d'arancia.

Fri. (*abbr of Friday*) ven.

Friday ['fraidi] *n* venerdì *m inv*, → Saturday.

fridge [frɪdʒ] *n* frigorifero *m*.

fried egg [fraid-] *n* uovo *m* al tegame.

fried rice [fraid-] *n* piatto cinese a base di riso fritto.

friend [frend] *n* amico *m* (-a *f*); **to be ~s with sb** essere amico di qn; **to make ~s with sb** fare amicizia con qn.

friendly ['frendlı] *adj* cordiale; **to be ~ with sb** essere amico di qn.

friendship ['frendʃɪp] *n* amicizia *f*.

fries [fraɪz] = **French fries**.

fright [fraɪt] *n* spavento *m*, paura *f*; **to give sb a ~** fare paura a qn.

frighten ['fraɪtn] *vt* spaventare, far paura a.

frightened ['fraɪtnd] *adj (scared)* spaventato(-a); **to be ~ (that) ...** *(worried)* avere paura che ...; **to be ~ of** avere paura di.

frightening ['fraɪtnɪŋ] *adj* spaventoso(-a).

frightful ['fraɪtful] *adj (very bad, unpleasant)* terribile.

frilly ['frɪlɪ] *adj* arricciato(-a).

fringe [frɪndʒ] *n* frangia *f*.

frisk [frɪsk] *vt* perquisire.

fritter ['frɪtər] *n* frittella *f*.

fro [frəʊ] *adv* → **to**.

frog [frɒg] *n* rana *f*.

from [frɒm] *prep* **1.** *(expressing origin, source)* da; **I'm ~ England** sono inglese; **I bought it ~ a supermarket** l'ho comprato al supermercato; **the train ~ Manchester** il treno (proveniente) da Manchester.

2. *(expressing removal, deduction)* da; **away ~ home** lontano da casa; **to take sthg (away) ~ sb** prendere qc a qn; **10% will be deducted ~ the total** dal totale verrà dedotto il 10%.

3. *(expressing distance)* da; **5 miles ~ London** a 5 miglia da Londra; **it's not far ~ here** non è lontano da (qui).

4. *(expressing position)* da; **~ here you can see the valley** da qui si vede la valle.

5. *(expressing starting time)* da; **open ~ nine to five** aperto dalle nove alle cinque; **~ next year** dall'anno prossimo.

6. *(expressing change)* da; **the price has gone up ~ £1 to £2** il prezzo è salito da 1 a 2 sterline.

7. *(expressing range)* da; **tickets are ~ £10** i biglietti vanno dalle 10 sterline in su.

8. *(as a result of)*: **I'm tired ~ walking all day** sono stanco per aver camminato tutto il giorno.

9. *(expressing protection)* da; **sheltered ~ the wind** al riparo dal vento.

10. *(in comparisons)*: **different ~** diverso da.

fromage frais [,frɒmɑːʒ'freɪ] *n* formaggio fresco cremoso.

front [frʌnt] *adj* anteriore ♦ *n* parte *f* anteriore; *(of weather)* fronte *m*; *(by the sea)* lungomare *m*; **in ~** *(further forward)* avanti; *(in the lead)* d'avanti; **in ~ of** davanti a.

front door *n* porta *f* principale.

frontier [frʌn'tɪər] *n* frontiera *f*.

front page *n* prima pagina *f*.

front seat *n* sedile *m* anteriore.

frost [frɒst] *n* gelo *m*.

frosty ['frɒstɪ] *adj (morning, weather)* gelato(-a).

froth [frɒθ] *n* spuma *f*.

frown [fraʊn] *n* fronte *f* aggrottata ♦ *vi* aggrottare la fronte.

froze [frəʊz] *pt* → **freeze**.

frozen ['frəʊzn] *pp* → **freeze** ♦ *adj* gelato(-a); *(food)* congelato(-a).

fruit [fruːt] *n (food)* frutta *f*; *(variety, single fruit)* frutto *m*; **a piece of ~** un frutto; **~s of the forest** frutti di bosco.

fruit cake n torta con frutta secca.

fruiterer [ˈfruːtərə] n (Br) fruttivendolo m (-a f).

fruit juice n succo m di frutta.

fruit machine n (Br) slot-machine f inv.

fruit salad n macedonia f.

frustrating [frʌˈstreɪtɪŋ] adj frustrante.

frustration [frʌˈstreɪʃn] n frustrazione f.

fry [fraɪ] vt soffriggere; (deep-fry) friggere.

frying pan [ˈfraɪɪŋ-] n padella f.

ft abbr = **foot, feet**.

fudge [fʌdʒ] n dolciume gommoso fatto con burro, latte e zucchero.

fuel [fjʊəl] n (for engine) carburante m; (for heating) combustibile m.

fuel pump n pompa f del carburante.

fulfil [fʊlˈfɪl] vt (Br) (promise) mantenere; (duty, role, need) adempiere; (conditions, request) soddisfare; (instructions) eseguire.

fulfill [fʊlˈfɪl] (Am) = **fulfil**.

full [fʊl] adj pieno(-a), (extent, fare) pieno(-a); (name) completo(-a) ◆ adv (directly) in pieno; I'm ~ (up) sono pieno; at ~ speed a tutta velocità; in ~ per esteso.

full board n pensione f completa.

full-cream milk n latte m intero.

full-length adj (skirt, dress) lungo(-a).

full moon n luna f piena.

full stop n punto m.

full-time adj & adv a tempo pieno.

fully [ˈfʊlɪ] adv (completely) completamente.

fully-licensed adj autorizzato a vendere alcolici.

fumble [ˈfʌmbl] vi (search clumsily) rovistare.

fun [fʌn] n divertimento m; it's good ~ è divertente; for ~ per divertimento; to have ~ divertirsi; to make ~ of prendere in giro.

function [ˈfʌŋkʃn] n (role) funzione f; (formal event) ricevimento m ◆ vi funzionare.

fund [fʌnd] n (of money) fondo m ◆ vt finanziare ◆ **funds** npl fondi mpl.

fundamental [ˌfʌndəˈmentl] adj fondamentale.

funeral [ˈfjuːnərəl] n funerale m.

funfair [ˈfʌnfeə] n luna park m inv.

funky [ˈfʌŋkɪ] adj (inf: music) funky (inv).

funnel [ˈfʌnl] n (for pouring) imbuto m; (on ship) fumaiolo m.

funny [ˈfʌnɪ] adj (amusing) divertente; (strange) strano(-a); to feel ~ (ill) sentirsi strano.

fur [fɜː] n pelliccia f.

fur coat n pelliccia f.

furious [ˈfjʊərɪəs] adj (angry) furioso(-a).

furnished [ˈfɜːnɪʃt] adj ammobiliato(-a).

furnishings [ˈfɜːnɪʃɪŋz] npl arredamento m.

furniture [ˈfɜːnɪtʃə] n mobilia f; a piece of ~ un mobile.

furry [ˈfɜːrɪ] adj peloso(-a).

further [ˈfɜːðə] → **far** ◆ adv (in distance) più lontano; (more) di più ◆ adj (additional) ulteriore; (more)

notice fino a nuovo avviso.

furthermore [fɜːðəˈmɔːʳ] *adv* inoltre.

furthest [ˈfɜːðɪst] → **far** ♦ *adj (most distant)* il più lontano (la più lontana) ♦ *adv (in distance)* il più lontano (possibile).

fuse [fjuːz] *n (of plug)* fusibile *m*; *(on bomb)* detonatore *m* ♦ *vi (plug, device)* saltare.

fuse box *n* scatola *f* dei fusibili.

fuss [fʌs] *n (agitation)* confusione *f*; *(complaints)* storie *fpl*.

fussy [ˈfʌsɪ] *adj (person)* difficile.

future [ˈfjuːtʃəʳ] *n* futuro *m* ♦ *adj* futuro(-a); **in ~** in futuro.

G

g *(abbr of gram)* g.

gable [ˈɡeɪbl] *n* timpano *m*.

gadget [ˈɡædʒɪt] *n* aggeggio *m*.

Gaelic [ˈɡeɪlɪk] *n* gaelico *m*.

gag [ɡæɡ] *n (inf: joke)* gag *f inv*.

gain [ɡeɪn] *n (improvement)* avanzamento *m*; *(profit)* guadagno *m* ♦ *vt* guadagnare; *(weight)* aumentare di; *(confidence, speed, popularity)* acquistare; *(achieve)* ottenere; *(subj: clock, watch)* andare avanti di ♦ *vi (get benefit)*: **to ~ from sthg** trarre vantaggio da qc.

gale [ɡeɪl] *n* burrasca *f*.

gallery [ˈɡælən] *n* galleria *f*.

gallon [ˈɡælən] *n (Br)* = 4,546 l, gallone *m*; *(Am)* = 3,791 l, gallone.

gallop [ˈɡæləp] *vi* galoppare.

gamble [ˈɡæmbl] *n* azzardo *m* ♦ *vi (bet money)* giocare d'azzardo.

gambling [ˈɡæmblɪŋ] *n* gioco *m* d'azzardo.

game [ɡeɪm] *n (gen, in tennis)* gioco *m*; *(of football, squash, cards)* partita *f*; *(wild animals, meat)* cacciagione *f* ❑ **games** *n (SCH)* = attività *fpl* sportive ♦ *npl (sporting event)* gare *fpl*.

gammon [ˈɡæmən] *n* coscia di maiale da cuocere.

gang [ɡæŋ] *n (of criminals)* banda *f*; *(of friends)* gruppo *m*.

gangster [ˈɡæŋstəʳ] *n* gangster *m inv*.

gangway [ˈɡæŋweɪ] *n (for ship)* passerella *f*; *(Br: in bus, aeroplane, theatre)* corridoio *m*.

gaol [dʒeɪl] *(Br)* = **jail**.

gap [ɡæp] *n (space)* buco *m*; *(of time)* intervallo *m*; *(difference)* divario *m*.

garage [ˈɡærɑːʒ, ˈɡærɪdʒ] *n (for keeping car)* garage *m inv*; *(Br: for petrol)* stazione *f* di servizio; *(for repairs)* autofficina *f*; *(Br: for selling cars)* concessionaria *f*.

garbage [ˈɡɑːbɪdʒ] *n (Am: refuse)* spazzatura *f*.

garbage can *n (Am)* pattumiera *f*.

garbage truck *n (Am)* camion *m inv* della nettezza urbana.

garden [ˈɡɑːdn] *n* giardino *m* ♦ *vi* fare giardinaggio ❑ **gardens** *npl (public park)* giardini *mpl* pubblici.

garden centre *n* vivaio *m*.

gardener [ˈɡɑːdnəʳ] *n* giardiniere *m* (-a *f*).

gardening [ˈɡɑːdnɪŋ] *n* giardinaggio *m*.

garden peas *npl* piselli *mpl*.

garlic ['gɑ:lɪk] *n* aglio *m*.

garlic bread *n* = bruschetta *f*.

garlic butter *n* burro *m* all'aglio.

garment ['gɑ:mənt] *n* indumento *m*.

garnish ['gɑ:nɪʃ] *n* guarnizione *f* ♦ *vt* guarnire.

gas [gæs] *n* gas *m inv*; (*Am: petrol*) benzina *f*.

gas cooker *n* (*Br*) cucina *f* a gas.

gas cylinder *n* bombola *f* del gas.

gas fire *n* (*Br*) stufa *f* a gas.

gasket ['gæskɪt] *n* guarnizione *f*.

gas mask *n* maschera *f* antigas.

gasoline ['gæsəli:n] *n* (*Am*) benzina *f*.

gasp [gɑ:sp] *vi* (*in shock*) rimanere senza fiato.

gas pedal *n* (*Am*) acceleratore *m*.

gas station *n* (*Am*) stazione *f* di servizio.

gas stove (*Br*) = **gas cooker**.

gas tank *n* (*Am*) serbatoio *m* della benzina.

gasworks ['gæswɜ:ks] (*pl inv*) *n* officina *f* del gas.

gate [geɪt] *n* (*to garden, field*) cancello *m*; (*at airport*) uscita *f*.

gâteau ['gætəʊ] (*pl* -x [-z]) *n* (*Br*) torta *f*.

gateway ['geɪtweɪ] *n* (*entrance*) entrata *f*.

gather ['gæðə'] *vt* (*collect*) raccogliere; (*speed*) acquistare; (*understand*) dedurre ♦ *vi* (*come together*) riunirsi.

gaudy ['gɔ:dɪ] *adj* vistoso(-a).

gauge [geɪdʒ] *n* (*for measuring*) indicatore *m*; (*of railway track*) scartamento *m* ♦ *vt* (*calculate*) misurare.

gauze [gɔ:z] *n* garza *f*.

gave [geɪv] *pt* → **give**.

gay [geɪ] *adj* (*homosexual*) gay (*inv*).

gaze [geɪz] *vi*: **to ~ at** fissare.

GB (*abbr of Great Britain*) GB.

GCSE *n* esami sostenuti a conclusione della scuola dell'obbligo.

---

i **GCSE**

Con questa abbreviazione si fa riferimento agli esami sostenuti dagli studenti inglesi, gallesi e irlandesi fra i 15 e i 16 anni d'età, a conclusione della scuola dell'obbligo. I "GCSEs" furono introdotti nel 1986 al posto degli "O levels", dai quali si differenziano in quanto la votazione finale dipende non solo dai risultati dell'esame ma anche dal profitto riportato durante il corso di studi in quella specifica disciplina. Gli studenti che intendono sostenere gli "A levels" devono superare i "GCSEs" in almeno cinque materie.

---

gear [gɪə'] *n* (*wheel*) ingranaggio *m*; (*speed*) marcia *f*; (*belongings*) roba *f*; (*equipment, clothes*) attrezzatura *f*; **in ~** con la marcia inserita.

gearbox ['gɪəbɒks] *n* cambio *m*.

gear lever *n* leva *f* del cambio.

gear shift (*Am*) = **gear lever**.

gear stick (*Br*) = **gear lever**.

geese [gi:s] *pl* → **goose**.

gel [dʒel] *n* gel *m inv*.

gelatine [ˌdʒelə'ti:n] *n* gelatina *f*.

gem [dʒem] n gemma f.

Gemini ['dʒemɪnaɪ] n Gemelli mpl.

gender ['dʒendəʳ] n genere m.

general ['dʒenərəl] adj generale; (idea, statement) generico(-a) ◆ n generale m; **in ~** in generale; (usually) in genere.

general anaesthetic n anestesia f totale.

general election n elezioni fpl politiche.

generally ['dʒenərəlɪ] adv generalmente.

general practitioner [-præk'tɪʃənəʳ] n medico m generico.

general store n drogheria f.

generate ['dʒenəreɪt] vt generare.

generation [,dʒenə'reɪʃn] n generazione f.

generator ['dʒenəreɪtəʳ] n generatore m.

generosity [,dʒenə'rɒsətɪ] n generosità f.

generous ['dʒenərəs] adj generoso(-a).

genitals ['dʒenɪtlz] npl genitali mpl.

genius ['dʒiːnjəs] n genio m.

gentle ['dʒentl] adj (careful) delicato(-a); (kind) gentile; (movement, breeze) leggero(-a).

gentleman ['dʒentlmən] (pl -men [-mən]) n signore m; (with good manners) gentiluomo m; '**gentlemen**' (men's toilets) 'uomini'.

gently ['dʒentlɪ] adv (carefully) delicatamente.

gents [dʒents] n (Br) toilette f inv degli uomini.

genuine ['dʒenjʊɪn] adj (authentic) autentico(-a); (sincere) sincero(-a).

geographical [dʒɪə'græfɪkl] adj geografico(-a).

geography [dʒɪ'ɒgrəfɪ] n geografia f.

geology [dʒɪ'ɒlədʒɪ] n geologia f.

geometry [dʒɪ'ɒmɪtrɪ] n geometria f.

Georgian ['dʒɔːdʒən] adj (architecture etc) georgiano(-a) (del periodo dei re Giorgio I–IV, 1714–1830).

geranium [dʒɪ'reɪnjəm] n geranio m.

German ['dʒɜːmən] adj tedesco(-a) ◆ n (person) tedesco m (-a f); (language) tedesco m.

German measles n rosolia f.

Germany ['dʒɜːmənɪ] n la Germania.

germs [dʒɜːmz] npl germi mpl.

gesture ['dʒestʃəʳ] n (movement) gesto m.

get [get] (pt & pp got, Am pp gotten) vt 1. (obtain) ottenere; (job, house) trovare; **I got some crisps from the shop** ho comprato delle patatine al negozio; **she got a job** ha trovato lavoro.
2. (receive) ricevere; **I got a book for Christmas** mi hanno regalato un libro per Natale; **you ~ a lot of rain here in winter** qui piove molto in inverno.
3. (means of transport) prendere; **let's ~ a taxi** prendiamo un taxi.
4. (fetch) andare a prendere; **could you ~ me the manager?** (in shop) mi può chiamare il direttore?; (on phone) mi può passare il direttore?
5. (illness) avere, prendere; **I've got a headache** ho mal di testa.
6. (cause to become, do): **to ~ sthg done** (do) fare qc; (have done) far

fare qc; **to ~ sb to do sthg** far fare qc a qn; **I can't ~ it open** non riesco ad aprirlo; **can I ~ my car repaired here?** posso far riparare qui la mia macchina?

7. (move): **to ~ sthg in/out** far entrare/uscire qc; **I can't ~ it through the door** non riesco a farlo passare dalla porta.

8. (understand) capire; **to ~ a joke** capire una barzelletta.

9. (time, chance) avere, trovare; **we didn't ~ the chance to see everything** non siamo riusciti a vedere tutto.

10. (answer) **I'll ~ it!** (phone) rispondo io!; (door) vado io!, → **have.**

◆ vi **1.** (become) diventare; **it's getting late** si sta facendo tardi; **to ~ bored** annoiarsi; **to ~ ready** prepararsi; **to ~ lost** perdersi; **~ lost!** (inf) vattene!

2. (arrive) arrivare; **when does the train ~ here?** a che ora arriva il treno?

3. (go): **to ~ to/from** andare a/da.

4. (manage): **to ~ to do sthg** riuscire a fare qc.

◆ aux vb: **to ~ delayed** essere trattenuto; **to ~ killed** essere ucciso.

❏ **get back** vi (return) ritornare; **get in** vi (arrive) arrivare; (enter) entrare; **get into** vt fus (enter) entrare in; **to ~ into the car** salire in macchina; **to ~ into bed** mettersi a letto; **to ~ into trouble** mettersi nei guai; **get off** vi (leave train, bus) scendere; (depart) partire; **get on** vi (enter train, bus) salire; (in relationship) andare d'accordo; **how are you getting on?** come va la vita?; **get out** vi (of car, bus, train) scendere; **get through** vi (on phone)

ottenere la comunicazione; **get up** vi alzarsi.

get-together n (inf) riunione f.

ghastly ['gɑ:stlɪ] adj (inf) terribile.

gherkin ['gɜ:kɪn] n cetriolino m.

ghetto blaster ['getəʊ,blɑ:stə^r] n (inf) stereo m portatile.

ghost [gəʊst] n fantasma m.

giant ['dʒaɪənt] adj gigantesco(-a) ◆ n (in stories) gigante m.

giblets ['dʒɪblɪts] npl rigaglie fpl.

giddy ['gɪdɪ] adj (dizzy): **I feel ~** mi gira la testa.

gift [gɪft] n regalo m; (talent) talento m.

gifted ['gɪftɪd] adj dotato(-a).

gift shop n negozio m di articoli da regalo.

gift voucher n (Br) buono m acquisto.

gig [gɪg] n (inf: concert) concerto m.

gigantic [dʒaɪ'gæntɪk] adj gigantesco(-a).

giggle ['gɪgl] vi ridacchiare.

gill [dʒɪl] n (measurement) = 0,142 l.

gimmick ['gɪmɪk] n trovata f.

gin [dʒɪn] n gin m inv; **~ and tonic** gin tonic.

ginger ['dʒɪndʒə^r] n zenzero m ◆ adj (colour) rosso(-a).

ginger ale n bibita analcolica gassata allo zenzero.

ginger beer n bibita analcolica allo zenzero.

gingerbread ['dʒɪndʒəbred] n torta o biscotto allo zenzero.

gipsy ['dʒɪpsɪ] n zingaro m (-a f).

giraffe [dʒɪ'rɑ:f] n giraffa f.

girdle ['gɜ:dl] n panciera f.

girl [gɜ:l] n (child) bambina f;

(young woman) ragazza f; *(daughter)* femmina f.

girlfriend ['gɜːlfrend] n *(of boy, man)* ragazza f; *(of girl, woman)* amica f.

girl guide n *(Br)* giovane f esploratrice.

girl scout *(Am)* = **girl guide**.

giro ['dʒaɪrəʊ] n *(system)* giroconto m.

give [gɪv] *(pt* **gave**, *pp* **given** ['gɪvn]) vt dare; *(a smile, speech)* fare; *(attention)* prestare; *(time)* dedicare; **to ~ sb sthg** dare qc a qn; *(as present)* regalare qc a qn; **to ~ sthg a push** dare una spinta a qc; **to ~ sb a kiss** dare un bacio a qn; **it took an hour, ~ or take a few minutes** c'è voluta un'ora, minuto più minuto meno; '~ **way**' 'dare la precedenza' □ **give away** vt sep *(get rid of)* dare via; *(reveal)* rivelare; **give back** vt sep restituire; **give in** vi arrendersi; **give off** vt fus emettere; **give out** vt sep *(distribute)* distribuire; **give up** vt sep *(cigarettes, chocolate)* rinunciare a; *(seat)* cedere ♦ vi *(admit defeat)* arrendersi; **to ~ up smoking** smettere di fumare.

glacier ['glæsɪə'] n ghiacciaio m.

glad [glæd] adj contento(-a); **to be ~ to do sthg** essere contento di fare qc.

gladly ['glædlɪ] adv *(willingly)* volentieri.

glamorous ['glæmərəs] adj affascinante.

glance [glɑːns] n sguardo m ♦ vi: **to ~ (at)** dare uno sguardo (a).

gland [glænd] n ghiandola f.

glandular fever ['glændjulə-] n mononucleosi f.

glare [gleə'] vi *(person)* lanciare sguardi truci; *(sun, light)* abbagliare.

glass [glɑːs] n *(material)* vetro m; *(container, glassful)* bicchiere m ♦ adj di vetro □ **glasses** npl occhiali mpl.

glassware ['glɑːsweə'] n oggetti mpl in vetro.

glen [glen] n *(Scot)* valle f.

glider ['glaɪdə'] n aliante m.

glimpse [glɪmps] vt intravedere.

glitter ['glɪtə'] vi luccicare.

global warming [ˌgləʊbl-ˈwɔːmɪŋ] n effetto m serra.

globe [gləʊb] n globo m; **the ~** *(Earth)* il globo.

gloomy ['gluːmɪ] adj cupo(-a).

glorious ['glɔːrɪəs] adj *(weather, sight)* magnifico(-a); *(victory, history)* glorioso(-a).

glory ['glɔːrɪ] n gloria f.

gloss [glɒs] n *(shine)* lucido m; **~ (paint)** vernice f lucida.

glossary ['glɒsərɪ] n glossario m.

glossy ['glɒsɪ] adj *(magazine)* patinato(-a); *(photo)* lucido(-a).

glove [glʌv] n guanto m.

glove compartment n vano m portaoggetti.

glow [gləʊ] n barlume m ♦ vi brillare.

glucose ['gluːkəʊs] n glucosio m.

glue [gluː] n colla f ♦ vt incollare.

gnat [næt] n pappataci m inv.

gnaw [nɔː] vt rosicchiare.

go [gəʊ] *(pt* **went**, *pp* **gone**, *pl* **goes**) vi **1.** *(move, travel, attend)* andare; **to ~ home** andare a casa; **to ~ to Italy** andare in Italia; **to ~ by bus** andare con l'autobus; **to ~ to school** andare a scuola; **to ~ for**

a walk andare a fare una passeggiata; **to ~ and do sthg** andare a fare qc; **to ~ shopping** andare a fare la spesa.

2. *(leave)* andarsene; *(bus, train)* partire; **it's time to ~** è ora d'andare; **~ away!** vattene!

3. *(become)* diventare; **she went pale** è impallidita; **the milk has gone sour** il latte è inacidito.

4. *(expressing future tense):* **to be going to do sthg** stare per fare qc; *(intend to do)* avere intenzione di fare qc; **I'm going to be sick** sto per vomitare; **I'm going to phone them tonight** ho intenzione di chiamarli stasera.

5. *(function)* funzionare; **the car won't ~** la macchina non parte.

6. *(stop working)* rompersi; **the fuse has gone** è saltato il fusibile.

7. *(time)* passare.

8. *(progress)* andare; **to ~ well** andar bene.

9. *(bell, alarm)* suonare.

10. *(match, be appropriate):* **to ~ (with)** andare (con).

11. *(be sold)* essere venduto(-a); **'everything must ~'** 'svendita totale'.

12. *(fit)* entrare.

13. *(lead)* andare, portare; **where does this path ~?** dove porta questo sentiero?

14. *(belong)* andare.

15. *(in phrases):* **to let ~ of sthg** *(drop)* lasciare (andare) qc; **to ~** *(Am: to take away)* da asportare; **there are only three weeks to ~** mancano solo tre settimane.

◆ *n* **1.** *(turn)* turno *m*; **it's your ~** tocca a te.

2. *(attempt)* prova *f*, tentativo *m*; **to have a ~ at sthg** provare qc; **'50p a**

~' *(in game)* '50 pence a partita'.

❑ **go ahead** *vi (take place)* aver luogo; **~ ahead!** fai pure!; **go back** *vi (return)* ritornare; **go down** *vi (decrease)* abbassarsi, scendere; *(sun)* tramontare; *(tyre)* sgonfiarsi; **go down with** *vt fus (inf: illness)* prendere; **go in** *vi (enter)* entrare; **go off** *vi (alarm, bell)* suonare; *(go bad)* andare a male; *(lights, heating)* spegnersi; **go on** *vi (happen)* succedere; *(lights, heating)* accendersi; *(continue):* **to ~ on doing sthg** continuare a fare qc; **go out** *vi (leave house)* uscire; *(light, fire, cigarette)* spegnersi; *(have relationship):* **to ~ out (with sb)** stare insieme (a qn); **to ~ out for a meal** andare a mangiare fuori; **go over** *vt fus (check)* controllare; **go round** *vi (revolve)* girare; *(be enough)* bastare per tutti; **go through** *vt fus (experience)* passare; *(spend)* spendere; *(search)* esaminare; **go up** *vi (increase)* aumentare; **go without** *vt fus* fare a meno di.

goal [gəʊl] *n (posts)* porta *f*; *(point scored)* goal *m inv*; *(aim)* scopo *m*.

goalkeeper ['gəʊl,ki:pə'] *n* portiere *m*.

goalpost ['gəʊlpəʊst] *n* palo *m*.

goat [gəʊt] *n* capra *f*.

gob [gɒb] *n (Br: inf: mouth)* bocca *f*.

god [gɒd] *n* dio *m* ❑ **God** *n* Dio *m*.

goddaughter ['gɒd,dɔ:tə'] *n* figlioccia *f*.

godfather ['gɒd,fɑ:ðə'] *n* padrino *m*.

godmother ['gɒd,mʌðə'] *n* madrina *f*.

gods [gɒdz] *npl:* **the ~** *(Br: inf: in*

theatre) il loggione.

godson ['gɒdsʌn] *n* figlioccio *m*.

goes [gəʊz] → **go**.

goggles ['gɒglz] *npl (for swimming)* occhialini *mpl; (for skiing)* occhiali *mpl* da neve.

going ['gəʊɪŋ] *adj (available)* disponibile; **the ~ rate** la tariffa corrente.

go-kart [-kɑ:t] *n* go-kart *m inv*.

gold [gəʊld] *n* oro *m* ♦ *adj* d'oro.

goldfish ['gəʊldfɪʃ] *(pl inv) n* pesce *m* rosso.

gold-plated [-'pleɪtɪd] *adj* placcato(-a) d'oro.

golf [gɒlf] *n* golf *m*.

golf ball *n* pallina *f* da golf.

golf club *n (place)* circolo *m* del golf; *(piece of equipment)* mazza *f* da golf.

golf course *n* campo *m* di golf.

golfer ['gɒlfə'] *n* golfista *mf*.

gone [gɒn] *pp* → **go** ♦ *prep (Br: past)*: **it's ~ ten** sono le dieci passate.

good [gʊd] *(compar better, superl best) adj* buono(-a); *(enjoyable)* bello(-a); *(skilled, well-behaved)* bravo(-a); *(kind)* gentile ♦ *n* bene *m*; **the weather's ~** fa bel tempo; **to have a ~ time** divertirsi; **to be ~ at sthg** saper fare qc bene; **a ~ ten minutes** dieci minuti buoni; **in ~ time** in anticipo; **to make ~ sthg** compensare qc; **for ~** per sempre; **for the ~ of** per il bene di; **to do sb ~** far bene a qn; **it's no ~** *(there's no point)* è inutile; **~ afternoon!** buon giorno!; **~ evening!** buona sera!; **~ morning!** buon giorno!; **~ night!** buona notte! ❑ **goods** *npl* merce *f*.

goodbye [gʊd'baɪ] *excl* arrivederci!

Good Friday *n* Venerdì *m* Santo.

good-looking [-'lʊkɪŋ] *adj* attraente.

goods train [gʊdz-] *n* treno *m* merci.

goose [gu:s] *(pl* geese*) n* oca *f*.

gooseberry ['gʊzbərɪ] *n* uva *f* spina.

gorge [gɔ:dʒ] *n* gola *f*.

gorgeous ['gɔ:dʒəs] *adj* stupendo(-a).

gorilla [gə'rɪlə] *n* gorilla *m inv*.

gossip ['gɒsɪp] *n (about someone)* pettegolezzi *mpl* ♦ *vi (about someone)* fare pettegolezzi; *(chat)* chiacchierare; **to have a ~** chiacchierare.

gossip column *n* cronaca *f* rosa.

got [gɒt] *pt & pp* → **get**.

gotten ['gɒtn] *pp (Am)* → **get**.

goujons ['gu:dʒɒnz] *npl (of fish)* frittelle *fpl*.

goulash ['gu:læʃ] *n* gulasch *m inv*.

gourmet ['gʊəmeɪ] *n* buongustaio *m* (-a *f)* ♦ *adj* per intenditori.

govern ['gʌvən] *vt (country, city)* governare.

government ['gʌvnmənt] *n* governo *m*.

gown [gaʊn] *n (dress)* abito *m* lungo.

GP *abbr* = **general practitioner**.

grab [græb] *vt (take hold of)* afferrare.

graceful ['greɪsfʊl] *adj (elegant)* aggraziato(-a).

grade [greɪd] *n (quality)* categoria *f; (in exam)* voto *m; (Am: year at school)* classe *f*.

gradient ['greidjənt] n pendenza f.

gradual ['grædjʊəl] adj graduale.

gradually ['grædjʊəlɪ] adv gradualmente.

graduate [n 'grædjʊət, vb 'grædjʊeɪt] n (from university) laureato m (-a f); (Am: from high school) diplomato m (-a f) ◆ vi (from university) laurearsi; (Am: from high school) diplomarsi.

graduation [grædjʊ'eɪʃn] n (ceremony at university) consegna f delle lauree; (Am: ceremony at school) consegna dei diplomi.

graffiti [grə'fiːtɪ] n graffiti mpl.

grain [greɪn] n (seed) chicco m; (crop) cereali mpl; (of sand, salt) granello m.

gram [græm] n grammo m.

grammar ['græmər] n grammatica f.

grammar school n ~(in UK) scuola secondaria più selettiva e tradizionale delle altre.

gramme [græm] = gram.

gramophone ['græməfəʊn] n grammofono m.

gran [græn] n (Br: inf) nonna f.

grand [grænd] adj (impressive) grandioso(-a) ◆ n (inf) (£1,000) mille sterline fpl; ($1,000) mille dollari mpl.

grandad ['grændæd] n (inf) nonno m.

grandchild ['grænt∫aɪld] (pl -children [-,t∫ɪldrən]) n nipote mf.

granddaughter ['græn,dɔːtər] n nipote f.

grandfather ['grænd,faːðər] n nonno m.

grandma ['grænmaː] n (inf)

nonna f.

grandmother ['græn,mʌðər] n nonna f.

grandpa ['grænpaː] n (inf) nonno m.

grandparents ['græn,peərənts] npl nonni mpl.

grandson ['grænsʌn] n nipote m.

granite ['grænɪt] n granito m.

granny ['grænɪ] n (inf) nonna f.

grant [graːnt] n (POL) sovvenzione f; (for study) borsa f di studio ◆ vt (fml: give) concedere; **to take sthg for ~ed** dare qc per scontato; **to take sb for ~ed** pensare di poter sempre contare su qn.

grapefruit ['greɪpfruːt] n pompelmo m.

grapefruit juice n succo m di pompelmo.

grapes [greɪps] npl uva f.

graph [graːf] n grafico m.

graph paper n carta f millimetrata.

grasp [graːsp] vt afferrare.

grass [graːs] n (plant) erba f; (lawn) prato m; **'keep off the ~'** 'non calpestare il prato'.

grasshopper ['graːs,hɒpər] n cavalletta f.

grate [greɪt] n grata f.

grated ['greɪtɪd] adj grattugiato(-a).

grateful ['greɪtfʊl] adj (person) grato(-a).

grater ['greɪtər] n grattugia f.

gratitude ['grætɪtjuːd] n gratitudine f.

gratuity [grə'tjuːɪtɪ] n (fml) mancia f.

grave[1] [greɪv] adj (mistake, news, concern) grave ◆ n tomba f.

grave² [grɑːv] *adj* (accent) grave.

gravel ['grævl] *n* ghiaia *f*.

graveyard ['greɪvjɑːd] *n* cimitero *m*.

gravity ['grævətɪ] *n* gravità *f*.

gravy ['greɪvɪ] *n* salsa ottenuta dal sugo di carne arrosto e resa più densa con della farina.

gray [greɪ] (Am) = **grey**.

graze [greɪz] *vt* (injure) scorticare, escoriare.

grease [griːs] *n* (for machine) olio *m*, lubrificante *m*; (animal fat) grasso *m*.

greaseproof paper ['griːsːpruːf-] *n* (Br) carta *f* oleata.

greasy ['griːsɪ] *adj* (food, skin, hair) grasso(-a); (tools, clothes) unto(-a).

great [greɪt] *adj* grande; (very good) eccellente, fantastico(-a); (that's) ~! fantastico!

Great Britain *n* la Gran Bretagna.

---

i GREAT BRITAIN

La Gran Bretagna è un'isola che comprende l'Inghilterra, la Scozia e il Galles. Non va confusa con il Regno Unito, che include l'Irlanda del Nord, o con le Isole Britanniche, di cui fanno parte anche la Repubblica d'Irlanda, l'Isola di Man, le Orcadi, le Shetlands e le Isole della Manica.

---

great-grandfather *n* bisnonno *m*.

great-grandmother *n* bisnonna *f*.

greatly ['greɪtlɪ] *adv* molto.

Greece [griːs] *n* la Grecia.

greed [griːd] *n* avidità *f*.

greedy ['griːdɪ] *adj* avido(-a).

Greek [griːk] *adj* greco(-a) ◆ *n* (person) greco *m* (-a *f*); (language) greco *m*.

Greek salad *n* insalata *f* greca (a base di pomodori, cetriolo, formaggio greco e olive nere).

green [griːn] *adj* verde; (environmentalist) ambientalista; (inf: inexperienced) inesperto(-a) ◆ *n* (colour) verde *m*; (in village) prato *m* pubblico; (on golf course) green *m inv* ❑ **greens** *npl* (vegetables) verdura *f*.

green beans *npl* fagiolini *mpl*.

green card *n* (Br: for car) carta *f* verde; (Am: work permit) permesso *m* di soggiorno.

green channel *n* uscita *f* di porto o aeroporto riservata ai passeggeri che non hanno niente da dichiarare.

greengage ['griːngeɪdʒ] *n* susina *f* Regina Claudia.

greengrocer's ['griːngrəʊsəz] *n* (shop) negozio *m* di frutta e verdura.

greenhouse ['griːnhaʊs, *pl* -haʊzɪz] *n* serra *f*.

greenhouse effect *n* effetto *m* serra.

green light *n* (go-ahead): to give sb the ~ dare il via libera a qn.

green pepper *n* peperone *m* verde.

Greens [griːnz] *npl*: **the ~** i Verdi.

green salad *n* insalata *f* verde.

greet [griːt] *vt* (say hello to) salutare.

greeting ['griːtɪŋ] *n* saluto *m*.

grenade [grəˈneɪd] *n* granata *f*.

grew [gruː] *pt* → **grow**.

grey [greɪ] adj grigio(-a) ◆ n grigio m; **to go ~** diventar grigio.

greyhound ['greɪhaʊnd] n levriero m.

grid [grɪd] n (grating) grata f; (on map etc) reticolato m.

grief [gri:f] n dolore m; **to come to ~** (plan) naufragare; (person) finire male.

grieve [gri:v] vi affliggersi.

grill [grɪl] n (on cooker) grill m inv; (for open fire) griglia f; (part of restaurant) area di un ristorante dove si cucina alla griglia ◆ vt cuocere ai ferri OR alla griglia.

grille [grɪl] n (AUT) griglia f.

grilled [grɪld] adj alla griglia, ai ferri.

grim [grɪm] adj (expression) severo(-a); (place) lugubre; (news) triste.

grimace [grɪˈmæs] n smorfia f.

grimy [ˈgraɪmɪ] adj sudicio(-a).

grin [grɪn] n (gran) sorriso m ◆ vi fare un gran sorriso.

grind [graɪnd] (pt & pp ground) vt (pepper, coffee) macinare.

grip [grɪp] n (hold) presa f; (of tyres) tenuta f di strada; (handle) impugnatura f; (bag) borsa f da viaggio ◆ vt (hold) afferrare.

gristle [ˈgrɪsl] n cartilagine f.

groan [grəʊn] n lamento m ◆ vi lamentarsi.

groceries [ˈgrəʊsərɪz] npl generi mpl alimentari.

grocer's [ˈgrəʊsəz] n (shop) drogheria f.

grocery [ˈgrəʊsərɪ] n (shop) drogheria f.

groin [grɔɪn] n inguine m.

groove [gru:v] n solco m.

grope [grəʊp] vi andare a tasto-

ni; **to ~ for sthg** cercare qc a tastoni.

gross [grəʊs] adj (weight, income) lordo(-a).

grossly [ˈgrəʊslɪ] adv (extremely) estremamente.

grotty [ˈgrɒtɪ] adj (Br: inf) squallido(-a).

ground [graʊnd] pt & pp → **grind** ◆ n (surface of earth) terra f; (soil) terreno m; (SPORT) campo m ◆ adj (coffee) macinato(-a) ◆ vt (Am: electrical connection) mettere a terra; **to be ~ed** (plane) essere trattenuto a terra; **on the ~** OR **per terra** ❑ **grounds** npl (of building) terreni mpl; (of coffee) fondi mpl; (reason) motivo m, ragione f.

ground floor n pianterreno m.

groundsheet [ˈgraʊndʃiːt] n telo m impermeabile.

group [gru:p] n gruppo m.

grouse [graʊs] (pl inv) n (bird) gallo m cedrone.

grovel [ˈgrɒvl] vi (be humble) umiliarsi.

grow [grəʊ] (pt grew, pp grown) vi (person, animal, plant) crescere; (fears, traffic) aumentare; (company, city) espandersi; (become) diventare ◆ vt (plant, crop) coltivare; (beard) farsi crescere; **to ~ old** invecchiare ❑ **grow up** vi crescere, diventare grande.

growl [graʊl] vi (dog) ringhiare.

grown [grəʊn] pp → **grow**.

grown-up adj adulto(-a) ◆ n adulto m (-a f).

growth [grəʊθ] n (increase) crescita f; (MED) tumore m.

grub [grʌb] n (inf: food) cibo m.

grubby [ˈgrʌbɪ] adj (inf) sporco(-a).

grudge [grʌdʒ] n rancore m ◆ vt: **to ~ sb sthg** invidiare qc a qn.

grueling [ˈgruəlɪŋ] (Am) = **gruelling**.

gruelling [ˈgruəlɪŋ] adj estenuante.

gruesome [ˈgruːsəm] adj raccapricciante.

grumble [ˈgrʌmbl] vi (complain) lagnarsi.

grumpy [ˈgrʌmpɪ] adj (inf) scorbutico(-a).

grunt [grʌnt] vi grugnire.

guarantee [ˌgærənˈtiː] n garanzia f ◆ vt garantire.

guard [gɑːd] n (of prisoner etc) guardia f; (Br: on train) capotreno mf; (protective cover) schermo m di protezione ◆ vt (watch over) sorvegliare; **to be on one's ~** stare in guardia.

guess [ges] n supposizione f ◆ vt & vi indovinare; **I ~ (so)** penso di sì; **have a ~!** indovina!

guest [gest] n (in home) ospite mf; (in hotel) cliente mf.

guesthouse [ˈgesthaʊs, pl -haʊzɪz] n pensione f.

guestroom [ˈgestrʊm] n camera f degli ospiti.

guidance [ˈgaɪdəns] n guida f, direzione f.

guide [gaɪd] n guida f ◆ vt guidare □ **Guide** n (Br) giovane esploratrice f.

guidebook [ˈgaɪdbʊk] n guida f.

guide dog n cane m guida.

guided tour [ˈgaɪdɪd-] n visita f guidata.

guidelines [ˈgaɪdlaɪnz] npl direttive fpl.

guilt [gɪlt] n colpa f.

guilty [ˈgɪltɪ] adj colpevole; **to feel ~** sentirsi in colpa.

guinea pig [ˈgɪnɪ-] n cavia f.

guitar [gɪˈtɑːʳ] n chitarra f.

guitarist [gɪˈtɑːrɪst] n chitarrista mf.

gulf [gʌlf] n (of sea) golfo m.

Gulf War n: **the ~** la guerra del Golfo.

gull [gʌl] n gabbiano m.

gullible [ˈgʌləbl] adj credulone(-a).

gulp [gʌlp] n (of drink) sorso m.

gum [gʌm] n gomma f da masticare; (adhesive) colla f □ **gums** npl gengive fpl.

gun [gʌn] n (pistol) pistola f; (rifle) fucile m; (cannon) cannone m.

gunfire [ˈgʌnfaɪəʳ] n sparatoria f.

gunshot [ˈgʌnʃɒt] n sparo m.

gust [gʌst] n (of wind) raffica f.

gut [gʌt] n (inf: stomach) stomaco m □ **guts** npl (inf: intestines) budella fpl; (courage): **to have ~s** avere fegato.

gutter [ˈgʌtəʳ] n (beside road) cunetta f; (of house) grondaia f.

guy [gaɪ] n (inf: man) tipo m □ **guys** npl (Am: inf: people) gente f.

Guy Fawkes Night [-ˈfɔːks-] n festa che si celebra il 5 novembre per ricordare il fallimento della Congiura delle polveri.

ⓘ GUY FAWKES NIGHT

Chiamata anche "Bonfire Night" (la notte dei falò), questa festa viene celebrata il 5 novembre di ogni anno con falò e fuochi artificiali, e segna l'anniversario della scoperta della Congiura delle polveri, complotto di ispirazione cattolica il cui obiettivo era l'uccisione di Giacomo I e la distruzione del Parlamento britannico (1605). Per l'occasione i bambini realizzano dei pupazzi raffiguranti Guy Fawkes, uno dei cospiratori, con i quali girano per le strade chiedendo soldi ai passanti. La sera, poi, i pupazzi vengono messi in cima ai falò e bruciati.

guy rope *n* cavo *m*.

gym [dʒɪm] *n* palestra *f*; *(school lesson)* ginnastica *f*.

gymnast ['dʒɪmnæst] *n* ginnasta *mf*.

gymnastics [dʒɪm'næstɪks] *n* ginnastica *f*.

gym shoes *npl* scarpe *fpl* da ginnastica.

gynaecologist [ˌgaɪnə'kɒlədʒɪst] *n* ginecologo *m* (-a *f*).

gypsy ['dʒɪpsɪ] = gipsy.

H

H *(abbr of hospital)* H ♦ *abbr* = hot.

habit ['hæbɪt] *n (custom)* abitudine *f*.

hacksaw ['hæksɔː] *n* seghetto *m*.

had [hæd] *pt & pp* → have.

haddock ['hædək] *(pl inv)* *n* eglefino *m (pesce simile al merluzzo)*.

hadn't ['hædnt] = had not.

haggis ['hægɪs] *n piatto tipico scozzese a base di avena e frattaglie di pecora*.

haggle ['hægl] *vi* mercanteggiare.

hail [heɪl] *n* grandine *f* ♦ *v impers* grandinare.

hailstone ['heɪlstəʊn] *n* chicco *m* di grandine.

hair [heəʳ] *n (on head)* capelli *mpl*; *(on animal)* pelo *m*; *(on human skin)* peli *mpl*; *(individual hair on head)* capello *m*; *(individual hair on skin)* pelo *m*; **to have one's ~ cut** tagliarsi i capelli.

hairband ['heəbænd] *n* cerchietto *m* per capelli.

hairbrush ['heəbrʌʃ] *n* spazzola *f* per capelli.

hairclip ['heəklɪp] *n* fermaglio *m* per capelli.

haircut ['heəkʌt] *n (style)* taglio *m* di capelli; **to have a ~** farsi tagliare i capelli.

hairdo ['heəduː] *(pl* -s*)* *n* acconciatura *f*, pettinatura *f*.

hairdresser ['heəˌdresəʳ] *n* parrucchiere *m* (-a *f*); **~'s (salon)** negozio *m* di parrucchiere; **to go to the ~'s** andare dal parrucchiere.

hairdryer ['heəˌdraɪəʳ] *n* asciugacapelli *m inv*, föhn *m inv*.

hair gel *n* gel *m inv* per capelli, gommina *f*.

hairgrip ['heəgrɪp] *n (Br)* molletta *f* (per capelli).

hairnet ['heənet] *n* retina *f* (per capelli).

hairpin bend ['heəpɪn-] *n* tornante *m*.

hair remover [-rɪˌmuːvəʳ] *n* crema *f* depilatoria.

hair rollers [-ˌrəʊləz] *npl* bigodini *mpl*.

hair slide *n* fermacapelli *m inv*.

hairspray ['heəspreɪ] *n* lacca *f* per capelli.

hairstyle ['heəstaɪl] n acconciatura f, pettinatura f.

hairy ['heəri] adj (person, chest, legs) peloso(-a).

half [Br hɑːf, Am hæf] (pl **halves**) n metà f inv; (of match) tempo m; (half pint) mezza pinta f; (child's ticket) biglietto m ridotto ◆ adj mezzo(-a) ◆ adv: ~ **cooked** cotto a metà; ~ **full** mezzo pieno; **I'm** ~ **Scottish** per metà sono scozzese; **a day and a** ~ un giorno e mezzo; **four and a** ~ quattro e mezzo; ~ **past seven** sette e mezza; ~ **as big as** la metà di; **an hour and a** ~ un'ora e mezza; ~ **an hour** mezz'ora; ~ **a dozen** mezza dozzina; ~ **price** a metà prezzo.

half board n mezza pensione f.

half-day n mezza giornata f.

half fare n mezza tariffa f.

half portion n mezza porzione f.

half-price adj a metà prezzo.

half term n (Br) vacanza a metà trimestre.

half time n intervallo m.

halfway [hɑːf'weɪ] adv (in space) a metà strada; (in time) a metà.

halibut ['hælɪbət] (pl inv) n halibut m inv.

hall [hɔːl] n (of house) ingresso m; (large room, building) sala f, salone m; (country house) maniero m.

hallmark ['hɔːlmɑːk] n (on silver, gold) marchio m.

hallo [hə'ləʊ] = **hello**.

hall of residence n casa f dello studente.

Halloween [,hæləʊ'iːn] n vigilia f d'Ognissanti.

---

i HALLOWEEN

Il 31 ottobre, la vigilia di Ognissanti, è, secondo la tradizione popolare, la notte dei fantasmi e delle streghe. In questa occasione i bambini giocano a "trick or treat", gioco che consiste nel recarsi mascherati a casa dei vicini minacciandoli di far loro uno scherzo ("trick") se questi non regalano loro soldi, caramelle e frutta (il "treat"). Altra tradizione associata alla celebrazione di Halloween sia in Gran Bretagna che negli Stati Uniti sono le lanterne di zucca, ottenute svuotando e intagliando un viso in grandi zucche gialle, all'interno delle quali vengono poste delle candele.

---

halt [hɔːlt] vi fermarsi ◆ n: **to come to a** ~ fermarsi.

halve [Br hɑːv, Am hæv] vt dimezzare.

halves [Br hɑːvz, Am hævz] pl → **half**.

ham [hæm] n (meat) prosciutto m (cotto).

hamburger ['hæmbɜːgə'] n (beefburger) hamburger m inv; (Am: mince) carne f macinata.

hamlet ['hæmlɪt] n paesino m.

hammer ['hæmə'] n martello m ◆ vt (nail) piantare.

hammock ['hæmək] n amaca f.

hamper ['hæmpə'] n cesta f.

hamster ['hæmstə'] n criceto m.

hamstring ['hæmstrɪŋ] n tendine m del ginocchio.

hand [hænd] n mano f; (of clock, watch, dial) lancetta f; **to give sb a** ~ dare una mano a qn; **to get out**

of ~ sfuggire di mano; **by** ~ a mano; **in** ~ *(time)* a disposizione; **on the one** ~ da una parte; **on the other** ~ d'altra parte ❏ **hand in** *vt sep* consegnare; **hand out** *vt sep* distribuire; **hand over** *vt sep (give)* consegnare.

handbag ['hændbæg] *n* borsetta *f*.

handbasin ['hændbeɪsn] *n* lavabo *m*.

handbook ['hændbʊk] *n* manuale *m*.

handbrake ['hændbreɪk] *n* freno *m* a mano.

hand cream *n* crema *f* per le mani.

handcuffs ['hændkʌfs] *npl* manette *fpl*.

handful ['hændfʊl] *n (amount)* manciata *f*.

handicap ['hændɪkæp] *n* handicap *m inv*.

handicapped ['hændɪkæpt] *adj* handicappato(-a) ◆ *npl*: **the ~** i portatori di handicap.

handkerchief ['hæŋkətʃɪf] *(pl* -chiefs OR -chieves [-tʃiːvz]) *n* fazzoletto *m*.

handle ['hændl] *n (of door, window)* maniglia *f*; *(of knife, pan, suitcase)* manico *m* ◆ *vt (touch)* toccare; *(deal with)* occuparsi di; **'~ with care'** 'fragile'.

handlebars ['hændlbɑːz] *npl* manubrio *m*.

hand luggage *n* bagaglio *m* a mano.

handmade [ˌhænd'meɪd] *adj* fatto(-a) a mano.

handout ['hændaʊt] *n (leaflet)* volantino *m*.

handrail ['hændreɪl] *n* corri-

mano *m*.

handset ['hændset] *n* ricevitore *m*; **'please replace the ~'** 'si prega di riporre il ricevitore'.

handshake ['hændʃeɪk] *n* stretta *f* di mano.

handsome ['hænsəm] *adj (man)* bello(-a).

handstand ['hændstænd] *n* verticale *f*.

handwriting ['hændˌraɪtɪŋ] *n* calligrafia *f*.

handy ['hændɪ] *adj (useful)* utile; *(convenient)* comodo(-a); *(good with one's hands)* abile; *(near)* vicino(-a), a portata di mano; **to come in ~** *(inf)* tornare utile.

hang [hæŋ] *(pt & pp* hung) *vt* appendere; *(execute: pt & pp* hanged) impiccare ◆ *vi (be suspended)* penzolare, pendere ◆ *n*: **to get the ~ of sthg** fare la mano a qc ❏ **hang about** *vi (Br: inf)* ciondolare; **hang around** *(inf)* = **hang about**; **hang down** *vi* penzolare; **hang on** *vi (inf: wait)* aspettare; **hang out** *vt sep (washing)* stendere ◆ *vi (inf)* stare; **hang up** *vi (on phone)* riagganciare.

hangar ['hæŋəʳ] *n* hangar *m inv*.

hanger ['hæŋəʳ] *n* gruccia *f*, stampella *f*.

hang gliding *n* deltaplano *m*.

hangover ['hæŋˌəʊvəʳ] *n* postumi *mpl* di sbornia.

hankie ['hæŋkɪ] *n (inf)* fazzoletto *m*.

happen ['hæpən] *vi* succedere, accadere; **I ~ed to catch sight of him** mi è capitato di vederlo.

happily ['hæpɪlɪ] *adv (luckily)* fortunatamente.

happiness ['hæpɪnɪs] *n* felicità *f*.

happy ['hæpɪ] *adj* felice; **to be ~ about** sthg essere contento(-a) di qc; **to be ~ to do** sthg *(willing)* fare qc volentieri; **to be ~ with** sthg essere soddisfatto di qc; **Happy Birthday!** buon compleanno!; **Happy Christmas!** buon Natale!; **Happy New Year!** buon anno!

happy hour *n (inf)* momento della giornata, di solito nel tardo pomeriggio, in cui, nei bar, le bevande vengono vendute a prezzo ridotto.

harassment ['hærəsmənt] *n* molestie *fpl*.

harbor ['hɑːbər] *(Am)* = **harbour.**

harbour ['hɑːbər] *n (Br)* porto *m*.

hard [hɑːd] *adj* duro(-a); *(difficult)* difficile; *(strenuous)* faticoso(-a); *(forceful)* forte; *(winter, frost)* rigido(-a); *(drugs)* pesante ♦ *adv (work)* duro; *(listen)* attentamente; *(hit)* con forza; *(rain)* a dirotto.

hardback ['hɑːdbæk] *n* edizione *f* rilegata.

hardboard ['hɑːdbɔːd] *n* pannello *m* di legno compresso.

hard-boiled egg [-bɔɪld-] *n* uovo *m* sodo.

hard disk *n* hard disk *m inv*, disco *m* rigido.

hardly ['hɑːdlɪ] *adv* a malapena, appena; **~ ever** quasi mai.

hardship ['hɑːdʃɪp] *n (difficult conditions)* privazioni *fpl*; *(difficult circumstance)* avversità *fpl*.

hard shoulder *n (Br)* corsia *f* d'emergenza.

hard up *adj (inf)* in bolletta.

hardware ['hɑːdweər] *n (tools, equipment)* ferramenta *fpl*; *(COMPUT)* hardware *m*.

hardwearing [,hɑːdˈweərɪŋ] *adj*

(Br) resistente.

hardworking [,hɑːdˈwɜːkɪŋ] *adj* instancabile.

hare [heər] *n* lepre *f*.

harm [hɑːm] *n (injury)* male *m*; *(damage)* danno *m* ♦ *vt (injure)* far male a; *(damage)* danneggiare.

harmful ['hɑːmful] *adj* nocivo(-a).

harmless ['hɑːmlɪs] *adj* innocuo(-a).

harmonica [hɑːˈmɒnɪkə] *n* armonica *f*.

harmony ['hɑːmənɪ] *n* armonia *f*.

harness ['hɑːnɪs] *n (for horse)* finimenti *mpl*; *(for child)* briglie *fpl*.

harp [hɑːp] *n* arpa *f*.

harsh [hɑːʃ] *adj (weather)* rigido(-a); *(conditions)* duro(-a); *(cruel)* severo(-a); *(sound)* sgradevole.

harvest ['hɑːvɪst] *n (of corn, fruit)* raccolto *m*; *(of grapes)* vendemmia *f*.

has [weak form həz, strong form hæz] → **have.**

hash browns [hæʃ-] *npl (Am)* frittelle *fpl* di patate.

hasn't ['hæznt] = **has not.**

hassle ['hæsl] *n (inf: problem)* seccatura *f*.

hastily ['heɪstɪlɪ] *adv (rashly)* precipitosamente.

hasty ['heɪstɪ] *adj (hurried)* affrettato(-a); *(rash)* precipitoso(-a).

hat [hæt] *n* cappello *m*.

hatch [hætʃ] *n (for food)* passavivande *m inv* ♦ *vi (egg)* schiudersi.

hatchback ['hætʃ,bæk] *n (car)* tre OR cinque porte *f inv*.

hatchet ['hætʃɪt] *n* accetta *f*.

hate [heɪt] *n* odio *m* ♦ *vt* odiare,

detestare; **to ~ doing sthg** detestare fare qc.

hatred ['heɪtrɪd] *n* odio *m*.

haul [hɔːl] *vt* trascinare ◆ *n*: **a long ~** un percorso lungo e faticoso.

haunted ['hɔːntɪd] *adj* (*house*) abitato(-a) da fantasmi.

have [hæv] (*pt & pp* **had**) *aux vb* 1. (*to form perfect tenses: gen*) avere; (*with many intransitive verbs*) essere; **I ~ finished** ho finito; **~ you been there? ~ no, I haven't** ci sei stato? – no; the train had already gone il treno era già partito.

2. (*must*): **to ~ (got) to do sthg** dover fare qc; **do you ~ to pay?** si deve pagare?
◆ *vt* 1. (*possess*): **to ~ (got)** avere; **do you ~ OR ~ you got a double room?** avete una camera doppia?; **she has (got) brown hair** ha i capelli castani.

2. (*experience*) avere; **to ~ a cold** avere il raffreddore; **we had a great time** ci siamo divertiti un mondo.

3. (*replacing other verbs*): **to ~ break-fast** fare colazione; **to ~ dinner** cenare; **to ~ lunch** pranzare; **to ~ a drink** bere qualcosa; **to ~ a shower** fare una doccia; **to ~ a swim** fare una nuotata; **to ~ a walk** fare una passeggiata.

4. (*cause to be*): **to ~ sthg done** far fare qc; **to ~ one's hair cut** farsi tagliare i capelli.

5. (*be treated in a certain way*): **I've had my wallet stolen** mi hanno rubato il portafoglio.

haversack ['hævəsæk] *n* zaino *m*.

havoc ['hævək] *n* caos *m*.

hawk [hɔːk] *n* falco *m*.

hawker ['hɔːkə'] *n* venditore *m*

(-trice *f*) ambulante.

hay [heɪ] *n* fieno *m*.

hay fever *n* raffreddore *m* da fieno.

haystack ['heɪˌstæk] *n* pagliaio *m*.

hazard ['hæzəd] *n* rischio *m*, pericolo *m*.

hazardous ['hæzədəs] *adj* rischioso(-a), pericoloso(-a).

hazard warning lights *npl* (*Br*) luci *fpl* di emergenza.

haze [heɪz] *n* foschia *f*.

hazel ['heɪzl] *adj* nocciola (*inv*).

hazelnut ['heɪzl,nʌt] *n* nocciola *f*.

hazy ['heɪzɪ] *adj* (*misty*) offuscato(-a).

he [hiː] *pron* lui, egli; **~'s tall** è alto.

head [hed] *n* (*of body*) testa *f*, capo *m*; (*of queue, page, bed*) cima *f*; (*of company, department, table*) capo *m*; (*head teacher of primary or lower secondary school*) direttore *m* (-trice *f*) di scuola; (*head teacher of upper secondary school*) preside *mf*; (*of beer*) schiuma *f* ◆ *vt* (*list*) essere in testa a; (*organization*) dirigere, essere a capo di ◆ *vi* dirigersi; **£10 a ~** 10 sterline a testa; **~s or tails?** testa o croce? □ **head for** *vt fus* dirigersi verso OR a.

headache ['hedeɪk] *n* (*pain*) mal *m* di testa; **to have a ~** avere mal di testa.

heading ['hedɪŋ] *n* intestazione *f*.

headlamp ['hedlæmp] (*Br*) = **headlight**.

headlight ['hedlaɪt] *n* fanale *m* anteriore.

headline ['hedlaɪn] *n (in newspaper)* titolo *m*; *(on TV, radio)* notizie *fpl* principali.

headmaster [,hed'mɑ:stəʳ] *n (of primary or lower secondary school)* direttore *m* di scuola; *(of upper secondary school)* preside *m*.

headmistress [,hed'mɪstrɪs] *n (of primary or lower secondary school)* direttrice *f* di scuola; *(of upper secondary school)* preside *f*.

head of state *n* capo *m* di Stato.

headphones ['hedfəʊnz] *npl* cuffie *fpl*.

headquarters [hed'kwɔ:təz] *npl (of company, bank)* sede *f* centrale; *(of police, army)* quartiere *m* generale.

headrest ['hedrest] *n* poggiatesta *m inv*.

headroom ['hedrʊm] *n (under bridge)* altezza *f* massima.

headscarf ['hedskɑ:f] *(pl -scarves* [-skɑ:vz]*) n* foulard *m inv*.

head start *n* vantaggio *m*.

head teacher *n (of primary or lower secondary school)* direttore *m* (-trice *f*) di scuola; *(of upper secondary school)* preside *mf*.

head waiter *n* capocameriere *m*.

heal [hi:l] *vt* curare ◆ *vi* guarire.

health [helθ] *n* salute *f*; **to be in good ~** essere in buona salute; **to be in poor ~** essere in cattive condizioni di salute; **your (very) good ~!** alla tua salute!

health centre *n* centro *m* sanitario.

health food *n* cibo *m* naturale.

health food shop *n* negozio *m* di prodotti naturali.

health insurance *n* assicurazione *f* contro le malattie.

healthy ['helθɪ] *adj* sano(-a).

heap [hi:p] *n* mucchio *m*; **~s of** *(inf)* un mucchio di.

hear [hɪəʳ] *(pt & pp* **heard** [hɜ:d]*) vt sentire; (case, evidence)* esaminare ◆ *vi* sentire; **to ~ about** sthg sapere OR sentire di qc; **to ~ from** sb ricevere notizie da qn; **to have heard of** aver sentito parlare di.

hearing ['hɪərɪŋ] *n (sense)* udito *m*; *(at court)* udienza *f*; **to be hard of ~** esser duro d'orecchi.

hearing aid *n* apparecchio *m* acustico.

heart [hɑ:t] *n* cuore *m*; **to know sthg (off) by ~** sapere qc a memoria; **to lose ~** scoraggiarsi ❑ **hearts** *npl (in cards)* cuori *mpl*.

heart attack *n* infarto *m*.

heartbeat ['hɑ:tbi:t] *n (rhythm)* battito *m* cardiaco.

heartburn ['hɑ:tbɜ:n] *n* bruciore *m* di stomaco.

heart condition *n*: **to have a ~** avere un disturbo cardiaco.

hearth [hɑ:θ] *n* focolare *m*.

hearty ['hɑ:tɪ] *adj (meal)* abbondante, sostanzioso(-a).

heat [hi:t] *n (warmth)* calore *m*; *(warm weather)* caldo *m*; *(of oven)* temperatura *f* ❑ **heat up** *vt sep* riscaldare.

heater ['hi:təʳ] *n (for room)* stufa *f*; *(radiator)* radiatore *m*; *(in car)* riscaldamento *m*; *(for water)* scaldabagno *m*.

heath [hi:θ] *n* brughiera *f*.

heather ['heðəʳ] *n* erica *f*.

heating ['hi:tɪŋ] *n* riscaldamento *m*.

heat wave n ondata f di caldo.

heave [hiːv] vt (push) spingere (con forza); (pull) tirare (con forza); (lift) sollevare (con forza).

Heaven ['hevn] n paradiso m.

heavily ['hevɪlɪ] adv (smoke, drink) molto; (rain) a dirotto.

heavy ['hevɪ] adj pesante; (rain, traffic) intenso(-a); (fighting) violento(-a); (losses, defeat) grave; **how ~ is it?** quanto pesa?; **to be a ~ smoker** essere un fumatore accanito.

heavy cream n (Am) panna molto densa ad alto contenuto di grassi.

heavy goods vehicle n (Br) veicolo m per trasporti pesanti.

heavy industry n industria f pesante.

heavy metal n heavy metal m.

heckle ['hekl] vt interrompere di continuo.

hectic ['hektɪk] adj frenetico(-a).

hedge [hedʒ] n siepe f.

hedgehog ['hedʒhɒg] n riccio m.

heel [hiːl] n (of person) calcagno m; (of shoe) tacco m.

hefty ['heftɪ] adj (person) robusto(-a); (fine) salato(-a).

height [haɪt] n altezza f; (peak period) apice m; **what ~ is it?** quanto è alto?

heir [eəʳ] n erede m.

heiress ['eərɪs] n erede f.

held [held] pt & pp → hold.

helicopter ['helɪkɒptəʳ] n elicottero m.

he'll [hiːl] = he will, = he shall.

Hell [hel] n inferno m.

hello [hə'ləʊ] excl (as greeting) ciao!; (more formal) buongiorno!;

(on phone) pronto!; (to attract attention) ehi!

helmet ['helmɪt] n casco m.

help [help] n aiuto m ♦ vt aiutare; (contribute to) contribuire a ♦ vi aiutare, essere d'aiuto ♦ excl aiuto!; **I can't ~ it** non ci posso fare niente; **to ~ sb (to) do sthg** aiutare qn a fare qc; **to ~ o.s. (to sthg)** servirsi (di qc); **can I ~ you?** (in shop) desidera? □ **help out** vi aiutare, dare una mano.

helper ['helpəʳ] n (assistant) aiutante mf; (Am: cleaner) uomo m (donna f) delle pulizie.

helpful ['helpful] adj (person) di grande aiuto; (useful) utile.

helping ['helpɪŋ] n porzione f.

helpless ['helplɪs] adj impotente; (child) indifeso(-a).

hem [hem] n orlo m.

hemophiliac [ˌhiːmə'fɪliæk] n emofiliaco m (-a f).

hemorrhage ['hemərɪdʒ] n emorragia f.

hen [hen] n gallina f.

hepatitis [ˌhepə'taɪtɪs] n epatite f.

her [hɜːʳ] adj il suo (la sua), i suoi (le sue) (pl) ♦ pron (direct) la; (indirect) le; (after prep, stressed) lei; **~ brother** suo fratello; **I know ~** la conosco; **it's ~** è lei; **send it to ~** mandaglielo, mandalo a lei; **tell ~** diglielo; **tell ~ that ...** dille che ...; **he's worse than ~** lui è peggio di lei.

herb [hɜːb] n erba f.

herbal tea ['hɜːbl-] n tè m inv d'erbe.

herd [hɜːd] n (of cattle) mandria f.

here [hɪəʳ] adv qui, qua; **~'s your book** eccoti il libro; **~ you are**

eccoti (qui OR qua).

heritage ['herɪtɪdʒ] n eredità f, patrimonio m.

heritage centre n centro informazioni in luoghi di interesse storico.

hernia ['hɜːnjə] n ernia f.

hero ['hɪərəʊ] (pl -es) n eroe m.

heroin ['herəʊɪn] n eroina f (droga).

heroine ['herəʊɪn] n eroina f.

heron ['herən] n airone m.

herring ['herɪŋ] n aringa f.

hers [hɜːz] pron il suo (la sua), i suoi (le sue) (pl); **a friend of** ~ un suo amico.

herself [hɜːˈself] pron (reflexive) si; (after prep) se stessa, sé; **she did it** ~ l'ha fatto da sola.

hesitant ['hezɪtənt] adj esitante.

hesitate ['hezɪteɪt] vi esitare.

hesitation [ˌhezɪˈteɪʃn] n esitazione f.

heterosexual [ˌhetərəʊˈsekʃʊəl] adj eterosessuale ◆ n eterosessuale mf.

hey [heɪ] excl (inf) ehi!

HGV abbr = heavy goods vehicle.

hi [haɪ] excl (inf) ciao!

hiccup ['hɪkʌp] n: **to have (the)** ~s avere il singhiozzo.

hide [haɪd] (pt hid [hɪd], pp hidden [hɪdn]) vt nascondere ◆ vi nascondersi ◆ n (of animal) pelle f.

hideous ['hɪdɪəs] adj raccapricciante.

hi-fi ['haɪfaɪ] n hi-fi m inv.

high [haɪ] adj alto(-a); (price, speed, temperature) alto, elevato(-a); (wind) forte; (sound, voice) acuto (-a), alto; (inf: from drugs) fatto(-a) ◆ n (weather front) anticiclone m ◆

adv alto, in alto; **how** ~ **is it?** quanto è alto?; **it's 10 metres** ~ è alto 10 metri.

high chair n seggiolone m.

high-class adj di lusso.

Higher ['haɪəʳ] n (Scot) esame sostenuto alla fine di studi secondari.

higher education n istruzione f universitaria.

high heels npl tacchi mpl alti.

high jump n salto m in alto.

Highland Games ['haɪlənd-] npl: **the** ~ gare sportive disputate all'aperto nelle Highlands scozzesi.

HIGHLAND GAMES

L'origine di queste manifestazioni sportive e musicali che hanno luogo in Scozia durante l'estate risale alle riunioni fra i diversi clan delle Highlands. I giochi odierni comprendono gare di corsa, di salto in lungo e di salto in alto, accanto a gare di danze tradizionali e di cornamusa. Un'altra competizione tipica di questa manifestazione è quella del lancio del tronco ("tossing the caber"), prova di forza che consiste nel lanciare un lungo tronco d'abete il più lontano possibile.

Highlands ['haɪləndz] npl: **the** ~ le Highlands fpl (regione montuosa nel nord della Scozia).

highlight ['haɪlaɪt] n (best part) clou m inv ◆ vt (emphasize) evidenziare ❏ **highlights** npl (of football match etc) sintesi f inv; (in hair) colpi mpl di sole.

highly ['haɪlɪ] adv (extremely) molto; (very well) molto bene; **to think** ~ **of sb** avere di grande stima di qn.

high-pitched [-'pɪtʃt] *adj* acuto (-a).

high-rise *adj* con tanti piani.

high school *n* (*in UK*) = scuola *f* secondaria inferiore e superiore; (*in US*) = scuola secondaria superiore.

high season *n* alta stagione *f*.

high-speed train *n* treno *m* ad alta velocità.

high street *n* (*Br*) strada *f* principale.

high tide *n* alta marea *f*.

highway ['haɪweɪ] *n* (*Am: between towns*) superstrada *f*; (*Br: any main road*) strada *f* principale.

Highway Code *n* (*Br*) codice *m* stradale.

hijack ['haɪdʒæk] *vt* dirottare.

hijacker ['haɪdʒækə'] *n* dirottatore *m* (-trice *f*).

hike [haɪk] *n* lunga camminata *f* ♦ *vi* fare una lunga camminata.

hiking ['haɪkɪŋ] *n*: **to go** ~ andare a fare lunghe camminate.

hilarious [hɪ'leərɪəs] *adj* spassoso(-a).

hill [hɪl] *n* collina *f*, colle *m*.

hillwalking ['hɪlwɔːkɪŋ] *n*: **to go** ~ fare lunghe camminate.

hilly ['hɪlɪ] *adj* collinoso(-a).

him [hɪm] *pron* (*direct*) lo; (*indirect*) gli; (*after prep, stressed*) lui; **I know** ~ lo conosco; **it's** ~ è lui; **send it to** ~ mandaglielo, mandalo a lui; **tell** ~ diglielo; **tell** ~ **that** ... digli che ...; **she's worse than** ~ lei è peggio di lui.

himself [hɪm'self] *pron* (*reflexive*) si; (*after prep*) se stesso, sé; **he did it** ~ l'ha fatto da solo.

hinder ['hɪndə'] *vt* ostacolare.

Hindu ['hɪnduː] (*pl* -s) *adj* indù (*inv*) ♦ *n* (*person*) indù *mf inv*.

hinge [hɪndʒ] *n* cardine *m*.

hint [hɪnt] *n* (*indirect suggestion*) accenno *m*, allusione *f*; (*piece of advice*) consiglio *m*; (*slight amount*) accenno, punta *f* ♦ *vi*: **to** ~ **at sthg** alludere a qc.

hip [hɪp] *n* fianco *m*.

hippopotamus [hɪpə'pɒtəməs] *n* ippopotamo *m*.

hippy ['hɪpɪ] *n* hippy *mf inv*.

hire ['haɪə'] *vt* (*car, bicycle, television*) noleggiare; **'for** ~**'** (*boats*) 'da noleggio'; (*taxi*) 'libero' □ **hire out** *vt sep* (*car, bicycle, television*) dare a noleggio.

hire car *n* (*Br*) vettura *f* a noleggio.

hire purchase *n* (*Br*) acquisto *m* rateale.

his [hɪz] *adj* il suo (la sua), i suoi (le sue) (*pl*) ♦ *pron* il suo (la sua), i suoi (le sue) (*pl*); ~ **brother** suo fratello; **a friend of** ~ un suo amico.

historical [hɪ'stɒrɪkəl] *adj* storico(-a).

history ['hɪstərɪ] *n* storia *f*; (*record*) passato *m*.

hit [hɪt] (*pt & pp* **hit**) *vt* colpire; (*bang*) sbattere, picchiare ♦ *n* (*record, play, film*) successo *m*.

hit-and-run *adj*: ~ **accident** incidente in cui l'automobilista colpevole non si ferma a prestare soccorso.

hitch [hɪtʃ] *n* (*problem*) contrattempo *m* ♦ *vt*: **to** ~ **a lift** farsi dare un passaggio ♦ *vi* fare l'autostop.

hitchhike ['hɪtʃhaɪk] *vi* fare l'autostop.

hitchhiker ['hɪtʃhaɪkə'] *n* autostoppista *mf*.

hive [haɪv] *n* (*of bees*) alveare *m*.

HIV-positive *adj* sieropositivo(-a).

hoarding ['hɔːdɪŋ] *n* (*Br: for adverts*) tabellone *m* per pubblicità.

hoarse [hɔːs] *adj* rauco(-a).

hoax [həʊks] *n* burla *f*.

hob [hɒb] *n* piano *m* di cottura.

hobby ['hɒbɪ] *n* hobby *m inv*, passatempo *m*.

hock [hɒk] *n* (*wine*) vino *m* bianco del Reno.

hockey ['hɒkɪ] *n* (*on grass*) hockey *m* su prato; (*Am: ice hockey*) hockey su ghiaccio.

hoe [həʊ] *n* zappa *f*.

Hogmanay ['hɒgmaneɪ] *n* (*Scot*) l'ultimo *m* dell'anno.

hold [həʊld] (*pt & pp* **held**) *vt* tenere; (*contain*) contenere; (*possess*) avere, possedere ♦ *vi* (*weather*) mantenersi; (*luck, offer*) permanere; (*on telephone*) restare in linea ♦ *n* (*grip*) presa *f*; (*of ship*) stiva *f*; (*of aircraft*) bagagliaio *m*; **to ~ sb prisoner** tenere prigioniero qn; **~ the line, please** resti in linea, per favore ❑ **hold back** *vt sep* (*restrain*) trattenere; (*keep secret*) tenere segreto; **hold on** *vi* (*wait*) aspettare, attendere; (*on telephone*) restare in linea; **to ~ on to sthg** (*grip*) tenersi (stretto) a qc; **hold out** *vt sep* (*hand*) porgere, tendere; **hold up** *vt sep* (*delay*) bloccare.

holdall ['həʊldɔːl] *n* (*Br*) borsone *m* da viaggio.

holder ['həʊldər] *n* (*of passport, licence*) titolare *mf*, proprietario *m* (-a *f*); (*container*) contenitore *m*.

holdup ['həʊldʌp] *n* (*delay*) ritardo *m*.

hole [həʊl] *n* (*in sock, wall*) buco *m*; (*in ground, golf*) buca *f*.

holiday ['hɒlɪdeɪ] *n* (*Br: period of time*) vacanze *fpl*; (*time off work*) ferie *fpl*; (*public holiday*) festa ♦ *vi* (*Br*) trascorrere le vacanze; **to be on ~** essere in vacanza; **to go on ~** andare in vacanza.

holidaymaker ['hɒlɪdɪˌmeɪkər] *n* (*Br*) villeggiante *mf*.

holiday pay *n* (*Br*) retribuzione *f* delle ferie.

Holland ['hɒlənd] *n* l'Olanda *f*.

hollow ['hɒləʊ] *adj* cavo(-a).

holly ['hɒlɪ] *n* agrifoglio *m*.

Hollywood ['hɒlɪwʊd] *n* Hollywood *f*.

---

i **HOLLYWOOD**

Quartiere di Los Angeles, Hollywood è, fin dal 1911, il cuore dell'industria cinematografica americana. Ha avuto il suo momento di maggior fulgore negli anni quaranta e cinquanta, quando gli immensi studi della Twentieth Century Fox, della Paramount e della Warner Brothers producevano centinaia di film all'anno, e resta tuttora una delle più grandi attrazioni turistiche d'America.

---

holy ['həʊlɪ] *adj* sacro(-a).

home [həʊm] *n* casa *f*; (*own country*) patria *f*; (*for old people*) istituto *m*, ricovero *m* ♦ *adv* a casa ♦ *adj* (*not foreign*) interno(-a), nazionale; (*cooking*) casereccio(-a); **at ~** (*in one's house*) a casa; **to make o.s. at ~** fare come se si fosse a casa propria; **to go ~** andare a casa; **to leave ~** (*for good*) andarsene di casa; ~ **address** indirizzo m di casa; ~ **number** numero m (telefonico) di casa.

home economics n economia f domestica.

home help n (Br) collaboratore m domestico (collaboratrice domestica f).

homeless ['həʊmlɪs] npl: **the** ~ i senzatetto.

homemade [ˌhəʊm'meɪd] adj (food) casereccio(-a).

homeopathic [ˌhəʊmɪəʊ'pæθɪk] adj omeopatico(-a).

Home Secretary n (Br) ministro m degli Interni.

homesick ['həʊmsɪk] adj: **to be** ~ avere nostalgia di casa.

homework ['həʊmwɜ:k] n compiti mpl a casa.

homosexual [ˌhɒmə'sekʃʊəl] adj omosessuale ◆ n omosessuale m.

honest ['ɒnɪst] adj (trustworthy) onesto(-a); (frank) sincero(-a), franco(-a).

honestly ['ɒnɪstlɪ] adv (truthfully) onestamente; (frankly) sinceramente, francamente.

honey ['hʌnɪ] n miele m.

honeymoon ['hʌnɪmu:n] n luna f di miele, viaggio m di nozze.

honor ['ɒnər] (Am) = **honour**.

honour ['ɒnər] n (Br) onore m.

honourable ['ɒnrəbl] adj onorevole.

hood [hʊd] n (of jacket, coat) cappuccio m; (on convertible car) capote f inv; (Am: car bonnet) cofano m.

hoof [hu:f] n zoccolo m.

hook [hʊk] n gancio m; (for fishing) amo m; **off the** ~ (telephone) staccato.

hooligan ['hu:lɪgən] n teppista mf, hooligan mf inv.

hoop [hu:p] n cerchio m.

hoot [hu:t] vi (driver) suonare il clacson.

Hoover® ['hu:vər] n (Br) aspirapolvere m inv.

hop [hɒp] vi (person) saltellare su una gamba.

hope [həʊp] n speranza f ◆ vt sperare; **to** ~ **for sthg** sperare in qc; **to** ~ **to do sthg** sperare di fare qc; **I** ~ **so** spero di sì.

hopeful ['həʊpfʊl] adj (optimistic) fiducioso(-a).

hopefully ['həʊpfəlɪ] adv (with luck) se tutto va bene.

hopeless ['həʊpləs] adj (without any hope) disperato(-a); **he's** ~! (inf) è un disastro!

hops [hɒps] npl luppolo m.

horizon [hə'raɪzn] n orizzonte m.

horizontal [ˌhɒrɪ'zɒntl] adj orizzontale.

horn [hɔ:n] n (of car) clacson m inv; (on animal) corno m.

horoscope ['hɒrəskəʊp] n oroscopo m.

horrible ['hɒrəbl] adj orribile.

horrid ['hɒrɪd] adj (very bad) orrendo(-a); (unkind) odioso(-a); (food, drink) pessimo(-a).

horrific [hɒ'rɪfɪk] adj orripilante, terrificante.

hors d'oeuvre [hɔ:'dɜ:vrə] n antipasto m.

horse [hɔ:s] n cavallo m.

horseback ['hɔ:sbæk] n: **on** ~ a cavallo.

horse chestnut n ippocastano m.

horse-drawn carriage

horse-drawn carriage *n* carrozza *f* a cavalli.

horsepower ['hɔːsˌpaʊəʳ] *n* cavallo *m* vapore.

horse racing *n* ippica *f*.

horseradish (sauce) ['hɔːsˌrædɪʃ-] *n* salsa *f* di rafano.

horse riding *n* equitazione *f*.

horseshoe ['hɔːsʃuː] *n* ferro *m* di cavallo.

hose [həʊz] *n* (hosepipe) tubo *m* per annaffiare.

hosepipe ['həʊzpaɪp] *n* tubo *m* per annaffiare.

hosiery ['həʊzɪərɪ] *n* calzetteria *f*.

hospitable [hɒ'spɪtəbl] *adj* ospitale.

hospital ['hɒspɪtl] *n* ospedale *m*; **in ~** all'ospedale.

hospitality [ˌhɒspɪ'tælətɪ] *n* ospitalità *f*.

host [həʊst] *n* (of party, event) ospite *m*; (of show, TV programme) conduttore *m* (-trice *f*).

hostage ['hɒstɪdʒ] *n* ostaggio *m*.

hostel ['hɒstl] *n* (youth hostel) ostello *m*.

hostess ['həʊstes] *n* (on aeroplane) hostess *f inv*; (of party, event) ospite *f*.

hostile [Br 'hɒstaɪl, Am 'hɒstl] *adj* ostile.

hostility [hɒ'stɪlətɪ] *n* ostilità *f*.

hot [hɒt] *adj* caldo(-a); (spicy) piccante; **to be ~** (person) aver caldo; **it's ~** fa caldo.

hot chocolate *n* cioccolata *f* calda.

hot-cross bun *n* panino dolce con uvetta e spezie tipico del periodo pasquale.

hot dog *n* hot dog *m inv* (panino imbottito con würstel e senape).

hotel [həʊ'tel] *n* hotel *m inv*, albergo *m*.

hot line *n* telefono *m* rosso.

hotplate ['hɒtpleɪt] *n* piastra *f*.

hotpot ['hɒtpɒt] *n* spezzatino di carne con patate.

hot-water bottle *n* borsa *f* dell'acqua calda.

hour ['aʊəʳ] *n* ora *f*; **I've been waiting for ~s** è un secolo che aspetto.

hourly ['aʊəlɪ] *adj* (per hour) orario(-a); (every hour) ogni ora ◆ *adv* (per hour) a ore; (every hour) ogni ora.

house [*n* haʊs, *pl* 'haʊzɪz, *vb* haʊz] *n* casa *f*; (SCH) uno dei gruppi in cui sono divisi gli alunni di una scuola media o superiore in occasione di competizioni sportive ecc. ◆ *vt* (person) alloggiare.

household ['haʊshəʊld] *n* famiglia *f*.

housekeeping ['haʊsˌkiːpɪŋ] *n* amministrazione *f* della casa.

House of Commons *n* (Br) Camera *f* dei Comuni.

House of Lords *n* (Br) Camera *f* dei Lord.

Houses of Parliament *npl* (Br: building) palazzo *m* del Parlamento.

---

i HOUSES OF PARLIAMENT

Il parlamento britannico comprende la Camera dei Comuni (House of Commons) e la Camera dei Lord (House of Lords). Ha sede a Londra, nel Palazzo di Westminster sulla riva del Tamigi. Gli edifici attuali risalgono alla metà del dician-novesimo secolo, quando vennero costruiti sulle macerie del palazzo originario, distrutto da un incendio nel 1834.

housewife ['hauswaif] (*pl* **-wives** [-waɪvz]) *n* casalinga *f*.

house wine *n* vino *m* della casa.

housewives *pl* → **housewife**.

housework ['hauswɜːk] *n* lavori *mpl* di casa.

housing ['hauzɪŋ] *n* alloggi *mpl*.

housing estate *n* (*Br*) complesso *m* residenziale.

housing project (*Am*) = **housing estate**.

hovercraft ['hɒvəkrɑːft] *n* hovercraft *m inv*.

hoverport ['hɒvəpɔːt] *n* porto *m* per hovercraft.

how [hau] *adv* **1.** (*asking about way or manner*) come; ~ **do you get there?** come ci si arriva?; ~ **does it work?** come funziona?; **tell me** ~ **to do it** dimmi come devo fare. **2.** (*asking about health, quality*) come; ~ **are you?** come stai?; ~ **are you doing?** come va?; ~ **are things?** come vanno le cose?; ~ **do you do?** piacere!; ~ **is your room?** com'è la tua camera? **3.** (*asking about degree, amount*): ~ **tall is he?** quanto è alto?; ~ **far is it?** quanto dista?; ~ **long will it take?** quanto tempo ci vorrà?; ~ **many?** quanti(-e)?; ~ **much?** quanto(-a)?; ~ **much is it?** quant'è?; ~ **old are you?** quanti anni hai? **4.** (*in phrases*): ~ **about some coffee?** cosa ne diresti di un caffè?; ~ **lovely!** che bello!

however [hau'evər] *adv* (*nevertheless*) tuttavia; ~ **difficult it is** per quanto sia difficile.

howl [haul] *vi* ululare.

HP *abbr* = **hire purchase**.

HQ *n* (*abbr of* **headquarters**) Q.G. *m*.

hub airport [hʌb-] *n* aeroporto *m* principale.

hubcap ['hʌbkæp] *n* coprimozzo *m*.

hug [hʌg] *vt* abbracciare ♦ *n*: **to give sb a** ~ abbracciare qn.

huge [hjuːdʒ] *adj* enorme.

hull [hʌl] *n* scafo *m*.

hum [hʌm] *vi* (*bee, machine*) ronzare; (*person*) canterellare.

human ['hjuːmən] *adj* umano(-a) ♦ *n*: ~ (**being**) essere *m* umano.

humanities [hjuː'mænətɪz] *npl* materie *fpl* umanistiche.

human rights *npl* diritti *mpl* dell'uomo.

humble ['hʌmbl] *adj* umile.

humid ['hjuːmɪd] *adj* umido(-a).

humidity [hjuː'mɪdətɪ] *n* umidità *f*.

humiliating [hjuː'mɪlɪeɪtɪŋ] *adj* umiliante.

humiliation [hjuːˌmɪlɪ'eɪʃn] *n* umiliazione *f*.

hummus ['huməs] *n* salsetta cremosa a base di ceci, aglio e pasta di sesamo.

humor ['hjuːmər] (*Am*) = **humour**.

humorous ['hjuːmərəs] *adj* (*story*) umoristico(-a); (*person*) spiritoso(-a).

humour ['hjuːmər] *n* umorismo *m*; **sense of** ~ senso *m* dell'umorismo.

hump [hʌmp] *n (bump)* dosso *m*; *(of camel)* gobba *f*.

humpbacked bridge ['hʌmp-bækt-] *n* ponte *m* a schiena d'asino.

hunch [hʌntʃ] *n* impressione *f*.

hundred ['hʌndrəd] *num* cento; **a ~ cento,** → **six**.

hundredth ['hʌndrətθ] *num* centesimo(-a), → **sixth**.

hundredweight ['hʌndrəd-weit] *n (in UK)* = 50,8 kg; *(in US)* = 45,4 kg.

hung [hʌŋ] *pt & pp* → **hang**.

Hungarian [hʌŋ'geəriən] *adj* ungherese ♦ *n (person)* ungherese *mf*; *(language)* ungherese *m*.

Hungary ['hʌŋgəri] *n* l'Ungheria *f*.

hunger ['hʌŋgər] *n* fame *f*.

hungry ['hʌŋgri] *adj* affamato(-a); **to be ~** avere fame.

hunt [hʌnt] *n (Br: for foxes)* caccia *f* ♦ *vt & vi* cacciare; **to ~ (for sb/sthg)** *(search)* cercare (qn/qc).

hunting ['hʌntɪŋ] *n* caccia *f*.

hurdle ['hɜ:dl] *n (SPORT)* ostacolo *m*.

hurl [hɜ:l] *vt (throw)* scaraventare, scagliare.

hurricane ['hʌrɪkən] *n* uragano *m*.

hurry ['hʌri] *vt (person)* mettere fretta a ♦ *vi* affrettarsi, sbrigarsi ♦ *n:* **to be in a ~** avere fretta; **to do sthg in a ~** fare qc in fretta ❑ **hurry up** *vi* sbrigarsi.

hurt [hɜ:t] *(pt & pp* **hurt)** *vt (injure)* fare male a; *(emotionally)* ferire ♦ *vi* fare male; **my arm ~s** mi fa male il braccio; **I ~ my arm** mi sono fatto male al braccio; **to ~ o.s.** farsi male.

husband ['hʌzbənd] *n* marito *m*.

hustle ['hʌsl] *n:* **~ and bustle** attività *f* febbrile.

hut [hʌt] *n* capanna *f*.

hyacinth ['haɪəsɪnθ] *n* giacinto *m*.

hydrofoil ['haɪdrəfɔɪl] *n* aliscafo *m*.

hygiene ['haɪdʒiːn] *n* igiene *f*.

hygienic [haɪ'dʒiːnɪk] *adj* igienico(-a).

hymn [hɪm] *n* inno *m*.

hypermarket ['haɪpə,mɑːkɪt] *n* ipermercato *m*.

hyphen ['haɪfn] *n* trattino *m*.

hypocrite ['hɪpəkrɪt] *n* ipocrita *mf*.

hypodermic needle [,haɪpə-'dɜːmɪk-] *n* ago *m* ipodermico.

hysterical [hɪs'terɪkl] *adj (person)* isterico(-a); *(inf: very funny)* esilarante.

I [aɪ] *pron* io; **I'm tall** sono alto.

ice [aɪs] *n* ghiaccio *m*; *(ice cream)* gelato *m*.

iceberg ['aɪsbɜːg] *n* iceberg *m inv*.

iceberg lettuce *n* lattuga *f* iceberg.

icebox ['aɪsbɒks] *n (Am: fridge)* frigorifero *m*.

ice-cold *adj* ghiacciato(-a).

ice cream *n* gelato *m*.

ice cube *n* cubetto *m* di ghiaccio.

ice hockey n hockey m su ghiaccio.

Iceland ['aɪslənd] n l'Islanda f.

ice lolly n (Br) ghiacciolo m.

ice rink n pista f di pattinaggio su ghiaccio.

ice skates npl pattini mpl da ghiaccio.

ice-skating n pattinaggio m su ghiaccio; **to go ~** andare a pattinare sul ghiaccio.

icicle ['aɪsɪkl] n ghiacciolo m.

icing ['aɪsɪŋ] n glassa f.

icing sugar n zucchero m a velo.

icy ['aɪsɪ] adj (covered with ice) ghiacciato(-a); (very cold) gelido(-a), gelato(-a).

I'd [aɪd] = I would, I had.

ID n (abbr of identification) documento m (d'identità).

ID card n carta f d'identità.

IDD code n prefisso m (teleselettivo) internazionale.

idea [aɪ'dɪə] n idea f; **I've no ~** non ne ho idea.

ideal [aɪ'dɪəl] adj ideale ♦ n ideale m.

ideally [aɪ'dɪəlɪ] adv idealmente; (suited) perfettamente.

identical [aɪ'dentɪkl] adj identico(-a).

identification [aɪ,dentɪfɪ'keɪʃn] n (document) documento m d'identità.

identify [aɪ'dentɪfaɪ] vt identificare.

identity [aɪ'dentətɪ] n identità f inv.

idiom ['ɪdɪəm] n (phrase) espressione f idiomatica.

idiot ['ɪdɪət] n idiota mf.

idle ['aɪdl] adj (lazy) ozioso(-a); (not working) inattivo(-a); (unemployed) disoccupato(-a) ♦ vi (engine) girare al minimo.

idol ['aɪdl] n (person) idolo m.

idyllic [ɪ'dɪlɪk] adj idilliaco(-a).

i.e. (abbr of id est) cioè.

if [ɪf] conj se; **~ I were you** se fossi in te; **~ not** (otherwise) se no.

ignition [ɪg'nɪʃn] n (AUT) accensione f.

ignorant ['ɪgnərənt] adj ignorante.

ignore [ɪg'nɔːr] vt ignorare.

ill [ɪl] adj (in health) malato(-a); (bad) cattivo(-a).

I'll [aɪl] = I will, I shall.

illegal [ɪ'liːgl] adj illegale.

illegible [ɪ'ledʒəbl] adj illeggibile.

illegitimate [ˌɪlɪ'dʒɪtɪmət] adj illegittimo(-a).

illiterate [ɪ'lɪtərət] adj analfabeta.

illness ['ɪlnɪs] n malattia f.

illuminate [ɪ'luːmɪneɪt] vt illuminare.

illusion [ɪ'luːʒn] n illusione f.

illustration [ˌɪlə'streɪʃn] n illustrazione f.

I'm [aɪm] = I am.

image ['ɪmɪdʒ] n immagine f.

imaginary [ɪ'mædʒɪnrɪ] adj immaginario(-a).

imagination [ɪ,mædʒɪ'neɪʃn] n immaginazione f.

imagine [ɪ'mædʒɪn] vt immaginare.

imitate ['ɪmɪteɪt] vt imitare.

imitation [ˌɪmɪ'teɪʃn] n imitazione f ♦ adj finto(-a).

immaculate [ɪˈmækjʊlət] adj (very clean) immacolato(-a), lindo(-a); (perfect) impeccabile.

immature [ˌɪməˈtjʊəˈ] adj immaturo(-a).

immediate [ɪˈmiːdjət] adj (without delay) immediato(-a).

immediately [ɪˈmiːdjətlɪ] adv (at once) immediatamente, subito ◆ conj (Br) non appena.

immense [ɪˈmɛns] adj immenso(-a).

immersion heater [ɪˈmɜːʃn] n scaldabagno m inv elettrico.

immigrant [ˈɪmɪgrənt] n immigrato m (-a f).

immigration [ˌɪmɪˈgreɪʃn] n (to country) immigrazione f; (section of airport, port) dogana f.

imminent [ˈɪmɪnənt] adj imminente.

immune [ɪˈmjuːn] adj: to be ~ to (MED) essere immune da.

immunity [ɪˈmjuːnətɪ] n (MED) immunità f.

immunize [ˈɪmjuːnaɪz] vt immunizzare.

impact [ˈɪmpækt] n impatto m.

impair [ɪmˈpeəˈ] vt danneggiare.

impatient [ɪmˈpeɪʃnt] adj impaziente; to be ~ to do sthg essere impaziente di fare qc.

imperative [ɪmˈperətɪv] n (GRAMM) imperativo m.

imperfect [ɪmˈpɜːfɪkt] n (GRAMM) imperfetto m.

impersonate [ɪmˈpɜːsəneɪt] vt (for amusement) imitare.

impertinent [ɪmˈpɜːtɪnənt] adj impertinente.

implement [n ˈɪmplɪmənt, vb ˈɪmplɪment] n attrezzo m; (for cooking) utensile m ◆ vt mettere in atto, realizzare.

implication [ˌɪmplɪˈkeɪʃn] n (consequence) implicazione f.

imply [ɪmˈplaɪ] vt (suggest) lasciar intendere, sottintendere.

impolite [ˌɪmpəˈlaɪt] adj scortese.

import [n ˈɪmpɔːt, vb ɪmˈpɔːt] n merce f d'importazione ◆ vt importare.

importance [ɪmˈpɔːtns] n importanza f.

important [ɪmˈpɔːtnt] adj importante.

impose [ɪmˈpəʊz] vt imporre ◆ vi approfittare; to ~ sthg on imporre qc a.

impossible [ɪmˈpɒsəbl] adj impossibile.

impractical [ɪmˈpræktɪkl] adj non pratico(-a).

impress [ɪmˈpres] vt fare una buona impressione a.

impression [ɪmˈpreʃn] n impressione f.

impressive [ɪmˈpresɪv] adj impressionante.

improbable [ɪmˈprɒbəbl] adj (event) improbabile; (story, excuse) inverosimile.

improper [ɪmˈprɒpəˈ] adj (incorrect, illegal) scorretto(-a); (rude) sconveniente.

improve [ɪmˈpruːv] vt & vi migliorare ❑ **improve on** vt fus migliorare.

improvement [ɪmˈpruːvmənt] n (in weather, health) miglioramento m; (to home) miglioria f.

improvise [ˈɪmprəvaɪz] vi improvvisare.

impulse ['ɪmpʌls] n impulso m; **on ~** d'impulso.

impulsive [ɪm'pʌlsɪv] adj impulsivo(-a).

in [ɪn] prep 1. (expressing place, position) in; **~ a box** in una scatola; **~ the bedroom** in camera da letto; **~ the street** per strada; **~ Scotland** in Scozia; **~ Sheffield** a Sheffield; **the United States** negli Stati Uniti; **~ here/there** qui/là dentro; **~ the sun** al sole; **~ the rain** sotto la pioggia; **~ the middle** al centro; **an article ~ the paper** un articolo sul giornale.
2. (participating in): **who's ~ the play?** chi recita nella commedia?
3. (expressing arrangement) in; **~ a row** in fila; **they come ~ packs of three** vengono venduti in pacchetti da tre.
4. (with time): **~ April** in aprile; **~ the afternoon** di OR nel pomeriggio; **at ten o'clock ~ the morning** alle dieci del mattino; **~ 1994** nel 1994; **it'll be ready ~ an hour** sarà pronto fra un'ora; **they're arriving ~ two weeks** arriveranno fra due settimane.
5. (expressing means): **to write ~ ink** scrivere a penna; **~ writing** per iscritto; **they were talking ~ English** parlavano in inglese.
6. (wearing): **the man ~ the blue jacket** l'uomo con la giacca blu; **dressed ~ white** vestito di bianco.
7. (expressing state): **a bad mood** di pessimo umore; **to be ~ a hurry** essere di fretta; **to cry ~ pain** gridare di dolore; **to be ~ pain** soffrire; **~ ruins** in rovina.
8. (with regard to): **a rise ~ prices** un aumento dei prezzi; **to be 50 metres ~ length** essere lungo 50 metri.
9. (with numbers, ratios): **one ~ ten** uno su dieci; **~ dozens** a dozzine.
10. (expressing age): **she's ~ her thirties** è sulla trentina.
11. (with colours): **it comes ~ green or blue** è disponibile in verde o in blu.
12. (with superlatives) di; **the best ~ the world** il migliore del mondo.
◆ adv 1. (inside) dentro; **you can go ~ now** ora può entrare; **come ~!** avanti!
(at home, work): **she's not ~** non c'è; **to stay ~** stare a casa.
3. (train, bus, plane): **the train's not ~ yet** il treno non è ancora arrivato.
4. (tide): **the tide is ~** c'è alta marea.
◆ adj (inf: fashionable) alla moda.

inability [ˌɪnə'bɪlətɪ] n: **~ (to do sth)** incapacità f (di fare qc).

inaccessible [ˌɪnək'sesəbl] adj inaccessibile.

inaccurate [ɪn'ækjurət] adj inesatto(-a), impreciso(-a).

inadequate [ɪn'ædɪkwət] adj inadeguato(-a).

inappropriate [ˌɪnə'prəuprɪət] adj non adatto(-a).

inauguration [ɪˌnɔːgju'reɪʃn] n inaugurazione f; (of president etc) insediamento m in carica.

incapable [ɪn'keɪpəbl] adj: **to be ~ of doing sth** essere incapace di fare qc.

incense ['ɪnsens] n incenso m.

incentive [ɪn'sentɪv] n incentivo m.

inch [ɪntʃ] n = 2,5 cm, pollice m.

incident ['ɪnsɪdənt] n episodio m, caso m.

incidentally [ˌɪnsɪˈdentəlɪ] adv a proposito.

incline [ˈɪnklaɪn] n pendio m.

inclined [ɪnˈklaɪnd] adj (sloping) inclinato(-a); **to be ~ to do sth** essere propenso(-a) a fare qc.

include [ɪnˈkluːd] vt includere, comprendere.

included [ɪnˈkluːdɪd] adj (in price) compreso(-a); **to be ~ in sth** essere compreso in qc.

including [ɪnˈkluːdɪŋ] prep compreso(-a).

inclusive [ɪnˈkluːsɪv] adj: **from the 8th to the 16th ~** dall'8 al 16 compreso; **~ of VAT** IVA compresa.

income [ˈɪŋkʌm] n reddito m.

income support n (Br) = sussidio m di indigenza.

income tax n imposta f sul reddito.

incoming [ˈɪnˌkʌmɪŋ] adj in arrivo.

incompetent [ɪnˈkɒmpɪtənt] adj incompetente.

incomplete [ˌɪnkəmˈpliːt] adj incompleto(-a).

inconsiderate [ˌɪnkənˈsɪdərət] adj sconsiderato(-a).

inconsistent [ˌɪnkənˈsɪstənt] adj incoerente.

incontinent [ɪnˈkɒntɪnənt] adj incontinente.

inconvenient [ˌɪnkənˈviːnjənt] adj scomodo(-a).

incorporate [ɪnˈkɔːpəreɪt] vt incorporare.

incorrect [ˌɪnkəˈrekt] adj (answer, number) sbagliato(-a); (information) inesatto(-a).

increase [n ˈɪnkriːs, vb ɪnˈkriːs] n aumento m ♦ vt & vi aumentare;

an ~ in sth un aumento di qc.

increasingly [ɪnˈkriːsɪŋlɪ] adv sempre più.

incredible [ɪnˈkredəbl] adj incredibile.

incredibly [ɪnˈkredəblɪ] adv (very) incredibilmente.

incur [ɪnˈkɜː] vt incorrere in.

indecisive [ˌɪndɪˈsaɪsɪv] adj indeciso(-a).

indeed [ɪnˈdiːd] adv (for emphasis) davvero; (certainly) certamente.

indefinite [ɪnˈdefɪnɪt] adj (time, number) indefinito(-a), indeterminato(-a); (answer, opinion) vago(-a).

indefinitely [ɪnˈdefɪnɪtlɪ] adv (closed, delayed) indefinitamente.

independence [ˌɪndɪˈpendəns] n indipendenza f.

independent [ˌɪndɪˈpendənt] adj indipendente.

independently [ˌɪndɪˈpendəntlɪ] adv indipendentemente.

independent school n (Br) scuola f privata.

index [ˈɪndeks] n (of book) indice m; (in library) catalogo m.

index finger n dito m indice.

India [ˈɪndjə] n l'India f.

Indian [ˈɪndjən] adj indiano(-a) ♦ n indiano m (-a f); **an ~ restaurant** un ristorante indiano.

Indian Ocean n: **the ~** l'oceano m Indiano.

indicate [ˈɪndɪkeɪt] vi (AUT) mettere la freccia ♦ vt indicare.

indicator [ˈɪndɪkeɪtə] n (AUT) indicatore m di direzione, freccia f.

indifferent [ɪnˈdɪfrənt] adj (uninterested) indifferente; (not very good) mediocre.

indigestion [ˌɪndɪˈdʒestʃn]

indigestione f.

indigo ['ɪndɪgəʊ] adj indaco (inv).

indirect [ˌɪndɪ'rekt] adj non diretto(-a).

individual [ˌɪndɪ'vɪdjʊəl] adj individuale ♦ n individuo m.

individually [ˌɪndɪ'vɪdjʊəlɪ] adv individualmente.

Indonesia [ˌɪndə'niːzjə] n l'Indonesia f.

indoor ['ɪndɔːʳ] adj (swimming pool) coperto(-a); (sports) praticato(-a) al coperto.

indoors [ˌɪn'dɔːz] adv dentro.

indulge [ɪn'dʌldʒ] vi: **to ~ in** sthg concedersi qc.

industrial [ɪn'dʌstrɪəl] adj industriale.

industrial estate n (Br) zona f industriale.

industry ['ɪndəstrɪ] n industria f.

inedible [ɪn'edɪbl] adj (unpleasant) immangiabile; (unsafe) non commestibile.

inefficient [ˌɪnɪ'fɪʃnt] adj inefficiente.

inequality [ˌɪnɪ'kwɒlətɪ] n disuguaglianza f.

inevitable [ɪn'evɪtəbl] adj inevitabile.

inevitably [ɪn'evɪtəblɪ] adv inevitabilmente.

inexpensive [ˌɪnɪk'spensɪv] adj poco costoso(-a).

infamous ['ɪnfəməs] adj infame.

infant ['ɪnfənt] n bambino m (-a f).

infant school n (Br) scuola f elementare (per bambini da 5 a 7 anni).

infatuated [ɪn'fætjʊeɪtɪd] adj: **to be ~ with** essere infatuato(-a) di.

infected [ɪn'fektɪd] adj infetto(-a).

infectious [ɪn'fekʃəs] adj contagioso(-a).

inferior [ɪn'fɪərɪəʳ] adj (person) inferiore; (goods, quality) scadente.

infinite ['ɪnfɪnət] adj infinito(-a).

infinitely ['ɪnfɪnətlɪ] adv infinitamente.

infinitive [ɪn'fɪnɪtɪv] n infinito m.

infinity [ɪn'fɪnətɪ] n (in space, MATH) infinito m.

infirmary [ɪn'fɜːmərɪ] n ospedale m.

inflamed [ɪn'fleɪmd] adj (MED) infiammato(-a).

inflammation [ˌɪnflə'meɪʃn] n (MED) infiammazione f.

inflatable [ɪn'fleɪtəbl] adj gonfiabile.

inflate [ɪn'fleɪt] vt gonfiare.

inflation [ɪn'fleɪʃn] n (of prices) inflazione f.

inflict [ɪn'flɪkt] vt infliggere.

in-flight adj durante il volo.

influence ['ɪnflʊəns] vt influenzare ♦ n: **~ (on)** influenza f (su).

inform [ɪn'fɔːm] vt informare.

informal [ɪn'fɔːml] adj (occasion, dress) informale.

information [ˌɪnfə'meɪʃn] n informazioni fpl; **a piece of ~** un'informazione.

information desk n banco m informazioni.

information office n ufficio m informazioni.

informative [ɪn'fɔːmətɪv] adj istruttivo(-a).

infuriating [ɪn'fjʊərɪeɪtɪŋ] adj molto irritante.

ingenious [ɪn'dʒiːnjəs] adj ingegnoso(-a).

ingredient [ɪnˈgriːdjənt] n ingrediente m.

inhabit [ɪnˈhæbɪt] vt abitare.

inhabitant [ɪnˈhæbɪtənt] n abitante mf.

inhale [ɪnˈheɪl] vi aspirare.

inhaler [ɪnˈheɪləʳ] n inalatore m.

inherit [ɪnˈherɪt] vt ereditare.

inhibition [ɪnhɪˈbɪʃn] n inibizione f.

initial [ɪˈnɪʃl] adj iniziale ♦ vt siglare ▫ **initials** npl iniziali fpl.

initially [ɪˈnɪʃəlɪ] adv inizialmente.

initiative [ɪˈnɪʃətɪv] n iniziativa f.

injection [ɪnˈdʒekʃn] n iniezione f.

injure [ˈɪndʒəʳ] vt (physically) ferire; to ~ o.s. ferirsi; to ~ one's arm ferirsi al braccio.

injured [ˈɪndʒəd] adj (physically) ferito(-a).

injury [ˈɪndʒərɪ] n (physical) ferita f.

ink [ɪŋk] n inchiostro m.

inland [adj ˈɪnlənd, adv ɪnˈlænd] adj interno(-a) ♦ adv nell'interno.

Inland Revenue n (Br) ≃ Fisco m.

inn [ɪn] n locanda f.

inner [ˈɪnəʳ] adj interno(-a), interiore.

inner city n quartieri vicino al centro di una città, generalmente sinonimo di problemi sociali.

inner tube n camera f d'aria.

innocence [ˈɪnəsəns] n innocenza f.

innocent [ˈɪnəsənt] adj innocente.

inoculate [ɪˈnɒkjuleɪt] vt: to ~ sb (against sthg) vaccinare qn (contro qc).

inoculation [ɪˌnɒkjuˈleɪʃn] n vaccinazione f.

input [ˈɪnput] (pt & pp input OR -ted) vt (COMPUT) immettere.

inquire [ɪnˈkwaɪəʳ] = **enquire**.

inquiry [ɪnˈkwaɪərɪ] = **enquiry**.

insane [ɪnˈseɪn] adj pazzo(-a), matto(-a).

insect [ˈɪnsekt] n insetto m.

insect repellent [-rəˈpelənt] n insettifugo m.

insensitive [ɪnˈsensətɪv] adj insensibile.

insert [ɪnˈsɜːt] vt inserire, introdurre.

inside [ɪnˈsaɪd] prep dentro, all'interno di ♦ adv dentro ♦ adj (internal) interno(-a) ♦ n: the ~ (interior) l'interno m; (AUT: in UK) la sinistra; (AUT: in Europe, US) la destra; ~ **out** (clothes) a rovescio.

inside lane n (AUT) (in UK) corsia f di sinistra; (in Europe, US) corsia f di destra.

inside leg n interno m gamba.

insight [ˈɪnsaɪt] n (glimpse) idea f.

insignificant [ˌɪnsɪgˈnɪfɪkənt] adj insignificante.

insinuate [ɪnˈsɪnjueɪt] vt insinuare.

insist [ɪnˈsɪst] vi insistere; to ~ o doing sthg insistere nel fare qc.

insole [ˈɪnsəʊl] n soletta f.

insolent [ˈɪnsələnt] adj insolente.

insomnia [ɪnˈsɒmnɪə] n insonnia f.

inspect [ɪnˈspekt] vt (object) ispezionare; (ticket, passport) controllare.

inspection [ɪn'spekʃn] n (of object) ispezione f; (of ticket, passport) controllo m.

inspector [ɪn'spektə'] n (on bus, train) controllore m; (in police force) ispettore m (-trice f).

inspiration [ˌɪnspə'reɪʃn] n ispirazione f.

instal [ɪn'stɔ:l] (Am) = install.

install [ɪn'stɔ:l] vt (Br) installare.

installment [ɪn'stɔ:lmənt] (Am) = instalment.

instalment [ɪn'stɔ:lmənt] n (payment) rata f; (episode) puntata f, parte f.

instance ['ɪnstəns] n (example, case) esempio m, caso m; for ~ per OR ad esempio.

instant ['ɪnstənt] adj (results, success) immediato(-a); (coffee) solubile ♦ n (moment) istante m.

instant coffee n caffè m inv solubile.

instead [ɪn'sted] adv invece; ~ of invece di.

instep ['ɪnstep] n collo m del piede.

instinct ['ɪnstɪŋkt] n istinto m.

institute ['ɪnstɪtjuːt] n istituto m.

institution [ˌɪnstɪ'tjuːʃn] n istituzione f.

instructions [ɪn'strʌkʃnz] npl istruzioni fpl.

instructor [ɪn'strʌktə'] n istruttore m (-trice f).

instrument ['ɪnstrumənt] n strumento m.

insufficient [ˌɪnsə'fɪʃnt] adj insufficiente.

insulating tape ['ɪnsjʊleɪtɪŋ-] n nastro m isolante.

insulation [ˌɪnsjʊ'leɪʃn] n (material) isolante m.

insulin ['ɪnsjʊlɪn] n insulina f.

insult [n 'ɪnsʌlt, vb ɪn'sʌlt] n insulto m ♦ vt insultare.

insurance [ɪn'ʃʊərəns] n assicurazione f.

insurance certificate n certificato m di assicurazione.

insurance company n compagnia f di assicurazione.

insurance policy n polizza f di assicurazione.

insure [ɪn'ʃʊə'] vt assicurare.

insured [ɪn'ʃʊəd] adj: to be ~ essere assicurato(-a).

intact [ɪn'tækt] adj intatto(-a).

intellectual [ˌɪntə'lektjʊəl] adj intellettuale ♦ n intellettuale mf.

intelligence [ɪn'telɪdʒəns] n (cleverness) intelligenza f.

intelligent [ɪn'telɪdʒənt] adj intelligente.

intend [ɪn'tend] vt (mean): to ~ to do sthg avere intenzione di fare qc; you weren't ~ed to know non dovevi saperlo.

intense [ɪn'tens] adj intenso(-a).

intensity [ɪn'tensəti] n intensità f.

intensive [ɪn'tensɪv] adj intensivo(-a).

intensive care n terapia f intensiva.

intent [ɪn'tent] adj: to be ~ on doing sthg essere deciso(-a) a fare qc.

intention [ɪn'tenʃn] n intenzione f.

intentional [ɪn'tenʃənl] adj intenzionale.

intentionally [ɪn'tenʃənəlɪ] adv intenzionalmente, apposta.

interchange [ˈɪntətʃeɪndʒ] n (on motorway) svincolo m.

Intercity® [ˌɪntəˈsɪtɪ] n (Br) intercity m inv.

intercom [ˈɪntəkɒm] n interfono m.

interest [ˈɪntrəst] n interesse m ◆ vt interessare; **to take an ~ in sthg** interessarsi di OR a qc.

interested [ˈɪntrəstɪd] adj interessato(-a); **to be ~ in sthg** interessarsi di qc.

interesting [ˈɪntrəstɪŋ] adj interessante.

interest rate n tasso m d'interesse.

interfere [ˌɪntəˈfɪəʳ] vi (meddle) immischiarsi; **to ~ with sthg** (damage) interferire con qc.

interference [ˌɪntəˈfɪərəns] n (on TV, radio) interferenza f.

interior [ɪnˈtɪərɪəʳ] adj interno(-a) ◆ n interno m.

intermediate [ˌɪntəˈmiːdjət] adj intermedio(-a).

intermission [ˌɪntəˈmɪʃn] n (at cinema, theatre) intervallo m.

internal [ɪnˈtɜːnl] adj interno(-a).

internal flight n volo m interno.

international [ˌɪntəˈnæʃənl] adj internazionale.

international flight n volo m internazionale.

interpret [ɪnˈtɜːprɪt] vi fare da interprete.

interpreter [ɪnˈtɜːprɪtəʳ] n interprete mf.

interrogate [ɪnˈterəgeɪt] vt interrogare.

interrupt [ˌɪntəˈrʌpt] vt interrompere.

intersection [ˌɪntəˈsekʃn] n (of roads) incrocio m.

interval [ˈɪntəvl] n intervallo m.

intervene [ˌɪntəˈviːn] vi (person, event) intervenire.

interview [ˈɪntəvjuː] n (on TV, in magazine) intervista f; (for job) colloquio m ◆ vt (on TV, in magazine) intervistare; (for job) fare un colloquio a.

interviewer [ˈɪntəvjuːəʳ] n (on TV, in magazine) intervistatore m (-trice f).

intestine [ɪnˈtestɪn] n intestino m.

intimate [ˈɪntɪmət] adj intimo(-a).

intimidate [ɪnˈtɪmɪdeɪt] vt intimidire.

into [ˈɪntʊ] prep (inside) in, dentro; (against) contro, in; (concerning) su; **4 ~ 20 goes 5 (times)** il 4 nel 20 ci sta 5 volte; **to translate ~ Italian** tradurre in italiano; **to change ~ sthg** trasformarsi in qc; **to be ~ sthg** (inf: like) essere appassionato di qc.

intolerable [ɪnˈtɒlrəbl] adj intollerabile.

intransitive [ɪnˈtrænzətɪv] adj intransitivo(-a).

intricate [ˈɪntrɪkət] adj intricato(-a).

intriguing [ɪnˈtriːgɪn] adj affascinante.

introduce [ˌɪntrəˈdjuːs] vt presentare; **I'd like to ~ you to Fred** ti presento Fred.

introduction [ˌɪntrəˈdʌkʃn] n (to book, programme) introduzione (to person) presentazione f.

introverted [ˈɪntrəˌvɜːtɪd] adj introverso(-a).

intruder [ɪn'truːdəʳ] *n* intruso *m* (-a *f*).

intuition [ˌɪntjuː'ɪʃn] *n* (feeling) intuizione *f*; (faculty) intuito *m*.

invade [ɪn'veɪd] *vt* invadere.

invalid [adj ɪn'vælɪd, *n* 'ɪnvəlɪd] *adj* (ticket, cheque) non valido(-a) ♦ *n* invalido *m* (-a *f*).

invaluable [ɪn'væljʊəbl] *adj* inestimabile.

invariably [ɪn'veərɪəblɪ] *adv* sempre, invariabilmente.

invasion [ɪn'veɪʒn] *n* invasione *f*.

invent [ɪn'vent] *vt* inventare.

invention [ɪn'venʃn] *n* invenzione *f*.

inventory ['ɪnventrɪ] *n* inventario *m*.

inverted commas [ɪn'vɜːtɪd-] *npl* virgolette *fpl*.

invest [ɪn'vest] *vt* investire ♦ *vi*: **to ~ in sthg** investire in qc.

investigate [ɪn'vestɪgeɪt] *vt* indagare.

investigation [ɪnˌvestɪ'geɪʃn] *n* indagine *f*.

investment [ɪn'vestmənt] *n* investimento *m*.

invisible [ɪn'vɪzɪbl] *adj* invisibile.

invitation [ˌɪnvɪ'teɪʃn] *n* invito *m*.

invite [ɪn'vaɪt] *vt* invitare; **to ~ sb to do sthg** (ask) invitare qn a fare qc; **to ~ sb round** invitare qn.

invoice ['ɪnvɔɪs] *n* fattura *f*.

involve [ɪn'vɒlv] *vt* (entail) richiedere, comportare; **what does it ~?** che cosa comporta?; **to be ~d in sthg** essere coinvolto in qc.

involved [ɪn'vɒlvd] *adj* (entailed) richiesto(-a), necessario(-a).

nwards ['ɪnwədz] *adv* verso

l'interno.

IOU *n* pagherò *m inv*.

IQ *n* Q.I. *m*.

Iran [ɪ'rɑːn] *n* l'Iran *m*.

Iraq [ɪ'rɑːk] *n* l'Iraq *m*.

Ireland ['aɪələnd] *n* l'Irlanda *f*.

iris ['aɪərɪs] (*pl* **-es**) *n* (flower) giaggiolo *m*, iris *f inv*.

Irish ['aɪrɪʃ] *adj* irlandese ♦ *n* (language) irlandese *m* ♦ *npl*: **the ~** gli irlandesi.

Irish coffee *n* Irish coffee *m inv* (caffè con whisky e panna).

Irishman ['aɪrɪʃmən] (*pl* **-men** [-mən]) *n* irlandese *m*.

Irish stew *n* spezzatino di agnello con patate e cipolle.

Irishwoman ['aɪrɪʃˌwʊmən] (*pl* **-women** [-ˌwɪmɪn]) *n* irlandese *f*.

iron ['aɪən] *n* (metal) ferro *m*; (for clothes) ferro da stiro; (golf club) mazza *f* da golf ♦ *vt* stirare.

ironic [aɪ'rɒnɪk] *adj* ironico(-a).

ironing board ['aɪənɪŋ-] *n* asse *f* da stiro.

ironmonger's ['aɪənˌmʌŋgəz] *n* (Br) ferramenta *f*.

irrelevant [ɪ'reləvənt] *adj* non pertinente, irrilevante.

irresistible [ˌɪrɪ'zɪstəbl] *adj* irresistibile.

irrespective [ˌɪrɪ'spektɪv]: **irrespective of** *prep* a prescindere da.

irresponsible [ˌɪrɪ'spɒnsəbl] *adj* irresponsabile.

irrigation [ˌɪrɪ'geɪʃn] *n* irrigazione *f*.

irritable ['ɪrɪtəbl] *adj* irritabile.

irritate ['ɪrɪteɪt] *vt* irritare.

irritating ['ɪrɪteɪtɪŋ] *adj* irritante.

IRS *n* (Am) = Fisco *m*.

is [ɪz] → be.

Islam ['ɪzlɑːm] n (religion) islamismo m.

island ['aɪlənd] n isola f.

isle [aɪl] n isola f.

isolated ['aɪsəleɪtɪd] adj isolato(-a).

Israel ['ɪzreɪəl] n Israele m.

issue ['ɪʃuː] n (problem, subject) questione f, problema m; (of newspaper, magazine) numero m ♦ vt (statement, passport, document) rilasciare; (stamps, bank notes) emettere.

it [ɪt] pron 1. (referring to specific thing: subject, after prep) esso(-a); (direct object) lo (la); (indirect object) gli (le); ~'s big è grande; she hit ~ l'ha colpito; give ~ to me dammelo; tell me about ~ parlamene; we went to ~ ci siamo andati. 2. (nonspecific): ~'s nice here si sta bene qui; ~'s me sono io; who is ~? chi è? 3. (used impersonally): ~'s hot fa caldo; ~'s six o'clock sono le sei; ~'s Sunday è domenica.

Italian [ɪ'tæljən] adj italiano(-a) ♦ n (person) italiano m (-a f); (language) italiano m; an ~ restaurant un ristorante italiano.

Italian Riviera n: the ~ la Riviera Ligure.

Italy ['ɪtəlɪ] n l'Italia f.

itch [ɪtʃ] vi (arm, leg) prudere; (person) avere prurito.

item ['aɪtəm] n (object) articolo m; (on agenda) punto m; news ~ notizia f.

itemized bill ['aɪtəmaɪzd-] n bolletta f con lettura dettagliata.

its [ɪts] adj il suo (la sua), i suoi (le sue) (pl).

it's [ɪts] = it is, it has.

itself [ɪt'self] pron (reflexive) si; (after prep), se stesso(-a) sé; the house ~ is fine la casa in sé va bene.

I've [aɪv] = I have.

ivory ['aɪvərɪ] n avorio m.

ivy ['aɪvɪ] n edera f.

J

jab [dʒæb] n (Br: inf: injection) puntura f.

jack [dʒæk] n (for car) cric m inv; (playing card) fante m.

jacket ['dʒækɪt] n (garment) giacca f; (of book) sopraccoperta f; (Am: of record) copertina f; (of potato) buccia f.

jacket potato n patata cotta al forno con la buccia.

jack-knife vi piegarsi su se stesso (camion).

Jacuzzi® [dʒə'kuːzɪ] n vasca f con idromassaggio.

jade [dʒeɪd] n giada f.

jail [dʒeɪl] n prigione f.

jam [dʒæm] n (food) marmellata f; (of traffic) ingorgo m; (inf: difficult situation) pasticcio m ♦ vt (pack tightly) stipare ♦ vi (get stuck) bloccarsi; the roads are jammed le strade sono intasate.

jam-packed ['-pækt] adj (inf) stipato(-a).

Jan. [dʒæn] (abbr of January) gen.

janitor ['dʒænɪtə'] n (Am & Scot) bidello m (-a f).

January ['dʒænjʊərɪ] n gennaio m, → September.

Japan [dʒə'pæn] n il Giappone.

Japanese [ˌdʒæpə'niːz] adj giapponese ♦ n (language) giapponese m ♦ npl: the ~ i giapponesi.

jar [dʒɑː'] n barattolo m, vasetto m.

javelin ['dʒævlɪn] n giavellotto m.

jaw [dʒɔː] n mascella f.

jazz [dʒæz] n jazz m.

jealous ['dʒeləs] adj geloso(-a).

jeans [dʒiːnz] npl jeans mpl.

Jeep® [dʒiːp] n jeep f inv.

Jello® ['dʒeləʊ] n (Am) gelatina f.

jelly ['dʒelɪ] n (dessert) gelatina f; (Am: jam) marmellata f.

jellyfish ['dʒelɪfɪʃ] (pl inv) n medusa f.

jeopardize ['dʒepədaɪz] vt mettere a repentaglio.

jerk [dʒɜːk] n (movement) strattone m, scossa f; (inf: idiot) imbecille mf.

jersey ['dʒɜːzɪ] (pl -s) n (garment) maglia f.

jet [dʒet] n (aircraft) aviogetto m; (of liquid, gas) getto m; (outlet) ugello m.

jetfoil ['dʒetfɔɪl] n aliscafo m.

jet lag n jetleg m.

jet-ski n acqua-scooter m inv.

jetty ['dʒetɪ] n molo m.

Jew [dʒuː] n ebreo m (-a f).

jewel ['dʒuːəl] n gioiello m ❑ jewels npl (jewellery) gioielli mpl.

jeweler's ['dʒuːələz] (Am) = jeweller's.

jeweller's ['dʒuːələz] n (Br)

gioielleria f.

jewellery ['dʒuːəlrɪ] n (Br) gioielli mpl.

jewelry ['dʒuːəlrɪ] (Am) = jewellery.

Jewish ['dʒuːɪʃ] adj ebreo(-a).

jigsaw (puzzle) ['dʒɪgsɔː-] n puzzle m inv.

jingle ['dʒɪŋgl] n (of advert) motivo m musicale di pubblicità.

job [dʒɒb] n lavoro m; to lose one's ~ perdere il lavoro.

job centre n (Br) ufficio m di collocamento.

jockey ['dʒɒkɪ] (pl -s) n fantino m (-a f).

jog [dʒɒg] vt (bump) urtare lievemente ♦ vi fare footing ♦ n: to go for a ~ andare a fare del footing.

jogging ['dʒɒgɪŋ] n footing m; to go ~ fare del footing.

join [dʒɔɪn] vt (club, organization) iscriversi a; (fasten together) unire; (other people, celebrations) unirsi a; (road, river) congiungersi con; (connect) collegare; to ~ a queue mettersi in fila ❑ join in vt fus prendere parte a ♦ vi partecipare.

joint [dʒɔɪnt] adj comune ♦ n (of body) articolazione f; (Br: of meat) taglio m di carne per arrosto; (in structure) giuntura f.

joke [dʒəʊk] n scherzo m; (story) barzelletta f ♦ vi scherzare.

joker ['dʒəʊkə'] n (playing card) jolly m inv, matta f.

jolly ['dʒɒlɪ] adj (cheerful) allegro(-a) ♦ adv (Br: inf: very) molto.

jolt [dʒəʊlt] n scossa f, sobbalzo m.

jot [dʒɒt] : jot down vt sep annotare in fretta.

journal ['dʒɜːnl] n (professional magazine) rivista f; (diary) diario m.

journalist ['dʒɜːnəlɪst] n giornalista mf.

journey ['dʒɜːnɪ] (pl -s) n viaggio m.

joy [dʒɔɪ] n gioia f.

joypad ['dʒɔɪpæd] n (of video game) comandi mpl.

joyrider ['dʒɔɪraɪdə'] n chi ruba un'auto per farci un giro e poi l'abbandona.

joystick ['dʒɔɪstɪk] n (of video game) joystick m inv.

judge [dʒʌdʒ] n giudice mf ♦ vt giudicare.

judg(e)ment ['dʒʌdʒmənt] n giudizio m.

judo ['dʒuːdəʊ] n judo m.

jug [dʒʌg] n brocca f, caraffa f.

juggernaut ['dʒʌgənɔːt] n (Br) grosso autotreno m, bestione m.

juggle ['dʒʌgl] vi fare giochi di destrezza (con palle, birilli, ecc.).

juice [dʒuːs] n succo m; (from meat) sugo m.

juicy ['dʒuːsɪ] adj (food) succoso(-a).

jukebox ['dʒuːkbɒks] n juke-box m inv.

Jul. (abbr of July) lug.

July [dʒuː'laɪ] n luglio m, → September.

jumble sale ['dʒʌmbl-] n (Br) vendita f di cose usate (a scopo di beneficenza).

ℹ **JUMBLE SALE**

L e "jumble sales" sono delle vendite dell'usato che si tengono

solitamente in sale parrocchiali o municipali. Libri, vestiti e casalinghi usati vengono venduti a prezzi bassissimi per raccogliere soldi, di solito per beneficenza.

jumbo ['dʒʌmbəʊ] adj (inf: big) gigante.

jumbo jet n jumbo-jet m inv.

jump [dʒʌmp] n salto m, balzo m ♦ vi saltare, balzare; (with fright) sussultare; (increase) salire ♦ vt (Am): to ~ the train/bus viaggiare sul treno/sull'autobus senza pagare; to ~ the queue (Br) saltare la fila.

jumper ['dʒʌmpə'] n (Br: pullover) maglione m, pullover m inv; (Am: dress) scamiciato m.

jump leads npl cavi mpl per batteria.

Jun. (abbr of June) giu.

junction ['dʒʌŋkʃn] n (of roads) incrocio m; (of railway lines) nodo m ferroviario; (on motorways) uscita f.

June [dʒuːn] n giugno m, → September.

jungle ['dʒʌŋgl] n giungla f.

junior ['dʒuːnjə'] adj (of lower rank) di grado inferiore, subalterno(-a); (Am: after name) junior ♦ n (younger person): to be sb's ~ essere più giovane di qn.

junior school n (Br) scuola f elementare (per bambini da 7 a 11 anni).

junk [dʒʌŋk] n (inf: unwanted things) cianfrusaglie fpl.

junk food n (inf) porcherie fpl.

junkie ['dʒʌŋkɪ] n (inf) drogato m (-a f).

junk shop n negozio m di rigattiere.

jury ['dʒʊərɪ] n giuria f.

just [dʒʌst] adv (recently, slightly) appena; (in the next moment) giusto; (exactly) proprio; (only) solo ♦ adj giusto(-a); **to be ~ about to do sth** stare per fare qc; **to have ~ done sth** avere appena fatto qc; **~ about** (almost) praticamente, quasi; (only) ~ per un pelo; **I've (only) ~ arrived** sono arrivato (appena) adesso; **I'm ~ coming** vengo (subito); **~ a minute!** (solo) un minuto!

justice ['dʒʌstɪs] n giustizia f.

justify ['dʒʌstɪfaɪ] vt giustificare.

jut [dʒʌt] : **jut out** vi sporgersi.

juvenile ['dʒuːvənaɪl] adj (young) giovanile; (childish) puerile; (crime) minorile.

K

kangaroo [ˌkæŋgə'ruː] n canguro m.

karate [kə'rɑːtɪ] n karate m.

kebab [kə'bæb] n: **(shish) ~** spiedino m di carne; **(doner) ~** pane azzimo imbottito con carne di agnello, insalata e salsa piccante.

keel [kiːl] n chiglia f.

keen [kiːn] adj (enthusiastic) entusiasta; (eyesight, hearing) acuto(-a); **to be ~ on sth** essere appassionato(-a) di qc; **to be ~ to do sth** avere voglia di fare qc.

keep [kiːp] (pt & pp **kept**) vt tenere; (promise) mantenere; (appointment) rispettare; (delay) trattenere

♦ vi (food) mantenersi; (remain) restare; **to ~ (on) doing sth** (continuously) continuare a fare qc; (repeatedly) fare qc di continuo; **to ~ sb from doing sth** impedire a qn di fare qc; **'~ back!'** state indietro!; **'~ in lane!'** 'restare in corsia'; **'~ left'** 'tenere la sinistra'; **'~ off the grass!'** 'vietato calpestare l'erba'; **'~ out!'** 'vietato l'accesso'; **'~ your distance!'** 'mantenere la distanza (di sicurezza)'; **to ~ clear (of)** stare lontano (da) ♦ keep up vt sep mantenere, continuare ♦ vi: **to ~ up (with)** tenersi al passo (con).

keep-fit n (Br) ginnastica f.

kennel ['kenl] n canile m.

kept [kept] pt & pp → **keep.**

kerb [kɜːb] n (Br) orlo m del marciapiede.

kerosene ['kerəsiːn] n (Am) cherosene m.

ketchup ['ketʃəp] n ketchup m.

kettle ['ketl] n bollitore m; **to put the ~ on** mettere l'acqua a bollire.

key [kiː] n chiave f; (of piano, typewriter) tasto m; (of map) legenda f ♦ adj chiave (inv).

keyboard ['kiːbɔːd] n tastiera f.

keyhole ['kiːhəʊl] n buco m della serratura.

keypad ['kiːpæd] n tastiera f.

key ring n portachiavi m inv.

kg (abbr of kilogram) kg.

kick [kɪk] n (of foot) calcio m ♦ vt dare calci a, prendere a calci.

kickoff ['kɪkɒf] n calcio m d'inizio.

kid [kɪd] n (inf) (child) bimbo m (-a f), bambino m (-a f); (young person) ragazzo m (-a f) ♦ vi (joke) scherzare.

kidnap ['kɪdnæp] vt rapire.

kidnaper ['kɪdnæpər] (Am) = **kidnapper**.

kidnapper ['kɪdnæpər] n (Br) rapitore m (-trice f).

kidney ['kɪdnɪ] (pl -s) n (organ) rene m; (food) rognone m.

kidney bean n fagiolo m comune.

kill [kɪl] vt (person) uccidere, ammazzare; (time) ammazzare; **my feet are ~ing me!** i piedi mi fanno un male!

killer ['kɪlər] n assassino m (-a f).

kilo ['kiːləʊ] (pl -s) n chilo m.

kilogram n ['kɪləgræm] n chilogrammo m.

kilometre ['kɪlə,miːtər] n chilometro m.

kilt [kɪlt] n kilt m inv.

kind [kaɪnd] adj gentile, buono(-a) ♦ n (sort, type) genere m, tipo m; **~ of** (Am: inf) un po'.

kindergarten ['kɪndə,gɑːtn] n asilo m infantile.

kindly ['kaɪndlɪ] adv: **would you ~ ...?** potrebbe ..., per favore?

kindness ['kaɪndnɪs] n gentilezza f, cortesia f.

king [kɪŋ] n re m inv.

kingfisher ['kɪŋ,fɪʃər] n martin m inv pescatore.

king prawn n gambero m.

king-size bed n letto largo 160 cm.

kiosk ['kiːɒsk] n (for newspapers etc) chiosco m, edicola f; (Br: phone box) cabina f (telefonica).

kipper ['kɪpər] n aringa f affumicata.

kiss [kɪs] n bacio m ♦ vt baciare.

kiss of life n respirazione f bocca a bocca.

kit [kɪt] n (set) attrezzatura f; (clothes) completo m; (for assembly) scatola f di montaggio.

kitchen ['kɪtʃɪn] n cucina f.

kitchen unit n mobile m componibile (da cucina).

kite [kaɪt] n (toy) aquilone m.

kitten ['kɪtn] n gattino m (-a f).

kitty ['kɪtɪ] n (of money) cassa f comune.

kiwi fruit ['kiːwiː] n kiwi m inv.

Kleenex® ['kliːneks] n fazzoletto m di carta.

km (abbr of kilometre) km.

km/h (abbr of kilometres per hour) km/h.

knack [næk] n: **to have the ~ of doing sthg** avere l'abilità di fare qc.

knackered ['nækəd] adj (Br: inf) stanco morto (stanca morta).

knapsack ['næpsæk] n zaino m.

knee [niː] n ginocchio m.

kneecap ['niːkæp] n rotula f.

kneel [niːl] (pt & pp **knelt** [nelt]) vi inginocchiarsi.

knew [njuː] pt → **know**.

knickers ['nɪkəz] npl (Br: underwear) mutandine fpl.

knife [naɪf] (pl **knives**) n coltello m.

knight [naɪt] n (in history) cavaliere m; (in chess) cavallo m.

knit [nɪt] vt fare a maglia.

knitted ['nɪtɪd] adj fatto(-a) a maglia.

knitting ['nɪtɪŋ] n lavoro m a maglia.

knitting needle n ferro m (da calza).

knitwear ['nɪtweə^r] *n* maglieria *f*.

knives [naɪvz] *pl* → knife.

knob [nɒb] *n* (on door etc) pomello *m*; (on machine) manopola *f*.

knock [nɒk] *n* (at door) colpo *m* ♦ *vt* (head, elbow) battere; (chair, table) battere contro ♦ *vi* (at door etc) bussare □ **knock down** *vt sep* (pedestrian) investire; (building) demolire; (price) ribassare; **knock out** *vt sep* (make unconscious) tramortire; (of competition) eliminare; **knock over** *vt sep* (glass, vase) rovesciare; (pedestrian) investire.

knocker ['nɒkə^r] *n* (on door) battente *m*.

knot [nɒt] *n* nodo *m*.

know [nəʊ] (*pt* knew, *pp* known) *vt* sapere; (person, place) conoscere; **to get to ~ sb** imparare a conoscere qc; **to ~ about sthg** (understand) saperne di qc; (have heard) sapere di qc; **to ~ how to do sthg** saper fare qc; **to ~ of** sapere di; **to be ~n as** essere noto come; **to let sb ~ sthg** far sapere qc a qn; **you ~** (for emphasis) sai.

knowledge ['nɒlɪdʒ] *n* conoscenza *f*; **to my ~** che io sappia.

known [nəʊn] *pp* → know.

knuckle ['nʌkl] *n* (of hand) nocca *f*; (of pork) garretto *m*.

Koran [kɒ'rɑːn] *n*: **the ~** il Corano.

l (abbr of litre) l.

L (abbr of learner) = P.

lab [læb] *n* (inf) laboratorio *m*.

label ['leɪbl] *n* cartellino *m*, etichetta *f*.

labor ['leɪbər] (Am) = labour.

laboratory [Br lə'bɒrətrɪ, Am 'læbrə,tɔːrɪ] *n* laboratorio *m*.

labour ['leɪbə^r] *n* (work) lavoro *m*; **to be in ~** (MED) avere le doglie.

labourer ['leɪbərə^r] *n* manovale *m*.

Labour Party *n* (Br) partito *m* laburista.

labour-saving *adj* che fa risparmiare fatica.

lace [leɪs] *n* (material) merletto *m*; (for shoe) laccio *m*.

lace-ups *npl* scarpe *fpl* con i lacci.

lack·[læk] *n* carenza *f* ♦ *vt* non avere ♦ *vi*: **to be ~ing** mancare.

lacquer ['lækə^r] *n* (for hair) lacca *f*; (paint) vernice *f*.

lad [læd] *n* (inf) ragazzo *m*.

ladder ['lædə^r] *n* (for climbing) scala *f*; (Br: in tights) smagliatura *f*.

ladies ['leɪdɪz] *n* (Br: toilet) toilette *f inv* per signore.

ladies room *n* (Am) = ladies.

ladieswear ['leɪdɪz,weə^r] *n* abbigliamento *m* da donna.

ladle ['leɪdl] *n* mestolo *m*.

lady ['leɪdɪ] *n* signora *f*.

ladybird ['leɪdɪbɜːd] *n* coccinella *f*.

ladybug n (Am) = **ladybird**.

lag [læg] vi (trade) ristagnare; **to ~ behind** (move more slowly) restare indietro.

lager ['lɑ:gə'] n birra f (chiara).

lagoon [lə'gu:n] n laguna f.

laid [leɪd] pt & pp → **lay**.

lain [leɪn] pp → **lie**.

lake [leɪk] n lago m.

Lake District n: **the ~** la regione dei laghi (nel nordovest dell'Inghilterra).

lamb [læm] n agnello m.

lamb chop n braciola f OR costoletta f d'agnello.

lame [leɪm] adj zoppo(-a).

lamp [læmp] n lampada f; (bicycle lamp) fanale m; (in street) lampione m.

lamppost ['læmppəʊst] n lampione m.

lampshade ['læmpʃeɪd] n paralume m.

land [lænd] n terra f ◆ vi (plane) atterrare; (passengers) sbarcare; (fall) cadere.

landing ['lændɪŋ] n (of plane) atterraggio m; (on stairs) pianerottolo m.

landlady ['lænd,leɪdɪ] n (of house) padrona f di casa; (of pub) proprietaria f.

landlord ['lændlɔ:d] n (of house) padrone m di casa; (of pub) proprietario m.

landmark ['lændmɑ:k] n punto m di riferimento.

landscape ['lændskeɪp] n paesaggio m.

landslide ['lændslaɪd] n (of earth, rocks) frana f.

lane [leɪn] n (narrow road) stradina f; (on road, motorway) corsia f; **'get in ~'** 'disporsi su più file'.

language ['læŋgwɪdʒ] n (of a people, country) lingua f; (system, words) linguaggio m.

lap [læp] n (of person) grembo m; (of race) giro m.

lapel [lə'pel] n risvolto m.

lapse [læps] vi (passport, membership) scadere.

lard [lɑ:d] n strutto m.

larder ['lɑ:də'] n dispensa f.

large [lɑ:dʒ] adj grande; (person, dog, sum) grosso(-a).

largely ['lɑ:dʒlɪ] adv in gran parte.

large-scale adj su vasta scala.

lark [lɑ:k] n allodola f.

laryngitis [,lærɪn'dʒaɪtɪs] n laringite f.

lasagne [lə'zænjə] n lasagne fpl.

laser ['leɪzə'] n laser m inv.

lass [læs] n (inf) ragazza f.

last [lɑ:st] adj ultimo(-a); (week, year, month) scorso(-a) ◆ adv (most recently) l'ultima volta; (after everything else) per ultimo ◆ vi (continue) durare ◆ pron: **the ~ to come** l'ultimo ad arrivare; **the ~ but one** il penultimo (la penultima); **the day before ~** l'altro ieri; **~ year** l'anno scorso; **the ~ year** l'ultimo anno; **at ~** finalmente; **to arrive ~** arrivare (per) ultimo; **it won't ~ til tomorrow** (food) non va fino a domani.

lastly ['lɑ:stlɪ] adv infine.

last-minute adj dell'ultimo momento.

latch [lætʃ] n serratura f a scatti **the door is on the ~** la porta non chiusa a chiave.

late [leɪt] *adj (not on time)* in ritardo; *(after usual time)* tardi *(inv)*; *(dead)* defunto(-a); *(morning, afternoon)* tardo(-a) ♦ *adv (not on time)* in ritardo; *(after usual time)* tardi; **in ~** June, **~ in** June verso la fine di giugno; **the train is running two hours ~** il treno viaggia con due ore di ritardo.

lately ['leɪtlɪ] *adv* ultimamente.

late-night *adj* aperto(-a) fino a tardi; **~ opening** apertura prolungata *(di negozi)*.

later ['leɪtə*r*] *adj (train)* successivo(-a) ♦ *adv*: **~ (on)** più tardi; **at a ~ date** in futuro.

latest ['leɪtɪst] *adj*: **the ~ fashion** l'ultima moda; **the ~ ultimo(-a); at the ~** al più tardi.

lather ['lɑ:ðə*r*] *n* schiuma *f*.

Latin ['lætɪn] *n* latino *m*.

Latin America *n* l'America *f* Latina.

Latin American *adj* latinoamericano(-a) ♦ *n* latinoamericano *m* (-a *f*).

latitude ['lætɪtju:d] *n (distance from Equator)* latitudine *f*.

latter ['lætə*r*] *n*: **the ~** quest'ultimo(-a).

laugh [lɑ:f] *n* risata *f* ♦ *vi* ridere; **to have a ~** *(Br: inf)* farsi due risate ❑ **laugh at** *vt fus (mock)* ridere di.

laughter ['lɑ:ftə*r*] *n* riso *m*.

launch [lɔ:ntʃ] *vt (boat)* varare; *(new product)* lanciare.

laund(e)rette [lɔ:n'dret] *n* lavanderia *f* (automatica).

laundry ['lɔ:ndrɪ] *n (washing)* bucato *m*; *(place)* lavanderia *f*.

lavatory ['lævətrɪ] *n* gabinetto *m*.

lavender ['lævəndə*r*] *n* lavanda *f*.

lavish ['lævɪʃ] *adj (meal, decoration)* sontuoso(-a).

law [lɔ:] *n* legge *f*; **to be against the ~** essere contro la legge.

lawn [lɔ:n] *n* prato *m*.

lawnmower ['lɔ:n,məʊə*r*] *n* tagliaerba *m inv*.

lawyer ['lɔ:jə*r*] *n (in court)* avvocato *m*; *(solicitor)* notaio *m*.

laxative ['læksətɪv] *n* lassativo *m*.

lay [leɪ] *(pt & pp* laid*)* *pt* → **lie** ♦ *vt (place)* poggiare; *(egg)* fare; **to ~ the table** apparecchiare la tavola ❑ **lay off** *vt sep (worker)* licenziare; **lay on** *vt sep (food, transport)* fornire; *(entertainment)* organizzare; **lay out** *vt sep (display)* disporre.

lay-by *(pl* lay-bys*)* *n* piazzola *f* di sosta.

layer ['leɪə*r*] *n* strato *m*.

layman ['leɪmən] *(pl* -men [-mən]*)* *n* profano *m* (-a *f*).

layout ['leɪaʊt] *n (of building)* struttura *f*; *(of streets)* tracciato *m*.

lazy ['leɪzɪ] *adj* pigro(-a).

lb *abbr* = **pound**.

lead¹ [li:d] *(pt & pp* led*)* *vt (take)* condurre; *(team, party, march)* guidare; *(procession)* aprire ♦ *vi (be winning)* condurre ♦ *n (for dog)* guinzaglio *m*; *(cable)* cavo *m*; **to ~ sb to do sthg** indurre qn a fare qc; **to ~ to** portare a; **to ~ the way** fare strada; **to be in the ~** essere in testa.

lead² [led] *n* piombo *m*; *(for pencil)* mina *f* ♦ *adj* di piombo.

leaded petrol ['ledɪd-] *n* benzina *f* con piombo.

leader ['li:də*r*] *n (of group)* capo

m; (of union, party) leader *mf inv; (in race)* chi è in testa.

leadership ['liːdəʃɪp] *n (position)* direzione *f*.

lead-free [led-] *adj* senza piombo.

leading ['liːdɪŋ] *adj (most important)* principale.

lead singer [liːd-] *n* cantante *mf* (solista).

leaf [liːf] *(pl* **leaves***) n. (of tree)* foglia *f*.

leaflet ['liːflɪt] *n* dépliant *m inv*.

league [liːg] *n (SPORT)* campionato *m; (association)* lega *f*.

leak [liːk] *n (hole)* buco *m; (of gas, water)* perdita *f* ♦ *vi (tank)* perdere; *(roof)* gocciolare.

lean [liːn] *(pt & pp* **leant** [lent] OR **-ed***) adj (meat)* magro(-a); *(person, animal)* asciutto(-a) ♦ *vi (bend)* piegarsi; *(building)* pendere ♦ *vt:* **to ~ sthg against sthg** appoggiare qc a qc; **to ~ on** appoggiarsi a □ **lean forward** *vi* sporgersi (in avanti); **lean over** *vi* sporgersi.

leap [liːp] *(pt & pp* **leapt** [lept] OR **-ed***) vi (jump)* balzare.

leap year *n* anno *m* bisestile.

learn [lɜːn] *(pt & pp* **learnt** OR **-ed***) vt* imparare; **to ~ (how) to do sthg** imparare a fare qc; **to ~ about sthg** *(hear about)* venire a sapere di qc; *(study)* studiare qc.

learner (driver) ['lɜːnə^r-] *n* guidatore *m* (-trice *f*) principiante.

learnt [lɜːnt] *pt & pp* → **learn**.

lease [liːs] *n* contratto *m* d'affitto ♦ *vt* affittare; **to ~ sthg from sb** affittare qc da qn; **to ~ sthg to sb** affittare qc a qn.

leash [liːʃ] *n* guinzaglio *m*.

least [liːst] *adv* meno (di tutti) ♦ *adj* meno ... di tutti ♦ *pron:* **(the) ~** meno di tutti; **at ~** almeno; **the ~ he could do** il minimo che potesse fare.

leather ['leðə^r] *n* cuoio *m*, pelle *f* □ **leathers** *npl (of motorcyclist)* tuta *f* in pelle da motociclista.

leave [liːv] *(pt & pp* **left***) vt* lasciare; *(school)* finire ♦ *vi (go away)* andarsene; *(train, bus)* partire ♦ *n (time off work)* permesso *m; to ~ a* **message** lasciare un messaggio, ♦ **left** □ **leave behind** *vt sep (not take away)* lasciare; **leave out** *vt sep* tralasciare.

leaves [liːvz] *pl* → **leaf**.

Lebanon ['lebənən] *n* il Libano.

lecture ['lektʃə^r] *n (at university)* lezione *f; (at conference)* conferenza *f*.

lecturer ['lektʃərə^r] *n* docente *mf* (universitario).

lecture theatre *n* aula *f (ad anfiteatro)*.

led [led] *pt & pp* → **lead**[1].

ledge [ledʒ] *n (of window)* davanzale *m*.

leek [liːk] *n* porro *m*.

left [left] *pt & pp* → **leave** ♦ *adj (not right)* sinistro(-a) ♦ *adv* a sinistra ♦ *n* sinistra *f;* **on the ~** a sinistra; **there are none** ~ sono finiti.

left-hand *adj (side)* sinistro(-a); *(lane)* di sinistra.

left-hand drive *n* guida *f* a sinistra.

left-handed [-'hændɪd] *adj (person)* mancino(-a); *(implement)* per mancini.

left-luggage locker *n (Br)* armadietto *m* per deposito bagagli.

left-luggage office n (Br) deposito m bagagli.

left-wing adj di sinistra.

leg [leg] n gamba f; (of animal) zampa f; (of lamb) coscia f d'agnello.

legal ['li:gl] adj legale.

legal aid n assistenza f legale gratuita.

legalize ['li:gəlaɪz] vt legalizzare.

legal system n sistema f legale.

legend ['ledʒənd] n leggenda f.

leggings ['legɪnz] npl fuseaux mpl, pantacollant mpl.

legible ['ledʒɪbl] adj leggibile.

legislation [,ledʒɪs'leɪʃn] n legislazione f.

legitimate [lɪ'dʒɪtɪmət] adj legittimo(-a).

leisure [Br 'leʒər, Am 'li:ʒər] n tempo m libero.

leisure centre n centro m sportivo.

leisure pool n piscina f.

lemon ['lemən] n limone m.

lemonade [,lemə'neɪd] n limonata f.

lemon curd [-kɜ:d] n (Br) sorta di marmellata a base di succo e scorza di limone, uova, burro e zucchero.

lemon juice n succo m di limone.

lemon meringue pie n dolce composto da una base di pasta frolla e uno strato di crema al limone rivestito di meringa.

lemon sole n limanda f (varietà di sogliola).

lemon tea n tè m al limone.

lend [lend] (pt & pp lent) vt prestare; to ~ sb sthg prestare

qc a qn.

length [leŋθ] n (in distance) lunghezza f; (in time) durata f; (of swimming pool) vasca f.

lengthen ['leŋθən] vt allungare.

lens [lenz] n lente f.

lent [lent] pt & pp → **lend**.

Lent [lent] n la Quaresima.

lentils ['lentlz] npl lenticchie fpl.

Leo (pl -s) n Leone m.

leopard ['lepəd] n leopardo m.

leopard-skin adj a pelle di leopardo.

leotard ['li:əta:d] n calzamaglia f.

leper ['lepər] n lebbroso m (-a f).

lesbian ['lezbɪən] adj lesbico(-a) ◆ n lesbica f.

less [les] adj, adv & pron meno; ~ than 20 meno di 20.

lesson ['lesn] n (class) lezione f.

let [let] (pt & pp let) vt (allow) lasciare; (rent out) affittare; **to ~ sb do sthg** lasciar fare qc a qn; **to ~ go of sthg** mollare qc; **to ~ sb have sthg** (give) dare qc a qn; **to ~ sb know sthg** far sapere qc a qn; **let's go!** andiamo!; **'to ~'** 'affittasi' ❑ **let in** vt sep (allow to enter) far entrare; **let off** vt sep (excuse): **to ~ sb off doing sthg** dispensare qn dal fare qc; **can you ~ me off at the station?** mi fa scendere alla stazione?; **let out** vt sep (allow to go out) far uscire.

letdown ['letdaʊn] n (inf) delusione f.

lethargic [lə'θa:dʒɪk] adj apatico(-a).

letter ['letər] n lettera f.

letterbox ['letəbɒks] n (Br) buca f delle lettere.

lettuce ['letɪs] n lattuga f.

leuk(a)emia [lu:'ki:mɪə] n leucemia f.

level ['levl] adj (flat) piano(-a); (horizontal) orizzontale ◆ n livello m; (storey) piano m; **to be ~ with** essere allo stesso livello di.

level crossing n (Br) passaggio m a livello.

lever [Br 'li:və, Am 'levər] n leva f.

liability [ˌlaɪə'bɪlətɪ] n (responsibility) responsabilità f.

liable ['laɪəbl] adj: **to be ~ to do** sthg avere la tendenza a fare qc; **to be ~ for** sthg rispondere di qc.

liaise [lɪ'eɪz] vi: **to ~ with** mantenere i contatti con.

liar ['laɪər] n bugiardo m (-a f).

liberal ['lɪbərəl] adj (tolerant) liberale; (generous) generoso(-a).

Liberal Democrat Party n Partito m Liberaldemocratico.

liberate ['lɪbəreɪt] vt liberare.

liberty ['lɪbətɪ] n libertà f inv.

Libra n Bilancia f.

librarian [laɪ'breərɪən] n bibliotecario m (-a f).

library ['laɪbrərɪ] n biblioteca f.

Libya ['lɪbɪə] n la Libia.

lice [laɪs] npl pidocchi mpl.

licence ['laɪsəns] n (Br: official document) licenza f ◆ vt (Am) = **license; driving ~** patente f (di guida); **TV ~** abbonamento m alla televisione.

license ['laɪsəns] vt (Br) autorizzare ◆ n (Am) = **licence**.

licensed ['laɪsənst] adj (restaurant, bar) munito di licenza per la vendita di alcolici.

licensing hours ['laɪsənsɪŋ-] npl (Br) orario in cui è consentita la vendita di alcolici.

lick [lɪk] vt leccare.

lid [lɪd] n (cover) coperchio m.

lie [laɪ] (pt lay, pp lain, cont lying) n bugia f ◆ vi (tell lie: pt & pp lied) mentire; (be horizontal) essere disteso; (lie down) sdraiarsi; (be situated) trovarsi; **to tell ~s** dire bugie; **to ~ about** sthg mentire su qc ❑ **lie down** vi sdraiarsi.

lieutenant [Br lef'tenənt, Am lu:'tenənt] n tenente m.

life [laɪf] (pl lives) n vita f.

life assurance n assicurazione f sulla vita.

life belt n salvagente m.

lifeboat ['laɪfbəʊt] n scialuppa f di salvataggio.

lifeguard ['laɪfgɑ:d] n bagnino m.

life jacket n giubbotto m di salvataggio.

lifelike ['laɪflaɪk] adj fedele.

life preserver [-prɪ'zɜ:vər] n (Am) (life belt) salvagente m; (life jacket) giubbotto m di salvataggio.

life-size adj a grandezza naturale.

lifespan ['laɪfspæn] n vita f.

lifestyle ['laɪfstaɪl] n stile m di vita.

lift [lɪft] n (Br: elevator) ascensore m ◆ vt (raise) sollevare, alzare ◆ vi (fog) alzarsi; **to give sb a ~** dare a qn un passaggio ❑ **lift up** vt sep sollevare, alzare.

light [laɪt] (pt & pp lit OR -ed) adj leggero(-a); (not dark) chiaro(-a); (traffic) scorrevole ◆ n luce f; (of bike) faro m ◆ vt (fire, cigarette) accendere; (room, stage) illuminare; **have you got a ~?** hai da accende re?; **to set ~ to** sthg dar fuoco a qc □ **lights** npl (traffic lights) semaforo m; **light up** vt sep (house, road) illuminare ♦ vi (inf: light a cigarette) accendersi una sigaretta.

light bulb n lampadina f.

lighter ['laɪtə'] n accendino m.

light-hearted ['-'hɑːtɪd] adj gioviale.

lighthouse ['laɪthaʊs, pl -hauzɪz] n faro m.

lighting ['laɪtɪŋ] n illuminazione f.

light meter n contatore m della luce.

lightning ['laɪtnɪŋ] n lampi mpl, fulmini mpl.

lightweight ['laɪtweɪt] adj (clothes, object) leggero(-a).

like [laɪk] prep come; (typical of) tipico di ♦ vt (want) volere; **I ~ it** mi piace; **I ~ them** mi piacciono; **I ~ going out** mi piace uscire; **I'd ~ to sit down** vorrei sedermi; **I'd ~ a drink** vorrei bere qualcosa; **what's it ~?** com'è?; **to look ~ sb** assomigliare a qn; **do it ~ this** fallo così; **it's not ~ him** non è da lui.

likelihood ['laɪklɪhʊd] n probabilità f.

likely ['laɪklɪ] adj probabile.

likeness ['laɪknɪs] n somiglianza f.

likewise ['laɪkwaɪz] adv allo stesso modo; **to do ~** fare lo stesso.

lilac ['laɪlək] adj lilla (inv).

Lilo® ['laɪləʊ] (pl -s) n (Br) materassino m (pneumatico).

lily ['lɪlɪ] n giglio m.

lily of the valley n mughetto m.

limb [lɪm] n arto m.

lime [laɪm] n (fruit) limetta f; **~ (juice)** succo m di limetta.

limestone ['laɪmstəun] n calcare m.

limit ['lɪmɪt] n limite m ♦ vt limitare; **the city ~s** i confini della città.

limited ['lɪmɪtɪd] adj (restricted) limitato(-a); (in company name) a responsabilità limitata.

limp [lɪmp] adj floscio(-a) ♦ vi zoppicare.

line [laɪn] n linea f; (row) fila f; (Am: queue) coda f, fila; (of words on page) riga f; (of poem, song) verso m; (for fishing) lenza f; (rope, washing line) corda f; (of business, work) settore m, ramo m ♦ vt (coat, drawers) foderare; **in ~** (aligned) allineato; **it's a bad ~** la linea è disturbata; **the ~ is engaged** la linea è occupata; **to drop sb a ~** (inf) mandare due righe a qn; **to stand in ~** (Am) stare in fila □ **line up** vt sep (arrange) organizzare ♦ vi allinearsi.

lined [laɪnd] adj (paper) rigato(-a), a righe.

linen ['lɪnɪn] n (cloth) lino m; (tablecloths, sheets) biancheria f.

liner ['laɪnə'] n (ship) nave f di linea.

linesman ['laɪnzmən] (pl -men [-mən]) n guardalinee m inv.

linger ['lɪŋgə'] vi (in place) attardarsi.

lingerie ['læ̃ʒərɪ] n biancheria f intima (femminile).

lining ['laɪnɪŋ] n (of coat, jacket) fodera f; (of brake) guarnizione f.

.**link** [lɪŋk] n (connection) collegamento m; (between countries, companies) relazione f ♦ vt (connect) collegare; **rail ~** collegamento ferroviario

rio; **road** ~ collegamento stradale.

lino ['laɪnəʊ] *n* (*Br*) linoleum *m*.

lion ['laɪən] *n* leone *m*.

lioness ['laɪənes] *n* leonessa *f*.

lip [lɪp] *n* (*of person*) labbro *m*.

lip salve [-sælv] *n* burro *m* di cacao.

lipstick ['lɪpstɪk] *n* rossetto *m*.

liqueur [lɪ'kjʊər] *n* liquore *m* (dolce).

liquid ['lɪkwɪd] *n* liquido *m*.

liquor ['lɪkər] *n* (*Am*) superalcolico *m*.

liquorice ['lɪkərɪs] *n* liquirizia *f*.

lisp [lɪsp] *n* difetto *f* di pronuncia (*relativo alla lettera* s).

list [lɪst] *n* lista *f*, elenco *m* ♦ *vt* elencare.

listen ['lɪsn] *vi*: **to** ~ **(to)** ascoltare.

listener ['lɪsnər] *n* (*on radio*) ascoltatore *m* (-trice *f*).

lit [lɪt] *pt & pp* → **light**.

liter ['liːtər] (*Am*) = **litre**.

literally ['lɪtərəlɪ] *adv* letteralmente.

literary ['lɪtərərɪ] *adj* letterario(-a).

literature ['lɪtrətʃər] *n* letteratura *f*; (*printed information*) materiale *m* illustrativo.

litre ['liːtər] *n* (*Br*) litro *m*.

litter ['lɪtər] *n* (*rubbish*) rifiuti *mpl*.

litterbin ['lɪtəbɪn] *n* (*Br*) cestino *m* dei rifiuti.

little ['lɪtl] *adj* piccolo(-a); (*not much*) poco(-a) ♦ *pron & adv* poco; **as** ~ **as possible** il meno possibile; ~ **by** ~ poco a poco ☐ **a little** *pron & adv* un po' ♦ *adj* un po' di.

little finger *n* mignolo *m*.

live[1] [lɪv] *vi* vivere; (*have home*) vivere, abitare; **to** ~ **with sb** vivere con qn ☐ **live together** *vi* vivere insieme.

live[2] [laɪv] *adj* (*alive*) vivo(-a); (*programme, performance*) dal vivo; (*wire*) sotto tensione ♦ *adv* in diretta.

lively ['laɪvlɪ] *adj* (*person*) vivace; (*place, atmosphere*) animato(-a).

liver ['lɪvər] *n* fegato *m*.

lives [laɪvz] *pl* → **life**.

living ['lɪvɪŋ] *adj* vivente ♦ *n*: **to earn a** ~ guadagnarsi da vivere; **what do you do for a** ~? che lavoro fa?

living room *n* soggiorno *m*.

lizard ['lɪzəd] *n* lucertola *f*.

load [ləʊd] *n* (*thing carried*) carico *m* ♦ *vt* caricare; ~**s of** (*inf*) un sacco di.

loaf [ləʊf] (*pl* **loaves**) *n*: **a** ~ **(of bread)** una pagnotta.

loan [ləʊn] *n* prestito *m* ♦ *vt* prestare.

loathe [ləʊð] *vt* detestare.

loaves [ləʊvz] *pl* → **loaf**.

lobby ['lɒbɪ] *n* (*hall*) atrio *m*.

lobster ['lɒbstər] *n* aragosta *f*.

local ['ləʊkl] *adj* locale; (*train*) regionale ♦ *n* (*inf*: *local person*) abitante *mf* del posto; (*Br*: *pub*) bar *m* vicino; (*Am*: *train*) regionale *m*; (*Am*: *bus*) autobus *m inv*.

local anaesthetic *n* anestesia *f* locale.

local call *n* chiamata *f* urbana.

local government *n* amministrazione *f* locale.

locate [Br ləʊ'keɪt, Am 'ləʊkeɪt] *vt* (*find*) localizzare; **to be** ~**d** essere situato.

location [ləʊˈkeɪʃn] *n* (place) posizione *f*.

loch [lɒk] *n* (Scot) lago *m*.

lock [lɒk] *n* (on door, drawer) serratura *f*; (for bike) lucchetto *m*; (on canal) chiusa *f* ♦ *vt* (door, drawer, car) chiudere a chiave; (keep safely) chiudere ♦ *vi* (become stuck) bloccarsi ❑ **lock in** *vt sep* chiudere dentro; **lock out** *vt sep* chiudere fuori; **lock up** *vt sep* (imprison) mettere dentro ♦ *vi* chiudere porte e finestre.

locker [ˈlɒkəʳ] *n* armadietto *m*.

locker room *n* (Am) spogliatoio *m*.

locket [ˈlɒkɪt] *n* medaglione *m*.

locomotive [ˌləʊkəˈməʊtɪv] *n* locomotiva *f*.

locum [ˈləʊkəm] *n* (doctor) medico *m* sostituto.

locust [ˈləʊkəst] *n* locusta *f*.

lodge [lɒdʒ] *n* (for skiers) rifugio *m*; (for hunters) casino *m* di caccia ♦ *vi* (stay) alloggiare; (get stuck) conficcarsi.

lodger [ˈlɒdʒəʳ] *n* pensionante *mf*.

lodgings [ˈlɒdʒɪŋz] *npl* camera *f* ammobiliata.

loft [lɒft] *n* soffitta *f*.

log [lɒg] *n* (piece of wood) ceppo *m*.

logic [ˈlɒdʒɪk] *n* logica *f*.

logical [ˈlɒdʒɪkl] *adj* logico(-a).

logo [ˈləʊgəʊ] *n* (*pl* -s) logo *m inv*.

loin [lɔɪn] *n* lombata *f*.

loiter [ˈlɔɪtəʳ] *vi* (remain) attardarsi; (walk around) bighellonare.

lollipop [ˈlɒlɪpɒp] *n* lecca lecca *m inv*.

lolly [ˈlɒlɪ] *n* (inf: lollipop) lecca lecca *m inv*; (Br: ice lolly) ghiac-

ciolo *m*.

Lombardy *n* la Lombardia.

London [ˈlʌndən] *n* Londra *f*.

Londoner [ˈlʌndənəʳ] *n* londinese *mf*.

lonely [ˈləʊnlɪ] *adj* (person) solo(-a); (place) isolato(-a).

long [lɒŋ] *adj* lungo(-a) ♦ *adv* molto; **it's 2 metres** ~ è lungo 2 metri; **it's two hours** ~ dura due ore; **how** ~ **is it?** (in length) quanto è lungo?; (in time) quanto dura?; a ~ **time** molto tempo; **all day** ~ tutto il giorno; **as** ~ **as** (provided that) purché; **for** ~ per molto tempo; **no** ~**er** non più; **so** ~! (inf) ciao! ❑ **long for** *vt fus* desiderare ardentemente.

long-distance *adj* (phone call) interurbano(-a).

long drink *n* long drink *m inv*.

long-haul *adj* su lunga distanza.

longitude [ˈlɒndʒɪtjuːd] *n* longitudine *f*.

long jump *n* salto *m* in lungo.

long-life *adj* (milk, fruit juice) a lunga conservazione; (battery) a lunga durata.

longsighted [ˌlɒŋˈsaɪtɪd] *adj* presbite.

long-term *adj* a lungo termine.

long wave *n* onde *fpl* lunghe.

longwearing [ˌlɒŋˈweərɪŋ] *adj* (Am) resistente.

loo [luː] *n* (*pl* -s) *n* (Br: inf) gabinetto *m*.

look [lʊk] *n* (glance) sguardo *m*, occhiata *f*; (appearance) aspetto *m* ♦ *vi* guardare; (seem) sembrare; **you don't** ~ **well** non hai una gran bella cera; **to** ~ **onto** (building, *room)* dare su; **to have a ~** dare un'occhiata; **(good) ~s** bellezza *f*; **I'm just ~ing** *(in shop)* sto solo guardando; **~ out!** attento! ❑ **look after** *vt fus* occuparsi di; **look at** *vt fus (observe)* guardare; *(examine)* vedere; **look for** *vt fus* cercare; **look forward to** *vt fus* non veder l'ora di; **look out for** *vt fus* cercare; **look round** *vt fus (city, museum)* visitare; *(shop)* fare un giro da ◆ *vi* girarsi; **look up** *vt sep (in dictionary, phone book)* cercare.

loony ['luːnɪ] *n (inf)* pazzo *m* (-a *f*).

loop [luːp] *n* cappio *m*.

loose [luːs] *adj (not fixed firmly)* allentato(-a); *(sweets, sheets of paper)* sciolto(-a); *(clothes)* largo(-a); **to let sb/sthg ~** lasciar libero qn/qc.

loosen ['luːsn] *vt* allentare.

lop-sided [-'saɪdɪd] *adj* storto(-a).

lord [lɔːd] *n* lord *m inv*.

lorry ['lɒrɪ] *n (Br)* camion *m inv*.

lorry driver *n (Br)* camionista *mf*.

lose [luːz] *(pt & pp lost) vt & vi* perdere; **to ~ weight** dimagrire.

loser ['luːzər] *n (in contest)* perdente *mf*.

loss [lɒs] *n* perdita *f*.

lost [lɒst] *pt & pp* → **lose** ◆ *adj (person)* perso(-a); **to get ~** *(lose way)* perdersi.

lost-and-found office *n (Am)* ufficio *m* oggetti smarriti.

lost property office *n (Br)* ufficio *m* oggetti smarriti.

lot [lɒt] *n (group of people)* gruppo *m*; *(at auction)* lotto *m*; *(Am: car park)* parcheggio *m*; **a ~ *(large***

amount) molto(-a), molti(-e) *(pl)*; *(to a great extent, often)* molto; **a ~ of** time molto tempo; **a ~ of** problems molti problemi; **~s (of)** molto(-a), molti(-e) *(pl)*, un sacco (di); **the ~** *(everything)* tutto quanto (tutta quanta).

lotion ['ləʊʃn] *n* lozione *f*.

lottery ['lɒtərɪ] *n* lotteria *f*.

loud [laʊd] *adj (music, noise)* forte; *(voice)* alto(-a); *(colour, clothes)* sgargiante.

loudspeaker [,laʊd'spiːkəʳ] *n* altoparlante *m*.

lounge [laʊndʒ] *n (in house)* salotto *m*, soggiorno *m*; *(at airport)* sala *f* partenze.

lounge bar *n (Br)* sala di un pub più confortevole e più cara del 'public bar' *m*.

lousy ['laʊzɪ] *adj (inf: poor-quality)* schifoso(-a).

lout [laʊt] *n* teppista *mf*.

love [lʌv] *n* amore *m*; *(in tennis)* zero *m* ◆ *vt* amare; **I ~ reading** mi piace molto leggere; **I'd ~ a coffee** mi andrebbe un caffè; **I'd ~ to help** vorrei tanto aiutare; **to be in ~ (with)** essere innamorato (di); **(with) ~ from** *(in letter)* con affetto.

love affair *n* relazione *f*.

lovely ['lʌvlɪ] *adj (very beautiful)* bello(-a); *(very nice)* delizioso(-a).

lover ['lʌvəʳ] *n (sexual partner)* amante *mf*; *(enthusiast)* appassionato *m* (-a *f*).

loving ['lʌvɪŋ] *adj* affettuoso(-a).

low [ləʊ] *adj* basso(-a); *(quantity)* piccolo(-a); *(supply)* scarso(-a); *(standard, quality, opinion)* scadente; *(depressed)* depresso(-a) ◆ *n (area of low pressure)* area *f* di bassa pressione; **we're ~ on petrol** abbiamo poca benzina.

low-alcohol *adj* a basso contenuto alcolico.

low-calorie *adj* ipocalorico(-a).

low-cut *adj* scollato(-a).

lower ['ləʊə^r] *adj* inferiore ◆ *vt* abbassare.

lower sixth *n (Br)* primo anno di studi superiori per studenti di 17 anni che prepareranno gli 'A levels'.

low-fat *adj* magro(-a).

low tide *n* bassa marea *f*.

loyal ['lɔɪəl] *adj* fedele.

loyalty ['lɔɪəltɪ] *n* fedeltà *f*.

lozenge ['lɒzɪndʒ] *n (sweet)* pasticca *f*, pastiglia *f*.

LP *n* LP *m inv*.

L-plate *n (Br)* targa indicante che chi guida la vettura non ha ancora preso la patente.

Ltd *(abbr of limited)* = Srl.

lubricate ['lu:brɪkeɪt] *vt* lubrificare.

luck [lʌk] *n* fortuna *f*; **bad** ~ sfortuna *f*; **good** ~! buona fortuna!; **with** ~ con un po' di fortuna.

luckily ['lʌkɪlɪ] *adv* fortunatamente.

lucky ['lʌkɪ] *adj* fortunato(-a); **to be** ~ essere fortunato.

ludicrous ['lu:dɪkrəs] *adj* ridicolo(-a).

lug [lʌg] *vt (inf)* trascinare.

luggage ['lʌgɪdʒ] *n* bagagli *mpl*.

luggage compartment *n* bagagliaio *m*.

luggage locker *n* armadietto *m* per deposito bagagli.

luggage rack *n (on train)* portabagagli *m*.

lukewarm ['lu:kwɔ:m] *adj* tiepido(-a).

lull [lʌl] *n* pausa *f*.

lullaby ['lʌləbaɪ] *n* ninnananna *f*.

lumbago [lʌm'beɪgəʊ] *n* lombaggine *f*.

lumber ['lʌmbə^r] *n (Am: timber)* legname *m*.

luminous ['lu:mɪnəs] *adj* fosforescente.

lump [lʌmp] *n (of coal, mud, butter)* pezzo *m*; *(of sugar)* zolletta *f*; *(on body)* nodulo *m*.

lump sum *n* compenso *m* forfettario.

lumpy ['lʌmpɪ] *adj (sauce)* grumoso(-a); *(mattress)* pieno(-a) di bozzi.

lunatic ['lu:nətɪk] *n* pazzo *m (*-a *f*).

lunch [lʌntʃ] *n* pranzo *m*; **to have** ~ pranzare.

luncheon ['lʌntʃən] *n (fml)* pranzo *m*.

luncheon meat *n* = carne di maiale *f* in scatola.

lunch hour *n* pausa *f* pranzo.

lunchtime ['lʌntʃtaɪm] *n* ora *f* di pranzo.

lung [lʌŋ] *n* polmone *m*.

lunge [lʌndʒ] *vi*: **to** ~ **at** gettarsi su.

lurch [lɜ:tʃ] *vi* barcollare.

lure [ljʊə^r] *vt* attirare.

lurk [lɜ:k] *vi (person)* stare in agguato.

lush [lʌʃ] *adj (grass, field)* rigoglioso(-a).

lust [lʌst] *n (sexual desire)* libidine *f*.

Luxembourg ['lʌksəmbɜ:g] *n* il Lussemburgo.

luxurious [lʌg'ʒʊərɪəs] *adj* di lusso.

luxury ['lʌkʃərɪ] *adj* di lusso ◆ *n*

lusso m.

lying ['laɪŋ] *cont* → lie.

lyrics ['lɪrɪks] *npl* parole *fpl*.

M

m *(abbr of metre)* m ♦ *abbr* = **mile**.

M *(Br: abbr of motorway)* A; *(abbr of medium)* M.

MA *n (abbr of Master of Arts) (titolare di)* master in materie umanistiche.

mac [mæk] *n (Br: inf: coat)* impermeabile m.

macaroni [,mækə'rəʊnɪ] *n* maccheroni *mpl*.

macaroni cheese *n* maccheroni *mpl* gratinati.

machine [mə'ʃiːn] *n* macchina f.

machinegun [mə'ʃiːngʌn] *n* mitragliatrice f.

machinery [mə'ʃiːnərɪ] *n* macchine *fpl*.

machine-washable *adj* lavabile in lavatrice.

mackerel ['mækrəl] *(pl inv)* n sgombro m.

mackintosh ['mækɪntɒʃ] *n (Br)* impermeabile m.

mad [mæd] *adj* pazzo(-a), matto(-a); *(angry)* arrabbiato(-a); *(uncontrolled)* furioso(-a); **to be ~ about** *(inf: like a lot)* andare pazzo per; **like ~** come un matto.

Madam ['mædəm] *n (form of address)* signora f.

made [meɪd] *pt & pp* → **make**.

madeira [mə'dɪərə] *n* madera f.

made-to-measure *adj* fatto (-a) su misura.

madness ['mædnɪs] *n* pazzia f.

magazine [,mægə'ziːn] *n (journal)* rivista f.

maggot ['mægət] *n* verme m.

magic ['mædʒɪk] *n* magia f.

magician [mə'dʒɪʃn] *n (conjurer)* mago m (-a f).

magistrate ['mædʒɪstreɪt] *n* magistrato m.

magnet ['mægnɪt] *n* calamita f.

magnetic [mæg'netɪk] *adj* magnetico(-a).

magnificent [mæg'nɪfɪsənt] *adj* magnifico(-a).

magnifying glass ['mægnɪfaɪŋ-] *n* lente f d'ingrandimento.

mahogany [mə'hɒgənɪ] *n* mogano m.

maid [meɪd] *n* cameriera f.

maiden name ['meɪdn-] *n* nome m da nubile.

mail [meɪl] *n* posta f ♦ *vt (Am)* spedire.

mailbox ['meɪlbɒks] *n (Am)* cassetta f delle lettere.

mailman ['meɪlmən] *(pl -men* [-mən]*) n (Am)* postino m.

mail order *n* vendita f per corrispondenza.

main [meɪn] *adj* principale.

main course *n* portata f principale.

main deck *n* ponte m principale, coperta f.

mainland ['meɪnlənd] *n*: **the ~ il** continente.

main line *n* linea f principale.

mainly ['meɪnlɪ] *adv* principalmente.

main road *n* strada *f* principale.

mains [meɪnz] *npl*: **the ~** le condutture.

main street *n (Am)* corso *m*.

maintain [meɪn'teɪn] *vt (keep)* mantenere; *(in good condition)* provvedere alla manutenzione di.

maintenance ['meɪntənəns] *n (of car, machine)* manutenzione *f*; *(money)* alimenti *mpl*.

maisonette [,meɪzə'net] *n (Br)* appartamento *m* (su due piani).

maize [meɪz] *n* granturco *m*, mais *m*.

major ['meɪdʒəʳ] *adj (important)* importante; *(most important)* principale ♦ *n (MIL)* maggiore *m* ♦ *vi (Am)*: **to ~ in** laurearsi in.

majority [mə'dʒɒrɪtɪ] *n* maggioranza *f*.

major road *n* strada *f* principale.

make [meɪk] *(pt & pp* **made)** *vt* 1. *(produce, manufacture)* fare; **to be made of** essere (fatto) di; **to ~ lunch/supper** preparare il pranzo/la cena; **made in Japan** fabbricato in Giappone.

2. *(perform, do)* fare; *(decision)* prendere; **to ~ a mistake** fare un errore; **to ~ a phone call** fare una telefonata.

3. *(cause to be)* rendere; **to ~ sthg better** migliorare qc; **to ~ sb happy** rendere felice qn.

4. *(cause to do, force)* fare; **to ~ sb do sthg** far fare qc a qn, costringere qn a fare qc; **it made her laugh** 'ha fatta ridere.

5. *(amount to, total)* fare; **that ~s £5** fanno 5 sterline.

6. *(calculate)*: **I ~ it £4** mi viene 4 sterline; **I ~ it seven o'clock** io faccio le sette.

7. *(earn)* fare; **to ~ a loss** registrare una perdita.

8. *(inf: arrive in time for)*: **I don't think we'll ~ the 10 o'clock train** non credo che ce la faremo per il treno delle 10.

9. *(friend, enemy)* farsi.

10. *(have qualities for)*: **this would ~ a lovely bedroom** sarebbe una camera (da letto) molto carina.

11. *(bed)* fare, rifare.

12. *(in phrases)*: **to ~ do (with)** arrangiarsi (con); **to ~ good (damage)** risarcire; **to ~ it** *(arrive on time, be able to go)* farcela.

♦ *n (of product)* marca *f*.

❑ **make out** *vt sep (cheque, receipt)* fare; *(form)* compilare; *(see, hear)* distinguere, capire; **make up** *vt sep (invent)* inventare; *(comprise)* costituire, comporre; *(difference)* coprire; **make up for** *vt fus* compensare.

makeshift ['meɪkʃɪft] *adj* di fortuna.

make-up *n (cosmetics)* trucco *m*.

malaria [mə'leərɪə] *n* malaria *f*.

Malaysia [mə'leɪzɪə] *n* la Malesia.

male [meɪl] *adj* maschile; *(child, animal)* maschio ♦ *n (animal)* maschio *m*.

malfunction [mæl'fʌŋkʃn] *vi (fml)* funzionare male.

malignant [mə'lɪgnənt] *adj (tumour)* maligno(-a).

mall [mɔːl] *n (shopping centre)* centro *m* commerciale.

i MALL

Lunga distesa di verde nel cuore di Washington DC, il Mall si estende dal Campidoglio al Lincoln Memorial. Lungo di esso si trovano i musei della Smithsonian Institution, gallerie d'arte, la Casa Bianca, il Washington Memorial e il Jefferson Memorial. Il muro ("the Wall"), sul quale sono incisi i nomi dei soldati morti o dispersi nella guerra del Vietnam, si trova all'estremità occidentale del Mall.

Nel Regno Unito il Mall è il nome del lungo viale alberato nel centro di Londra, che porta da Buckingham Palace a Trafalgar Square.

mallet ['mælɪt] *n* maglio *m*.

malt [mɔːlt] *n* malto *m*.

maltreat [ˌmælˈtriːt] *vt* maltrattare.

malt whisky *n* whisky *m inv* di malto.

mammal ['mæml] *n* mammifero *m*.

man [mæn] (*pl* **men**) *n* uomo *m* ◆ *vt* (*office*) dotare di personale; (*phones*) rispondere a.

manage ['mænɪdʒ] *vt* (*company, business*) dirigere; (*suitcase*) farcela a portare; (*job*) riuscire a fare; (*food*) farcela a mangiare ◆ *vi* (*cope*) farcela; **can you ~ Friday?** venerdì ti andrebbe bene?; **to ~ to do sthg** riuscire a fare qc.

management ['mænɪdʒmənt] *n* direzione *f*.

manager ['mænɪdʒəʳ] *n* (*of business, bank, shop*) direttore *m*; (*of sports team*) allenatore *m*.

manageress [ˌmænɪdʒəˈres] *n* (*of business, bank, shop*) direttrice *f*.

managing director ['mænɪdʒɪŋ-] *n* amministratore *m* delegato.

mandarin ['mændərɪn] *n* mandarino *m*.

mane [meɪn] *n* criniera *f*.

maneuver [məˈnuːvər] (*Am*) = **manoeuvre**.

mangetout [ˌmɒnʒˈtuː] *n* pisello *m* mangiatutto.

mangle ['mæŋgl] *vt* (*body*) straziare.

mango ['mæŋgəʊ] (*pl* **-es** OR **-s**) *n* mango *m*.

Manhattan [mænˈhætən] *n* Manhattan *f*.

i MANHATTAN

Quartiere centrale di New York, è diviso in tre zone principali: Downtown, Midtown e Upper Manhattan. Vi si trovano alcuni tra i grattacieli più famosi del mondo, quali l'Empire State Building e il Chrysler Building, e luoghi celebri quali Central Park, la Quinta Strada (Fifth Avenue), Broadway e il Greenwich Village.

manhole ['mænhəʊl] *n* pozzo *m* d'ispezione.

maniac ['meɪnɪæk] *n* (*inf*) pazzo *m* (-a *f*).

manicure ['mænɪkjʊəʳ] *n* manicure *f inv*.

manifold ['mænɪfəʊld] *n* (*AUT*) collettore *m*.

manipulate [məˈnɪpjʊleɪt] *vt* (*person*) manipolare; (*machine, controls*) manovrare.

mankind [ˌmænˈkaɪnd] n l'umanità f.

manly ['mænlɪ] adj virile.

man-made adj artificiale.

manner ['mænəʳ] n (way) modo m ▫ **manners** npl maniere fpl.

manoeuvre [məˈnuːvəʳ] n (Br) manovra f ◆ vt (Br) manovrare.

manor ['mænəʳ] n grande casa f di campagna.

mansion ['mænʃn] n casa f signorile.

manslaughter ['mænˌslɔːtəʳ] n omicidio m colposo.

mantelpiece ['mæntlpiːs] n mensola f del caminetto.

manual ['mænjʊəl] adj manuale ◆ n manuale m.

manufacture [ˌmænjʊˈfæktʃəʳ] n fabbricazione f ◆ vt (produce) fabbricare.

manufacturer [ˌmænjʊˈfæktʃərəʳ] n fabbricante m.

manure [məˈnjʊəʳ] n concime m.

many ['menɪ] (compar **more**, superl **most**) adj molti(-e) ◆ pron molti mpl (-e fpl); **how** ~? quanti(-e)?; **so** ~ così tanti(-e); **too** ~ troppi(-e); **take as** ~ **as** you like prendine quanti ne vuoi; **twice as** ~ as il doppio di.

map [mæp] n (of country) carta f geografica; (of town) pianta f.

Mar. (abbr of March) mar.

marathon ['mærəθn] n maratona f.

marble ['mɑːbl] n (stone) marmo m; (glass ball) bilia f, pallina f (di vetro).

march [mɑːtʃ] n (demonstration) marcia f ◆ vi (walk quickly) avanzare con passo deciso.

March [mɑːtʃ] n marzo m, →

September.

mare [meəʳ] n giumenta f.

margarine [ˌmɑːdʒəˈriːn] n margarina f.

margin ['mɑːdʒɪn] n margine m.

marina [məˈriːnə] n porto m turistico.

marinated ['mærɪneɪtɪd] adj marinato(-a).

marital status ['mærɪtl-] n stato m civile.

mark [mɑːk] n (spot) macchia f; (cut, symbol) segno m; (SCH) voto m; (of gas oven) numero corrispondente a una certa temperatura ◆ vt (blemish) macchiare; (put symbol on) segnare; (correct) correggere; (show position of) indicare.

marker pen ['mɑːkə-] n (grosso) pennarello m.

market ['mɑːkɪt] n mercato m.

marketing ['mɑːkɪtɪŋ] n marketing m.

marketplace ['mɑːkɪtpleɪs] n (place) piazza f del mercato.

markings ['mɑːkɪŋz] npl (on road) segnaletica f orizzontale.

marmalade ['mɑːməleɪd] n marmellata f di agrumi.

marquee [mɑːˈkiː] n padiglione m.

marriage ['mærɪdʒ] n matrimonio m.

married ['mærɪd] adj sposato(-a); **to get** ~ sposarsi.

marrow ['mærəʊ] n (vegetable) zucca f.

marry ['mærɪ] vt sposare ◆ vi sposarsi.

marsh [mɑːʃ] n palude f.

martial arts [ˌmɑːʃl-] npl arti fpl marziali.

marvellous ['mɑːvələs] adj (Br)

meraviglioso(-a).

marvelous ['mɑːvələs] *(Am)* = marvellous.

marzipan ['mɑːzɪpæn] *n* marzapane *m*.

mascara [mæsˈkɑːrə] *n* mascara *m inv*.

masculine ['mæskjʊlɪn] *adj* maschile; *(woman)* mascolino(-a).

mashed potatoes [mæʃt-] *npl* purè *m inv* di patate.

mask [mɑːsk] *n* maschera *f*.

masonry ['meɪsnrɪ] *n* muratura *f*.

mass [mæs] *n (large amount)* massa *f*; *(RELIG)* messa *f*; **~es (of)** *(inf: lots)* un sacco (di).

massacre ['mæsəkə'] *n* massacro *m*.

massage [*Br* 'mæsɑːʒ, *Am* məˈsɑːʒ] *n* massaggio *m* ♦ *vt* massaggiare.

masseur [mæˈsɜː'] *n* massaggiatore *m*.

masseuse [mæˈsɜːz] *n* massaggiatrice *f*.

massive ['mæsɪv] *adj* enorme.

mast [mɑːst] *n (on boat)* albero *m*.

master ['mɑːstə'] *n (at school)* insegnante *m*; *(of servant, dog)* padrone *m* ♦ *vt (learn)* imparare a fondo.

masterpiece ['mɑːstəpiːs] *n* capolavoro *m*.

mat [mæt] *n (small rug)* tappetino *m*; *(on table)* sottopiatto *m*.

match [mætʃ] *n (for lighting)* fiammifero *m*; *(game)* partita *f*, incontro *m* ♦ *vt (in colour, design)* intonarsi a OR con; *(be the same as)* corrispondere a; *(be as good as)* uguagliare ♦ *vi (in colour, design)* intonarsi.

matchbox ['mætʃbɒks] *n* scatola *f* di fiammiferi.

matching ['mætʃɪŋ] *adj* intonato(-a).

mate [meɪt] *n (inf: friend)* amico *m* (-a *f*) ♦ *vi* accoppiarsi.

material [məˈtɪərɪəl] *n* materiale *m*; *(cloth)* stoffa *f* ❑ **materials** *npl (equipment)* occorrente *m*.

maternity leave [məˈtɜːnɪ-] *n* congedo *m* di maternità.

maternity ward [məˈtɜːnɪ-] *n* reparto *m* maternità.

math [mæθ] *(Am)* = **maths**.

mathematics [,mæθəˈmætɪks] *n* matematica *f*.

maths [mæθs] *n (Br)* matematica *f*.

matinée ['mætɪneɪ] *n* matinée *f inv*.

matt [mæt] *adj* opaco(-a).

matter ['mætə'] *n (issue, situation)* questione *f*; *(physical material)* materia *f* ♦ *vi* importare; **it doesn't ~** non importa; **no ~ what happens** qualsiasi cosa accada; **there's something the ~ with my car** c'è qualcosa che non va con la mia macchina; **what's the ~?** che cosa c'è (che non va)?; **as a ~ of course** come è naturale; **as a ~ of fact** in realtà.

mattress ['mætrɪs] *n* materasso *m*.

mature [məˈtjʊə'] *adj (person, behaviour)* maturo(-a); *(cheese, wine)* stagionato(-a).

mauve [məʊv] *adj (color)* malva *(inv)*.

max. [mæks] *(abbr of maximum)* max.

maximum ['mæksɪməm] *adj* massimo(-a) ♦ *n* massimo *m*.

may [meɪ] *aux vb* **1.** *(expressing possibility)*: **it ~ be done as follows** si può procedere come segue; **it ~ rain** può darsi che piova; **they ~ have got lost** può darsi che si siano persi.

2. *(expressing permission)*: **~ I smoke?** posso fumare?; **you ~ sit, if you wish** può sedersi, se vuole.

3. *(when conceding a point)*: **it ~ be a long walk, but it's worth it** sarà anche lontano a piedi, ma ne vale la pena.

May [meɪ] *n* maggio *m*, → **September**.

maybe ['meɪbiː] *adv* forse.

mayonnaise [ˌmeɪə'neɪz] *n* maionese *f*.

mayor [meəʳ] *n* sindaco *m*.

mayoress ['meərɪs] *n* sindaco *m* (donna).

maze [meɪz] *n* labirinto *m*.

me [miː] *pron* mi; *(after prep, stressed)* me; **she knows ~** (lei) mi conosce; **it's ~** sono io; **send it to ~** mandalo a me; **tell ~** dimmi; **he's worse than ~** lui è peggio di me.

meadow ['medəʊ] *n* prato *m*.

meal [miːl] *n* pasto *m*.

mealtime ['miːltaɪm] *n* ora *f* di mangiare.

mean [miːn] *(pt & pp* **meant)** *adj (miserly)* avaro(-a), gretto(-a); *(unkind)* scortese, villano(-a) ♦ *vt (signify, matter)* significare, voler dire; *(intend, be serious about)* intendere; *(be a sign of)* significare; **I didn't ~ it** non dicevo sul serio; **to ~ to do sthg** avere l'intenzione di fare qc; **the bus was meant to leave**

at 8.30 l'autobus sarebbe dovuto partire alle 8.30; **it's meant to be good** dovrebbe essere buono.

meaning ['miːnɪŋ] *n* significato *m*, senso *m*.

meaningless ['miːnɪŋlɪs] *adj (irrelevant)* insignificante.

means [miːnz] *(pl inv) n (method)* mezzo *m* ♦ *npl (money)* mezzi *mpl*; **by all ~!** ma certo!; **by ~ of** per mezzo di.

meant [ment] *pt & pp* → **mean.**

meantime ['miːntaɪm]: **in the meantime** *adv* nel frattempo.

meanwhile ['miːnwaɪl] *adv* nel frattempo.

measles ['miːzlz] *n* morbillo *m*.

measure ['meʒəʳ] *vt* misurare ♦ *n (step, action)* misura *f*, provvedimento *m*; *(of alcohol)* dose *f*; **the room ~s 10 m²** la stanza misura 10 m².

measurement ['meʒəmənt] *n* misura *f*.

meat [miːt] *n* carne *f*; **red ~** carne rossa; **white ~** carne bianca.

meatball ['miːtbɔːl] *n* polpetta *f* (di carne).

mechanic [mɪ'kænɪk] *n* meccanico *m*.

mechanical [mɪ'kænɪkl] *adj (device)* meccanico(-a).

mechanism ['mekənɪzm] *n* meccanismo *m*.

medal ['medl] *n* medaglia *f*.

media ['miːdjə] *n or npl*: **the ~** i *(mass)* media.

medical ['medɪkl] *adj* medico(-a) ♦ *n* visita *f* medica.

medication [ˌmedɪ'keɪʃn] *n* medicine *fpl*.

medicine ['medsɪn] *n* medicina f.

medicine cabinet n armadietto m dei medicinali.

medieval [ˌmedɪ'iːvl] adj medievale.

mediocre [ˌmiːdɪ'əʊkəʳ] adj mediocre.

Mediterranean [ˌmedɪtə'reɪnjən] n: the ~ (region) la regione del Mediterraneo; the ~ (Sea) il (Mare) Mediterraneo.

medium ['miːdjəm] adj medio (-a); (sherry) semisecco(-a).

medium-dry adj semisecco(-a).

medium-sized [-saɪzd] adj di misura media.

medley ['medlɪ] n: a ~ of cold meats affettati mpl misti.

meet [miːt] (pt & pp met) vt incontrare; (get to know) fare la conoscenza di, conoscere; (go to collect) andare a prendere; (need, requirement) soddisfare; (cost, expenses) far fronte a ♦ vi incontrarsi; (get to know each other) conoscersi ❑ **meet up** vi incontrarsi; **meet with** vt fus incontrare.

meeting ['miːtɪŋ] n (for business) incontro m.

meeting point n (at airport, station) punto m d'incontro.

melody ['melədɪ] n melodia f.

melon ['melən] n melone m.

melt [melt] vi sciogliersi; (metal) fondersi.

member ['membəʳ] n membro m.

Member of Congress [-'kɒŋgres] n membro m del Congresso (Americano).

Member of Parliament n

= deputato m (-a f).

membership ['membəʃɪp] n (state of being a member) appartenenza f; (members) (numero dei) membri mpl.

memorial [mɪ'mɔːrɪəl] n monumento m.

memorize ['meməraɪz] vt memorizzare.

memory ['memərɪ] n memoria f; (thing remembered) ricordo m.

men [men] pl → **man**.

menacing ['menəsɪŋ] adj minaccioso(-a).

mend [mend] vt accomodare, aggiustare; (clothes) rammendare.

menopause ['menəpɔːz] n menopausa f.

men's room n (Am) gabinetto m degli uomini.

menstruate ['menstrʊeɪt] vi avere le mestruazioni.

menswear ['menzweəʳ] n abbigliamento m da uomo.

mental ['mentl] adj mentale.

mental hospital n ospedale m psichiatrico.

mentally handicapped ['mentlɪ-] adj mentalmente handicappato(-a) ♦ npl: **the** ~ i portatori di handicap mentale.

mentally ill ['mentlɪ-] adj malato(-a) di mente.

mention ['menʃn] vt accennare a; **don't** ~ **it!** non c'è di che!

menu ['menjuː] n menu m inv; **children's** ~ menu per bambini.

merchandise ['mɜːtʃəndaɪz] n mercanzia f, merce f.

merchant marine [ˌmɜːtʃənt-mə'riːn] (Am) = **merchant navy**.

merchant navy [ˌmɜːtʃənt-

(Br) marina *f* mercantile.

mercury ['mɜːkjʊri] *n* mercurio *m*.

mercy ['mɜːsɪ] *n* pietà *f*.

mere [mɪəʳ] *adj* semplice; **a ~ £5** solo 5 sterline.

merely ['mɪəlɪ] *adv* soltanto.

merge [mɜːdʒ] *vi (combine)* fondersi, unirsi; **'merge'** *(Am: AUT)* segnale che indica agli automobilisti che si immettono su un'autostrada di disporsi sulla corsia di destra.

merger ['mɜːdʒəʳ] *n* fusione *f*.

meringue [məˈræŋ] *n (egg white)* meringa *f*; *(cake)* meringa alla panna.

merit ['merɪt] *n* merito *m*.

merry ['merɪ] *adj* allegro(-a); **Merry Christmas!** Buon Natale!

merry-go-round *n* giostra *f*.

mess [mes] *n (untidiness)* disordine *m*, confusione *f*; *(difficult situation)* pasticcio *m*; **in a ~** *(untidy)* in disordine ☐ **mess about** *vi (inf) (have fun)* divertirsi; *(behave foolishly)* fare lo scemo; **to ~ about with sthg** *(interfere)* intromettersi in qc; **mess up** *vt sep (inf: ruin, spoil)* mandare a monte.

message ['mesɪdʒ] *n* messaggio *n*.

messenger ['mesɪndʒəʳ] *n* messaggero *m (-a f)*.

messy ['mesɪ] *adj* disordinato(-a).

met [met] *pt & pp* → **meet**.

metal ['metl] *adj* metallico(-a), di metallo ◆ *n* metallo *m*.

metalwork ['metlwɜːk] *n (craft)* lavorazione *f* dei metalli.

meter ['miːtəʳ] *n (device)* contatore *m*; *(Am)* = **metre**.

method ['meθəd] *n* metodo *m*.

methodical [mɪˈθɒdɪkl] *adj* metodico(-a).

meticulous [mɪˈtɪkjʊləs] *adj* meticoloso(-a).

metre ['miːtəʳ] *n (Br)* metro *m*.

metric ['metrɪk] *adj* metrico(-a).

mews [mjuːz] *(pl inv) n (Br)* stradina o cortile di antiche scuderie trasformate in appartamenti.

Mexican ['meksɪkən] *adj* messicano(-a) ◆ *n* messicano *m (-a f)*.

Mexico ['meksɪkəʊ] *n* il Messico.

mg *(abbr of milligram)* mg.

miaow [miːˈaʊ] *vi (Br)* miagolare.

mice [maɪs] *pl* → **mouse**.

microchip ['maɪkrəʊtʃɪp] *n* microcircuito *m* integrato, microchip *m inv*.

microphone ['maɪkrəfəʊn] *n* microfono *m*.

microscope ['maɪkrəskəʊp] *n* microscopio *m*.

microwave (oven) ['maɪkrəweɪv-] *n* forno *m* a microonde.

midday [ˌmɪdˈdeɪ] *n* mezzogiorno *m*.

middle ['mɪdl] *n* mezzo *m*, parte *f* centrale ◆ *adj (central)* di mezzo; **in the ~ of the road** in mezzo alla strada; **in the ~ of April** a metà aprile; **to be in the ~ of doing sthg** stare facendo qc.

middle-aged *adj* di mezza età.

middle-class *adj* borghese.

Middle East *n*: **the ~** il Medio Oriente.

middle name *n* secondo nome *m*.

middle school *n (in UK)* scuola *f* media *(per ragazzi dagli 8 ai 13 anni)*.

midge [mɪdʒ] *n* pappataci *m inv*.

midget ['mɪdʒɪt] n nano m (-a f).

Midlands ['mɪdləndz] npl: the ~ le contee dell'Inghilterra centrale.

midnight ['mɪdnaɪt] n mezzanotte f.

midsummer ['mɪd'sʌməʳ] n piena estate f.

midway ['mɪd'weɪ] adv (in space) a metà strada; (in time) a metà.

midweek [adj 'mɪd'wi:k, adv mɪd'wi:k] adj di metà settimana ◆ adv a metà settimana.

midwife ['mɪdwaɪf] n (pl -wives [-waɪvz]) n levatrice f.

midwinter ['mɪd'wɪntəʳ] n pieno inverno m.

might [maɪt] aux vb 1. (expressing possibility): we ~ go to Wales this year forse andremo in Galles quest'anno; I suppose they ~ still come può ancora darsi che arrivino; they ~ have been killed avrebbero potuto rimanere uccisi.

2. (fml: expressing permission): ~ I have a few words? posso parlarle un attimo?

3. (when conceding a point): it ~ be expensive, but it's good quality sarà anche caro, ma è di buona qualità.

4. (would): I'd hoped you ~ come too speravo che venissi anche tu.

◆ n (physical strength) forza f.

migraine ['mi:greɪn, 'maɪgreɪn] n emicrania f.

Milan [mɪ'læn] n Milano f.

mild [maɪld] adj (cheese, person) dolce; (detergent, taste) delicato(-a); (effect, flu) leggero(-a); (weather, climate) mite; (curiosity, surprise) lieve ◆ n (Br: beer) birra f leggera.

mile [maɪl] n miglio m; it's ~s away è lontanissimo.

mileage ['maɪlɪdʒ] n distanza f in miglia, = chilometraggio m.

mileometer [maɪ'lɒmɪtəʳ] n = contachilometri m inv.

military ['mɪlɪtrɪ] adj militare.

milk [mɪlk] n latte m ◆ vt (cow) mungere.

milk chocolate n cioccolato m al latte.

milkman ['mɪlkmən] (pl -men [-mən]) n lattaio m.

milk shake n frappé m inv.

milky ['mɪlkɪ] adj (drink) con tanto latte.

mill [mɪl] n (flour-mill) mulino m; (for pepper, coffee) macinino m; (factory) fabbrica f.

milligram ['mɪlɪgræm] n milligrammo m.

millilitre ['mɪlɪ,li:təʳ] n millilitro m.

millimetre ['mɪlɪ,mi:təʳ] n millimetro m.

million ['mɪljən] n milione m; ~s of (fig) milioni m.

millionaire [,mɪljə'neəʳ] n = miliardario m (-a f).

mime [maɪm] vi mimare.

min. [mɪn] (abbr of minute, minimum) min.

mince [mɪns] n (Br) carne f macinata.

mincemeat ['mɪnsmi:t] n (sweet filling) miscuglio a base di uvetta e spezie; (Am: mince) carne f macinata.

mince pie n pasticcino con ripieno a base di uvetta e spezie che si mangia durante il periodo natalizio.

mind [maɪnd] n mente f ◆ vt (be careful of) fare attenzione a; (look after) badare a ◆ vi: I don't ~ non m'importa; do you ~ if ...? le dispiace se ...?; never ~! (don't worry)

non preoccuparti!, non importa!;
it slipped my ~ mi è sfuggito di
mente; **to my ~** secondo me, a
mio parere; **to bear sthg in ~** tenere presente qc; **to change one's ~**
cambiare idea; **to have sthg in ~**
avere in mente qc; **to have sthg on
one's ~** essere preoccupato per qc;
to make one's ~ up decidersi; **do
you ~ the noise!** le dà fastidio il
rumore?; **I wouldn't ~ a drink** non
mi dispiacerebbe bere qualcosa;
'~ the gap!' (on underground) annuncio che avverte i viaggiatori sulla
metropolitana di fare attenzione alla buca
tra le carrozze e il marciapiede.

mine[1] [maɪn] pron il mio (la mia),
i miei (le mie) (pl); **a friend of ~** un
mio amico.

mine[2] [maɪn] n (for coal etc) miniera f; (bomb) mina f.

miner ['maɪnəʳ] n minatore m.

mineral ['mɪnərəl] n minerale m.

mineral water n acqua f
minerale.

minestrone [ˌmɪnɪ'strəʊnɪ] n
minestrone m.

mingle ['mɪŋgl] vi mescolarsi.

miniature ['mɪnətʃəʳ] adj in
miniatura ◆ n (bottle) bottiglia f
mignon.

minibar ['mɪnɪbɑːʳ] n minibar m
inv.

minibus ['mɪnɪbʌs] (pl -es) n
minibus m inv.

minicab ['mɪnɪkæb] n (Br) radiotaxi m inv.

minimal ['mɪnɪml] adj mini-
mo(-a).

minimum ['mɪnɪməm] adj mini-
mo(-a) ◆ n minimo m.

miniskirt ['mɪnɪskɜːt] n minigonna f.

minister ['mɪnɪstəʳ] n (in government) ministro m; (in church) pastore m.

ministry ['mɪnɪstrɪ] n (of government) ministero m.

minor ['maɪnəʳ] adj minore, di
secondaria importanza ◆ n (fml)
minorenne mf.

minority [maɪ'nɒrətɪ] n minoranza f.

minor road n strada f secondaria.

mint [mɪnt] n (sweet) caramella f
alla menta; (plant) menta f.

minus ['maɪnəs] prep (in subtraction) meno; **it's ~ 10 (degrees C)** è
meno 10 (gradi).

minuscule ['mɪnəskjuːl] adj
minuscolo(-a).

minute[1] ['mɪnɪt] n minuto m; **any
~** da un momento all'altro; **just a
~!** (solo) un minuto!

minute[2] [maɪ'njuːt] adj minusco-
lo(-a).

minute steak [ˌmɪnɪt-] n fettina f (di carne).

miracle ['mɪrəkl] n miracolo m.

miraculous [mɪ'rækjʊləs] adj
miracoloso(-a).

mirror ['mɪrəʳ] n specchio m; (on
car) specchietto m.

misbehave [ˌmɪsbɪ'heɪv] vi comportarsi male.

miscarriage [ˌmɪs'kærɪdʒ] n
aborto m spontaneo.

miscellaneous [ˌmɪsə'leɪnjəs]
adj (things) vario(-a); (collection)
misto(-a).

mischievous ['mɪstʃɪvəs] adj
birichino(-a).

misconduct [ˌmɪs'kɒndʌkt] n
condotta f scorretta.

miser ['maɪzə'] n avaro m (-a f).

miserable ['mɪzrəbl] adj (unhappy) infelice; (place, news, weather) deprimente; (amount) misero(-a).

misery ['mɪzərɪ] n (unhappiness) tristezza f; (poor conditions) miseria f.

misfire [,mɪs'faɪə'] vi (car) perdere colpi.

misfortune [mɪs'fɔ:tʃu:n] n (bad luck) sfortuna f.

mishap ['mɪshæp] n disavventura f.

misjudge [,mɪs'dʒʌdʒ] vt giudicare male.

mislay [,mɪs'leɪ] (pt & pp **-laid**) vt smarrire.

mislead [,mɪs'li:d] (pt & pp **-led**) vt trarre in inganno.

miss [mɪs] vt perdere; (not notice) non vedere; (fail to hit) mancare ♦ vi sbagliare; **I ~ you** mi manchi ❏ **miss out** vt sep saltare, omettere ♦ vi: **to ~ out on sthg** perdersi qc.

Miss [mɪs] n Signorina f.

missile [Br 'mɪsaɪl, Am 'mɪsl] n (weapon) missile m; (thing thrown) oggetto m (scagliato).

missing ['mɪsɪŋ] adj (lost) scomparso(-a); (after accident) disperso(-a); **to be ~** (not there) mancare.

missing person n persona f scomparsa.

mission ['mɪʃn] n missione f.

missionary ['mɪʃənrɪ] n missionario m (-a f).

mist [mɪst] n foschia f.

mistake [mɪ'steɪk] (pt **-took**, pp **-taken**) n sbaglio m, errore m ♦ vt (misunderstand) fraintendere; **by ~** per sbaglio; **to make a ~** fare uno sbaglio; **to ~ sb/sthg for** scambiare qn/qc per.

Mister ['mɪstə'] n Signor m.

mistook [mɪ'stʊk] pt → **mistake**.

mistress ['mɪstrɪs] n (lover) amante f; (Br: teacher) insegnante f.

mistrust [,mɪs'trʌst] vt diffidare di.

misty ['mɪstɪ] adj nebbioso(-a).

misunderstanding [,mɪsʌndə'stændɪŋ] n malinteso m.

misuse [,mɪs'ju:s] n cattivo uso m.

mitten ['mɪtn] n muffola f, manopola f.

mix [mɪks] vt mescolare ♦ n (for cake, sauce) (miscuglio) preparato m ♦ vi (socially): **to ~ with people** veder gente; **to ~ sthg with sthg** mescolare qc a OR con qc ❏ **mix up** vt sep (confuse) confondere; (put into disorder) mescolare.

mixed [mɪkst] adj (school) misto(-a).

mixed grill n grigliata f mista.

mixed salad n insalata f mista.

mixed vegetables npl verdure fpl miste.

mixer ['mɪksə'] n (for food) frullatore m; (drink) bevanda analcolica usata nella preparazione di cocktail.

mixture ['mɪkstʃə'] n (combination) mescolanza f.

mix-up n (inf) confusione f.

ml (abbr of millilitre) ml.

mm (abbr of millimetre) mm.

moan [məʊn] vi (in pain, grief) gemere; (inf: complain) lamentarsi.

moat [məʊt] n fossato m.

mobile ['məʊbaɪl] adj mobile.

mobile phone n telefono cellulare, telefonino m.

mock [mɒk] adj finto(-a) ♦ vt deridere, prendersi gioco di ♦

(Br: exam) esercitazione *f* d'esame.

mode [məʊd] *n* modo *m*.

model ['mɒdl] *n* modello *m*; *(fashion model)* modello *m* (-a *f*).

moderate ['mɒdərət] *adj* moderato(-a).

modern ['mɒdən] *adj* moderno(-a).

modernized ['mɒdənaɪzd] *adj* rimodernato(-a).

modern languages *npl* lingue *fpl* moderne.

modest ['mɒdɪst] *adj* modesto(-a).

modify ['mɒdɪfaɪ] *vt* modificare.

mohair ['məʊheəʳ] *n* mohair *m*.

moist [mɔɪst] *adj* umido(-a).

moisture ['mɔɪstʃəʳ] *n* umidità *f*.

moisturizer ['mɔɪstʃəraɪzəʳ] *n* idratante *m*.

molar ['məʊləʳ] *n* molare *m*.

mold [məʊld] *(Am)* = **mould**.

mole [məʊl] *n (animal)* talpa *f*; *(spot)* neo *m*.

molest [mə'lest] *vt* molestare.

mom [mɒm] *n (Am: inf)* mamma *f*.

moment ['məʊmənt] *n* momento *m*; **at the ~** al momento; **for the ~** per il momento.

Mon. *(abbr of Monday)* lun.

monarchy ['mɒnəkɪ] *n*: **the ~** la monarchia.

monastery ['mɒnəstrɪ] *n* monastero *m*.

Monday ['mʌndɪ] *n* lunedì *m inv*, → **Saturday**.

money ['mʌnɪ] *n* denaro *m*, soldi *mpl*.

money belt *n* marsupio *m*.

money order *n* vaglia *m inv* (postale).

mongrel ['mʌŋgrəl] *n* cane *m* ba-

stardo.

monitor ['mɒnɪtəʳ] *n (computer screen)* monitor *m inv* ◆ *vt (check, observe)* controllare.

monk [mʌŋk] *n* monaco *m*.

monkey ['mʌŋkɪ] *(pl* **monkeys**) *n* scimmia *f*.

monkfish ['mʌŋkfɪʃ] *n* bottatrice *f*.

monopoly [mə'nɒpəlɪ] *n* monopolio *m*.

monorail ['mɒnəʊreɪl] *n* monorotaia *f*.

monotonous [mə'nɒtənəs] *adj* monotono(-a).

monsoon [mɒn'su:n] *n* monsone *m*.

monster ['mɒnstəʳ] *n* mostro *m*.

month [mʌnθ] *n* mese *m*; **every ~** ogni mese; **in a ~'s time** fra un mese.

monthly ['mʌnθlɪ] *adj* mensile ◆ *adv* mensilmente, ogni mese.

monument ['mɒnjʊmənt] *n* monumento *m*.

mood [mu:d] *n* umore *m*; **to be in a (bad) ~** essere di cattivo umore; **to be in a good ~** essere di buon umore.

moody ['mu:dɪ] *adj (in a bad mood)* di malumore; *(changeable)* lunatico(-a), volubile.

moon [mu:n] *n* luna *f*.

moonlight ['mu:nlaɪt] *n* chiaro *m* di luna.

moor [mɔːʳ] *n* brughiera *f* ◆ *vt* ormeggiare.

moose [mu:s] *(pl inv)* *n* alce *m*.

mop [mɒp] *n (for floor)* lavapavimenti *m inv* ◆ *vt (floor)* lavare con lo straccio ❏ **mop up** *vt sep (clean up)* asciugare con uno straccio.

moped [ˈməupəd] n ciclomotore m.

moral [ˈmɒrəl] adj morale ◆ n (lesson) morale f.

morality [məˈrælɪt] n moralità f.

more [mɔːʳ] adj 1. (a larger amount of) più; **there are ~ tourists than usual** ci sono più turisti del solito. 2. (additional) altro(-a); **are there any ~ cakes?** ci sono altri pasticcini?; **I'd like two ~ bottles** vorrei altre due bottiglie; **there's no ~ wine** non c'è più vino. 3. (in phrases): **~ and more** sempre più.

◆ adv 1. (in comparatives) più; **it's ~ difficult than before** è più difficile di prima; **speak ~ clearly** parla più chiaramente. 2. (to a greater degree) di più; **we ought to go to the cinema ~** dovremmo andare più spesso al cinema. 3. (in phrases): **not ... any ~** non ... più; **I don't go there any ~** non ci vado più; **once ~** ancora una volta, un'altra volta; **~ or less** più o meno; **we'd be ~ than happy to help** saremmo più che lieti di dare una mano.

◆ pron 1. (a larger amount) più; **I've got ~ than you** ne ho più di te; **~ than 20 types of pizza** oltre 20 tipi di pizza. 2. (an additional amount): **is there any ~?** ce n'è ancora?; **there's no ~** non ce n'è più.

moreover [mɔːˈrəuvəʳ] adv (fml) inoltre.

morning [ˈmɔːnɪŋ] n mattina f, mattino m; **two o'clock in the ~** le due di notte; **good ~!** buon giorno!; **in the ~** (early in the day) di mattina; (tomorrow morning) domattina.

morning-after pill n pillola f del giorno dopo.

morning sickness n nausea f mattutina.

Morocco [məˈrɒkəu] n il Marocco.

moron [ˈmɔːrɒn] n (inf) deficiente mf.

Morse (code) [mɔːs-] n alfabeto m Morse.

mortgage [ˈmɔːgɪdʒ] n mutuo m (ipotecario).

mosaic [məˈzeɪɪk] n mosaico m.

Moslem [ˈmɒzləm] = Muslim.

mosque [mɒsk] n moschea f.

mosquito [məˈskiːtəu] (pl -es) n zanzara f.

mosquito net n zanzariera f.

moss [mɒs] n muschio m.

most [məust] 1. adj (the majority of) la maggior parte di; **~ people agree** la maggior parte della gente è d'accordo. 2. (the largest amount of): **I drank (the) ~ beer** sono quello che ha bevuto più birra.

◆ adv 1. (in superlatives) più; **the ~ expensive hotel in town** l'albergo più caro della città. 2. (to the greatest degree) di più, maggiormente; **I like this one ~** questo è quello che mi piace di più. 3. (fml: very) molto, estremamente; **they were ~ welcoming** sono stati estremamente accoglienti.

◆ pron 1. (the majority) la maggior parte; **~ of the villages** la maggior parte dei paesi; **~ of the time** la maggior parte del tempo. 2. (the largest amount): **she earns (the) ~** è quella che guadagna di più.

3. *(in phrases):* **at ~ al** massimo; **to make the ~ of sthg** sfruttare al massimo qc.

mostly ['məʊstlɪ] *adv* per lo più.

MOT *n* (Br: test) revisione annuale obbligatoria degli autoveicoli di più di tre anni.

motel [məʊ'tel] *n* motel *m inv*.

moth [mɒθ] *n* farfalla *f* notturna.

mother ['mʌðəʳ] *n* madre *f*.

mother-in-law *n* suocera *f*.

mother-of-pearl *n* madreperla *f*.

motif [məʊ'tiːf] *n* motivo *m*.

motion ['məʊʃn] *n* (movement) movimento *m*, moto *m* ◆ *vi:* **to ~ to sb** fare cenno a qn.

motionless ['məʊʃənlɪs] *adj* immobile.

motivate ['məʊtɪveɪt] *vt* (encourage) motivare, stimolare.

motive ['məʊtɪv] *n* motivo *m*.

motor ['məʊtəʳ] *n* (engine) motore *m*.

Motorail® ['məʊtəreɪl] *n* treno *m* auto-cuccette.

motorbike ['məʊtəbaɪk] *n* moto *f inv*.

motorboat ['məʊtəbəʊt] *n* motoscafo *m*.

motorcar ['məʊtəkɑːʳ] *n* automobile *f*.

motorcycle ['məʊtəˌsaɪkl] *n* motocicletta *f*.

motorcyclist ['məʊtəˌsaɪklɪst] *n* motociclista *mf*.

motorist ['məʊtərɪst] *n* automobilista *mf*.

motor racing *n* corse *fpl* automobilistiche.

motorway ['məʊtəweɪ] *n* (Br)

autostrada *f*.

motto ['mɒtəʊ] *(pl* **-s)** *n* motto *m*.

mould [məʊld] *n* (Br) (shape) forma *f*, stampo *m*; (substance) muffa *f* ◆ *vt* (Br) formare, modellare.

mouldy ['məʊldɪ] *adj* (Br) ammuffito(-a).

mound [maʊnd] *n* (hill) monticello *m*, collinetta *f*; (pile) mucchio *m*.

mount [maʊnt] *n* (for photo) supporto *m*; (mountain) monte *m* ◆ *vt* (horse) montare a OR su; (photo) sistemare ◆ *vi* (increase) aumentare.

mountain ['maʊntɪn] *n* montagna *f*.

mountain bike *n* mountain bike *f inv*.

mountaineer [ˌmaʊntɪ'nɪəʳ] *n* alpinista *mf*.

mountaineering [ˌmaʊntɪ'nɪərɪŋ] *n*: **to go ~** fare alpinismo.

mountainous ['maʊntɪnəs] *adj* montagnoso(-a).

Mount Rushmore [-'rʌʃmɔːʳ] *n* il monte Rushmore.

ⓘ MOUNT RUSHMORE

I ritratti giganti dei presidenti degli Stati Uniti Washington, Jefferson, Lincoln e Theodore Roosevelt, scolpiti nella roccia granitica, hanno trasformato il monte Rushmore, nel Dakota del Sud, in monumento nazionale e grande centro di attrazione turistica.

---

mourning ['mɔːnɪŋ] *n*: **to be in ~** essere in lutto.

mouse [maʊs] *(pl* **mice)** *n* (animal) topo *m*; (COMPUT) mouse *m*.

moussaka [muːˈsɑːkə] *n* piatto

tipico della cucina greca e turca, composto da strati di carne macinata, melanzane e besciamella.

mousse [muːs] *n* mousse *f inv.*

moustache [məˈstɑːʃ] *n* (Br) baffi *mpl.*

mouth [mauθ] *n* bocca *f; (of cave, tunnel)* entrata *f,* imboccatura *f; (of river)* foce *f,* bocca.

mouthful [ˈmauθful] *n (of food)* boccone *m; (of drink)* sorsata *f.*

mouthorgan [ˈmauθˌɔːɡən] *n* armonica *f* (a bocca).

mouthpiece [ˈmauθpiːs] *n (of telephone)* microfono *m; (of musical instrument)* bocchino *m.*

mouthwash [ˈmauθwɒʃ] *n* collutorio *m.*

move [muːv] *n* mossa *f; (change of house)* trasloco *m* ♦ *vt (shift)* muovere, spostare; *(emotionally)* commuovere ♦ *vi (shift)* muoversi, spostarsi; **to ~ (house)** cambiare casa, traslocare; **to make a ~** *(leave)* andarsene ☐ **move along** *vi* circolare, andare avanti; **move in** *vi (to house)* andare/venire ad abitare; **move off** *vi (train, car)* partire; **move on** *vi (after stopping)* ripartire; **move out** *vi (from house)* sgombrare; **move over** *vi* spostarsi; **move up** *vi (make room)* spostarsi.

movement [ˈmuːvmənt] *n* movimento *m.*

movie [ˈmuːvɪ] *n* film *m inv.*

movie theater *n (Am)* cinema *m inv.*

moving [ˈmuːvɪŋ] *adj (emotionally)* commovente.

mow [məʊ] *vt:* **to ~ the lawn** tagliare l'erba (del prato).

mozzarella [ˌmɒtsəˈrelə] *n* moz-

zarella *f.*

MP *n (abbr of Member of Parliament)* = deputato *m* (-a *f*).

mph *(abbr of miles per hour)* miglia all'ora.

Mr [ˈmɪstə] *abbr* Sig.

Mrs [ˈmɪsɪz] *abbr* Sig.ra.

Ms [mɪz] *abbr abbreviazione che comprende sia Mrs che Miss.*

MSc *n (abbr of Master of Science)* (degree) master *m inv* in materie scientifiche.

much [mʌtʃ] *(compar* more, *superl* most) *adj* molto(-a); **I haven't got ~ money** non ho molti soldi; **as ~ food as you can eat** tanto cibo quanto ne riesci a mangiare; **how ~ time is left?** quanto tempo resta?; **they have so ~ money** hanno tanti di quei soldi; **we have too ~ work** abbiamo troppo lavoro.
♦ *adv* 1. *(to a great extent)* molto; **it's ~ better** è molto meglio; **I like it very ~** mi piace moltissimo; **it's not ~ good** *(inf)* non è un granché; **thank you very ~** grazie tante.
2. *(often)* spesso, molto; **we don't go there ~** non ci andiamo spesso.
♦ *pron* molto; **I haven't got ~** non ne ho molto; **as ~ as you like** quanto ne vuoi; **how ~ is it?** quant'è?; **quanto costa?**

muck [mʌk] *n (dirt)* sudiciume *m* ☐ **muck about** *vi (Br) (inf) (have fun)* divertirsi; *(waste time)* gingillarsi; **muck up** *vt sep (Br: inf)* pasticciare.

mud [mʌd] *n* fango *m.*

muddle [ˈmʌdl] *n:* **to be in a ~** *(confused)* essere confuso; *(in a mess)* essere in disordine.

muddy [ˈmʌdɪ] *adj* fangoso(-a).

mudguard [ˈmʌdɡɑːd] *n* parafango *m*.

muesli ['mju:zli] *n* muesli *m*.

muffin ['mʌfin] *n (roll)* panino *m* soffice *(mangiato caldo, con burro)*; *(cake)* pasticcino *m* soffice.

muffler ['mʌflə'] *n (Am: silencer)* marmitta *f*.

mug [mʌg] *n (cup)* tazza *f* (cilindrica) ◆ *vt* aggredire e derubare.

mugging ['mʌgɪŋ] *n* aggressione *f (a scopo di rapina)*.

muggy ['mʌgɪ] *adj* afoso(-a).

mule [mju:l] *n* mulo *m*.

multicoloured ['mʌltɪ,kʌləd] *adj* multicolore.

multiple ['mʌltɪpl] *adj* multiplo(-a).

multiplex cinema ['mʌltɪpleks-] *n* cinema *m inv* multisala.

multiplication [,mʌltɪplɪ'keɪʃn] *n* moltiplicazione *f*.

multiply ['mʌltɪplaɪ] *vt* moltiplicare ◆ *vi* moltiplicarsi.

multistorey (car park) [,mʌltɪ'stɔ:rɪ-] *n* parcheggio *m* multipiano.

mum [mʌm] *n (Br: inf)* mamma *f*.

mummy ['mʌmɪ] *n (Br: inf: mother)* mamma *f*.

mumps [mʌmps] *n* orecchioni *mpl*.

munch [mʌntʃ] *vt* sgranocchiare.

municipal [mju:'nɪsɪpl] *adj* municipale.

mural ['mju:ərəl] *n* dipinto *m* murale.

murder ['mɜ:də'] *n* assassinio *m*, omicidio *m* ◆ *vt* assassinare.

murderer ['mɜ:dərə'] *n* assassino *m (-a f)*, omicida *mf*.

muscle ['mʌsl] *n* muscolo *m*.

museum [mju:'zi:əm] *n* museo *m*.

mushroom ['mʌʃrʊm] *n* fungo *m*.

music ['mju:zɪk] *n* musica *f*.

musical ['mju:zɪkl] *adj* musicale; *(person)* portato(-a) per la musica ◆ *n* musical *m inv*.

musical instrument *n* strumento *m* musicale.

musician [mju:'zɪʃn] *n* musicista *mf*.

Muslim ['mʊzlɪm] *adj* musulmano(-a) ◆ *n* musulmano *m (-a f)*.

mussels ['mʌslz] *npl* cozze *fpl*.

must [mʌst] *aux vb* dovere ◆ *n (inf)*: it's a ~ è d'obbligo; I ~ go devo andare; the room ~ be vacated by ten la camera deve essere lasciata entro le dieci; you ~ have seen it devi averlo visto; you ~ see that film devi vedere quel film; you ~ be joking! stai scherzando!

mustache ['mʌstæʃ] *(Am)* = **moustache**.

mustard ['mʌstəd] *n* senape *f*, mostarda *f*.

mustn't ['mʌsənt] = **must not**.

mutter ['mʌtə'] *vt* borbottare.

mutton ['mʌtn] *n* carne *f* di montone.

mutual ['mju:tʃʊəl] *adj (feeling)* reciproco(-a), mutuo(-a); *(friend, interest)* comune.

muzzle ['mʌzl] *n (for dog)* museruola *f*.

my [maɪ] *adj* il mio (la mia), i miei (le mie) *(pl)*; ~ **brother** mio fratello.

myself [maɪ'self] *pron (reflexive)* mi; *(after prep)* me; I did it ~ l'ho fatto da solo.

mysterious [mɪ'stɪərɪəs] *adj* misterioso(-a).

mystery ['mɪstərɪ] *n* mistero *m*.

myth [mɪθ] *n* mito *m*.

N

N *(abbr of North)* N.

nag [næg] *vt* tormentare.

nail [neɪl] *n (of finger, toe)* unghia *f; (metal)* chiodo *m* ◆ *vt (fasten)* inchiodare.

nailbrush ['neɪlbrʌʃ] *n* spazzolino *m* da unghie.

nail file *n* limetta *f* per unghie.

nail scissors *npl* forbicine *fpl* da unghie.

nail varnish *n* smalto *m* per unghie.

nail varnish remover [-rə-'mu:və^r] *n* acetone *m*, solvente *m* per unghie.

naive [naɪˈiːv] *adj* ingenuo(-a).

naked ['neɪkɪd] *adj (person)* nudo(-a).

name [neɪm] *n* nome *m* ◆ *vt (baby, animal)* chiamare; *(place)* denominare; *(identify)* dire il nome di, nominare; *(date, price)* fissare; **first ~** nome di battesimo; **last ~** cognome *m*; **what's your ~?** come si chiama?; **my ~ is … mi** chiamo …

namely ['neɪmlɪ] *adv* cioè, vale a dire.

nan bread [næn-] *n* pane indiano *schiacciato e soffice.*

nanny ['nænɪ] *n (childminder)* bambinaia *f; (inf: grandmother)* nonna *f.*

nap [næp] *n*: **to have a ~** fare un pisolino.

napkin ['næpkɪn] *n* tovagliolo *m.*

Naples ['neɪplz] *n* Napoli *f.*

nappy ['næpɪ] *n* pannolino *m.*

nappy liner *n* pannolino *m.*

narcotic [nɑːˈkɒtɪk] *n* narcotico *m.*

narrow ['nærəʊ] *adj (road, gap)* stretto(-a) ◆ *vi (road, gap)* restringersi.

narrow-minded [-ˈmaɪndɪd] *adj* di idee ristrette.

nasty ['nɑːstɪ] *adj (person, comment, taste)* cattivo(-a); *(accident, moment, feeling)* brutto(-a).

nation ['neɪʃn] *n* nazione *f.*

national ['næʃənl] *adj* nazionale ◆ *n* cittadino *m* (-a *f*).

national anthem *n* inno *m* nazionale.

National Health Service *n* = Servizio *m* Sanitario Nazionale.

National Insurance *n (Br: contributions)* = Previdenza *f* Sociale.

nationality [ˌnæʃəˈnælətɪ] *n* nazionalità *f inv.*

national park *n* parco *m* nazionale.

---

i NATIONAL PARK

Come in Italia, anche in Gran Bretagna e negli Stati Uniti i parchi nazionali sono delle vaste zone protette per la loro bellezza naturale. Aperti al pubblico, sono sempre dotati di campeggi attrezzati. Fra i più famosi parchi della Gran Bretagna ricordiamo Snowdonia, il distretto dei Laghi e il Peak District, mentre Yellowstone e Yosemite sono fra i più famosi parchi nazionali americani.

---

nationwide ['neɪʃənwaɪd] *adj* su scala nazionale.

native ['neɪtɪv] adj (customs, population) indigeno(-a); (country) d'origine ♦ n nativo m (-a f); **a ~ speaker of English** una persona di madrelingua inglese.

Native American adj indiano(-a) (d'America) ♦ n indiano m (-a f) (d'America).

NATO ['neɪtəʊ] n NATO f.

natural ['nætʃrəl] adj (charm) naturale; (ability) innato(-a); (swimmer, actor) nato(-a).

natural gas n metano m, gas m naturale.

naturally ['nætʃrəlɪ] adv (of course) naturalmente.

natural yoghurt n yogurt m inv naturale.

nature ['neɪtʃə'] n natura f.

nature reserve n riserva f naturale.

naughty ['nɔːtɪ] adj (child) birichino(-a).

nausea ['nɔːzɪə] n nausea f.

navigate ['nævɪgeɪt] vi (in boat, plane) calcolare la rotta; (in car) fare da navigatore.

navy ['neɪvɪ] n (ships) marina f (militare) ♦ adj: ~ **(blue)** blu scuro (inv).

NB (abbr of nota bene) N.B.

near [nɪə'] adv vicino ♦ adj (place, object) vicino(-a); (relation) prossimo(-a) ♦ prep: ~ **(to)** (edge, object, place) vicino a, presso; **in the ~ future** nel prossimo futuro.

nearby [nɪə'baɪ] adv vicino ♦ adj vicino(-a).

nearly ['nɪəlɪ] adv quasi.

near side n (for right-hand drive) destra f; (for left-hand drive) sinistra f.

neat [niːt] adj (room) ordinato(-a);

(writing) chiaro(-a); (work) preciso(-a); (whisky, vodka etc) liscio(-a).

neatly ['niːtlɪ] adv (placed, arranged) in modo ordinato; (written) in modo chiaro.

necessarily [,nesə'serɪlɪ, Br 'nesəsrɪlɪ] adv: **not ~ non** necessariamente.

necessary ['nesəsrɪ] adj necessario(-a); **it is ~ to do it** è necessario farlo.

necessity [nɪ'sesɪtɪ] n necessità f inv □ **necessities** npl necessità fpl.

neck [nek] n collo m.

necklace ['neklɪs] n collana f.

nectarine ['nektərɪn] n pescanoce f.

need [niːd] n bisogno m ♦ vt avere bisogno di; **to ~ to do sthg** dover fare qc; **you don't ~ to go** non c'è bisogno che tu ci vada.

needle ['niːdl] n ago m; (for record player) puntina f.

needlework ['niːdlwɜːk] n (SCH) cucito m.

needn't ['niːdənt] = **need not**.

needy ['niːdɪ] adj bisognoso(-a).

negative ['negətɪv] adj negativo(-a) ♦ n (in photography) negativo m; (GRAMM) negazione f.

neglect [nɪ'glekt] vt trascurare.

negligence ['neglɪdʒəns] n negligenza f.

negotiations [nɪ,gəʊʃɪ'eɪʃnz] npl negoziati mpl, trattative fpl.

negro ['niːgrəʊ] (pl -es) n negro m (-a f).

neighbour ['neɪbə'] n vicino m (-a f).

neighbourhood ['neɪbəhʊd] n quartiere m, vicinato m.

neighbouring ['neɪbərɪŋ] adj

vicino(-a), confinante.

neither ['naɪðə', 'niːðə'] *adj:* ~ **bag is big enough** nessuna delle due borse è abbastanza grande ♦ *pron:* ~ **of us** nessuno(-a) di noi (due) ♦ *conj:* ~ **do I** neanch'io, nemmeno io; ~ ... **nor** ... né ... né ...

neon light ['niːɒn-] *n* luce *f* al neon.

nephew ['nefjuː] *n* nipote *m*.

nerve [nɜːv] *n (in body)* nervo *m*; *(courage)* coraggio *m*; **what a** ~! che faccia tosta!

nervous ['nɜːvəs] *adj* nervoso(-a).

nervous breakdown *n* esaurimento *m* nervoso.

nest [nest] *n* nido *m*.

net [net] *n* rete *f* ♦ *adj* netto(-a).

netball ['netbɔːl] *n* specie di pallacanestro femminile.

Netherlands ['neðələndz] *npl:* **the** ~ i Paesi Bassi.

nettle ['netl] *n* ortica *f*.

network ['netwɜːk] *n* rete *f*.

neurotic [,njʊə'rɒtɪk] *adj* nevrotico(-a).

neutral ['njuːtrəl] *adj (country, person)* neutrale; *(in colour)* neutro(-a) ♦ *n (AUT):* **in** ~ in folle.

never ['nevə'] *adv* non ...) mai; **she's** ~ **late** non è mai in ritardo; **I** ~ **knew he was married** non sapevo che fosse sposato; ~ **mind!** non preoccuparti!

nevertheless [,nevəðə'les] *adv* tuttavia, ciononostante.

new [njuː] *adj* nuovo(-a).

newly ['njuːlɪ] *adv* di recente.

new potatoes *npl* patate *fpl* novelle.

news [njuːz] *n (information)* noti-

zie *fpl; (on TV)* telegiornale *m; (on radio)* giornale *m* radio; **a piece of** ~ una notizia.

newsagent ['njuːˌzeɪdʒənt] *n (shop)* giornalaio *m*.

newspaper ['njuːz,peɪpə'] *n* giornale *m*.

New Year *n* anno *m* nuovo.

ℹ️ NEW YEAR

Anche in Gran Bretagna la notte di San Silvestro è celebrata con feste, in casa o fuori. Allo scoccare della mezzanotte, la fine dell'anno vecchio e l'arrivo di quello nuovo vengono tradizionalmente salutati cantando "Auld Lang Syne". La notte di fine anno riveste un'importanza del tutto particolare in Scozia, dove è nota come "Hogmanay". Così come in Italia, il giorno di Capodanno è un giorno festivo in tutta la Gran Bretagna.

New Year's Day *n* Capodanno.

New Year's Eve *n* l'ultimo *m* dell'anno, San Silvestro *m*.

New Zealand [-'ziːlənd] *n* la Nuova Zelanda.

next [nekst] *adj* prossimo(-a); *(room, house)* accanto ♦ *adv (afterwards)* dopo; *(on next occasion)* di nuovo; **when does the** ~ **bus leave?** quando parte il prossimo autobus?; ~ **to** *(by the side of)* accanto a; ~ **the week after** ~ la settimana dopo la prossima.

next door *adv* accanto.

next of kin [-kɪn] *n* parente *m* prossimo (parente prossima *f*).

NHS *n (abbr of National Heal*

Service) = S.S.N. *m.*

nib [nɪb] *n* pennino *m.*

nibble ['nɪbl] *vt (eat)* mangiucchiare; *(bite)* mordicchiare.

nice [naɪs] *adj (taste, meal)* buono(-a); *(day, clothes, house)* bello(-a); *(person, gesture)* simpatico(-a), gentile; *(feeling, job)* piacevole; **to have a ~ time** divertirsi; **~ to see you!** piacere di rivederti!

nickel ['nɪkl] *n (metal)* nichel *m;* *(Am: coin)* moneta da cinque centesimi di dollaro.

nickname ['nɪkneɪm] *n* soprannome *m.*

niece [niːs] *n* nipote *f.*

night [naɪt] *n* notte *f;* *(evening)* sera *f;* **at ~** *(not in daytime)* di notte; *(in evening)* di sera; **by ~** di notte; **last ~** *(yesterday evening)* ieri sera; *(very late)* ieri notte.

nightclub ['naɪtklʌb] *n* locale *m* notturno.

nightdress ['naɪtdres] *n* camicia *f* da notte.

nightie ['naɪtɪ] *n (inf)* camicia *f* da notte.

nightlife ['naɪtlaɪf] *n* vita *f* notturna.

nightly ['naɪtlɪ] *adv* ogni notte; *(every evening)* ogni sera.

nightmare ['naɪtmeəʳ] *n* incubo *m.*

night safe *n* cassa *f* continua.

night school *n* scuola *f* serale.

nightshift ['naɪtʃɪft] *n* turno *m* di notte.

nil [nɪl] *n (SPORT)* zero *m.*

Nile [naɪl] *n:* **the ~** il Nilo.

nine [naɪn] *num* nove, → **six.**

nineteen [,naɪn'tiːn] *num* diciannove; **~ ninety-five** millenovecentonovantacinque, → **six.**

nineteenth [,naɪn'tiːnθ] *num* diciannovesimo(-a), → **sixth.**

ninetieth ['naɪntɪɪθ] *num* novantesimo(-a), → **sixth.**

ninety ['naɪntɪ] *num* novanta, → **six.**

ninth [naɪnθ] *num* nono(-a), → **sixth.**

nip [nɪp] *vt (pinch)* pizzicare.

nipple ['nɪpl] *n (of breast)* capezzolo *m;* *(of bottle)* tettarella *f.*

nitrogen ['naɪtrədʒən] *n* azoto *m.*

no [nəʊ] *adv* no ♦ *adj* nessuno(-a) ♦ *n* no *m inv;* **I've got ~ time** non ho tempo; **I've got ~ money left** non ho più soldi.

noble ['nəʊbl] *adj* nobile.

nobody ['nəʊbədɪ] *pron* nessuno.

nod [nɒd] *vi (in agreement)* annuire.

noise [nɔɪz] *n* rumore *m.*

noisy ['nɔɪzɪ] *adj* rumoroso(-a).

nominate ['nɒmɪneɪt] *vt (choose)* nominare; *(suggest)* proporre come candidato.

non-alcoholic *adj* analcolico(-a).

none [nʌn] *pron* nessuno *m* (-a *f);* **there's ~ left** non ce n'è più.

nonetheless [,nʌnðə'les] *adv* tuttavia, nondimeno.

non-fiction *n* opere *fpl* non narrative *(saggistica, ecc.).*

non-iron *adj:* **'non-iron'** 'lava e indossa', 'non stiro'.

nonsense ['nɒnsəns] *n* sciocchezze *fpl,* fesserie *fpl.*

non-smoker *n* non fumatore *m* (-trice *f).*

non-stick *adj* antiaderente.

non-stop *adj (flight)* diretto(-a); *(talking, arguing)* continuo(-a) ♦ *adv (fly)* senza scalo; *(run, rain)* ininterrottamente, senza sosta.

noodles ['nu:dlz] *npl* taglierini *mpl.*

noon [nu:n] *n* mezzogiorno *m.*

no-one *n* = nobody.

nor [nɔ:ʳ] *conj* neanche, nemmeno; ~ **do I** neanch'io, nemmeno io, → **neither.**

normal ['nɔ:ml] *adj* normale.

normally ['nɔ:məlɪ] *adv* normalmente.

north [nɔ:θ] *n* nord *m*, settentrione *m* ♦ *adj* del nord ♦ *adv* (fly, walk) verso nord; (be situated) a nord; **in the ~ of England** nel nord dell'Inghilterra.

North America *n* l'America *f* del Nord.

northbound ['nɔ:θbaʊnd] *adj* diretto(-a) a nord.

northeast *n* nord-est *m.*

northern ['nɔ:ðən] *adj* settentrionale, del nord.

Northern Ireland *n* l'Irlanda *f* del Nord.

North Pole *n* Polo *m* Nord.

North Sea *n* Mare *m* del Nord.

northwards ['nɔ:θwədz] *adv* verso nord.

northwest *n* nord-ovest *m.*

Norway ['nɔ:weɪ] *n* la Norvegia.

Norwegian [nɔ:'wi:dʒən] *adj* norvegese ♦ *n* (person) norvegese *mf*; (language) norvegese *m.*

nose [nəʊz] *n* (of person) naso *m*; (of animal, plane) muso *m*; (of rocket) punta *f.*

nosebleed ['nəʊzbli:d] *n* emorragia *f* nasale.

no-smoking area *n* zona *f* non fumatori.

nostril ['nɒstrəl] *n* narice *f.*

nosy ['nəʊzɪ] *adj* curioso(-a).

not [nɒt] *adv* non; **she's ~ there** non c'è; ~ **yet** non ancora; ~ **at all** (pleased, interested) per niente; (in reply to thanks) di niente, prego.

notably ['nəʊtəblɪ] *adv* (in particular) in particolare.

note [nəʊt] *n* nota *f*; (message, bank note) biglietto *m* ♦ *vt* (notice) notare; (write down) annotare; **to take ~s** prendere appunti.

notebook ['nəʊtbʊk] *n* taccuino *m.*

noted ['nəʊtɪd] *adj* celebre.

notepaper ['nəʊtpeɪpəʳ] *n* carta *f* da lettere.

nothing ['nʌθɪŋ] *pron* niente, nulla; **he did ~** non ha fatto niente; ~ **new/interesting** niente di nuovo/interessante; **for ~** per niente.

notice ['nəʊtɪs] *vt* notare, accorgersi di ♦ *n* (written announcement) avviso *m*; (warning) preavviso *m*; **to take ~ of** fare caso a; **to hand in one's ~** dare il preavviso, licenziarsi.

noticeable ['nəʊtɪsəbl] *adj* evidente.

notice board *n* tabellone *m* per avvisi.

notion ['nəʊʃn] *n* idea *f.*

notorious [nəʊ'tɔ:rɪəs] *adj* famigerato(-a).

nougat ['nu:gɑ:] *n* torrone *m.*

nought [nɔ:t] *n* zero *m.*

noun [naʊn] *n* nome *m*, sostantivo *m.*

nourishment ['nʌrɪʃmənt] *n* nutrimento *m.*

Nov. (abbr of November) nov.

novel ['nɒvl] *n* romanzo *m* ♦ *a* nuovo(-a).

novelist ['nɒvəlɪst] *n* romanziere *m* (-a *f*).

November [nə'vembə'] *n* novembre *m*, → **September**.

now [nau] *adv* ora, adesso ♦ *conj*: ~ **(that)** adesso che, ora che; **just** ~ proprio ora; **right** ~ *(at the moment)* in questo momento; *(immediately)* subito; **by** ~ ormai; **from** ~ **on** d'ora in poi.

nowadays ['nauədeɪz] *adv* oggigiorno.

nowhere ['nəuweə'] *adv* da nessuna parte, in nessun posto.

nozzle ['nɒzl] *n* boccaglio *m*.

nuclear ['nju:klɪə'] *adj* nucleare.

nude [nju:d] *adj* nudo(-a).

nudge [nʌdʒ] *vt* dare un colpetto di gomito a.

nuisance ['nju:sns] *n*: **it's a real ~!** è una vera seccatura!; **he's such a ~!** è un tale scocciatore!

numb [nʌm] *adj* intorpidito(-a).

number ['nʌmbə'] *n* numero *m* ♦ *vt (give number to)* numerare.

numberplate ['nʌmbəpleɪt] *n* targa *f*.

numeral ['nju:mərəl] *n* numero *m*, cifra *f*.

numerous ['nju:mərəs] *adj* numeroso(-a).

nun [nʌn] *n* suora *f*.

nurse [nɜ:s] *n* infermiera *f* ♦ *vt (look after)* avere cura di, curare; **male** ~ infermiere *m*.

nursery ['nɜ:srɪ] *n (in house)* stanza *f* dei bambini; *(for plants)* vivaio *m*.

nursery (school) *n* scuola *f* materna.

nursery slope *n* pista *f* per sciatori principianti.

nursing ['nɜ:sɪŋ] *n (profession)* professione *f* d'infermiera.

nut [nʌt] *n (to eat)* frutta *f* secca *(noci, nocciole, ecc.)*; *(of metal)* dado *m*.

nutcrackers ['nʌt,krækəz] *npl* schiaccianoci *m inv*.

nutmeg ['nʌtmeg] *n* noce *f* moscata.

nylon ['naɪlɒn] *n* nailon *m* ♦ *adj* di nailon.

o' [ə] *abbr* = **of**.

O *n (zero)* zero *m*.

oak [əuk] *n* quercia *f* ♦ *adj* di quercia.

OAP *abbr* = **old age pensioner**.

oar [ɔ:'] *n* remo *m*.

oatcake ['əutkeɪk] *n* biscotto *m* di farina d'avena.

oath [əuθ] *n (promise)* giuramento *m*.

oatmeal ['əutmi:l] *n* farina *f* d'avena.

oats [əuts] *npl* avena *f*.

obedient [ə'bi:djənt] *adj* ubbidiente.

obey [ə'beɪ] *vt (person, command)* ubbidire a; *(regulations)* osservare.

object [*n* 'ɒbdʒɪkt, *vt* ɒb'dʒekt] *n (thing)* oggetto *m*; *(purpose)* scopo *m*; *(GRAMM)* complemento *m* oggetto ♦ *vi*: **to** ~ **(to)** *(disapprove of)* disapprovare; *(oppose)* opporsi (a), protestare (contro).

objection [əb'dʒekʃn] *n* obie-

188

zione f.

objective [əb'dʒektɪv] n obiettivo m.

obligation [ɒblɪ'geɪʃn] n obbligo m, dovere m.

obligatory [ə'blɪgətrɪ] adj obbligatorio(-a).

oblige [ə'blaɪdʒ] vt: to ~ sb to do sthg obbligare qn a fare qc.

oblique [ə'bli:k] adj obliquo(-a).

oblong ['ɒblɒŋ] adj oblungo(-a), rettangolare ♦ n rettangolo m.

obnoxious [əb'nɒkʃəs] adj odioso(-a).

oboe ['əubəu] n oboe m.

obscene [əb'si:n] adj osceno(-a).

obscure [əb'skjuə'] adj oscuro(-a).

observant [əb'zɜ:vnt] adj dotato(-a) di spirito d'osservazione.

observation [ˌɒbzə'veɪʃn] n osservazione f.

observatory [əb'zɜ:vətrɪ] n osservatorio m.

observe [əb'zɜ:v] vt (watch, see) osservare.

obsessed [əb'sest] adj ossessionato(-a).

obsession [əb'seʃn] n ossessione f.

obsolete ['ɒbsəli:t] adj obsoleto(-a).

obstacle ['ɒbstəkl] n ostacolo m.

obstinate ['ɒbstənət] adj ostinato(-a).

obstruct [əb'strʌkt] vt (road, path) ostruire.

obstruction [əb'strʌkʃn] n (in road, path) ostruzione f.

obtain [əb'teɪn] vt ottenere.

obtainable [əb'teɪnəbl] adj ottenibile.

obvious ['ɒbvɪəs] adj ovvio(-a), evidente.

obviously ['ɒbvɪəslɪ] adv ovviamente.

occasion [ə'keɪʒn] n occasione f; (important event) avvenimento m.

occasional [ə'keɪʒənl] adj saltuario(-a), occasionale.

occasionally [ə'keɪʒnəlɪ] adv saltuariamente, di tanto in tanto.

occupant ['ɒkjupənt] n occupante mf.

occupation [ˌɒkju'peɪʃn] n lavoro m; (on form) occupazione f.

occupied ['ɒkjupaɪd] adj (toilet) occupato(-a).

occupy ['ɒkjupaɪ] vt occupare.

occur [ə'kɜ:'] vi (happen) accadere, avvenire; (exist) trovarsi, essere presente.

occurrence [ə'kʌrəns] n (event) evento m, caso m.

ocean ['əuʃn] n oceano m; the ~ (Am: sea) il mare.

o'clock [ə'klɒk] adv: it's one ~ è l'una; it's seven ~ sono le sette; at one ~ all'una; at seven ~ alle sette.

Oct. (abbr of October) ott.

October [ɒk'təubə'] n ottobre m, → September.

octopus ['ɒktəpəs] n polpo m, piovra f.

odd [ɒd] adj (strange) strano(-a) (number) dispari (inv); (not matching) spaiato(-a); (occasional) saltuario(-a), occasionale; 60 ~ miles una sessantina di miglia; some ~ bits of paper vari pezzetti di carta; ~ jobs lavori mpl occasionali.

odds [ɒdz] npl (in betting) quota (chances) probabilità fpl; ~ and ends un po' di tutto.

odor ['əʊdər] (Am) = **odour**.

odour ['əʊdə] n (Br) odore m.

of [ɒv] prep 1. (gen) di; **the handle ~ the door** la maniglia della porta; **a group ~ schoolchildren** un gruppo di scolari; **a great love ~ art** un grande amore per l'arte.
2. (expressing amount) di; **a piece ~ cake** una fetta di torta; **a fall ~ 20%** un ribasso del 20%; **a town ~ 50,000 people** una città di 50 000 abitanti.
3. (made from) di, in; **a house ~ stone** una casa di pietra; **it's made ~ wood** è di OR in legno.
4. (referring to time) di; **the summer ~ 1969** l'estate del 1969; **the 26th ~ August** il 26 agosto.
5. (indicating cause) di; **he died ~ cancer** è morto di cancro.
6. (on the part of) da parte di; **that was very kind ~ you** è stato molto gentile da parte tua.
7. (Am: in telling the time): **it's ten ~ four** sono le quattro meno dieci.

off [ɒf] adv 1. (away): **to drive ~** partire; **to get ~** (from bus, train, plane, boat) scendere; **we're ~ to Austria next week** partiamo per l'Austria la settimana prossima.
2. (expressing removal): **to cut sthg ~** tagliare qc; **to take sthg ~** togliere qc.
3. (so as to stop working): **to turn sthg ~** (TV, radio, engine) spegnere qc; (tap) chiudere qc.
4. (expressing distance or time away): **it's 10 miles ~** è a 10 miglia (da qui); **it's two months ~** mancano due mesi; **it's a long way ~** è lontano.
5. (not at work): **I'm ~ next Tuesday** martedì prossimo non lavoro; **I'm taking a week ~** prendo una setti-

mana di ferie.
♦ prep 1. (away from) da; **to get ~ sthg** scendere da qc; **~ the coast** al largo della costa; **just ~ the main road** poco lontano dalla strada principale.
2. (indicating removal) da; **take the lid ~ the jar** togli il tappo dal barattolo; **they've taken £20 ~ the price** mi hanno fatto uno sconto di 20 sterline.
3. (absent from): **to be ~ work** essere assente dal lavoro.
4. (inf: from) da; **I bought it ~ her** l'ho comprato da lei.
5. (inf: no longer liking): **I'm ~ my food** non ho appetito, non mi va di mangiare.
♦ adj 1. (food) andato(-a) a male.
2. (TV, radio, engine) spento(-a); (tap) chiuso(-a).
3. (cancelled) annullato(-a).
4. (not available) esaurito(-a).

offence [ə'fens] n (Br) (minor crime) infrazione f; (serious crime) reato m; **to take ~ (at)** offendersi (per).

offend [ə'fend] vt (upset) offendere.

offender [ə'fendə'] n (criminal) delinquente mf.

offense [ə'fens] (Am) = **offence**.

offensive [ə'fensɪv] adj (insulting) offensivo(-a).

offer ['ɒfə'] n offerta f ♦ vt offrire; **on ~** (at reduced price) in offerta; **to ~ to do sthg** offrirsi di fare qc; **to ~ sb sthg** offrire qc a qn.

office ['ɒfɪs] n (room) ufficio m.

office block n palazzo m di uffici.

officer ['ɒfɪsə'] n (MIL) ufficiale m; (policeman) agente m (di polizia).

official [əˈfɪʃl] *adj* ufficiale ◆ *n* funzionario *m* (-a *f*).

officially [əˈfɪʃəlɪ] *adv* ufficialmente.

off-licence *n* (Br) negozio *m* di bevande alcoliche.

off-peak *adj* (train) delle ore non di punta; (ticket) a tariffa ridotta.

off sales *npl* (Br) vendita *f* di bevande alcoliche da asporto.

off-season *n* bassa stagione *f*.

offshore [ˈɒfʃɔːᵊ] *adj* (breeze) di terra.

off side *n* (for right-hand drive) lato *m* destro; (for left-hand drive) lato sinistro.

off-the-peg *adj* confezionato(-a).

often [ˈɒfn, ˈɒftn] *adv* spesso; **how ~ do the buses run?** ogni quanto passano gli autobus?; **every so ~** ogni tanto.

oh [əʊ] *excl* oh!

oil [ɔɪl] *n* olio *m*; (fuel) petrolio *m*.

oilcan [ˈɔɪlkæn] *n* oliatore *m*.

oil filter *n* filtro *m* dell'olio.

oil rig *n* piattaforma *f* petrolifera.

oily [ˈɔɪlɪ] *adj* unto(-a).

ointment [ˈɔɪntmənt] *n* unguento *m*, pomata *f*.

OK [ˌəʊˈkeɪ] *adv* (inf) (expressing agreement) va bene, d'accordo; (satisfactorily, well) bene ◆ *adj* (of average quality) non male; **is that ~?** va bene?; **are you ~?** tutto bene?

okay [ˌəʊˈkeɪ] = **OK**.

old [əʊld] *adj* vecchio(-a); (person) vecchio, anziano(-a); **how ~ are you?** quanti anni hai?; **I'm 36 years ~** ho 36 anni; **to get ~** invecchiare.

old age *n* vecchiaia *f*.

old age pensioner *n* pensionato *m* (-a *f*).

O-level *n* esame oggi sostituito dal 'GCSE'.

olive [ˈɒlɪv] *n* oliva *f*.

olive oil *n* olio *m* d'oliva.

Olympic Games [əˈlɪmpɪk-] *npl* giochi *mpl* olimpici, Olimpiadi *fpl*.

omelette [ˈɒmlɪt] *n* frittata *f*, omelette *f inv*; **mushroom ~** frittata ai funghi.

ominous [ˈɒmɪnəs] *adj* sinistro(-a).

omit [əˈmɪt] *vt* omettere.

on [ɒn] *prep* 1. (expressing position, location) su; **it's ~ the table** è sul tavolo; **a picture ~ the wall** un quadro alla parete; **the exhaust ~ the car** il tubo di scappamento dell'automobile; **~ my right** alla mia destra; **~ the right** a OR sulla destra; **we stayed ~ a farm** ci siamo fermati in una fattoria; **a hotel ~ George Street** un albergo in George Street.
2. (with forms of transport): **~ the train/plane** in treno/aereo; **to get ~ a bus** salire su un autobus.
3. (expressing means, method): **~ foot** a piedi; **~ the radio** alla radio; **~ TV** in TV, alla televisione; **~ the piano** al piano.
4. (using): **it runs ~ unleaded petrol** va a benzina verde; **to be ~ medication** prendere medicine.
5. (about): **a book ~ Germany** un libro sulla Germania.
6. (expressing time): **~ arrival** all'arrivo; **~ Tuesday** martedì; **25th August** il 25 agosto.
7. (with regard to) su; **a tax ~ imports** una tassa sulle import...

zioni; **the effect ~ Britain** l'effetto sulla Gran Bretagna.

8. *(describing activity, state)* in; **~ holiday** in vacanza; **~ offer** in offerta; **~ sale** in vendita.

9. *(in phrases):* **do you have any money ~ you?** *(inf)* hai un po' di soldi con te?; **the drinks are ~ me** offro io da bere.

♦ *adv* **1.** *(in place, covering):* **to have sthg ~** *(clothes)* indossare qc; **put the lid ~** mettici il coperchio; **to put one's clothes ~** vestirsi.

2. *(film, play, programme):* **the news is ~** c'è il telegiornale; **what's ~ at the cinema?** cosa danno al cinema?

3. *(with transport):* **to get ~** salire.

4. *(functioning):* **to turn sthg ~** *(TV, radio, engine)* accendere qc; *(tap)* aprire qc.

5. *(taking place):* **how long is the festival ~?** quanto (tempo) dura il festival?

6. *(further forward):* **to drive ~** continuare a guidare.

7. *(in phrases):* **do you have anything ~ tonight?** fai qualcosa stasera?

♦ *adj* *(TV, engine, light)* acceso(-a); *(tap)* aperto(-a).

once [wʌns] *adv* una volta ♦ *conj* una volta che, non appena; **at ~** *(immediately)* subito; *(at the same time)* insieme, contemporaneamente; **for ~** per una volta; **~ more** ancora una volta.

oncoming ['ɒn,kʌmɪŋ] *adj* *(traffic)* che procede in senso opposto.

one [wʌn] *num* uno(-a) ♦ *adj* *(only)* unico(-a) ♦ *pron* uno(-a); **~ thirty-~** trentuno; **~ fifth** un quinto; **that ~** quello(-a); **which ~?** quale?; **this ~** questo(-a); **I want ~** voglio uno; **the ~ I told you**

about quello di cui ti ho detto; **~ of my friends** uno dei miei amici; **~ day** un giorno.

one-piece (swimsuit) *n* costume *m* intero.

oneself [wʌn'self] *pron (reflexive)* si; *(after prep)* se stesso(-a), sé.

one-way *adj* *(street)* a senso unico; *(ticket)* di sola andata.

onion ['ʌnjən] *n* cipolla *f*.

onion bhaji [-'bɑːdʒi] *n* polpetta a base di cipolla e spezie varie, fritta e servita come antipasto nella cucina indiana.

onion rings *npl* rondelle *fpl* di cipolle fritte.

only ['əʊnlɪ] *adj* solo(-a), unico (-a) ♦ *adv* solo, soltanto; **he's an ~ child** è figlio unico; **I ~ want one** ne voglio solo uno; **we've ~ just arrived** siamo appena arrivati; **there's ~ just enough** ce n'è appena a sufficienza; **'members ~'** 'riservato ai soci'; **not ~** non solo.

onto ['ɒntu:] *prep (with verbs of movement)* su; **to get ~ sb** *(telephone)* chiamare qn.

onward ['ɒnwəd] *adv* = **onwards** ♦ *adj:* **the ~ journey** il proseguimento.

onwards ['ɒnwədz] *adv (forwards)* in avanti; **from now ~** da ora in poi; **from October ~** da ottobre in poi.

opal ['əʊpl] *n* opale *m* o *f*.

opaque [əʊ'peɪk] *adj (not transparent)* opaco(-a).

open ['əʊpn] *adj* aperto(-a) ♦ *vt* aprire ♦ *vi* *(door, lock, meeting)* aprirsi; *(shop, office, bank)* aprire; *(play, film)* cominciare; **are you ~ at the weekend?** siete aperti il fine settimana?; **wide ~** spalancato(-a);

in the ~ (air) all'aperto □ **open onto** vt fus dare su; **open up** vi aprire.

open-air adj all'aperto.

opening ['əʊpnɪŋ] n apertura f; (opportunity) opportunità f inv.

opening hours npl orario m di apertura.

open-minded [-'maɪndɪd] adj aperto(-a).

open-plan adj senza pareti divisorie.

open sandwich n tartina f.

opera ['ɒpərə] n opera f.

opera house n teatro m dell'opera.

operate ['ɒpəreɪt] vt (machine) azionare, far funzionare ♦ vi (work) funzionare, agire; **to ~ on sb** operare qn.

operating room ['ɒpəreɪtɪŋ-] n (Am) = operating theatre.

operating theatre ['ɒpəreɪtɪŋ-] n (Br) sala f operatoria.

operation [ˌɒpə'reɪʃn] n operazione f; **to be in ~** (law, system) essere in vigore; **to have an ~** operarsi.

operator ['ɒpəreɪtə[r]] n (on phone) centralinista mf.

opinion [ə'pɪnjən] n opinione f, parere m; **in my ~** a mio parere, secondo me.

opponent [ə'pəʊnənt] n avversario m (-a f).

opportunity [ˌɒpə'tju:nətɪ] n opportunità f inv, occasione f.

oppose [ə'pəʊz] vt opporsi a.

opposed [ə'pəʊzd] adj: **to be ~ to** essere contrario(-a) a.

opposite ['ɒpəzɪt] adj (facing) di fronte; (totally different) opposto

(-a), contrario(-a) ♦ prep di fronte a ♦ n: **the ~ (of)** il contrario (di).

opposition [ˌɒpə'zɪʃn] n opposizione f; (SPORT) avversari mpl.

opt [ɒpt] vt: **to ~ to do sthg** scegliere di fare qc.

optician's [ɒp'tɪʃns] n (shop) ottico m.

optimist ['ɒptɪmɪst] n ottimista mf.

optimistic [ˌɒptɪ'mɪstɪk] adj ottimistico(-a).

option ['ɒpʃn] n (alternative) scelta f, alternativa f; (optional extra) optional m inv.

optional ['ɒpʃənl] adj facoltativo(-a).

or [ɔ:[r]] conj o, oppure; (otherwise) se no, altrimenti; (after negative): **I can't read ~ write** non so (né) leggere né scrivere.

oral ['ɔ:rəl] adj orale ♦ n orale m.

orange ['ɒrɪndʒ] adj arancione ♦ n (fruit) arancia f; (colour) arancione m.

orange juice n succo m d'arancia.

orange squash n (Br) aranciata f non gassata.

orbit ['ɔ:bɪt] n orbita f.

orbital (motorway) ['ɔ:bɪtl-] n (Br) raccordo m anulare.

orchard ['ɔ:tʃəd] n frutteto m.

orchestra ['ɔ:kɪstrə] n orchestra f.

ordeal [ɔ:'di:l] n (durissima) esperienza f, travaglio m.

order ['ɔ:də[r]] n ordine m; (in restaurant, for goods) ordinazione f ♦ vt & vi ordinare; **in ~ to** allo scopo di, per; **out of ~** (not working) guasto; **in working ~** funzionante; **~ sb to do sthg** ordinare a qn di fare qc.

order form *n* modulo *m* d'ordinazione.

ordinary ['ɔ:dənrɪ] *adj* ordinario(-a), comune.

ore [ɔ:r] *n* minerale *m* (grezzo).

oregano [ˌɒrɪ'gɑ:nəʊ] *n* origano *m*.

organ ['ɔ:gən] *n* organo *m*.

organic [ɔ:'gænɪk] *adj (food)* biologico(-a).

organization [ˌɔ:gənaɪ'zeɪʃn] *n* organizzazione *f*.

organize ['ɔ:gənaɪz] *vt* organizzare.

organizer ['ɔ:gənaɪzər] *n (person)* organizzatore *m* (-trice *f*); *(diary)* agenda *f*.

oriental [ˌɔ:rɪ'entl] *adj* orientale.

orientate ['ɔ:rɪenteɪt] *vt*: **to ~ o.s.** orientarsi.

origin ['ɒrɪdʒɪn] *n* origine *f*.

original [ə'rɪdʒənl] *adj (first)* originario(-a); *(novel)* originale.

originally [ə'rɪdʒənəlɪ] *adv (formerly)* originariamente.

originate [ə'rɪdʒəneɪt] *vi*: **to ~ (from)** avere origine (da).

ornament ['ɔ:nəmənt] *n (object)* soprammobile *m*.

ornamental [ˌɔ:nə'mentl] *adj* ornamentale.

ornate [ɔ:'neɪt] *adj* molto ornato(-a).

orphan ['ɔ:fn] *n* orfano *m* (-a *f*).

orthodox ['ɔ:θədɒks] *adj* ortodosso(-a).

ostentatious [ˌɒstən'teɪʃəs] *adj* ostentoso(-a); *(action, behaviour)* ostentato(-a).

ostrich ['ɒstrɪtʃ] *n* struzzo *m*.

other ['ʌðər] *adj* altro(-a) ♦ *pron* altro(-a) ♦ *adv*: **~ than** a parte; **the ~ (one)** l'altro; **the ~ day** l'altro

giorno; **one after the ~** uno dopo l'altro.

otherwise ['ʌðəwaɪz] *adv* altrimenti.

otter ['ɒtər] *n* lontra *f*.

ought [ɔ:t] *aux vb* dovere; **you ~ to have gone** avresti dovuto andarci; **you ~ to see a doctor** dovresti andare dal dottore; **the car ~ to be ready by Friday** la macchina dovrebbe essere pronta per venerdì.

ounce [aʊns] *n (unit of measurement)* = 28,35 g, oncia *f*.

our [aʊər] *adj* il nostro (la nostra), i nostri (le nostre) *(pl)*; **~ mother** nostra madre.

ours [aʊəz] *pron* il nostro (la nostra), i nostri (le nostre) *(pl)*; **a friend of ~** un nostro amico.

ourselves [aʊə'selvz] *pron (reflexive)* ci; *(after prep)* noi stessi (-e), noi; **we did it ~** l'abbiamo fatto da soli.

out [aʊt] *adj* **1.** *(light, cigarette)* spento(-a).
2. *(wrong)* inesatto(-a); **the bill's £10 ~** c'è un errore di 10 sterline nel conto.
♦ *adv* **1.** *(outside)* fuori; **to get ~ (of)** *(car)* scendere (da); **to go ~ (of)** uscire (da); **it's cold ~** fa freddo fuori.
2. *(not at home, work)* fuori; **to go ~** uscire, andare fuori.
3. *(so as to be extinguished)*: **to turn sthg ~** spegnere qc; **put your cigarette ~** spegni la sigaretta.
4. *(expressing removal)*: **to pour sthg ~** versare qc; **to take sthg ~ (of)** tirar fuori qc (da); *(from bank)* ritirare qc (da).
5. *(outwards)*: **to stick ~** sporgere.
6. *(expressing distribution)*: **to hand sthg ~** distribuire qc.

7. (in phrases): **to stay ~ of the sun** evitare il sole; **made ~ of wood** in OR di legno; **five ~ of ten women** cinque donne su dieci; **I'm ~ of cigarettes** ho finito le sigarette.

outback ['aʊtbæk] n: **the ~** l'outback m, l'entroterra m australiano.

outboard (motor) ['aʊtbɔːd] n motore m fuoribordo.

outbreak ['aʊtbreɪk] n (of fighting) scoppio m; (of disease) epidemia f.

outburst ['aʊtbɜːst] n scoppio m.

outcome ['aʊtkʌm] n esito m, risultato m.

outcrop ['aʊtkrɒp] n affioramento m.

outdated [,aʊt'deɪtɪd] adj antiquato(-a).

outdo [,aʊt'duː] (pt -did, pp -done) vt fare meglio di, superare.

outdoor ['aʊtdɔːʳ] adj all'aperto.

outdoors [aʊt'dɔːz] adv all'aperto, fuori.

outer ['aʊtəʳ] adj esterno(-a).

outer space n spazio m cosmico.

outfit ['aʊtfɪt] n (clothes) completo m.

outing ['aʊtɪŋ] n gita f.

outlet ['aʊtlet] n (pipe) scarico m, sbocco m; **'no ~'** (Am) 'strada senza uscita'.

outline ['aʊtlaɪn] n profilo m.

outlook ['aʊtlʊk] n (for future) prospettiva f; (of weather) previsioni fpl; (attitude) modo m di vedere.

out-of-date adj (old-fashioned) superato(-a); (passport, licence) scaduto(-a).

outpatients'   (depart-

ment) ['aʊt,peɪʃnts-] n reparto m pazienti esterni.

output ['aʊtpʊt] n (of factory) produzione f; (COMPUT: printout) output m inv, tabulato m.

outrage ['aʊtreɪdʒ] n (cruel act) atrocità f inv.

outrageous [aʊt'reɪdʒəs] adj (shocking) scandaloso(-a).

outright [aʊt'raɪt] adv (tell, deny) apertamente; (own) completamente.

outside [adv ,aʊt'saɪd, adj, prep & n 'aʊtsaɪd] adv fuori, all'esterno ◆ prep fuori di ◆ adj esterno(-a) ◆ n: **the ~** (of building, car, container) l'esterno m; (AUT: in UK) la destra; (AUT: in Europe, US) la sinistra; **an ~ line** una linea esterna; **~ of** (Am) (on the outside of) fuori di; (apart from) all'infuori di.

outside lane n corsia f di sorpasso.

outsize ['aʊtsaɪz] adj (clothes) di taglia forte.

outskirts ['aʊtskɜːts] npl periferia f.

outstanding [,aʊt'stændɪŋ] adj (remarkable) eccellente; (problem) rilevante; (debt) da pagare, in sospeso.

outward ['aʊtwəd] adj (journey) di andata; (external) esteriore.

outwards ['aʊtwədz] adv verso l'esterno, in fuori.

oval ['əʊvl] adj ovale.

ovation [əʊ'veɪʃn] n ovazione f.

oven ['ʌvn] n forno m.

oven glove n guanto m da forno.

ovenproof ['ʌvnpruːf] adj da forno.

oven-ready adj pronto(-a) per forno.

mettere in forno.

over ['əʊvə'] *prep* **1.** *(above)* sopra; su; **a bridge ~ the river** un ponte sul fiume.

2. *(across)* oltre, al di là di; **with a view ~ the park** con vista sul parco; **to walk ~ sthg** attraversare qc a piedi; **it's just ~ the road** è proprio qui di fronte.

3. *(covering)* su; **put a plaster ~ the wound** mettere un cerotto sulla ferita.

4. *(more than)* più di; **it cost ~ £1,000** è costato più di 1 000 sterline.

5. *(during)* durante; **~ the past two years** negli ultimi due anni.

6. *(with regard to)* su; **an argument ~ the price** una discussione sul prezzo.

7. *(in phrases)*: **all ~ the world/ country** in tutto il mondo/paese.
   ◆ *adv* **1.** *(downwards)*: **to fall ~** cadere; **to bend ~** piegarsi (in avanti).

2. *(referring to position, movement)*: **to fly ~ to Canada** andare in Canada in aereo; **~ here** qui; **~ there** là.

3. *(round to other side)*: **to turn sthg ~** rigirare qc.

4. *(more)*: **children aged 12 and ~** ragazzi dai 12 anni in su.

5. *(remaining)*: **to be (left) ~** restare.

6. *(to one's house)*: **to invite sb ~ for dinner** invitare qn a cena; **we have some friends coming ~** verranno da noi OR a trovarci degli amici.
   ◆ *adj (finished)*: **to be ~** essere finito(-a).

overall [*adv* ,əʊvə'rɔːl, *n* 'əʊvərɔːl] *(in general)* complessivamente, nell'insieme ◆ *n* (Br: *coat*) grembiule *m*; (Am: *boiler suit*) tuta *f* (da lavoro); **how much does it cost ~?** quanto costa in tutto? ❑ **overalls** *npl* (Br: *boiler suit*) tuta *f* (da lavoro); (Am: *dungarees*) salopette *f inv*.

overboard ['əʊvəbɔːd] *adv (from ship)* in mare.

overbooked [,əʊvə'bʊkt] *adj*: **to be ~** avere più prenotazioni dei posti disponibili.

overcame [,əʊvə'keɪm] *pt* → overcome.

overcast [,əʊvə'kɑːst] *adj* coperto(-a).

overcharge [,əʊvə'tʃɑːdʒ] *vt* far pagare un prezzo eccessivo a.

overcoat ['əʊvəkəʊt] *n* cappotto *m*.

overcome [,əʊvə'kʌm] *(pt* -came, *pp* -come) *vt (defeat)* sopraffare; *(problem)* superare.

overcooked [,əʊvə'kʊkt] *adj* troppo cotto(-a).

overcrowded [,əʊvə'kraʊdɪd] *adj* sovraffollato(-a).

overdo [,əʊvə'duː] *(pt* -did, *pp* -done) *vt (exaggerate)* esagerare con; **to ~ it** esagerare.

overdone [,əʊvə'dʌn] *pp* → overdo ◆ *adj (food)* troppo cotto(-a).

overdose ['əʊvədəʊs] *n* overdose *f inv*.

overdraft ['əʊvədrɑːft] *n* scoperto *m* (di conto).

overdue [,əʊvə'djuː] *adj (bus, flight)* in ritardo; *(rent, payment)* in arretrato.

over easy *adj* (Am: *egg)*: **eggs ~** uova al tegamino fritte da entrambe le parti.

overexposed [,əʊvərɪk'spəʊzd] *adj (photograph)* sovraesposto(-a).

overflow [*vb* ,əʊvə'fləʊ,

overgrown ['əʊvəˈbɒk] vi (container, bath) traboccare; (river) strariparare ◆ n (pipe) troppopieno m.

overgrown [,əʊvəˈgrəʊn] adj (garden, path) ricoperto(-a) di erbacce.

overhaul [,əʊvəˈhɔːl] n (of machine, car) revisione f.

overhead [adj 'əʊvəhed, adv ,əʊvəˈhed] adj aereo(-a) ◆ adv in alto, al di sopra.

overhead locker n (on plane) scomparto m in alto.

overhear ['əʊvəˈhɪər] (pt & pp -heard) vt sentire (per caso).

overheat [,əʊvəˈhiːt] vi surriscaldarsi.

overland ['əʊvəlænd] adv via terra.

overlap [,əʊvəˈlæp] vi sovrapporsi.

overleaf [,əʊvəˈliːf] adv a tergo.

overload [,əʊvəˈləʊd] vt sovraccaricare.

overlook [vb ,əʊvəˈlʊk, n 'əʊvəlʊk] vt (subj: building, room) dare su; (miss) lasciarsi sfuggire, trascurare ◆ n: (scenic) ~ (Am) punto m panoramico.

overnight [adv ,əʊvəˈnaɪt, adj 'əʊvənaɪt] adv (during the night) durante la notte; (until next day) per la notte ◆ adj (train, journey) di notte.

overnight bag n piccola borsa f da viaggio.

overpass ['əʊvəpɑːs] n cavalcavia m inv.

overpowering [,əʊvəˈpaʊərɪŋ] adj (heat, smell) opprimente, soffocante.

oversaw [,əʊvəˈsɔː] pt → oversee.

overseas [adv ,əʊvəˈsiːz, adj 'əʊvəsiːz] adv all'estero (oltremare) ◆ adj straniero(-a); (trade) estero(-a).

oversee [,əʊvəˈsiː] (pt -saw, pp -seen) vt sovrintendere a.

overshoot [,əʊvəˈʃuːt] (pt & pp -shot) vt (turning, motorway exit) oltrepassare.

oversight ['əʊvəsaɪt] n svista f.

oversleep [,əʊvəˈsliːp] (pt & pp -slept) vi non svegliarsi (all'ora prevista).

overtake [,əʊvəˈteɪk] (pt -took, pp -taken) vt & vi sorpassare; 'no overtaking' 'divieto di sorpasso'.

overtime ['əʊvətaɪm] n straordinario m.

overtook [,əʊvəˈtʊk] pt → overtake.

overture ['əʊvə,tjʊər] n (MUS) ouverture f inv.

overturn [,əʊvəˈtɜːn] vi rovesciarsi.

overweight [,əʊvəˈweɪt] adj sovrappeso (inv).

overwhelm [,əʊvəˈwelm] vt sopraffare.

owe [əʊ] vt dovere; to ~ sb sthg dovere qc a qn; owing to a causa di.

owl [aʊl] n gufo m.

own [əʊn] adj proprio(-a) ◆ vt possedere ◆ pron: my ~ il mio (la mia), i miei (le mie) (pl); a room of my ~ una stanza (solo) per me; on my ~ da solo; to get one's ~ back prendersi la rivincita ❑ **own up** vi: to ~ up to sthg ammettere qc.

owner ['əʊnər] n proprietario n (-a f).

ownership ['əʊnəʃɪp] n proprietà f, possesso m.

ox [ɒks] (*pl* **oxen** [ˈɒksən]) *n* bue *m*.

oxtail soup [ˈɒksteɪl-] *n* minestra *f* di coda di bue.

oxygen [ˈɒksɪdʒən] *n* ossigeno *m*.

oyster [ˈɔɪstəʳ] *n* ostrica *f*.

oz *abbr* = **ounce**.

ozone-friendly [ˈəʊzəʊn-] *adj* che non danneggia l'ozono.

P

p (*abbr of* **page**) p., pag. ♦ *abbr* = **penny**, **pence**.

pace [peɪs] *n* passo *m*.

pacemaker [ˈpeɪsˌmeɪkəʳ] *n* (*for heart*) pacemaker *m inv*.

Pacific [pəˈsɪfɪk] *n*: **the ~ (Ocean)** il Pacifico, l'Oceano *m* Pacifico.

pacifier [ˈpæsɪfaɪəʳ] *n* (*Am: for baby*) succhiotto *m*.

pacifist [ˈpæsɪfɪst] *n* pacifista *mf*.

pack [pæk] *n* (*of washing powder*) pacco *m*; (*of cigarettes, crisps*) pacchetto *m*; (*Br: of cards*) mazzo *m*; (*rucksack*) zaino *m* ♦ *vt* (*suitcase, bag*) preparare; fare; (*clothes, camera etc*) mettere in valigia; (*to package*) impacchettare, imballare ♦ *vi* (*for journey*) fare i bagagli OR le valigie; **a ~ of lies** un mucchio di bugie; **to ~ sthg into sthg** stipare qc in qc; **to ~ one's bags** fare i bagagli OR le valigie ❑ **pack up** *vi* (*pack clothes*) fare la valigia; (*tidy up*) riordinare; (*Br: inf: machine, car*) guastarsi.

package [ˈpækɪdʒ] *n* pacchetto *m* ♦ *vt* imballare.

package holiday *n* vacanza *f* organizzata.

package tour *n* viaggio *m* organizzato.

packaging [ˈpækɪdʒɪŋ] *n* (*material*) imballaggio *m*, confezione *f*.

packed [pækt] *adj* (*crowded*) stipato(-a).

packed lunch *n* pranzo *m* al sacco.

packet [ˈpækɪt] *n* pacchetto *m*; **it cost a ~** (*Br: inf*) è costato un mucchio di soldi.

packing [ˈpækɪŋ] *n* (*material*) imballaggio *m*; **to do one's ~** fare i bagagli OR le valigie.

pad [pæd] *n* (*of paper*) blocco *m*; (*of cloth, cotton wool*) tampone *m*; (*for protection*) imbottitura *f*.

padded [ˈpædɪd] *adj* (*jacket, seat*) imbottito(-a).

padded envelope *n* busta *f* imbottita.

paddle [ˈpædl] *n* (*pole*) pagaia *f* ♦ *vi* (*wade*) sguazzare; (*in canoe*) remare (*con la pagaia*).

paddling pool [ˈpædlɪŋ-] *n* piscina *f* per bambini.

paddock [ˈpædək] *n* (*at racecourse*) paddock *m inv*.

padlock [ˈpædlɒk] *n* lucchetto *m*.

page [peɪdʒ] *n* (*of book, newspaper*) pagina *f* ♦ *vt* chiamare.

paid [peɪd] *pt & pp* → **pay** ♦ *adj* (*holiday, work*) pagato(-a).

pain [peɪn] *n* dolore *m*; **to be in ~** avere dolore, soffrire; **he's such a ~!** (*inf*) è un tale rompiscatole! ❑ **pains** *npl* (*trouble*) disturbo *m*.

painful [ˈpeɪnful] *adj* doloroso(-a).

painkiller [ˈpeɪnˌkɪləʳ] *n* analgesico m, antidolorifico m.

paint [peɪnt] n vernice f, colore m
♦ vt & vi dipingere; **to ~** one's nails
dipingersi le unghie ❏ **paints** npl
(tubes, pots etc) colori mpl.

paintbrush ['peɪntbrʌʃ] n pennello m.

painter ['peɪntə^r] n (artist) pittore m (-trice f); (decorator) imbianchino m.

painting ['peɪntɪŋ] n (picture) dipinto m, quadro m; (artistic activity) pittura f; (by decorator) tinteggiatura f.

pair [peə^r] n (of two things) paio m;
in ~s a coppie, a due a due; **a ~ of
pliers** un paio di pinze; **a ~ of scissors** un paio di forbici; **a ~ of
shorts** un paio di calzoncini; **a ~ of
tights** un paio di collant; **a ~ of
trousers** un paio di pantaloni.

pajamas [pə'dʒɑːməz] (Am) =
pyjamas.

Pakistan [Br ˌpɑːkɪ'stɑːn, Am
ˌpækə'stæn] n il Pakistan.

Pakistani [Br ˌpɑːkɪ'stɑːnɪ, Am
ˌpækə'stænɪ] adj pakistano(-a) ♦ n
pakistano m (-a f).

pakora [pə'kɔːrə] npl frittelle piccanti a base di verdura e spezie varie
servite come antipasto nella cucina
indiana.

pal [pæl] n (inf) amico m (-a f).

palace ['pælɪs] n palazzo m.

palatable ['pælətəbl] adj (food,
drink) gustoso(-a).

palate ['pælət] n palato m.

pale [peɪl] adj pallido(-a).

pale ale n birra f chiara.

palm [pɑːm] n (of hand) palmo m;
~ (tree) palma f.

palpitations [ˌpælpɪ'teɪʃnz] npl

palpitazioni fpl.

pamphlet ['pæmflɪt] n opuscolo m.

pan [pæn] n (saucepan) pentola f;
(frying pan) padella f.

pancake ['pænkeɪk] n crêpe f inv.

pancake roll n involtino m primavera.

panda ['pændə] n panda m inv.

panda car n (Br) auto f inv della polizia.

pane [peɪn] n vetro m.

panel ['pænl] n (of wood) pannello
m; (group of experts) gruppo m di
esperti; (on TV, radio) giuria f.

paneling ['pænəlɪŋ] (Am) = **panelling**.

panelling ['pænəlɪŋ] n (Br) rivestimento m a pannelli.

panic ['pænɪk] (pt & pp **-ked**, cont
-king) n panico m ♦ vi farsi prendere dal panico.

panniers ['pænɪəz] npl (for bicycle) borse fpl da bicicletta.

panoramic [ˌpænə'ræmɪk] adj
panoramico(-a).

pant [pænt] vi ansare.

panties ['pæntɪz] npl (inf)
mutandine fpl.

pantomime ['pæntəmaɪm] n
(Br) spettacolo natalizio per bambini.

ⓘ PANTOMIME

Spettacolo teatrale comico per
bambini, in cui si alternano parti
recitate a parti cantate, la cui trama
generalmente si ispira a favole famose e viene
rappresentato nel periodo natalizio.
Di solito il ruolo dell'eroe è interpretato da una giovane attrice, mentre
un attore comico interpreta la parte
della vecchia signora, la "dame".

pantry ['pæntrɪ] n dispensa f.

pants [pænts] npl (Br: underwear) mutande fpl; (Am: trousers) pantaloni mpl.

panty hose ['pæntɪ-] npl (Am) collant m inv.

papadum ['pæpədəm] = **poppa+dom**.

paper ['peɪpəʳ] n (material) carta f; (newspaper) giornale m; (exam) esame m (scritto) ♦ adj di carta ♦ vt tappezzare (con carta da parati); **a piece of** ~ un pezzo di carta ❑ **papers** npl (documents) documenti mpl.

paperback ['peɪpəbæk] n libro m in brossura.

paper bag n sacchetto m di carta.

paperboy ['peɪpəbɔɪ] n ragazzo che recapita i giornali a domicilio.

paper clip n graffetta f.

papergirl ['peɪpəgɜːl] n ragazza che recapita i giornali a domicilio.

paper handkerchief n fazzoletto m di carta.

paper shop n giornalaio m.

paperweight ['peɪpəweɪt] n fermacarte m inv.

paprika ['pæprɪkə] n paprica f.

par [pɑːʳ] n (in golf) norma f.

paracetamol [ˌpærə'siːtəmɒl] n paracetamolo m.

parachute ['pærəʃuːt] n paracadute m inv.

parade [pə'reɪd] n (procession) parata f; (of shops) fila f di negozi.

paradise ['pærədaɪs] n paradiso m.

paraffin ['pærəfɪn] n cherosene m.

paragraph ['pærəgrɑːf] n paragrafo m.

parallel ['pærəlel] adj: ~ (to) parallelo(-a) (a).

paralysed ['pærəlaɪzd] adj (Br) paralizzato(-a).

paralyzed ['pærəlaɪzd] (Am) = **paralysed**.

paramedic [ˌpærə'medɪk] n paramedico m.

paranoid ['pærənɔɪd] adj paranoico(-a).

parasite ['pærəsaɪt] n parassita m.

parasol ['pærəsɒl] n parasole m inv.

parcel ['pɑːsl] n pacco m, pacchetto m.

parcel post n servizio m pacchi postali.

pardon ['pɑːdn] excl: ~? prego!; ~ (me)! mi scusi!; **I beg your** ~! (apologizing) scusi!; **I beg your** ~? (asking for repetition) prego?

parent ['peərənt] n genitore m.

parish ['pærɪʃ] n (of church) parrocchia f; (village area) = comune m.

park [pɑːk] n parco m ♦ vt & vi parcheggiare.

park and ride n parcheggio decentrato presso una stazione di mezzi pubblici locali.

parking ['pɑːkɪŋ] n parcheggio m; 'no ~' 'sosta vietata'.

parking brake n (Am) freno m a mano.

parking lot n (Am) parcheggio m, posteggio m.

parking meter n parchimetro m.

parking space n posto m per parcheggiare.

parking ticket n multa f per sosta vietata.

parkway ['pɑːkweɪ] n (Am) viale con alberi o piante nella banchina spartitraffico.

parliament ['pɑːləmənt] n parlamento m.

Parmesan (cheese) [pɑːmɪ-ˈzæn] n parmigiano m, grana m.

parrot ['pærət] n pappagallo m.

parsley ['pɑːslɪ] n prezzemolo m.

parsnip ['pɑːsnɪp] n pastinaca f.

parson ['pɑːsn] n curato m, parroco m.

part [pɑːt] n parte f; (of machine, car) pezzo m; (of serial) puntata f; (Am: in hair) scriminatura f ♦ adv in parte ♦ vi (couple) separarsi; **in this ~ of Italy** in questa zona dell'Italia; **to form ~ of** costituire parte di; **to play a ~ in** avere un ruolo in; **to take ~ in** prendere parte a; **for my ~** da parte mia; **for the most ~** per lo più, in generale; **in these ~s** da queste parti.

partial ['pɑːʃl] adj (not whole) parziale; **to be ~ to sthg** avere un debole per qc.

participant [pɑːˈtɪsɪpənt] n partecipante mf.

participate [pɑːˈtɪsɪpeɪt] vi: **to ~ (in)** partecipare (a).

particular [pəˈtɪkjʊləʳ] adj particolare; (fussy) esigente; **in ~** in particolare, specialmente; **nothing in ~** niente di particolare ❑ **particulars** npl (details) particolari mpl.

particularly [pəˈtɪkjʊləlɪ] adv particolarmente, soprattutto.

parting ['pɑːtɪŋ] n (Br: in hair) scriminatura f.

partition [pɑːˈtɪʃn] n (wall) tramezzo m.

partly ['pɑːtlɪ] adv parzialmente, in parte.

partner ['pɑːtnəʳ] n (husband) marito m; (wife) moglie f; (lover, in

game, dance) compagno m (-a f); (COMM) socio m (-a f).

partnership ['pɑːtnəʃɪp] n associazione f; (COMM) società f inv.

partridge ['pɑːtrɪdʒ] n pernice f.

part-time adj & adv part time.

party ['pɑːtɪ] n (for fun) festa f; (POL) partito m; (group of people) gruppo m; **to have a ~** fare una festa.

pass [pɑːs] vt passare; (move past) oltrepassare, passare davanti a; (test, exam) passare, superare; (overtake) sorpassare; (law) approvare ♦ vi passare ♦ n (document) lasciapassare m inv, permesso m; (in mountain) passo m; (in exam) sufficienza f; (SPORT) passaggio m; **to ~ sb sthg** passare qc a qn ❑ **pass by** vt (building, window etc) passare davanti a ♦ vi passare; **pass on** vt sep (message) passare; **pass out** vi (faint) svenire; **pass up** vt sep (opportunity) lasciarsi sfuggire.

passable ['pɑːsəbl] adj (road) transitabile; (satisfactory) passabile.

passage ['pæsɪdʒ] n (corridor) passaggio m, corridoio m; (in book) brano m, passo m; (sea journey) traversata f.

passageway ['pæsɪdʒweɪ] n corridoio m.

passenger ['pæsɪndʒəʳ] n passeggero m (-a f).

passerby [ˌpɑːsəˈbaɪ] n passante mf.

passing place ['pɑːsɪŋ-] n (for cars) piazzola f.

passion ['pæʃn] n passione f.

passionate ['pæʃənət] adj (showing strong feeling) appassionato(-a); (sexually) passionale.

pawn

passive ['pæsɪv] *n* passivo *m*.

passport ['pɑ:spɔ:t] *n* passaporto *m*.

passport control *n* controllo *m* passaporti.

passport photo *n* fototessera *f*.

password ['pɑ:swɜ:d] *n* (for computer) password *f* inv, parola *f* d'accesso.

past [pɑ:st] *adj* passato(-a); (last) ultimo(-a); (former) ex (inv) ♦ prep (in times) dopo; (further than) oltre, al di là di; (in front of) davanti a ♦ adv oltre ♦ *n* (former time) passato *m*; ~ (tense) (GRAMM) passato; the ~ month il mese scorso; twenty ~ four le quattro e venti; to run ~ passare di corsa; in the ~ in passato.

pasta ['pæstə] *n* pasta *f*.

paste [peɪst] *n* (spread) pasta *f*, crema *f* (da spalmare); (glue) colla *f*.

pastel ['pæstl] *n* (for drawing) pastello *m*; (colour) colore *m* pastello.

pasteurized ['pɑ:stʃəraɪzd] *adj* pastorizzato(-a).

pastille ['pæstɪl] *n* pastiglia *f*.

pastime ['pɑ:staɪm] *n* passatempo *m*.

pastry ['peɪstrɪ] *n* pasta *f*.

pasture ['pɑ:stʃəʳ] *n* pascolo *m*.

pasty ['pæstɪ] *n* (Br) pasticcio *m*.

pat [pæt] *vt* dare un colpetto affettuoso) a.

patch [pætʃ] *n* (for clothes) toppa *f* (of colour, cloud, damp) macchia *f*; (for skin) cerotto *m*; (for eye) benda *f*; **a bad ~** (fig) un brutto periodo.

pâté ['pæteɪ] *n* pâté *m* inv.

patent [Br 'peɪtənt, Am 'pætənt] *n* revetto *m*.

path [pɑ:θ] *n* (in park, country) sentiero *m*, viottolo *m*; (in garden) vialetto *m*.

pathetic [pə'θetɪk] *adj* (pej: useless) penoso(-a).

patience ['peɪʃns] *n* (quality) pazienza *f*; (Br: card game) solitario *m*.

patient ['peɪʃnt] *adj* paziente ♦ *n* paziente *mf*, malato *m* (-a *f*).

patio ['pætɪəʊ] *n* terrazza *f*.

patriotic [Br ,pætrɪ'ɒtɪk, Am ,peɪtrɪ'ɒtɪk] *adj* patriottico(-a).

patrol [pə'trəʊl] *vt* pattugliare ♦ *n* (group) pattuglia *f*.

patrol car *n* auto *f* inv di pattuglia.

patron ['peɪtrən] *n* (fml: customer) cliente *mf*; '~s only' 'riservato ai clienti'.

patronizing ['pætrənaɪzɪŋ] *adj* (person) che tratta con aria di superiorità.

pattern ['pætn] *n* (of shapes, colours) disegno *m*, motivo *m*; (for sewing) modello *m*.

patterned ['pætənd] *adj* fantasia (inv).

pause [pɔ:z] *n* pausa *f* ♦ *vi* fare una pausa, soffermarsi.

pavement ['peɪvmənt] *n* (Br: beside road) marciapiede *m*; (Am: roadway) pavimentazione *f*.

pavilion [pə'vɪljən] *n* edificio annesso a campo sportivo, adibito a spogliatoio.

paving stone ['peɪvɪŋ-] *n* lastra *f* di pietra.

pavlova [pæv'ləʊvə] *n* dolce composto da due strati di meringa farciti da panna montata e frutta.

paw [pɔ:] *n* zampa *f*.

pawn [pɔ:n] *vt* impegnare, dare

in pegno ♦ *n (in chess)* pedone *m*.

pay [peɪ] *(pt & pp* **paid)** *vt* pagare ♦ *vi (give money)* pagare; *(be profitable)* rendere ♦ *n* paga *f*, stipendio *m*; **to ~ sb for sthg** pagare qn per qc; **to ~ money into an account** versare dei soldi su un conto; **to ~ attention (to)** fare attenzione (a); **to ~ sb a visit** fare visita a qn; **to ~ by credit card** pagare con la carta di credito □ **pay back** *vt sep (money)* restituire; *(person)* rimborsare; **pay for** *vt fus (purchase)* pagare; **pay in** *vt sep (cheque, money)* versare; **pay out** *vt sep (money)* sborsare; **pay up** *vi* saldare il debito.

payable ['peɪəbl] *adj (bill)* pagabile; **~ to** *(cheque)* pagabile a, intestato(-a) a.

payment ['peɪmənt] *n (of money, bill)* pagamento *m; (amount)* pagamento, versamento *m*.

payphone ['peɪfəʊn] *n* telefono *m* pubblico.

PC *n (abbr of personal computer)* PC *m inv* ♦ *abbr (Br)* = **police constable**.

PE *abbr* = **physical education**.

pea [piː] *n* pisello *m*.

peace [piːs] *n* pace *f*; **to leave sb in ~** lasciare qn in pace; **~ and quiet** pace e tranquillità.

peaceful ['piːsfʊl] *adj (place, day, feeling)* tranquillo(-a), calmo(-a); *(demonstration)* pacifico(-a).

peach [piːtʃ] *n* pesca *f*.

peach melba [-'melbə] *n* pesche *fpl* melba.

peacock ['piːkɒk] *n* pavone *m*.

peak [piːk] *n (of mountain)* cima *f*, vetta *f; (of hat)* visiera *f; (fig: highest point)* apice *m*, culmine *m*.

peak hours *npl* ore *fpl* di punta.

peak rate *n* tariffa *f* ore di punta.

peanut ['piːnʌt] *n* arachide *f*, nocciolina *f* americana.

peanut butter *n* burro *m* di arachidi.

pear [peəʳ] *n* pera *f*.

pearl [pɜːl] *n* perla *f*.

peasant ['peznt] *n* contadino *m* (-a *f*).

pebble ['pebl] *n* ciottolo *m*.

pecan pie ['piːkæn-] *n* torta *f* noci pecan.

peck [pek] *vi (bird)* beccare.

peculiar [pɪ'kjuːlɪəʳ] *adj (strange)* strano(-a), singolare; **to be ~ to** *(exclusive)* essere peculiare di.

peculiarity [pɪˌkjuːlɪ'ærətɪ] *n (special feature)* particolarità *f inv*.

pedal ['pedl] *n* pedale *m* ♦ *vi* pedalare.

pedal bin *n* pattumiera *f* a pedale.

pedalo ['pedələʊ] *(pl* -s) *n* moscone *m* a pedali, pedalò® *m inv*.

pedestrian [pɪ'destrɪən] *n* pedone *m* (-a *f*).

pedestrian crossing *n* passaggio *m* pedonale.

pedestrianized [pɪ'destrɪənaɪzd] *adj* riservato(-a) ai pedoni.

pedestrian precinct *n (Br)* zona *f* pedonale.

pedestrian zone *(Am)* = **pedestrian precinct**.

pee [piː] *vi (inf)* fare la pipì ♦ *n*: **to have a ~** *(inf)* fare la pipì.

peel [piːl] *n* buccia *f; (of orange, lemon)* scorza *f* ♦ *vt (fruit, vegetable)* sbucciare ♦ *vi (paint)* staccarsi; *(skin)* spellarsi.

peep [piːp] *n*: to have a ~ dare una sbirciatina.

peer [pɪəʳ] *vi*: to ~ at fissare, scrutare.

peg [peg] *n (for tent)* picchetto *m*; *(hook)* attaccapanni *m inv*; *(for washing)* molletta *f*.

pelican crossing ['pelɪkən-] *n (Br)* passaggio pedonale con semaforo a comando manuale.

pelvis ['pelvɪs] *n* bacino *m*.

pen [pen] *n (for writing)* penna *f*; *(for animals)* recinto *m*.

penalty ['penltɪ] *n (fine)* multa *f*, sanzione *f*; *(in football)* rigore *m*.

pence [pens] *npl* penny *m inv*; it costs 20 ~ costa 20 penny.

pencil ['pensl] *n* matita *f*.

pencil case *n* portamatite *m inv*.

pencil sharpener *n* temperamatite *m inv*.

pendant ['pendənt] *n* pendente *m*, ciondolo *m*.

pending ['pendɪŋ] *prep (fml)* in attesa di.

penetrate ['penɪtreɪt] *vt* penetrare.

penfriend ['penfrend] *n* amico *m* (-a *f*) per corrispondenza.

penguin ['peŋgwɪn] *n* pinguino *m*.

penicillin [ˌpenɪ'sɪlɪn] *n* penicillina *f*.

peninsula [pə'nɪnsjulə] *n* penisola *f*.

penis ['piːnɪs] *n* pene *m*.

penknife ['pennaɪf] *(pl* -knives) *n* temperino *m*.

penny ['penɪ] *(pl* pennies) *n (in UK)* penny *m inv*; *(in US)* centesimo *m*.

pension ['penʃn] *n* pensione *f*.

pensioner ['penʃənəʳ] *n* pensionato *m* (-a *f*).

penthouse ['penthaus, *pl* -hauzɪz] *n* superattico *m*.

penultimate [pe'nʌltɪmət] *adj* penultimo-(a).

people ['piːpl] *npl (persons)* persone *fpl*; *(in general)* gente *f* ♦ *n (nation)* popolo *m*; the ~ *(citizens)* il popolo.

pepper ['pepəʳ] *n (spice)* pepe *m*; *(vegetable)* peperone *m*.

peppercorn ['pepəkɔːn] *n* grano *m* di pepe.

peppermint ['pepəmɪnt] *adj* alla menta (piperita) ♦ *n (sweet)* caramella *f* di menta.

pepper pot *n* pepiera *f*.

pepper steak *n* bistecca *f* al pepe.

Pepsi® ['pepsɪ] *n* Pepsi *f inv*.

per [pɜːʳ] *prep* per, a; ~ **person** a persona; ~ **week** alla settimana; £20 ~ **night** 20 sterline a notte.

perceive [pə'siːv] *vt* percepire.

per cent *adv* per cento.

percentage [pə'sentɪdʒ] *n* percentuale *f*.

perch [pɜːtʃ] *n (for bird)* posatoio *m*, asticella *f*.

percolator ['pɜːkəleɪtəʳ] *n* caffettiera *f* a filtro.

perfect [*adj & n* 'pɜːfɪkt, *vb* pə'fekt] *adj* perfetto-(a) ♦ *vt* perfezionare ♦ *n*: the ~ (**tense**) il passato prossimo.

perfection [pə'fekʃn] *n*: to do sthg to ~ fare qc alla perfezione.

perfectly ['pɜːfɪktlɪ] *adv (very well)* perfettamente, alla perfezione.

perform [pə'fɔːm] *vt (task, opera-*

tion) eseguire, fare; *(play)* rappresentare; *(concert)* eseguire ♦ *vi (actor)* recitare; *(singer)* cantare.

performance [pəˈfɔːməns] *n (of play, concert, film)* spettacolo *m; (by actor)* interpretazione *f; (musician)* esecuzione *f; (of car)* prestazioni *fpl.*

performer [pəˈfɔːməʳ] *n* artista *mf.*

perfume [ˈpɜːfjuːm] *n* profumo *m.*

perhaps [pəˈhæps] *adv* forse.

perimeter [pəˈrɪmɪtəʳ] *n* perimetro *m.*

period [ˈpɪərɪəd] *n* periodo *m; (SCH)* lezione *f; (menstruation)* mestruazioni *fpl; (Am: full stop)* punto *m* ♦ *adj (costume, furniture)* d'epoca.

periodic [ˌpɪərɪˈɒdɪk] *adj* periodico(-a).

period pains *npl* dolori *mpl* mestruali.

periphery [pəˈrɪfərɪ] *n* periferia *f.*

perishable [ˈperɪʃəbl] *adj* deperibile.

perk [pɜːk] *n* vantaggio *m.*

perm [pɜːm] *n* permanente *f* ♦ *vt:* **to have one's hair ~ed** farsi la permanente.

permanent [ˈpɜːmənənt] *adj* permanente.

permanent address *n* residenza *f.*

permanently [ˈpɜːmənəntlɪ] *adv* permanentemente.

permissible [pəˈmɪsəbl] *adj (fml)* permissibile, ammissibile.

permission [pəˈmɪʃn] *n* permesso *m.*

permit [*vb* pəˈmɪt, *n* ˈpɜːmɪt] *vt* permettere ♦ *n* permesso *m;* **to ~ sb to do sthg** permettere a qn di fare qc; **'~ holders only'** 'solo auto-

rizzati'.

perpendicular [ˌpɜːpənˈdɪkjuləʳ] *adj* perpendicolare.

persevere [ˌpɜːsɪˈvɪəʳ] *vi* perseverare.

persist [pəˈsɪst] *vi* persistere; **to ~ in doing sthg** ostinarsi a fare qc.

persistent [pəˈsɪstənt] *adj* persistente; *(person)* ostinato(-a).

person [ˈpɜːsn] *(pl* **people)** *n* persona *f;* **in ~** di persona.

personal [ˈpɜːsənl] *adj* personale.

personal assistant *n* segretario *m* (-a *f)* personale.

personal belongings *npl* effetti *mpl* personali.

personal computer *n* personal computer *m inv.*

personality [ˌpɜːsəˈnælətɪ] *n* personalità *f inv.*

personally [ˈpɜːsnəlɪ] *adv* personalmente.

personal property *n* beni *mpl* mobili.

personal stereo *n* walkman® *m inv.*

personnel [ˌpɜːsəˈnel] *npl* personale *m.*

perspective [pəˈspektɪv] *n* prospettiva *f.*

Perspex® [ˈpɜːspeks] *n (Br)* = plexiglas® *m inv.*

perspiration [ˌpɜːspəˈreɪʃn] *n* traspirazione *f,* sudore *m.*

persuade [pəˈsweɪd] *vt:* **to ~ sb (to do sthg)** persuadere qn (a fare qc); **to ~ sb that ...** persuadere qn che ...

persuasive [pəˈsweɪsɪv] *adj* persuasivo(-a), convincente.

pervert [ˈpɜːvɜːt] *n* pervertì-

m (-a *f*).

pessimist ['pesɪmɪst] *n* pessimista *mf*.

pessimistic [.pesɪ'mɪstɪk] *adj* pessimistico(-a).

pest [pest] *n (insect)* insetto *m* nocivo; *(animal)* animale *m* nocivo; *(inf: person)* peste *f*.

pester ['pestə^r] *vt* tormentare.

pesticide ['pestɪsaɪd] *n* pesticida *m*.

pet [pet] *n* animale *m* domestico; **the teacher's ~** il favorito dell'insegnante.

petal ['petl] *n* petalo *m*.

pet food *n* cibo *m* per animali (domestici).

petition [pɪ'tɪʃn] *n (letter)* petizione *f*.

petits pois *npl* pisellini *mpl*.

petrified ['petrɪfaɪd] *adj (frightened)* impietrito(-a) (dalla paura).

petrol ['petrəl] *n (Br)* benzina *f*.

petrol can *n (Br)* tanica *f* per la benzina.

petrol cap *n (Br)* tappo *m* del serbatoio.

petrol gauge *n (Br)* indicatore *m* di livello della benzina.

petrol pump *n (Br)* pompa *f* di benzina.

petrol station *n (Br)* stazione *f* di rifornimento.

petrol tank *n (Br)* serbatoio *m* della benzina.

pet shop *n* negozio *m* di animali.

petticoat ['petɪkəʊt] *n* sottoveste *f*.

petty ['petɪ] *adj (pej: person, rule)* meschino(-a).

petty cash *n* piccola cassa *f*.

pew [pju:] *n* panca *f* (di chiesa).

pewter ['pju:tə^r] *adj* di peltro.

PG *(abbr of parental guidance)* sigla che contraddistingue i film non vietati ai minori, per i quali è però consigliato l'accompagnamento dei genitori.

pharmacist ['fɑ:məsɪst] *n* farmacista *mf*.

pharmacy ['fɑ:məsɪ] *n (shop)* farmacia *f*.

phase [feɪz] *n* fase *f*.

PhD *n (degree)* = dottorato *m* di ricerca.

pheasant ['feznt] *n* fagiano *m*.

phenomena [fɪ'nɒmɪnə] *pl* → **phenomenon**.

phenomenal [fɪ'nɒmɪnl] *adj* fenomenale.

phenomenon [fɪ'nɒmɪnən] *(pl* **-mena)** *n* fenomeno *m*.

Philippines ['fɪlɪpi:nz] *npl*: **the ~** le Filippine.

philosophy [fɪ'lɒsəfɪ] *n* filosofia *f*.

phlegm [flem] *n (in throat)* catarro *m*.

phone [fəʊn] *n* telefono *m* ◆ *vt (Br)* telefonare a ◆ *vi (Br)* telefonare; **to be on the ~** *(talking)* essere al telefono; *(connected)* avere il telefono ◘ **phone up** *vt sep* telefonare a, chiamare ◆ *vi* telefonare.

phone book *n* elenco *m* telefonico.

phone booth *n* cabina *f* telefonica.

phone box *n (Br)* cabina *f* telefonica.

phone call *n* telefonata *f*.

phonecard ['fəʊnkɑ:d] *n* scheda *f* telefonica.

phone number *n* numero *m* di telefono.

photo ['fəʊtəʊ] *(pl* **-s)** *n* foto *f* inv.

to take a ~ of fare una foto a.
photo album *n* album *m inv*
portafotografie.
photocopier [ˌfəʊtəʊˈkɒpɪəʳ] *n*
fotocopiatrice *f*.
photocopy [ˈfəʊtəʊˌkɒpɪ] *n* fotocopia *f* ♦ *vt* fotocopiare.
photograph [ˈfəʊtəgrɑːf] *n*
fotografia *f* ♦ *vt* fotografare.
photographer [fəˈtɒgrəfəʳ] *n*
fotografo *m* (-a *f*).
photography [fəˈtɒgrəfɪ] *n*
fotografia *f*.
phrase [freɪz] *n* espressione *f*.
phrasebook [ˈfreɪzbʊk] *n* voca-
bolarietto *m* con frasi tipiche.
physical [ˈfɪzɪkl] *adj* fisico(-a) ♦ *n*
visita *f* medica.
physical education *n* educazione *f* fisica.
physically handicapped
[ˈfɪzɪklɪ-] *adj* handicappato fisico
(handicappata fisica).
physics [ˈfɪzɪks] *n* fisica *f*.
physiotherapy [ˌfɪzɪəʊˈθerəpɪ]
n fisioterapia *f*.
pianist [ˈpɪənɪst] *n* pianista *mf*.
piano [pɪˈænəʊ] (*pl* **-s**) *n* pianoforte *m*.
pick [pɪk] *vt* (*select*) scegliere;
(*fruit, flowers*) cogliere ♦ *n* (*pickaxe*)
piccone *m*; **to ~ a fight** attaccar
briga; **to ~ one's nose** mettersi le
dita nel naso; **to take one's ~** scegliere ❑ **pick on** *vt fus* prendersela
con, prendere di mira; **pick out** *vt
sep* (*select*) scegliere; (*see*) individuare, riconoscere; **pick up** *vt sep*
(*lift up*) raccogliere; (*collect*) passare
a prendere; (*learn*) imparare; (*habit*)
prendere; (*bargain*) trovare; (*hitchhiker*) far salire; (*inf: woman, man*)
rimorchiare ♦ *vi* (*improve*) ripren-

dersi; **to ~ up the phone** (*answer*)
rispondere al telefono.
pickaxe [ˈpɪkæks] *n* piccone *m*.
pickle [ˈpɪkl] *n* (*Br: food*) sottaceti
mpl; (*Am: pickled cucumber*) cetriolo
m sottaceto.
pickled onion [ˈpɪkld-] *n* cipollina *f* sottaceto.
pickpocket [ˈpɪkˌpɒkɪt] *n* borsaiolo *m*.
pick-up (truck) *n* camioncino *m*.
picnic [ˈpɪknɪk] *n* picnic *m inv*.
picnic area *n* area *per picnic*.
picture [ˈpɪktʃəʳ] *n* (*painting*)
quadro *m*; (*drawing*) disegno *m*;
(*photograph*) fotografia *f*; (*on TV*)
immagine *f*; (*film*) film *m inv* ❑ **pictures** *npl*: **the ~s** (*Br*) il cinema.
picture frame *n* cornice *f*.
picturesque [ˌpɪktʃəˈresk] *adj*
pittoresco(-a).
pie [paɪ] *n* (*savoury*) pasticcio *m*;
(*sweet*) torta *f*.
piece [piːs] *n* pezzo *m*; **a 20p ~**
un pezzo da 20 penny; **a ~ of
advice** un consiglio; **a ~ of clothing**
un capo di vestiario; **a ~ of furniture** un mobile; **to fall to ~s** andare in pezzi; **in one ~** tutto intero.
pier [pɪəʳ] *n* molo *m*.
pierce [pɪəs] *vt* forare, perforare;
to have one's ears ~d farsi i buchi
alle orecchie.
pig [pɪg] *n* maiale *m*, porco *m*.
pigeon [ˈpɪdʒɪn] *n* piccione *m*.
pigeonhole [ˈpɪdʒɪnhəʊl] *n*
casella *f*.
pigskin [ˈpɪgskɪn] *adj* di cinghiale.
pigtails [ˈpɪgteɪlz] *npl* trecce *fpl*.
pike [paɪk] *n* (*fish*) luccio *m*.

pilau rice ['pɪlaʊ-] n riso m pilaf.

pilchard ['pɪltʃəd] n sardina f.

pile [paɪl] n (heap) mucchio m; (neat stack) pila f ♦ vt ammucchiare; ~s of (inf: a lot) mucchi di □ **pile up** vt sep ammucchiare ♦ vi (accumulate) ammucchiarsi.

piles [paɪlz] npl (MED) emorroidi fpl.

pileup ['paɪlʌp] n tamponamento m a catena.

pill [pɪl] n pillola f.

pillar ['pɪlə²] n colonna f.

pillar box n (Br) cassetta f delle lettere.

pillion ['pɪljən] n: **to ride ~** viaggiare sul sellino posteriore.

pillow ['pɪləʊ] n cuscino m.

pillowcase ['pɪləʊkeɪs] n federa f.

pilot ['paɪlət] n pilota mf.

pilot light n fiamma f pilota.

pimple ['pɪmpl] n foruncolo m.

pin [pɪn] n (for sewing, safety pin) spillo m; (drawing pin) puntina f; (Am: brooch, badge) spilla f ♦ vt (fasten) attaccare con uno spillo; **a two-~ plug** una spina bipolare; **~s and needles** formicolìo m.

pinafore ['pɪnəfɔː²] n (apron) grembiule m; (Br: dress) scamiciato m.

pinball ['pɪnbɔːl] n flipper m inv.

pincers ['pɪnsəz] npl (tool) tenaglie fpl.

pinch [pɪntʃ] vt (squeeze) pizzicare, dare un pizzicotto a; (Br: inf: steal) fregare ♦ n (of salt) pizzico m.

pine [paɪn] n pino m ♦ adj di pino.

pineapple ['paɪnæpl] n ananas m inv.

pink [pɪŋk] adj rosa (inv) ♦ n (colour) rosa m inv.

pinkie ['pɪŋkɪ] n (Am) mignolo m.

PIN number n numero m di codice segreto.

pint [paɪnt] n (in UK) = 0,568 l, pinta f; (in US) = 0,473 l, pinta; **a ~ (of beer)** (Br) = una birra grande.

pip [pɪp] n (of fruit) seme m.

pipe [paɪp] n (for smoking) pipa f; (for gas, water) tubo m.

pipe cleaner n scovolino m.

pipeline ['paɪplaɪn] n conduttura f; (for oil) oleodotto m.

pipe tobacco n tabacco m da pipa.

pirate ['paɪrət] n pirata m.

Pisces ['paɪsiːz] n Pesci mpl.

piss [pɪs] vi (vulg) pisciare ♦ n: **to have a ~** (vulg) pisciare; **it's ~ing down** (vulg) piove a dirotto.

pissed [pɪst] adj (Br: vulg: drunk) sbronzo(-a); (Am: vulg: angry) incazzato(-a).

pissed off adj (vulg) incazzato(-a).

pistachio [pɪ'stɑːʃɪəʊ] (pl -s) n pistacchio m ♦ adj al pistacchio.

pistol ['pɪstl] n pistola f.

piston ['pɪstən] n pistone m.

pit [pɪt] n (hole) buca f, fossa f; (coalmine) miniera f (di carbone); (for orchestra) fossa dell'orchestra; (Am: in fruit) nocciolo m.

pitch [pɪtʃ] n (Br: SPORT) campo m ♦ vt (throw) lanciare; **to ~ a tent** piantare una tenda.

pitcher ['pɪtʃə²] n brocca f.

pitfall ['pɪtfɔːl] n insidia f, pericolo m.

pith [pɪθ] n (of orange) parte f interna della scorza.

pitta (bread) ['pɪtə-] n tipo di schiacciata f di origine mediorientale.

pitted ['pɪtd] *adj (olives)* snocciolato(-a).

pity ['pɪtɪ] *n (compassion)* pietà *f*; **to have ~ on sb** avere pietà di qn; **it's a ~ that ...** è un peccato che ...; **what a ~!** che peccato!

pivot ['pɪvət] *n* perno *m*.

pizza ['pi:tsə] *n* pizza *f*.

pizzeria [,pi:tsə'ri:ə] *n* pizzeria *f*.

Pl. *(abbr of Place)* abbreviazione di *strada in alcuni indirizzi*.

placard ['plækɑ:d] *n* cartello *m*.

place [pleɪs] *n (location)* posto *m*, luogo *m*; *(house, flat)* casa *f*; *(seat, proper position, in race, list)* posto ◆ *vt (put)* collocare, mettere; *(an order, bet)* fare; **in the first ~** *(firstly)* in primo luogo; **to take ~** avere luogo, avvenire; **to take sb's ~** *(replace)* prendere il posto di qn; **all over the ~** dappertutto; **in ~ of** al posto di.

place mat *n (heat-resistant)* sottopiatto *m*; *(linen)* tovaglietta *f*.

placement ['pleɪsmənt] *n (work experience)* stage *m inv*.

place of birth *n* luogo *m* di nascita.

plague [pleɪg] *n* peste *f*.

plaice [pleɪs] *(pl inv)* platessa *f*.

plain [pleɪn] *adj (simple)* semplice; *(in one colour)* in tinta unita; *(clear)* chiaro(-a); *(paper)* non rigato(-a); *(pej: not attractive)* scialbo(-a) ◆ *n* pianura *f*.

plain chocolate *n* cioccolato *m* fondente.

plainly ['pleɪnlɪ] *adv* chiaramente.

plait [plæt] *n* treccia *f* ◆ *vt* intrecciare.

plan [plæn] *n (scheme, project)* piano *m*, progetto *m*; *(drawing)* pianta *f* ◆ *vt (organize)* programmare, progettare; **have you any ~s for tonight?** hai qualche programma per stasera?; **according to ~** secondo i piani; **to ~ to do sthg, to ~ on doing sthg** progettare di fare qc.

plane [pleɪn] *n (aeroplane)* aereo *m*; *(tool)* pialla *f*.

planet ['plænɪt] *n* pianeta *m*.

plank [plæŋk] *n* asse *f*, tavola *f*.

plant [plɑ:nt] *n* pianta *f*; *(factory)* stabilimento *m*, fabbrica ◆ *vt* piantare; **'heavy ~ crossing'** 'uscita mezzi pesanti'.

plantation [plæn'teɪʃn] *n* piantagione *f*.

plaque [plɑ:k] *n* placca *f*.

plaster ['plɑ:stər] *n (Br: for cut)* cerotto *m*; *(for walls)* intonaco *m*; **in ~** *(arm, leg)* ingessato.

plaster cast *n (for broken bones)* ingessatura *f*.

plastic ['plæstɪk] *n* plastica *f* ◆ *adj* di plastica.

plastic bag *n* sacchetto *m* di plastica.

Plasticine® ['plæstɪsi:n] *n (Br)* plastilina® *f*.

plate [pleɪt] *n (for food)* piatto *m*; *(of metal, glass)* piastra *f*.

plateau ['plætəʊ] *n* altopiano *m*.

plate-glass *adj* di vetro fisso.

platform ['plætfɔ:m] *n (at railway station)* marciapiede *m* (di binario); *(raised structure)* piattaforma *f*; *(stage)* palco *m*; **~ 12** binario 12.

platinum ['plætɪnəm] *n* platino *m*.

platter ['plætər] *n (CULIN)* piatto *m (di affettati, frutti di mare assortiti, ecc.)*.

play [pleɪ] *vt (sport, game)* giocare a; *(musical instrument, music)* suonare; *(opponent)* giocare contro; *(CD, tape, record)* mettere (su); *(role, character)* interpretare ◆ vi giocare; *(musician)* suonare ◆ n *(in theatre, on TV)* dramma m, commedia f; *(button on CD, tape recorder)* play m ❑ **play back** vt sep *(tape)* riascoltare; *(video)* rivedere; **play up** vi *(machine, car)* fare i capricci.

player ['pleɪə*] n *(of sport, game)* giocatore m *(-trice f)*; *(of musical instrument)* suonatore m *(-trice f)*.

playful ['pleɪfʊl] adj scherzoso(-a), giocoso(-a).

playground ['pleɪgraʊnd] n *(in school)* cortile m per la ricreazione; *(in park etc)* parco m giochi.

playgroup ['pleɪgruːp] n asilo m infantile.

playing card ['pleɪɪŋ-] n carta f da gioco.

playing field ['pleɪɪŋ-] n campo n sportivo.

playroom ['pleɪrʊm] n stanza f dei giochi.

playschool ['pleɪskuːl] = play-group.

playtime ['pleɪtaɪm] n ricreazio-e f.

playwright ['pleɪraɪt] n dram-aturgo m *(-a f)*.

plc *(Br: abbr of public limited compa-y)* = S.r.l. *(quotata in borsa)*.

pleasant ['plez'nt] adj piacevole, adevole; *(person)* simpatico(-a).

please [pliːz] adv per favore, per acere ◆ vt far piacere a; ~ **take a** at prego, si sieda; **yes ~**! sì, gra-!; **whatever you ~** quello che ti ~e.

pleased [pliːzd] adj conten-, to be ~ with essere conten-li; ~ **to meet you!** piacere!

pleasure ['pleʒə*] n piacere m; **with ~** con piacere; **it's a ~**! non c'è di che!, prego!

pleat [pliːt] n piega f.

pleated ['pliːtɪd] adj pieghetta-to(-a).

plentiful ['plentɪfʊl] adj abbondante.

plenty ['plentɪ] pron: **there's ~** ce n'è in abbondanza; **~ of** un sacco di.

pliers ['plaɪəz] npl pinze fpl.

plimsoll ['plɪmsəl] n *(Br)* scarpa f da tennis.

plonk [plɒŋk] n *(Br: inf: wine)* vino m da poco.

plot [plɒt] n *(scheme)* complotto m; *(of story, film, play)* trama f; *(of land)* appezzamento m.

plough [plaʊ] n *(Br)* aratro m ◆ vt *(Br)* arare.

ploughman's (lunch) ['plaʊ-mænz-] n *(Br)* piatto a base di formaggi, sottaceti e pane, spesso servito nei pub.

plow [plaʊ] *(Am)* = **plough**.

ploy [plɔɪ] n tattica f.

pluck [plʌk] vt *(eyebrows)* depilare; *(chicken)* spennare.

plug [plʌg] n *(electrical)* spina f; *(for bath, sink)* tappo m ❑ **plug in** vt sep attaccare (a una presa).

plughole ['plʌghəʊl] n buco m *(della vasca, ecc.)*.

plum [plʌm] n susina f, prugna f.

plumber ['plʌmə*] n idraulico m.

plumbing ['plʌmɪŋ] n *(pipes)* tubature fpl.

plump [plʌmp] adj grassoc-cio(-a).

plunge [plʌndʒ] vi *(fall)* precipitare, cadere; *(dive)* tuffarsi; *(de-*

crease) precipitare.

plunge pool *n* piscina *f* piccola.

plunger ['plʌndʒə^r] *n (for unblocking pipe)* sturalavandini *m inv*.

pluperfect (tense) [ˌpluː-ˈpɜːfɪkt] *n*: **the ~** il piucchepperfetto.

plural ['plʊərəl] *n* plurale *m*; **in the ~** al plurale.

plus [plʌs] *prep* più ♦ *adj*: **30 ~** più di 30.

plush [plʌʃ] *adj* lussuoso(-a).

plywood ['plaɪwʊd] *n* compensato *m*.

p.m. *(abbr of post meridiem)*: **at 3 ~** alle 3 del pomeriggio; **at 10 ~** alle 10 di sera.

PMT *n (abbr of premenstrual tension)* sindrome *f* premestruale.

pneumatic drill [nju:ˈmætɪk-] *n* martello *m* pneumatico.

pneumonia [nju:ˈməʊnjə] *n* polmonite *f*.

poached egg [pəʊtʃt-] *n* uovo *m* in camicia.

poached salmon [pəʊtʃt-] *n* salmone *m* bollito.

poacher ['pəʊtʃə^r] *n* bracconiere *m*.

PO Box *n (abbr of Post Office Box)* C.P.

pocket ['pɒkɪt] *n* tasca *f* ♦ *adj* tascabile.

pocketbook ['pɒkɪtbʊk] *n (notebook)* taccuino *m*; *(Am: handbag)* borsetta *f*.

pocket money *n (Br)* paghetta *f*, settimana *f*.

podiatrist [pəˈdaɪətrɪst] *n (Am)* pedicure *mf*, callista *mf*.

poem ['pəʊɪm] *n* poesia *f*.

poet ['pəʊɪt] *n* poeta *m* (-essa *f*).

poetry ['pəʊɪtrɪ] *n* poesia *f*.

point [pɔɪnt] *n* punto *m*; *(tip)* punta *f*; *(Br: electric socket)* presa *f* ♦ *vi*: **to ~** indicare; **five ~ seven** cinque virgola sette; **what's the ~?** a che serve?; **there's no ~** è inutile; **to be on the ~ of doing sthg** essere sul punto di fare qc □ **points** *npl (Br: on railway)* scambio *m*; **point out** *vt sep (object, person)* indicare; *(fact, mistake)* far notare.

pointed ['pɔɪntɪd] *adj (in shape)* appuntito(-a).

pointless ['pɔɪntlɪs] *adj* inutile.

point of view *n* punto *m* di vista.

poison ['pɔɪzn] *n* veleno *m* ♦ *vt* avvelenare.

poisoning ['pɔɪznɪŋ] *n* avvelenamento *m*, intossicazione *f*.

poisonous ['pɔɪznəs] *adj* velenoso(-a).

poke [pəʊk] *vt (with finger, stick, elbow)* dare un colpetto a.

poker ['pəʊkə^r] *n (card game, poker m.*

Poland ['pəʊlənd] *n* la Polonia.

polar bear ['pəʊlə-] *n* orso *n* bianco.

Polaroid® ['pəʊlərɔɪd] *n (photograph)* foto *f inv* polaroid®; *(camera)* polaroid® *f inv*.

pole [pəʊl] *n (of wood)* palo *m*.

Pole [pəʊl] *n (person)* polacco (-a *f*).

police [pəˈliːs] *npl*: **the ~** la po zia.

police car *n* auto *f inv* de polizia.

police force *n* forze *fpl* di po zia OR dell'ordine.

policeman [pə'li:smən] (*pl* **-men** [-mən]) *n* poliziotto *m*.

police officer *n* agente *m* di polizia.

police station *n* posto *m* di polizia.

policewoman [pə'li:s,wʊmən] (*pl* **-women** [-,wɪmɪn]) *n* donna *f* poliziotto.

policy ['pɒləsɪ] *n* (*approach, attitude*) politica *f*; (*for insurance*) polizza *f*.

policy-holder *n* assicurato *m* (-a *f*).

polio ['pəʊlɪəʊ] *n* polio *f*.

polish ['pɒlɪʃ] *n* (*for cleaning*) lucido *m*, cera *f* ◆ *vt* lucidare.

Polish ['pəʊlɪʃ] *adj* polacco(-a) ◆ *n* (*language*) polacco *m* ◆ *npl*: **the ~** i polacchi.

polite [pə'laɪt] *adj* cortese, gentile.

political [pə'lɪtɪkl] *adj* politico(-a).

politician [,pɒlɪ'tɪʃn] *n* politico *m*.

politics ['pɒlətɪks] *n* politica *f*.

poll [pəʊl] *n* (*survey*) sondaggio *m* (d'opinioni); **the ~s** (*election*) le elezioni.

pollen ['pɒlən] *n* polline *m*.

Poll Tax *n* (*Br*) tassa comunale pro capite.

pollute [pə'lu:t] *vt* inquinare.

pollution [pə'lu:ʃn] *n* inquinamento *m*.

polo neck ['pəʊləʊ-] *n* (*Br: jumper*) maglione *m* a collo alto.

polyester [,pɒlɪ'estə'] *n* poliestere *m*.

polystyrene [,pɒlɪ'staɪri:n] *n* polistirolo *m*.

polytechnic [,pɒlɪ'teknɪk] *n* =

politecnico *m*.

polythene bag ['pɒlɪθi:n-] *n* sacchetto *m* di plastica.

pomegranate ['pɒmɪˌɡrænɪt] *n* melagrana *f*.

pompous ['pɒmpəs] *adj* pomposo(-a).

pond [pɒnd] *n* stagno *m*.

pontoon [pɒn'tu:n] *n* (*Br: card game*) ventuno *m*.

pony ['pəʊnɪ] *n* pony *m inv*.

ponytail ['pəʊnɪteɪl] *n* coda *f* di cavallo.

pony-trekking [-,trekɪŋ] *n* (*Br*) escursione *f* a dorso di pony.

poodle ['pu:dl] *n* barboncino *m*.

pool [pu:l] *n* pozza *f*; (*for swimming*) piscina *f*; (*game*) biliardo *m* a buca ◆ **pools** *npl* (*Br*): **the ~s** = il totocalcio.

poor [pɔ:'] *adj* povero(-a); (*bad*) mediocre, scadente ◆ *npl*: **the ~** i poveri.

poorly ['pɔ:lɪ] *adv* malamente, male ◆ *adj* (*Br: ill*): **to be ~** poco bene.

pop [pɒp] *n* (*music*) musica *f* pop ◆ *vt* (*inf: put*) mettere ◆ *vi* (*balloon*) scoppiare; **my ears popped** mi si sono stappate le orecchie ❑ **pop in** *vi* (*Br: visit*) fare un salto.

popcorn ['pɒpkɔ:n] *n* popcorn *m*.

Pope [pəʊp] *n*: **the ~** il papa.

pop group *n* gruppo *m* pop.

poplar (tree) ['pɒplə'-] *n* pioppo *m*.

pop music *n* musica *f* pop.

poppadom ['pɒpədəm] *n* pane indiano molto sottile e croccante.

popper ['pɒpə'] *n* (*Br*) bottone *m* a pressione.

poppy ['pɒpɪ] *n* papavero *m*.

212

Popsicle

Popsicle® ['pɒpsɪkl] n (Am) ghiacciolo m.

pop socks npl gambaletti mpl.

pop star n pop star f inv.

popular ['pɒpjʊləʳ] adj popolare; (fashionable) in voga.

popularity [,pɒpjʊ'lærətɪ] n popolarità f.

populated ['pɒpjʊleɪtɪd] adj popolato(-a).

population [,pɒpjʊ'leɪʃn] n popolazione f.

porcelain ['pɔːsəlɪn] n porcellana f.

porch [pɔːtʃ] n (entrance) portico m; (Am: outside house) veranda f.

pork [pɔːk] n carne f di maiale.

pork chop n braciola f OR costoletta f di maiale.

pork pie n pasticcio m di maiale.

pornographic [,pɔːnə'græfɪk] adj pornografico(-a).

porridge ['pɒrɪdʒ] n porridge m, farinata f d'avena.

port [pɔːt] n porto m.

portable ['pɔːtəbl] adj portatile.

porter ['pɔːtəʳ] n (at hotel, museum) portiere m; (at station, airport) facchino m.

porthole ['pɔːthəʊl] n oblò m inv.

portion ['pɔːʃn] n porzione f.

portrait ['pɔːtreɪt] n ritratto m.

Portugal ['pɔːtʃʊgl] n il Portogallo.

Portuguese [,pɔːtʃʊ'giːz] adj portoghese ◆ n (language) portoghese m ◆ npl: **the** ~ i portoghesi.

pose [pəʊz] vt (problem, threat) porre ◆ vi (for photo) posare.

posh [pɒʃ] adj (inf) (person, accent) snob inv, raffinato(-a); (hotel, res-

taurant) elegante, di lusso.

position [pə'zɪʃn] n posizione f; (fml: job) posto m; '~ **closed**' (in bank, post office etc) 'sportello chiuso'.

positive ['pɒzətɪv] adj positivo(-a); (certain, sure) sicuro(-a), certo(-a).

possess [pə'zes] vt possedere.

possession [pə'zeʃn] n (thing owned) bene m.

possessive [pə'zesɪv] adj possessivo(-a).

possibility [,pɒsə'bɪlətɪ] n possibilità f inv.

possible ['pɒsəbl] adj possibile; it's ~ **that we may be late** può darsi che facciamo tardi; **would it be** ~ ...? sarebbe possibile ...?; **as much as** ~ il più possibile; **if** ~ se possibile.

possibly ['pɒsəblɪ] adv (perhaps) forse.

post [pəʊst] n (system, letters, delivery) posta f; (pole) palo m; (fml: job) posto m ◆ vt (letter, parcel) spedire (per posta); **by** ~ per posta.

postage ['pəʊstɪdʒ] n affrancatura f, spese fpl postali; ~ **and packing** spese di spedizione (postale); ~ **paid** franco di porto, affrancatura pagata.

postage stamp n (fml) francobollo m.

postal order ['pəʊstl-] n vaglia m inv postale.

postbox ['pəʊstbɒks] n (Br) cassetta f delle lettere.

postcard ['pəʊstkɑːd] n cartolina f.

postcode ['pəʊstkəʊd] n (Br) codice m (di avviamento) postale.

poster ['pəʊstəʳ] n manifesto m

poster *m inv*.

poste restante [ˌpəʊst-rɛsˈtɑːnt] *n (Br)* fermo posta *m*.

post-free *adv* in franchigia postale, con affrancatura pagata.

postgraduate [ˌpəʊst-ˈgrædʒʊət] *n* laureato(-a) che frequenta un corso di specializzazione.

postman [ˈpəʊstmən] *(pl* **-men** [-mən]*) n* postino *m*.

postmark [ˈpəʊstmɑːk] *n* timbro *m* postale.

postmen *pl* → postman.

post office *n (building)* ufficio *m* postale; **the Post Office** = le Poste e Telecomunicazioni.

postpone [ˌpəʊstˈpəʊn] *vt* rinviare, rimandare.

posture [ˈpɒstʃəʳ] *n* postura *f*.

postwoman [ˈpəʊstˌwʊmən] *(pl* **-women** [-ˌwɪmɪn]*) n* postina *f*.

pot [pɒt] *n (for cooking)* pentola *f*; *(for jam, paint)* vasetto *m*, barattolo *m*; *(for coffee)* caffettiera *f*; *(for tea)* teiera *f*; *(inf: cannabis)* erba *f*; **a ~ of tea** un tè *(servito in una teiera).*

potato [pəˈteɪtəʊ] *(pl* **-es***) n* patata *f*.

potato salad *n* patate *fpl* in insalata.

potential [pəˈtenʃl] *adj* potenziale ♦ *n* potenziale *m*.

pothole [ˈpɒthəʊl] *n (in road)* buca *f*.

pot plant *n* pianta *f* da vaso.

pot scrubber *n* [ˈskrʌbəʳ] *n* paglietta *f*.

potted [ˈpɒtɪd] *adj (meat, fish)* in vasetto, in scatola; *(plant)* in vaso.

pottery [ˈpɒtərɪ] *n (clay objects)* ceramiche *fpl*; *(craft)* ceramica *f*.

potty [ˈpɒtɪ] *n (inf)* vasino *m*.

pouch [paʊtʃ] *n (for money, tobacco)* borsellino *f*.

poultry [ˈpəʊltrɪ] *n & npl* pollame *m*.

pound [paʊnd] *n (unit of money)* sterlina *f*; *(unit of weight)* = 453,6 g, libbra *f* ♦ *vi (heart)* battere forte; *(head)* martellare.

pour [pɔːʳ] *vt* versare ♦ *vi (flow)* riversarsi; **it's ~ing (with rain)** sta piovendo a dirotto ◻ **pour out** *vt sep (drink)* versare.

poverty [ˈpɒvətɪ] *n* povertà *f*, miseria *f*.

powder [ˈpaʊdəʳ] *n* polvere *f*; *(cosmetic)* cipria *f*.

power [ˈpaʊəʳ] *n (control, authority)* potere *m*; *(ability)* capacità *f inv*; *(strength, force)* potenza *f*; *(energy)* energia *f*; *(electricity)* corrente *f* ♦ *vt* azionare; **to be in ~** essere al potere.

power cut *n* interruzione *f* di corrente.

power failure *n* interruzione *f* di corrente.

powerful [ˈpaʊəfʊl] *adj* potente.

power point *n (Br)* presa *f* di corrente.

power station *n* centrale *f* elettrica.

power steering *n* servosterzo *m*.

practical [ˈpræktɪkl] *adj* pratico(-a).

practically [ˈpræktɪklɪ] *adv (almost)* praticamente.

practice [ˈpræktɪs] *n (training)* pratica *f*; *(training session)* allenamento *m*, esercizio *m*; *(of doctor, lawyer)* studio *m*; *(regular activity, custom)* consuetudine *f* ♦ *vt (Am)* = **practise; out of ~** fuori allenamento.

practise ['præktɪs] *vt (sport, music, technique)* allenarsi a, esercitarsi a OR in ♦ *vi (train)* allenarsi, esercitarsi; *(doctor, lawyer)* esercitare ♦ *n (Am)* = **practice**.

praise [preɪz] *n* elogio *m*, lode *f* ♦ *vt* elogiare, lodare.

pram [præm] *n (Br)* carrozzina *f*.

prank [præŋk] *n* burla *f*.

prawn [prɔːn] *n* gamberetto *m*.

prawn cocktail *n* cocktail *m inv* di gamberetti.

prawn crackers *npl* nuvolette *fpl* di drago.

pray [preɪ] *vi* pregare; **to ~ for sthg** *(fig)* pregare per qc, invocare qc.

prayer [preəʳ] *n* preghiera *f*.

precarious [prɪ'keəriəs] *adj* precario(-a).

precaution [prɪ'kɔːʃn] *n* precauzione *f*.

precede [prɪ'siːd] *vt (fml)* precedere.

preceding [prɪ'siːdɪŋ] *adj* precedente.

precinct ['priːsɪŋkt] *n (Br: for shopping)* centro *m* commerciale *(chiuso al traffico)*; *(Am: area of town)* circoscrizione *f*.

precious ['preʃəs] *adj* prezioso(-a).

precious stone *n* pietra *f* preziosa.

precipice ['presɪpɪs] *n* precipizio *m*.

precise [prɪ'saɪs] *adj* preciso(-a).

precisely [prɪ'saɪslɪ] *adv* precisamente.

predecessor ['priːdɪsesəʳ] *n* predecessore *m*.

predicament [prɪ'dɪkəmənt] *n* situazione *f* difficile.

predict [prɪ'dɪkt] *vt* predire.

predictable [prɪ'dɪktəbl] *adj* prevedibile.

prediction [prɪ'dɪkʃn] *n* predizione *f*.

preface ['prefɪs] *n* prefazione *f*.

prefect ['priːfekt] *n (Br: at school)* studente *m* (-essa *f*) con funzioni disciplinari.

prefer [prɪ'fɜːʳ] *vt*: **to ~ sthg (to)** preferire qc (a); **to ~ to do sthg** preferire fare qc.

preferable ['prefrəbl] *adj* preferibile.

preferably ['prefrəblɪ] *adv* preferibilmente.

preference ['prefərəns] *n* preferenza *f*.

prefix ['priːfɪks] *n* prefisso *m*.

pregnancy ['pregnənsɪ] *n* gravidanza *f*.

pregnant ['pregnənt] *adj* incinta.

prejudice ['predʒudɪs] *n* pregiudizio *m*.

prejudiced ['predʒudɪst] *adj*: **~ (against)** prevenuto(-a) (contro); **~ (in favour of)** bendisposto(-a) (verso).

preliminary [prɪ'lɪmɪnərɪ] *adj* preliminare.

premature ['premətjuəʳ] *adj* prematuro(-a).

premier ['premjəʳ] *adj* primo(-a) ♦ *n* primo ministro *m*.

premiere ['premɪeəʳ] *n* prima *f*.

premises ['premɪsɪz] *npl* locali *mpl*; **on the ~** sul posto.

premium ['priːmjəm] *n (for insurance)* premio *m*.

premium-quality *adj (meat*

di prima qualità.

preoccupied [pri:'ɒkjupaɪd] adj preoccupato(-a).

prepacked [pri:'pækt] adj pre-confezionato(-a).

prepaid ['pri:peɪd] adj (envelope) con affrancatura pagata.

preparation [ˌprepə'reɪʃn] n preparazione f □ **preparations** npl (arrangements) preparativi mpl.

preparatory school [prɪ-'pærətrɪ-] n (in UK) scuola f elementare privata; (in US) scuola f secondaria privata (che prepara agli studi universitari).

prepare [prɪ'peəʳ] vt preparare ♦ vi prepararsi.

prepared [prɪ'peəd] adj (ready) preparato(-a), pronto(-a); **to be ~ to do sthg** essere disposto(-a) a fare qc.

preposition [ˌprepə'zɪʃn] n preposizione f.

prep school [prep-] = preparatory school.

prescribe [prɪ'skraɪb] vt prescrivere.

prescription [prɪ'skrɪpʃn] n (paper) ricetta f; (medicine) medicine fpl.

presence ['prezns] n presenza f; **in sb's ~** in presenza di qn.

present [adj & n 'preznt, vb prɪ'zent] adj (in attendance) presente; (current) attuale ♦ n (gift) regalo m ♦ vt presentare; (offer) offrire; **the ~ (tense)** il (tempo) presente; **at ~** al momento, attualmente; **the ~** il presente; **to ~ sb to sb** presentare qn a qn.

presentable [prɪ'zentəbl] adj presentabile.

presentation [ˌprezn'teɪʃn] n

(way of presenting) presentazione f; (ceremony) consegna f (ufficiale).

presenter [prɪ'zentəʳ] n (of TV, radio programme) presentatore m (-trice f).

presently ['prezntlɪ] adv (soon) fra poco, a momenti; (now) attualmente.

preservation [ˌprezə'veɪʃn] n tutela f, protezione f.

preservative [prɪ'zɜ:vətɪv] n conservante m.

preserve [prɪ'zɜ:v] n (jam) marmellata f ♦ vt (conserve) mantenere; (keep) preservare, proteggere; (food) conservare.

president ['prezɪdənt] n presidente mf.

press [pres] vt (push) premere, pigiare; (iron) stirare ♦ n: **the ~** la stampa; **to ~ sb to do sthg** insistere perché qn faccia qc.

press conference n conferenza f stampa.

press-stud n bottone m a pressione, automatico m.

press-ups npl flessioni fpl (sulle braccia).

pressure ['preʃəʳ] n pressione f.

pressure cooker n pentola f a pressione.

prestigious [pre'stɪdʒəs] adj prestigioso(-a).

presumably [prɪ'zju:məblɪ] adv presumibilmente.

presume [prɪ'zju:m] vt (assume) presumere, supporre.

pretend [prɪ'tend] vt: **to ~ to do sthg** far finta di fare qc.

pretentious [prɪ'tenʃəs] adj pretenzioso(-a).

pretty ['prɪtɪ] adj grazioso(-a),

carino(-a) ◆ *adv (inf) (quite)* piuttosto, abbastanza; *(very)* assai.

prevent [prɪˈvɛnt] *vt* evitare; **to ~ sb/sthg from doing sthg** impedire a qn/qc di fare qc.

prevention [prɪˈvɛnʃn] *n* prevenzione *f*.

preview [ˈpriːvjuː] *n* anteprima *f*.

previous [ˈpriːvjəs] *adj* precedente.

previously [ˈpriːvjəslɪ] *adv (formerly)* precedentemente, in precedenza; *(earlier, before)* prima.

price [praɪs] *n* prezzo *m* ◆ *vt* fissare il prezzo di.

priceless [ˈpraɪslɪs] *adj* inestimabile, senza prezzo.

price list *n* listino *m* prezzi.

pricey [ˈpraɪsɪ] *adj (inf)* costoso(-a).

prick [prɪk] *vt* pungere.

prickly [ˈprɪklɪ] *adj (plant, bush)* spinoso(-a).

prickly heat *n* sudamina *f*.

pride [praɪd] *n (satisfaction, self-respect)* orgoglio *m*; *(arrogance)* superbia *f* ◆ *vt*: **to ~ o.s. on sthg** vantarsi di qc.

priest [priːst] *n* prete *m*, sacerdote *m*.

primarily [ˈpraɪmərɪlɪ] *adv* principalmente.

primary school [ˈpraɪmərɪ-] *n* scuola *f* elementare.

prime [praɪm] *adj (chief)* fondamentale; *(beef, cut)* di prima qualità.

prime minister *n* primo ministro *m*.

primitive [ˈprɪmɪtɪv] *adj* primitivo(-a).

primrose [ˈprɪmrəʊz] *n* primula *f*.

prince [prɪns] *n* principe *m*.

Prince of Wales *n* Principe *m* di Galles.

princess [prɪnˈsɛs] *n* principessa *f*.

principal [ˈprɪnsəpl] *adj* principale ◆ *n (of school)* direttore *m* (-trice *f*); *(of university)* rettore *m* (-trice *f*).

principle [ˈprɪnsəpl] *n* principio *m*; **in ~** in linea di principio.

print [prɪnt] *n (words)* caratteri *mpl*; *(photo, of painting)* stampa *f*; *(mark)* impronta *f* ◆ *vt (book, newspaper, photo)* stampare; *(publish)* pubblicare; *(write)* scrivere a stampatello; **out of ~** = esaurito ❑ **print out** *vt sep* stampare.

printed matter [ˈprɪntɪd-] *n* stampe *fpl*.

printer [ˈprɪntəʳ] *n (machine)* stampante *f*; *(person)* tipografo *m* (-a *f*).

printout [ˈprɪntaʊt] *n* stampato *m*.

prior [ˈpraɪəʳ] *adj (previous)* precedente; **~ to** *(fml)* precedente.

priority [praɪˈɒrɪtɪ] *n (important thing)* elemento *m* prioritario; **to have ~ over** avere la priorità rispetto a.

prison [ˈprɪzn] *n* prigione *f*.

prisoner [ˈprɪznəʳ] *n* prigioniero *m* (-a *f*).

prisoner of war *n* prigioniero *m* (-a *f*) di guerra.

prison officer *n* guardia *f* carceraria.

privacy [ˈprɪvəsɪ] *n* privacy *f*.

private [ˈpraɪvɪt] *adj* privato(-a); *(confidential)* confidenziale; *(place, bathroom)* in camera ◆ *n (MIL)* soldato *m* semplice; **in ~** in privato.

private health care n assistenza f medica privata.

private property n proprietà f privata.

private school n scuola f privata.

privilege ['prɪvɪlɪdʒ] n privilegio m; it's a ~! è un onore!

prize [praɪz] n premio m.

prize-giving ['-gɪvɪŋ] n premiazione f.

pro [prəʊ] (pl -s) n (inf: professional) professionista mf □ **pros** npl: **the ~s and cons** i pro e i contro.

probability [ˌprɒbə'bɪlətɪ] n probabilità f.

probable ['prɒbəbl] adj probabile.

probably ['prɒbəblɪ] adv probabilmente.

probation officer [prə'beɪʃn-] n persona incaricata di seguire i criminali in libertà vigilata.

problem ['prɒbləm] n problema m; **no ~!** (inf) non c'è problema!

procedure [prə'si:dʒər] n procedura f.

proceed [prə'si:d] vi (fml) procedere; **'~ with caution'** 'procedere con cautela'.

proceeds ['prəʊsi:dz] npl ricavato m.

process ['prəʊses] n processo m; **to be in the ~ of doing sthg** star facendo qc.

processed cheese ['prəʊsest-] n formaggio m fuso.

procession [prə'seʃn] n processione f.

prod [prɒd] vt (poke) pungolare.

produce [prə'dju:s] vt produrre; (cause) creare ♦ n prodotti mpl

agricoli.

producer [prə'dju:sər] n produttore m (-trice f).

product ['prɒdʌkt] n prodotto m.

production [prə'dʌkʃn] n produzione f.

productivity [ˌprɒdʌk'tɪvətɪ] n produttività f.

profession [prə'feʃn] n professione f.

professional [prə'feʃənl] adj (relating to work) professionale; (not amateur) professionista ♦ n professionista mf.

professor [prə'fesər] n professore m (-essa f).

profile ['prəʊfaɪl] n profilo m.

profit ['prɒfɪt] n profitto m ♦ vi: **to ~ (from)** trarre profitto (da).

profitable ['prɒfɪtəbl] adj (financially) rimunerativo(-a); (useful) vantaggioso(-a).

profiteroles [prə'fɪtərəʊlz] npl profiterole m inv.

profound [prə'faʊnd] adj profondo(-a).

program ['prəʊgræm] n (COMPUT) programma m; (Am) = **programme** ♦ vt (COMPUT) programmare.

programme ['prəʊgræm] n (Br) programma m.

progress [n 'prəʊgres, vb prə'gres] n (improvement) progresso m; (forward movement) moto m ♦ vi (work, talks, student) progredire; (day, meeting) andare avanti; **to make ~** (improve) fare progressi; (in journey) avanzare; **in ~** in corso.

progressive [prə'gresɪv] adj (forward-looking) progressista.

prohibit [prə'hɪbɪt] vt proibire;

'**smoking strictly ~ed**' 'è severamente vietato fumare'.

project ['prɒdʒekt] n progetto m; (at school) ricerca f.

projector [prə'dʒektə^r] n proiettore m.

prolong [prə'lɒŋ] vt prolungare.

prom [prɒm] n (Am: dance) ballo m (per studenti).

promenade [.prɒmə'nɑːd] n (Br: by the sea) lungomare m inv.

prominent ['prɒmɪnənt] adj (person) importante; (noticeable) evidente.

promise ['prɒmɪs] n promessa f ◆ vt & vi promettere; **to show ~** promettere (bene); **I ~!** te lo prometto; **I ~ (that) I'll come** prometto che verrò; **to ~ sb sthg** promettere qc a qn; **to ~ to do sthg** promettere di fare qc.

promising ['prɒmɪsɪŋ] adj promettente.

promote [prə'məut] vt (in job) promuovere.

promotion [prə'məuʃn] n promozione f.

prompt [prɒmpt] adj (quick) pronto(-a) ◆ adv: **at six o'clock ~** alle sei in punto.

prone [prəun] adj: **to be ~ to sthg** essere incline a qc; **to be ~ to do sthg** essere incline a fare qc.

prong [prɒŋ] n (of fork) dente m.

pronoun ['prəunaun] n pronome m.

pronounce [prə'nauns] vt (word) pronunciare.

pronunciation [prə.nʌnsɪ'eɪʃn] n pronuncia f.

proof [pruːf] n (evidence) prova f; **to be 12% ~** (alcohol) avere 12

gradi.

prop [prɒp]: **prop up** vt sep (support) sostenere.

propeller [prə'pelə^r] n elica f.

proper ['prɒpə^r] adj (suitable) adatto(-a); (correct) giusto(-a); (socially acceptable) decoroso(-a).

properly ['prɒpəli] adv (suitably) adeguatamente; (correctly) correttamente.

property ['prɒpəti] n proprietà f inv.

proportion [prə'pɔːʃn] n proporzione f; (in art) proporzioni fpl.

proposal [prə'pəuzl] n (suggestion) proposta f.

propose [prə'pəuz] vt (suggest) proporre ◆ vi: **to ~ (to sb)** fare una proposta di matrimonio (a qn).

proposition [.prɒpə'zɪʃn] n (offer) proposta f.

proprietor [prə'praɪətə^r] n (fml) proprietario m (-a f).

prose [prəuz] n (not poetry) prosa f; (SCH) traduzione f (dalla madrelingua).

prosecution [.prɒsɪ'kjuːʃn] n (JUR: charge) azione f giudiziaria.

prospect ['prɒspekt] n (possibility) prospettiva f; **I don't relish the ~** non mi attira la prospettiva; **prospects** npl (for the future) prospettive fpl.

prospectus [prə'spektəs] n (pl -es) n prospetto m.

prosperous ['prɒspərəs] adj prospero(-a).

prostitute ['prɒstɪtjuːt] n prostituta f.

protect [prə'tekt] vt proteggere; **to ~ sb/sthg from** proteggere qn/qc da; **to ~ sb/sthg against**

teggere qn/qc da.

protection [prə'tekʃn] *n* protezione *f*.

protection factor *n* fattore *m* di protezione.

protective [prə'tektɪv] *adj (person)* protettivo(-a); *(clothes)* di protezione.

protein ['prəʊti:n] *n* proteina *f*.

protest [*n* 'prəʊtest, *vb* prə'test] *n* protesta *f* ♦ *vt* (Am: protest against) protestare contro ♦ *vi:* **to ~ (against)** protestare (contro).

Protestant ['prɒtɪstənt] *n* protestante *mf*.

protester [prə'testə'] *n* dimostrante *mf*.

protractor [prə'træktə'] *n* goniometro *m*.

protrude [prə'tru:d] *vi* sporgere.

proud [praud] *adj (pleased)* orgoglioso(-a); *(pej: arrogant)* superbo(-a); **to be ~ of** essere orgoglioso di.

prove [pru:v] *(pp* **-d** OR **proven** [pru:vn]) *vt (show to be true)* dimostrare; *(turn out to be)* dimostrarsi.

proverb ['prɒvɜ:b] *n* proverbio *m*.

provide [prə'vaɪd] *vt* fornire; **to ~ sb with sthg** fornire qc a qn □ **provide for** *vt fus (person)* provvedere a.

provided (that) [prə'vaɪdɪd-] *conj* purché.

providing (that) [prə'vaɪdɪŋ-] = **provided (that)**.

province ['prɒvɪns] *n* regione *f*.

provisional [prə'vɪʒənl] *adj* provvisorio(-a).

provisions [prə'vɪʒnz] *npl* provviste *fpl*.

provocative [prə'vɒkətɪv] *adj*

provocatorio(-a).

provoke [prə'vəʊk] *vt* provocare.

prowl [praul] *vi* muoversi furtivamente.

prune [pru:n] *n* prugna *f* secca ♦ *vt (tree, bush)* potare.

PS *(abbr of postscript)* P.S.

psychiatrist [saɪ'kaɪətrɪst] *n* psichiatra *mf*.

psychic ['saɪkɪk] *adj* dotato(-a) di poteri paranormali.

psychological [ˌsaɪkə'lɒdʒɪkl] *adj* psicologico(-a).

psychologist [saɪ'kɒlədʒɪst] *n* psicologo *m* (-a *f*).

psychology [saɪ'kɒlədʒɪ] *n* psicologia *f*.

psychotherapist [ˌsaɪkəʊ'θerəpɪst] *n* psicoterapeuta *mf*.

pt *(abbr of pint)* pt.

PTO *(abbr of please turn over)* v.r.

pub [pʌb] *n* pub *m inv*.

---

i **PUB**

Vera e propria istituzione, i pub sono al centro della vita sociale in Gran Bretagna. Soggetti fino a poco tempo fa a rigide restrizioni d'orario, oggi possono generalmente restare aperti dalle 11 alle 23 (e fino a più tardi in Scozia). Le restrizioni relative all'ingresso dei minori di sedici anni variano da regione a regione e da pub a pub mentre rimane il divieto di vendere alcolici ai minorenni. Oltre a una grande varietà di birre e altre bevande alcoliche e non, i pub offrono una discreta scelta di piatti tipici.

puberty ['pju:bəti] *n* pubertà *f*.

public ['pʌblɪk] *adj* pubblico(-a).

◆ *n*: the ~ il pubblico; **in ~** in pubblico.

publican ['pʌblɪkən] *n* (*Br*) gestore *m* (-trice *f*) di un pub.

publication [,pʌblɪ'keɪʃn] *n* pubblicazione *f*.

public bar *n* (*Br*) sala di un pub, in cui le bevande costano meno.

public convenience *n* (*Br*) gabinetti *mpl* pubblici.

public footpath *n* (*Br*) sentiero *m*.

public holiday *n* giorno *m* festivo.

public house *n* (*Br: fml*) pub *m inv*.

publicity [pʌb'lɪsɪtɪ] *n* pubblicità *f*.

public school *n* (*in UK*) scuola *f* privata; (*in US*) scuola statale.

public telephone *n* telefono *m* pubblico.

public transport *n* trasporti *mpl* pubblici.

publish ['pʌblɪʃ] *vt* pubblicare.

publisher ['pʌblɪʃəʳ] *n* (*person*) editore *m* (-trice *f*); (*company*) casa *f* editrice.

publishing ['pʌblɪʃɪŋ] *n* (*industry*) editoria *f*.

pub lunch *n* pranzo semplice e a basso costo servito in un pub.

pudding ['pʊdɪŋ] *n* (*sweet dish*) budino *m*; (*Br: course*) dessert *m inv*.

puddle ['pʌdl] *n* pozzanghera *f*.

puff [pʌf] *vi* (*breathe heavily*) ansare ◆ *n* (*of air, smoke*) sbuffo *m*; **to ~ at** tirare una boccata di.

puff pastry *n* pasta *f* sfoglia.

pull [pʊl] *vt* tirare; (*trigger*) premere ◆ *vi* tirare ◆ *n*: **to give sthg a ~** dare una tirata a qc; **to ~ a face** fare una smorfia; **to ~ a muscle** farsi uno strappo muscolare; **'pull'** (*on door*) 'tirare' ❑ **pull apart** *vt sep* (*machine, book*) fare a pezzi; **pull down** *vt sep* (*lower*) abbassare; (*demolish*) demolire; **pull in** *vi* (*train*) arrivare; (*car*) accostare; **pull out** *vt sep* (*tooth, cork, plug*) estrarre ◆ *vi* (*train*) partire; (*car*) entrare in corsia; (*withdraw*) ritirarsi; **pull over** *vi* (*car*) accostare; **pull up** *vt sep* (*socks, trousers, sleeve*) tirare su ◆ *vi* (*stop*) fermarsi.

pulley ['pʊlɪ] (*pl* **pulleys**) *n* carrucola *f*.

pull-out *n* (*Am: beside road*) piazzola *f* (di sosta).

pullover ['pʊl,əʊvəʳ] *n* pullover *m inv*.

pulpit ['pʊlpɪt] *n* pulpito *m*.

pulse [pʌls] *n* (*MED*) polso *m*.

pump [pʌmp] *n* pompa *f* ❑ **pumps** *npl* (*sports shoes*) scarpe *fpl* da ginnastica; **pump up** *vt sep* gonfiare.

pumpkin ['pʌmpkɪn] *n* zucca *f*.

pun [pʌn] *n* gioco *m* di parole.

punch [pʌntʃ] *n* (*blow*) pugno *m*; (*drink*) punch *m inv* ◆ *vt* (*hit*) sferrare un pugno a; (*ticket*) forare.

Punch and Judy show [-'dʒuːdɪ-] *n* spettacolo *m* di burattini.

punctual ['pʌŋktʃʊəl] *adj* puntuale.

punctuation [,pʌŋktʃʊ'eɪʃn] *n* punteggiatura *f*.

puncture ['pʌŋktʃəʳ] *vt* forare ◆ *n*: **to get a ~** forare (una gomma).

punish ['pʌnɪʃ] *vt*: **to ~ sb** (for sthg) punire qn (per qc).

punishment ['pʌnɪʃmənt] *n* punizione *f*.

punk [pʌŋk] *n* (*person*) punk *m inv*; (*music*) musica *f* punk.

punnet ['pʌnɪt] *n* (Br) cestino *m*.

pupil ['pjuːpl] *n* (student) alunno *m* (-a *f*); (of eye) pupilla *f*.

puppet ['pʌpɪt] *n* burattino *m*.

puppy ['pʌpɪ] *n* cucciolo *m*.

purchase ['pɜːtʃəs] *vt* (fml) acquistare ◆ *n* (fml) acquisto *m*.

pure [pjʊə*r*] *adj* puro(-a).

puree ['pjʊəreɪ] *n* purè *m inv*.

purely ['pjʊəlɪ] *adv* (only) soltanto.

purity ['pjʊərətɪ] *n* purezza *f*.

purple ['pɜːpl] *adj* viola (*inv*).

purpose ['pɜːpəs] *n* scopo *m*; **on ~** apposta.

purr [pɜː*r*] *vi* (cat) fare le fusa.

purse [pɜːs] *n* (Br: for money) portamonete *m inv*; (Am: handbag) borsa *f*.

pursue [pə'sjuː] *vt* (follow) inseguire; (study) continuare; (matter, inquiry) approfondire.

pus [pʌs] *n* pus *m*.

push [pʊʃ] *vt* spingere; (button, doorbell) premere; (product) pubblicizzare ◆ *vi* spingere ◆ *n*: **to give sb/sthg a ~** dare una spinta a qn/qc; **to ~ sb into doing sthg** spingere qn a fare qc; **'push'** (on door) 'spingere' ❑ **push in** *vi* (in queue) passare avanti; **push off** *vi* (inf: go away) andarsene.

push-button telephone *n* telefono *m* a tastiera.

pushchair ['pʊʃtʃeə*r*] *n* (Br) passeggino *m*.

pushed [pʊʃt] *adj* (inf): **to be ~ (for time)** essere a corto di tempo.

push-ups *npl* flessioni *fpl* (sulle braccia).

put [pʊt] (*pt & pp* put) *vt* mettere; (responsibility) dare; (pressure)

esercitare; (express) esprimere; (a question) porre; (estimate) stimare; **to ~ a child to bed** mettere a letto un bambino; **to ~ money into sthg** investire soldi in qc ❑ **put aside** *vt sep* (money) mettere da parte; **put away** *vt sep* (tidy up) mettere via; **put back** *vt sep* (replace) mettere a posto; (postpone) posporre; (clock, watch) mettere indietro; **put down** *vt sep* (on floor, table) posare; (passenger) far scendere; (Br: animal) abbattere; (deposit) dare in acconto; **put forward** *vt sep* (clock, watch) mettere avanti; (suggest) suggerire; **put in** *vt sep* (insert) inserire; (install) installare; **put off** *vt sep* (postpone) rimandare; (distract) distrarre; (repel) disgustare; (passenger) far scendere; **put on** *vt sep* (clothes, glasses, make-up) mettersi; (weight) mettere su; (television, light, radio) accendere; (CD, tape, record) mettere; (play, show) mettere in scena; **put out** *vt sep* (cigarette, fire, light) spegnere; (publish) pubblicare; (hand, arm, leg) stendere; (inconvenience) disturbare; **to ~ one's back out** farsi male alla schiena; **put together** *vt sep* (assemble) montare; (combine) mettere insieme; **put up** *vt sep* (tent, statue, building) erigere; (umbrella) aprire; (a notice, sign) mettere; (price, rate) aumentare; (provide with accommodation) ospitare ◆ *vi* (Br: in hotel) alloggiare; **put up with** *vt fus* sopportare.

putter ['pʌtə*r*] *n* (club) putter *m inv*.

putting green ['pʌtɪŋ-] *n* campo *m* da minigolf.

putty ['pʌtɪ] *n* stucco *m*.

puzzle ['pʌzl] *n* (game) rompica-

po m; (jigsaw) puzzle m inv; (mystery) enigma m ◆ vt confondere.

puzzling ['pʌzlɪŋ] adj sconcertante.

pyjamas [pə'dʒɑːməz] npl (Br) pigiama m.

pylon ['paɪlən] n traliccio m.

pyramid ['pɪrəmɪd] n piramide f.

Pyrenees [,pɪrə'niːz] npl: **the ~** i Pirenei.

Pyrex® ['paɪreks] n pyrex® m.

Q

quail [kweɪl] n quaglia f.

quail's eggs npl uova fpl di quaglia.

quaint [kweɪnt] adj pittoresco(-a).

qualification [,kwɒlɪfɪ'keɪʃn] n (diploma) qualifica f; (ability) qualità f inv.

qualified ['kwɒlɪfaɪd] adj (having qualifications) qualificato(-a).

qualify ['kwɒlɪfaɪ] vi (for competition) qualificarsi; (pass exam) abilitarsi.

quality ['kwɒlətɪ] n qualità f inv ◆ adj di qualità.

quarantine ['kwɒrəntiːn] n quarantena f.

quarrel ['kwɒrəl] n lite f ◆ vi litigare.

quarry ['kwɒrɪ] n (for stone, sand) cava f.

quart [kwɔːt] n (in UK) = 1,136 l, = litro m; (in US) = 0,946 l, =

litro.

quarter ['kwɔːtər] n (fraction) quarto m; (Am: coin) quarto di dollaro; (4 ounces) quarto di libbra; (three months) trimestre m; (part of town) quartiere m; **(a) ~ to five** (Br) le cinque meno un quarto; **(a) ~ of five** (Am) le cinque meno un quarto; **(a) ~ past five** (Br) le cinque e un quarto; **(a) ~ after five** (Am) le cinque e un quarto; **(a) ~ of an hour** un quarto d'ora.

quarterpounder [,kwɔːtə'paʊndər] n grosso hamburger m inv.

quartet [kwɔː'tet] n quartetto m.

quartz [kwɔːts] adj (watch) al quarzo.

quay [kiː] n banchina f.

queasy ['kwiːzɪ] adj (inf): **to feel ~** avere la nausea.

queen [kwiːn] n regina f.

queer [kwɪər] adj (strange) strano(-a); (inf: homosexual) omosessuale; **to feel ~** (ill) sentirsi male.

quench [kwentʃ] vt: **to ~ one's thirst** dissetarsi.

query ['kwɪərɪ] n quesito m.

question ['kwestʃn] n (query, in exam, on questionnaire) domanda f; (issue) questione f ◆ vt (person) interrogare; **it's out of the ~** è fuori discussione.

question mark n punto m interrogativo.

questionnaire [,kwestʃə'neər] n questionario m.

queue [kjuː] n (Br) coda f ◆ vi (Br) fare la coda ❑ **queue up** vi (Br) fare la coda.

quiche [kiːʃ] n torta f salata.

quick [kwɪk] adj rapido(-a) ◆ ad rapidamente.

quickly [ˈkwɪklɪ] *adv* rapidamente.

quid [kwɪd] (*pl inv*) *n* (*Br: inf*) sterlina *f*.

quiet [ˈkwaɪət] *adj* silenzioso(-a); (*calm, peaceful*) tranquillo(-a) ◆ *n* quiete *f*; **in a ~ voice** a bassa voce; **keep ~!** silenzio!; **to keep ~** (*not say anything*) tacere; **to keep ~ about sthg** tenere segreto qc.

quieten [ˈkwaɪətn]: **quieten down** *vi* calmarsi.

quietly [ˈkwaɪətlɪ] *adv* silenziosamente; (*calmly*) tranquillamente.

quilt [kwɪlt] *n* (*duvet*) piumino *m*; (*eiderdown*) trapunta *f*.

quince [kwɪns] *n* mela *f* cotogna.

quirk [kwɜːk] *n* stranezza *f*.

quit [kwɪt] (*pt & pp* **quit**) *vi* (*resign*) dimettersi; (*give up*) smettere ◆ *vt* (*Am: school, job*) lasciare; **to ~ doing sthg** smettere di fare qc.

quite [kwaɪt] *adv* (*fairly*) abbastanza; (*completely*) proprio; **not ~** non proprio; **~ a lot (of)** un bel po' (di).

quiz [kwɪz] (*pl* **-zes**) *n* quiz *m inv*.

quota [ˈkwəʊtə] *n* quota *f*.

quotation [kwəʊˈteɪʃn] *n* (*phrase*) citazione *f*; (*estimate*) preventivo *m*.

quotation marks *npl* virgolette *fpl*.

quote [kwəʊt] *vt* (*phrase, writer*) citare ◆ *n* (*phrase*) citazione *f*; (*estimate*) preventivo *m*; **he ~d me a price of £50** mi ha dato un prezzo indicativo di 50 sterline.

R

rabbit [ˈræbɪt] *n* coniglio *m*.

rabies [ˈreɪbiːz] *n* rabbia *f*.

RAC *n* = ACI *m*.

race [reɪs] *n* (*competition*) gara *f*; (*ethnic group*) razza *f* ◆ *vi* (*compete*) gareggiare; (*go fast*) correre; (*engine*) imballarsi ◆ *vt* (*compete against*) gareggiare con.

racecourse [ˈreɪskɔːs] *n* ippodromo *m*.

racehorse [ˈreɪshɔːs] *n* cavallo *m* da corsa.

racetrack [ˈreɪstræk] *n* (*for horses*) ippodromo *m*.

racial [ˈreɪʃl] *adj* razziale.

racing [ˈreɪsɪŋ] *n*: (**horse**) **~** corse *fpl* (di cavalli).

racing car *n* automobile *f* da corsa.

racism [ˈreɪsɪzm] *n* razzismo *m*.

racist [ˈreɪsɪst] *n* razzista *mf*.

rack [ræk] *n* (*for coats*) attaccapanni *m inv*; (*for plates*) scolapiatti *m inv*; (*for bottles*) portabottiglie *m inv*; (*luggage*) **~** portabagagli *m inv*; **~ of lamb** carrè *m inv* di agnello.

racket [ˈrækɪt] *n* (*for tennis, badminton, squash*) racchetta *f*; (*noise*) baccano *m*.

racquet [ˈrækɪt] *n* racchetta *f*.

radar [ˈreɪdɑː^r] *n* radar *m inv*.

radiation [ˌreɪdɪˈeɪʃn] *n* (*nuclear*) radiazione *f*.

radiator [ˈreɪdɪeɪtə^r] *n* radiatore *m*.

radical [ˈrædɪkl] *adj* radicale.

radii [ˈreɪdɪaɪ] *pl* → **radius**.

radio ['reɪdɪəʊ] (pl -s) n radio f inv ♦ vt (person) chiamare via radio; **on the ~** alla radio.

radioactive [ˌreɪdɪəʊ'æktɪv] adj radioattivo(-a).

radio alarm n radiosveglia f.

radish ['rædɪʃ] n ravanello m.

radius ['reɪdɪəs] (pl radii) n raggio m.

raffle ['ræfl] n lotteria f.

raft [rɑːft] n (of wood) zattera f; (inflatable) materassino m (gonfiabile).

rafter ['rɑːftə'] n travicello m.

rag [ræg] n (old cloth) straccio m.

rage [reɪdʒ] n rabbia f.

raid [reɪd] n raid m inv; (robbery) scorreria f ♦ vt (subj: police) fare irruzione in; (subj: thieves) fare razzia in.

rail [reɪl] n (bar) sbarra f; (for curtain) asta f; (on stairs) corrimano m inv; (for train, tram) rotaia f ♦ adj ferroviario(-a); **by ~** in treno.

railcard ['reɪlkɑːd] n (Br) (for young people) tessera per riduzione ferroviaria; (for pensioners) = carta d'argento.

railings ['reɪlɪŋz] npl ringhiera f.

railroad ['reɪlrəʊd] (Am) = railway.

railway ['reɪlweɪ] n ferrovia f.

railway line n (route) linea f ferroviaria; (track) binario m.

railway station n stazione f ferroviaria.

rain [reɪn] n pioggia f ♦ v impers piovere; **it's ~ing** sta piovendo.

rainbow ['reɪnbəʊ] n arcobaleno m.

raincoat ['reɪnkəʊt] n impermeabile m.

raindrop ['reɪndrɒp] n goccia f di pioggia.

rainfall ['reɪnfɔːl] n precipitazione f.

rainy ['reɪnɪ] adj piovoso(-a).

raise [reɪz] vt sollevare; (increase) aumentare; (money) raccogliere; (child, animals) allevare ♦ n (Am: pay increase) aumento m.

raisin ['reɪzn] n uva f passa.

rake [reɪk] n (gardening tool) rastrello m.

rally ['rælɪ] n (public meeting) comizio m; (motor race) rally m inv; (in tennis, badminton, squash) serie di scambi della palla.

ram [ræm] n montone m ♦ vt (bang into) speronare.

Ramadan [ˌræmə'dæn] n Ramadan m inv.

ramble ['ræmbl] n camminata f.

ramp [ræmp] n (slope) rampa f; (in roadworks) dislivello m; (Am: to freeway) rampa f d'accesso; **'ramp'** (Br: bump) 'fondo dissestato'.

ramparts ['ræmpɑːts] npl bastioni mpl.

ran [ræn] pt → run.

ranch [rɑːntʃ] n ranch m inv.

ranch dressing n (Am) maionese piuttosto liquida e piccante.

rancid ['rænsɪd] adj rancido(-a).

random ['rændəm] adj a caso ♦ n: **at ~** a caso.

rang [ræŋ] pt → ring.

range [reɪndʒ] n (of radio, telescope) portata f; (of aircraft) raggio m; (for shooting) campo m di tiro; (of prices, temperatures, goods) gamma f; (of hills, mountains) catena f; (cooker) cucina f economica ♦ vi (vary, variare).

ranger ['reɪndʒə'] n (of park

forest) guardia *f* forestale.

rank [ræŋk] *n (in armed forces, police)* rango *m* ◆ *adj (smell, taste)* rancido(-a).

ransom ['rænsəm] *n* riscatto *m*.

rap [ræp] *n (music)* rap *m inv*.

rape [reɪp] *n* stupro *m* ◆ *vt* stuprare.

rapid ['ræpɪd] *adj* rapido(-a) □ **rapids** *npl* rapide *fpl*.

rapidly ['ræpɪdlɪ] *adv* rapidamente.

rapist ['reɪpɪst] *n* stupratore *m*.

rare [reəʳ] *adj (not common)* raro(-a); *(meat)* al sangue.

rarely ['reəlɪ] *adv* raramente.

rash [ræʃ] *n* eruzione *f* cutanea ◆ *adj* impulsivo(-a).

rasher ['ræʃəʳ] *n* fettina *f* di pancetta.

raspberry ['rɑːzbərɪ] *n* lampone *m*.

rat [ræt] *n* ratto *m*.

ratatouille [rætə'tuːɪ] *n* ratatouille *f inv*.

rate [reɪt] *n (level)* tasso *m*; *(charge)* tariffa *f*; *(speed)* ritmo *m* ◆ *vt (consider)* reputare; *(deserve)* meritare; **~ of exchange** tasso di cambio; **at any ~** in ogni caso; **at this ~** di questo passo.

rather ['rɑːðəʳ] *adv (quite)* piuttosto; **I'd ~ not** preferirei di no; **would you ~ …?** preferisci …?; **~ than** piuttosto che; **~ a lot** molto.

ratio ['reɪʃɪəʊ] *(pl* **-s**) *n* rapporto *m*.

ration ['ræʃn] *n (share)* razione *f* □ **rations** *npl (food)* razioni *fpl*.

rational ['ræʃnl] *adj* razionale.

rattle ['rætl] *n (of baby)* sonaglio *m* ◆ *vi* sbatacchiare.

rave [reɪv] *n (party)* rave *m inv*.

raven ['reɪvn] *n* corvo *m*.

ravioli [ˌrævɪ'əʊlɪ] *n* ravioli *mpl*.

raw [rɔː] *adj (uncooked)* crudo(-a); *(unprocessed)* grezzo(-a).

raw material *n* materia *f* prima.

ray [reɪ] *n* raggio *m*.

razor ['reɪzəʳ] *n* rasoio *m*.

razor blade *n* lametta *f (da barba)*.

Rd *abbr* = **Road**.

re [riː] *prep* in merito a.

RE *n (abbr of religious education)* religione *f (materia)* .

reach [riːtʃ] *vt* raggiungere ◆ *n*: **out of ~** lontano; **within ~ of the beach** a poca distanza dalla spiaggia □ **reach out** *vi*: **to ~ out (for)** allungarsi (per raggiungere).

react [rɪ'ækt] *vi* reagire.

reaction [rɪ'ækʃn] *n* reazione *f*.

read [riːd] *(pt & pp* **read** [red]) *vt* leggere; *(subj: sign, note)* dire; *(subj: meter, gauge)* segnare ◆ *vi* leggere; **to ~ about sthg** leggere di qc □ **read out** *vt sep* leggere ad alta voce.

reader ['riːdəʳ] *n (of newspaper, book)* lettore *m* (-trice *f*).

readily ['redɪlɪ] *adv (willingly)* prontamente; *(easily)* facilmente.

reading ['riːdɪŋ] *n (of books, papers)* lettura *f*; *(of meter, gauge)* valore *m* indicato.

reading matter *n* qualcosa da leggere.

ready ['redɪ] *adj* pronto(-a); **to be ~ for sthg** *(prepared)* essere preparato(-a) per qc; **to be ~ to do sthg** *(willing)* essere pronto a fare qc; *(likely)* essere sul punto di fare qc; **to get ~** prepararsi; **to get sthg ~** preparare qc.

ready cash n contante m.

ready-cooked [-kukt] adj precotto(-a).

ready-to-wear adj confezionato(-a).

real ['riəl] adj vero(-a); (world) reale ♦ adv (Am) davvero.

real ale n (Br) birra rossa prodotta secondo metodi tradizionali.

real estate n proprietà fpl immobiliari.

realistic [ˌriə'lıstık] adj realistico(-a).

reality [rı'ælətı] n realtà f inv; in ~ in realtà.

realize ['riəlaız] vt rendersi conto di; (ambition, goal) realizzare; to ~ (that) ... rendersi conto che OR di ...

really ['riəlı] adv veramente; (in reality) realmente; do you like it? - no, not ~ ti piace? - veramente no; ~! (expressing surprise) davvero!

realtor ['riəltər] n (Am) agente mf immobiliare.

rear [rıər] adj posteriore ♦ n (back) retro m inv.

rearrange [ˌriːə'reındʒ] vt spostare.

rearview mirror ['rıəvjuː-] n specchietto m retrovisore.

rear-wheel drive n trazione f posteriore.

reason ['riːzn] n motivo m; for some ~ per qualche motivo.

reasonable ['riːznəbl] adj ragionevole; (quite big) buono(-a).

reasonably ['riːznəblı] adv (quite) piuttosto.

reasoning ['riːznıŋ] n ragionamento m.

reassure [ˌriːə'ʃɔːr] vt rassicurare.

reassuring [ˌriːə'ʃɔːrıŋ] adj rassicurante.

rebate ['riːbeıt] n rimborso m.

rebel [n 'rebl] n ribelle mf ♦ vi [rı'bel] ribellarsi.

rebound [rı'baʊnd] vi (ball) rimbalzare.

rebuild [ˌriː'bıld] (pt & pp rebuilt [ˌriː'bılt]) vt ricostruire.

rebuke [rı'bjuːk] vt rimproverare.

recall [rı'kɔːl] vt (remember) ricordare.

receipt [rı'siːt] n (for goods, money) ricevuta f; on ~ of al ricevimento di.

receive [rı'siːv] vt ricevere.

receiver [rı'siːvər] n (of phone) ricevitore m.

recent ['riːsnt] adj recente.

recently ['riːsntlı] adv recentemente.

receptacle [rı'septəkl] n (fml) ricettacolo m.

reception [rı'sepʃn] n (in hotel) reception f inv; (at hospital) accettazione f; (party) ricevimento m; (welcome) accoglienza f; (of TV, radio) ricezione f.

reception desk n banco m della reception.

receptionist [rı'sepʃənıst] n receptionist mf inv.

recess ['riːses] n (in wall) nicchia f; (Am: SCH) intervallo m.

recession [rı'seʃn] n recessione f.

recipe ['resıpı] n ricetta f.

recite [rı'saıt] vt (poem) recitare; (list) elencare.

reckless ['reklıs] adj avventato(-a).

reckon ['rekn] vt (inf: think) pen

sare ❑ **reckon on** vt fus aspettarsi; **reckon with** vt fus (expect) aspettarsi.

reclaim [rɪ'kleɪm] vt (baggage) ritirare.

reclining seat [rɪ'klaɪnɪŋ-] n sedile m reclinabile.

recognition [ˌrekəg'nɪʃn] n riconoscimento m.

recognize ['rekəgnaɪz] vt riconoscere.

recollect [ˌrekə'lekt] vt ricordare.

recommend [ˌrekə'mend] vt raccomandare; **to ~ sb to do sthg** consigliare a qn di fare qc.

recommendation [ˌrekəmen'deɪʃn] n (suggestion) indicazione f.

reconsider [ˌriːkən'sɪdər] vt riconsiderare.

reconstruct [ˌriːkən'strʌkt] vt ricostruire.

record [n 'rekɔːd, vb rɪ'kɔːd] n (MUS) disco m; (best performance, highest level) record m inv; (account) nota f ♦ vt (keep account of) annotare; (on tape) registrare.

recorded delivery [rɪ'kɔːdɪd-] n (Br) = raccomandata f.

recorder [rɪ'kɔːdər] n (tape recorder) registratore m; (instrument) flauto m diritto.

recording [rɪ'kɔːdɪŋ] n registrazione f.

record player n giradischi m inv.

record shop n negozio m di dischi.

recover [rɪ'kʌvər] vt (stolen goods, lost property) recuperare ♦ vi riprendersi.

recovery [rɪ'kʌvərɪ] n (from illness) guarigione f.

recovery vehicle n (Br) carro m attrezzi.

recreation [ˌrekrɪ'eɪʃn] n divertimento m.

recreation ground n parco m (giochi).

recruit [rɪ'kruːt] n recluta mf ♦ vt (staff) assumere.

rectangle ['rektæŋgl] n rettangolo m.

rectangular [rek'tæŋgjʊlər] adj rettangolare.

recycle [ˌriː'saɪkl] vt riciclare.

red [red] adj rosso(-a) ♦ n (colour) rosso m; **in the ~** in rosso.

red cabbage n cavolo m rosso.

Red Cross n Croce f Rossa.

redcurrant ['redkʌrənt] n ribes m inv.

redecorate [ˌriː'dekəreɪt] vt rimbiancare.

redhead ['redhed] n rosso m (-a f).

red-hot adj (metal) rovente.

redial [ˌriː'daɪəl] vi rifare il numero.

redirect [ˌriːdɪ'rekt] vt (letter) spedire a un nuovo indirizzo; (traffic, plane) dirottare.

red pepper n peperone m rosso.

reduce [rɪ'djuːs] vt ridurre ♦ vi (Am: slim) dimagrire.

reduced price [rɪ'djuːst-] n prezzo m ridotto.

reduction [rɪ'dʌkʃn] n riduzione f.

redundancy [rɪ'dʌndənsɪ] n (Br) licenziamento m (per esubero).

redundant [rɪ'dʌndənt] adj (Br): **to be made ~** essere licenziato(-a).

red wine n vino m rosso.

reed [riːd] n canna f.

reef [ri:f] n scogliera f.

reek [ri:k] vi puzzare.

reel [ri:l] n (of thread) rocchetto m; (on fishing rod) mulinello m.

refectory [rɪ'fektərɪ] n refettorio m.

refer [rɪ'fɜ:ʲ]: **refer to** vt fus (speak about) fare riferimento a; (relate to) riferirsi a; (consult) consultare.

referee [,refə'ri:] n (SPORT) arbitro m (-a f).

reference ['refrəns] n (mention) riferimento m; (letter for job) lettera f di referenze ♦ adj (book, library) di consultazione; **with ~ to** con riferimento a.

referendum [,refə'rendəm] n referendum m inv.

refill [n 'ri:fɪl, vb ri:'fɪl] n (for pen) ricambio m; (inf: drink) rifornimento m ♦ vt riempire.

refinery [rɪ'faɪnərɪ] n raffineria f.

reflect [rɪ'flekt] vt & vi riflettere.

reflection [rɪ'flekʃn] n (image) riflesso m.

reflector [rɪ'flektəʲ] n catarifrangente m.

reflex ['ri:fleks] n riflesso m.

reflexive [rɪ'fleksɪv] adj riflessivo(-a).

reform [rɪ'fɔ:m] n riforma f ♦ vt riformare.

refresh [rɪ'freʃ] vt rinfrescare.

refreshing [rɪ'freʃɪŋ] adj (drink, breeze, sleep) rinfrescante; (change) piacevole.

refreshments [rɪ'freʃmənts] npl rinfreschi mpl.

refrigerator [rɪ'frɪdʒəreɪtəʲ] n frigorifero m.

refugee [,refjʊ'dʒi:] n rifugiato

m (-a f).

refund [n 'ri:fʌnd, vb rɪ'fʌnd] n rimborso m ♦ vt rimborsare.

refundable [rɪ'fʌndəbl] adj rimborsabile.

refusal [rɪ'fju:zl] n rifiuto m.

refuse[1] [rɪ'fju:z] vt (not accept) rifiutare; (not allow) negare ♦ vi rifiutare; **to ~ to do sthg** rifiutare di fare qc.

refuse[2] ['refju:s] n (fml) rifiuti mpl.

refuse collection ['refju:s-] n (fml) raccolta f dei rifiuti.

regard [rɪ'gɑ:d] vt (consider) considerare ♦ n: **with ~ to** riguardo a; **as ~s** per quanto riguarda □

regards npl (in greetings) saluti mpl; **give them my ~s** li saluti da parte mia.

regarding [rɪ'gɑ:dɪŋ] prep riguardo a.

regardless [rɪ'gɑ:dlɪs] adv lo stesso; **~ of** senza tener conto di.

reggae ['regeɪ] n reggae m inv.

regiment ['redʒɪmənt] n reggimento m.

region ['ri:dʒən] n regione f; **in the ~ of** circa.

regional ['ri:dʒənl] adj regionale.

register ['redʒɪstəʲ] n registro m ♦ vt registrare; (subj: machine, gauge) segnare ♦ vi (put one's name down) iscriversi; (at hotel) firmare il registro.

registered ['redʒɪstəd] adj (letter, parcel) assicurato(-a).

registration [,redʒɪ'streɪʃn] n (for course, at conference) iscrizione f

registration (number) n (of car) numero m di targa.

registry office ['redʒɪstrɪ-] n anagrafe f.

regret [rɪ'gret] n (thing regretted) rimpianto m ◆ vt rimpiangere; **I ~ telling** her mi dispiace (di) avervelo detto; **we ~ any inconvenience caused** ci scusiamo per il disagio causato.

regrettable [rɪ'gretəbl] adj spiacevole.

regular ['regjʊlə'] adj regolare; (normal, in size) normale; (customer, reader) abituale ◆ n (customer) mf abituale.

regularly ['regjʊləlɪ] adv regolarmente.

regulate ['regjʊleɪt] vt regolare.

regulation [,regjʊ'leɪʃn] n (rule) norma f.

rehearsal [rɪ'hɜːsl] n prova f.

rehearse [rɪ'hɜːs] vt provare.

reign [reɪn] n regno m ◆ vi regnare.

reimburse [,riːɪm'bɜːs] vt (fml) rimborsare.

reindeer ['reɪn,dɪə'] (pl inv) n renna f.

reinforce [,riːɪn'fɔːs] vt (wall, handle) rinforzare; (argument, opinion) rafforzare.

reinforcements [,riːɪn'fɔːsmənts] npl rinforzi mpl.

reins [reɪnz] npl briglie fpl.

reject [rɪ'dʒekt] vt (proposal, request, coin) respingere; (applicant, plan) scartare.

rejection [rɪ'dʒekʃn] n rifiuto m.

rejoin [,riː'dʒɔɪn] vt (motorway) riprendere.

relapse [rɪ'læps] n ricaduta f.

relate [rɪ'leɪt] vt (connect) collegare ◆ vi: to ~ to (be connected with) essere collegato a; (concern) riguardare.

related [rɪ'leɪtɪd] adj (of same family) imparentato(-a); (connected) collegato(-a).

relation [rɪ'leɪʃn] n (member of family) parente mf; (connection) rapporto m; **in ~ to** in rapporto a ❑ **relations** npl parenti mpl.

relationship [rɪ'leɪʃnʃɪp] n rapporto m, relazione f.

relative ['relətɪv] adj relativo(-a) ◆ n parente mf.

relatively ['relətɪvlɪ] adv relativamente.

relax [rɪ'læks] vi (person) rilassarsi.

relaxation [,riːlæk'seɪʃn] n (of person) relax m.

relaxed [rɪ'lækst] adj rilassato(-a).

relaxing [rɪ'læksɪŋ] adj rilassante.

relay ['riːleɪ] n (race) staffetta f.

release [rɪ'liːs] vt (set free) liberare; (let go of) mollare; (record, film) far uscire; (handbrake, catch) togliere ◆ n (record, film) uscita f.

relegate ['relɪgeɪt] vt: to be ~d (SPORT) essere retrocesso.

relevant ['reləvənt] adj (connected) pertinente; (important) importante; (appropriate) appropriato(-a).

reliable [rɪ'laɪəbl] adj (person, machine) affidabile.

relic ['relɪk] n (object) reperto m (archeologico).

relief [rɪ'liːf] n (gladness) sollievo m; (aid) aiuto m.

relief road n strada f di smaltimento.

relieve [rɪ'liːv] vt (pain, headache) alleviare.

relieved [rɪ'liːvd] adj sollevato(-a).

religion [rɪˈlɪdʒn] n religione f.

religious [rɪˈlɪdʒəs] adj religioso(-a).

relish [ˈrelɪʃ] n (sauce) salsa f.

reluctant [rɪˈlʌktənt] adj riluttante.

rely [rɪˈlaɪ] : **rely on** vt fus (trust) contare su; (depend on) dipendere da.

remain [rɪˈmeɪn] vi rimanere ☐ **remains** npl resti mpl.

remainder [rɪˈmeɪndəʳ] n resto m.

remaining [rɪˈmeɪnɪŋ] adj restante.

remark [rɪˈmɑːk] n commento m ♦ vt commentare.

remarkable [rɪˈmɑːkəbl] adj notevole.

remedy [ˈremɪdɪ] n rimedio m.

remember [rɪˈmembəʳ] vt (recall) ricordare; (not forget) ricordarsi (di) ♦ vi (recall) ricordarsi; **to ~ doing sthg** ricordarsi di aver fatto qc; **to ~ to do sthg** ricordarsi di fare qc.

remind [rɪˈmaɪnd] vt: **to ~ sb of sthg** ricordare qc a qn; **to ~ sb to do sthg** ricordare a qn di fare qc.

reminder [rɪˈmaɪndəʳ] n (for bill, library book) sollecito m.

remittance [rɪˈmɪtns] n rimessa f.

remnant [ˈremnənt] n resto m.

remote [rɪˈməut] adj remoto(-a).

remote control n telecomando m.

removal [rɪˈmuːvl] n (taking away) rimozione f.

removal van n camion m inv dei traslochi.

remove [rɪˈmuːv] vt togliere; (clothes) togliersi.

renew [rɪˈnjuː] vt rinnovare.

renovate [ˈrenəveɪt] vt rinnovare.

renowned [rɪˈnaund] adj rinomato(-a).

rent [rent] n affitto m ♦ vt (flat) affittare; (car, TV) noleggiare.

rental [ˈrentl] n (fee) affitto m.

repaid [riːˈpeɪd] pt & pp → **repay.**

repair [rɪˈpeəʳ] vt riparare ♦ n: **in good ~** in buone condizioni ☐ **repairs** npl riparazioni fpl.

repair kit n (for bicycle) borsetta f degli attrezzi.

repay [riːˈpeɪ] (pt & pp **repaid**) vt restituire.

repayment [riːˈpeɪmənt] n (of loan) rimborso m.

repeat [rɪˈpiːt] vt ripetere; (gossip, news) riferire ♦ n (on TV, radio) replica f.

repetition [ˌrepɪˈtɪʃn] n ripetizione f.

repetitive [rɪˈpetɪtɪv] adj ripetitivo(-a).

replace [rɪˈpleɪs] vt rimpiazzare; (put back) mettere a posto.

replacement [rɪˈpleɪsmənt] n (substitute) sostituto m (-a f).

replay [ˈriːpleɪ] n (rematch) partita f ripetuta; (on TV) replay m inv.

reply [rɪˈplaɪ] n risposta f ♦ vt & vi rispondere.

report [rɪˈpɔːt] n (account) relazione f; (in newspaper, on TV, radio) servizio m; (Br: SCH) = scheda f ♦ vt (announce) riportare; (theft, disappearance, person) denunciare ♦ vi (give account) riferire; (for newspaper, TV, radio) fare un servizio; **to ~ sb (go to)** presentarsi a qn.

report card n = scheda f (sco

lastica).

reporter [rɪˈpɔːtəʳ] *n* reporter *mf inv*.

represent [repɾɪˈzent] *vt* rappresentare.

representative [repɾɪˈzentətɪv] *n* rappresentante *mf*.

repress [rɪˈpres] *vt (feelings)* reprimere; *(people)* opprimere.

reprieve [rɪˈpriːv] *n (delay)* sospensione *f*.

reprimand [ˈrepɾɪmɑːnd] *vt* rimproverare.

reproach [rɪˈprəʊtʃ] *vt* rimproverare.

reproduction [riːprəˈdʌkʃn] *n* riproduzione *f*.

reptile [ˈreptaɪl] *n* rettile *m*.

republic [rɪˈpʌblɪk] *n* repubblica *f*.

Republican [rɪˈpʌblɪkən] *n* repubblicano *m* (-a *f*) ♦ *adj* repubblicano(-a).

repulsive [rɪˈpʌlsɪv] *adj* repellente.

reputable [ˈrepjʊtəbl] *adj* di buona reputazione.

reputation [repjʊˈteɪʃn] *n* reputazione *f*.

reputedly [rɪˈpjuːtɪdlɪ] *adv* per quanto si dice.

request [rɪˈkwest] *n* richiesta *f* ♦ *vt* chiedere; **to ~ sb to do sthg** chiedere a qn di fare qc; **available on ~** (disponibile) su richiesta.

request stop *n (Br)* fermata *f* a richiesta.

require [rɪˈkwaɪəʳ] *vt (subj: person)* avere bisogno di; *(subj: situation)* richiedere; **passengers are ~d to show their tickets** i passeggeri sono pregati di presentare i biglietti.

requirement [rɪˈkwaɪəmənt] *n (condition)* requisito *m*; *(need)* esigenza *f*.

resat [riːˈsæt] *pt & pp* → **resit**.

rescue [ˈreskjuː] *vt* salvare.

research [rɪˈsɜːtʃ] *n* ricerca *f*.

resemblance [rɪˈzembləns] *n* somiglianza *f*.

resemble [rɪˈzembl] *vt* somigliare a.

resent [rɪˈzent] *vt* risentirsi per.

reservation [rezəˈveɪʃn] *n (booking)* prenotazione *f*; *(doubt)* riserva *f*; **to make a ~** fare una prenotazione.

reserve [rɪˈzɜːv] *n* riserva *f* ♦ *vt (book)* prenotare; *(save)* riservare.

reserved [rɪˈzɜːvd] *adj* riservato(-a).

reservoir [ˈrezəvwɑːʳ] *n* bacino *m* (idrico).

reset [riːˈset] *(pt & pp* **reset***) vt (watch, device)* rimettere; *(meter)* azzerare.

reside [rɪˈzaɪd] *vi (fml)* risiedere.

residence [ˈrezɪdəns] *n (fml)* residenza *f*; **place of ~** *(fml)* luogo *m* di residenza.

residence permit *n* permesso *m* di soggiorno.

resident [ˈrezɪdənt] *n (of country)* residente *mf*; *(of hotel)* cliente *mf*; *(of area, house)* abitante *mf*; **'~s only'** *(for parking)* 'parcheggio riservato ai residenti'.

residential [rezɪˈdenʃl] *adj (area)* residenziale.

residue [ˈrezɪdjuː] *n* residuo *m*.

resign [rɪˈzaɪn] *vi* dare le dimissioni ♦ *vt*: **to ~ o.s. to sthg** rassegnarsi a qc.

resignation [rezɪgˈneɪʃn] *n (from*

job) dimissioni *fpl.*

resilient [rɪˈzɪlɪənt] *adj (person)* che ha buone capacità di ripresa.

resist [rɪˈzɪst] *vt (fight against)* opporre resistenza a; *(temptation)* resistere a; **I can't ~ chocolate** non so resistere al cioccolato; **to ~ doing sthg** trattenersi dal fare qc.

resistance [rɪˈzɪstəns] *n (refusal to accept)* opposizione *f; (fighting)* resistenza *f.*

resit [ˌriːˈsɪt] *(pt & pp resat) vt* ridare.

resolution [ˌrezəˈluːʃn] *n (promise)* proposito *m.*

resolve [rɪˈzɒlv] *vt (solve)* risolvere.

resort [rɪˈzɔːt] *n (for holidays)* luogo *m* di villeggiatura; **as a last ~** come ultima risorsa □ **resort to** *vt fus* ricorrere a; **to ~ doing sthg** ricorrere a fare qc.

resource [rɪˈsɔːs] *n* risorsa *f.*

resourceful [rɪˈsɔːsful] *adj* pieno(-a) di risorse.

respect [rɪˈspekt] *n* rispetto *m* ◆ *vt* rispettare; **in some ~s** sotto certi aspetti; **with ~ to** per quanto riguarda.

respectable [rɪˈspektəbl] *adj (person, job etc)* rispettabile; *(acceptable)* decente.

respective [rɪˈspektɪv] *adj* rispettivo(-a).

respond [rɪˈspɒnd] *vi* rispondere.

response [rɪˈspɒns] *n* risposta *f.*

responsibility [rɪˌspɒnsəˈbɪlətɪ] *n* responsabilità *f inv.*

responsible [rɪˈspɒnsəbl] *adj* responsabile; **to be ~ (for)** *(accountable)* essere responsabile (di).

rest [rest] *n (relaxation)* riposo *m;*

(support) sostegno *m* ◆ *vi (relax)* riposarsi; **the ~ (remainder)** il resto; **to have a ~** riposarsi; **to ~ against** appoggiarsi contro.

restaurant [ˈrestərɒnt] *n* ristorante *m.*

restaurant car *n (Br)* carrozza *f* ristorante.

restful [ˈrestful] *adj* riposante.

restless [ˈrestlɪs] *adj (bored, impatient)* insofferente; *(fidgety)* agitato(-a).

restore [rɪˈstɔːr] *vt (building, painting)* restaurare; *(order)* ripristinare.

restrain [rɪˈstreɪn] *vt* controllare.

restrict [rɪˈstrɪkt] *vt* limitare.

restricted [rɪˈstrɪktɪd] *adj* limitato(-a).

restriction [rɪˈstrɪkʃn] *n* restrizione *f.*

rest room *n (Am)* toilette *f inv.*

result [rɪˈzʌlt] *n* risultato *m* ◆ *vi:* **to ~ in** avere come conseguenza; **as a ~ of** in seguito a.

resume [rɪˈzjuːm] *vi* riprendere.

résumé [ˈrezjuːmeɪ] *n (summary)* riassunto *m; (Am: curriculum vitae)* curriculum vitae *m inv.*

retail [ˈriːteɪl] *n* vendita *f* al dettaglio ◆ *vt (sell)* vendere al dettaglio ◆ *vi:* **to ~ at** essere venduto a.

retailer [ˈriːteɪlər] *n* dettagliante *mf.*

retail price *n* prezzo *m* al dettaglio.

retain [rɪˈteɪn] *vt (fml)* conservare.

retaliate [rɪˈtælɪeɪt] *vi* fare rappresaglie.

retire [rɪˈtaɪər] *vi (stop working)* andare in pensione.

retired [rɪˈtaɪəd] *adj* in pensione.

retirement [rɪˈtaɪəmənt] *n (leav-*

ing job) pensionamento m; *(period after retiring*) periodo m dopo il pensionamento.

retreat [rɪ'triːt] vi *(move away)* indietreggiare ♦ n *(place)* rifugio m.

retrieve [rɪ'triːv] vt *(get back)* recuperare.

return [rɪ'tɜːn] n ritorno m; *(Br: ticket)* biglietto m (di) andata e ritorno ♦ vt *(put back)* rimettere; *(give back)* restituire; *(ball, serve)* rimandare ♦ vi ritornare; *(happen again)* ricomparire ♦ adj *(journey)* di ritorno; **to ~ sthg (to sb)** *(give back)* restituire qc a qn; **by ~ of post** *(Br)* a giro di posta; **many happy ~s!** cento di questi giorni!; **in ~ (for)** in cambio di.

return flight n *(journey back)* volo m di ritorno.

return ticket n *(Br)* biglietto m (di) andata e ritorno.

reunite [ˌriːjuː'naɪt] vt riunire.

reveal [rɪ'viːl] vt rivelare.

revelation [ˌrevə'leɪʃn] n rivelazione f.

revenge [rɪ'vendʒ] n vendetta f.

reverse [rɪ'vɜːs] adj inverso(-a) ♦ n *(AUT)* retromarcia f; *(of coin)* rovescio m; *(of document)* retro m ♦ vt *(decision)* ribaltare ♦ vi *(car, driver)* fare marcia indietro; **in ~** in ordine inverso; **the ~** *(opposite)* l'inverso; **to ~ the car** fare marcia indietro; **to ~ the charges** *(Br)* fare una telefonata a carico del destinatario.

reverse-charge call n *(Br)* telefonata f a carico del destinatario.

review [rɪ'vjuː] n *(of book, record, etc)* recensione f; *(examination)* esame m ♦ vt *(Am: for exam)* ri-

passare.

revise [rɪ'vaɪz] vt rivedere ♦ vi *(Br: for exam)* ripassare.

revision [rɪ'vɪʒn] n *(Br: for exam)* ripasso m.

revive [rɪ'vaɪv] vt *(person)* rianimare; *(economy)* far riprendere; *(custom)* riportare in uso.

revolt [rɪ'vəʊlt] n rivolta f.

revolting [rɪ'vəʊltɪŋ] adj disgustoso(-a).

revolution [ˌrevə'luːʃn] n rivoluzione f.

revolutionary [ˌrevə'luːʃnəri] adj rivoluzionario(-a).

revolver [rɪ'vɒlvəʳ] n revolver m inv.

revolving door [rɪ'vɒlvɪŋ-] n porta f girevole.

revue [rɪ'vjuː] n rivista f *(spettacolo)*.

reward [rɪ'wɔːd] n ricompensa f ♦ vt ricompensare.

rewind [ˌriː'waɪnd] *(pt & pp rewound* [ˌriː'waʊnd]*)* vt riavvolgere.

rheumatism ['ruːmətɪzm] n reumatismo m.

rhinoceros [raɪ'nɒsərəs] *(pl inv OR* **-es***)* n rinoceronte m.

rhubarb ['ruːbɑːb] n rabarbaro m.

rhyme [raɪm] n *(poem)* rima f ♦ vi fare rima.

rhythm ['rɪðm] n ritmo m.

rib [rɪb] n *(of body)* costola f.

ribbon ['rɪbən] n nastro m.

rice [raɪs] n riso m.

rice pudding n budino m di riso *(dolce)*.

rich [rɪtʃ] adj ricco(-a) ♦ npl: **the ~** i ricchi; **to be ~ in sthg** essere ricco di qc.

ricotta cheese [rɪ'kɒtə-]

ricotta *f*.

rid [rɪd] *vt*: **to get ~ of** sbarazzarsi di.

ridden ['rɪdn] *pp* → **ride**.

riddle ['rɪdl] *n* indovinello *m*.

ride [raɪd] (*pt* **rode**, *pp* **ridden**) *n* (*on horse*) cavalcata *f*; (*in vehicle*, *on bike*) giro *m* ♦ *vi* (*on horse*) andare a cavallo; (*on bike*) andare in bicicletta; (*in vehicle*) viaggiare ♦ *vt*: **to ~ a horse** andare a cavallo; **to go for a ~** (*in car*) andare a fare un giro.

rider ['raɪdə'] *n* (*on horse*) persona *f* a cavallo; (*on bike*) ciclista *mf*.

ridge [rɪdʒ] *n* (*of mountain*) cresta *f*; (*raised surface*) increspatura *f*.

ridiculous [rɪ'dɪkjʊləs] *adj* ridicolo(-a).

riding ['raɪdɪŋ] *n* equitazione *f*.

riding school *n* scuola *f* d'equitazione.

rifle ['raɪfl] *n* fucile *m*.

rig [rɪg] *n* (*oil rig at sea*) piattaforma *f*; (*on land*) pozzo *m* petrolifero ♦ *vt* (*fix*) manipolare.

right [raɪt] *adj* **1.** (*correct*) giusto(-a), corretto(-a); **to be ~** (*person*) avere ragione; **to be ~ to do sthg** fare bene a fare qc; **have you got the ~ time?** ha l'ora esatta?; **that's ~!** esatto!; **is this the ~ way?** è la strada giusta?
2. (*fair*) giusto(-a); **that's not ~!** non è giusto!
3. (*on the right*) destro(-a); **the ~ side of the road** il lato destro della strada.
♦ *n* **1.** (*side*): **the ~** la destra.
2. (*entitlement*) diritto *m*; **to have the ~ to do sthg** avere il diritto di fare qc.
♦ *adv* **1.** (*towards the right*) a destra;

turn ~ at the post office all'ufficio postale giri a destra.
2. (*correctly*) bene, correttamente; **am I pronouncing it ~?** lo pronuncio bene?
3. (*for emphasis*) proprio; **~ here** proprio qui; **I'll be ~ back** torno subito; **~ away** subito.

right angle *n* angolo *m* retto.

right-hand *adj* di destra.

right-hand drive *n* guida *f* a destra.

right-handed [-'hændɪd] *adj* (*person*) destrimano(-a); (*implement*) per destrimani.

rightly ['raɪtlɪ] *adv* (*correctly*) correttamente; (*justly*) giustamente.

right of way *n* (AUT) diritto *m* di precedenza; (*path*) sentiero *m*.

right-wing *adj* di destra.

rim [rɪm] *n* (*of cup*) bordo *m*; (*of glasses*) montatura *f*; (*of wheel*) cerchione *m*.

rind [raɪnd] *n* (*of fruit*) buccia *f*; (*of bacon*) cotenna *f*; (*of cheese*) crosta *f*.

ring [rɪŋ] (*pt* **rang**, *pp* **rung**) *n* anello *m*; (*of people*) cerchio *m*; (*sound*) trillo *m*; (*on cooker*) fornello *m*; (*for boxing*) ring *m inv*; (*in circus*) pista *f* ♦ *vt* (Br: *on phone*) telefonare a; (*bell*) suonare ♦ *vi* (*bell*, *telephone*) suonare; (Br: *make phone call*) telefonare; **to give sb a ~** fare una telefonata a qn; **to ~ the bell** suonare il campanello ❑ **ring back** *sep* (Br) ritelefonare a ♦ *vi* (Br) ritelefonare; **ring off** *vi* (Br) mettere giù (il telefono); *vt sep* (Br) telefonare a ♦ *vi* (Br) telefonare.

ringing tone ['rɪŋɪŋ-] *n* segnale *m* di libero.

ring road *n* circonvallazione

rink [rɪŋk] n pista f di pattinaggio.

rinse [rɪns] vt sciacquare □ **rinse out** vt sep sciacquare.

riot [raɪət] n sommossa f.

rip [rɪp] n strappo m ♦ vt strappare ♦ vi strapparsi □ **rip up** vt sep strappare.

ripe [raɪp] adj (fruit, vegetable) maturo(-a); (cheese) stagionato(-a).

ripen [raɪpn] vi maturare.

rip-off n (inf) fregatura f.

rise [raɪz] (pt rose, pp risen [rɪzn]) vi alzarsi; (sun, moon) sorgere; (increase) aumentare ♦ n aumento m; (slope) salita f.

risk [rɪsk] n rischio m ♦ vt rischiare; **to take a ~** correre un rischio; **at your own ~** a suo rischio (e pericolo); **to ~ doing sthg** rischiare di fare qc; **to ~ it** arrischiarsi.

risky [rɪskɪ] adj rischioso(-a).

risotto [rɪzɒtəʊ] (pl -s) n risotto m.

ritual [rɪtʃʊəl] n rituale m.

rival [raɪvl] adj rivale ♦ n rivale mf.

river [rɪvər] n fiume m.

river bank n sponda f del fiume.

riverside [rɪvəsaɪd] n riva f del fiume.

Riviera [rɪvɪˈeərə] n: **the (Italian)** ~ la riviera (ligure).

roach [rəʊtʃ] n (Am: cockroach) scarafaggio m.

road [rəʊd] n strada f; **by ~** in macchina.

road book n atlante m stradale.

road map n carta f stradale.

road safety n sicurezza f sulle strade.

roadside [rəʊdsaɪd] n: **the ~** il bordo della strada.

road sign n segnale m stradale.

road tax n tassa f di circolazione.

roadway [rəʊdweɪ] n carreggiata f.

road works npl lavori mpl stradali.

roam [rəʊm] vi vagabondare.

roar [rɔːr] n (of crowd) strepito m; (of plane) rombo m ♦ vi (lion) ruggire; (crowd) strepitare; (traffic) rombare.

roast [rəʊst] n arrosto m ♦ vt arrostire ♦ adj arrosto (inv); ~ **beef** roast beef m; ~ **chicken** pollo m arrosto; ~ **lamb** arrosto di agnello; ~ **pork** arrosto di maiale; ~ **potatoes** patate fpl arrosto.

rob [rɒb] vt (house, bank) svaligiare; (person) derubare; **to ~ sb of sthg** derubare qn di qc.

robber [rɒbər] n rapinatore m (-trice f).

robbery [rɒbərɪ] n rapina f.

robe [rəʊb] n (Am: bathrobe) accappatoio m.

robin [rɒbɪn] n pettirosso m.

robot [rəʊbɒt] n robot m inv.

rock [rɒk] n roccia f; (Am: stone) pietra f; (music) rock m; (Br: sweet) bastoncini mpl di zucchero ♦ vt (baby) cullare; (boat) far rollare; **on the ~s** (drink) con ghiaccio.

rock climbing n roccia f (sport); **to go ~** fare scalate.

rocket [rɒkɪt] n (missile) missile m; (space rocket, firework) razzo m.

rocking chair [rɒkɪŋ-] n sedia f a dondolo.

rock 'n' roll [rɒkən'rəʊl] n rock

and roll *m*.

rocky ['rɒkɪ] *adj* roccioso(-a).

rod [rɒd] *n* (pole) asta *f*; (for fishing) canna *f* (da pesca).

rode [rəʊd] *pt* → **ride**.

roe [rəʊ] *n* uova *fpl* di pesce.

role [rəʊl] *n* ruolo *m*.

roll [rəʊl] *n* (of bread) panino *m*; (of film) rullino *m*; (of paper) rotolo *m* ♦ *vi* (ball, rock) rotolare; (ship) rollare ♦ *vt* (ball, rock) far rotolare; (cigarette) arrotolare; (dice) tirare □ **roll over** *vi* (person, animal) rivoltarsi; (car) ribaltarsi; **roll up** *vt sep* arrotolare.

roller coaster ['rəʊlə͵kəʊstə'] *n* otto *m* volante.

roller skate ['rəʊlə-] *n* pattino *m* a rotelle.

roller-skating ['rəʊlə-] *n* pattinaggio *m* a rotelle.

rolling pin ['rəʊlɪŋ-] *n* matterello *m*.

Roman ['rəʊmən] *adj* romano(-a) ♦ *n* romano *m* (-a *f*).

Roman Catholic *n* cattolico *m* romano (cattolica romana *f*).

romance [rəʊ'mæns] *n* (love) amore *m*; (love affair) avventura *f*; (novel) romanzo *m* sentimentale.

Romania [ru:'meɪnjə] *n* la Romania.

romantic [rəʊ'mæntɪk] *adj* romantico(-a).

Rome [rəʊm] *n* Roma *f*.

romper suit ['rɒmpə-] *n* pagliaccetto *m*.

roof [ru:f] *n* tetto *m*; (of cave) volta *f*.

roof rack *n* portapacchi *m inv*.

room [ru:m, rʊm] *n* stanza *f*, camera *f*; (space) spazio *m*.

room number *n* numero *m* di stanza.

room service *n* servizio *m* in camera.

room temperature *n* temperatura *f* ambiente.

roomy ['ru:mɪ] *adj* spazioso(-a).

root [ru:t] *n* radice *f*.

rope [rəʊp] *n* corda *f* ♦ *vt* legare.

rose [rəʊz] *pt* → **rise** ♦ *n* (flower) rosa *f*.

rosé ['rəʊzeɪ] *n* vino *m* rosé.

rosemary ['rəʊzmərɪ] *n* rosmarino *m*.

rot [rɒt] *vi* marcire.

rota ['rəʊtə] *n* turni *mpl*.

rotate [rəʊ'teɪt] *vi* ruotare.

rotten ['rɒtn] *adj* (food, wood) marcio(-a); (inf: not good) schifoso(-a); **I feel ~** (ill) mi sento uno schifo.

rouge [ru:ʒ] *n* fard *m inv*.

rough [rʌf] *adj* (surface, skin, cloth) ruvido(-a); (sea) burrascoso(-a); (person) rude; (approximate) approssimativo(-a); (conditions) disagiato(-a); (area, town) brutto(-a); (wine) scadente ♦ *n* (on golf course) rough *m*; **to have a ~ time** passarsela male.

roughly ['rʌflɪ] *adv* (approximately) approssimativamente; (push, handle) sgarbatamente.

roulade [ru:'lɑ:d] *n* rotolo *m*.

roulette [ru:'let] *n* roulette *f*.

round [raʊnd] *adj* rotondo(-a); (cheeks) paffuto(-a).

♦ *n* **1.** (of drinks) giro *m*; **it's my ~** tocca a me offrire (questo giro).

2. (of sandwiches) tramezzini *mpl*.

3. (of toast) fetta *f*.

4. (of competition) turno *m*.

5. (in golf) partita f; (in boxing) round m inv, ripresa f.

6. (of policeman, postman, milkman) giro m.

♦ adv 1. (in a circle): **to go ~** girare; **to spin ~** ruotare.

2. (surrounding): **all (the way) ~** tutt'intorno.

3. (near): **~ about** nei dintorni.

4. (to one's house): **to ask some friends ~** invitare (a casa propria) degli amici; **we went ~ to her place** siamo andati da lei OR a casa sua.

5. (continuously): **all year ~** tutto l'anno.

♦ prep 1. (surrounding, circling) intorno a; **to go ~ the corner** girare l'angolo; **we walked ~ the lake** abbiamo fatto il giro del lago a piedi.

2. (visiting): **to go ~ a museum** visitare un museo; **to show sb ~ sthg** far fare il giro di qc a qn.

3. (approximately) circa, pressappoco; **~ (about) 100** circa 100; **~ ten o'clock** verso le dieci.

4. (near): **~ here** da queste parti.

5. (in phrases): **it's just ~ the corner** (nearby) è qui vicino; **the clock** 24 ore su 24.

round off vt sep (meal, day) terminare.

roundabout ['raundəbaut] n (Br) (in road) isola f rotazionale; (in playground, at fairground) giostra f.

rounders ['raundəz] n (Br) gioco a squadre simile al baseball.

round trip n viaggio m di andata e ritorno.

route [ru:t] n (way) strada f; (of bus, train) percorso m; (of plane) rotta f ♦ vt (change course of) dirottare.

routine [ru:'ti:n] n routine f inv

adj di routine.

row[1] [rəu] n (line) fila f ♦ vt & vi remare; **in a ~** (in succession) di fila.

row[2] [rau] n (argument) lite f; (inf: noise) baccano m; **to have a ~** litigare.

rowboat ['rəubəut] (Am) = **rowing boat**.

rowdy ['raudɪ] adj turbolento(-a).

rowing ['rəuɪŋ] n canottaggio m.

rowing boat n (Br) barca f a remi.

royal ['rɔɪəl] adj reale.

royal family n famiglia f reale.

i **ROYAL FAMILY**

A capo della famiglia reale inglese è oggi la Regina Elisabetta. Altri membri di spicco della famiglia reale sono il principe consorte Filippo (Duca di Edimburgo), la Regina Madre, i figli Carlo (Principe di Galles), Andrea e Edoardo, e la figlia Anna. Quando uno o più membri della famiglia reale presenziano cerimonie ufficiali viene eseguito l'inno nazionale. La presenza della regina a palazzo è segnalata dalla Union Jack (la bandiera del Regno Unito).

royalty ['rɔɪəltɪ] n (royal family) reali mpl.

RRP (abbr of recommended retail price) prezzo m consigliato.

rub [rʌb] vt & vi strofinare; **to ~ sb's back** massaggiare la schiena a qn; **my shoes are rubbing** mi fanno male le scarpe ❏ **rub in** vt sep (lotion, oil) far penetrare sfregando; **rub out** vt sep cancellare.

rubber

rubber ['rʌbə'] *adj* di gomma ◆ *n* gomma *f*; (*Am: inf: condom*) preservativo *m*.

rubber band *n* elastico *m*.

rubber gloves *npl* guanti *mpl* di gomma.

rubber ring *n* ciambella *f*.

rubbish ['rʌbɪʃ] *n* spazzatura *f*; (*inf: nonsense*) cretinate *fpl*.

rubbish bin *n* (Br) pattumiera *f*.

rubbish dump *n* (Br) discarica *f*.

rubble ['rʌbl] *n* macerie *fpl*.

ruby ['ru:bɪ] *n* rubino *m*.

rucksack ['rʌksæk] *n* zaino *m*.

rudder ['rʌdə'] *n* timone *m*.

rude [ru:d] *adj* (*person*) sgarbato(-a); (*behaviour, joke, picture*) volgare.

rug [rʌg] *n* (*for floor*) tappeto *m*; (*Br: blanket*) coperta *f*.

rugby ['rʌgbɪ] *n* rugby *m*.

ruin ['ru:ɪn] *vt* rovinare ❑ **ruins** *npl* rovine *fpl*.

ruined ['ru:ɪnd] *adj* (*building*) in rovina; (*clothes, meal, holiday*) rovinato(-a).

rule [ru:l] *n* (*law*) regola *f* ◆ *vt* (*country*) governare; **to be the ~** (*normal*) essere la regola; **against the ~s** contro le regole; **as a ~** di regola ❑ **rule out** *vt sep* escludere.

ruler ['ru:lə'] *n* (*of country*) capo *m* di Stato; (*for measuring*) righello *m*.

rum [rʌm] *n* rum *m inv*.

rumor ['ru:mə'] (*Am*) = **rumour**.

rumour ['ru:mə'] *n* (Br) voce *f*.

rump steak [,rʌmp-] *n* bistecca *f* di girello.

run [rʌn] (*pt* ran, *pp* run) *vi* 1. (*on foot*) correre; **we had to ~ for the bus** abbiamo dovuto fare una corsa per prendere l'autobus.

2. (*train, bus*) fare servizio; **the bus ~s every hour** c'è un autobus ogni ora; **the train is running an hour late** il treno ha un'ora di ritardo.

3. (*operate*) funzionare; **to ~ on sthg** andare a qc.

4. (*tears, liquid, river*) scorrere; **to ~ through** (*river, road*) passare per; **the path ~s along the coast** il sentiero corre lungo la costa; **she left the tap running** ha lasciato il rubinetto aperto.

5. (*play, event*) durare; **'now running at the Palladium'** 'in cartellone al Palladium'.

6. (*nose*) gocciolare, colare; (*eyes*) lacrimare.

7. (*colour, dye, clothes*) stingere.

◆ *vt* 1. (*on foot*) correre.

2. (*compete in*): **to ~ a race** partecipare a una corsa.

3. (*business, hotel*) dirigere.

4. (*bus, train*): **we're running a special bus to the airport** mettiamo a disposizione una navetta per andare all'aeroporto.

5. (*take in car*) dare un passaggio a; **I'll ~ you home** ti do un passaggio (fino) a casa.

6. (*water*) far correre.

◆ *n* 1. (*on foot*) corsa *f*; **to go for a ~** andare a fare una corsa.

2. (*in car*) giro *m*; **to go for a ~** andare a fare un giro (in macchina).

3. (*for skiing*) pista *f*.

4. (*Am: in tights*) smagliatura *f*.

5. (*in phrases*): **in the long ~** alla lunga.

❑ **run away** *vi* scappare; **run down** *vt sep* (*run over*) investire; (*criticize*) criticare ◆ *vi* (*battery*) scaricarsi; **run into** *vt fus* (*meet*) incontrare per caso; (*hit*) sbattere contro; (*problem, difficulty*) inco[...]

trare; **run out** *vi (be used up)* esaurirsi; **run out of** *vt fus* finire, esaurire; **run over** *vt sep (hit)* investire.

runaway [ˈrʌnəweɪ] *n* fuggiasco *m (-a f)*.

rung [rʌŋ] *pp* → **ring ♦** *n (of ladder)* piolo *m*.

runner [ˈrʌnəʳ] *n (person)* corridore *m; (for door, drawer)* guida *f; (for sledge)* pattino *m*.

runner bean *n* fagiolo *m* rampicante.

runner-up [pl **runners-up**] *n* secondo *m* classificato (seconda classificata *f*).

running [ˈrʌnɪŋ] *n (SPORT)* corsa *f; (management)* amministrazione *f* **♦** *adj:* **three days** ~ tre giorni di fila; **to go** ~ andare a correre.

running water *n* acqua *f* corrente.

runny [ˈrʌnɪ] *adj (sauce, egg, omelette)* troppo liquido(-a); *(nose)* che cola; *(eye)* che lacrima.

runway [ˈrʌnweɪ] *n* pista *f (di volo)*.

rural [ˈrʊərəl] *adj* rurale.

rush [rʌʃ] *n (hurry)* fretta *f; (of crowd)* grosso afflusso *m* **♦** *vi (move quickly)* precipitarsi; *(hurry)* affrettarsi **♦** *vt (work)* fare in fretta; *(food)* mangiare in fretta; *(transport quickly)* portare d'urgenza; **to be in a** ~ avere fretta; **there's no** ~! non c'è fretta!; **don't** ~ **me!** non mettermi fretta!

rush hour *n* ora *f* di punta.

Russia [ˈrʌʃə] *n* la Russia.

Russian [ˈrʌʃn] *adj* russo(-a) **♦** *n (person)* russo *m (-a f); (language)* russo *m*.

rust [rʌst] *n* ruggine *f* **♦** *vi* arrugginirsi.

rustic [ˈrʌstɪk] *adj* rustico(-a).

rustle [ˈrʌsl] *vi* frusciare.

rustproof [ˈrʌstpruːf] *adj* inossidabile.

rusty [ˈrʌstɪ] *adj* arrugginito(-a).

RV *n (Am: abbr of recreational vehicle)* camper *m inv*.

rye [raɪ] *n* segale *f*.

rye bread *n* pane *m* di segale.

S

S *(abbr of south, small)* S.

saccharin [ˈsækərɪn] *n* saccarina *f*.

sachet [ˈsæʃeɪ] *n* bustina *f*.

sack [sæk] *n (bag)* sacco *m* **♦** *vt* licenziare; **to get the** ~ essere licenziato.

sacrifice [ˈsækrɪfaɪs] *n (fig)* sacrificio *m*.

sad [sæd] *adj* triste.

saddle [ˈsædl] *n* sella *f*.

saddlebag [ˈsædlbæg] *n* bisaccia *f*.

sadly [ˈsædlɪ] *adv (unfortunately)* sfortunatamente; *(unhappily)* tristemente.

sadness [ˈsædnɪs] *n* tristezza *f*.

s.a.e. *n (Br: abbr of stamped addressed envelope)* busta affrancata e completa d'indirizzo.

safari park [səˈfɑːrɪ-] *n* zoosafari *m inv*.

safe [seɪf] *adj* sicuro(-a); *(out of harm)* salvo(-a); *(valuables)* al sicuro **♦** *n* cassaforte *f*; **a** ~ **place** un posto sicuro; **(have a)** ~ **journey!** buon viaggio!; ~ **and sound** sano(-a) e salvo(-a).

safe-deposit box n cassetta f di sicurezza.

safely ['seɪflɪ] adv (not dangerously) senza pericolo; (arrive) senza problemi; (out of harm) al sicuro.

safety ['seɪftɪ] n sicurezza f.

safety belt n cintura f di sicurezza.

safety pin n spilla f da balia.

sag [sæg] vi avvallarsi.

sage [seɪdʒ] n (herb) salvia f.

Sagittarius [,sædʒɪ'teərɪəs] n Sagittario m.

said [sed] pt & pp → **say**.

sail [seɪl] n vela f ♦ vi (boat, ship) navigare; (person) andare in barca; (depart) salpare ♦ vt: **to ~ a boat** condurre una barca; **to set ~** salpare.

sailboat ['seɪlbəʊt] (Am) = **sailing boat**.

sailing ['seɪlɪŋ] n (activity) vela f; (departure) partenza f; **to go ~** fare della vela.

sailing boat n barca f a vela.

sailor ['seɪlər] n marinaio m.

saint [seɪnt] n santo m (-a f).

sake [seɪk] n: **for my/their ~** per il mio/il loro bene; **for God's ~!** per l'amor di Dio!

salad ['sæləd] n insalata f.

salad bar n (Br: area in restaurant) tavolo m delle insalate; (restaurant) locale specializzato in insalate.

salad bowl n insalatiera f.

salad cream n (Br) salsa per l'insalata, simile alla maionese.

salad dressing n condimento m per l'insalata.

salami [sə'lɑːmɪ] n salame m.

salary ['sælərɪ] n stipendio m.

sale [seɪl] n (selling) vendita f; (at reduced prices) svendita f; **'for ~'** 'vendesi'; **on ~** in vendita ❑ **sales** npl (COMM) vendite fpl; **the ~s** (at reduced prices) i saldi.

sales assistant ['seɪlz-] n commesso m (-a f).

salesclerk ['seɪlzklɑːrk] (Am) = **sales assistant**.

salesman ['seɪlzmən] (pl **-men** [-mən]) n (in shop) commesso m; (rep) rappresentante m.

sales rep(resentative) n rappresentante mf.

saleswoman ['seɪlz,wʊmən] (pl **-women** [-,wɪmɪn]) n (in shop) commessa f.

saliva [sə'laɪvə] n saliva f.

salmon ['sæmən] (pl inv) n salmone m.

salon ['sælɒn] n (hairdresser's) salone m.

saloon [sə'luːn] n (Br: car) berlina f; (Am: bar) saloon m inv; **~ (bar)** (Br) sala f interna.

salopettes [,sælə'pets] npl salopette f inv.

salt [sɔːlt, sɒlt] n sale m.

saltcellar ['sɔːlt,selər] n (Br) saliera f.

salted peanuts ['sɔːltɪd-] npl noccioline fpl salate.

salt shaker [-,ʃeɪkər] (Am) = **saltcellar**.

salty ['sɔːltɪ] adj salato(-a).

salute [sə'luːt] n saluto m ♦ vi fare il saluto.

same [seɪm] adj stesso(-a) ♦ pron: **the ~** lo stesso (la stessa); **they look the ~** sembrano uguali; **I have the ~ as her** prendo lo stesso che ha preso lei; **you've got the**

book as me hai lo stesso libro che ho io; **it's all the ~ to me** per me è tutto uguale.

samosa [sə'məʊsə] n fagottino fritto triangolare, ripieno di carne o verdure, tipico della cucina indiana.

sample ['sɑ:mpl] n campione m ♦ vt assaggiare.

sanctions ['sæŋkʃnz] npl sanzioni fpl.

sanctuary ['sæŋktʃʊərɪ] n (for birds, animals) riserva f.

sand [sænd] n sabbia f ♦ vt (wood) smerigliare ❑ **sands** npl spiaggia f.

sandal ['sændl] n sandalo m.

sandcastle ['sænd,kɑ:sl] n castello m di sabbia.

sandpaper ['sænd,peɪpə] n carta f vetrata.

sandwich ['sænwɪdʒ] n tramezzino m.

sandwich bar n paninoteca f.

sandy ['sændɪ] adj (beach) sabbioso(-a); (hair) color sabbia (inv).

sang [sæŋ] pt → sing.

sanitary ['sænɪtrɪ] adj (conditions, measures) sanitario(-a); (hygienic) igienico(-a).

sanitary napkin (Am) = **sanitary towel**

sanitary towel n (Br) assorbente m igienico.

sank [sæŋk] pt → sink.

sapphire ['sæfaɪə] n zaffiro m.

sarcastic [sɑ:'kæstɪk] adj sarcastico(-a).

sardine [sɑ:'di:n] n sardina f.

Sardinia [sɑ:'dɪnjə] n la Sardegna.

SASE n (Am: abbr of self-addressed stamped envelope) busta affrancata e completa del proprio indirizzo.

sat [sæt] pt & pp → sit.

Sat. (abbr of Saturday) sab.

satchel ['sætʃəl] n cartella f.

satellite ['sætəlaɪt] n (in space) satellite m; (at airport) zona f satellite.

satellite dish n antenna f parabolica.

satellite TV n televisione f via satellite.

satin ['sætɪn] n raso m.

satisfaction [,sætɪs'fækʃn] n soddisfazione f.

satisfactory [,sætɪs'fæktərɪ] adj soddisfacente.

satisfied ['sætɪsfaɪd] adj soddisfatto(-a).

satisfy ['sætɪsfaɪ] vt soddisfare.

satsuma [sæt'su:mə] n (Br) mandarino m.

saturate ['sætʃəreɪt] vt (with liquid) impregnare.

Saturday ['sætədɪ] n sabato m; **it's ~** è sabato; **morning** sabato mattina; **on ~** sabato; **on ~** il OR di sabato; **last ~** sabato scorso; **this ~** questo sabato; **next ~** sabato prossimo; **~ week, a week on ~** sabato a otto.

sauce [sɔ:s] n salsa f.

saucepan ['sɔ:spən] n casseruola f.

saucer ['sɔ:sə] n piattino m.

Saudi Arabia [,saʊdɪə'reɪbjə] n l'Arabia f Saudita.

sauna ['sɔ:nə] n sauna f.

sausage ['sɒsɪdʒ] n salsiccia f.

sausage roll n rustico m con salsiccia.

sauté [Br 'səʊteɪ, Am səʊ'teɪ] adj saltato(-a).

savage ['sævɪdʒ] adj selvaggio(-a).

save [seɪv] vt (rescue, COMPUT) salvare; (money, time) risparmiare; (reserve) tenere; (SPORT) parare ◆ n parata f ❏ **save up** vi risparmiare; **to ~ up (for sthg)** mettere da parte i soldi (per qc).

saver ['seɪvəʳ] n (Br: ticket) biglietto m ridotto.

savings ['seɪvɪŋz] npl risparmi mpl.

savings and loan association n (Am) = istituto m di credito fondiario.

savings bank n cassa f di risparmio.

savory ['seɪvərɪ] (Am) = **savoury**.

savoury ['seɪvərɪ] adj (Br: not sweet) salato(-a).

saw [sɔ:] (Br pt -ed, pp sawn, Am pt & pp -ed) pt → **see** ◆ n (tool) sega f ◆ vt segare.

sawdust ['sɔ:dʌst] n segatura f.

sawn [sɔ:n] pp → **saw**.

saxophone ['sæksəfəun] n sassofono m.

say [seɪ] (pt & pp said) vt dire; (subj: clock, meter) segnare ◆ n: **to have a ~ in sthg** avere voce in capitolo riguardo a qc; **could you ~ that again?** può ripetere, per favore?; **~ we met at nine?** diciamo che ci vediamo alle nove?; **what did you ~?** che cosa hai detto?

saying ['seɪɪŋ] n detto m.

scab [skæb] n (on skin) crosta f.

scaffolding ['skæfəldɪŋ] n impalcatura f.

scald [skɔ:ld] vt scottare.

scale [skeɪl] n scala f; (of fish, snake) squama f; (in kettle) incrostazione f ❏ **scales** npl (for weighing) bilancia f.

scallion ['skæljən] n (Am) cipol-

lina f.

scallop ['skɒləp] n pettine m (mollusco).

scalp [skælp] n cuoio m capelluto.

scampi ['skæmpɪ] n gamberoni mpl impanati e fritti.

scan [skæn] vt (consult quickly) scorrere ◆ n (MED) esame m eseguito con scanner.

scandal ['skændl] n scandalo m.

Scandinavia [ˌskændɪ'neɪvjə] n la Scandinavia.

scar [skɑ:ʳ] n cicatrice f.

scarce ['skeəs] adj scarso(-a).

scarcely ['skeəslɪ] adv (hardly) a malapena.

scare ['skeəʳ] vt spaventare.

scarecrow ['skeəkrəu] n spaventapasseri m inv.

scared ['skeəd] adj spaventato(-a).

scarf [skɑ:f] (pl **scarves**) n (woollen) sciarpa f; (for women) foulard m inv.

scarlet ['skɑ:lət] adj scarlatto(-a).

scarves [skɑ:vz] pl → **scarf**.

scary ['skeərɪ] adj (inf) terrificante.

scatter ['skætəʳ] vt spargere ◆ vi sparpagliarsi.

scene [si:n] n scena f; (view) vista f; **the music** = il mondo della musica; **to make a ~** fare una scenata.

scenery ['si:nərɪ] n (countryside) paesaggio m; (in theatre) scenario m.

scenic ['si:nɪk] adj pittoresco(-a).

scent [sent] n odore m; (perfume, profumo m.

sceptical ['skeptɪkl] adj (Br) scettico(-a).

schedule [Br 'ʃedju:l, Am

'skedʒul] n (of work, things to do) tabella f di marcia; (timetable) orario m; (list) tabella ◆ vt programmare; **according to** ~ secondo la tabella di marcia; **behind** ~ in ritardo sulla tabella di marcia; **on** ~ puntualmente.

scheduled flight [Br 'ʃedjuːld-, Am 'skedʒuld-] n volo m di linea.

scheme [skiːm] n (plan) piano m; (pej: dishonest plan) intrigo m.

scholarship ['skɒləʃɪp] n (award) borsa f di studio.

school [skuːl] n scuola f; (university department) facoltà f inv; (Am: university) università f inv ◆ adj scolastico(-a); **at** ~ a scuola.

schoolbag ['skuːlbæg] n cartella f.

schoolbook ['skuːlbʊk] n libro m di testo.

schoolboy ['skuːlbɔɪ] n scolaro m.

school bus n scuolabus m inv.

schoolchild ['skuːltʃaɪld] n (pl -children [-tʃɪldrən]) n scolaro m (-a f).

schoolgirl ['skuːlgɜːl] n scolara f.

schoolmaster ['skuːlmɑːstər] n (Br) maestro m.

schoolmistress ['skuːlmɪstrɪs] n (Br) maestra f.

schoolteacher ['skuːltiːtʃər] n insegnante mf.

school uniform n divisa f.

science ['saɪəns] n scienza f; (SCH) scienze fpl.

science fiction n fantascienza f.

scientific [ˌsaɪənˈtɪfɪk] adj scientifico(-a).

scientist ['saɪəntɪst] n scienziato (-a f).

scissors ['sɪzəz] npl: **(a pair of)** ~ un paio di forbici fpl.

scold [skəʊld] vt sgridare.

scone [skɒn] n pasta rotonda con uvette che si mangia con burro e marmellata durante il tè.

scoop [skuːp] n (for ice cream, flour) paletta f; (of ice cream) pallina f; (in media) scoop m inv.

scooter ['skuːtər] n (motor vehicle) scooter m inv.

scope [skəʊp] n (possibility) opportunità fpl; (range) portata f.

scorch [skɔːtʃ] vt bruciare.

score [skɔːr] n (total, final result) punteggio m; (current position) situazione f ◆ vt (SPORT) segnare; (in test) totalizzare ◆ vi (SPORT) segnare.

scorn [skɔːn] n disprezzo m.

Scorpio ['skɔːpɪəʊ] n Scorpione m.

scorpion ['skɔːpjən] n scorpione m.

Scot [skɒt] n scozzese mf.

scotch [skɒtʃ] n scotch m inv (whiskey).

Scotch broth n minestra a base di brodo di carne, verdure e orzo perlato.

Scotch tape® n (Am) scotch m inv.

Scotland ['skɒtlənd] n la Scozia.

Scotsman ['skɒtsmən] n (pl -men [-mən]) n scozzese m.

Scotswoman ['skɒtswʊmən] n (pl -women [-wɪmɪn]) n scozzese f.

Scottish ['skɒtɪʃ] adj scozzese.

scout [skaʊt] n (child) scout mf inv.

---

[i] **SCOUTS**

G li "scouts" sono membri della Scouting Association, fondata in Gran Bretagna nel 1908 da Lord Baden-Powell, allo scopo di promuovere lo spirito di avventura e il senso di responsabilità e disciplina fra i più giovani. I ragazzi fra gli 11 e i 16 anni sono organizzati in piccoli gruppi che, sotto la guida di un adulto, imparano tecniche di sopravvivenza all'aperto e di pronto soccorso. I ragazzi sotto gli 11 anni possono iscriversi ai "Cub Scouts" (Lupetti). Organizzazioni equivalenti per le ragazze sono le "Guides" e le "Brownies" (Coccinelle).

scowl [skaʊl] vi aggrottare le ciglia.

scrambled eggs [ˌskræmbld-] npl uova fpl strapazzate.

scrap [skræp] n (of paper, cloth) pezzo m; (old metal) rottami mpl (di metallo).

scrapbook ['skræpbʊk] n album m inv.

scrape [skreɪp] vt (rub) raschiare; (scratch) graffiare.

scrap paper n (Br) carta f da brutta copia.

scratch [skrætʃ] n graffio m ◆ vt (cut, mark) graffiare; (rub) grattare; **to be up to ~** essere all'altezza della situazione; **to start from ~** cominciare da zero.

scratch paper (Am) = scrap paper.

scream [skri:m] n strillo m ◆ vi strillare.

screen [skri:n] n schermo m; (hall in cinema) sala f; (panel) paravento m ◆ vt (film) proiettare; (TV programme) trasmettere.

screening ['skri:nɪŋ] n (of film) proiezione f.

screen wash n detergente m per il parabrezza.

screw [skru:] n vite f ◆ vt (fasten) avvitare; (twist) torcere.

screwdriver ['skru:ˌdraɪvər] n cacciavite m inv.

scribble ['skrɪbl] vi scarabocchiare.

script [skrɪpt] n (of play, film) copione m.

scrub [skrʌb] vt strofinare.

scruffy ['skrʌfɪ] adj trasandato(-a).

scrumpy ['skrʌmpɪ] n sidro f ad alta gradazione alcolica tipico del sudovest dell'Inghilterra.

scuba diving ['sku:bə-] n immersioni fpl (con autorespiratore).

sculptor ['skʌlptər] n scultore m.

sculpture ['skʌlptʃər] n scultura f.

sea [si:] n mare m; **by ~** via mare; **by the ~** sul mare.

seafood ['si:fu:d] n frutti mpl di mare.

seafront ['si:frʌnt] n lungomare m.

seagull ['si:gʌl] n gabbiano m.

seal [si:l] n (animal) foca f; (on bottle, container, official mark) sigillo m ◆ vt (envelope, container) sigillare.

seam [si:m] n (in clothes) cucitura f.

search [sɜ:tʃ] n ricerca f ◆ vt perquisire ◆ vi: **to ~ for** cercare.

seashell ['si:ʃel] n conchiglia f.

seashore ['si:ʃɔ:r] n riva f del mare.

seasick ['si:sɪk] adj: **to be ~** avere il mal di mare.

seaside ['si:saɪd] n: **the ~** il mare.

seaside resort n località f inv balneare.

season ['si:zn] n stagione f ◆ vt condire; **in ~** (fruit, vegetables) d stagione; (holiday) in alta stagione out of ~ *(fruit, vegetables)* fuori stagione; *(holiday)* in bassa stagione.

seasoning ['si:znɪŋ] *n* condimento *m*.

season ticket *n* abbonamento *m*.

seat [si:t] *n (place, chair)* posto *m*; *(in parliament)* seggio *m* ◆ *vt*: **the minibus ~s 12** il minibus ha 12 posti a sedere; **'please wait to be ~ed'** cartello che avvisa i clienti di un ristorante di attendere il cameriere per essere condotti al tavolo.

seat belt *n* cintura *f* di sicurezza.

seaweed ['si:wi:d] *n* alghe *fpl.*

secluded [sɪ'klu:dɪd] *adj* appartato(-a).

second ['sekənd] *n* secondo *m* ◆ *num* secondo(-a); ~ **gear** seconda *f* □ **seconds** *npl (goods)* merce *f* di seconda scelta; *(inf: of food)* bis *m inv*, → **sixth**.

secondary school ['sekəndrɪ-] *n* ≃ scuola *f* media inferiore e superiore.

second-class *adj (ticket)* di seconda classe; *(stamp)* per posta ordinaria sul territorio nazionale; *(inferior)* di seconda categoria.

second-hand *adj* di seconda mano.

Second World War *n*: **the ~** la seconda guerra mondiale.

secret ['si:krɪt] *adj* segreto(-a) ◆ *n* segreto *m*.

secretary [*Br* 'sekrətrɪ, *Am* 'sekrə,terɪ] *n* segretario *m* (-a *f*).

Secretary of State *n (Am: foreign minister)* segretario *m* di Stato, ≃ ministro *m* degli Esteri; *(Br: government minister)* ministro.

section ['sekʃn] *n* sezione *f.*

sector ['sektəʳ] *n* settore *m.*

secure [sɪ'kjʊəʳ] *adj (safe, protected)* sicuro(-a); *(firmly fixed)* saldamente assicurato(-a); *(free from worry)* tranquillo(-a) ◆ *vt (fix)* assicurare; *(fml: obtain)* assicurarsi.

security [sɪ'kjʊərətɪ] *n (protection)* sicurezza *f*; *(freedom from worry)* tranquillità *f.*

security guard *n* guardia *f* giurata.

sedative ['sedətɪv] *n* sedativo *m.*

seduce [sɪ'dju:s] *vt* sedurre.

see [si:] *(pt* saw, *pp* seen) *vt* vedere; *(accompany)* accompagnare ◆ *vi* vedere; **I ~** *(understand)* capisco; **to ~ if one can do sthg** vedere se si può fare qc; **to ~ to sthg** *(deal with)* occuparsi di qc; *(repair)* riparare qc; **~ you!** arrivederci!; **~ you later!** a più tardi!; **~ you soon!** a presto!; **~ p 14** vedi pag. 14 □ **see off** *vt sep (say goodbye to)* (andare a) salutare.

seed [si:d] *n* seme *m.*

seedy ['si:dɪ] *adj* squallido(-a).

seeing (as) ['si:ɪŋ-] *conj* visto che.

seek [si:k] *(pt & pp* sought) *vt (fml) (look for)* cercare; *(request)* chiedere.

seem [si:m] *vi* sembrare ◆ *v impers*: **it ~s (that) ...** sembra (che) ...

seen [si:n] *pp* → **see.**

seesaw ['si:sɔ:] *n* altalena *f.*

segment ['segmənt] *n (of fruit)* spicchio *m.*

seize [si:z] *vt (grab)* afferrare; *(drugs, arms)* sequestrare □ **seize up** *vi* bloccarsi.

seldom ['seldəm] *adv* raramente.

select [sɪ'lekt] vt scegliere ◆ adj selezionato(-a).

selection [sɪ'lekʃn] n selezione f.

self-assured [ˌselfə'ʃʊəd] adj sicuro(-a) di sé.

self-catering [ˌself'keɪtərɪŋ] adj (flat) con uso di cucina.

self-confident [ˌself-] adj sicuro(-a) di sé.

self-conscious [ˌself-] adj timido(-a).

self-contained [ˌselfkən'teɪnd] adj (flat) autosufficiente.

self-defence [ˌself-] n autodifesa f.

self-employed [ˌself-] adj che lavora in proprio.

selfish ['selfɪʃ] adj egoista.

self-raising flour [ˌself'reɪzɪŋ-] n (Br) farina f con lievito.

self-rising flour [ˌself'raɪzɪŋ-] (Am) = **self-raising flour**.

self-service [ˌself-] adj self-service (inv).

sell [sel] (pt & pp **sold**) vt & vi vendere; **to ~ for** essere venduto per; **to ~ sthg** vendere qc a qn.

sell-by date n data f di scadenza.

seller ['selər] n (person) venditore m (-trice f).

Sellotape® ['seləteɪp] n (Br) nastro m adesivo.

semester [sɪ'mestər] n semestre m.

semicircle ['semɪˌsɜːkl] n semicerchio m.

semicolon [ˌsemɪ'kəʊlən] n punto m e virgola.

semidetached [ˌsemɪdɪ'tætʃt] adj bifamiliare.

semifinal [ˌsemɪ'faɪnl] n semifinale f.

seminar ['semɪnɑː] n seminario m.

semolina [ˌsemə'liːnə] n semolino m.

send [send] (pt & pp **sent**) vt (letter, parcel, goods) spedire, mandare; (person) mandare; (TV or radio signal) trasmettere; **to ~ sthg to sb** mandare qc a qn ❑ **send back** vt sep (faulty goods) rimandare; **send off** vt sep (letter, parcel) spedire; (SPORT) espellere ◆ vi: **to ~ off (for sthg)** ordinare (qc) per corrispondenza.

sender ['sendər] n mittente mf.

senile ['siːnaɪl] adj senile.

senior ['siːnɪər] adj di grado superiore ◆ n (Br: SCH) studente m più grande; (Am: SCH) studente dell'ultimo anno di scuola superiore o università.

senior citizen n anziano m (-a f).

sensation [sen'seɪʃn] n sensazione f; **to cause a ~** fare colpo.

sensational [sen'seɪʃənl] adj (very good) fantastico(-a).

sense [sens] n senso m; (common sense) buonsenso m; (of word, expression) senso, significato m ◆ vt sentire, percepire; **to make ~** avere senso; **~ of direction** senso dell'orientamento; **~ of humour** senso dell'umorismo.

sensible ['sensəbl] adj (person) ragionevole, assennato(-a); (clothes, shoes) pratico(-a).

sensitive ['sensɪtɪv] adj sensibile; (subject, issue) delicato(-a).

sent [sent] pt & pp → **send**.

sentence ['sentəns] n (GRAMM) proposizione f; (for crime) sentenza f, condanna f ◆ vt condannare.

sentimental [ˌsentɪ'mentl] ad

(pej) sentimentale.

Sep. *(abbr of September)* set.

separate *[adj* 'seprət, *vb* 'sepəreɪt] *adj* separato(-a); *(different)* diverso(-a) ♦ *vt* separare ♦ *vi* separarsi ❑ **separates** *npl (Br)* coordinati *mpl.*

separately ['seprətlɪ] *adv* separatamente.

separation [,sepə'reɪʃn] *n* separazione *f.*

September [sep'tembəʳ] *n* settembre *m*; **at the beginning of ~** all'inizio di settembre; **at the end of ~** alla fine di settembre; **during ~** durante il mese di settembre; **every ~** ogni anno a settembre; **in ~** a settembre; **last ~** lo scorso settembre; **next ~** il prossimo settembre; **this ~** a settembre (di quest'anno); **2 ~ 1995** *(in letters etc)* 2 settembre 1995.

septic ['septɪk] *adj* infetto(-a).

septic tank *n* fossa *f* settica.

sequel ['siːkwəl] *n (to book, film)* seguito *m.*

sequence ['siːkwəns] *n (series)* serie *f inv*; *(order)* ordine *m.*

sequin ['siːkwɪn] *n* lustrino *m*, paillette *f inv.*

sergeant ['sɑːdʒənt] *n (in police force)* = brigadiere *m*; *(in army)* sergente *m.*

serial ['sɪərɪəl] *n (on TV, radio)* sceneggiato *m*, serial *m inv*; *(in magazine)* romanzo *m* a puntate.

series ['sɪərɪz] *(pl inv)* *n* serie *f inv.*

serious ['sɪərɪəs] *adj* serio(-a); *(illness, problem)* grave, serio; **are you ~?** dici sul serio?

seriously ['sɪərɪəslɪ] *adv (really)* seriamente; *(badly)* gravemente.

sermon ['sɜːmən] *n* sermone *m.*

servant ['sɜːvənt] *n* domestico *m* (-a *f*).

serve [sɜːv] *vt* servire ♦ *vi (SPORT)* servire; *(work)* prestare servizio ♦ *n (SPORT)* servizio *m*; **to ~ as** *(be used for)* servire da; **the town is ~d by two airports** la città è servita da due aeroporti; **'~s two'** *(on packaging, menu)* 'per due persone'; **it ~s you right!** ben ti sta!

service ['sɜːvɪs] *n* servizio *m*; *(at church)* rito *m*; *(of car)* revisione *f* ♦ *vt (car)* revisionare; **'~ included'** 'servizio incluso'; **'~ not included'** 'servizio escluso'; **to be of ~ to sb** *(fml)* essere d'aiuto a qn ❑ **services** *npl (on motorway)* stazione *f* di servizio; *(of person)* servigi *mpl.*

service area *n* area *f* di servizio.

service charge *n* servizio *m.*

service department *n* servizio *m* clienti.

service station *n* stazione *f* di servizio.

serviette [,sɜːvɪ'et] *n* tovagliolo *m.*

serving ['sɜːvɪŋ] *n (helping)* porzione *f.*

serving spoon *n* cucchiaio *m* da portata.

sesame seeds ['sesəmɪ-] *npl* semi *mpl* di sesamo.

session ['seʃn] *n* seduta *f*; **a drinking ~** una bevuta.

set [set] *(pt & pp* set) *adj* **1.** *(price, time)* fisso(-a); **a ~ lunch** un menu fisso.

2. *(text, book)* assegnato(-a).

3. *(situated)* situato(-a).

♦ *n* **1.** *(of tools etc)* serie *f inv*; *(of cutlery, dishes)* servizio *m*; **chess ~**

gioco m degli scacchi.

2. *(TV):* **a (TV)** ~ un apparecchio televisivo, un televisore.

3. *(in tennis)* set m inv.

4. *(of play)* scenario m.

5. *(at hairdresser's):* **a shampoo and ~** uno shampoo e messa in piega. ♦ vt **1.** *(put)* mettere, posare; **to ~ the table** apparecchiare.

2. *(cause to be):* **to ~ a machine going** avviare una macchina; **to ~ fire to sthg** dar fuoco a qc.

3. *(clock, alarm, controls)* regolare; **~ the alarm for 7 a.m.** metti la sveglia alle 7.

4. *(price, time)* fissare.

5. *(a record)* stabilire.

6. *(homework, essay)* dare.

7. *(play, film, story):* **to be ~** essere ambientato(-a). ♦ vi **1.** *(sun)* tramontare.

2. *(glue)* fare presa; *(jelly)* rapprendersi.

❑ **set down** vt sep *(Br: passengers)* far scendere; **set off** vt sep *(alarm)* far scattare ♦ vi *(on journey)* mettersi in viaggio; **set out** vt sep *(arrange)* disporre ♦ vi *(on journey)* mettersi in viaggio; **set up** vt sep *(barrier)* erigere; *(equipment)* installare.

set meal n menu m inv fisso.

set menu n menu m inv fisso.

settee [se'ti:] n divano m.

setting ['setɪŋ] n *(on machine)* posizione f; *(physical surroundings)* scenario m; *(atmosphere)* ambiente m.

settle ['setl] vt *(argument)* sistemare, appianare; *(bill)* saldare, regolare; *(stomach, nerves)* calmare; *(arrange, decide on)* stabilire, decidere ♦ vi *(start to live)* stabilirsi; *(come to rest)* posarsi; *(sediment, dust)* depositarsi ❑ **settle down** vi

(calm down) calmarsi; *(sit comfortably)* accomodarsi; **settle up** vi *(pay bill)* saldare il conto.

settlement ['setlmənt] n *(agreement)* accordo m; *(place)* insediamento m.

seven ['sevn] num sette, → **six**.

seventeen [,sevn'ti:n] num diciassette, → **six**.

seventeenth [,sevn'ti:nθ] num diciassettesimo(-a), → **sixth**.

seventh ['sevnθ] num settimo(-a), → **sixth**.

seventieth ['sevntjəθ] num settantesimo(-a), → **sixth**.

seventy ['sevntɪ] num settanta, → **six**.

several ['sevrəl] adj & pron parecchi(-chie), diversi(-e).

severe [sɪ'vɪə^r] adj *(conditions, damage, illness)* grave; *(criticism, person, punishment)* severo(-a); *(pain)* violento(-a), forte.

sew [səʊ] *(pp* sewn) vt & vi cucire.

sewage ['su:ɪdʒ] n acque fpl di scarico.

sewing ['səʊɪŋ] n *(activity)* cucito m; *(things sewn)* lavoro m.

sewing machine n macchina f da cucire.

sewn [səʊn] pp → **sew**.

sex [seks] n *(gender)* sesso m; *(sexual intercourse)* rapporto m sessuale; **to have ~ (with)** avere rapporti sessuali (con).

sexist ['seksɪst] n sessista mf.

sexual ['sekʃʊəl] adj sessuale.

sexy ['seksɪ] adj sexy (inv).

shabby ['ʃæbɪ] adj trasandato(-a).

shade [ʃeɪd] n *(shadow)* ombra f; *(lampshade)* paralume m; *(of colour* sfumatura f, tonalità f inv ◆ vt (protect) fare ombra a ❑ **shades** npl (inf: sunglasses) occhiali mpl da sole.

shadow [ˈʃædəʊ] n ombra f.

shady [ˈʃeɪdɪ] adj (place) ombroso(-a); (inf: person, deal) losco(-a).

shaft [ʃɑːft] n (of machine) albero m; (of lift) pozzo m.

shake [ʃeɪk] (pt shook, pp shaken [ˈʃeɪkn]) vt (tree, rug, person) scuotere; (bottle, dice) agitare; (shock) scuotere, turbare ◆ vi tremare; to ~ hands (with sb) dare OR stringere la mano (a qn); to ~ one's head (saying no) scuotere la testa.

shall [weak form ʃəl, strong form ʃæl] aux vb **1.** (expressing future): **I** ~ **be ready soon** sarò pronto tra poco. **2.** (in questions): ~ **I buy some wine?** devo comprare del vino?; ~ **we listen to the radio?** vogliamo ascoltare la radio?; **where** ~ **we go?** dove andiamo?, dove vogliamo andare? **3.** (fml: expressing order): **payment** ~ **be made within a week** il pagamento dovrà essere effettuato entro una settimana.

shallot [ʃəˈlɒt] n scalogno m.

shallow [ˈʃæləʊ] adj poco profondo(-a).

shallow end n (of swimming pool) lato m meno profondo.

shambles [ˈʃæmblz] n macello m, casino m.

shame [ʃeɪm] n vergogna f; **it's a** ~ è un peccato; **what a** ~! che peccato!

shampoo [ʃæmˈpuː] (pl **-s**) n shampoo m inv.

shandy [ˈʃændɪ] n bevanda a base di birra e limonata.

shape [ʃeɪp] n forma f; **to be in good/bad** ~ essere in/fuori forma.

share [ʃeəʳ] n (part) parte f; (in company) azione f ◆ vt dividere ❑ **share out** vt sep dividere.

shark [ʃɑːk] n squalo m, pescecane m.

sharp [ʃɑːp] adj (knife, razor) affilato(-a); (pin, nails) appuntito(-a); (teeth) aguzzo(-a); (clear) nitido(-a); (quick, intelligent) acuto(-a), scaltro (-a); (rise, change, bend) brusco(-a); (painful) acuto, lancinante; (food, taste) aspro(-a) ◆ adv (exactly) in punto.

sharpen [ˈʃɑːpn] vt (pencil) temperare; (knife) affilare.

shatter [ˈʃætəʳ] vt (break) frantumare ◆ vi frantumarsi.

shattered [ˈʃætəd] adj (Br: inf: tired) distrutto(-a).

shave [ʃeɪv] vt radere, rasare ◆ vi radersi, rasarsi ◆ n: **to have a** ~ farsi la barba.

shaver [ˈʃeɪvəʳ] n rasoio m elettrico.

shaver point n presa f per rasoio elettrico.

shaving brush [ˈʃeɪvɪŋ-] n pennello m da barba.

shaving cream [ˈʃeɪvɪŋ-] n crema f da barba.

shaving foam [ˈʃeɪvɪŋ-] n schiuma f da barba.

shawl [ʃɔːl] n scialle m.

she [ʃiː] pron lei; ~**'s tall** è alta.

sheaf [ʃiːf] (pl **sheaves**) n (of paper, notes) fascio m.

shears [ʃɪəz] npl cesoie fpl.

sheaves [ʃiːvz] pl → **sheaf**.

shed [ʃed] (pt & pp shed) n capanno m ◆ vt (tears, blood) versare.

she'd [weak form ʃɪd, strong form ʃi:d] = she had, she would.

sheep [ʃi:p] (pl inv) n pecora f.

sheepdog ['ʃi:pdɒg] n cane m pastore.

sheepskin ['ʃi:pskɪn] adj di pelle di pecora.

sheer [ʃɪəʳ] adj (pure, utter) puro(-a); (cliff) a picco, a strapiombo; (stockings) velato(-a).

sheet [ʃi:t] n (for bed) lenzuolo m; (of paper) foglio m; (of glass, metal) lastra f; (of wood) pannello m.

shelf [ʃelf] (pl shelves) n scaffale m.

shell [ʃel] n (of egg, nut, animal) guscio m; (on beach) conchiglia f; (bomb) granata f.

she'll [ʃi:l] = she will, she shall.

shellfish ['ʃelfɪʃ] n (food) frutti mpl di mare.

shell suit n (Br) tuta f in acetato.

shelter ['ʃeltəʳ] n riparo m, rifugio m; (at bus stop) pensilina f ♦ vt (protect) proteggere, riparare ♦ vi proteggersi, ripararsi; **to take ~** mettersi al riparo.

sheltered ['ʃeltəd] adj (place) riparato(-a).

shelves [ʃelvz] pl → shelf.

shepherd ['ʃepəd] n pastore m.

shepherd's pie ['ʃepədz-] n tortino a base di carne macinata coperta da uno spesso strato di purè di patate.

sheriff ['ʃerɪf] n (in US) sceriffo m.

sherry ['ʃerɪ] n sherry m inv.

she's [ʃi:z] = she is, she has.

shield [ʃi:ld] n scudo m ♦ vt proteggere.

shift [ʃɪft] n (change) cambiamento m; (period of work) turno m ♦ vt spostare ♦ vi (move) spostarsi,

(change) mutare, cambiare.

shin [ʃɪn] n stinco m.

shine [ʃaɪn] (pt & pp **shone**) vi brillare, splendere ♦ vt (shoes) lucidare, lustrare; (torch) puntare.

shiny ['ʃaɪnɪ] adj scintillante, lucido(-a).

ship [ʃɪp] n nave f; **by ~** (travel) con la nave; (send, transport) via mare.

shipwreck ['ʃɪprek] n (accident) naufragio m; (wrecked ship) relitto m.

shirt [ʃɜ:t] n camicia f.

shit [ʃɪt] n (vulg) merda f ♦ excl (vulg) merda!

shiver ['ʃɪvəʳ] vi rabbrividire.

shock [ʃɒk] n (surprise) shock m inv; (force) urto m, scossa f ♦ vt (surprise) colpire, scioccare; (horrify) scioccare; **to be in ~** (MED) essere sotto shock.

shock absorber [-əb‚zɔ:bəʳ] n ammortizzatore m.

shocking ['ʃɒkɪŋ] adj (very bad) terribile.

shoe [ʃu:] n scarpa f.

shoelace ['ʃu:leɪs] n stringa f.

shoe polish n lucido m da scarpe.

shoe repairer's [-rɪ‚peərəz] n calzolaio m.

shoe shop n negozio m di calzature.

shone [ʃɒn] pt & pp → shine.

shook [ʃʊk] pt → shake.

shoot [ʃu:t] (pt & pp **shot**) vt (kill, injure) sparare a; (gun) sparare; (arrow) tirare, scoccare; (film) girare ♦ vi (with gun) sparare; (move quickly) sfrecciare; (SPORT) tirare ♦ n (of plant) germoglio m.

shop [ʃɒp] *n* negozio *m* ♦ *vi* fare acquisti.

shop assistant *n* (Br) commesso *m* (-a *f*).

shop floor *n* (place) area di una fabbrica dove lavorano gli operai.

shopkeeper [ˈʃɒpˌkiːpəˀ] *n* negoziante *mf*.

shoplifter [ˈʃɒpˌlɪftəˀ] *n* taccheggiatore *m* (-trice *f*).

shopper [ˈʃɒpəˀ] *n* cliente *mf*, acquirente *mf*.

shopping [ˈʃɒpɪŋ] *n* spesa *f*; **to do the ~** fare la spesa; **to go ~** andare a fare spese.

shopping bag *n* borsa *f* per la spesa.

shopping basket *n* sporta *f* per la spesa.

shopping centre *n* centro *m* commerciale.

shopping list *n* lista *f* della spesa.

shopping mall *n* centro *m* commerciale.

shop steward *n* rappresentante *mf* sindacale.

shop window *n* vetrina *f*.

shore [ʃɔː] *n* riva *f*; **on ~** a terra.

short [ʃɔːt] *adj* (not tall) basso(-a); (letter, speech) corto(-a), breve; (hair, skirt) corto; (in time, distance) breve ♦ *adv* (cut hair) corti ♦ *n* (drink) bicchierino *m*; (film) cortometraggio *m*; **to be ~ of** (time, money) essere a corto di qc; **to be ~ for sthg** (be abbreviation of) essere abbreviazione di qc; **to be ~ of breath** essere senza fiato; **in ~** in breve □ **shorts** *npl* (short trousers) calzoncini *mpl*, pantaloncini *mpl*; (Am: underpants) boxer *mpl*.

shortage [ˈʃɔːtɪdʒ] *n* carenza *f*.

shortbread [ˈʃɔːtbred] *n* biscotto *m* di pasta frolla.

short-circuit *vi* fare cortocircuito.

shortcrust pastry [ˈʃɔːtkrʌst-] *n* pasta *f* frolla.

short cut *n* scorciatoia *f*.

shorten [ˈʃɔːtn] *vt* accorciare.

shorthand [ˈʃɔːthænd] *n* stenografia *f*.

shortly [ˈʃɔːtlɪ] *adv* (soon) presto, fra poco; **~ before** poco prima di.

shortsighted [ˌʃɔːtˈsaɪtɪd] *adj* miope.

short-sleeved [-ˌsliːvd] *adj* a maniche corte.

short-stay car park *n* parcheggio *m* a tempo limitato.

short story *n* racconto *m*, novella *f*.

short wave *n* onde *fpl* corte.

shot [ʃɒt] *pt & pp* → **shoot** ♦ *n* (of gun) sparo *m*; (in football, tennis, golf etc) tiro *m*; (photo) foto *f* inv; (in film) ripresa *f*; (inf: attempt) prova *f*, tentativo *m*; (drink) bicchierino *m*.

shotgun [ˈʃɒtgʌn] *n* fucile *m* da caccia.

should [ʃʊd] *aux vb* **1.** (expressing desirability): **we ~ leave now** ora dovremmo OR sarebbe meglio andare.

2. (asking for advice): **~ I go too?** devo andarci anch'io?

3. (expressing probability): **she ~ be home soon** dovrebbe arrivare a momenti.

4. (ought to): **they ~ have won the match** avrebbero dovuto vincere la partita.

5. (fml: in conditionals): **~ you need anything, call reception** se dovesse aver bisogno di qualcosa, chiami la reception.

6. *(fml: expressing wish):* **I ~ like to come with you** mi piacerebbe venire con voi.

shoulder [ˈʃəʊldə*] *n* spalla *f; (Am: of road)* corsia *f* d'emergenza.

shoulder pad *n* spallina *f*.

shouldn't [ˈʃʊdnt] = **should not.**

should've [ˈʃʊdəv] = **should have.**

shout [ʃaʊt] *n* grido *m*, urlo *m* ◆ *vt & vi* gridare, urlare □ **shout out** *vt sep* gridare.

shove [ʃʌv] *vt (push)* spingere; *(put carelessly)* ficcare, cacciare.

shovel [ˈʃʌvl] *n* pala *f*.

show [ʃəʊ] *(pp* **-ed** OR **shown)** *n (at theatre, on TV)* spettacolo *m; (on radio)* programma *m; (exhibition)* mostra *f* ◆ *vt* mostrare; *(represent, depict)* raffigurare; *(accompany)* accompagnare; *(film, TV programme)* dare ◆ *vi (be visible)* vedersi, essere visibile; *(film)* essere in programmazione; **to ~ sthg to sb** mostrare qc a qn; **to ~ sb how to do sthg** mostrare a qn come fare qc □ **show off** *vi* mettersi in mostra; **show up** *vi (come along)* farsi vivo, arrivare; *(be visible)* risaltare.

shower [ˈʃaʊə*] *n (for washing)* doccia *f; (of rain)* acquazzone *m* ◆ *vi* fare la doccia; **to have a ~** fare la doccia.

shower gel *n* gel *m inv* per la doccia.

shower unit *n* blocco *m* doccia.

showing [ˈʃəʊɪŋ] *n (of film)* proiezione *f*.

shown [ʃəʊn] *pp* → **show.**

showroom [ˈʃəʊrʊm] *n* salone *m* d'esposizione.

shrank [ʃræŋk] *pt* → **shrink.**

shrimp [ʃrɪmp] *n* gamberetto *m*.

shrine [ʃraɪn] *n* santuario *m*.

shrink [ʃrɪŋk] *(pt* **shrank**, *pp* **shrunk)** *n (inf: psychoanalyst)* strizzacervelli *mf inv* ◆ *vi (clothes)* restringersi; *(number, amount)* ridursi, diminuire.

shrub [ʃrʌb] *n* arbusto *m*.

shrug [ʃrʌg] *n* scrollata *f* di spalle ◆ *vi* scrollare le spalle.

shrunk [ʃrʌŋk] *pp* → **shrink.**

shuffle [ˈʃʌfl] *vt (cards)* mischiare ◆ *vi (walk)* camminare strascicando i piedi.

shut [ʃʌt] *(pt & pp* **shut)** *adj* chiuso(-a) ◆ *vt* chiudere ◆ *vi (door, mouth, eyes)* chiudersi; *(shop, restaurant)* chiudere □ **shut down** *vt sep* chiudere i battenti; **shut up** *vi (inf: stop talking)* tacere, stare zitto; **~ up!** chiudi il becco!

shutter [ˈʃʌtə*] *n (on window)* imposta *f; (on camera)* otturatore *m*.

shuttle [ˈʃʌtl] *n (plane, bus etc)* navetta *f*.

shuttlecock [ˈʃʌtlkɒk] *n* volano *m*.

shy [ʃaɪ] *adj* timido(-a).

Sicily [ˈsɪsɪlɪ] *n* la Sicilia.

sick [sɪk] *adj (ill)* malato(-a); **to be ~** *(vomit)* vomitare; **to feel ~** *(nauseous)* avere la nausea; **to be ~ of** *(fed up with)* essere stufo(-a) di.

sick bag *n* sacchetto di emergenz[a] per viaggiatori che soffrono di nausea [e] vomito.

sickness [ˈsɪknɪs] *n (illness)* ma[...] lattia *f*.

sick pay *n* indennità *f* per ma[...] lattia.

side [saɪd] *n* lato *m; (of road, pitc[h)*...]

margine m; (of river) sponda f; (team) squadra f; (in argument) parte f; (Br: TV channel) canale m ◆ adj (door, pocket) laterale; **at the ~ of** a fianco di; (road) al margine di; (river) sulla riva di; **on the other ~** dall'altra parte; **on this ~** da questo lato; **~ by ~** fianco a fianco.

sideboard ['saɪdbɔːd] n credenza f.

sidecar ['saɪdkɑːʳ] n sidecar m inv.

side dish n contorno m.

side effect n effetto m collaterale.

sidelight ['saɪdlaɪt] n (Br: of car) luce f di posizione.

side order n contorno m.

side salad n insalata f di contorno.

side street n traversa f.

sidewalk ['saɪdwɔːk] n (Am) marciapiede m.

sideways ['saɪdweɪz] adv (move) di lato, di fianco; (look) di traverso.

sieve [sɪv] n setaccio m.

sigh [saɪ] n sospiro m ◆ vi sospirare.

sight [saɪt] n (eyesight) vista f; (thing seen) spettacolo m; **at first ~** a prima vista; **to catch ~ of** intravedere; **in ~** in vista; **to lose ~ of** perdere di vista; **to be out of ~** non essere visibile ❑ **sights** npl (of city, country) luoghi mpl di maggiore interesse.

sightseeing ['saɪtsiːɪŋ] n: **to go ~** fare un giro turistico.

sign [saɪn] n (in shop, station) insegna f; (next to road) segnale m, cartello m; (symbol, indication) segno m; (signal) segnale ◆ vt & vi firmare; **there's no ~ of her** non c'è traccia di lei ❑ **sign in** vi (at hotel, club)

firmare il registro (all'arrivo).

signal ['sɪgnl] n segnale m; (Am: traffic lights) semaforo m ◆ vi (in car, on bike) segnalare.

signature ['sɪgnətʃəʳ] n firma f.

significant [sɪg'nɪfɪkənt] adj (large) considerevole; (important) importante.

signpost ['saɪnpəʊst] n cartello m stradale.

sikh [siːk] n Sikh mf inv.

silence ['saɪləns] n silenzio m.

silencer ['saɪlənsəʳ] n (Br: AUT) marmitta f.

silent ['saɪlənt] adj silenzioso(-a).

silk [sɪlk] n seta f.

sill [sɪl] n davanzale m.

silly ['sɪlɪ] adj sciocco(-a), stupido(-a).

silver ['sɪlvəʳ] n (substance) argento m; (coins) monete fpl d'argento ◆ adj d'argento.

silver foil n stagnola f, carta f argentata.

silver-plated [-'pleɪtɪd] adj placcato(-a) d'argento.

similar ['sɪmɪləʳ] adj simile; **to be ~ to** essere simile a.

similarity [sɪmɪ'lærətɪ] n (resemblance) somiglianza f; (similar point) affinità f inv.

simmer ['sɪməʳ] vi cuocere a fuoco lento.

simple ['sɪmpl] adj semplice.

simplify ['sɪmplɪfaɪ] vt semplificare.

simply ['sɪmplɪ] adv semplicemente.

simulate ['sɪmjʊleɪt] vt simulare.

simultaneous [Br ˌsɪml'teɪnjəs, Am ˌsaɪml'teɪnjəs] adj simultaneo(-a).

simultaneously [Br ˌsɪməl-
'teɪnjəslɪ, Am ˌsaɪməl'teɪnjəslɪ] adv
simultaneamente.

sin [sɪn] n peccato m ◆ vi peccare.

since [sɪns] adv da allora ◆ prep
da ◆ conj (in time) da quando, da
che; (as) dato che, poiché; **ever ~**
prep fin da ◆ conj da che, fin da
quando.

sincere [sɪn'sɪəʳ] adj sincero(-a).

sincerely [sɪn'sɪəlɪ] adv sinceramente; **Yours ~** Distinti saluti.

sing [sɪŋ] (pt sang, pp sung) vt &
vi cantare.

singer ['sɪŋəʳ] n cantante mf.

single ['sɪŋgl] adj solo(-a); (man)
celibe; (woman) nubile ◆ n (Br: ticket) biglietto m di sola andata;
(record) 45 giri m inv; **every ~** ogni
❏ **singles** n (SPORT) singolo m ◆ adj
(bar, club) per single.

single bed n letto m a una piazza.

single cream n (Br) panna f
liquida.

single parent n genitore m
single.

single room n camera f singola.

single track road n strada f a
una carreggiata.

singular ['sɪŋgjʊləʳ] n singolare
m; **in the ~** al singolare.

sinister ['sɪnɪstəʳ] adj sinistro(-a).

sink [sɪŋk] (pt sank, pp sunk) n
lavandino m ◆ vi (in water, mud)
affondare; (decrease) calare, diminuire.

sink unit n blocco m lavello.

sinuses ['saɪnəsɪz] npl seni mpl
paranasali.

sip [sɪp] n sorso m ◆ vt sorseg-
giare.

siphon ['saɪfn] n sifone m ◆ vt
travasare.

sir [sɜːʳ] n signore m; **Dear Sir**
Egregio Signore; **Sir Richard Blair**
Sir Richard Blair.

siren ['saɪərən] n sirena f.

sirloin steak [ˌsɜːlɔɪn-] n bistecca f di lombo.

sister ['sɪstəʳ] n sorella f; (Br:
nurse) caposala f.

sister-in-law n cognata f.

sit [sɪt] (pt & pp sat) vi sedere; (be
situated) trovarsi ◆ vt (to place) far
sedere; (Br: exam) sostenere, dare;
to be sitting essere seduto ❏ **sit
down** vi sedersi; **to be sitting
down** essere seduto; **sit up** vi (after
lying down) tirarsi su a sedere; (stay
up late) stare a piedi fino a tardi.

site [saɪt] n luogo m; (building site)
cantiere m.

sitting room ['sɪtɪŋ-] n salotto m.

situated ['sɪtjʊeɪtɪd] adj: **to be ~**
essere situato(-a).

situation [ˌsɪtjʊ'eɪʃn] n (state of
affairs) situazione f; (fml: location)
ubicazione f; **'~s vacant'** 'offerte di
lavoro'.

six [sɪks] num adj & n sei; **to be ~
(years old)** avere sei anni; **it's ~
(o'clock)** sono le sei; **a hundred and
~** centosei; **~ Hill Street** Hill Street
(numero) sei; **it's minus ~
(degrees)** è meno sei.

sixteen [sɪks'tiːn] num sedici, -
six.

sixteenth [sɪks'tiːnθ] num sed-
cesimo(-a), → **sixth**.

sixth [sɪksθ] num adj, adv & pro-
sesto(-a) ◆ num n sesto m; **the ~ (
September)** il sei (di settembre).

sixth form n (Br) ultimi due an-

facoltativi della scuola superiore.

sixth-form college *n (Br) istituto che prepara agli esami dell'ultimo anno di scuola superiore.*

sixtieth [ˈsɪkstɪəθ] *num* sessantesimo(-a), → **sixth**.

sixty [ˈsɪkstɪ] *num* sessanta, → **six**.

size [saɪz] *n* dimensioni *fpl; (of clothes, hats)* taglia *f,* misura *f; (of shoes)* numero *m;* **what ~ do you take?** che taglia porta?; **what ~ is this?** che taglia è?

sizeable [ˈsaɪzəbl] *adj* notevole.

skate [skeɪt] *n (ice skate, roller skate)* pattino *m; (fish: pl inv)* razza *f* ♦ *vi* pattinare.

skateboard [ˈskeɪtbɔːd] *n* skateboard *m inv.*

skater [ˈskeɪtəʳ] *n* pattinatore *m* (-trice *f*).

skating [ˈskeɪtɪŋ] *n:* **to go ~** andare a pattinare.

skeleton [ˈskelɪtn] *n* scheletro *m.*

skeptical [ˈskeptɪkl] *(Am)* = **sceptical**.

sketch [sketʃ] *n (drawing)* schizzo *m; (humorous)* sketch *m inv,* scenetta *f* ♦ *vt* schizzare.

skewer [ˈskjʊəʳ] *n* spiedo *m.*

ski [skiː] *(pt & pp* **skied,** *cont* **kiing)** *n* sci *m inv* ♦ *vi* sciare.

ski boots *npl* scarponi *mpl* da sci.

kid [skɪd] *n* slittamento *m,* sbandamento *m* ♦ *vi* slittare, sbandare.

kier [ˈskiːəʳ] *n* sciatore *m* (-trice *f*).

kiing [ˈskiːɪŋ] *n* sci *m;* **to go ~** andare a sciare; **a ~ holiday** una vacanza sulla neve.

kilful [ˈskɪlfʊl] *adj (Br)* abile.

ki lift *n* sciovia *f.*

skill [skɪl] *n (ability)* abilità *f inv; (technique)* tecnica *f.*

skilled [skɪld] *adj (worker, job)* qualificato(-a); *(driver, chef)* provetto(-a).

skillful [ˈskɪlfʊl] *(Am)* = **skilful**.

skimmed milk [ˈskɪmd-] *n* latte *m* scremato.

skin [skɪn] *n* pelle *f; (on fruit, vegetable)* buccia *f; (on milk)* pellicola *f.*

skin freshener [-ˌfreʃnəʳ] *n* tonico *m.*

skinny [ˈskɪnɪ] *adj* magrissimo(-a).

skip [skɪp] *vi (with rope)* saltare la corda; *(jump)* saltellare ♦ *vt (omit)* saltare ♦ *n (container)* cassonetto *m.*

ski pants *npl* pantaloni *mpl* da sci.

ski pass *n* ski-pass *m inv.*

ski pole *n* racchetta *f* da sci.

skipping rope [ˈskɪpɪŋ-] *n* corda *f* per saltare.

skirt [skɜːt] *n* gonna *f.*

ski slope *n* pista *f* da sci.

ski tow *n* ski-lift *m inv.*

skittles [ˈskɪtlz] *n* birilli *mpl.*

skull [skʌl] *n* cranio *m.*

sky [skaɪ] *n* cielo *m.*

skylight [ˈskaɪlaɪt] *n* lucernario *m.*

skyscraper [ˈskaɪˌskreɪpəʳ] *n* grattacielo *m.*

slab [slæb] *n (of stone, concrete)* lastra *f.*

slack [slæk] *adj (rope)* non tirato(-a); *(careless)* negligente; *(not busy)* calmo(-a); *(period)* morto(-a).

slacks [slæks] *npl* pantaloni *mpl.*

slam [slæm] *vt & vi* sbattere.

slander [ˈslɑːndəʳ] *n* calunnia *f; (in law)* diffamazione *f.*

slang [slæŋ] n slang m, gergo m.

slant [slɑ:nt] n (slope) pendenza f ♦ vi pendere.

slap [slæp] n (smack) schiaffo m ♦ vt schiaffeggiare.

slash [slæʃ] vt (cut) tagliare; (face) sfregiare; (fig: prices) ridurre ♦ n (written symbol) barra f.

slate [sleɪt] n (rock) ardesia f; (on roof) tegola f di ardesia.

slaughter ['slɔ:tər] vt (people, team) massacrare; (animal) macellare.

slave [sleɪv] n schiavo m (-a f).

sled [sled] = sledge.

sledge [sledʒ] n slitta f.

sleep [sli:p] n sonno m ♦ vi dormire ♦ vt: **the house ~s six** la casa ha sei posti letto; **did you ~ well?** hai dormito bene?; **I couldn't get to ~** non riuscivo a prender sonno; **to go to ~** addormentarsi; **to ~ with sb** andare a letto con qn.

sleeper ['sli:pər] n (train) treno m con vagoni letto; (sleeping car) vagone m letto; (Br: on railway track) traversina f; (Br: earring) campanella f.

sleeping bag ['sli:pɪŋ-] n sacco m a pelo.

sleeping car ['sli:pɪŋ-] n vagone m letto.

sleeping pill ['sli:pɪŋ-] n sonnifero m.

sleeping policeman ['sli:pɪŋ-] n (Br) piccolo dosso stradale che ha la funzione di rallentare il traffico.

sleepy ['sli:pɪ] adj insonnolito(-a); **I'm ~** ho sonno.

sleet [sli:t] n nevischio m ♦ v impers: **it's ~ing** sta nevischiando.

sleeve [sli:v] n (of garment) manica f; (of record) copertina f.

sleeveless ['sli:vlɪs] adj senza maniche.

slept [slept] pt & pp → sleep.

slice [slaɪs] n fetta f ♦ vt affettare, tagliare a fette.

sliced bread [,slaɪst-] n pane m a cassetta.

slide [slaɪd] (pt & pp slid [slɪd]) n (in playground) scivolo m; (of photograph) diapositiva f; (Br: hair slide) fermacapelli m inv ♦ vi (slip) scivolare.

sliding door [,slaɪdɪŋ-] n porta f scorrevole.

slight [slaɪt] adj (minor) lieve; **the ~est** il minimo (la minima); **not in the ~est** niente affatto.

slightly ['slaɪtlɪ] adv (a bit) leggermente; **I know him ~** lo conosco appena.

slim [slɪm] adj (person, waist) snello(-a) ♦ vi dimagrire.

slimming ['slɪmɪŋ] n dimagrimento m.

sling [slɪŋ] (pt & pp slung) vt (inf: throw) buttare ♦ n: **to have one's arm in a ~** portare il braccio al collo.

slip [slɪp] vi scivolare ♦ n (mistake) errore m; (of paper) foglietto m (petticoat) sottoveste f; **to slip up** (make a mistake) fare un errore.

slipper ['slɪpər] n pantofola f.

slippery ['slɪpərɪ] adj scivolo so(-a).

slip road n (Br) raccordo autostradale.

slit [slɪt] n fessura f.

slob [slɒb] n (inf) sciattone m (-a f)

slogan ['sləʊgən] n slogan m inv

slope [sləʊp] n (incline) pendio m; (hill) fianco m; (for skiing) pista f da sci ♦ vi (hill, path) scendere; (floor, roof, shelf) essere inclinato.

sloping ['sləʊpɪŋ] adj (floor, roof, shelf) inclinato(-a); (hill) degradante.

slot [slɒt] n (for coin) fessura f; (groove) scanalatura f.

slot machine n (vending machine) distributore m automatico; (for gambling) slot-machine f inv.

Slovakia [sləˈvækɪə] n la Slovacchia.

slow [sləʊ] adj lento(-a); (business) fiacco(-a) ♦ adv lentamente; 'slow' (sign on road) 'rallentare'; a ~ train un accelerato; to be ~ (clock) essere indietro ❑ **slow down** vt sep & vi rallentare.

slowly ['sləʊlɪ] adv lentamente.

slug [slʌg] n (animal) lumaca f.

slum [slʌm] n (building) baracca f ❑ **slums** npl (district) bassifondi mpl.

slung [slʌŋ] pt & pp → **sling**.

slush [slʌʃ] n neve f in parte sciolta.

sly [slaɪ] adj (cunning) astuto(-a); (deceitful) scaltro(-a).

smack [smæk] n (slap) schiaffo m ♦ vt schiaffeggiare.

small [smɔːl] adj piccolo(-a); (in height) basso(-a).

small change n spiccioli mpl.

smallpox ['smɔːlpɒks] n vaiolo m.

smart [smɑːt] adj (elegant, posh) elegante; (clever) intelligente.

smart card n carta f intelligente.

smash [smæʃ] n (SPORT) smash m, schiacciata f; (inf: car crash)

scontro m ♦ vt (plate, window) frantumare ♦ vi (plate, vase etc) frantumarsi.

smashing ['smæʃɪŋ] adj (Br: inf) fantastico(-a).

smear test ['smɪə-] n striscio m, pap-test m inv.

smell [smel] (pt & pp -ed OR smelt) n odore m; (bad odour) puzza f ♦ vt (sniff at) annusare; (detect) sentire odore di ♦ vi avere un odore; (have bad odour) puzzare; to ~ of sthg (pleasant) profumare di qc; (unpleasant) puzzare di qc.

smelly ['smelɪ] adj puzzolente.

smelt [smelt] pt & pp → **smell**.

smile [smaɪl] n sorriso m ♦ vi sorridere.

smoke [sməʊk] n fumo m ♦ vt & vi fumare; to have a ~ fumare una sigaretta.

smoked [sməʊkt] adj affumicato(-a).

smoked salmon n salmone m affumicato.

smoker ['sməʊkəʳ] n (person) fumatore m (-trice f).

smoking ['sməʊkɪŋ] n fumo m; 'no ~' 'vietato fumare'.

smoking area n area f per fumatori.

smoking compartment n scompartimento m per fumatori.

smoky ['sməʊkɪ] adj (room) fumoso(-a).

smooth [smuːð] adj (surface, skin, road) liscio(-a); (takeoff, landing) dolce, morbido(-a); (flight, journey, life) tranquillo(-a); (mixture, liquid) vellutato(-a), omogeneo(-a); (wine, beer) amabile; (pej: suave) mellifluo(-a) ❑ **smooth down** vt sep lisciare.

smother ['smʌðəʳ] vt (cover) coprire.

smudge [smʌdʒ] n sbavatura f.

smuggle ['smʌgl] vt contrabbandare.

snack [snæk] n spuntino m, snack m inv.

snack bar n snack-bar m inv, tavola f calda.

snail [sneɪl] n chiocciola f.

snake [sneɪk] n (animal) serpente m.

snap [snæp] vt (break) spezzare ◆ vi (break) spezzarsi ◆ n (inf: photo) foto f inv; (Br: card game) rubamazzo m.

snare [sneəʳ] n (trap) trappola f.

snatch [snætʃ] vt strappare.

sneakers ['sni:kəz] npl (Am) scarpe fpl da ginnastica.

sneeze [sni:z] vi starnuto m ◆ vi starnutire.

sniff [snɪf] vi tirar su col naso ◆ vt (smell) annusare.

snip [snɪp] vt tagliare.

snob [snɒb] n snob mf inv.

snog [snɒg] vi (Br: inf) pomiciare.

snooker ['snu:kəʳ] n snooker m (specie di biliardo giocato con 22 palle).

snooze [snu:z] n pisolino m.

snore [snɔːʳ] vi russare.

snorkel ['snɔːkl] n respiratore m (subacqueo).

snout [snaʊt] n muso m, grugno m.

snow [snəʊ] n neve f ◆ v impers: it's ~ing sta nevicando.

snowball ['snəʊbɔːl] n palla f di neve.

snowdrift ['snəʊdrɪft] n cumulo m di neve.

snowflake ['snəʊfleɪk] n fiocco m di neve.

snowman ['snəʊmæn] (pl -men [-men]) n pupazzo m di neve.

snowplough ['snəʊplaʊ] n spazzaneve m inv.

snowstorm ['snəʊstɔːm] n bufera f di neve.

snug [snʌg] adj (person) comodo(-a); (place) accogliente.

so [səʊ] adv 1. (emphasizing degree) così, talmente; it's ~ difficult (that ...) è così difficile (che ...).
2. (referring back): I don't think ~ credo di no; I'm afraid ~ temo proprio di sì; if ~ se è così, in tal caso.
3. (also): ~ do I anch'io.
4. (in this way) così, in questo modo.
5. (expressing agreement): ~ there is proprio così, già.
6. (in phrases): or ~ all'incirca; ~ as per, così da; ~ that affinché, perché.
◆ conj 1. (therefore) quindi, perciò; nobody answered ~ we went away non rispondeva nessuno perciò ce ne siamo andati.
2. (summarizing) allora; ~ what have you been up to? allora come vanno le cose?
3. (in phrases): ~ what? (inf) e allora?; ~ there! (inf) ecco!

soak [səʊk] vt (leave in water) mettere a bagno OR a mollo; (make very wet) impregnare, infradiciare ◆ vi: to ~ through sthg infiltrarsi in qc □ **soak up** vt sep assorbire.

soaked [səʊkt] adj fradicio(-a).

soaking ['səʊkɪŋ] adj fradicio(-a).

soap [səʊp] n sapone m.

soap opera n soap opera f inv.

telenovela f.

soap powder n detersivo m in polvere.

sob [sɒb] n singhiozzo m ◆ vi singhiozzare.

sober ['səʊbə'] adj (not drunk) sobrio(-a).

soccer ['sɒkə'] n calcio m.

sociable ['səʊʃəbl] adj socievole.

social ['səʊʃl] adj (problem, conditions, class) sociale.

social club n circolo m sociale.

socialist ['səʊʃəlɪst] adj socialista ◆ n socialista mf.

social life n vita f sociale.

social security n previdenza f sociale.

social worker n assistente mf sociale.

society [sə'saɪətɪ] n società f inv; (organization, club) associazione f, società.

sociology [,səʊsɪ'ɒlədʒɪ] n sociologia f.

sock [sɒk] n calzino m.

socket ['sɒkɪt] n (for plug) presa f; (for light bulb) portalampada m inv.

sod [sɒd] n (Br: vulg: nasty person) stronzo m (-a f).

soda ['səʊdə] n (soda water) seltz n inv; (Am: fizzy drink) spuma f.

soda water n acqua f di seltz.

sofa ['səʊfə] n divano m, sofà m inv.

sofa bed n divano m letto.

soft [sɒft] adj (bed, ground, skin) [off]ice, morbido(-a); (breeze, tap, [s]ound) leggero(-a).

[s]oft cheese n formaggio m [m]olle.

[s]oft drink n analcolico m.

[s]oftware ['sɒftweə'] n software m [inv].

soil [sɔɪl] n (earth) suolo m.

solarium [sə'leərɪəm] n solarium m inv.

solar panel ['səʊlə-] n pannello m solare.

sold [səʊld] pt & pp → **sell**.

soldier ['səʊldʒə'] n soldato m, militare m.

sold out adj esaurito(-a).

sole [səʊl] adj (only) solo(-a), unico(-a); (exclusive) esclusivo(-a) ◆ n (of shoe) suola f; (of foot) pianta f; (fish: pl inv) sogliola f.

solemn ['sɒləm] adj (person) serio(-a); (occasion) solenne.

solicitor [sə'lɪsɪtə'] n (Br) ≃ notaio m.

solid ['sɒlɪd] adj solido(-a); (not hollow) pieno(-a); (gold, silver, oak) massiccio(-a); (uninterrupted) ininterrotto(-a); **three hours ~** tre ore intere.

solo ['səʊləʊ] (pl -s) n assolo m; **'~ m/cs'** (traffic sign) 'riservato ai motocicli'.

soluble ['sɒljʊbl] adj solubile.

solution [sə'luːʃn] n soluzione f.

solve [sɒlv] vt risolvere.

some [sʌm] adj **1.** (certain amount of): ~ **meat** della carne; ~ **money** del denaro; **I had** ~ **difficulty getting here** ho avuto qualche difficoltà ad arrivare qui.
2. (certain number of): ~ **sweets** delle caramelle; ~ **boys** dei ragazzi; ~ **people** della gente; **I've known him for** ~ **years** lo conosco da anni.
3. (not all) certi(-e); ~ **jobs are better paid than others** certi lavori sono pagati meglio di altri.
4. (in imprecise statements): **she married** ~ **writer (or other)** ha sposato

un certo scrittore; **they're staying in ~ posh hotel** stanno in un albergo di lusso.
♦ *pron* 1. *(certain amount)* un po'; **can I have ~?** me ne dai un po'?; **~ of the money** una parte dei soldi.
2. *(certain number)* alcuni(-e), certi(-e); **can I have ~?** me ne dai qualcuno?; **~ (of them)** left early alcuni (di loro) sono andati via presto.
♦ *adv (approximately)* circa; **there were ~ 7,000 people there** c'erano circa 7 000 persone.

somebody ['sʌmbədɪ] = **someone**.

somehow ['sʌmhaʊ] *adv (some way or other)* in qualche modo, in un modo o nell'altro; *(for some reason)* per qualche motivo.

someone ['sʌmwʌn] *pron* qualcuno.

someplace ['sʌmpleɪs] *(Am)* = **somewhere**.

somersault ['sʌməsɔːlt] *n* capriola *f*, salto *m* mortale.

something ['sʌmθɪŋ] *pron* qualcosa; **it's really ~** è veramente eccezionale; **or ~** (*inf*) o qualcosa del genere; **~ like** all'incirca, pressappoco.

sometime ['sʌmtaɪm] *adv*: **~ in May** in maggio.

sometimes ['sʌmtaɪmz] *adv* a volte.

somewhere ['sʌmweəʳ] *adv (in or to unspecified place)* da qualche parte, in qualche posto; *(approximately)* all'incirca.

son [sʌn] *n* figlio *m*.

song [sɒŋ] *n* canzone *f*.

son-in-law *n* genero *m*.

soon [suːn] *adv* presto; **how ~ can**

you do it? fra quanto può farlo?; **~ as** (non) appena; **as ~ as possible** al più presto possibile; **~ after** poco dopo; **~ er or later** prima o poi.

soot [sʊt] *n* fuliggine *f*.

soothe [suːð] *vt* calmare; *(pain)* alleviare.

sophisticated [sə'fɪstɪkeɪtɪd] *adj (refined, chic)* sofisticato(-a), raffinato(-a); *(complex)* sofisticato, complesso(-a).

sorbet ['sɔːbeɪ] *n* sorbetto *m*.

sore [sɔːʳ] *adj (painful)* dolorante; *(Am: inf: angry)* incavolato(-a) ♦ *n* piaga *f*; **to have a ~ throat** avere mal di gola.

sorry ['sɒrɪ] *adj*: **I'm ~!** scusa! **I'm ~ I'm late** scusa il ritardo; **~?** *(asking for repetition)* scusa?; **to feel ~ for sb** dispiacersi per qn; **I'm ~ you can't come** mi dispiace che tu non venga; **I'm ~ about the mess** scusa il disordine.

sort [sɔːt] *n* tipo *m* ♦ *vt* ordinare; **~ of** *(more or less)* più o meno; **it's ~ of difficult** è piuttosto difficile ❑ **sort out** *vt sep (classify)* ordinare; *(resolve)* chiarire.

so-so *adj & adv (inf)* così così.

soufflé ['suːfleɪ] *n* soufflé *m inv*.

sought [sɔːt] *pt & pp* → **seek**.

soul [səʊl] *n (spirit)* anima *f*; *(soul music)* musica *f* soul.

sound [saʊnd] *n* suono *m*; *(noise, rumore m; (volume)* volume *m* ♦ *vt (horn, bell)* suonare ♦ *vi (alarm, bell voice)* suonare; *(seem to be)* sembrare ♦ *adj (building, structure)* solido(-a); *(heart)* sano(-a); *(advice idea)* valido(-a); **to ~ like** sembrare; *(seem to be)* sembrare, aver l'aria di.

soundproof ['saʊndpruːf] *a*

insonorizzato(-a).

soup [su:p] n zuppa f, minestra f.

soup spoon n cucchiaio m da minestra.

sour ['sauə'] adj (taste) aspro(-a); (milk) acido(-a); **to go ~** inacidire.

source [sɔ:s] n (supply, origin) fonte f; (cause) causa f; (of river) sorgente f.

sour cream n panna f acida.

south [sauθ] n sud m, meridione m ♦ adj del sud ♦ adv (fly, walk) verso sud; (be situated) a sud; **in the ~ of England** nel sud dell'Inghilterra.

South Africa n il Sudafrica.

South America n l'America f del sud, il Sudamerica.

southbound ['sauθbaund] adj diretto(-a) a sud.

southeast [,sauθ'i:st] n sud-est m.

southern ['sʌðən] adj meridionale, del sud.

South Pole n Polo m Sud.

southwards ['sauθwədz] adv verso sud.

southwest [,sauθ'west] n sudovest m.

souvenir [,su:və'nɪə'] n souvenir m inv, ricordo m.

Soviet Union [səuvɪət-] n: **the ~** l'Unione f Sovietica.

sow[1] [səu] (pp **sown** [səun]) vt (seeds) seminare.

sow[2] [sau] n (pig) scrofa f.

soya [ˈsɔɪə] n soia f.

soya bean n seme m di soia.

soy sauce [,sɔɪ-] n salsa f di soia.

spa [spɑ:] n terme fpl.

space [speɪs] n spazio m; (empty space) posto m; (room) spazio, posto; (period) periodo m ♦ vt di-

stanziare.

spaceship ['speɪsʃɪp] n astronave f.

space shuttle n shuttle m inv.

spacious ['speɪʃəs] adj spazioso(-a).

spade [speɪd] n (tool) vanga f, badile m ♦ **spades** npl (in cards) picche fpl.

spaghetti [spə'getɪ] n spaghetti mpl.

Spain [speɪn] n la Spagna.

span [spæn] pt → **spin** ♦ n (of time) periodo m, arco m di tempo.

Spaniard ['spænjəd] n spagnolo m (-a f).

spaniel ['spænjəl] n spaniel m inv.

Spanish ['spænɪʃ] adj spagnolo(-a); (language) spagnolo m.

spank [spæŋk] vt sculacciare.

spanner ['spænə'] n chiave f (arnese).

spare [speə'] adj (kept in reserve) di riserva; (not in use) in più ♦ n (spare part) ricambio m, (spare wheel) ruota f di scorta ♦ vt: **to ~ sb sthg** (money) dare qc a qn; **can you ~ me ten minutes?** hai dieci minuti?; **with ten minutes to ~** con dieci minuti di anticipo.

spare part n pezzo m di ricambio.

spare ribs npl costine fpl di maiale.

spare room n camera f degli ospiti.

spare time n tempo m libero.

spare wheel n ruota f di scorta.

spark [spɑ:k] n scintilla f.

sparkling ['spɑ:klɪŋ] adj (mineral water, soft drink) frizzante.

sparkling wine n vino m frizzante.

spark plug n candela f.

sparrow ['spærəʊ] n passero m.

spat [spæt] pt & pp = **spit**.

speak [spiːk] (pt **spoke**, pp **spoken**) vt (language) parlare; (say) dire ♦ vi parlare; who's ~ing? (on phone) chi parla?; can I ~ to Sarah? - ~ing! (on phone) posso parlare con Sarah? - sono io!; to ~ to sb about sthg parlare a qn di qc ❏ **speak up** vi (more loudly) parlare più forte.

speaker ['spiːkəʳ] n (at conference) oratore m (-trice f); (loudspeaker, of stereo) altoparlante m; **an English ~** una persona che parla inglese.

spear [spɪəʳ] n lancia f.

special ['speʃl] adj speciale ♦ n: **'today's ~'** 'piatto del giorno'.

special delivery n (Br) = espresso m.

special effects npl effetti mpl speciali.

specialist ['speʃəlɪst] n (doctor) specialista mf.

speciality [ˌspeʃɪ'ælətɪ] n specialità f inv.

specialize ['speʃəlaɪz] vi: **to ~ (in)** specializzarsi (in).

specially ['speʃəlɪ] adv (specifically) specialmente; (on purpose) appositamente; (particularly) particolarmente.

special offer n offerta f speciale.

special school n (Br) = scuola f speciale.

specialty ['speʃltɪ] (Am) = **speciality**.

species ['spiːʃiːz] n specie f inv.

specific [spə'sɪfɪk] adj (particular) specifico(-a).

specification [ˌspesɪfɪ'keɪʃn] n

(of machine, car) caratteristiche fpl tecniche.

specimen ['spesɪmən] n (MED) campione m; (example) esemplare m.

specs [speks] npl (inf) occhiali mpl.

spectacle ['spektəkl] n (sight) scena f.

spectacles ['spektəklz] npl occhiali mpl.

spectacular [spek'tækjʊləʳ] adj spettacolare.

spectator [spek'teɪtəʳ] n spettatore m (-trice f).

sped [sped] pt & pp = **speed**.

speech [spiːtʃ] n (ability to speak) parola f; (manner of speaking) modo m di parlare; (talk) discorso m.

speech impediment [-ɪmˌpedɪmənt] n difetto m di pronuncia.

speed [spiːd] (pt & pp **-ed** OR **sped**) n velocità f inv; (fast rate) alta velocità; (of film) sensibilità f inv; (bicycle gear) marcia f ♦ vi (move quickly) andare velocemente; (drive too fast) andare a velocità eccessiva; **'reduce ~ now'** 'rallentare' ❏ **speed up** vi accelerare.

speedboat ['spiːdbəʊt] n fuoribordo m inv.

speeding ['spiːdɪŋ] n eccesso m di velocità.

speed limit n limite m di velocità.

speedometer [spɪ'dɒmɪtəʳ] n tachimetro m.

spell [spel] (Br pt & pp **-ed** OR **spelt**, Am pt & pp **-ed**) vt (word, name) scrivere; (subj: letters) formare la parola n (period) periodo m; (magic) incantesimo m.

spelling ['spelɪŋ] n (correct order) ortografia f.

spelt [spelt] *pt & pp* (*Br*) → **spell**.

spend [spend] (*pt & pp* **spent** [spent]) *vt* (*money*) spendere; (*time*) passare.

sphere [sfɪəʳ] *n* sfera *f*.

spice [spaɪs] *n* spezia *f* ♦ *vt* condire con delle spezie.

spicy ['spaɪsɪ] *adj* piccante.

spider ['spaɪdəʳ] *n* ragno *m*.

spider's web *n* ragnatela *f*.

spike [spaɪk] *n* (*metal*) punta *f*.

spill [spɪl] (*Br pt & pp* **-ed** OR **spilt**, *Am pt & pp* **-ed**) *vt* versare ♦ *vi* versarsi.

spin [spɪn] (*pt* **span** OR **spun**, *pp* **spun**) *vt* (*wheel*) far girare; (*washing*) centrifugare ♦ *vi* (*on ball*) effetto *m*; **to go for a ~** (*inf*) andare a fare un giro in macchina.

spinach ['spɪnɪdʒ] *n* spinaci *mpl*.

spine [spaɪn] *n* spina *f* dorsale; (*of book*) costa *f*.

spinster ['spɪnstəʳ] *n* zitella *f*.

spiral ['spaɪərəl] *n* spirale *f*.

spiral staircase *n* scala *f* a chiocciola.

spire [spaɪəʳ] *n* guglia *f*.

spirit ['spɪrɪt] *n* spirito *m*; (*mood*) umore *m* □ **spirits** *npl* (*Br: alcohol*) superalcolici *mpl*.

spit [spɪt] (*Br pt & pp* **spat**, *Am pt & pp* **spit**) *vi* (*person*) sputare; (*fire, food*) scoppiettare ♦ *n* (*saliva*) saliva *f*; (*for cooking*) spiedo *m* ♦ *v impers*: **it's spitting** pioviggina.

spite [spaɪt] : **in spite of** *prep* nonostante.

spiteful ['spaɪtful] *adj* malevolo(-a).

splash [splæʃ] *n* (*sound*) tonfo *m* ♦ *vt* schizzare.

splendid ['splendɪd] *adj* splendido(-a).

splint [splɪnt] *n* stecca *f*.

splinter ['splɪntəʳ] *n* scheggia *f*.

split [splɪt] (*pt & pp* **split**) *n* (*tear*) strappo *m*; (*crack, in skirt*) spacco *m* ♦ *vt* (*wood, stone*) spaccare; (*tear*) strappare; (*bill, cost, profits, work*) dividere ♦ *vi* (*wood, stone*) spaccarsi; (*tear*) strapparsi □ **split up** *vi* (*couple*) lasciarsi; (*group*) dividersi.

spoil [spɔɪl] (*pt & pp* **-ed** OR **spoilt**) *vt* (*ruin*) rovinare; (*child*) viziare.

spoke [spəʊk] *pt* → **speak** ♦ *n* raggio *m*.

spoken ['spəʊkn] *pp* → **speak**.

spokesman ['spəʊksmən] (*pl* **-men** [-mən]) *n* portavoce *m inv*.

spokeswoman ['spəʊks,wʊmən] (*pl* **-women** [-,wɪmɪn]) *n* portavoce *f inv*.

sponge [spʌndʒ] *n* (*for cleaning, washing*) spugna *f*.

sponge bag *n* (*Br*) nécessaire *m inv* (da viaggio).

sponge cake *n* pan *m* di Spagna.

sponsor ['spɒnsəʳ] *n* (*of event, TV programme*) sponsor *m inv*.

sponsored walk [,spɒnsəd-] *n* marcia *f* di beneficenza.

spontaneous [spɒn'teɪnjəs] *adj* spontaneo(-a).

spoon [spuːn] *n* cucchiaio *m*.

spoonful ['spuːnful] *n* cucchiaiata *f*.

sport [spɔːt] *n* sport *m inv*.

sports car [spɔːts-] *n* automobile *f* sportiva.

sports centre [spɔːts-] *n* centro *m* sportivo.

sports jacket [spɔːts-] *n* giacca

f sportiva.

sportsman ['spɔːtsmən] (*pl* **-men** [-mən]) *n* sportivo *m*.

sports shop [spɔːts-] *n* negozio *m* di articoli sportivi.

sportswoman ['spɔːtsˌwʊmən] (*pl* **-women** [-ˌwɪmɪn]) *n* sportiva *f*.

spot [spɒt] *n* (*of paint, rain*) goccia *f*; (*on clothes*) macchia *f*; (*on skin*) brufolo *m*; (*place*) posto *m* ◆ *vt* notare; **on the** ~ (*at once*) immediatamente; (*at the scene*) sul posto.

spotless ['spɒtlɪs] *adj* pulitissimo(-a).

spotlight ['spɒtlaɪt] *n* riflettore *m*.

spotty ['spɒtɪ] *adj* brufoloso(-a).

spouse [spaʊs] *n* (*fml*) coniuge *mf*.

spout [spaʊt] *n* beccuccio *m*.

sprain [spreɪn] *vt* (*ankle, wrist*) slogarsi.

sprang [spræŋ] *pt* → **spring**.

spray [spreɪ] *n* (*aerosol*) spray *m* inv; (*for perfume*) vaporizzatore *m*; (*droplets*) spruzzi *mpl* ◆ *vt* spruzzare.

spread [spred] (*pt & pp* **spread**) *vt* (*butter, jam, glue*) spalmare; (*map, tablecloth, blanket*) stendere; (*legs, fingers, arms*) distendere; (*disease, news, rumour*) diffondere ◆ *vi* diffondersi ◆ *n* (*food*) crema *f* da spalmare ❑ **spread out** *vi* (*disperse*) disperdersi.

spring [sprɪŋ] (*pt* **sprang**, *pp* **sprung**) *n* (*season*) primavera *f*; (*coil*) molla *f*; (*in ground*) sorgente *f* ◆ *vi* (*leap*) balzare; **in (the)** ~ in primavera.

springboard ['sprɪŋbɔːd] *n* trampolino *m*.

spring-cleaning [-'kliːnɪŋ] *n* pulizie *fpl* di Pasqua.

spring onion *n* cipollina *f*.

spring roll *n* involtino *m* primavera.

sprinkle ['sprɪŋkl] *vt*: **to** ~ **sthg with sugar** spolverizzare qc di zucchero; **to** ~ **sthg with water** spruzzare dell'acqua su qc.

sprinkler ['sprɪŋklər] *n* (*for fire*) sprinkler *m inv*; (*for grass*) irrigatore *m*.

sprint [sprɪnt] *vi* (*run fast*) scattare ◆ *n* (*race*): **the 100-metres** ~ i 100 metri piani.

Sprinter® ['sprɪntər] *n* (*Br: train*) treno usato su brevi distanze.

sprout [spraʊt] *n* (*vegetable*) cavoletto *m* di Bruxelles.

spruce [spruːs] *n* abete *m*.

sprung [sprʌŋ] *pp* → **spring** ◆ *adj* (*mattress*) a molle.

spud [spʌd] *n* (*inf*) patata *f*.

spun [spʌn] *pt & pp* → **spin**.

spur [spɜːr] *n* (*for horse rider*) sperone *m*; **on the** ~ **of the moment** d'impulso.

spurt [spɜːt] *vi* sprizzare.

spy [spaɪ] *n* spia *f*.

squall [skwɔːl] *n* burrasca *f*.

squalor ['skwɒlər] *n* squallore *m*.

square [skweər] *adj* (*in shape*) quadrato(-a) ◆ *n* (*shape*) quadrato *m*; (*in town*) piazza *f*; (*on chessboard*) scacco *m*; **2** ~ **metres** 2 metri quadrati; **it's 2 metres** ~ misura 2 metri per 2; **we're (all)** ~ **now** (*not owing money*) adesso siamo pari.

squash [skwɒʃ] *n* (*game*) squash *m*; (*Am: vegetable*) zucca *f*; (*Br: drink*): **orange/lemon** ~ sciroppo *m* di arancia/limone ◆ *vt* schiacciare.

squat [skwɒt] *adj* tozzo(-a) ◆ *vi* (*crouch*) accovacciarsi.

squeak [skwiːk] *vi* (*door, whee*

cigolare; *(mouse)* squittire.

squeeze [skwiːz] *vt (tube, orange)* spremere; *(hand)* stringere ◆ *vi:* **to ~ in** infilarsi.

squid [skwɪd] *n* calamaro *m.*

squint [skwɪnt] *n* strabismo *m* ◆ *vi:* **to ~ at** guardare con gli occhi socchiusi.

squirrel [Br 'skwɪrəl, Am 'skwɜːrəl] *n* scoiattolo *m.*

squirt [skwɜːt] *vi* schizzare.

St *(abbr of Street)* V.; *(abbr of Saint)* S.

stab [stæb] *vt (with knife)* pugnalare.

stable ['steɪbl] *adj* stabile ◆ *n* stalla *f.*

stack [stæk] *n (pile)* pila *f;* **~s of** *(inf: lots)* un mucchio di.

stadium ['steɪdjəm] *n* stadio *m.*

staff [stɑːf] *n (workers)* personale *m.*

stage [steɪdʒ] *n (phase)* stadio *m; (in theatre)* palcoscenico *m.*

stagger ['stægər] *vt (arrange in stages)* scaglionare ◆ *vi* barcollare.

stagnant ['stægnənt] *adj* stagnante.

stain [steɪn] *n* macchia *f* ◆ *vt* macchiare.

stained glass [.steɪnd-] *n* vetro colorato.

stainless steel ['steɪnlɪs-] *n* acciaio *m* inossidabile.

staircase ['steəkeɪs] *n* scala *f.*

stairs [steəz] *npl* scale *fpl.*

stairwell ['steəwel] *n* tromba *f* delle scale.

stake [steɪk] *n (share)* quota *f; (in gambling)* posta *f; (post)* palo *m;* **at stake** in gioco.

stale [steɪl] *adj (food)* stantio(-a).

stalk [stɔːk] *n* gambo *m.*

stall [stɔːl] *n (in market, at exhibi-*

tion) banco *m* ◆ *vi (car, engine)* spegnersi □ **stalls** *npl* (Br: *in theatre)* platea *f.*

stamina ['stæmɪnə] *n* resistenza *f.*

stammer ['stæmər] *vi* balbettare.

stamp [stæmp] *n (for letter)* francobollo *m; (in passport, on document)* timbro *m* ◆ *vt (passport, document)* timbrare ◆ *vi:* **to ~ on sthg** pestare qc.

stamp-collecting [-kə.lektɪŋ] *n* filatelia *f.*

stamp machine *n* distributore *m* di francobolli.

stand [stænd] *(pt & pp* **stood)** *vi (be on feet)* stare in piedi; *(be situated)* trovarsi; *(get to one's feet)* alzarsi ◆ *vt (place)* mettere; *(bear)* sopportare; *(withstand)* tollerare ◆ *n (stall)* banco *m; (for umbrellas)* portaombrelli *m inv; (for coats)* attaccapanni *m inv; (on bike, motorbike)* cavalletto *m; (at sports stadium)* tribuna *f;* **newspaper ~** edicola *f;* **to be ~ing** stare in piedi; **to ~ sb a drink** offrire da bere a qn; **'no ~ing'** *(Am: aut)* 'divieto di sosta' □ **stand back** *vi* tirarsi indietro; **stand for** *vt fus (mean)* stare per; *(tolerate)* tollerare; **stand in** *vi:* **to ~ in for sb** sostituire qn; **stand out** *vi* spiccare; **stand up** *vi (be on feet)* stare in piedi; *(get to one's feet)* alzarsi ◆ *vt sep (inf: boyfriend, girlfriend etc)* tirare un bidone a; **stand up for** *vt fus* difendere.

standard ['stændəd] *adj (normal)* standard *(inv)* ◆ *n (level)* livello *m; (norm)* standard *m inv;* **up to ~** soddisfacente □ **standards** *npl (principles)* principi *mpl.*

standard-class *adj* (Br: *on train)* di seconda classe.

standby ['stændbaɪ] *adj (ticket)*

stand-by (inv).

stank [stæŋk] pt → **stink**.

staple ['steɪpl] n (for paper) punto m metallico.

stapler ['steɪplə*] n cucitrice f.

star [stɑ:*] n stella f ◆ vt (subj: film, play etc) avere come protagonista ❑ **stars** npl (horoscope) oroscopo m.

starboard ['stɑ:bəd] adj di tribordo.

starch [stɑ:tʃ] n amido m.

stare [steə*] vi: to ~ at fissare.

starfish ['stɑ:fɪʃ] (pl inv) n stella f marina.

starling ['stɑ:lɪŋ] n storno m.

Stars and Stripes n: the ~ la bandiera a stelle e strisce.

---

i STARS AND STRIPES

È uno dei tanti nomi con i quali viene comunemente indicata la bandiera americana, oltre a "Old Glory", "Star-Spangled Banner" e "Stars and Bars". Le 50 stelle ("stars") rappresentano i 50 stati che attualmente fanno parte degli Stati Uniti, mentre le 13 strisce ("stripes") rosse e bianche rappresentano i 13 stati che formavano originariamente l'Unione. Gli americani sono molto orgogliosi della loro bandiera e non è perciò raro vederla sventolare dalle case di molti privati cittadini.

start [stɑ:t] n (beginning) inizio m; (starting place) partenza f ◆ vt cominciare, iniziare; (car, engine) mettere in moto; (company, club) fondare ◆ vi cominciare; (car, engine, on journey) partire; **prices ~ at** OR **from £5** i prezzi partono da 5

sterline; **to ~ doing sthg** OR **to do sthg** cominciare a fare qc; **to ~ with** ... per cominciare ... ❑ **start out** vi (on journey) partire; (be originally) cominciare; **start up** vt sep (car, engine) mettere in moto; (business) intraprendere; (shop) aprire.

starter ['stɑ:tə*] n (Br: of meal) antipasto m; (of car) starter m inv; **for ~s** (in meal) per antipasto.

starter motor n motorino m di avviamento.

starting point ['stɑ:tɪŋ-] n punto m di partenza.

startle ['stɑ:tl] vt far trasalire.

starvation [stɑ:'veɪʃn] n fame f.

starve [stɑ:v] vi (have no food) morire di fame; **I'm starving!** muoio di fame!

state [steɪt] n stato m ◆ vt (declare) dichiarare; (specify) specificare; **the State** lo Stato; **the States** gli Stati Uniti.

statement ['steɪtmənt] n (declaration) dichiarazione f; (from bank) estratto m conto.

state school n scuola f statale.

statesman ['steɪtsmən] (pl -men [-mən]) n statista m.

static ['stætɪk] n (on radio, TV) scarica f (elettrostatica).

station ['steɪʃn] n stazione f.

stationary ['steɪʃnərɪ] adj stazionario(-a).

stationer's ['steɪʃnəz] n (shop) cartoleria f.

stationery ['steɪʃnərɪ] n cancelleria f.

station wagon n (Am) station wagon f inv.

statistics [stə'tɪstɪks] npl (facts) statistiche fpl.

statue ['stætʃuː] n statua f.
Statue of Liberty n: the ~ la Statua della Libertà.

ℹ️ STATUE OF LIBERTY

Su un'isoletta al largo del porto di New York si erge la Statua della Libertà, scultura gigante di una donna che regge nella mano destra una fiaccola. Fu donata agli Stati Uniti dalla Francia nel 1884 ed è aperta al pubblico.

---

status ['steɪtəs] n (legal position) stato m; (social position) condizione f sociale; (prestige) prestigio m.
stay [steɪ] n (time spent) soggiorno m ♦ vi (remain) rimanere m; (as guest) alloggiare; (Scot: reside) abitare; **to ~ the night** passare la notte ▪ **stay away** vi: **to ~ away (from)** (not attend) non andare (a); (not go near) stare lontano (da); **stay in** vi rimanere a casa; **stay out** vi (from home) rimanere fuori; **stay up** vi rimanere alzato.

STD code n prefisso m.

steady ['stedɪ] adj (not shaking, firm) stabile; (gradual, stable) costante; (job) fisso(-a) ♦ vt (stop from shaking) tenere fermo.

steak [steɪk] n (type of meat) carne di manzo; (piece of meat) bistecca f; (piece of fish) trancia f.

steak and kidney pie n pasticcio di carne di manzo e rognone.

steakhouse ['steɪkhaʊs, pl -hauzɪz] n ristorante m specializzato in bistecche.

steal [stiːl] (pt stole, pp stolen) vt rubare; **to ~ sthg from sb** rubare qc a qn.

steam [stiːm] n vapore m ♦ vt (food) cuocere a vapore.
steamboat ['stiːmbəʊt] n battello m a vapore.
steam engine n locomotiva f a vapore.
steam iron n ferro m a vapore.
steel [stiːl] n acciaio m ♦ adj di acciaio.
steep [stiːp] adj (hill, path) ripido(-a); (increase, drop) notevole.
steeple ['stiːpl] n campanile m.
steer ['stɪəʳ] vt (car, boat, plane) condurre.
steering ['stɪərɪŋ] n sterzo m.
steering wheel n volante m.
stem [stem] n stelo m.
step [step] n (stair) gradino m; (rung) piolo m; (pace) passo m; (measure) misura f; (stage) mossa f ♦ vi: **to ~ on sthg** calpestare qc; **'mind the ~'** 'attenti al gradino' ▪ **steps** npl (stairs) scala f; **step aside** vi (move aside) farsi da parte; **step back** vi (move back) tirarsi indietro.

step aerobics n step m.
stepbrother ['step,brʌðəʳ] n fratellastro m.
stepdaughter ['step,dɔːtəʳ] n figliastra f.
stepfather ['step,fɑːðəʳ] n patrigno m.
stepladder ['step,lædəʳ] n scala f (a pioli).
stepmother ['step,mʌðəʳ] n matrigna f.
stepsister ['step,sɪstəʳ] n sorellastra f.
stepson ['stepsʌn] n figliastro m.
stereo ['sterɪəʊ] (pl -s) adj stereofonico(-a) ♦ n (hi-fi) stereo m inv.

sterile *(stereo sound)* stereofonia f.

sterile ['sterail] *adj* sterile.

sterilize ['steralaiz] *vt* sterilizzare.

sterling ['stɜ:lɪŋ] *adj (pound)* sterlina ♦ *n* sterlina f.

sterling silver *n* argento m di buona lega.

stern [stɜ:n] *adj* severo(-a) ♦ *n* poppa f.

stew [stju:] *n* stufato m.

steward ['stjʊəd] *n (on plane, ship)* steward m *inv; (at public event)* membro m del servizio d'ordine.

stewardess ['stjʊədɪs] *n* hostess f *inv*.

stewed [stju:d] *adj (fruit)* cotto(-a).

stick [stɪk] *(pt & pp* **stuck)** *n (of wood)* bastone m; *(of chalk)* pezzetto m; *(of celery)* bastoncino m ♦ *vt (glue)* attaccare; *(push, insert)* ficcare; *(inf: put)* ficcare ♦ *vi (become attached)* attaccarsi; *(jam)* incastrarsi ◻ **stick out** *vi (protrude)* sporgere; *(be noticeable)* saltare agli occhi; **stick to** *vt fus (decision, promise)* mantenere; *(principles)* tener fede a; **stick up** *vt sep (poster, notice)* attaccare ♦ *vi* sporgere; **stick up for** *vt fus* difendere.

sticker ['stɪkə'] *n* adesivo m.

sticking plaster ['stɪkɪŋ-] *n* cerotto m.

stick shift *n (Am: car)* auto f con cambio manuale.

sticky ['stɪkɪ] *adj (substance, hands, weather)* appiccicoso(-a); *(label, tape)* adesivo(-a).

stiff [stɪf] *adj* duro(-a); *(back, neck, person)* rigido(-a) ♦ *adv:* **to be bored ~** *(inf)* essere annoiato a morte.

stile [staɪl] *n* gradini per scavalcare un recinto.

stiletto heels [stɪ'letəʊ-] *npl* tacchi mpl a spillo.

still [stɪl] *adv* ancora; *(despite that)* comunque ♦ *adj (motionless)* immobile; *(quiet, calm)* calmo(-a); *(not fizzy)* non gassato(-a); **we've ~ got ten minutes** abbiamo ancora dieci minuti; **~ more** ancora di più; **to stand ~** stare fermo.

Stilton ['stɪltn] *n* stilton m *(formaggio simile al gorgonzola).*

stimulate ['stɪmjʊleɪt] *vt (encourage)* stimolare.

sting [stɪŋ] *(pt & pp* **stung)** *vt* pungere ♦ *vi (skin, eyes)* pizzicare.

stingy ['stɪndʒɪ] *adj (inf)* tirchio(-a).

stink [stɪŋk] *(pt* **stank** OR **stunk,** *pp* **stunk)** *vi (smell bad)* puzzare.

stipulate ['stɪpjʊleɪt] *vt* stipulare.

stir [stɜ:'] *vt* mescolare.

stir-fry *n* piatto m saltato ♦ *vt* saltare (in padella).

stirrup ['stɪrəp] *n* staffa f.

stitch [stɪtʃ] *n (in sewing, knitting)* punto m; **to have a ~** *(stomach pain)* avere una fitta ◻ **stitches** *npl (for wound)* punti *mpl*.

stock [stɒk] *n (of shop, business)* stock m *inv; (supply)* scorta f; *(FIN)* azioni *fpl; (in cooking)* brodo m; **in ~** *(have in stock)* avere in magazzino; **in ~** in magazzino; **out of ~** esaurito.

stock cube *n* dado m (per brodo).

Stock Exchange *n* Borsa valori.

stocking ['stɒkɪŋ] *n* calza f.

stock market n borsa f valori.

stodgy ['stɒdʒɪ] adj (food) pesante.

stole [stəʊl] pt → **steal**.

stolen ['stəʊln] pp → **steal**.

stomach ['stʌmək] n (organ) stomaco m; (belly) pancia f.

stomachache ['stʌməkeɪk] n mal m di stomaco.

stomach upset [-'ʌpset] n disturbo m di stomaco.

stone [stəʊn] n (substance) pietra f; (in fruit) nocciolo m; (measurement: pl inv) = 6,35 kg; (gem) pietra preziosa ♦ adj di pietra.

stonewashed ['stəʊnwɒʃt] adj délavé (inv).

stood [stʊd] pt & pp → **stand**.

stool [stuːl] n (for sitting on) sgabello m.

stop [stɒp] n (for bus, train) fermata f; (in journey) tappa f ♦ vt (cause to cease) porre fine a; (car, machine) fermare; (prevent) impedire ♦ vi fermarsi; **to ~ sb/sthg from doing sthg** impedire a qn/qc di fare qc; **to ~ doing sthg** smettere di fare qc; **to put a ~ to sthg** porre fine a qc; '**stop**' (road sign) 'stop'; '**stopping at ...**' (train, bus) 'ferma a ...' □ **stop off** vi fare una sosta.

stopover ['stɒp,əʊvə^r] n sosta f.

stopper ['stɒpə^r] n tappo m.

stopwatch ['stɒpwɒtʃ] n cronografo m.

storage ['stɔːrɪdʒ] n immagazzinaggio m.

store [stɔː^r] n (shop) negozio m; (supply) scorta f ♦ vt immagazzinare.

storehouse ['stɔːhaʊs, pl -haʊzɪz] n magazzino m.

storeroom ['stɔːrʊm] n stanzino m.

storey ['stɔːrɪ] (pl -s) n (Br) piano m.

stork [stɔːk] n cicogna f.

storm [stɔːm] n tempesta f.

stormy ['stɔːmɪ] adj (weather) burrascoso(-a).

story ['stɔːrɪ] n (account, tale) storia f; (news item) notizia f; (Am) = **storey**.

stout [staʊt] adj (fat) corpulento(-a) ♦ n (drink) birra f scura.

stove [stəʊv] n (for cooking) cucina f; (for heating) stufa f.

straight [streɪt] adj (not curved) diritto(-a); (hair, drink) liscio(-a); (consecutive) di seguito ♦ adv (in a straight line) dritto; (upright) in posizione eretta; (directly, without delay) direttamente; **~ ahead** sempre diritto; **~ away** subito.

straightforward [,streɪt'fɔːwəd] adj (easy) semplice.

strain [streɪn] n (force) sforzo m; (tension, nervous stress) tensione f; (injury) distorsione f ♦ vt (muscle, eyes) sforzare; (food) scolare; (tea) filtrare.

strainer ['streɪnə^r] n colino m.

strait [streɪt] n stretto m.

strange [streɪndʒ] adj (unusual) strano(-a); (unfamiliar) sconosciuto(-a).

stranger ['streɪndʒə^r] n (unfamiliar person) sconosciuto m (-a f); (person from different place) forestiero m (-a f).

strangle ['stræŋgl] vt strangolare.

strap [stræp] n (of bag, camera) tracolla f; (of watch, shoe) cinturino m; (of dress) bretella f.

strapless ['stræplɪs] adj senza
spalline.
strategy ['strætɪdʒɪ] n (plan)
strategia f.
Stratford-upon-Avon [stræt-
fədəpɒn'eɪvn] n Stratford-upon-
Avon.

---

i **STRATFORD-UPON-AVON**

Questa cittadina nella contea del
Warwickshire è famosa per
aver dato i natali al grande dramma-
turgo e poeta William Shakespeare
(1564-1616). Oggi è un importante
centro del teatro britannico e sede
della Royal Shakespeare Company,
che vi allestisce opere di Shakespeare e di altri drammaturghi.

---

straw [strɔ:] n paglia f; (for drinking) cannuccia f.
strawberry ['strɔ:bərɪ] n fragola
f.
stray [streɪ] adj (animal) randa-
gio(-a) ◆ vi vagare.
streak [stri:k] n (stripe, mark)
striscia f; (period) periodo m.
stream [stri:m] n (river) ruscello
m; (of traffic, people, blood) flusso m.
street [stri:t] n via f, strada f.
streetcar ['stri:tkɑ:ʳ] n (Am)
tram m inv.
street light n lampione m.
street plan n piantina f.
strength [streŋθ] n forza f; (of
structure) robustezza f; (influence)
potere m; (strong point) punto m di
forza; (of feeling, smell) intensità f;
(of drink) gradazione f alcolica.
strengthen ['streŋθn] vt (structure) rafforzare.
stress [stres] n (tension) stress m

inv; (on word, syllable) accento m ◆
vt (emphasize) sottolineare; (word,
syllable) accentare.
stretch [stretʃ] n (of land, water)
distesa f; (of time) periodo m ◆ vt
tendere; (body) stirare ◆ vi (land,
sea) estendersi; (person, animal) sti-
rarsi; **to ~ one's legs** (fig) sgranchirsi le gambe ❑ **stretch out** vt sep
(hand) tendere ◆ vi (lie down) distendersi.
stretcher ['stretʃəʳ] n barella f.
strict [strɪkt] adj (person) seve-
ro(-a); (rule, instructions) rigido(-a);
(exact) stretto(-a).
strictly ['strɪktlɪ] adv strettamente; **~ speaking** per essere pre-
cisi.
stride [straɪd] n falcata f.
strike [straɪk] (pt & pp struck) n
(of employees) sciopero m ◆ vt (fml:
hit) colpire; (fml: collide with) urtare;
(a match) accendere ◆ vi (refuse to
work) scioperare; (happen suddenly)
colpire; **the clock struck eight**
l'orologio ha battuto le otto.
striking ['straɪkɪŋ] adj (noticeable)
impressionante; (attractive) appariscente.
string [strɪŋ] n spago m; (of
pearls, beads) filo m; (of musical instrument, tennis racket) corda f;
(series) serie f inv; **a piece of ~** un
pezzo di spago.
strip [strɪp] n striscia f ◆ vt (pain,
wallpaper) togliere ◆ vi (undress)
spogliarsi.
stripe [straɪp] n striscia f.
striped [straɪpt] adj a strisce.
strip-search vt perquisi
(facendo spogliare).
strip show n spogliarello m.
stroke [strəʊk] n (MED) colpo

(in tennis) battuta *f; (in golf)* tiro *m; (swimming style)* stile *m* ♦ *vt* accarezzare; **a ~ of luck** un colpo di fortuna.

stroll [strəʊl] *n* passeggiata *f.*

stroller ['strəʊlə*r*] *n (Am: pushchair)* passeggino *m.*

strong [strɒŋ] *adj* forte; *(structure, bridge, chair)* robusto(-a); *(feeling, smell)* intenso(-a).

struck [strʌk] *pt & pp* → **strike**.

structure ['strʌktʃə*r*] *n* struttura *f.*

struggle ['strʌgl] *n (great effort)* sforzo *m* ♦ *vi (fight)* lottare; *(in order to get free)* divincolarsi; **to ~ to do sthg** sforzarsi di fare qc.

stub [stʌb] *n (of cigarette)* mozzicone *m; (of cheque, ticket)* matrice *f.*

stubble ['stʌbl] *n (on face)* barba *f* ispida.

stubborn ['stʌbən] *adj (person)* ostinato(-a).

stuck [stʌk] *pt & pp* → **stick** ♦ *adj (jammed)* incastrato(-a); *(unable to continue, stranded)* bloccato(-a).

stud [stʌd] *n (on boots)* borchia *f; (fastener)* bottone *m* automatico; *(earring)* miniorecchino *m.*

student ['stju:dnt] *n* studente *m* (-essa *f*).

student card *n* carta *f* dello studente.

students' union [,stju:dnts-] *n (place)* circolo *m* studentesco.

studio ['stju:dɪəʊ] *(pl -s) n* studio *m.*

studio apartment *(Am) =* **studio flat**.

studio flat *n (Br)* miniappartamento *m.*

study ['stʌdɪ] *n (learning)* studio *m* ♦ *vt & vi* studiare.

stuff [stʌf] *n (inf)* roba *f* ♦ *vt (put roughly)* ficcare; *(fill)* riempire.

stuffed [stʌft] *adj (food)* ripieno(-a); *(inf: full up)* pieno(-a); *(dead animal)* imbalsamato(-a).

stuffing ['stʌfɪŋ] *n (food)* ripieno *m; (of pillow, cushion)* imbottitura *f.*

stuffy ['stʌfɪ] *adj (room, atmosphere)* che sa di chiuso.

stumble ['stʌmbl] *vi (when walking)* inciampare.

stump [stʌmp] *n (of tree)* ceppo *m.*

stun [stʌn] *vt (shock)* sbalordire.

stung [stʌŋ] *pt & pp* → **sting**.

stunk [stʌŋk] *pt & pp* → **stink**.

stunning ['stʌnɪŋ] *adj (very beautiful)* favoloso(-a); *(very surprising)* sbalorditivo(-a).

stupid ['stju:pɪd] *adj* stupido(-a).

sturdy ['stɜ:dɪ] *adj* robusto(-a).

stutter ['stʌtə*r*] *vi* balbettare.

sty [staɪ] *n (pigsty)* porcile *m; (on eye)* orzaiolo *m.*

style [staɪl] *n* stile *m* ♦ *vt (hair)* acconciare.

stylish ['staɪlɪʃ] *adj* elegante.

stylist ['staɪlɪst] *n (hairdresser)* acconciatore *m* (-trice *f*).

sub [sʌb] *n (inf) (substitute)* riserva *f; (Br: subscription)* quota *f* (d'iscrizione).

subdued [səb'dju:d] *adj (person)* abbacchiato(-a); *(lighting, colour)* smorzato(-a).

subject [*n* 'sʌbdʒekt, *vb* səb'dʒekt] *n (topic)* argomento *m; (at school, university)* materia *f; (GRAMM)* soggetto *m; (fml: of country)* cittadino *m* (-a *f*) ♦ *vt:* **to ~ sb to sthg** sottoporre qn a qc; **'~ to availability'** 'fino ad esaurimento'; **they are ~ to an additional charge** sono suscettibili di soprapprezzo.

subjunctive [səb'dʒʌŋktɪv] *n* congiuntivo *m*.

submarine [ˌsʌbmə'riːn] *n* sottomarino *m*.

submit [səb'mɪt] *vt* presentare ♦ *vi* sottomettersi.

subordinate [sə'bɔːdɪnət] *adj* subordinato(-a).

subscribe [səb'skraɪb] *vi* (to magazine, newspaper) abbonarsi.

subscription [səb'skrɪpʃn] *n* abbonamento *m*.

subsequent [ˈsʌbsɪkwənt] *adj* successivo(-a).

subside [səb'saɪd] *vi* (ground) cedere; (noise, feeling) smorzarsi.

substance [ˈsʌbstəns] *n* sostanza *f*.

substantial [səb'stænʃl] *adj* (large) sostanziale.

substitute [ˈsʌbstɪtjuːt] *n* (person) sostituto *m* (-a *f*); (thing) surrogato *m*; (SPORT) riserva *f*.

subtitles [ˈsʌbˌtaɪtlz] *npl* sottotitoli *mpl*.

subtle [ˈsʌtl] *adj* (difference, change) sottile; (person, plan) astuto(-a).

subtract [səb'trækt] *vt* sottrarre.

subtraction [səb'trækʃn] *n* sottrazione *f*.

suburb [ˈsʌbɜːb] *n* sobborgo *m*; the ~s la periferia.

subway [ˈsʌbweɪ] *n* (Br: for pedestrians) sottopassaggio *m*; (Am: underground railway) metropolitana *f*.

succeed [sək'siːd] *vi* (be successful) avere successo ♦ *vt* (fml: follow) succedere a; to ~ in doing sthg riuscire a fare qc.

success [sək'ses] *n* successo *m*.

successful [sək'sesful] *adj* (plan, attempt) riuscito(-a); (film, book, politician) di successo; to be ~ (person) riuscire.

succulent [ˈsʌkjʊlənt] *adj* succulento(-a).

such [sʌtʃ] *adj* tale ♦ *adv*: ~ a lot così tanto; it's ~ a lovely day è una giornata così bella; ~ good luck una tale fortuna; ~ a thing should never have happened una cosa simile non sarebbe mai dovuta accadere; ~ as come.

suck [sʌk] *vt* succhiare.

sudden [ˈsʌdn] *adj* improvviso(-a); all of a ~ all'improvviso.

suddenly [ˈsʌdnlɪ] *adv* improvvisamente.

sue [suː] *vt* citare in giudizio.

suede [sweɪd] *n* pelle *f* scamosciata.

suffer [ˈsʌfər] *vt* (defeat, injury) subire ♦ *vi* soffrire; to ~ from (illness) soffrire di.

suffering [ˈsʌfrɪŋ] *n* sofferenza *f*.

sufficient [sə'fɪʃnt] *adj* (fml) sufficiente.

sufficiently [sə'fɪʃntlɪ] *adv* (fml) sufficientemente.

suffix [ˈsʌfɪks] *n* suffisso *m*.

suffocate [ˈsʌfəkeɪt] *vi* soffocare.

sugar [ˈʃʊɡər] *n* zucchero *m*.

suggest [sə'dʒest] *vt* suggerire; to ~ doing sthg suggerire di fare qc.

suggestion [sə'dʒestʃn] *n* (proposal) suggerimento *m*; (hint, accenno *m*.

suicide [ˈsuːɪsaɪd] *n* suicidio *m*; to commit ~ suicidarsi.

suit [suːt] *n* (clothes) completo *m* (in cards) seme *m*; (JUR) causa *f* ♦ *vt*

(subj: clothes, colour, shoes) star bene
a; *(be convenient for)* andare bene a;
(be appropriate for) addirsi a; **to be
~ed to** essere adatto a.

suitable ['su:təbl] *adj* adatto(-a);
to be ~ for essere adatto a.

suitcase ['su:tkeɪs] *n* valigia f.

suite [swi:t] *n (set of rooms)* suite f
inv; (furniture): **a three-piece ~** un
divano e due poltrone *(coordinati)*.

sulk [sʌlk] *vi* mettere il broncio.

sultana [sʌl'tɑ:nə] *n (Br)* uva f
sultanina.

sultry ['sʌltrɪ] *adj (weather, climate)* caldo umido (calda umida).

sum [sʌm] *n* somma f □ **sum up**
vt sep riassumere.

summarize ['sʌməraɪz] *vt* riassumere.

summary ['sʌmərɪ] *n* riassunto m.

summer ['sʌməʳ] *n* estate f; **in
(the) ~** d'estate; **~ holidays** vacanze fpl estive.

summertime ['sʌmətaɪm] *n*
estate f.

summit ['sʌmɪt] *n (of mountain)*
cima f; *(meeting)* summit m inv.

summon ['sʌmən] *vt (send for)*
convocare; *(JUR)* citare.

sumptuous ['sʌmptʃʊəs] *adj*
sontuoso(-a).

sun [sʌn] *n* sole m ♦ *vt:* **to ~ o.s.**
prendere il sole; **to catch the ~**
prendere il sole; **in the ~** al sole;
out of the ~ al riparo dal sole.

Sun. *(abbr of Sunday)* dom.

sunbathe ['sʌnbeɪð] *vi* prendere
il sole.

sunbed ['sʌnbed] *n* lettino m.

sun block *n* crema f solare a
protezione totale.

sunburn ['sʌnbɜ:n] *n* scottatura f.

sunburnt ['sʌnbɜ:nt] *adj* scotta-
to(-a).

sundae ['sʌndeɪ] *n* gelato m guarnito
con frutta o cioccolato, nocciole e panna
montata.

Sunday ['sʌndɪ] *n* domenica f, →
Saturday.

Sunday school *n* = scuola f di
catechismo.

sundress ['sʌndres] *n* prendisole
m inv.

sundries ['sʌndrɪz] *npl (on bill)*
varie fpl.

sunflower ['sʌnˌflaʊəʳ] *n* girasole m.

sunflower oil *n* olio m di semi
di girasole.

sung [sʌŋ] *pt* → **sing**.

sunglasses ['sʌnˌglɑ:sɪz] *npl*
occhiali mpl da sole.

sunhat ['sʌnhæt] *n* cappello m
(per il sole).

sunk [sʌŋk] *pp* → **sink**.

sunlight ['sʌnlaɪt] *n* luce f del
sole.

sun lounger [-ˌlaʊndʒəʳ] *n
(chair)* lettino m.

sunny ['sʌnɪ] *adj (day)* di sole;
(weather) bello(-a); *(room, place)*
soleggiato(-a); **it's ~** c'è il sole.

sunrise ['sʌnraɪz] *n* alba f.

sunroof ['sʌnru:f] *n* tettuccio m
apribile.

sunset ['sʌnset] *n* tramonto m.

sunshine ['sʌnʃaɪn] *n* luce f del
sole; **in the ~** al sole.

sunstroke ['sʌnstrəʊk] *n* insolazione f.

suntan ['sʌntæn] *n* abbronzatura f.

suntan cream *n* crema f
abbronzante.

suntan lotion *n* lozione f

abbronzante.

super ['suːpə[r]] *adj* fantastico(-a)
♦ *n* (petrol) super *f* inv.

superb [suːˈpəːb] *adj* splendido(-a).

superficial [ˌsuːpəˈfɪʃl] *adj* superficiale.

superfluous [suːˈpəːfluəs] *adj* superfluo(-a).

Superglue® ['suːpəgluː] *n* colla *f* a presa rapida.

superior [suːˈpɪərɪə[r]] *adj* superiore ♦ *n* superiore *mf*.

supermarket ['suːpəˌmɑːkɪt] *n* supermercato *m*.

supernatural [ˌsuːpəˈnætʃrəl] *adj* soprannaturale.

Super Saver® *n* (Br: rail ticket) *biglietto ferroviario a tariffa ridotta, con condizioni particolari.*

superstitious [ˌsuːpəˈstɪʃəs] *adj* superstizioso(-a).

superstore ['suːpəstɔː[r]] *n* grande supermercato *m*.

supervise ['suːpəvaɪz] *vt* sorvegliare.

supervisor ['suːpəvaɪzə[r]] *n* (of workers) sovrintendente *mf*.

supper ['sʌpə[r]] *n* (evening meal) cena *f*; (before bed) spuntino *m*.

supple ['sʌpl] *adj* agile.

supplement [*n* 'sʌplɪmənt, *vb* 'sʌplɪment] *n* supplemento *m*; (of diet) integratore *m* alimentare ♦ *vt* integrare.

supplementary [ˌsʌplɪˈmentəri] *adj* supplementare.

supply [səˈplaɪ] *n* (store) scorta *f*; (providing) approvvigionamento *m*; (of electricity, gas etc) erogazione *f* ♦ *vt* fornire; **to ~ sb with sthg** fornire qc a qn □ **supplies** *npl* scorte *fpl*.

support [səˈpɔːt] *n* (for cause, candidate) appoggio *m*; (object, encouragement) sostegno *m* ♦ *vt* (cause, campaign, person) appoggiare; (SPORT) tifare per; (hold up) sostenere; (financially) mantenere.

supporter [səˈpɔːtə[r]] *n* (SPORT) tifoso *m* (-a *f*); (of cause, political party) sostenitore *m* (-trice *f*).

suppose [səˈpəuz] *vt* (assume, imagine); (think) credere ♦ *conj* = **supposing**; **I ~ so** penso di sì; **you were ~d to be home at six o'clock** dovevate essere a casa all[...] sei; **it's ~d to be the best** è ritenu[...] to il migliore.

supposing [səˈpəuzɪŋ] *conj* supponendo che.

supreme [suˈpriːm] *adj* eccezio[...] nale.

surcharge ['sɜːtʃɑːdʒ] *n* sovra[...] prezzo *m*.

sure [ʃuə[r]] *adj* sicuro(-a) ♦ *a[...]* (inf: yes) certo!; (Am: inf: certain[...] certamente; **to be ~ of o.s.** esser[...] sicuro di sé; **to make ~ that** [...] assicurarsi che ...; **for ~** di sicur[...]

surely ['ʃuəlɪ] *adv* sicuramente.

surf [sɜːf] *n* (foam) spuma *f* ♦ *v[...]* fare surf.

surface ['sɜːfɪs] *n* superficie *f*.

surface area *n* superfic[...] (esterna).

surface mail *n* posta *f* ord[...] ria.

surfboard ['sɜːfbɔːd] *n* tavo[...] da surf.

surfing ['sɜːfɪŋ] *n* surf *m*; **to** [...] andare a fare surf.

surgeon ['sɜːdʒən] *n* chirurg[...]

surgery ['sɜːdʒərɪ] *n* (treat[...] chirurgia *f*; (Br: building) ambu[...] rio *m*; (Br: period) orario *m* d'a[...]

latorio.

surname ['sɜːneɪm] n cognome m.

surplus ['sɜːpləs] n eccedenza f.

surprise [sə'praɪz] n sorpresa f ◆ vt sorprendere.

surprised [sə'praɪzd] adj sorpreso(-a).

surprising [sə'praɪzɪŋ] adj sorprendente.

surrender [sə'rendə'] vi arrendersi ◆ vt (fml: hand over) consegnare.

surround [sə'raʊnd] vt circondare.

surrounding [sə'raʊndɪŋ] adj circostante □ **surroundings** npl dintorni mpl.

survey ['sɜːveɪ] n (investigation) studio m; (poll) sondaggio m; (of land) rilevamento m (topografico); (Br: of house) sopralluogo m.

surveyor [sə'veɪə'] n (Br: of houses) perito m; (of land) agrimensore m.

survival [sə'vaɪvl] n sopravvivenza f.

survive [sə'vaɪv] vi sopravvivere ◆ vt sopravvivere a.

survivor [sə'vaɪvə'] n sopravvissuto m (-a f).

suspect [vb sə'spekt, n & adj 'sʌspekt] vt sospettare ◆ n sospetto ◆ adj sospetto(-a); **to ~ sb of sthg** sospettare qn di qc.

suspend [sə'spend] vt sospendere.

suspender belt [sə'spendə-] n gigalze m inv.

suspenders [sə'spendəz] npl (Br: stockings) giarrettiere fpl; (Am: trousers) bretelle fpl.

suspense [sə'spens] n suspense f.

suspension [sə'spenʃn] n so-

spensione f.

suspicion [sə'spɪʃn] n (mistrust, idea) sospetto m; (trace) accenno m.

suspicious [sə'spɪʃəs] adj (behaviour, situation) sospetto(-a); **to be ~ of** (distrustful) sospettare di.

swallow ['swɒləʊ] n (bird) rondine f ◆ vt & vi ingoiare.

swam [swæm] pt → **swim**.

swamp [swɒmp] n palude f.

swan [swɒn] n cigno m.

swap [swɒp] vt (possessions, places) scambiare; (ideas, stories) scambiarsi; **to ~ sthg for sthg** scambiare qc con qc.

swarm [swɔːm] n (of bees) sciame m.

swear [sweə'] (pt **swore**, pp **sworn**) vi (use rude language) imprecare; (promise) giurare ◆ vt: **to ~ to do sthg** promettere di fare qc.

swearword ['sweəwɜːd] n parolaccia f.

sweat [swet] n sudore m ◆ vi sudare.

sweater ['swetə'] n maglione m.

sweatshirt ['swetʃɜːt] n felpa f.

swede [swiːd] n (Br) rapa f svedese.

Swede [swiːd] n svedese mf.

Sweden ['swiːdn] n la Svezia.

Swedish ['swiːdɪʃ] adj svedese ◆ n (language) svedese m ◆ npl: **the ~** gli svedesi.

sweep [swiːp] (pt & pp **swept**) vt (with brush, broom) scopare.

sweet [swiːt] adj dolce; (kind) gentile, carino(-a) ◆ n (Br) (candy) caramella f; (dessert) dolce m.

sweet-and-sour adj (pork) in agrodolce; (sauce) agrodolce.

sweet corn n granturco m.

sweetener ['swiːtnə'] n (for

drink) dolcificante *m*.

sweet potato *n* patata *f* americana.

sweet shop *n* (Br) negozio *m* di dolciumi.

swell [swel] (*pp* **swollen**) *vi* (*ankle, arm etc*) gonfiarsi.

swelling ['swelɪŋ] *n* gonfiore *m*.

swept [swept] *pt & pp* → **sweep**.

swerve [swɜːv] *vi* (*vehicle*) sterzare.

swig [swɪg] *n* (*inf*) sorsata *f*.

swim [swɪm] (*pt* **swam**, *pp* **swum**) *n* nuotata *f*, bagno *m* ♦ *vi* (*in water*) nuotare; **to go for a** ~ andare a fare il bagno.

swimmer ['swɪmə^r] *n* nuotatore *m* (-trice *f*).

swimming ['swɪmɪŋ] *n* nuoto *m*; **to go** ~ andare in piscina.

swimming baths *npl* (Br) piscina *f* coperta.

swimming cap *n* cuffia *f*.

swimming costume *n* (Br) costume *m* da bagno.

swimming pool *n* piscina *f*.

swimming trunks *npl* costume *m* da bagno (*da uomo*).

swimsuit ['swɪmsuːt] *n* costume *m* da bagno.

swindle ['swɪndl] *n* truffa *f*.

swing [swɪŋ] (*pt & pp* **swung**) *n* (*for children*) altalena *f* ♦ *vt & vi* (*from side to side*) dondolare.

swipe [swaɪp] *vt* (*credit card etc*) far passare nel lettore magnetico.

Swiss [swɪs] *adj* svizzero(-a) ♦ *n* (*person*) svizzero *m* (-a *f*) ♦ *npl*: **the** ~ gli svizzeri.

Swiss cheese *n* formaggio *m* svizzero.

swiss roll *n* rotolo *m* di pan di Spagna farcito di marmellata.

switch [swɪtʃ] *n* (*for light, power, television set*) interruttore *m* ♦ *vt* (*change*) cambiare; (*exchange*) scambiare ♦ *vi* cambiare ❑ **switch off** *vt sep* spegnere; **switch on** *vt sep* accendere.

switchboard ['swɪtʃbɔːd] *n* centralino *m*.

Switzerland ['swɪtsələnd] *n* la Svizzera.

swivel ['swɪvl] *vi* girarsi.

swollen ['swəʊln] *pp* → **swell** ♦ *adj* (*ankle, arm etc*) gonfio(-a).

swop [swɒp] = **swap**.

sword [sɔːd] *n* spada *f*.

swordfish ['sɔːdfɪʃ] (*pl inv*) *n* pesce *m* spada.

swore [swɔː^r] *pt* → **swear**.

sworn [swɔːn] *pp* → **swear**.

swum [swʌm] *pp* → **swim**.

swung [swʌŋ] *pt & pp* → **swing**.

syllable ['sɪləbl] *n* sillaba *f*.

syllabus ['sɪləbəs] *n* programma *m*

symbol ['sɪmbl] *n* simbolo *m*.

sympathetic [,sɪmpə'θetɪk] *a* (*understanding*) comprensivo(-a).

sympathize ['sɪmpəθaɪz] *vi*: ~ **(with)** (*feel sorry*) provare com passione (per); (*understand*) capir

sympathy ['sɪmpəθɪ] *n* (*unde standing*) comprensione *f*.

symphony ['sɪmfənɪ] *n* sinfonia

symptom ['sɪmptəm] *n* sintomo

synagogue ['sɪnəgɒg] *n* sinag ga *f*.

synthesizer ['sɪnθəsaɪzə^r] *n* s tetizzatore *m*.

synthetic [sɪn'θetɪk] *adj* sint co(-a).

syringe [sɪ'rɪndʒ] *n* siringa *f*.

syrup ['sɪrəp] n (for fruit etc) sciroppo m.

system ['sɪstəm] n sistema m; (hi-fi, computer, for heating etc) impianto m.

ta [tɑ:] excl (Br: inf) grazie!

tab [tæb] n (of cloth, paper etc) etichetta f; (bill) conto m; **put it on my ~** lo metta sul mio conto.

table ['teɪbl] n (piece of furniture) tavolo m; (of figures etc) tavola f.

tablecloth ['teɪblklɒθ] n tovaglia f.

tablemat ['teɪblmæt] n sottopiatto m.

tablespoon ['teɪblspu:n] n cucchiaio m da tavola.

tablet ['tæblɪt] n (pill) compressa f; (of chocolate) tavoletta f; **~ of soap** saponetta f.

table tennis n ping-pong® m.

table wine n vino m da tavola.

tabloid ['tæblɔɪd] n tabloid m inv.

tack [tæk] n (nail) puntina f.

tackle ['tækl] n (in football) tackle m (in rugby) placcaggio m; (for fishing) attrezzatura f ♦ vt (in football) contrastare; (in rugby) placcare; (deal with) affrontare.

tacky ['tæki] adj (inf: jewellery, design etc) pacchiano(-a).

taco ['tækəʊ] n (pl **-s**) n taco m piadicciatina a base di farina di grano farcita di carne o fagioli, tipica della cucina messicana.

tact [tækt] n tatto m.

tactful ['tæktful] adj discreto(-a).

tactics ['tæktɪks] npl tattica f.

tag [tæg] n (label) etichetta f.

tagliatelle [ˌtægljə'teli] n tagliatelle fpl.

tail [teɪl] n coda f □ **tails** n (of coin) croce f ♦ npl (formal dress) frac m inv.

tailgate ['teɪlgeɪt] n (of car) portellone m.

tailor ['teɪləʳ] n sarto m.

Taiwan [ˌtaɪ'wɑːn] n Taiwan f.

take [teɪk] (pt **took**, pp **taken**) vt
1. (gen) prendere.
2. (carry, drive) portare.
3. (do, make) fare; **to ~ a bath/shower** fare un bagno/una doccia; **to ~ an exam** OR **sustenere un esame**; **to ~ a decision** prendere una decisione.
4. (time, effort) volerci, richiedere; **how long will it ~?** quanto ci vorrà?; **it won't ~ long** non ci vorrà molto tempo.
5. (size in clothes, shoes) portare, avere; **what size do you ~?** (clothes) che taglia porta?; (shoes) che misura porta?
6. (subtract) sottrarre, togliere.
7. (accept) accettare; **do you ~ traveller's cheques?** accettate traveller's cheques?; **to ~ sb's advice** seguire il consiglio di qn.
8. (contain) contenere.
9. (control, power) assumere; **to ~ charge of** assumere la direzione di.
10. (tolerate) sopportare.
11. (assume) **I ~ it that ...** suppongo che ...
12. (rent) prendere in affitto. □ **take apart** vt sep (dismantle) smontare; **take away** vt sep (re-

move) portare via; *(subtract)* togliere; **take back** vt sep *(return)* riportare; *(statement)* ritrattare; **take down** vt sep *(picture, decorations)* togliere; **take in** vt sep *(include)* includere; *(understand)* capire; *(deceive)* abbindolare; *(clothes)* restringere; **take off** vi *(plane)* decollare ◆ vt sep *(remove)* togliere; *(as holiday)*: **to ~ a week off** prendere una settimana di ferie; **take out** vt sep *(from container, pocket)* tirare fuori; *(loan, insurance policy)* ottenere; *(go out with)* portare fuori; **take over** vi assumere il comando; vt sep **to ~** prendere le consegne da qn; **take up** vt sep *(hobby)* dedicarsi a; *(use up)* prendere; *(trousers, dress)* accorciare.

takeaway ['teɪkəweɪ] n *(Br)* *(shop) locale che prepara piatti pronti da asporto; (food) cibo m da asporto.*

taken ['teɪkn] pp → **take**.

takeoff ['teɪkɒf] n *(of plane)* decollo m.

takeout ['teɪkaʊt] *(Am)* = **takeaway**.

takings ['teɪkɪŋz] npl incasso m.

talcum powder ['tælkəm-] n borotalco® m.

tale [teɪl] n *(story)* storia f; *(account)* racconto m.

talent ['tælənt] n talento m.

talk [tɔːk] n *(conversation)* conversazione f; *(speech)* discorso m ◆ vi parlare; **to ~ to sb (about sthg)** parlare con qn (di qc); **to ~ with sb** parlare con qn ◆ **talks** npl negoziati mpl.

talkative ['tɔːkətɪv] adj loquace.

tall [tɔːl] adj alto(-a); **how ~ are you?** quanto sei alto?; **I'm five and a half feet ~** sono alto un

metro e 65.

tame [teɪm] adj *(animal)* addomesticato(-a).

tampon ['tæmpɒn] n tampone m.

tan [tæn] n *(suntan)* abbronzatura f ◆ vi abbronzarsi ◆ adj *(colour)* marrone chiaro *(inv)*.

tangerine [,tændʒə'riːn] n *(fruit)* mandarino m.

tank [tæŋk] n *(container)* serbatoio m; *(vehicle)* carro m armato.

tanker ['tæŋkə'] n *(truck)* autocisterna f.

tanned [tænd] adj *(suntanned)* abbronzato(-a).

tap [tæp] n *(for water)* rubinetto m ◆ vt *(hit)* dare un colpetto a.

tape [teɪp] n *(cassette, video)* cassetta f; *(in cassette)* nastro m; *(adhesive material)* nastro m adesivo; *(strip of material)* fettuccia f ◆ vt *(record)* registrare; *(stick)* attaccare con nastro adesivo.

tape measure n metro m.

tape recorder n registratore m.

tapestry ['tæpɪstrɪ] n arazzo m.

tap water n acqua f di rubinetto.

tar [tɑː'] n *(for roads)* catrame m; *(in cigarettes)* condensato m.

target ['tɑːgɪt] n bersaglio m.

tariff ['tærɪf] n *(price list)* tariffario m; *(Br: menu)* listino m prezzi; *(customs)* tariffa f doganale.

tarmac ['tɑːmæk] n *(at airport)* pista f □ **Tarmac**® n *(on road)* asfalto m.

tarpaulin [tɑː'pɔːlɪn] n telone m.

tart [tɑːt] n *(sweet)* crostata f.

tartan ['tɑːtn] n *(design)* scozzese m; *(cloth)* tartan m.

tartare sauce [,tɑːtə-] n sals

tartara.

task [tɑ:sk] *n* compito *m*.

taste [teɪst] *n* gusto *m*; *(flavour)* gusto, sapore *m* ◆ *vt* *(sample)* assaggiare; *(detect)* sentire il gusto di ◆ *vi*: **to ~ of sthg** sapere di qc; **it ~s bad** ha un cattivo sapore; **it ~s good** ha un buon sapore; **to have a ~ of sthg** *(food, drink)* assaggiare qc; *(fig: experience)* provare qc; **bad ~** cattivo gusto; **good ~** buon gusto.

tasteful ['teɪstful] *adj* di buon gusto.

tasteless ['teɪstlɪs] *adj* *(food)* insipido(-a); *(comment, decoration)* di cattivo gusto.

tasty ['teɪstɪ] *adj* gustoso(-a).

tattoo [tə'tu:] *(pl* **-s**) *n* *(on skin)* tatuaggio *m*; *(military display)* parata *f*.

taught [tɔ:t] *pt & pp* → **teach**.

Taurus ['tɔ:rəs] *n* Toro *m*.

taut [tɔ:t] *adj* teso(-a).

tax [tæks] *n* *(on income)* imposta *f*, tasse *fpl*; *(on import, goods)* tassa *f* ◆ *vt* *(goods, person)* tassare.

tax disc *n* *(Br)* = bollo *m*.

tax-free *adj* esentasse *(inv)*.

taxi ['tæksɪ] *n* taxi *m inv* ◆ *vi (plane)* rullare.

taxi driver *n* tassista *mf*.

taxi rank *n* *(Br)* posteggio *m* dei taxi.

taxi stand *(Am)* = **taxi rank**.

T-bone steak *n* costata *f* alla fiorentina.

tea [ti:] *n* tè *m inv*; *(evening meal)* cena *f*.

tea bag *n* bustina *f* di tè.

teacake ['ti:keɪk] *n* panino dolce all'uvetta.

teach [ti:tʃ] *(pt & pp* **taught**) *vt* *(subject)* insegnare; *(person)* insegnare a ◆ *vi* insegnare; **to ~ sb sthg, to ~ sthg to sb** insegnare qc a qn; **to ~ sb (how) to do sthg** insegnare a qn a fare qc.

teacher ['ti:tʃə'] *n* insegnante *mf*; *(in primary school)* maestro *m* (-a *f*); *(in secondary school)* professore *m* (-essa *f*).

teaching ['ti:tʃɪŋ] *n* insegnamento *m*.

tea cloth = **tea towel**.

teacup ['ti:kʌp] *n* tazza *f* da tè.

team [ti:m] *n* squadra *f*.

teapot ['ti:ppt] *n* teiera *f*.

tear[1] [teə'] *(pt* **tore**, *pp* **torn**) *vt* *(rip)* strappare ◆ *vi* *(rip)* strapparsi; *(move quickly)* precipitarsi ◆ *n* *(rip)* strappo *m* ❑ **tear up** *vt sep* strappare.

tear[2] [tɪə'] *n* lacrima *f*.

tearoom ['ti:rum] *n* sala *f* da tè.

tease [ti:z] *vt* prendere in giro.

tea set *n* servizio *m* da tè.

teaspoon ['ti:spu:n] *n* cucchiaino *m*.

teaspoonful ['ti:spu:n,ful] *n* cucchiaino *m*.

teat [ti:t] *n* *(of animal)* capezzolo *m*; *(Br: of bottle)* tettarella *f*.

teatime ['ti:taɪm] *n* ora *f* del tè.

tea towel *n* strofinaccio *m*.

technical ['teknɪkl] *adj* tecnico(-a).

technical drawing *n* disegno *m* tecnico.

technicality [,teknɪ'kælətɪ] *n* *(detail)* dettaglio *m* tecnico.

technician [tek'nɪʃn] *n* tecnico *m* (-a *f*).

technique [tek'ni:k] *n* tecnica *f*.

technological [ˌteknəˈlɒdʒɪkl] adj tecnologico(-a).

technology [tekˈnɒlədʒɪ] n tecnologia f.

teddy (bear) [ˈtedɪ-] n orsacchiotto m.

tedious [ˈtiːdjəs] adj noioso(-a).

tee [tiː] n tee m inv.

teenager [ˈtiːnˌeɪdʒəʳ] n adolescente mf.

teeth [tiːθ] pl → tooth.

teethe [tiːð] vi: to be teething mettere i denti.

teetotal [tiːˈtəʊtl] adj astemio(-a).

telegram [ˈtelɪgræm] n telegramma m.

telegraph [ˈtelɪgrɑːf] n telegrafo m ♦ vt telegrafare.

telegraph pole n palo m del telegrafo.

telephone [ˈtelɪfəʊn] n telefono m ♦ vt (person) telefonare a ♦ vi telefonare; **to be on the ~** (talking) essere al telefono; (connected) avere il telefono.

telephone booth n cabina f telefonica.

telephone box n cabina f telefonica.

telephone call n telefonata f.

telephone directory n elenco m telefonico.

telephone number n numero m di telefono.

telephonist [tɪˈlefənɪst] n (Br) centralinista mf.

telephoto lens [ˌtelɪˈfəʊtəʊ-] n teleobiettivo m.

telescope [ˈtelɪskəʊp] n telescopio m.

television [ˈtelɪˌvɪʒn] n televisione f; (set) televisore m; **on (the) ~** (broadcast) alla televisione.

telex [ˈteleks] n telex m inv.

tell [tel] (pt & pp told) vt dire; (story, joke) raccontare; (distinguish) distinguere ♦ vi: **I can ~** si vede; **can you ~ me the time?** sa dirmi l'ora?; **to ~ sb sthg** dire qc a qn; **to ~ sb about sthg** raccontare qc a qn; **to ~ sb how to do sthg** dire a qn come fare qc; **to ~ sb to do sthg** dire a qn di fare qc ❑ **tell off** vt sep rimproverare.

teller [ˈteləʳ] n (in bank) cassiere m (-a f).

telly [ˈtelɪ] n (Br: inf) tele f.

temp [temp] n impiegato m straordinario (impiegata f straordinaria) ♦ vi avere un impiego temporaneo.

temper [ˈtempəʳ] n (character) carattere m; **to be in a ~** essere in collera; **to lose one's ~** andare in collera.

temperature [ˈtemprətʃəʳ] n temperatura f; **to have a ~** avere la febbre.

temple [ˈtempl] n (building) tempio m; (of forehead) tempia f.

temporary [ˈtempərərɪ] adj temporaneo(-a).

tempt [tempt] vt tentare; **to be ~ed to do sthg** essere tentato di fare qc.

temptation [tempˈteɪʃn] n tentazione f.

tempting [ˈtemptɪŋ] adj allettante.

ten [ten] num dieci, → six.

tenant [ˈtenənt] n inquilino m (-f).

tend [tend] vi: **to ~ to do sthg** tendere a fare qc.

tendency ['tendənsı] *n* tendenza *f*.

tender ['tendə*r*] *adj* tenero(-a); (sore) dolorante ♦ *vt* (fml: pay) presentare.

tendon ['tendən] *n* tendine *m*.

tenement ['tenəmənt] *n* caseggiato *m*.

tennis ['tenıs] *n* tennis *m*.

tennis ball *n* palla *f* da tennis.

tennis court *n* campo *m* da tennis.

tennis racket *n* racchetta *f* da tennis.

tenpin bowling ['tenpın-] (Br) bowling *m*.

tenpins ['tenpınz] (Am) = **tenpin bowling**.

tense [tens] *adj* teso(-a) ♦ *n* (GRAMM) tempo *m*.

tension ['tenʃn] *n* tensione *f*.

tent [tent] *n* tenda *f*.

tenth [tenθ] *num* decimo(-a), → **sixth**.

tent peg *n* picchetto *m* da tenda.

tepid ['tepıd] *adj* (water) tiepido(-a).

tequila [tı'ki:lə] *n* tequila *f*.

term [tɜ:m] *n* (word, expression) termine *m*; (at school, university) trimestre *m*; **in the long ~** a lungo andare; **in the short ~** a breve scadenza; **in ~s of** per quanto riguarda; **in business ~s** al punto di vista commerciale □ **terms** *npl* (of contract) condizioni *f pl*.

terminal ['tɜ:mınl] *adj* (illness) terminale ♦ *n* (for buses) capolinea *m*; (at airport) terminal *m inv*; (COMPUT) terminale *m*.

terminate ['tɜ:mıneıt] *vi* (train, bus) fare capolinea.

terminus ['tɜ:mınəs] *n* (of buses) capolinea *m*; (of trains) stazione *f* terminale.

terrace ['terəs] *n* (patio) terrazza *f*; **the ~s** (at football ground) le gradinate.

terraced house ['terəst-] *n* (Br) casa *f* a schiera.

terrible ['terəbl] *adj* terribile; (very ill): **to feel ~** stare malissimo.

terribly ['terəblı] *adv* (extremely) terribilmente; (very badly) malissimo.

terrier ['terə*r*] *n* terrier *m inv*.

terrific [tə'rıfık] *adj* (inf) (very good) fantastico(-a); (very great) grande.

terrified ['terıfaıd] *adj* terrorizzato(-a).

territory ['terətrı] *n* (political area) territorio *m*; (terrain) terreno *m*.

terror ['terə*r*] *n* terrore *m*.

terrorism ['terərızm] *n* terrorismo *m*.

terrorist ['terərıst] *n* terrorista *mf*.

terrorize ['terəraız] *vt* terrorizzare.

test [test] *n* (at school) prova *f*; (check) controllo *m*; (MED) esame *m* ♦ *vt* (check) controllare; (give exam to) esaminare; (try) provare; **driving ~** esame di guida.

testicles ['testıklz] *npl* testicoli *mpl*.

tetanus ['tetənəs] *n* tetano *m*.

text [tekst] *n* testo *m*.

textbook ['tekstbʊk] *n* libro *m* di testo.

textile ['tekstaıl] *n* tessuto *m*.

texture ['tekstʃə*r*] *n* consistenza *f*; (of fabric) trama *f*.

Thai [taı] *adj* tailandese.

Thailand [ˈtaɪlænd] *n* la Tailandia.

Thames [temz] *n*: **the ~** il Tamigi.

than [*weak form* ðən, *strong form* ðæn] *prep* di ♦ *conj* che; **you're better ~ me** sei più bravo di me; **I'd rather stay in ~ go out** preferisco restare a casa piuttosto che uscire; **more ~ six** più di sei.

thank [θæŋk] *vt*: **to ~ sb (for sthg)** ringraziare qn (per qc) ▫ **thanks** *npl* ringraziamenti *mpl* ♦ *excl* grazie!; **~s to** grazie a; **many ~s** grazie infinite.

Thanksgiving [ˈθæŋksgɪvɪn] *n* festa *f* del Ringraziamento *(festa nazionale americana).*

---

i THANKSGIVING

L e origini di questa festa nazionale, celebrata ogni anno negli Stati Uniti il quarto giovedì di novembre, risalgono al 1621, anno in cui i Padri Pellegrini resero grazie al Signore per il primo raccolto dal loro arrivo dall'Inghilterra. Il tacchino arrosto e la torta di zucca sono i due piatti tipici serviti durante il pranzo della festa del Ringraziamento.

---

thank you *excl* grazie!; **~ very much!** tante OR mille grazie!; **no ~!** no, grazie!

that [ðæt, *weak form of pron senses* 3, 4 & *conj* ðət] *(pl* **those)** *adj* 1. *(referring to thing, person mentioned)* quel/quello (quella/quell'), quegli/quei (quelle) *(pl)*; **~ book** quel libro; **who's ~ man?** chi è quell'uomo?; **those chocolates are delicious**

quei cioccolatini sono buonissimi. 2. *(referring to thing, person further away)* quello(-a) là; **I prefer ~ book** preferisco quel libro; **I'll have ~ one** prendo quello là.
♦ *pron* 1. *(referring to thing mentioned)* ciò; **what's ~?** che cos'è (quello)?; **I can't do ~** non posso farlo; **who's ~?** chi è quello?; **is ~ Lucy?** è Lucy?
2. *(referring to thing, person further away)* quello(-a), quelli(-e) *(pl)*.
3. *(introducing relative clause)* che; **a shop ~ sells antiques** un negozio che vende oggetti d'antiquariato; **the film ~ I saw** il film che ho visto.
4. *(introducing relative clause: after prep)* cui; **the person ~ I was telling you about** la persona di cui ti stavo parlando; **the place ~ I'm looking for** il posto che sto cercando.
♦ *adv* tanto, così; **it wasn't bad/good** non era così cattivo/buono.
♦ *conj* che; **tell him ~ I'm going to be late** digli che farò tardi.

thatched [θætʃt] *adj (roof)* paglia.

that's [ðæts] = **that is.**

thaw [θɔː] *vi (snow, ice)* sciogliersi
♦ *vt (frozen food)* scongelare.

the [*weak form* ðə, *before vowel strong form* ðiː] *definite article* 1. *(g*il/lo (la), i/gli (le); **~ book** il libro; **~ man** l'uomo; **~ mirror** lo specchi~ **woman** la donna; **~ island** l'is~ **men** gli uomini; **~ girls** le rag ze; **~ Wilsons** i Wilsons.
2. *(with an adjective to form a nou* **~ British** i britannici; **~ you** giovani.
3. *(in dates):* **Friday ~ nineteent** May venerdì diciannove maggi **twelfth ~ forties** il dodici; **~ forties** is.

quaranta.

4. *(in titles):* **Elizabeth ~ Second** Elisabetta Seconda.

theater ['θɪətə'] *n (Am) (for plays, drama)* = **theatre**; *(for films)* cinema *m inv.*

theatre ['θɪətə'] *n (Br) (for plays)* teatro *m.*

theft [θeft] *n* furto *m.*

their [ðeə'] *adj* il loro (la loro), i loro (le loro) *(pl).*

theirs [ðeəz] *pron* il loro (la loro), i loro (le loro) *(pl);* **a friend of ~** un loro amico.

them *[weak form* ðəm, *strong form* ðem] *pron (direct)* li (le); *(indirect)* gli; *(after prep with people)* loro; *(after prep with things)* essi(-e); **I know ~** li conosco; **it's ~** sono loro; **send it to ~** mandaglielo; **tell ~** diglielo; **he's worse than ~** è peggio di loro.

theme [θi:m] *n* tema *m.*

theme park *n* parco *m* di divertimenti.

themselves [ðəm'selvz] *pron (reflexive)* si; *(after prep)* se stessi (se stesse), sé; **they did it ~** l'hanno fatto da soli.

then [ðen] *adv* allora; *(next, afterwards)* dopo, poi; **from ~ on** da allora in poi; **until ~** fino ad allora.

theory ['θɪərɪ] *n* teoria *f;* **in ~** in teoria.

therapist ['θerəpɪst] *n* terapeuta *mf.*

therapy ['θerəpɪ] *n* terapia *f.*

there [ðeə'] *adv (at, in, to that place)* lì, là ♦ *pron* ~ **is/are** c'è/ci sono; **is anyone ~?** c'è nessuno?; **is ~, please?** *(on phone)* c'è Bob, per cortesia?; **we're going ~ tomorrow** ci andiamo domani; **over ~**

laggiù; ~ **you are** *(when giving)* ecco a lei.

thereabouts [ˌðeərə'bauts] *adv:* **or ~** o giù di lì.

therefore ['ðeəfɔː'] *adv* perciò.

there's [ðeəz] = **there is.**

thermal underwear [ˌθɜːml-] *n* biancheria *f* termica.

thermometer [θə'mɒmɪtə'] *n* termometro *m.*

Thermos (flask)® ['θɜːməs-] *n* thermos® *m inv.*

thermostat ['θɜːməstæt] *n* termostato *m.*

these [ðiːz] *pl* → **this.**

they [ðeɪ] *pron* essi (esse); *(referring to people)* loro; ~**'re tall** sono alti.

thick [θɪk] *adj (in size)* spesso(-a); *(hair)* folto(-a); *(sauce, smoke)* denso(-a); *(fog)* fitto(-a); *(inf: stupid)* tonto(-a); **it's one metre ~** ha uno spessore di un metro.

thicken ['θɪkn] *vt (sauce, soup)* rendere più denso ♦ *vi (mist, fog)* infittirsi.

thickness ['θɪknɪs] *n* spessore *m.*

thief [θiːf] *n (pl* **thieves** [θiːvz]*)* ladro *m (-a f).*

thigh [θaɪ] *n* coscia *f.*

thimble ['θɪmbl] *n* ditale *m.*

thin [θɪn] *adj* sottile; *(person, animal)* magro(-a); *(soup, sauce)* liquido(-a).

thing [θɪŋ] *n* cosa *f;* **the ~** is il fatto è □ **things** *npl (clothes, possessions)* cose *fpl;* **how are ~s?** *(inf)* come vanno le cose?

thingummyjig ['θɪŋəmɪdʒɪg] *n (inf)* coso *m.*

think [θɪŋk] *(pt & pp* **thought***)* *vt* pensare ♦ *vi* pensare; **to ~ that**

third

pensare che; **to ~ about** pensare a; **to ~ of** pensare a; **to ~ of doing sth** pensare di fare qc; **I ~ so** penso di sì; **I don't ~ so** penso di no; **do you ~ you could …?** potrebbe …?; **I'll think about it** ci penserò; **I can't ~ of his address** non mi viene in mente il suo indirizzo; **to ~ highly of sb** avere una buona opinione di qn □ **think over** vt sep riflettere su; **think up** vt sep escogitare.

third [θɜːd] num terzo(-a), → sixth.

third party insurance n assicurazione f contro terzi.

Third World n: the ~ il Terzo Mondo.

thirst [θɜːst] n sete f.

thirsty [ˈθɜːstɪ] adj: **to be ~** avere sete.

thirteen [ˌθɜːˈtiːn] num tredici, → six.

thirteenth [ˌθɜːˈtiːnθ] num tredicesimo(-a), → sixth.

thirtieth [ˈθɜːtɪəθ] num trentesimo(-a), → sixth.

thirty [ˈθɜːtɪ] num trenta, → six.

this [ðɪs] (pl **these**) adj **1.** (referring to thing, person mentioned) questo(-a); **these chocolates are delicious** questi cioccolatini sono buonissimi; **~ morning** stamattina; **~ week** questa settimana.
2. (referring to thing, person nearer) questo(-a); **I prefer ~ book** preferisco questo libro; **I'll have ~ one** prendo questo.
3. (inf: when telling a story): **there was ~ man …** c'era un tizio …
♦ pron **1.** (referring to thing, person mentioned) questo(-a); **~ is for you** questo è per te; **what are these?**

che cosa sono questi?; **~ is David Gregory** (introducing someone) questo è David Gregory; (on telephone) sono David Gregory.
2. (referring to thing, person nearer) questo(-a).
♦ adv: **it was ~ big** era grande così.

thistle [ˈθɪsl] n cardo m.

thorn [θɔːn] n spina f.

thorough [ˈθʌrə] adj (check, search) accurato(-a); (person) preciso(-a).

thoroughly [ˈθʌrəlɪ] adv (completely) a fondo.

those [ðəʊz] pl → that.

though [ðəʊ] conj benché, sebbene ♦ adv tuttavia; **even ~** anche se.

thought [θɔːt] pt & pp → think
♦ n pensiero m; (idea) idea f.

thoughtful [ˈθɔːtful] adj (quiet and serious) pensieroso(-a); (considerate) premuroso(-a).

thoughtless [ˈθɔːtlɪs] adj sconsiderato(-a).

thousand [ˈθaʊznd] num mille; OR **one ~** mille; **~s of** migliaia d → six.

thrash [θræʃ] vt (inf: defeat heavily) battere.

thread [θred] n (of cotton etc) fi m ♦ vt (needle) infilare.

threadbare [ˈθredbeə] adj l goro(-a).

threat [θret] n minaccia f.

threaten [ˈθretn] vt minacciare **to ~ to do sth** minacciare di fa qc.

threatening [ˈθretnɪŋ] adj r naccioso(-a).

three [θriː] num tre, → six.

three-D n: **in ~** tridimens

nale.

three-piece suite n divano m e due poltrone coordinate.

three-quarters ['kwɔ:təz] n tre quarti mpl; ~ **of an hour** tre quarti d'ora.

threshold ['θreʃhəʊld] n (fml) soglia f.

threw [θru:] pt → **throw**.

thrifty ['θrɪftɪ] adj parsimonioso(-a).

thrilled [θrɪld] adj contentissimo(-a).

thriller ['θrɪlə'] n thriller m inv.

thrive [θraɪv] vi (plant, animal, person) crescere bene; (business, tourism, place) prosperare.

throat [θrəʊt] n gola f.

throb [θrɒb] vi (noise, engine) vibrare; **my head is throbbing** ho un mal di testa lancinante.

throne [θrəʊn] n trono m.

throttle ['θrɒtl] n (of motorbike) valvola f a farfalla.

through [θru:] prep attraverso; (because of) grazie a; (from beginning to end) per tutta la durata di; (across all of) per tutto(-a) ♦ adv (to other side) attraverso; (from beginning to end) dall'inizio alla fine ♦ adj: to be ~ (with sthg) (finished) avere finito (con qc); **you're** ~ (on phone) è in linea; **Monday** ~ **Thursday** (Am) dal lunedì al giovedì; to go ~ (to somewhere else) passare; to let sb ~ far passare qn; I slept ~ the entire film ho dormito per tutto il film; ~ **traffic** traffico m attraversamento; a ~ **train** un treno diretto; 'no ~ road' (Br) 'strada senza uscita'.

throughout [θru:'aʊt] prep (day, morning, year) per tutto(-a);

(place, country, building) in tutto(-a) ♦ adv (all the time) per tutto il tempo; (everywhere) dappertutto.

throw [θrəʊ] (pt **threw**, pp **thrown** [θrəʊn]) vt gettare; (ball, javelin) lanciare; (dice) tirare; to ~ **sthg in the bin** gettare qc nel cestino □ **throw away** vt sep (get rid of) buttare OR gettare via; **throw out** vt sep (get rid of) buttare OR gettare via; (person) buttare fuori; **throw up** vi (inf: vomit) rimettere.

thru [θru:] (Am) = **through**.

thrush [θrʌʃ] n (bird) tordo m.

thud [θʌd] n tonfo m.

thug [θʌɡ] n delinquente mf.

thumb [θʌm] n pollice m ♦ vt: to ~ **a lift** fare l'autostop.

thumbtack ['θʌmtæk] n (Am) puntina f da disegno.

thump [θʌmp] n (punch) pugno m; (sound) tonfo m ♦ vt picchiare.

thunder ['θʌndə'] n tuono m.

thunderstorm ['θʌndəstɔ:m] n temporale m.

Thurs. (abbr of Thursday) gio.

Thursday ['θɜ:zdɪ] n giovedì m inv, → **Saturday**.

thyme [taɪm] n timo m.

Tiber ['taɪbə'] n: the ~ il Tevere.

tick [tɪk] n (written mark) segno m; (insect) zecca f ♦ vt spuntare ♦ vi (clock, watch) fare tic tac □ **tick off** vt sep (mark off) spuntare.

ticket ['tɪkɪt] n (for travel, cinema, theatre, match) biglietto m; (label) etichetta f; (speeding ticket, parking ticket) multa f.

ticket collector n controllore m.

ticket inspector n controllore m.

ticket machine n distributore m automatico di biglietti.

ticket office n biglietteria f.

tickle ['tɪkl] vt fare il solletico a.

ticklish ['tɪklɪʃ] adj: to be ~ soffrire il solletico.

tick-tack-toe n (Am) tris m (gioco).

tide [taɪd] n (of sea) marea f.

tidy ['taɪdɪ] adj (room, desk, person) ordinato(-a); (hair, clothes) in ordine □ **tidy up** vt sep riordinare, mettere in ordine.

tie [taɪ] (pt & pp **tied**, cont **tying**) n (around neck) cravatta f; (draw) pareggio m; (Am: on railway track) traversa f ◆ vt (fasten) legare; (laces) allacciare; (knot) fare ◆ vi (draw) pareggiare □ **tie up** vt sep (fasten) legare; (laces) annodare.

tied up ['taɪd-] adj occupato(-a).

tiepin ['taɪpɪn] n fermacravatta m inv.

tier [tɪəʳ] n (of seats) fila f.

tiger ['taɪgəʳ] n tigre f.

tight [taɪt] adj stretto(-a); (rope) teso(-a); (chest) chiuso(-a); (inf: drunk) sbronzo(-a) ◆ adv (hold) stretto(-a).

tighten ['taɪtn] vt stringere.

tightrope ['taɪtrəʊp] n corda f (sulla quale si esibiscono i funamboli).

tights [taɪts] npl collant m inv; a pair of ~ un paio di collant.

tile [taɪl] n (for roof) tegola f; (for floor, wall) mattonella f, piastrella f.

till [tɪl] n (for money) cassa f ◆ prep fino a ◆ conj finché non.

tiller ['tɪləʳ] n barra f del timone.

tilt [tɪlt] vt inclinare ◆ vi inclinarsi.

timber ['tɪmbəʳ] n (wood) legna-me m; (of roof) trave f.

time [taɪm] n tempo m; (measured by clock) ora f; (of train, flight, bus) orario m; (moment) momento m; (occasion) volta f ◆ vt (measure) cronometrare; (arrange) programmare; to ~ sthg well fare qc al momento giusto; I haven't got the ~ non ho tempo; it's ~ to go è ora di andare; what's the ~? che ore sono?; two ~s two due per due; two at a ~ due per volta; five ~s as much cinque volte tanto; in a month's ~ fra un mese; to have a good ~ divertirsi; all the ~ sempre; every ~ ogni volta; from ~ to ~ di tanto in tanto; for the ~ being per il momento; in ~ (arrive) in tempo; in good ~ per tempo; last ~ l'ultima volta; most of the ~ la maggior parte del tempo; on ~ puntuale; some of the ~ parte del tempo; this ~ questa volta.

time difference n differenza di fuso orario.

time limit n termine m massimo.

timer ['taɪməʳ] n timer m inv.

time share n multiproprietà inv.

timetable ['taɪmˌteɪbl] n orari m; (of events) calendario m.

time zone n fuso m orario.

timid ['tɪmɪd] adj (shy) timido(-a); (easily frightened) pauroso(-a).

tin [tɪn] n (metal) stagno m; (container) scatola f ◆ adj di latta.

tinfoil ['tɪnfɔɪl] n stagnola f.

tinned food [tɪnd-] n (Br) ci m in scatola.

tin opener [-ˌəʊpnəʳ] n (Br) ap scatole m inv.

tinsel ['tɪnsl] n fili mpl argen

(per decorare l'albero di Natale).

tint [tɪnt] *n* tinta *f*.

tinted glass [ˌtɪntɪd-] *n* vetro *m* colorato.

tiny ['taɪnɪ] *adj* molto piccolo(-a).

tip [tɪp] *n (point, end)* punta *f*; *(to waiter, taxi driver etc)* mancia *f*; *(piece of advice)* suggerimento *m*; *(rubbish dump)* discarica *f* ◆ *vt (waiter, taxi driver etc)* dare la mancia a; *(tilt)* inclinare; *(pour)* versare ❑ **tip over** *vt sep* rovesciare ◆ *vi* rovesciarsi.

tire ['taɪər] *vi* stancarsi ◆ *n (Am)* = **tyre**.

tired ['taɪəd] *adj* stanco(-a); **to be ~ of** *(fed up with)* essere stanco di.

tired out *adj* esausto(-a).

tiring ['taɪərɪŋ] *adj* faticoso(-a).

tissue ['tɪʃuː] *n (handkerchief)* fazzolettino *m* di carta.

tissue paper *n* carta *f* velina.

tit [tɪt] *n (vulg: breast)* tetta *f*.

title ['taɪtl] *n* titolo *m*.

T-junction *n* incrocio *m* a T.

to [unstressed before consonant tə, unstressed before vowel tu, stressed tuː] *prep* **1.** *(indicating direction)* a; **to go ~ Milan** andare a Milano; **to go ~ France** andare in Francia; **to go ~ school** andare a scuola; **to go ~ the office** andare in ufficio.

2. *(indicating position)* a; **~ the left/right** a sinistra/destra.

3. *(expressing indirect object)* a; **to give sthg ~ sb** dare qc a qn; **to listen ~ the radio** ascoltare la radio.

4. *(indicating reaction, effect)* a; **to be favourable ~ sthg** essere favorevole a qc; **~ my surprise** con mia grande sorpresa.

5. *(until)* fino a; **to count ~ ten** contare fino a dieci; **we work from**

nine **~ five** lavoriamo dalle nove alle cinque.

6. *(indicating change of state)*: **to turn ~ sthg** trasformarsi in qc; **it could lead ~ trouble** potrebbe causare problemi.

7. *(Br: in expressions of time)*: **it's ten ~ three** sono le tre meno dieci; **at quarter ~ seven** alle sette meno un quarto.

8. *(in ratios, rates)*: **40 miles ~ the gallon** = 100 chilometri con 7 litri; **there are sixteen ounces ~ the pound** sedici once fanno una libbra.

9. *(of, for)*: **the keys ~ the car** le chiavi dell'automobile; **a letter ~ my daughter** una lettera a mia figlia.

10. *(indicating attitude)* con, verso; **to be rude ~ sb** essere scortese con qn.

◆ *with infinitive* **1.** *(forming simple infinitive)*: **~ walk** camminare; **~ laugh** ridere.

2. *(following another verb)*: **to begin ~ do sthg** cominciare a fare qc; **to try ~ do sthg** cercare di fare qc.

3. *(following an adjective)*: **difficult ~ do** difficile da fare; **ready ~ go** pronto a partire.

4. *(indicating purpose)* per; **we came here ~ look at the castle** siamo venuti qui per visitare il castello.

toad [təʊd] *n* rospo *m*.

toadstool ['təʊdstuːl] *n* fungo *m* velenoso.

toast [təʊst] *n (bread)* pane *m* tostato; *(when drinking)* brindisi *m inv* ◆ *vt (bread)* tostare; **a piece** OR **slice of ~** una fetta di pane tostato.

toasted sandwich ['təʊstɪd-] *n* toast *m inv*.

toaster ['təʊstər] *n* tostapane

m inv.

toastie ['təʊstɪ] = **toasted sand-wich**.

tobacco [tə'bækəʊ] *n* tabacco *m*.

tobacconist's [tə'bækənɪsts] *n (shop)* tabaccaio *m*.

toboggan [tə'bɒgən] *n* toboga *m inv.*

today [tə'deɪ] *n* oggi *m* ◆ *adv* oggi.

toddler ['tɒdlə] *n* bambino *m* (-a *f*) *(che muove i primi passi).*

toe [təʊ] *n (of person)* dito *m* del piede.

toe clip *n* puntapiedi *m inv.*

toenail ['təʊneɪl] *n* unghia *f* del piede.

toffee ['tɒfɪ] *n (sweet)* caramella *f* mou *(inv).*

together [tə'geðə] *adv* insieme; ~ **with** insieme a.

toilet ['tɔɪlɪt] *n (room)* gabinetto *m; (bowl)* water *m inv;* **to go to the** ~ andare al gabinetto; **where's the** ~? dov'è il gabinetto?

toilet bag *n* nécessaire *m inv* da toilette.

toilet paper *n* carta *f* igienica.

toiletries ['tɔɪlɪtrɪz] *npl* prodotti *mpl* cosmetici.

toilet roll *n* rotolo *m* di carta igienica.

toilet water *n* acqua *f* di colonia.

token ['təʊkn] *n (metal disc)* gettone *m.*

told [təʊld] *pt & pp* → **tell**.

tolerable ['tɒlərəbl] *adj (fairly good)* passabile; *(bearable)* sopportabile.

tolerant ['tɒlərənt] *adj* tollerante.

tolerate ['tɒləreɪt] *vt* tollerare.

toll [təʊl] *n (for road, bridge)* pedaggio *m.*

tollbooth ['təʊlbuːθ] *n* casello *m.*

toll-free *adj (Am):* ~ **number** = numero *m* verde.

tomato [Br tə'mɑːtəʊ, Am tə'meɪtəʊ] *(pl* -es) *n* pomodoro *m.*

tomato juice *n* succo *m* di pomodoro.

tomato ketchup *n* ketchup *m.*

tomato puree *n* conserva *f* di pomodoro.

tomato sauce *n* sugo *m* di pomodoro.

tomb [tuːm] *n* tomba *f.*

tomorrow [tə'mɒrəʊ] *n* domani *m* ◆ *adv* domani; **the day after** ~ dopodomani; ~ **afternoon** domani pomeriggio; ~ **morning** domani mattina; ~ **night** domani sera.

ton [tʌn] *n (in Britain)* = 1016 kg; *(in U.S.)* = 907 kg; *(metric tonne)* tonnellata *f;* ~**s of** *(inf)* un sacco di.

tone [təʊn] *n (of voice)* tono *m; (on phone)* segnale *m; (of colour)* tonalità *f inv.*

tongs [tɒŋz] *npl (for hair)* arricciacapelli *m inv; (for sugar)* mollette *fpl*

tongue [tʌŋ] *n* lingua *f.*

tonic ['tɒnɪk] *n (tonic water)* acqua *f* tonica; *(medicine)* ricostituente *m.*

tonic water *n* acqua *f* tonica.

tonight [tə'naɪt] *n (night)* quest notte *f; (evening)* questa sera *f* ◆ *adv (night)* stanotte; *(evening)* questa notte *(evening)* stasera, questa sera.

tonne [tʌn] *n* tonnellata *f.*

tonsillitis [ˌtɒnsɪ'laɪtɪs] *n* tonsillite *f.*

too [tuː] *adv (excessively)* troppo *(also)* anche; **it's** ~ **late to go out**

troppo tardi per uscire; **~ many** troppi(-e); **~ much** troppo(-a).

took [tʊk] *pt* → **take.**

tool [tu:l] *n* attrezzo *m.*

tool kit *n* attrezzi *mpl.*

tooth [tu:θ] (*pl* **teeth**) *n* dente *m.*

toothache ['tu:θeɪk] *n* mal *m* di denti.

toothbrush ['tu:θbrʌʃ] *n* spaz-zolino *m* da denti.

toothpaste ['tu:θpeɪst] *n* denti-fricio *m.*

toothpick ['tu:θpɪk] *n* stuzzica-denti *m.*

top [tɒp] *adj (highest)* più alto(-a); *(step, stair)* ultimo(-a); *(best)* miglio-re; *(most important)* più importante ♦ *n (of stairs, hill, page)* cima *f;* *(of table)* piano *m;* *(of class, league)* primo *m* (-a *f*); *(for bottle, tube, pen)* tappo *m;* *(for jar, box)* coperchio *m;* *(of pyjamas, bikini)* sopra *m inv;* *(blouse)* camicetta *f;* *(T-shirt)* ma-glietta *f;* **at the ~ (of)** *(stairs, list, mountain)* in cima (a); **on ~ of** *(table etc)* sopra, su; *(in addition to)* oltre a; **at ~ speed** a tutta velocità; **~ gear** = quinta *f* □ **top up** *vt sep (glass, drink)* riempire ♦ *vi (with petrol)* fare il pieno.

top floor *n* ultimo piano *m.*

topic ['tɒpɪk] *n* argomento *m.*

topical ['tɒpɪkl] *adj* d'attualità.

topless ['tɒplɪs] *adj:* **to go ~** met-tersi in topless.

topped [tɒpt] *adj:* **~ with** *(cream etc)* ricoperto(-a) di.

topping ['tɒpɪŋ] *n* guarnizione *f* (*su pizza ecc.*).

torch [tɔ:tʃ] *n (Br: electric light)* torcia *f* elettrica.

tore [tɔ:r] *pt* → **tear**[1].

torment [tɔ:'ment] *vt (annoy)* tormentare.

torn [tɔ:n] *pp* → **tear**[1] ♦ *adj (rip-ped)* strappato(-a).

tornado [tɔ:'neɪdəʊ] (*pl* **-es** OR **-s**) *n* tornado *m.*

torrential rain [təˌrenʃl-] *n* pioggia *f* torrenziale.

tortoise ['tɔ:təs] *n* tartaruga *f.*

tortoiseshell ['tɔ:təʃel] *n* tarta-ruga *f.*

torture ['tɔ:tʃər] *n* tortura *f* ♦ *vt* torturare.

Tory ['tɔ:rɪ] *n* membro *m* del partito conservatore britannico.

toss [tɒs] *vt (throw)* lanciare; *(salad, vegetables)* mescolare; **to ~ a coin** fare testa o croce.

total ['təʊtl] *adj* totale ♦ *n* totale *m;* **in ~** in totale.

touch [tʌtʃ] *n (sense)* tatto *m;* *(small amount)* tantino *m;* *(detail)* tocco *m* ♦ *vt* toccare ♦ *vi* toccarsi; **to get in ~ (with sb)** mettersi in contatto (con qn); **to keep in ~ (with sb)** tenersi in contatto (con qn) □ **touch down** *vi (plane)* atter-rare.

touching ['tʌtʃɪŋ] *adj* toccante.

tough [tʌf] *adj* duro(-a); *(resilient)* tenace; *(hard, strong)* resistente.

tour [tʊər] *n (journey)* viaggio *m;* *(of city, castle etc)* visita *f;* *(of pop group, theatre company)* tournée *f inv* ♦ *vt* visitare; **on ~** in tournée.

tourism ['tʊərɪzm] *n* turismo *m.*

tourist ['tʊərɪst] *n* turista *mf.*

tourist class *n* classe *f* turisti-ca.

tourist information of-fice *n* ufficio *m* d'informazione turistica.

tournament [ˈtɔːnəmənt] *n* torneo *m*.

tour operator *n* operatore *m* turistico (operatrice turistica *f*).

tout [taʊt] *n* bagarino *m*.

tow [təʊ] *vt* rimorchiare.

toward [təˈwɔːd] *(Am)* = towards.

towards [təˈwɔːdz] *prep* (*Br*) verso; (*with regard to*) nei confronti di; (*to help pay for*) per.

towaway zone [ˈtəʊəweɪ-] *n* (*Am*) zona *f* rimozione forzata.

towel [ˈtaʊəl] *n* asciugamano *m*.

toweling [ˈtaʊəlɪŋ] *(Am)* = towelling.

towelling [ˈtaʊəlɪŋ] *n* (*Br*) spugna *f*.

towel rail *n* portasciugamano *m*.

tower [ˈtaʊəʳ] *n* torre *f*.

tower block *n* (*Br*) grattacielo *m*.

Tower Bridge *n* Tower Bridge (*famoso ponte levatoio di Londra*).

TOWER BRIDGE

Costruito in stile gotico nel diciannovesimo secolo, questo ponte sul Tamigi è costituito da due caratteristici ponti levatoi gemelli che si alzano per permettere il passaggio delle navi più grandi.

Tower of London *n*: the ~ la Torre di Londra.

TOWER OF LONDON

Situata sulla riva nord del Tamigi, la Torre di Londra è una fortezza che risale all'undicesimo secolo e fu residenza reale fino al diciassettesimo secolo. Oggi è un'attrazione turistica aperta al pubblico e ospita al suo interno un museo.

---

town [taʊn] *n* città *f*; (*town centre*) centro *m* (città).

town centre *n* centro *m* (città).

town hall *n* comune *m*.

towpath [ˈtəʊpɑːθ, *pl* -pɑːðz] *n* alzaia *f*.

towrope [ˈtəʊrəʊp] *n* cavo *m* di rimorchio.

tow truck *n* (*Am*) carro *m* attrezzi.

toxic [ˈtɒksɪk] *adj* tossico(-a).

toy [tɔɪ] *n* giocattolo *m*.

toy shop *n* negozio *m* di giocattoli.

trace [treɪs] *n* traccia *f* ♦ *vt* (*find*) rintracciare.

tracing paper [ˈtreɪsɪŋ-] *n* carta *f* da ricalco.

track [træk] *n* (*path*) sentiero *m*; (*of railway*) binario *m*, rotaie *fpl*; (*SPORT*) pista *f*; (*song*) pezzo *m* □ **track down** *vt sep* trovare.

tracksuit [ˈtræksuːt] *n* tuta *f* da ginnastica.

tractor [ˈtræktəʳ] *n* trattore *m*.

trade [treɪd] *n* (*COMM*) commercio *m*; (*job*) mestiere *m* ♦ *vt* scambiare ♦ *vi* commerciare.

trade-in *n* permuta *f*.

trademark [ˈtreɪdmɑːk] *n* marchio *m* di fabbrica.

trader [ˈtreɪdəʳ] *n* commerciante *mf*.

tradesman [ˈtreɪdzmən] (*pl* -men [-mən]) *n* (*deliveryman*) addetto *m* alle consegne; (*shopkeeper*) commerciante *mf*.

trade union *n* sindacato *m*.

tradition [trə'dɪʃn] *n* tradizione *f*.

traditional [trə'dɪʃənl] *adj* tradizionale.

traffic ['træfɪk] (*pt & pp* **-ked**) *n* (*cars etc*) traffico *m* ♦ *vi*: **to ~ in** trafficare in.

traffic circle *n* (*Am*) rotatoria *f*.

traffic island *n* salvagente *m*.

traffic jam *n* ingorgo *m*.

traffic lights *npl* semaforo *m*.

traffic warden *n* (*Br*) = vigile *m* urbano (*addetto al controllo dei divieti e limiti di sosta*).

tragedy ['trædʒədɪ] *n* tragedia *f*.

tragic ['trædʒɪk] *adj* tragico(-a).

trail [treɪl] *n* (*path*) sentiero *m*; (*marks*) tracce *fpl* ♦ *vi* (*be losing*) essere in svantaggio.

trailer ['treɪlə²] *n* (*for boat, luggage*) rimorchio *m*; (*Am: caravan*) roulotte *f inv*; (*for film, programme*) trailer *m inv*.

train [treɪn] *n* (*on railway*) treno *m* ♦ *vt* (*teach*) formare; (*animal*) addestrare ♦ *vi* (*SPORT*) allenarsi; **by ~** in treno.

train driver *n* macchinista *m*.

trainee [treɪ'niː] *n* (*for profession*) tirocinante *mf*; (*for trade*) apprendista *mf*.

trainer ['treɪnə²] *n* (*of athlete etc*) allenatore *m* (-trice *f*) ❑ **trainers** *npl* (*Br: shoes*) scarpe *fpl* da ginnastica.

training ['treɪnɪŋ] *n* (*instruction*) formazione *f*, addestramento *m*; (*exercises*) allenamento *m*.

training shoes *npl* (*Br*) scarpe *fpl* da ginnastica.

tram [træm] *n* (*Br*) tram *m inv*.

tramp [træmp] *n* vagabondo *m* (-a *f*).

trampoline ['træmpəliːn] *n* trampolino *m*.

trance [trɑːns] *n* trance *f*.

tranquilizer ['træŋkwɪlaɪzə²] (*Am*) = **tranquillizer**.

tranquillizer [træŋkwɪlaɪzə²] *n* (*Br*) tranquillante *m*.

transaction [træn'zækʃn] *n* transazione *f*.

transatlantic [ˌtrænzət'læntɪk] *adj* transatlantico(-a).

transfer [*n* 'trænsfɜː², *vb* træns-'fɜː²] *n* trasferimento *m*; (*of power, property*) passaggio *m*; (*picture*) decalcomania *f*; (*Am: ticket*) biglietto *che dà la possibilità di cambiare autobus, treno ecc. senza pagare alcun supplemento* ♦ *vt* trasferire ♦ *vi* (*change bus, plane etc*) cambiare; '**~s**' (*in airport*) 'transiti'.

transfer desk *n* banco *m* transiti.

transform [træns'fɔːm] *vt* trasformare.

transfusion [træns'fjuːʒn] *n* trasfusione *f*.

transistor radio [træn'zɪstə²] *n* transistor *m inv*.

transit ['trænzɪt] : **in transit** *adv* in transito.

transitive ['trænzɪtɪv] *adj* transitivo(-a).

transit lounge *n* sala *f* transiti.

translate [træns'leɪt] *vt* tradurre.

translation [træns'leɪʃn] *n* traduzione *f*.

translator [træns'leɪtə²] *n* traduttore *m* (-trice *f*).

transmission [trænz'mɪʃn] *n* trasmissione *f*.

transmit

transmit [trænz'mɪt] *vt* trasmettere.

transparent [træns'pærənt] *adj* trasparente.

transplant [ˈtrænsplɑ:nt] *n* trapianto *m*.

transport [*n* 'trænspɔ:t, *vb* træn'spɔ:t] *n* (cars, trains, planes etc) trasporti *mpl*; (moving) trasporto *m* ◆ *vt* trasportare.

transportation [ˌtrænspɔ:ˈteɪʃn] *n* (Am) (cars, trains, planes etc) trasporti *mpl*; (moving) trasporto *m*.

trap [træp] *n* trappola *f* ◆ *vt*: **to be trapped** (stuck) essere intrappolato.

trapdoor [ˌtræpˈdɔ:ʳ] *n* botola *f*.

trash [træʃ] *n* (Am: waste material) spazzatura *f*.

trashcan [ˈtræʃkæn] *n* (Am) pattumiera *f*.

trauma [ˈtrɔ:mə] *n* (bad experience) trauma *m*.

traumatic [trɔ:ˈmætɪk] *adj* traumatico(-a).

travel [ˈtrævl] *n* viaggi *mpl* ◆ *vt* (distance) percorrere ◆ *vi* viaggiare.

travel agency *n* agenzia *f* di viaggi.

travel agent *n* agente *mf* di viaggi; ~'s (shop) agenzia *f* di viaggi.

Travelcard [ˈtrævlkɑ:d] *n* biglietto che dà accesso ai mezzi pubblici di Londra per un'intera giornata.

travel centre *n* (in railway, bus station) ufficio informazioni e biglietteria.

traveler [ˈtrævlər] (Am) = **traveller**.

travel insurance *n* assicurazione *f* viaggio.

traveller [ˈtrævlə̯ʳ] *n* (Br) viaggiatore *m* (-trice *f*).

traveller's cheque *n* traveller's cheque *m inv*.

travelsick [ˈtrævəlsɪk] *adj*: **to be ~** (in car) soffrire il mal d'auto; (on boat) soffrire il mal di mare; (on plane) soffrire il mal d'aria.

trawler [ˈtrɔ:lə̯ʳ] *n* peschereccio *m*.

tray [treɪ] *n* vassoio *m*.

treacherous [ˈtretʃərəs] *adj* (person) infido(-a); (roads, conditions) insidioso(-a).

treacle [ˈtri:kl] *n* (Br) melassa *f*.

tread [tred] (*pt* trod, *pp* trodden) *n* (of tyre) battistrada *m inv* ◆ *vi*: **to ~ on sthg** calpestare qc.

treasure [ˈtreʒə̯ʳ] *n* tesoro *m*.

treat [tri:t] *vt* trattare; (patient, illness) curare ◆ *n* regalo *m*; **to ~ sb to sthg** offrire qc a qn.

treatment [ˈtri:tmənt] *n* (MED) cure *fpl*; (of person) trattamento *m*; (of subject) trattazione *f*.

treble [ˈtrebl] *adj* triplo(-a).

tree [tri:] *n* albero *m*.

trek [trek] *n* escursione *f*.

tremble [ˈtrembl] *vi* tremare.

tremendous [trɪˈmendəs] *adj* (very large) enorme; (inf: very good) formidabile.

trench [trentʃ] *n* fosso *m*.

trend [trend] *n* (tendency) tendenza *f*; (fashion) moda *f*.

trendy [ˈtrendɪ] *adj* (inf) alla moda.

trespasser [ˈtrespəsə̯ʳ] *n*: **'~s will be prosecuted'** 'vietato l'accesso; i trasgressori saranno puniti a termini di legge'.

trial [ˈtraɪəl] *n* (JUR) processo *m*; (test) prova *f*; **a ~ period** un periodo di prova.

triangle ['traɪæŋgl] n triangolo m.

triangular [traɪ'æŋgjʊlər] adj triangolare.

tribe [traɪb] n tribù f inv.

tributary ['trɪbjʊtrɪ] n tributario m, affluente m.

trick [trɪk] n trucco m; (conjuring trick) gioco m di prestigio ◆ vt imbrogliare, ingannare; **to play a ~ on sb** giocare un brutto tiro a qn.

trickle ['trɪkl] vi (liquid) gocciolare, colare.

tricky ['trɪkɪ] adj difficile.

tricycle ['traɪsɪkl] n triciclo m.

trifle ['traɪfl] n (dessert) zuppa f inglese.

trigger ['trɪgər] n grilletto m.

trim [trɪm] n (haircut) spuntata f ◆ vt (hair, beard) spuntare; (hedge) regolare.

trinket ['trɪŋkɪt] n ciondolo m, gingillo m.

trio ['triːəʊ] (pl -s) n trio m.

trip [trɪp] n (journey) viaggio m; (short) gita f, escursione f ◆ vi inciampare ❑ **trip up** vi inciampare.

triple ['trɪpl] adj triplo(-a).

tripod ['traɪpɒd] n treppiedi m inv.

triumph ['traɪəmf] n trionfo m.

trivial ['trɪvɪəl] adj (pej) insignificante, banale.

trod [trɒd] pt → **tread**.

trodden ['trɒdn] pp → **tread**.

trolley ['trɒlɪ] (pl -s) n (Br: in supermarket, at airport, for food etc) carrello m; (Am: tram) tram m inv.

trombone [trɒm'bəʊn] n trombone m.

troops [truːps] npl truppe fpl.

trophy ['trəʊfɪ] n trofeo m.

tropical ['trɒpɪkl] adj tropicale.

trot [trɒt] vi (horse) trottare ◆ n: **on the ~** (inf) di fila.

trouble ['trʌbl] n problemi mpl ◆ vt (worry) preoccupare; (bother) disturbare; **to be in ~** essere nei guai; **to get into ~** mettersi nei guai; **to take the ~ to do sthg** darsi la pena di fare qc; **it's no ~** non si preoccupi; (in reply to thanks) di niente.

trough [trɒf] n (for drinking) abbeveratoio m.

trouser press ['traʊzər-] n stiracalzoni m inv.

trousers ['traʊzəz] npl pantaloni mpl; **a pair of ~** un paio di pantaloni.

trout [traʊt] (pl inv) n trota f.

trowel ['traʊəl] n (for gardening) paletta f.

truant ['truːənt] n: **to play ~** marinare la scuola.

truce [truːs] n tregua f.

truck [trʌk] n (lorry) camion m inv, autocarro m.

true [truː] adj vero(-a).

truly ['truːlɪ] adv: **yours ~** distinti saluti.

trumpet ['trʌmpɪt] n tromba f.

trumps [trʌmps] npl atout m inv.

truncheon ['trʌntʃən] n sfollagente m inv.

trunk [trʌŋk] n (of tree) tronco m; (Am: of car) bagagliaio m; (case, box) baule m; (of elephant) proboscide f.

trunk call n (Br) interurbana f.

trunk road n (Br) strada f statale.

trunks [trʌŋks] npl costume m da bagno da uomo.

trust [trʌst] n (confidence) fiducia f ◆ vt (believe, have confidence in) fidarsi di, aver fiducia in; *(fml: hope)* sperare.

trustworthy ['trʌst͵wɜ:ðɪ] *adj* degno(-a) di fiducia.

truth [tru:θ] *n (true facts)* verità *f*; *(quality of being true)* veridicità *f*.

truthful ['tru:θful] *adj (statement, account)* veritiero(-a); *(person)* sincero(-a).

try [traɪ] *n (attempt)* tentativo *m*, prova *f* ♦ *vt* provare; *(JUR)* giudicare ♦ *vi* provare; **to ~ to do sthg** provare a fare qc □ **try on** *vt sep (clothes)* provare, provarsi; **try out** *vt sep* provare.

T-shirt *n* maglietta *f*.

tub [tʌb] *n (of margarine etc)* vaschetta *f*; *(inf: bath)* vasca *f* (da bagno).

tube [tju:b] *n (container)* tubetto *m*; *(Br: inf: underground)* metropolitana *f*; *(pipe)* tubo *m*; **by ~** in metropolitana.

tube station *n (Br: inf)* stazione *f* della metropolitana.

tuck [tʌk] : **tuck in** *vt sep (shirt)* mettersi dentro; *(child, person)* rimboccare le coperte a ♦ *vi (inf)* mangiare di buon appetito.

tuck shop *n (Br)* piccolo negozio di merendine, caramelle ecc., presso una scuola.

Tudor ['tju:dər] *adj* Tudor *(inv)* (sedicesimo secolo).

Tues. *(abbr of Tuesday)* mar.

Tuesday ['tju:zdɪ] *n* martedì *m inv*, → **Saturday**.

tuft [tʌft] *n* ciuffo *m*.

tug [tʌg] *vt* tirare ♦ *n (boat)* rimorchiatore *m*.

tuition [tju:'ɪʃn] *n* lezioni *fpl*.

tulip ['tju:lɪp] *n* tulipano *m*.

tumble-dryer ['tʌmbldraɪər] *n* asciugabiancheria *m inv*.

tumbler ['tʌmblər] *n (glass)* bicchiere *m (senza stelo)*.

tummy ['tʌmɪ] *n (inf)* pancia *f*.

tummy upset *n (inf)* disturbi *mpl* di pancia.

tumor ['tu:mər] *(Am)* = **tumour**.

tumour ['tju:mər] *n (Br)* tumore *m*.

tuna (fish) [*Br* 'tju:nə, *Am* 'tu:nə] *n (food)* tonno *m*.

tuna melt *n (Am)* crostino di tonno e formaggio fuso.

tune [tju:n] *n (melody)* melodia *f* ♦ *vt (radio, TV)* sintonizzare; *(engine)* mettere a punto; *(instrument)* accordare; **in ~** intonato; *(instrument)* accordato; **out of ~** *(person)* stonato; *(instrument)* scordato.

tunic ['tju:nɪk] *n* tunica *f*.

Tunisia [tju:'nɪzɪə] *n* la Tunisia.

tunnel ['tʌnl] *n* tunnel *m inv*, galleria *f*.

turban ['tɜ:bən] *n* turbante *m*.

turbo ['tɜ:bəʊ] *(pl -s)* *n (car)* turbo *m inv*.

turbulence ['tɜ:bjʊləns] *n (when flying)* turbolenza *f*.

turf [tɜ:f] *n (grass)* tappeto *m* erboso.

Turin [tjʊ'rɪn] *n* Torino *f*.

Turk [tɜ:k] *n* turco *m* (-a *f*).

turkey ['tɜ:kɪ] *(pl -s)* *n* tacchino *m*.

Turkey *n* la Turchia.

Turkish ['tɜ:kɪʃ] *adj* turco(-a) ♦ *n (language)* turco *m* ♦ *npl*: **the ~** turchi.

Turkish delight *n* dolciume fatto di gelatina e ricoperto di zucchero a velo.

turn [tɜ:n] *n (in road)* curva *f*; *(a*

knob, key, switch) giro *m*; (*go, chance*) turno *m* ◆ *vt* girare; (*a bend*) prendere; (*become*) diventare; (*cause to become*) far diventare ◆ *vi* girare; (*person*) girarsi; (*milk*) andare a male; **to ~ into sthg** (*become*) diventare qc; **to ~ sthg into sthg** trasformare qc in qc; **to ~ left/right** girare a sinistra/a destra; **it's your ~** tocca a te; **at the ~ of the century** all'inizio del secolo; **to take it in ~s to do sthg** fare qc a turno; **to ~ sthg inside out** rigirare qc □ **turn back** *vt sep* (*person, car*) mandare indietro ◆ *vi* tornare indietro; **turn down** *vt sep* (*radio, volume, heating*) abbassare; (*offer, request*) rifiutare; **turn off** *vt sep* (*light, TV, engine*) spegnere; (*water, gas, tap*) chiudere ◆ *vi* (*leave road*) girare, svoltare; **turn on** *vt sep* (*light, TV, engine*) accendere; (*water, gas, tap*) aprire; **turn out** *vt fus* (*be in the end*) rivelarsi ◆ *vt sep* (*light, fire*) spegnere ◆ *vi* (*come, attend*) affluire; **to ~ out to be sthg** risultare essere qc; **turn over** *vi* (*in bed*) girarsi, rigirarsi; (*Br: change channels*) cambiare canale ◆ *vt sep* girare; **turn round** *vt sep* (*car, table etc*) girare ◆ *vi* (*person*) girarsi, voltarsi; **turn up** *vt sep* (*radio, volume, heating*) alzare ◆ *vi* comparire.

turning ['tɜːnɪŋ] *n* (*off road*) svolta *f*.

turnip ['tɜːnɪp] *n* rapa *f*.

turn-up *n* (*Br: on trousers*) risvolto *m*.

turps [tɜːps] *n* (*Br: inf*) trementina *f*.

turquoise ['tɜːkwɔɪz] *adj* turchese.

turtle ['tɜːtl] *n* tartaruga *f* (acquatica).

turtleneck ['tɜːtlnek] *n* maglione *m* a collo alto.

Tuscany ['tʌskənɪ] *n* la Toscana.

tutor ['tjuːtə'] *n* (*private teacher*) insegnante *m* privato (insegnante *f* privata).

tuxedo [tʌk'siːdəʊ] (*pl* -**s**) *n* (*Am*) smoking *m inv*.

TV *n* tivù *f inv*, TV *f inv*; **on ~** alla tivù.

tweed [twiːd] *n* tweed *m*.

tweezers ['twiːzəz] *npl* pinzette *fpl*.

twelfth [twelfθ] *num* dodicesimo(-a), → **sixth**.

twelve [twelv] *num* dodici, → **six**.

twentieth ['twentɪəθ] *num* ventesimo(-a); **the ~ century** il ventesimo secolo, → **sixth**.

twenty ['twentɪ] *num* venti, → **six**.

twice [twaɪs] *adv* due volte; **it's ~ as good** è due volte meglio; **~ as much** il doppio.

twig [twɪg] *n* ramoscello *m*.

twilight ['twaɪlaɪt] *n* crepuscolo *m*.

twin [twɪn] *n* gemello *m* (-a *f*).

twin beds *npl* letti *mpl* gemelli.

twine [twaɪn] *n* spago *m*.

twin room *n* stanza *f* a due letti.

twist [twɪst] *vt* (*wire*) torcere, piegare; (*rope, hair*) attorcigliare; (*bottle top, lid, knob*) girare; **to ~ one's ankle** slogarsi la caviglia.

twisting ['twɪstɪŋ] *adj* (*road, river*) tortuoso(-a).

two [tuː] *num* due, → **six**.

two-piece *adj* (*swimsuit, suit*) a due pezzi (*inv*).

type [taɪp] *n* (*kind*) tipo *m* ◆ *vt* &

vi bàttere a macchina.

typewriter ['taɪp̩raɪtə'] *n* macchina *f* da scrivere.

typhoid ['taɪfɔɪd] *n* tifoidea *f*.

typical ['tɪpɪkl] *adj* tipico(-a).

typist ['taɪpɪst] *n* dattilografo *m* (-a *f*).

tyre ['taɪə'] *n* (*Br*) gomma *f*, pneumatico *m*.

U *adj* (*Br: film*) per tutti.

UFO *n* (*abbr of unidentified flying object*) UFO *m inv*.

ugly ['ʌglɪ] *adj* brutto(-a).

UHT *adj* (*abbr of ultra heat treated*) UHT.

UK *n*: the ~ il Regno Unito.

ulcer ['ʌlsə'] *n* ulcera *f*.

Ulster ['ʌlstə'] *n* l'Ulster *m*.

ultimate ['ʌltɪmət] *adj* (*final*) finale; (*best, greatest*) ideale.

ultraviolet [ˌʌltrə'vaɪələt] *adj* ultravioletto(-a).

umbrella [ʌm'brelə] *n* ombrello *m*.

umpire ['ʌmpaɪə'] *n* arbitro *m*.

UN *n* (*abbr of United Nations*): the ~ l'ONU *f*.

unable [ʌn'eɪbl] *adj*: to be ~ to do sthg non poter fare qc.

unacceptable [ˌʌnək'septəbl] *adj* inaccettabile.

unaccustomed [ˌʌnə'kʌstəmd] *adj*: to be ~ to sthg non essere abituato(-a) a qc.

unanimous [juː'nænɪməs] *adj* unanime.

unattended [ˌʌnə'tendɪd] *adj* (*baggage*) incustodito(-a).

unattractive [ˌʌnə'træktɪv] *adj* (*person, idea*) poco attraente; (*place*) privo(-a) di attrattiva.

unauthorized [ˌʌn'ɔːθəraɪzd] *adj* non autorizzato(-a).

unavailable [ˌʌnə'veɪləbl] *adj* non disponibile.

unavoidable [ˌʌnə'vɔɪdəbl] *adj* inevitabile.

unaware [ˌʌnə'weə'] *adj*: to be ~ of sthg/that ignorare qc/che.

unbearable [ʌn'beərəbl] *adj* insopportabile.

unbelievable [ˌʌnbɪ'liːvəbl] *adj* incredibile.

unbutton [ˌʌn'bʌtn] *vt* sbottonare.

uncertain [ʌn'sɜːtn] *adj* incerto(-a).

uncertainty [ʌn'sɜːtntɪ] *n* incertezza *f*.

uncle [ʌŋkl] *n* zio *m*.

unclean [ʌn'kliːn] *adj* sporco(-a).

unclear [ʌn'klɪə'] *adj* non chiaro(-a).

uncomfortable [ʌn'kʌmftəbl] *adj* (*person, chair*) scomodo(-a); (*fig: awkward*) a disagio.

uncommon [ʌn'kɒmən] *adj* (*rare*) raro(-a).

unconscious [ʌn'kɒnʃəs] *adj* (*after accident*) privo(-a) di sensi; (*unaware*) inconsapevole.

unconvincing [ˌʌnkən'vɪnsɪŋ] *adj* poco convincente.

uncooperative [ˌʌnkəʊ'ɒpərətɪv] *adj* poco disposto(-a) a collaborare.

uncork [ʌnˈkɔːk] vt stappare.

uncouth [ʌnˈkuːθ] adj villano(-a), grossolano(-a).

uncover [ʌnˈkʌvər] vt scoprire.

under [ˈʌndər] prep sotto; (less than) meno di, al di sotto di; (according to) secondo; **children ~ ten** bambini sotto i dieci anni; **~ the circumstances** date le circostanze; **to be ~ pressure** essere sotto pressione.

underage [ʌndərˈeɪdʒ] adj minorenne.

undercarriage [ˈʌndəˌkærɪdʒ] n carrello m.

underdone [ʌndəˈdʌn] adj poco cotto(-a).

underestimate [ʌndərˈestɪmeɪt] vt sottovalutare.

underexposed [ʌndərɪkˈspəʊzd] adj (photograph) sottoesposto(-a).

undergo [ʌndəˈgəʊ] (pt -went, pp -gone) vt subire.

undergraduate [ʌndəˈɡrædjʊət] n studente m universitario (studentessa f universitaria).

underground [ˈʌndəɡraʊnd] adj (below earth's surface) sotterraneo(-a); (secret) clandestino(-a) ♦ n (Br: railway) metropolitana f.

undergrowth [ˈʌndəɡrəʊθ] n sottobosco m.

underline [ʌndəˈlaɪn] vt sottolineare.

underneath [ʌndəˈniːθ] prep & adv sotto ♦ n sotto m.

underpants [ˈʌndəpænts] npl mutande fpl, slip m inv.

underpass [ˈʌndəpɑːs] n sottopassaggio m.

undershirt [ˈʌndəʃɜːt] n (Am) maglietta f.

underskirt [ˈʌndəskɜːt] n sottoveste f.

understand [ʌndəˈstænd] (pt & pp -stood) vt capire; (believe) credere ♦ vi capire; **I don't ~** non capisco; **to make o.s. understood** farsi capire.

understanding [ʌndəˈstændɪŋ] adj comprensivo(-a) ♦ n (agreement) accordo m; (knowledge) conoscenza f; (interpretation) interpretazione f; (sympathy) comprensione f.

understatement [ʌndəˈsteɪtmənt] n: **that's an ~!** è dir poco!

understood [ʌndəˈstʊd] pt & pp → **understand**.

undertake [ʌndəˈteɪk] (pt -took, pp -taken) vt intraprendere; **to ~ to do sthg** impegnarsi a fare qc.

undertaker [ˈʌndəteɪkər] n impresario di pompe funebri.

undertaking [ʌndəˈteɪkɪŋ] n (promise) promessa f; (task) impresa f.

undertook [ʌndəˈtʊk] pt → **undertake**.

underwater [ʌndəˈwɔːtər] adj subacqueo(-a) ♦ adv sott'acqua.

underwear [ˈʌndəweər] n biancheria f intima.

underwent [ʌndəˈwent] pt → **undergo**.

undesirable [ʌndɪˈzaɪərəbl] adj indesiderato(-a).

undo [ʌnˈduː] (pt -did, pp -done) vt (coat, shirt) sbottonare; (shoelaces) slacciare; (tie) sciogliere il nodo di; (parcel) sfare.

undone [ʌnˈdʌn] adj (coat, shirt) sbottonato(-a); (shoelaces) slacciato(-a).

undress [ʌn'dres] *vi* spogliarsi ♦ *vt* spogliare.

undressed [ʌn'drest] *adj* spogliato(-a); **to get ~** spogliarsi.

uneasy [ʌn'iːzɪ] *adj* a disagio.

uneducated [ʌn'edjukeɪtɪd] *adj* non istruito(-a).

unemployed [ʌnɪm'plɔɪd] *adj* disoccupato(-a) ♦ *npl*: **the ~ i** disoccupati.

unemployment [ʌnɪm'plɔɪmənt] *n* disoccupazione *f*.

unemployment benefit *n* sussidio *m* di disoccupazione.

unequal [ʌn'iːkwəl] *adj (not the same)* disuguale; *(not fair)* iniquo(-a).

uneven [ʌn'iːvn] *adj (surface, speed, beat)* irregolare; *(share, distribution)* ineguale.

uneventful [ʌnɪ'ventful] *adj* tranquillo(-a).

unexpected [ʌnɪk'spektɪd] *adj* inaspettato(-a).

unexpectedly [ʌnɪk'spektɪdlɪ] *adv* inaspettatamente.

unfair [ʌn'feəʳ] *adj* ingiusto(-a).

unfairly [ʌn'feəlɪ] *adv* ingiustamente.

unfaithful [ʌn'feɪθful] *adj* infedele.

unfamiliar [ʌnfə'mɪljəʳ] *adj* sconosciuto(-a); **to be ~ with** non conoscere bene.

unfashionable [ʌn'fæʃnəbl] *adj* fuori moda.

unfasten [ʌn'fɑːsn] *vt (seatbelt, belt, laces)* slacciare; *(knot)* sfare, sciogliere.

unfavourable [ʌn'feɪvrəbl] *adj* sfavorevole.

unfinished [ʌn'fɪnɪʃt] *adj* incompiuto(-a).

unfit [ʌn'fɪt] *adj (not healthy)* non in forma; **to be ~ for sthg** *(not suitable)* essere inadatto(-a) a qc.

unfold [ʌn'fəʊld] *vt* spiegare *(tovaglia, cartina)*.

unforgettable [ʌnfə'getəbl] *adj* indimenticabile.

unforgivable [ʌnfə'gɪvəbl] *adj* imperdonabile.

unfortunate [ʌn'fɔːtʃnət] *adj (unlucky)* sfortunato(-a); *(regrettable)* infelice; **it is ~ that** è un peccato che.

unfortunately [ʌn'fɔːtʃnətlɪ] *adv* sfortunatamente.

unfriendly [ʌn'frendlɪ] *adj* poco amichevole.

unfurnished [ʌn'fɜːnɪʃt] *ad[j]* non ammobiliato(-a).

ungrateful [ʌn'greɪtful] *ad[j]* ingrato(-a).

unhappy [ʌn'hæpɪ] *adj (sad)* infelice; *(not pleased)* insoddisfatto(-a); **to be ~ about sthg** esser[e] insoddisfatto di qc.

unharmed [ʌn'hɑːmd] *adj* i[n]denne.

unhealthy [ʌn'helθɪ] *adj (perso[n])* malaticcio(-a); *(food, smoking)* da noso(-a) per la salute; *(place)* ma[l]sano(-a).

unhelpful [ʌn'helpful] *adj (pe[r]son)* poco disponibile; *(advice, structions)* inutile.

unhurt [ʌn'hɜːt] *adj* indenne.

unhygienic [ʌnhaɪ'dʒiːnɪk] *ad[j]* non igienico(-a).

unification [ˌjuːnɪfɪ'keɪʃn] *n* u[ni]ficazione *f*.

uniform ['juːnɪfɔːm] *n* uniform[e]

unimportant [ˌʌnɪmˈpɔːtənt]
adj senza importanza.

unintelligent [ˌʌnɪnˈtelɪdʒənt]
adj poco intelligente.

unintentional [ˌʌnɪnˈtenʃənl]
adj involontario(-a).

uninterested [ʌnˈɪntrəstɪd] adj
indifferente.

uninteresting [ʌnˈɪntrəstɪŋ] adj
poco interessante, noioso(-a).

union [ˈjuːnjən] n (of workers) sindacato m.

Union Jack n: the ~ la bandiera
nazionale del Regno Unito.

unique [juːˈniːk] adj unico(-a); to
be ~ to essere proprio(-a) di.

unisex [ˈjuːnɪseks] adj unisex (inv).

unit [ˈjuːnɪt] n unità f inv; (department, building) reparto m; (piece of
furniture) elemento m; (machine)
apparecchio m.

unite [juːˈnaɪt] vt unire ♦ vi unir-
i.

United Kingdom [juːˈnaɪtɪd-]
: the ~ il Regno Unito.

United Nations [juːˈnaɪtɪd-]
pl: the ~ le Nazioni Unite.

**United States (of Ameri-
a)** [juːˈnaɪtɪd-] npl: the ~ gli Stati
niti (d'America).

nity [ˈjuːnətɪ] n unità f.

niversal [ˌjuːnɪˈvɜːsl] adj univer-
le.

niverse [ˈjuːnɪvɜːs] n universo m.

niversity [ˌjuːnɪˈvɜːsətɪ] n uni-
rsità f inv.

njust [ʌnˈdʒʌst] adj ingiu-
o(-a).

nkind [ʌnˈkaɪnd] adj scortese.

nknown [ʌnˈnəʊn] adj scono-
uto(-a).

leaded (petrol) [ʌnˈledɪd-]

n benzina f senza piombo.

unless [ənˈles] conj a meno che
non; ~ it rains a meno che non
piova.

unlike [ʌnˈlaɪk] prep a differenza
di; that's ~ her non è da lei.

unlikely [ʌnˈlaɪklɪ] adj improbabile; he is ~ to arrive before six è
improbabile che arrivi prima delle
sei.

unlimited [ʌnˈlɪmɪtɪd] adj illimi-
tato(-a); ~ mileage = chilometraggio illimitato.

unlisted [ʌnˈlɪstɪd] adj (Am:
phone number): to be ~ non essere
sull'elenco telefonico.

unload [ʌnˈləʊd] vt scaricare.

unlock [ʌnˈlɒk] vt aprire.

unlucky [ʌnˈlʌkɪ] adj (unfortunate)
sfortunato(-a); (bringing bad luck)
che porta sfortuna.

unmarried [ʌnˈmærɪd] adj non
sposato(-a).

unnatural [ʌnˈnætʃrəl] adj (unusual) inconsueto(-a); (behaviour,
person) poco naturale.

unnecessary [ʌnˈnesəsərɪ] adj
inutile.

unobtainable [ˌʌnəbˈteɪnəbl]
adj (product) non disponibile;
(phone number) non ottenibile.

unoccupied [ʌnˈɒkjupaɪd] adj
(place, seat) libero(-a).

unofficial [ˌʌnəˈfɪʃl] adj non ufficiale; (strike) non autorizzato(-a).

unpack [ʌnˈpæk] vt (bags, suitcase) disfare ♦ vi disfare le valigie.

unpleasant [ʌnˈpleznt] adj
(smell, weather, etc) sgradevole; (person) spiacevole, antipatico(-a).

unplug [ʌnˈplʌg] vt staccare.

unpopular [ʌnˈpɒpjʊlə*] adj

impopolare.

unpredictable [ˌʌnprɪˈdɪktəbl] *adj* imprevedibile.

unprepared [ˌʌnprɪˈpeəd] *adj* impreparato(-a).

unprotected [ˌʌnprəˈtektɪd] *adj* senza protezione.

unqualified [ʌnˈkwɒlɪfaɪd] *adj* (*person*) non qualificato(-a).

unreal [ʌnˈrɪəl] *adj* irreale.

unreasonable [ʌnˈriːznəbl] *adj* irragionevole.

unrecognizable [ʌnrekəɡˈnaɪzəbl] *adj* irriconoscibile.

unreliable [ˌʌnrɪˈlaɪəbl] *adj* inaffidabile.

unrest [ʌnˈrest] *n* agitazione *f*.

unroll [ʌnˈrəʊl] *vt* srotolare.

unsafe [ʌnˈseɪf] *adj* (*dangerous*) pericoloso(-a); (*in danger*) in pericolo.

unsatisfactory [ˌʌnsætɪsˈfæktərɪ] *adj* insoddisfacente.

unscrew [ʌnˈskruː] *vt* (*lid, top*) svitare.

unsightly [ʌnˈsaɪtlɪ] *adj* brutto(-a).

unskilled [ˌʌnˈskɪld] *adj* (*worker*) non qualificato(-a).

unsociable [ʌnˈsəʊʃəbl] *adj* poco socievole.

unsound [ʌnˈsaʊnd] *adj* (*building, structure*) poco saldo(-a); (*argument*) non regge.

unspoiled [ʌnˈspɔɪlt] *adj* (*place, beach*) incontaminato(-a).

unsteady [ʌnˈstedɪ] *adj* instabile; (*hand*) malfermo(-a).

unstuck [ʌnˈstʌk] *adj*: to come ~ (*label, poster etc*) staccarsi.

unsuccessful [ˌʌnsəkˈsesfʊl] *adj* che non ha successo.

unsuitable [ʌnˈsuːtəbl] *adj* inadatto(-a), inadeguato(-a); (*moment*) inopportuno(-a).

unsure [ʌnˈʃɔː] *adj*: to be ~ (about) non essere sicuro(-a) (di).

unsweetened [ʌnˈswiːtnd] *adj* senza zucchero.

untidy [ʌnˈtaɪdɪ] *adj* (*person*) disordinato(-a); (*room, desk*) in disordine.

untie [ʌnˈtaɪ] (*cont* **untying** [ʌnˈtaɪŋ]) *vt* (*person*) slegare; (*knot*) sciogliere, sfare.

until [ənˈtɪl] *prep* fino a ♦ *conj* finché; (*after negative, in past*) prima che, prima di; **it won't be ready ~ Thursday** non sarà pronto prima di giovedì.

untrue [ʌnˈtruː] *adj* falso(-a).

untrustworthy [ʌnˈtrʌstˌwɜːðɪ] *adj* non è degno(-a) di fiducia.

untying *cont* → **untie**.

unusual [ʌnˈjuːʒl] *adj* insolito(-a).

unusually [ʌnˈjuːʒəlɪ] *adv* (*more than usual*) insolitamente.

unwell [ʌnˈwel] *adj* indisposto(-a); **to feel ~** sentirsi bene.

unwilling [ʌnˈwɪlɪŋ] *adj*: **to be ~ to do sth** non voler fare qc.

unwind [ʌnˈwaɪnd] (*pt & pp unwound* [ʌnˈwaʊnd]) *vt* svolgere ♦ *vi* (*relax*) rilassarsi, distendersi.

unwrap [ʌnˈræp] *vt* aprire.

unzip [ʌnˈzɪp] *vt* aprire (la cerniera di).

up [ʌp] *adv* 1. (*towards higher position*) su, in alto; **to go ~** salire; **walked ~ to the top** siamo saliti fino in cima; **to pick sth ~** raccogliere qc.
2. (*in higher position*) su, in alto

she's ~ in her bedroom è su nella sua stanza; ~ there lassù.

3. (into upright position): **to stand** ~ alzarsi; **to sit** ~ (from lying position) tirarsi su a sedere; (sit straight) stare seduto diritto.

4. (to increased level): **prices are going** ~ i prezzi stanno salendo.

5. (northwards): ~ **in Scotland** in Scozia.

6. (in phrases): **to walk** ~ **and down** andare su e giù; ~ **to ten people** fino a dieci persone; **are you** ~ **to travelling?** te la senti di viaggiare?; **what are you** ~ **to?** cosa stai combinando?; **it's** ~ **to you** sta a te decidere; ~ **until ten o'clock** fino alle dieci.

♦ **prep 1.** (towards higher position): **to walk** ~ **a hill** salire su per una collina; **I went** ~ **the stairs** sono salito per le scale.

2. (in higher position) in cima a; ~ **a hill** in cima ad una collina; ~ **a ladder** in cima ad una scala.

3. (at end of): **they live** ~ **the road from us** abitano un po' più su di noi.

♦ **adj 1.** (out of bed) alzato(-a); **I was up at six today** mi sono alzato alle sei oggi.

2. (at an end): **time's** ~ tempo scaduto.

3. (rising): **the** ~ **escalator** la scala mobile per salire.

♦ **n:** ~**s and downs** alti e bassi *mpl*.

update [ʌp'deɪt] *vt* aggiornare.

uphill [ʌp'hɪl] *adj* in salita.

upholstery [ʌp'həʊlstərɪ] *n* tappezzeria f.

upkeep ['ʌpkiːp] *n* manutenzione f.

up-market *adj* rivolto(-a) alla fascia alta del mercato.

upon [ə'pɒn] *prep* (fml: on) su; ~ **hearing the news** ... dopo aver appreso la notizia ...

upper ['ʌpəʳ] *adj* superiore ♦ *n* (of shoe) tomaia f.

upper class *n:* **the** ~ i ceti alti.

uppermost ['ʌpəməʊst] *adj* (highest) il più alto (la più alta).

upper sixth *n* (Br: SCH) secondo anno del corso biennale che prepara agli 'A levels'.

upright ['ʌpraɪt] *adj* (person) diritto(-a); (object) verticale ♦ *adv* diritto.

upset [ʌp'set] (pt & pp **upset**) *adj* (distressed) addolorato(-a) ♦ *vt* (distress) addolorare, sconvolgere; (cause to go wrong) scombussolare; (knock over) rovesciare; **to have an** ~ **stomach** avere disturbi intestinali.

upside down [ʌpsaɪd-] *adj* capovolto(-a); (person) a testa in giù ♦ *adv* sottosopra.

upstairs [ʌp'steəz] *adj* di sopra ♦ *adv* (on a higher floor) di sopra, al piano superiore; **to go** ~ andare di sopra.

up-to-date *adj* (modern) moderno(-a); (well-informed) aggiornato(-a).

upwards ['ʌpwədz] *adv* (to a higher place) verso l'alto, in su; (to a higher level) verso l'alto; ~ **of 100 people** più di 100 persone.

urban ['ɜːbən] *adj* urbano(-a).

urban clearway [-'klɪəweɪ] *n* (Br) strada con divieto di sosta.

Urdu ['ʊədu:] *n* urdu *m*.

urge [ɜːdʒ] *vt:* **to** ~ **sb to do sthg** esortare qn a fare qc.

urgent ['ɜːdʒənt] *adj* urgente.

urgently ['ɜːdʒəntlɪ] *adv* (immediately) d'urgenza, urgentemente.

urinal [juə'raɪnl] n (bowl) orinale m; (place) vespasiano m.

urinate ['juərɪneɪt] vi (fml) urinare.

urine ['juərɪn] n urina f.

us [ʌs] pron ci; (after prep) noi; **they know** ~ ci conoscono; **it's** ~ siamo noi; **send it to** ~ mandacelo; **tell** ~ dicci; **they're worse than** ~ sono peggio di noi.

US n (abbr of United States): **the** ~ gli USA.

USA n (abbr of United States of America): **the** ~ gli USA.

usable ['ju:zəbl] adj utilizzabile.

use [n ju:s, vb ju:z] n uso m ◆ vt usare; (run on) andare a; **to be of** ~ essere utile, servire; **to have the** ~ **of sthg** avere accesso a qc; **to make** a ~ **of sthg** sfruttare qc; **'out of** ~ 'guasto'; **to be in** ~ essere in uso; **it's no** ~ non serve a niente; **what's the** ~? a che scopo?; **to** ~ **sthg as** sthg usare qc come qc; **'** ~ **before** ...' (food, drink) 'da consumarsi preferibilmente entro ...' ❑ **use up** vt sep consumare.

used [adj ju:zd, aux vb ju:st] adj (towel, glass etc) sporco(-a); (car) usato(-a) ◆ aux vb: **I** ~ **to live near here** una volta abitavo qui vicino; **I** ~ **to go there every day** una volta ci andavo tutti i giorni; **to be** ~ **to sthg** essere abituato(-a) a qc; **to get** ~ **to sthg** abituarsi a qc.

useful ['ju:sful] adj utile.

useless ['ju:slɪs] adj inutile; (inf: very bad): **he's** ~ non è buono a nulla.

user ['ju:zə'] n utente mf.

usher ['ʌʃə'] n (at cinema, theatre) maschera f.

usherette [ʌʃə'ret] n maschera f.

USSR n: **the (former)** ~ **l'(ex) URSS** f.

usual ['ju:ʒəl] adj solito(-a); **as** ~ (in the normal way) come al solito.

usually ['ju:ʒəlɪ] adv di solito.

utensil [ju:'tensl] n utensile m.

utilize ['ju:tɪlaɪz] vt (fml) utilizzare.

utmost ['ʌtməʊst] adj estremo(-a) ◆ n: **to do one's** ~ fare tutto il possibile.

utter ['ʌtə'] adj totale ◆ vt (word) proferire, pronunciare; (cry) emettere.

utterly ['ʌtəlɪ] adv completamente, del tutto.

U-turn n (in vehicle) inversione f a U.

vacancy ['veɪkənsɪ] n (job) posto m vacante; **'vacancies'** 'si affittano camere'; **'no vacancies'** 'completo'.

vacant ['veɪkənt] adj libero(-a).

vacate [və'keɪt] vt (fml: room, house) lasciare libero.

vacation [və'keɪʃn] n (Am) (period of time) vacanze fpl; (time off work) ferie fpl ◆ vi (Am) passare vacanze; **to go on** ~ andare in vacanza.

vacationer [və'keɪʃənə'] n (Am) villeggiante mf.

vaccination [ˌvæksɪ'neɪʃn] n vaccinazione f.

vaccine [Br 'væksi:n, Am væk'si:n] n vaccino m.

vacuum ['vækjʊəm] vt pulire con l'aspirapolvere.

vacuum cleaner n aspirapolvere m inv.

vague [veɪg] adj vago(-a); (shape, outline) indistinto(-a).

vain [veɪn] adj (pej: conceited) vanitoso(-a); **in ~** invano.

Valentine card ['væləntaɪn-] n biglietto che si manda per San Valentino alla persona che si ama o di cui si è innamorati.

Valentine's Day ['væləntaɪnz-] n San Valentino.

valet ['væleɪ, 'vælɪt] n (in hotel) chi si occupa del servizio lavanderia e stiratura.

valet service n (in hotel) servizio m di lavanderia; (for car) servizio di lavaggio.

valid ['vælɪd] adj (ticket, passport) valido(-a).

validate ['vælɪdeɪt] vt (ticket) convalidare.

Valium® ['vælɪəm] n valium® m.

valley ['vælɪ] n valle f.

valuable ['væljʊəbl] adj (jewellery, object) di valore; (advice, help) prezioso(-a) □ **valuables** npl oggetti mpl di valore.

value ['vælju:] n (financial) valore m; (usefulness) utilità f; **a ~ pack** una confezione formato famiglia; **to be good ~ (for money)** essere conveniente □ **values** npl (principles) valori mpl.

valve [vælv] n valvola f.

van [væn] n furgone m.

vandal ['vændl] n vandalo m (-a f).

vandalize ['vændəlaɪz] vt vandalizzare.

vanilla [və'nɪlə] n vaniglia f.

vanish ['vænɪʃ] vi svanire, scomparire.

vapor ['veɪpər] (Am) = **vapour**.

vapour ['veɪpər] n (Br) vapore m.

variable ['veərɪəbl] adj variabile.

varicose veins ['værɪkəʊs-] npl vene fpl varicose.

varied ['veərɪd] adj vario(-a).

variety [və'raɪətɪ] n varietà f inv.

various ['veərɪəs] adj vari(-e).

varnish ['vɑːnɪʃ] n vernice f ◆ vt verniciare.

vary ['veərɪ] vi & vt variare.

vase [Br vɑːz, Am veɪz] n vaso m.

Vaseline® ['væsəliːn] n vasellina f.

vast [vɑːst] adj vasto(-a).

vat [væt] n tino m.

VAT [væt, viːeɪ'tiː] n (abbr of value added tax) IVA f.

vault [vɔːlt] n (in bank) camera f blindata; (in church) cripta f.

VCR n (abbr of video cassette recorder) videoregistratore m.

VDU n (abbr of visual display unit) monitor m inv.

veal [viːl] n vitello m.

veg [vedʒ] abbr = **vegetable**.

vegan ['viːgən] adj vegetaliano(-a) ◆ n vegetaliano m (-a f).

vegetable ['vedʒtəbl] n verdura f.

vegetable oil n olio m vegetale.

vegetarian [,vedʒɪ'teərɪən] adj vegetariano(-a) ◆ n vegetariano m (-a f).

vegetation [,vedʒɪ'teɪʃn] n vegetazione f.

vehicle ['viːəkl] n veicolo m.

veil [veɪl] n velo m.

vein [veɪn] n vena f.

Velcro® ['velkrəʊ] n velcro m.

velvet ['velvɪt] n velluto m.

vending machine ['vendɪŋ-] n distributore m automatico.

venetian blind [vɪˌniːʃn-] n veneziana f.

Venice ['venɪs] n Venezia f.

venison ['venɪzn] n carne m di cervo.

vent [vent] n (for air, smoke etc) presa f d'aria.

ventilation [ˌventɪˈleɪʃn] n ventilazione f.

ventilator ['ventɪleɪtəʳ] n ventilatore m.

venture ['ventʃəʳ] n impresa f ♦ vi (go) avventurarsi.

venue ['venjuː] n luogo m (di partita, concerto ecc.).

veranda [vəˈrændə] n veranda f.

verb [vɜːb] n verbo m.

verdict ['vɜːdɪkt] n verdetto m.

verge [vɜːdʒ] n (of road, lawn, path) bordo m; 'soft ~s' 'banchina non transitabile'.

verify ['verɪfaɪ] vt verificare.

vermin ['vɜːmɪn] n roditori che portano malattie e distruggono raccolti.

vermouth [vɜːˈmuːθ] n vermut m inv.

versa → vice versa.

versatile ['vɜːsətaɪl] adj versatile.

verse [vɜːs] n (of song, poem) strofa f; (poetry) versi mpl.

version ['vɜːʃn] n versione f.

versus ['vɜːsəs] prep contro.

vertical ['vɜːtɪkl] adj verticale.

vertigo ['vɜːtɪgəʊ] n: to suffer from ~ soffrire di vertigini.

very ['verɪ] adv molto ♦ adj: at the ~ bottom proprio in fondo; ~ much molto; not ~ big non molto grande; my ~ own room una stanza tutta per me; ~ rich ricchissimo, molto ricco; it's the ~ thing I need è proprio quello di cui avevo bisogno.

vessel ['vesl] n (fml: ship) vascello m.

vest [vest] n (Br: underwear) maglietta f; (sleeveless) canottiera f; (Am: waistcoat) gilè m inv.

Vesuvius [vɪˈsuːvjəs] n Vesuvio m.

vet [vet] n (Br) veterinario m.

veteran ['vetrən] n (of war) vecchio combattente m.

veterinarian [ˌvetərɪˈneərɪən] (Am) = vet.

veterinary surgeon ['vetərɪnrɪ-] (Br: fml) = vet.

VHF n (abbr of very high frequency) VHF f.

VHS n (abbr of video home system) VHS m.

via ['vaɪə] prep (place) via; (by means of) tramite.

viaduct ['vaɪədʌkt] n viadotto m.

vibrate [vaɪˈbreɪt] vi vibrare.

vibration [vaɪˈbreɪʃn] n vibrazione f.

vicar ['vɪkəʳ] n pastore m.

vicarage ['vɪkərɪdʒ] n presbiterio m.

vice [vaɪs] n (moral fault) vizio m; (crime) crimine m; (Br: tool) morsa f.

vice-president n vice-presidente mf.

vice versa [ˌvaɪsɪˈvɜːsə] adv vice versa.

vicinity [vɪˈsɪnətɪ] n: in the ~ nelle vicinanze.

vicious ['vɪʃəs] adj (attack) vio

lento(-a); *(animal)* feroce; *(comment)* cattivo(-a), maligno(-a).

victim ['vɪktɪm] *n* vittima *f*.

Victorian [vɪk'tɔ:rɪən] *adj* vittoriano(-a).

victory ['vɪktərɪ] *n* vittoria *f*.

video ['vɪdɪəʊ] *(pl* **-s)** *n (video recording)* video *m inv*; *(videotape)* videocassetta *f*; *(video recorder)* videoregistratore *m* ◆ *vt (using video recorder)* videoregistrare; *(using camera)* filmare; ~ su videocassetta.

video camera *n* videocamera *f*.

video game *n* videogioco *m*.

video recorder *n* videoregistratore *m*.

video shop *n* videoteca *f*.

videotape ['vɪdɪəʊteɪp] *n* videocassetta *f*.

Vietnam [Br ˌvjet'næm, Am ˌvjet'nɑːm] *n* il Vietnam.

view [vjuː] *n* vista *f*; *(opinion)* opinione *f* ◆ *vt (house)* vedere; *(situation)* considerare; **in my ~** secondo me; **in ~ of** *(considering)* considerato; **to come into ~** apparire.

viewer ['vjuːər] *n (of TV)* telespettatore *m* (-trice *f*).

viewfinder ['vjuːˌfaɪndər] *n* mirino *m*.

viewpoint ['vjuːpɔɪnt] *n (opinion)* punto *m* di vista; *(place)* punto *f* osservazione.

vigilant ['vɪdʒɪlənt] *adj (fml)* vigile.

villa ['vɪlə] *n* villa *f*.

village ['vɪlɪdʒ] *n* paese *m*.

villager ['vɪlɪdʒər] *n* abitante *mf* paese.

villain ['vɪlən] *n (of book, film)* cattivo *m*; *(criminal)* malvivente *mf*.

vinaigrette [ˌvɪnɪ'gret] *n* condimento per insalata a base di olio, aceto, sale, pepe ed erbe aromatiche.

vine [vaɪn] *n (grapevine)* vite *f*; *(climbing plant)* rampicante *m*.

vinegar ['vɪnɪgər] *n* aceto *m*.

vineyard ['vɪnjəd] *n* vigna *f*.

vintage ['vɪntɪdʒ] *adj (wine)* d'annata *f* ◆ *n (year)* annata *f*.

vinyl ['vaɪnɪl] *n* vinile *m*.

viola [vɪ'əʊlə] *n* viola *f*.

violence ['vaɪələns] *n* violenza *f*.

violent ['vaɪələnt] *adj* violento(-a).

violet ['vaɪələt] *adj* viola *(inv)* ◆ *n (flower)* viola *f*.

violin [ˌvaɪə'lɪn] *n* violino *m*.

VIP *n (abbr of very important person)* vip *mf inv*.

virgin ['vɜːdʒɪn] *n* vergine *f*.

Virgo ['vɜːgəʊ] *(pl* **-s)** *n* Vergine *f*.

virtually ['vɜːtʃʊəlɪ] *adv* praticamente.

virtual reality [ˌvɜːtʃʊəl-] *n* realtà *f* virtuale.

virus ['vaɪrəs] *n* virus *m inv*.

visa ['viːzə] *n* visto *m*.

viscose ['vɪskəʊs] *n* viscosa *f*.

visibility [ˌvɪzɪ'bɪlɪtɪ] *n* visibilità *f*.

visible ['vɪzəbl] *adj* visibile.

visit ['vɪzɪt] *vt (person)* andare a trovare; *(place)* visitare ◆ *n* visita *f*.

visiting hours ['vɪzɪtɪŋ-] *npl* orario *m* delle visite.

visitor ['vɪzɪtər] *n (to person)* visita *f*; *(to place)* visitatore *m* (-trice *f*).

visitor centre *n (at tourist attraction)* punto accoglienza per i visitatori di musei ec.

visitors' book *n* registro *m*

dei visitatori.
visitor's passport n (Br)
passaporto m provvisorio.
visor [vaɪzəʳ] n visiera f.
vital [vaɪtl] adj vitale.
vitamin [Br 'vɪtəmɪn, Am 'vaɪtəmɪn] n vitamina f.
vivid [vɪvɪd] adj vivido(-a).
V-neck n (design) scollo m a V.
vocabulary [vəˈkæbjʊləɪ] n vocabolario m.
vodka [vɒdkə] n vodka f.
voice [vɔɪs] n voce f.
volcano [vɒlˈkeɪnəʊ] (pl -es OR -s) n vulcano m.
volleyball [vɒlɪbɔːl] n pallavolo f.
volt [vəʊlt] n volt m inv.
voltage [vəʊltɪdʒ] n voltaggio m.
volume [vɒljuːm] n volume m.
voluntary [vɒləntrɪ] adj volontario(-a).
volunteer [vɒlənˈtɪəʳ] n volontario m (-a f) ♦ vt: to ~ to do sthg offrirsi di fare qc.
vomit [vɒmɪt] n vomito m ♦ vi vomitare.
vote [vəʊt] n voto m; (number of votes) voti mpl ♦ vi: to ~ (for) votare (per).
voter [vəʊtəʳ] n elettore m (-trice f).
voucher [vaʊtʃəʳ] n buono m.
vowel [vaʊəl] n vocale f.
voyage [vɔɪdʒ] n viaggio m (per mare).
vulgar [vʌlgəʳ] adj volgare.
vulture [vʌltʃəʳ] n avvoltoio m.

W

W (abbr of west) O.
wad [wɒd] n (of paper, banknotes) fascio m; (of cotton) batuffolo m.
waddle [wɒdl] vi camminare come una papera.
wade [weɪd] vi camminare (a fatica).
wading pool [weɪdɪŋ-] n (Am) piscina f per bambini.
wafer [weɪfəʳ] n (biscuit) cialda f.
waffle [wɒfl] n (pancake) cialda dalla caratteristica superficie a quadretti che si mangia con sciroppo d'acero, panna o frutta ♦ vi (inf) parlare molto e dire poco.
wag [wæg] vt agitare.
wage [weɪdʒ] n salario m ☐ **wages** npl salario m.
wagon [wægən] n (vehicle) carro m; (Br: of train) vagone m.
waist [weɪst] n vita f.
waistcoat [weɪskəʊt] n gilè m inv.
wait [weɪt] n attesa f ♦ vi aspettare; to ~ for sb to do sthg aspettare che qn faccia qc; I can't ~! no vedo l'ora! ☐ **wait for** vt fus aspe...
waiter [weɪtəʳ] n cameriere m.
waiting room [weɪtɪŋ-] n sala d'attesa OR d'aspetto.
waitress [weɪtrɪs] n cameriera f.
wake [weɪk] (pt woke, pp woke... vt svegliare ♦ vi svegliarsi ☐ **wak... up** vt sep svegliare ♦ vi s...
Waldorf salad [wɔːldɔːf-] n

insalata a base di mele, sedano e noci, condita con maionese.

Wales [weɪlz] n il Galles.

walk [wɔ:k] n (journey, path) passeggiata f ◆ vi camminare ◆ vt (distance) percorrere a piedi; (dog) portare a spasso; **to go for a ~** andare a fare una passeggiata; **it's a short ~ a piedi è vicino; to take the dog for a ~** portare a spasso il cane; **'walk'** (Am) 'avanti'; **'don't ~'** (Am) 'alt' □ **walk away** vi andarsene; **walk in** vi entrare; **walk out** vi (leave angrily) andarsene.

walker ['wɔ:kər] n camminatore m (-trice f).

walking boots ['wɔ:kɪŋ-] npl scarponcini mpl.

walking stick ['wɔ:kɪŋ-] n bastone m.

Walkman® ['wɔ:kmən] n walkman® m.

wall [wɔ:l] n muro m; (internal) parete f, muro.

wallet ['wɒlɪt] n (for money) portafoglio m.

wallpaper ['wɔ:l,peɪpər] n carta f da parati.

wally ['wɒlɪ] n (Br: inf) cretino m (-a f).

walnut ['wɔ:lnʌt] n (nut) noce f.

waltz [wɔ:ls] n valzer m inv.

wander ['wɒndər] vi vagare.

want [wɒnt] vt volere; (need) aver bisogno di; **to ~ to do sthg** voler fare qc; **to ~ sb to do sthg** volere che qn faccia qc.

war [wɔ:r] n guerra f.

ward [wɔ:d] n (in hospital) reparto m.

warden ['wɔ:dn] n (of park) guardiano m; (of youth hostel) custode mf.

wardrobe ['wɔ:drəʊb] n (cupboard) armadio m; (clothes) guardaroba m inv.

warehouse ['weəhaʊs, pl -haʊzɪz] n magazzino m.

warm [wɔ:m] adj caldo(-a); (person, smile) cordiale; (welcome) caloroso(-a) ◆ vt scaldare, riscaldare; **to be ~** (person) avere caldo; **it's ~** (weather) è OR fa caldo □ **warm up** vt sep scaldare, riscaldare ◆ vi (get warmer) scaldarsi, riscaldarsi; (do exercises) riscaldarsi; (machine, engine) scaldare.

war memorial n monumento m ai caduti.

warmth [wɔ:mθ] n calore m.

warn [wɔ:n] vt avvertire, avvisare; **to ~ sb about sthg** avvisare qn di qc; **to ~ sb not to do sthg** avvertire qn di non fare qc.

warning ['wɔ:nɪŋ] n (of danger) avvertimento m; (advance notice) preavviso m.

warranty ['wɒrəntɪ] n (fml) garanzia f.

warship ['wɔ:ʃɪp] n nave f da guerra.

wart [wɔ:t] n verruca f.

was [wɒz] pt → **be**.

wash [wɒʃ] vt lavare ◆ vi lavarsi ◆ n: **to give sthg a ~** dare una lavata a qc; **to have a ~** lavarsi; **to one's hands/face** lavarsi le mani/il viso □ **wash up** vi (Br: do washing-up) lavare i piatti; (Am: clean o.s.) lavarsi.

washable ['wɒʃəbl] adj lavabile.

washbasin ['wɒʃ,beɪsn] n lavabo m.

washbowl ['wɒʃbəʊl] n (Am) lavabo m.

washer ['wɒʃər] n (ring) rondella f.

washing [wɒʃɪŋ] n bucato m.
washing line n corda f del bucato.
washing machine n lavatrice f.
washing powder n detersivo m in polvere.
washing-up n (Br): **to do the ~** fare i piatti.
washing-up bowl n (Br) bacinella f.
washing-up liquid n (Br) detersivo m liquido per piatti.
washroom [wɒʃrum] n (Am) bagno m, gabinetto m.
wasn't [wɒznt] = was not.
wasp [wɒsp] n vespa f.
waste [weɪst] n (rubbish) rifiuti mpl ♦ vt sprecare; **a ~ of money** uno spreco di denaro; **a ~ of time** una perdita di tempo.
wastebin [weɪstbɪn] n cestino m (dei rifiuti).
waste ground n terreno m abbandonato.
wastepaper basket [,weɪst-'peɪpə-] n cestino m (per la carta straccia).
watch [wɒtʃ] n (wristwatch) orologio m ♦ vt (observe) guardare; (spy on) sorvegliare; (be careful with) fare attenzione a ♦ **watch out** vi (be careful) stare attento, fare attenzione; to ~ **out for** (look for) cercare.
watchstrap [wɒtʃstræp] n cinturino m dell'orologio.
water [wɔːtə°] n acqua f ♦ vt (plants, garden) annaffiare ♦ vi (eyes) lacrimare; **it makes my mouth ~** mi fa venire l'acquolina in bocca.
water bottle n borraccia f.
watercolour [wɔːtə,kʌlə°] n

acquerello m.
watercress [wɔːtəkres] n crescione m.
waterfall [wɔːtəfɔːl] n cascata f.
watering can [wɔːtərɪŋ-] n annaffiatoio m.
watermelon [wɔːtə,melən] n cocomero m, anguria f.
waterproof [wɔːtəpruːf] adj impermeabile.
water purification tablets [-pjuːərɪfɪkeɪʃn-] npl compresse fpl per la disinfezione dell'acqua.
water skiing n sci m nautico.
watersports [wɔːtəspɔːts] npl sport mpl acquatici.
water tank n cisterna f.
watertight [wɔːtətaɪt] adj stagno(-a).
watt [wɒt] n watt m inv; **a 60-~ bulb** una lampadina da 60 watt.
wave [weɪv] n onda f; (of crime, violence) ondata f ♦ vt (hand) agitare; (flag) sventolare ♦ vi (to attract attention) fare un cenno (con la mano); (when greeting, saying goodbye) salutare con la mano.
wavelength [weɪvleŋθ] n lunghezza f d'onda.
wavy [weɪvɪ] adj (hair) ondulato(-a).
wax [wæks] n (for candles) cera f (in ears) cerume m.
way [weɪ] n (manner, means) modo m; (route) strada f; (direction) parte direzione f; (distance travelled) tragitto m; **which ~ is the station?** d che parte è la stazione?; **the tow is out of our ~** la città non è sull nostra strada; **to be in the ~** esse re d'intralcio; **to be on the ~** (pe son) stare arrivando; (meal) essere in arrivo; **to get out of sb's ~** l

sciar passare qn; **to get under ~** cominciare; **a long ~ away** lontano; **to lose one's ~** smarrirsi; **on the ~ back** al ritorno; **on the ~ there** all'andata; **that ~** *(like that)* in quel modo; *(in that direction)* da quella parte; **this ~** *(like this)* in questo modo; *(in this direction)* da questa parte; **'give ~'** 'dare la precedenza'; **'~ in'** 'entrata'; **'~ out'** 'uscita'; **no ~!** *(inf)* neanche per sogno!

WC *n (abbr of water closet)* W.C. *m inv.*

we [wi:] *pron* noi; **~'re fine** stiamo bene.

weak [wi:k] *adj* debole; *(drink)* leggero(-a); *(soup)* liquido(-a).

weaken ['wi:kn] *vt* indebolire.

weakness ['wi:knɪs] *n* debolezza *f.*

wealth [welθ] *n* ricchezza *f.*

wealthy ['welθɪ] *adj* ricco(-a).

weapon ['wepən] *n* arma *f.*

wear [weəʳ] *(pt* **wore,** *pp* **worn)** *vt* portare, indossare ♦ *n (clothes)* abbigliamento *m*; **~ and tear** usura *f* ❑ **wear off** *vi* passare; **wear out** *vi* consumarsi.

weary ['wɪərɪ] *adj* stanco(-a).

weasel ['wi:zl] *n* donnola *f.*

weather ['weðəʳ] *n* tempo *m*; **what's the ~ like?** che tempo fa?; **to be under the ~** *(inf)* sentirsi poco bene.

weather forecast *n* previsioni *fpl* del tempo.

weather forecaster [-fɔ:-kɑ:stəʳ] *n* meteorologo *m (-a f).*

weather report *n* bollettino *m* meteorologico.

weather vane [-veɪn] *n* banderuola *f.*

weave [wi:v] *(pt* **wove,** *pp* **woven)** *vt* tessere.

web [web] *n (of spider)* ragnatela *f.*

Wed. *(abbr of Wednesday)* mer.

wedding ['wedɪŋ] *n* matrimonio *m.*

wedding anniversary *n* anniversario *m* di matrimonio.

wedding dress *n* abito *m* da sposa.

wedding ring *n* fede *f.*

wedge [wedʒ] *n (of cake)* fetta *f*; *(of wood etc)* cuneo *m.*

Wednesday ['wenzdɪ] *n* mercoledì *m inv,* → **Saturday.**

wee [wi:] *adj (Scot)* piccolo(-a) ♦ *n (inf)* pipì *f.*

weed [wi:d] *n* erbaccia *f.*

week [wi:k] *n* settimana *f*; **a ~ today** oggi a otto; **in a ~'s time** fra una settimana.

weekday ['wi:kdeɪ] *n* giorno *m* feriale.

weekend [,wi:k'end] *n* fine settimana *m inv.*

weekly ['wi:klɪ] *adj* settimanale ♦ *adv* ogni settimana ♦ *n* settimanale *m.*

weep [wi:p] *(pt & pp* **wept)** *vi* piangere.

weigh [weɪ] *vt* pesare; **how much does it ~?** quanto pesa?

weight [weɪt] *n* peso *m*; **to lose ~** dimagrire; **to put on ~** ingrassare ❑ **weights** *npl (for weight training)* pesi *mpl.*

weightlifting ['weɪt,lɪftɪŋ] *n* sollevamento *m* pesi.

weight training *n* allenamento *m* ai pesi.

weir [wɪəʳ] *n* chiusa *f.*

weird [wɪəd] *adj* strano(-a).

welcome ['welkəm] *adj (guest)* benvenuto(-a); *(appreciated)* gradito(-a) ♦ *n* accoglienza *f* ♦ *vt (greet)* dare il benvenuto a; *(be grateful for)* gradire ♦ *excl* benvenuto!; **you're ~ to help yourself** si serve pure; **to make sb feel ~** far sentire qn benaccetto; **you're ~!** prego!

weld [weld] *vt* saldare.

welfare ['welfeə^r] *n (happiness, comfort)* benessere *m*; *(Am: money)* sussidio *m*.

well [wel] *(compar* **better**, *superl* **best)** *adj* bene ♦ *adv* bene; *(a lot)* molto ♦ *n* pozzo *m*; **to get ~** guarire; **to go ~** andar bene; **~ done!** bravo!; **it may ~ happen** è assai probabile che accada; **it's ~ worth it** ne vale ben la pena; **as ~** *(in addition)* anche; **as ~ as** *(in addition)* oltre a.

we'll [wi:l] = **we shall, we will**.

well-behaved [-bɪ'heɪvd] *adj* educato(-a).

well-built *adj* aitante.

well-done *adj (meat)* ben cotto(-a).

well-dressed [-'drest] *adj* vestito(-a) bene.

wellington (boot) ['welɪŋtən-] *n* stivale *m* di gomma.

well-known *adj* noto(-a).

well-off *adj (rich)* ricco(-a).

well-paid *adj* ben pagato(-a).

welly ['welɪ] *n (Br: inf)* stivale *m* di gomma.

Welsh [welʃ] *adj* gallese ♦ *n (language)* gallese *m* ♦ *npl*: **the ~** i gallesi.

Welshman ['welʃmən] *(pl* **-men** [-mən]**)** *n* gallese *m*.

Welsh rarebit [-'reəbɪt] *n* crostino *di formaggio fuso.*

Welshwoman ['welʃ,wʊmən] *(pl*

-women [-,wɪmɪn]**)** *n* gallese *f*.

went [went] *pt* → **go**.

wept [wept] *pt & pp* → **weep**.

were [wɜ:^r] *pt* → **be**.

we're [wɪə^r] = **we are**.

weren't [wɜ:nt] = **were not**.

west [west] *n* ovest *m*, occidente *m* ♦ *adj* dell'ovest ♦ *adv (fly, walk)* verso ovest; *(be situated)* a ovest; **in the ~ of England** nell'Inghilterra occidentale.

westbound ['westbaʊnd] *adj* diretto(-a) a ovest.

West Country *n*: **the ~** l'Inghilterra *f* sud-occidentale.

West End *n*: **the ~** *(of London)* zona occidentale del centro di Londra, celebre per i suoi negozi, cinema e teatri.

western ['westən] *adj* occidentale ♦ *n (film)* western *m inv*.

West Indies [-ˈɪndiːz] *npl* le Indie Occidentali.

Westminster ['westmɪnstə^r] *n* quartiere nel centro di Londra.

---

i **WESTMINSTER**

In questo quartiere di Londra, situato lungo il Tamigi, si trovano sia il Palazzo del Parlamento che l'Abbazia di Westminster. Il termine "Westminster" designa, per estensione, il Parlamento stesso.

Westminster Abbey l'abbazia *f* di Westminster.

---

i **WESTMINSTER ABBEY**

Situata nel quartiere londinese di Westminster, questa è la chie-

dove ha luogo l'incoronazione dei sovrani britannici. Vi sono sepolti molti personaggi famosi e una parte della chiesa, il "Poet's Corner" ("l'angolo dei poeti"), ospita le tombe di poeti e scrittori di chiara fama, tra i quali Chaucer, Dickens e Hardy.

westwards ['westwədz] *adv* verso ovest.

wet [wet] (*pt* & *pp* **wet** OR **-ted**) *adj* (*soaked, damp*) bagnato(-a); (*rainy*) piovoso(-a) ◆ *vt* bagnare; **to get ~** bagnarsi; '~ **paint**' 'vernice fresca'.

wet suit *n* muta *f*.

we've [wi:v] = **we have**.

whale [weɪl] *n* balena *f*.

wharf [wɔ:f] (*pl* **-s** OR **wharves** [wɔ:vz]) *n* banchina *f*.

what [wɒt] *adj* **1.** (*in questions*) che, quale; ~ **colour is it?** di che colore è?; **he asked me ~ colour it was** mi ha chiesto di che colore era. **2.** (*in exclamations*): ~ **a surprise!** che sorpresa!; ~ **a beautiful day!** che bella giornata!

◆ *pron* **1.** (*in direct questions*) cosa; ~ **is going on?** (che) cosa succede?; ~ **are they doing?** (che) cosa fanno?; ~ **is that?** (che) cos'è?; ~ **is it called?** come si chiama?; ~ **are they talking about?** (che) cosa parlano?; ~ **is it for?** a (che) cosa serve? **2.** (*in indirect questions, relative clauses*) cosa; **she asked me ~ had happened** m'ha chiesto cos'era successo; **she asked me ~ I had seen** mi ha chiesto cosa avevo visto; **she asked me ~ I was thinking about** m'ha chiesto a cosa pensavo; ~ **worries me is ...** ciò che mi preoccupa ...; **I didn't see ~ happened** non ho visto cos'è successo; **you can't have ~ you want** non puoi avere quello che vuoi. **3.** (*in phrases*): ~ **for?** a che scopo?, perché?; ~ **about going out for a meal?** cosa ne diresti di mangiare fuori?

◆ *excl* come?

whatever [wɒt'evə¹] *pron*: **take ~ you want** prendi quello che vuoi; **I do, I'll lose** qualsiasi cosa faccia, perderò; ~ **that may be** quale che sia.

wheat [wi:t] *n* grano *m*, frumento *m*.

wheel [wi:l] *n* ruota *f*; (*steering wheel*) volante *m*.

wheelbarrow ['wi:l,bærəʊ] *n* carriola *f*.

wheelchair ['wi:l,tʃeə¹] *n* sedia *f* a rotelle.

wheelclamp [,wi:l'klæmp] *n* bloccaruota *m inv*.

wheezy ['wi:zɪ] *adj* ansante.

when [wen] *adv* quando ◆ *conj* quando; (*although, seeing as*) sebbene, mentre; ~ **it's ready** quando è pronto; ~ **I've finished** quando avrò finito.

whenever [wen'evə¹] *conj* ogni volta che; ~ **you like** quando vuoi.

where [weə¹] *adv* & *conj* dove; **this is ~ you'll be sleeping** è qui che dormirà.

whereabouts ['weərəbaʊts] *adv* dove ◆ *npl*: **his ~ are unknown** nessuno sa dove si trovi.

whereas [weər'æz] *conj* mentre.

wherever [weər'evə¹] *conj* dovunque; ~ **you like** dove vuoi; ~ **that may be** dove che sia.

whether ['weðə¹] *conj* se; ~ **you**

like it or not ti piaccia o no.

which [wɪtʃ] *adj (in questions)* quale; ~ **room do you want?** quale stanza vuole?; ~ **one?** quale?; **she asked me** ~ **room I wanted** mi ha chiesto quale stanza volevo.

♦ *pron* 1. *(in questions)* quale; ~ **is the cheapest?** qual è il più economico?; ~ **do you prefer?** quale preferisci?; **he asked me** ~ **was the best** mi ha chiesto quale era il migliore; **he asked me** ~ **I preferred** mi ha chiesto quale preferivo.
2. *(introducing relative clause)* che; **the house** ~ **is on the corner** la casa che è all'angolo; **the television** ~ **I bought** il televisore che ho comprato.
3. *(introducing relative clause: after prep)* il quale (la quale); **the settee on** ~ **I'm sitting** il divano su cui siedo; **the book about** ~ **we were talking** il libro di cui stavamo parlando.
4. *(referring back)* il che, cosa che; **he's late,** ~ **annoys me** è in ritardo, il che mi secca molto.

whichever [wɪtʃ'evə'] *pron* quello(-a), quelli(-e) *(pl)* che ♦ *adj*: **take** ~ **chocolate you like best** prendi il cioccolatino che preferisci; ~ **chocolate you take** qualsiasi cioccolatino tu prenda.

while [waɪl] *conj* mentre; *(although)* sebbene ♦ *n*: **a** ~ un po' (di tempo); **for a** ~ per un po'; **in a** ~ fra un po'.

whim [wɪm] *n* capriccio *m*.

whine [waɪn] *vi* gemere; *(complain)* frignare.

whip [wɪp] *n* frusta *f* ♦ *vt (with whip)* frustare.

whipped cream [wɪpt-] *n* panna *f* montata.

whirlpool [ˈwɜːlpuːl] *n (Jacuzzi)* vasca *f* per idromassaggi.

whisk [wɪsk] *n (utensil)* frusta *f*, frullino *m* ♦ *vt (eggs, cream)* sbattere.

whiskers [ˈwɪskəz] *npl (of person)* favoriti *m*; *(of animal)* baffi *m*.

whiskey [ˈwɪskɪ] *(pl -s) n* whisky *m inv (irlandese o americano)*.

whisky [ˈwɪskɪ] *n* whisky *m inv (scozzese)*.

WHISKY

L iquore scozzese ottenuto dal malto d'orzo, il whisky viene sempre invecchiato in botti di legno e le sue diverse caratteristiche dipendono dai metodi di produzione e dai tipi di acqua usati. Il whisky di puro malto ("single malt"), spesso prodotto in piccole distillerie regionali, è comunemente considerato migliore rispetto alle varietà miscelate ("blended"), di solito meno costose.

---

whisper [ˈwɪspə'] *vt & vi* sussurrare.

whistle [ˈwɪsl] *n (instrument)* fischietto *m*; *(sound)* fischio *m* ♦ *vi* fischiare.

white [waɪt] *adj* bianco(-a); *(tea)* con latte ♦ *n* bianco *m*; *(person)* bianco *m* (-a *f*); ~ **coffee** caffè *m inv* con latte.

white bread *n* pane *m* bianco.

White House *n*: **the** ~ la Casa *f* Bianca.

white sauce *n* besciamella *f*.

white spirit *n* acquaragia *f*.

whitewash [ˈwaɪtwɒʃ] *vt* imbiancare.

white wine *n* vino *m* bianco.

whiting ['waɪtɪŋ] (pl inv) n merlango m.

Whitsun ['wɪtsn] n Pentecoste f.

who [hu:] pron (in questions) chi; (in relative clauses) che.

whoever [hu:'evə'] pron chiunque; ~ it is chiunque sia.

whole [həʊl] adj intero(-a) ◆ n: the ~ of the journey tutto il viaggio; on the ~ nel complesso; the ~ time tutto il tempo.

wholefoods ['həʊlfu:dz] npl prodotti mpl integrali.

wholemeal bread ['həʊlmi:l-] n (Br) pane m integrale.

wholesale ['həʊlseɪl] adv (COMM) all'ingrosso.

wholewheat bread ['həʊlwi:t] n (Am) = wholemeal bread.

whom [hu:m] pron (fml: in questions) chi; (in relative clauses) che; to ~? a chi?; the person to ~ I wrote la persona alla quale ho scritto.

whooping cough ['hu:pɪŋ-] n pertosse f.

whose [hu:z] adj & pron: ~ jumper is this? di chi è questo maglione?; she asked ~ jumper it was ha chiesto di chi era il maglione; this is the woman ~ son is a priest questa è la donna il cui figlio è un prete; ~ is this? di chi è questo?

why [waɪ] adv & conj perché; ~ not? perché no?; ~ not do it tomorrow? perché non farlo domani?

wick [wɪk] n (of candle, lighter) stoppino m.

wicked ['wɪkɪd] adj (evil) malvagio(-a); (mischievous) malizioso(-a).

wicker ['wɪkə'] adj di vimini.

wide [waɪd] adj largo(-a); (open-ended) ampio(-a); (range, variety)

vasto(-a); (difference, gap) grande ◆ adv: to open sthg ~ spalancare qc; how ~ is the road? quanto è larga la strada?; it's 12 metres ~ è largo 12 metri; ~ open spalancato.

widely ['waɪdlɪ] adv (known) generalmente; (travel) molto.

widen ['waɪdn] vt (make broader) allargare ◆ vi (gap, difference) aumentare.

widespread ['waɪdspred] adj molto diffuso(-a).

widow ['wɪdəʊ] n vedova f.

widower ['wɪdəʊə'] n vedovo m.

width [wɪdθ] n larghezza f.

wife [waɪf] (pl wives) n moglie f.

wig [wɪg] n parrucca f.

wild [waɪld] adj (animal, plant) selvatico(-a); (land, area) selvaggio(-a); (uncontrolled) sfrenato(-a); (crazy) folle; to be ~ about (inf) andare pazzo(-a) per.

wild flower n fiore m di campo.

wildlife ['waɪldlaɪf] n flora e fauna f.

will[1] [wɪl] aux vb 1. (expressing future tense): I ~ see you next week ci vediamo la settimana prossima; ~ you be here next Friday? sarai qui venerdì prossimo?; yes I ~ sì; no I won't no.

2. (expressing willingness): I won't do it mi rifiuto di farlo.

3. (expressing polite question): ~ you have some more tea? vuole ancora un po' di tè?

4. (in commands, requests): ~ you please be quiet! volete tacere!; close that window, ~ you? chiudi la finestra, per favore.

will[2] n (document) testamento m; against one's ~ contro la propria volontà.

willing ['wılıŋ] *adj*: to be ~ to do sthg essere disposto(-a) a fare qc.

willingly ['wılıŋlı] *adv* volentieri.

willow ['wıləʊ] *n* salice *m*.

win [wın] (*pt & pp* won) ◆ *n* vittoria *f* ◆ *vt* vincere; (*support, approval, friends*) guadagnarsi ◆ *vi* vincere.

wind[1] [wınd] *n* vento *m*; (*in stomach*) aria *f*.

wind[2] [waınd] (*pt & pp* wound) *vi* (*road, river*) snodarsi ◆ *vt*: to ~ sthg round sthg avvolgere qc intorno a qc ❑ **wind up** *vt sep* (*Br: inf: annoy*) dare sui nervi a; (*car window*) tirare su, chiudere; (*clock, watch*) caricare.

windbreak ['wındbreık] *n* frangivento *m*.

windmill ['wındmıl] *n* mulino *m* a vento.

window ['wındəʊ] *n* (*of house*) finestra *f*; (*of shop*) vetrina *f*; (*of car*) finestrino *m*.

window box *n* cassetta *f* per fiori.

window cleaner *n* lavavetri *mf*.

windowpane ['wındəʊ,peın] *n* vetro *m*.

window seat *n* (*on plane*) posto *m* finestrino.

window-shopping *n*: to go ~ andare a guardare le vetrine.

windowsill ['wındəʊsıl] *n* davanzale *m*.

windscreen ['wındskri:n] *n* (*Br*) parabrezza *m inv*.

windscreen wipers *npl* (*Br*) tergicristalli *mpl*.

windshield ['wındʃi:ld] *n* (*Am*) parabrezza *m inv*.

Windsor Castle ['wınzə-] *n* il

castello di Windsor.

WINDSOR CASTLE

Situato nell'omonima cittadina della contea del Berkshire, questo castello risale all'undicesimo secolo, quando Guglielmo il Conquistatore ne iniziò la costruzione. È una delle residenze ufficiali del sovrano britannico ed è parzialmente aperto al pubblico.

---

windsurfing ['wınd,sɜ:fıŋ] *n* windsurf *m*; to go ~ fare del windsurf.

windy ['wındı] *adj* ventoso(-a); it's ~ c'è vento.

wine [waın] *n* vino *m*.

wine bar *n* (*Br*) = enoteca *f*.

wineglass ['waınglɑ:s] *n* bicchiere *m* da vino.

wine list *n* lista *f* dei vini.

wine tasting [-'teıstıŋ] *n* degustazione *f* dei vini.

wine waiter *n* sommelier *m inv*.

wing [wıŋ] *n* ala *f*; (*Br: of car*) fiancata *f* ❑ **wings** *npl*: the ~s (*in theatre*) le quinte.

wink [wıŋk] *vi* strizzare l'occhio.

winner ['wınə*] *n* vincitore (-trice *f*).

winning ['wınıŋ] *adj* vincente.

winter ['wıntə*] *n* inverno; (the) ~ d'inverno.

wintertime ['wıntətaım] *n* inverno *m*.

wipe [waıp] *vt* pulire; to ~ one' hands/feet pulirsi le mani/le scarp ❑ **wipe up** *vt sep* (*liquid*) asciuga (*dirt*) pulire ◆ *vi* (*dry the dishe* asciugare i piatti.

wiper ['waɪpə^r] *n (windscreen wiper)* tergicristallo *m*.

wire ['waɪə^r] *n* filo *m* di ferro; *(electrical)* filo *m* (elettrico) ◆ *vt (plug)* collegare.

wireless ['waɪəlɪs] *n* radio *f inv*.

wiring ['waɪərɪŋ] *n* impianto *m* elettrico.

wisdom tooth ['wɪzdəm-] *n* dente *m* del giudizio.

wise [waɪz] *adj* saggio(-a).

wish [wɪʃ] *n (desire)* desiderio *m* ◆ *vt (desire)* desiderare; **best ~es** *(in letter)* cordiali saluti; **I ~ you'd told me earlier!** perché non me l'hai detto prima!; **I ~ I was younger** vorrei tanto essere più giovane; **to ~ for sthg** desiderare qc; **to ~ to do sthg** *(fml)* desiderare fare qc; **to ~ sb luck/happy birthday** augurare buona fortuna/buon compleanno a qn; **if you ~** *(fml)* se vuole.

witch [wɪtʃ] *n* strega *f*.

with [wɪð] *prep* **1**. *(gen)* con; **come ~ me** vieni con me; **a man ~ a beard** un uomo con la barba; **a room ~ a bathroom** una camera con bagno.

2. *(at house of)* da, a casa di; **we stayed ~ friends** siamo stati da amici.

3. *(indicating emotion)* di, per; **to tremble ~ fear** tremare di paura.

4. *(indicating opposition)*: **to argue ~** litigare con qn; **to fight ~** combattere contro qn.

5. *(indicating covering, contents)* di; **to ~ sthg ~ sthg** riempire qc di qc; **topped ~ cream** ricoperto di panna.

withdraw [wɪð'drɔː] *(pt* **-drew**, *pp* **-drawn**) *vt (take out)* ritirare;

(money) prelevare ◆ *vi (from race, contest)* ritirarsi.

withdrawal [wɪð'drɔːəl] *n (from bank account)* prelievo *m*.

withdrawn [wɪð'drɔːn] *pp* → withdraw.

withdrew [wɪð'druː] *pt* → withdraw.

wither ['wɪðə^r] *vi* appassire.

within [wɪ'ðɪn] *prep (inside)* all'interno di; *(not exceeding)* entro ◆ *adv* all'interno, dentro; **~ walking distance** raggiungibile a piedi; **~ 10 miles of ...** a non più di 10 miglia da ...; **it arrived ~ a week** è arrivato nel giro di una settimana; **~ the next week** entro la prossima settimana.

without [wɪ'ðaʊt] *prep* senza; **~ doing sthg** senza fare qc.

withstand [wɪð'stænd] *(pt & pp* **-stood**) *vt* resistere a.

witness ['wɪtnɪs] *n* testimone *mf* ◆ *vt (see)* assistere a.

witty ['wɪtɪ] *adj* arguto(-a).

wives [waɪvz] *pl* → wife.

wobbly ['wɒblɪ] *adj (table, chair)* traballante.

wok [wɒk] *n* padella larga e profonda usata nella cucina cinese.

woke [wəʊk] *pt* → wake.

woken ['wəʊkn] *pp* → wake.

wolf [wʊlf] *(pl* **wolves** ['wʊlvz]) *n* lupo *m*.

woman ['wʊmən] *(pl* **women**) *n* donna *f*.

womb [wuːm] *n* utero *m*.

women ['wɪmɪn] *pl* → woman.

won [wʌn] *pt & pp* → win.

wonder ['wʌndə^r] *vi (ask o.s.)* chiedersi, domandarsi ◆ *n (amazement)* meraviglia *f*; **to ~ if** domandarsi se; **I ~ if I could ask you a favour?** potrei chiederle un favore?

wonderful ['wʌndəful] *adj* meraviglioso(-a).

won't [wəʊnt] = **will not**.

wood [wʊd] *n (substance)* legno *m; (small forest)* bosco *m; (golf club)* mazza *f* di legno.

wooden ['wʊdn] *adj* di legno.

woodland ['wʊdlənd] *n* terreno *m* boschivo.

woodpecker ['wʊd,pekəʳ] *n* picchio *m*.

woodwork ['wʊdwɜːk] *n (SCH)* falegnameria *f*.

wool [wʊl] *n* lana *f*.

woolen ['wʊlən] *(Am)* = **woollen**.

woollen ['wʊlən] *adj (Br)* di lana.

woolly ['wʊlɪ] *adj* di lana.

wooly ['wʊlɪ] *(Am)* = **woolly**.

Worcester sauce ['wʊstəʳ-] *n* salsa *f* Worcester.

word [wɜːd] *n* parola *f*; **in other ~s** in altre parole; **to have a ~ with sb** parlare con qn.

wording ['wɜːdɪŋ] *n* formulazione *f*.

word processing ['-prəʊsesɪŋ] *n* videoscrittura *f*.

word processor ['-prəʊsesəʳ] *n* sistema *m* di videoscrittura.

wore [wɔːʳ] *pt →* **wear**.

work [wɜːk] *n* lavoro *m; (painting, novel etc)* opera *f* ♦ *vi* lavorare; *(operate, have desired effect)* funzionare; *(take effect)* fare effetto ♦ *vt (machine, controls)* far funzionare; **out of ~** senza lavoro; **to be at ~** *(at workplace)* essere al lavoro; **to be off ~** *(on holiday)* essere in ferie; *(ill)* essere

in malattia; **the ~s** *(inf:* everything) tutto quanto; **how does it ~?** come funziona?; **it's not ~ing** non funziona ❑ **work out** *vt sep (price, total)* calcolare; *(understand)* capire; *(solution)* trovare; *(method, plan)* mettere a punto ♦ *vi (result, be successful)* funzionare; *(do exercise)* fare ginnastica; **it ~s out at £20 each** *(bill, total)* fa 20 sterline a testa.

worker ['wɜːkəʳ] *n* lavoratore *m* (-trice *f*).

working class ['wɜːkɪŋ-] *n*: **the ~** la classe operaia.

working hours ['wɜːkɪŋ-] *npl* orario *m* di lavoro.

workman ['wɜːkmən] *(pl* -men [-mən]) *n* operaio *m*.

work of art *n* opera *f* d'arte.

workout ['wɜːkaʊt] *n* allenamento *m*.

work permit *n* permesso *m* di lavoro.

workplace ['wɜːkpleɪs] *n* posto *m* di lavoro.

workshop ['wɜːkʃɒp] *n (for repairs)* officina *f*.

work surface *n* piano *m* di lavoro.

world [wɜːld] *n* mondo *m* ♦ *ad[j]* mondiale; **the best in the ~** il migliore del mondo.

worldwide [,wɜːld'waɪd] *adv* i[n] tutto il mondo.

worm [wɜːm] *n* verme *m*.

worn [wɔːn] *pp →* **wear** ♦ *adj (clothes, carpet)* consumato(-a).

worn-out *adj (clothes, shoes etc)* consumato(-a); *(tired)* esausto(-a).

worried ['wʌrɪd] *adj* preoccupato(-a).

worry ['wʌrɪ] *n* preoccupazione

◆ *vt* preoccupare ◆ *vi*: **to ~ (about)** preoccuparsi (per).

worrying [ˈwʌrɪɪŋ] *adj* preoccupante.

worse [wɜːs] *adj* peggiore ◆ *adv* peggio; **to get ~** peggiorare; **~ off** *(in worse position)* in una situazione peggiore; *(poorer)* più povero.

worsen [ˈwɜːsn] *vi* peggiorare.

worship [ˈwɜːʃɪp] *n* culto *m* ◆ *vt* adorare.

worst [wɜːst] *adj* peggiore ◆ *adv* peggio ◆ *n*: **the ~** il peggiore (la peggiore).

worth [wɜːθ] *prep*: **how much is it ~?** quanto vale?; **it's ~ £50** vale 50 sterline; **it's ~ seeing** vale la pena vederlo; **it's not ~ it** non ne vale la pena; **£50 ~ of traveller's cheques** traveller's cheques per un valore di 50 sterline.

worthless [ˈwɜːθlɪs] *adj* di nessun valore.

worthwhile [ˌwɜːθˈwaɪl] *adj*: **to be ~** valere la pena.

worthy [ˈwɜːðɪ] *adj* *(winner, cause)* degno(-a); **to be ~ of sthg** essere degno di qc.

would [wʊd] *aux vb* **1.** *(in reported speech)*: **she said she ~ come** ha detto che sarebbe venuta.

2. *(indicating condition)*: **what ~ you do?** tu cosa faresti?; **what ~ you have done?** tu cosa avresti fatto?; **I ~ be most grateful** le sarei molto grato.

3. *(indicating willingness)*: **she ~n't go** non ci è voluta andare; **he ~ do anything for her** farebbe qualsiasi cosa per lei.

4. *(in polite questions)*: **~ you like a drink?** vuole qualcosa da bere?; **~ you mind closing the window?** le spiacerebbe chiudere la finestra?

5. *(indicating inevitability)*: **he ~ say that** era ovvio che dicesse così.

6. *(giving advice)*: **I ~ report it if I were you** se fossi in voi lo riferirei.

7. *(expressing opinions)*: **I ~ prefer ...** preferirei ...; **I ~ have thought (that) ...** avrei pensato che ...

wound[1] [wuːnd] *n* ferita *f* ◆ *vt* ferire.

wound[2] [waʊnd] *pt & pp* → **wind**[2].

wove [wəʊv] *pt* → **weave**.

woven [ˈwəʊvn] *pp* → **weave**.

wrap [ræp] *vt* *(package)* incartare; **to ~ sthg round sthg** avvolgere qc intorno a qc **wrap up** *vt sep* *(package)* incartare ◆ *vi* *(dress warmly)* coprirsi bene.

wrapper [ˈræpəʳ] *n* *(for sweets)* carta *f*.

wrapping [ˈræpɪŋ] *n* involucro *m*.

wrapping paper *n* *(for present)* carta *f* da regalo; *(for parcel)* carta da pacchi.

wreath [riːθ] *n* corona *f*.

wreck [rek] *n* *(of plane, car)* rottame *m*; *(of ship)* relitto *m* ◆ *vt* *(destroy)* distruggere; *(spoil)* rovinare; **to be ~ed** *(ship)* fare naufragio.

wreckage [ˈrekɪdʒ] *n* *(of plane, car)* rottami *mpl*; *(of building)* macerie *fpl*.

wrench [rentʃ] *n* *(Br: monkey wrench)* chiave *f* inglese; *(Am: spanner)* chiave.

wrestler [ˈresləʳ] *n* lottatore *m* (-trice *f*).

wrestling [ˈreslɪŋ] *n* lotta *f* libera.

wretched [ˈretʃɪd] *adj* *(miserable)* infelice; *(very bad)* orrendo.

wring [rɪŋ] *(pt & pp* **wrung**) *vt* *(clothes, cloth)* strizzare.

wrinkle ['rɪŋkl] *n* ruga *f*.

wrist [rɪst] *n* polso *m*.

wristwatch ['rɪstwɒtʃ] *n* orologio *m* da polso.

write [raɪt] (*pt* wrote, *pp* written) *vt* scrivere; (*cheque, prescription*) fare; (*Am: send letter to*) scrivere a ◆ *vi* scrivere; **to ~ to sb** (*Br*) scrivere a qn □ **write back** *vi* rispondere; **write down** *vt sep* scrivere; **write off** *vt sep* (*Br: inf: car*) distruggere ◆ *vi*: **to ~ off for sthg** richiedere qc per posta; **write out** *vt sep* (*list, essay*) scrivere; (*cheque, receipt*) fare.

write-off *n* (*vehicle*) rottame *m*.

writer ['raɪtə'] *n* (*author*) scrittore *m* (-trice *f*).

writing ['raɪtɪŋ] *n* (*handwriting*) scrittura *f*; (*written words*) scritto *m*; (*activity*) scrivere *m*.

writing desk *n* scrivania *f*.

writing pad *n* blocchetto *m* per appunti.

writing paper *n* carta *f* da lettere.

written ['rɪtn] *pp* → write ◆ *adj* (*exam, notice, confirmation*) scritto(-a).

wrong [rɒŋ] *adv* male ◆ *adj* (*incorrect, unsuitable*) sbagliato(-a); (*bad, immoral*): **it's ~ to steal** non si deve rubare; **what's ~?** cosa c'è che non va?; **what's ~ with her?** cos'ha?; **something's ~ with the car** la macchina ha qualcosa che non va; **to be ~** (*person*) sbagliarsi; **to be in the ~** essere in torto; **to get sthg ~** sbagliare qc; **to go ~** (*machine*) non funzionare più; **'~ way'** (*Am*) cartello che segnala agli automobilisti il senso vietato.

wrongly ['rɒŋlɪ] *adv* (*accused*) ingiustamente; (*informed*) male.

wrong number *n*: **to get the ~** sbagliare numero.

wrote [rəʊt] *pt* → write.

wrought iron [rɔːt] *n* ferro *m* battuto.

wrung [rʌŋ] *pt & pp* → wring.

XYZ

xing (*Am: abbr of crossing*): **'ped ~'** 'passaggio pedonale'.

XL (*abbr of extra-large*) XL.

Xmas ['eksməs] *n* (*inf*) Natale *m*.

X-ray *n* (*picture*) radiografia *f* ◆ *vt* fare una radiografia a; **to have an ~** farsi una radiografia.

yacht [jɒt] *n* yacht *m inv*.

yard [jɑːd] *n* (*unit of measurement*) = 91,44 cm, iarda *f*; (*enclosed area*) cortile *m*; (*Am: behind house*) giardino *m*.

yard sale *n* (*Am*) vendita di oggetti di seconda mano organizzata da un privato nel giardino di casa.

yarn [jɑːn] *n* (*thread*) filato *m*.

yawn [jɔːn] *vi* (*person*) sbadigliare.

yd *abbr* = yard.

yeah [jeə] *adv* (*inf*) sì.

year [jɪə'] *n* anno *m*; **next ~** l'anno prossimo; **this ~** quest'anno; **I'm 15 ~s old** ho 15 anni; **I haven't seen her for ~s** (*inf*) sono anni che non la vedo.

yearly ['jɪəlɪ] *adj* annuale, annuo(-a).

yeast [jiːst] *n* lievito *m*.

yell [jel] *vi* urlare.

yellow [ˈjeləʊ] *adj* giallo(-a) ◆ *n* giallo *m*.

yellow lines *npl* strisce *fpl* gialle (che regolano la sosta dei veicoli).

YELLOW LINES

In Gran Bretagna le linee gialle, singole o doppie, sul bordo della strada indicano restrizioni relative alla sosta dei veicoli. Un'unica linea gialla indica il divieto di sosta dalle ore 8 alle ore 18.30 dei giorni feriali, mentre una linea doppia indica il divieto di sosta permanente. La sosta è consentita quindi solo sulle linee gialle singole dopo le 18.30, oppure tutta la domenica.

Yellow Pages® *n*: the ~ le Pagine gialle.

yes [jes] *adv* sì; **to say ~** dire di sì.

yesterday [ˈjestədɪ] *n* ieri *m* ◆ *adv* ieri; **the day before ~** l'altro ieri; **~ afternoon** ieri pomeriggio; **~ morning** ieri mattina.

yet [jet] *adv* ancora ◆ *conj* ma; **have they arrived ~?** sono già arrivati?; **the best one ~** il migliore fino a questo momento; **not ~** non ancora; **I've ~ to do it** devo ancora farlo; **~ again** ancora una volta; **~ another delay** ancora un altro ritardo.

yew [juː] *n* tasso *m* (pianta).

yield [jiːld] *vt* dare, rendere ◆ *vi* (break, give way) cedere; **'yield'** (Am: AUT) 'dare la precedenza'.

YMCA *n* associazione cristiana dei giovani (che offre alloggi a buon prezzo).

yob [jɒb] *n* (Br: inf) teppista *mf*.

yoga [ˈjəʊgə] *n* yoga *m*.

yoghurt [ˈjɒgət] *n* yogurt *m inv*.

yolk [jəʊk] *n* tuorlo *m*, rosso *m* d'uovo.

York Minster [jɔːkˈmɪnstəʳ] *n* la cattedrale di York.

YORK MINSTER

Capolavoro dell'architettura gotica, nella città romana di York, nel nord dell'Inghilterra, questa cattedrale risale al dodicesimo secolo ed è famosa per le sue mura in pietra chiara e per il suo rosone. Danneggiata gravemente da un fulmine nel 1984, è stata parzialmente restaurata.

Yorkshire pudding [ˈjɔːkʃəʳ] *n* focaccia soffice servita tradizionalmente con arrosti di manzo.

you [juː] *pron* **1.** (subject: singular) tu; (subject: polite form) lei; (subject: plural) voi; **~ Italians** voi italiani. **2.** (direct object: singular) ti; (direct object: polite form) la; (direct object: plural) vi; **I called ~, not him** ho chiamato te, non lui. **3.** (indirect object: singular) ti; (indirect object: polite form) le; (indirect object: plural) vi. **4.** (after prep: singular) te; (after prep: polite form) lei; (after prep: plural) voi; **I'm shorter than ~** sono più basso di te/lei/voi. **5.** (indefinite use) si; **~ never know** non si sa mai; **swimming is good for ~** nuotare fa bene.

young [jʌŋ] *adj* giovane ◆ *npl*: **the ~** i giovani.

younger [ˈjʌŋgəʳ] *adj* (brother, sister) minore, più giovane.

youngest [ˈjʌŋgəst] *adj* (brother,

sister) minore, più giovane.

youngster [ˈjʌŋstə*r*] *n* giovane *mf*.

your [jɔː*r*] *adj* **1.** *(singular subject)* il tuo (la tua), i tuoi (le tue) *(pl)*; *(singular subject: polite form)* il suo (la sua), i suoi (le sue) *(pl)*; *(plural subject)* il vostro (la vostra), i vostri (le vostre) *(pl)*; ~ **dog** il tuo/suo/vostro cane; ~ **house** la tua/sua/vostra casa; ~ **children** i tuoi/suoi/vostri bambini; ~ **mother** tua/sua/vostra madre.
2. *(indefinite subject)*: **it's good for ~ health** fa bene alla salute.

yours [jɔːz] *pron (referring to singular subject)* il tuo (la tua), i tuoi (le tue) *(pl)*; *(polite form)* il suo (la sua), i suoi (le sue) *(pl)*; *(referring to plural subject)* il vostro (la vostra), i vostri (le vostre) *(pl)*; **a friend of ~** un tuo/suo/vostro amico; **are these shoes ~?** queste scarpe sono tue/sue/vostre?

yourself [jɔːˈself] *(pl* -**selves***) pron* **1.** *(reflexive: singular)* ti; *(reflexive: polite form)* si; *(reflexive: plural)* vi. **2.** *(after prep: singular)* te; *(after prep: polite form)* sé; *(after prep: plural)* voi. **3.** *(emphatic use: singular)* tu stesso(-a); *(emphatic use: polite form)* lei stesso(-a); *(emphatic use: plural)* voi stessi(-e); **did you do it ~?** *(singular)* l'hai fatto da solo?

youth [juːθ] *n (period of life)* gioventù *f*; *(quality)* giovinezza *f*; *(young man)* giovane *m*.

youth club *n* circolo *m* gio-

vanile.

youth hostel *n* ostello *m* della gioventù.

Yugoslavia [ˌjuːgəˈslɑːvɪə] *n* la Jugoslavia.

yuppie [ˈjʌpɪ] *n* yuppie *mf inv*.

YWCA *n* associazione cristiana delle giovani che offre alloggi a buon prezzo.

zebra [*Br* ˈzebrə, *Am* ˈziːbrə] *n* zebra *f*.

zebra crossing *n (Br)* strisce *fpl* pedonali.

zero [ˈzɪərəʊ] *(pl* -**es***) n* zero *m*; **five degrees below ~** cinque gradi sotto zero.

zest [zest] *n (of lemon, orange)* scorza *f*.

zigzag [ˈzɪgzæg] *vi* procedere a zigzag.

zinc [zɪŋk] *n* zinco *m*.

zip [zɪp] *n (Br)* cerniera *f* OR chiusura *f* lampo *(inv)* ◆ *vt* chiudere la cerniera di ❑ **zip up** *vt sep* chiudere la cerniera di.

zip code *n (Am)* codice *m* di avviamento postale.

zipper [ˈzɪpə*r*] *n (Am)* cerniera OR chiusura *f* lampo *(inv)*.

zit [zɪt] *n (inf)* brufolo *m*.

zodiac [ˈzəʊdɪæk] *n* zodiaco *m*.

zone [zəʊn] *n* zona *f*.

zoo [zuː] *(pl* -**s***) n* zoo *m inv*.

zoom (lens) [zuːm-] *n* zoom *m inv*.

zucchini [zuːˈkiːnɪ] *(pl inv) n (Am)* zucchine *fpl*.

Dépôt légal : Mai 1997
Imprimé en Grande-Bretagne par
Caledonian International Book Manufacturing